THE COMPLETE ENCYCLOPEDIA OF HOCKEY

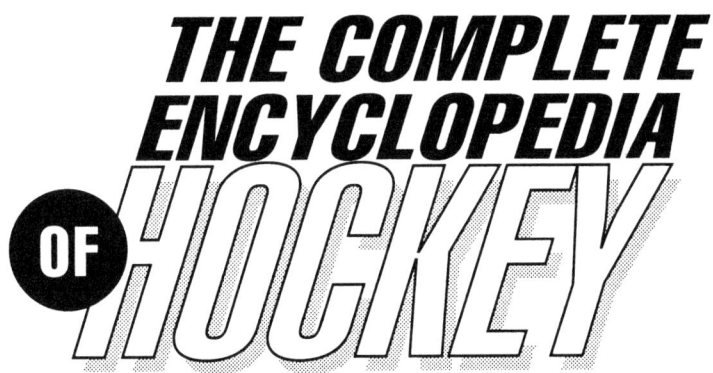

THE COMPLETE ENCYCLOPEDIA OF HOCKEY

FOURTH EDITION EXPANDED & UPDATED

edited by
ZANDER HOLLANDER

an Associated Features book

VISIBLE INK™
PRESS

DETROIT   WASHINGTON, D.C.   LONDON

Published by **Visible Ink Press**™
a division of Gale Research Inc.
835 Penobscot Building
Detroit, MI 48226-4094

Visible Ink Press™ is a trademark of Gale Research Inc.

Technical Design Services Manager: Arthur Chartow
Art Director: Cynthia Baldwin
Cover Design: Mark C. Howell
Interior Design: Business Graphic Services

Cover photo of Wayne Gretzky, Photography Ink.
Back cover photo of Kelly Buchberger, Photography Ink.

ISBN 0-8103-9419-7

CONTENTS

In one of his last official acts, outgoing NHL president John A. Ziegler presents the Stanley Cup to Pittsburgh's 1991–92 champions.

FOREWORD

The timing could not be better—the 100th Anniversary of the Stanley Cup and the publication of the fourth edition of *The Complete Encyclopedia of Hockey*.

Like the sport itself, this present volume has come a long way since the first one in 1970. But the core of the material has always been excellent, as noted by my predecessor, Clarence Campbell, who wrote in the introduction to that first edition, "This is a truly remarkable combination of accurate historical information about the NHL from its inception . . . about the many stars of the game, as well as leading officials; interesting incidents and anecdotes about the Stanley Cup and the current official and team records.

"The writing is superb, which by generous use of direct quotes makes the events and the personalities both lively and exciting. The book is extensively illustrated, which adds to its interest and authenticity."

This new edition brings us the same scholarship and readability. Of course, it is right up to date with over 4,200 players now listed, an increase of over 1,400 over the last edition in 1983. These new player listings are accompanied by improvements in career statistics, with the inclusion of playoff statistics and penalty minutes columns; more complete goaltender data; and the addition of each player's height and weight.

The *Complete Encyclopedia of Hockey* also adds to the team records section over its previous editions and includes information from the Entry Drafts since their inception.

With over 270 vintage and current photographs, including 50 new photos, it is visual as well as informational.

The *Complete Encyclopedia of Hockey* is a comprehensive documentation of all the ingredients that make our game the most exciting sport in the world. It will be a valuable and welcome addition to the reference library of every hockey fan, journalist, broadcaster and even those of us in the hockey business. I applaud the editor and his contributors for their efforts.

John A. Ziegler, Jr.
Former President
National Hockey League

To the pioneers,
the peewees
and the pros

INTRODUCTION

Ever since 1893, when Lord Stanley of Preston, the Earl of Derby and Governor-General of Canada, invested 10 pounds (about $49 at the time) in a squat, punch-bowl-shaped trophy to symbolize amateur hockey supremacy, men have spent fortunes and lifetimes pursuing that elusive piece of silverware.

The Stanley Cup's 100-year history is nearly as legendary and exciting as the game of hockey itself. At various times, Lord Stanley's Cup has been tossed into a graveyard, drop-kicked into a canal, dumped out of an automobile and stolen from its showcase. Each time, however, the sacred Cup has been rescued.

For the NHL, it has served as the holy grail for 75 years as hockey has grown from a simple game on the frozen lakes and ponds of Canada to one played on artificial ice in huge indoor arenas across the whole of North America and in other sectors of the world. Today NHL teams perform for stadium crowds that reach almost 20,000 and before additional millions on television.

Created in response to a need for a single comprehensive work on the sport of hockey, the first edition of *The Complete Encyclopedia of Hockey* was published in 1970. So far as is known, it was the first hockey encyclopedia. Its goal then, as now, was to include not only the vital facts and figures but the drama, the history, and the heroics that have made the game so special.

This fourth edition traces the sport from its beginning and covers every NHL season, including the climactic Cup playoffs. It profiles the outstanding players of all time, including for the first time Mario Lemieux, Mark Messier, and Ray Bourque, who join Wayne Gretzky among the actives along with such immortals as Bobby Hull, Gordie Howe, and Bobby Orr.

A changing of the guard in recent years is marked by first-time champions in Calgary and Pittsburgh, which made it two in a row in 1991-92. And the chapter on "Hockey's Memorable Moments" now includes the night the New York Islanders won their fourth straight Stanley Cup, and the game in which The Great Gretzky broke Howe's all-time scoring record.

The heart of the *Encyclopedia* remains the All-Time NHL Player Register, which contains additional vital statistics and has increased almost triple-fold from the 1,500 players who appeared in the first edition.

Since there is more to the complete story of hockey than the NHL, and the other major leagues of the past, I've covered the Olympic Games, world championships, and collegiate championships—all another part of the ice.

Zander Hollander

ACKNOWLEDGMENTS

Hockey is a team game and it took a talented, dedicated team of writers and researchers to produce The *Complete Encyclopedia of Hockey*. This one couldn't have been achieved without the monumental efforts of contributing editor Eric Compton of *Newsday* (N.Y.) and Lee Stowbridge, once of the New York *Daily News*. They updated the vastly expanded All-Time NHL Player Register.

And then there is Tim Moriarty. Where was Tim 22 years ago? Covering the NHL for *Newsday* and writing "The Greatest Players" chapter in the first edition of the encyclopedia. The iron man of the team, Tim has revised the old and written the new in the second, third, and now fourth editions. The editor also acknowledges 1992 contributors Doug Gould, formerly of the *New York Post* (season roundups, 1983–84—1991–92) and Rich Chere of the *Newark* (N.J.) *Star-Ledger* (new "Memorable Moments"). Others who helped were Bill Chadwick, ex-referee and member of the Hall of Fame; the NHL's John Halligan, a valued factor from the beginning; Phyllis Hollander, David Salamie, Martin Connors, Stu Hackel, Benny Ercolani, Gary Meagher, Susan Elliott, Greg Inglis, and the Hall of Fame's Phil Pritchard.

A thank-you, too, for the support of former NHL president John A. Ziegler.

The years may play games with one's memory, but the editor remembers those who contributed to the earlier editions: co-editor Hal Bock of Associated Press, Ben Olan of Associated Press, Reyn Davis of the *Winnipeg Free Press*, Pat Calabria of *Newsday*, Larry Fox, Jerry Ahrens, Art Friedman, and Jeff Shermack.

Others who contributed over the years include Maurice (Lefty) Reid, former curator and secretary of the Hall of Fame, Red Fisher of *The Gazette*, Don Andrews, Frank Kelly, Bill Himmelman, David Rosen, Richard Sherwin, Frank Polnaszek, and the team publicity directors of the NHL.

An encyclopedia depends in part on what has been written before—in newspapers, magazines, books. Among the books that proved helpful were: *The Trail of the Stanley Cup* by Charles L. Coleman; *50 Years of Hockey* by Bryan McFarlane; *The Stanley Cup* by Henry Roxborough; *The Hockey Encyclopedia* by Stan Fischler and Shirley Walton Fischler; The *NHL's Official Guide and Record Book;* and individual team media guides.

And last, but far more than least, editor Larry Baker of Gale Research smoothed the way by driving the Zamboni.

PHOTO CREDITS

Photographs appearing in *The Complete Encyclopedia of Hockey* were received from the following sources:

Bruce Bennett: 140, 141, 148, 150, 151, 152, 155 (both), 156, 158, 159 (both), 160, 161, 162, 166, 168, 170, 173, 174, 176, 184, 187, 188, 194, 216, 248, 270, 274, 297, 311, 312 (right), 321, 327, 328, 332, 335, 344

Paul Bereswill: 116, 378

Cliff Boutelle: 213, 324, 333

Detroit Red Wings: 211

Michael DiGirolamo/B. Bennett Studios: 164, 175

John Giamundo/B. Bennett Studios: 557

Hockey Hall of Fame: 3, 4, 6, 8, 9, 11 (both), 12, 13, 14, 15, 16, 19, 20, 21, 22, 23, 25, 26, 28, 31, 32, 33 (both), 35, 36, 37, 39, 42, 43, 44, 45, 47, 49, 50, 51, 54, 58, 60, 61, 62, 63, 64, 65, 67, 69 (right), 70, 71, 72, 75, 83, 85, 86, 88, 90 (right), 92, 196, 199, 206, 208, 210, 222, 227, 234, 238, 240, 241, 242 (both), 254, 260, 306, 307, 308 (both), 314, 316, 317, 319, 322, 326, 334, 357 (right)

Nancy Hogue: 130

Mitch Jaspon/B. Bennett Studios: 205

Scotty Kilpatrick: 90 (left), 102, 201, 221, 304

La Presse: 80

Madison Square Garden: 97, 202, 323

Brian Miller/B. Bennett Studios: 171, 249

Larry Morris: 105

National Hockey League: 69 (left), 132, 312 (left), 349, 350, 351, 352, 353 (both), 354, 355 (right), 356, 357 (left), 358, 359 (both), 360, 361

New York Rangers: 53, 57, 318, 355 (left)

Richard Pilling: 127, 131, 134, 135, 144, 145, 146, 153, 154, 204, 215, 218, 228

Public Archives of Canada: facing page 1

Dick Raphael: 114

Ken Regan: 94, 104, 182, 192

Robert Shaver: 119, 124, 126, 128, 136, 143, 225, 246, 266, 320, 329

Barton Silverman: 100, 107, 108, 190, 230, 236, 309

Toronto Maple Leafs: 331

UPI: 30, 40, 41, 46, 66, 74, 77, 78, 81, 84, 93, 98, 101, 110, 112, 115, 121, 122, 123, 133, 142, 147, 232, 233, 243, 244, 245, 261, 265, 268, 277, 296, 376, 380, 382, 384, 385, 386, 389, 392, 554

Wide World: foreword, 48, 68, 76, 96, 138, 177, 178, 179, 180, 209, 219, 224, 247, 258, 264, 272, 303, 310, 390, 393, 394, 395, 396, 397

Brian Winkler/B. Bennett Studios: 198

NHL FAMILY TREE

| '17 | '18 | '19 | '20 | '21 | '22 | '23 | '24 | '25 | '26 | '27 | '28 | '29 | '30 | '31 | '32 | '33 | '34 | '35 | '36 | '37 | '38 | '39 | '40 | '41 | '42 | '43 | '44 | '45 | '46 | '47 | '48 | '49 | '50 | '51 | '52 | |

Montreal Canadiens (1917–Present)

Montreal Wanderers (1917–1918)

Ottawa Senators (1917–31) (1932–34)   St. Louis Eagles (1934–35)

Toronto Arenas (1917–19) • Toronto St. Pats (1919–26) • Toronto Maple Leafs (1926–Present)

Quebec Bulldogs (1919–20) Hamilton Tigers (1920–25)   New York Americans (1925–41)   Brooklyn Americans (1941–42)

Boston Bruins (1924–Present)

Montreal Maroons (1924–38)

Pittsburgh Pirates (1925–30)   Philadelphia Quakers (1930–31)

New York Rangers (1926–Present)

Detroit Cougars (1926–30)   Detroit Falcons (1930–32) • Detroit Red Wings (1932–Present)

Chicago Black Hawks (1926–Present)

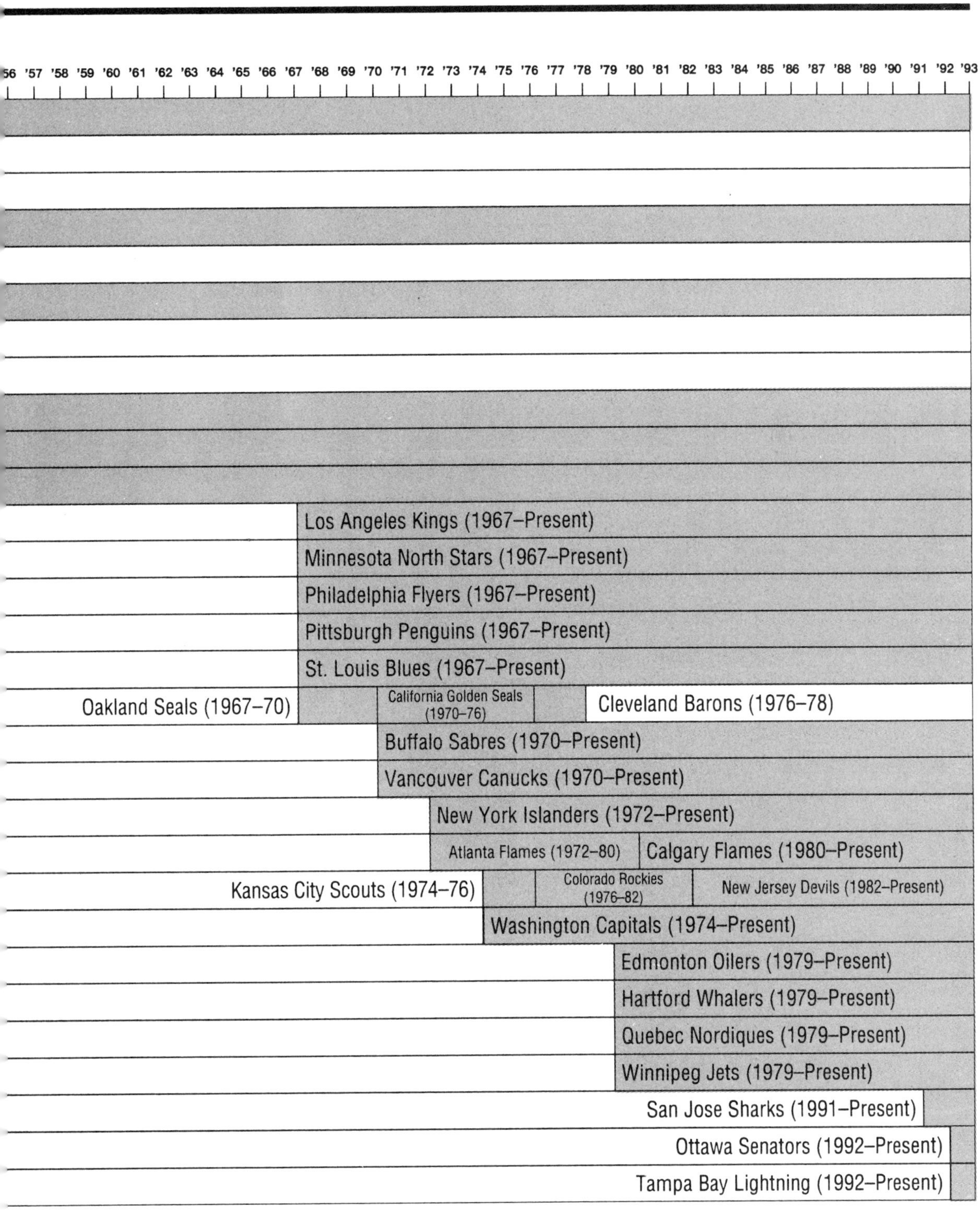

'56 '57 '58 '59 '60 '61 '62 '63 '64 '65 '66 '67 '68 '69 '70 '71 '72 '73 '74 '75 '76 '77 '78 '79 '80 '81 '82 '83 '84 '85 '86 '87 '88 '89 '90 '91 '92 '93
Los Angeles Kings (1967–Present)
Minnesota North Stars (1967–Present)
Philadelphia Flyers (1967–Present)
Pittsburgh Penguins (1967–Present)
St. Louis Blues (1967–Present)
Oakland Seals (1967–70)
California Golden Seals (1970–76)
Cleveland Barons (1976–78)
Buffalo Sabres (1970–Present)
Vancouver Canucks (1970–Present)
New York Islanders (1972–Present)
Atlanta Flames (1972–80)
Calgary Flames (1980–Present)
Kansas City Scouts (1974–76)
Colorado Rockies (1976–82)
New Jersey Devils (1982–Present)
Washington Capitals (1974–Present)
Edmonton Oilers (1979–Present)
Hartford Whalers (1979–Present)
Quebec Nordiques (1979–Present)
Winnipeg Jets (1979–Present)
San Jose Sharks (1991–Present)
Ottawa Senators (1992–Present)
Tampa Bay Lightning (1992–Present)

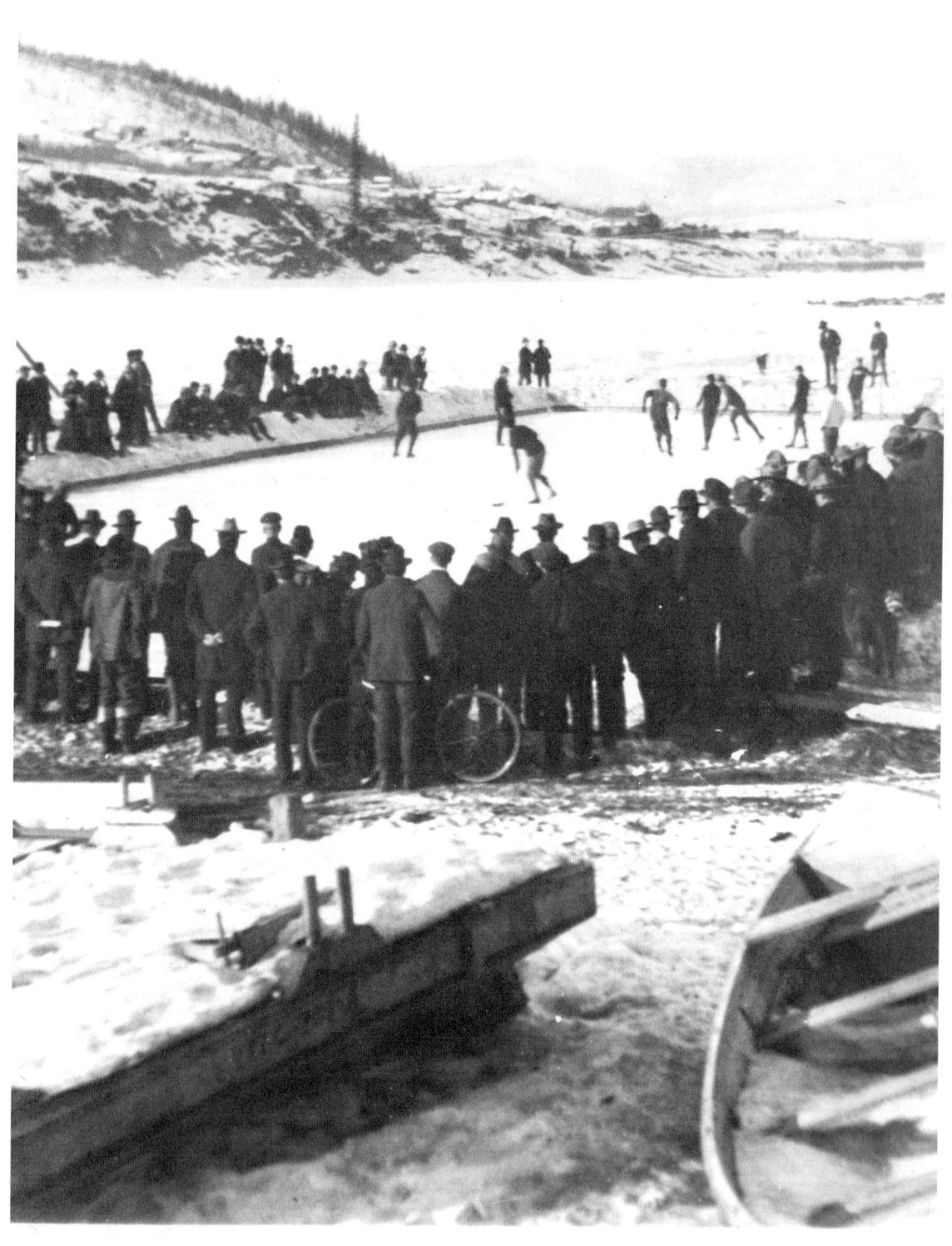

HOW IT ALL BEGAN
1917–1924

The family tree of the National Hockey League has its roots in the years around the turn of the century with branches spreading from the eastern provinces of Quebec and Ontario clear across the vast prairie land of Canada to the west and British Columbia.

It is rich with legendary hockey names— Frank and Lester Patrick, Edouard (Newsy) Lalonde, Fred (Cyclone) Taylor, Frank Nighbor, Joe Malone—men who built the game from pastime to profession and nurtured it from the frozen ponds in small mining towns to packed big-city arenas.

Hockey began as a seven-man game with upright posts embedded in the ice for goals. There were no nets, no blue lines, no red lines and no faceoff circles on the ice. But by the time the pioneers got through with it, the game closely resembled the sport we know today.

The Amateur Hockey Association of Canada and the Ontario Hockey Association were among the first organized hockey leagues in Canada. Players and teams freely shifted from league to league in those early years.

Finally, in 1910, there were two major leagues operating in competition with each

« *Hockey in the Yukon, circa 1900.*

other. The Canadian Hockey Association listed Ottawa, Quebec and three Montreal teams— the Shamrocks, the Nationals and All-Montreal. The National Hockey Association had teams in Cobalt, Haileybury and Renfrew and two in Montreal—the Wanderers and the Canadiens.

The bidding war for players was spirited. The Patrick brothers signed with Renfrew for $3,000 each and the same club lured Cyclone Taylor away from Ottawa and offered an Edmonton player $1,000 to come east for a single game.

Aware that the war would ruin them, the two leagues came to an understanding and merged into the single National Hockey Association, a seven-team league composed of Renfrew, Cobalt, Haileybury, Ottawa and three Montreal teams—the Shamrocks, the Wanderers and the Canadiens.

The Patrick brothers went west that year and organized their own league—the Pacific Coast Hockey Association, with franchises in Vancouver, Victoria and New Westminster. The Patricks were veterans of the teamhopping in the East and started player raids of their own to lure established stars to their new league. Many, including Taylor, Lalonde and Nighbor, went west.

With top talent migrating to it, the Pacific Coast Hockey Association gained stature and eventually a series was started, pitting the PCHA and NHA champions against each other in a playoff for the Stanley Cup.

In 1912, the NHA introduced six-man hockey and added numbers to players' jerseys. A year before, hockey's traditional two 30-minute periods had been switched to three periods of 20 minutes each. Slowly but surely, the sport was changing.

In 1913, the PCHA introduced blue lines, dividing the ice into three sections. It was the same year that, for the first time, assists as well as goals were credited to a player's scoring totals.

A year later, the NHA followed suit, crediting assists as well as goals. The Eastern circuit also allowed referees to start dropping the puck on faceoffs instead of placing it between the two sticks, thus saving a lot of bruised knuckles.

And in the West, a referee named Mickey Ion, destined to become one of the greatest officials in the history of the game, began picking an All-Star team—a custom which added considerable interest to the game.

In 1914, Canada went to war and with the conflict came problems for hockey. Many players were called up to serve in the Army and some were given deferments conditional upon their not playing hockey.

Train schedules were disrupted, causing cancellation of some games. The NHA clubs turned over the entire proceeds of their exhibition games to patriotic causes and a portion of the regular-season income to the Red Cross.

By 1917, the NHA had evolved into a six-team circuit composed of the Montreal Wanderers, Montreal Canadiens, Ottawa, Toronto, Quebec and the Northern Fusiliers—an Army team representing the 228th Battalion of the Canadian Army.

When the 228th was ordered overseas, it was forced to withdraw from the league, leaving five teams and an unbalanced schedule. After considerable bickering, it was decided that Eddie Livingstone's Toronto team would also be dropped and its players redistributed.

There is some evidence that Livingstone was not the most popular man among his fellow owners and it was their desire to rid themselves of him that led to the creation of the new league—the National Hockey League.

1917–18

Tired of intra-league squabbling, much of which had centered around the Toronto franchise and its combative owner, Eddie Livingstone, NHA owners met in Montreal's Windsor Hotel on November 22, 1917, to settle their problems once and for all.

Their solution was a simple one. They simply created their own league and left Livingstone in the NHA all by himself. The new circuit would be called the National Hockey League, with franchises going to Ottawa, the Montreal Wanderers, Montreal Canadiens and Toronto, provided Livingstone was not included in that team's operation. Quebec was also granted a franchise, but chose not to play that first year and its players were divided among the other four teams in what turned out to be the NHL's first intra-league draft.

Major Frank Robinson, president of the NHA, bowed out and Frank Calder, secretary-treasurer of the NHA, was elected president of the new league. A 22-game schedule, running from December 19 through March 10, was adopted.

Joe Malone, Quebec's best player, wound up with the Canadiens and on opening night he scored five goals as Montreal whipped Ottawa, 7–4. Malone, playing in only 20 games, won the first NHL scoring crown with 44 goals—a pace that has never been matched.

The Wanderers opened at home with a 10–9 victory over Toronto in a game that attracted only 700 fans. That was the only victory the Wanderers ever managed in the NHL. They dropped five straight games and then, on January 2, 1918, a $150,000 fire

burned Westmount Arena to the ground, leaving them without a home rink.

The Canadiens, who had shared the Arena with the Wanderers, moved into the 3,250-seat Jubilee rink for the remainder of the season but the Wanderers dropped out of the league with owner Sam Lichtenhein apparently happy to be out of what had been a losing venture.

Vancouver's Fred (Cyclone) Taylor was the Pacific Coast Hockey League's scoring champion in 1917–18.

Frank Calder was appointed president of the newly formed National Hockey League in 1917.

A major rule change was adopted during the NHL's first season that was to affect the art of goaltending forever. Until then, goalies had been forced to stand up to defend their nets and in 1914 a rule was added by the NHA imposing $2 fines on goalies who sprawled on the ice to make a save. Now the rule was changed and goalies were permitted to assume any position they wished.

If the rule helped, the statistics don't show it. The legendary Georges Vezina of the Canadiens led the league with 84 goals allowed in 21 games—a 4.0 average that is not very good by today's standards. In addition to Malone, the top shooters were Ottawa's Cy Denneny with 36 goals in 22 games, Reg Noble of Toronto with 28 in 20 and Newsy Lalonde of the Canadiens, who had 23 goals in 14 games.

The Canadiens, first-half champions, and Toronto, winners of the second half, played off for the NHL title with Toronto taking the two-game, total-goals playoff, 10–7.

In the West, the PCHA, cut back to three teams by the departure of Spokane, had a tight race almost all season. But Seattle finally finished two games in front of Vancouver and four up on Portland.

Vancouver's Cyclone Taylor led the league with 32 goals, including one game-winner against Seattle scored with his back to the goal. It was a routine play for Taylor, who boasted that he once scored a goal in the NHA by skating backwards through the whole Ottawa team.

In the two-game total-goals playoff between the top two teams, Vancouver defeated Seattle, 3–2. The Millionaires traveled east to face Toronto for the Stanley Cup and split the first four games. Then the Arenas captured the deciding fifth game and the Cup, 2–1, as Corbett Denneny scored the winning goal.

1917–18

The Canadiens' Joe Malone was the first NHL scoring champion, with 44 goals in 20 games in 1917–18.

FINAL STANDINGS

First Half

	W	L	T	PTS	GF	GA
Montreal C	10	4	0	20	81	47
Toronto	8	6	0	16	71	75
Ottawa	5	9	0	10	67	79
Montreal W.	1	5	0	2	17	35

Montreal Wanderers forced to withdraw from league after home rink burned down on January 2, 1918.

Second Half

	W	L	T	PTS	GF	GA
Toronto	5	3	0	10	37	34
Ottawa	4	4	0	8	35	35
Montreal C.	3	5	0	6	34	37

Toronto defeated Montreal Canadiens in playoffs and won regular-season championship.

LEADING SCORERS

	G
Malone, Montreal C.	44
Denneny, Ottawa	36
Noble, Toronto	28
Lalonde, Montreal C.	23
Denneny, Toronto	20
Pitre, Montreal C.	17
Cameron, Toronto	17
Darragh, Ottawa	14
Hyland, Montreal W-Ottawa	14
Gerard, Ottawa	13
Skinner, Toronto	13

No records of assists were compiled.

1918-19

The demise of the Wanderers the year before had left the NHL with just three teams—the Montreal Canadiens, Toronto Arenas and Ottawa Senators. There was, though, a possibility that Quebec, which had not operated in 1917–18, might join the league for its second season.

President Frank Calder, reelected for a five-year term, drew up two schedules for the new season—one for a three-team league, one for a four-team league.

When Quebec's ownership failed to meet an NHL deadline for declaring its intentions, the league suspended the franchise and went with the three-team schedule. With the end of World War I, it was expected that many players would be returning from the Army. But few were discharged in time and when the season started, the teams had much the same personnel as the year before.

The NHL adopted several important rule changes including the adoption of the PCHA's blue-line idea. This divided the ice surface into three zones with forward passing permitted in the 40-foot-wide center area. Kicking the puck was also allowed and assists were added to regular-season statistics. Penalty rules were reshuffled. A minor penalty would leave a team shorthanded for three minutes, a major penalty would cost five minutes and for a match penalty, no substitute would be allowed for the penalized player.

The 18-game regular season started on December 21 with Ottawa beating Montreal, 5–2. The Canadiens bounced back to lose only two more games and captured the first-half championship. Ottawa, a so-so 5–5 in the first half, won seven of eight games and took the second-half title.

Toronto, heavily favored after winning the Stanley Cup the year before, started in reverse, dropping six of its first seven games. The Arenas never righted themselves and finished in last place in both halves.

Newsy Lalonde, the Canadiens' fiery player-manager, won the scoring title with 21 goals and Ottawa's Clint Benedict was the top goalie with two shutouts and a 3.0 average in 18 games.

In the playoff between the Canadiens and Ottawa, Montreal dominated. Lalonde's team won the first three games, dropped the fourth and then wrapped up the series in the fifth game. The format had been changed from total goals in two games to a best-of-seven series.

In the PCHA, Portland's franchise was transferred to Victoria with Lester Patrick set as the team's player-manager. Lester's younger brother, Frank, was serving his sixth term as president of the league.

Seattle beat Vancouver in the opening game and held onto the league lead for six weeks before the defending champion Vancouver Millionaires took over. Vancouver won the regular-season title by one game and Cyclone Taylor again was the scoring champ with 23 goals—one more than Seattle's Bernie Morris.

There was a celebrated fight between Cully Wilson of Seattle and Vancouver's mild-mannered Mickey MacKay in which Wilson's cross-check broke MacKay's jaw. The incident cost Wilson a $50 fine, match penalty and eventual suspension from the league.

In the two-game, total-goals playoff, Seattle defeated Vancouver, 7–5, scoring six goals in the first game. That set up the Stanley Cup series against Montreal.

The NHL champion Canadiens dropped two of the first three games, played a scoreless tie in the fourth and then tied the series by winning the fifth. But the deciding sixth game was never played. The Canadiens' ranks had been shredded by the great influenza epidemic which covered the continent. Bad Joe Hall, a defenseman, was hospitalized, and four

others, including Lalonde, were confined to their hotel by the disease. The series was ended with no Cup winner—the only time in history that has happened. Hall never recovered. He died in a Seattle hospital.

1918–19

FINAL STANDINGS

First Half

	W	L	T	PTS	GF	GA
Montreal	7	3	0	14	57	50
Ottawa	5	5	0	10	39	40
Toronto	3	7	0	6	43	49

Second Half

	W	L	T	PTS	GF	GA
Ottawa	7	1	0	14	32	14
Montreal	3	5	0	6	31	28
Toronto	2	6	0	4	22	43

Montreal defeated Ottawa in playoffs and won regular-season championship.

LEADING SCORERS	G	A	PTS
Lalonde, Montreal C.	23	9	32
Cleghorn, Montreal C.	23	6	29
Nighbor, Ottawa	18	4	22
Denneny, Ottawa	18	4	22
Pitre, Montreal C.	14	4	18
Skinner, Toronto	12	3	15
Noble, Toronto	11	3	14
Cameron, Toronto-Ottawa	11	3	14
Darragh, Ottawa	12	1	13
Randall, Ottawa	7	6	13

1919–20

The player shuttle created between East and West when the Patrick brothers organized the Pacific Coast Hockey Association was in full swing.

Moving west from the NHL was a youngster used sparingly the year before by Toronto. But Jack Adams would one day be back and make his mark as a player, coach and executive in the NHL.

Alf Skinner and Rusty Crawford also jumped to the PCHA while Cully Wilson, a rough, tough right wing, who was banned from the coast league for his overly aggressive play, showed up in the NHL with Toronto. His style stayed the same and he was the most penalized player in the league that season, spending 79 minutes sitting out infractions.

« *Joe Hall starred on defense for the Canadiens before dying of influenza in the spring of 1919.*

Toronto's management, disturbed over the team's disappointing performance the year before, undertook a rebuilding job. The first step was to change the club's nickname from the Arenas to the St. Patricks, perhaps in an attempt to attract the luck of the Irish.

The Quebec Bulldogs operated their franchise and reclaimed players who had been assigned to other teams for the NHL's first two seasons. The most dominant was Joe Malone, who had won the scoring title in the league's first year of operation and now returned to Quebec from the Montreal Canadiens.

Malone was the standout on what was a dismal Quebec team. On January 31, he went on a tear of seven goals in a single game against Toronto, setting an NHL record that still stands. He almost matched that performance a little more than one month later when he scored six times against Ottawa in the final game of the season.

Malone finished the season with 39 goals and nine assists for 48 points and his second scoring title in three years. But despite his brilliance, Quebec won only four games all year and finished last. Newsy Lalonde of the Canadiens gave Malone a run for the scoring title with 37 goals and six assists for 43 points.

Ottawa's Clint Benedict was the top goalie, posting a 2.7 goals-against average and five shutouts for the 24-game season. No other netminder in the league recorded a single shutout that year.

With World War I over, Canadiens began paying more attention to hockey and crowds began growing in size. On February 21, Ottawa's game at Toronto attracted 8,500—a record.

Ottawa won both halves of the NHL's split schedule, eliminating the need for the play-offs. The Senators would represent the NHL in the battle for the Stanley Cup against either Seattle, the PCHA champion, or second-place Vancouver. Frank Foyston of Seattle had won the PCHA scoring crown and he led a 6–0 romp in the second game that gave Seattle the two-game, total-goals playoff over the Millionaires, 7–3.

Seattle's Frank Foyston won the PCHA scoring title in 1919–20.

Seattle traveled east to play Ottawa for the Cup but when the team arrived, there was a problem. Seattle's red, white and green uniforms closely resembled Ottawa's red, white and black. The conflict was resolved when the Senators agreed to change to white sweaters.

Ottawa took the Cup in five games—the last two played on Toronto's artificial ice after hot weather turned Ottawa's natural surface to slush.

1919–20

FINAL STANDINGS

First Half	W	L	T	PTS	GF	GA
Ottawa	9	3	0	18	59	23
Montreal	8	4	0	16	62	51
Toronto	5	7	0	10	52	62
Quebec	2	10	0	4	44	81
Second Half						
Ottawa	10	2	0	20	62	41
Toronto	7	5	0	14	67	44
Montreal	5	7	0	10	67	62
Quebec	2	10	0	4	47	96

LEADING SCORERS

	G	A	PTS
Malone, Quebec	39	9	48
Lalonde, Montreal C.	36	6	42
Denneny, Toronto	23	12	35
Nighbor, Ottawa	26	7	33
Noble, Toronto	24	7	31
Darragh, Ottawa	22	5	27
Arbour, Montreal C.	22	4	26
Wilson, Toronto	21	5	26
Broadbent, Ottawa	19	4	23
Cleghorn, Montreal C.	19	3	22
Pitre, Montreal C.	15	7	22

1920–21

Quebec's dismal showing the season before left the team's owners disenchanted and the Bulldogs faded from the NHL picture for the second and final time.

Percy Thompson of Hamilton, Ontario, purchased the franchise for $5,000, moved the club to Hamilton and changed the nickname to the Tigers. It was obvious that the same players who had failed in Quebec would not do much better in Hamilton and an SOS was sent out to the other teams in the league, asking for player help.

The last time that had happened was in 1917, the NHL's first season, when the undermanned Montreal Wanderers appealed for help. The other clubs refused then and the

Victoria's Ernie (Moose) Johnson was known as the man with the longest reach in hockey.

result was Montreal's eventual dropout from the league. It was perhaps with this in mind that the NHL responded favorably to Hamilton's plight.

Toronto contributed George (Goldie) Prodgers, Joe Matte and Cecil (Babe) Dye, Montreal ticketed Bill Couture to the Tigers and Joe Malone led the leftovers from Quebec which included Eddie Carpenter, George Carey and Tom McCarthy.

The makeshift team stung the Canadiens with a 5–0 shutout in its home opener on December 22. Dye scored two goals and Toronto promptly reclaimed him from Hamilton and shipped Mickey Roach to take his place with the Tigers.

The move turned out to be a smart one because Dye scored more goals than anyone in the league, finishing with 35. He had 37 total points, four less than Newsy Lalonde of the

Canadiens, whose 33 goals and eight assists for 41 points led the league. It was Lalonde's second scoring title and both times he won because his assists gave him more total points than the leading goal-scorer.

After the opening victory, Hamilton slipped badly and finished in the cellar for both halves of the season, managing only six victories in 24 games. Ottawa won the first-half title with an 8–2 record, three games better than Toronto's 5–5. But the Senators, saddled by a seven-game losing streak, slipped to third in the second half, behind both Toronto and the Canadiens.

Despite the second-half slump, Ottawa's Clint Benedict finished as the top goalie with a 3.1 goals-against average and two shutouts. In the NHL playoffs against second-half champ Toronto, Benedict and the Senators regained their touch. Ottawa shut out the St. Pats, 5–0,

in the opener and came back with a 2–0 whitewashing to sweep the series.

Vancouver won the PCHA title by one-half game over Seattle—the difference being a 4–4 tie which Seattle played at Victoria on March 4, Moose Johnson Night. Johnson, a veteran defenseman, was honored before the game and then the teams played through three overtimes before agreeing to let the game end as a tie.

In the two-game playoff, Vancouver romped, outscoring Seattle, 13–2. The Millionaires then met Ottawa for the Stanley Cup. The opening game attracted a record 11,000 fans. The teams split the first four games and then Ottawa won the fifth, 2–1, for the Cup.

1920–21

FINAL STANDINGS

First Half

	W	L	T	PTS	GF	GA
Ottawa	8	2	0	16	49	23
Toronto	5	5	0	10	39	47
Montreal	4	6	0	8	37	51
Hamilton	3	7	0	6	34	38

Second Half

	W	L	T	PTS	GF	GA
Toronto	10	4	0	20	66	53
Montreal	9	5	0	18	75	48
Ottawa	6	8	0	12	48	52
Hamilton	3	11	0	6	58	94

Ottawa defeated Toronto in playoffs and won regular-season championship.

LEADING SCORERS

	G	A	PTS
Lalonde, Montreal C.	33	8	41
Denneny, Ottawa	34	5	39
Dye, Toronto	35	2	37
Malone, Hamilton	30	4	34
Cameron, Toronto	18	9	27
Noble, Toronto	20	6	26
Prodgers, Hamilton	18	8	26
Denneny, Toronto	17	6	23
Nighbor, Ottawa	18	3	21
Berlinquette, Montreal C.	12	9	21

1921–22

This was a year of major changes for hockey in both the East and the West. The NHL dropped the split schedule and its first- and second-half champions, substituting instead a single schedule with playoffs between the top two teams. The PCHA introduced the penalty shot which was awarded to a player who was interfered with after breaking in alone on the goalie. There was a new league in the West and some new owners in the East.

George Kennedy, one of the founders of the NHL and owner of the Montreal club, died in 1921 and his widow sold the club to Joe Cattarinich and Leo Dandurand for $11,000. Cattarinich and Dandurand were anxious to get Sprague Cleghorn, a defenseman who had starred for the Wanderers, back to Montreal and they accomplished this in a roundabout fashion.

The NHL, still trying to help the Hamilton club, devised the plan which eventually brought Cleghorn to the Canadiens. Players with the Wanderers when the club dissolved in 1918, said the NHL, became the property of the league. Cleghorn was one of these players and the NHL simply claimed him from Ottawa and assigned him to Hamilton. Provided with this windfall, the Tigers promptly offered Cleghorn to the Canadiens, who, they knew, were anxious to get him.

A neat package was arranged with Billy Couture and Cleghorn going to Montreal in exchange for Harry Mummery, Amos Arbour and Cully Wilson. It was the first major, multiple-player trade in the NHL.

The trade reunited Sprague Cleghorn with his brother, Odie, and the two ran wild one week in January. Each scored four goals on January 14 against Hamilton and they combined for six goals against Ottawa a few days later. Interestingly, this spree came shortly after Newsy Lalonde walked out on the team, claiming he couldn't get along with his new bosses. Frank Calder, president of the league, mediated the dispute and, after missing four games, Lalonde returned. But his days in Montreal were numbered.

On February 1, Sprague Cleghorn almost wiped out the Ottawa team singlehandedly. He cut Eddie Gerard and Cy Denneny and charged Frank Nighbor. All three Ottawa players missed two games because of injuries and Cleghorn drew a match foul plus a $15 fine. Ottawa police tried to arrest him for assault in the wake of his one-man war.

Odie Cleghorn (right) was a star forward on the Canadiens and his older brother, Sprague, was a teammate on defense. »

Despite Cleghorn's rambunctious play, Montreal finished third behind Ottawa and Toronto. Harry (Punch) Broadbent of Ottawa established a record with at least one goal in 16 consecutive games and a total of 25 during the streak. He finished as the leading scorer with 32 goals and 46 points.

Toronto defeated Ottawa, 5–4, in the first game of the total-goals playoff and then battled the Senators to a scoreless tie in the second to clinch the Stanley Cup berth.

In the West, Jack Adams, playing center for Vancouver, led the PCHA in scoring with 25 goals. But Seattle, with Frank Foyston and Jim

Riley scoring 16 goals each, finished in first place.

In Victoria, a combative goalie named Norm Fowler was thrown out of two games within 10 days for fighting and the team's manager, Lester Patrick, made his debut as a goalie.

Vancouver won the playoff with goalie Hugh Lehman turning in a pair of 1–0 shutouts over Seattle.

A new league, the Western Canada Hockey League, with clubs in Calgary, Edmonton, Saskatoon and Regina, had been formed and its players included Red Dutton, Bill Cook and Dick Irvin. Regina finished second but knocked off pennant winner Edmonton in the playoff and challenged Vancouver for the right to represent the West in the Stanley Cup series against Toronto. Regina took the first game, 2–1, but Vancouver recovered with a 4–0 victory in the second game to clinch the playoff.

In the Stanley Cup series, Vancouver and Toronto split the first four games and then Babe Dye fired four goals, pacing a 5–1 St. Pats' victory that clinched the series and the Cup in the fifth contest.

1921–22

FINAL STANDINGS

	W	L	T	PTS	GF	GA
Ottawa	14	8	2	30	106	84
Toronto	13	10	1	27	98	97
Montreal	12	11	1	25	88	94
Hamilton	7	17	0	14	88	105

Toronto defeated Ottawa in playoffs and won regular-season championship.

LEADING SCORERS

	G	A	PTS
Broadbent, Ottawa	32	14	46
Denneny, Ottawa	27	12	39
Dye, Toronto	30	7	37
Malone, Hamilton	25	7	32
Cameron, Toronto	19	8	27
Denneny, Toronto	19	7	26
Noble, Toronto	17	8	25
S. Cleghorn, Montreal C.	21	3	24
O. Cleghorn, Montreal C.	17	7	24
Reise, Hamilton	9	14	23

1922–23

The split between Newsy Lalonde and Leo Dandurand could not be mended and eventually Montreal dealt its great star to Saskatoon of

Little Aurel Joliat came to the Canadiens in a big trade in 1922–23.

Toronto's Babe Dye had a five-goal game en route to the 1922–23 scoring title.

the new Western League. In return, the Canadiens received the rights to an amateur named Aurel Joliat, a slightly built left wing who belonged to Saskatoon but was playing with Iroquois Falls.

Joliat weighed about 140 pounds and was hardly an imposing athlete. The thought that Montreal had traded one of hockey's early greats for this little guy placed an extra burden on Joliat. But he was equal to it and was to develop into an outstanding NHL player.

In another trade, Montreal sent Bert Corbeau and Edmond Bouchard to Hamilton for Joe Malone, then in the twilight of his career. Vancouver swapped Jack Adams to Toronto for Corbett Denneny.

Joliat scored two goals in his first game for Montreal but Babe Dye had five for Toronto and the St. Pats beat the Canadiens, 7–2. It was the start of a fine season for Dye, who was to win the scoring title with 26 goals and 11 assists for 37 points.

Ottawa won the regular-season title, edging Montreal with Toronto finishing third. Clint Benedict again led the goalies with a 2.3 goals-against average and four shutouts in 24 games. It was the fifth straight year that he was the top goaltender.

Perhaps the most significant event of the season took place in Toronto's Mutual Street Arena in March 1923. That was when a young man named Foster Hewitt, sitting in an airless glass booth erected in three seat spaces and talking into an upright telephone, broadcast radio's first hockey game.

It was the start of a new era for the sport.

In the playoffs, Ottawa blanked the Canadiens, 2–0, in the first game and won the Cup berth on the basis of total goals although it lost the second game, 2–1. Billy Couture and Sprague Cleghorn played viciously in the opener, injuring several Ottawa players with their sticks and elbows. Owner Leo Dandurand was so disturbed at the display that he suspended both of them for the second game, without waiting for the league to act.

Lalonde flourished in the dual role of player-manager with Saskatoon and led the Western League in scoring with 29 goals in 26 games. But his team finished last, with Edmonton taking the regular-season title as well as the two-game, total-goals playoff over Regina.

The PCHA eliminated the position of rover and adopted six-man hockey which had been played in the East for some time. Victoria's Frank Fredrickson led the scorers with 41 goals in 30 games but Vancouver finished first and beat Victoria in the playoffs.

Ottawa, its ranks thinned by injuries, went west for the Stanley Cup playoffs and eliminated Vancouver in four games and then took Edmonton in two straight to clinch it. After watching the gritty show put on by the undermanned Senators, Frank Patrick, president of the PCHA, called them the greatest team he had ever seen.

1922–23

FINAL STANDINGS						
	W	L	T	PTS	GF	GA
Ottawa	14	9	1	29	77	54
Montreal C.	13	9	2	28	73	61
Toronto	13	10	1	27	82	88
Hamilton	6	18	0	12	81	110

Ottawa defeated Montreal Canadiens in playoffs and won regular-season championship.

LEADING SCORERS	G	A	PTS
Dye, Toronto	26	11	37
Denneny, Ottawa	21	10	31
Adams, Toronto	19	9	28
B. Boucher, Montreal C.	23	4	27
O. Cleghorn, Montreal C.	19	7	26
Roach, Hamilton	17	8	25
B. Boucher, Ottawa	15	9	24
Joliat, Montreal C.	13	9	22
Noble, Toronto	12	10	22
Wilson, Hamilton	16	3	19

1923–24

Until this year, hockey players had no individual trophy for which to compete. There was the scoring championship, of course, and the satisfaction of playing for the Stanley Cup winner for some, but no single award that a player could go after and call his own.

This all changed in 1924 when Dr. David Hart, father of Cecil Hart, a manager-coach of the Montreal Canadiens, contributed a trophy to the league. The Hart Trophy was to be awarded to the Most Valuable Player in the league and the first one went to Frank Nighbor, Ottawa's smooth-skating center.

Nighbor, whose pokecheck repeatedly relieved opponents of the puck, won the award by a single vote over Sprague Cleghorn, the Canadiens' boisterous defenseman.

It was ironic that Nighbor and Cleghorn were the top contestants for the first Hart Trophy. Their styles were a study in contrasts. Nighbor was a gentlemanly sort who rarely was involved in trouble on the ice while

Cleghorn seemed to cause a ruckus wherever he went.

In fact, Cleghorn's rough play caused an NHL meeting at midseason to consider his suspension. The Ottawa club claimed Cleghorn was trying to injure opponents deliberately, citing a spearing incident against Cy Denneny. The charges were rejected by the league and in Montreal's next game against Ottawa, Cleghorn charged Lionel Hitchman

Cy Denneny of Ottawa fell down a well, but climbed out and won the 1923–24 scoring crown.

into the boards and received a one-game suspension.

Ottawa's Denneny won the scoring crown with 22 goals despite a bizarre experience near the end of the season. The Ottawa club was on its way to Montreal for a game when the team train became snowbound. The Sena-

Frank Nighbor of Ottawa won the NHL's first Hart Trophy as the Most Valuable Player in 1923–24.

tors were stuck all night and Denneny, scrounging about for some food, somehow fell down a well. Luckily he emerged without injury. The game, of course, had to be postponed.

Georges Vezina of Montreal led the goalies with a 2.0 goals-against average and three shutouts, barely edging Clint Benedict. Ottawa took the regular-season title but Montreal beat the Senators in the total-goals playoff, 5–2, with a newcomer, Howie Morenz, starring.

In the PCHA, Seattle dropped eight straight games but came out of the slump and managed to win the regular-season crown. Mickey MacKay of Vancouver led the scorers with 23 goals and teammate Hugh Lehman was the top goalie with a 2.7 goals-against average for the 30-game season.

Calgary took the Western title and Bill Cook of Saskatoon was the scoring champ with 26 goals. Regina's Red McCusker had a 2.2 goals-against average, best among the goaltenders.

Vancouver eliminated Seattle in the PCHA playoff and Calgary ousted Regina in the Western series. Then Calgary earned a bye into the Stanley Cup finals by beating Vancouver in the three-game series before both teams came east to face Montreal.

The Canadiens whipped Vancouver, 3–2 and 2–1, in the semifinals and then defeated Calgary for the Cup, winning 6–1 and 3–0.

1923–24

FINAL STANDINGS

	W	L	T	PTS	GF	GA
Ottawa	16	8	0	32	74	54
Montreal C.	13	11	0	26	59	48
Toronto	10	14	0	20	59	85
Hamilton	9	15	0	18	63	68

Montreal defeated Ottawa in playoffs and won regular-season championship.

LEADING SCORERS

	G	A	PTS
Denneny, Ottawa	22	1	23
B. Boucher, Montreal C.	16	6	22
Joliat, Montreal C.	15	5	20
Dye, Toronto	17	2	19
G. Boucher, Ottawa	14	5	19
Burch, Hamilton	16	2	18
Clancy, Ottawa	9	8	17
Morenz, Montreal C.	13	3	16
Adams, Toronto	13	3	16
Noble, Toronto	12	3	15

THE YANKS ARE COMING
1924–1929

By 1924, the four-team National Hockey League had taken hold and fans were attracted to games in ever larger numbers. Hockey's popularity had grown to the point where NHL brass was seriously considering expansion into the United States. The Pacific Coast Hockey Association had been successfully operating American franchises at Seattle and Portland and there was reason to believe that a team in eastern U.S. would enjoy similar success.

There was no problem in finding a market for expanding the prospering league. Bids for franchises came from New York, Boston, Philadelphia and Pittsburgh. And Montreal interests were seeking a second team for that city. The league decided to move slowly on expansion, a policy that would continue for many years.

The groundwork for adding new teams was laid in 1924 when Thomas J. Duggan was granted options to operate two United States franchises. Duggan interested Boston sportsman Charles Adams and on October 12, 1924, final plans were made at Montreal's Windsor Hotel.

Adams would operate the Boston team with Art Ross, an NHL referee, chosen to manage

« *Reg Noble had to trade in his Toronto St. Pats' jersey for a Montreal Maroons' model.*

the club. Donat Raymond and Thomas Strachan were granted a second Montreal franchise and New York would get a team for the 1926 season. The price for a new franchise was $15,000.

The league was clearly moving forward and the best proof of that was to look at the stars. Men like Newsy Lalonde and Joe Malone, who had come to the NHL as established players, were gone and in their place was a new breed featuring Aurel Joliat and Howie Morenz, who started their professional careers in the NHL and established themselves as first-line players in that league.

But with expansion came problems for the National Hockey League and its struggle to survive was to undergo a severe test in its very first year of international operation.

1924–25

With the addition of the new Boston team, called the Bruins, and the Montreal Maroons, the NHL also expanded its schedule, upping the total from 24 to 30 games. And this change was to cause a minor rebellion and a player strike late in the season.

Hamilton's Red Green, one of the three players who scored five goals in a single game this season, was at the center of the squabble. The Tigers had won the regular-season race and under a new playoff plan, the first-place finishers were to meet the winners of a series between the second- and third-place teams.

But Green, acting as a spokesman for the Hamilton players, pointed out that he had signed a two-year contract the season before which called for a 24-game schedule and that now he had already played 30 and was being asked to play even more for the same salary. Green and his teammates wanted $200 each to play against the winner of the semifinal series between Toronto and the Montreal Canadiens. The Hamilton players went on strike.

Frank Calder, the NHL president, refused to yield and declared that the semifinal winner would represent the league in the Stanley Cup playoffs. On April 17, the NHL suspended the Hamilton players and fined them $200 each for their action.

The Maroons and Bruins had assembled teams composed mostly of the amateurs and old pros. Montreal came up with Clint Benedict and Harry Broadbent from Ottawa, Louis Berlinquette from Saskatoon and Reg Noble from Toronto, among others. Alf Skinner, Bernie Morris and Norm Fowler, all lured from the West, turned up with Boston.

The Bruins opened at home with a victory over the Maroons but then dropped 11 straight games. The Maroons inaugurated their new home, the Montreal Forum, by losing to their crosstown rivals, the Canadiens.

Toronto's Babe Dye won the scoring title with 38 goals and 44 points and Georges Vezina of the Canadiens was the top goalie with a 1.9 goals-against average and five shutouts. Billy Burch of Hamilton won the Hart Trophy as the league's MVP and a new award donated by Lady Byng, the wife of Canada's governor general, went to Frank Nighbor, the Hart winner the year before. The Lady Byng Trophy was awarded the player who best combined sportsmanship with effective play.

The Canadiens beat Toronto, 3–2 and 2–0, in the playoffs and because of Hamilton's stand, Montreal advanced to the Stanley Cup finals against Victoria, which had joined the WCHL with Vancouver when Seattle bowed out of the PCHA, leaving that league with just two teams.

Victoria finished third behind Saskatoon and Calgary and knocked both clubs off in the WCHL playoffs, with Jack Walker starring. Victoria defeated Montreal in the first two playoff games as Walker scored four goals. The Canadiens won the third game and then Walker set up two goals by Frank Fredrickson that gave the Westerners the fourth game and the Cup.

1924-25

FINAL STANDINGS

	W	L	T	PTS	GF	GA
Hamilton	19	10	1	39	90	60
Toronto	19	11	0	38	90	84
Montreal C.	17	11	2	36	93	56
Ottawa	17	12	1	35	83	66
Montreal M.	9	19	2	20	45	65
Boston	6	24	0	12	49	119

Montreal Canadiens defeated Toronto and Hamilton in playoffs and won the regular-season title.

LEADING SCORERS

	G	A	PTS
Dye, Toronto	38	6	44
Denneny, Ottawa	27	15	42
Joliat, Montreal C.	29	11	40
Morenz, Montreal C.	27	7	34
B. Boucher, Montreal C.	18	13	31
Adams, Toronto	21	8	29
Burch, Hamilton	20	4	24
R. Green, Hamilton	19	4	23
Day, Toronto	10	12	22
Herberts, Boston	17	5	22

1925-26

The Hamilton club was sold to a New York group which paid $75,000 for the franchise. The team was renamed the Americans and rented a new sports palace, Madison Square Garden, for its home ice.

The Amerks drew 17,000 fans on opening night in the Garden and big-league hockey became an instant success in New York.

A seventh team was added to the circuit with Odie Cleghorn, the longtime Canadiens' star, named to the NHL Board of Governors to represent the new team, the Pittsburgh Pirates.

Albert (Battleship) Leduc, a Canadiens' defenseman, scored against the New York Americans on the opening night of a new Madison Square Garden in 1925.

Cleghorn would also serve as playing-manager of the Pirates. The team, made up essentially of players from the United States Amateur League, fared remarkably well, with Cleghorn's rapid line changes always keeping fresh legs on the ice.

Pittsburgh spoiled the home opener of the Canadiens with a 1–0 victory and Montreal lost more than just a hockey game in that one. Midway through the game, the Canadiens' great goalie, Georges Vezina, collapsed on the ice from a high fever. Vezina, who had never missed a game in 15 years with the Canadiens, was suffering from tuberculosis and died four months later.

There were new stars around the league. Ottawa's Alex Connell had an amazing 15 shutouts and 1.2 goals-against average in 36 games and the Maroons introduced Nels Stewart, who played both center and defense, and won the scoring title with 34 goals in his rookie season. Stewart also captured the Hart Trophy and Frank Nighbor took the Lady Byng Trophy for the second consecutive year.

Ottawa won the regular-season title with two of the league's newest teams, the Maroons and the Pirates, finishing second and third. Boston was fourth and the New York Americans fifth, leaving the bottom two spots to Toronto and the Canadiens.

The Maroons eliminated Pittsburgh in the two-game, total-goals playoff, 6–4, and then whipped champion Ottawa as Clint Benedict shut out his former teammates, 1–0, in the final game.

In the West, the troubles of the old PCHA seemed to spread to the WCHL. Regina's franchise was shifted to Portland and the name Canada was dropped from the league's title, making it the Western Hockey League.

Bill Cook of Saskatoon and Dick Irvin of Portland tied for the scoring lead with 31 goals apiece and a youngster named Eddie Shore was a formidable force on defense with Edmonton, which edged Saskatoon for the regular-season title. Third-place Victoria eliminated Saskatoon and Edmonton in the playoffs and advanced to the Stanley Cup finals against the Montreal Maroons.

Nels Stewart and Clint Benedict dominated the final series as the Maroons captured the Cup. Stewart scored six goals in four games and Benedict shut out the Westerners three times.

The 1926 series was to mark the last time any league other than the NHL competed for the Stanley Cup. The floundering WHL folded its tent. Its players drifted east to the still-expanding National League, which was getting ready to add three more American teams.

1925–26

FINAL STANDINGS						
	W	L	T	PTS	GF	GA
Ottawa	24	8	4	52	77	42
Montreal M.	20	11	5	45	91	73
Pittsburgh	19	16	1	39	82	70
Boston	17	15	4	38	92	85
New York A.	12	20	4	28	68	89
Toronto	12	21	3	27	92	114
Montreal C.	11	24	1	23	79	108

LEADING SCORERS	G	A	PTS
Stewart, Montreal M.	34	8	42
Denneny, Ottawa	24	12	36
Herberts, Boston	26	5	31
Cooper, Boston	28	3	31
Morenz, Montreal C.	23	3	26
Joliat, Montreal C.	17	9	26
Adams, Toronto	21	5	26
Burch, New York A.	22	3	25
Smith, Ottawa	16	9	25
Nighbor, Ottawa	12	13	25

1926–27

Writers called this era the Golden Age of Sports, and the NHL was about to make itself a solid part of the scene which included baseball's Babe Ruth, tennis' Bill Tilden, football's Red Grange, boxing's Jack Dempsey and golf's Bobby Jones.

The success of the New York Americans at Madison Square Garden inspired the Garden owners to seek a franchise of their own, and they were awarded one. The team, called the Rangers, was one of three new clubs added to the NHL, the others being the Detroit Cougars and the Chicago Black Hawks. With the Western and Pacific Coast Leagues now defunct, there were plenty of players available.

The 10-team league was split into two divisions, the American and the Canadian. The four Canadian teams—Ottawa, Toronto, the

Rookie Nels Stewart of the Montreal Maroons won the scoring championship and MVP trophy in 1925–26.

Montreal Maroons and Montreal Canadiens—
and New York's Americans comprised the
Canadian Division. The American Division
listed the three new teams—the Rangers,
Detroit and Chicago—along with Pittsburgh
and Boston.

The players came from professional as well
as amateur ranks. A package deal was arranged
with the Western loop in which whole rosters
of players became available for a total of
$25,000 per club.

Bill Cook and his brother Bun both wound
up in New York, where Conn Smythe was
assembling the Rangers. Eddie Shore went to
Boston, where he would become perhaps the
greatest defenseman in NHL history. Detroit
came up with Frank Foyston and Frank Fredrickson while Dick Irvin and Mickey MacKay
landed in Chicago.

Smythe had a falling-out with the Garden
management and was dismissed before the
Rangers ever played a game. Lester Patrick was
brought in from the West to run the New York
team. Smythe went home to his native Toronto, determined to get even with the New York
brass. The last-place St. Pats were in trouble
and up for sale and Smythe raised $160,000
and made the deal. The club's name was
changed to the Maple Leafs and flourished
under Smythe's shrewd control.

In Montreal, the owners of the Canadiens
donated a trophy to the league in the memory
of Georges Vezina to be awarded annually to
the goaltender on the team which was the
least-scored-upon in the league. George Hainsworth, Vezina's successor with the Canadiens,
won the first one.

Howie Morenz took the Canadian Division
scoring title with 32 points, including 25
goals. Bill Cook of the Rangers scored 33 goals
and won the American Division scoring race
with 37 points. Herb Gardiner of the Canadiens was named the MVP and Hart Trophy
winner while Billy Burch of the New York
Americans got the Lady Byng.

Ottawa won the Canadian Division and the
Rangers took the American Division regular-
season titles. Six teams qualified for the
Stanley Cup playoffs with Ottawa and Boston

Duncan (Mickey) MacKay, a star forward from
the Vancouver Millionaires, joined the Chicago
Blackhawks in 1926–27.

The great Ranger line: (from left) Bill Cook, Frank Boucher and Bun Cook.

reaching the finals and the Senators winning in four games.

1926-27

FINAL STANDINGS

Canadian Division

	W	L	T	PTS	GF	GA
Ottawa	30	10	4	64	86	69
Montreal C.	28	14	2	58	99	67
Montreal M.	20	20	4	44	71	68
New York A.	17	25	2	36	82	91
Toronto	15	24	5	35	79	94

American Division

	W	L	T	PTS	GF	GA
New York R.	25	13	6	56	95	72
Boston	21	20	3	45	97	89
Chicago	19	22	3	41	115	116
Pittsburgh	15	26	3	33	79	108
Detroit	12	28	4	28	76	105

LEADING SCORERS

	G	A	PTS
Bill Cook, New York R.	33	4	37
Irvin, Chicago	18	18	36
Morenz, Montreal C.	25	7	32
Frederickson, Detroit-Boston	18	13	31
Dye, Chicago	25	5	30
Bailey, Toronto	15	13	28
Boucher, New York R.	13	15	28
Burch, New York A.	19	8	27
Oliver, Boston	18	6	24
Keats, Boston-Detroit	16	8	24

1927-28

There have been many hexes in sports history but none so mysterious as the eerie Curse of Muldoon which shackled the Chicago Black Hawks for 40 years. It was in 1927 that Pete Muldoon administered it.

Muldoon had been brought in to coach the new Chicago team when the NHL added three franchises in 1926. The team had done moderately well, winning 19 games in a 44-game season and finishing third to qualify for the playoffs. They were the highest-scoring team in the league with 115 goals but also allowed more goals than anyone else, 116.

So Muldoon was understandably distressed when Hawks' owner Fred McLaughlin dismissed him at the start of the 1927–28 season. In fact, Muldoon was said to be so distressed, he placed his curse on McLaughlin and the

Hawks. As comeuppance for his unjust dismissal, Muldoon told McLaughlin, Chicago would never win an NHL title.

Sour grapes one might say, but it's a fact that for 40 years the Hawks never did win the regular-season championship and only when they finally did make it was the curse wiped out.

Muldoon's successors didn't do nearly as well with the Hawks as he had done in their first season. Barney Stanley and Hugh Lehman split the job and Chicago managed only seven victories all season, finishing a dismal last in the American Division race won by Boston. The Canadiens finished first in the Canadian Division.

The individual stars were Hart Trophy winner Howie Morenz, the scoring champ with 33 goals and 51 total points, and Frank Boucher of the Rangers, who led the American Division with 35 points and won the Lady Byng Trophy.

George Hainsworth again won the goalie's Vezina Trophy but the most outstanding goaltending job was turned in by Alex Connell of Ottawa, who set a record with six straight shutouts and 446 minutes, nine seconds of scoreless hockey. Connell became the center of contention the night Lester Patrick went in to play goal.

The Rangers had advanced to the Stanley Cup final by eliminating Pittsburgh and Boston while the Montreal Maroons knocked off Ottawa and the Canadiens. The Maroons won the first game of the finals, 2–0.

Early in the second period of the next game, Nels Stewart fired a shot that caught Ranger goalie Lorne Chabot in the eye. Chabot could not continue and Patrick asked Eddie Gerard, manager of the Maroons, for permission to use Ottawa's Connell, who was in the stands watching the game, as a replacement.

Gerard refused and when Patrick asked permission to use a minor leaguer who was also in the stands, Gerard again refused. Patrick, seething, returned to the Ranger dressing room to tell his club what had happened.

"What do we do now?" he asked.

Ottawa's Alex Connell set an NHL record by registering six consecutive shutouts in 1927–28.

"How about you playing goal?" suggested Frank Boucher, half-kidding, half-serious.

Patrick, 44, had retired as a player several years earlier. But he mulled over Boucher's suggestion and said, "Okay, I'll do it."

The Rangers protected Lester like a piece of fine china. Patrick made 18 saves, allowed one goal and New York won the game in overtime.

After losing the next game, New York came back to win the final two games and the Stanley Cup.

1927-28

FINAL STANDINGS
Canadian Division

	W	L	T	PTS	GF	GA
Montreal C.	26	11	7	59	116	48
Montreal M.	24	14	6	54	96	77
Ottawa	20	14	10	50	78	57
Toronto	18	18	8	44	89	88
New York A.	11	27	6	28	63	128

American Division

	W	L	T	PTS	GF	GA
Boston	20	13	11	51	77	70
New York R.	19	16	9	47	97	79
Pittsburgh	19	17	8	46	67	76
Detroit	19	19	6	44	88	79
Chicago	7	34	3	17	68	134

LEADING SCORERS

	G	A	PTS
Morenz, Montreal C.	33	18	51
Joliat, Montreal C.	28	11	39
Boucher, New York R.	23	12	35
Hay, Detroit.	22	13	35
Stewart, Montreal M.	27	7	34
Gagne, Montreal C.	20	10	30
Bun Cook, New York R.	14	14	28
Carson, Toronto.	20	6	26
Finnigan, Ottawa	20	5	25
Bill Cook, New York R.	18	6	24
Keats, Chicago-Detroit	14	10	24

1928-29

A rule designed to hype hockey offenses was introduced in 1928, but instead it became the year of the goalie around the NHL. The new rule allowed forward passing in all three zones on the ice—that is, the defensive zone, the area between the blue lines, and the offensive zone. There was still no red line in the game and the ice was divided by only the two blue lines.

Previously, forward passing was allowed only in a team's defensive zone or center ice, but never in the offensive area. Eventually, the rule change would affect the game and open play up, but not this season.

In Montreal, little George Hainsworth almost obliterated the memory of the great Georges Vezina. In 44 games, goaltender Hainsworth recorded an incredible 22 shutouts.

Hainsworth allowed 43 goals all year—an average of less than one per game. The highest-scoring team in the league was Boston, winner of the American Division race. The Bruins scored a total of 89 goals—a shade over two per game.

One of Hainsworth's shutouts came against Ottawa on December 22, 1928, a special date for Montreal and for hockey. It marked the first NHL broadcast of a Montreal game and started an era that brought hockey into the home regularly. Arthur Dupont, founder of radio station CJAD, handled the French broadcast and columnist Elmer Ferguson did the English.

"The hockey people looked upon radio with a great deal of suspicion," noted Dupont. "They feared that if stories of the games came into the home without cost, it would ruin the attendance. So we were limited to a brief description of the third period and afterwards a summary of the entire game."

As it developed, of course, broadcasts increased hockey interest and now the radio-television industry plays a major role in the sport.

With the goalies dominating play, Toronto's Ace Bailey captured the scoring crown with 32 points—22 of them on goals. Carson Cooper of Detroit was the top scorer in the American Division with 18 goals and 27 points.

Hainsworth easily won the Vezina Trophy, but another goalie, Roy Worters of the New York Americans, took the Hart as MVP. The Rangers' Frank Boucher won the Lady Byng.

A new playoff arrangement matched the first-place, second-place and third-place teams in each division against each other. The winners of the series between second-place teams and the series between the third-place finishers clashed in the semifinal with that winner advancing to the Stanley Cup finals against the winner of the series between the two first-place clubs.

Toronto eliminated Detroit in two straight games and the Rangers knocked off the Americans in two straight. Then New York beat Toronto to advance to the finals against Bos-

Ace Bailey of Toronto took scoring honors in »
1928-29.

BOSTON BRUINS
WORLD CHAMPIONS
Stanley Cup Winners
AMERICAN DIVISION CHAMPIONS · PRINCE OF WALES TROPHY WINNERS
SEASON 1928-29

"DUTCH" KLEIN "BILL" CARSON GEO. OWEN   HARRY OLIVER   WIN GREEN, *trainer*   MYLES LANE   NORMAN "DUTCH" GAINOR   AUBREY "DIT" CLAPPER
PERCY GALBRAITH   EDDIE SHORE   "MICKEY" McKAY   ART ROSS, *mgr.*   FRED HITCHMAN   CY DENNENY   RALPH "COONEY" WEILAND
"TINY" THOMPSON

FINAL STANDING N.H.L., 1928-29							
AMERICAN DIVISION						Goals	
	P	W	L	D	Pts.	For	Agst.
BOSTON	44	26	13	5	57	89	52
N.Y. RANGERS	44	21	13	10	52	72	65
DETROIT	44	19	16	9	47	72	63
PITTSBURGH	44	9	27	8	26	46	80
CHICAGO	44	7	29	8	22	33	85

· Playoffs ·

— N.H.L. CHAMPIONSHIP —
SERIES "A"
MARCH 19 .. BOSTON 1, CANADIENS 0
MARCH 21 .. BOSTON 1, CANADIENS 0
MARCH 23 .. BOSTON 3, CANADIENS 2
SERIES "B" (2 GAMES - TOTAL GOALS)
MARCH 19 .. N.Y. RANGERS 0, N.Y. AMERICANS 0
MARCH 21 .. N.Y. RANGERS 1, N.Y. AMERICANS 0
SERIES "C" (2 GAMES - TOTAL GOALS)
MARCH 19 .. TORONTO 3, DETROIT 1
MARCH 21 .. TORONTO 4, DETROIT 1
SERIES "D" (2 OUT OF 3 GAMES)
MARCH 24 .. N.Y. RANGERS 1, TORONTO 0
MARCH 26 .. N.Y. RANGERS 2, TORONTO 1
STANLEY CUP (FINAL - 2 OUT OF 3 GAMES)
SERIES "E"
MARCH 28 .. BOSTON 2, N.Y. RANGERS 0
MARCH 29 .. BOSTON 2, N.Y. RANGERS 1

FINAL STANDING N.H.L., 1928-29							
CANADIAN DIVISION						Goals	
	P	W	L	D	Pts.	For	Agst.
CANADIENS	44	22	7	15	59	71	43
N.Y. AMERICANS	44	19	13	12	50	53	53
TORONTO	44	21	18	5	47	85	69
OTTAWA	44	14	17	13	41	54	67
MONTREAL	44	15	20	9	39	67	65

Charles F. Adams, PRESIDENT

Arthur H. Ross, VICE PRES. & GEN. MGR.

Ralph F. Burkard, TREASURER

Frank Ryan, PUBLICITY DIRECTOR

ton, which had eliminated the Canadiens. The Bruins won the Cup in two games as rookie goalie Tiny Thompson turned in his third playoff shutout in five games. Thompson allowed three goals in the five games, a playoff goals-against average of 0.60.

1928–29

	G	A	PTS
Bailey, Toronto	22	10	32
Stewart, Montreal M.	21	8	29
Cooper, Detroit	18	9	27
Morenz, Montreal C.	17	10	27
Blair, Toronto	12	15	27
Boucher, New York R.	10	16	26
Oliver, Boston	17	6	23
Bill Cook, New York R.	15	8	23
Ward, Montreal M.	14	8	22
Finnigan, Ottawa	15	4	19

FINAL STANDINGS

Canadian Division

	W	L	T	PTS	GF	GA
Montreal C.	22	7	15	59	71	43
New York	19	13	12	50	53	53
Toronto	21	18	5	47	85	69
Ottawa	14	17	13	41	54	67
Montreal M	15	20	9	39	67	65

American Division

	W	L	T	PTS	GF	GA
Boston	26	13	5	57	89	52
New York R.	21	13	10	52	72	65
Detroit	19	16	9	47	72	63
Pittsburgh	9	27	8	26	46	80
Chicago	7	29	8	22	33	85

3

A NEW WORLD
OF OFFENSE
1929–1942

The NHL had taken a firm hold in the 1920s, expanding from four teams to 10 and emerging as the sport's universally recognized major league. But in the '30s, problems would arise. There was the American Depression and the shock waves traveled right through the Canadian sport which had franchises in five United States cities. And there was the complaint that hockey was too defensive a game . . . that the offenses were stymied.

Lester Patrick, boss of the New York Rangers, agreed with the detractors to some extent.

"I believe in keeping the game wide open," said Patrick at the height of the debate over whether to remove all restrictions on forward passing. "Our followers are entitled to action . . . not for a few brief moments, but for three full 20-minute periods of a game.

"The open style of play calls for better stickhandling and speedier skating. What better system could the coaches and managers adopt to preserve and further popularize the fastest game in the world."

« *The Montreal Maroons' Clint Benedict: Hockey's first masked goalie.*

The NHL eventually went along with Patrick's ideas and, predictably, the game opened up considerably. The economic problems, however, caused several club shifts and a couple of franchise casualties.

But stickhandling and speed, the two qualities Patrick talked about, combined to give hockey a loyal core of fans that grew and grew, despite the Depression. The sport had its rough moments, it is true, but the game's brass, from NHL president Frank Calder on down, pulled it through the periods of crisis.

1929–30

It would take more than a Depression to stop Conn Smythe, who was determined to build the Toronto Maple Leafs into an NHL power, if for no other reason than to prove to Madison Square Gardens's owners just how valuable a man they had lost when they fired him three years before.

Smythe needed a bigger arena for his club but raising the money to build one was a problem. So Smythe solved the financial question by turning to the trade unions and

builders for help. As partial payment of wages, the workmen would receive stock in Maple Leaf Gardens.

The solution worked out beautifully for all parties. Smythe got his new arena and his shareholders had a part in what would become a highly successful sports and entertainment center.

But the Maple Leafs spent their next-to-last season in the old Arena Gardens and it was less than a success. They finished fourth in the Canadian Division even though they introduced a good-looking rookie named Charlie Conacher, who was destined for NHL stardom.

The new rules allowing passing in all three zones added scoring punch throughout the

league and Boston's Cooney Weiland was the leading pointmaker with 73, including 43 goals. The Bruins, with Weiland setting the pace, were the highest-scoring team in the league and their goalie, Tiny Thompson, allowed the fewest goals. The combination gave Boston a fantastic 38 victories in 44 games, including one record stretch of 14 straight victories. Naturally, the Bruins won the American Division title.

Hec Kilrea of Ottawa was the leading scorer in the Canadian Division with 58 points, three more than Nels Stewart of the Montreal Maroons, who won the Hart Trophy as MVP. Tiny Thompson broke George Hainsworth's three-year hold on the Vezina Trophy and Frank Boucher took the Lady Byng again.

While the Bruins won their division crown by 30 points, Ottawa and the two Montreal teams staged a three-way battle for Canadian Division honors. The Maroons and Canadiens both finished with 51 points and Ottawa had 50. The Maroons were recognized as the first-place team because they had more victories (23) than the Canadiens (21).

That was a break for the Canadiens because it meant the Maroons would have to face Boston's powerhouse in the opening Stanley Cup series. Sure enough, the Bruins eliminated the Maroons in four games while the Canadiens got past Chicago in the two-game, total-goals playoff. The Rangers eliminated Ottawa but then the Canadiens took the Rangers and stunned the Bruins, winning the Cup finale in two straight games.

Clint Benedict, the Maroons' great goalie, made hockey history by using the first face mask ever that season. It happened after Howie Morenz of the Canadiens had broken Benedict's nose with a shot. Benedict didn't stay with the protection, however, and it would be almost three decades before a goalie would try a mask again.

The 1929–30 scoring title went to Ralph (Cooney) Weiland of Boston.

《 Chicago's Johnny Gottselig chases puck in 1929 match against the Montreal Maroons.

Roy Worters of the New York Americans was the 1930–31 Vezina Trophy winner.

1929–30

FINAL STANDINGS

Canadian Division

	W	L	T	PTS	GF	GA
Montreal M.	23	16	5	51	141	114
Montreal C.	21	14	9	51	142	114
Ottawa	21	15	8	50	138	118
Toronto	17	21	6	40	116	124
New York A.	14	25	5	33	113	161

American Division

	W	L	T	PTS	GF	GA
Boston	38	5	1	77	179	98
Chicago	21	18	5	47	117	111
New York R.	17	17	10	44	136	143
Detroit	14	24	6	34	117	133
Pittsburgh	5	36	3	13	102	185

LEADING SCORERS

	G	A	PTS
Weiland, Boston	43	30	73
Boucher, New York R.	26	36	62
Clapper, Boston	41	20	61
Bill Cook, New York R.	29	30	59
Kilrea, Ottawa	36	22	58
Stewart, Montreal M.	39	16	55
Morenz, Montreal C.	40	10	50
Himes, New York A.	28	22	50
Lamb, Ottawa	29	20	49
Gainor, Boston	18	31	49

1930–31

The saga of how he financed Maple Leaf Gardens proved how determined Conn Smythe could be. In 1930, he decided that one of the things his Maple Leafs needed for improvement was a player of King Clancy's ability.

Smythe asked how much it would take to get Clancy away from Ottawa. A couple of players and cash . . . say about $35,000 . . . he was told.

The players Smythe had. The cash was another story. He had most of his assets tied up in the construction of the Leafs' new home. But if $35,000 was what he needed to get Clancy, Smythe decided he'd come up with it.

He raised some capital from friends, giving himself a little room to maneuver. Then he bet

The Detroit Falcons' Ebbie Goodfellow led the American Division with 48 points in 1930–31.

Herb Drury was a center for the Quakers, who lasted for one season, 1930–31, in Philadelphia.

the bundle on a longshot horse—his own Rare Jewel. Naturally, the horse won and Smythe had the price for Clancy.

Smythe's wheeling and dealing was typical of the problems of Depression-burdened owners. The Pittsburgh club was forced to move to Philadelphia because of poor attendance. The Pirates changed their name to the Quakers but were doomed anyway. They lasted just that season in Philadelphia.

In Detroit, the club changed its nickname from the Cougars to the Falcons in an effort to lift sagging interest. But with money in short supply, especially in the automobile capital, there was little left over to spend on watching hockey games.

Another step to inject interest around the league was the introduction of an All-Star team. The first squad selected was a study in immortals. The forward line included Howie Morenz of the Canadiens at center, his linemate Aurel Joliat at left wing and Bill Cook of the New York Rangers at right wing. The defensemen were Boston's Eddie Shore and King Clancy of Toronto. Charlie Gardiner of Chicago was picked as the goalie.

Morenz led the league in scoring with 28 goals and 51 points and won the Hart Trophy as the MVP. Frank Boucher took his fourth straight Lady Byng and Roy Worters of the New York Americans edged out Gardiner for the Vezina Trophy. Detroit's Ebbie Goodfellow led the American Division scorers with 48 points.

In the playoffs, division champs Boston and the Montreal Canadiens went five games before the Canadiens won. Three of the games went into overtime. Chicago eliminated Toronto and then whipped the Rangers, who had knocked off the Maroons.

In the final round, the Canadiens won their second straight Cup, coming from behind to beat the Black Hawks in the five-game playoffs.

Just as the Pittsburgh-Philadelphia franchise was in trouble in the American Division, the Canadian Division's Ottawa team had fallen on lean days. The Senators won just 10 games,

finished in last place and requested and were granted a one-year leave of absence from the league.

1930-31

FINAL STANDINGS

Canadian Division

	W	L	T	PTS	GF	GA
Montreal	26	10	8	60	129	89
Toronto	22	13	9	53	118	99
Montreal M.	20	18	6	46	105	106
New York A.	18	16	10	46	76	74
Ottawa	10	30	4	24	91	142

American Division

	W	L	T	PTS	GF	GA
Boston	28	10	6	62	143	90
Chicago	24	17	3	51	108	78
New York R.	19	16	9	46	106	87
Detroit	16	21	7	39	102	105
Philadelphia	4	36	4	12	76	184

LEADING SCORERS

	G	A	PTS
Morenz, Montreal C.	28	23	51
Goodfellow, Detroit	25	23	48
Conacher, Toronto	31	12	43
Bill Cook, New York R.	30	12	42
Bailey, Toronto	23	19	42
Primeau, Toronto	9	32	41
Stewart, Montreal M.	25	14	39
Boucher, New York R.	12	27	39
Weiland, Boston	25	13	38
Bun Cook, New York R.	18	17	35
Joliat, Montreal C.	13	22	35

1931-32

The departure of Ottawa and Philadelphia left the NHL with eight clubs, four in each division. The schedule was increased to 48 games per club in an effort to increase team income during the dreary Depression days.

It was a gala night in Toronto on November 12 when Conn Smythe proudly unveiled his new Maple Leaf Gardens. A crowd of 13,542 packed the arena for the game between Toronto and Chicago. But the Black Hawks, who had never won a game in Toronto before, spoiled the party by upsetting the Leafs, 3–1.

The anger that burned within Smythe against New York and the Ranger organization could not be extinguished until he built the Leafs into a powerhouse. This was to be the year for him to get even, although it didn't start out that way. Toronto slumped into last place after one month and Smythe hired Dick Irvin to replace Art Duncan as coach. Irvin had been fired by Chicago the year before but

Morenz won his second straight Hart Trophy as the MVP while Primeau ended Frank Boucher's four-year domination of the Lady Byng award. Charlie Gardiner of Chicago won the Vezina again and was named the All-Star goalie for the second time.

Jackson, a left wing, and Morenz, a center, both made the All-Star team along with right wing Bill Cook of the New York Rangers, whose 34 goals and 48 points led American Division scorers. The defensemen selected were Boston's Eddie Shore and bald-headed Ching Johnson of the Rangers, who delighted in breaking up the rushes of Montreal's Aurel Joliat by sweeping the little guy's cap off his head.

Toronto finished second behind the Canadiens in the Canadian Division while the Rangers won the American Division crown. Now, if only the playoffs worked out properly, Smythe thought, he'd finally have a chance at his revenge.

After Chicago's Charlie Gardiner shut out Toronto in the first game, the Leafs exploded for a 6–1 victory to eliminate the Black Hawks on total goals. The Maroons beat Detroit in the other quarterfinal while, happily for Smythe, the Rangers advanced to the finals by eliminating the Canadiens.

Toronto got past the Maroons in the two-game, total-goals semifinal and now it was the Leafs and the Rangers for the Stanley Cup. Conacher, Primeau, Hap Day and the other Leafs ran wild, beating the Rangers in three straight games and scoring six goals in each of them. The Stanley Cup was the ultimate ornament to adorn Smythe's new Maple Leaf Gardens. Conn's revenge was served!

Toronto's Joe Primeau ended Frank Boucher's hold on the Lady Byng Trophy in 1931–32.

when he took over the Leafs, they acted like a brand-new club.

Toronto soared from last to first place with Charlie Conacher, Harvey Jackson and Joe Primeau providing the fire-power. Jackson won the Canadian Division scoring title with 53 points, three more than Primeau. Conacher finished fourth with 48 and only Howie Morenz managed to squeeze his way between the Toronto trio with 49 points.

1931–32

FINAL STANDINGS

Canadian Division	W	L	T	PTS	GF	GA
Montreal C.	25	16	7	57	128	111
Toronto	23	18	7	53	155	127
Montreal	19	22	7	45	142	139
New York A.	16	24	8	40	95	142
American Division						
New York R.	23	17	8	54	134	112
Chicago	18	19	11	47	86	101
Detroit	18	20	10	46	95	108
Boston	15	21	12	42	122	117

LEADING SCORERS	G	A	PTS
Jackson, Toronto	28	25	53
Primeau, Toronto	13	37	50
Morenz, Montreal C.	24	25	49
Bill Cook, New York R.	34	14	48
Conacher, Toronto	34	14	48
Trottier, Montreal M.	26	18	44
Smith, Montreal M.	11	33	44
Siebert, Montreal M.	21	18	39
Clapper, Boston	17	22	39
Joliat, Montreal C.	15	24	39

1932–33

In an effort to tighten belts during the height of the Depression, NHL owners decided

A former Canadiens' star, Newsy Lalonde returned to coach his old team in 1932–33.

to put a ceiling of $70,000 on club payrolls with no single player to be paid more than $7,500. That represented a 10 percent slice for most teams and the players staged a small revolution over the move.

There were big-name holdouts all over the league, including Frank Boucher of the Rangers, Reg Noble and Hap Emms of Detroit, the Canadiens' Aurel Joliat, Lorne Chabot of Toronto and Hooley Smith of the Montreal Maroons. President Frank Calder was given permission to suspend the dissidents but eventually all of the holdouts fell into line.

Seat prices were slashed, too. The top price was $3 and fans could get into most arenas for as little as 50 cents.

Ottawa returned to the league after a one-year hiatus with Cy Denneny as its coach. Other great former players also turned up as coaches: Newsy Lalonde with the Canadiens and Jack Adams in Detroit, where the team was about to adopt its third name, the Red Wings. In New York, Colonel John Hammond, who was instrumental in bringing hockey to Madison Square Garden, first with the Americans and then with the Rangers, resigned. As a result, coach Lester Patrick took on the added titles of general manager and vice president of the Rangers.

Before the season started, the Rangers sold goalie John Ross Roach to Detroit for $11,000. It was a worthwhile investment for the Cougars-Falcons-Red Wings. Roach was named the All-Star goalie on a team that included Bill Cook and Frank Boucher of the Rangers, and Baldy Northcott of the Montreal Maroons up front, and a defense of Boston's Eddie Shore and the Rangers' Ching Johnson.

Cook took the scoring title with 50 points, 28 of them goals, Boucher reclaimed the Lady Byng and Shore became the first fulltime defenseman to win the Hart Trophy. Boston's Tiny Thompson took the Vezina.

The Bruins and Detroit ended with identical records of 25–15–8 in the American Division with Boston recognized as the champion because the Bruins had scored more goals (124) than the Red Wings (111). Toronto won the Canadian Division race.

NIGHT 8.30 "CLANCY NIGHT"

The King

The World's Best

MAPLE LEAF GARDENS   MARCH 17TH 1934

Toronto fans stepped out to honor their King Clancy.

In the playoffs, the Maple Leafs eliminated the Bruins in five games. It was one of the most memorable playoff series as four of the games went into overtime and the final one lasted six extra periods.

Detroit eliminated the Montreal Maroons and the Rangers ousted the Canadiens in the quarterfinals. Then New York finished Detroit off and went up against the bone-weary Leafs in the final series.

With Toronto softened up by the prolonged series against Boston, the Rangers had an easy time, winning in four games. The heroes were the Cook brothers, Bill and Bun, and their center, Frank Boucher, all of whom had been signed for New York by Toronto's boss, Conn Smythe.

1932–33

FINAL STANDINGS

Canadian Division

	W	L	T	PTS	GF	GA
Toronto	24	18	6	54	119	111
Montreal M.	22	20	6	50	135	119
Montreal C.	18	25	5	41	92	115
New York A.	15	22	11	41	91	118
Ottawa	11	27	10	32	88	131

American Division

	W	L	T	PTS	GF	GA
Boston	25	15	8	58	124	88
Detroit	25	15	8	58	111	93
New York R.	23	17	8	54	135	107
Chicago	16	20	12	44	88	101

LEADING SCORERS

	G	A	PTS
Bill Cook, New York R.	28	22	50
Jackson, Toronto	27	17	44
Northcott, Montreal M.	22	21	43
Smith, Montreal M.	20	21	41
Haynes, Montreal M.	16	25	41
Joliat, Montreal C.	18	21	39
Barry, Boston	24	13	37
Bun Cook, New York R.	22	15	37
Stewart, Boston	18	18	36
Morenz, Montreal C.	14	21	35

1933–34

Eddie Shore was the epitome of a hockey bad man. He was a no-nonsense guy who was the scourge of the Bruins' blue line—the most feared defenseman in hockey. And in December 1933, Shore was part of one of the most dramatic incidents in the game's history.

The Bruins were at home against Toronto, with the Maple Leafs leading, 1–0, when a pair of quick penalties left Toronto two men short. Dick Irvin sent defensemen King Clancy and Red Horner and forward Ace Bailey out to kill the time.

Bailey, a former scoring champ, was an excellent puckcarrier and stickhandler—just what the Leafs needed with the Bruins enjoying a two-man edge. He won a faceoff and dodged Boston skaters, protecting the puck for a full minute before another faceoff was called because Ace was not advancing the puck.

Bailey won the second faceoff as well, again stickhandled for awhile and finally shot the puck into the Bruins' end, forcing Boston to retreat. Shore picked the rubber up and started up ice. Clancy met him and dumped him, regaining the puck for Toronto. As Shore slowly got up, he saw Bailey, still winded from his earlier one-man show, in front of him.

Eddie set sail for the Leaf star, caught him from behind and flipped him with his shoulder. Bailey hit the ice with a dull thud and lay motionless, seriously injured. When Shore grinned at Horner, skating to Bailey's aid, Red decked the Bruin defenseman with an uppercut.

Bailey hovered between life and death for several days with a severe head injury. He finally pulled through but never played hockey again. In February, Maple Leaf Gardens hosted a benefit game for Bailey between Toronto and a team of NHL All-Stars. The meeting at center ice between Bailey and Shore was shrouded in silence until the two embraced. That hug brought a thunderous roar from the crowd and eased the tension that had been building before the meeting.

"I know it was an accident," said Bailey, exonerating Shore.

Toronto's Kid Line—Harvey (Busher) Jackson, Joe Primeau, and Charlie Conacher—was challenging the Cooks and Frank Boucher of the Rangers as the top scoring line in the league. The Toronto unit finished 1–2–3 in scoring in the Canadian Division with Conacher leading the league with 52 points including 32 goals, Primeau scoring 46 points and Jackson 38. Boucher's 44 points led American Division scorers.

Conacher, Primeau and Boucher were named to the NHL All-Star team along with defensemen Clancy of Toronto and Lionel Conacher, Charlie's brother, of Chicago, and Black Hawk goalie Charlie Gardiner. Aurel Joliat of the Canadiens was the MVP and Boucher, as usual, won the Lady Byng. The Vezina went to Chicago's Gardiner, who starred in the playoffs and led the Hawks to the Stanley Cup.

Toronto finished first in the Canadian Division but lost in the playoffs to Detroit, the American Division pennant winners. Chicago eliminated the Canadiens and then the Montreal Maroons, who had finished off the Rangers.

Chicago took the Stanley Cup from Detroit in four games. Two of them went into double overtime with Gardiner shutting out the Red Wings in the last one.

In the celebration that followed the victory, Chicago's Roger Jenkins wheeled Gardiner through the city's Loop section in a wheelbarrow, never dreaming his buddy would be dead from a brain hemorrhage a scant eight weeks later.

1933–34

FINAL STANDINGS

Canadian Division

	W	L	T	PTS	GF	GA
Toronto	26	13	9	61	174	119
Montreal C.	22	20	6	50	99	101
Montreal M.	19	18	11	49	117	122
New York A.	15	23	10	40	104	132
Ottawa	13	29	6	32	115	143

American Division

	W	L	T	PTS	GF	GA
Detroit	24	14	10	58	113	98
Chicago	20	17	11	51	88	83
New York R.	21	19	8	50	120	113
Boston	18	25	5	41	111	130

LEADING SCORERS	G	A	PTS
Conacher, Toronto	32	20	52
Primeau, Toronto	14	32	46
Boucher, New York R	14	30	44
Barry, Boston	21	17	38
Dillon, New York R	13	26	39
Stewart, Boston	21	17	38
Jackson, Toronto	20	18	38
Joliat, Montreal C	22	15	37
Smith, Montreal M	18	19	37
Thompson, Chicago	20	16	36

1934–35

The Ottawa franchise, still floundering after two more last-place finishes, was shifted to St. Louis, where the team was christened the Eagles. In a shift almost as momentous, the legendary Howie Morenz was dealt to Chicago.

Morenz and Montreal had been synonymous and the great center never acclimated himself to his new team. He finished the season with a mere eight goals, far down in the American Division scoring list. Syd Howe, who split the season between Detroit and St. Louis, led the American Division scorers with 47 points while Charlie Conacher of Toronto and his linemate, Busher Jackson, were 1–2 in Canadian Division scoring. Conacher won the title with 57 points and Jackson finished second with 44.

The penalty shot, long a popular feature of Western League hockey, was introduced in the NHL, which now had several Western figures in its coaching ranks. There was Lester Patrick in New York, Dick Irvin in Toronto, Jack Adams in Detroit and Lester's brother, Frank Patrick, in Boston.

Scotty Bowman, purchased by Detroit along with Howe for $50,000 from St. Louis in midseason, was the first player ever to score on a penalty shot in the NHL. It came against Alex Connell, the Montreal Maroons' great goalie.

A couple of new names made their first appearances on the All-Star team. They were goalie Lorne Chabot, acquired by Chicago from Toronto to replace the deceased Gardiner, and defenseman Earl Seibert of the New York Rangers. Also chosen were Boston's Eddie Shore on defense and a forward line of

Ranger Frank Boucher took permanent possession of the original Lady Byng Trophy in 1934–35.

Toronto's Charlie Conacher won the scoring crown and led the Maple Leafs to the top of the Canadian Division in 1934-35.

Charlie Conacher and Busher Jackson from Toronto and Frank Boucher of the Rangers.

Chabot won the Vezina Trophy and Shore took the Hart Trophy. Frank Boucher won the Lady Byng for the seventh time in eight years and was awarded permanent possession of the trophy, which would be replaced by a new one.

Toronto, with the Conacher-Jackson-Joe Primeau "Kid Line" dominating the league, easily won the Canadian Division title while Boston squeezed past Chicago by one point to take the American Division.

In the playoffs, the Maple Leafs dropped the opener to Boston and then beat the Bruins three straight to advance to the Stanley Cup finals. Meanwhile, the Montreal Maroons eliminated Chicago on consecutive shutouts by Alex Connell and then knocked off the Rangers, who had topped the Canadiens.

In the final round, it was a matchup of two hot goalies—Connell of the Maroons and George Hainsworth of Toronto, who had allowed Boston just two goals in four games in the opening round. Connell proved to be hotter, giving up only four goals as the Maroons captured the Stanley Cup with three straight victories.

1934–35

FINAL STANDINGS

Canadian Division

	W	L	T	PTS	GF	GA
Toronto	30	14	4	64	157	111
Montreal M.	24	19	5	53	123	92
Montreal C.	19	23	6	44	110	145
New York A.	12	27	9	33	100	142
St. Louis	11	31	6	28	86	144

American Division

	W	L	T	PTS	GF	GA
Boston	26	16	6	58	129	112
Chicago	26	17	5	57	118	88
New York R.	22	20	6	50	137	139
Detroit	19	22	7	45	127	114

LEADING SCORERS

	G	A	PTS
Conacher, Toronto	36	21	57
Howe, Detroit-St. Louis	22	25	47
Aurie, Detroit	17	29	46
Boucher, New York R.	13	32	45
Jackson, Toronto	22	22	44
Lewis, Detroit	16	27	43
Chapman, New York A.	9	34	43
Barry, Boston	20	20	40
Schriner, New York A.	18	22	40
Stewart, Boston	21	18	39
Thompson, Chicago	16	23	39

Boston's Tiny Thompson recorded an historic goalie assist in 1935–36.

1935–36

The St. Louis franchise was dissolved only one year after being moved from Ottawa. This reduced the NHL to eight teams, four in each division. The Eagles' players were distributed to other clubs around the league and there were some good ones available. Boston probably came up with the best in Bill Cowley, who developed into a star.

Carl Voss, who had started in the league with the New York Rangers three seasons earlier, continued to move from club to club. Voss had already played with the New York Rangers, Detroit, Ottawa and St. Louis and that season moved on to the New York Americans after the Eagles folded. He would also play for the Montreal Maroons and Chicago Black Hawks before ending his career after six years in the NHL.

The Americans boasted the league's top scorer, second-year man Dave (Sweeney) Schriner, a left wing, who had 45 points, including 19 goals. The leading scorer in the American Division was Detroit's Marty Barry, with 21 goals and a total of 40 points.

Schriner was named to the All-Star team along with Toronto's Charlie Conacher and Hooley Smith of the Montreal Maroons, Boston defensemen Eddie Shore and Babe Siebert and Tiny Thompson, the Bruins' goalie.

Thompson also won the Vezina Trophy and wrote his name in the record book as the first goalie to assist on a scoring play. It happened on a goal by defenseman Siebert, who scored after taking a pass from the goalie.

Eddie Shore won the Hart Trophy, his third MVP award in four years, while Chicago's Doc Romnes took the Lady Byng. The Black Hawks

also had the league's hottest rookie, an American-born goalie named Mike Karakas, who stepped in when Lorne Chabot was injured and played so well that the Hawks sold Chabot to the Maroons. Chicago also dealt Howie Morenz to the Rangers, a move that still left the great center homesick for Montreal.

The Montreal Maroons won the Canadian Division race by two points over Toronto while Detroit had an easier time, taking the American Division by six points over Boston. The opening game of the Stanley Cup playoffs between the Maroons and Red Wings was a memorable one.

The goalies, Detroit's Norm Smith and Lorne Chabot of the Maroons, played shutout hockey through the 60-minute regulation game and the scoreless tie lasted through five periods of overtime. Finally, with $3\frac{1}{2}$ minutes remaining in the sixth extra period, Modere (Mud) Bruneteau put a shot past Chabot. The Arena clock read 2:25 A.M. and the goal ended 176 minutes, 30 seconds of play. It remains the longest game ever played.

The Red Wings went on to win the next two games, eliminating the Maroons. Toronto ousted Boston and then downed the Americans, who had beaten Chicago. Then Detroit took the Maple Leafs in the four-game finale to capture the Stanley Cup.

1935–36

Defenseman Eddie Shore of the Bruins was MVP in 1935–36.

FINAL STANDINGS

Canadian Division

	W	L	T	PTS	GF	GA
Montreal M	22	16	10	54	114	106
Toronto	23	19	6	52	126	106
New York A.	16	25	7	39	109	122
Montreal C.	11	26	11	33	82	123

American Division

	W	L	T	PTS	GF	GA
Detroit	24	16	8	56	124	103
Boston	22	20	6	50	92	83
Chicago	21	19	8	50	93	92
New York R.	19	17	12	50	91	96

LEADING SCORERS

	G	A	PTS
Schriner, New York A.	19	26	45
Barry, Detroit	21	19	40
Thompson, Chicago	17	23	40
Thoms, Toronto	23	15	38
Conacher, Toronto	23	15	38
Smith, Montreal M.	19	19	38
Romnes, Chicago	13	25	38
Chapman, New York A.	10	28	38
Lewis, Detroit	14	23	37
Northcott, Montreal M.	15	21	36

1936–37

It was a year for the great lines. Two immortal ones broke up and another one was reunited, but with a tragic outcome.

In New York, the famous Bill Cook-Frank Boucher-Bun Cook unit was finished when the Rangers sold Bun Cook to Boston. The trio had scored more than 1,000 points playing together for the Rangers ever since the team came into the league a decade earlier. In Toronto, Joe Primeau announced his retirement, breaking up the Kid Line he had comprised along with Charlie Conacher and Busher Jackson.

In Montreal, the Canadiens brought Howie Morenz back from his two years of exile in Chicago and New York and no one was happier about the move than the veteran center.

Reunited with is old linemates, Aurel Joliat and Johnny Gagnon, Morenz played inspired hockey. He had scored 20 points at midseason when tragedy struck. Going into a corner after the puck, Morenz got his skates caught in a rut in the ice and snapped a bone in his leg.

The accident and his ability to overcome it weighed heavily on Morenz' mind as he lay in a Montreal hospital. Two months later, on March 8, his heart gave out and he died.

The funeral services were held at center ice in the Montreal Forum and 25,000 fans, many of them in tears, filed past his bier to pay their last respects to one of hockey's truly great stars.

The New York Americans, with owner Bill Dwyer in deep financial trouble, had their franchise taken over by the league. NHL president Frank Calder was to act as advisor to the club.

Calder also introduced a trophy to be awarded annually to the league's top rookie. The first one went to Toronto's Syl Apps, a pole vaulter at the 1936 Berlin Olympics who turned pro with the Leafs after returning from the Games. Apps finished second in the Canadian Division scoring race with 45 points, one less than Sweeney Schriner of the New York Americans, who captured his second straight

The Hart Trophy was awarded to the Canadiens' Babe Siebert in 1936–37.

scoring crown. Detroit's Marty Barry led American Division scorers with 44 points.

The Red Wings dominated the All-Star team, gaining four of the six spots. Detroit's Larry Aurie was named at right wing, Marty Barry at center, Ebbie Goodfellow at one defense post and Norm Smith at goal. Toronto's Busher Jackson at left wing and defenseman Babe Siebert of the Montreal Canadiens were the only non-Red Wings named. Siebert won the Hart Trophy, Barry the Lady Byng and Smith the Vezina.

The Canadiens edged the Montreal Maroons for the Canadian Division title while Detroit won the American Division race. In the playoffs, the Red Wings beat the Canadiens in the first two games, then dropped two straight before winning the decisive fifth game.

The New York Rangers first eliminated Toronto and then the Maroons, who had beaten Boston. In the Stanley Cup finals, Marty Barry and substitute goalie Earl Robertson helped the Red Wings come from behind with two straight victories to capture the five-game series.

1936–37

FINAL STANDINGS

Canadian Division

	W	L	T	PTS	GF	GA
Montreal C.	24	18	6	54	115	111
Montreal M.	22	17	9	53	126	110
Toronto	22	21	5	49	119	115
New York A.	15	29	4	34	122	161

American Division

Detroit	25	14	9	59	128	102
Boston	23	18	7	53	120	110
New York R.	19	20	9	47	117	106
Chicago	14	27	7	35	99	131

LEADING SCORERS

	G	A	PTS
Schriner, New York A.	21	25	46
Apps, Toronto	16	29	45
Barry, Detroit	17	27	44
Aurie, Detroit	23	20	43
Jackson, Toronto	21	19	40
Gagnon, Montreal C.	20	16	36
Gracie, Montreal M.	11	25	36
Stewart, Boston-New York A.	23	12	35
Thompson, Chicago	17	18	35
Cowley, Boston	13	22	35

1937–38

Clem Loughlin had set a longevity record by lasting three seasons in the revolving door for

Toronto's Syl Apps, a former Olympic pole vaulter, was the 1936–37 Rookie of the Year.

coaches operated by Chicago's boss, Major Fred McLaughlin. In 10 years, McLaughlin had employed an even dozen coaches—11 of them over the first seven seasons. When Loughlin was shown to the exit door in 1937, he was replaced by a baseball umpire and hockey referee named Bill Stewart, who would pilot Chicago to its first Stanley Cup.

A baseball umpire? Well, McLaughlin was like that, often depending for advice in running his hockey club with distinctly un-hockey types. Stewart, at least, did have some refereeing in his background.

In Boston, the Bruins assembled a new line destined for a long run of glory. Milt Schmidt was the center and his wingmen were Bobby Bauer and Woody Dumart—The Kraut Line.

Lester Patrick, coach of the New York Rangers, brought up his son, Muzz, to join his brother, Lynn, and give the Rangers three Patricks. New York also added a rookie named Bryan Hextall who was to star during the war years and later see both his sons play in the NHL.

Toronto's Gordie Drillon won the scoring title with 52 points, 26 of them goals. Drillon was part of considerable confusion caused by the similarity in name with another fine right wing, Cecil Dillon of the Rangers. In fact, both were selected to the All-Star team—the only time in history that two players were chosen for the same position on the first team.

The other All-Stars were left wing Paul Thompson of Chicago, who led American Division scorers with 44 points, Boston's Bill Cowley at center, defensemen Eddie Shore of the Bruins and Babe Siebert of the Montreal Canadiens and Boston's Tiny Thompson, Paul's brother, in goal.

Shore recaptured the MVP Hart Trophy, his fourth in six years, Drillon was the Lady Byng winner and Tiny Thompson took the Vezina for the fourth time. Chicago's Cully Dahlstrom won the Calder Trophy as the top rookie.

Toronto and Boston won the division championships and the Maple Leafs whipped the Bruins in three straight games to advance to the final round of the Stanley Cup playoffs.

The Rangers' Cecil Dillon shared an All-Star berth with Toronto's Gordie Drillon in 1937–38.

Meanwhile, in an intra-city showdown, the New York Americans eliminated the Rangers and reached the semifinals against Chicago, which had come from behind to beat the Montreal Canadiens. The Black Hawks ousted the Americans and found themselves up against Toronto's powerhouse for the Stanley Cup.

Against Toronto, the Hawks were simply in over their heads. They had won just 14 of 48 games during the regular season and made the playoffs by only two points. Toronto, on the other hand, had won or tied 33 of their 48 games and had easily won the Canadian Division.

What was worse, Mike Karakas, Chicago's goalie, came up with an injured toe before the opening game. Coach Bill Stewart was not about to repeat Lester Patrick's feat of playing goal. Instead, he asked permission of the Leafs to use Dave Kerr, the Rangers' goalie. Conn Smythe refused and the Hawks wound up with Alfie Moore, a minor leaguer, in the nets, but not before Stewart and Smythe engaged in a brief jostling match outside the dressing room.

The Hawks won the opener, 3–1, and Moore thumbed his nose at the Leafs' bench. In the second game, with Moore ruled ineligible by NHL president Frank Calder, the Hawks came up with Paul Goodman, another minor leaguer who was fished out of a movie theater just two hours before the game began. He was beaten by the Leafs, 5–1, to even the series.

In the third game, Karakas returned and the Hawks won, 2–1, on Doc Romnes' goal with 4:05 left in the game. The Leafs argued that the shot had hit the post but were overruled by referee Clarence Campbell, a man who one day would become president of the NHL.

The Hawks won the fourth game and the Cup, making Stewart the toast of Chicago—for about nine months.

1937–38

FINAL STANDINGS

Canadian Division	W	L	T	PTS	GF	GA
Toronto	24	15	9	57	151	127
New York A.	19	18	11	49	110	111
Montreal C.	18	17	13	49	123	128
Montreal M.	12	30	6	30	101	149

American Division	W	L	T	PTS	GF	GA
Boston	30	11	7	67	142	89
New York R.	27	15	6	60	149	96
Chicago	14	25	9	37	97	139
Detroit	12	25	11	35	99	133

LEADING SCORERS	G	A	PTS
Drillon, Toronto	26	26	52
Apps, Toronto	21	29	50
Thompson, Chicago	22	22	44
Mantha, Montreal C.	23	19	42
Dillon, New York R.	21	18	39
Schriner, New York A.	21	17	38
Thoms, Toronto	14	24	38
Smith, New York R.	14	23	37
Stewart, New York A.	19	17	36
N. Colville, New York R.	17	19	36

《 *Lorne Carr of the New York Americans gets congratulations after a winning goal against Chicago in the 1938 playoffs.*

Hector (Toe) Blake of the Canadiens won scoring and MVP honors in 1938–39.

A NEW WORLD OF OFFENSE   47

Rookie Frank Brimsek of the Bruins totaled 10 shutouts in 1938–39.

1938–39

For years the Maroons were fighting a losing battle attracting fan support while the Canadiens enjoyed far more popularity in Montreal. Finally, the Maroons asked permission to shift to St. Louis. The league refused but did grant the franchise a one-year leave of absence to regroup its forces. But when they sold most of their players to other clubs, it became apparent that the Maroons were through for good.

The demise of the Maroons left seven teams still operating and they were grouped in a single division with six clubs qualifying for the rather crowded playoffs. Only Chicago, whose Bill Stewart was dismissed in midseason and replaced by Paul Thompson, missed.

In Boston, manager Art Ross took a dramatic step. He sold goalie Tiny Thompson, a Bruins' favorite for a decade, to Detroit. The reason was Ross' conviction that a youngster from

Eveleth, Minn., was ready for the NHL. And Frank Brimsek really was ready.

Brimsek had played the Bruins' first two games while Thompson recovered from an eye ailment. Then Tiny returned and Brimsek was farmed out to Providence. But Thompson was 33 and Ross was anxious to create a spot for the promising rookie who had succeeded Chicago's Mike Karakas at Eveleth High School. On November 28, the deal was made, with the Bruins receiving $15,000 from the Red Wings. Brimsek returned two days later.

The Canadiens beat him, 2–0, in his first game and then Brimsek produced three. straight shutouts. His shutout streak extended to 231 minutes, 54 seconds, breaking Thompson's modern mark of 224:47.

After Brimsek's sensational streak was broken, he started another one. Three more shutouts—one against Thompson and the Red

WORLDS CHAMPIONS
1938 · 1939
and
NATIONAL HOCKEY LEAGUE CHAMPIONS
Winners of STANLEY CUP and PRINCE of WALES Trophy

BRUINS

Wings—gave him six in seven games and another unbelievable streak of 220 minutes, 24 seconds of scoreless hockey.

The Boston fans, never easy to please, were unhappy to lose Thompson but Brimsek's fantastic debut made him an instant hero. He turned in 10 shutouts in 41 games, earning the Vezina Trophy as top goalie, the Calder Trophy as top rookie, a spot on the All-Star team and the nickname "Mr. Zero."

The other All-Stars were defensemen Eddie Shore and Dit Clapper of Boston, Toronto's center, Syl Apps, right wing Gordie Drillon of the Maple Leafs and left wing Hector (Toe) Blake of the Montreal Canadiens. Blake was the scoring champion with 47 points, including 24 goals, and captured the Hart Trophy while Clint Smith of the New York Rangers won the Lady Byng.

The Bruins won the regular-season title by 16 points over the Rangers and then the two clubs staged one of the most memorable playoff battles in history. Boston took the first three games—two of them on overtime goals by Mel Hill, an obscure 10-goal scorer during the regular season. Then the Rangers roared back to win three straight and tie the series. In the seventh game, Hill struck again, beating the Rangers eight minutes into the third overtime period and earning forever the nickname of "Sudden Death" Hill.

Toronto ripped through the New York Americans and Detroit, which had eliminated the Canadiens. In the finals, the Bruins whipped the Leafs in five games to claim their first Stanley Cup in a decade.

Woody Dumart played left wing on the Bruins' high-scoring Kraut Line.

1938–39

FINAL STANDINGS						
	W	L	T	PTS	GF	GA
Boston	36	10	2	74	156	76
New York R.	26	16	6	58	149	105
Toronto	19	20	9	47	114	107
New York A.	17	21	10	44	119	157
Detroit	18	24	6	42	107	128
Montreal	15	24	9	39	115	146
Chicago	12	28	8	32	91	132

Davey Kerr of the Rangers won the Vezina 》 *Trophy and led the Stanley Cup champions in 1939–40.*

LEADING SCORERS	G	A	PTS
Blake, Montreal	24	23	47
Schriner, New York A.	13	31	44
Cowley, Boston	8	34	42
Smith, New York R.	21	20	41
Barry, Detroit	13	28	41
Apps, Toronto	15	25	40
Anderson, New York A.	13	27	40
Gottselig, Chicago	16	23	39
Haynes, Montreal	5	33	38
Conacher, Boston	26	11	37
Carr, New York A.	19	18	37
N. Colville, New York R.	18	19	37
Watson, New York R.	15	22	37

1939–40

The guns of Europe began firing before the 1939 hockey season got underway and before long the NHL would feel the manpower squeeze of world conflict. But, for the time being at least, the league's operations were not affected by the events overseas.

Ironically, the hottest line in the league was Boston's Milt Schmidt, Woody Dumart and Bobby Bauer, tabbed the "Kraut Line" because of their Germanic extractions. But the name proved a bit unpopular at this sensitive time so the "Kraut Line" was re-christened the "Kitchener Kids" because the trio all hailed from the Kitchener, Ontario, area.

Schmidt, the center, led the league in scoring with 52 points, 22 of them on goals. Dumart and Bauer tied for second with 43 points apiece.

The All-Star team had Schmidt at center, Bryan Hextall of the Rangers at right wing and Montreal's Toe Blake at left wing. The defensemen were Aubrey (Dit) Clapper of the Bruins and Detroit's Ebbie Goodfellow. Davey Kerr of the Rangers was the goalie.

Goodfellow won the Hart Trophy and Bobby Bauer the Lady Byng. Kerr won the Vezina and a 28-year-old Ranger rookie, Kilby MacDonald, took the Calder.

For the first time since they came into the league, the Bruins had to get along without the great Eddie Shore patrolling their blue line. Shore had become owner and manager of the minor league Springfield Indians and was available only for Boston's home games. The Bruins quickly tired of this arrangement and sold Eddie to the New York Americans. Shore finished the season with the Amerks and then retired to build the Springfield club into a rewarding financial operation.

Even without Shore, the Bruins finished first in the regular-season race, again beating out the Rangers. But New York got revenge for the heartbreaking playoff loss of the year before by eliminating Boston in the Stanley Cup series, four games to two.

Toronto got by Chicago and Detroit eliminated the New York Americans in other playoff matchups. When the Maple Leafs and Red Wings met in the semifinals it turned into a little war. A 15-minute brawl marred the final game with every player on the ice and 17 who left the opposing benches joining in.

"The Wings are a bunch of hoodlums," declared the Toronto management. To which Jack Adams, manager of the Red Wings, replied, "We're just sorry we can't play the Leafs seven nights in a row."

In the Stanley Cup finale, the Rangers beat Toronto in six games, three of the New York victories coming in overtime. That wiped out the bad overtime memories Boston's "Sudden Death" Hill had left the year before.

1939–40

FINAL STANDINGS

	W	L	T	PTS	GF	GA
Boston	31	12	5	67	170	98
New York R.	27	11	10	64	136	77
Toronto	25	17	6	56	134	110
Chicago	23	19	6	52	112	120
Detroit	16	26	6	38	90	126
New York A.	15	29	4	34	106	140
Montreal	10	33	5	25	90	167

LEADING SCORERS	G	A	PTS
Schmidt, Boston	22	30	52
Dumart, Boston	22	21	43
Bauer, Boston	17	26	43
Drillon, Toronto	21	19	40
Cowley, Boston	13	27	40
Hextall, New York R.	24	15	39
N. Colville, New York R.	19	19	38
Howe, Detroit	14	23	37
Blake, Montreal	17	19	36
Armstrong, New York A.	16	20	36

1940–41

Dick Irvin left Toronto and moved into the coaching job at Montreal, hoping to rebuild the Canadiens, who had fallen on lean times.

Irvin would do such a successful job that his teams of the early 1940s were hockey's most dynamic squads. And the reason for much of his success was a scouting job he did for the Canadiens shortly before becoming the club's coach. It was on that trip that he discovered a junior hockey player named Maurice Richard, who was destined to become one of the greatest scorers in hockey history.

Before the season started, Irvin predicted a fourth-place finish for Montreal—three notches higher than they had finished the year before. Asked his thoughts about the league's top rookie, he placed the name of his own Johnny Quilty in a sealed envelope.

Quilty made it but the Canadiens didn't. Montreal finished sixth but Quilty captured the Calder Trophy as the league's best rookie. Boston's Bill Cowley won the scoring title with 62 points—only 17 of them goals. Cowley also was the MVP and Bobby Bauer of

the Bruins won his second straight Lady Byng. Turk Broda of Toronto won the Vezina, edging out Detroit's Johnny Mowers on the final night of the season. It marked the first time a Maple Leaf had been the NHL's top goaltender.

The All-Star team had Broda in goal, Boston's Dit Clapper and Toronto's Wally Stanowski on defense, Cowley at center, Bryan Hextall of the Rangers and Sweeney Schriner, now with Toronto, on the wings.

The Bruins were the class of the league again and captured their fourth straight regular-season title. They set two records, going 15 games without a loss on the road over one stretch and 23 without a setback over another.

Boston finished five points in front of Toronto and knocked off the Maple Leafs in the opening round of the Stanley Cup playoffs. Detroit eliminated the Rangers and then Chicago, which had disposed of Montreal in the opening round.

The Rangers celebrate their Stanley Cup triumph in 1940.

In the Cup finals, the Bruins swept past the Red Wings in four straight games with Milt Schmidt and Eddie Wiseman, the player they had obtained from the Americans in the Eddie Shore deal the year before, starring.

War clouds had convinced players and executives around the league that it would not be long before the events in Europe and the Pacific would affect the NHL. Conn Smythe, owner of the Maple Leafs, advised all of his players to volunteer for military training and most of the club joined the Toronto Scottish Reserve. Other players around the league followed suit and soon many of them were trading shoulder pads and hockey sticks for field packs and rifles.

1940–41

FINAL STANDINGS

	W	L	T	PTS	GF	GA
Boston	27	8	13	67	168	102
Toronto	28	14	6	62	145	99
Detroit	21	16	11	53	112	102
New York R.	21	19	8	50	143	125
Chicago	16	25	7	39	112	139
Montreal	16	26	6	38	121	147
New York A.	8	29	11	27	99	186

LEADING SCORERS

	G	A	PTS
Cowley, Boston	17	45	62
Hextall, New York R.	26	18	44
Drillon, Toronto	23	21	44
Apps, Toronto	20	24	44
L. Patrick, New York R.	20	24	44
Howe, Detroit	20	24	44
N. Colville, New York R.	14	28	42
Wiseman, Boston	16	24	40
Bauer, Boston	17	22	39
Schriner, Toronto	24	14	38
R. Conacher, Boston	24	14	38
Schmidt, Boston	13	25	38

1941–42

The National Hockey League season was less than one month old in December 1941, when suddenly hockey didn't seem very important anymore. It was on the morning of December 7 that Japanese bombs poured down on United States ships anchored in Pearl Harbor and plunged the U.S. into World War II.

《 *MVP and scoring champ in 1940–41 was Boston's Bill Cowley.*

On the night of December 7, the New York Rangers defeated Boston, 5–4, Chicago nipped the Americans, who had changed the designation of their franchise from New York to Brooklyn, 5–4, and Detroit edged Montreal, 3–2. But nobody cared about the results that night.

The next morning, many of the same fans who had packed hockey arenas the night before lined up for recruiting stations as America went to war. Hockey players, too, did their part.

Of the 14 players listed in the Ranger lineup the night of December 7, 10 eventually wound up in uniform. It was the same throughout the league as the service rolls swelled with top NHL talent. The names included Muzz and Lynn Patrick, Sid Abel, Boston's "Kraut Line" of Milt Schmidt, Woody Dumart and Bobby Bauer, Terry and Ken Reardon, Howie Meeker, Black Jack Stewart, goalies Jim Henry and Chuck Rayner and scores of others.

But, as it had 25 years before when confronted by another world conflict, the NHL continued through World War II without a single interruption in its schedule.

On the day that Japan attacked Pearl Harbor, Bryan Hextall of the Rangers and Toronto's Gordie Drillon shared the NHL scoring lead. Hextall went on to capture the championship with 56 points, two points more than his teammate Lynn Patrick. Both Rangers made the All-Star team along with Toronto center Syl Apps, defensemen Tommy Anderson of the Brooklyn Americans and Earl Seibert of Chicago and goalie Frankie Brimsek of Boston.

Anderson won the Hart Trophy as MVP, Apps took the Lady Byng, Brimsek captured the Vezina Trophy and Grant Warwick of the Rangers was the Calder Trophy winner.

Red Dutton's troubled Americans weathered one of the longest holdouts in hockey history when Busher Jackson could not reach terms with the club. Finally, in desperation, Dutton shipped Jackson to Boston for $7,500 in January. Dutton also traded Lorne Carr to Toronto for four players. But nothing worked right for the Amerks. When they finished last

and their cross-town rivals, the Rangers, won the regular-season title, it marked the end of the Americans. They dropped out of the league at the conclusion of the season.

Toronto eliminated the first-place Rangers in the opening round of the playoffs while Detroit eliminated the Canadiens and then the Bruins, who had knocked out Chicago. That set up a final-round meeting between the Red Wings and Maple Leafs—one of the most amazing series in Stanley Cup history.

Detroit stunned the favored Leafs by winning the first three games—two of them at Toronto. Billy Taylor of the Leafs kidded newsmen before the next game, saying, "Don't worry about us, we'll beat them four straight."

Few observers, except perhaps Taylor, were prepared for what followed. The Leafs shook up their lineup and with seldom-used Don Metz and Ernie Dickens supplying the spark, won the next four games and the Stanley Cup.

It was Taylor who set up Sweeney Schriner's second goal of the game and the final one of the series in Toronto's 3–1 victory in the seventh game.

1941-42

FINAL STANDINGS

	W	L	T	PTS	GF	GA
New York	29	17	2	60	177	143
Toronto	27	18	3	57	158	136
Boston	25	17	6	56	160	118
Chicago	22	23	3	47	145	155
Detroit	19	25	4	42	140	147
Montreal	18	27	3	39	134	173
Brooklyn	16	29	3	35	133	175

LEADING SCORERS

	G	A	PTS
Hextall, New York	24	32	56
L. Patrick, New York	32	22	54
Grosso, Detroit	23	30	53
Watson, New York	15	37	52
Abel, Detroit	18	31	49
Blake, Montreal	17	28	45
Thoms, Chicago	15	30	45
Drillon, Toronto	23	18	41
Apps, Toronto	18	23	41
Anderson, Brooklyn	12	29	41

Ranger Bryan Hextall skated off with the scoring title in 1941–42. »

A SOLID SIX
1942–1967

With the exit of the Americans, the NHL was down to six teams—Detroit, Chicago, Montreal, New York Rangers, Boston and Toronto. This solid foundation would remain intact until the ambitious expansion program of the NHL's second half-century.

The war years would bring important changes to the NHL. Before the conflict was over, Frank Boucher, the creative center of the Rangers, who now coached the New York club, was to suggest the adoption of a red line at center ice to speed up the game. Overtime periods would be done away with in the interest of maintaining tight wartime travel schedules.

And Montreal's Maurice Richard emerged as the game's first superscorer. The Rocket, as Richard became known, was to be the key man on one of the most devastating teams in hockey history—the Canadiens of the mid-1950s. They were so proficient that they forced a rule change to keep them from utterly dominating the sport.

In Detroit, a young man named Gordie Howe arrived on the scene with little advance

« *Bloodied Jimmy Orlando of Detroit looks for support from referee King Clancy after a fight with Toronto's Gaye Stewart in 1943.*

notice and established himself as hockey's greatest scorer and its longevity king. It was Howe and Richard who ruled the game in the fifties along with the Canadiens and the Red Wings.

And then came the 1960s and Bobby Hull, the dynamic blond bomber of the Chicago Black Hawks, who epitomized hockey's next era of bigger, stronger, faster players.

The period would see the shifting of the league's administration from president Frank Calder, who had been head man since the NHL's inception in 1917, to Red Dutton and then to Clarence Campbell, the ex-referee, who would be at the helm when big-league hockey swung into its most successful era.

1942–43

Numerous NHL players and executives were in the service by the time the 1942 season began and early in the season a major rule change was enacted. Because of the tight train schedules during the war, NHL teams had to be precise about the length of games. Thus, they eliminated overtime.

Until then, when a game was tied at the end of three regulation periods, the teams played a

The Maple Leafs' Gaye Stewart was Rookie of the Year in 1942–43.

president Frank Calder suffered a heart attack. Two weeks later, the man who had been at the head of the league since its inception in 1917 was dead. The Governors chose Dutton as president pro tem with the understanding that Clarence Campbell, the man Calder had chosen as his successor, would eventually take over.

Chicago's Bentley brothers, Doug and Max, battled Bill Cowley of Boston for the scoring title. Doug Bentley finally won the crown with 73 points, including 33 goals. Cowley had 72 points and Max Bentley 70.

Cowley and Doug Bentley made the All-Star team along with Toronto's Lorne Carr, Black Jack Stewart of Detroit and Earl Seibert of Chicago on defense, and Johnny Mowers of Detroit in goal. Cowley also won the Hart Trophy while Mowers took the Vezina. The Lady Byng went to Max Bentley and Gaye Stewart of Toronto won the Calder.

In Montreal, the Canadiens introduced Maurice Richard, a young right winger, who scored five goals in 16 games before a broken ankle put him out of action.

Detroit won the regular-season title by four points over Boston while Toronto finished third and the Canadiens made it to fourth place—their highest finish in five seasons—and the final playoff spot in the six-team league. The Red Wings eliminated the Maple Leafs and Boston dropped the Canadiens in the Stanley Cup semifinals. Then, with Carl Liscombe and Sid Abel starring, Detroit flashed past the Bruins in four straight games to capture the Cup.

1942–43

FINAL STANDINGS

	W	L	T	PTS	GF	GA
Detroit	25	14	11	61	169	124
Boston	24	17	9	57	195	176
Toronto	22	19	9	53	198	159
Montreal	19	19	12	50	181	191
Chicago	17	18	15	49	179	180
New York	11	31	8	30	161	253

Chicago's Doug Bentley (73 points) beat out brother Max (70) and Boston's Bill Cowley (72) for scoring honors in 1942–43. »

10-minute overtime period in an attempt to break the deadlock. Unlike Stanley Cup overtimes, the extra periods were not sudden death but lasted a full 10 minutes. Therefore, it was possible to have goals scored during overtime but for the game to still end in a tie.

Referee Bill Chadwick, a leading NHL official of the 1940s, felt the elimination of the extra period was a good thing for hockey. "Overtimes benefitted the stronger teams," he said. "It gave them 10 more minutes to wear down weaker competition. If a weak club held a stronger one to a tie for 60 minutes, it ought to be worth something."

With the Americans out of the league, the schedule was increased from 48 to 50 games. Red Dutton, the Amerks' head man, was disconsolate at the demise of his club but he was to be back in hockey much faster than he expected.

On his way to a meeting of the league's Board of Governors in Toronto in January,

LEADING SCORERS	G	A	PTS
D. Bentley, Chicago	33	40	73
Cowley, Boston	27	45	72
M. Bentley, Chicago	26	44	70
L. Patrick, New York	22	39	61
Carr, Toronto	27	33	60
Taylor, Toronto	18	42	60
Hextall, New York	27	32	59
Blake, Montreal	23	36	59
Lach, Montreal	18	40	58
O'Connor, Montreal	15	43	58

1943–44

The war had ravaged NHL rosters, leaving only youngsters, service rejects or over-age veterans. The situation was so desperate that in New York, coach Frank Boucher of the Rangers attempted a comeback at the age of 42.

Detroit's Syd Howe set an NHL record with six goals against the Rangers on February 3, 1944.

Boucher's return at center ice lasted 15 games and he averaged almost a point per game for hapless New York.

It was Boucher and Art Ross, Boston's manager, who pushed for, and eventually got, legislation introducing the center red line. The mid-ice divider was introduced at the start of the 1943 season in an effort to speed up the game. Boucher explained the reasoning behind it.

"My thought was that hockey had become a see-saw affair," said Boucher. "Defending teams were jammed in their own end for minutes because they couldn't pass their way out against the new five-man attack."

Before the red line was introduced, players could not pass the puck out of their defensive zone but had to carry it out themselves. This was difficult with five opposing skaters to weave through and Boucher suggested a solution.

"Why not allow teams to pass their way out of trouble, say up to mid-ice," he reasoned. "Use a red line to divide the ice. It would open the dam for the defending team and restore end-to-end play."

The idea was adopted and speeded up the game considerably.

Boston's Herbie Cain won the scoring race with 36 goals and 82 points but missed the first All-Star team. Chicago's Doug Bentley, Lorne Carr of Toronto and Bill Cowley of Boston were named to the All-Star forward line, with Toronto's Babe Pratt and Earl Seibert of Chicago on defense and Montreal's Bill Durnan in goal. Pratt was the Hart Trophy winner, Clint Smith of Chicago took the Lady Byng, Durnan won the Vezina and Toronto's Gus Bodnar captured the Calder.

And in Montreal, coach Dick Irvin assembled a new line. He used Elmer Lach, who

Toronto's Babe Pratt was the MVP in 1943–44.

spoke only English, at center; Toe Blake, fluent in French and English, on left wing, and young Maurice Richard, the darling of the French-Canadian fans, on the right side. The unit was tagged the Punch Line and produced 82 goals—32 of them by the fiery Richard.

With Durnan doing an outstanding job in goal and the Punch Line racing through the league, Montreal dropped just five games and won the regular-season championship by 15 points over Detroit. It was the start of a dynasty.

There were two notable goal-scoring feats. Detroit's Syd Howe blasted six goals in a 12–2 romp over the Rangers, setting a modern mark for most goals in a single game. And Toronto's Gus Bodnar, a rookie, set a record for the fastest goal by a first-year man when he scored just 15 seconds after hitting the ice in his debut, also against the Rangers.

In the Stanley Cup playoffs, Richard really took off. The Rocket scored all five goals in the Canadiens' second-game victory and Montreal finished off Toronto in the opening round before sweeping past Chicago in four straight games for the Cup. Richard set a Cup record with 12 goals in the nine playoff games.

1943–44

FINAL STANDINGS

	W	L	T	PTS	GF	GA
Montreal	38	5	7	83	234	109
Detroit	26	18	6	58	214	177
Toronto	23	23	4	50	214	174
Chicago	22	23	5	49	178	187
Boston	19	26	5	43	223	268
New York	6	39	5	17	162	310

LEADING SCORERS

	G	A	PTS
Cain, Boston	36	46	82
D. Bentley, Chicago	38	39	77
Carr, Toronto	36	38	74
Liscombe, Detroit	36	37	73
Lach, Montreal	24	48	72
Smith, Chicago	23	49	72
Cowley, Boston	30	41	71
Mosienko, Chicago	32	38	70
Jackson, Boston	28	41	69
Bodnar, Toronto	22	40	62

1944-45

"Terrible Ted" Lindsay broke in with the Red Wings in 1944–45.

Maurice Richard's playoff explosion the year before set the stage for the Montreal star's greatest season. The Rocket zoomed through the NHL's 50-game schedule at an incredible goal-per-game pace, scoring a record 50 times. He had 15 goals in one nine-game stretch, including five goals in one game. Ten times during the season he scored two or more goals in a single game.

Richard was the first to score 50 goals in a season and the only one ever to do it in a 50-game season. His accomplishment is often compared to the record he erased—Joe Malone's 44 goals in a 22-game season in 1917–18, the NHL's first year of operation. Malone's record was established in the era before forward passing; Richard's came in the modern era. Critics often pointed out that Richard's feat came against watered-down teams weakened by the war but the fact remains that the Rocket was the first man to hit the magic 50.

Richard's linemates also flourished from his record spree and the Punch Line finished 1–2–3 in scoring. Center Elmer Lach led all scorers with 80 points, Richard finished second with 73 points and left wing Toe Blake was third with 67.

The Canadiens dominated the league, winning the regular-season title again, this time by 13 points. Five Montreal players—Richard, Lach, Blake, defenseman Butch Bouchard and goalie Bill Durnan made the All-Star team with only Detroit defenseman Flash Hollett breaking the Canadiens' monopoly. Lach was the MVP, Chicago's Bill Mosienko won the Lady Byng Trophy, Durnan took the Vezina and Toronto's Frank McCool captured the Calder.

The Canadiens had lost only eight regular-season games in 1944–45 and a total of just 14 games (one in the playoffs) in two seasons while winning two straight league titles and the Stanley Cup. They were, quite naturally, favored to take the Cup again.

Montreal's Emil (Butch) Bouchard was an All-Star defenseman in 1944–45. »

Kraut Liners Milt Schmidt (left) and Woody Dumart (14) backcheck against the Rangers in 1945–46.

But Toronto stung Montreal with two quick victories in the opening round of the playoffs and eliminated the Canadiens in six games. Detroit wiped out a two-game Boston edge and whipped the Bruins in their semifinal series. That set up a final round between the Maple Leafs and Red Wings.

Detroit almost erased the memory of the embarassing Cup loss to the Leafs three years earlier, when they had blown a three-game lead. This time, it was Toronto which won the first three games—all of them shutouts by rookie goalie Frank McCool.

Suddenly the Red Wings bounced back, just as the Leafs had done in 1942. Detroit won three straight games and it looked like history was about to repeat. But Toronto finally halted the storybook comeback by winning the seventh game on defenseman Babe Pratt's goal.

1944–45

FINAL STANDINGS						
	W	L	T	PTS	GF	GA
Montreal	38	8	4	80	228	121
Detroit	31	14	5	67	218	161
Toronto	24	22	4	52	183	161
Boston	16	30	4	36	179	219
Chicago	13	30	7	33	141	194
New York	11	29	10	32	154	247

LEADING SCORERS	G	A	PTS
Lach, Montreal	26	54	80
Richard, Montreal	50	23	73
Blake, Montreal	29	38	67
Cowley, Boston	25	40	65
Kennedy, Toronto	29	25	54
Mosienko, Chicago	28	26	54
Carveth, Detroit	26	28	54
DeMarco, New York	24	30	54
Smith, Chicago	23	31	54
S. Howe, Detroit	17	36	53

1945–46

With World War II drawing to a close, hockey players began returning to the sport.

Boston's All-Star backliner John Crawford wore this helmet to protect his bald head.

Players came back throughout the season, causing a constant shuffle of rosters throughout the NHL.

Many had lost the best hockey years of their lives while in service and found it difficult to make moves that once were second nature to them. Four years of war had robbed many of that vital extra measure of speed that separated the average players from the stars.

Some clubs, the Rangers among them, felt a sense of responsibility to the returnees and stuck with them until it became all too apparent that they just weren't able to keep up with the NHL pace anymore.

Chicago's Max Bentley got back in time to start the season with the Black Hawks and proved that his service years had not affected his hockey ability.

Bentley won the scoring title with 31 goals and 61 points and earned the Hart Trophy as the league's MVP.

Bentley was picked as the All-Star center on a team that included Montreal's Maurice Richard at right wing, Gaye Stewart of Toronto at left wing, Montreal's Butch Bouchard and Boston's Jack Crawford on defense and Montreal goalie Bill Durnan, who won his third straight Vezina Trophy. The Lady Byng went to Montreal's Toe Blake and Edgar Laprade of the Rangers won the Calder Trophy as the NHL's best rookie.

Richard did not come close to the record goal-scoring pace he had maintained the year before and finished with 27—less than three other players, including his linemate, Toe Blake.

Despite the Rocket's reduced output, the Canadiens won their third straight regular-season title, this time by five points over Boston. But they at least looked mortal, losing 17 games—just one less than they had dropped in combined regular-season and Stanley Cup play for the previous two years.

The NHL had a new look for the service returnees. In addition to the powerful Canadiens, who had been little more than also-rans when the war started, there was the red line and a new system of three officials—two linesmen as well as a referee—for every game. Goal lights were made mandatory.

In the playoffs, the Punch Line carried the Canadiens to their second Stanley Cup in three years. Blake and Richard had seven goals each and Elmer Lach added five and 12 assists as Montreal shredded Chicago in four games and Boston in five to clinch the Cup.

1945–46

FINAL STANDINGS

	W	L	T	PTS	GF	GA
Montreal	28	17	5	61	172	134
Boston	24	18	8	56	167	156
Chicago	23	20	7	53	200	178
Detroit	20	20	10	50	146	159
Toronto	19	24	7	45	174	185
New York	13	28	9	35	144	191

LEADING SCORERS

	G	A	PTS
M. Bentley, Chicago	31	30	61
Stewart, Toronto	37	15	52
Blake, Montreal	29	21	50
Smith, Chicago	26	24	50
Richard, Montreal	27	21	48
Mosienko, Chicago	18	30	48
DeMarco, New York	20	27	47
Lach, Montreal	13	34	47
Kaleta, Chicago	19	27	46
Taylor, Toronto	23	18	41
Horeck, Chicago	20	21	41

Goalie Turk Broda of Toronto stops bid for a goal by Boston's Bep Guidolin in 1946–47.

1946–47

Red Dutton had successfully steered the NHL through the war years and before the 1946–47 season he announced his retirement. The new NHL president was Clarence Campbell, a former referee, a Rhodes scholar, a lieutenant colonel in the Canadian Army and on the legal staff at the Nuremberg Trials. All this was experience that would serve Campbell well at one time or another in the ensuing years.

In Montreal, Tommy Gorman announced his retirement as general manager of the Canadiens and his replacement was Frank Selke, who for many years had played a key role in Conn Smythe's Toronto operation. Selke's move to Montreal reunited him with another ex-Smythe employee, Canadiens' coach Dick Irvin.

Detroit introduced a slope-shouldered, raw-boned right wing who would one day become hockey's top star. But Gordie Howe was just another rookie and his seven-goal season hardly portended greatness.

The league increased its schedule from 50 to 60 games and introduced a system of bonuses for All-Star selection and individual trophy winners. From then on, in addition to the honor of being selected, each player would get a $1,000 bonus from the league. In addition, the NHL boosted to $127,000 the regular-season and Stanley Cup playoff pools, making it more profitable than ever before for individuals and teams to do well.

Montreal's power-laden Canadiens reaped most of the benefits from the NHL's new affluence. They won their fourth straight regular-season title and gained four of the six

Former referee Clarence S. Campbell took over the NHL presidency in the fall of 1946.

first-team All-Star berths. Goalie Bill Durnan, defensemen Butch Bouchard and Kenny Reardon and right winger Maurice Richard were the Canadiens' All-Star selections. Milt Schmidt of Boston at center and Doug Bentley of Chicago at left wing completed the team.

Durnan won his fourth Vezina Trophy in a row—the first goalie to turn that trick. Richard took the Hart Trophy and Boston's Bobby Bauer was the Lady Byng winner. The Calder Trophy went to Toronto's Howie Meeker, who had been so badly wounded during the war that he was told he would never be able to play hockey again.

Chicago's Max Bentley won his second straight scoring title with 72 points—one more than Richard, who fired 45 goals. Interestingly, Richard earned the MVP designation in a season when he scored five goals less than his record 50. The year he scored 50, the Rocket's linemate, Elmer Lach, was the MVP.

Defenseman Ken Reardon of Montreal was voted to the All-Star team in 1946–47.

The Toronto Maple Leafs: Stanley Cup champions in 1946–47.

The Canadiens breezed past Boston in the five-game opening series of the Stanley Cup playoffs and then faced Toronto, which had knocked off Detroit in five games. The Canadiens won the opener of the final series, 6–0, prompting goalie Bull Durnan to scoff at the Leafs. "How did these guys get in the playoffs anyway?" needled Durnan. He soon found out.

Toronto bounced back with three straight victories that left Montreal on the brink of elimination. The Canadiens won the fifth game but the Leafs took game No. 6 and the Stanley Cup. It was in the midst of the final series that a high-sticking episode cost Richard a $250 fine and a one-game suspension by Campbell—the first of several scrapes involving the fiery Canadiens' star and the placid president of the league.

1946–47

FINAL STANDINGS

	W	L	T	PTS	GF	GA
Montreal	34	16	10	78	189	138
Toronto	31	19	10	72	209	172
Boston	26	23	11	63	190	175
Detroit	22	27	11	55	190	193
New York	22	32	6	50	167	186
Chicago	19	37	4	42	193	274

LEADING SCORERS

	G	A	PTS
M. Bentley, Chicago	29	43	72
Richard, Montreal	45	26	71
Taylor, Detroit	17	46	63
Schmidt, Boston	27	35	62
Kennedy, Toronto	28	32	60
D. Bentley, Chicago	21	34	55
Bauer, Boston	30	24	54
R. Conacher, Detroit	30	24	54
Mosienko, Chicago	25	27	52
Dumart, Boston	24	28	52

Montreal's Elmer Lach was the 1947–48 scoring leader.

1947–48

The NHL pension plan was born in 1947, with contributions by both the players and the league. In an effort to build pension revenue, an annual All-Star game was initiated, pitting the previous season's All-Star squad against the winners of the Stanley Cup. The game was to be played just before the beginning of the regular season.

Toronto's Maple Leaf Gardens hosted the first All-Star affair and a crowd of 14,169 paid $25,865 to watch the All-Stars defeat Toronto, 4–3. Financially, the game was off to a good start. But the opening classic was marred when Bill Mosienko of Chicago fractured his left ankle.

The Maple Leafs were anxious to retain the Stanley Cup they had won the previous spring and Conn Smythe decided the best way to achieve that was to get Max Bentley into a Toronto uniform. That would not be easy since Bentley had won two straight scoring championships and, along with his brother Doug, provided Chicago with a very healthy gate attraction.

But the Black Hawks' farm system had not produced much in the way of NHL talent and Chicago was short of bodies. That gave Smythe the opening he needed. The Maple Leaf boss assembled an attractive package of Gus Bodnar, Gaye Stewart, Bob Goldham, Bud Poile and Ernie Dickens which the Hawks could not turn down. Bentley and Cy Thomas went to the Leafs in the seven-player swap.

Smythe's bold move paid off. The Leafs soared to the top of the league and won the regular-season title as Bentley contributed 54 points, including 26 goals. The scoring title, however, went to Montreal's Elmer Lach, who had 31 goals and 61 points. The season marked the breakup of the Canadiens' potent Punch Line, on which Lach was the center. Toe Blake, the left wing, suffered a broken ankle in January which ended his playing career.

A combination of circumstances, not the least of them injuries to Blake and others, dropped the Canadiens to fifth place and out of the playoffs.

Buddy O'Connor, traded by Montreal to New York before the season, won both the Hart and Lady Byng trophies—the first player to capture both in the same season. Toronto's Turk Broda took the Vezina and Detroit's Jimmy McFadden was the Calder winner.

In Detroit, the Red Wings assembled a line of Sid Abel at center, Ted Lindsay on left wing and Gordie Howe on the right side and tabbed

it the Production Line. And it produced handsomely with 63 goals—33 of them by Lindsay.

The league was rocked late in the season by a gambling scandal which led to lifetime suspensions of two players—Billy Taylor of the Rangers and Don Gallinger of Boston. President Clarence Campbell emphasized that no games had been fixed and that Gallinger and Taylor were punished for betting on games. A similar charge had resulted in a midseason suspension for Babe Pratt two seasons earlier but Pratt was reinstated after missing nine games.

Detroit dominated the All-Star team with Ted Lindsay at left wing and Bill Quackenbush

and Jack Stewart on defense. The other choices were goalie Turk Broda of Toronto and line-mates Elmer Lach and Maurice Richard of Montreal.

While the Wings led in All-Star picks, it was the Maple Leafs who dominated the Stanley Cup playoffs. Toronto whipped Boston in five games and then clinched its second straight Cup by beating Detroit in four straight. In the final series, the Leafs held the Red Wings' vaunted Production Line to a single goal.

1947–48

FINAL STANDINGS

	W	L	T	PTS	GF	GA
Toronto	32	15	13	77	182	143
Detroit	30	18	12	72	187	148
Boston	23	24	13	59	167	168
New York	21	26	13	55	176	201
Montreal	20	29	11	51	147	169
Chicago	20	34	6	46	195	225

LEADING SCORERS

	G	A	PTS
Lach, Montreal	30	31	61
O'Connor, New York	24	36	60
D. Bentley, Chicago	20	37	57
Stewart, Toronto-Chicago	27	29	56
M. Bentley, Chicago-Toronto	26	28	54
Poile, Toronto-Chicago	25	29	54
Richard, Montreal	28	25	53
Apps, Toronto	26	27	53
Lindsay, Detroit	33	19	52
R. Conacher, Chicago	22	27	49

1948–49

When he first saw Sid Abel, Ted Lindsay and Gordie Howe on a line together, Jack Adams knew the Detroit trio would be something special. And he was right. Starting in 1948, the Production Line led the Red Wings to one of the most successful eras in NHL history—seven straight league titles.

Abel, Lindsay and Howe meshed together like precision gears and Adams, the genial Detroit general manager, marveled at the trio's uncanny anticipation. "They could score goals in their sleep," Adams once remarked. "They

« *Toronto's Turk Broda (right) won the Vezina Trophy in 1947–48, breaking a string of four straight Vezinas by Montreal's Bill Durnan.*

always seem to know where the play will develop."

Abel, the center, was the playmaker. Lindsay, at left wing, was a fierce checker and competitor who was deadly in the corners. And right winger Howe had a marvelous shot and could control the puck for what seemed like minutes on end.

Howe, only 21, was Adams' pet. The Detroit boss had almost lost the shy youngster in his first training camp when someone forgot to furnish him with a Red Wing jacket which Adams had promised. When made aware of the problem, Adams produced the jacket in record time and Howe stayed with the Wings.

Injuries limited Howe to 40 games in 1948–49 and he scored just 12 goals. But Abel and Lindsay kept the Production Line output healthy with 54 goals between them. Goalie Harry Lumley had a 2.42 goals-against average and six shutouts as the Red Wings won the regular-season title by nine points over Boston. But the best goaltending job was turned in by Montreal's Bill Durnan, who won his fifth Vezina Trophy in six years with a 2.10 goals-against average and 10 shutouts. Durnan had four shutouts in a row over one stretch and established a modern record by not allowing a goal for 309 minutes, 21 seconds.

Roy Conacher of Chicago and teammate Doug Bentley staged an exciting battle for the scoring title, with Conacher finally winning it. He finished with 68 points, two more than Bentley.

Conacher was chosen as the left wing on the All-Star team with Maurice Richard of Montreal at right wing and Sid Abel of Detroit at center. Two Detroit defensemen, Jack Stewart and Bill Quackenbush, and Montreal's goalie, Durnan, completed the team. Despite his limited output, Gordie Howe made the second All-Star squad.

Abel won the Hart Trophy and Quackenbush became the first defenseman to take the Lady Byng. Penti Lund of the Rangers won the Calder Trophy.

In the playoffs, the Production Line riddled Montreal, scoring 12 of Detroit's 17 goals,

Ranger Don Raleigh lifts one past Vezina Trophy winner Bill Durnan of Montreal in 1948–49.

eight of them by Howe. That put the Red Wings in the Stanley Cup finals against Toronto, which had beaten Boston in five games.

Turk Broda, the Leafs' great goalie, was more than a match for the Production Line. Broda allowed just five goals in four games and Sid Smith's hat trick in the second game set the tone as Toronto won the Cup in four straight.

The victory, marking the Leafs' second four-game sweep in two seasons, made them the first NHL team to take three straight Stanley Cups.

1948–49

FINAL STANDINGS

	W	L	T	PTS	GF	GA
Detroit	34	19	7	75	195	145
Boston	29	23	8	66	178	163
Montreal	28	23	9	65	152	126
Toronto	22	25	13	57	147	161
Chicago	21	31	8	50	173	211
New York	18	31	11	47	133	172

LEADING SCORERS

	G	A	PTS
R. Conacher, Chicago	26	42	68
D. Bentley, Chicago	23	43	66
Abel, Detroit	28	26	54
Lindsay, Detroit	26	28	54
J. Conacher, Detroit-Chicago	26	23	49
Ronty, Boston	20	29	49
Watson, Toronto	26	19	45
Reay, Montreal	22	23	45
Bodnar, Chicago	19	26	45
Peirson, Boston	22	21	43

1949–50

Detroit's Production Line, with a healthy Gordie Howe rejoining Sid Abel and Ted Lindsay, tore through the league and finished 1-2-3 in the scoring race, matching the feat which Boston's Kraut Line, Montreal's Punch Line and Toronto's Kid Line had previously performed.

Lindsay won the scoring title with 78 points, Abel finished with 69 and Howe had

Chicago's Roy Conacher, upholding family tradition, was an All-Star in 1948–49.

68. The trio combined for an amazing 215 points, including 92 goals—35 of them by Howe.

Despite Howe's brilliant season, he had to settle for a second-team All-Star berth. For the second straight year the right wing spot on the first team went to Montreal's Maurice Richard, who scored 43 goals, the most in the league. The intense rivalry would continue through the early 1950s with the two men occupying the two All-Star berths eight times over a nine-year period.

Throughout the league, fans argued the relative merits of the two right wingers and the extended debate created quite a feud between the Canadiens and Red Wings. Once, in a ruckus on the ice, Howe knocked Richard down. When the Rocket got up, Abel rubbed salt in the wound with a taunt. Richard wheeled and teed off on Abel, breaking his nose with a punch.

The other All-Stars in 1950 were Lindsay and Abel, defensemen Kenny Reardon of Montreal and Gus Mortson of Toronto and goaltender Bill Durnan of Montreal.

It was Durnan's sixth All-Star selection in seven seasons and he also captured his sixth Vezina Trophy. They were also his last, for he stunned Montreal by quitting in the midst of the Stanley Cup playoffs, saying that the pressure of big-league goaltending had simply become too much.

Two other goalies won individual awards that season. Chuck Rayner of the Rangers was the Hart winner and Jack Gelineau, a rookie who beat Frank Brimsek out of the Boston netminding job, took the Calder Trophy. The Lady Byng winner was Edgar Laprade of the Rangers.

Detroit finished first in the regular-season race and met Toronto in one Stanley Cup semifinal while the Rangers tangled with the Canadiens in the other. Going into the series, the Red Wings had dropped 11 straight playoff games to the Leafs and been eliminated three straight years by Toronto.

In the opening game of the series, a devastating injury almost cost Gordie Howe his life.

Frank Brimsek, playing his last year as a Blackhawk, stops a shot by the Bruins' Red Sullivan in 1949–50.

Ted Kennedy sidestepped a Howe check and Gordie plunged face-first into the boards. He suffered a concussion, a broken nose, a fractured right cheekbone and a scratched eyeball.

The Wings, beaten by 5–0 in that opener and deprived of their top scorer, gallantly bounced back and defeated the Maple Leafs in seven games. The Rangers hung three straight defeats on the Canadiens and then Bill Durnan went to Dick Irvin before the fourth game and asked that the Montreal coach use rookie Gerry McNeil in his place. McNeil won the fourth game but New York finished Montreal off in the fifth.

In the Stanley Cup finals, the Rangers led three games to two and were leading, 4–3, in the third period of the sixth game. But goals by Ted Lindsay and Sid Abel gave the Red Wings the game and tied the series. In the seventh game, Pete Babando's overtime goal sank New York and delivered the Stanley Cup to Detroit.

1949–50

FINAL STANDINGS

	W	L	T	PTS	GF	GA
Detroit	37	19	14	88	229	164
Montreal	29	22	19	77	172	150
Toronto	31	27	12	74	176	173
New York	28	31	11	67	170	189
Boston	22	32	16	60	198	228
Chicago	22	38	10	54	203	244

LEADING SCORERS

	G	A	PTS
Lindsay, Detroit	23	55	78
Abel, Detroit	34	35	69
Howe, Detroit	35	33	68
M. Richard, Montreal	43	22	65
Ronty, Boston	23	36	59
R. Conacher, Chicago	25	31	56
D. Bentley, Chicago	20	33	53
Peirson, Boston	27	25	52
Prystai, Chicago	29	22	51
Guidolin, Chicago	17	34	51

Maple Leafs (from left) Sid Smith, Max Bentley and Bill Barilko celebrate playoff victory over the Bruins en route to the 1950–51 Stanley Cup championship.

1950–51

Jack Adams was never a stand-pat general manager and although Detroit had won two straight titles, the Red Wings' boss shook them up before the 1950–51 season. He engineered a mammoth nine-player trade with Chicago—the biggest deal in NHL history.

Shuttled off to Chicago were forwards Al Dewsbury, Don Morrison and Pete Babando, defenseman Jack Stewart and goalie Harry Lumley. Babando's overtime goal had won the Stanley Cup for the Wings the season before, Stewart had made the first All-Star team three times and Lumley had turned in a 2.35 goals-against average the season before.

In return, Adams got defenseman Bob Goldham, forwards Gaye Stewart and Metro Prystai and goalie Jim Henry. Perhaps the main reason for making the trade was to give Terry Sawchuk a clear shot at the Red Wings' goalie job.

Sawchuk was not yet 21 when he became the Red Wings' regular goalie. The youngster did a spectacular job in his rookie season, with a 1.98 goals-against average and a league-leading 11 shutouts. He was the easy winner of the Calder Trophy and was named to the first All-Star team.

The other All-Stars included Detroit's Gordie Howe, who won the scoring championship with 88 points and scored 43 goals—one more than his right wing rival, Montreal's Maurice Richard. The other forwards were Howe's linemate, Ted Lindsay on left wing, and Boston's Milt Schmidt at center. Red Kelly of Detroit and Bill Quackenbush of Boston were picked as the defensemen.

Schmidt won the Hart Trophy and Kelly took the Lady Byng, becoming the second Red Wing defenseman in three years to win the trophy for gentlemanly play. In spite of Saw-

chuk's incredible first-year statistics, he was not the Vezina Trophy winner. That honor went to Al Rollins, who split Toronto's netminding with veteran Turk Broda. Rollins played 40 games compared to Sawchuk's 70 and had a 1.75 goals-against average.

The Red Wings finished first with 44 victories and 13 ties, accumulating a record 101 points. But they were only six points up on Toronto, which won 41 games. It was a busy season for President Clarence Campbell. He slapped three-game suspensions and $300 fines each on Ted Lindsay of Detroit and Bill Ezinicki of Boston for a midseason brawl. Gus Mortson of Toronto used his stick on Chicago's Adam Brown in March and it cost him a two-game suspension and $200 fine. Maurice Richard, still steaming over a game miscon-

duct penalty he had drawn from referee Hugh McLean the night before, grabbed McLean in New York's Picadilly Hotel and as a result of the confrontation, Campbell fined the Rocket $500.

In the Stanley Cup opening round, the Canadiens were decided underdogs to the Red Wings. But Montreal won the first two games—both of them on overtime goals by Maurice Richard. Detroit squared the series by taking the next two but Montreal came right back and eliminated the Red Wings by winning the fifth and sixth games.

Toronto took Boston in five games and advanced to the finals against Montreal. The Maple Leafs and Canadiens set a record of sorts as all five games of their series went into overtime.

In the fifth game, Toronto was trailing, 2–1, in the final period when coach Joe Primeau yanked goalie Turk Broda to make room for an extra attacker. The maneuver paid off with Tod Sloan's game-tying goal with just 32 seconds remaining.

Less than three minutes into overtime, defenseman Bill Barilko won the game and the Cup for the Leafs with a goal. It was the last one he ever scored. Two months later, he was killed in a plane crash.

1950–51

FINAL STANDINGS

	W	L	T	PTS	GF	GA
Detroit	44	13	13	101	236	139
Toronto	41	16	13	95	212	138
Montreal	25	30	15	65	173	184
Boston	22	30	18	62	178	197
New York	20	29	21	61	169	201
Chicago	13	47	10	36	171	280

LEADING SCORERS

	G	A	PTS
Howe, Detroit	43	43	86
M. Richard, Montreal	42	24	66
M. Bentley, Toronto	21	41	62
Abel, Detroit	23	38	61
Schmidt, Boston	22	39	61
Kennedy, Toronto	18	43	61
Lindsay, Detroit	24	35	59
Sloan, Toronto	31	25	56
Kelly, Detroit	17	37	54
Smith, Toronto	30	21	51
Gardner, Toronto	23	28	51

« *Montreal's Doug Harvey, an All-Star, starts up ice in 1951–52 against Boston.*

1951–52

Detroit won its fourth straight regular-season championship, but the most exciting moments of the season came on March 23 in a meaningless game between New York and Chicago. That was the night Bill Mosienko made hockey history.

The Rangers and Black Hawks were out of the race for a playoff berth when they met that night at Madison Square Garden. New York was fifth and Chicago last. The Rangers, who had used Chuck Rayner and Emile Francis in goal during most of the season, went with Lorne Anderson in this particular game.

Mosienko, one of Chicago's top scorers, was playing on a line with Gus Bodnar and George Gee. At 6:09 of the third period, Bodnar fed the puck to Mosienko and the right wing fired a goal. The puck was brought back for a faceoff and at 6:20 the combination clicked again. Then another faceoff and at 6:30 another goal by Mosienko. Three goals in 21 seconds earned him a spot in the record book for the quickest hat trick in NHL history.

In Detroit, the Red Wings were dreaming about the Stanley Cup. And it was no idle dream, either. The Wings had ripped through the regular season, rolling up 100 points— just one point under the record they had established the season before. They finished 22 points ahead of second-place Montreal.

Gordie Howe won his second straight scoring title with 86 points, the same number he had posted the year before. He scored 47 goals, making a serious run at Maurice Richard's record of 50. Howe was chosen MVP and named to the right wing spot on the All-Star team. The other All-Stars were Detroit's Ted Lindsay at left wing, Montreal's Elmer Lach at center, Red Kelly of Detroit and Doug Harvey of Montreal on defense and Detroit's Terry Sawchuk in goal.

Sawchuk took the Vezina Trophy with a 1.94 goals-against average and a league-leading 12 shutouts. Toronto's Sid Smith won the Lady Byng and Montreal's Bernie Geoffrion, nicknamed Boom Boom for his jet-powered

slap shots, took the Calder Trophy as the top rookie.

Montreal battled through seven games before eliminating Boston in the Stanley Cup semifinals. The Canadiens took the deciding game when Maurice Richard skated through four Bruins and then fought off Bill Quackenbush, the last defender, before beating Jim Henry for the tie-breaking goal with four minutes to play. The significant thing about the goal is that Richard remembers very little about it. He had spent the second period of the game in the clinic at the Montreal Forum having six stitches put in his head after being pelted by Leo Labine.

"I was dizzy and a few times when I got the puck I didn't know whether I was skating toward our goal or their goal," Richard said.

Detroit goalie Terry Sawchuk gets help from teammate Marcel Pronovost in holding off Boston's Milt Schmidt in 1952–53.

Richard's heroics got the Canadiens into the final round but the Rocket couldn't help against the Red Wing juggernaut. Howe and Ted Lindsay scored five goals between them and Sawchuk turned in his third and fourth shutouts of the playoffs as Detroit swept to the Stanley Cup in four straight games. In eight playoff games, Sawchuk allowed only five goals—an incredible 0.62 goals-against average.

1951–52

FINAL STANDINGS

	W	L	T	PTS	GF	GA
Detroit	44	14	12	100	215	133
Montreal	34	26	10	78	195	164
Toronto	29	25	16	74	168	157
Boston	25	29	16	66	162	176
New York	23	34	13	59	192	219
Chicago	17	44	9	43	158	241

❰❰ *Boston's Jim Henry congratulates Montreal's Maurice Richard after the Canadiens eliminated the Bruins in the 1952 semifinals.*

LEADING SCORERS

	G	A	PTS
Howe, Detroit	47	39	86
Lindsay, Detroit	30	39	69
Lach, Montreal	15	50	65
Raleigh, New York	19	42	61
Smith, Toronto	27	30	57
Geoffrion, Montreal	30	24	54
Mosienko, Chicago	31	22	53
Abel, Detroit	17	36	53
Kennedy, Toronto	19	33	52
Schmidt, Boston	21	29	50
Peirson, Boston	20	30	50

1952–53

Detroit's Production Line was broken up before the 1952–53 season when Sid Abel asked to be traded to Chicago. The Black Hawks wanted Abel as coach and Jack Adams, the Detroit general manager, did not stand in the way of his veteran center.

Abel's replacement was Alex Delvecchio, who flourished playing between Gordie Howe

and Ted Lindsay. He scored 59 points, including 43 assists. The switch in centers made little difference to right winger Howe and left winger Lindsay. They finished 1-2 in scoring for the second straight year with Gordie accumulating 95 points and making his most serious run at Maurice Richard's 50-goal record, finishing with 49. Lindsay had 71 points, including 32 goals.

The departure of Abel didn't seem to hurt the Red Wings, who won their fifth straight regular-season title, but it had a major effect on Chicago, the club Abel took over. Doubling as a player-coach, Abel piloted the Black Hawks to a third-place tie with Boston for Chicago's first playoff berth in seven years.

The scoring crown was Howe's third straight and he became the first man in NHL history to put three together. Similarly, the Red Wings made NHL history with their fifth straight league title. Boston twice and Montreal once had strung four regular-season titles together, but no team had ever managed five.

Howe and Lindsay were named right wing and left wing on the first All-Star team for the third straight year. The other All-Stars were Boston center Fleming Mackell, defensemen Red Kelly of Detroit and Doug Harvey of Montreal and goalie Terry Sawchuk of Detroit.

Howe won his second consecutive Hart Trophy as MVP, Kelly was the Lady Byng winner and Sawchuk, with a 1.90 average, won the Vezina. The Calder Trophy went to New York goalie Lorne (Gump) Worsley—the third goalie in four years to be honored as the NHL's top rookie.

Early in the season, Maurice Richard scored his 324th career goal, tying the NHL record held by another Montreal great, Nels Stewart. On November 8, he scored No. 325 to set the new standard. On the same night, Richard's center, Elmer Lach, scored the 200th goal of his career.

In the playoffs, the powerful Red Wings, who had breezed to the Stanley Cup in eight straight games the year before, ruled as heavy favorites. They battered Boston, 7–0, in the opening game and looked like a sure thing to

repeat as champions. But some clutch scoring by Ed Sandford and heroic goaltending by Sugar Jim Henry gave the Bruins a six-game first-round victory over Detroit.

Chicago held a three-to-two edge in games against Montreal in the other semifinal when Gerry McNeil went to coach Dick Irvin of the Canadiens and suggested that he use Jacques Plante, a rookie, in goal. It was a repeat of Bill Durnan's action during the playoffs in 1950 when he had gone to Irvin and asked to be replaced by McNeil. Plante allowed the Black Hawks one goal in two games and the Canadiens advanced to the final round against Boston.

With Plante and McNeil dividing the netminding, Montreal whipped the Bruins in five games to capture the Stanley Cup.

1952–53

FINAL STANDINGS

	W	L	T	PTS	GF	GA
Detroit	36	16	18	90	222	133
Montreal	28	23	19	75	155	148
Boston	28	29	13	69	152	172
Chicago	27	28	15	69	169	175
Toronto	27	30	13	67	156	167
New York	17	37	16	50	152	211

LEADING SCORERS

	G	A	PTS
Howe, Detroit	49	46	95
Lindsay, Detroit	32	39	71
M. Richard, Montreal	28	33	61
Hergesheimer, New York	30	29	59
Delvecchio, Detroit	16	43	59
Ronty, New York	16	38	54
Prystai, Detroit	16	34	50
Kelly, Detroit	19	27	46
Olmstead, Montreal	17	28	45
Mackell, Boston	27	17	44
McFadden, Chicago	23	21	44

1953–54

The Chicago Black Hawks slipped back into the NHL's cellar after their one-season move into the playoffs and established a record for futility in 1953–54. They managed only 12 victories and lost 51 times. Both are NHL records for 70-game seasons.

Ironically, the Black Hawks did achieve one important honor that season. Goalie Al Rollins was named the Most Valuable Player in the league. The award might very well have been for heroism in the face of a season-long

Toronto's Harry Lumley blanked 13 opponents and won the Vezina Trophy in 1953–54.

barrage of enemy shots. Four of the 12 Chicago victories were shutouts by Rollins and the 242 goals allowed by the Black Hawks were the most in the league.

Even more ironic is the fact that Harry Lumley, whom Chicago had traded to Toronto for Rollins and three other players the year before, won the Vezina Trophy, a spot on the All-Star team and a line in the NHL record book with 13 shutouts, the most ever. But the MVP was Rollins.

Gordie Howe and the Detroit Red Wings again ruled the league. Howe won an unprecedented fourth straight scoring title with 81 points and the Red Wings captured a record sixth consecutive regular-season championship.

Howe and his Detroit linemate, Ted Lindsay, made the first All-Star team for the fourth straight year. Montreal center Ken Mosdell,

defensemen Doug Harvey of Montreal and Red Kelly of Detroit and Lumley, Toronto's goalie, completed the team. It was the third straight All-Star berth for Kelly and Harvey.

Kelly also won his third Lady Byng Trophy in four years and captured a new award, the James Norris Trophy, as the league's top defenseman. The trophy was presented by the four children of the late former owner-president of the Detroit Red Wings. Camille Henry of New York took the Calder Trophy.

Detroit needed just five games to eliminate Toronto, and Montreal took Boston in four straight in the opening rounds of the Stanley Cup playoffs.

Then the Canadiens and Red Wings went at each other in the final round in a memorable series that stretched over seven games. The Red Wings, with Gordie Howe, Ted Lindsay and Alex Delvecchio starring, won three of the

Montreal goalie Jacques Plante and teammate Butch Bouchard are down but not out as they block scoring attempt by the Rangers' Don Raleigh in 1954–55.

first four contests. Then Canadiens' coach Dick Irvin changed goalies, recalling 31-year-old Gerry McNeil from the minors to replace Jacques Plante.

McNeil shut out the Red Wings in the fifth game, which Montreal won on an overtime goal by Ken Mosdell. Then he beat them, 4–1, to even the series at three games apiece.

The seventh game went into overtime tied at 1–1. With 4½ minutes gone in the extra period, Detroit's Tony Leswick lofted a shot toward McNeil. Doug Harvey, the Canadiens' superlative defenseman, lifted his glove to flick the puck away. Instead, it glanced off Harvey's glove, over McNeil's shoulder and into the Montreal net, giving Detroit the Stanley Cup.

The Canadiens stormed off the ice instead of congratulating the Red Wings as custom dictated. "If I had shaken hands," stormed coach Dick Irvin, "I wouldn't have meant it. I refuse to be a hypocrite."

1953–54

FINAL STANDINGS

	W	L	T	PTS	GF	GA
Detroit	37	19	14	88	191	132
Montreal	35	24	11	81	195	141
Toronto	32	24	14	78	152	131
Boston	32	28	10	74	177	181
New York	29	31	10	68	161	182
Chicago	12	51	7	31	133	242

LEADING SCORERS

	G	A	PTS
Howe, Detroit	33	48	81
M. Richard, Montreal	37	30	67
Lindsay, Detroit	26	36	62
Geoffrion, Montreal	29	25	54
Olmstead, Montreal	15	37	52
Kelly, Detroit	16	33	49
Reibel, Detroit	15	33	48
Sanford, Boston	16	31	47
Mackell, Boston	15	32	47
Mosdell, Montreal	22	24	46
Ronty, New York	13	33	46

1954–55

Montreal was piecing together a powerful young team to make a run at Detroit's domination of the NHL. There was tall Jean Beliveau, the slick center from Quebec whom the Canadiens wanted so badly they purchased the rights to an entire amateur league to get him. There was flamboyant Boom Boom Geoffrion, a hard-shooting right winger. There was cool Doug Harvey, perhaps the finest defenseman in the league since Eddie Shore. There was colorful Jacques Plante in goal. And there was the Rocket—Maurice Richard.

The Rocket was always No. 1 with the Canadiens' fans. He was the heart of the club. The fiery Frenchman with the Gallic glare was long on talent and short on temper. It was the latter that got him in trouble, costing him the scoring title and leading to the riot of Ste. Catherine Street which rocked the hockey world in March 1955.

Richard, Geoffrion and Beliveau were racing for the scoring title when the Rocket's temper sabotaged him. It was March 13 in Boston when Richard lost his poise, attacked Hal Laycoe of the Bruins with his stick and took a punch at linesman Cliff Thompson.

Clarence Campbell, the league president, was outraged by Richard's behavior and suspended the star for the final three games of the regular season as well as the entire playoffs. Campbell showed up at the Montreal Forum on March 17 to watch the Canadiens play Detroit in a battle for first place. When the president took his seat, he was greeted with some hooting as well as a shower of peanuts and programs. Then a tear gas bomb was thrown on the ice at about the same moment that a fan approached Campbell's box with hand extended as if to shake, and then whacked the president.

Outside the building, more trouble was brewing. As fans poured out of the besieged Forum, they turned into a mob, rumbling down Ste. Catherine Street, Montreal's main avenue, and looting stores.

The next day, Richard went on the radio to plead in French for calm. "I will take my

General manager Jack Adams guided Detroit to its seventh Stanley Cup in 1954–55.

punishment," he said, "and come back next year to help the club and the younger players to win the Stanley Cup."

The suspension left Richard with 74 points and Geoffrion edged past him with 75 to win the scoring crown. Beliveau finished third with 73. Richard was named to the All-Star team along with Beliveau at center and Sid Smith of Toronto at left wing. The defensemen, again, were Doug Harvey of Montreal and Red Kelly of Detroit with Toronto's Harry Lumley in goal.

Smith won the Lady Byng Trophy while Terry Sawchuk of Detroit took the Vezina with a league-leading 12 shutouts and a 1.94 average. It was the fifth straight season in which his goals-against average was less than two per game. The Norris Trophy went to Harvey, the Hart Trophy to Toronto's Ted Kennedy and the Calder to Ed Litzenberger of Chicago.

Detroit edged Montreal for the regular-season title, winning its seventh straight crown by just two points. In the Stanley Cup semifinals, the Red Wings whipped Toronto in four straight and the Canadiens needed five games to eliminate Boston.

In an effort to beat the Red Wings, Montreal coach Dick Irvin alternated his goalies, Jacques Plante and Charlie Hodge. But the Wings, winning all their games at home and none in Montreal, took the series and the Cup, four games to three, as Alex Delvecchio scored twice in the seventh game.

1954–55

FINAL STANDINGS

	W	L	T	PTS	GF	GA
Detroit	42	17	11	95	204	134
Montreal	41	18	11	93	228	157
Toronto	24	24	22	70	147	135
Boston	23	26	21	67	169	188
New York	17	35	18	52	150	210
Chicago	13	40	17	43	161	235

LEADING SCORERS

	G	A	PTS
Geoffrion, Montreal	38	37	75
M. Richard, Montreal	38	36	74
Beliveau, Montreal	37	36	73
Reibel, Detroit	25	41	66
Howe, Detroit	29	33	62
Sullivan, Chicago	19	42	61
Olmstead, Montreal	10	48	58
Smith, Toronto	33	21	54
Mosdell, Montreal	22	32	54
Lewicki, New York	29	24	53

1955–56

There were important personnel changes around the league in 1955–56—both on the players' benches and behind them. After 14 seasons as coach of the Canadiens, Dick Irvin left Montreal and moved on to Chicago, where the challenge of rebuilding the Black Hawks seemed enormous. Irvin's replacement was Toe Blake, left wing on the old Punch Line. In New York, Phil Watson, always a firebrand, took over as coach, replacing Muzz Patrick, who in turn took over from Frank Boucher as the Rangers' general manager.

《 *Montreal goalie Jacques Plante hurdles a fallen Maple Leaf in 1955–56, the year Plante's 1.86 goals-against average netted him the Vezina Trophy.*

Detroit shook up its Stanley Cup champions and a series of trades left the Red Wings with only nine players from the squad that had captured the Cup the previous spring. In the biggest trade, Jack Adams swapped four players, including goalie Terry Sawchuk, to Boston for five Bruins. The Sawchuk deal was made because the Red Wing management felt that Terry's nerves were getting the best of him and also because Adams had a ready-made replacement in young Glenn Hall.

Adams also consummated an eight-player trade with Chicago as the Black Hawks feverishly tried to move out of the league's lower echelon. They didn't make it, but the Rangers did. New scoring punch from a group of recently-graduated junior players including Andy Bathgate, Dean Prentice and Ron Murphy, as well as a stiffened defense supplied by Bill Gadsby, Harry Howell and the fans' favorite, Louie Fontinato, vaulted New York to third place—its highest finish in 14 years.

Fontinato, a rookie, accumulated 202 minutes in penalties—spending the equivalent of more than 10 periods sitting out infractions. The New York fans loved his brawling and nicknamed him Louie the Leaper.

In Montreal, Blake added three rookies— Henri Richard, the younger brother of Maurice, defenseman Jean Guy Talbot and forward Claude Provost. The Canadiens were clearly the class of the league and finished with 100 points, losing only 15 of their 70 games. Three of the top four scorers were Canadiens, including the champion, Jean Beliveau, who had 47 goals among his 88 points.

Beliveau was named to the All-Star team along with teammates Maurice Richard, Doug Harvey and Jacques Plante. Beliveau and Richard were joined on the forward line by Detroit's Ted Lindsay while Bill Gadsby of New York won the other defense spot alongside Harvey and in front of goaltender Plante.

Plante won the Vezina Trophy with a 1.86 goals-against average, Harvey took the Norris Trophy and Beliveau was named MVP. Detroit's Earl (Dutch) Reibel won the Lady Byng while Glenn Hall, Sawchuk's replacement at Detroit, was the Calder Trophy winner.

Montreal finished off New York in five games and Detroit eliminated Toronto, also in five, in the opening rounds of the Stanley Cup playoffs. Then, with Beliveau, Bernie Geoffrion, Richard and Bert Olmstead supplying the firepower, Montreal beat Detroit in five games to win its first Stanley Cup in a decade.

1955–56

FINAL STANDINGS

	W	L	T	PTS	GF	GA
Montreal	45	15	10	100	222	131
Detroit	30	24	16	76	183	148
New York	32	28	10	74	204	203
Toronto	24	33	13	61	153	181
Boston	23	34	13	59	147	185
Chicago	19	39	12	50	155	216

LEADING SCORERS

	G	A	PTS
Beliveau, Montreal	47	41	88
Howe, Detroit	38	41	79
M. Richard, Montreal	38	33	71
Olmstead, Montreal	14	56	70
Sloan, Toronto	37	29	66
Bathgate, New York	19	47	66
Geoffrion, Montreal	29	33	62
Reibel, Detroit	17	39	56
Delvecchio, Detroit	25	26	51
Creighton, New York	20	31	51
Gadsby, New York	9	42	51

1956–57

Montreal's powerhouse Canadiens became the scourge of the league with a collection of the finest shooters ever to occupy a single team's roster at the same time. Maurice Richard, Jean Beliveau, Boom Boom Geoffrion, Bert Olmstead, Dickie Moore and the others were all expert marksmen. And when coach Toe Blake assembled a power play to take advantage of an enemy penalty, the Canadiens' shooters could turn a game around.

Blake used Geoffrion and Doug Harvey at the points on power plays because of their hard, accurate shots. Up front he would employ Richard at right wing, Beliveau at center and Moore or Olmstead at left wing. The effect was devastating. The Canadiens often would score two or three goals on a single penalty because at the time the rules required a penalized player to spend his full

« *The Canadiens' Henri Richard splits Ranger defensemen Lou Fontinato (on ice) and Harry Howell in 1956–57.*

two minutes in the penalty box, regardless of how often the team with the manpower edge scored.

But the Canadiens made a travesty of the rule and eventually it had to be changed, specifically because of Montreal's proficiency. Starting in 1956–57, as soon as the team with the manpower edge scored, the penalized player was allowed to return to the ice and restore his team to full strength.

Detroit's assessment of Terry Sawchuk's nerves proved accurate when the ex-Red Wing goalie walked out on the Bruins in midseason, saying he was ill. The Bruins put in a hurry-up call to Springfield of the American League and came up with Don Simmons to replace Sawchuk. Ironically, on the day he left Boston, Sawchuk was named to the All-Star team for the first half of the season. With Terry sitting out the second half, Glenn Hall, his replacement at Detroit, captured the final All-Star designation.

The other All-Stars were Detroit's Red Kelly and Montreal's Doug Harvey on defense, Jean Beliveau of Montreal at center and Detroit's Ted Lindsay and Gordie Howe on the wings.

Howe won his fifth scoring championship with 89 points, including 44 goals and also captured the Hart Trophy as MVP. The Lady Byng went to New York's Andy Hebenton, while Montreal's Jacques Plante took the Vezina, Larry Regan of Boston won the Calder and Harvey captured the Norris.

Detroit won its eighth regular-season crown in nine years, beating out the Canadiens by six points. But the Red Wings were upset by Boston's determined Bruins in the Stanley Cup semifinal series. Detroit bowed when Boston rallied for three goals in the third period to win the deciding seventh contest.

Montreal eliminated New York in five games with Geoffrion exploding for three goals in the third engagement. The Canadiens faced the Bruins for the Stanley Cup and Richard set the tone by exploding for four goals in the 5–1 opening-game victory. The Rocket scored three times in the second period and Simmons, the victim of the assault,

The Blackhawks unveiled dynamic Bobby Hull in 1957–58.

Toronto's Frank Mahovlich won the Calder Trophy in 1957–58 and became known as "The Big M."

said simply, "It was humiliating." It took the Canadiens just five games to clinch the Cup.

1956–57

FINAL STANDINGS

	W	L	T	PTS	GF	GA
Detroit	38	20	12	88	198	157
Montreal	35	23	12	82	210	155
Boston	34	24	12	80	195	174
New York	26	30	14	66	184	227
Toronto	21	34	15	57	174	192
Chicago	16	39	15	47	169	225

LEADING SCORERS

	G	A	PTS
Howe, Detroit	44	45	89
Lindsay, Detroit	30	55	85
Beliveau, Montreal	33	51	84
Bathgate, New York	27	50	77
Litzenberger, Chicago	32	32	64
M. Richard, Montreal	33	29	62
McKenney, Boston	21	39	60
Moore, Montreal	29	29	58
H. Richard, Montreal	18	36	54
Ullman, Detroit	16	36	52

1957–58

Two marvelously talented rookie left wings broke into the NHL in 1957–58. Toronto's Frank Mahovlich won the Calder Trophy as the top rookie, but it was Chicago's Bobby Hull who was to emerge as one of the game's most dynamic stars.

In Detroit, Jolly Jack Adams was again active in the player market. He took Terry Sawchuk back from the Bruins in exchange for Johnny Bucyk and made room for his returning goaltender by swapping Glenn Hall and Ted Lindsay to Chicago for four players. It was rumored that part of the reason Adams unloaded Lindsay was the veteran left wing's active participation in the formation of an NHL Players' Association.

It was the best of times and it was the worst of times for Montreal's Maurice Richard. On October 19, he scored his 500th regular-sea-

son goal, but less than one month later he collided with Toronto's Marc Reaume and his Achilles tendon was almost completely severed. For a time, it was feared that the 36-year-old Rocket's career might be over.

In February, the Canadiens again were jolted by an injury. This time it was Boom Boom Geoffrion, leading the league in goals at the time. The Boomer ran into teammate Andre Pronovost during a workout and ruptured a bowel. He was given the last rites of the Roman Catholic Church before major stomach surgery saved his life.

Despite the injuries, the Canadiens carried on and finished first, 19 points ahead of the surprising Rangers, who had uncovered a new scoring star in Andy Bathgate. Part of the reason for the Canadiens' success was left winger Dickie Moore, who played the last five weeks of the season with a cast on his right wrist but still won the scoring championship with 84 points as well as an All-Star berth.

Despite the Rocket's injury, there was a Richard on the All-Star team. Brother Henri, the Pocket Rocket, who finished second to Moore in scoring with 80 points, was picked as the center. Gordie Howe of Detroit was on right wing, with Bill Gadsby of New York and Doug Harvey of Montreal as the defensemen and Chicago's Glenn Hall in goal.

Howe won Most Valuable Player honors and Harvey took the Norris Trophy as the top defenseman for the fourth straight year. Camille Henry of the Rangers won the Lady Byng, Montreal's Jacques Plante, who had started using a mask in practice, was the Vezina winner and Toronto's Frank Mahovlich took the Calder. Mahovlich had 20 goals and 16 assists compared to Bobby Hull's 13 goals and 34 assists.

Maurice Richard, who had missed 42 regular-season games after his injury and had scored only 15 goals all year, was the spark that drove the Canadiens to their third straight Stanley Cup. Montreal swept Detroit in four games with Richard's hat trick in the final contest leading a last-period comeback that erased a two-goal deficit and gave the Canadiens a 4–3 victory.

Boston, which had eliminated New York in six games, was tied at two games apiece with Montreal when the Rocket's overtime goal in the fifth game put the Canadiens in the driver's seat. Montreal finished off Boston in the sixth game as Richard completed the 10 playoff games with 11 goals.

1957–58

FINAL STANDINGS

	W	L	T	PTS	GF	GA
Montreal	43	17	10	96	250	158
New York	32	25	13	77	195	188
Detroit	29	29	12	70	176	207
Boston	27	28	15	69	199	194
Chicago	24	39	7	55	163	202
Toronto	21	38	11	53	192	226

LEADING SCORERS

	G	A	PTS
Moore, Montreal	36	48	84
H. Richard, Montreal	28	52	80
Bathgate, New York	30	48	78
Howe, Detroit	33	44	77
Horvath, Boston	30	36	66
Litzenberger, Chicago	32	30	62
Mackell, Boston	20	40	60
Beliveau, Montreal	27	32	59
Delvecchio, Detroit	21	38	59
McKenney, Boston	28	30	58

1958–59

Conn Smythe never was a very good loser and when his Toronto Maple Leafs slipped into the NHL cellar, he decided it was time for action. Smythe sought out George (Punch) Imlach, director of player personnel for Boston, and offered him a front-office spot with the Leafs. Imlach accepted, provided that the position was that of general manager. The Leafs had no one doing that particular job, so Smythe agreed.

A week after he was named general manager, Imlach decided that Billy Reay, Toronto's coach, wasn't doing a good enough job. Imlach went on a talent hunt and lured the best man available—Punch Imlach.

The Maple Leafs had several new faces besides Imlach's. They had swapped Jim Morrison to Boston for defenseman Allan Stanley and signed another new defenseman in 21-year-old Carl Brewer. Bert Olmstead was acquired from Montreal and Imlach picked up a 33-year-old journeyman goalie, Johnny Bower, from Cleveland of the American League.

Montreal's Jean Beliveau (4) makes one of his league-leading 45 goals against Toronto's Johnny Bower in 1958–59.

They all played a role in Toronto's helter-skelter stretch run to a playoff spot. With 20 games left to play, the Maple Leafs were in the cellar. On the final night of the regular season they won their fifth straight game while New York was losing its sixth in the last seven. As a result, Toronto sneaked into the fourth and final playoff spot, one point ahead of the embarrassed Rangers, who had to refund thousands of dollars worth of useless playoff tickets.

Montreal easily captured the regular-season title, beating Boston by 18 points. Detroit, meanwhile, had fallen on lean times and dipped all the way into the league basement despite a 32-goal season by Gordie Howe.

Dickie Moore of Montreal won his second straight scoring title with a record 96 points and earned the left wing spot on the All-Star team. Three other Canadiens also made the

All-Stars, with Jacques Plante in goal, Jean Beliveau at center and Tom Johnson on defense. Johnson beat out teammate Doug Harvey, who missed the first team after seven straight selections. Right winger Andy Bathgate and defenseman Bill Gadsby of the Rangers completed the squad.

Bathgate won the Hart Trophy, Plante took his fourth straight Vezina and Johnson ended Harvey's four-year monopoly of the Norris Trophy. Montreal's Ralph Backstrom captured the Calder Trophy and Alex Delvecchio of Detroit was the Lady Byng winner.

Maurice Richard of Montreal missed 28 games with a fractured ankle and was virtually useless to the Canadiens in the playoffs. But his loss made little difference to the Montreal powerhouse. The Canadiens eliminated Chicago in six games and ousted Toronto, which had eliminated Boston, in five games for an

The Rocket, Montreal's Maurice Richard, battles Chicago's Elmer
(Moose) Vasko in 1959–60.

unprecedented fourth consecutive Stanley Cup.

1958–59

FINAL STANDINGS

	W	L	T	PTS	GF	GA
Montreal	39	18	13	91	258	158
Boston	32	29	9	73	205	215
Chicago	28	29	13	69	197	208
Toronto	27	32	11	65	189	201
New York	26	32	12	64	201	217
Detroit	25	37	8	58	167	218

LEADING SCORERS

	G	A	PTS
Moore, Montreal	41	55	96
Beliveau, Montreal	45	46	91
Bathgate, New York	40	48	88
Howe, Detroit	32	46	78
Litzenberger, Chicago	33	44	77
Geoffrion, Montreal	22	44	66
Sullivan, New York	21	42	63
Hebenton, New York	33	29	62
McKenney, Boston	32	30	62
Sloan, Chicago	27	35	62

1959–60

The pressures of modern hockey had taken their toll on goaltenders. There was Montreal's Bill Durnan, who retired prematurely because of nerves; Montreal's Gerry McNeil, another early retiree, and Terry Sawchuk, who left Boston in midseason when he began seeing too much rubber. Montreal's Jacques Plante was determined not to let that happen to him.

Plante had been using a mask in practice for two years after fracturing first one and then the other cheekbone during workouts. Jacques had approached coach Toe Blake about wearing the mask during a game but Blake would not allow it.

Then, on November 1, 1959, a shot by New York's Andy Bathgate crunched into Plante's

profile, inflicting a gash that took seven stitches.

When Plante subsequently emerged from the dressing room carrying a mask, he looked like a creature from outer space. How could he follow the puck through the mask's tiny eye slits? The answer was that Plante somehow saw it. That night, he beat the Rangers, 3–1,

for Montreal's eighth straight game without a loss. The Canadiens tacked 10 more on to that streak as fans around the league flocked to see the masked marvel at work.

Plante captured his fifth consecutive Vezina Trophy, but the All-Star goalie berth went to Chicago's Glenn Hall. Chicago's Bobby Hull won the scoring race in an exciting battle with

Boston's Bronco Horvath. Hull finished with 39 goals and 81 points—one point more than Horvath—and was the left wing on the All-Star team.

Gordie Howe of Detroit was the All-Star right wing with Montreal's Jean Beliveau at center. The defensemen were Marcel Pronovost of Detroit and Doug Harvey of Montreal. Howe won the Hart Trophy as MVP, Don McKenney of Boston was the Lady Byng winner, Harvey took the Norris and Chicago's Bill Hay, who centered for Hull, won the Calder.

The Canadiens won their third straight regular-season title, beating Toronto by 13 points. Then Montreal eliminated Chicago in four games in the opening round of the playoffs, with Plante turning in shutouts in the last two.

The Maple Leafs, perhaps inspired by a pile of 1,250 dollar bills that coach Punch Imlach placed in the middle of the dressing room floor as a reminder of the difference between winning and losing, eliminated Detroit in six games.

But Montreal swept past Toronto in the finals in four straight games, to win the Stanley Cup in the minimum of eight games.

1959–60

FINAL STANDINGS

	W	L	T	PTS	GF	GA
Montreal	40	18	12	92	255	178
Toronto	35	26	9	79	199	195
Chicago	28	29	13	69	191	180
Detroit	26	29	15	67	186	197
Boston	28	34	8	64	220	241
New York	17	38	15	49	187	247

LEADING SCORERS

	G	A	PTS
Hull, Chicago	39	42	81
Horvath, Boston	39	41	80
Beliveau, Montreal	34	40	74
Bathgate, New York	26	48	74
H. Richard, Montreal	30	43	73
Howe, Detroit	28	45	73
Geoffrion, Montreal	30	41	71
McKenney, Boston	20	49	69
Stasiuk, Boston	29	39	68
Prentice, New York	32	34	66

1960–61

An era came to an end in 1960 when Montreal's Maurice Richard retired. After 18

« *The 1960–61 Rookie of the Year was Dave Keon of Toronto.*

professional seasons and 544 goals, the Rocket was off the ice. But that didn't keep his name out of the hockey headlines.

That was because for the first time since 1953, when Gordie Howe scored 49 times, there was a genuine threat to the Rocket's record of 50 goals in a season. It would be more correct to say there were two threats, but Frank Mahovlich's early-season pace obscured Bernie Geoffrion's run at the Rocket's mark.

By midseason, Mahovlich, Toronto's hard-skating left wing, had 37 goals and seemed a cinch to top 50. Geoffrion, on the other hand, missed six games with injuries and had only 29 goals going into the final six weeks of the season. And 14 of those had come over one 11-game stretch.

The defenses keyed on Mahovlich over those final weeks and Toronto's Big M finished with 48 goals. Geoffrion, a streaky player, hit another hot spell, exploding for 18 goals in 13 games and scoring his 50th of the season in the Canadiens' 68th game—ironically against Mahovlich's team, the Maple Leafs.

Geoffrion did not score in either of the last two games of the regular season, but won the scoring title with his 50 goals and 45 assists for 95 points. He was the All-Star right wing with Toronto's Mahovlich at left wing and Jean Beliveau of Montreal at center. The defensemen were Doug Harvey of Montreal and Marcel Pronovost of Detroit with Toronto's Johnny Bower in goal.

Bower ended Jacques Plante's five-year hold on the Vezina Trophy while Geoffrion earned the Hart Trophy and Harvey won the Norris for the sixth time. Dave Keon of Toronto was the Calder winner and Red Kelly, switched from defense to center after being traded to Toronto, won his fourth Lady Byng.

The Canadiens captured their fourth straight regular-season championship, beating out Toronto by two points. And Montreal was favored to continue its string of five consecutive Stanley Cups when it opened the playoffs against third-place Chicago.

But the Black Hawks intimidated the Canadiens with some tough body work and got

consecutive shutouts from goalie Glenn Hall in the fifth and sixth games to beat Montreal, four games to two. The turning point may have come in the third game, won in triple overtime by Chicago on Murray Balfour's goal. Montreal coach Toe Blake was so incensed at the officiating of Dalton McArthur that he rushed on the ice and took a swing at the referee. That sortie cost Toe $2,000.

Detroit knocked out Toronto in five games, setting up the final for the Stanley Cup between the third-place Black Hawks and fourth-place Red Wings. Unflattering remarks about the officiating cost coach Rudy Pilous and general manager Tommy Ivan of the Black Hawks $500 between them but the fines didn't hurt too much because Chicago took the Cup in six games.

1960–61

FINAL STANDINGS

	W	L	T	PTS	GF	GA
Montreal	41	19	10	92	254	188
Toronto	39	19	12	90	234	176
Chicago	29	24	17	75	198	180
Detroit	25	29	16	66	195	215
New York	22	38	10	54	204	248
Boston	15	42	13	43	176	254

LEADING SCORERS

	G	A	PTS
Geoffrion, Montreal	50	45	95
Beliveau, Montreal	32	58	90
Mahovlich, Toronto	48	36	84
Bathgate, New York	29	48	77
Howe, Detroit	23	49	72
Ullman, Detroit	28	42	70
Kelly, Toronto	20	50	70
Moore, Montreal	35	34	69
H. Richard, Montreal	24	44	68
Delvecchio, Detroit	27	35	62

1961–62

In August, the Hockey Hall of Fame erected on the Canadian National Exhibition grounds at Toronto, was officially opened. Built at a cost of $500,000, the hockey shrine honored 89 players, executives and referees from hockey's past.

But it was a player very much of the present who created the excitement, Chicago's blond bombshell, Bobby Hull. A scoring champion two years earlier at the age of 21, Hull boasted

Gordie Howe of Detroit displays the puck and stick that marked his 500th regular-season goal on March 14, 1962.

a slap shot clocked at better than 100 miles per hour.

Hull started his record run slowly and had only 16 goals after 40 games. But then, like Geoffrion had done the year before, when he tied Maurice Richard's record of 50 goals, Bobby went on a tear. Fourteen goals in nine games, including four in one night, left him 20 goals away from the record with 20 games to play. He needed an average of one goal per game and he got them. He was blanked in only four of the Hawks' final 20 games but made up for those scoreless nights with four two-goal games. He scored his 50th on the final night of the season in New York.

His 84 points gave Hull a tie for the scoring championship with New York's Andy Bathgate. Both received $1,000 from the league

Toronto's Ron Stewart attempts to bunt the »
puck past Chicago's Glenn Hall.

but Hull took the Art Ross Trophy emblematic of the scoring title because he had 22 more goals.

New York, led by Bathgate and player-coach Doug Harvey, acquired from Montreal in a trade for defensemen Lou Fontinato, made it to the playoffs for the first time in four seasons, barely beating out Detroit. A goal on a penalty shot by Bathgate against the Red Wings in New York virtually clinched the spot for New York. In the same game, Gordie Howe, killing a Detroit penalty, scored the 500th regular-season goal of his NHL career.

Bathgate was chosen at right wing on the All-Star team and Hull at left wing. The center was slender Stan Mikita of Chicago, who

Montreal's Jacques Plante, turning away a shot by Detroit's Parker MacDonald, wound up the 1961–62 season with his sixth Vezina Trophy.

finished the season with 77 points, tied for third with Howe behind Hull and Bathgate. Jean Guy Talbot of Montreal and Harvey of New York were picked on defense and Montreal's Jacques Plante in goal. It was the 10th time in 11 years that Harvey had been selected as a first-team All-Star defensemen. In the other year he made the second team.

Harvey took his seventh Norris Trophy while Plante captured the Hart Trophy as well as his sixth Vezina. The Calder Trophy went to Montreal's Bobby Rousseau and Toronto's Dave Keon took the Lady Byng.

Montreal captured its fifth straight regular-season title, but again the Canadiens went up against the rambunctious Black Hawks in the playoffs. Montreal, playing at home, won the first two games, but Chicago rebounded to take four straight games with Mikita and Hull the key men.

Toronto eliminated New York in six games, winning the pivotal fifth one in double over-time on Red Kelly's goal despite a superb performance by New York goalie Gump Worsley, who stopped 56 shots.

The Leafs went on to win the Stanley Cup in six games against Chicago, the series turning on an 8–4 romp in the fifth game in which Toronto's Bob Pulford scored three goals.

1961–62

FINAL STANDINGS

	W	L	T	PTS	GF	GA
Montreal	42	14	14	98	259	166
Toronto	37	22	11	85	232	180
Chicago	31	26	13	75	217	186
New York	26	32	12	64	195	207
Detroit	23	33	14	60	184	219
Boston	15	47	8	38	177	306

LEADING SCORERS	G	A	PTS
Hull, Chicago	50	34	84
Bathgate, New York	28	56	84
Howe, Detroit	33	44	77
Mikita, Chicago	25	52	77
Mahovlich, Toronto	33	38	71
Delvecchio, Detroit	26	43	69
Backstrom, Montreal	27	38	65
Ullman, Detroit	26	38	64
Hay, Chicago	11	52	63
Provost, Montreal	33	29	62

1962–63

Punch Imlach, coach of the Toronto Maple Leafs, was tired of playing bridesmaid to Montreal's bride. For three straight seasons Imlach had finished second behind the Canadiens. It wasn't Imlach's idea of success.

Punch realized he had to strengthen his defense and he decided the man who could do it was a youngster named Kent Douglas, who was playing at Springfield in the American League. Owner Eddie Shore, himself a former defenseman of considerable repute, demanded a high price. It cost Imlach five players to get Douglas in a Leaf uniform but the move paid off. Douglas became the first defenseman to win the Calder Trophy as the outstanding rookie. And the Maple Leafs put on a late surge to catch Chicago and win the regular-season title. Toronto finished one point ahead of the Black Hawks in the NHL's closest race in years. Only five points separated the Leafs in first place and Detroit in fourth.

Gordie Howe of Detroit won his sixth scoring championship with 38 goals and 86 points. Howe was also the MVP and right wing on the All-Star team. The other All-Stars were Toronto's Frank Mahovlich on left wing, Chicago's Stan Mikita at center, Pierre Pilote of Chicago and Carl Brewer of Toronto on defense and Glenn Hall of Chicago in goal.

Hall won the Vezina Trophy but had his iron-man streak of consecutive regular-season games ended at 502 when a back ailment forced him out of a game in early November. It was the first game Hall had missed since coming into the league in 1954.

In Detroit, Jack Adams ended 35 years of association with the Red Wings to become president of the Central Hockey League,

where the NHL clubs had some of their most promising players developing.

But Adams' absence didn't bother Detroit fans. They were too fascinated by Howe's scoring heroics and the antics of defenseman Howie Young, who accumulated an unbelievable record 273 minutes in penalties—the equivalent of more than 4½ games.

The Red Wings kept their rooters happy in the opening round of the playoffs, eliminating Chicago in six games. Even the individual heroics of Bobby Hull, who scored eight goals despite a lame shoulder, a broken nose and a 10-stitch cut on his face, couldn't save the Black Hawks.

Montreal, weakened by late-season injuries to defensemen Lou Fontinato and Tom Johnson, bowed to Toronto in five games. Then the Maple Leafs took Detroit in five to win the Stanley Cup for the second straight year.

1962–63

FINAL STANDINGS

	W	L	T	PTS	GF	GA
Toronto	35	23	12	82	221	180
Chicago	32	21	17	81	194	178
Montreal	28	19	23	79	225	183
Detroit	32	25	13	77	200	194
New York	22	36	12	56	211	233
Boston	14	39	17	45	198	281

LEADING SCORERS	G	A	PTS
Howe, Detroit	38	48	86
Bathgate, New York	35	46	81
Mikita, Chicago	31	45	76
Mahovlich, Toronto	36	37	73
Richard, Montreal	23	50	73
Beliveau, Montreal	18	49	67
Bucyk, Boston	27	39	66
Delvecchio, Detroit	20	44	64
B. Hull, Chicago	31	31	62
Oliver, Boston	22	40	62

1963–64

Detroit's Gordie Howe entered his 19th National Hockey League season with 540 goals—just four away from the career record held by his great rival, Montreal's Maurice Richard. Howe and the other Red Wings were affected by the record as his teammates continually sought to set him up, often ignoring their own scoring chances.

On October 27, playing in Detroit's Olympia Stadium against Richard's old team, the

Canadiens, Howe tied the record at 544. The goal came despite tenacious checking by Montreal's Gilles Tremblay, who held Howe to two shots on goal all night. Defenseman Bill Gadsby earned his 400th NHL assist on Howe's historic goal.

Now, with his 544th in the books, Howe went for the record-breaker. Again the tension gripped both him and his teammates every time he took the ice. Finally, after two weeks of frustration, the break came. On November 10 at Detroit, Howe was killing a penalty against Montreal when he and Bill McNeill broke into Canadiens' ice. Gadsby flashed up the left side to make it a three-man rush and Howe fired the record-breaker.

Detroit's Terry Sawchuk blocks shot as Toronto's George Armstrong (10) and Red Wing Bill Gadsby (4) look for the rebound.

"I knew he would get it," conceded Maurice Richard after Howe had shattered his record. "He's a great player. How about that, scoring both goals (his 544th and 545th) against my old team!"

Like his record of 50 goals in 50 games, however, Richard could point out that it took him 978 games to reach 544, while Howe needed 1,132 games to achieve 545.

Chicago teammates Bobby Hull and Stan Mikita staged an exciting battle in the scoring race. Hull's booming shot produced a league-leading 43 goals, four more than Mikita. But the stick of Chicago center had 50 assists and 89 points to win the scoring championship.

« *Concentration is the key for Montreal's Jean Beliveau as he faces off against the Rangers' Lou Angotti in 1963–64.*

For the second straight year the Black Hawks finished one point away from first place, this time behind Montreal. Many Chicago observers thought back to 1927 and the curse Pete Muldoon was alleged to have put on Chicago when he was fired as coach.

The Hawks dominated the All-Star balloting with Mikita, Hull and Ken Wharram named up front along with teammates Pierre Pilote on defense and Glenn Hall in goal. It was only the second time in history that one team had placed five men on the first All-Star squad. The only non-Black Hawk chosen was defenseman Tim Horton of Toronto.

Montreal's Jean Beliveau won the Hart Trophy, Ken Wharram of Chicago took the Lady Byng, Pierre Pilote of Chicago won the Norris, Jacques Laperriere of Montreal cap-

Ted Lindsay of Detroit scores the final goal of his career, No. 379, against Boston's Jack Norris, in the spring of 1965.

tured the Calder and Charlie Hodge of Montreal, who took over when Jacques Plante was traded to New York, won the Vezina.

In February, Punch Imlach pulled off another major trade, dealing five players to New York for Andy Bathgate and Don McKenney. Eventually, the trade worked out in the Rangers' favor but its immediate effect was to help the Maple Leafs to their third straight Stanley Cup.

Bathgate and McKenney combined for nine goals and 12 assists between them as the Leafs eliminated Montreal in seven games and won the Cup in seven against Detroit.

1963–64

FINAL STANDINGS

	W	L	T	PTS	GF	GA
Montreal	36	21	13	85	209	167
Chicago	36	22	12	84	218	169
Toronto	33	25	12	78	192	172
Detroit	30	29	11	71	191	204
New York	22	38	10	54	186	242
Boston	18	40	12	48	170	212

LEADING SCORERS

	G	A	PTS
Mikita, Chicago	39	50	89
B. Hull, Chicago	43	44	87
Beliveau, Montreal	28	50	78
Bathgate, New York-Toronto	19	58	77
Howe, Detroit	26	47	73
Wharram, Chicago	39	32	71
Oliver, Boston	24	44	68
Goyette, New York	24	41	65
Gilbert, New York	24	40	64
Keon, Toronto	23	37	60

1964–65

NHL teams made two important front-office changes in 1964–65. First, in Montreal, Frank Selke retired as managing director of the Canadiens and was succeeded by Sammy Pollock, an organization man who had worked his way up through the Canadiens' vast network of farm teams. And in New York, Emile Francis succeeded Muzz Patrick as general manager of the Rangers. Francis, a journeyman goaltender in his playing days, had spent five years

tutoring the top Ranger junior prospects at the club's Guelph, Ontario, farm. Included among his students were Rod Gilbert and Jean Ratelle, two developing Ranger stars.

Detroit, fed up with the penalty-drawing antics of Howie Young, had traded the defenseman to Chicago for a minor-league goalie named Roger Crozier. The Red Wings, anxious to protect the young prospect, exposed veteran Terry Sawchuk to the draft, thinking his age, 34, would deter any claim. But Punch Imlach, who had remarkable success with elderly players at Toronto, most notably goalie Johnny Bower, claimed Sawchuk. That made Crozier the Red Wings' regular goalie and he didn't disappoint.

A shrimp at 5-foot-8 and 160 pounds, Crozier displayed remarkable reflexes. He sprung at shots as though his life depended on them. It may have been a carryover from his childhood. He was one of 14 children and that can cause plenty of scrambling.

Crozier's 2.42 goals-against average earned him the Calder Trophy and a berth on the All-Star team. And, combined with the goal-scoring of Norm Ullman, Alex Delvecchio and Gordie Howe, Crozier's performance led Detroit to its first regular-season title since 1957. Ullman scored 42 goals and finished second in the scoring race behind Chicago's Stan Mikita, who had 87 points. Howe had 29 goals and 76 points—third in the scoring race—and Delvecchio posted 25 goals and 67 points.

Ullman was the All-Star center, beating out Mikita. Chicago's Bobby Hull was picked at left wing and Claude Provost of Montreal at right wing. The defensemen were Pierre Pilote of Chicago and Jacques Laperriere of Montreal, with Crozier in goal.

Toronto's goaltending was split down the middle with Johnny Bower playing 34 games and Terry Sawchuk 36. When the Maple Leafs finished with the fewest goals scored against them, the goalies refused to accept the Vezina Trophy unless both their names were inscribed on it and unless both received an equal cash award. The league agreed and the two-goalie system became a permanent part of the Vezina award.

Chicago's Hull won both the Lady Byng and the Hart Trophy—the first man to take the two awards in the same year since the Rangers' Buddy O'Connor in 1947–48. Pierre Pilote was the Norris winner for the third straight season.

Hull, who had 37 goals in his first 35 games, fell victim to injuries and the worst slump of his career and finished with 39 goals for the season. But Bobby exploded during the playoffs, scoring eight goals in the seven-game semifinal victory over Detroit. The Hawks won the sixth and seventh games to take the series.

But the Canadiens, who had survived a brutal warlike series to eliminate Toronto in the semifinals, silenced Hull in the finals. Hull scored only two goals as Montreal whipped Chicago in seven games to win the Stanley Cup. Gump Worsley's seventh-game shutout clinched it.

A new award, the Conn Smythe Trophy, honoring the outstanding player of the playoffs, went to Montreal captain Jean Beliveau, who scored eight goals in 13 playoff games.

1964–65

FINAL STANDINGS

	W	L	T	PTS	GF	GA
Detroit	40	23	7	87	224	175
Montreal	36	23	11	83	211	185
Chicago	34	28	8	76	224	176
Toronto	30	26	14	74	204	173
New York	20	38	12	52	179	246
Boston	21	43	6	48	166	253

LEADING SCORERS

	G	A	PTS
Mikita, Chicago	28	59	87
Ullman, Detroit	42	41	83
Howe, Detroit	29	47	76
B. Hull, Chicago	39	32	71
Delvecchio, Detroit	25	42	67
Provost, Montreal	27	37	64
Gilbert, New York	25	36	61
Pilote, Chicago	14	45	59
Bucyk, Boston	26	29	55
Backstrom, Montreal	25	30	55
Esposito, Chicago	23	32	55

1965–66

In response to considerable pressure to expand the size of the league, the NHL decided in October 1965 to add six new teams by 1967. Four months later, franchises were awarded to Los Angeles, Oakland, Minneapo-

lis-St. Paul, Pittsburgh and Philadelphia. A sixth franchise was granted to St. Louis in April. The cost of joining the league would be $2 million per team.

On the ice, Bobby Hull of the Black Hawks made the big noise again. For years Hull had threatened the 50-goal mark he shared with Maurice Richard and Bernie Geoffrion. But something always stalled his drive. This time, nothing could stop him.

Hull opened the season with two hat tricks in the first week and had 15 goals in 11 games. A pair of four-goal games and three straight two-goal nights kept him on target. Hull had 44 goals in 45 games—a fantastic goal-per-game average. He hit the magic 50 mark in Chicago's 57th game. Then, he and the Hawks, feeling the record pressure, went scoreless for three games. Finally, on March 12 in Chicago, Hull scored No. 51 against New York goalie

Rangers climb over the glass to aid general manager Emile Francis, who was involved in a fracas in the stands in a 1965 game against Detroit.

Cesare Maniago, setting off a 7½ minute demonstration by ecstatic Chicago fans. Ironically, Maniago, then playing for Toronto, had been the victim of Bernie Geoffrion's record-tying 50th goal in 1961.

Hull finished with 54 goals and a record 97 points, winning the Hart Trophy and the left wing spot on the All-Star team for the fifth time. Detroit's Gordie Howe was picked at right wing for the ninth time and Chicago's Stan Mikita made it at center for the fourth time. Jacques Laperriere of Montreal and Pierre Pilote of Chicago were the defensemen, Pilote for the fourth straight year. Chicago's "Mr. Goalie," Glenn Hall, made the team for the sixth time.

《 *Chicago's Bobby Hull strikes back at one of his defensive shadows, Boston's Ed Westfall.*

Detroit's Alex Delvecchio won the Lady Byng Trophy, Brit Selby of Toronto took the Calder and Laperriere broke Pilote's three-year grip on the Norris. The Vezina went to Montreal goalies Gump Worsley and Charlie Hodge.

The Black Hawks, led by Hull, made another run at the top but again fell short, finishing eight points behind Montreal. Toronto was third and Detroit, pennant winners the year before, slipped to fourth.

Montreal and Toronto seemed to declare war on each other in the opening round of the playoffs. Twenty-six penalties were doled out in the second game and that was topped by record totals of 35 penalties and 154 minutes in the next game. The fights were a standoff but the Canadiens won the hockey games, sweeping four straight.

Detroit eliminated the Black Hawks, four games to two, and when the Red Wings stung the Canadiens by winning the first two games of the final series in Montreal, it appeared that Red Wing defenseman Bill Gadsby, playing in his 20th and final season, might finally drink champagne from the Stanley Cup. But it was not to be. The Canadiens roared back with four straight victories to win their second consecutive Cup. However, Roger Crozier, Detroit's heroic goalie, was awarded the Conn Smythe Trophy as the outstanding player of the playoffs.

1965–66

FINAL STANDINGS

	W	L	T	PTS	GF	GA
Montreal	41	21	8	90	239	173
Chicago	37	25	8	82	240	187
Toronto	34	25	11	79	208	187
Detroit	31	27	12	74	221	194
Boston	21	43	6	48	174	275
New York	18	41	11	47	195	261

LEADING SCORERS

	G	A	PTS
B. Hull, Chicago	54	43	97
Mikita, Chicago	30	48	78
Rousseau, Montreal	30	48	78
Beliveau, Montreal	29	48	77
Howe, Detroit	29	46	75
Ullman, Detroit	31	41	72
Delvecchio, Detroit	31	38	69
Nevin, New York	29	33	62
Richard, Montreal	22	39	61
Oliver, Boston	18	42	60

1966–67

The National Hockey League celebrated its 50th anniversary season by signing a $3.5-million television contract with the Columbia Broadcasting System providing for Game-of-the-Week coverage.

After laboring for 40 years under the Curse of Muldoon, which had been cast by their first coach after he felt he was unjustly fired, the Chicago Black Hawks finally broke the spell and won their first NHL regular-season title.

The Hawks won convincingly, beating Montreal by 17 points. Bobby Hull reached the 50-goal plateau for the third time in his fabulous career, finishing with 52. But the scoring crown went to teammate Stan Mikita, who set a record with 62 assists and tied Hull's mark of 97 points in a season.

The surprise team of the year was the Rangers, who flirted with first place and could have finished as high as second going into the final weekend of the season. The key men were Rod Gilbert, Phil Goyette, goalie Ed Giacomin, who had been acquired from the minors for four players two seasons earlier, and Bernie Geoffrion, lured out of retirement by general manager-coach Emile Francis. Gilbert had 28 goals, Goyette's 49 assists were second only to Mikita, Giacomin was the All-Star goalie and Geoffrion contributed 17 goals on the ice and a winning spirit in the dressing room.

Joining Giacomin on the All-Star team were New York defenseman Harry Howell, a 15-year veteran enjoying his finest season, Chicago defenseman Pierre Pilote, picked for the fifth straight year, and three Black Hawk forwards—Hull, Mikita and Ken Wharram.

Mikita, the scoring champion, also won the Hart Trophy and the Lady Byng, becoming the first triple-crown winner in NHL history. Chicago goalies Glenn Hall and Denis DeJordy shared the Vezina Trophy while Harry Howell won the Norris and 18-year-old Bobby Orr of Boston took the Calder.

The expansion teams were busily assembling front-office staffs to scout the established teams and their farm systems for the upcoming stocking draft. Philadelphia hired Bud Poile as general manager and Keith Allen as coach. Pittsburgh came up with Jack Riley as general manager and Red Sullivan as coach. Minnesota gave both jobs to Wren Blair and St. Louis did the same with Lynn Patrick. Oakland would give both posts to Bert Olmstead and Los Angeles would name Larry Regan as general manager and Red Kelly as coach.

In the playoffs, Montreal staged a five-goal third-period rally to wipe out a Ranger lead in the first game and then burst by the demoralized New Yorkers in four straight games. Terry Sawchuk, who had achieved a landmark with his 100th career shutout during the season, led Toronto past Chicago in six games and the Maple Leafs faced the Canadiens for the Cup.

Again, it was Sawchuk's sparkling goaltending and some opportunistic scoring by Jim

Pappin, Pete Stemkowski, Bob Pulford and Dave Keon that pulled the Maple Leafs through. Toronto won its 11th Stanley Cup in six games with the Smythe Trophy going to Keon.

1966–67

FINAL STANDINGS

	W	L	T	PTS	GF	GA
Chicago	41	17	12	94	264	170
Montreal	32	25	13	77	202	188
Toronto	32	27	11	75	204	211
New York	30	28	12	72	188	189
Detroit	27	39	4	58	212	241
Boston	17	43	10	44	182	253

LEADING SCORERS

	G	A	PTS
Mikita, Chicago	35	62	97
B. Hull, Chicago	52	28	80
Ullman, Detroit	26	44	70
Wharram, Chicago	31	34	65
Howe, Detroit	25	40	65
Rousseau, Montreal	19	44	63
Esposito, Chicago	21	40	61
Goyette, New York	12	49	61
Mohns, Chicago	25	35	60
Richard, Montreal	21	34	55
Delvecchio, Detroit	17	38	55

Boston's Bobby Orr was an obvious choice as Rookie of the Year in 1966–67.

COAST-TO-COAST
1967–1979

It was the most ambitious undertaking ever attempted by a major sport, and many predicted it wouldn't work. But the National Hockey League went ahead with its expansion program anyway, and in a span of 11 years grew from six to 17 teams.

The biggest increase came at the start of the 1967–68 season, when the league doubled in size to 12 franchises. For the first time, hockey became a coast-to-coast sport, as teams were placed in Los Angeles and Oakland. The four other new teams were also in the U.S.— Minnesota, Philadelphia, Pittsburgh and St. Louis.

The Montreal Canadiens continued their championship tradition in the first two seasons of expansion play, but then a young defenseman named Bobby Orr and a sharpshooting center named Phil Esposito brought the Boston Bruins into the limelight, winning the Stanley Cup in two out of the next three seasons.

Teams were added in 1970 (Buffalo and Vancouver), 1972 (New York Islanders and Atlanta) and 1974 (Kansas City and Washington), bringing the league total to 18 teams.

« *Terry Sawchuk of Los Angeles halts scoring attempt by the New York Rangers' Orland Kurtenbach in 1967–68.*

The Philadelphia Flyers made league history when they became the first expansion team to win the Cup in 1973–74, but after another year at the top, the Flyers gave way to a restoration of the Canadiens' dynasty as Montreal, led by super-scorer Guy Lafleur and goalie Ken Dryden, won the Cup four years in a row.

Along the way, competition from the rival World Hockey Association sent players' salaries soaring; Clarence Campbell stepped down as NHL president after serving for 31 years, replaced in 1977 by John A. Ziegler, Jr., and the league was pared to 17 teams when the franchises in Cleveland and Minnesota merged in 1978.

1967–68

On June 6, 1967, the most ambitious expansion program in sports history became a reality. The league doubled in size with six new teams stocked with 20 players each drafted from the established teams, and added as the NHL's West Division. The six older clubs became the East Division and a 74-game schedule was adopted.

Some good names were available and chosen by the six new clubs. Goalie Glenn Hall

Boston's Bobby Orr breaks his stick as he knocks puck away from New York's Phil Goyette.

went to the St. Louis Blues and goalie Terry Sawchuk to the Los Angeles Kings. The Pittsburgh Penguins came up with high-scoring Andy Bathgate. The first player drafted was forward Dave Balon, chosen by the Minnesota North Stars. Defensemen Bob Baun and Kent Douglas both were chosen by the San Francisco-Oakland entry, called the California Seals. The Philadelphia Flyers drafted goaltenders Doug Favell and Bernie Parent.

The first meeting between an established team and an expansion team came on opening night when the Montreal Canadiens nipped the Pittsburgh Penguins, 2-1, as Jean Beliveau scored the 400th goal of his career.

For the season, expansion clubs won 40 games, lost 86 and tied 18 against the established teams. Los Angeles, coached by Red Kelly, was 10-12-2 for the best West record against the East. Of the established teams,

Toronto had the most trouble with the new division. The Maple Leafs were under .500 with a 10-11-3 record and that figured importantly in their tumble to fifth place—their first season out of the playoffs in a decade. New York enjoyed the best record against the West, 17-4-3, and this helped the Rangers to a second-place finish.

In midseason the California entry decided to shed its San Francisco image and was renamed the Oakland Seals. Of the six new teams, the Seals had the toughest time at the gate and there was repeated talk about a possible shift of the franchise to Vancouver, British Columbia. But the Seals remained in Oakland.

Both divisions produced exciting races. Montreal finished four points ahead of the charging Rangers. New York's attack was led by Rod Gilbert and Jean Ratelle, who had

played hockey together since their childhood days in Montreal. Gilbert scored 29 goals and Ratelle 32. Gilbert had four goals one night at Montreal and set an NHL record with 16 shots on net in that game. Philadelphia edged Los Angeles by one point for the West crown but the big scorer in the division was Minnesota's Wayne Connelly, who had 35 goals.

Chicago's Stan Mikita captured his fourth scoring title in five seasons with 40 goals and 87 points and repeated as a triple trophy winner, adding the Hart and Lady Byng to his scoring championship. Gump Worsley and Rogatien Vachon of Montreal shared the Vezina Trophy while Boston's Bobby Orr took the Norris and teammate Derek Sanderson won the Calder.

Worsley was the All-Star goalie with Orr and Toronto's Tim Horton on defense and Stan Mikita and Bobby Hull of Chicago and Detroit's Gordie Howe up front. Howe celebrated his 40th birthday on the final night of the season and finished with 39 goals, his highest total in 12 seasons. Hull had 44, his lowest total in three seasons.

The new Stanley Cup playoff format provided for intra-division playoffs involved the first four teams and then a Cup final between the survivors. In the East, Montreal breezed through Boston in four straight and then took Chicago in five after the Black Hawks had rallied from a two-game deficit to eliminate the Rangers. In the West, Minnesota and St. Louis emerged victorious in a pair of exciting seven-game series against Los Angeles and Philadelphia. Then the Blues struggled through seven games to beat off the North Stars.

In the final, Montreal swept four straight games, winning the Cup. Twice the expansion Blues forced the Canadiens into overtime and each of the four games was decided by one goal. Glenn Hall, the St. Louis goalie, won the Smythe Trophy for his playoff performance.

"The expansion," NHL president Clarence Campbell said, "was successful beyond our fondest hopes."

It was a year of triumph and tragedy. The triumph was successful doubling in size of the league. The tragedy was the death in January of Bill Masterton, a Minnesota forward, who struck his head on the ice after a collision and never regained consciousness. It was the first game-related fatality in NHL history.

1967–68

FINAL STANDINGS

East Division

	W	L	T	PTS	GF	GA
Montreal	42	22	10	94	236	167
New York	39	23	12	90	226	183
Boston	37	27	10	84	259	216
Chicago	32	26	16	80	212	222
Toronto	33	31	10	76	209	176
Detroit	27	35	12	66	245	257

West Division

	W	L	T	PTS	GF	GA
Philadelphia	31	32	11	73	173	179
Los Angeles	31	33	10	72	200	224
St. Louis	27	31	16	70	177	191
Minnesota	27	32	15	69	191	226
Pittsburgh	27	34	13	67	195	216
Oakland	15	42	17	47	153	219

LEADING SCORERS	G	A	PTS
Mikita, Chicago	40	47	87
Esposito, Boston	35	49	84
Howe, Detroit	39	43	82
Ratelle, New York	32	46	78
Gilbert, New York	29	48	77
B. Hull, Chicago	44	31	75
Ullman, Detroit-Toronto	35	37	72
Delvecchio, Detroit	22	48	70
Bucyk, Boston	30	39	69
Wharram, Chicago	27	42	69

1968–69

In his 23rd NHL season at the age of 40, Gordie Howe scored more points than he ever had before. Detroit's wonder man finished the season with an incredible 103 points, eight more than his previous high.

It was good enough for third place in the scoring race. That's because 1968–69 went down in NHL history as the year of the scorer, with records falling all around the league.

Chicago's Bobby Hull shattered the 50-goal plateau for the fourth time and pushed his own single season mark to an almost unbelievable 58 goals. He finished with 107 scoring points for second place in the scoring race.

The man of the year was Phil Esposito, a tall, almost gangly center, who set Boston and the NHL on its collective ear. Esposito, who had centered for Hull when Bobby scored 54

Red Berenson of St. Louis scores the first of his six goals against the Philadelphia Flyers on November 7, 1968.

goals, shattered all scoring records with an amazing 126 points including 49 goals.

Esposito, Hull and Howe all soared past the 100-point mark, easily smashing the NHL single-season point record of 97 shared by Hull and teammate Stan Mikita. In fact, Mikita scored 97 points this year and was considered a disappointment to the Black Hawks.

The record-making wasn't confined to the established East Division teams either. In November, Red Berenson, a castoff, scored six goals for St. Louis, tying the single-game record set a quarter of a century earlier by Syd Howe of Detroit.

The St. Louis club, led by Berenson, raced to the West Division championship, winning it by a whopping 19 points. Jacques Plante, drafted from New York and lured out of retirement by the Blues, joined Glenn Hall in goal and the two veterans shared the Vezina Trophy for fewest goals allowed.

In the East, Montreal and Boston battled down to the final weekend before the Canadiens clinched first place for rookie coach Claude Ruel, who took over when Toe Blake retired.

The Canadiens and Bruins swept past New York and Toronto in four straight games as the Stanley Cup playoffs got underway. Then Montreal beat Boston in six games—three of the victories coming on overtime goals—to qualify for the Cup finals.

St. Louis shattered Philadelphia in four games and repeated the sweep against Los Angeles, which had ousted Oakland in seven. But in the finals, the Blues were no match for Montreal. The powerful Canadiens swept to their 16th Stanley Cup in the minimum of four games, repeating their 1967–68 sweep of St. Louis.

Esposito, who led all playoff scorers with 18 points, won the Hart Trophy as MVP and

was named center on the All-Star team. The other All-Stars were Hull and Howe, Boston's Bobby Orr, who broke all scoring records for defensemen with 21 goals, Toronto's Tim Horton and St. Louis goalie Glenn Hall.

Orr won the Norris Trophy as the outstanding defenseman while Detroit's Alex Delvecchio took the Lady Byng and Danny Grant of the Minnesota North Stars won the Calder as Rookie of the Year.

1968–69

FINAL STANDINGS

East Division

	W	L	T	PTS	GF	GA
Montreal	46	19	11	103	271	202
Boston	42	18	16	100	303	221
New York	41	26	9	91	231	196
Toronto	35	26	15	85	234	217
Detroit	33	31	12	78	239	221
Chicago	34	33	9	77	280	246

West Division

	W	L	T	PTS	GF	GA
St. Louis	37	25	14	88	204	157
Oakland	29	36	11	69	219	251
Philadelphia	20	35	21	61	174	225
Los Angeles	24	42	10	58	185	260
Pittsburgh	20	45	11	51	189	252
Minnesota	18	43	15	51	189	270

LEADING SCORERS

	G	A	PTS
Esposito, Boston	49	77	126
B. Hull, Chicago	58	49	107
Howe, Detroit	44	59	103
Mikita, Chicago	30	67	97
Hodge, Boston	45	45	90
Cournoyer, Montreal	43	44	87
Delvecchio, Detroit	25	58	83
Berenson, St. Louis	35	47	82
Beliveau, Montreal	33	49	82
Mahovlich, Detroit	49	29	78

1969–70

It had been 29 long, frustrating years between champagne sips out of the Stanley Cup for the Boston Bruins. But with a super player like Bobby Orr in the lineup, it was only a matter of time before the Bruins returned to the top. This was the year.

Orr shattered all scoring records for defensemen, exploding for 33 goals, 87 assists and 120 points. He became the first defenseman in history to win the scoring title, only the fourth player ever to go over 100 points and fell just six short of the record of 126 established by his teammate, Phil Esposito, the year before.

Esposito finished with 99 points for second place in the scoring race. But the family pride was protected by Phil's younger brother, Chicago's Tony, who won the Calder Trophy as Rookie of the Year and the Vezina as the Black Hawks allowed fewer goals than any other team in the league.

Tony Esposito was drafted by Chicago from Montreal and took the league by storm. He turned in a record-breaking 15 shutouts and led the Hawks from a last-place finish in 1969 to first place in 1970. The East Division race was not decided until the final night of the season and then with some bizarre developments.

New York had led the East for $3\frac{1}{2}$ months but wilted under an avalanche of injuries, dropping from the lead March 1. Boston and Chicago took over, battling head-to-head for the top spot. Meanwhile, New York, Detroit and Montreal battled it out for the other three playoff berths.

In the West, St. Louis clinched its second consecutive title early and watched with interest as Philadelphia tied its way out of the playoffs. The Flyers set a record with 24 deadlocks and, although tied with Oakland in points, lost the final playoff spot in the West because the Seals had more victories.

The same thing happened in the East, where Boston and Chicago tied in points but the Black Hawks had more victories and were awarded first place. The Rangers beat out the Canadiens for fourth on the basis of more goals scored. The two teams finished with identical won-lost-tied marks and only a nine-goal binge on the final day allowed New York to make it.

Montreal's elimination ended a 22-year string of playoff appearances and marked the first time in history that no Canadian team was in the playoffs.

Boston captured the Cup, beating New York, Chicago and St. Louis and winning the last 10 games in a row. St. Louis eliminated Minnesota and Pittsburgh before being swept out in the finals for the third straight year.

Orr became the first man in history to win four individual trophies in a single season,

The Esposito brothers go head-to-head: Boston's Phil against Chicago's Tony in 1969–70.

taking the Ross as scoring champ, the Norris as best defenseman, the Hart as regular-season MVP and the Smythe as playoff MVP. Tony Esposito captured the Calder and Vezina and Phil Goyette of St. Louis won the Lady Byng.

The Esposito brothers—Chicago's goalie, Tony, and Boston's center, Phil—made the All-Star team along with Gordie Howe of Detroit, Bobby Hull of Chicago, and defensemen Brad Park of New York and the incredible Orr.

1969–70

FINAL STANDINGS

East Division

	W	L	T	PTS	GF	GA
Chicago	45	22	9	99	250	170
Boston	40	17	19	99	277	216
Detroit	40	21	15	95	246	199
New York	38	22	16	92	246	189
Montreal	38	22	16	92	244	201
Toronto	29	34	13	71	222	242

West Division

St. Louis	37	27	12	86	224	179
Pittsburgh	26	38	12	64	182	238
Minnesota	19	35	22	60	224	257
Oakland	22	40	14	58	169	243
Philadelphia	17	35	24	58	197	225
Los Angeles	14	52	10	38	168	290

LEADING SCORERS

	G	A	PTS
Orr, Boston	33	87	120
Esposito, Boston	43	56	99
Mikita, Chicago	39	47	86
Goyette, St. Louis	29	49	78
Tkaczuk, New York	27	50	77
Ratelle, New York	32	42	74
Berenson, St. Louis	33	39	72
Parise, Minnesota	24	48	72
Howe, Detroit	31	40	71
Mahovlich, Detroit	38	32	70
Balon, New York	33	37	70
McKenzie, Boston	29	41	70

1970–71

Goaltending has always been a tough way to earn a living but it never was tougher than during the 1970–71 season when the Boston

Ken Dryden had appeared in only six regular-season NHL games when he led Montreal to the Stanley Cup in 1971.

Bruins assembled what may have been the greatest scoring machine in the history of hockey.

The cast was headed by Phil Esposito, the bull of a center who had set a single-season scoring record two years earlier when he totaled 126 points. Espo attacked his record with a vengeance and shattered it with an avalanche of goals and assists. He finished with 152 points, an all-time record that was split exactly down the middle with 76 goals and 76 assists. The 76 goals, a truly remarkable achievement, shattered Bobby Hull's old single-season record by 18.

Esposito thus became the fourth man in NHL history to soar past the 50-goal mark. Not long after he made it, teammate Johnny Bucyk also shot past 50, making the Bruins the first team ever to have two 50-goal scorers on the same team. Bucyk finished with 51 goals and

116 points but that total was only third in the NHL scoring race. Squeezed between scoring champion Esposito and Bucyk was Boston's fantastic defenseman, Bobby Orr, who totaled 139 points, 19 more than he had the year before when he won the scoring crown.

Fourth place in the scoring race belonged to another Bruin, Esposito's linemate, Ken Hodge, who also went over 100 points. Two more Boston players, Wayne Cashman and Johnny McKenzie, finished seventh and eighth, completing a remarkable Bruin domination of the league's top scorers.

Boston finished with a record 399 goals for the season, an average of better than five goals per game. With that kind of attack, it was no surprise that the Bruins zoomed to the East Division championship, losing only 14 games all season. The West crown went to the Chicago Black Hawks, shifted to the expansion

division in a realignment of teams when two new teams, Buffalo and Vancouver, were added to the East.

In the playoffs, defending champion Boston and its awesome scoring machine ranked as heavy favorites. But the Bruins ran into a hot goalie, Montreal rookie Ken Dryden, and the Canadiens eliminated Boston in seven games—a stunning first-round upset. Montreal then knocked off Minnesota to advance to the final round. Chicago eased its way past Philadelphia and then struggled in seven games, three of them stretching into overtime, before eliminating New York. That sent the Canadiens against the Black Hawks for the Cup and Montreal won it in a pulsating seven-game showdown.

Dryden, who had played only six regular-season games before the playoffs, emerged as the Canadiens' hero and won the Smythe Trophy as the Cup's MVP. The regular-season MVP was Orr, who also won his fourth straight Norris Trophy as the best defenseman. The Calder Trophy for Rookie of the Year went to Buffalo center Gilbert Perreault and the Lady Byng for clean play was awarded to Boston's Bucyk. Goalies Ed Giacomin and Gilles Villemure of the defensive-minded Rangers shared the Vezina Trophy as New York allowed fewer goals than any other team.

Esposito, Hodge, Bucyk and Orr made the All-Star team along with Montreal defenseman J. C. Tremblay and Ranger goalie Giacomin.

The year was otherwise notable in that it was presumed to be the valedictory for two of the NHL's greatest stars, Detroit's Gordie Howe and Montreal's Jean Beliveau. Howe scored 23 goals for a 25-year career total of 786. Beliveau scored 25, finishing his 18-year career with 507.

Defensive play of young Brad Park, alongside Chicago's Dennis Hull here, helped the Rangers reach the Stanley Cup finals in 1972.

1970–71

FINAL STANDINGS

East Division

	W	L	T	PTS	GF	GA
Boston	57	14	7	121	399	207
New York	49	18	11	109	259	177
Montreal	42	23	13	97	291	216
Toronto	37	33	8	82	248	211
Buffalo	24	39	15	63	217	291
Vancouver	24	46	8	56	229	296
Detroit	22	45	11	55	209	308

West Division

	W	L	T	PTS	GF	GA
Chicago	49	20	9	107	277	184
St. Louis	34	25	19	87	223	208
Philadelphia	28	33	17	73	207	225
Minnesota	28	34	16	72	191	223
Los Angeles	25	40	13	63	239	303
Pittsburgh	21	37	20	62	221	240
California	20	53	5	45	199	320

LEADING SCORERS

	G	A	PTS
Esposito, Boston	76	76	152
Orr, Boston	37	102	139
Bucyk, Boston	51	65	116
Hodge, Boston	43	62	105
B. Hull, Chicago	44	52	96
Ullman, Toronto	34	51	85
Cashman, Boston	21	58	79
McKenzie, Boston	31	47	77
Keon, Toronto	38	38	76
Beliveau, Montreal	25	51	76
Stanfield, Boston	24	52	76

1971–72

There has always been considerable debate over whether there is more prestige for a team to win a National Hockey League regular-season title or to capture the postseason Stanley Cup playoffs instead. Coming out on top of the six-month, 78-game regular-season grind is a test of staying power, but the tension and excitement of the playoffs for Lord Stanley's battered old mug have a way of stealing the thunder. People tend to remember the Stanley Cup champions longer.

The Boston Bruins solved this all very simply in 1971–72. They just won everything available to them. Led by the scoring tandem of center Phil Esposito and defenseman Bobby Orr, the Bruins zoomed to a first-place finish in the East Division, finishing 10 points ahead of the New York Rangers and losing just 13 games, a record for the 78-game season. It was the second straight regular-season crown for the boisterous Bruins. But the season before, they had been submarined in the first round of the playoffs by Montreal. This time there was

no Stanley Cup slip. Boston zipped to the Cup, losing only three of 15 postseason games.

Esposito and Orr finished 1-2 in the scoring race for the third straight season. Esposito won the title with 133 points, including 66 goals. Orr finished second with 117 points, including 37 goals, matching his total of the year before. Both made the All-Star team along with Ranger defenseman Brad Park, right wing Rod Gilbert of the Rangers, left wing Bobby Hull of Chicago and Chicago goalie Tony Esposito (Phil's brother).

The scoring title was the third in four years for Esposito, but he couldn't break the stranglehold Orr was establishing on the Hart Trophy as Most Valuable Player. Bobby won the MVP award for the third straight year and also took his fifth consecutive Norris Trophy as the league's finest defenseman. The Lady Byng Trophy for clean and effective play went to Jean Ratelle of the New York Rangers, and Montreal's Ken Dryden, playoff hero a year earlier, took the Calder Trophy as Rookie of the Year. Dryden, despite his previous season's playoff heroics, was still eligible for the rookie award based on his limited regular-season duty the year before. Chicago's Tony Esposito and Gary Smith shared the Vezina Trophy as the Black Hawks achieved the league's best defensive record.

There was considerable talk around the hockey world about the establishment of another league to challenge the NHL. Most NHL officials shrugged off the talk as just that. But there was some scurrying around by the league's expansion committee and a quite sudden decision was made to add two new franchises for 1972–73. One would go to Long Island and the other to Atlanta. The development of the World Hockey Association and the establishment of those two new NHL franchises were linked. The key was a handsome new building on Long Island, the Nassau Veterans Memorial Coliseum. The WHA was eyeing the arena to house its New York team. But the NHL moved faster and placed a franchise in the building first. It was the first of many skirmishes between the two leagues.

1971-72

FINAL STANDINGS

East Division

	W	L	T	PTS	GF	GA
Boston	54	13	11	119	330	204
New York	48	17	13	109	317	192
Montreal	46	16	16	108	307	205
Toronto	33	31	14	80	209	208
Detroit	33	35	10	76	261	262
Buffalo	16	43	19	51	203	289
Vancouver	20	50	8	48	203	297

West Division

	W	L	T	PTS	GF	GA
Chicago	46	17	15	107	256	166
Minnesota	37	29	12	86	212	191
St. Louis	28	39	11	67	208	247
Pittsburgh	26	38	14	66	220	258
Philadelphia	26	38	14	66	200	236
California	21	39	18	60	216	288
Los Angeles	20	49	9	49	206	305

LEADING SCORERS

	G	A	PTS
Esposito, Boston	66	67	133
Orr, Boston	37	80	117
Ratelle, New York	46	63	109
Hadfield, New York	50	56	106
Gilbert, New York	43	54	97
F. Mahovlich, Montreal	43	53	96
B. Hull, Chicago	50	43	93
Cournoyer, Montreal	47	36	83
Bucyk, Boston	32	51	83
Clarke, Philadelphia	35	46	81
Lemaire, Montreal	32	49	81

1972-73

The summer before the National Hockey League's 1972–73 season was unlike any the league had ever experienced. The offseason had always offered a serene time of recuperation for players and executives. But this summer, there was frenzied activity at all levels.

First, there was the matter of the World Hockey Association. The new league asserted itself with 12 franchises and stocked rosters by signing players whose NHL contracts were expiring. The lure of large bonuses and new challenges drew about 70 former NHL performers. The most important was Chicago star Bobby Hull, who signed a 10-year contract for $2.75 million with the new Winnipeg Jets. Hull received $1 million up front, an unprecedented bonus put together by all the franchises in the league. They knew how important an established star like Bobby would be to the new league.

Stung by the defections, the NHL went to court and sued. The legal steps prevented Hull and some others from playing early in the season but injunctions later permitted them to perform in the WHA.

While the WHA was sniping at the NHL on one front, the older league took on an international series against Russia's world champions, a long awaited test of the best professionals against the best of the so-called amateurs. Many confident observers predicted an NHL sweep of the eight-game series as Team Canada (composed only of NHL players) began training in August. The first four games were to be played in early September in Canada starting in Montreal and then moving on to Toronto, Winnipeg and Vancouver. The last four would be played in Moscow later in the month.

The Russians stunned the Canadians, winning two and tying another of the four games in Canada. When the series moved to Moscow, Team Canada finally pulled itself together and managed to win three times, taking the World Series of hockey by the barest of margins. Paul Henderson's goal in the final minute of the final game produced the deciding victory.

WHA defections hurt many NHL teams. The newly-franchised New York Islanders, for example, lost seven of their 20 expansion draft choices to the new league and wound up setting an all-time futility record with 60 losses in their first season.

Montreal and Chicago won their division races and the Canadiens again captured the Stanley Cup, finishing off Chicago in six games. Boston's Phil Esposito captured his third straight scoring title and fourth in five years, leading the scorers with 130 points, including 55 goals.

Bobby Orr won the Norris Trophy as the NHL's best defenseman for a record sixth straight year. The Hart Trophy as Most Valuable Player went to Philadelphia's Bobby Clarke, a remarkable young center who became the first West Division player to take that award. Gil Perreault of Buffalo won the Lady Byng Trophy for clean and effective play and

Philadelphia center Bobby Clarke became the))
first player from the West Division to be
named MVP in 1972–73.

the Calder Trophy as Rookie of the Year went to Steve Vickers of the New York Rangers.

Three Canadiens, goalie Ken Dryden, defenseman Guy Lapointe and left winger Frank Mahovlich, made the All-Star team along with Boston's Orr on defense, Esposito at center and Mickey Redmond of Detroit at right wing.

1972-73

FINAL STANDINGS

East Division

	W	L	T	PTS	GF	GA
Montreal	52	10	16	120	329	184
Boston	51	22	5	107	330	235
New York R.	47	23	8	102	297	208
Buffalo	37	27	14	88	257	219
Detroit	37	29	12	86	265	243
Vancouver	22	47	9	53	233	339
New York I.	12	60	6	30	170	347

West Division

	W	L	T	PTS	GF	GA
Chicago	42	27	9	93	284	225
Philadelphia	37	30	11	85	296	256
Minnesota	37	30	11	85	254	230
St. Louis	32	34	12	76	233	251
Pittsburgh	32	37	9	73	257	265
Los Angeles	31	36	11	73	232	245
Atlanta	25	38	15	65	191	239
California	16	46	16	48	213	323

LEADING SCORERS

	G	A	PTS
Esposito, Boston	55	75	130
Clarke, Philadelphia	37	67	104
Orr, Boston	39	72	101
MacLeish, Philadelphia	50	50	100
Lemaire, Montreal	44	51	95
Ratelle, New York	41	53	94
Redmond, Detroit	52	41	93
Bucyk, Boston	40	53	93
F. Mahovlich, Montreal	38	55	93
Pappin, Chicago	41	51	92

1973-74

Ever since 1967, when the National Hockey League orchestrated its most ambitious expansion program by doubling in size from six to twelve teams, the magic word had been parity. The lords of the NHL lived for the day when the expansion infants could compete on an even keel with the established teams. They longed to be able to say that on any given night, any team could beat any other team.

For a long time, that just wasn't so. The expansion teams always seemed a stride or two behind the established clubs. And on those rare occasions when a new club rose up to kayo one of its big brothers, the loss was considered a total disaster. The expansion teams were whipping boys. Parity was a dream for the distant future.

Then, in 1973-74, along came the Broad Street Bullies, alias Philadelphia Flyers. The team of tough guys was led by Bobby Clarke, a diabetic center with a choir-boy expression, and goalie Bernie Parent, who was the first NHL player to jump to the World Hockey Association, and also one of the first to jump back.

The Flyers lived by the coaching creed of scholarly-looking Fred Shero, who often said, "If you can't beat 'em in the alley, you can't beat 'em on the ice." First Philadelphia would win the alley fight, then repeat on the ice. "We take the most direct route to the puck," philosophized Clarke, captain of the Bullies, "and we arrive in ill humor."

Most of the Flyers were acquired by general manager Keith Allen through clever trades. In one of his deals, Allen swapped goalie Parent to Toronto to bring a forward named Rick MacLeish to Philadelphia. Parent studied for two seasons under his goaltending idol, Jacques Plante, then fled to the WHA. MacLeish, meanwhile, developed into a 50-goal scorer for the talented young Flyers.

When Parent grew disenchanted with the WHA, he let it be known that he wanted to return to the older league. Allen immediately swung a deal for his rights with Toronto and then signed the goalie to a multiyear contract with Philadelphia.

Back with the Flyers, Parent found some old friends in veteran defensemen Joe Watson and Ed Van Impe, both leftovers from the original Philadelphia expansion team, and some new friends in tough Andre Dupont and Barry Ashbee, acquired through trades, and youngsters Jim Watson and Tom Bladon, draft choices. Together, the defensemen and Parent gave the Flyers the stingiest defense in the NHL. The goalie played in a backbreaking 73 games and compiled a sparkling 1.89 average with 12 shutouts—by far the best individual netminding numbers in the NHL.

The Flyers won the West Division crown by a comfortable seven points over Chicago—the first time the established Black Hawks had

missed winning the crown in four seasons in the expansionist West Division. In the East, Boston, led by scoring champion Phil Esposito, finished a fat 14 points ahead of runnerup Montreal. Esposito won his fourth straight scoring title and fifth in the last six years with 145 points.

En route to their division crown, the Flyers led the NHL with a staggering 1,750 penalty minutes, 600 minutes more than the next most penalized team. Of the total, a record 348 minutes belonged to the club's No. 1 hatchetman, Dave Schultz.

In the opening round of the playoffs, Philadelphia wiped out the surprising Atlanta Flames in four straight games and Boston did the same to Toronto. Chicago went five to eliminate Los Angeles while the New York Rangers knocked off the defending Stanley Cup champion Montreal Canadiens in six games.

The semifinals were a struggle. The Bruins eliminated Chicago in six games and Philadelphia had to go seven to beat New York. That was a landmark victory. It marked the first time an expansion team had eliminated an established club in the playoffs. Parity, it seemed, was on its way. Two weeks later, it arrived.

Paced by Parent, the Flyers defeated the Bruins in the six-game championship round and brought the Stanley Cup to Philadelphia. The clincher was a 1-0 shutout spun by Parent with the only goal scored, ironically, by MacLeish, the man for whom the goalie once was traded.

Parent, whose airtight goaltending earned him the Conn Smythe Trophy as the Most

The Flyers, led by Dave (The Hammer) Schultz, fought their way to the Stanley Cup in 1974.

Bobby Clarke sipped from the Cup after the Flyers became the first expansion team to win the championship in 1974.

Valuable Player of the playoffs, and Chicago's Tony Esposito were co-winners of the Vezina Trophy as the netminders with the lowest goals-against average during the regular season.

Boston's Phil Esposito won the Hart Trophy as the league's MVP, while teammate Bobby Orr was the winner of the Norris Trophy as the NHL's top defenseman for a record seventh consecutive season.

New York Islander defenseman Denis Potvin won the Calder as Rookie of the Year. Boston's John Bucyk got the Lady Byng for sportsmanship and ability.

1973–74

FINAL STANDINGS

East Division

	W	L	T	PTS	GF	GA
Boston	52	17	9	113	349	221
Montreal	45	24	9	99	293	240
New York R.	40	24	14	94	300	251
Toronto	35	27	16	86	274	230
Buffalo	32	34	12	76	242	250
Detroit	20	39	10	68	255	319
Vancouver	24	43	11	59	224	296
New York I.	19	41	18	56	182	247

Los Angeles defenseman Bob Murdoch loses his stick but not his hold on Atlanta's Eric Vail in 1974–75. »

West Division						
Philadelphia	50	16	12	112	273	164
Chicago	41	14	23	105	272	164
Los Angeles	33	33	12	78	233	231
Atlanta	30	34	14	74	214	238
Pittsburgh	28	41	9	65	242	273
St. Louis	26	40	12	64	206	248
Minnesota	23	38	17	63	235	275
California	13	55	10	36	195	342

LEADING SCORERS	G	A	PTS
Esposito, Boston	68	77	145
Orr, Boston	32	90	122
Hodge, Boston	30	59	89
Cashman, Boston	30	59	89
Clarke, Philadelphia	35	52	87
Martin, Buffalo	52	34	86
Apps, Pittsburgh	24	61	85
Sittler, Toronto	38	46	84
L. MacDonald, Pittsburgh	43	39	82
Park, New York R.	25	57	82
D. Hextall, Minnesota	20	62	82

1974–75

The addition of two new franchises and realignment of the 18 teams into four divisions set the stage for a season in which the Philadelphia Flyers would be seeking a repeat of their stunning Stanley Cup success.

The new entries were the Kansas City Scouts and the Washington Capitals, and the divisions, named for hockey notables, were the James Norris and Jack Adams in the Prince of Wales Conference and the Lester Patrick and Conn Smythe in the Clarence Campbell Conference.

If the newest members of the league quickly became discouraged en route to last-place finishes in their divisions, at least they could take heart in the gallant strides made by the New York Islanders. An expansion team just three years earlier, the Islanders climbed into a second-place tie with the rival New York Rangers behind the Flyers in the Patrick Division and then found themselves matched against the Rangers in the best-of-three first-round playoff series.

The teams split the first two games and in an electrifying finish the Islanders won out when J. P. Parise scored a goal in just 11 seconds of overtime—a league record.

The Islanders lost the first three games of the quarterfinal round against Pittsburgh, but

« Bernie Parent's net play helped the Flyers knock off Buffalo in the Cup finals in 1975.

rallied to win the last four, becoming the first team in 33 years to win a series after losing the first three games. In the semifinal against the Flyers, the Islanders lost the decisive seventh game after again tying a series with three straight triumphs.

Philadelphia went on to defeat the Buffalo Sabres in six games in the finals, becoming the first team to win the Stanley Cup two years in a row since Montreal won in 1968 and 1969.

Influenced by the success of the Flyers' roughhouse tactics, more players began to fight and violence in the game increased. Two players were charged with assault for their involvement in fighting incidents. Dave Forbes of the Boston Bruins was put on trial for punching Henry Boucha of the Minnesota North Stars, but the trial ended in a hung jury and the charges were dropped. And Detroit's Dan Maloney was charged with assaulting Brian Glennie of Toronto. But there were still victories scored by the most graceful players of the generation.

Boston defenseman Bobby Orr won his second scoring title with 135 points, ending the four-year stranglehold on the award by teammate Phil Esposito. It was the sixth straight season either Orr or Esposito had won the scoring championship.

Philadelphia's Bobby Clarke, the feisty center, won the Hart Trophy as Most Valuable Player for the second time in three years while Orr won the Norris as best defenseman for the seventh straight time. The Lady Byng for gentlemanly play went to Los Angeles center Marcel Dionne. Atlanta Flames left wing Eric Vail won the Calder as Rookie of the Year and goalie Bernie Parent of the Flyers won the Vezina.

Parent also won the Conn Smythe as playoff MVP and was named to the All-Star team with teammate Clarke. Others on the team were defensemen Orr and Islander Denis Potvin and wingers Guy Lafleur of Montreal and Richard Martin of Buffalo.

1974–75

FINAL STANDINGS

Prince of Wales Conference

Norris Division

	W	L	T	PTS	GF	GA
Montreal	47	14	19	113	374	225
Los Angeles	42	17	21	105	269	185
Pittsburgh	37	28	15	89	326	289
Detroit	23	45	12	58	259	335
Washington	8	67	5	21	181	446

Adams Division

	W	L	T	PTS	GF	GA
Buffalo	49	16	15	113	354	240
Boston	40	26	14	94	345	245
Toronto	31	33	16	78	280	309
California	19	48	13	51	212	316

Clarence Campbell Conference

Patrick Division

	W	L	T	PTS	GF	GA
Philadelphia	51	18	11	113	293	181
New York R.	37	29	14	88	319	276
New York I.	33	25	22	88	264	221
Atlanta	34	31	15	83	243	233

Smythe Division

	W	L	T	PTS	GF	GA
Vancouver	38	32	10	86	271	254
St. Louis	35	31	14	84	269	267
Chicago	37	35	8	82	268	241
Minnesota	23	50	7	53	221	341
Kansas City	15	54	11	41	184	328

LEADING SCORERS

	G	A	PTS
Orr, Boston	46	89	135
Esposito, Boston	61	66	127
Dionne, Detroit	47	74	121
Lafleur, Montreal	53	66	119
P. Mahovlich, Montreal	35	82	117
Clarke, Philadelphia	27	89	116
Robert, Buffalo	40	60	100
Gilbert, New York	36	61	97
Perreault, Buffalo	39	57	96
Martin, Buffalo	52	43	95

The Flower, Guy Lafleur, led the Canadiens to their 19th Stanley Cup in 1976.

1975–76

For years, the argument had reigned: could swifter, more inventive players challenge the dominance of the stronger, more aggressive teams and the style that had been popularized by the Philadelphia Flyers? The answer, it seemed, was an emphatic yes.

The Flyers' string of successes was ended not by a more violent team, but by a faster one. The Montreal Canadiens did not have anyone as powerful as Dave Schultz, the Flyer who perennially led the league in penalty minutes. But Montreal did have Guy Lafleur, a slender, graceful right wing whose name translated from French was, appropriately enough, "The Flower."

Lafleur led Montreal back into the championship ranks. After being dethroned by Philadelphia, the two-time winner, Montreal won

the Stanley Cup for the 19th time. Like Lafleur, the Canadiens were simply overwhelming. They finished the season with 58 victories and 127 points—both records. They had only 11 defeats, just one more than the record they held for fewest losses in one season. They led the league in virtually ever offensive and defensive category and they did it with one of the lowest penalty-minute totals of any team—an average of 12.2 a game—half of what the Flyers averaged.

In the playoffs, they won 12 of 13 games, sweeping Philadelphia in four games in the finals. In all but three of those games, the Canadiens held their opponent to three goals or fewer. Lafleur, who won the scoring title with 125 points, had 17 points in the playoffs.

Toronto's Darryl Sittler posted 100 points in » *1975–76, including a 10-point night against the Bruins on February 7, 1976.*

This was a season marked by the trade that brought Bruin Phil Esposito to the Rangers and Brad Park to Boston. It was also a year in which Boston's Bobby Orr, operated on again because of his ailing left knee, played only 10 games. And Toronto's Darryl Sittler set a mark for most points in a game when he recorded six goals and four assists against Boston.

Philadelphia tied a league record by going unbeaten in 23 straight games (17-0-6) and the Kansas City Scouts, in their second season, set a record for futility by going 27 games without a victory (0-21-6).

Although Philadelphia was toppled as Stanley Cup champion, the Flyers did have Bobby Clarke, the winner of the Hart Trophy as Most

Valuable Player. It was the third time in four years Clarke had won the award and he became only the second center, along with the legendary Howie Morenz, to win it a third time.

New York Islander center Bryan Trottier was the winner of the Calder as Rookie of the Year; Montreal goalie Ken Dryden won the Vezina and Jean Ratelle won the Lady Byng for gentlemanly play. Philadelphia's Reggie Leach, despite his team's defeat in the finals, was the Conn Smythe Trophy winner as playoff MVP after scoring a playoff record 19 goals.

Lafleur, Dryden, Clarke and Park made the All-Star team along with defenseman Denis

Potvin of the New York Islanders and left wing Bill Barber of Philadelphia.

1975–76

FINAL STANDINGS
Prince of Wales Conference
Norris Division

	W	L	T	PTS	GF	GA
Montreal	58	11	11	127	337	174
Los Angeles	38	33	9	85	263	265
Pittsburgh	35	33	12	82	339	303
Detroit	26	44	10	62	226	300
Washington	11	59	10	32	224	394

Adams Division

Boston	48	15	17	113	313	237
Buffalo	46	21	13	105	339	240
Toronto	34	31	15	83	294	276
California	27	42	11	65	250	278

Clarence Campbell Conference
Patrick Division

Philadelphia	51	13	16	118	348	209
New York I.	42	21	17	101	297	190
Atlanta	35	33	12	82	262	237
New York R.	29	42	9	67	262	333

Smythe Division

Chicago	32	30	18	82	254	261
Vancouver	33	32	15	81	271	272
St. Louis	29	37	14	72	249	290
Minnesota	20	53	7	47	195	303
Kansas City	12	56	12	36	190	351

LEADING SCORERS

	G	A	PTS
Lafleur, Montreal	56	69	125
Clarke, Philadelphia	30	89	119
Perreault, Buffalo	44	69	113
Barber, Philadelphia	50	62	112
Larouche, Pittsburgh	53	58	111
Ratelle, New York R.-Boston	36	69	105
P. Mahovlich, Montreal	34	71	105
Pronovost, Pittsburgh	52	52	104
Sittler, Toronto	41	59	100
Apps, Pittsburgh	32	67	99

1976–77

If there was any doubt that the Montreal Canadiens had been restored to the National Hockey League's most privileged class, it was quickly dispelled in the 1976–77 season. Coming off their Stanley Cup success of the season before, it seemed there was little the Canadiens could do to improve upon their resounding record.

Guy Lafleur, who already had begun to establish himself as the most recognizable—and the most coveted—player of his generation was soon surrounded by invaluable help-

« The Canadiens' Larry Robinson, checking Buffalo's Gil Perreault, was the NHL's best defenseman in 1976–77.

mates. The Canadiens, in fact, were so rich in talent that they all but saved the All-Star selections for themselves.

In one of the most lopsided voting totals ever, the Canadiens placed four of their members on the first team—right wing Lafleur, defenseman Larry Robinson, goalie Ken Dryden and Lafleur's linemate, left wing Steve Shutt. The only players to interrupt the Montreal domination were Los Angeles center Marcel Dionne and Toronto defenseman Borje Salming. Not only that, but one more Canadien, defenseman Guy Lapointe, was named to the second team.

Who could argue with the choices? The Canadiens won a record 60 games, lost a mere eight, and set another record with the total of 132 points. The Philadelphia Flyers, the team with the second-best overall record, had 20 fewer points. And the Los Angeles Kings, second to Montreal in the Norris Division, were 49 points behind. Not since the league broke into four divisions had one team so easily commanded a season.

In their own palace, the Montreal Forum, the Canadiens lost only once in 40 games, tying the modern NHL record for fewest losses at home. But while the Canadiens were obviously delighted to be in their home, two other teams found new homes to start the season when the league approved a pair of franchise shifts.

The Kansas City Scouts, struggling both on the ice and in the accounting department, were sold to Denver oilman Jack Vickers, who moved the team to his home city and renamed the club the Colorado Rockies. Alas, the changes were merely cosmetic. The Rockies won only 20 games and finished with just 54 points, the second-worst total in the league.

The Cleveland Barons did not fare much better. Transplanted from Oakland, where they were known as the Seals in the NHL's six-team expansion of 1967, the Barons played in suburban Richfield in a cavernous arena that was located next to a sprawling farm. Encouraged by only a few fans willing to make the journey there, the Barons won only 25 games.

Montreal charged through the playoffs, losing only two games—both to the New York Islanders in a semifinal series—and swept the Boston Bruins in the finals when Jacques Lemaire scored an overtime goal at 4:32 in the fourth game. Montreal was once more led by Lafleur, who had finished the regular season with a league-leading 136 points, 56 of them goals.

Not surprisingly, the Canadiens swept most of the NHL postseason awards. Lafleur, besides being the Art Ross winner as scoring champion, won the Hart Trophy as Most Valuable Player and the Conn Smythe as the playoff MVP. Robinson won the Norris as best defenseman, while Willi Plett of Atlanta won the Calder as Rookie of the Year. Dionne won the Lady Byng for good conduct for the second time in three years.

1976–77

FINAL STANDINGS

Prince of Wales Conference

Norris Division

	W	L	T	PTS	GF	GA
Montreal	60	8	12	132	387	171
Los Angeles	34	31	15	83	271	241
Pittsburgh	34	33	13	81	240	252
Washington	24	42	14	62	221	307
Detroit	16	55	9	41	183	309

Adams Division

Boston	49	23	8	106	312	240
Buffalo	48	24	8	104	301	220
Toronto	33	32	15	81	301	285
Cleveland	25	42	13	63	240	292

Clarence Campbell Conference

Patrick Division

Philadelphia	48	16	16	112	323	213
New York I.	47	21	12	106	288	193
Atlanta	34	34	12	80	264	265
New York R.	29	37	14	72	272	310

Smythe Division

St. Louis	32	39	9	73	239	276
Minnesota	23	39	18	64	240	310
Chicago	26	43	11	63	240	298
Vancouver	25	42	13	63	235	294
Colorado	20	46	14	54	226	307

LEADING SCORERS

	G	A	PTS
Lafleur, Montreal	56	80	136
Dionne, Los Angeles	53	69	122
Shutt, Montreal	60	45	105
MacLeish, Philadelphia	49	48	97
Perreault, Buffalo	39	56	95
Young, Minnesota	29	66	95
Ratelle, Boston	33	61	94
McDonald, Toronto	46	44	90
Sittler, Toronto	38	52	90
Clarke, Philadelphia	27	63	90

The 1976–77 Lady Byng Trophy went to Marcel Dionne of Los Angeles.

1977–78

While the Montreal Canadiens again were the dominant force in 1977–78, at least one team served notice that it was on its way to the top. In fact, the team, the New York Islanders, turned out to be the only one that had been able to win a playoff game from the Canadiens the previous two years—and it won three of them.

The rise of the Islanders really was no surprise. It had been coming for some time. The Islanders had been known for their defense, but finally were able to add a gifted scorer, Mike Bossy, to give them the goal-getting punch they needed. It happened that the young man was born and raised in Montreal and had played outstanding junior hockey on the city's outskirts in Laval.

Yet, for some reason, Bossy had gone untouched in the first round of the amateur draft until the Islanders made him the 15th player

Mike Bossy of the New York Islanders broke in with a bang in 1977–78 when he scored a rookie-record 53 goals.

chosen. Six other right wings already had been taken, but Bossy was confident he could help the Islanders. And when contract negotiations with his new club temporarily collapsed, Bossy boldly told general manager Bill Torrey: "I'll score 50 goals for you."

Torrey laughed. No Islander had ever scored that many goals. No rookie had ever scored that many goals. But Bossy had the last laugh. By the time he ended his rookie year, he had 53 goals and was sixth in the scoring race with 91 points, the most ever by a first-year right wing. The Islanders, with center Bryan Trottier and defenseman Denis Potvin, had three of the first six scorers in the league.

The Islanders won their first Patrick Division title, dethroning Philadelphia, and clearly were one of the most imposing threats to end Montreal's Stanley Cup reign. But the Islanders were not the only team to make a vast

improvement during the season. Detroit vaulted from the league's worst record to a second-place finish behind Montreal in the Norris Division.

Still, the Canadiens again led the league during the season with 129 points, and with 59 victories failed by one to equal their own league record of 60 set the year before. The Boston Bruins, the other threat to the Canadiens, had 113 points, two more than the Islanders.

But in a stunning playoff upset, the Islanders were eliminated by the Toronto Maple Leafs when Lanny McDonald scored at 4:13 of overtime in the seventh game.

After sweeping the upstart Toronto team in the semifinals, the Canadiens faced the Bruins for the second year in a row in the final round. Boston had failed to win even a single game in

John A. Ziegler, Jr., became the fourth president of the NHL in 1977, succeeding Clarence Campbell, who had served 31 years.

Clark Gillies, a left wing, and Lafleur were the other selections. Bossy won the Calder Trophy as Rookie of the Year, Lafleur won the Hart as MVP for the second straight season, Potvin regained the Norris as best defenseman and Los Angeles' Butch Goring won the Lady Byng for gentlemanly play.

Off the ice, John A. Ziegler, Jr., became the fourth president in the 61-year history of the NHL, succeeding Clarence Campbell, who had been president since 1946. A Michigan-born lawyer, Ziegler played amateur hockey and was a quarterback in football and a shortstop in baseball as a Detroit schoolboy. His bachelor and law degrees were achieved at the University of Michigan.

1977-78

FINAL STANDINGS

Prince of Wales Conference

Norris Division

	W	L	T	PTS	GF	GA
Montreal	59	10	11	129	359	183
Detroit	32	34	14	78	252	266
Los Angeles	31	34	15	77	243	245
Pittsburgh	25	37	18	68	254	321
Washington	17	49	14	48	195	321

Adams Division

Boston	51	18	11	113	333	218
Buffalo	44	19	17	105	288	215
Toronto	41	29	10	92	271	237
Cleveland	22	45	13	57	230	325

Clarence Campbell Conference

Patrick Division

New York I.	48	17	15	111	334	210
Philadelphia	45	20	15	105	296	200
Atlanta	34	27	19	87	274	252
New York R.	30	37	13	73	279	280

Smythe Division

Chicago	32	29	19	83	230	220
Colorado	19	40	21	59	257	305
Vancouver	20	43	17	57	239	320
St. Louis	20	47	13	53	195	304
Minnesota	18	53	9	45	218	325

LEADING SCORERS

	G	A	PTS
Lafleur, Montreal	60	72	132
Trottier, New York I.	46	77	123
Sittler, Toronto	45	72	117
Lemaire, Montreal	36	61	97
D. Potvin, New York I.	30	64	94
Bossy, New York I.	53	38	91
O'Reilly, Boston	29	61	90
Perreault, Buffalo	41	48	89
Clarke, Philadelphia	21	68	89
McDonald, Toronto	47	40	87
Paiement, Colorado	31	56	87

the championship series the year before. This time they managed to win two as the Canadiens captured the Cup for the third consecutive year. While Montreal still had the dependable scoring of Guy Lafleur, who during the season won his third straight scoring title with 132 points, it also had a mighty defense. The Canadiens allowed only 12 goals in the final series against Boston.

A major factor was the play of goaltender Ken Dryden, who shared the Vezina Trophy as the league's outstanding goalie with Michel Larocque. Another reason for the Canadiens' success was Larry Robinson, the defenseman who was the Conn Smythe Trophy winner as the Most Valuable Player in the playoffs.

But while Dryden was named to the All-Star team, Robinson was supplanted by Denis Potvin of the Islanders and Brad Park of the Bruins. Trottier, the Islander center; teammate

The Bruins' John Wensink won this battle, but his teammates
lost the war when they were eliminated by Montreal in the 1978 finals.

1978–79

New York is a city of extremes and its fans are no different. They can be fiercely loyal and terribly impatient. They can jeer with witless vengeance and cheer with boundless passion. And for the honor of doing any of those, they will pay handsomely for their tickets.

Some even paid as much as $500 a ticket when the Rangers galvanized the city in a glorious march to the Stanley Cup finals, a march orchestrated by coach Fred Shero in his first year at the helm. "Freddie the Fog" had been hired away from the Philadelphia Flyers and almost immediately transformed the downtrodden Rangers into a success.

With the help of Swedish stars Ulf Nilsson and Anders Hedberg, who signed contracts for $300,000 a year apiece after defecting from the World Hockey Association, Shero confirmed his reputation as a genius. Although the Rangers finished in third place in the Patrick Division, they finished only four points behind second-place Philadelphia.

Not only did the Rangers then knock off Shero's old team in the quarterfinals, but they faced the rival New York Islanders in the semifinals, an electrifying series that was a scalper's delight.

The Islanders had become the first expansion team ever to lead the league in points. They had Bryan Trottier, who led the league in scoring with 134 points, and Mike Bossy, who scored 69 goals, the second-highest total ever, including goals in 10 straight games to equal the modern NHL record. The Rangers had spirit.

Seeking their first Stanley Cup since 1940, the Rangers upset the Islanders in six games and went on to meet the defending champion Montreal Canadiens. Finally, the magic van-

Things were looking up for the Rangers (Pat Hickey, right) after they stunned the regular-season champion Islanders in the 1979 playoffs.

ished. After winning the opening game, the Rangers failed to win another and Montreal won its fourth straight title.

The Rangers had to console themselves while the stunned Islanders could take heart only in a spate of postseason awards. Trottier won the Hart Trophy as Most Valuable Player and teammate Denis Potvin was given the Norris as best defenseman. Minnesota center Bobby Smith won the Calder as Rookie of the Year, Atlanta's Bob MacMillan won the Lady Byng as the most gentlemanly player and Montreal left wing Bob Gainey was named winner of the Conn Smythe as playoff MVP.

Three Islanders—Trottier, Potvin and left wing Clark Gillies—were named to the All-Star team, along with right wing Guy Lafleur of Montreal and teammates Ken Dryden, goalie, and Larry Robinson, defenseman.

1978–79

FINAL STANDINGS

Prince of Wales Conference

Norris Division

	W	L	T	PTS	GF	GA
Montreal	52	17	11	115	337	204
Pittsburgh	36	31	13	85	281	279
Los Angeles	34	34	12	80	292	286
Washington	24	41	15	63	273	338
Detroit	23	41	16	62	252	295

Adams Division

Boston	43	23	14	100	316	270
Buffalo	36	28	16	88	280	263
Toronto	34	33	13	81	267	252
Minnesota	28	40	12	68	257	289

Clarence Campbell Conference

Patrick Division

New York I.	51	15	14	116	358	214
Philadelphia	40	25	15	95	281	248
New York R.	40	29	11	91	316	292
Atlanta	41	31	8	90	327	280

Smythe Division

Chicago	29	36	15	73	244	277
Vancouver	25	42	13	63	217	291
St. Louis	18	50	12	48	249	348
Colorado	15	53	12	42	210	331

Ken Dryden led the Canadiens to their fourth straight Cup in 1979 and then retired to pursue a career in law.

LEADING SCORERS	G	A	PTS
Trottier, New York I	47	87	134
Dionne, Los Angeles	59	71	130
Lafleur, Montreal	52	77	129
Bossy, New York I	69	57	126
MacMillan, Atlanta	37	71	108
Chouinard, Atlanta	50	57	107
D. Potvin, New York I.	31	70	101
Federko, St. Louis	31	64	95
Taylor, Los Angeles	43	48	91
Gillies, New York I.	35	56	91

MERGER AND THE GRETZKY EXPLOSION 1979–1988

The costly war with the World Hockey Association finally came to an end in 1979, when the two professional leagues reached agreement on a merger. The NHL jumped from 17 to 21 franchises with the addition of four WHA clubs—the Quebec Nordiques, Edmonton Oilers, Winnipeg Jets and Hartford Whalers. The merger, along with the signings of several European stars, changed the game dramatically.

The days of the Philadelphia Flyers' overly physical style were dwindling as the games became free-skating and wide-open. As a result, scoring totals skyrocketed. Leading the surge was Edmonton's Wayne Gretzky, who set every scoring record imaginable and became the sport's No. 1 attraction.

The Montreal Canadiens' domination was terminated in the first year of the merger as parity enabled the expansion teams of the 1970s to rise to the top. In the forefront were the New York Islanders, who ruled the game in the early 1980s. Paced by all-around center Bryan Trottier and sniper Mike Bossy, the

« *The merger with the WHA brought superstar Wayne Gretzky to the NHL in 1979.*

Islanders could play either style—physical or finesse—with equal ability.

The Islanders would be succeeded by The Great Gretzky's Oilers, who made it into the winners' circle in a span that saw them win the Stanley Cup four times in five years.

More and more teams scouted Europe in search of talent. The Nordiques signed three Czechoslovakian brothers, the Stastnys, all of whom became stars, and other Europeans defected soon after. The league, once almost exclusively made up of Canadians, took on an international flavor.

1979–80

Clearly, the 1979–80 season was an historic one for the National Hockey League. Armistice with the World Hockey Association was achieved when the NHL agreed to absorb four of the WHA teams and in return the WHA agreed to pay off its other teams and cease operation.

With the addition of the surviving Quebec Nordiques, Winnipeg Jets, Edmonton Oilers

Islander goalie Billy Smith chugs champagne from the Cup after conquest of the Flyers in 1980.

and Hartford Whalers, the 21-team league moved to a balanced 80-game schedule. Each team would play every other team four times, with the top 16 point-getters earning playoff spots.

Two of the new teams—Edmonton and Hartford—made the playoffs, but both were near the bottom of the league and it was obvious that by and large the talent was spread thin among the old WHA squads; indeed, the NHL had stripped the incoming teams of many of their best players in a reentry draft, with each of the four WHA teams permitted to protect only two goalies and two skaters.

One notable exception was that of a thin, pimpled 19-year-old named Wayne Gretzky, the Edmonton Oiler who was the most exciting and productive player in all of hockey. Before the merger, the Oilers struck an agreement that called for Gretzky remaining their property. It was, to say the least, a wise move.

In his first NHL season, although he technically did not qualify as a rookie because of his WHA service, Gretzky scored 51 goals and tied for the league lead in points with 137 along with Los Angeles' Marcel Dionne. But Gretzky only managed to help the Oilers claim the 16th and final playoff spot.

The biggest success of the season was that of the New York Islanders. Upset in the playoffs a year earlier and having struggled through the 1979–80 season, finally finishing fifth in points, the Islanders became only the second expansion team, along with the Philadelphia Flyers, to win a Stanley Cup. It came eight years after the team's birth in the 1972 expansion draft.

To do it, the Islanders made one of the most pivotal trades in history, landing center Butch Goring from Los Angeles right at the March trading deadline. With Goring in the lineup,

the Islanders finished the season unbeaten in their last 12 games. They went on to defeat Goring's old team in the first round, Boston in the quarterfinals and Buffalo in the semifinals.

That earned the Islanders their first berth ever in the finals against divisional rival Philadelphia. And the Islanders managed to win the opening game when Denis Potvin scored a rare power-play goal in overtime. The Islanders went on to win the series in six games on Bobby Nystrom's overtime goal.

Gretzky was the Hart Trophy winner as Most Valuable Player and winner of the Lady Byng for gentlemanly play. Montreal's Larry Robinson won the Norris as best defenseman, Boston defenseman Ray Bourque won the Calder as Rookie of the Year and Islander center Bryan Trottier won the Smythe as playoff MVP.

Robinson, Bourque and Dionne were named to the All-Star team, along with Montreal right wing Guy Lafleur and Los Angeles left wing Charlie Simmer.

1979–80

FINAL STANDINGS

Prince of Wales Conference

Norris Division

	W	L	T	PTS	GF	GA
Montreal	47	20	13	107	328	240
Los Angeles	30	36	14	74	290	313
Pittsburgh	30	37	13	73	251	303
Hartford	27	34	19	73	303	312
Detroit	26	43	11	63	268	306

Adams Division

	W	L	T	PTS	GF	GA
Buffalo	47	17	16	110	318	201
Boston	46	21	13	105	310	234
Minnesota	36	28	16	88	311	253
Toronto	35	40	5	75	304	327
Quebec	25	44	11	61	248	313

Clarence Campbell Conference

Patrick Division

	W	L	T	PTS	GF	GA
Philadelphia	48	12	20	116	327	254
New York I.	39	28	13	91	281	247
New York R.	38	32	10	86	308	284
Atlanta	35	32	13	83	282	269
Washington	27	40	13	67	261	293

Smythe Division

	W	L	T	PTS	GF	GA
Chicago	34	27	19	87	241	251
St. Louis	34	34	12	80	266	278
Vancouver	27	37	16	70	256	281
Edmonton	28	39	13	69	301	322
Winnipeg	20	49	11	51	214	314
Colorado	19	48	13	51	234	308

LEADING SCORERS	G	A	PTS
Dionne, Los Angeles	53	84	137
Gretzky, Edmonton	51	86	137
Lafleur, Montreal	50	75	125
Perreault, Buffalo	40	66	106
Rogers, Hartford	44	61	105
Trottier, New York I.	42	62	104
Simmer, Los Angeles	56	45	101
Stoughton, Hartford	56	44	100
Sittler, Toronto	40	57	97
MacDonald, Edmonton	46	48	94
Federko, St. Louis	38	56	94

1980–81

The New York Islanders began the 1980–81 season as Stanley Cup defenders, but there were skeptics who felt the championship was a fluke and their reign would be short-lived.

How wrong they were! Not even Edmonton's Wayne Gretzky could steal the Islanders' thunder, although he tried mightily. Gretzky, proving his share of the scoring championship the season before in his first NHL campaign was no mistake, broke Phil Esposito's scoring record by recording an astonishing 164 points—29 more than his nearest rival—including 109 assists to break a record held by none other than Bobby Orr.

But the swift center could only lead his Edmonton team to a 15th-place finish overall in the regular-season standings. The Oilers did upset Montreal in the first round of the playoffs, but then fell in the quarterfinals to the Islanders, the team that would go on to win it all again.

There seemed to be nothing the Islanders lacked. While Gretzky piled up points, Islander Mike Bossy stockpiled goals. He scored 68 of them, one below his career high and the third-highest total in history. But Bossy's first 50 goals came in his first 50 games, tying the record set by Maurice (Rocket) Richard 38 years before and unequaled since.

Even the way Bossy, a sharp-shooting right wing, grabbed a piece of the record was dramatic. He had 48 in 49 games and appeared to be falling short when the final minutes in the 50th game against the Quebec Nordiques began to tick away. But Bossy scored twice in the last four minutes, the

who scored five goals in the finals, including three in one game.

For his record performance, Gretzky won the Hart Trophy as Most Valuable Player for the second straight season. Pittsburgh's Randy Carlyle won the Norris as best defenseman and teammate Rick Kehoe won the Lady Byng for sportsmanship. Peter Stastny, a native of Czechoslovakia and a member of the Quebec Nordiques, won the Calder as Rookie of the Year.

Bossy, Gretzky and Carlyle were named to the All-Star team along with Los Angeles left wing Charlie Simmer, St. Louis goalie Mike Liut and defenseman Denis Potvin of the New York Islanders.

Of any losers during the season, the Winnipeg Jets would have had to rate at the top—or the bottom. They went a record 30 games without winning a game. Overall, they were 9-57-14.

Butch Goring sparked the Islanders to a second Cup and was named playoff MVP in 1981.

second time with under two minutes remaining, to earn another line in the record book.

Bossy still wasn't finished. He scored a playoff record 35 points and helped the Islanders sweep the rival New York Rangers in four games in the semifinals and dispatch the Minnesota North Stars in just five games in the finals, a convincing show that finally earned the Islanders respect. But the Conn Smythe Trophy as playoff MVP went to Butch Goring,

1980-81

FINAL STANDINGS

Prince of Wales Conference

Norris Division

	W	L	T	PTS	GF	GA
Montreal	45	22	13	103	332	232
Los Angeles	43	24	13	99	337	290
Pittsburgh	30	37	13	73	302	345
Hartford	21	41	18	60	292	372
Detroit	19	43	18	56	252	339

Adams Division

	W	L	T	PTS	GF	GA
Buffalo	39	20	21	99	327	250
Boston	37	30	13	87	316	272
Minnesota	35	28	17	87	291	263
Quebec	30	32	18	78	314	318
Toronto	28	37	15	71	322	367

Clarence Campbell Conference

Patrick Division

	W	L	T	PTS	GF	GA
New York I.	48	18	14	110	355	260
Philadelphia	41	24	15	97	313	249
Calgary	39	27	14	92	329	298
New York R.	30	36	14	74	312	317
Washington	26	36	18	70	286	317

Smythe Division

	W	L	T	PTS	GF	GA
St. Louis	45	18	17	107	352	281
Chicago	31	33	16	78	304	315
Vancouver	28	32	20	76	289	301
Edmonton	29	35	16	74	328	327
Colorado	22	45	13	57	258	344
Winnipeg	9	57	14	32	246	400

Pittsburgh's Randy Carlyle won the Norris Trophy as the league's top defenseman in 1980–81.

LEADING SCORERS	G	A	PTS
Gretzky, Edmonton	55	109	164
Dionne, Los Angeles	58	77	135
K. Nilsson, Calgary	49	82	131
Bossy, New York I.	68	51	119
Taylor, Los Angeles	47	65	112
P. Stastny, Quebec	39	70	109
Simmer, Los Angeles	56	49	105
Rogers, Hartford	40	65	105
Federko, St. Louis	31	73	104
Richard, Quebec	52	51	103
Middleton, Boston	44	59	103
Trottier, New York I.	31	72	103

1981–82

He stood a lean and bony 165 pounds, barely reached 5-11 on his tiptoes and with his thin, innocent face looked more like a schoolboy than the greatest player of his generation—maybe the greatest of any generation. Edmonton's Wayne Gretzky was 21 years old and no one had ever done what he did in 1981–82.

Having already shattered the scoring record a year earlier, Gretzky went on to destroy it, amassing 212 points, an incredible 65 more than anyone else and 107 more than his closest teammate. Included in Gretzky's total was a record 92 goals, which broke Phil Esposito's record by 16, and a record 120 assists.

The New York Islanders won their third straight Stanley Cup and won a record 15 consecutive games in the process, but it was clearly the season of No. 99, known to his Edmonton fans as "The Kid."

Gretzky became the National Hockey League's first million-dollar-a-year performer, negotiating the record pact shortly after scoring 50 goals in his first 39 games, breaking the record set by Maurice (Rocket) Richard 39 years earlier and equaled by New York Islander Mike Bossy the year before.

The Great Gretzky meets Goldie Hawn and Burt Reynolds after his record-setting goal.

Taking a cue from their slender center, the Oilers vaulted from 15th place in 1980–81 to a second-place finish overall in the point standings, behind only the champion Islanders. But the Oilers were upset in the first round of the playoffs by Los Angeles, the team with the worst record of any of the 16 playoff entrants.

Edmonton's ouster only served to make the Islanders' march to their third straight title that much easier. They became only the third franchise, joining Toronto and Montreal, to win as many as three consecutive Stanley Cups.

Bossy, the quick right wing, led the Islanders in the playoffs, earning the Conn Smythe

« *A snap of the wrist and Wayne Gretzky breaks the NHL record for goals. It was No. 77 and it came against Buffalo's Don Edwards on February 24, 1982.*

Trophy as playoff MVP after scoring 17 goals, seven of them in a four-game finals sweep of Vancouver, tying a 26-year-old record set by Jean Beliveau.

Bossy and Gretzky were named to the All-Star team with Edmonton left wing Mark Messier, Islander goalie Bill Smith and defensemen Ray Bourque of Boston and Doug Wilson of Chicago.

To no one's surprise, Gretzky was the first unanimous choice as Hart Trophy winner as the Most Valuable Player, joining Bobby Orr as the only player to win the award three straight seasons.

Wilson won the Norris as best defenseman, Boston right wing Rick Middleton won the Lady Byng for sportsmanship and Winnipeg center Dale Hawerchuk won the Calder as Rookie of the Year.

In his first season as a Bruin, goalie Pete Peeters posted a streak of 31 games without a defeat and won the Vezina Trophy.

1981–82

FINAL STANDINGS

Prince of Wales Conference

Patrick Division

	W	L	T	PTS	GF	GA
New York I.	54	16	10	118	385	250
New York R.	39	27	14	92	316	306
Philadelphia	38	31	11	87	325	313
Pittsburgh	31	36	13	75	310	337
Washington	26	41	13	65	319	338

Adams Division

Montreal	46	17	17	109	360	223
Boston	43	27	10	96	323	285
Buffalo	39	26	15	93	307	273
Quebec	33	31	16	82	356	345
Hartford	21	41	18	60	264	351

Clarence Campbell Conference

Norris Division

Minnesota	37	23	20	94	346	288
Winnipeg	33	33	14	80	319	332
St. Louis	32	40	8	72	315	349
Chicago	30	38	12	72	332	363
Toronto	20	44	16	56	298	380
Detroit	21	47	12	54	270	351

❮❮ *Peter Stastny and brothers Anton (left) and Marian (middle) led Quebec into the semifinals in the 1982 playoffs.*

Smythe Division

Edmonton	48	17	15	111	417	295
Vancouver	30	33	17	77	290	286
Calgary	29	34	17	75	334	345
Los Angeles	24	41	15	63	314	369
Colorado	18	49	13	49	241	362

LEADING SCORERS

	G	A	PTS
Gretzky, Edmonton	92	120	212
Bossy, New York I.	64	83	147
P. Stastny, Quebec	46	93	139
Maruk, Washington	60	76	136
Trottier, New York I.	50	79	129
D. Savard, Chicago	32	87	119
Dionne, Los Angeles	50	67	117
Smith, Minnesota	43	71	114
Ciccarelli, Minnesota	55	52	107
Taylor, Los Angeles	39	67	106

1982–83

As the teams went deeper into the 1982–83 season, the question seemed to be not whether the New York Islanders could win another Stanley Cup championship, but rather which team would succeed them. The Islanders

*Islander goalie Billy Smith, MVP of the 1983 Stanley Cup
playoffs, frustrated Wayne Gretzky (99) and his Edmonton teammates.*

slumped and suffered during the season, but
when the playoffs ended, the Islanders possessed their fourth straight title, earning themselves a slice of immortality.

They became only the second franchise to
win that many consecutive championships,
joining the five-time winners from Montreal
(1956–60) and the Canadiens' four-time winners (1976–79). While there were record-
setting performances by individuals on other
teams, they seemed to pale in comparison to
the Islanders' fourth championship in just
their 11th season of existence.

Not even Wayne Gretzky, who again led the
league in scoring with 196 points, could stop
the Islanders' charge to the Cup. Gretzky was
held without a goal and with just four assists as
the Islanders swept the Edmonton Oilers in
four games in the final series. The Islanders
were led by goalie Billy Smith, who won the

Conn Smythe Trophy as playoff MVP, and Mike
Bossy, who set an NHL playoff record with five
game-winning goals in one season.

Bossy also tied Guy Lafleur's regular-season
record of six straight 50-goal seasons and
became the first player to score 60 goals three
straight years. Marcel Dionne of Los Angeles
became the first player to score 100 points in
seven consecutive seasons, breaking the mark
held by Lafleur and Bobby Orr. Boston goalie
Pete Peeters went 31 games without a loss,
one shy of the record held by his coach, Gerry
Cheevers, and the Oilers set a record by
scoring 424 goals.

Still, the biggest accomplishment belonged
to the Islanders. They finished a disappointing
sixth in points during the season, the worst
finish ever for a Cup winner, but defeated
Washington in the preliminary round of the
playoffs and the New York Rangers in the

Held scoreless in the Islanders' sweep to their fourth consecutive Stanley Cup, a dejected Wayne Gretzky accepts the reality of defeat in the third period of the final game.

Patrick Division finals. After disposing of the Rangers, the Islanders met Boston, the team that led the league during the season with 110 points.

Following a six-game elimination of the Bruins in the Prince of Wales Conference final, the Islanders finished off the Oilers for their second straight finals sweep, adding it to the one the previous year against Vancouver. Smith was the hero. He shut out the Oilers in the opening game, 2-0, the first goalie to blank them since he did it two years earlier. He held the high-scoring Oilers to just six goals in the series while running his career playoff record to 73-24.

That represented vindication for both Smith and the Islanders. Smith failed to win a game for two months during the regular season and the Islanders went through a stretch when they could not assemble back-to-back victories

for two months. The four Stanley Cups put the Islanders fifth among all NHL teams and with his 97th career playoff victory, Islander coach Al Arbour moved right behind Scotty Bowman (111) and Dick Irvin (100), who lead the all-time list.

But not all the records set were glowing ones. Islander Billy Carroll, a center, set an all-time record for forwards by playing in 69 straight games without scoring a goal. And the Canadiens suffered their third straight preliminary-round elimination, which hadn't happened in the long and regal history of the franchise.

Besides winning the Ross Trophy for leading the league in scoring, Gretzky also was awarded his fourth straight MVP award, the most times anyone has ever won the trophy consecutively. Peeters got the Vezina Trophy for best regular-season goaltender, Washington's Rod Langway captured the Norris Trophy for top defenseman and Bossy took the Lady Byng Trophy for sportsmanship and high standard of playing ability. Philadelphia's Bobby Clarke won the Selke Trophy as best defensive forward and Chicago's Steve Larmer was Rookie of the Year.

The Oilers placed two players, Gretzky and Mark Messier, on the All-Star team. Joining them were Bossy, Peeters, Langway and Philadelphia's Mark Howe.

1982-83

FINAL STANDINGS
Prince of Wales Conference

Adams Division
	W	L	T	PTS	GF	GA
Boston	50	20	10	110	327	228
Montreal	42	24	14	98	350	286
Buffalo	38	29	13	89	318	285
Quebec	34	34	12	80	343	336
Hartford	19	54	7	45	261	403

Patrick Division
Philadelphia	49	23	8	106	326	240
New York I.	42	26	12	96	302	226
Washington	39	25	16	94	306	283
New York R.	35	35	10	80	306	287
New Jersey	17	49	14	48	230	338
Pittsburgh	18	53	9	45	257	394

Clarence Campbell Conference

Norris Division
Chicago	47	23	10	104	338	268
Minnesota	40	24	16	96	321	290
Toronto	28	40	12	68	293	330
St. Louis	25	40	15	65	285	316
Detroit	21	44	15	57	263	344

Smythe Division						
Edmonton	47	21	12	106	424	315
Calgary	32	34	14	78	321	317
Vancouver	30	35	15	75	303	309
Winnipeg	33	39	8	74	311	333
Los Angeles	27	41	12	66	308	365

LEADING SCORERS	G	A	PTS
Gretzky, Edmonton	71	125	196
P. Stastny, Quebec	47	77	124
Savard, Chicago	35	85	120
Bossy, New York I.	60	58	118
Dionne, Los Angeles	56	51	107
Pederson, Boston	46	61	107
Messier, Edmonton	48	58	106
Goulet, Quebec	57	48	105
Anderson, Edmonton	48	56	104
Nilsson, Calgary	46	58	104
Kurri, Edmonton	45	59	104

1983–84

In his first four years in the NHL, Edmonton's Wayne Gretzky lived an everyday hockey existence that to all other players was fantasy. Yet he still had not realized his dream—taking a victory lap with the Stanley Cup hoisted above his shoulders.

Indeed, a season earlier in the Cup finals, he had been reduced to a mere mortal for the first time in his career, held to just four assists in the Islanders' sweep of his Oilers.

From the outset of the 1983–84 season, it became apparent Gretzky would do everything possible to help earn the Oilers another shot. He scored in the Oilers' opener and in every game his club played in October, November and into December. On December 18, he scored a pair of goals and assists against Winnipeg to reach the 100-point mark in only his 34th game, breaking his own league mark.

The streak continued until January 27, 1984, when Kings' goaltender Markus Mattson held the Oilers to a couple of goals in a 4-2 decision, snapping Gretzky's string at an incredible 51 games during which he amassed 153 points, including 61 goals.

His final totals of 87-118-205 left him 79 points ahead of his nearest challenger—teammate Paul Coffey—in the scoring race. The pair helped Edmonton to a 57-18-5 record and

« Edmonton's Mark Messier (11) was the playoff MVP as the Oilers won their first Stanley Cup, ending the Islanders' "Drive for Five."

119 points. The Oilers also established an all-time mark with 446 goals, a record 36 of them shorthanded, and set another record with three 50-plus goal scorers (Gretzky, Glenn Anderson with 54 and Jari Kurri with 52).

Gretzky and the Oilers were not the only ones to create headlines or set records. Buffalo rookie goaltender Tom Barrasso, an 18-year-old who was drafted out of high school the previous June, collected both the Vezina Trophy as top netminder and the Calder for rookie honors and earned a spot on the first All-Star team. He finished the season with a 26-12-3 record and a league-leading 2.84 goals-against average.

An unusual record was set October 30 in Philadelphia when four brothers appeared in the same game. Duane and Brent Sutter of the Islanders relived their "Hayloft Hockey" days with twin brothers Ron and Rich, who were rookies with the Flyers. That brought to six the number of Sutters in the league, with Brian playing for St. Louis and Darryl with Chicago.

The Olympic Saddledome opened in Calgary, Quebec's Michel Goulet scored more points (121) than any left wing in one season, and on November 25 an NHL-record crowd of 21,019 jammed Joe Louis Arena in Detroit to watch the Red Wings defeat the Penguins, 7-4.

Fans in every arena got a little more for their money when, for the first time since November 21, 1942, overtime was reinstated. The five-minute, sudden-death format made its debut on October 5 when the Jets and Red Wings tied at 6-6. The first overtime goal came three nights later in the Capital Centre when the Islanders' Bob Bourne scored at 2:01 to beat Washington, 8-7. It was the first regular-season overtime goal since November 10, 1942, when the Rangers' Lynn Patrick tallied his team's fifth goal at 7:11 in a 5-3 victory. In those days, the extra session ran a full 10 minutes, no matter how many goals were scored.

While most of the early attention in the playoffs was focused on whether Al Arbour's Islanders could win their fifth straight Cup or if Edmonton could finally fulfill its promise, St. Louis and Minnesota kept everyone enter-

All-Star Rod Langway of Washington was voted the league's leading defenseman in 1983–84.

opening game at Nassau Coliseum, giving a superior defensive performance in front of Grant Fuhr to beat the Islanders and Bill Smith, 1-0.

The Isles, physically battered in their previous series, rebounded with a 6-1 victory, but after that, it was Edmonton in a rout. With Gretzky and Mark Messier leading the attack, the Oilers reeled off three consecutive triumphs (7-2, 7-2, 5-2) to wrap up their first Stanley Cup. Gretzky's 35 points topped playoff scorers and Messier, with 26 points and sensational pivotal goals in Games 3 and 4, wound up with the Conn Smythe Trophy as playoff MVP.

Washington's Rod Langway (the Norris Trophy winner), Boston's Ray Bourque, Gretzky, Goulet and the Islanders' Mike Bossy joined Barrasso on the All-Star team and Washington's Doug Jarvis won the Selke Trophy. The Flyers' Bobby Clarke announced his retirement on May 15.

The biggest winners among the losers appeared to be the Penguins, who finished with 38 points, three fewer than the Devils, giving them the chance to select junior phenom Mario Lemieux in the 1984 June entry draft.

tained in their Norris Division final, the North Stars winning the seventh game after six minutes of overtime on a goal by Steve Payne.

The Islanders' "Drive for Five," as they tried to match the Canadiens' feat of winning five straight titles (the Habs accomplished it in the old six-team league when it required only two postseason series victories per year), got off to a rocky start. They trailed, 2-1, in a best-of-five Patrick Division semifinal series with the Rangers, but eventually survived when Ken Morrow scored at 8:56 of overtime to win the fifth and deciding game. They got by the Capitals in five games and overcame a 2-0 deficit to oust the Canadiens in six games, winning their NHL-record 19th straight playoff series to make the finals for a fifth straight year.

The Oilers, who needed just 12 games to make it to the championship round, took a page from the Islanders' style book in the

1983–84

FINAL STANDINGS

Prince of Wales Conference

Adams Division

	W	L	T	PTS	GF	GA
Boston	49	25	6	104	336	261
Buffalo	48	25	7	103	315	257
Quebec	42	28	10	94	360	278
Montreal	35	40	5	75	286	295
Hartford	28	42	10	66	288	320

Patrick Division

New York I.	50	26	4	104	357	269
Washington	48	27	5	101	308	226
Philadelphia	44	26	10	98	350	290
New York R.	42	29	9	93	314	304
New Jersey	17	56	7	41	231	350
Pittsburgh	16	58	6	38	254	390

Clarence Campbell Conference

Norris Division

Minnesota	39	31	10	88	345	344
St. Louis	32	41	7	71	293	316
Detroit	31	42	7	69	298	323
Chicago	30	42	8	68	277	311
Toronto	26	45	9	61	303	387

Smythe Division

Edmonton	57	18	5	119	446	314
Calgary	34	32	14	82	311	314
Vancouver	32	39	9	73	306	328
Winnipeg	31	38	11	73	340	374
Los Angeles	23	44	13	59	309	376

Buffalo's Tom Barrasso was Rookie of the Year and winner of the Vezina Trophy as No. 1 goaltender in 1983–84.

LEADING SCORERS	G	A	PTS
Gretzky, Edmonton	87	118	205
Coffey, Edmonton	40	86	126
Goulet, Quebec	56	65	121
P. Stastny, Quebec	46	73	119
Bossy, New York I.	51	67	118
Pederson, Boston	39	77	116
Kurri, Edmonton	52	61	113
Trottier, New York I.	40	71	111
Federko, St. Louis	41	66	107
Middleton, Boston	47	58	105

1984–85

The spotlight that had been glowing solely on Wayne Gretzky finally broke into a prism with the emergence of teammate Jari Kurri as a superstar and with the much-hyped arrival in Pittsburgh of Mario Lemieux, the youngster who had broken all of Guy Lafleur's Quebec Major Junior Hockey League scoring records in 1983–84 with 133 goals and 282 points with the Laval Voisins.

Gretzky was in a race for the goal-scoring crown all season with Kurri, his sharpshooting right wing who became only the third player in history (after Phil Esposito and Gretzky) to reach the 70-goal plateau. Kurri finished with 71 goals, two behind Gretzky, who ran away with the Art Ross Trophy, scoring 208 points, 73 more than runnerup Kurri. The pair helped the Oilers go a record 15 games from the start of the season without a loss (12-0-3).

Of course, another season in the NHL meant another milestone for Gretzky. It came on December 19, when he picked up an assist for his 1,000th career point in only his 424th game, demolishing Guy Lafleur's 720-game record of being the fastest player to reach that total.

Lemieux got off to a slow start, but began to make his presence felt as the season progressed. Lemieux got little help from teammates on a club that managed only 53 points, the next-to-worst record in the league. By the time April arrived, Lemieux had become only

the third rookie (Peter Stastny and Dave Hawerchuk were the others) ever to reach the 100-point plateau. He finished with 43 goals and 57 assists and won the Calder Trophy as the league's top rookie.

Washington's Bobby Carpenter also was finally fulfilling expectations, as his 53 goals made him the first U.S.-born player ever to score 50 in a season.

The same night that Gretzky was scoring his 1,000th point, Buffalo coach Scotty Bowman was rewriting the record book, recording his 691st victory behind the bench in a career with the Canadiens and Sabres. That eclipsed

former Montreal-Chicago-Toronto coach Dick Irvin. In the meantime, the Rangers were playing musical chairs with coaches, dismissing 1980 U.S. Olympic coach Herb Brooks, with general manager Craig Patrick taking over and later selecting Ted Sator.

The Islanders gave indication that a sixth consecutive appearance in the Cup finals was not likely when they finished the season in third place in the Patrick Division with 86 points, their poorest showing in 11 years.

The league's best record belonged to the resurgent Philadelphia Flyers, whose 53-20-7 mark for 113 points was four better than the defending Cup champion Oilers, whom they would meet in the finals. Philadelphia was led by goaltender Pelle Lindbergh, who led the league with 40 victories (40-17-7), and on offense by Tim Kerr, who contributed 54 goals.

The playoffs were full of memorable moments and records. One mark was set in the opening second of the postseason when Detroit's Brad Park stepped on the ice, making it the 17th consecutive year in which he participated in the playoffs.

After dropping the first two games in overtime in their opening series against Washington, the Islanders rebounded with a 2-1 victory, then scored four times in the third period to win, 6-4, in Game 4. Bill Smith's goaltending and Brent Sutter's game-winning goal were the keys to a 2-1 victory in Game 5 as the Isles became the first team in history to win a five-game series after losing the first two.

There were no more miracles in the following round, however, when they ran up against the Flyers, who had swept the Rangers in an opening round that featured Kerr's record four goals in the second period of Game 3. The Flyers promptly defeated the Islanders in five games and then dispatched Quebec in six.

But Philadelphia didn't have enough weapons to stay with Edmonton. After losing the

« Wayne Gretzky celebrates two Cups in a row for Edmonton in 1985.

Pittsburgh's Mario Lemieux responded to his pre-NHL fanfare with a 100-point performance on the way to Rookie of the Year honors in 1984–85.

Philadelphia's Pelle Lindbergh, the embattled goalie here under the Islanders' John Tonelli, emerged as winner of the Vezina Trophy in 1984–85.

opener, 4-1, the Oilers ran off four straight wins to earn their second consecutive Cup.

Gretzky captured one of the few awards that had eluded him to that point—the Conn Smythe Trophy as playoff MVP, completing the postseason with a record for assists (30) and points (47). Kurri's 19 goals equaled the NHL mark.

Left wing John Ogrodnick became the first Red Wing in 12 years to be named to the first All-Star team, joining Lindbergh (Vezina), Edmonton's Paul Coffey (Norris), Boston's Ray Bourque, Gretzky and Kurri (Lady Byng). Buffalo's Craig Ramsey won the Selke Trophy as best defensive forward.

1984–85

FINAL STANDINGS

Prince of Wales Conference
Adams Division

	W	L	T	PTS	GF	GA
Montreal	41	27	12	94	309	262
Quebec	41	30	9	91	323	275
Buffalo	38	28	14	90	290	237
Boston	36	34	10	82	303	287
Hartford	30	41	9	69	268	318

Patrick Division

	W	L	T	PTS	GF	GA
Philadelphia	53	20	7	113	348	241
Washington	46	25	9	101	322	240
New York I.	40	34	6	86	345	312
New York R.	26	44	10	62	295	345
New Jersey	22	48	10	54	264	346
Pittsburgh	24	51	5	53	276	385

Clarence Campbell Conference
Norris Division

	W	L	T	PTS	GF	GA
St. Louis	37	31	12	86	299	288
Chicago	38	35	7	83	309	299
Detroit	27	41	12	66	313	357
Minnesota	25	43	12	62	268	321
Toronto	20	52	8	48	253	358

Smythe Division

	W	L	T	PTS	GF	GA
Edmonton	49	20	11	109	401	298
Winnipeg	43	27	10	96	358	332
Calgary	41	27	12	94	363	302
Los Angeles	34	32	14	82	339	326
Vancouver	25	46	9	59	284	401

LEADING SCORERS	G	A	PTS
Gretzky, Edmonton	73	135	208
Kurri, Edmonton	71	64	135
Hawerchuk, Winnipeg	53	77	130
Dionne, Los Angeles	46	80	126
Coffey, Edmonton	37	84	121
Bossy, New York I.	58	59	117
Ogrodnick, Detroit	55	50	105
Savard, Chicago	38	67	105
Federko, St. Louis	30	73	103
Gartner, Washington	50	52	102
B. Sutter, New York I.	42	60	102

1985–86

Bobby Orr had been out of hockey for seven years, but fans kept being reminded of his greatness throughout the 1985–86 season as several of his single-season and career records for defensemen were eclipsed.

The first Orr mark to fall came on December 20 when the Islanders' Denis Potvin, in his 13th season, earned his 915th career point, surpassing Orr's total, which was accumulated

Oiler defenseman Paul Coffey shone in a record-breaking 1985–86 campaign that landed his second consecutive Norris Trophy.

in 12 seasons with the Bruins and Black Hawks. Just 39 days later, Potvin again replaced Orr at the top of a scoring list when he netted his 271st career goal.

Oiler backliner Paul Coffey tallied his 46th and 47th goals on April 2, snapping Orr's once untouchable record. Coffey finished the season at 48-90-138, one point shy of Orr's standard for defensemen.

Eight of Coffey's points came on March 14 when he tied the NHL mark for defensemen established by Philadelphia's Tom Bladon and also equaled a backliner's record for assists in one game with six. Coffey added one more record for defensemen by collecting points in 28 consecutive games.

There was change, triumph and tragedy during the regular season. The league announced that fans would vote for the starting teams in the All-Star Game. In addition, the

A 20-year-old rookie goaltender, Montreal's Patrick Roy achieved MVP honors in the playoffs as Montreal captured the Stanley Cup in 1986.

Philadelphia's Tim Kerr set a single-season record with 34 power-play goals.

set a one-season mark with 34 powerplay goals; by Minnesota center Neal Broten, who became the first U.S.-born player to record 100 or more points (105), and by Buffalo's Gilbert Perreault, who scored his 500th career goal in March.

The experts predicted that the playoffs would be another futile exercise for everyone except the Oilers. It didn't work out that way. In fact, the Oilers never got out of the Smythe Division. After dispatching the Canucks in three straight, the Oilers faced arch-rival Calgary, which had been bolstered three months earlier when it received Joey Mullen, Terry Johnson and Rik Wilson from St. Louis for Eddy Beers, Gino Cavallini and Charlie Bourgeois in a blockbuster trade.

The Flames, relying on rookie goaltender Mike Vernon, won the opener, 4-1, and the teams alternated victories from that point, forcing a seventh game at Northlands Coliseum. The contest was tied at two with 5:14 gone in the third period when one of the strangest plays in postseason history occurred. Rookie Oiler defenseman Steve Smith, pressured near his own net, tried to backpass to defensive partner Don Jackson. Instead, the puck ticked off goalie Grant Fuhr's left skate and slid into the net. Calgary center Perry Berezan got credit for the goal. The stunned Oilers never got the equalizer and their two-year reign as Stanley Cup champions ended in bizarre fashion.

There were other early-round surprises. The Islanders were swept for the first time in their history, ousted in three games by Washington and Adams Division winner Quebec was bounced in the same number by fourth-place Hartford.

All but the Rangers-Capitals division final went seven games, the most thrilling between the Whalers and Canadiens when Montreal's Claude Lemieux scored at 5:55 of overtime of the seventh game.

The Blues forced the Flames to a seventh game in the Campbell Conference finals, losing 2-1, while the Canadiens ousted the Rangers in five games to set up the first all-Canadian final since Montreal and Toronto met

league created a new award—the President's Trophy—presented to the team with the NHL's overall best record, along with a check for $100,000 to be split among the players.

The Oilers gobbled up the cash, finishing with 119 points, matching their previous club record. The Flyers placed second with 110 points and overcame the grief and shock of losing their All-Star goaltender Pelle Lindbergh, who was killed when he drove his Porsche at high speed into a wall in November.

Of course, it was Wayne Gretzky who played a major role in keeping the Oilers at the top in the regular season. He ended the season with NHL records of 215 points and 163 assists. Gretzky took the Art Ross Trophy for a sixth straight year, finishing 74 points ahead of Pittsburgh's Mario Lemieux.

Gretzky's figures dwarfed other notable accomplishments by the Flyers' Tim Kerr, who

in 1967. Calgary won the Cup final opener at home and went into overtime in Game 2. But Brian Skrudland's goal at nine seconds (the fastest overtime goal in playoff history) evened the series.

Montreal won the next three games to cop the Stanley Cup, the club's 23rd championship. Rookie goaltender Patrick Roy became the youngest Conn Smythe Trophy winner at age 20 after compiling a 15-5 record and 1.92 goals-against average.

Coffey copped the Norris Trophy for the second straight season while Ranger goaltender John Vanbiesbrouck won the Vezina, Calgary defenseman Gary Suter the Calder, Chicago center Troy Murray the Selke and the Islanders' Mike Bossy the Lady Byng for the third time. Gretzky, Vanbiesbrouck, Bossy, Coffey, Philadelphia's Mark Howe and Quebec's Michel Goulet were first-team All-Stars.

1985–86

FINAL STANDINGS

Prince of Wales Conference

Adams Division

	W	L	T	PTS	GF	GA
Quebec	43	31	6	92	330	289
Montreal	40	33	7	87	330	280
Boston	37	31	12	86	311	288
Hartford	40	36	4	84	332	302
Buffalo	37	37	6	80	296	291

Patrick Division

	W	L	T	PTS	GF	GA
Philadelphia	53	23	4	110	335	241
Washington	50	23	7	107	315	272
New York I.	39	29	12	90	327	284
New York R.	36	38	6	78	280	276
Pittsburgh	34	38	8	76	313	305
New Jersey	28	49	3	59	300	374

Clarence Campbell Conference

Norris Division

	W	L	T	PTS	GF	GA
Chicago	39	33	8	86	351	349
Minnesota	38	33	9	85	327	305
St. Louis	37	34	9	83	302	291
Toronto	25	48	7	57	311	386
Detroit	17	57	6	40	266	415

Smythe Division

	W	L	T	PTS	GF	GA
Edmonton	56	17	7	119	426	310
Calgary	40	31	9	89	354	315
Winnipeg	26	47	7	59	295	372
Vancouver	23	44	13	59	282	333
Los Angeles	23	49	8	54	284	389

LEADING SCORERS	G	A	PTS
Gretzky, Edmonton	52	163	215
Lemieux, Pittsburgh	48	93	141
Coffey, Edmonton	48	90	138
Kurri, Edmonton	68	63	131
Bossy, New York I.	61	62	123
P. Stastny, Quebec	41	81	122
Savard, Chicago	47	69	116
Naslund, Montreal	43	67	110
Hawerchuk, Winnipeg	46	59	105
N. Broten, Minnesota	29	76	105

1986–87

From the moment the six-team league ballooned to 12 in 1967, there appeared to be a noticeable talent imbalance in the NHL. There always were powerhouse teams, clubs capable of competing against each other, but there also were too many teams each season that had absolutely no chance of winning the Cup or even able to keep games close on the majority of nights.

But in 1986–87, the league finally appeared to have achieved parity, with all but three of the 21 teams finishing with 70 or more points. Just two teams, league-leading Edmonton (106) and Washington (100) reached the century mark.

None of the teams in the Norris Division managed to reach the .500 level but they staged an exciting race for first place, with St. Louis finishing on top with a 32-33-15 record for 79 points, just nine more than last-place Minnesota. The Blues trailed Detroit by one point going into the season's final game, but defenseman Rob Ramage scored with 71 seconds remaining in overtime to enable St. Louis to leapfrog over Detroit into first place.

A milestone occurred during the season's opening week when, on October 9, the Kings' Marcel Dionne picked up an assist in a 4-3 loss to St. Louis, giving him 1,600 career points, the second player in league history (behind Gordie Howe) to attain that plateau.

Exactly one week later, the Islanders' Denis Potvin earned his 684th career assist, breaking Brad Park's record for defensemen. It happened 13 years to the day after Potvin had been credited with his first NHL assist and point.

The Flyers' Ron Hextall stood tall, winning the Vezina Trophy and the Smythe Trophy, the latter despite playing for the losers in the 1987 Cup final won by Edmonton.

A record set by Hartford's Doug Jarvis took almost as long to realize. The day after Christmas, the former Montreal and Washington center played in his 915th consecutive game, breaking Garry Unger's ironman mark. Jarvis, playing in his first full season with the Whalers, helped his team edge the Canadiens by one point to win its first Adams Division title.

New Year's Day brought more than hangovers. The Capitals sent Bobby Carpenter and a 1989 second-round draft pick to the Rangers for Kelly Miller, Mike Ridley and Bob Crawford. Just 68 days later, Carpenter was packing again, this time headed to Los Angeles for Dionne, Jeff Crossman and a future draft choice.

When the regular season ended, Wayne Gretzky had run away with the Hart Trophy for an eighth straight year with 183 points, pacing the league in both goals (62) and assists (121) and finishing 75 points ahead of teammate and runnerup Jari Kurri.

The closely contested campaign gave promise to a wide-open battle for the Stanley Cup. It also promised to be the longest road ever for the eventual champion because the best-of-five opening round was expanded to best-of-seven. That set the stage for one of the most remarkable playoff series in history—between the Islanders and Capitals. After splitting the first two games, the Caps beat the Islanders twice to open a 3-1 lead. But the Isles took the next two, forcing a seventh game.

A goal by Bryan Trottier with 5:23 remaining in regulation enabled the Isles to tie the game at 2-2. Both the Isles' Kelly Hrudey and Caps' rookie goaltender Bob Mason kicked out everything from that point as the game went into overtime after overtime. Finally, six hours and 15 minutes of agony for both teams ended in ecstasy for the Islanders when Pat LaFontaine rang a shot off the right post and into the cords at 8:15 of the fourth extra session, ending the longest game in 44 years and the fifth-longest game in NHL history.

Almost lost in the euphoria over winning the marathon at 1:55 A.M. on Easter Sunday was the fact that the Islanders had become only the third team in history to win a series after trailing 3-1. The 1942 Maple Leafs and 1975 Islanders each rebounded from 3-0 deficits.

A week later, the Isles found themselves again trailing 3-1 in a series, this time the Patrick Division final against the Flyers. Again they rallied to tie the series, but the Flyers dominated, 5-1, in Game 7. Meanwhile, De-

Left wing Luc Robitaille gave the Kings cause for cheer as he earned Rookie of the Year honors in 1986–87.

Quebec left wing Michel Goulet made the first All-Star team for the third time in 1986–87.

troit rebounded from a 3-1 deficit to oust Toronto, with Glen Hanlon limiting the Leafs to just two goals in the final three games.

Edmonton avoided that kind of drama, cruising past the Kings (including a postseason record 13 goals in a 13-3 victory), Jets and Red Wings in 15 games to earn a spot in the Cup finals. The Flyers defeated the Canadiens in six games in the Wales Conference finals, winning all three games in Montreal but needlessly expended some energy in extra-curricular activities in the process.

The league had passed an instigator rule before the season began, allowing officials to assess an additional minor penalty to a player who starts an altercation. But before the opening faceoff for the Wales Conference finale, without any officials on ice, Montreal's Claude Lemieux tried to take his customary warmup-ending shot into the opponent's net.

Philadelphia's Ed Hospodar jumped Lemieux and a fight began. Players in various stages of undress came out of the locker rooms and the brawl continued for 11 minutes before the referee and linesmen were alerted and able to restore order.

With the exception of goaltender Ron Hextall's vicious slash of Edmonton's Kent Nilsson, the Flyers stuck to hockey in the finals and earned the begrudging respect of even their harshest critics when they kept coming back. After losing the first two games and trailing, 3-0, halfway through Game 3, the Flyers exploded for a 5-3 victory. Although they fell in Game 4, they survived, 4-3, in Game 5 and then scored twice in a 1:24 span to erase a 2-1 deficit in Game 6. But the Oilers took the final, 3-1, to prevail in the first seven-game final since Montreal and Chicago met in 1971.

Gretzky scored just five goals in the Oilers' 21-game postseason journey, but had a play-

off-high 34 points. However, the losers' Hextall was awarded the Conn Smythe Trophy, joining Detroit goaltender Roger Crozier (1966) and the Flyers' Reggie Leach (1976) as the only MVPs from losing teams.

Hextall, who won a league-leading 37 games, copped the Vezina, Boston's Ray Bourque the Norris and Luc Robitaille of the Kings the Calder. Bourque, Hextall, Gretzky and Kurri joined Quebec's Michel Goulet and Philadelphia's Mark Howe as first-team All-Stars.

1986-87

FINAL STANDINGS

Prince of Wales Conference

Adams Division

	W	L	T	PTS	GF	GA
Hartford	43	30	7	93	287	270
Montreal	41	29	10	92	277	241
Boston	39	34	7	85	301	276
Quebec	31	39	10	72	267	276
Buffalo	28	44	8	66	280	308

Patrick Division

	W	L	T	PTS	GF	GA
Philadelphia	46	26	8	100	310	245
Washington	38	32	10	86	285	278
New York I.	35	33	12	82	279	281
New York R.	34	38	8	76	307	323
Pittsburgh	30	38	12	72	297	290
New Jersey	29	45	6	64	293	368

Clarence Campbell Conference

Norris Division

	W	L	T	PTS	GF	GA
St. Louis	32	33	15	79	281	293
Detroit	34	36	10	78	260	274
Chicago	29	37	14	72	290	310
Toronto	32	42	6	70	286	319
Minnesota	30	40	10	70	296	314

Smythe Division

	W	L	T	PTS	GF	GA
Edmonton	50	24	6	106	372	284
Calgary	46	31	3	95	318	289
Winnipeg	40	32	8	88	279	271
Los Angeles	31	41	8	70	318	341
Vancouver	29	43	8	66	282	314

LEADING SCORERS

	G	A	PTS
Gretzky, Edmonton	62	121	183
Kurri, Edmonton	54	54	108
Lemieux, Pittsburgh	54	53	107
Messier, Edmonton	37	70	107
Gilmour, St. Louis	42	63	105
Ciccarelli, Minnesota	52	51	103
Hawerchuk, Winnipeg	47	53	100
Goulet, Quebec	49	47	96
Kerr, Philadelphia	58	37	95
Bourque, Boston	23	72	95

1987-88

The man who engraved the Hart and Art Ross Trophies through the 1980s had one of the easiest jobs in the world. Every June, all he would have to do is pull out a stencil with the

Indicating the time had come, Pittsburgh's Mario Lemieux broke Wayne Gretzky's stranglehold on MVP and scoring honors in 1987–88.

name Gretzky on it and etch away. But someone new had to be lettered in after the 1987–88 season.

For the first time since entering the NHL in 1979, Wayne Gretzky was not the league MVP. For the first time since his second season, the Oiler center was not the league's scoring champion. Both honors went to Pittsburgh's Mario Lemieux, who finished his fourth season with 70 goals and 168 points, 30 points and 19 points ahead of Gretzky, who missed 16 games because of injury. Lemieux's wins broke a string of eight straight MVP awards and seven consecutive scoring titles for Gretzky.

Lemieux's scoring prowess still was not enough to get the Penguins into the playoffs. In a remarkable finish, all six teams in the Patrick Division finished with records of better than .500. The Islanders won the division with 88 points and the Penguins finished last

Grant Fuhr of the championship Oilers played in a record number of games for a goaltender and was named to the All-Star team in 1987–88.

defenseman held out in a contract dispute and was traded to Pittsburgh on November 24, 1987, in a seven-player deal.

Philadelphia's Ron Hextall made history on December 8 when he became the first goaltender in NHL history to actually shoot a puck into a net. Bill Smith of the Islanders had been the first goaltender to be credited with scoring a goal (November 28, 1979, in Denver), but he was simply the last Islander to touch the puck before Colorado's Rob Ramage put it into his own net.

Another goaltender, Edmonton's Grant Fuhr, set a record by playing in 75 games, two more than Bernie Parent played for the Flyers in 1973–74.

There were other significant milestones in the season. On December 19, Boston's Ken Linseman and St. Louis center Doug Gilmour made history when they scored goals two seconds apart. On January 14, the Islanders' Denis Potvin became the first defenseman ever to score 300 goals when he tallied in an 8-5 victory over Quebec. Calgary's Hakan Loob became the first Swedish 50-goal scorer in the NHL and teammate Joe Nieuwendyk, the Calder Trophy winner, challenged Mike Bossy's rookie goal-scoring record of 53, falling two short.

Amid all the celebrations came a note of sadness. Just three days before the February 9 All-Star Game in St. Louis was to honor him, former Blues player and coach Barclay Plager passed away from cancer.

Meanwhile, there were hurrahs in arenas where fans had been quiet for some time. In Detroit, the Red Wings finished on top of the Norris Division, the first time they had finished first since the 1964–65 season, and their 41-28-11 record (93 points) was their best in 18 years. Jacques Demers won the Jack Adams Award as Coach of the Year for an unprecedented second straight season.

And in New Jersey, the Devils produced a miracle finish to make the playoffs for the first time since moving from Colorado in 1982. They needed a victory on the final night in Chicago to jump over both the Penguins and Rangers into fourth place in the Patrick Divi-

with 81. Calgary edged Montreal by two points for the league's best record at 48-23-9.

Individuals making headlines included Marcel Dionne, who was now wearing a Rangers' uniform. Dionne collected his 700th career goal on Halloween night to join Gordie Howe (801) and Phil Esposito (717) as the only players ever to reach that milestone. One week later, Dionne notched his 1,000th career assist, joining Gretzky and Howe in that exclusive club.

Actually, Gretzky had joined the club only three days earlier when he picked up the milestone assist in Montreal. Then, on March 1, 1988, Gretzky got the big one against Los Angeles, garnering his 1,050th assist to pass Howe and move into first place on the all-time list.

Gretzky didn't combine with Paul Coffey on any of his points in 1987–88. The All-Star

Joe Nieuwendyk of Calgary nailed down the Calder Trophy as 1987–88 Rookie of the Year with prolific goal-scoring.

score a shorthanded goal in overtime since Harvey (Busher) Jackson did it for the Bruins against the Canadiens in 1943. But the Devils rebounded to oust the Islanders in six games and face the Caps in the Patrick Division finals. Washington made it that far via Dale Hunter's fourth overtime playoff goal, coming in 5:57 of the extra session in Game 7 against the Flyers.

The Capitals went seven again against the Devils, but this time the magic belonged to New Jersey. In Game 3, the Devils' Patrik Sundstrom exploded for a playoff-record eight points (3-5-8), breaking Gretzky's mark of seven points, set on three occasions.

It was in the Wales Conference finals against the Bruins that the Devils really rocked the NHL. Their coach, the volatile Jim Schoenfeld, angered over the officiating in Game 3, confronted referee Don Koharski as the official left the ice. When others tried to keep the two apart in the corridor leading from the ice to the locker rooms, Koharski was bumped and fell.

The NHL immediately suspended Schoenfeld, but the Devils got a court injunction to get the coach behind the bench for Game 4. Game officials then refused to work the game and off-ice officials were quickly rounded up. Amid threats of lawsuits and countersuits, the Bruins went on to win the series in seven games and earn a berth in the Cup finals for the first time in 10 years.

There they faced the defending champion Oilers, who won the first three games and hoped to wrap up the series at Boston Garden. With the game tied at 3-3 at 16:37 of the second period, the lights went out. The power failure continued, the game was suspended and the series shifted back to Edmonton, where it ended as the Oilers won, 6-3, for their fourth Stanley Cup in five seasons.

Gretzky's record 31 assists in one playoff year highlighted his winning of his second Conn Smythe Trophy. The Selke Trophy went to Montreal's Guy Carbonneau and the Lady Byng to Montreal's Mats Naslund. Boston's Ray Bourque, the Norris Trophy winner, was named a first-team All-Star for the sixth time, but everyone else on the 1987–88 team was

sion and got it with John MacLean scoring in Chicago with seconds left in regulation time and then again late in the five-minute overtime. The Devils' entry into the postseason set up one of the most bizarre playoff adventures in league annals.

It started in their first-round series with the Islanders. The Devils were shocked at home when Brent Sutter became the first player to

making his All-Star debut. Lemieux replaced Gretzky, joining newcomers Loob, Fuhr, Los Angeles' Luc Robitaille and Washington defenseman Scott Stevens.

1987–88

FINAL STANDINGS

Prince of Wales Conference

Adams Division

	W	L	T	PTS	GF	GA
Montreal	45	22	13	103	298	238
Boston	44	30	6	94	300	251
Buffalo	37	32	11	85	283	305
Hartford	35	38	7	77	249	267
Quebec	32	43	5	69	271	306

Patrick Division

New York I.	39	31	10	88	308	267
Washington	38	33	9	85	281	249
Philadelphia	38	33	9	85	292	292
New Jersey	38	36	6	82	295	296
New York R.	36	34	10	82	300	283
Pittsburgh	36	35	9	81	319	316

Clarence Campbell Conference

Norris Division

Detroit	41	28	11	93	322	269
St. Louis	34	38	8	76	278	294
Chicago	30	41	9	69	284	328
Toronto	21	49	10	52	273	345
Minnesota	19	48	13	51	242	349

Smythe Division

Calgary	48	23	9	105	397	305
Edmonton	44	25	11	99	363	288
Winnipeg	33	36	11	77	292	310
Los Angeles	30	42	8	68	318	359
Vancouver	25	46	9	59	272	320

LEADING SCORERS

	G	A	PTS
Lemieux, Pittsburgh	70	98	168
Gretzky, Edmonton	40	109	149
Savard, Chicago	44	87	131
Hawerchuk, Winnipeg	44	77	121
Robitaille, Los Angeles	53	58	111
P. Stastny, Quebec	46	65	111
Messier, Edmonton	37	74	111
Carson, Los Angeles	55	52	107
Loob, Calgary	50	56	106
Goulet, Quebec	48	58	106

CROWNING NEW CHAMPIONS 1988–1992

An era dawned in which fans in many NHL cities dared to dream that this would be the year their heroes would drink from the Stanley Cup. For now, no one club dominated the league. The Islanders had faded, the Canadiens moved back into the pack, the Flyers changed direction and a surprising dismemberment of the Oilers' star-studded roster was about to begin with one of the most shocking trades in sports history.

It was an era in which Calgary and Pittsburgh would win their first championships, when the Rangers would capture a division crown for the first time in almost a half-century, and when the long downtrodden Norris Division would rise to challenge for the Cup.

New stars were about to emerge, most notably Brett Hull, the son of a Hall of Fame left wing, who would challenge some of the standards set by Wayne Gretzky and Mario Lemieux.

《 *Introducing . . . the new king of Kings . . . Wayne Gretzky.*

1988–89

Hockey was thrust onto the front pages across North America on August 9, 1988, with one of the biggest trades in his history of professional sports.

Oilers' owner Peter Pocklington, reportedly in need of money, traded the greatest asset in hockey, Wayne Gretzky, to the Kings. Mike Krushelnyski and Marty McSorley joined Gretzky in Los Angeles in exchange for Jimmy Carson, Martin Gelinas, three first-round draft picks (1989, '91 and '93) and an estimated $15-20 million.

Another immortal had a change of address—after almost four years out of hockey. Guy Lafleur, who left the Canadiens in November 1984, signed as a free agent with the New York Rangers. Lafleur, who had only recently been inducted into the Hall of Fame, had 18 goals and 45 points in 67 games and scored a goal in an emotional return to Montreal.

Playing shorthanded didn't seem as much a disadvantage as usual during the season. On October 17, the Calgary Flames scored two shorthanded goals in four seconds, setting a record and tying the record for the fastest two

goals by one team in any situation. Doug Gilmour and Paul Ranheim had the goals as the Flames tied the Nordiques, 8-8, in Quebec. Less than a month later, the Oilers' Esa Tikkanen scored two shorthanded goals in 12 seconds, breaking the league record set by former Oiler Pat Hughes.

Calgary's Joe Nieuwendyk tied the NHL mark for most goals in one period (four) on January 11, 1989, scoring the four in the second period of an 8-3 win over Winnipeg. Nieuwendyk finished with his second straight 51-goal season, joining Gretzky and Mike Bossy as the only players to score 50 goals in each of their first two seasons.

Perhaps the most amazing individual feat came on New Year's Eve when Pittsburgh's Mario Lemieux, on his way to a second straight scoring title (85-114-199), tallied goals in every possible fashion in an 8-6 victory over New Jersey. Lemieux scored at even strength, on a power play, while the Penguins were shorthanded, on a penalty shot, and, finally, into an empty net.

An average of more than 19,700 fans per game at Joe Louis Arena watched Detroit win in the Norris Division behind center Steve Yzerman, who set club records in goals (65), assists (90) and points (155). Yzerman finished third in scoring behind Lemieux and Gretzky (54-114-168).

Gretzky combined with Bernie Nicholls (70 goals) to lead the Kings to a second-place finish in the Smythe, with Gretzky winning the Hart Trophy as MVP for the ninth time in 10 years. Calder Trophy winner Brian Leetch of the Rangers set the NHL mark for rookie defensemen with 23 goals and Montreal goaltender Patrick Roy, the Vezina Trophy winner, was unbeatable on Forum ice with a 25-0-3 mark. That helped the Canadiens finish second overall, their 115 points two behind the Flames.

Fittingly, the Oilers faced the Kings in the opening round of the playoffs. Edmonton, in a quest for a third straight Cup and fifth in six years, took a 3-1 lead in the series. But the Kings stormed back to win three straight games as Kelly Hrudey helping hold the Oilers to six goals.

Calgary had its own problems in its first-round matchup with Vancouver, which, despite finishing the season 43 points behind the Flames, took the series to overtime of a seventh game. Joel Otto rescued Calgary with a goal at 19:21 of the first overtime period. The Flames went on to sweep the Kings and then oust Chicago in five in the Campbell Conference finals to advance to their second Cup final in four seasons.

In the Wales Conference, Philadelphia's Ron Hextall, who a year earlier became the first goaltender to actually score a goal, became the first goalie to score in the playoffs as he hit an empty net in an 8-5 victory over Washington. The Capitals, who had just won their first Patrick Division title, were eliminated in six games.

The Flyers' next opponent was the Penguins, whose sweep of the Rangers in the opening round was their first postseason series victory since 1979. Lemieux tied Patrik Sundstrom's playoff record of eight points in a game with a five-goal, three-assist outburst in Game 5. This included four goals in the first period of a 10-7 victory, but the Flyers took the final two games to prevail. In the Wales final, Montreal bounced Philadelphia in six games to set up its second Cup matchup with Calgary in four seasons.

The Canadiens took a 2-1 edge by winning Game 3 on Ryan Walter's goal in the second overtime, but goaltender Mike Vernon and the Flames' defense held Montreal to just six goals in the next three games. Calgary won the finale, 4-2, the franchise's first championship and the first time in history that a visiting team had won the Cup in Montreal.

Calgary's Al MacInnis, whose 31 points led all playoff scorers, became the fourth defenseman to win the Conn Smythe Trophy, while Vernon tied Grant Fuhr's record with 16 playoff victories.

« *Defenseman Al MacInnis took playoff MVP honors as Calgary celebrated its first Stanley Cup championship in 1989.*

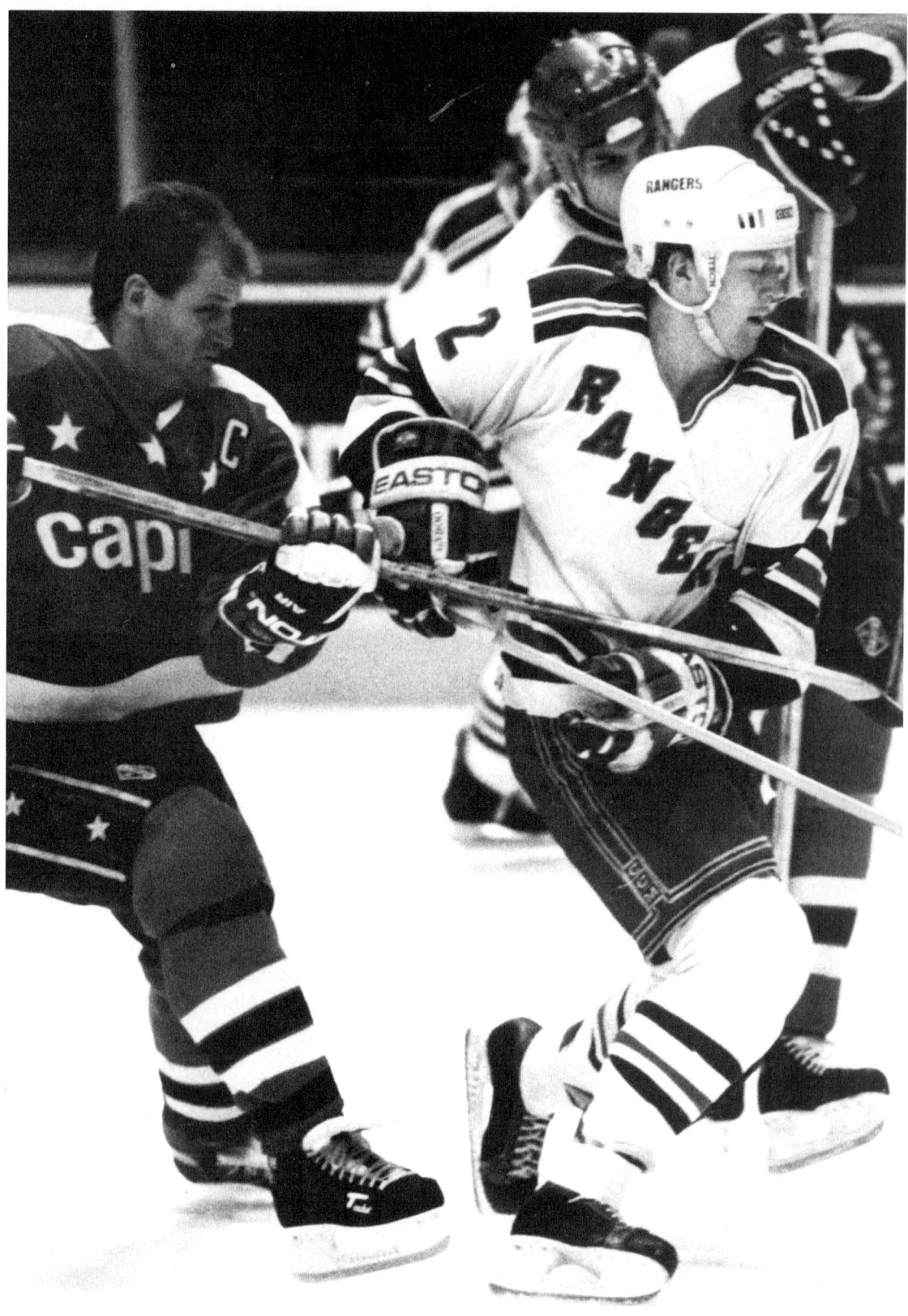

Other trophy winners included Montreal's Chris Chelios (Norris), Montreal's Guy Carbonneau (Selke) and Calgary's Joe Mullen (Lady Byng). Named as first-team All-Stars were Roy, defensemen Chelios and Edmonton's Paul Coffey and forwards Mullen, Lemieux and Luc Robitaille of Los Angeles.

1988–89

FINAL STANDINGS

Prince of Wales Conference

Adams Division

	W	L	T	PTS	GF	GA
Montreal	53	18	9	115	315	218
Boston	37	29	14	88	289	256
Buffalo	38	35	7	83	291	299
Hartford	37	38	5	79	299	290
Quebec	27	46	7	61	269	342

Patrick Division

	W	L	T	PTS	GF	GA
Washington	41	29	10	92	305	259
Pittsburgh	40	33	7	87	347	349
New York R.	37	35	8	82	310	307
Philadelphia	36	36	8	80	307	285
New Jersey	27	41	12	66	281	325
New York I.	28	47	5	61	265	325

Clarence Campbell Conference

Norris Division

	W	L	T	PTS	GF	GA
Detroit	34	34	12	80	313	316
St. Louis	33	35	12	78	275	285
Minnesota	27	37	16	70	258	278
Chicago	27	41	12	66	297	335
Toronto	28	46	6	62	259	342

Smythe Division

	W	L	T	PTS	GF	GA
Calgary	54	17	9	117	354	226
Los Angeles	42	31	7	91	376	335
Edmonton	38	34	8	84	325	306
Vancouver	33	39	8	74	251	253
Winnipeg	26	42	12	64	300	355

LEADING SCORERS

	G	A	PTS
Lemieux, Pittsburgh	85	114	199
Gretzky, Los Angeles	54	114	168
Yzerman, Detroit	65	90	155
Nicholls, Los Angeles	70	80	150
Brown, Pittsburgh	49	66	115
Coffey, Pittsburgh	30	83	113
J. Mullen, Calgary	51	59	110
Kurri, Edmonton	44	58	102
Carson, Edmonton	49	51	100
Robitaille, Los Angeles	46	52	98

1989–90

The man now called Hollywood home, so, naturally, it was with a flair for the dramatic that Los Angeles King Wayne Gretzky handled his pursuit of Hall-of-Famer Gordie Howe's NHL career scoring mark of 1,850 points.

« It was a record year for Ranger defenseman Brian Leetch, 1988–89 Rookie of the Year.

The big moment came on October 15, 1989, in a most-fitting venue, Edmonton, where the former Oiler came into the game trailing Howe's record by one point and quickly tied it by earning an assist on Bernie Nicholls' first-period goal. But, as the game progressed, it appeared the historic point would not come on this night. Just 53 seconds remained in regulation time when, with the Oilers holding a 5-4 lead, Gretzky swooped in and beat Edmonton goaltender Bill Ranford, setting the NHL's new career scoring record. Gretzky took it one step further by scoring the game-winner in overtime to end a remarkable evening.

Two more records were set in an Oilers-Kings game later in the season. On February 28 in Los Angeles, the clubs were whistled for an unprecedented 86 penalties. The Oilers had a record 45, which included 27 minors, seven majors, six misconducts, four game misconducts and one match penalty.

Gretzky went on to regain the scoring crown he had lost to Mario Lemieux for two years, compiling 40-102-142 totals in 73 games. As for Lemieux, he missed 31 games with a back problem but still managed 45 goals (a record 13 shorthanded) and 123 points. The Pittsburgh center finished fourth in scoring, behind Lemieux, the Oilers' Mark Messier and Detroit's Steve Yzerman.

In Toronto, former Devils' coach Doug Carpenter took over behind the bench, the Leafs' ninth head coach of the decade, matching the number of changes in Los Angeles, where Tom Webster assumed a similar position. Nothing could help Quebec, which managed just 31 points, the fewest since Washington had 21 in 1974–75, its first season. The Nordiques finished 51 points behind fourth-place Hartford in the Adams Division.

It was a different story in New York, where a well-traveled Roger Neilson guided the Rangers to first place in the Patrick, the first time since 1941–42 that the club had finished on top of any division. But that was as far as the team got. The Rangers were bounced in the second round by Washington, ending their

The pucks say it all for Wayne Gretzky and Gordie Howe.

quest for the Stanley Cup they last won a half-century ago.

A new star was emerging in St. Louis, where Brett Hull, the son of Hall of Famer Bobby Hull, set a right-wing record with a league-leading 72 goals, breaking Jari Kurri's mark by one.

Because no one team dominated the league during the regular season (Boston led with just 101 points), it promised to be one of the most wide-open battles for the Cup in years.

There were knowing nods in Edmonton when the Gretzky-less Oilers fell behind, 3-1, in their Smythe Division opening-round matchup with Winnipeg. But the Oilers won a pair of one-goal games and emerged with a 4-1 victory in Game 7 to advance against the Kings. They swept that series, with Joe Murphy scoring the series winner in overtime.

Meanwhile, the Oilers' Campbell Conference finals opponent, Chicago, needed 14

games to get by Minnesota and St. Louis. The Oilers eliminated the Blackhawks in six games.

In the battle for the Cup, the Oilers went up against the Bruins for the second time in three years. The Bruins had overcome a pesky Hartford club in seven games, needed five to knock off Montreal and then swept Washington in the Capitals' first-ever conference final appearance.

In the final, the Bruins were facing an old teammate in goaltender Bill Ranford, who had played for Boston until traded on March 8, 1988, for Andy Moog. He became the Oilers' No. 1 goaltender when shoulder surgery sidelined Grant Fuhr early in the season.

The Oilers featured 1989–90 regular-season »
MVP Mark Messier (left) and they prevailed
over the Bruins (Dave Poulin, 19) for the
Stanley Cup.

Ranford was magnificent in the playoffs, at one point going a span of 154:24 without surrendering a goal. And he was brilliant in Game 1 of the finals when he and Moog battled into a third overtime of a 2-2 thriller. Then, after 55:13 of overtime play, the Oilers' Petr Klima, acquired earlier in the season from Detroit, ended the game and, most likely, the Bruins' chances. Boston was outscored, 17-5, the rest of the way, managing only a 2-1 victory in Game 3. The Oilers earned their fifth Cup in seven years, tying them with the Bruins for the third-most titles in league history, but still far behind Montreal's 21.

Ranford was the clear choice for the Conn Smythe Trophy as playoff MVP. Gretzky regained the Ross Trophy and his old teammate, Messier, won the Hart as regular-season MVP. The Vezina went to Montreal's Patrick Roy, the Norris to Boston's Ray Bourque, the Selke to St. Louis' Rick Meagher, the Lady Byng to Hull and the Calder to the Flames' Sergei Makarov.

Roy, Bourque and Messier joined Hull, Calgary's Al MacInnis and the Kings' Luc Robitaille as first-team All-Stars.

1989-90

FINAL STANDINGS

Prince of Wales Conference

Adams Division

	W	L	T	PTS	GF	GA
Boston	46	25	9	101	289	232
Buffalo	45	27	8	98	286	248
Montreal	41	28	11	93	288	234
Hartford	38	33	9	85	275	268
Quebec	12	61	7	31	240	407

Patrick Division

	W	L	T	PTS	GF	GA
New York R.	36	31	13	85	279	267
New Jersey	37	34	9	83	295	288
Washington	36	38	6	78	284	275
New York I.	31	38	11	73	281	288
Pittsburgh	32	40	8	72	318	359
Philadelphia	30	39	11	71	290	297

Clarence Campbell Conference

Norris Division

	W	L	T	PTS	GF	GA
Chicago	41	33	6	88	316	294
St. Louis	37	34	9	83	295	279
Toronto	38	38	4	80	337	358
Minnesota	36	40	4	76	284	291
Detroit	28	38	14	70	288	323

Smythe Division

	W	L	T	PTS	GF	GA
Calgary	42	23	15	99	348	265
Edmonton	38	28	14	90	315	283
Winnipeg	37	32	11	85	298	290
Los Angeles	34	39	7	75	338	337
Vancouver	25	41	14	64	245	306

LEADING SCORERS

	G	A	PTS
Gretzky, Los Angeles	40	102	142
Messier, Edmonton	45	84	129
Yzerman, Detroit	62	65	127
Lemieux, Pittsburgh	45	78	123
Hull, St. Louis	72	41	113
Nicholls, L.A.-N.Y.R.	39	73	112
P. Turgeon, Buffalo	40	66	106
LaFontaine, New York I.	54	51	105
Coffey, Pittsburgh	29	74	103
Sakic, Quebec	39	63	102
Oates, St. Louis	23	79	102

1990-91

It was an ominous beginning for the Pittsburgh Penguins when Mario Lemieux, one of the NHL's marquee players, underwent surgery for a herniated disc in July. Without their superstar, the Penguins' outlook was at best viewed as bleak.

There would be other stars, of course, who would make the headlines and the one who stood out over all was Brett Hull of the St. Louis Blues, who exploded for 86 goals, the third-highest total in history behind Wayne Gretzky's 92 (1981-82) and 87 (1983-84). Hull's performance, plus that of defenseman Scott Stevens, the million-dollar free-agent signee who came from the Washington Capitals, helped lead the Blues to a 105-point season, the second-best mark in the league, one point behind Chicago.

The player who put the Blackhawks on top for the first time in 24 years was rookie goaltender Ed Belfour, who had a dream season. Belfour not only won the Calder Trophy as Rookie of the Year, he also captured the Vezina Trophy with a league-leading 43 victories (43-19-7), the top goals-against average (2.47) and the leading save percentage (.910). Belfour also came within one game of Grant Fuhr's record of appearing in 75 games as the Blackhawks finished 49-23-8.

Calgary was a rude host at the Saddledome, winning 17 and tying one in a span from December 29, 1990, to March 14, 1991. Chris Nilan was rude in his own right to the visiting Whalers on March 31 when he set an NHL record with 10 penalties. As one might imagine, Nilan was not around for the final buzzer after accumulating six minors, a pair of ma-

jors, a 10-minute misconduct and a game misconduct.

Minnesota was fighting, too—fighting for its life early in the season. The North Stars got off to a terrible start under new general manager Bobby Clarke and first-year coach Bob Gainey. The question seemed not whether the team could make the playoffs, but if it could avoid finishing with the league's worst record.

But the North Stars began to come together before midseason and finished comfortably ahead of Toronto with a 27-39-14 record. Still, their 68 points were far behind 14 other playoff qualifiers and 38 points less than Chicago, their first-round opponent.

But Cinderella came to the ball dressed in the green, white, gold and black colors of the North Stars, and the most unlikely postseason adventure since the 1975 Islanders' odyssey was about to unfold.

Minnesota began in Chicago with Brian Propp's overtime goal for a 4-3 victory before dropping the next two games. But the Black-hawks didn't come close the rest of the series, scoring just two goals over the next three games. Suddenly, the NHL regular-season champions were gone.

Next up was equally fearsome St. Louis with Hull, Stevens and 20 more victories than the Stars. The Blues had beaten Detroit in the opening round, including a two-team playoff-record 298 penalty minutes in Game 5, a 6-1 St. Louis victory. Perhaps worn out by the rough stuff, the Blues were stunned by Minnesota in six games. Now all the Stars had to do to reach the finals was knock off defending and five-time champion Edmonton.

The Oilers had struggled through the first two rounds. It took an overtime goal by Esa Tikkanen to give the Oilers a 5-4 victory in Game 7 of their Smythe Division semifinal against the Flames. They followed that with a memorable series against the Kings, who had gotten by Vancouver in six games.

Luc Robitaille's overtime goal gave the Kings a 4-3 decision over the Oilers in the opener, but Edmonton came back on Petr

Soviet import Sergei Makarov of Calgary was Rookie of the Year in 1990–91.

High-scoring Brett Hull of the St. Louis Blues won the Hart
Trophy in his fourth season.

Klima's overtime goal for a 4-3 victory in the
second game. Game 3 went into a second
overtime before Tikkanen gave the Oilers a
4-3 win. Edmonton won the fourth game, 4-2,
in regulation and the Kings avoided elimination in Game 5, winning, 5-2. But the Oilers
wrapped it up—appropriately once more in
overtime—when Craig MacTavish scored for a
4-3 verdict.

But there would be no sixth Stanley Cup for
Edmonton. The North Stars eliminated the
Oilers in six games to make it back to the
finals 10 years after their only appearance,
when they had lost in five games to the
Islanders.

Minnesota's opponent? Pittsburgh, the team
that had been counted out when Lemieux had
his surgery. Indeed, the Penguins, making

their first-ever trip to the finals, had weathered
the absence of Lemieux, who did not return
until late in the season and played in only 26
games. Mark Recchi (113 points) had picked
up the scoring slack during the regular season
and helped the Penguins win the division title.

Lemieux's comeback, combined with the
play of Recchi, Kevin Stevens and Tom Barrasso, sparked the Penguins in the playoffs.
Losing at least the first game of every series
they played, Pittsburgh made it to the final the
hard way. New Jersey was the first victim in a
seven-game series. The Penguins took four
straight from Washington after their Game 1
loss and they came back from two defeats to
oust Boston in six behind the superb goaltending of Barrasso, who had been injured.

Mario Lemieux's comeback enabled Pittsburgh ❱❱
to win its first Stanley Cup in 1991.

Chicago's Ed Belfour was Rookie of the Year and winner of the Vezina Trophy in 1990–91.

Of course, the Penguins lost the first game, 5-4, to Minnesota in the finals. They won the next, 4-1, but dropped Game 3, 3-1. Then they won three in a row, 5-3, 6-4 and 8-0—demolishing the North Stars in the finale with the largest final-round margin of victory in this century.

The Conn Smythe Trophy went to Lemieux, who had a 16-goal, 44-point playoff, the second-highest total in league annals. Hull received the Hart Trophy, the first player other than Gretzky and Lemieux to be voted MVP since 1979, when Bryan Trottier won.

Ray Bourque won the Norris for the fourth time and Gretzky the Ross for the ninth time with a 41-122-163 mark, 32 points better than Hull. Gretzky also was the recipient of the Lady Byng for a second time after being runnerup five times. Chicago's Dirk Graham won the Selke.

The All-Star team was made up of Belfour, Bourque, Gretzky, Hull, Robitaille and Calgary's Al MacInnis.

1990–91

FINAL STANDINGS

Prince of Wales Conference

Adams Division

	W	L	T	PTS	GF	GA
Boston	44	24	12	100	299	264
Montreal	39	30	11	89	273	249
Buffalo	31	30	19	81	292	278
Hartford	31	38	11	73	238	276
Quebec	16	50	14	46	236	354

Patrick Division

	W	L	T	PTS	GF	GA
Pittsburgh	41	33	6	88	342	305
New York R.	36	31	13	85	297	265
Washington	37	36	7	81	258	258
New Jersey	32	33	15	79	272	264
Philadelphia	33	37	10	76	252	267
New York I.	25	45	10	60	223	290

The St. Louis Blues' Brett Hull was again the goal-scoring champion and an obvious All-Star selection in 1991–92.

Clarence Campbell Conference

Norris Division

Chicago	49	23	8	106	284	211
St. Louis	47	22	11	105	310	250
Detroit	34	38	8	76	273	298
Minnesota	27	39	14	68	256	266
Toronto	23	46	11	57	241	318

Smythe Division

Los Angeles	46	24	10	102	340	254
Calgary	46	26	8	100	344	263
Edmonton	37	37	6	80	272	272
Vancouver	28	43	9	65	243	315
Winnipeg	26	43	11	63	260	288

LEADING SCORERS

	G	A	PTS
Gretzky, Los Angeles	41	122	163
Hull, St. Louis	86	45	131
Oates, St. Louis	25	90	115
Recchi, Pittsburgh	40	73	113
Cullen, Pitt.-Hart.	39	71	110
Sakic, Quebec	48	61	109
Yzerman, Detroit	51	57	108
Fleury, Calgary	51	53	104
MacInnis, Calgary	28	75	103
Larmer, Chicago	44	57	101

1991–92

It was the most tumultuous season in the 75-year history of the NHL, marked by the tragic death of a coach, a future superstar's refusal to sign, an expansion team, a strike, a back-to-back Stanley Cup triumph and the ouster of the league president.

In early August, it was learned that Pittsburgh Penguins' coach Bob Johnson, who had led the team to its first Stanley Cup championship just three months earlier, was suffering from incurable brain cancer. Johnson, one of hockey's greatest good-will ambassadors, passed away on November 26.

Scotty Bowman, who had guided Montreal to five Cup titles in the 1970s, took over as the Penguins' head coach.

There would be no sign of Eric Lindros, the 19-year-old center with the potential impact of Wayne Gretzky and Mario Lemieux. The No. 1 draft pick in 1991, Lindros rejected a contract with the Quebec Nordiques and decided to sit out the NHL season. He got his

Down but not permanently out, Pittsburgh's Mario Lemieux suffered a broken hand in the Patrick Division final series against the Rangers, but came back to lead the Penguins to their second straight Stanley Cup championship.

ice time playing junior hockey and on the Canadian team that captured a silver medal in the 1992 Olympic Games.

The league had a new look for the first time since four teams from the WHA were absorbed in 1979 as the San Jose Sharks began operations at San Francisco's Cow Palace. Midway through the season, the expansion Tampa Bay Lightning and Ottawa Senators met their final payment obligations and were granted permanent membership in the NHL, with the teams to begin play in the 1992-93 season.

The Sharks' merchandising program proved more successful than the club's on-ice exploits, as fans across the continent sported clothing and artifacts bearing the logo of a team that finished with a 17-58-5 record, just 3-35-2 on the road.

Losses for the Sharks obviously meant victories for the rest of the league. By season's end, 18 of the 22 teams finished with at least 70 points, another indication of relative parity.

At the top of the list were the New York Rangers, who acquired Mark Messier for Bernie Nichols and two minor leaguers on October 4 as the dismantling of the Edmonton Oiler Stanley-Cup dynasty continued. Messier, who contributed 107 points and invaluable leadership on the way to winning the MVP award, spurred the Rangers to a 50-25-5 mark for 105 points and the President's Trophy as the league's regular-season champion, the first time in 50 years the club had attained that status.

There also was a resurrection in Vancouver as the Canucks established a franchise record

Jaromir Jagr, a key to the Cup in 1991–92, shares a happy moment with teammate Mario Lemieux (right) as they cap the sweep of the Blackhawks in the finale.

with a 46-26-12 mark and first place in the Smythe Division. Detroit captured the Norris-Division crown while Montreal, employing an air-tight defense, built an insurmountable lead in the first half of the season and coasted to a first-place finish in the Adams Divison.

Eight coaching changes would come before the end of June 1992 as vacancies occurred in Buffalo, Montreal, Toronto, New Jersey, Los Angeles, Boston, St. Louis and Hartford.

Players moved, too. Calgary's Doug Gilmour was the principal name in a 10-player deal between the Flames and Maple Leafs in early January. The Penguins, struggling through much of the regular season, were part of a three-team deal on the eve of the March trading deadline with defenseman Paul Coffey going to Los Angeles and high-scoring Mark Recchi to Philadelphia. In return, the Pen-

guins obtained forward Rick Tocchet and defenseman Kjell Samuelsson.

It appeared all the maneuvering was in vain when, on April 1, after long and fruitless months of negotiation, the NHL Players Association went on strike. The major issues included licensing and endorsements, free agency, salary arbitration and pension contributions.

The walkout, which threatened to bring a cancellation of the playoffs, was settled after 10 days with NHL president John Ziegler and NHLPA executive director Bob Goodenow, guided by moderates in both camps, forging a new collective bargaining agreement. Among the results were an increase to an 84-game season to generate additional revenue beginning in 1992-93, a less restrictive free-agency system and an almost three-fold increase in the playoff bonus pool to $9 million in 1993.

The regular season resumed with teams completing the final week. That enabled the Islanders' Al Arbour to pass Dick Irvin as the leader in NHL games coached at 1,438, the record coming on April 15 in the Islanders' final game, a 7-0 victory over the Devils.

Despite missing 16 games because of injuries, the Penguins' Lemieux captured the scoring crown for a third time, finishing with 44-87-131, eight points more than teammate Kevin Stevens (54-69-123). The Kings' Gretzky, the defending scoring champion, ranked third with 31-90-121 while St. Louis' Brett Hull again ran away with the goal-scoring race with 70, 16 more than runnerup Stevens. Ranger defenseman Brian Leetch led all backliners with 22-80-102 while teammate Tony Amonte paced rookies with 35 goals and 69 points.

Montreal's Patrick Roy boasted the league's best goals-against average at 2.36 while Vancouver's Kirk McLean (38-17-9) and Detroit's Tim Cheveldae (38-23-9) paced the league in goaltending victories.

The playoffs began with six of the eight first-round series going the full seven games, including all four in the Wales Conference. Pittsburgh came back from a 3-1 deficit to beat Washington. Vancouver did the same against

Ending a guessing game, celebrated draftee Eric Lindros proudly sports his Philadelphia Flyers' cap.

Winnipeg and Detroit survived the same deficit against Minnesota.

Game 6 of the Red Wings-North Stars series was one of the most memorable with the teams staging the first playoff scoreless tie after regulation play since the Islanders beat Chicago, 1-0, on a Mike Bossy goal in April 1979. But Sergei Federov's game-winning goal 18 minutes into the first overtime also proved historic because it was confirmed only after a video review by league official Wally Harris, the first time the video-replay procedure directly determined the outcome of a game.

The Penguins lost Lemieux when his left hand was broken by an Adam Graves slash five minutes into Game 2 of their Patrick Division final series with the Rangers. Joe Mullen also was lost with a leg injury, but Pittsburgh still managed to advance in six games while the Bruins were ousting the Canadiens in four

games, their first sweep of the Habs in 64 years.

Chicago was rolling, establishing a one-year playoff record with 11 consecutive victories by winning the last three games against the Blues in six games and sweeping the Wings and Oilers. Pittsburgh, sparked by the stick-handling and scoring prowess of Czechoslovakian second-year star Jaromir Jagr, beat the Bruins in four straight to earn the other berth in the finals.

That's where Chicago's streak ended. The Penguins, with Lemieux returning and goaltender Tom Barrasso making the key saves, swept the Blackhawks to equal Chicago's record 11-game playoff winning streak. Lemieux finished with 16 goals and 34 points in 15 postseason games to earn his second straight MVP award as Pittsburgh won its second straight Cup championship.

Trophy winners included Roy (Vezina and Jennings), Messier (Hart, as regular-season MVP, and Pearson), Lemieux (Ross and Smythe), Montreal's Guy Carbonneau (Selke), the New York Rangers' Brian Leetch (Norris), Vancouver rookie Pavel Bure (Calder), Gretzky (Lady Byng), Boston's Ray Bourque (Clancy), the New York Islanders' Mark Fitzpatrick (Masterton) and Vancouver's Pat Quinn (Adams). Roy, Leetch, Bourque, Messier, Hull and Kevin Stevens made the All-Star team.

In a major development in June, president Ziegler, under growing criticism from a vocal group of owners, announced his resignation, ending his 15-year tenure.

On the player front, the charismatic Lindros, a 6-foot-5, 225-pound center, landed with Philadelphia, following a tug-of-war between the Flyers and the Rangers, both teams having claimed a deal with Quebec. An arbitrator upheld the trade that provided the Nordiques with five players, a first-round draft pick and $15 million. Lindros wound up signing a six-year contract estimated at $15-20 million.

1991–92

FINAL STANDINGS

Clarence Campbell Confernce

Norris Division

	W	L	T	PTS	GF	GA
Detroit	43	25	12	98	320	256
Chicago	36	29	15	87	257	236
St. Louis	36	33	11	83	279	266
Minnesota	32	42	6	70	246	278
Toronto	30	43	7	67	234	294

Smythe Division

Vancouver	42	26	12	96	285	250
Los Angeles	35	31	14	84	287	296
Edmonton	36	34	10	82	295	297
Winnipeg	33	32	15	81	251	244
Calgary	31	37	12	74	296	305
San Jose	17	58	5	39	219	359

Prince of Wales Conference

Adams Division

Montreal	41	28	11	93	267	207
Boston	36	32	12	84	270	275
Buffalo	31	37	12	74	289	299
Hartford	26	41	13	65	247	283
Quebec	20	48	12	52	255	318

Patrick Division

New York R.	50	25	5	105	321	246
Washington	45	27	8	98	330	275
Pittsburgh	39	32	9	87	343	308
New Jersey	38	31	11	87	289	259
New York I.	34	35	11	79	291	299
Philadelphia	32	37	11	75	252	273

LEADING SCORERS

	G	A	PTS
Lemieux, Pittsburgh	44	87	131
Stevens, Pittsburgh	54	69	123
Gretzky, Los Angeles	31	90	121
Hull, St. Louis	70	39	109
Robitaille, Los Angeles	44	63	107
Messier, New York R.	35	72	107
Roenick, Chicago	53	50	103
Yzerman, Detroit	45	58	103
Leetch, New York R.	22	80	102
Oates, St. Louis and Boston	20	79	99

THE GREATEST PLAYERS

Selection of hockey's all-time greatest players is a pursuit that inevitably inspires lively debate among followers of the game. Older fans cling to their memories and their heroes of yore; younger rooters, who never got to see the stars of the past, understandably make a case for the moderns.

In an attempt at historic balance in determining the best forwards, best defensemen and best goalies, opinions were sought from former and current players, coaches, writers and broadcasters. They span the NHL almost from its beginnings.

In the end, it was the editor who made the final selections of the players whose profiles appear in this chapter.

THE FORWARDS
They Make the Headlines

JEAN BELIVEAU

The Montreal Canadiens purchased an entire hockey league in order to make Jean Beliveau a member of their team. It happened

《 *Jean Beliveau*

in 1953 while Beliveau was completing his third season for the Quebec Aces of the Quebec Senior League. The league was classified as "amateur," although its players received modest salaries. Modest, that is, except for Jean Beliveau. His annual salary was $20,000.

Beliveau, like many amateur tennis players in those days, claimed he couldn't afford to turn professional. It got to be extremely embarrassing for the Canadiens, who owned the negotiating rights to the young star. The fans were clamoring for big Jean in Montreal, but he wouldn't budge from Quebec City.

Then, in the most unusual measure ever taken to obtain a player, the Canadiens purchased the entire Quebec Senior League and the pro rights to all its players. The new owners turned the league professional, leaving Beliveau with no choice but to join Montreal. He received a $20,000 bonus for signing and a five-year, $105,000 contract, a fantastic salary for a 23-year-old rookie.

Jean Beliveau, though, was worth every Canadian penny the Montreal club paid him. He was the highest-scoring center in NHL history with 1,219 points when he retired. He finished with 507 goals in 1971 after 18 NHL

seasons. That year, Beliveau had led the Canadiens to their 10th Stanley Cup since he joined the team.

To watch Beliveau in action was to marvel at the deceptive grace of this big bear on skates. A Gulliver in the icy world of comparative Lilliputians, he was 6-foot-3 and weighed 210 pounds. He didn't appear to skate quickly, but few could keep up with him. He had all the right instincts and all the right shots.

Rival players were awed by Beliveau's size and strength when he broke into the NHL. Bill Ezinicki, a vicious bodychecker in his glory days with Toronto and Boston, remembers the first time he lined up Beliveau for one of his patented hip checks. "It was like running into the side of a big oak tree," Ezinicki recalled. "I bounced right off the guy and landed on the seat of my pants."

In those days, Beliveau had only one flaw in his makeup. His disposition was better suited to the priesthood than the savage atmosphere of the hockey rink. He was crosschecked, hooked, and belted in every NHL rink. He didn't hit back because, he said, "I want to play hockey." He maintained that attitude until his third season with the Canadiens when he decided to retaliate. He wound up among the league's penalty leaders, a fact he wasn't proud of, but he also won the league's scoring title.

No longer did rival ruffians pick on Jean Beliveau. He had arrived—as a player and as a man—in the NHL. Other honors followed. In his 18 years with the Canadiens he was named to the All-Star team 10 times and twice won the Hart Trophy as the league's Most Valuable Player.

Toe Blake, Beliveau's coach for 13 years, summed up big Jean's value to the Canadiens this way: "In all the time he's been in hockey I've never heard anybody say a bad word against him. As a hockey player and a gentleman, Jean Beliveau is pretty hard to beat."

MIKE BOSSY

The scenario rarely changed. Mike Bossy would carry the puck into the right faceoff

« *Mike Bossy*

circle or into the slot or into No-Man's Land in front of the net. Then he would shoot, quicker than a wink. Poof! The puck was in the net.

That was how Bossy scored many of the 573 goals he accumulated during his 10-year career with the New York Islanders.

Bossy was only 31 when he was forced to retire because of a chronic back problem. It is ironic that a man who endured battles with the likes of Tiger Williams was put out of commission by the same kind of injury that could be suffered by a couch potato reaching for a TV remote control.

The beginning of the end came at training camp in 1986. Bossy had finished a skating drill and bent over to catch his breath. When he stood up, there was a stabbing pain in his lower back. Rest, heat, ice and every imaginable treatment nursed Bossy through a season he never should have played in 1986–87. With the pain and physical limitations, the thin-faced right winger registered the only sub-50-goal season of his career.

Why did Bossy push himself over the pain threshold time and again? "The pride, the feeling that I didn't want to wimp out," he said. "I went through my junior and professional career being thought of as a wimp because I wouldn't fight. I had to prove that I wasn't a wimp."

Bossy sat out the entire 1987–88 season, hoping that he would be able to resume his career. But he finally announced his retirement—through misty eyes—on October 21, 1988. "My back won the battle," he said.

The legacy Bossy left behind is awesome. He scored 50 goals or more in nine consecutive seasons—over 60 in five of those. The 53 goals he scored in his first season, 1977–78, was a rookie record. He was selected to the All-Star team eight times, earned one Conn Smythe Trophy as playoff MVP (1982), won the Lady Byng for sportsmanship three times and helped the Islanders win four consecutive Stanley Cup championships.

It seems inconceivable that 14 NHL teams passed up the chance to pick Bossy in the first round of the 1977 amateur draft, allowing

general manager Bill Torrey to make the Montreal-born youngster an Islander.

At the time, he was considered a one-dimensional sharpshooter. He later developed into an exquisite passer and playmaker. And nobody, not even Wayne Gretzky, could match Bossy's quick release when he took aim at rival goalies. Most players wait until the puck has settled on their stick before they shoot. Not Bossy.

"I felt the quicker I got the shot away, the better chance I had to score," he said. "I tried to pick a spot, high or low, but other than that I didn't think about it. I just shot."

Bossy had been shooting that way since he tied on his first pair of skates as a five-year-old. He was a pure shooter who once scored 21 goals in a single game while playing youth hockey in the Montreal suburb of Laval.

He was a homesick 20-year-old when he joined the Islanders in 1977. He had married his teen-age sweetheart, Lucie, that summer and had to leave home without her. She eventually joined him and Bossy went on to his rookie-record season.

When hockey violence became an issue, Bossy always took a stand. "I didn't fight because I thought fighting was senseless," he said. "I was tougher than a lot of tough guys in the league. I didn't drop my gloves and I probably took as much abuse as anybody. But this was my way of saying that I was as tough as they were."

Bossy did get into one high-sticking duel with Dean Hopkins of the Los Angeles Kings in 1981. "I was teed off because Hopkins cross-checked me from behind," Bossy explained.

The notorious Tiger Williams shadowed Bossy during the final round of the 1982 Stanley Cup playoffs against the Vancouver Canucks, and attempted to provoke Bossy. It didn't work.

Following his retirement, Bossy returned to his home in a Montreal suburb and became involved in public relations. He was elected to the Hockey Hall of Fame in 1991.

PHIL ESPOSITO

On the night of January 9, 1981, Phil Esposito faced one of the toughest assignments of his life—his farewell address as a player. He was about to play his final game for the New York Rangers against the Buffalo Sabres at Madison Square Garden. A center-ice ceremony before the game was meant to be brief, but the crowd of 17,501 gave Esposito a lengthy standing ovation and chanted "ESPO! ESPO!!"

As the applause rumbled down from the mezzanine, Esposito nodded and smiled, then raised his hands. "Please," he said. "I've been preparing for this for 10 years." The crowd roared and Esposito continued. "My world seemed to shatter when I was traded here from Boston. But after the initial shock, which took a long time, I fell in love with New York."

That was it. After 1,282 games covering 18 National Hockey League seasons, Phil Esposito was retiring as the second-highest scorer in history. He failed to score a goal that night, but he did pick up an assist. It raised his career total to 1,590 points on 717 goals and 873 assists. Only Gordie Howe had more goals (801) and more points (1,850).

Howe was at the Garden that night as the keynote speaker and presented Esposito with a number "77" sweater.

Esposito was a month shy of his 39th birthday at the time of his retirement. "I couldn't handle the pressure any more," he told friends. "It really affected me . . . For my whole life as a hockey player, I told myself if I wasn't satisfied, I should do something else. This year I wasn't satisfied . . . I gave it all I had, but I had nothing left to give."

Born in Sault Ste. Marie, Ontario, Esposito grew up shooting pucks at his kid brother, Tony. "He was younger," explained Phil, "so he had to be the goalie." They would play the same roles years later in the NHL.

The Black Hawks sponsored the minor hockey program in Sault Ste. Marie, and in those days that was enough for an NHL club to gain the rights to local hockey talent. That's how Phil filtered into the Chicago Black Hawks' system. He spent two years in the

minors before being called up to Chicago midway through the 1963–64 season.

Three goals in 27 NHL games gave no clue to the kind of scoring that Esposito would one day produce. A bit clumsy on his skates, Phil's major asset was his strength, and the Hawks used him to center superstar Bobby Hull. In the next three seasons, he scored 71 goals, many of them on rebounds of Hull bombs.

In 1967, the Hawks went shopping for a tough defenseman and asked Boston about Gilles Marotte. The talks expanded and finally on May 15, the deal was completed. Marotte, center Pit Martin and minor-league goalie Jack Norris went to Chicago, with Esposito and two other forwards, Ken Hodge and Fred Stanfield, moving to the Bruins.

In $8\frac{1}{2}$ seasons with Boston, Espo won five scoring championships and finished second twice. He was the first man to go over 100 points in a single season and he passed the 50-goal plateau five times. He enjoyed his greatest season in 1970–71 when he established records for most goals (76) and most points (152). Both records later were erased by Wayne Gretzky.

It is no coincidence that the Bruins ended a 29-year wait and won two Stanley Cups following the arrival of Esposito. The first Cup came in 1970 and, en route to it, Boston eliminated Chicago in four games. The scoring star for Boston was Esposito and it was accomplished at the expense of his goaltending brother, Tony, who had wound up with the Hawks after graduating from Michigan Tech.

Fans in Boston and New York were shocked when the Bruins traded Esposito to the Rangers in a five-player deal early in the 1975–76 season. The 6-foot-1, 212-pound center was shocked, too. He displayed only flashes of his old form with the Rangers—notably in the 1979 Stanley Cup playoffs when he sparked New York into the finals against the Montreal Canadiens. The Canadiens won the series in five games.

Following his retirement, Esposito became an analyst on telecasts of Ranger games. He served as general manager of the Rangers for three years (1986–89) and during that time

Phil Esposito

Wayne Gretzky

had two brief flings as interim coach. He spearheaded a group that was granted an NHL franchise in Tampa, Fla., in 1990 and was named president of the expansion team.

WAYNE GRETZKY

He looks too thin, too fragile to be playing professional hockey. Five feet, 11 inches and 170 pounds. A comic claimed he could wear a long fur coat on Halloween and go out disguised as a pipe cleaner. When he joins teammates for those stress and strength tests, he invariably finishes near the bottom.

But don't let Wayne Gretzky's looks deceive you. When it comes to scoring goals and setting up goals, he is at the top of the class.

Jean Beliveau and Phil Esposito were bigger. Maurice (Rocket) Richard, Gordie Howe and Bobby Hull were stronger. However, none of these former superstars ever enjoyed the type of season Gretzky had while playing for the Edmonton Oilers in 1981–82. Gretzky scored 50 goals in his first 39 games that season, smashing a record first set by Richard and later matched by Mike Bossy of the New York Islanders.

Gretzky went on from there to wipe out Esposito's single-season, goal-scoring record. Esposito scored 76 in 78 games in 1970–71. Gretzky eclipsed that mark in his 64th game and finished the season with an astounding 92 goals, 120 assists and 212 points.

Then, to prove that season wasn't a fluke, Gretzky broke two of his own records in 1985–86 when he collected 163 assists and 215 points.

"Wayne is a natural goal-scorer, just like I was," Rocket Richard said. "He's moving all the time and it seems the players trying to check him can't catch him."

"Ever try to catch a feather?" said Dennis Sobchuk, a former Gretzky teammate. "That's what Wayne is like."

Bruce MacGregor, the Oilers' assistant general manager, likened Gretzky to Howe, MacGregor's teammate on the Detroit Red Wings in the sixties. "I see a lot of similarities between Wayne and Gordie," MacGregor said. "When you walked through a hotel lobby with Gordie, people buzzed. It's the same with Wayne."

People have been buzzing about Gretzky since his early days in his hometown of Brantford, Ontario. When he was 10, he scored 378 goals in 85 games!

Gretzky was only 17 when he signed his first pro contract with the Indianapolis Racers of the old World Hockey Association in 1978. When the Racers ran out of money after only eight games, he was sold to the Oilers.

Gretzky totaled 46 goals and 110 points in his first pro season. The WHA folded in 1979 and the Oilers were granted an NHL franchise. Gretzky recalls his NHL baptism with a wry smile. "Everywhere I went they thought I would get killed because of my size," he said. "I heard a lot of talk then that I'd never get 110 points like I did in the WHA." He did better than that, totaling 137 points on 51 goals and 86 assists.

There was no stopping Gretzky. During the next nine seasons, (1980–88), he led the league in scoring seven times, won the Hart (MVP) Trophy seven times and captained the Oilers to four Stanley Cup championships.

Then came that day of infamy for Oiler fans: August 9, 1988, when Gretzky was traded to the Los Angeles Kings for $15 million, three players and three first-round draft picks. In return, the Kings received Gretzky and three other players.

It was the most spectacular trade in the history of the NHL—maybe of all sports. Gretzky was misty-eyed at a press conference held to announce the trade. "I hate to leave," he said. "Sometimes in life you do things that you don't want to do."

Gretzky's record-breaking didn't stop when he changed uniforms. The slender center became the NHL's all-time leading scorer on October 15, 1989, when he wiped out Howe's total of 1,850 points. Ironically, Gretzky broke the record in Edmonton's Northlands Coliseum—his home for 10 seasons.

The record-breaking point was produced when Gretzky scored a goal with 53 seconds left in regulation time to tie the score. He then scored in overtime to give the Kings a 4–3 victory over the Oilers.

Gretzky was earning an estimated $3 million at this stage of his career; it included close to $1 million in endorsements. Friends and foes agreed he was earning every cent.

Early in the 1990–91 season, Gretzky scored his 2,000th career point. He was then closing in on his 30th birthday. Asked if he thought he might eventually reach 3,000 points, Gretzky said: "That might be tough. Barring injury and staying healthy, I can probably average 150 points a year, which means seven more years. I don't know if I'll play seven more years."

Gretzky was giving no signs of slowing down when he led the league in scoring for the ninth time in 1990–91 and increased his career goal total to 718.

He added 31 goals in 1991–92 and was third in scoring with 121 points (Mario Lemieux led with 131, followed by his Penguin teammate, Kevin Stevens, 123).

With 749 goals, he has only one more significant individual record to chase: Howe's 801 career goals. Gretzky admits to some reluctance over knocking his boyhood idol off the top of another list. "I wish I could stop at 800," he says.

GORDIE HOWE

Gordie Howe, looking a little uncomfortable in a tuxedo, was grinning as he approached the speaker's rostrum in the Canadian Room of the Royal York Hotel in Toronto. The occasion was the 1982 Hockey Hall of Fame dinner, and Howe was there to receive

THE COMPLETE ENCYCLOPEDIA OF HOCKEY

the initial presentation of the Milestone Award, instituted by the National Hockey League to honor players and coaches who have achieved milestones during their careers.

Howe glanced about the room, packed with almost 900 diners, and was still grinning as he began his acceptance speech. He recalled how he had dreamed during his youth of playing in the NHL. "I would have been happy to play just one season," he said. Now the audience was laughing—not at Howe but with him.

Gordie Howe was the most durable player in the history of pro hockey. He played not one season but 32—26 in the NHL and six in the World Hockey Association.

The dictionary defines durability as "the ability to withstand decay or wear." It is the word that best describes Howe and his fabulous career. The six-foot, 205-pound right wing from the wheat fields of Saskatchewan started his career with the Detroit Red Wings at the age of 18 in 1946. He finished it with the Hartford Whalers at the age of 52 in 1980.

Howe's statistics for his pro career are astounding. Including playoff games, he totaled 2,421 games, 1,071 goals, 1,518 assists, 2,589 points and 2,418 penalty minutes.

He was hailed throughout the hockey world as a seemingly indestructible man of steel. Howe's career—and his life—were almost snuffed out in his third season with the Red Wings. He collided with Toronto's Ted Kennedy during a 1950 Stanley Cup playoff game, crashed head-on into the sideboards and suffered a severe brain injury. He hovered between life and death while surgeons operated to relieve pressure on his brain.

The injury left him with a slight facial tic; there are times when his dark eyes blink uncontrollably. His teammates called him "Blinky," and it was a mark of Howe's class that he never resented the nickname. He frequently startled newsmen with remarks like "Old Blinky was flying tonight" or "Did you see old Blinky miss that goal in the second period?"

《 *Gordie Howe*

Even in the twilight of his career, Howe remained an amazing athlete—the complete hockey player. He was big and tough and sometimes a little rough. He could still shoot with the best NHL marksmen; he could set up plays; he acted as the triggerman on power plays; he killed penalties.

Jean Beliveau of the Montreal Canadiens claimed "Gordie Howe is the best hockey player I have ever seen." It is an interesting assessment from a man who once was a teammate of Maurice (Rocket) Richard. But even Richard admits, "Howe was a better all-around player than I was."

Blessed with a powerful body, Howe would have made an ideal heavyweight boxer. He had the sloping shoulders of a fighter, his neck thick and his muscular arms dangling loosely like the limbs of an oak tree. He had his share of fights on the ice, the most memorable taking place in 1959 when he tangled with Lou Fontinato of the New York Rangers. Fontinato's nose was broken, and his whole face needed considerable repairs.

Howe, though, was no troublemaker. He just kept rolling along, content to score goals and accumulate records and honors. He was named to the NHL's All-Star team 21 times. He won the league's scoring title six times and was a six-time winner of the Hart Trophy as the league's MVP.

He ended his 25-year career with the Red Wings in 1971, sat out two years, then made an historic return in 1973 in order to play with sons Marty and Mark in the WHA.

Gordie Howe was with the Hartford Whalers when they joined three other WHA teams in the NHL in 1979. He played in all 80 games in the Whalers' first season in the NHL, then retired for the second time.

BOBBY HULL

It started from the instant he cradled the puck on the curved blade of his stick. One . . . two strides . . . and he was in full flight, skating and slamming his way across the neutral zone and into enemy territory. By this time a chorus of sound enveloped

Bobby Hull

the rink, rising into a long, drawn-out OO-OOHH! as this whirlwind on skates fired one of his patented slap shots.

The puck, traveling at more than 100 miles per hour, invariably wound up high in the net and Bobby Hull had scored another goal.

This scene was enacted and reenacted on an average of 40 times a season from the time of Hull's arrival in the NHL in 1957. In the 23 years that followed, nobody scored nearly as many goals or caused nearly as much excitement as this ruggedly handsome, blond-haired muscleman from the little Ontario town of Point Anne.

Hull was only 18 years old when he quit the junior ranks to turn pro with the Chicago Black Hawks. His great magnetism and goal-scoring ability turned a franchise which was losing money into the richest in the NHL. And as the Hawks grew in wealth, so did Bobby Hull. He became the league's first $100,000-

a-year player when he signed a four-year, $400,000 contract at the start of the 1968–69 season. Other income from endorsements, several purebred cattle farms he owned and league awards and playoff money swelled his earnings that season to approximately $200,000.

In 1972, he accepted a $1,000,000 offer from the World Hockey Association to play for the Winnipeg Jets. Despite missing 15 games because of court suits initiated by the NHL aimed at blocking his move to the new league, Hull reached the 50-goal plateau for the sixth time in his career.

Hull enjoyed his greatest season in 1974–75 when he scored a record 77 goals in 78 games and totaled 142 points for Winnipeg. He was playing then on a line with two Swedish imports, center Ulf Nilsson and right wing Anders Hedberg. "They make the game

fun for me," Hull said. "They're also my legs."

Hull's strong legs started to weaken in 1979, the year the Jets were admitted into the NHL. He also was experiencing shoulder problems. He ended his eight-year stay in Winnipeg late in the 1979–80 season when the Jets traded him to the Hartford Whalers. Gordie Howe also was winding up his career with the Whalers, and the two greats played on the same line in a handful of games.

Hull was the highest-scoring left wing in hockey history with 1,018 goals and 2,017 points when he retired in 1980. He was 41. He joined the New York Rangers at their training camp in 1981, attempting a comeback. But he was released before the start of the regular season and he returned to his farm in Ontario.

What made Bobby Hull so great? He combined some of the talents of his most famed predecessors—the speed of Howie Morenz, the goal-scoring instincts of Maurice Richard, the strength and control of Gordie Howe— into a blend of the perfect hockey player.

He was the fastest skater in hockey (28.3 miles per hour with the puck, 29.7 m.p.h. without it). He had the fastest shot: his slapshot was clocked at 118.3 m.p.h., nearly 35 m.p.h. above the league average. And then there were the Hull muscles. He didn't have an ounce of excess baggage on his 5-foot-10, 195-pound frame.

Hull totaled only 31 goals in his first two seasons with the Black Hawks, then developed the slapshot that was the bane of all goalies. He scored 50 goals in the 1961–62 season to equal a league record and progressively increased the mark to 58 in 1968–69. In his first 15 NHL seasons, he totaled 604 goals, won the league scoring championship three times and played left wing on the NHL All-Star team 10 times.

The supreme compliment came from Stan Mikita, the former Black Hawks' center. "To say that Bobby was a great hockey player is to labor the point," Mikita said. "He was all of that, of course. But the thing I admired about him was the way he handled people. He

always enjoyed signing autographs for fans and was a genuine nice guy."

MARIO LEMIEUX

Mario Lemieux had heard the whispers almost from the time he broke into the National Hockey League with the Pittsburgh Penguins in 1984. He was accused of being a floater, a player who didn't go all out every night, a man with no leadership qualities.

All those whispers were finally put to rest on a balmy May night in 1991 when Lemieux hoisted the Stanley Cup over his head and skated it around the perimeter of the Met Center in Bloomington, Minn.

The Penguins had wiped out the Minnesota North Stars in a six-game final series to claim their first Stanley Cup championship. And the man who contributed the most to Pittsburgh's march to victory was their captain, Mario Lemieux.

The 6-foot-4, 210-pound center played as if he were on a mission, and the rest of the Penguins took their cue from him. He totaled 12 points in five games against the North Stars and finished the playoffs with 44 points, three shy of the playoff record set by Wayne Gretzky in 1985. And he skated off with the Conn Smythe Trophy as MVP of the playoffs.

Lemieux had shown courage and determination in the way he came back from back surgery in July 1990, followed by an infection in September. He spent two months flat on his back in a hospital bed, fighting off deep-seated fears that he would never play again.

In 1991–92, he was challenged anew. Injuries caused him to miss 16 games, but he won his third scoring championship. In the playoffs, he suffered a broken left hand when slashed by the Rangers' Adam Graves in Game 2 of the Patrick Division finals. He missed the rest of that series, but came back against Chicago to bring the Penguins their second consecutive Cup. In the process, he again was playoff MVP.

In French, the words *le mieux* mean "the best." Born in hockey-mad Montreal, Lemieux has had to live with the label for years. In his

Mario Lemieux

final year of junior hockey in 1983–84, he scored an amazing 133 goals and 149 assists for 282 points, all records, while playing for Laval of the Quebec Major Junior League.

It was obvious throughout that season that Lemieux was going to be selected first overall in the 1984 amateur draft. The Penguins finished with the worst record in the NHL and won the right to draft Lemieux.

The Penguins opened the 1984–85 season in Boston. On his first shift, Lemieux stripped the puck from All-Star defenseman Ray Bourque, skated in alone on goalie Pete Peeters and beat him to score his first NHL goal on his first shot.

By season's end Lemieux had become the third rookie in NHL history to score at least 100 points (43 goals and 57 assists). He propelled the Penguins' season point total from 38 in 1983–84 to 51 and sparked an attendance jump from 273,500 to 400,707.

And, of course, he won the Calder Trophy as the NHL's Rookie of the Year.

"It was tough," Lemieux says of his first year in the pros. "There was a lot of pressure, playing against older guys with a lot more experience. But it went very well and I thought I had some pretty good games."

A major event for Lemieux was the 1985 NHL All-Star Game at Calgary. The rookie teenager dazzled teammates, opponents, experts and fans with two goals and an assist in sparking the Wales Conference team to a 6–4 victory. He skated away with the keys to a new car, his prize for being named the MVP of the game.

"It was a great feeling to play in the All-Star Game in my first year in the league," Lemieux recalled. "That was my type of game—almost no hitting and a lot of skating and passing."

Skating and passing. Nobody does it better than Lemieux. He is extremely quick and

mobile for a man his size. He has the ability to thread perfect passes through tangles of legs and skates, and he is big enough to reach around a forechecker to make his play.

Anticipation is another Lemieux talent. "Before I get the puck, I look where the players are and try to determine where they will be after," he said. "I try to get a crowd to go after me, then pass to who's open. It's easy."

It did look easy for Lemieux during the 1987–88 season when he emerged as the NHL's leading scorer with 70 goals and 168 points. The first indication Lemieux would have a magical season came during the Canada Cup tournament. He had a tournament-high 11 goals, including four game-winners.

The 1988 All-Star Game in St. Louis provided another forum for Lemieux. He totaled an unprecedented six points that included three goals, the most notable being the game-winner in overtime.

For an encore, Lemieux produced another great season in 1988–89. He led the league in goals (85), assists (114) and points (199).

Great players are measured by their ability to win championships. Lemieux could lift people out of their seats, yet he couldn't seem to lift his teammates to greater heights. The Penguins made the playoffs just once in Lemieux's first six seasons.

Now, all those frustrations have ended for Mario Lemieux.

TED LINDSAY

No man on skates was ever too big or too tough for Ted Lindsay to challenge. He was small (5-foot-8 and 160 pounds), but he always carried a big stick. And he used that stick—and his fists—to cut down some of the biggest, meanest men in the National Hockey League.

His tormentors called him "Scarface" or "Terrible Ted." Lindsay didn't mind. The scar tissue on his thin but rugged face represented his badge of courage. He stopped counting the stitches when they reached 400. And the nickname "Terrible" only applied to his repu-

tation for getting into trouble, because as a player he was magnificent.

Lindsay broke into the NHL in 1944, making the big jump from the junior ranks to the Detroit Red Wings at the age of 19. Playing left wing on Detroit's memorable Production Line with Gordie Howe and Sid Abel, Lindsay helped the Red Wings win eight regular-season league titles (including seven in a row) and four Stanley Cup championships in the late 1940s and early '50s.

A member of nine All-Star teams and the league's leading scorer in 1949–50, Lindsay retired in 1960 after 16 years of service, 13 with the Red Wings and the last three with the Chicago Black Hawks. He totaled 365 goals and 458 assists, a league high for left wings until Bobby Hull passed the goals figure in 1968.

Lindsay had established a partnership with another former Detroit player, Marty Pavelich, in a plastics firm late in his playing career. Now he was able to devote all his time to this prosperous business. But he missed the excitement of the brawling world of hockey.

After four years of retirement, he returned to the Red Wings as a player. He was 39 years old. Asked why he would risk possible injury by attempting a comeback at that age, Lindsay said, "It's certainly not the money. I'm well off. I just had this desire to wind up my career with the Red Wings."

The Red Wings—and their fans—welcomed Lindsay back with open arms. He launched his comeback against the Toronto Maple Leafs in Detroit's opening game of the 1964–65 season. A crowd of 14,323, largest ever to see a Detroit home opener, greeted the old battler and he responded by dealing out several vicious bodychecks to assorted Maple Leafs. Ted Lindsay was back, and soon the whole league knew it.

In a game at Montreal he drew a $25 fine for spearing Ted Harris, a rugged defenseman who towered seven inches over Lindsay and outweighed him by 40 pounds. Claude Larose, a Montreal youngster with a reputation for being reasonably talented with his fists, tried to even matters. Lindsay gripped his stick with

both hands and slashed Larose across the legs. Larose, 17 years Lindsay's junior, hobbled away in pain.

Lindsay's comeback lasted only one season, but it was a season in which the Red Wings led the league for the first time in eight years. They wouldn't have done it without old man Lindsay, who scored 14 goals and, coinciden- tally, was among the league leaders in penal- ties. Clarence Campbell, the president of the National Hockey League who had earlier scoffed at Lindsay's return, called it one of the most amazing comebacks in professional sports.

A year later, Ted Lindsay was inducted into the Hockey Hall of Fame.

MARK MESSIER

He has all the attributes of a hockey superstar: swift skater, strong, heavy shot, tenacious forechecker, rugged backchecker. And then there's Mark Messier's eyes!

"When he gets mad, it's like he's in another world," said former Ranger defenseman Barry Beck. "He'll look at you with those big eyes and they'll be going around in circles."

It's a look that, combined with a well-practiced elbow, has dismantled many a rival.

In 1987, Messier was a member of the NHL squad that played the Soviets in the Rendez-Vous All-Star series. "We're sitting in the locker room before the first game," said Dave Poulin of the Boston Bruins, "and Mark stood up and outlined what we were going to do in the warmup. He said, 'Anybody have any problems with that?'"

"I glanced around the room and I saw Rod Langway, Wayne Gretzky, all those people who were leaders. We looked at each other like, 'Nope, no problems at all.' Mark just took over."

It was his leadership qualities, buttressed by his all-around play that inspired the New York Rangers to acquire him from the Edmonton Oilers at the start of the 1991–92 season. In one of hockey's most stunning trades, the Rangers shipped three players—Bernie Nicholls, Steven Rice and Louie DeBrusk—to Edmonton for Messier.

The 6-foot-1, 210-pound center arrived in New York with five Stanley Cup rings, one regular-season MVP award, one playoff MVP award and three first-team All-Star selections—all of which had accumulated during 12 seasons with the Oilers.

The 30-year-old Messier had demanded a trade and was delighted to be in New York. "I'm looking forward to a new challenge," he said. "I'm starting a new career."

In his first game in Ranger blue, Messier sparked the team to a 2–1 overtime victory over the Canadiens in Montreal. It was the Rangers' first triumph in the Forum in eight years.

He went on to become the Rangers' leader as they won the Patrick Division with a 105-point total, tops in the league. He wound up with his second MVP award. But the repeat-bound Penguins ended it all for Messier and the Rangers in the division final.

Messier is a native of Edmonton who grew up in Portland, Ore., where his father was a defenseman for the Portland Buckaroos of the Western Hockey League. "My father was one tough hockey player," he said.

Messier was only 17 when he turned pro with Indianapolis of the World Hockey Association in 1978. He had played only five games when the team folded. Messier finished his first pro season with Cincinnati of the WHA and was hardly a sensation. He scored only one goal the entire season and that on a flip shot from center ice.

Glen Sather, the general manager-coach of the Oilers, picked Messier in the second round of the 1979 draft, bringing the 18-year-old hometown lad directly into the NHL. "He was no sure thing, but he could skate and he worked hard," said Sather.

After scoring 33 points in his first season and 63 the next year, Messier blossomed into a 50-goal scorer as the Oilers exploded as an NHL power in 1981–82.

He played in Wayne Gretzky's shadow during those early years in Edmonton. But one can argue that the Oilers didn't get to the top until Messier was ready to put them there. He had a bad shoulder when the Oilers reached the Cup finals for the first time in 1983. They went down in four straight to the Islanders.

But the next year he was healthy and helped the Oilers end the Islanders' four-year reign as champions. The teams split the first two games of the Cup finals. The Oilers were trailing, 2–1, in Game 3 when Messier went the length of the ice to blow a goal past Billy Smith. It was a spectacular goal and the Oilers went on to win their first Cup in a five-game series. Messier won the Conn Smythe Trophy as playoff MVP.

« *Ted Lindsay*

Mark Messier

After Gretzky was traded to Los Angeles in 1988, he was named Oiler captain. He enjoyed his most productive season in 1989–90 (129 points), helping the Oilers win their fifth Cup in seven years and winning the Hart Trophy as league MVP.

HOWIE MORENZ

Babe Ruth and Bobby Jones, Bill Tilden and Jack Dempsey—these were the men who dominated America's Golden Age of Sport in the Roaring Twenties. During that same period of bathtub gin and flappers and ragtime jazz, Canada had its own hero. He was Howie Morenz of the Montreal Canadiens, the greatest hockey player of his generation.

To the French-speaking fans of the Province of Quebec, Howie Morenz was *L'homme-eclair*. In English he was the same thing: the top man.

Morenz was a center for the Canadiens for 12 years and near the end of his career played with the Chicago Black Hawks and the New York Rangers. Once, in a 44-game season, he scored 40 goals—a remarkable achievement. He totaled 270 goals during his National Hockey League career and was among the first group of players admitted to the Hockey Hall of Fame in 1945.

A happy-go-lucky man with large, smiling eyes, a receding hairline and a heavy beard, Morenz was a typical sports hero of the 1920s. He was colorful and glamorous, hockey's fastest man on skates and a fiery competitor. Toe Blake, the most successful coach in the history of the Canadiens, was a rookie player with Montreal when Morenz was approaching the end of the line. He remembers Morenz: "He was an inspiration for all of us . . . a man with remarkable skills who laughed hard and played hard."

Dazzling speed and guile were Morenz's trademarks. A contemporary of his, Ott Heller of the Rangers, once remarked: "When Howie skates full speed, everyone else on the ice seems to be skating backward." Morenz's shot was equally impressive. Once he broke a goalie's nose with one of his bullet-like drives. Another time his shot caught a netminder square in the forehead, flipping him over on his back.

Although he never played at more than 165 pounds, Morenz bodychecked with the ferocity of a giant. He was so swift, so skillful and so fearless that the wildly nationalistic French-Canadians of Montreal were undisturbed when they discovered his secret sin: Howie Morenz was of German ancestry.

He was born in the Ontario village of Mitchell in 1902, moving with his family to Stratford, Ontario, at the age of 14. He attracted the attention of the Canadiens when he scored nine goals in an amateur game in Montreal in 1922. The following year he turned pro with the Canadiens for a $1,000 bonus and quickly earned the nickname of "The Stratford Streak."

Off the ice, Morenz's pace was just as fast. He sang and played the ukulele. He was a clothes horse; he changed his suits twice and sometimes three times a day. He wore spats. He was a charming and cosmopolitan young man living swiftly in the charming, cosmopolitan city of Montreal.

Then, suddenly, he was no longer quite so young. After 11 seasons with the Canadiens he was traded, first to Chicago in 1934 and then to the New York Rangers the following year. In 1936, he was repurchased by the Canadiens. On the night of January 28, 1937, in the midst of a fine comeback, Morenz broke four bones in his left leg and ankle in a game against Chicago. Five weeks later, the bones were knitting well when he fell to the cold floor of a Montreal hospital. An embolism had stopped his heart.

Howie Morenz was dead at the age of 34. The funeral service was held at center ice in the Montreal Forum, where thousands of fans wept openly for "Le Grand Morenz."

Howie Morenz

MAURICE (ROCKET) RICHARD

Long after Maurice Richard retired in 1960, there were National Hockey League goalies who would sit around in locker rooms, coffee shops and taprooms and recall what it was like to face the old Rocket from Montreal.

Glenn Hall, who was an All-Star netminder with Detroit and Chicago before winding up with the St. Louis Blues, had a rather unique memory of Richard. "What I remember most about the Rocket were his eyes," Hall says. "When he came flying toward you with the puck on his stick, his eyes were all lit up, flashing and gleaming like a pinball machine. It was terrifying."

Richard terrified goalies like Hall for 18 seasons, all with the Montreal Canadiens. He totaled 544 regular-season goals, a record until Gordie Howe wiped it out in 1963. He was the first to score 50 goals in one season (1944–45), and he is the only one to have reached that figure in a 50-game schedule.

There was nothing quite so dramatic as a Richard goal. He would run, not glide, down the ice, cut in from right wing as he neared the cage and then use either a forehand or backhand shot to fool rival goalies. That was another of Richard's great, unmatched talents. He was ambidextrous, a right wing with an unorthodox left-hand shot.

"The Rocket did everything by instinct and with brute strength," said Frank Selke Sr., who was the Canadiens' general manager during Richard's record-breaking years. "He was the greatest opportunist the game has ever known."

Bill Chadwick, a former referee and a member of the Hockey Hall of Fame, was another Richard admirer. "He was the greatest scorer I ever saw from the blue line in," Chadwick said. "And his strength was amazing. I saw him carry defensemen on his back right up to the goal mouth and score."

Richard learned the rudiments of the game as a teenager in Montreal's Lafontaine Park in the years preceding World War II. He was a prolific scorer in the city's Park League, but appeared too injury-prone to become a real star. He broke an ankle while playing amateur hockey, then fractured a wrist. He was finally promoted to the Canadiens in 1942, but was sidelined early by another broken ankle. "It looks as if we have a brittle-boned player on our hands," sighed Tommy Gorman, then the Canadiens' general manager.

Gorman even considered releasing Richard, but the Rocket became stronger as he reached manhood, shook off his injuries and developed into a small bull on skates. He stood a shade under six feet and weighed 190 pounds at the height of his career. Many teams used two players to "shadow" the Rocket. He considered it a compliment. And when they got in his way, he would simply bowl them over and then glare at them with those dark, menacing eyes.

He had a mean temper that got him into frequent scrapes with players and officials. His suspension by NHL president Clarence Campbell in 1955 for carving up a Boston player with his stick and punching a linesman precipitated a riot in the Montreal Forum.

All of Richard's transgressions, though, were forgotten when he was rushed into the Hockey Hall of Fame in 1961. This honor normally wasn't bestowed on a player until at least the third year of his retirement. Maurice Richard had only been retired for nine months!

MILT SCHMIDT

He would glide behind the Boston net to pick up the puck and then start up ice. As he reached center ice he was under a full head of steam, his cowlick flying, his neck outthrust, his prominent nose sticking out like the prow of a ship. And he never had to look down at the puck, which he was shifting back and forth, left to right, right to left, on the end of his stick.

When he crossed the blue line and entered enemy territory he would skate around or barge through rival defensemen until he was close enough to the net to release his famed

Maurice Richard »

Milt Schmidt

wrist shot. Then, bingo! The puck was in the cage and all Boston went wild.

This was Milt Schmidt in action, the kid from Kitchener, the center of the much-feared Kraut Line, who in 16 years as a player for the Bruins scored 229 goals and ranked among the most fiery competitors in the history of the National Hockey League.

One of his greatest admirers was Art Ross, who coached and managed the Bruins during Schmidt's big years. "Schmidt was the fastest playmaker of all time," Ross said. "By that I mean no player ever skated at full tilt the way he did and was still able to make the play."

It was Ross who scouted Schmidt and signed him to a Bruins' contract in 1935. Milt played one season of minor-league hockey at Providence, then moved up to the Bruins and was reunited with two of his old school pals, Bobby Bauer and Woody Dumart. That was the beginning of the Kraut Line, so named because

all three came from the Kitchener-Waterloo area of Ontario, which was predominantly German in origin.

With Schmidt as their center and leader, the Krauts led the Bruins to four straight regular-season NHL championships beginning in 1938. Boston also won two Stanley Cup titles during that same period.

Injuries frequently slowed Schmidt but never stopped him from playing. "That's the only trouble with Milt," Ross once said. "If he would not put so much of his heart and soul into his play, he wouldn't be injured so much."

In one Stanley Cup playoff series against Toronto, when both his knees were so banged up from repeated injuries that he couldn't bend them, he had his legs taped from the ankle to the thigh and then had himself lifted off the table and onto his skates.

Referees, normally impartial, were amazed at Schmidt's courage. "Milt had more guts than any player I ever saw," said Bill Chadwick. Red Storey, another retired referee, said, "I'd take five Milt Schmidts, put my grandmother in the nets and we'd beat any team."

Schmidt was named to the NHL All-Star team four times and won the league's Most Valuable Player award in 1951 at the age of 33. He served as the Bruins' coach following his retirement as a player in 1955, then became the club's general manager.

He claimed he received his greatest thrill in 1952 when he scored the 250th goal of his career. It was Milt Schmidt Night at Boston Garden and Bauer came out of retirement for that one game to play alongside his old Kraut linemates. "That was a great night," Schmidt said. "The goal and the ovation we got from the fans . . . I'll never forget it."

Hockey fans—in Boston and everywhere— will never forget Milt Schmidt either.

BRYAN TROTTIER

Hall of Fame referee Bill Chadwick once described Bryan Trottier as the greatest hockey player he has ever seen. Other observers of the sport claim that Trottier, in his prime, was as great as Wayne (The Great) Gretzky.

No less an authority than Gordie Howe has always favored Trottier in any Gretzky vs. Trottier debate. "I feel Bryan does more things for his team," Howe said in a 1984 interview. "He could play with any man and on any team in any era."

Trottier has always scoffed at any comparison with Gretzky. "I just wish I had some of Wayne's tools," he says with typical modesty.

A storied performer since breaking into the NHL with the Islanders in 1975, Trottier won the Calder Trophy as the league's top rookie in 1976. Three years later, the gifted center captured the Art Ross Trophy as the leading scorer and the Hart Trophy as Most Valuable Player.

Trottier owns six Stanley Cup rings, four with the Islanders. When the team released Trottier after 15 years of service in 1990,

Islanders' general manager Bill Torrey called it "a painful decision" and had to choke back tears.

But it was not the end of the ice for Trottier, whose playing had been reduced to such a point that he was benched for the Isles' final game against the New York Rangers in their 1990 playoff series. A glorious era had ended for Trottier, but he signed as a free agent with the Pittsburgh Penguins and helped them win back-to-back Stanley Cups in 1991 and 1992.

Trottier was born and raised in Val Marie, Saskatchewan, a small farming and cattle-raising community close to the Montana border. He was 17 when the Islanders made him their second pick (behind Clark Gillies) in the 1974 amateur draft. Torrey shipped Trottier back to junior hockey for a season.

He was deemed ready for the Islanders after totaling 144 points for Lethbridge of the Western League in 1974–75. His coach at Lethbridge was Earl Ingarfield, a former center with the New York Rangers, who refined Trottier's talents as a center.

In his second NHL game, Trottier scored three goals and equaled a club single-game record with five points. He went on to set two league records for a rookie—most assists (63) and most points (95).

With Trottier, the Islanders finally had a center who could neutralize the other team's big guns. He was a scorer who could play defense and could win critical faceoffs. A 5-foot-11, 195-pounder, he proved a fierce and relentless checker. Once he slammed Rangers' defenseman Barry Beck, a much bigger man, into the boards with such force, a reporter at Madison Square Garden quipped, "I think the building just moved two feet."

When Mike Bossy, with his sniper's rifle, joined the Islanders in 1977, he and Trottier soon became a lethal scoring combination.

"Right off the bat, Trots knew what I was going to do and there was that chemistry . . . like we'd played together all our lives," Bossy said.

"It was eerie at times," Trottier said. "I would start a sentence and Mike would finish

Brian Trottier

it. We always knew what the other was thinking.''

Bossy was elected to the Hockey Hall of Fame in 1991. His longtime linemate and buddy should join him in the near future.

THE DEFENDERS
Behind the Blue Line

RAY BOURQUE

Harry Sinden, general manager of the Boston Bruins, remembers the first time he saw Ray Bourque play hockey. ''It was an All-Star junior tournament in Canada, and Ray was easily the best player on the ice,'' Sinden said. ''He impressed me as being the perfect size for a hockey player.

''Some people look at racehorses and know just by looking which ones will be great, and I'm supposed to know that about hockey players. I looked at Ray Bourque and I said, 'We've got us a champion here.' I was right, too.''

Ever since the Montreal native reached puberty, expectations have been high. In 1979, when he broke into the National Hockey League as an enormously talented 18-year-old rookie, the Bruins needed a star. Bourque was it.

He then was being hailed as ''the best thing to come along since Bobby Orr.'' The comparison quickly became odious—Bourque's game is as cautious as Orr's was flashy—but Bourque ignored the hype and responded by winning the Calder Trophy as the league's best rookie. On the way, he was also selected for the All-Star first team, the only non-goalie ever to receive both honors.

That was just the beginning of Bourque's record-setting career. In the 1990–91 season, he won his fourth Norris Trophy and was an All-Star selection for the 12th consecutive season. What's more, he is the Bruins' all-time leading scorer, with 1,015 points.

Mike Milbury, the Bruins' assistant GM, played with and coached Bourque. ''Ray is the

Ray Bourque

best I've ever played with or seen on defense," Milbury said. "Maybe Paul Coffey is more explosive offensively, but in a tight game, you couldn't ask for a better player."

Indefatigable is the word that best describes Bourque. He frequently logs between 35 and 40 minutes a game.

"It bothers me to watch Ray play that much," Sinden said. "But he is blessed with what it takes to do it."

Bourque was born in the proletarian community of St. Laurent, Quebec, in 1960. He began playing hockey five years later. His formal education ended at 15 when he dropped out of high school to devote all his time to his junior team, the Verdun Black Hawks.

Bourque was the eighth player taken in the 1979 NHL draft, having scored 22 goals and 93 points in his final season with Verdun.

After signing his first pro contract with the Bruins, Bourque bought his father, Raymond Sr., a new car. His dad had been clocking 30,000 miles a year on a 10-year-old Buick following his son through the hockey provinces.

Ray Sr. still gets weepy recalling his son's gift. "I'll tell you this," Ray Sr. said. "The NHL didn't swell Ray's head. He comes over to help me take out the garbage every week of the summer."

Bourque's debut with the Bruins was spectacular. He had a goal and two assists in his first NHL game. Ray recalled the goal with characteristic self-deprecation. "I think it was Bobby Schmautz who passed the puck to me along the left boards," he said. "There was a screen, so I shot, a little wrist shot, and it hit a couple of skates and trickled in."

There would be bigger goals later. Bourque enjoyed his greatest season in 1983–84 when he totaled 31 goals and 65 assists for 96 points.

Bourque, who is 5-foot-11 and 210 pounds, is very difficult to move off the puck once he gets going. He is so stable on the ice that he seems to carve a wake behind him.

Terry O'Reilly, Bourque's former teammate and coach, said: "Ray combines speed and maneuverability and puckhandling ability. He's a terrific stickhandler and he can stop on a dime. And with that stocky, powerful body, I've seldom seen him knocked off his feet."

Bourque never complains about the extra ice time he gets. "I want to play," he said. "I want to make things happen. I'm tired sometimes, but I'm still able to do the job."

Sinden admitted that Bourque had some "defensive deficiencies" when he joined the Bruins. "But that was because he so dominated the junior game, he had the puck all the time. He didn't need to work hard on defense. These days, when Raymond is on his game, there isn't a better defensive player in the league."

Bourque is the Bruins' captain in every way, which is amazing for someone who was introverted and spoke far more French than English when he first joined the team. Now he is the elder statesman who leads by both example and discourse.

Bourque is known to sportswriters as one of the most accessible and patient of athletes. He seems incapable of talking down to someone. And among the young fans who sometimes haunt practice sessions, he is known as a player who not only signs autographs but also has some friendly remark to offer.

"Off the ice, I'm completely and totally different," Bourque said. "I don't talk much. I love to be around kids, though, because with kids everything's honest and innocent."

FRANK (KING) CLANCY

The setting was Toronto's Maple Leaf Gardens just before the outbreak of World War II. The hometown Maple Leafs were involved in a rough game with Montreal, and referee Frank (King) Clancy was finding it difficult controlling the tempers of the players and the fans. When one rinkside customer went so far as to compare Clancy with the less personable end of a horse, the referee, always quick with a quip, bellowed, "If it wasn't for a horse you wouldn't have had me playing in this joint for six years."

King Clancy

It was a classic stopper. And Clancy, of course, was right. A horse did figure in his trade from Ottawa to Toronto in 1930. It developed this way: Conn Smythe, the owner of the Maple Leafs, made a hefty bet on a horse named Rare Jewel at longshot odds that year and collected $14,000. He used his winnings as a down payment to acquire Clancy from Ottawa. The total price was $35,000 and two players—a record hockey transaction in those days.

Clancy was worth it, too. He helped spark the Maple Leafs to the Stanley Cup in his second year with the club and went on to lead them to two regular-season NHL titles before retiring as a player in 1936.

In his 16 years as one of the NHL's greatest rushing defensemen (he spent his first 10 seasons with Ottawa), Clancy totaled 136 goals and assisted on 145. He was named to four All-Star teams, starting with the first one in 1930. Those are impressive credentials for a man who once was considered too puny to play hockey.

Clancy, born in Ottawa in 1902, entered the NHL as a 150-pound teenager. Most rival defensemen outweighed him by at least 30 pounds. But Clancy made up for his lack of heft with great speed and agility. And he never backed away from a brawl, although he admits he won only one fight, against Boston's Eddie Shore, of all people. "I socked Eddie once as he was getting to his feet and skated like mad to the other end of the rink," he said.

Boston fans used to ride Clancy the most. He recalled one night when a Bostonian seated behind the Toronto bench needled him until he could stand it no longer. He turned to the fan and said, "You think you're pretty tough, buddy. Okay, stay around after the game and we'll see how tough you are."

Teammate Charlie Conacher overheard Clancy's challenge and grinned. "King, you'll be the next heavyweight champion of the world if you can handle that fan," Conacher said. "Didn't you recognize him? He's Jack Sharkey, the heavyweight champion of the world."

Clancy didn't keep his appointment with the champ.

The colorful Irishman with the dented nose and bellowing voice served as a coach both before and after his 11-year service as an NHL referee. His last coaching job was a three-year tenure with his beloved Maple Leafs (1954–56). He later was named an assistant to general manager-coach Punch Imlach of the Leafs.

"I'm sort of a good-will ambassador," he explained.

Hockey never had a better one than King Clancy.

VICTOR (DIT) CLAPPER

There are various yardsticks by which a player can be measured for greatness in professional hockey. One is the number of goals he scores. Another is longevity. In both areas, Dit Clapper had few peers.

An even-tempered, six-foot, 200-pounder from Hastings, Ontario, Clapper was the National Hockey League's first 20-year man. He played all those 20 years with the Boston Bruins, the first 10 as a right wing, the last 10 as a defenseman. He wound up his playing career in 1947 with 228 goals, a very respectable total for a man who drifted between two positions.

Clapper arrived in the NHL with the oddest nickname in hockey. His parents christened him Aubrey Victor and called him Vic. "I couldn't say Vic," Clapper once explained. "I lisped and the name came out Dit. It stuck, sort of."

It was a name that stuck in the minds of selectors for the Hockey Hall of Fame. In 1947, Dit Clapper became the first active player to be named to the Hall. He had earned it. The late Bobby Bauer, one of Clapper's teammates on those great Boston clubs in the years preceding World War II, once hailed Dit as "the athlete's type of athlete. He was a big guy, but he used his heft to stop fights."

Clapper was a top-notch lacrosse player as a teenager, but he gave up that sport to play junior hockey in Toronto. He signed his first pro contract with the Bruins at the age of 19 in 1926, played half a season in the minors, then moved up to Boston in 1927.

Although a defenseman up to that time, Clapper was converted into a right wing by the Bruins and eventually wound up on Boston's Dynamite Line with Cooney Weiland and Dutch Gainor. In his second full season with Boston, the Bruins won the NHL regular-season title and the Stanley Cup. The next year the

Dit Clapper

Bruins finished first again and Clapper enjoyed his greatest season, totaling 41 goals and 20 assists.

In 1937, Clapper returned to his old position on defense. He sparked the Bruins to four more league titles and two more Stanley Cup championships. These were Boston's glory years in the NHL. The Bruins had Frank Brimsek, the original "Mr. Zero," in goal, the famed Kraut Line of Bauer, Milt Schmidt and

Woody Dumart to lead the attack, and good old Dit Clapper on defense.

Clapper was named to the first All-Star team in three successive years (1939-40-41). In 1942, he suffered a severed Achilles tendon in a game at Toronto. It was thought he would never play again, but he made a remarkable recovery and two years later was named to the All-Star team for the sixth time.

Boston fans will never forget Clapper's retirement ceremony on February 12, 1947. He stood at center ice in Boston Garden, wearing his familiar No. 5 jersey and looking as handsome as ever. Then, while a capacity crowd of 14,000 looked on approvingly, he received $7,500 in gifts. It was only part payment for all the thrills Dit Clapper had given his devoted followers for 20 glorious years.

DOUG HARVEY

Most hockey players are content to master only a few facets of the game. Doug Harvey literally controlled every part of it during his great years as a defenseman for the Montreal Canadiens.

Pacemaking is what set him apart from his contemporaries. He could slow down or speed up the tempo of most games with his extraordinary talents.

If the Canadiens wanted to kill time, Harvey would bring the puck up ice slowly, maneuvering his way past forechecking forwards until he reached the blue line. Then he would weave back and forth along the line, sliding soft passes to teammates and never becoming rattled.

If the Canadiens were trailing and attempting to beat the clock, it was Harvey who invariably led their fast-break up ice. And once the puck was in the enemy zone, he would station himself at the left point, waiting for a return pass and protecting against a possible breakaway by a rival player.

Harvey performed all these functions in a calm, almost lackadaisical fashion. He never seemed to fully extend himself, yet he was the unchallenged leader of the powerful Cana-

Doug Harvey

diens when they swept to an unprecedented five straight Stanley Cup championships from 1956 through 1960.

A native of Montreal, Harvey turned to hockey only after rejecting tempting offers from pro football and baseball scouts. It was the right choice—for him and for the Canadiens. During 13 seasons with Montreal he was named to the first All-Star team nine times and once to the second team. He earned the Norris

Trophy as the league's outstanding defenseman six times.

The only fault most experts found with Harvey was a minor one: he didn't shoot enough. (The most goals he scored in a season was nine.) He claimed he would rather finesse his way to within shooting range and set up a goal for a teammate than try one of his own slapshots. "I didn't have a bonus for goals," he once said, "so why not set up the guys who needed them?"

A hero to every youngster in Montreal, Harvey encountered trouble with the Canadiens' front office when he became involved with the organization of the NHL Players' Association. In 1961 he was traded to the New York Rangers and became their player-coach, leading the league's one-time patsies into the Stanley Cup playoffs for the first time in four years. During that same 1961–62 season he won his seventh Norris Trophy and once again was named to the All-Star team.

Harvey surrendered the coaching position after one season—he disliked the responsibility—but remained with the Rangers as a player for another 18 months. "When I was a coach, I couldn't be one of the boys," he said. "This way if I want a beer with them, I get a beer."

He then drifted to the minors, playing in Baltimore, St. Paul, Quebec City, Pittsburgh and Kansas City. He returned to the NHL with the St. Louis Blues during the 1968 Stanley Cup playoffs and, ironically, wound up playing against his old Montreal club in the final round.

Although he was then 45 years old, Harvey remained with St. Louis for the 1968–69 season as a defenseman and assistant coach. The next year he became defensive coach for Los Angeles before retiring.

CHING JOHNSON

More than a decade after his retirement as a player, Ching Johnson was serving as a linesman in a game in Washington, D.C., between the New York Rovers and the Washington Lions of the Eastern Hockey League. The game

Ching Johnson

was spirited and Johnson was kept busy trying to keep up with the flow of action.

Suddenly, a Washington player slithered into the open in the New York zone. Johnson, fat and fifty, forgot his role. For that split-second, he wasn't an official any longer. He was the defenseman he once was with the New York Rangers and his goal was in danger. He cut over in front of the onrushing Washington forward and crunched him to the ice with a solid bodycheck.

Johnson later apologized. "You know, I just can't explain it," he said. "Here was that guy racing for the goal and I just had to stop him. Why? Instinct, I guess. The old habit was too deep within me. I forgot where I was and what I was doing."

Something like this could happen only to Ching Johnson, a star for 11 years with the Rangers. He was one of the New York club's pioneer players, joining the team when it was organized in 1926 and staying on until 1937.

His fearlessness, his one-man sorties on the opposition's net, were something to behold.

Year after year, he handled his duties on the Ranger defense even when his large body (he was a 210-pound, six-footer) was racked with pain. But he ignored the skate cuts, the welts and the bruises while he went about his business of protecting the New York goal. His rugged face was creased by a permanent pixie-like grin. He smiled when he knocked people down and he smiled when he, himself, was sent sprawling to the ice.

The hockey wars Johnson engaged in were mild compared to his service with a Canadian Army trench mortar outfit in France in World War I. He was gassed at Passchandaelle, recovered and returned home to Winnipeg, where he launched his hockey career with a semipro team.

"I was a big, awkward kid then," he once recalled. "I couldn't skate very well. I looked like an elephant on skates. But after a while I started to get the hang of it."

Johnson moved from the semipros of Winnipeg to the old Central League. He was pushing 30 when he joined Bill and Bun Cook, Frank Boucher and Taffy Abel on that first Ranger team. "I told the Rangers I was 28 when I joined them," he said, "but I was almost two years older. That's why I demanded a three-year contract. I didn't think I could last any longer."

He lasted 12 years in New York, completing his NHL career by playing one season with the Americans in 1938. He bowed out with fine credentials—a member of two Stanley Cup championship teams and a four-time member of the league All-Stars. He was admitted into the Hockey Hall of Fame in 1958.

LEONARD PATRICK (RED) KELLY

The key lyrics in that old song, "Has Anybody Here Seen Kelly?" have always served to remind fans of the most versatile All-Star in the history of the National Hockey League. He is Leonard Patrick Kelly. And if he

Red Kelly »

wasn't the Kelly mentioned in the song, he should have been, for "his hair is red and his eyes are blue and he is Irish through and through."

NHL fans first saw Red Kelly in 1947 when he joined the Detroit Red Wings as a pink-cheeked youth of 19, fresh from the junior ranks. A native of Toronto, he was ignored by the Maple Leafs when one of their scouts predicted he wasn't good enough to last 20 games in the NHL. It was a poor prediction. Kelly lasted 20 years.

Kelly spent the first 12½ years of his NHL career with Detroit. During that time the Red Wings won eight regular-season championships and four Stanley Cup titles. Kelly was a defenseman then, the best rushing defenseman in the league. He was the first winner of the Norris Trophy, awarded annually to the league's outstanding defenseman, in 1954. He was named to the All-Star team six times and was a three-time winner of the Lady Byng (good sportsmanship) Trophy.

All these honors came Kelly's way while he was playing at Detroit. Then, late in the 1959–60 season, he returned home. The Maple Leafs, convinced that they had made a mistake in letting him get away the first time, talked the Red Wings into a trade after Kelly had balked at being peddled to the New York Rangers.

Kelly will never forget his first game in a Toronto uniform. "I was finally where I'd always wanted to be," he recalled. "When the people stood up and clapped and cheered me, I felt so tight I nearly burst."

The Maple Leafs, aware of Kelly's great playmaking ability, converted him into a center. He turned out to be just as valuable at his new position. In his first full season with Toronto, he propelled the previously disorganized Maple Leafs into the Stanley Cup finals, where they were finally stopped by the Chicago Black Hawks.

Toronto coach Punch Imlach called Kelly "my ace in the hole." The flaming redhead's greatest contribution to the Maple Leafs was the remarkable change he brought about in Frank Mahovlich, a brooding young man with

great talent who increased his goal output from 18 to 48 the first season he played on a line with Kelly.

Kelly's style was so economical he almost appeared lazy. He was a worker, though. He served two terms in the Canadian Parliament while playing for Toronto, but the extra duties as a legislator didn't hamper his play. He scored 119 goals in 7½ seasons with the Maple Leafs, giving him a career total of 281, and he sipped champagne from the Stanley Cup four more times.

Following retirement as a player in 1967, Kelly became coach of the Los Angeles Kings. The Kings were picked by everybody to finish last, but Kelly—then the only pilot in the NHL without previous coaching experience—led his team to second place in the West. He moved to Pittsburgh for 1969–70 and the Penguins finished second.

Red stayed as coach of the Penguins for the next 2½ seasons, piloting them to one more playoff berth before moving on to Toronto for a four-year stay.

BOBBY ORR

He was always looked upon as the boy next door, the one with the winning smile and the gracious manner. Square-jawed and thick-necked, there was never an ounce of fat on his 5-foot-11 frame. And he was looked upon in many quarters as the best defenseman in hockey history.

Bobby Orr was something special. "All Bobby did was change the face of hockey all by himself," said a former teammate, Phil Esposito.

Orr revolutionized the role of the defenseman with his slick passing and playmaking and end-to-end dashes. He also was responsible in part for elevating the salary structure of National Hockey League players.

Orr signed a record bonus contract with the Boston Bruins at the age of 18 in 1966 and four years later he became the first defenseman in NHL history to win the scoring title when he led the Bruins to the Stanley Cup championship.

Bobby Orr

Appropriately enough, it was Orr's overtime goal that won the fourth and final game of the playoffs for the Bruins and brought them their first Stanley Cup in 29 years. It was his ninth goal and 20th point of the playoffs, both records. During the regular season, Bobby had made history with record-cracking totals of 33 goals, 87 assists and 120 points to win the scoring title.

The Bruins discovered Orr in 1962 playing midget hockey in his home town of Parry Sound, Ontario. He was only 14 but he had everything even then. Boston moved him into junior hockey at Oshawa and in three years playing defense there, he averaged 33 goals per season, an amazing output at the time.

It cost Boston $75,000 for a two-year agreement to get young Bobby's name on an NHL contract, the best investment the team ever made.

Orr won the Calder Trophy as Rookie of the Year in 1967. "Bobby was a star from the moment they played the National Anthem in his first NHL game," said Harry Sinden, Orr's first coach in Boston. Veteran Harry Howell won the Norris Trophy as the best defenseman that year and was delighted. "I'm glad I won it now," said Howell, then 36, "because it's going to belong to Orr from now on."

Howell's prediction was fulfilled. Orr won the Norris Trophy eight straight years and in 1970 he became the first man in history to nail down four individual trophies in a single season. He took the Norris as top defenseman, the Art Ross Trophy for scoring, the Hart Trophy as the Most Valuable Player in the regular season and the Conn Smythe Trophy as MVP in the playoffs.

Orr repeated as playoff MVP in 1972 when he led the Bruins to the Stanley Cup championship again. He also won his third consecutive Hart Trophy as regular-season MVP, becoming the first man in NHL history to win it more than two straight times.

Orr scored a career-high 46 goals and won his second scoring title with 135 points in 1974–75. He also was named to the All-Star first team for the eighth consecutive year. However, constant knee problems were slow-

ing him down. He ended his 10-year association with the Bruins in 1976, became a free
agent and signed a $3-million, five-year con-
tract with the Chicago Black Hawks.

He sat out the 1977–78 season after under-
going his sixth knee operation, attempted a
comeback the following year but was forced to
quit after appearing in six games. His last
game was on November 1, 1978, against the
Vancouver Canucks in Chicago. "My knees
can't handle playing anymore," he said. He
was 30 years old.

Orr held or shared 12 individual records at
the time of his retirement. He totaled 270
goals and 915 points in 657 games—remarkable figures for a defenseman. He was voted
into the Hockey Hall of Fame in 1979.

Orr received his greatest accolade, though,
when the *Boston Globe* conducted a poll to
determine the greatest athlete in the city's
history. It was not Ted Williams, Carl Yas-
trzemski, Bob Cousy or Bill Russell. The
winner was Bobby Orr.

BRAD PARK

Misfortune and heartbreak walked hand in
hand with Brad Park during most of his career.
Yet he overcame all to become a standout
defenseman in the National Hockey League.
He played on knees that had no cartilage and
on ankles weakened by fractures, and became
a hero to fans in two cities.

His heart was broken on a November day in
1975 when the New York Rangers traded him
and Jean Ratelle to the Boston Bruins for Phil
Esposito and Carol Vadnais. Park, who had
been the Rangers' captain and the darling of
the gallery gods at Madison Square Garden,
quickly shook off the shock of that trade and
eventually became the darling of the gallery
gods at Boston Garden.

Misfortune seized Park early in life. He was
only 17 when he suffered torn cartilage in his
left knee while playing in a Junior A game.
The following season he required surgery for
ligament damage in his right knee. He fractured his right ankle in his second season with
the Rangers in 1969.

Park's knee problems followed him to
Boston. In his first season with the Bruins, he
caught his left skate in a hole on the ice
against the Islanders in Nassau Coliseum and
required surgery to remove torn cartilage.
Park's fourth and last cartilage (two in each
knee) was removed during the 1978–79 season, but his right-knee problems persisted.

He considered retiring in 1980, changed
his mind and enjoyed an injury-free season in
1980–81. "Brad had a sensational season,"
said Harry Sinden, the Bruins' general manager. "There wasn't a better defenseman in the
NHL."

On December 11, 1980, Park became only
the second defenseman in NHL history to
collect 500 assists. The first was Bobby Orr,
who was Park's teammate for a brief period
during the 1975–76 season. When they skated
onto the ice for a Boston power play, taking up
positions on opposite points, rivals shud-
dered.

Park always was a dangerous point man.
During the 1981–82 and 1982–83 seasons, he
scored 13 of his 24 goals on power plays and
he completed 1982–83 with 600 career assists, fifth-highest among active playmakers in
the NHL.

Park grew up in the Toronto Maple Leafs'
junior system and was drafted by the Rangers
in 1966 when the Leafs, through an oversight,
left him unprotected in the amateur draft.
King Clancy, a Toronto vice president, used to
moan over that mistake. "I don't know how
we ever let that boy get away," he said.

Park was barely 20 years old when he
showed up at the Rangers' training camp in
1968. He was the last player cut before the
season started and was sent to the American
League for more seasoning. But his minor-
league career lasted just 17 games. The Rangers lost Harry Howell with an injury and Park
was called up as his replacement. Park never
saw the minors again.

Early in his rookie season, Park cracked the
NHL record book when he assisted on four
goals in a game against Pittsburgh. Later in the
season, he scored his first NHL goal—the final
one in a 9–0 romp over the Bruins. Delighted

Brad Park

by the goal, he leaped high in the air and landed ingloriously on his backside. When he picked himself up and brushed himself off, Park grinned and said, "I'm okay. That first goal was worth it."

Park was named to the All-Star first team five times and twice to the second team. He appeared in the Stanley Cup playoffs for 17 consecutive years from 1969 through 1985. He was signed as a free agent by the Detroit Red Wings in 1983, played two more seasons and had a brief fling as coach of the Red Wings in 1986. He was elected to the Hockey Hall of Fame in 1988.

DENIS POTVIN

It was in early September 1973 when a 19-year-old rookie with a friendly smile arrived at the New York Islanders' training camp in Peterborough, Ontario. He hit speeds of more than 100-miles-an-hour in traveling from his Ottawa home in the new Mercedes Benz convertible purchased after he signed his first pro contract two months earlier.

Denis Potvin obviously was a young man in a hurry. While playing amateur hockey for Ottawa of the Ontario Hockey League, he had smashed all of Bobby Orr's league records for a defenseman. It was only natural that observers were comparing Potvin to Orr, then a Boston Bruins superstar.

"I'm not Bobby Orr and I know it," Potvin said. "You can't compare us because our styles are different. I can't skate as well as Orr, but I feel there are a couple of things I might do better, like hitting. That's a big part of my game . . . I just hope I can accomplish some of the things Orr has done, but in my own way."

Potvin's feats during his 15 seasons in the National Hockey League are well chronicled: three-time winner of the Norris Trophy as the

NHL's best defenseman, five times a first-team All-Star, and captain of four Stanley Cup championship teams with the Islanders.

Along the way, Potvin broke two of Orr's career records for a defenseman: most goals and most points. When he retired in 1988, he owned all the NHL's major scoring records for a defenseman: most goals (310), most assists (742) and most points (1,052).

So much for the numbers.

Off the ice? Intelligent, articulate, insightful, urbane—adjectives that fit Potvin like a tight pair of skates. Yet he found it difficult at times to win the respect of fans and foes.

"I don't think people looked at me as a hero-type—like a Wayne Gretzky. I was an opponent people didn't like. That's the way I'll be remembered," Potvin said.

There were times when he didn't get along with his own teammates. He acknowledges that. "I suppose," he once said, "I'm subject to a lot of prejudice and jealousy because of what I accomplished. I'm arrogant at times. But I think that's because I'm honest with people. I tell them what I think and they don't always like that. I have a great deal of confidence in myself."

Potvin never lacked confidence—not even as a 14-year-old growing up in Ottawa. At that tender age he joined the Ottawa team of the OHL and was pitted against players five or six years older.

He had completed five seasons of junior hockey when the Islanders made him the No. 1 pick in the 1973 amateur draft. Some of the Islanders' veterans greeted Potvin's arrival with skepticism, but they soon realized that he had the makings of superstar.

"Denis kind of strutted into camp," said Al Arbour, the coach who took it upon himself to humble the player without diminishing his ego. "I had to blend a very strong-willed individual into a team concept, but it's no secret that we built our team around Denis."

Potvin took years to accept the method behind Arbour's manipulations. "I lived pretty

« *Denis Potvin*

much on the edge back then," Potvin said. "My emotions were on a tightrope and Al saw that and capitalized. He made me perform like a madman."

With Arbour wielding the whip, Potvin totaled 17 goals and 54 points in his first season with the Isles and won the Calder Trophy as the NHL's Rookie of the Year. He kept improving with each season and had his finest year in 1978–79 when he scored 31 goals and 101 points.

Potvin, who carried 205 pounds on a six-foot frame, was a devastating bodychecker. In 1986, he bore down on Washington's Bengt Gustaffson, breaking the Swede's leg with a clean, crunching check. And fans won't forget Potvin's career-ending check on the New York Rangers' Ulf Nilsson in 1979.

Potvin was blessed with other talents. He was an excellent passer and quarterbacked the Islanders' power play from his spot at the left point.

Nagging injuries started to catch up with him, beginning in 1978 when he missed 49 games after surgery to correct stretched ligaments in a thumb. He later missed three months with a broken toe, then was sidelined for two months with a pulled groin muscle.

After 15 years of unconditional hard labor—all with the Islanders—Potvin retired in 1988. He was only 34. "I feel I have nothing else to prove," he said.

Potvin remained in New York after his retirement. He spent several years working in commercial real estate and then became a financial advisor.

He was elected to the Hockey Hall of Fame in 1991, with the induction ceremonies held in Ottawa, his hometown. "This is the place I always want to come home to," he said. "I can't think of a better way to come back."

LARRY ROBINSON

Larry Robinson, who developed into a king among defensemen in the National Hockey League, did not have a regal background. He was a farm kid from eastern Ontario who

Larry Robinson

remembers getting up at dawn and stumbling into the hen house to pick up eggs.

He was born in 1951 in the hamlet of Winchester, about 30 miles from Ottawa, but the family home was in Marvelville, a town of about 2,000. His dairy-farming family also worked the soil around another locale ignored by many mapmakers—Metcalf, Ontario.

But everybody wanted to know about Marvelville. "Marvelville's population is about . . . " Robinson liked to say with a pause. "Well, if a dog dies, everybody knows about it."

From those beginnings, Robinson became an All-Star with the Montreal Canadiens. He is considered the prototype defenseman of modern hockey. Big (6-foot-3 and 212 pounds), strong, tough, mobile. He skates and handles the puck well enough to be a forward, a spot he occasionally plays.

Robinson enjoyed his greatest season in 1976–77 when he totaled 19 goals and 85 assists and won the Norris Trophy as the league's outstanding defenseman. The following year, he won the Smythe Trophy as the MVP of the Stanley Cup playoffs. He sipped champagne from the Stanley Cup for the fourth straight year in 1979 and was named to the All-Star team for the third time in 1980.

Success did not spoil Larry Robinson. "When I think back to when I was a kid, I never dreamed of anything like this, like the things I have now," he admitted. "When I watched the NHL players on TV, I never thought of a hockey player as a person making a lot of money. You know what I got when I turned pro? Well, it was $7,100 a year."

He went on from there to earn $600,000 a year. However, there were times when it appeared he would never make it to the NHL.

Eddie Shore

Most pro prospects are placed on a Junior A team when they are 15 or 16, but not Robinson. He spent two years playing Tier Two in Brockville, Ontario, before moving up to the Kitchener Rangers of the Ontario Hockey Association.

Those were rough times for Robinson, then 19 years old. "I got $60 a week for playing hockey," he told Toronto reporter Al Strachan. "But I was married and that wasn't enough to feed a family. I had a job during the day working for a beverage company. I'd get up at seven and deliver soda pop all day. I'd finish about four and we'd practice at 5:30. That job paid me $80 a week.

"Then there were the games at night. It was pretty hectic. We really scraped and scraped. In the summer, I worked on road construction. I was worried. I didn't want to live like that all my life, but what would happen if I didn't make it in hockey? What was I going to do?"

Robinson's worries eased slightly when the Canadiens made him their fourth pick (20th overall) in the 1971 amateur draft. He spent his first two seasons as a pro with Nova Scotia of the American League. Midway though his third season at Nova Scotia, he was called up to Montreal as a replacement for the injured Pierre Bouchard. He never returned to the minors.

Robinson concluded 17 seasons with the Canadiens in 1989 and signed as a free agent with the Los Angeles Kings. He was then 38 years old. "This is too tough a game and too tough a league to play in if there isn't a little fun in it," he said. "Well, it still is fun for me."

It must be. Robinson played 56 games with the Kings in 1991–92, bringing his total to 1,384 games in 20 seasons.

EDDIE SHORE

All the hockey greats—past and present— were gathered in a midtown New York restaurant for the annual Lester Patrick awards dinner in the spring of 1970. At a table near the rear of the room, the Patrick winner with

the scarred features of a retired boxer was discussing hockey and how it had changed in recent years.

"The accent is on speed now," Eddie Shore said. "I guess it's better for the fans, but I liked it better in the old days. Then it was pretty much a 50–50 proposition. You socked the other guy and the other guy socked you."

Indeed, Shore had socked a lot of guys and caught a few socks in return during a brilliant 14-year career as the meanest defenseman in the National Hockey League.

Shore came out of Edmonton, Alberta, in 1929 to join the Boston Bruins. He infused them with a spirit and color which promptly lifted them from last place to second place in the NHL's American Division. Previously ignored by Bostonians, the Bruins also developed a loyal following—all because of Shore. He was a drawing card wherever he went because of his free-swinging style, his cold and brutal attacks on rival players, and his brilliance on defense. He was the most applauded player of his time—and received the most boos, too.

Hammy Moore, who was the Boston trainer during Shore's heyday, once described Eddie's style of attack. "He was the only player I ever saw who had the whole arena standing every time he rushed down the ice," Moore said. "When Shore carried the puck you were always sure something would happen. He would either end up bashing somebody, get into a fight or score a goal."

Shore totaled 108 NHL goals, a respectable number for a defenseman, before retiring in 1940. He was named the league's Most Valuable Player four times and was voted to the All-Star team seven times.

But there are even more impressive statistics. He accumulated the astounding total of 978 stitches on his rugged body. He had his nose broken 14 times, his jaw shattered five times and he lost most of his teeth.

Shore's most celebrated fight occurred on December 12, 1933, in Toronto and it was one he always regretted. Red Horner of the Maple Leafs started it by slamming Shore into

the boards. Shore picked himself up and went after Horner. He flew down the ice and, mistaking Ace Bailey for Horner, flattened Bailey with a vicious check.

Bailey's head struck the ice and he was taken to a hospital with a fractured skull. His life was saved by delicate brain surgery, but he was never able to play hockey again.

The memory of that near-tragedy haunted Shore for many years. But he continued to play great defense for the Bruins and then the New York Americans before finally hanging up his skates and becoming fulltime owner of the Springfield Indians of the American Hockey League.

As a club owner, Shore remained a fighter. He fought with his players at contract time and with other owners in the committee rooms. Eddie Shore won most of those fights, too.

He was elected to the Hockey Hall of Fame in 1947.

JACK STEWART

Jack Stewart did more to perfect the art of the teeth-rattling bodycheck than any defenseman in the history of the National Hockey League.

There were bigger men in the league when Stewart was patrolling the backline for the Detroit Red Wings in the 1930s and '40s, but none hit with the shattering force of this 5-foot-11, 185-pound wheat farmer from Pilot Mound, Manitoba.

The late Jack Adams, who coached Stewart during most of his 10 years with Detroit, was always impressed by his star defenseman's strength. "He was one of the strongest guys I've ever seen in a hockey uniform," Adams remarked. "He worked hard on his farm all summer and that probably accounted for it."

Frank Boucher, the former coach and general manager of the New York Rangers, was another Stewart admirer. "Jack played defense a lot like Ching Johnson, my old teammate," Boucher said. "He went all out in every game. And he was tough. Hockey was no tea party to Jack Stewart."

Jack Stewart

Stewart also was responsible for the development of other great Detroit defensemen both before and after World War II. Bill Quackenbush and Red Kelly attained stardom while paired with Stewart. "Jack did all the heavy work," said Lynn Patrick, the former coach of the Boston Bruins who claimed he received the hardest bodychecks of his career from Stewart. "He was always advising the other defensemen and if they made an error, Jack was there to back them up."

Hockey fans will always remember Stewart for his bodychecking, but he was a good blocking defenseman as well. He could clear the puck out of his zone quickly and rarely made a bad pass. He could also skate faster than most spectators realized, but they came to see him hit.

It was this penchant for flattening rival skaters that eventually produced a series of injuries and forced Stewart's retirement. After 10 seasons at Detroit, during which he was named to five All-Star teams and was a member of two Stanley Cup championship teams, Stewart was traded to the Chicago Black Hawks in 1950.

Shortly after joining the Hawks, Stewart was sidelined with a slipped disc in his back. Surgery followed and it appeared then that the man known as "Black Jack" had played his last game. But Stewart wasn't ready to quit. He spent long hours exercising, even while flat on his back in the hospital, and promised, "I'll be back, maybe next year."

He did come back the following season, but couldn't shake the injury jinx. In a game against the Rangers, Stewart suffered a fractured skull in a collision with teammate Clare Martin and New York's Edgar Laprade. That did it. Midway through the 1951–52 season, Stewart retired.

Ebbie Goodfellow, the Black Hawks' coach, was saddened by Stewart's loss. "We're going to miss Jack," he said. "He was a great one." The selection committee of the Hockey Hall of Fame agreed when it voted Stewart into the Hall in 1964.

THE GOALIES
The Last Man

FRANKIE BRIMSEK

No player ever made a more spectacular debut in the National Hockey League than Frankie Brimsek, the frozen-faced "Mr. Zero" of the Boston Bruins.

In his first eight games as Boston's regular netminder in December 1938, Brimsek turned in six shutouts, wiped out a league record for consecutive scoreless minutes, and helped the Boston citizenry forget the sadness that enveloped them when Tiny Thompson was sold to Detroit.

The Bruins elevated Brimsek from their Providence, Rhode Island, farm club after Thompson, a great favorite with Boston fans, had been peddled to the Red Wings for $15,000. "I'll never forget my debut in

Boston," Brimsek recalled. "Thompson was a popular guy and a great goalie. I could feel the coolness of the fans as soon as I joined the club. They were waiting for me to kick one."

Brimsek, though, turned that Boston coolness into hand-clapping warmth in less than a month. After losing to the Montreal Canadiens, 2–0, in his first game as Thomp-son's replacement, Brimsek posted three consecutive shutouts. He added three more shutouts in Boston's next four games to surpass Thompson's scoreless record with 231 minutes and 54 seconds of flawless netminding.

The Bruins' followers now were ready to run Brimsek against old Jim Curley for mayor of Boston. Another factor that contributed to

Brimsek's popularity—at least with fans in the United States—was his birthplace. He was born and raised in Eveleth, Minn., and thereby became an oddity in pro hockey—an American-born All-Star.

From Boston's Back Bay to the fish wharves of San Francisco, Brimsek was hailed as hockey's "Mr. Zero." He climaxed his first year with the Bruins by sparking them to the regular-season title and the Stanley Cup championship. He won the Vezina Trophy as the league's most proficient goalie, the Calder (Rookie of the Year) Trophy and a berth on the NHL's first All-Star team.

The Bruins won two more regular-season titles and another Stanley Cup behind Brimsek's goaltending in the next three years. He entered the U.S. Coast Guard in 1943 and served two years aboard a patrol craft in the South Pacific. He returned to the Bruins from his World War II duty in 1945 and found it difficult to regain his old form in goal.

Brimsek reasoned that his years aboard ship had "tied up" his legs. "I was a little shaky when I got back," he admitted. "My legs and my nerves were shot."

After putting in four postwar seasons with Boston, Brimsek asked the Bruins to trade him to Chicago, where he would be closer to his Minnesota home, his family and business interests. The Bruins complied and traded him to the Black Hawks in 1949. He played one season for Chicago and then retired.

In 1966, the selection committee of the Hockey Hall of Fame remembered "Mr. Zero" and made him a member of that exclusive club.

WALTER (TURK) BRODA

Professional hockey can thank an anonymous school principal for launching the career of one of the outstanding clutch goaltenders of all time.

It all began for Walter (Turk) Broda when he was a chubby youngster in Brandon, Manitoba, where he was born on May 15, 1914.

《 Frank Brimsek

One day the principal at his public school announced he was organizing a hockey team. Young Broda, called "Turkey Egg" because of the freckles on his face, tried out for a defense position. It was a bad choice.

"I'm sorry," his principal said, "we have all the defensemen we need." Broda started to leave the ice. "Wait a minute," the principal said. "We need a goaltender, Walter. Get into the goal."

Turk Broda was a goaltender from that day. He started his pro career in the Detroit organization and landed with Toronto through sheer luck. Conn Smythe, the Toronto club owner, was seeking a replacement for Hall of Famer George Hainsworth in 1936 when he scouted a minor-league playoff game between the Detroit Olympias and the Windsor (Ontario) Bulldogs.

Smythe had received glowing reports on the Windsor goalie, Earl Robertson. But when the Olympias trounced Windsor, 8–1, the Maple Leafs' boss forgot all about Robertson. "I like the fellow tending goal for the other team," Smythe said. The other goalie was Broda.

Smythe wasted no time purchasing Broda from Detroit for $8,000. Early in the 1936–37 season, Turk replaced Hainsworth as the Maple Leafs' regular goalie. He held the job for 14 seasons, during which he helped Toronto win five Stanley Cup championships. He twice won the Vezina Trophy as the National Hockey League's top netminder and earned berths on three All-Star teams.

Broda was always at his best when the pressure was greatest, especially in playoff games. He allowed only 211 goals (a 2.08 average) in 101 playoff games. In the 1949 championship playoffs he gave up only four goals as the Maple Leafs swept Detroit in four straight games. In the 1951 playoffs he was again brilliant, allowing only nine goals in eight games.

A happy-go-lucky man of Polish extraction, Broda was inclined to be overweight, a condition which frequently aroused the ire of Smythe. Early in the 1949–50 season, when the Leafs failed to win in six games, Smythe called the chubby Broda into his office. "I'm

Turk Broda

not running a fat man's team,'' the owner said. ''I'm taking you out of the nets and you're not coming back until you get down to 190 pounds.'' At the time Broda scaled almost 200.

The goalie knew Smythe wasn't kidding. He launched a crash diet. He turned his back on desserts. He went to a gym and was steamed, boiled and pounded. It was a Herculean effort for Broda, who regained his job after missing only one game.

After retiring as a player in 1952, Broda turned to coaching. He was elected to the Hockey Hall of Fame in 1967.

KEN DRYDEN

During a timeout, he would stand in front of the net, leaning forward slightly, and using his large goalie stick as a support post. He grasped the top of the stick with his catching glove and folded his blocker over it. When he

was tired, he would lower his head so that his chin rested on his forearms.

That was Ken Dryden's at-ease stance. Once play resumed and the action moved into the Montreal Canadiens' end of the rink, Dryden was a crouched panther, waiting to repulse the next enemy attack. And because he was a big man at 6-foot-4 and 205 pounds, he covered a lot of net. ''He's a bleeping octopus,'' is the way Phil Esposito once described Dryden.

Ken Dryden also was a rarity among goalies—an articulate scholar-athlete. He worked his way through Cornell University on a partial hockey scholarship, then worked his way through law school with his earnings as an All-Star goalie with the Canadiens. He took a

Ken Dryden »

sabbatical from the Canadiens during the 1973–74 season to fulfill his law school requirements, working with a Toronto law firm which paid him $137 a week.

Some members of the hockey establishment were surprised when Dryden retired in 1979 at the age of 31. He was then at the peak of his career and earning $200,000 a year. Why retire? "This was a decision I had to make some time in my life," Dryden said. "I'm certain that I would have enjoyed playing a couple of more years. But this seems the most appropriate time to move on to new challenges."

It was expected Dryden would enter law practice or politics following his retirement. Instead, he took his wife Lynda and two children to England, settled down in a brownstone house in Cambridge and wrote a book on his hockey experiences. He had much to write about. Consider some of his accomplishments:

● He made his debut with the Canadiens at the tail end of the 1970–71 season, allowed only nine goals in six games, then sparked the Canadiens to the Stanley Cup championship and won the Smythe Trophy as the MVP of the playoffs.

● He won the Calder (Rookie of the Year) Trophy at the end of the 1971–72 season.

● In seven-plus seasons with the Canadiens, he totaled 46 shutouts and had a 2.24 goals-allowed average. His average for 112 playoff games was 2.40.

● He played in every playoff game, helping the Canadiens win six Stanley Cups, four in succession.

● He was named to the NHL All-Star team five times, led the league in shutouts four times and won or shared the Vezina Trophy five times.

Scotty Bowman, who was Dryden's coach at Montreal, always used one word to describe Dryden—consistent. "Ken would lose one game, but he rarely lost two in a row," Bowman said. "Oh, he was so consistent."

It was Dryden's intellect, though, that set him apart from his teammates and rivals. His postgame analyses were masterpieces of logic, language and, often, self-deprecating humor.

Once, while being interviewed by Frank Orr of the Toronto Star, he commented on his love affair with hockey. "It's a beautiful thing with its rhythms and patterns, its esthetics, although I never felt I contributed much in that way. I never liked to watch myself in game films. Before I saw myself on TV, I always figured I was Nureyev on skates, dipping and darting across the goal crease. Then I saw myself on TV and realized I was a dump truck. I was an elephant on wheels."

Dump truck? Elephant? Hardly.

Ken Dryden was what Phil Esposito labelled him—a bleeping octopus.

BILL DURNAN

Bill Durnan's career as a National Hockey League goaltender was short in terms of service and sweet in terms of personal satisfaction.

He broke into the NHL in 1943 as a 29-year-old rookie with the Montreal Canadiens and, after seven brilliant seasons, was forced to quit the club in the middle of the 1950 Stanley Cup playoffs because of frayed nerves. But in that comparatively short time he established records which still stand.

During the 1948–49 season, Durnan set the league's modern record for the longest shutout sequence when he held the opposition scoreless for 309 minutes and 21 seconds. He was the first goalie to win the Vezina Trophy four consecutive years (1944 through 1947). Turk Broda of Toronto interrupted his string in 1948, but Durnan won the trophy for the next two years, giving him a record six in seven years.

Durnan's appearances on the league's All-Star first team matched his Vezina Trophy accomplishments. He made the squad as a rookie in 1944 and repeated each year except for 1948 when Broda again prevented him from fashioning a seven-year sweep.

Looking back on his career, Durnan once attributed his great success to the fact that he was ambidextrous.

Bill Durnan

"It was a tremendous asset and I owe that gift to Steve Faulkner, one of my coaches in a church league in Toronto when I was just a youngster," he said. "Steve showed me how to switch the stick from one hand to the other. It wasn't easy at first because I was so young and the stick seemed so heavy. But Steve kept after me and gradually the stick became lighter and I could switch it automatically."

This ability to use either hand to catch flying pucks or to bat them away with his stick was perfected by Durnan during a long career in the amateur ranks. By the time he finally turned pro with the Canadiens he was an accomplished netminder who rarely permitted a rebound in front of his cage.

In his rookie year with Montreal, Durnan gave up only 109 goals in 50 games. That was the same season (1943–44) that Maurice Richard scored his record 50 goals. Sparked by Durnan's netminding and Richard's scoring,

the Canadiens lost only five of 50 games in winning the NHL pennant and then skated off with the Stanley Cup.

A big, friendly man who packed 200 pounds on his 6-foot-2 frame, Durnan soon found that the pressures that eventually engulf every major-league goalie were ruining his health. "It got so bad that I couldn't sleep on the night before a game," he said. "I couldn't keep my meals down. I felt that nothing was worth that kind of agony."

Injuries—another occupational hazard of goalies—also bothered Durnan. Late in the 1949–50 season, he suffered a severely-gashed head from an opponent's skate. He recovered in time for the playoffs, but midway through a semifinal series against the New York Rangers he asked to be replaced in the nets.

Bill Durnan had played his last game. In a short span of seven years in the NHL he had

accomplished great feats and won many awards. His most cherished came in 1964 when he was named to the Hockey Hall of Fame.

TONY ESPOSITO

Tony Esposito becomes rueful when he recalls what it was like growing up in Sault Ste. Marie, Ontario, with his brother Phil. "It was always 'Phil did this' and 'Phil did that' and it used to make me feel awful inferior," the younger Esposito said.

That was back in the late 1950s when the Espositos were teenagers. Everybody was predicting hockey stardom for Phil Esposito, while Tony's future was slightly blurred. He even quit hockey for one year and concentrated on high school football.

Tony Esposito shrugged off that inferior feeling once he reached the National Hockey League. For while Phil was setting scoring records with the Boston Bruins, his brother developed into an All-Star goalie with the Chicago Black Hawks. In time, they became one of hockey's most famous brother combinations.

The road Tony Esposito followed to stardom took several twists—all of them fortuitous. When he graduated from high school, he turned down a football scholarship to a major U.S. college ("I can't even remember the name of the school now") and accepted a hockey scholarship to Michigan Tech. He helped Michigan Tech win the NCAA championship in 1965, was named to the All-America team and was drafted by the Montreal Canadiens.

Esposito turned pro in 1967 and spent a season with the Vancouver team of the Western League. The following season, he was with Houston of the Central League when the Canadiens encountered a manpower shortage among their goalies. Gump Worsley was hospitalized and Rogie Vachon suffered a broken hand. Esposito was called up from Houston. He made his first NHL start against brother Phil

« Tony Esposito

and the Bruins at Boston Garden on December 5, 1968.

It was a classic confrontation—the first time the Espositos opposed each other since their street-hockey days in Sault Ste. Marie. "I think I was more nervous than Tony that night," Phil recalled. "In fact, it was probably the most frightful game of my entire career. I had been a pro since 1962 and was in my sixth season in the NHL. I was an established player, getting ready to shoot pucks at my own brother, who had been in the league only a week."

In the Montreal dressing room, coach Claude Ruel was advising Tony Esposito to relax. "But how could I relax?" Tony said. "I was about to face the Bruins and my own brother, who was then tearing the league apart. I wondered how I would react if Phil skated in on me and fired one of his wicked shots."

It didn't take Phil long to test his brother. He scored with eight minutes gone in the opening period, added a third-period goal, and the game ended in a 2–2 tie. Poetic justice.

Two months later, Tony Esposito was back in the minors—even though he had allowed only 32 goals in 13 appearances with the Canadiens. But during the NHL meetings in Montreal, on June 11, 1969, the Black Hawks plucked Tony off Montreal's unprotected list for the $30,000 draft price. It was one of the best investments the Black Hawks ever made.

Tony enjoyed a brilliant first season with Chicago. He won the Vezina Trophy with a 2.17 goals-allowed average, established a league record with 15 shutouts, was named to the All-Star team and won the Calder (Rookie of the Year) Trophy.

He went on to earn a share of the Vezina on two other occasions, was named to the first or second All-Star team four more times, and helped the Black Hawks win four straight division titles (a total of nine through 1983).

Tony Esposito also earned a reputation as a workhorse (he averaged 60 games a season) and as a solid playoff performer (3.09 average

Glenn Hall

in 99 games). He retired in 1984 and was elected to the Hall of Fame in 1988.

Esposito was named general manager of the Pittsburgh Penguins in 1988 and was succeeded by Craig Patrick midway through the 1989–90 season.

GLENN HALL

Glenn Hall once offered a terse explanation of what it is like to be a major-league goaltender. "Playing goal is a winter of torture for me," he said. "I often look at those guys who can whistle and laugh before a game and shake my head. You'd think they didn't have a care in the world. Me? I'm plain miserable before every game."

Hall's main problem was a nervous stomach. Early in his career he used to become physically ill just sitting in the locker room waiting for a game to start. The attacks became

less frequent as he grew older, but the butterflies were always there.

Despite these pregame seizures of anxiety, Hall once played 502 consecutive games in the National Hockey League. He launched the streak in his first full season in the league in 1955–56 when he played all 70 games with the Detroit Red Wings. He didn't miss a game with Detroit the following season, then moved on to Chicago, where he put in five additional 70-game campaigns before the string was finally snapped in November 1962.

Hall was born and raised in Humboldt, Saskatchewan, a railway center, where he learned to tend goal on outdoor rinks. He turned pro with the old Indianapolis team in the American Hockey League in 1951, then put in three seasons with Edmonton of the Western League before moving up to the Red Wings. He was an immediate success with

Detroit, winning the Calder Trophy as the NHL's top rookie in 1956.

After two seasons with the Red Wings, he was sent to the Black Hawks in the same celebrated six-player trade that put Hall of Famer Ted Lindsay in a Chicago uniform. During 10 years with the Black Hawks, Hall won the Vezina Trophy as the league's outstanding goalie three times and was named to the All-Star first team five times.

He reached his peak in the spring of 1961 when the Black Hawks won the Stanley Cup championship for the first time in 23 years. In the semifinals against Montreal he was at his acrobatic best, holding the Canadiens scoreless for 135 minutes and 26 seconds at one stage of the series. And that Montreal team boasted such feared sharpshooters as Jean Beliveau, Bernie Geoffrion, Dickie Moore and Henri Richard.

At the end of each season, Hall would advise the Black Hawks that he was considering retiring, but the lure of a fatter contract would always prompt him to change his mind. Then, once the season had started, he would have further doubts. "Plenty of times I'm tempted to climb into my car and head for home," he confessed.

When the St. Louis Blues plucked Hall from Chicago in hockey's first expansion draft in 1967, he was ready to quit again and become a gentleman farmer in Edmonton, Alberta. He was then 36 years old. However, the promise of the largest salary ever paid a goaltender at that time—an estimated $45,000—encouraged him to leave his 160-acre farm for St. Louis.

Hall's great goaltending led the expansion club into the finals of the 1968 Stanley Cup playoffs against Montreal. The Blues were defeated in four straight games, all of which were decided by one goal. But Hall won the Conn Smythe Trophy as the outstanding performer in the playoffs.

Then, in 1968–69 he teamed with Jacques Plante to win his third Vezina Trophy and earned his 11th All-Star team berth in 14 NHL seasons. He hung up his skates at the end of the 1970–71 season.

JACQUES PLANTE

From a 50-cents-per-game goaltender with a factory team in Quebec to a $35,000-a-year All-Star in the National Hockey League was the road Jacques Plante traveled during a playing career that spanned more than two decades.

It all started back in Plante's home town of Shawinigan Falls, Quebec, when he was 15 years old. "I was playing goal for a factory team," he recalled. "We didn't get paid, so one day my father suggested that I ask the coach for some money. The coach agreed to give me 50 cents a game if I didn't tell any of the other players about it.

"Even 50 cents meant a lot to me in those days. I was the oldest of 11 children. We couldn't afford a radio . . . or luxuries of any kind. The only time we had soft drinks was at Christmas."

Plante went on from there to earn $85 a week as a netminder for Quebec City in a junior amateur league and turned pro with the Montreal Royals in the old Quebec Senior League at the age of 22 in 1951. He made his NHL debut the following season with the Montreal Canadiens in a Stanley Cup playoff game at Chicago.

That first game with the Canadiens is still stamped in Plante's memory. "I was so nervous I couldn't tie my skates," he said. But he shut out the Black Hawks, 3–0. Jacques Plante was on his way to becoming one of the highest-salaried goalies in pro hockey.

He spent 10 glorious years with the Canadiens, helping them to five straight Stanley Cup championships (1956 through 1960). He won the Vezina Trophy as the league's top netminder a record-tying six times (five in a row) and was a member of the NHL All-Star team six times. In 1962, he became only the fourth goaltender in NHL history to win the Hart (Most Valuable Player) Trophy.

Plante's flair for the dramatic and his inventiveness also marked his career at Montreal. He became a roving goalie early in his career ("One of the amateur teams I played for was so bad I had to always chase the puck behind

Jacques Plante

the cage''), and he perfected this art with the Canadiens.

He also will be remembered as the man who popularized the goalie mask in the NHL. It happened in a game against the New York Rangers on November 1, 1959. Struck in the face by an Andy Bathgate shot, he went to the dressing room, had the wound stitched, and then returned to the ice wearing a cream-colored plastic face mask. Before long, most pro goalies adopted the mask as part of their equipment.

Plante was traded to New York in 1963, spent a year and a half with the Rangers and then retired to become a salesman with a Canadian brewery. In 1968, the St. Louis Blues offered him $35,000 to make a comeback. The lanky French-Canadian, approaching his 40th birthday, couldn't resist the offer. He packed his pads and his mask and moved to St. Louis, where he shared the goaltending with 37-year-old Glenn Hall. Together, they won the Vezina Trophy and led the Blues to two consecutive West titles.

Then he was sold to Toronto in 1970 and spent three seasons with the Maple Leafs. In March 1973, Boston, looking for playoff help, purchased the 44-year-old goalie from the Leafs. He ended his career with Edmonton in the WHA in 1974–75.

TERRY SAWCHUK

Terry Sawchuk used to quote that old nursery rhyme which insisted ''Sticks and stones may break my bones, but names will never harm me.'' Only in Sawchuk's case it was sticks and pucks which broke his bones. And the names that people called him did hurt.

In more than two decades of professional hockey, Sawchuk overcame the following inju-

Terry Sawchuk

ries and ailments to earn his place among hockey's top 10 goalies: a broken right arm that didn't heal properly and wound up inches shorter than his left arm, severed hand tendons, a fractured instep, infectious mononucleosis, punctured lungs, ruptured discs, bone chips in his elbows that required three operations, a ruptured appendix and innumerable cuts on his face and body, one of which almost cost him the sight in his right eye.

But the injury that hurt the most involved his pride. It happened in 1956 when he left the Boston Bruins in midseason after his bout with mononucleosis. "Those Boston reporters called me everything in the book, including a quitter," he said. "It was so bad I threatened to sue four newspapers for libel. I didn't go through with it, though. I guess those guys have to make a living, too."

He experienced his first pains of anguish when he was 10 years old back home in Winnipeg, Manitoba. His older brother, Mike, a goalie, developed a heart murmur and died. Terry inherited Mike's goalie pads and seven

years later (1947) he broke into professional hockey as a fuzzy-cheeked netminder with Omaha of the United States Hockey League. He won the league's rookie award that season, spent the next two years in the American Hockey League and then joined Detroit in 1950.

Sawchuk's unorthodox, gorilla-like crouch in the nets immediately captured the imagination of Detroit fans. It also helped him capture many awards. He won the Vezina Trophy, awarded to the NHL's most proficient goaltender, three times and shared a fourth. His goals-against average was less than two per game in each of his first five seasons with Detroit.

The Red Wings traded Sawchuk to the Bruins in 1955, reacquired him two years later and then lost him to Toronto in the draft in 1964. He was picked up by Los Angeles in the 1967 expansion draft and a year later returned to Detroit, then went to New York for the 1969–70 season.

Hailed as the only NHL goalie to record more than 100 career shutouts, Sawchuk credited most of his success to his crouching

style. "When I'm crouching low, I can keep better track of the puck through the players' legs on screen shots," he explained.

Ironically, this doughty figure who had survived many injuries on the ice died as a result of an off-the-ice incident in May 1970.

GEORGES VEZINA

Goaltending, as Georges Vezina knew it in the first quarter of the century, was a different art than it is today. He played when a netminder was not permitted to sprawl on the ice to block shots. So Georges Vezina stood straight and tall in front of his net during a brilliant 15-year career with the Montreal Canadiens from 1910 to 1925.

Vezina was a product of the northlands of Quebec. He was born in 1887 in the lumber city of Chicoutimi on the Saguenay River. He was 23 years old and playing goal for an amateur team in Chicoutimi when he first came to the attention of the Canadiens.

It was in February 1910, when the Canadiens made an exhibition tour of the Province of Quebec. They were then kingpins of the National Association of Hockey, a forerunner of the National Hockey League. A game was arranged between Montreal's great pros and the Chicoutimi amateurs led by Vezina. However, the gangling, six-foot netminder didn't play like an amateur. He shut out the powerful Canadiens. In the fall of that same year, Vezina was playing for Montreal.

He went on to become one of Montreal's most valuable and loved players. With Vezina guarding the nets, the Canadiens won the NHA championship twice, the NHL regular-season title three times and the Stanley Cup twice.

The most impressive part of Vezina's game was his coolness. In time, he became known throughout the NHL as the "Chicoutimi Cucumber." Even while the action swirled around him, he moved with a tireless, quiet dignity. In one historic game between Montreal and Ottawa, with the league championship

《 *Georges Vezina*

awaiting the victor, the poker-faced Vezina turned back 78 of 79 shots.

He was also known as Montreal's "Silent Habitant," a man of few words who never complained. His whole life revolved around his large family (he was the father of 22 children), yet even those in his own household did not know he was fighting for his life when he played his last game on November 28, 1925.

The Canadiens' opponent in the old Mt. Royal Arena in Montreal that night was Pittsburgh. After a scoreless first period, Vezina left the ice bleeding from the mouth. He collapsed in the dressing room, returned for the start of the second period, then collapsed again and had to leave the game. Only then did his family and friends learn he had tuberculosis. Four months later, at the age of 39, he passed away.

The memory of Georges Vezina, the quiet man, is perpetuated in the trophy awarded each year to the NHL's outstanding goaltender. It is an impressive trophy—almost as impressive as the Hall of Famer it honors.

LORNE (GUMP) WORSLEY

A friend once asked Gump Worsley why he never wore a mask while tending goal in the slapshot world of the National Hockey League. The Gumper smiled impishly and answered, "My face is my mask."

Worsley was an enigma. He thought nothing of standing up barefaced against the booming shots NHL players fired his way. But try and get him in an airplane and Worsley would break out in a cold sweat. The Gumper had an abiding distrust of air travel.

An unlikely looking athlete, the crew-cut, pint-sized goalie brought a perfect temperament to his job. He was a cherubic happy-go-lucky soul who never let his nerve-wracking job get the best of him . . . until his team had to fly from one city to another.

Worsley's fear of flying dated back to his amateur hockey days when he was with the New York Rovers. On a return flight from Milwaukee, one of the plane's engines caught

Gump Worsley

fire and forced an emergency landing. The players survived but Worsley's psyche didn't. After that experience, the Gump suffered terribly every time he stepped into a plane. He would sit on the aisle, clench the armrests as tightly as he could and hang on for dear life. "It's the one time I don't talk," said Worsley. "I'm too scared to say anything.

Worsley was born in Montreal and grew up in a tough end of town where his buddies decided he looked like comic-strip character Andy Gump and tagged him with that nickname. Gump was 20 when he turned pro and two years later he found himself guarding goal for the otherwise defenseless New York Rangers.

Night after distressing night, Worsley would skate out to meet 40-shot and 50-shot onslaughts from the opposition. Once a newsman asked the New York goalie which team gave him the most trouble. Worsley never

broke stride, answering quickly, "The Rangers."

New York's coach in those days was fiery Phil Watson. After a bad performance by his club, Watson started blasting his players publicly. He accused Worsley, a plump little soul, of having "a beer belly." Gump bristled at that crack. "He should know better than that," snapped the goalie. "He knows I only drink Scotch."

Worsley's career took an odd twist in 1963 when, after a decade in the shooting gallery at New York, he was traded to Montreal's defense-oriented Canadiens. After his experiences with the Rangers, this was a piece of cake for the Gumper. He subsequently shared two Vezina Trophies and helped the Canadiens to four Stanley Cups.

Worsley was pushing 35 and had been playing pro hockey for 15 years when he

sipped champagne from the Stanley Cup for the first time in 1965. He was not supposed to start in the final game for the Canadiens against the Black Hawks, but coach Toe Blake changed his mind at the last minute and inserted Worsley into the lineup. Gump responded by shutting out the Hawks, 4–0.

"Nothing has ever matched that thrill," Worsley said. "The first Cup victory is always the biggest moment in a hockey player's life. Many a thought raced through my mind that night as we shook hands at center ice. I remembered the old days with the Rangers and the trips back to the minors and I was glad I didn't quit before I got a chance to play with a championship team."

Early in the 1969–70 season, Worsley suffered a nervous breakdown and was idle for several months. Then Minnesota obtained the rights to negotiate with the 40-year-old goalie and he was lured back in February 1970. Playing with the enthusiasm of a rookie, Worsley helped the North Stars into the play-offs for three straight years.

He finally donned a mask during parts of the North Stars' 1973–74 season—his last as a player. His professional career spanned 24 seasons. He had a 2.91 goals-allowed average for 860 regular-season games in the NHL (43 shutouts) and was elected to the Hockey Hall of Fame in 1980.

THE STANLEY CUP

Lord Stanley, the Canadian Governor-General who donated the Stanley Cup in 1893, ironically never saw a Cup game.

One of his aides, Lord Kilcoursie, had more than a passing role in Lord Stanley's decision to initiate the Cup. Lord Kilcoursie played hockey with Lord Stanley's sons and his deep interest in the sport had spread to his boss.

Lord Stanley's guidelines for presenting the Cup were simple enough. It was to go to the leading hockey club in Canada.

In 1893, the first Cup went to the Montreal Amateur Athletic Association team, champion of the Amateur Hockey Association of Canada. There was no playoff; Montreal AAA had simply won the most games in the regular season.

In 1894, Montreal AAA defeated the Montreal Victorias, 3–2, and then the Ottawa Generals, 3–1, in a one-game final of the first-ever playoffs to capture the Cup. But Lord Stanley was gone. He had returned to his native England.

He designated two Ottawa sportsmen—Sheriff Sweetland and P.D. Ross—as trustees of the Cup, and they sifted through the various challenges from leagues all over Canada which wanted their chance to play for the trophy.

In those early days, hockey was an amateur sport played by seven-man teams on outdoor rinks built for curling. Two portable poles, embedded in the ice with no net between them, constituted the goals, and goal judges stood behind these makeshift targets with no padding to protect them. Conditions were truly primitive and it was an appropriate setting for the most fantastic Cup challenge in history—that of Dawson City in 1905.

The Ottawa Silver Seven were the Cup holders from 1903 through 1906, successfully defending it against nine challenges from all parts of Canada. But none of the challengers could match the 1905 Yukon team's effort.

Colonel Joe Boyle, a wealthy Dawson City prospector, bankrolled the team's 23-day journey to Ottawa. The happy-go-lucky gold diggers traveled by dog sled, boat and train to cover the 4,400 miles. They made 46 miles by dogs the first day and 41 the second. Some of the players were forced to remove their boots because of blistered feet on the third day, with the temperature dropping to 20 below zero.

They missed a boat connection at Skagway by two hours and had to wait five days at the docks before catching another boat from Seattle to Vancouver. Then they took a train on to

Ottawa. They arrived in Ottawa, January 12, 1905, a day before the best-of-three series against the Silver Seven was to begin.

It was all for naught. The team that traveled the farthest to try for the Cup suffered the most lopsided elimination. The Klondikers lost the first game, 9–2, and the second and final game, 23–3. Frank McGee of Ottawa scored an unbelievable 14 goals in the second-game rout—eight of them in a span of eight minutes, twenty seconds. What makes it truly unbelievable is that McGee was blind in one eye.

The year before the Klondike challenge, Ottawa had beaten off the Brandon Wheat Kings and the only notable thing about that

challenge was the fact that Brandon goalie Doug Morrison incurred a penalty and was replaced in the nets by a teammate, Lester Patrick. A quarter of a century later, Patrick, then 44 and coach of the New York Rangers, would duplicate the feat and take over in goal during another Stanley Cup game.

The prestige of fielding a winning hockey team—possibly a Stanley Cup winner—was quite tantalizing to Canadian communities and the better players found themselves being offered fat contracts. Hockey's amateur posture was disappearing, and soon the Stanley Cup's would, too.

By 1907 the Eastern Canadian Amateur Hockey Association had deleted the "Amateur" from its name. And in 1910 when the National Hockey Association—forerunner of the National Hockey League—came into existence, the Stanley Cup became the goal of professional hockey teams.

When Lester Patrick and his brother Frank moved westward to organize the Pacific Coast Hockey League in 1913, a Stanley Cup series matching East and West was inaugurated. After the PCHL went out of business in 1927, the trophy became exclusively an NHL award.

Although there were no American teams in the NHL until 1924, it was seven years earlier that a U.S. team first captured the cherished Cup. In 1917, the Seattle Metropolitans, coached by Pete Muldoon, beat the Montreal Canadiens in the Cup series and transported the Cup below the border for the first time.

Through the years, the Cup has had varied adventures. It has been the most sought and at the same time most neglected trophy in sport.

Shortly after the turn of the century, following one of the Ottawa Silver Seven's several successful defenses, some members of the team were lugging the trophy back from a victory banquet. For kicks no doubt, it was suggested by one of the players that he could successfully boot the mug into Rideau Canal. And just to prove his point, he did.

« The Montreal Shamrocks won their first Stanley Cup in 1899.

Ottawa right wing Jack Darragh played on four Stanley Cup championship teams, the first in 1911.

Goalie Paddy Moran helped the Quebec Bulldogs win back-to-back Cups in 1912 and 1913.

Russell (Barney) Stanley wears a Calgary Tigers' uniform here, but in 1915 he played for the Cup-winning Vancouver Millionaires.

Strong defense of Red Kelly (left) enabled Detroit to defeat Montreal for the Cup in 1954.

The next day, when they realized what they had done, the Ottawa players rushed back to Rideau. Luckily the canal had been frozen over, and there, slightly the worse for wear but still intact, sat the Stanley Cup.

Shortly after that, the Cup did a brief turn as a flower pot. That happened when the Montreal team gathered around the silver mug for a picture in a local photographer's studio. When the posing was over, the players left the studio, and the Cup as well.

The photographer's mother found the deserted silverware and, not knowing its significance, filled it with earth and planted geraniums. Eventually, the photographer discovered it and rescued Lord Stanley's Cup.

In 1924, the Montreal Canadiens were celebrating their Cup victory at a downtown hotel when it was suggested that the celebration be moved to owner Leo Dandurand's home. A group of players, the Cup in tow, started out driving for Dandurand's home when a tire blew out. In the course of changing the tire, the Cup somehow was removed from the car and placed on the sidewalk. When the repairs were completed, the celebrants took off for Dandurand's again.

It wasn't until the Canadiens reached their destination that they missed the Cup. They scurried back to the spot and, sure enough, sitting there undisturbed, waiting for them, was the Cup.

Another time, an official of the Kenora Thistles stormed out of a meeting of hockey executives with the Cup under his arm. Angered over the refusal of his colleagues to authorize the use of two borrowed players during a Cup series, he was prepared to act drastically.

"Where are you going with the Cup?" he was asked. He replied quite simply: "I'm going to throw it in the Lake of Woods."

There are those who swear he would have, too, had compromise not been reached on the use of the two disputed players.

Once, during the Ottawa Silver Seven's Cup reign, one member of the team decided to cap off a celebration by taking the mug home with him to show to his mother. The idea wasn't terribly popular with his teammates and in the ensuing scuffle, the Cup was tossed over a cemetery fence.

In 1962, the Cup was on display in the lobby of the Chicago Stadium while the Black Hawks and Montreal Canadiens battled for it

on the ice inside the arena. When Chicago took a commanding edge in the game, a Montreal fan left his seat. He went to the lobby, broke into the showcase, lifted out the Cup and was on his way out the door before he was stopped. He, too, had a simple explanation.

"I was taking it back to Montreal, where it belongs," he said.

Stanley Cup play is hockey's World Series. Through the years it has been packed with individual and team heroics that live on and even tend to expand as the years go by. The stories include some of hockey's most cherished lore.

• **1919**—The only time no decision was reached. The Montreal Canadiens had traveled west to play Seattle for the Cup and the teams split the first five games (one tie). But the great flu epidemic had riddled the ranks of the Montreal team, leaving five players bedridden. The series was halted because of the wave of illness and no Cup champion was declared. Joe Hall, one of the Canadiens' stars, never recovered and died in a Seattle hospital.

• **1922**—When Lester Patrick, boss of the Vancouver team, allowed crippled Toronto to use defenseman Eddie Gerard as an emergency replacement. Gerard starred in two straight Toronto victories that cost Vancouver the Cup. Six years later, Patrick, the New York Ranger coach, went to Gerard, then general manager of the Montreal Maroons, and asked permission to use a borrowed goaltender when regular Lorne Chabot was injured. Gerard refused and Patrick, at age 44, went in to play goal, won the game and the inspired Rangers went on to take the Cup.

• **1936**—When the longest game in hockey history was played. Modere Bruneteau, a rookie who had scored only two goals during the regular season for Detroit, broke the scoreless tie against the Montreal Maroons with the only goal of the night at 16:30 of the

« *Gump Worsley in goal and Jacques Laperriere on defense were major factors as Montreal swept Boston in 1968. Phil Esposito (7) and Ted Green (right) are the Bruins.*

Henri Richard grasps hockey's Holy Grail after Montreal downed Chicago in the 1973 finals.

sixth overtime period, ending 176 minutes, 30 seconds of scoreless hockey.

• **1939**—When Mel (Sudden Death) Hill of Boston personally slew the Rangers. Hill, a Ranger reject, scored the winning overtime goal in three of the Bruins' four victories over New York that year.

• **1942**—When the Detroit Red Wings beat Toronto in the first three games and with their mouths watering for a taste of Stanley Cup champagne, went into an incredible collapse, losing four straight, the series and the Cup.

• **1951**—When Toronto beat Montreal in five games, all of them going into overtime. The winning goal in the final game was scored by defenseman Bill Barilko, who was in midair when his shot went in. It was the last goal he ever scored. A few months later, Barilko died in a plane wreck.

• **1952**—When Detroit swept through to the Stanley Cup in eight straight games and

It's all over: Bobby Nystrom has just beaten Philadelphia goalie Pete Peeters with the overtime goal that brought the New York Islanders their first Stanley Cup in 1980.

goalie Terry Sawchuk allowed a total of just five goals for an astounding 0.62 Stanley Cup average. Sawchuk's feat overshadowed Montreal's Maurice Richard, who emerged from a first-aid room with six stitches holding his forehead together to score the Canadiens' winning goal against Boston in the semifinals.

● **1964**—When Toronto defenseman Bob Baun was carried off the ice on a stretcher during the sixth game against Detroit when his right leg crumpled under him. Baun demanded that the doctors pump some pain-killer into the leg and he skated out to score the winning, sudden-death goal. Only after the Leafs took game No. 7 and the Cup, did the defenseman consent to have X-rays taken. That's when they found a broken bone in his ankle.

《 *Captain Bobby Clarke leads triumphant Flyers after Philadelphia ousted Buffalo for the Cup in 1975.*

● **1980**—When the Islanders' Bob Nystrom scored in overtime of the sixth game to defeat Philadelphia and bring the New York area its first Stanley Cup in four decades. The Islanders won six of seven overtime games in the march to their first Cup.

● **1981**—When Butch Goring, who scored five goals in the finals, three in one game, to become playoff MVP, and record-setting Mike Bossy wrapped up the Islanders' second straight Cup in a five-game series against Minnesota.

● **1982**—When Mike Bossy scored 17 goals in the playoffs, seven in a four-game finals wipeout of Vancouver, to make it three Cups in a row for the Islanders.

● **1983**—When Islander goalie Billy Smith, who hadn't won a game for two months in the regular season, caught fire in the

It's no-holds-barred for Calgary's Doug Risebrough (left) and Montreal's Mats Naslund in the 1986 finals. The Canadiens settled things by winning four in a row after losing the first game.

playoffs. He limited the Oilers to six goals in the finals as the Islanders swept the series for their fourth straight Cup.

• **1984**—When Edmonton, led by Wayne Gretzky and Mark Messier, and in only its fifth NHL season, captured the Cup for the first time, breaking the Islanders' string of four.

• **1985**—When Wayne Gretzky won his first Conn Smythe Trophy as playoff MVP as Edmonton downed Philadelphia for its second straight Stanley Cup.

• **1986**—When Montreal won its first Cup since 1979, defeating Calgary in five games. Mats Naslund topped the Canadiens in playoff scoring and 20-year-old goaltender Patrick Roy, Rookie of the Year, became the youngest winner of the Conn Smythe Trophy as playoff MVP.

• **1987**—When the Islanders' Pat LaFontaine scored the game-winning goal in the fourth overtime of Game 7 of the Patrick Division semifinal against Washington. But it was Edmonton which emerged as the Cupholder over Philadelphia in seven games.

• **1988**—When the lights went out in Boston Garden and Game 4 against Edmonton had to be suspended with the score 3–3. The lights shone brightly for the Oilers when the series went back to Edmonton, where Wayne Gretzky led the way to a sweep of the Bruins.

• **1989**—When Calgary, paced by goaltender Mike Vernon and defenseman Al MacInnis, captured its first Cup, vanquishing Montreal in six games.

• **1990**—When ex-Bruin goaltender Bill Ranford got his chance with Edmonton in the

Bill Ranford's saves earned him MVP honors as Edmonton vanquished Boston for the Cup in 1990.

playoffs and wound up as the MVP after stopping his old Boston team in the finals.

• **1991**—When Mario Lemieux capped a spectacular comeback from injury by leading Pittsburgh to its first Cup. Vanquishing Minnesota in the finals, the Penguins did it all after losing the first game of every playoff series.

• **1992**—When the Penguins, with Mario Lemieux, who came back after breaking his hand in the Patrick Division finals, and Jaromir Jagr leading the way, swept the Blackhawks to win their second Cup in a row.

STANLEY CUP WINNERS

Season	Champions	Manager	Coach
1892–93	Montreal A.A.A.	————	
1894–95	Montreal Victorias		Mike Grant*
1895–96	Winnipeg Victorias		
1896–97	Montreal Victorias		Mike Grant*
1897–98	Montreal Victorias		F. Richardson
1898–99	Montreal Shamrocks	————	H. J. Trihey*
1899–1900	Montreal Shamrocks	————	H. J. Trihey*
1900–01	Winnipeg Victorias	————	
1901–02	Montreal A.A.A.	————	R. R. Boon*
1902–03	Ottawa Silver Seven	————	A. T. Smith
1903–04	Ottawa Silver Seven	————	A. T. Smith
1904–05	Ottawa Silver Seven	————	A. T. Smith
1905–06	Montreal Wanderers	————	————
# 1906–07	Kenora Thistles (January)	F. A. Hudson	Tommy Phillips*
# 1906–07	Montreal Wanderers (March)	R. R. Boon	Cecil Blachford
1907–08	Montreal Wanderers	R. R. Boon	Cecil Blachford
1908–09	Ottawa Senators	————	Bruce Stuart*
1909–10	Montreal Wanderers	R. R. Boon	Pud Glass*
1910–11	Ottawa Senators	————	Bruce Stuart*
1911–12	Quebec Bulldogs	M. J. Quinn	C. Nolan
** 1912–13	Quebec Bulldogs	M. J. Quinn	Joe Marlowe*
1913–14	Toronto Blue Shirts	Jack Marshall	Scotty Davidson*
1914–15	Vancouver Millionaires	Frank Patrick	Frank Patrick
1915–16	Montreal Canadiens	George Kennedy	George Kennedy
1916–17	Seattle Metropolitans	Pete Muldoon	Pete Muldoon
1917–18	Toronto Arenas	Charlie Querrie	Dick Carroll
*** 1918–19	No champion		

Season	Team	Manager	Coach
1919–20	Ottawa Senators	Tommy Gorman	Pete Green
1920–21	Ottawa Senators	Tommy Gorman	Pete Green
1921–22	Toronto St. Pats	Charlie Querrie	Eddie Powers
1922–23	Ottawa Senators	Tommy Gorman	Pete Green
1923–24	Montreal Canadiens	Leo Dandurand	Leo Dandurand
1924–25	Victoria Cougars	Lester Patrick	Lester Patrick
1925–26	Montreal Maroons	Eddie Gerard	Eddie Gerard
1926–27	Ottawa Senators	Dave Gill	Dave Gill
1927–28	New York Rangers	Lester Patrick	Lester Patrick
1928–29	Boston Bruins	Art Ross	Cy Denneny
1929–30	Montreal Canadiens	Cecil Hart	Cecil Hart
1930–31	Montreal Canadiens	Cecil Hart	Cecil Hart
1931–32	Toronto Maple Leafs	Conn Smythe	Dick Irvin
1932–33	New York Rangers	Lester Patrick	Lester Patrick
1933–34	Chicago Black Hawks	Tommy Gorman	Tommy Gorman
1934–35	Montreal Maroons	Tommy Gorman	Tommy Gorman
1935–36	Detroit Red Wings	Jack Adams	Jack Adams
1936–37	Detroit Red Wings	Jack Adams	Jack Adams
1937–38	Chicago Black Hawks	Bill Stewart	Bill Stewart
1938–39	Boston Bruins	Art Ross	Art Ross
1939–40	New York Rangers	Lester Patrick	Frank Boucher
1940–41	Boston Bruins	Art Ross	Cooney Weiland
1941–42	Toronto Maple Leafs	Conn Smythe	Hap Day
1942–43	Detroit Red Wings	Jack Adams	Jack Adams
1943–44	Montreal Canadiens	Tommy Gorman	Dick Irvin
1944–45	Toronto Maple Leafs	Conn Smythe	Hap Day
1945–46	Montreal Canadiens	Tommy Gorman	Dick Irvin
1946–47	Toronto Maple Leafs	Conn Smythe	Hap Day
1947–78	Toronto Maple Leafs	Conn Smythe	Hap Day
1948–49	Toronto Maple Leafs	Conn Smythe	Hap Day
1949–50	Detroit Red Wings	Jack Adams	Tommy Ivan
1950–51	Toronto Maple Leafs	Conn Smythe	Joe Primeau
1951–52	Detroit Red Wings	Jack Adams	Tommy Ivan
1952–53	Montreal Canadiens	Frank Selke	Dick Irvin
1953–54	Detroit Red Wings	Jack Adams	Tommy Ivan
1954–55	Detroit Red Wings	Jack Adams	Jimmy Skinner
1955–56	Montreal Canadiens	Frank Selke	Toe Blake
1956–57	Montreal Canadiens	Frank Selke	Toe Blake
1957–58	Montreal Canadiens	Frank Selke	Toe Blake
1958–59	Montreal Canadiens	Frank Selke	Toe Blake
1959–60	Montreal Canadiens	Frank Selke	Toe Blake
1960–61	Chicago Black Hawks	Tommy Ivan	Rudy Pilous
1961–62	Toronto Maple Leafs	Punch Imlach	Punch Imlach
1962–63	Toronto Maple Leafs	Punch Imlach	Punch Imlach
1963–64	Toronto Maple Leafs	Punch Imlach	Punch Imlach
1964–65	Montreal Canadiens	Sam Pollock	Toe Blake
1965–66	Montreal Canadiens	Sam Pollock	Toe Blake
1966–67	Toronto Maple Leafs	Punch Imlach	Punch Imlach
1967–68	Montreal Canadiens	Sam Pollock	Toe Blake
1968–69	Montreal Canadiens	Sam Pollock	Claude Ruel
1969–70	Boston Bruins	Milt Schmidt	Harry Sinden
1970–71	Montreal Canadiens	Sam Pollock	Al MacNeil
1971–72	Boston Bruins	Milt Schmidt	Tom Johnson
1972–73	Montreal Canadiens	Sam Pollock	Scotty Bowman
1973–74	Philadelphia Flyers	Keith Allen	Fred Shero
1974–75	Philadelphia Flyers	Keith Allen	Fred Shero
1975–76	Montreal Canadiens	Sam Pollock	Scotty Bowman
1976–77	Montreal Canadiens	Sam Pollock	Scotty Bowman
1977–78	Montreal Canadiens	Sam Pollock	Scotty Bowman
1978–79	Montreal Canadiens	Irving Grundman	Scotty Bowman
1979–80	New York Islanders	Bill Torrey	Al Arbour
1980–81	New York Islanders	Bill Torrey	Al Arbour
1981–82	New York Islanders	Bill Torrey	Al Arbour
1982–83	New York Islanders	Bill Torrey	Al Arbour
1983–84	Edmonton Oilers	Glen Sather	Glen Sather
1984–85	Edmonton Oilers	Glen Sather	Glen Sather
1985–86	Montreal Canadiens	Serge Savard	Jean Perron
1986–87	Edmonton Oilers	Glen Sather	Glen Sather
1987–88	Edmonton Oilers	Glen Sather	Glen Sather
1988–89	Calgary Flames	Cliff Fletcher	Terry Crisp
1989–90	Edmonton Oilers	Glen Sather	John Muckler
1990–91	Pittsburgh Penguins	Craig Patrick	Bob Johnson
1991–92	Pittsburgh Penguins	Craig Patrick	Scotty Bowman

* Indicates captain. In the early years the teams were frequently run by the captain.

** Victoria defeated Quebec in challenge series. No official recognition.

*** In the spring of 1919 the Montreal Canadiens traveled to Seattle to meet Seattle, PCHL champions. After five games had been played—teams were tied at two wins each and one tie—the series was called off by the local Department of Health because of the influenza epidemic that hospitalized a number of Montreal players, including Joe Hall, who died from it.

Split season

STANLEY CUP PLAYOFF RECORDS

TEAM

Most Stanley Cup championships—22, Montreal Canadiens.

Most final series appearances—32, Montreal Canadiens.

Most years in playoffs—67, Montreal Canadiens.

Most consecutive Stanley Cup championships—5, Montreal Canadiens (1956–60).

Most consecutive final series appearances—10, Montreal (1951–60).

Most consecutive playoff appearances—25, Boston (1968–92).

Most goals, both teams, one series—69, Edmonton 44, Chicago 25, six games, 1985 conference finals.

Most goals, one team, one series—44, Edmonton, vs. Chicago, 1985.

Most goals, both teams, four-game series—36, three times, most recently Edmonton 25, Chicago 11, conference final, 1983.

Most goals, one team, four-game series—28, Boston, vs. St. Louis, semifinal, 1972.

Most goals, both teams, five-game series–52, Edmonton 32, Los Angeles 20, 1987 division semifinal.

Most goals, one team, five-game series—35, Edmonton, vs. Calgary, 1983 division final.

Most goals, both teams, six-game series—69, Edmonton 44, Chicago 25, 1985 conference final.

Most goals, one team, six-game series—44, Edmonton, vs. Chicago, 1985 conference final.

Most goals, both teams, seven-game series—60, Edmonton 33, Calgary 27, 1984 division final.

Most goals, one team, seven-game series—33, three times, most recently, Edmonton, vs. Calgary, 1984 division final.

Fewest goals, both teams, four-game series—9, Toronto 7, Boston 2, 1935 semifinal.

Fewest goals, one team, four-game series—2, Boston, vs. Toronto, 1935 semifinal; Montreal, vs. Detroit, 1952 final.

Fewest goals, both teams, five-game series—11, Montreal Maroons 6, New York Rangers 5, 1928 final.

Fewest goals, one team, five-game series—5, New York Rangers, vs. Montreal Maroons, 1928 final.

Fewest goals, both teams, six-game series—22, Toronto 17, Boston 5, 1951 semifinal.

Fewest goals, one team, six-game series—5, Boston, vs. Toronto, 1951 semifinal.

Fewest goals, both teams, seven-game series—18, Toronto 9, Detroit 9, 1945 final.

Fewest goals, one team, seven-game series—9, Toronto, vs. Detroit, 1945 final; Detroit, vs. Toronto, 1945 Stanley Cup final.

Most goals, both teams, one game—18, Los Angeles 10, Edmonton 8, 1982 division semifinal.

Most goals, one team, one game—13, Edmonton, vs. Los Angeles (3), April 9, 1987.

Most goals, both teams, one period—9, New York Rangers 6, Philadelphia 3, third period, April 24, 1979; Los Angeles 5, Calgary 4, second period, April 10, 1990.

Most goals, one team, one period—7, Montreal Canadiens, vs. Toronto, third period, March 30, 1944, in 11–0 win.

Longest overtime—116 minutes, 30 seconds, Detroit vs. Montreal Maroons at Montreal, March 24–25, 1936. Mud Bruneteau scored at 16:30 of sixth overtime period.

Shortest overtime—9 seconds, Montreal at Calgary, May 18, 1986. Montreal's Brian Skrudland scored to give Canadiens 3–2 win.

Most overtime games, one season—16, 1982 (71 games played).

Fewest overtime games, one season—0, 1963 (16 games played).

Most overtime-game wins, one team, one play-off season—6, New York Islanders, 1980.

Most overtime games, final series—5, Toronto vs. Montreal, 1951.

Most overtime games, semifinal series—4, three times, most recently, St. Louis vs. Minnesota, 1968.

Most consecutive playoff game wins—12, Edmonton (May 15, 1984 to May 9, 1985).

Most consecutive wins, one playoff year—11, Chicago and Pittsburgh, 1992.

Longest playoff losing streak—16 games, Chicago, 1975–80.

Most shutouts, one playoff year, all teams—12, 1992.

Fewest shutouts, one playoff year, all teams—0, 1959 (18 games played).

Most shutouts, both teams, one series—5, Toronto 3, Detroit 2, 1945 final; Toronto 3, Detroit 2, 1950 semifinal.

Most penalties, both teams, one series—219, New Jersey 119 vs. Washington 110, 1988 division final, seven games.

Most penalty minutes, both teams, one series—656, New Jersey 351 vs. Washington 305, 1988 division final, seven games.

Most penalties, one team, one series—119, New Jersey, vs. Washington, 1988 division final.

Most penalty minutes, one team, one series—351, New Jersey, vs. Washington, 1988 division final.

Most penalty minutes, both teams, one game—298, Detroit 152, St. Louis 146, at St. Louis, April 12, 1991.

Most penalties, both teams, one game—66, Detroit 33, St. Louis 33, at St. Louis, April 12, 1991.

Most penalties, one team, one game—33, Detroit and St. Louis, at St. Louis, April 12, 1991.

Most penalty minutes, one team, one game—152, Detroit, at St. Louis, April 12, 1991.

Most penalties, both teams, one period—43, New York Rangers 24, Los Angeles 19, at Los Angeles, first period, April 9, 1981.

Most penalty minutes, both teams, one period—248, New York Islanders 124, Boston 124, at Boston, first period, April 17, 1980.

Most penalties and most penalty minutes, one team, one period—24 penalties, 125 minutes, New York Rangers, at Los Angeles, first period, April 9, 1981.

Most power-play goals, one team, one playoff year—35, Minnesota, 1991.

Most power-play goals, one team, one series—15, New York Islanders, vs. Philadelphia, 1980 final; Minnesota, vs. Chicago, 1991 division semifinal.

Most power-play goals, one team, one game—6, Boston, vs. Toronto, in 10-0 win April 2, 1969.

Most power-play goals, both teams, one game—8, Minnesota 4, St. Louis 4, at Minnesota, April 24, 1991.

Fastest two goals, both teams—5 seconds, Pittsburgh at Buffalo, first period, April 14, 1979. Gil Perreault scored for Buffalo at 12:59 and Jim Hamilton for Pittsburgh at 13:04.

Fastest two goals, one team—5 seconds, Detroit, vs. Chicago, second period, April 11, 1965. Norm Ullman scored at 17:35 and 17:40.

Fastest three goals, both teams—21 seconds, Chicago at Edmonton, third period, May 7, 1985. Chicago's Behn Wilson scored at 19:22, Edmonton's Jari Kurri scored at 19:36 and Edmonton's Glenn Anderson scored at 19:43.

Fastest three goals, one team—23 seconds, Toronto, vs. Atlanta, first period, April 12, 1979. Darryl Sittler scored at 4:04 and again at 4:16 and then Ron Ellis scored at 4:27.

Fastest four goals, one team—2 minutes, 35 seconds, Montreal, vs. Toronto, third period, March 30, 1944. Toe Blake scored at 7:58 and 8:37, Maurice Richard at 9:17 and Ray Getliffe at 10:33 in 11-0 win.

Fastest five goals, one team—3 minutes, 36 seconds, Montreal, vs. Toronto, third period, March 30, 1944. Toe Blake scored at 7:58 and 8:37, Maurice Richard at 9:17, Ray Getliffe at 10:33 and Buddy O'Connor at 11:34 in 11-0 win.

Most shorthanded goals, one team, one playoff year—10, Edmonton, 1983 (16 games).

Most shorthanded goals, one team, one series—5, Edmonton, vs. Calgary, 1983 seven-game division final; New York Rangers, vs. Philadelphia, 1979 five-game quarterfinal.

Most shorthanded goals, one team, one game—3, Boston, at Minnesota, April 11, 1981; New York Islanders, at New York Rangers, April 17, 1983.

Most shorthanded goals, one team, one period—2, 18 times, most recently New York Islanders, at New Jersey, third period, April 14, 1988.

INDIVIDUAL

Most years in playoffs—20, Gordie Howe, Detroit and Hartford; Larry Robinson, Montreal and Los Angeles.

Most consecutive years in playoffs—20, Larry Robinson, Montreal and Los Angeles, 1973-92.

Most playoff games—227, Larry Robinson, Montreal and Los Angeles.

Most points in playoffs—306, Wayne Gretzky, Edmonton and Los Angeles, 95 goals, 211 assists.

Most goals in playoffs—95, Wayne Gretzky, Edmonton and Los Angeles.

Most assists in playoffs—211, Wayne Gretzky, Edmonton and Los Angeles.

Most overtime goals in playoffs—6, Maurice Richard, Montreal.

Most penalty minutes in playoffs—564, Dale Hunter, Quebec and Washington.

Most shorthanded goals in playoffs—13, Mark Messier, Edmonton and New York Rangers.

Most power-play goals in playoffs—35, Mike Bossy, New York Islanders.

Most shutouts in playoffs—15, Clint Benedict, Ottawa and Montreal Maroons.

Most playoff games, goaltender—132, Bill Smith, New York Islanders.

Most points, one playoff year—47, Wayne Gretzky, Edmonton, 1985.

Most goals, one playoff year—19, Reggie Leach, Philadelphia, 1976; Jari Kurri, Edmonton, 1985.

Most assists, one playoff year—31, Wayne Gretzky, Edmonton, 1988.

Most points by a defenseman, one playoff year—37, Paul Coffey, Edmonton, 1985.

Most points by a rookie, one playoff year—21, Dino Ciccarelli, Minnesota, 1981.

Most goals by a defenseman, one playoff year—12, Paul Coffey, Edmonton, 1985.

Most goals by a rookie, one playoff year—14, Dino Ciccarelli, Minnesota, 1981.

Most power-play goals, one playoff year—9, Mike Bossy, New York Islanders, 1981; Cam Neely, Boston, 1991.

Most shorthanded goals, one playoff year—3, five times, most recently Wayne Presley, Chicago, 1989.

Most assists by a defenseman, one playoff year—25, Paul Coffey, Edmonton, 1985.

Most wins by a goaltender, one playoff year—16, Grant Fuhr, Edmonton, 1988;

Mike Vernon, Calgary, 1989; Bill Ranford, Edmonton, 1990, Tom Barrasso, Pittsburgh, 1992.

Most shutouts, one playoff year—4, seven times; most recently, Ken Dryden, Montreal, 1977.

Most consecutive shutouts—3, Clint Benedict, Montreal Maroons, 1926; Frank McCool, Toronto, 1945.

Most points in final series—13, Wayne Gretzky, Edmonton, vs. Boston, 1988.

Most goals in final series—9, Babe Dye, Toronto, vs. Vancouver, 1922.

Most assists in final series—10, Wayne Gretzky, Edmonton, vs. Boston, 1988.

Most points, one game—8, Patrik Sundstrom, New Jersey, vs. Washington, April 22, 1988 (three goals, five assists); Mario Lemieux, Pittsburgh vs. Philadelphia, April 25, 1989 (five goals, three assists).

Most goals, one game—5, Newsy Lalonde, Montreal, vs. Ottawa, March 1, 1919; Maurice Richard, Montreal, vs. Toronto, March 23, 1944; Darryl Sittler, Toronto, vs. Philadelphia, April 22, 1976; Reggie Leach, Philadelphia, vs. Boston, May 6, 1976; Mario Lemieux, Pittsburgh, vs. Philadelphia, April 25, 1989.

Most assists, one game—6, Mikko Leinonen, New York Rangers, vs. Philadelphia, April 8, 1982; Wayne Gretzky, Edmonton, vs. Los Angeles, April 9, 1987.

Most points by a defenseman, one game—6, Paul Coffey, Edmonton, vs. Chicago, May 14, 1985 (one goal, five assists).

Most penalty minutes, one game—42, Dave Schultz, Philadelphia, at Toronto, April 22, 1976.

Most points, one period—4, 11 times, most recently, Mario Lemieux, Pittsburgh vs. Washington, second period, April 23, 1992.

Most goals, one period—4, Tim Kerr, Philadelphia, at New York Rangers, second period, April 13, 1985; Mario Lemieux, Pittsburgh, vs. Philadelphia, first period, April 25, 1989.

Most assists, one period—3, 56 times, most recently, Chris Chelios, Chicago vs. Edmonton, third period, May 18, 1992.

Fastest two goals—5 seconds, Norm Ullman, Detroit, vs. Chicago, April 11, 1965.

Fastest goal from start of game—6 seconds, Don Kozak, Los Angeles, vs. Boston, April 17, 1977.

Fastest goal from start of period—6 seconds, Don Kozak, Los Angeles, vs. Boston, April 17, 1977; Pelle Eklund, Philadelphia, at Pittsburgh, April 25, 1989.

Most three-goal-or-more-games—7, Maurice Richard, Montreal; Wayne Greztky, Edmonton and Los Angeles; Jari Kurri, Edmonton and Los Angeles.

Most three-goal-or-more games, one playoff year—4, Jari Kurri, Edmonton, 1985.

Most three-goal-or-more games, one playoff series—3, Jari Kurri, Edmonton, vs. Chicago, 1985 conference final.

10

HOCKEY'S MEMORABLE MOMENTS

In the more than a half century of the National Hockey League, there have been many memorable moments—individual feats, team performances and rare games. The editor has chosen these unforgettable happenings on ice.

April 7, 1928
MAROONS VS. RANGERS

The New York Rangers entered the finals of the 1928 Stanley Cup playoffs at a distinct disadvantage. Because of previous commitments, their own arena, Madison Square Garden, was unavailable and the entire series had to be played on the home ice of the Montreal Maroons. Montreal took advantage of the situation and won the first game of the best-of-five series, 2–0.

After a scoreless first period in the second game, the outlook appeared even more grim for the orphaned New Yorkers. A few minutes into the second session, Nels Stewart, the big Maroon center who was the greatest scorer of his time, skated in slowly on the New York

《 *At age 44, Lester Patrick donned the goalie's pads in a memorable Stanley Cup game.*

goal and let loose a blistering shot that hit the goalie, Lorne Chabot, in the left eye.

Chabot fell unconscious, with blood dripping down his cheek. The crowd of 12,000 in Montreal's Forum sat silently as he was carried off on a stretcher.

There was no such thing as a substitute goalie in those days. Lester Patrick, a once-great defenseman who served as manager and coach of the Rangers, had only 10 minutes to find a replacement.

Alex Connell, a big-league goalie for Ottawa, was in the stands, but Eddie Gerard, the Maroons' manager, refused to let him play. "If I let you take Connell, it could cost me. Suckers were born yesterday and you're talking to the wrong man. I can't hear you," Gerard laughed.

So Patrick returned to his players and told them they would have to finish the game with a goalie from their own squad. It took Frank Boucher, the irrepressible center, to break the gloom. "How about you playing goal?" he asked.

Patrick, 44 years old and long since retired as a player, demurred. "I'm too old," he protested. But he and his players knew that he had had at least some goaltending experience.

Back in hockey's dark ages, goaltenders when penalized had to serve time in the penalty box like any other player. And one of the other members of the team had to take over goal. On the rare occasions when this was necessary, Patrick drew the assignment. Surveying the desperate situation this night of April 7, 1928, Patrick knew he would have to do it again.

Patrick was actually trembling as his players helped him into more elaborate goalie equipment than he had ever worn before, and, on shaky legs, he skated onto the ice to kick out a few of the easy test shots his players made sure he couldn't miss.

Then he announced he was ready and the Rangers went out to play the most inspired game of their lives. They flattened every Montreal player who dared skate near the nets guarded by their white-haired leader and, 30 seconds into the third period, took a 1–0 lead on a goal by Bill Cook. However, with six minutes to play, Montreal tied the game on a shot by Stewart and it went into overtime.

Frustrated at being stymied by an old man and with the crowd cheering the visitors, the enraged Maroons mounted attack after attack on the Ranger goal. But, after 7:05 of overtime, the clever Boucher stole the puck, broke in alone and scored the winner.

Patrick, in tears, was half-dragged and half-carried off the ice by his players to a tremendous ovation from the crowd.

He didn't attempt an encore. A rookie, Joe Miller, was in goal when the Rangers won two of the next three games to capture the Stanley Cup—the perfect ending for the series in which the gallant Lester Patrick had provided their finest hour.

March 24–25, 1936
RED WINGS VS. MAROONS

The clock in Montreal's Forum the night of March 24, 1936, showed 8:34 P.M. when the referee dropped the puck to start the first-round Stanley Cup playoff series between the Montreal Maroons, champion of the National Hockey League's Canadian Division, and the Detroit Red Wings, titlist in the American Division.

Playoffs games, especially in the early going, usually are played close to the vest and nobody was surprised when the first period was scoreless and marked only by three minor penalties.

The second period was more of the same, the only excitement being a mild scuffle that drew two-minute penalties for Marty Barry of the Wings and Jimmy Ward of the Maroons. The third period also was scoreless and the fans were getting restless.

After a brief intermission, the teams went into a 20-minute sudden-death overtime session. No score. Then a second overtime period. No score. And a third. And a fourth. Near the end of the fifth overtime, Barry, the Detroit center, set up left winger Herb Lewis with a perfect pass. Lewis appeared to have Maroon goalie Lorne Chabot beaten, but his shot hit the post and bounced out.

That flurry finished the action in the fifth overtime, which amounted to the eighth 20-minute period. After 4:46 of the sixth overtime, the Red Wings and Maroons owned the record for the longest Cup playoff game. They broke the mark of 144 minutes, 46 seconds set in 1933 when Toronto defeated Boston, 1–0.

In that game, after about 100 minutes of overtime, league president Frank Calder had refused a request that the game be resumed the following night. Calder, however, was willing to toss a coin to decide the winner, but his plan was vetoed by the Maple Leafs.

The Red Wings and Maroons knew they had to play to a decision. The break didn't come until 16:30 had elapsed in the sixth overtime, or just short of three regulation games. Detroit goalie Norm Smith repulsed a Maroon rush with his 90th save and Hec Kilrea headed up ice in a two-man dash with rookie Mud Bruneteau. Bruneteau, who had scored only two goals all season, managed to skate past the weary Maroon defense. As Lionel Conacher lost his footing on the rough ice, Mud took a pass from Kilrea, faked Chabot, who had stopped 66 shots, out of position and poked home the winner into an open net.

At 2:25 A.M. on March 25, five hours and 51 minutes after play had begun, hockey's longest game ended. The defeat seemed to take something out of the Maroons, who lost the next two games and were eliminated from the playoffs while the Red Wings went on to win the Stanley Cup.

March 23, 1944
CANADIENS VS. MAPLE LEAFS

Stanley Cup playoff games usually emphasize defense. The checking is tight and rough. In the short series with a lot at stake, errors can be fatal. The Montreal Canadiens had run away with the regular-season championship of 1943–44. They lost only five games out of 50 on the schedule (with seven ties) and finished 25 points ahead of second-place Detroit.

The Stanley Cup series opened in Montreal with the Canadiens playing third-place Toronto. In a close-checking game, the Maple Leafs won the opener, 3–1. The two teams met again two nights later, March 23, 1944, in Montreal's Forum as the fans wondered how long the Leafs could hold off the powerful Canadiens, namely Maurice (Rocket) Richard.

Bob Davidson, a big, close-checking forward for the Leafs, always drew the assignment of guarding Richard. The Rocket, a 23-year-old French-Canadian, was only in his second season in the National Hockey League but already merited special attention. Davidson and the Leafs were successful through a scoreless first period. But in the second period the home team broke loose.

Taking passes from Toe Blake and defensemen Mike McMahon, Richard wheeled in and beat Leaf goalie Paul Bibeault for the first goal of the game at 1:48. Seventeen seconds later Richard scored again on assists from his famous linemates, Blake and Elmer Lach.

Now that Montreal had a two-goal lead, Toronto had to abandon its conservative checking game. The Leafs needed goals. They got one from Reg Hamilton after 8:50 of the second period, but Richard matched that with

his third goal of the night on assists from Lach and Blake at 16:46. The fiery-tempered Richard achieved his hat trick in a single period even though he twice had been set down for two-minute penalties.

The crowd gave its idol an ovation as he left the ice after the second period, but there was more to come. The Canadiens were determined not to sit on their two-goal lead. The fabulous Flying Frenchmen came out flying for the final period. After only a minute of play, Richard again was set up by Lach and Blake on the famous Punch Line, and he scored his fourth goal. And, at 8:34 he scored a fifth. The final score of the game was Richard 5, Toronto 1.

After NHL games at the Forum, the three top stars of the contest are honored. This time the crowd of 12,500 was able to give a continuous ovation. Star No. 3, Star No. 2 and Star No. 1—all Maurice Richard! Richard's five goals—a Stanley Cup record that would not be equaled until 32 years later, by Darryl Sittler and Reggie Leach—demoralized the Leafs, who lost the next three games as well, the final by an 11–0 score.

"I didn't know until after the game that the five goals set a record," Richard said. "I only had six or seven shots on net all game and each goal was scored in a different way. The funny thing is that when we beat the Leafs 11–0, I only scored two goals.

"The Leafs always were a close-checking club and they used to put Bob Davidson out to check me every game. Sometimes he stayed so close to me that I got angry and that night, I guess, I took it out on him—and the puck."

April 21, 1951
MAPLE LEAFS VS. CANADIENS

Bill Barilko never really seemed destined for fame. Curly-haired and good-looking, he was a 190-pound defenseman for the Toronto Maple Leafs. Only 19 when the Leafs called him up from the minors at the end of the 1946–47 season, Barilko quickly established

Toronto's Bill Barilko (5) scored the winning goal to clinch the Stanley Cup in 1951. It was his last goal.

himself as a defensive defenseman, the kind who doesn't score goals, doesn't make All-Star teams and doesn't get his picture in the papers very often.

Only among rival players, whom he delighted in belting into the boards, did Barilko gain any real measure of fame and respect. He never scored more than seven goals in a season as a major leaguer and his most outstanding statistic was the 147 minutes in penalties he amassed in 1947–48, his first full year in the NHL. That penalty total led the NHL and for most of his short career he was up among the penalty leaders.

But, while he wasn't a star, Barilko was no slouch, either, and in each of his first three seasons he played an important role as the Maple Leafs won the Stanley Cup. The Leafs lost in the first round of the 1950 playoffs to Detroit, the eventual winner, and in 1951

Toronto found itself back in the finals against the Montreal Canadiens.

The Maple Leafs won the Cup, four games to one, but the series was not as one-sided as it appeared. Every game was decided in a sudden-death overtime.

Barilko was a key figure in the first game. Near the end of regulation time, Maurice Richard fired what seemed a sure goal at an open Toronto net, only to see Barilko dive full-length to block the shot and preserve the 2–2 tie. Sid Smith then scored the winner for Toronto after 5:51 of overtime. The second game went to Montreal, 3–2, after 2:55 of overtime on a goal by Maurice Richard.

The series moved to Montreal for the next two games and Toronto took both. Ted Kennedy won the first game, 2–1, after 4:47 of overtime and Harry Watson the second, 3–2, after 5:15.

The Leafs returned home to a joyous greeting at Maple Leaf Gardens as they prepared to clinch the Cup in the fifth game on April 21, 1951. For once it didn't look as if the game would go into overtime. With a minute to go, Montreal held a 2–1 lead. But Toronto coach Joe Primeau pulled his goalie and, with an extra skater on the ice, the Leafs got a goal from Tod Sloan with 32 seconds left to force the game into overtime.

After only 2:53, it was sudden death for the Canadiens. Barilko, who hadn't recorded a goal or an assist in the series, took a pass from Howie Meeker at mid-ice and in blind desperation fired a shot at the goal and he crossed the blue line. He actually flung himself in the air with the force of his effort and the puck skipped past Montreal goalie Gerry McNeil. The Stanley Cup returned to Toronto.

After the season, Barilko went home to Timmons, a mining town in northern Ontario. For the first time he was a national hero. He didn't get to enjoy it for long. That August, he and a friend, Dr. Henry Hudson, flew into northern Canada on a fishing trip in the doctor's private plane. They were never heard from again.

Some 15 years later, what was believed to be the wreckage of their plane was discovered, reviving briefly memories of the low-scoring but hard-hitting defenseman who once won a Stanley Cup for Toronto.

March 23, 1952
BLACK HAWKS VS. RANGERS

Bill Mosienko, a 30-year-old right winger for the Chicago Black Hawks, and Lorne Anderson, a 20-year-old goalie for the amateur New York Rovers, each had a hope as the 1952 hockey season went into its final days before the Stanley Cup playoffs. Mosienko, looking at the NHL record book with some friends, remarked, "Gee, it would be nice to have my name in there with some of the hockey greats." Anderson's wish was more simple: to play in the National Hockey League.

The dream came true for both, but for Anderson it was more like a nightmare.

The Rangers faced their final three games of the season already eliminated from the play-offs, Cincinnati, a minor-league team, had owned the rights to Ranger goalie Emile (Cat) Francis, so the NHL regular was shipped down to help that American Hockey League team in its playoff quest. As a result, the Rangers called up Anderson to finish the season.

The New Yorkers won Anderson's first game, 6–4, over Boston, but lost the second, 6–3, to Detroit. The final game of the 1952 season was played on March 23 with the Rangers and Black Hawks performing before a mere 3,254 fans in Madison Square Garden.

This was what is called a "brother-in-law" game. The final placings had long since been decided and nobody wanted to get hurt. With virtually no checking, referee George Gravel did not call a single penalty in the entire 60-minute game.

However, that's not to say there wasn't plenty of action. The Black Hawks' Gus Bodnar scored first with Mosienko getting an assist. Then the Rangers scored three times before the visitors tallied again—and it was still only the first period! The Rangers scored twice more for a 5–2 lead after two periods and expanded this margin to 6–2 in the opening minutes of the third as Ed Slowinski completed the three-goal hat trick.

But then, in a shocking explosion, Mosienko, the speedy 5-foot-6 right winger, made hockey history.

In almost leisurely but precise fashion, the Hawks formed for the attack. Bodnar, the center, passed off to Mosienko and his little winger beat the defenseman to rap home a goal from in front of the net. The time was 6:09 of the third period.

After the goal, there was a faceoff at center ice. Bodnar won the draw and hit the streaking Mosienko just as Bill was crossing the blue line. Mosienko took the pass, shot and scored. The time was 6:20 of the third period. Only 11 seconds had elapsed.

Three goals in 21 seconds put Chicago's Bill Mosienko into ecstasy and the record book.

Again there was a faceoff, again Bodnar controlled the puck, but this time he passed off to George Gee on the left wing. Gee carried over the Ranger blue line, spotted Mosienko breaking toward the net and laid a perfect pass on the right winger's stick. Mosienko fired it past Anderson and, as the red light flashed again, the clock showed 6:30 had elapsed. Mosienko had scored three goals in 21 seconds. No player—or team—had ever scored three times in such a short period of time. Mosienko's dream had come true. He landed in the record book, breaking the old mark by 43 seconds as the Hawks scored twice more to win, 7–6.

Mosienko went on to play three more full seasons for the Black Hawks and retired at age 32 after the 1954–55 campaign with a career total of 258 goals.

As for the unfortunate Anderson, who had surrendered 17 goals in his brief trial, he never played in another big-league game.

November 1, 1959
CANADIENS VS. RANGERS

By 1959, Jacques Plante's reputation as one of the greatest hockey goaltenders of all time was firmly established. He had already won four Vezina Trophies, the award that annually goes to the top goalie in the National Hockey League. And his success as a roving goalie for the Montreal Canadiens had revolutionized the techniques of playing his position.

Montreal's bloodied Jacques Plante dons a »
mask for the first time in 1959 against the Rangers.

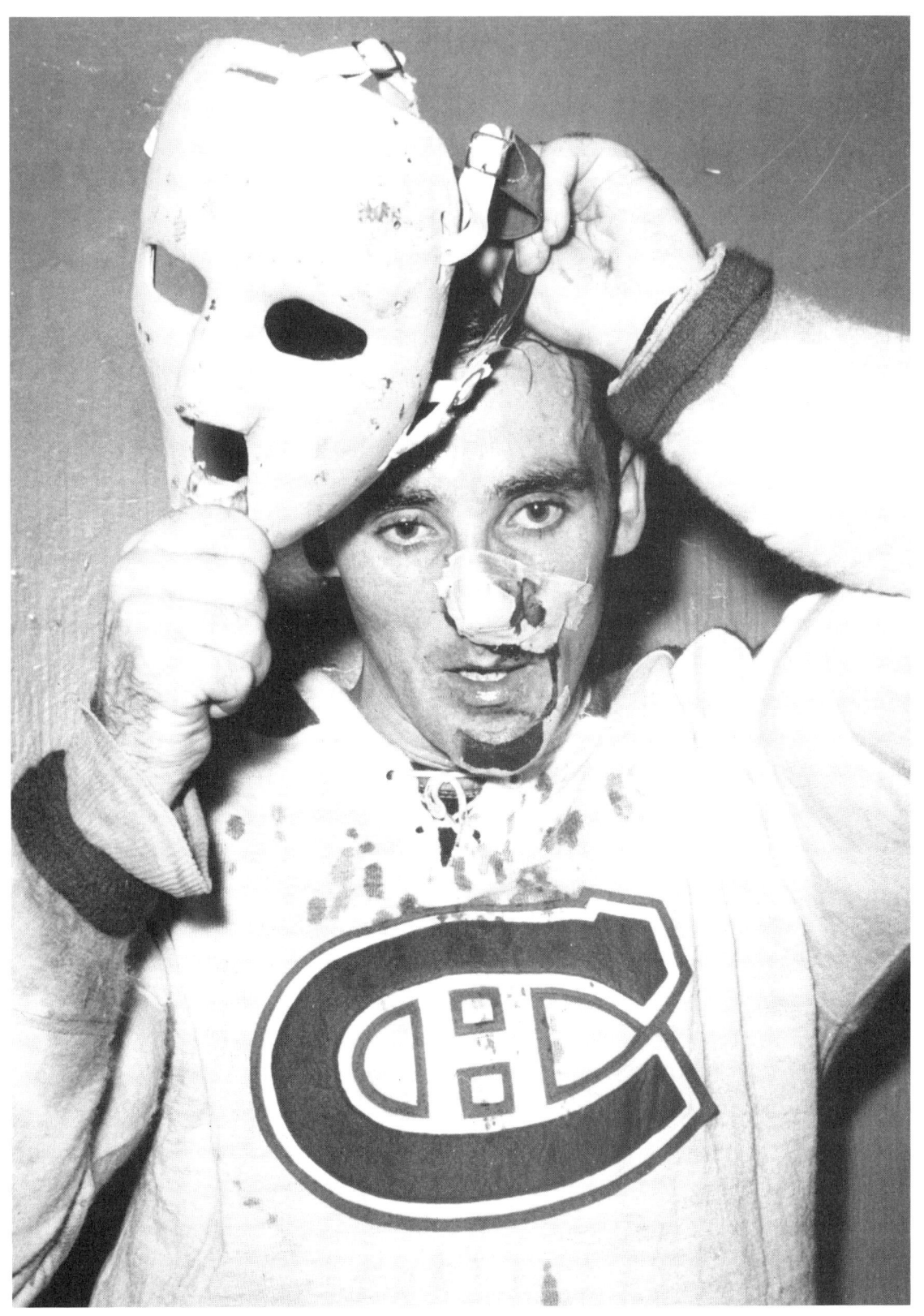

But, as he skated out on the ice against the Rangers in New York on November 1, 1959, he also had some other souvenirs of his dangerous profession: the scars of 200 stitches in his face, a nose broken four times, a fractured skull and two broken cheekbones.

The fractured cheekbones had come in each of Plante's first two big-league seasons. Both times he was hurt in practice from a shot by a teammate. After the second injury he had a plastic mask designed and he wore it in workouts.

The mask was a bit awkward, but during the 1958–59 season, Plante learned that a mask had been developed that would fit snugly against his face. It was just what he wanted, for now the blind spots of the old mask were eliminated. Before the season, Plante asked coach Toe Blake if he could wear the mask during games.

It was not unprecedented: Clint Benedict of the Montreal Maroons had worn one briefly in 1929, but discarded it. Goalies were traditionally barefaced after that and Blake was a traditionalist. He turned down Plante.

However, in less than two months, tradition was broken. It happened in this game against the Rangers, scoreless for eight minutes until Andy Bathgate, the New Yorkers' hardest shooter, let loose a 25-foot backhander from the left of the net.

Plante, screened by the mass of players, never saw the puck until it smashed into his face, ripping open his cheek and nose. He fell to the ice, blood staining his uniform and the Garden ice. But he recovered with a towel held against his face. It took seven stitches to close the wound.

All that time, NHL teams did not carry a spare goalie. It was up to the home club to have someone on hand who could fill in during an emergency. Some teams called on their assistant trainer; others, in Canada especially, would have available the teenage goalie from their junior team in the same city. The Rangers used a fortyish and pudgy weekend amateur named Joe Schaefer. When Schaefer had to play, it really was an emergency.

That was the situation as Plante sat up on the first-aid table. Twenty minutes had elapsed. The game had to resume. Plante looked at Blake, "I won't go back on unless I can wear the mask," he said grimly. Blake, who had fought the new device so stubbornly, had to agree. And hockey history was made.

Fortunately, Plante played well with the mask. The Canadiens beat the Rangers, 3–1, with the losers' only goal coming in the final period. Montreal had arrived at the Garden with an unbeaten streak of seven. They made it eight against the Rangers and finally extended it to 18 before losing to Toronto, 1–0. In the last 11 games of the streak, or all the time he wore the mask, Plante gave up only 13 goals.

The Montreal management reluctantly went along with Plante. "I had to show good results to keep the mask," he later commented, and he did, winning three more Vezina Trophies. And masks for goalies eventually became commonplace.

November 10, 1963
RED WINGS VS. CANADIENS

It was like Babe Ruth's 714 home runs. When Maurice Richard retired from the National Hockey League in 1960 with 544 goals in regular-season play, nobody was even close. And nobody, Rocket's French-Canadien fans insisted, would ever approach his scoring record.

But when the 1963–64 campaign began, Gordie Howe, Detroit's durable right winger, was close. He started the season with 540 and it seemed only a matter of time until he passed the Rocket. Only an injury could stop the husky, slope-shouldered Howe from overtaking Richard.

On October 27, 1963, Howe and the Red Wings were playing host to the Canadiens. Gordie had 543 goals and the proud Habitants were determined that Howe would not join the Rocket in the record book at their expense. Toe Blake, coach of the Canadiens, made sure that a line centered by Richard's brother, Henri, was always on ice against

Howe's line. It was more than a psychological ploy. When Henri was on the ice, he controlled the puck. And Howe couldn't score without it.

Then Blake assigned Gilles Tremblay, a Montreal winger, to forget about scoring himself and to concentrate on shadowing Howe.

The strategy almost worked. Howe was limited to only two shots all game. But the second was a goal. At 11:04 of the third period, Howe got a step on Tremblay and deflected Bruce MacGregor's goal-mouth pass past Montreal netminder Gump Worsley. It wasn't a picture goal, but it counted and Jean Beliveau, captain of the Canadiens, gravely skated over to shake Howe's hand.

However, the battle was only half over for Howe, then 34 and in his 18th pro season. Now he had to break the record and, game after game, the pressure mounted. Detroit had lost to Montreal, 6–4, the night Howe tied Richard after failing to score in 10 previous games, and the whole team suffered as the Red Wings tried to help their captain register No. 545.

But there was nothing coach Sid Abel could do. The Wings lost three of their next five games. Howe's nervous twitch became more pronounced, and newsmen and photographers ran out of clean shirts as they followed Howe from city to city in hope of recording the monumental goal.

Two weeks later, they found themselves back in Detroit's glistening Olympia Stadium. Another sellout crowd of more than 15,000 jammed the building—and again Montreal provided the opposition. The only major change was that instead of Gump Worsley, the Canadiens had little Charlie Hodge in goal.

Again the Canadiens were determined to protect the Rocket's record and again they concentrated solely on stopping Howe. The first period was scoreless but Detroit scored twice in 47 seconds to take a 2–0 lead after 5½ minutes of the second period. At the 13:57 mark, Alex Faulkner of the Wings was penalized five minutes for high-sticking and the redoubtable Howe came along with Billy McNeill to help kill the penalty.

The Canadiens mounted one of their fierce power assaults when McNeill dug out the puck from against the boards deep in the Detroit zone. Howe moved behind him and yelled, "Get along!" The little winger took off down the right wing and swung to the middle of the ice as he crossed into Montreal territory with Howe behind him to the right and defenseman Bill Gadsby on the left wing. As they approached the Canadiens' goal, McNeill slid the puck to Howe, who, with one motion, swiped a 15-foot shot just off the ice past Hodge and into the cage.

As the red light flashed with 15:06 gone in the period, Hodge slammed his stick against the top of the cage and skated to the sidelines. He knew there would be a prolonged ovation after what McNeill called a "perfect goal."

It was also perfect as Howe passed the Rocket by scoring when his team was short a man. And, unlike the night he tied the record, it came when his team was winning, not losing. To Howe, that was as important as any record.

March 12, 1966
BLACK HAWKS VS. RANGERS

Maurice (Rocket) Richard of the Montreal Canadiens became the first player in National Hockey League history to score 50 goals during the 1944–45 season. Then, in 1960–61, Bernie (Boom-Boom) Geoffrion of the same team did it, too. And the following year Bobby Hull of the Chicago Black Hawks also turned the trick in the final game of the season.

Now it was the end of the 1965–66 campaign. Hull, the Golden Jet, had missed five games because of torn knee ligaments but he already had his 50 after 57 games of the 70-game schedule.

The sky seemed the limit for Hull, then 27 years old and a handsome, husky, muscular picture athlete. But game 58 passed, and Hull didn't score; then game 59 and game 60 and still the powerful left winger appeared anchored at 50 goals.

Chicago's Bobby Hull netted his record-setting 51st goal against the Rangers in 1966.

On the night of March 12, Hull skated out on the ice of massive Chicago Stadium as 21,000 fans—4,000 more than listed capacity—watched to see if he could make his 51st goal against the fifth-place New York Rangers.

The first period was scoreless and then the Rangers scored twice in the second 20 minutes to take a 2–0 lead as the rest of the Black Hawks seemed to be standing around waiting for Hull to get his record.

As the third period opened, Hull assisted on a goal by teammate Chico Maki and then, with 4:05 gone, Harry Howell of the Rangers was sent off with a two-minute penalty for slashing.

Back on the ice went Hull as perhaps hockey's most explosive point man on the power play. Howell had been in the penalty box almost a minute and a half when the Hawks gathered to start another rush against the undermanned Rangers. Bill Hay and Lou

Angotti fed the puck up to Hull and then watched, almost as spectators, as the Golden Jet moved slowly to his left, stopped, crossed the New York blue line and then, as his teammates swooped toward the net, fired a deceptively swift wrist shot at Ranger goalie Cesare Maniago.

Eric Nesterenko, another Black Hawks forward, was near the goal-mouth at the time and he tipped Maniago's stick as the Ranger goalie, who had also given up Geoffrion's 50th goal, tried vainly to make a split save.

As the puck zipped past Maniago and the red light flashed to signify a score, the crowd erupted into what was to be a 7½ minute ovation. But Hull, for a moment, stood still, nerves tingling. If Nesterenko had tipped the puck on its way past Maniago, he, not Hull, would get the goal.

But the official scorer settled all doubts. Hull had his 51st goal after 5:34 of the third period. He skated over to the section where his wife was sitting and whispered to her through the protective glass, "Well, I did it." Then, as he skated around the ice to acknowledge the applause, Hull reached down and put on one of the dozens of hats that frenzied fans had skimmed onto the ice.

It was a glorious moment for Hull. A couple of weeks earlier, the normally placid star had exploded into a fistfight with a close-checking rival. He had considered quitting because of the pressure of the 51-goal quest. But now the tensions were past. The Hawks went on to win the game, 4–2, and Bobby proceeded to score three more goals during the rest of the season to put the record at 54. But, as Hull could testify, the 51st was the hardest.

March 2, 1969
BRUINS VS. PENGUINS

The National Hockey League was founded in 1917 and for more than 50 years no player had ever scored 100 points in a single season.

For awhile, the scoring mark belonged to Dickie Moore, a shifty left wing who totaled 96 points for Montreal in 1958–59. Then, in

Boston's Phil Esposito snapped Stan Mikita's one-season scoring mark on March 1, 1969. The next night, he became the first player to crack the 100-point barrier.

1965–66, Chicago's Bobby Hull boosted the mark to 97 and a year later, another Black Hawks player, Stan Mikita, also reached 97.

Mikita's 97 points came in the last year that the NHL operated with just six teams. The next year, six new clubs were added and even though scoring predictably increased, it was spread around more. Mikita repeated as scoring champion, but his total fell to 87 points, 10 below the standard he shared with Hull.

That same year, Chicago swapped a center named Phil Esposito to Boston. Espo had been Hull's center in Bobby's 97-point season and was considered a caddy for the great left wing. But he proved to more than that. Much more.

Esposito gave Mikita a battle for the scoring crown that year, finishing with 84 points, only three less than the Chicago pivot. The next year, Espo exploded, scoring points at a record-setting pace. It became apparent in February that the NHL's 100-point plateau was going to be broken by the sad-eyed center who set up shop in front of goalies and refused to be moved out of there.

With linemates Ken Hodge on the right and Ron Murphy on the left, Esposito flourished. As the season turned into March, its final month, he had 97 points. On March 1, in a game against the New York Rangers, Esposito cracked the mark with point No. 98. He had been stopped on 10 shots in the first two periods by goalie Ed Giacomin before finally slipping a shorthanded goal past the New York netminder. Later, he assisted on a goal by Bobby Orr for his 99th point.

That set the stage for Pittsburgh's visit to Boston Garden the next night. The Penguins were determined to keep Espo off the score-

Toronto's Darryl Sittler exploded for 10 points against Boston.

board. He was going to get point No. 100 some place, but Pittsburgh didn't want to be the victim.

"Joe Daley was the Pittsburgh goaltender and he did a good job over the first two periods," Esposito would recount. "I had two shots and no goals."

As the Bruins returned to the ice for the game's final 20 minutes, a youngster shouted to Esposito. "Please get that one-hundredth point, Phil. I want to be able to say I saw it."

Esposito obliged. With only 17 seconds gone in the period, passes from Ted Green and Hodge sprung Espo, cutting in from the left side. "Daley moved to his right," recalled Esposito, "and hit the ice. I spilled it underneath him."

The fans showered Espo with all kinds of debris, including a football helmet, saluting the historic 100th point. Espo added 26 more points that year for the first of four scoring championships in five seasons. In each of those years, he scored more than 100 points and in 1970–71 he reached his high with 152 points, including 76 goals.

Both records would stand for a decade—until a young man named Wayne Gretzky surfaced as an unprecedented scoring machine.

February 7, 1976
MAPLE LEAFS VS. BRUINS

It did not figure to be an exciting game. In fact, it shaped up as a mismatch. The Boston Bruins came into Maple Leaf Gardens on the night of February 7, 1976, as the hottest team in the National Hockey League. They were unbeaten in seven games and had lost only one of the previous 17 outings. And now they were about to face the Maple Leafs, who had won but one of their last seven games.

A day earlier, Harold Ballard, the Leafs' bombastic owner, claimed he was "determined to find a sensational center" to play between the team's top wingers, Lanny Mc-Donald and Errol Thompson. "We'd set off a

time bomb if we had a helluva center in there,'' Ballard said.

Coach Red Kelly had inserted Darryl Sittler into the spot earlier in the week—mainly because Sittler also had been in a slump with only five goals in his previous 17 games. It turned out to be a dynamite move.

Sittler, performing before a sellout crowd of 16,485, rewrote the NHL record book that night, scoring six goals (on 10 shots) and adding four assists in the Leafs' 11–4 thumping of the Bruins and a rookie goalie named Dave Reece.

Sittler's 10 points smashed the one-game NHL standard of eight, set by Maurice (Rocket) Richard of the Montreal Canadiens in 1944 (five goals, three assists), and equaled by teammate Bert Olmstead (four goals, four assists) 10 years later. Sittler's six goals tied the ''modern era'' record set by Syd Howe of Detroit in 1944 and matched by Red Berenson of St. Louis in 1968.

Joe Malone set the all-time one-game goal mark with seven while playing for the Quebec Bulldogs in 1920. However, an unofficial split exists in NHL history, created by the 1943 introduction of the center red line, which loosely divides the early and modern eras.

Sittler, 25 years old at the time of his epic performance, was numbed by it all. ''It was a night when every time I had the puck something seemed to happen,'' he said. ''Sure, I got some bounces, and I don't think it was one of their goalie's greatest nights.''

Oddly, Sittler did not score a goal in the opening period, but he did pick up two assists. In the second period, he had three goals and two assists. He completed his big night with three more goals in the final period. It was the first time an NHL player scored hat tricks in consecutive periods.

Dave Reece, the sad rookie who served as Sittler's sleeve, was never to be permitted to forget that memorable night. He appeared in 13 other games for the Bruins that season, then drifted back to the minor leagues.

February 24, 1982
SABRES VS. OILERS

Phil Esposito was shadowing Wayne Gretzky. Everywhere that Gretzky went, Esposito was sure to follow. The trail began in Edmonton, then it was on to Detroit and, finally, it was time to shuffle off to Buffalo.

The date was February 24, 1982, and the Edmonton Oilers, led by the Great Gretzky, were playing the Buffalo Sabres in Memorial Auditorium. Esposito was the most interested spectator in the capacity crowd of 16,433 that night. Eleven years earlier, he had scored a record 76 goals in 78 games while playing for the Boston Bruins.

Gretzky had equaled Espo's record against the Red Wings in Detroit at the start of the Oilers' road trip. Now it was three nights later and Esposito squirmed in his seat as the Oilers and the Sabres carried a 3–3 tie into the final 10 minutes. Gretzky had taken seven shots at Buffalo goalie Don Edwards without scoring. Would Wayne have to wait another night for the record-breaker?

Then, with less than seven minutes left to play, Gretzky stole the puck from Buffalo's Steve Patrick just inside the Sabres' blue line. As Gretzky skated into the slot, Buffalo defenseman Richie Dunn attempted to slow him down by hooking his stick across Gretzky's arms. Gretzky brushed the stick away and shot the puck low, from about 12 feet. It went between Edwards' legs, and the record was broken.

Esposito came onto the ice to congratulate the 21-year-old center. ''Attaway, Wayne,'' Esposito said. ''Now I can get back to New York.''

A year earlier, Esposito had retired as a player and became a television commentator for Ranger games. He knew from the moment Gretzky arrived on the NHL scene that his record was in jeopardy. So did Patsy Esposito, Phil's father. The elder Esposito had seen Gretzky play amateur hockey in Sault Ste. Marie, Ontario, where Phil was born and raised, and predicted then that Gretzky would be a record-breaker.

Gretzky did not stop at goal No. 77 against the Sabres. He added two more in the final two minutes, giving him 79 in 64 games. He completed the season with an astounding 92 goals, 120 assists and 212 points.

Gretzky received a telegram of congratulations from Ronald Reagan, President of the United States. That impressed him. He was also impressed by the fact that Don Edwards, the man who surrendered the record goal, skated the length of the ice to shake his hand.

Gretzky predicted his record also would be broken eventually. "Maybe I'll break it," he said with a grin.

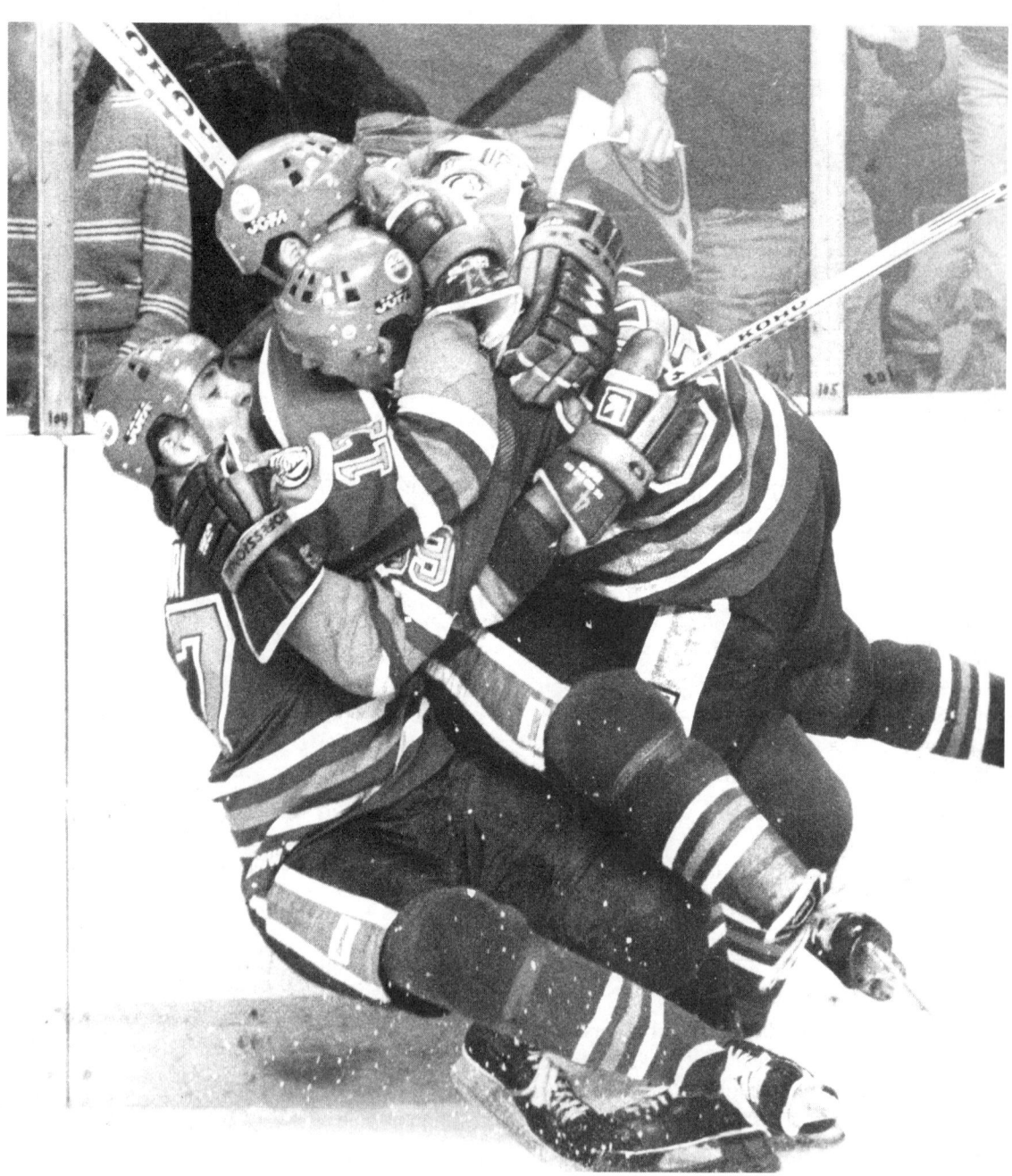

May 17, 1983
OILERS VS. ISLANDERS

For 65 years there was only one true dynasty in the National Hockey League and that was the Montreal Canadiens. They had won 19 Cups, including four straight Cups coming into the spring of 1983.

The New York Islanders—with a star-studded corps led by Denis Potvin, Mike Bossy, Bryan Trottier and Billy Smith—had won three consecutive Cups starting in 1980 under the leadership of general manager Bill Torrey and head coach Al Arbour. Only the Toronto Maple Leafs, Detroit Red Wings and the Islanders, apart from the Canadiens, had ever won three in a row.

But the Islanders' opponent in the '83 Cup finals was the Edmonton Oilers—not Montreal, not Toronto, not Detroit. These Oilers were led by Wayne Gretzky and they were determined to snap the Islander streak.

"We've had young players who grew up together," Torrey said. "All of them being together all this time has been important. They got knocked off together in the playoffs by Toronto in 1978 and then by the Rangers in 1979, but ever since they've won together."

In the opening game, goalie Billy Smith posted a 2–0 shutout in Edmonton and incurred the wrath of Oiler fans when he slashed Glenn Anderson. Oilers' coach Glen Sather demanded that Smith be suspended and on the day of Game 2 an Edmonton newspaper ran a full-page color photo of a human eye with the headline: "Evil Eye on Smith."

Jeered by the Edmonton crowd which held up hundreds of Evil Eyes, Smith was again sharp as the Islanders skated to a 6–3 victory that sent them back home with a 2–0 advantage in the best-of-seven series.

The Islanders romped in Game 3, 5–1, and their fans were ready to celebrate when Game 4 began on May 17. Trottier, John Tonelli and Bossy scored goals in the first period as the

« *His Edmonton teammates mob Wayne Gretzky after he broke Phil Esposito's goal-scoring record.*

Isles took a 3–0 lead. But Edmonton's Jari Kurri scored on a Gretzky setup just 35 seconds into the second period and Mark Messier tallied with 21 seconds remaining to cut the Isles' lead to 3–2.

Smith, the Islander goalie, and his Edmonton counterpart, Andy Moog, didn't yield a goal for nearly 19 minutes of the third period. The Oilers removed Moog for an extra skater and Islander defenseman Ken Morrow found the open net at 18:51 to give his team a 4–2 victory and its fourth consecutive Cup.

Smith had turned aside 24 of 26 shots in the clincher and he finished with a 13–3 record and 2.68 goals-against average in the playoffs. He was an overwhelming choice for MVP.

The home crowd of 15,317 thrilled to the song "We Are the Champions," and the knowledge that the Islanders had a dynasty of their own.

April 25, 1989
FLYERS VS. PENGUINS

In the 48 hours leading up to the evening of April 25, 1989, the Pittsburgh Penguins wondered if captain Mario Lemieux's strained neck would permit him to play against the Philadelphia Flyers in Game 5 of the Patrick Division finals.

Lemieux had been knocked out of action in Game 4 after butting heads with teammate Randy Cunneyworth. Lemieux was in considerable pain the next morning. Although his condition improved in the hours prior to the fifth game, there was the question of risking further injury by rushing Lemieux back into the lineup.

He did not participate in the morning skate and only tested his neck during the pregame skate. A crowd of 16,025 at Pittsburgh's Civic Arena and his concerned teammates awaited the decision.

The news was good. Lemieux said he would play and the Flyers soon discovered he couldn't be stopped. Just 2:15 into the opening period, Lemieux skated in on a breakaway and tucked a backhander past Philadelphia

goaltender Ron Hextall. At 3:45, Lemieux deflected a pass across the crease and into the net for a 2–0 lead. Before the game was seven minutes old, he completed a hat trick by picking up a loose puck and firing a snap shot through Hextall's pads.

"Once I got the first goal, I thought we could have a big night," Lemieux said later.

"There was not a lot of pain and I had my range of motion back."

It was the Flyers who had the pain. In the second period, Lemieux stole the puck from Hextall and scored his fourth goal, lifting up the goalie's stick to take the puck and flipping it inside the far post.

Lemieux set up all three Pittsburgh goals in the second period as the Penguins opened up a 9–3 lead after 40 minutes of play. Topping off the lopsided game, Lemieux made the record book when he added an empty-net goal, his fifth of the game, for a 10–3 Penguin rout.

"Considering that he was hurt, we definitely didn't expect it from him," said Hextall, the vanquished goalie.

Lemieux's feat enabled him to tie Patrik Sundstrom's record for most points (eight) in a Stanley Cup playoff game. Sundstrom had set the mark with the New Jersey Devils in a 10–4 victory over the Washington Capitals on April 22, 1988. Sundstrom had three goals and five assists in that contest.

Lemieux's five goals equaled the NHL record for goals in a playoff game held by Reggie Leach (Philadelphia), Darryl Sittler (Toronto), Maurice Richard (Montreal Canadiens) and Newsy Lalonde (Montreal Canadiens).

May 25, 1989
FLAMES VS. CANADIENS

For 16 years, ever since the birth of the Flames' franchise in Atlanta, general manager Cliff Fletcher had been saying, "Wait till next year." He'd reiterated it in Atlanta and then in Calgary when the team moved there in May 1980.

They'd never won the Stanley Cup and, as with every player, coach, general manager and fan, this was the ultimate goal. Fletcher, a native of the Montreal suburb of Ville St. Laurent, had spent 10 years working part-time for the Montreal Canadiens before moving on to the St. Louis Blues and the Flames.

And now the Cup was within grasp as Calgary and Montreal met in the finals in 1989. The teams split the first two games and the Canadiens appeared to be on the way to yet another Cup when Ryan Walter's goal gave

« *Calgary veteran Lanny McDonald earned the right to hold the Cup aloft in 1989.*

Montreal a 4–3 victory in the second overtime in Game 3.

However, Al MacInnis' third-period game-winner (4–2) again evened the series in Game 4. A crowd of 20,002 at the Olympic Saddledome watched the Flames score a 3–2 victory in Game 5, sending the teams back to Montreal. If Montreal lost, it would be the first Canadiens' team ever to lose the Cup on home ice.

After sitting out three games, 16-year veteran Lanny McDonald returned to the Flames' lineup on May 25 for Game 6. "Lanny was rested," coach Terry Crisp explained. "When you put Lanny McDonald in your lineup and the 'C' back on his chest, you could feel the dressing room start to go. We felt he would give us an emotional lift."

It went beyond that. After the Flames' Colin Patterson and Montreal's Claude Lemieux exchanged goals, McDonald put the Flames ahead, 2–1, in the second period. Doug Gilmour's power-play goal at 11:02 of the third period made it 3–1.

Then Rick Green's goal at 11:53 brought the Canadiens within a goal. But it was Gilmour who ended Montreal's hopes when he scored an empty-net goal at 18:57 for a 4–2 victory and the first Cup in Calgary history.

MacInnis, who scored at least one point in 17 consecutive playoff games for Calgary, won the Conn Smythe Trophy as MVP of the playoffs.

Two days later, the Flames were cheered at a victory parade in the rain. "Next year" had finally arrived for Cliff Fletcher and Calgary.

October 15, 1989
KINGS VS. OILERS

It was as inevitable as the cold winds of an Alberta winter, yet Wayne Gretzky somehow managed to make it as thrilling as the first gush from an Edmonton oil well.

For more than a decade, Gretzky had pursued Gordie Howe's record as the National Hockey League's all-time leading scorer. Now, Howe's standard of 1,850 career points was about to fall.

Fittingly, The Great One saved his feat for Edmonton's Northlands Coliseum, where he had played for 10 seasons before the August 9, 1988, trade to the Los Angeles Kings. A sellout crowd of 17,503 cheered wildly as Gretzky returned to the scene of so many triumphs.

At the 4:32 mark of the opening period, Gretzky tied Howe's record with an assist on a goal by Bernie Nicholls. From the right wing boards, No. 99 passed the puck to defenseman Tom Laidlaw between the faceoff circles. Laidlaw found Nicholls just outside the goal crease for a shot that beat goaltender Bill Ranford.

The drama began to build. The Oilers, who would go on to win the Stanley Cup that season, shut Gretzky down at that point and it appeared the crowd might go home disappointed. With 3:29 remaining in the third period, Gretzky fed the puck to teammate Luc Robitaille, who gave it to Nicholls for a shot on goal. Nicholls' wrist shot had Ranford beaten, but the puck glanced off the post. So close.

Now time was running out. The Kings had removed goalie Mario Gosselin for an extra skater, but Mark Messier won the draw with Nichols. He got the puck back to defenseman Kevin Lowe, who was unable to clear the zone.

Steve Duchesne kept the puck in the offensive zone, driving it in deep. The disc hopped over Lowe's stick and bounced off King forward Dave Taylor's knee to Gretzky in front. The crowd gasped as Gretzky struck for the record-breaking goal. There were 53 seconds left in the game.

The crowd exploded as "1851" flashed on the scoreboard and the game was stopped while a red carpet was rolled onto the ice for a fitting ceremony. Gretzky was hugged by his

« *The Kings' Wayne Gretzky revels in his record-smashing accomplishment—No. 1851!*

father, Walter, before receiving gifts from Messier representing the Oilers, Robitaille and Taylor representing the Kings, and NHL president John Ziegler.

"This is the greatest feeling in the world," Gretzky said. "It will be the highlight of my life."

When the game, now tied at 4–4, resumed, Gretzky added to the magic of the evening. There was no score in the time that remained, but after 3:24 of sudden-death overtime, Gretzky beat Ranford for No. 1,852 and a 5–4 Kings' victory.

Howe, who had remained close to the events for eight days as Gretzky pursued his record, was gracious when it was finally broken.

"I am so proud of the fact that we have gotten along over the years," Howe said. "He calls me his friend and that's one of the greatest things in my life. I feel more gain than loss. I lost a record, but I have gained a lot of friends."

"Wayne finished it and he finished it with style," said Nicholls.

May 25, 1991
PENGUINS VS. NORTH STARS

In Pittsburgh, May had traditionally been the month when sports fans debated how well the Steelers had done in the NFL draft and how far the Pirates might go in the National League East. The Penguins had always packed up in April because they rarely made the playoffs.

But on the night of May 25, 1991, a city known for its Super Bowl champions (four) and World Series winners (five) sat glued to television and radio to find out if the Penguins could bring their very first Stanley Cup championship home from Minnesota.

After getting past the New Jersey Devils, Washington Capitals and Boston Bruins, the Penguins faced a North Stars' team with as much of a Cinderella story as their own. The Penguins lost the first game of the Cup finals

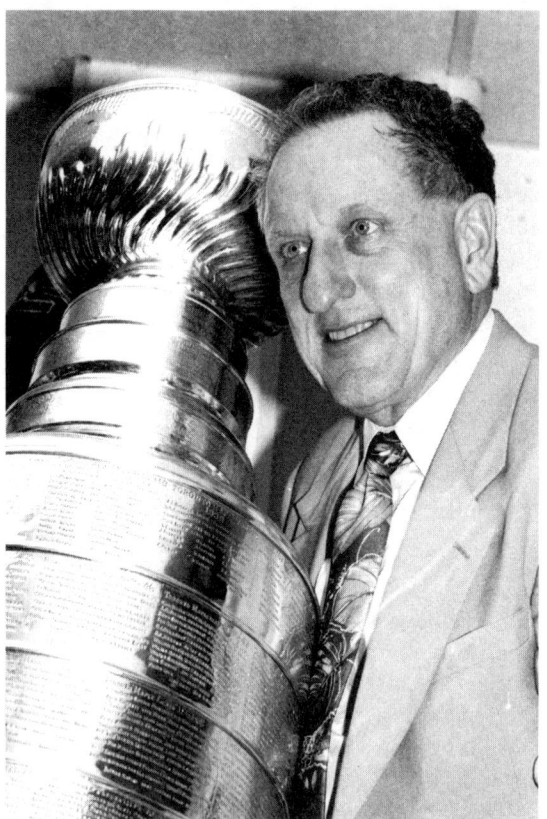

Badger Bob Johnson led Lemieux & Co. to the summit in the spring of 1991. The Penguins' coach didn't have a chance to repeat. Johnson died of brain cancer in the fall of 1991.

on their home ice and went to Minnesota after a split.

A loss at the Met Center in Bloomington, Minn., in Game 3 appeared to suggest the end of Pittsburgh. Mario Lemieux did not play because of back spasms and it was uncertain if he would be able to return in the series. The Penguins had endured most of the 1990–91 season without their captain, but the playoffs became a different story.

To the delight of his teammates, Lemieux was healthy enough to play in Game 4 and he was magnificent. He scored one goal and set up another as the Pens evened the finals with a 5–3 triumph.

Returning to Pittsburgh's Civic Arena for the fifth game, Mark Recchi ended a four-game scoring slump with two goals as the Pens skated to a 6–4 victory. They were now just

one victory away from what had once seemed impossible.

Penguins' forward Troy Loney recalled the feeling in the visitors' dressing room before Game 6. "The guys were so nervous, so ready, so keyed up that it was scary," Loney said. "I could see we were going to win it, that we were going to win the Cup. You could feel it."

No one felt it more than Lemieux. He was unstoppable. Ulf Samuelsson broke the ice with a wrist shot from the left point that gave Pittsburgh a 1–0 lead at 2:00 of the first period and Lemieux took a Larry Murphy pass off the boards, broke in alone and scored a shorthanded goal at 12:19 for a 2–0 lead. Joey Mullen scored 55 seconds later and it was 3–0.

Bob Errey scored on a Jaromir Jagr rebound midway through the second period, followed by goals from Ron Francis and Mullen again. Jim Paek and Murphy added third-period goals for an 8–0 rout and Pittsburgh finally had its first Stanley Cup. It was the largest margin of victory for a final-series game in this century.

Goalie Tom Barrasso played the final game with a bad groin injury, but finished the playoffs with a 12–7 record and 2.60 goals-against average. Lemieux wound up with an aching back and the Conn Smythe Trophy as the Most Valuable Player of the playoffs. He led all scorers with 16 goals and 28 assists for 44 points in 23 games.

When the final seconds had ticked off the Met Center clock, the Penguins swarmed onto the ice to celebrate with head coach Bob Johnson and general manager Craig Patrick.

Even Recchi, who had been carried off the ice one hour before after being knocked unconscious by a Jim Johnson check, was able to join the party.

"It can't get any better than this," he said. "It's an unbelievable thrill that so many players never get to experience."

"Boy, I'm so proud right now for the city of Pittsburgh," Loney said. "It's been a 20-year struggle for our fans, but they stuck with us. This is the reward. For all of us."

Although the clincher was played in Minnesota, Pittsburgh fans had their own celebration, clogging downtown streets and, at 3:30 A.M., greeting the champions at Greater Pittsburgh International Airport.

Two days later, they cheered as Lemieux raised the Cup at Point State Park. Before the celebration was over, the Cup would sit in the grass on Barrasso's front lawn and be dunked in the swimming pool at Lemieux's home.

11

THE ALL-STAR GAME

The National Hockey League's All-Star Game has been played in several formats since its inception in 1947, thanks to expansion and a closer relationship between the NHL and the Soviet Union.

The original format of the game pitted the Stanley Cup champions from the preceding season playing a team composed of All-Stars from the five other teams. These players were selected in a vote of hockey writers and broadcasters.

The Stanley Cup champion vs. All-Star team format remained until 1951, when it was changed to a true All-Star Game in which the First Team All-Stars from the previous season would play the Second Team All-Stars. That system was used for only two seasons, though, as in 1953 the league reverted to its Stanley Cup winners vs. All-Stars formula.

The game was played just before the start of the regular season and it would remain that way until expansion brought a change in 1967. The NHL's addition of six teams had resulted in two six-team divisions, called the

《 *All-Star veterans (from left) Phil Esposito, Bobby Orr, Gordie Howe and Bobby Hull share a laugh at the 1970 All-Star Game banquet in St. Louis.*

East and West, and the All-Star Game, the first to be played in midseason, pitted the champion Montreal Canadiens against stars from the other 11 teams. The following season, the All-Star Game became a contest between the East All-Stars and West All-Stars, with the Eastern players representing the six original NHL franchises and the Western stars the six expansion franchises.

The addition of the Atlanta Flames and New York Islanders in 1972 did not affect the All-Star Game, but the expansion to Vancouver and Buffalo did two years later. That was when the NHL split into four divisions, with two divisions in the newly formed Wales Conference and two in the Campbell Conference. It has been Wales vs. Campbell since then, except in 1979, when a group of NHL All-Stars played a Soviet Union All-Star squad in a three-game Challenge Cup series, and in 1987, when the NHL stars and Soviet stars met in Rendez-Vous '87, a two-game series that replaced the All-Star Game.

Since 1985, the starting six players on the two conference teams have been selected in a pool of fans, while the remainder of each squad is chosen by the two All-Star coaches. One requirement is that each of the NHL teams has at least one representative.

Players on the winning team receive $1,000 each. The losers get $750 each.

FIRST GAME

October 13, 1947 at Toronto
All-Stars 4, Toronto 3

Left wing Doug Bentley of the Chicago Black Hawks broke a 3–3 tie by drilling a shot past goalie Turk Broda in the second minute of the third period to give the All-Stars a 4–3 victory over the Maple Leafs.

Maurice Richard of Montreal and Syl Apps of the Leafs also starred. Richard assisted on the game-winning goal and scored once himself while Apps collected a goal and an assist.

Bill Mosienko, Chicago right wing, suffered a fractured left ankle when he was checked into the boards early in the second period.

All-Stars: Goal—Durnan (Montreal), Brimsek (Boston). Defense—Bouchard (Montreal), Reardon (Montreal), Stewart (Detroit), Quackenbush (Detroit). Forwards—M. Bentley (Chicago), D. Bentley (Chicago), Mosienko (Chicago), Warwick (New York), M. Richard (Montreal), Laprade (New York), Lindsay (Detroit), Dumart (Boston), Schmidt (Boston), Bauer (Boston), Leswick (New York), Coach—Dick Irvin (Montreal).

Toronto: Goal—Broda. Defense—Goldham, Stanowski, Mortson, Thomson, Barilko. Forwards—Watson, N. Metz, Poile, Kennedy, Apps, Ezinicki, Lynn, Meeker, Stewart, Klukay, Mackell. Coach—Hap Day.

Referee—King Clancy. Linesmen—Ed Mepham, Jim Primeau.

First Period: 1. Toronto, Watson (Ezinicki) 12:29. Penalties—Mortson, Leswick, Ezinicki 2, Reardon.

Second Period: 2. Toronto Ezinicki (Apps, Watson) 1:03. 3. All-Stars, M. Bentley (Reardon) 4:39. 4. Toronto, Apps (Watson, Mortson) 5:01. 5. All-Stars, Warwick (Laprade, Reardon) 17:35. Penalties—Lynn, Reardon 2.

Third Period: 6. All-Stars, M. Richard (unassisted) 0:28. 7. All-Stars, D. Bentley (Schmidt, M.

Richard) 1:26. Penalties—Mortson 2, Bouchard, Ezinicki, Schmidt.

Attendance—14,138.

SECOND GAME

November 3, 1948 at Chicago
All-Stars 3, Toronto 1

Goals by Gaye Stewart, Ted Lindsay and Woody Dumart enabled the All-Stars to defeat the Maple Leafs, 3–1. Dumart accounted for the most spectacular tally when he skated the length of the ice and put the puck past goalie Turk Broda at 3:06 of the second period.

Dumart's goal gave the All-Stars a 2–0 lead. Max Bentley scored for Toronto two minutes later. Stewart, however, added an insurance goal for the visitors with only 28 seconds remaining in the second period. Only eight penalties were handed out by referee Bill Chadwick.

All-Stars: Goal—Brimsek (Boston), Durnan (Montreal). Defense—Stewart (Detroit), Quackenbush (Detroit), N. Colville (New York), Reardon (Montreal), Bouchard (Montreal). Forwards—Lindsay (Detroit), D. Bentley (Chicago), M. Richard (Montreal), Laprade (New York), Howe (Detroit), Stewart (Chicago), Dumart (Boston), Schmidt (Boston), Lach (Montreal), Leswick (New York), Poile (Chicago). Coach—Tommy Ivan (Detroit).

Toronto: Goal—Broda. Defense—Thomson, Mortson, Boesch, Barilko, Mathers, Juzda. Forwards—H. Watson, M. Bentley, Klukay, Kennedy, Meeker, Ezinicki, Lynn, Costello, Mackell, Gardner. Coach—Hap Day.

Referee—Bill Chadwick. Linesman—Sam Babcock, Mush March.

First Period: No scoring. Penalties—Ezinicki, Reardon.

Second Period: 1. All-Stars, Lindsay (M. Richard, Lach) 1:35. 2. All-Stars, Dumart (unassisted) 3:06. 3. Toronto, M. Bentley (Costello) 5:13. 4. All-Stars, Stewart (D. Bentley) 19:32. Penalties—Mortson, Howe (major), Stewart, Bouchard, Juzda.

Third Period: No scoring. Penalty—Bouchard.

THIRD GAME

October 10, 1949 at Toronto
All-Stars 3, Toronto 1

Bob Goldham, a Chicago defenseman, registered the tying goal and assisted on the winner by Paul Ronty as the All-Stars defeated the Maple Leafs, 3–1, for their third straight victory over the Stanley Cup champions.

In the 15th minute of the second period, Goldham, after a rink-long dash, passed neatly to Boston's Ronty, who put the All-Stars ahead, 2–1. Goldham had tied the score with two minutes left in the opening period after Bill Barilko had found the nets for the Leafs three minutes earlier.

All-Stars: Goal—Durnan (Montreal), Rayner (New York). Defense—Stewart (Detroit), Goldham (Chicago), Egan (New York), Quackenbush (Boston), Harmon (Montreal), Reardon (Montreal). Forwards—O'Connor (New York), R. Conacher (Chicago), D. Bentley (Chicago), Mosienko (Chicago), M. Richard (Montreal), Laprade (New York), Abel (Detroit), Howe (Detroit), Lindsay (Detroit), Leswick (New York), Ronty (Boston). Coach—Tommy Ivan (Detroit).

Toronto: Goal—Broda. Defense—Thomson, Boesch, Juzda, Barilko. Forwards—Watson, M. Bentley, Klukay, Meeker, Lynn, Mackell, Kennedy, Gardner, Timgren, Dawes, Smith. Coach—Hap Day.

Referee—Bill Chadwick. Linesman—Ed Mepham, Jim Primeau.

First Period: 1. Toronto, Barilko (Watson, Gardner) 15:22. 2. All-Stars, Goldham (Laprade) 18:03. Penalties—M. Richard, Meeker, Thomson, Howe.

Second Period: 3. All-Stars, Ronty (Goldham) 14:42. Penalties—Harmon, Thomson, Boesch, Egan, Smith.

Third Period: 4. All-Stars, D. Bentley (Quackenbush) 2:38. Penalties—None.

Attendance—13,541.

FOURTH GAME

October 8, 1950 at Detroit
Detroit 7, All-Stars 1

Left wing Ted Lindsay scored three goals in leading the Red Wings to a 7–1 triumph over the All-Stars, snapping the Stars' three-year winning streak.

Lindsay beat goalie Chuck Rayner of the Rangers only 19 seconds after the opening faceoff. He scored again with three minutes remaining in the first period and registered No. 3 with five minutes left in the game.

Terry Sawchuk, a rookie, also was a standout for the Red Wings. He made 25 saves in goal, several of them spectacular stops.

All-Stars: Goal—Rayner (New York), Broda (Toronto). Defense—Stewart (Chicago), Mortson (Toronto), Thomson (Toronto), Harmon (Montreal), Quackenbush (Boston), Bouchard (Montreal). Forwards—D. Bentley (Chicago), Mosienko (Chicago), M. Richard (Montreal), Laprade (New York), Kennedy (Toronto), Leswick (New York), Ronty (Boston), Smith (Toronto), Peirson (Boston). Coach—Lynn Patrick (Boston).

Detroit: Goal—Sawchuk. Defense—Goldham, Kelly, Reise, Fogolin, Pronovost. Forwards—Lindsay, Gee, Howe, Peters, Stewart, Abel, McFadden, Prystai, Pavelich, Carveth, Black, Couture. Coach—Tommy Ivan.

Referee—George Gravel. Linesmen—George Hayes, Doug Young.

First Period: 1. Detroit, Lindsay (Howe) 0:19. 2. Detroit, Lindsay (Abel) 17:12. Penalties—M. Richard, Leswick 2, Abel, Pronovost, D. Bentley.

Second Period: 3. Detroit, Howe (Lindsay, Kelly) 11:12. 4. Detroit, Peters (Prystai, Kelly) 18:36. 5. Detroit, Pavelich (Prystai, Peters) 19:44. Penalty—Couture.

Third Period: 6. Detroit, Prystai (Pavelich) 7:36. 7. Detroit, Lindsay (unassisted) 14:28. 8. All-Stars, Smith (Peirson) 18:27. Penalties—Peters, Stewart.

Attendance—9,166.

FIFTH GAME

October 9, 1951 at Toronto
First Team All-Stars 2, Second Team All-Stars 2

Ken Mosdell's goal midway through the third period and two fistfights highlighted a 2–2 tie between the First and Second All-Star teams.

Mosdell, a Montreal forward, forged the deadlock for the Second Team when he converted passes from Tod Sloan and Gus Mortson at 9:25 of the final session.

The fisticuffs involved Detroit's Gordie Howe and Montreal's Maurice Richard in one match and Detroit's Ted Lindsay and Toronto's Ted Kennedy in the other.

First Team: Goal—Sawchuk (Detroit), Lumley (Chicago). Defense—Kelly (Detroit), Quackenbush (Boston), Eddolls (New York), Fogolin (Chicago), Dewsbury (Chicago). Forwards—Schmidt (Boston), Howe (Detroit), Lindsay (Detroit), Raleigh (New York), Peirson (Boston), Sandford (Boston), Sinclair (New York), D. Bentley (Chicago), Stewart (New York), Bodnar (Chicago). Coach—Joe Primeau (Toronto).

Second Team: Goal—Rayner (New York), McNeil (Montreal). Defense—Thomson (Toronto), Reise (Detroit), Bouchard (Montreal), Harvey (Montreal), Mortson (Toronto). Forwards—Kennedy (Toronto), Abel (Detroit), M. Richard (Montreal), Smith (Toronto), M. Bentley (Toronto), Sloan (Toronto), Watson (Toronto), Mosdell (Montreal), Meger (Montreal), Curry (Montreal). Coach—Dick Irvin (Montreal).

Referee—Bill Chadwick. Linesmen—Sam Babcock, Bill Morrison.

First Period: 1. First Team, Howe (Lindsay, Schmidt) 7:59. Penalties—Curry, Eddolls, Sloan.

Second Period: 2. Second Team, Sloan (Watson, M. Bentley) 2:26. 3. First Team, Peirson (Stewart, Raleigh) 16:49. Penalties—Raleigh, Lindsay.

Third Period: 4. Second Team, Mosdell (Sloan, Mortson) 9:25. Penalties—Lindsay, Howe.

Attendance—11,469.

SIXTH GAME

October 5, 1952 at Detroit
First Team All-Stars 1, Second Team All-Stars 1

Maurice (Rocket) Richard, taking a pass from defenseman Hy Buller, scored at 1:36 of the third period to give the Second Team All-Stars a 1–1 tie with the First Team.

Marty Pavelich of Detroit had put the First Team in front at 9:57 of the second period after taking passes from Bill Mosienko and Dave Creighton.

After Richard, Montreal's great right wing, tied the score, each team had several scoring opportunities but no success against goalies Terry Sawchuk of Detroit and Gerry McNeil of Montreal.

First Team: Goal—Sawchuk (Detroit). Defense—Kelly (Detroit), Harvey (Montreal), Mortson (Chicago), Quackenbush (Boston), Reise (New York), Goldham (Detroit). Forwards—Lach (Montreal), Howe (Detroit), Lindsay (Detroit), Creighton (Boston), Sandford (Boston), Pavelich (Detroit), Mosienko (Chicago), Leswick (Detroit), Sinclair (Detroit). Coach—Tommy Ivan (Detroit).

Second Team: Goal—Henry (Boston), McNeil (Montreal). Defense—Thomson (Toronto), Buller (New York), Johnson (Montreal), Flaman (Toronto), Bouchard (Montreal). Forwards—Schmidt (Boston), M. Richard (Montreal), Smith (Toronto), Watson (Toronto), Geoffrion (Montreal), Sloan (Toronto), Curry (Montreal), Reay (Montreal), Mosdell (Montreal), Megar (Montreal). Coach—Dick Irvin (Montreal).

Referee—Bill Chadwick. Linesmen—Doug Young, George Hayes.

First Period: No scoring. Penalties—Buller, Thomson, M. Richard.

Second Period: 1. First Team, Pavelich (Mosienko, Creighton) 9:57. Penalties—Bouchard, Thomson 2.

Third Period: 2. Second Team, M. Richard (Buller) 1:36. Penalty—Lach.

Attendance—10,680.

SEVENTH GAME

October 3, 1953 at Montreal
All-Stars 3, Montreal 1

Wally Hergesheimer of the New York Rangers scored two power-play goals in the opening period and paced the All-Stars to a 3–1 victory over the Canadiens.

Both of Hergesheimer's tallies came on plays originated by Detroit defenseman Red Kelly. Maurice Richard put Montreal on the scoreboard in the fifth minute of the third period. However, Detroit's Alex Delvecchio put the game out of reach with a goal into an empty net with 33 seconds left to play.

Kelly and Montreal's Bert Olmstead received major penalties for fighting in the third period.

All-Stars: Goal—Sawchuk (Detroit). Defense—Kelly (Detroit), Quackenbush (Boston), Gadsby (Chicago), Thomson (Toronto), Reise (New York), Mortson (Chicago). Forwards—Howe (Detroit), Lindsay (Detroit), Delvecchio (Detroit), Sandford (Boston), Smith (Toronto), Prystai (Detroit), Hergesheimer (New York), Mosienko (Chicago), Ronty (New York), Watson (Toronto). Coach—Lynn Patrick (Boston).

Montreal: Goal—McNeil. Defense—Harvey, St. Laurent, Bouchard, Johnson, MacPherson. Forwards—Moore, Curry, Olmstead, Beliveau, Geoffrion, Gamble, M. Richard, MacKay, Lach, McCormack, Mosdell, Meger, Davis, Mazur. Coach—Dick Irvin.

Referee—Red Storey. Linesmen—Sam Babcock, Doug Davies.

First Period: 1. All-Stars, Hergesheimer (Ronty, Kelly) 4:06. 2. All-Stars, Hergesheimer (Kelly) 5:25. Penalties—MacPherson, Lindsay.

Second Period: No scoring. Penalties—Mortson, St. Laurent, Howe, Richard.

Third Period: 3. Montreal, M. Richard (Harvey, Beliveau) 4:30. 4. All-Stars, Delvecchio (unassisted) 19:27. Penalties—Kelly, Olmstead, Smith.

Attendance—14,153.

EIGHTH GAME

October 2, 1954 at Detroit
Detroit 2, All-Stars 2

Toronto's Gus Mortson and Boston's Doug Mohns fired second-period goals that enabled the All-Stars to gain a 2–2 deadlock with the Red Wings.

The game was featured by the stellar goaltending of Terry Sawchuk, who played all 60 minutes for the Wings, and Toronto's Harry Lumley and Chicago's Al Rollins, who split the netminding chores for the Stars.

Alex Delvecchio and Gordie Howe collected Detroit's goals, Delvecchio midway in the opening period and Howe 10 minutes later.

All-Stars: Goal—Lumley (Toronto), Rollins (Chicago). Defense—Harvey (Montreal), Mortson (Chicago), Horton (Toronto), Gadsby (Chicago), Howell (New York), Quackenbush (Boston). Forwards—Geoffrion ((Montreal), Mackell (Boston), Smith (Toronto), M. Richard (Montreal), Kennedy (Toronto), Beliveau (Montreal), Sandford (Boston), Raleigh (New York), Mosdell (Montreal), Ronty (New York), Mohns (Boston). Coach—King Clancy (Toronto).

Detroit: Goal—Sawchuk. Defense—Goldham, Pronovost, Kelly, Woit, Allen. Forwards—Lindsay, Leswick, Howe, Prystai, Skov, Reibel, Delvecchio, Wilson, Dineen, Poile, Bonin. Coach—Jim Skinner.

Referee—Bill Chadwick. Linesmen—George Hayes, Bill Morrison.

First Period: 1. Detroit, Delvecchio (Lindsay, Reibel) 9:50. 2. Detroit, Howe (Reibel, Kelly) 19:55. Penalties—Mortson, Bonin 2, Mackell, Howell.

Second Period: 3. All-Stars, Mortson (Gadsby, Kennedy) 4:19. 4. All-Stars, Mohns (Beliveau) 13:10. Penalties—Dineen, Bonin, Howell, Sandford, Mohns.

Third Period: No scoring. Penalties—Lindsay, Mortson, Woit.

Attendance—10,689.

NINTH GAME

October 2, 1955 at Detroit
Detroit 3, All-Stars 1

Earl (Dutch) Reibel scored twice as the Red Wings extended their unbeaten streak on home ice to 26 games by downing the All-Stars, 3–1.

The Wings, who finished the 1954–55 season with 19 victories and six ties at the Olympia, took the lead 57 seconds into the second period when Gordie Howe beat Toronto's Harry Lumley. Reibel made it 2–0 five minutes later. Doug Harvey of Montreal scored the Stars' only goal at 16:38 of the third period.

With a minute left in the game, All-Star coach Dick Irvin replaced goalie Terry Sawchuk with an extra forward and Reibel slid a long shot into the empty cage.

All-Stars: Goal—Lumley (Toronto), Sawchuk (Boston). Defense—Harvey (Montreal), Flaman (Boston), Morrison (Toronto), Stanley (Chicago), Martin (Chicago). Forwards—Beliveau (Montreal), M. Richard (Montreal), Smith (Toronto), Mosdell (Montreal), Geoffrion (Montreal), Lewicki (New York), Sullivan (Chicago), Litzenberger (Chicago), Stewart (Toronto), Labine (Boston), Watson (Chicago). Coach—Dick Irvin (Chicago).

Detroit: Goal—Hall. Defense—Goldham, Pronovost, Kelly, Godfrey, Hillman, Hollingworth. Forwards—Lindsay, Reibel, Howe, Delvecchio, Pavelich, Sandford, Chevrefils, Dineen, Toppazzini, Bucyk, Corcoran. Coach—Jim Skinner.

First Period: No scoring. Penalties—Flaman, Corcoran, Geoffrion, Stewart, Bucyk, Stanley, Morrison.

Second Period: 1. Detroit, Howe (Reibel, Delvecchio) 0:57. 2. Detroit, Reibel (Howe, Lindsay) 5:43. Penalties—Corcoran, Hollingworth.

Third Period: 3. All-Stars, Harvey (Beliveau, Smith) 16:38. 4. Detroit, Reibel (Goldham, Lindsay) 19:33. Penalties—Hollingworth, Harvey.

Attendance—10,111.

TENTH GAME

October 9, 1956 at Montreal
Montreal 1, All-Stars 1

The Canadiens and All-Stars played to a 1–1 tie in a game that marked the introduction of the new power-play regulation.

Maurice Richard clicked on a power play for Montreal only 33 seconds after the Rangers' Red Sullivan had been penalized for holding in the 15th minute of the second period.

Sullivan came out of the penalty box immediately after Richard's tally. Before the rule change, a player serving a minor penalty had to spend the full two minutes in the penalty box even if his team was scored against while shorthanded.

Detroit's Ted Lindsay evened the score four minutes after Richard's tally.

All-Stars: Goal—Hall (Detroit), Sawchuk (Boston). Defense—Gadsby (New York), Kelly (Detroit), Flaman (Boston), Mortson (Chicago), Morrison (Toronto), Bolton (Toronto). Forwards—Lindsay (Detroit), Sloan (Toronto), Howe (Detroit), Delvecchio (Detroit), Labine (Boston), Duff (Toronto), Armstrong (Toronto), Mickoski (Chicago), Wilson (Chicago), Hergesheimer (Chicago), Creighton (New York), Sullivan (New York). Coach—Jim Skinner (Detroit).

Montreal: Goal—Plante. Defense-Harvey, St. Laurent, Johnson, Turner, Talbot. Forwards—Beliveau, Geoffrion, Olmstead, Curry, Leclair, M. Richard, Moore, H. Richard, Marshall, Provost. Coach—Toe Blake.

Referee—Red Storey. Linesmen—Doug Davies, Bill Roberts.

First Period: No scoring. Penalties—Flaman, Beliveau 2.

Second Period: 1. Montreal, M. Richard (Olmstead, Harvey) 14:58. 2. All-Stars, Lindsay (Mortson) 18:48. Penalties—Mortson, Sullivan.

Third Period: No scoring. Penalties—Labine, Mortson.

Attendance—13,095.

ELEVENTH GAME

October 5, 1957 at Montreal
All-Stars 5, Montreal 3

Gordie Howe of the Detroit Red Wings and Dean Prentice of the New York Rangers each scored in the third period to give the All-Stars a 5–3 triumph over the Canadiens.

Howe broke a 3–3 tie at 8:11 and Prentice registered an insurance marker with 3:10 left in the game.

The Canadiens had taken a 3–2 lead in the second period on goals by Bert Olmstead and Stan Smrke, but the Rangers' Andy Bathgate tied it for the Stars at 18:14 of the second period on assists from Prentice and Chicago's Ed Litzenberger.

All-Stars: Goal—Hall (Chicago). Defense—Kelly (Detroit), Flaman (Boston), Gadsby (New York), Morrison (Toronto), M. Pronovost (Detroit), Stanley (Boston). Forwards—Howe (Detroit), Lindsay (Chicago), Litzenberger (Chicago), Chevrefils (Boston), Bathgate (New York), Duff (Toronto), Delvecchio (Detroit), Prentice (New York), Migay (Toronto), Armstrong (Toronto), McKenney (Boston). Coach—Milt Schmidt (Boston).

Montreal: Goal—Plante. Defense—Harvey, St. Laurent, Johnson, Turner, Talbot. Forwards—Beliveau, M. Richard, Curry, Olmstead, Smrke, Moore, Provost, H. Richard, Bonin, Goyette, A. Pronovost, Marshall. Coach—Toe Blake.

Referee—Red Storey. Linesmen—Doug Davis, Bill Morrison.

First Period: 1. All-Stars, Kelly (unassisted) 1:06. 2. Montreal, M. Richard (H. Richard, Moore) 10:53. 3. All-Stars, Stanley (Prentice, Migay) 19:55. Penalties—Migay, Talbot, Howe 2, Harvey.

Second Period: 4. Montreal, Olmstead (Johnson) 0:33. 5. Montreal, Smrke (Bonin) 9:13. 6. All-Stars, Bathgate (Prentice, Litzenberger) 18:14. Penalties—Talbot, Chevrefils, Johnson.

Third Period: 7. All-Stars, Howe (Chevrefils, Morrison) 8:11. 8. All-Stars, Prentice (Bathgate, Litzenberger) 16:50. Penalties—Flaman 2, Olmstead.

Attendance—13,003.

TWELFTH GAME

October 4, 1958 at Montreal
Montreal 6, All-Stars 3

Maurice Richard scored Montreal's first and final goals as the Canadiens defeated the All-Stars, 6–3, and ended a three-year non-winning streak for the Stanley Cup champions.

Referee Eddie Powers handed out six minor penalties and four led to goals. Andy Bathgate of the Rangers scored twice for the All-Stars while Bob Pulford of Toronto notched the visitors' other goal.

The Canadiens' Bernie (Boom Boom) Geoffrion suffered pulled neck and chest muscles from a bodycheck by Detroit's Red Kelly.

All-Stars: Goal—Hall (Chicago). Defense—Gadsby (New York), Flaman (Boston), M. Pronovost (Detroit), Mohns (Boston), Kelly (Detroit), St. Laurent (Chicago). Forwards—Howe (Detroit), Bathgate (New York), Henry (New York), Sullivan (New York), Delvecchio (Detroit), Toppazzini (Boston), Harris (Toronto), Duff (Toronto), Litzenberger (Chicago), McKenney (Boston), Pulford (Toronto). Coach—Milt Schmidt (Boston).

Montreal: Goal—Plante. Defense—Harvey, Johnson, Turner, Talbot, Cushenan. Forwards—Beliveau, Geoffrion, Backstrom, M. Richard, Moore, Provost, McDonald, H. Richard, Bonin, Goyette, Marshall, A. Pronovost. Coach—Toe Blake.

Referee—Eddie Powers. Linesmen—George Hayes, Bill Morrison.

First Period: 1. Montreal, M. Richard (Harvey, Moore) 9:19. 2. Montreal, Geoffrion (H. Richard) 16:20. Penalties—Henry, Harvey.

Second Period: 3. Montreal, Marshall (Provost) 2:33. 4. Montreal, H. Richard (Talbot, Moore) 5:08. 5. All-Stars, Pulford (Toppazzini, Harris) 11:39. Penalty—Turner.

Third Period: 6. All-Stars, Bathgate (Litzenberger, Henry) 3:55. 7. Montreal, McDonald (Provost, Marshall) 7:43. 8. All-Stars, Bathgate (Pulford, Sullivan) 13:54. 9. Montreal, M. Richard (Moore, H. Richard) 16:04. Penalties—Mohns, Duff, Provost.

Attendance—13,989.

THIRTEENTH GAME

October 3, 1959 at Montreal
Montreal 6, All-Stars 1

Big Jean Beliveau scored twice and defenseman Doug Harvey collected three assists as the Canadiens trounced the All-Stars, 6–1.

The Stars were considerably weakened by the absence of holdouts Bobby Hull, Tod Sloan and Pierre Pilote of Chicago and Bob Pulford, Dick Duff and Tim Horton of Toronto. They had not signed contracts for the season and therefore were ineligible to play.

Leading by 2–1 going into the third period, Montreal buried the Stars under a four-goal avalanche in the final 20 minutes. The marksmen were Beliveau, Dickie Moore, Henri Richard and Andre Pronovost.

All-Stars: Goal—Sawchuk (Detroit). Defense—M. Pronovost (Detroit), Gadsby (New York), Flaman (Boston), Brewer (Toronto), Mohns (Boston). Forwards—Bathgate (New York), Howe (Detroit), Delvecchio (Detroit), Sullivan (New York), Toppazzini (Boston), Mahovlich (Toronto), Olmstead (Toronto), Litzenberger (Chicago), McKenney (Boston), Armstrong (Toronto). Coach—Punch Imlach (Toronto).

Montreal: Goal—Plante. Defense—Johnson, Harvey, Turner, Langlois, J.C. Tremblay. Forwards—Beliveau, Moore, H. Richard, Geoffrion, Backstrom, Hicke, M. Richard, Provost, McDonald, Bonin, Goyette, Marshall, A. Pronovost. Coach—Toe Blake.

Referee—Frank Udvari. Linemen—George Hayes, Bob Frampton.

First Period: No scoring. Penalties—None.

Second Period: 1. Montreal, Beliveau (Hicke, Harvey) 4:25. 2. Montreal, McDonald (Backstrom, Geoffrion) 13:43. 3. All-Stars, McKenney (Litzenberger) 18:30. Penalties—None.

Third Period: 4. Montreal, Moore (H. Richard, Johnson) 7:44. 5. Montreal, H. Richard (Moore, Harvey) 9:31. 6. Montreal, Beliveau (Hicke, Bonin) 11:54. 7. Montreal, Pronovost (Harvey) 15:51. Penalties—Tremblay, Bathgate, Turner.

Attendance—13,818.

FOURTEENTH GAME

October 1, 1960 at Montreal
All-Stars 2, Montreal 1

Andy Hebenton took a pass from his New York Ranger teammate, Red Sullivan, and beat goalie Jacques Plante at 15:51 of the second period to give the All-Stars a 2–1 victory over the Canadiens.

Frank Mahovlich of Toronto got the other Stars' goal in the opening minutes of the second period and Claude Provost tied the score for the Canadiens 11 minutes later.

This was the first All-Star game in which Maurice Richard, the Canadiens' brilliant right wing, did not participate. He had announced his retirement as a player the previous month.

All-Stars: Goal—Hall (Chicago). Defense—M. Pronovost (Detroit), Stanley (Toronto), Pilote (Chicago), Gadsby (New York), Kelly (Toronto), Armstrong (Boston). Forwards—Howe (Detroit), Hull (Chicago), Horvath (Boston), Stasiuk (Boston), Ullman (Detroit), Bathgate (New York), Hay (Chicago), Hebenton (New York), Sullivan (New York), McKenney (Boston), Mahovlich (Toronto), Pulford (Toronto). Coach—Punch Imlach (Toronto).

Montreal: Goal—Plante. Defense—Harvey, Langlois, Johnson, Turner, Talbot. Forwards—Beliveau, Geoffrion, Bonin, Backstrom, Hicke, Moore, Provost, H. Richard, Marshall, A. Pronovost. Coach—Toe Blake.

Referee—Eddie Powers. Linesmen—George Hayes, Neil Armstrong.

First Period: No scoring. Penalty—Talbot.

Second Period: 1. All-Stars, Mahovlich (Pilote, Kelly) 0:40. 2. Montreal, Provost (Backstrom, A. Pronovost) 11:40. 3. All-Stars, Hebenton (Sullivan) 15:51. Penalties—Sullivan, Hull, Johnson.

Third Period: No scoring. Penalties—Hicke, Gadsby, Pilote, Harvey.

Attendance—13,949.

FIFTEENTH GAME

October 7, 1961 at Chicago
All-Stars 3, Chicago 1

Teammates Gordie Howe and Alex Delvecchio of the Detroit Red Wings each scored one goal and assisted on another to lead the All-Stars to a 3–1 triumph over the Black Hawks.

Delvecchio opened the scoring in the 12th minute of the opening period and Howe closed it in the 12th minute of the second session. Norm Ullman, another Red Wing, assisted on both tallies.

Eric Nesterenko beat Toronto goalie Johnny Bower for Chicago's only tally at 6:26 of the second period.

All-Stars: Goal—Bower (Toronto), Worsley (New York). Defense—Harvey (New York), Pronovost (Detroit), Boivin (Boston), Stanley (Toronto), Brewer (Toronto), Mohns (Boston). Forwards—Richard (Montreal), McKenney (Boston), Ullman (Detroit), Bathgate (New York), Geoffrion (Montreal), Howe (Detroit), Provost (Montreal), Mahovlich (Toronto), Moore (Montreal), Delvecchio (Detroit), Goyette (Montreal). Coach—Sid Abel (Detroit).

Chicago: Goal—Hall. Defense—Turner, Pilote, Vasko, Evans, Fleming, St. Laurent. Forwards—Hall, Balfour, Horvath, Murphy, Hay, Melnyk, McDonald, Nesterenko, Hull, Wharram, Maki, Mikita. Coach—Rudy Pilous.

Referee—Frank Udvari. Linesmen—George Hayes, Neil Armstrong.

First Period: 1. All-Stars, Delvecchio (Ullman, Howe) 11:37. Penalties—Mahovlich, Hay, Vasko.

Second Period: 2. All-Stars, McKenney (Pronovost, Bathgate) 2:37. 3. Chicago, Nesterenko (Pilote, Hull) 6:26. 4. All-Stars, Howe (Delvecchio, Ullman) 11:38. Penalties—Goyette, Nesterenko 3, McKenney, Mahovlich 2.

Third Period: No scoring. Penalties—Pilote, Richard, Hull.

Attendance—14,534.

SIXTEENTH GAME

October 6, 1962 at Toronto
Toronto 4, All-Stars 1

The Maple Leafs erupted for all their goals in the opening period against Montreal goalie Jacques Plante and went on to defeat the All-Stars, 4–1, for their first victory in the annual classic.

Dick Duff, Bob Pulford, Frank Mahovlich and Eddie Shack beat Plante, who had captured the Vezina Trophy the previous season.

Detroit's Gordie Howe scored the only goal for the Stars. It was his seventh in the competition and enabled him to tie the record held by the retired Maurice Richard.

All-Stars: Goal—Plante (Montreal), Hall (Chicago), Worsley (New York). Defense—Harvey (New York), Talbot (Montreal), Pilote (Chicago), Mohns (Boston), Boivin (Boston). Forwards—McKenney (Boston), Howe (Detroit), Hull (Chicago), Geoffrion (Montreal), Bathgate (New York), Ullman (Detroit), Delvecchio (Detroit), Backstrom (Montreal), Prentice (New York). Coach—Rudy Pilous (Chicago).

Toronto: Goal—Bower. Defense—Brewer, Horton, Douglas, Baun, Hillman, Stanley. Forwards—Kelly, Mahovlich, Nevin, Duff, Armstrong, Stewart, Keon, Harris, Pulford, Shack, MacMillan, Litzenberger. Coach—Punch Imlach.

Referee—Eddie Powers. Linesmen—Matt Pavelich, Ron Wicks.

First Period: 1. Toronto, Duff (Armstrong, Douglas) 5:22. 2. All-Stars, Howe (Delvecchio, Pilote) 7:26. 3. Toronto, Pulford (Stewart) 10:45. 4. Toronto, Mahovlich (Stanley) 13:03. 5. Toronto, Shack (Keon) 19:32. Penalties—Mohns, Nevin, McKenney, Brewer, Shack, Howe.

Second Period: No scoring. Penalties—Kelly, Howe, Brewer.

Third Period: No scoring. Penalties—Baun, Boivin, Shack.

Attendance—14,197.

SEVENTEENTH GAME

October 5, 1963 at Toronto
Toronto 3, All-Stars 3

Frank Mahovlich, Toronto's big left wing, scored two goals and collected an assist as the Leafs played a 3–3 tie with the All-Stars.

The Leafs held the lead three times, but each time the Stars rallied for a deadlock. Mahovlich scored his team's first two goals and Ed Litzenberger's tally put Toronto in front, 3–2, at 2:56 of the third period. Just 27 seconds later, Detroit defenseman Marcel Pronovost drilled the puck home from the point.

All-Stars: Goal—Hull (Chicago), Sawchuk (Detroit). Defense—Pilote (Chicago), Vasko (Chicago), Howell (New York), Johnson (Boston), Pronovost (Detroit). Forwards—Howe (Detroit), Richard (Montreal), Bathgate (New York), Hull (Chicago), Delvecchio (Detroit), Ullman (Detroit), Prentice (Boston), Oliver (Boston), Henry (New York), Bucyk (Boston), Geoffrion (Montreal), Provost (Montreal), Beliveau (Montreal). Coach—Sid Abel (Detroit).

Toronto: Goal—Bower, Simmons. Defense—Baun, Horton, Hillman, Douglas, Stanley. Forwards—Mahovlich, Shack, Kelly, Harris, Pulford, Nevin, Keon, Litzenberger, MacMillan, Stewart, Duff, Armstrong. Coach—Punch Imlach.

Referee—Frank Udvari. Linesmen—Matt Pavelich, Neil Armstrong.

First Period: 1. Toronto, Mahovlich (Armstrong, Baun) 2:22. 2. All-Stars, Richard (Henry, Howe) 4:08. 3. Toronto, Mahovlich (Keon, Litzenberger) 12:11. 4. All-Stars, Hull (Geoffrion) 19:27. Penalties—Stanley, Howell, Duff.

Second Period: No scoring. Penalties—Pronovost, Horton 2, Baun, Hull.

Third Period: 5. Toronto, Litzenberger (Mahovlich, Kelly) 2:56. 6. All-Stars, Pronovost (Bucyk, Oliver) 3:23. Penalty—Stanley.

Attendance—14,003.

EIGHTEENTH GAME

October 10, 1964 at Toronto
All-Stars 3, Leafs 2

Montreal's Jean Beliveau scored the tie-breaking goal with six minutes remaining in the second period and led the All-Stars to a 3–2 victory over the Maple Leafs.

Beliveau's goal snapped a 1–1 deadlock. Gordie Howe of Detroit and Bobby Hull of Chicago assisted on the play.

Murray Oliver of Boston put the Stars in front, 3–1, in the seventh minute of the third period, offsetting a Leafs' goal by Jim Pappin later in the session.

All-Stars: Goal—Hall (Chicago), Hodge (Montreal). Defense—Vasko (Chicago), Pilote (Chicago), Laperriere (Montreal), Howell (New York), Boivin (Boston). Forwards—Beliveau (Montreal), Howe (Detroit), B. Hull (Chicago), Delvecchio (Detroit), Gilbert (New York), Oliver (Boston), Henry (New York), Mikita (Chicago), Bucyk (Boston), Provost (Montreal). Coach—Sid Abel (Detroit).

Toronto: Goal—Bower, Sawchuk. Defense—Horton, Douglas, Baun, Brewer, Hillman. Forwards—Pulford, Stewart, Shack, Keon, McKenney, Armstrong, Harris, Ehman, Pappin, Ellis, Bathgate, Mahovlich. Coach—Punch Imlach.

Referee—Frank Udvari. Linesmen—Ron Wicks, Neil Armstrong.

First Period: No scoring. Penalties—Bathgate, Howell, Baun, Douglas, Oliver.

Second Period: 1. All-Stars, Boivin (Laperriere, Oliver) 10:47. 2. Toronto, Douglas (Bathgate, Mahovlich) 11:45. 3. All-Stars, Beliveau (Hull, Howe) 13:51. Penalties—Laperriere, Mikita, Baun, Howell, Hodge (served by Gilbert).

Third Period: 4. All-Stars, Oliver (Bucyk, Howell) 6:11. 5. Toronto, Pappin (Ehman) 13:35. Penalties—Stewart, Pilote, Douglas, Provost.

Attendance—14,200.

NINETEENTH GAME

October 20, 1965 at Montreal
All-Stars 5, Montreal 2

Gordie Howe of Detroit shattered the career All-Star game record for goals by scoring his eighth and ninth while leading the All-Stars to a 5–2 victory over the Canadiens.

The veteran right winger, who also assisted on two other scores, broke the mark of seven goals he shared with the Canadiens' Maurice Richard. Howe broke another All-Star record by lifting his career-point total to 16. He played on a line with Norm Ullman, also of Detroit, and Chicago's Bobby Hull.

All-Stars: Goal—Hall (Chicago), Crozier (Detroit), Johnston (Boston). Defense—Gadsby (Detroit), Pilote (Chicago), Howell (New York), Pronovost (Toronto), Green (Boston), Baun (Toronto). Forwards—Ullman (Detroit), Howe (Detroit), Hull (Chicago), Ellis (Toronto), Hadfield (New York), Gilbert (New York), Oliver (Boston), Bucyk (Boston), Mahovlich (Toronto), Nesterenko (Chicago), Delvecchio (Detroit), Mohns (Chicago). Coach—Billy Reay (Chicago).

Montreal: Goal—Hodge, Worsley. Defense—J. C. Tremblay, Harris, Laperriere, Talbot, Harper. Forwards—Beliveau, Rousseau, Duff, Backstrom, Larose, Provost, Richard, Balon, G. Tremblay, Ferguson, Berenson. Coach—Toe Blake.

Referee—Art Skov. Linesman—Matt Pavelich, Neil Armstrong.

First Period: No scoring. Penalties—Harris 2, Gadsby, Beliveau, Larose, Pronovost.

Second Period: 1. Montreal, Beliveau (Duff, Rousseau) 6:48. 2. Montreal, Laperriere (Backstrom, Larose) 11:00. 3. All-Stars, Ullman (Hull, Howe) 12:40. 4. All-Stars, Hull (Howe, Oliver) 16:35. 5. All-Stars, Howe (Ullman, Baun) 19:19. Penalty—Balon.

Third Period: 6. All-Stars, Bucyk (Gadsby, Oliver) 10:01. 7. All-Stars, Howe (unassisted) 18:39. Penalties—Ellis, Ferguson, Howell 2.

Attendance—13,351.

TWENTIETH GAME

January 18, 1967 at Montreal
Montreal 3, All-Stars 0

John Ferguson, Montreal's aggressive left wing, scored twice as the Canadiens blanked the All-Stars, 3–0, in a dull, listless contest, the first annual All-Star Game played in mid-season.

Speedy Henri Richard put the Canadiens in front at 14:03 of the opening period when he converted passes from Bobby Rousseau and Terry Harper to beat Chicago's Glenn Hall, who was in the Stars' nets.

Ferguson scored less than two minutes later and again with only eight seconds remaining in the game.

All-Stars: Goal—Hall (Chicago), Giacomin (New York). Defense—Stanley (Toronto), Howell (New York), Stapleton (Chicago), Neilson (New York), Pilote (Chicago). Forwards—Ullman (Detroit), Mikita (Chicago), Keon (Toronto), Oliver (Boston), Howe (Detroit), Gilbert (New York), Nevin (New York), B. Hull (Chicago), Mahovlich (Toronto), Bucyk (Boston), Delvecchio (Detroit). Coach—Sid Abel (Detroit).

Montreal: Goal—Hodge, Bauman. Defense—Laperriere, Talbot, Harper, J. C. Tremblay, Harris, Roberts. Forwards—Richard, Beliveau, Backstrom, Balon, Provost, Larose, Cournoyer, Rousseau, Rochefort, Duff, G. Tremblay, Ferguson. Coach—Toe Blake.

Referee—Vern Buffey. Linesmen—Matt Pavelich, Neil Armstrong.

First Period: 1. Montreal, Richard (Rousseau, Harper) 14:03. 2. Montreal, Ferguson (Larose) 15:59. Penalties—None.

Second Period: No scoring. Penalties—Howell, Richard, Ferguson.

Third Period: 3. Montreal, Ferguson (Richard, Rousseau) 19:52. Penalties—None.

Attendance—14,284.

TWENTY-FIRST GAME

January 16, 1968 at Toronto
Toronto 4, All-Stars 3

The Maple Leafs came from behind on second-period goals by Allan Stanley and Pete Stemkowski to defeat the All-Stars, 4–3, before a record All-Star crowd of 15,740.

The Stars took a 2–1 lead on Ken Wharram's goal in the opening minute of the second period. But Stanley, on passes from Stemkowski and Wayne Carleton, tied the score seven minutes later and Stemkowski put the Leafs in front to stay at 16:36.

A moment of silence was observed before the start of the game in tribute to Bill Masterton, the Minnesota forward who died the previous day from a head injury received in a game three days earlier.

All-Stars: Goal—Giacomin (New York), Hall (St. Louis). Defense—Pilote (Chicago), Howell (New York), Orr (Boston), Laperriere (Montreal), Baun (Oakland), J. C. Tremblay (Montreal). Forwards—Mikita (Chicago), B. Hull (Chicago), Beliveau (Montreal), Ullman (Detroit), Howe (Detroit), Bucyk (Boston), Schinkel (Pittsburgh), Rochefort (Philadelphia), Balon (Minnesota), Marshall (New York). Coach—Toe Blake (Montreal).

Toronto: Goal—Gamble, A. Smith. Defense—Rupp, Horton, L. Hillman, Pronovost, Stanley. Forwards—Keon, Mahovlich, Ellis, Armstrong, Oliver, Stemkowski, Walton, Pappin, Pulford, Conacher, Carleton. Coach—Punch Imlach.

Referee—Bill Friday. Linesmen—Brent Castleman and Pat Shetler.

First Period: 1. Toronto, Oliver (Mahovlich, L. Hillman) 5:56. 2. All-Stars, Mikita (Hull, J. C. Tremblay) 19:53. Penalty—Stemkowski.

Second Period: 3. All-Stars, Wharram (Mikita) 0:35. 4. Toronto, Stanley (Stemkowski, Carleton) 7:56. 5. Toronto, Stemkowski (Carleton, Rupp) 16:36. Penalty—Howe.

Third Period: 6. All-Stars, Ellis (Mahovlich, L. Hillman) 3:31. 7. All-Stars, Ullman (Howe, Orr) 8:23. Penalties—Howe, Walton.

Attendance—15,740.

TWENTY-SECOND GAME

January 21, 1969 at Montreal
East 3, West 3

For the first time, the All-Star Game pitted a squad from the new NHL West Division against one from the established East Division.

Claude Larose of Minnesota scored a goal with less than three minutes to play to give the underdog West a 3–3 standoff against the powerful East.

East All-Stars: Goal—Giacomin (New York), Cheevers (Boston). Defense—Orr (Boston), J. C. Tremblay (Montreal), Harris (Montreal), Green (Boston), Horton (Toronto), Stapleton (Chicago). Forwards—Beliveau (Montreal), Nevin (New York), Howe (Detroit), D. Hull (Chicago), Esposito (Boston), Ullman (Toronto), Rousseau (Montreal), B. Hull (Chicago), Gilbert (New York), Mikita (Chicago), Mahovlich (Detroit). Coach—Toe Blake (Montreal).

West All-Stars: Goal—Hall (St. Louis), Parent (Philadelphia), Plante (St. Louis). Defense—Van Impe (Philadelphia), Arbour (St. Louis), Harvey (St. Louis), Vasko (Minnesota), Picard (St. Louis), Vadnais (Oakland), White (Los Angeles). Forwards—Berenson (St. Louis), O'Shea (Minnesota), Hicke (Oakland), Hampson (Oakland), Schinkel (Pittsburgh), Roberts (St. Louis), Larose (Minnesota), McDonald (St. Louis), Grant (Minnesota). Coach—Scotty Bowman (St. Louis).

Referee—John Ashley. Linesmen—Neil Armstrong, Matt Pavelich.

First Period: 1. West, Berenson (Harvey, Picard) 4:43. 2. East, Mahovlich (Rousseau, Stapleton) 17:32. Penalty—Vadnais.

Second Period: 3. West, Roberts (Berenson, Picard) 1:53. Penalties—Horton, White.

Third Period: 4. East, Mahovlich (Harris, Gilbert) 3:11. 5. East, Nevin (Ullman) 7:20. 6. West, Larose (Grant, O'Shea) 17:07. Penalties—White, Harvey.

Attendance—16,256.

TWENTY-THIRD GAME

January 20, 1970 at St. Louis
East 4, West 1

Chicago's Bobby Hull scored one goal and set up another by Gordie Howe of Detroit as the East All-Stars completely dominated the play and whipped the West, 4–1.

The East set a record with 44 shots on goal, including 20 in the last period, all of which were stopped by Jacques Plante of St. Louis. All of the East goals came in the first 30 minutes against Philadelphia's Bernie Parent. The West had just 17 shots, a record low.

Each team scored in the first 37 seconds with Jacques Laperriere hitting for the East and Pittsburgh's Dean Prentice for the West. The two goals were the fastest in All-Star history.

East All-Stars: Goal—Giacomin (New York), T. Esposito (Chicago). Defense—Orr (Boston), Laperriere (Montreal), Neilson (New York), Park (New York), Savard (Montreal), Brewer (Detroit). Forwards—P. Esposito (Boston), Bucyk (Boston), Howe (Detroit), Ratelle (New York), Tkaczuk (New York), Ellis (Toronto), Keon (Toronto), Lemaire (Montreal), B. Hull (Chicago), Gilbert (New York), McKenzie (Boston), Mahovlich (Detroit). Coach—Claude Ruel (Montreal).

West All-Stars: Goal—Hall (St. Louis), Parent (Philadelphia), Plante (St. Louis). Defense—Arbour (St. Louis), White (Los Angeles), Woytowich (Pittsburgh), Howell (Oakland), B. Plager (St. Louis), Vadnais (Oakland). Forwards—Berenson (St. Louis), St. Marseille (St. Louis), Clarke (Philadelphia), Goyette (St. Louis), Parise (Minnesota), Prentice (Pittsburgh), Roberts (St. Louis), O'Shea (Minnesota), Larose (Minnesota), McDonald (St. Louis), Goldsworthy (Minnesota), Grant (Minnesota), Sabourin (St. Louis). Coach—Scotty Bowman (St. Louis).

Referee—Art Skov. Linesmen—Matt Pavelich, Claude Bechard.

First Period: 1. East, Laperriere (unassisted) 0:20. 2. West, Prentice (Berenson, Woytowich) 0:37. 3. East, Howe (B. Hull, Lemaire) 7:20. Penalties—Park, St. Marseille.

Second Period: 4. East, B. Hull (Brewer) 3:26. 5. East, Tkaczuk (McKenzie, Bucyk) 9:37. Penalties—Woytowich.

Third Period: No scoring. Penalties—Woytowich.

Attendance—16,587.

TWENTY-FOURTH GAME

January 19, 1971 at Boston
West 2, East 1

The Chicago Black Hawks had moved from the East to the West Division at the start of the 1970–71 season and the expansion division reaped an immediate benefit in the All-Star game.

Black Hawk teammates Bobby Hull and Chico Maki scored goals in the first $4\frac{1}{2}$ minutes and that was enough for a 2–1 West victory over the East. Montreal's Yvan Cournoyer got one goal for the East at 6:19 of the first period but the game was scoreless after that.

A crowd of 14,790 paid a record $79,000 to watch the defense-dominated game.

East All-Stars: Goal—Giacomin (New York), Villemure (New York). Defense—Park (New York), Tremblay (Montreal), Orr (Boston), Tallon (Vancouver), Neilson (New York), Smith (Boston). Forwards-Bucyk (Boston), P. Esposito (Boston), Hodge (Boston), Howe (Detroit), Westfall (Boston), Perreault (Buffalo), Cournoyer (Montreal), Keon (Toronto), Balon (New York), Ratelle (New York), P. Mahovlich (Montreal), F. Mahovlich (Montreal). Coach—Harry Sinden (Boston).

West All-Stars: Goal—Wakely (St. Louis), T. Esposito (Chicago). Defense—White (Chicago), Magnuson (Chicago), Harris (Minnesota), Roberts (St. Louis), B. Plager (St. Louis), Stapleton (Chicago). Forwards—Martin (Chicago), Berenson (St. Louis), B. Hull (Chicago), D. Hull (Chicago), Sabourin (St. Louis), Ecclestone (St. Louis), Clarke (Philadelphia), C. Maki (Chicago), Flett (Los Angeles), Grant (Minnesota), Mikita (Chicago), Polis (Pittsburgh). Coach—Scotty Bowman (St. Louis).

Referee—Bill Friday. Linesmen—Neil Armstrong, John D'Amico.

First period: 1. West, C. Maki (unassisted) 0:36. 2. West, R. Hull (Flett) 4:38. 3. East, Cournoyer (D. Smith, Balon) 6:19. Penalties—Harris, F. Mahovlich, R. Hull.

Second period: No scoring. Penalties—Bucyk.

Third period: No scoring. Penalties—Stapleton, Magnuson.

Attendance—14,790.

TWENTY-FIFTH GAME

January 25, 1972 at Minnesota
East 3, West 2

Behind, 2-0, on West goals by Bobby Hull and Simon Nolet, the East Division All-Stars roared back to tie the score on second-period goals by Jean Ratelle and Johnny McKenzie. Then Phil Esposito's third-period score gave the East the victory in the silver anniversary game.

A crowd of 15,423 braved sub-zero Minnesota temperatures to watch the clash of the two divisions. Esposito scored the winning goal against Gump Worsley, goaltender for the host Minnesota North Stars.

East All-Stars: Goal—Dryden (Montreal), Villemure (New York). Defense—Park (New York), Tremblay (Montreal), Orr (Boston), Seiling (New York), Smith (Boston). Forwards—Berenson (Detroit), R. Martin (Buffalo), P. Esposito (Boston), Gilbert (New York), Tallon (Vancouver), Perreault (Buffalo), Hadfield (New York), Cournoyer (Montreal), Henderson (Toronto), McKenzie (Boston), Ratelle (New York), F. Mahovlich (Montreal). Coach—Al MacNeil (Montreal).

West All-Stars: Goal—Worsley (Minnesota), T. Esposito (Chicago). Defense—White (Chicago), Magnuson (Chicago), Harris (Minnesota), Vadnais (California), Mohns (Minnesota), Stapleton (Chicago), Forwards—Unger (St. Louis), Goldsworthy (Minnesota), B. Hull (Chicago), D. Hull (Chicago), Lonsberry (Los Angeles), P. Martin (Chicago), Clarke (Philadelphia), C. Maki (Chicago), Nolet (Philadelphia), Mikita (Chicago),

Polis (Pittsburgh). Coach—Billy Reay (Chicago).

Referee—Bruce Hood. Linesmen—Matt Pavelich, Claude Bechard.

First period: 1. West, B. Hull (P. Martin, C. Maki) 17:01. Penalty—Hadfield.

Second period: 2. West, Nolet (D. Hull) 1:11. 3. East, Ratelle (Tremblay, Gilbert) 3:48. 4. East, McKenzie (Park, Seiling) 18:45. Penalty—White.

Third period: 5. East, P. Esposito (Smith, Orr) 1:09. Penalties—White, P. Esposito, Tremblay, Mohns.

Attendance—15,423.

TWENTY-SIXTH GAME

January 30, 1973 at New York
East 5, West 4

Greg Polis, who arrived only hours before gametime following the birth of his first child in Pittsburgh, emerged as the star of the game, first ever at New York's Madison Square Garden.

Polis scored two goals for the West and drove off with the car awarded to the game's Most Valuable Player. The East, however, drove off with the victory with Bobby Schmautz scoring the decisive goal with only six minutes left to play.

A record All-Star crowd of 17,500 watched the game.

East All-Stars: Goal—Giacomin (New York R.), Villemure (New York R.). Defense—Savard (Montreal), Park (New York R.), G. Bergman (Detroit), Orr (Boston), Lapointe (Montreal), Smith (Boston). Forwards—R. Martin (Buffalo), P. Esposito (Boston), Hodge (Boston), Schmautz (Vancouver), Cournoyer (Montreal), Keon (Toronto), Robert (Buffalo), Westfall (New York I.), Ratelle (New York R.), Henderson (Toronto), Lemaire (Montreal), F. Mahovlich (Montreal). Coach—Tom Johnson (Boston).

West All-Stars: Goal—T. Esposito (Chicago), Vachon (Los Angeles). Defense—White (Chicago), Harper (Los Angeles), Marotte (Los An-

geles), Gibbs (Minnesota), B. Plager (St. Louis), Manery (Atlanta). Forwards—P. Martin (Chicago), Pappin (Chicago), Unger (St. Louis), D. Hull (Chicago), Parise (Minnesota), Dornhoefer (Philadelphia), Clarke (Philadelphia), Berry (Los Angeles), Mikita (Chicago), Polis (Pittsburgh), J. Johnston (California), MacDonald (Pittsburgh). Coach—Billy Reay (Chicago).

Referee—Lloyd Gilmour. Linesmen—Neil Armstrong, John D'Amico.

First period: No scoring. Penalties—Orr, Bergman.

Second period: 1. West, Polis (Clarke, MacDonald) 0:55. 2. East, Robert (Park) 3:56. 3. East, F. Mahovlich (unassisted) 16:27. 4. East, Henderson (P. Esposito, Hodge) 19:12. 5. West, P. Martin (D. Hull, Pappin) 19:29. Penalty—Hodge.

Third period: 6. East, Lemaire (F. Mahovlich) 3:19. 7. West, Polis (unassisted) 4:27. 8. West, Harper (Mikita) 9:27. 9. East, Schmautz (Savard) 13:59. Penalty—White.

Attendance—17,500.

TWENTY-SEVENTH GAME

January 29, 1974 at Chicago
West 6, East 4

Stan Mikita, with a goal and two assists, and Garry Unger, with a goal and assist, led the expansionist West to a come-from-behind 6–4 triumph over the East.

The East jumped to a 2–0 lead in the first period but the West roared back to score three unanswered goals in the second. Unger, voted the game's Most Valuable Player, scored what proved to be the winning goal at 7:54 of the final period. The 10 goals were the most scored in an All-Star contest.

A capacity crowd of 16,426 attended the game at Chicago Stadium.

West All-Stars: Goal—Parent (Philadelphia), Esposito (Chicago). Defense—White (Chicago), Van Impe (Philadelphia), Burrows (Pittsburgh), Plager (St. Louis), Watson (Philadelphia), Awrey (St. Louis). Forwards—Berry (Los Angeles), Unger (St. Louis), P. Martin (Chicago), Hull (Chi-

cago), Goldsworthy (Minnesota), McDonough (Atlanta), Pappin (Chicago), Clarke (Philadelphia), Johnston (California), Mikita (Chicago), MacDonald (Pittsburgh), Hextall (Minnesota). Coach—Billy Reay (Chicago).

East All-Stars: Goal—Gilbert (Boston), Dryden (Buffalo). Defense—Park (New York R.), Potvin (New York I.), Guevremont (Vancouver), Robinson (Montreal), McKenny (Toronto), Smith (Boston). Forwards—R. Martin (Buffalo), Esposito (Boston), Hodge (Boston), Ullman (Toronto), Schmautz (Vancouver), Berenson (Detroit), Cournoyer (Montreal), Cashman (Boston), Richard (Montreal), Westfall (New York I.), Redmond (Detroit), F. Mahovlich (Montreal). Coach—Scotty Bowman (Montreal).

Referee—Art Skov. Linesmen—Matt Pavelich, Willard Norris.

First period: 1. East, Mahovlich (Cournoyer, Ullman) 3:33. 2. East, Cournoyer (Ullman) 16:20. Penalty—Martin.

Second period: 3. West, Berry (Mikita) 5:59. 4. West, McDonough (Clarke, MacDonald) 13:55. 5. West, MacDonald (Plager, Awrey) 19:07. Penalties—Hextall, Berenson.

Third period: 6. West, Mikita (Unger, White) 2:25. 7. West, Unger (White, Mikita) 7:54. 8. East, Potvin 9:55. 9. East, Redmond (Berenson) 14:55. 10. West, P. Martin (Pappin) 19:13. Penalty—Plager.

Attendance—16,426.

TWENTY-EIGHTH GAME

January 21, 1975 at Montreal
Wales Conference 7,
Campbell Conference 1

NHL expansion turned the All-Star game into a battle of conferences: the Prince of Wales Conference against the Clarence Campbell Conference. In this first such pairing, Wales won easily, 7–1, at the Montreal Forum before a capacity crowd of 16,080.

Syl Apps Jr., son of a former NHL great, scored twice for Wales and was voted the game's MVP. Apps was the first son of an NHL All-Star to appear in an All-Star game.

Campbell All-Stars: Goal—Parent (Philadelphia), Smith (Vancouver). Defense—Park (New York R.), Van Impe (Philadelphia), Jarrett (Chicago), D. Potvin (New York I.), Pratt (Vancouver), Watson (Philadelphia). Forwards—Barber (Philadelphia), Unger (St. Louis), Pappin (Chicago), Vickers (New York R.), Gilbert (New York R.), Bennett (Atlanta), Lysiak (Atlanta), Clarke (Philadelphia), Nolet (Kansas City), Westfall (New York I.), Mikita (Chicago), Hextall (Minnesota). Coach—Fred Shero (Philadelphia).

Wales All-Stars: Goal—Vachon (Los Angeles), Dryden (Montreal). Defense—Harper (Los Angeles), Murdoch (Los Angeles), Orr (Boston), Korab (Buffalo), Lapointe (Montreal), Vadnais (Boston). Forwards—Luce (Buffalo), Esposito (Boston), Martin (Buffalo), Dionne (Detroit), Robert (Buffalo), Dupere (Washington), Pronovost (Pittsburgh), Lafleur (Montreal), Johnston (California), O'Reilly (Boston), Apps (Pittsburgh), Sittler (Toronto). Coach—Bep Guidolin (Boston-Kansas City).

Referee—Wally Harris. Linesmen—Leon Stickle, Claude Bechard.

First period: 1. Wales, Apps (Johnston, Vadnais) 9:38. 2. Wales, Luce (O'Reilly, Dupere) 12:02. 3. Wales, Sittler (Lafleur) 14:22. 4. Campbell, Potvin (Unger) 19:41. Penalties—None.

Second period: 5. Wales, Esposito (Lafleur, Murdoch) 19:16. Penalties—Vickers, Luce, Harper, Korab.

Third period: 6. Wales, Apps (Robert, Martin) 3:25. 7. Wales, O'Reilly (unassisted) 5:43. 8. Wales, Orr (Lafleur, Sittler) 7:19. Penalties—Watson, Clarke.

Attendance—16,080.

TWENTY-NINTH GAME

January 20, 1976 at Philadelphia
Wales Conference 7,
Campbell Conference 5

Montreal's Pete Mahovlich collected a goal and three assists to pace Wales to a 7–5 victory over Campbell in the highest-scoring All-Star Game ever played.

It was a close game until midway of the second period, when Campbell coach Fred Shero inserted Philadelphia's Wayne Stephenson in goal. Wales scored on its first three shots against Stephenson to open a 6–1 lead. They coasted the rest of the way before a crowd of 16,436 at the Philadelphia Spectrum. Mahovlich was voted MVP.

Campbell All-Stars: Goal—Resch (New York I.), Stephenson (Philadelphia). Defense—Vadnais (New York R.), Russell (Chicago), D. Potvin (New York I.), Dupont (Philadelphia), Marks (Chicago), Watson (Philadelphia). Forwards—Unger (St. Louis), Vickers (New York R.), Paiement (Kansas City), Ververgaert (Vancouver), Barber (Philadelphia), Goldsworthy (Minnesota), Harris (New York I.), Bennett (Atlanta), Lysiak (Atlanta), Trottier (New York I.), MacLeish (Philadelphia), Leach (Philadelphia). Coach—Fred Shero (Philadelphia).

Wales All-Stars: Goal—Thomas (Toronto), Dryden (Montreal). Defense—Park (Boston), Robinson (Montreal), Burrows (Pittsburgh), Lapointe (Montreal), Korab (Buffalo), Salming (Toronto). Forwards—Larouche (Pittsburgh), Clement (Washington), Martin (Buffalo), Pronovost (Pittsburgh), Lafleur (Montreal), Ramsay (Buffalo), MacAdam (California), Sheppard (Boston), Dionne (Los Angeles), Shutt (Montreal), Mahovlich (Montreal), Maloney (Detroit). Coach—Floyd Smith (Buffalo).

Referee—Lloyd Gilmour. Linesmen—John D'Amico, Neil Armstrong.

First period: 1. Wales, Martin (Mahovlich, Lafleur) 6:01. 2. Campbell, Bennett (Dupont) 16:59. 3. Wales, Mahovlich (Lapointe, Lafleur) 18:31. 4. Wales, Park (Mahovlich, Martin) 19:00. Penalties—None.

Second period: 5. Wales, MacAdam (Maloney) 9:34. 6. Wales, Lafleur (Mahovlich, Martin) 11:54. 7. Wales, Dionne (unassisted) 13:51. 8. Wales, Maloney (Larouche, MacAdam) 16:59. Penalty—Barber.

Third period: 9. Campbell, Ververgaert (Trottier, Harris) 4:33. 10. Campbell, Ververgaert (Trottier, Harris) 4:43. 11. Campbell, D. Potvin (unassisted) 14:17. 12. Campbell, Vickers (Unger, D. Potvin) 14:46. Penalty—Marks.

Attendance—16,436.

THIRTIETH GAME

January 25, 1977 at Vancouver
Wales Conference 4,
Campbell Conference 3

Rick Martin of Buffalo scored two third-period goals, including the game-winner with under two minutes to play, as Wales won their third straight over Campbell, 4–3, at the Pacific Coliseum in Vancouver.

Martin, voted MVP, scored at the four-minute mark to give the Wales a 3–2 lead. After Phil Esposito tied it with a goal at 12:23, Martin beat Chico Resch from in close with 1:56 remaining for the winning score before a crowd of 15,613.

Campbell All-Stars: Goal—Parent (Philadelphia), Resch (New York I.). Defense—Snepsts (Vancouver), Bladon (Philadelphia), Russell (Chicago), D. Potvin (New York I.), Joe Watson (Philadelphia), Jim Watson (Philadelphia). Forwards—Gilbert (New York R.), Unger (St. Louis), Paiement (Colorado), Lysiak (Atlanta), Dornhoefer (Philadelphia), Murdoch (New York R.), Clarke (Philadelphia), Young (Minnesota), MacLeish (Philadelphia), Nystrom (New York I.), Vail (Atlanta), Esposito (New York R.). Coach—Fred Shero (Philadelphia).

Wales All-Stars: Goal—Dryden (Montreal), Desjardins (Buffalo). Defense—Turnbull (Toronto), Lapointe (Montreal), Schoenfeld (Buffalo), Savard (Montreal), Robinson (Montreal), Salming (Toronto), Park (Boston). Forwards—Martin (Buffalo), McNab (Boston), McDonald (Toronto), Lafleur (Montreal), Perreault (Buffalo), Pronovost (Pittsburgh), Libett (Detroit), Charron (Washington), MacAdam (Cleveland), Gainey (Montreal), Dionne (Los Angeles). Coach—Scotty Bowman (Montreal).

Referee—Ron Wicks. Linesmen—Matt Pavelich, Ron Finn.

First period: 1. Campbell, Vail (Potvin) 2:54. 2. Wales, McDonald (Gainey, McNab) 6:22. Penalties—Campbell bench, Dornhoefer, Lapointe.

Second period: 3. Campbell, MacLeish (Nystrom, Potvin) 11:56. 4. Wales, McDonald (Perreault, Robinson) 19:27. Penalties—Potvin, Lapointe, Paiement, Joe Watson.

Third period: 5. Wales, Martin (Dionne, Robinson) 4:00. 6. Campbell, Esposito (Gilbert, Dornhoefer) 12:23. 7. Wales, Martin (Dionne, Lafleur) 18:04. Penalties—Russell, Salming.

Attendance—15,607.

THIRTY-FIRST GAME

January 24, 1978 at Buffalo
Wales Conference 3,
Campbell Conference 2

Wales continued its domination of the All-Star classic, defeating Campbell, 3–2, for the fourth straight year.

Buffalo's Gil Perreault scored at 3:55 of sudden-death overtime for the winning score, but the MVP award went to New York Islander goalie Billy Smith, who stopped 16 shots in the first 30 minutes of action. A crowd of 16,433 attended the game at the Buffalo Auditorium.

Campbell All-Stars: Goal—Smith (New York I.), Stephenson (Philadelphia). Defense—Dailey (Philadelphia), Bladon (Philadelphia), Vadnais (New York R.), D. Potvin (New York I.), Watson (Philadelphia), Beck (Colorado). Forwards—Barber (Philadelphia), Bossy (New York I.), Paiement (Colorado), Gillies (New York I.), Clement (Atlanta), Ververgaert (Vancouver), Unger (St. Louis), Boldirev (Chicago), Clarke (Philadelphia), Trottier (New York I.), Esposito (New York R.), Eriksson (Minnesota). Coach—Fred Shero (Philadelphia).

Wales All-Stars: Goal—Dryden (Montreal), Vachon (Los Angeles). Defense—Savard (Montreal), Robinson (Montreal), Salming (Toronto), Park (Boston), Larson (Detroit). Forwards—Pronovost (Pittsburgh), Shutt (Montreal), Martin (Buffalo), McDonald (Toronto), Lafleur (Montreal), Perreault (Buffalo), Sirois (Washington), Cournoyer (Montreal), Dionne (Los Angeles), Maruk (Cleveland), O'Reilly (Boston), Gainey

(Montreal), Sittler (Toronto). Coach—Scotty Bowman (Montreal).

Referee—Bruce Hood. Linesmen—John D'Amico, Leon Stickle.

First period: 1. Campbell, Barber (unassisted) 1:25. 2. Campbell, Potvin (Clarke) 12:12. Penalties—Salming, Gillies.

Second period: 3. Wales, Sittler (Robinson, Park) 19:32. Penalties—Dailey, Smith, McDonald, Vadnais.

Third period: 4. Wales, Martin (Dionne, O'Reilly) 18:21. Penalties—None.

Overtime: 5. Wales, Perreault (Shutt, Salming) 3:55. Penalties—None.

Attendance—16,433.

THIRTY-SECOND GAME

February 5, 1980 at Detroit
Wales Conference 6,
Campbell Conference 3

After a year's absence due to the Challenge Cup series against the Soviet Union, the All-Star Game was returned to its regular format. And, as usual, Wales won, this time by a 6–3 count before 21,002 fans at Joe Louis Arena in Detroit. It was the fifth straight triumph for Wales.

Reggie Leach, who scored a goal and assist for Campbell, was voted MVP, but it was 51-year-old Gordie Howe who stole the show. Howe, playing in his final All-Star game, had an assist on the Wales' final goal and earned a long ovation from the largest crowd ever to attend an NHL game.

Campbell All-Stars: Goal—Peeters (Philadelphia), Esposito (Chicago). Defense—Lindgren (Vancouver), McEwen (Colorado), Picard (Washington), Greschner (New York R.), Watson (Philadelphia), Barnes (Philadelphia). Forwards—Barber (Philadelphia), Lukowich (Winnipeg), McDonald (Edmonton), Nilsson (Atlanta), MacLeish (Philadelphia), Bossy (New York I.), Trottier (New York I.), Federko (St. Louis), Propp (Philadelphia), Leach (Philadelphia), Esposito (New York R.), Gretzky (Edmonton). Coach—Al Arbour (New York I.).

Wales All-Stars: Goal—Edwards (Buffalo), Meloche (Minnesota). Defense—Stackhouse (Pittsburgh), Hartsburg (Minnesota), Schoenfeld (Buffalo), Robinson (Montreal), Burrows (Toronto), Larson (Detroit). Forwards—Ratelle (Boston), Cloutier (Quebec), Howe (Hartford), Lafleur (Montreal), Perreault (Buffalo), Murphy (Los Angeles), Goring (Los Angeles), Dionne (Los Angeles), Gainey (Montreal), Gare (Buffalo), Payne (Minnesota), Sittler (Toronto). Coach—Scotty Bowman (Montreal).

Referee—Dave Newell. Linesmen—John D'Amico, Ray Scapinello.

First period: 1. Wales, Robinson (unassisted) 3:58. 2. Wales, Payne (Murphy, Goring) 4:19. 3. Campbell, Leach (McEwen) 7:15. Penalty—Hartsburg.

Second period: 4. Campbell, Nilsson (Federko, MacLeish) 6:03. Penalties—None.

Third period: 5. Campbell, Propp (P. Esposito, Leach) 4:14. 6. Wales, Stackhouse (Sittler, Lafleur) 11:40. 7. Wales, Hartsburg (Cloutier, Ratelle) 12:40. 8. Wales, Larson (Payne, Perreault) 13:12. 9. Wales, Cloutier (Howe) 16:06. Penalties—None.

Attendance—21,002.

THIRTY-THIRD GAME

February 10, 1981 at Los Angeles
Campbell Conference 4,
Wales Conference 1

Campbell finally got into the win column as it posted a 4–1 victory over Wales. The triumph snapped the Wales' five-game victory streak.

Although outshot, 43–25, Campbell got outstanding goaltending from Mike Liut and Pete Peeters. Liut, voted MVP, stopped 18 shots in the first period and seven more in the middle period before Peeters relieved him.

A crowd of 16,005 watched the game played at the Los Angeles Forum.

Campbell All-Stars: Goal—Liut (St. Louis), Peeters (Philadelphia). Defense—Dailey (Philadelphia), Wilson (Philadelphia), Ramage (Colorado), Potvin (New York I.), Murray (Chicago),

McCarthy (Vancouver). Forwards—Barber (Philadelphia), Babych (St. Louis), Gartner (Washington), Bourne (New York I.), Lukowich (Winnipeg), Nilsson (Calgary), Holmgren (Philadelphia), Johnstone (New York R.), Williams (Vancouver), Bossy (New York I.), Federko (St. Louis), Gretzky (Edmonton). Coach—Pat Quinn (Philadelphia).

Wales All-Stars: Goal—Lessard (Los Angeles), Beaupre (Minnesota). Defense—Langway (Montreal), Picard (Toronto), Howe (Hartford), Bourque (Boston), Carlyle (Pittsburgh), Larson (Detroit). Forwards—Simmer (Los Angeles), Middleton (Boston), Kehoe (Pittsburgh), Smith (Minnesota), Dionne (Los Angeles), Rogers (Hartford), Taylor (Los Angeles), Ogrodnick (Detroit), Gare (Buffalo), Shutt (Montreal), Gainey (Montreal), P. Stastny (Quebec). Coach—Scotty Bowman (Buffalo).

Referee—Bryan Lewis. Linesmen—Jim Christison, Gerard Gauthier.

First period: 1. Campbell, Nilsson (Barber, Holmgren) :45. 2. Campbell, Barber (Johnstone) 8:02. Penalties—Bourne, Williams.

Second period: 3. Campbell, Babych (Johnstone, Federko) 16:12. Penalties—None.

Third period: 4. Wales, Ogrodnick (Howe, Kehoe) 6:13. 5. Campbell, Wilson (Bossy, Gretzky) 10:18. Penalties—None.

Attendance—16,005.

THIRTY-FOURTH GAME

February 9, 1982 at Landover, Md.
Wales Conference 4,
Campbell Conference 2

Mike Bossy scored late in the second period to snap a 2–2 tie and then added an insurance goal early in the third period to send Wales to a 4–2 decision over the Campbell Conference Stars at Landover, Maryland.

While MVP Bossy was providing the offense, goaltenders Michel Dion and Don Edwards combined to stop 29 shots and help Wales win for the sixth time in seven games. A capacity crowd of 18,130 was on hand.

Campbell All-Stars: Goal—Fuhr (Edmonton), Meloche (Minnesota). Defense—Hartsburg (Minnesota), Coffey (Edmonton), Wilson (Chicago), Manno (Toronto), Rautakallio (Calgary), Snepsts (Vancouver). Forwards—Gretzky (Edmonton), Savard (Chicago), Smith (Minnesota), Taylor (Los Angeles), Hawerchuk (Winnipeg), Ciccarelli (Minnesota), Lever (Colorado), Vaive (Toronto), Messier (Edmonton), Secord (Chicago), Sutter (St. Louis), Ogrodnick (Detroit). Coach—Glen Sonmor (Minnesota).

Wales All-Stars: Goal—Dion (Pittsburgh), Edwards (Buffalo). Defense—Ramsey (Buffalo), Bourque (Boston), Robinson (Montreal), Carlyle (Pittsburgh), Beck (New York R.), Langway (Montreal). Forwards—Trottier (New York I.), P. Stastny (Quebec), Acton (Montreal), Maruk (Washington), Stoughton (Hartford), Bossy (New York I.), Propp (Philadelphia), Middleton (Boston), Duguay (New York R.), Barber (Philadelphia), Tardif (Quebec), Tonelli (New York I.). Coach—Al Arbour (New York I.).

Referee—Wally Harris. Linesmen—Ron Finn, Swede Knox.

First period: 1. Campbell, Vaive (Sutter) 2:32. 2. Wales, Bourque (Maruk, Carlyle) 12:03. 3. Wales, Tardif (Middleton, Stastny) 13:27. Penalties—Tardif, Hartsburg.

Second period: 4. Campbell, Gretzky (Coffey, Ciccarelli) 0:26. 5. Wales, Bossy (Beck, Tonelli) 17:10. Penalties—Hawerchuk, Tardif.

Third period: 6. Wales, Bossy (Robinson) 1:19. Penalty—Stoughton.

Attendance—18,130.

THIRTY-FIFTH GAME

February 8, 1983 at Uniondale, N.Y.
Campbell Conference 9,
Wales Conference 3

Wayne Gretzky scored four goals in the final period, shattering four All-Star Game records and helping the Campbell Conference post a 9–3 victory over the Wales Conference at Nassau Coliseum.

Gretzky's outburst helped the Campbell turn a close 3–2 game into a rout and hand the

A super sombrero is fitting for Wayne Gretzky after he scores four goals in the 1983 All-Star Game.

Wales only their second loss in eight games. A capacity crowd of 15,230 witnessed Gretzky's feat, which won him MVP honors.

Campbell All-Stars: Goal—Bannerman (Chicago), Garrett (Vancouver). Defense—Huber (Detroit), Hartsburg (Minnesota), Murray (Chicago), Coffey (Edmonton), Wilson (Chicago), Babych (Winnipeg). Forwards—Broten (Minnesota), McDonald (Calgary), B. Sutter (St. Louis), Kurri (Edmonton), Messier (Edmonton), McCarthy (Minnesota), Vaive (Toronto), Dionne (Los Angeles), Savard (Chicago), Ciccarelli (Minnesota), Secord (Chicago), Gretzky (Edmonton). Coach—Roger Neilson (Vancouver).

Wales All-Stars: Goal—Peeters (Boston), Lindbergh (Philadelphia). Defense—Potvin (New York I.), Bourque (Boston), Howe (Philadelphia), Langevin (New York I.), Ramsey (Buffalo), Langway (Washington). Forwards—Francis (Hartford), Pederson (Boston), Walter (Montreal), Maloney (New York R.), Goulet (Quebec), Kehoe (Pittsburgh), Trottier (New York I.), Bossy (New York I.), M. Stastny (Quebec), P. Stastny (Quebec), Marini (New Jersey), Sittler (Philadelphia). Coach—Al Arbour (New York I.).

Referee—Bob Myers. Linesmen—Ryan Bozak, Leon Stickle.

First period: 1. Wales, Goulet (P. Stastny) 3:41. 2. Campbell, Babych (McDonald, Sutter) 11:37. 3. Wales, Bourque (unassisted) 19:01. Penalties—Sutter, Langevin.

Second period: 4. Campbell, Ciccarelli (Broten, Secord) 3:01. 5. Campbell, McCarthy (Ciccarelli, Murray) 14:51. Penalties—None.

Third period: 6. Campbell, Gretzky (Kurri, Coffey) 6:20. 7. Campbell, McDonald (Sutter, Dionne) 7:29. 8. Campbell, Gretzky (Messier, Kurri) 10:31. 9. Wales, Maloney (Marini) 14:04.

The Rangers' Don Maloney won a car and a plaque as MVP of the 1984 All-Star Game.

10. Campbell, Gretzky (Wilson, Messier) 15:32. 11. Campbell, Vaive (unassisted) 17:15. 12. Campbell, Gretzky (Messier) 19:18. Penalties—Ramsey.

Attendance—15,230.

THIRTY-SIXTH GAME

January 31, 1984 at East Rutherford, N.J.
Wales Conference 7,
Campbell Conference 6

Don Maloney of the New York Rangers tied an All-Star record with three assists and also had a goal as the Wales Conference outlasted the Campbell Conference, 7–6, at Meadowlands Arena in the highest-scoring All-Star Game ever.

Maloney won a $14,000 sports car as the game's MVP. The Wales' Mark Johnson and the Campbell's Rick Vaive also tied the All-Star Game record with three assists before a capacity crowd of 18,939.

Campbell All-Stars: Goal—Bannerman (Chicago), Fuhr (Edmonton). Defense—Babych (Winnipeg), Coffey (Edmonton), Lowe (Edmonton), Maxwell (Minnesota), Ramage (St. Louis), Wilson (Chicago). Forwards—Anderson (Edmonton), Bellows (Minnesota), Gretzky (Edmonton), McDonald (Calgary), Messier (Edmonton), Nicholls (Los Angeles), Ogrodnick (Detroit), Yzerman (Detroit), Rota (Vancouver), Savard (Chicago), Simmer (Los Angeles), Vaive (Toronto). Coach—Glen Sather (Edmonton).

Wales All-Stars: Goal—Peeters (Boston), Resch (New Jersey). Defense—Bourque (Boston), Cirella (New Jersey), Housley (Buffalo), Langway (Washington), O'Connell (Boston), Potvin (New York I.). Forwards—Kerr (Philadelphia), Bullard (Pittsburgh), Goulet (Quebec), Johnson (Hartford), Larouche (New York R.), Maloney (New York R.), Middleton (Boston), Naslund (Montreal), Pederson (Boston), Perreault (Buffalo), Propp (Philadelphia), P. Stastny (Quebec). Coach—Al Arbour (New York I.)

Referee—Bruce Hood. Linesmen—Ray Scapinello, John D'Amico.

First period: 1. Wales, Cirella (P. Stastny) 8:51. 2. Wales, Potvin (Kerr, Goulet) 9:30. 3. Wales, Middleton (Pederson, Housley) 14:49. 4. Wales, Naslund (Maloney, Potvin) 16:40. 5. Wales, Larouche (Johnson, Maloney) 17:14. Penalties—Housley.

Second period: 6. Campbell, Savard (Vaive, Rota) 1:23. 7. Campbell, Rota (Vaive, Savard) 5:51. 8. Campbell, Ogrodnick (Yzerman) 6:42. 9. Wales, Larouche (Maloney, Johnson) 17:34. Penalties—None.

Third period: 10. Wales, Maloney (Johnson, Cirella) 7:24. 11. Campbell, Babych (Ogrodnick) 8:11. 12. Campbell, Gretzky (Vaive, Simmer) 11:23. 13. Campbell, Bellows (Wilson) 17:37. Penalties—Maxwell, Resch.

Attendance—18,939.

THIRTY-SEVENTH GAME

February 12, 1985 at Calgary
Wales Conference 6,
Campbell Conference 4

Rookie Mario Lemieux had three points—including a game-clinching score in the third period—as the Wales Conference defeated the Campbell Conference, 6–4, before a crowd of 16,683 at Calgary's Olympic Saddledome.

Ray Bourque of the Wales stars set an All-Star Game record with four assists and tied a record with four points, but the 18-year-old Lemieux was voted the game's Most Valuable Player. It was his goal that gave the Wales a 5–3 lead that they protected down the stretch.

Campbell All-Stars: Goal—Fuhr (Edmonton), Moog (Edmonton). Defense—Carlyle (Winnipeg), Coffey (Edmonton), Lowe (Edmonton), MacInnis (Calgary), Reinhart (Calgary), Wilson (Chicago). Forwards—Anderson (Edmonton), Dionne (Los Angeles), Frycer (Toronto), Krushelnyski (Edmonton), Gradin (Vancouver), Gretzky (Edmonton), Hawerchuk (Winnipeg), Kurri (Edmonton), MacLean (Winnipeg), Payne (Minnesota), Brian Sutter (St. Louis), Ogrodnick (Detroit). Coach—Glen Sather (Edmonton).

Wales All-Stars: Goal—Barrasso (Buffalo), Lindbergh (Philadelphia). Defense—Bourque (Boston), Chelios (Montreal), Langway (Washington), Ramsey (Buffalo), Russell (New Jersey), Stevens (Washington). Forwards—Bossy (New York I.), Carpenter (Washington), Francis (Hartford), Kerr (Philadelphia), Gartner (Washington), Goulet (Quebec), Hedberg (New York R.), Lemieux (Pittsburgh), Muller (New Jersey), Brent Sutter (New York I.), Tonelli (New York I.), Trottier (New York I.). Coach—Al Arbour (New York I.).

Referee—Andy vanHellemond. Linesmen—Gerard Gauthier, Bob Hodges.

First period: 1. Wales, Francis (Kerr) 1:40. 2. Wales, Kerr (Goulet, Bourque) 5:31. 3. Campbell, Dionne (Ogrodnick, MacInnis) 6:33. 4. Campbell, Frycer (Krushelnyski, Carlyle) 16:35. Penalties—Muller.

Second period: 5. Wales, Hedberg (Lemieux, Langway) 13:46. 6. Wales, Lemieux (Muller, Bourque) 17:47. Penalties—None.

Third period: 7. Campbell, Gretzky (Krushelnyski) 10:09. 8. Wales, Lemieux (Bourque) 11:09. 9. Campbell, Carlyle (Krushelnyski) 17:09. 10. Wales, Gartner (Bourque) 19:51. Penalties—Russell, Dionne.

Attendance—16,683.

THIRTY-EIGHTH GAME

February 4, 1986 at Hartford
Wales Conference 4,
Campbell Conference 3

New York Islander teammates Mike Bossy and Bryan Trottier combined on a two-on-one in overtime to give the Wales Conference a 4–3 win over the Campbell Conference before a sellout crowd of 15,100 at the Civic Arena in Hartford.

Trottier took a pass from Bossy and beat goaltender Andy Moog from in close to give the Wales Conference the victory in only the second overtime All-Star Game in history. The MVP award went to Campbell goalie Grant Fuhr, who stopped all 15 shots he faced.

Campbell All-Stars: Goal—Fuhr (Edmonton), Moog (Edmonton). Defense—Lowe (Edmonton), Fogolin (Edmonton), Ramage (St. Louis), Coffey (Edmonton), Suter (Calgary), Wilson (Chicago). Forwards—Anderson (Edmonton), Hawerchuk (Winnipeg), Messier (Edmonton), Broten (Minnesota), Tanti (Vancouver), Clark (Toronto), Kurri (Edmonton), Taylor (Los Angeles), Savard (Chicago), M. Hunter (St. Louis), Ogrodnick (Detroit), Gretzky (Edmonton). Coach—Glen Sather (Edmonton).

Wales All-Stars: Goal—Gosselin (Quebec), Froese (Philadelphia). Defense—Mark Howe (Philadelphia), Langway (Washington), Ramsey (Buffalo), Bourque (Boston), Robinson (Montreal), Routsalainen (New York R.). Forwards—Lemieux (Pittsburgh), Muller (New Jersey), Gartner (Washington), Kerr (Philadelphia), Turgeon (Hartford), Bossy (New York I.), Trottier (New York I.), Goulet (Quebec), P. Stastny (Quebec), Poulin (Philadelphia), Propp (Philadelphia), Naslund (Montreal). Coach—Mike Keenan (Philadelphia).

Referee—Ron Wicks. Linesmen—John D'Amico, Gord Broseker.

First period: No scoring. Penalties—Suter, Gartner.

Second period: 1. Campbell, Tanti (unassisted) 7:56. 2. Wales, Propp (Naslund, Bourque) 17:56. Penalties—None.

Third period: 3. Wales, Stastny (Robinson, Turgeon) 4:45. 4. Campbell, Gretzky (Coffey, Savard) 17:09. 5. Wales, Propp (Robinson) 17:38. 6. Campbell, Hawerchuk (Savard, Coffey) 19:17. Penalties—Lowe, Turgeon, Messier, Gartner.

Overtime: 7. Wales, Trottier (Bossy) 3:05. Penalties—None.

Attendance—15,100.

THIRTY-NINTH GAME

February 9, 1988 at St. Louis
Wales Conference 6,
Campbell Conference 5

Mario Lemieux's third goal of the game, an overtime tally at 1:08 of sudden death, lifted the Wales Conference All-Stars to a 6–5 victory over the Campbell Conference All-Star at The Arena in St. Louis. It was the fourth victory in a row for the Wales squad in the midseason classic.

Lemieux, the game's MVP, also added three assists to set an All-Star Game record with six points, two more than any player had ever scored. Wales teammate Mats Naslund also broke the record with five points, all assists, in the game.

Campbell All-Stars: Goal—Fuhr (Edmonton), Vernon (Calgary). Defense—MacInnis (Calgary), McCrimmon (Calgary), Lowe (Edmonton), Ramage (St. Louis), Iafrate (Toronto), Suter (Calgary). Forwards—Adams (Vancouver), Gretzky (Edmonton), Anderson (Edmonton), Kurri (Edmonton), Savard (Chicago), Yzerman (Detroit), Bellows (Minnesota), Probert (Detroit), Nieuwendyk (Calgary), Messier (Edmonton), Hawerchuk (Winnipeg), Robitallie (Los Angeles). Coach—Glen Sather (Edmonton).

Wales All-Stars: Goal—Hextall (Philadelphia), Roy (Montreal). Defense—Howe (Philadelphia), Potvin (New York I.), Coffey (Philadelphia), K. Samuelsson (Philadelphia), Bourque (Boston), Robinson (Montreal). Forwards—Neely (Boston), Muller (New Jersey), Dineen (Hartford), Gartner (Washington), LaFontaine (New York I.), Goulet (Quebec), Poulin (Philadelphia), Ruuttu (Buffalo), Naslund (Montreal), Stastny (Quebec), Sandstrom (New York R.), Lemieux (Pittsburgh). Coach—Mike Keenan (Philadelphia).

Referee—Denis Morel. Linesmen—Kevin Collins, Randy Mitton.

First period: 1. Campbell, Hawerchuk (Nieuwendyk, Bellows) 3:25. 2. Wales, Sandstrom (Lemieux, Naslund) 14:45. 3. Campbell, Gretzky (Probert) 18:46. Penalties—Potvin.

Second period: 4. Wales, Gartner (Lemieux) 4:28. 5. Wales, Stastny (Lemieux, Naslund) 10:08. 6. Wales, Lemieux (Naslund) 11:34. 7. Campbell, Robitaille (Savard, Lowe) 15:09. Penalties—LaFontaine, McCrimmon.

Third period: 8. Campbell, Savard (Robitaille, Anderson) 5:19. 9. Wales, Lemieux (Naslund, Dineen) 8:07. 10. Campbell, Robitaille (Anderson, Savard) 16:28. Penalties—Bellows.

Overtime: 1. Wales, Lemieux (Naslund, Dineen) 1:08. Penalties—None.

Attendance—17,878.

FORTIETH GAME

February 7, 1989 at Edmonton
Campbell Conference 9,
Wales Conference 5

Luc Robitaille, Jimmy Carson and Mark Messier scored goals in the final eight minutes as the Campbell Conference broke a four-game All-Star losing streak with a 9–5 victory over the Wales Conference at the Northlands Coliseum in Edmonton.

Wayne Gretzky, who had been traded from Edmonton to Los Angeles before the start of the season, celebrated his return by getting a goal and two assists and winning Most Valuable Player honors.

Campbell All-Stars: Goal—Fuhr (Edmonton), Vernon (Calgary). Defense—Ellett (Winnipeg), Manson (Chicago), Lowe (Edmonton), Suter (Calgary), Reinhart (Calgary), Duchesne (Los Angeles). Forwards—Gretzky (Los Angeles), J. Mullen (Calgary), Nicholls (Los Angeles), Leeman (Toronto), Messier (Edmonton), Carson (Edmonton), Ciccarelli (Minnesota), Hull (St. Louis), Kurri (Edmonton), Yzerman (Detroit), Robitaille (Los Angeles), Nieuwendyk (Calgary). Coach—Glen Sather (Edmonton).

Wales All-Stars: Goal—Lemelin (Boston), Burke (New Jersey). Defense—Stevens (Washington), Bourque (Boston), Coffey (Pittsburgh), Housley (Buffalo), Wesley (Boston), Robinson (Montreal). Forwards—Lemieux (Pittsburgh), LaFontaine (New York I.), Dineen (Hartford), Neely (Boston), MacLean (New Jersey), Smith (Montreal), Poddubny (Quebec), Brown (Pittsburgh), Tocchet (Philadelphia), B. Mullen (New York R.), Ridley (Washington), McPhee (Montreal). Coach—Terry O'Reilly (Boston).

Referee—Ron Hoggarth. Linesmen—Ron Asselstine, Wayne Bonney.

First period: 1. Campbell, Kurri (Gretzky, Robitaille) 1:07. 2. Campbell, Gretzky (Duchesne) 4:33. 3. Wales, Neely (Lemieux, Stevens) 9:47. 4. Wales, Poddubny (Ridley, Robinson) 10:38. Penalties—Messier.

Second period: 5. Wales, Wesley (LaFontaine, B. Mullen) 3:16. 6. Campbell, J. Mullen (Messier, Nieuwendyk) 7:57. 7. Campbell, Yzerman (Duchesne, Ciccarelli) 17:21. 8. Campbell, Leeman (Carson) 17:35. Penalties—Bourque.

Third period: 9. Wales, Poddubny (Tocchet, Robinson) 4:40. 10. Campbell, J. Mullen (Manson) 6:53. 11. Wales, Ridley (Bourque, Tocchet) 9:35. 12. Campbell, Robitaille (Kurri, Gretzky) 12:18. 13. Campbell, Carson (Leeman, Hull) 14:35. 14. Campbell, Messier (Nieuwendyk, J. Mullen) 17:14. Penalties—None.

Attendance—17,503.

FORTY-FIRST GAME

January 21, 1990 at Pittsburgh
Wales Conference 12,
Campbell Conference 7

Playing in front of his hometown fans in Pittsburgh, Mario Lemieux scored four goals and skated off with his third Most Valuable Player award as the Wales Conference won a 12–7 shootout that was by far the highest-scoring All-Star Game in history.

Lemieux scored his first goal just 21 seconds into the game and had a hat trick before the first period was over. He tied Wayne Gretzky's record for goals in an All-Star Game with his fourth early in the third period.

Campbell All-Stars: Goal—McLean (Vancouver), Vernon (Calgary). Defense—MacInnis (Calgary), Lowe (Edmonton), Duchesne (Los Angeles), Iafrate (Toronto), Wilson (Chicago), Cavallini (St. Louis). Forwards—Gretzky (Los Angeles), Nieuwendyk (Calgary), Robitaille (Los Angeles) Mullen (Calgary), Nicholls (Los Angeles), Smail (Winnipeg), Messier (Edmonton), Gartner (Minnesota), Hull (St. Louis), Kurri (Edmonton), Yzerman (Detroit), Larmer (Chicago). Coach—Terry Crisp (Calgary).

Wales All-Stars: Goal—Puppa (Buffalo), Roy (Montreal). Defense—Leetch (New York R.), Hatcher (Washington), Housley (Buffalo), Coffey (Pittsburgh), Chelios (Montreal), Bourque (Boston). Forwards—Neely (Boston), Muller (New Jersey), Francis (Hartford), LaFontaine (New York I.), Sakic (Quebec), Turgeon (Buffalo), Andreychuk (Buffalo), Tocchet (Philadelphia), Propp (Philadelphia), Corson (Montreal), Lemieux (Pittsburgh), Richer (Montreal). Coach—Pat Burns (Montreal).

Referee—Kerry Fraser. Linesmen—Bob Hodges, Dan McCourt.

First period: 1. Wales, Lemieux (Propp, Neely) :21. 2. Wales, Andreychuk (unassisted) 5:13. 3. Wales, Turgeon (Francis) 9:22. 4. Campbell, Messier (Hull, Smail) 11:01. 5. Wales, Lemieux (Housley) 13:00. 6. Campbell, Yzerman (unassisted) 14:31. 7. Wales, Tocchet (Bourque, Muller) 16:55. 8. Wales, Lemieux (Coffey) 17:37. 9. Wales, Turgeon (Francis, Andreychuk) 18:52. Penalties—None.

Second period: 10. Wales, Muller (Coffey, Sakic) 8:47. 11. Campbell, MacInnis (Lowe) 9:03. 12. Campbell, Mullen (Nicholls) 13:00. 13. Wales, Corson (LaFontaine) 16:43. Penalties—Roy, Iafrate.

Third period: 14. Wales, Lemieux (Neely) 1:07. 15. Wales, Neely (Sakic, Hatcher) 11:20. 16. Campbell, Robitaille (Yzerman, Hull) 15:09. 17. Campbell, Robitaille (Hull, Yzerman) 16:11. 18. Wales, Muller (Tocchet) 17:50. 19. Campbell, Smail (Mullen, Nieuwendyk) 19:35. Penalties—Neely, Smail.

Attendance—16,236.

FORTY-SECOND GAME

January 19, 1991 at Chicago
Campbell Conference 11,
Wales Conference 5

Vincent Damphousse, playing in his first All-Star Game, tied a record with four goals, three coming in the third period, as the Campbell Conference stars routed the Wales stars, 11–5, at Chicago Stadium.

Damphousse, the only Toronto Maple Leafs' representative, scored midway through the first period to give Campbell a 2–1 lead. He then took over in the final 11:06, beating Wales' goaltender Andy Moog to tie Wayne Gretzky and Mario Lemieux for most goals in an All-Star Game and win Most Valuable Player honors.

Campbell All-Stars: Goal—Vernon (Calgary), Ranford (Edmonton). Defense—MacInnis (Calgary), S. Stevens (St. Louis), Chelios (Chicago), Housley (Winnipeg), Suter (Calgary), S. Smith (Edmonton). Forwards—Oates (St. Louis), Fleury (Calgary), Damphousse (Toronto), Robitaille (Los Angeles), Messier (Edmonton), Gagner (Minnesota), B. Smith (Minnesota), Yzerman (Detroit), Roenick (Chicago), Larmer (Chicago), Gretzky (Los Angeles), Sandstrom (Los Angeles), Linden (Vancouver). Coach—John Muckler (Edmonton).

Wales All-Stars: Goal—Roy (Montreal), Moog (Boston). Defense—Leetch (New York R.), Hatcher (Washington), Coffey (Pittsburgh), Krupp (Buffalo), Galley (Boston), Bourque (Boston). Forwards—LaFontaine (New York I.), Turcotte (New York R.), Neely (Boston), Sakic (Quebec), Recchi (Pittsburgh), Tocchet (Philadelphia), Cullen (Pittsburgh), Verbeek (Hartford), K. Stevens (Pittsburgh), Christian (Boston), Savard (Montreal), Lafleur (Quebec), MacLean (New Jersey). Coach—Mike Milbury (Boston).

Referee—Terry Gregson. Linesmen—Jerry Pateman, Dan Schachte.

First period: 1. Campbell, Gagner (Larmer, Roenick) 6:17. 2. Wales, LaFontaine (Turcotte) 9:17. 3. Campbell, Damphousse (Oates) 11:36. Penalties—None.

Second period: 4. Wales, LaFontaine (Hatcher) 1:33. 5. Campbell, Suter (unassisted) 5:23. 6. Campbell, Gretzky (Sandstrom) 9:10. 7. Campbell, Oates (Yzerman) 9:48. 8. Campbell, Fleury (Messier, Chelios) 14:40. 9. Wales, Tocchet (Verbeek, Sakic) 15:36. 10. Campbell, Roenick (S. Smith, Oates) 17:07. Penalties—None.

Third period: 11. Wales, MacLean (Cullen, Bourque) 2:29. 12. Campbell, Chelios (Larmer, Roenick) 5:23. 13. Campbell, Damphousse (Oates, Housley) 8:54. 14. Campbell, Damphousse (Housley, Oates) 11:40. 15. Wales, K. Stevens (Tocchet) 13:56. 16. Campbell, Damphousse (unassisted) 17:14. Penalties—Housley 2.

Attendance—18,472.

FORTY-THIRD GAME

January 18, 1992 at Philadelphia
Campbell Conference 10,
Wales Conference 6

Brett Hull scored twice and assisted on another to power the Campbell Conference to a 10–6 swamping of Wales. Playing on a line with Wayne Gretzky, who had a goal and two assists, Hull posted his two goals in a six-goal second period that scorched Wales' goaltender Don Beaupre.

Hull won a car as MVP of the game, played before a crowd of 17,380 at the Spectrum in Philadelphia. For 40-year-old defenseman Lar-

ry Robinson, playing for Campbell, it marked his 10th All-Star appearance.

Campbell All-Stars: Goal—Belfour (Chicago), Cheveldae (Detroit), McLean (Vancouver). Defense—Chelios (Chicago), Ellett (Toronto), Housley (Winnipeg), MacInnis (Calgary), Robinson (Los Angeles), Tinordi (Minnesota), Wilson (San Jose). Forwards—Bellows (Minnesota), Damphousse (Edmonton), Fleury (Calgary), Hull (St. Louis), Linden (Vancouver), Gretzky (Los Angeles), Fedorov (Detroit), Oates (St. Louis), Roberts (Calgary), Robitaille (Los Angeles), Roenick (Chicago), Yzerman (Detroit). Coach—Bob Gainey (Minnesota).

Wales All-Stars: Goal—Beaupre (Washington), Richter (New York R.), Roy (Montreal). Defense—Bourque (Boston), Coffey (Pittsburgh), Desjardins (Montreal), Hatcher (Washington), Leetch (New York R.), S. Stevens (New Jersey). Forwards—Brind'Amour (Philadelphia), Burridge (Washington), Cullen (Hartford), Ferraro (New York I.), Jagr (Pittsburgh), Lemieux (Pittsburgh), Messier (New York R.), Mogilny (Buffalo), Muller (Montreal), Nolan (Quebec), Sakic (Quebec), K. Stevens (Pittsburgh), Trottier (Pittsburgh). Coach—Scotty Bowman (Pittsburgh).

Referee—Don Koharski. Linesmen—Mark Vines, Mark Pare.

First period: 1. Campbell, Linden (Roenick, Tinordi) 7:53. 2. Wales, K. Stevens (Lemieux, Jagr) 11:20. 3. Campbell, Gretzky (Hull, Robitaille) 14:56. Penalties—None.

Second period: 4. Campbell, Hull (Gretzky, Robitaille) :42. 5. Wales, S. Stevens (Mogilny, Messier) 5:37. 6. Campbell, Bellows (Fedorov, MacInnis) 7:40. 7. Campbell, Roenick (Ellett) 8:13. 8. Campbell, Fleury (Robinson) 11:06. 9. Campbell, Hull (Gretzky, Robitaille) 11:59. 10. Campbell, Fleury (Damphousse, Oates) 17:33. 11. Wales, Nolan (Sakic, Bourque) 19:30. Penalties—None.

Third period: 12. Wales, Trottier (Hatcher) 4:03. 13. Campbell, Bellows (Fedorov) 4:50. 14. Wales, Mogilny (Desjardins) 5:28. 15. Campbell, Roberts (Linden) 18:42. 16. Wales, Burridge (Sakic, Nolan) 19:13. Penalties—None.

Attendance—17,380.

ALL-STAR GAME RECORDS
TEAM

Most goals, both teams, one game—19, Wales 12, Campbell 7, 1990.

Fewest goals, both teams, one game—2, All-Stars 1, Montreal 1, 1956; First Team All-Stars 1, Second Team All-Stars 1, 1952.

Most goals, one team, one game—12, Wales, 1990.

Fewest goals, one team, one game—0, All-Stars vs. Montreal, 1967.

Most shots, both teams, one game—87, Wales 45, Campbell 42, 1990.

Fewest shots, both teams, one game—52, Wales 40, Campbell 12, 1978.

Most shots, one team, one game—45, Wales, 1990.

Fewest shots, one team, one game—12, Campbell, 1978.

Most power-play goals, both teams, one game—3, three times, most recently Montreal 2, All-Stars 1, 1958.

Fewest power-play goals, both teams, one game—0, 14 times, most recently 1992.

Fastest two goals, both teams, from start of game—37 seconds, Jacques Laperriere, East, and Dean Prentice, West, 1970.

Fastest two goals, both teams—10 seconds, Dennis Ververgaert, Campbell, 1976.

Fastest three goals, both teams—1:25, 1992.

Fastest four goals, both teams—4:21, 1990.

Fastest two goals, one team, from start of game—4:19, Wales, 1980.

Fastest two goals, one team—10 seconds, Campbell, 1976.

Fastest three goals, one team—1:32, Wales, 1980.

Fastest four goals, one team—4:19, Campbell, 1992.

Most goals, both teams, one period—9, Wales 7, Campbell 2, first period, 1990.

Most goals, one team, one period—7, Wales, first period, 1990.

MVP honors went to Brett Hull of the St. Louis Blues in the 1992 All-Star Game.

Most shots, both teams, one period—36, Campbell, 22, Wales, 14, third period, 1990.

Most shots, one team, one period—22, Campbell, third period, 1990.

Fewest shots, both teams, one period—9, West 7, East 2, third period, 1971; Wales 5, Campbell 4, second period, 1980.

Fewest shots, one team, one period—2, East, third period, 1971; Campbell, second period, 1978.

INDIVIDUAL

Most games played—23, Gordie Howe, Detroit and Hartford.

Most goals, career—12, Wayne Gretzky, Edmonton and Los Angeles.

Most goals, one game—4, Wayne Gretzky, Campbell, 1983; Mario Lemieux, Wales, 1990; Vincent Damphousse, Campbell, 1991.

Most goals, one period—4, Wayne Gretzky, Campbell, third period, 1983.

Most assists, career—9, Gordie Howe, Detroit and Hartford; Ray Bourque, Boston; Larry Robinson, Los Angeles.

Most assists, one game—5, Mats Naslund, Wales Conference, 1988.

Most assists, one period—3, Mark Messier, Campbell Conference, third period, 1983.

Most points, career—19, Gordie Howe, Detroit and Hartford.

Most points, one game—6, Mario Lemieux, Wales Conference, 1988.

Most points, one period—4, Wayne Gretzky, Campbell Conference, third period, 1983.

12

THE OFFICIALS

When constabulary duty's to be done
A Policeman's lot is not a happy one.
          —Pirates of Penzance, Act. II

It is safe to assume that Sir William Gilbert of the operatic composing team of Gilbert and Sullivan never met an ice hockey referee. He was born in Victorian London in 1838 and died in 1911, long before hockey was introduced to his country. If he were living today, he presumably would show the same compassion for referees that he did for policemen.

The lot of the hockey referee isn't a happy one either. His constabulary duties consist of bringing discipline and control to 60 minutes of speed and confusion on ice. Players skim along the frozen surface at 20 to 30 miles an hour; there are violent collisions at great speed; sticks are swung like clubs, and pucks whiz over the ice and through the air at upwards of 100 mph.

This is the referee's work day:

He skates between 15 and 20 miles in an average game. He must match the fastest player stride for stride and be on top of every

« *A referee's life has its risks, as Frank Udvari discovered. He held on for dear life as Gordie Howe crashed an opponent into the boards in the mid-1950s.*

play. The players' bench disgorges fresh skaters as though they were traveling through a revolving door, but the harried referee gets no rest, except between periods.

And then there are the hazards of the job. While he is trying to control the game and the players, the referee may be tripped, jammed into the corners of the rink, boarded, draped over the protective glass, slashed by a skate, hit by a flying puck or pelted with programs, fruit, vegetables, eggs, overshoes—or squid.

Squid? "You better believe it," said Bill Chadwick, the only American-born referee to be named to the Hockey Hall of Fame. "I was working a Stanley Cup playoff game in Detroit in 1952 when a fan tossed something at me which missed and landed on the ice. I went over to pick it up, but after one look I spun around and skated off in a hurry. I thought at first it was a baby octopus. I found out later it was a squid. But octopus or squid, it sure scared the hell out of me."

Bryan Lewis, the NHL's director of officiating, was a referee for 18 years. He recalls being hit with every conceivable object. "Referees don't wear much protective equipment, so no matter where you get hit, it hurts," he said. "I got hit in the back by a thrown egg

Mickey Ion (left) and Cooper Smeaton, both members of the Hockey Hall of Fame, spell out who's in charge.

once and it swelled up the exact size of an egg. I also had plenty of cuts from pucks bouncing off me."

Referees also have been victims of assaults by players. Lewis was once punched by Barry Ashbee of the Philadelphia Flyers during a game in Pittsburgh. "Did it hurt?" said Lewis. "You bet. But Ashbee got hit, too, with an eight-game suspension."

Andy vanHellemond, who has refereed more games than any man in the history of the NHL, remembers the 1981–82 season for two reasons: he was twice assaulted by players. He was punched in the chest by Paul Holmgren of the Philadelphia Flyers during a regular-season game and was swatted in the head by Terry O'Reilly of the Boston Bruins at the conclusion of a Boston-Quebec playoff game.

VanHellemond recalls the O'Reilly assault more vividly because it occurred in the play-offs. "As the game ended, O'Reilly started a fight with Dale Hunter [of the Nordiques]," vanHellemond said. "O'Reilly was real hot. 'I'm going to cut your eyes out,' he told Hunter.

"I tried to intercede, and O'Reilly said, 'Get out of my way or I'll go right through you.' Then he swung but it was more like a swat than a punch and he caught me on the side of my head."

Holmgren drew a five-game suspension for his assault and O'Reilly was suspended for 10 games. The rules dealing with abuse of officials have been tightened in recent years and can carry 25-game suspensions.

Fear grips most referees—as it does the policeman on the beat. Referees of yore like Chadwick, Red Storey, Cooper Smeaton, Mickey Ion, King Clancy and Mike Rodden were

Referee Bill Chadwick, calling a penalty on the Canadiens' Murph Chamberlain, blew his whistle for 16 years in the NHL.

threatened with physical violence while serving in the NHL.

They learned to live with this fear and eventually wound up in the Hockey Hall of Fame because they had courage—courage to render a decision and make it stick in the face of taunts from players, coaches and hostile fans.

Clancy earned his berth in the Hall of Fame as a fighting defenseman. But he is also remembered as a fighting referee, a 150-pound bantam rooster of a man who never allowed himself to be intimidated by a player or coach, a club owner or a fan.

In Clancy's mind, Mickey Ion was hockey's most outstanding referee. "When Mickey refereed a game, he was in complete charge," said Clancy in an interview conducted before his death in 1986. "There's never been anyone to equal him. One night in Boston, Mickey

was knocked over the boards and landed in a fan's lap. Boston scored while he was scrambling back over the boards, but Mickey didn't allow the goal. He wasn't on the ice and he said nobody was allowed to score unless he was there to see it."

Clancy, who served as a referee for 11 years following his retirement as a player in 1936, never forgot the instructions Ion gave him and Rabbit McVeigh before they worked their first Stanley Cup playoff game in 1938.

"Mickey came into the officials' room and started lecturing us," Clancy said. "He said, 'Crack down on those players right from the start. And remember this: There are 15,000 idiots out there, including the players. You two guys are the only sane ones in the building.' And, you know, there were times when I think Mickey was right."

Mike Rodden worked 1,187 NHL games.

Red Storey refereed from 1951 through 1959.

Referee Art Skov wants no part of complaining Canadien Jean Beliveau.

VanHellemond refereed his first NHL game in 1972 and broke Bill Chadwick's longevity record (1,200 regular-season games) early in the 1991–92 season. The best advice van-Hellemond received came from retired referee Frank Udvari.

"Frank told me to be consistent and not try to be someone else," vanHellemond said. "He also told me that acceptance was important and to guard against antagonizing people. It was good advice."

Terry Gregson, an NHL referee since 1981, admits that "a man's personality is extremely important" in his job. "You have to show quiet confidence but not arrogance," he said.

In the early days of pro hockey, referees were picked haphazardly. Retired and active players assisted in the officiating and were not paid. The first referees of the Stanley Cup playoffs were chosen from among the executives of the competing leagues.

Ion and Smeaton got their starts as referees before the first World War. They were paid—sometimes. "We got paid by the game," Smeaton recalled. "But if one of the bosses didn't like your work just once, you didn't come back. And you didn't get paid either."

The starting salary for NHL referees these days is $40,000 a year. Veteran referees can earn up to $150,000 a year through the league's bonus structure and work in the Stanley Cup playoffs.

The referee was the sole official in Smeaton's day. "There were no linesmen to help out," he said. "I had to call the offsides, the penalties, break up the fights and do the arguing."

Modern-day referees share the work load with two linesmen. And beginning with the 1991–92 season, referees were able to rely on video replays—but only on disputed goals.

Scotty Morrison, who was referee-in-chief for more than two decades and is now chairman of the Hockey Hall of Fame, had to go by the book when the referees and linesmen went on strike before the 1969 season.

"I'm all for it," vanHellemond said when the replays were introduced. "I know I don't feel good when I wave off a goal that is questionable. Now we have help and that should make it a better game."

Bill Chadwick recalled other problems he encountered early in his whistle-blowing career.

"When I first started refereeing [in 1941], you were more or less at the mercy of the club owners," he said. "You'd have a waiting line outside your door after every period. The owners would be there and the coaches, too. You couldn't keep 'em out. They'd walk in, give you hell and walk out.

"The referee had nobody to turn to for support. There was no referee-in-chief. All we had was the league president and he was only

an intermediary. Then Clarence Campbell took over as president [in 1947] and he backed us up because he knew our problems. He had been a referee."

It was during Red Dutton's reign as NHL president that Chadwick endured his most trying experience with mob violence. He was working a playoff game between the Canadiens and the Black Hawks in Chicago Stadium in 1943. One of his calls infuriated the Chicago fans, who went on a wild rampage, littering the ice with debris while crying for Chadwick's scalp.

The harassed referee ducked for cover, then dispatched a courier to Dutton in his front row box, asking what he should do. Dutton's answer was starkly brief: "You got yourself into this, now get yourself out."

Nobody officiated more playoff games than Matt Pavelich, the first linesman elected to the Hockey Hall of Fame.

"I needed a police escort to get out of the building that night," Chadwick said. "The next game I worked there, I was picked up at my hotel by detectives, who escorted me to the Stadium and back to the hotel after the game. Those Chicago fans really gave me a hard time."

Why so much abuse? "In no other sport are referees charged so much with the responsibility of who wins and loses," said Udvari, an NHL referee for 16 years. "That's why we're such a focal point for criticism."

The NHL even encourages referee identification. Although it has long been said that the best officiated games are the ones in which the referees go unnoticed, the NHL in 1977 began putting the names of officials on the back of their jerseys. Officials in other sports are usually identified by numbers.

So hockey fans are more conscious of the whistle-blowers and their respective reputa-

tions. Indeed, "Who's the ref?" is one of the first questions asked at any NHL game.

Many referees, past and present, readily admit the job has one other serious drawback. It deals with non-fraternizing. The loneliness of the long-distance runner is minor compared to the life of a referee, who is prohibited from mingling with players, club officials or fans.

Referees are not allowed to register at the same hotel as players and are advised not to frequent the same restaurants.

"It takes a certain type of person to accept that nonfraternization," Gregson said. "If you're gregarious . . . well, refereeing is not an ideal position for you."

Chadwick claimed it was even tougher when he was officiating. "The referees now have some companionship," he said. "They travel with the linesmen or arrange to meet them in various cities. In my day, the referee traveled alone and lived alone."

Nearly two decades as a referee prepared Bryan Lewis for his current position as the NHL's director of officiating.

"You couldn't associate with the players, but I always talked to them. I figured if they talked to me off the ice, I had a better chance of dealing with them in tight situations on the ice. The big thing is to get the respect of the players."

There is no way referees can stop players from talking to them. Ron Hoggarth, who turned to refereeing while he was "a starving student" at McMaster University in Hamilton, Ontario, and has been on the NHL staff since 1971, recalls an incident that occurred in the finals of the Stanley Cup playoffs in 1983.

"The Islanders were playing the Oilers at Nassau Coliseum and the crowd went wild when I called three penalties in a row against the Islanders," Hoggarth said. "After I called the third one, Denis Potvin [the Islanders' captain] skated up to me and said, 'Hey, Hoggarth, how can you sleep through this noise?'"

Andy vanHellemond is regarded as one of the NHL's best modern referees.

NHL referees are under constant scrutiny by supervisors—most of whom are retired officials. The referees are rated at midseason and at the end of the regular season. The ratings are then used to determine playoff assignments.

Chadwick is enjoying his retirement years in a home on the eastern tip of Long Island, N.Y. He attends many games involving the Rangers and the Islanders. And, of course, he critiques the work of the referees.

"The only problem I've noticed among the current referees is a tendency to fluctuate," he said. "Some call every infraction at the start of a game and then loosen up or vice versa. A good referee has to be consistent."

Scotty Morrison, chairman of the Hockey Hall of Fame, who served as the NHL's referee-in-chief for 21 years, points out that referees have shorter careers than officials of other sports. "In hockey, the demands are so strenu-ous that referees are retiring at the age of 45 or 46," he said. "Beyond that, they just can't keep up with the play."

However, referees like Ron Hoggarth rue the day when they will take away his whistle.

"It gets more difficult to be away from home so much and you get tired of the travel, the restaurants and the hotels," he said. "But I love the game and the roar of the crowd."

13

HOCKEY HALL OF FAME

Winning the Stanley Cup is the ultimate team honor in hockey. Making the Hall of Fame represents the supreme individual achievement.

It is the Hall of Fame that since 1945 has perpetuated the memories of the greatest players, the sports founders, club executives, referees and linesmen. It also honors the writers and broadcasters.

It wasn't until August 26, 1961, that the Hall of Fame had a home. That was the day John F. Diefenbaker, Prime Minister of Canada, stood before a new structure on the grounds of the Canadian National Exhibition in Toronto and announced, "I now officially proclaim the opening of the Hockey Hall of Fame building."

Here have been housed the artifacts, photographs and other treasures of the game. After more than 30 years, the Hall of Fame has outgrown itself and will move into another venue in the spring of 1993—the historic Bank of Montreal's Upper Canadian headquarters at the center of Front and Yonge Streets in the heart of Toronto.

《 *The historic Bank of Montreal edifice is retained as the anchor of the new Hockey Hall of Fame and Museum.*

The new Hall of Fame and Museum will feature state-of-the-art technical exhibits and, among other attractions, an invitation to visitors to electronically challenge the greatest hockey players of all time, a theater for screening hockey films and a library that will include videos of special interest to players and coaches.

Originally it took five years after retirement for a player or a referee to be eligible for membership. However, in exceptional cases the period could be shortened. Under present rules the waiting period is three years.

Players and referees are elected by a Selection Committee headed by Dan Gallivan and made up of former players, writers and officials. Builders are elected by a committee led by Ian P. (Scotty) Morrison, Chairman of the Hall of Fame Board of Directors.

A committee from the Professional Hockey Writers' Association selects the writers, winners of the Elmer Ferguson Memorial Award, and a committee from the NHL Broadcasters' Association selects the broadcasters, winners of the Foster Hewitt Memorial Award.

PLAYERS

Sidney Gerald (Sid) Abel: Starred on Red Wings' Production Line (with Gordie Howe and Ted Lindsay) in the 1940s. Later coached Wings to seven playoff berths in 10 seasons behind the bench. *Elected 1964.*

John James (Jack) Adams: Star forward for the Toronto Arenas, Toronto St. Pats and Ottawa Senators. Later coached and served as general manager of the Detroit Red Wings. *Elected 1959.*

Sylvanus (Syl) Apps: A center who was the first winner of the Calder Trophy as the Rookie of the Year for 1936–37. Played entire big-league career with Toronto Maple Leafs. *Elected 1961.*

George Armstrong: One of the greatest clutch players in Toronto history. When the Leafs won four Stanley Cups in the 1960s, George had 20 goals and 20 assists in the 45 playoff games the team played. *Elected 1975.*

Irwin W. (Ace) Bailey: Right wing played only 7½ years in NHL due to fractured skull that ended career. Led league with 22 goals in 44 games in 1928–29 and was one of league's top penalty-killers. *Elected 1975.*

Dan Bain: Never played professional hockey. Was a standout center for the Winnipeg Victorias, an amateur team, in the late 1890s and early 1900s. *Elected 1945.*

Hobart (Hobey) Baker: An all-around legend at Princeton University before the first World War, he was known as a one-man hockey team. Also starred in football. Later played for the St. Nicholas amateur hockey team. *Elected 1945.*

William (Bill) Barber: Left wing tallied 420 goals and 883 points for Philadelphia from 1973 to 1984. Scored goal that sent 1976 Canada Cup final game into overtime. *Elected 1991.*

Martin A. (Marty) Barry: A center on the productive Detroit Red Wing line of the mid-1930s which included Larry Aurie and Herbie Lewis. Also played for New York Americans and Boston Bruins. *Elected 1965.*

Andrew James (Andy) Bathgate: Averaged nearly a point a game in 17-year career despite playing with a badly damaged knee. Starred for

《 A kaleidoscope of masks traces the evolution of a goalie's best friend.

Hobey Baker never played pro hockey but he made the Hall of Fame following a brilliant career at Princeton.

Andy Bathgate starred for 17 years in the NHL and averaged nearly a point a game.

the New York Rangers in 1950s and 1960s. Was league MVP in 1958–59, when he had 88 points. *Elected 1978.*

Jean Beliveau: Scored 507 goals in 18 seasons with the Montreal Canadiens as one of the most respected players in hockey history. Played on 10 Stanley Cup championship teams. *Elected 1972.*

Clint Benedict: A goalie on five winning Stanley Cup teams, four with Ottawa and one with the Montreal Maroons. Allowed only three goals in a four-game Cup series while with the Maroons in 1926–27. *Elected 1965.*

Douglas Wagner (Doug) Bentley: Left wing on the crack Chicago Black Hawk line with brother Max Bentley and Bill Mosienko. Played for the Hawks from 1939 to 1951. *Elected 1964.*

Maxwell (Max) Bentley: A clever center and a fine stickhandler for the Chicago Black Hawks

and Toronto Maple Leafs. Was voted the NHL's Most Valuable Player in 1945–46. *Elected 1966.*

Hector (Toe) Blake: A left wing for the Montreal Maroons and Montreal Canadiens. Was member of great Canadiens' line that included Maurice Richard and Elmer Lach. Later coached Canadiens to eight Stanley Cup crowns. *Elected 1966.*

Leo Joseph Boivin: Although just a 5-foot-7 defenseman, he set standard for bone-jarring checks. Played 1,150 games over 19 seasons, including 10 with Boston from 1955–65. *Elected 1986.*

Richard (Dickie) Boon: Played for amateur teams in the Montreal area in the late 1890s and for the Montreal Wanderers in 1904 and 1905. *Elected 1952.*

Michael Dean (Mike) Bossy: Scored 50-or-more goals in each of first nine seasons, totaling 573 and 1,126 points in 10 years with Islanders. Right wing set NHL rookie mark with 53 goals in 1977–78. Conn Smythe winner in 1982. *Elected 1991.*

Emile (Butch) Bouchard: A Montreal Canadiens' defenseman for 14 years, starting in 1941–42. Named to NHL's first All-Star team three times. *Elected 1966.*

Frank Boucher: A center on the famous New York Ranger line that also included the Cook brothers, Bill and Bun. Winner of record seven Lady Byng Trophies. Also was a Ranger coach and general manager. *Elected 1958.*

George (Buck) Boucher: An older brother of Frank Boucher, he was a leading defenseman for the Ottawa Senators and Montreal Maroons from 1917 to 1929. *Elected 1960.*

John W. Bower: Didn't make his mark on a full-time basis until he was 34, when he became the work-horse goalie as Maple Leafs won four Stanley Cups in the 1960s. Had 37 career shutouts. *Elected 1976.*

Russell (Dubbie) Bowie: Was a rover for the Montreal Victorias for 10 years in the early

Turk Broda was a champ in the nets and at ▶▶ *the dinner table.*

1900s. Had career total of 234 goals. *Elected 1945.*

Frank Brimsek: A native of Eveleth, Minn., he was nicknamed "Mr. Zero" because he twice had three consecutive shutouts as a goalie for the Boston Bruins. Starred in the late 1930s and early 1940s. *Elected 1966.*

Walter (Turk) Broda: Played goal 16 seasons for the Toronto Maple Leafs. Had reputation for excellence in important games. *Elected 1967.*

Harry L. (Punch) Broadbent: As a forward he played for four Stanley Cup-winning teams, three as a member of the Ottawa Senators and one with the Montreal Maroons. *Elected 1962.*

Johnny Bucyk played 21 years with the Boston Bruins and helped them win two Stanley Cups.

John P. Bucyk: Played for 23 years in NHL, 21 of them with the Boston Bruins. Left wing scored 556 goals and helped Bruins win two Stanley Cups (1970, 1972). Two-time Lady Byng winner. *Elected 1981.*

William (Billy) Burch: Born in Yonkers, N.Y., in 1900, he became star center of the New York Americans in the 1920s. Led his team in scoring five times. *Elected 1974.*

Harold (Hugh) Harry Cameron: Was famous for rushes up ice while playing defense for the Toronto Arenas, Ottawa Senators, Toronto St. Pats and Montreal Canadiens. *Elected 1962.*

Gerald Michael (Gerry) Cheevers: In Boston goal for Cup titles in 1970 and 1972. Compiled 230-94-74 record with 2.89 GAA. Coached Bruins to 204-126-46 record from 1980–84. *Elected 1985.*

Francis (King) Clancy: Was outstanding scoring defenseman for the Ottawa Senators and Toronto Maple Leafs. Also was an NHL referee and a coach for the Leafs and Montreal Maroons. *Elected 1958.*

Aubry (Dit) Clapper: Played right wing and right defense for the Boston Bruins. Spent 20 years as a player in the NHL and also coached the Bruins. *Elected 1947.*

Robert Earle (Bobby) Clarke: Feisty center overcame diabetes to amass 1,210 points in 1,144 games in 15 seasons with Philadelphia. Won Hart Trophy three times. First expansion-team player to record 100-point season. *Elected 1987.*

Sprague Cleghorn: A defenseman, he played 18 years for Ottawa, Toronto, the Montreal Canadiens and Boston Bruins before retiring in 1928. *Elected 1958.*

Neil Colville: Center on New York Rangers' standout line of late 1930s and 1940s that included brother Mac Colville and Alex Shibicky. Later played as a defenseman for the Rangers. *Elected 1967.*

William (Bill) Cook: A big, strong sharpshooter from the right wing position, he played for 12 years with the New York Rangers. One of original Rangers, who came into NHL in 1926. *Elected 1962.*

Gerry Cheevers figured in two of Boston's Stanley Cup championships and later coached the Bruins.

Charlie (Chuck) Conacher: A husky, hard-shooting right wing, he played for 10 years for the Toronto Maple Leafs. Was a member of standout line of Conacher-Joe Primeau-Harvey Jackson. Also played for Detroit and New York Americans. *Elected 1961.*

Alex Connell: As a goalie for the Ottawa Senators, he once posted a record 446 minutes, six seconds without being scored on. The streak included six consecutive shutouts. *Elected 1958.*

Art Coulter: Prototype defensive defenseman with Black Hawks and Rangers in the 1930s. Scored only 30 goals in 11 NHL seasons but was on three Cup winners. *Elected 1974.*

Yvan Cournoyer: Blazing speed gave him nickname "The Roadrunner" during 15-year career with the Canadiens. Played on 10 Stanley Cup winners and scored 25 or more goals 12 straight seasons. *Elected 1982.*

Bill Cowley: A clever center, he starred for the Boston Bruins in the late 1930s and early 1940s. Scored 195 goals in 13 NHL seasons. *Elected 1968.*

Samuel Russell (Rusty) Crawford: A fast-skating forward, he played amateur and professional hockey from 1906 through 1929. The Ottawa Senators and Toronto Arenas were among his teams. *Elected 1962.*

John Proctor (Jack) Darragh: A clever stick-handler and a speedy skater from the right-wing position, he was also noted for an effective backhand shot. Played mostly for the Ottawa Senators. *Elected 1962.*

Allan (Scotty) Davidson: A rugged, powerful defenseman, he starred for Kingston and Toronto before the formation of the NHL. Was shifted to forward toward the end of his career. *Elected 1950.*

Toronto's Happy Day coached the Leafs to five Stanley Cups after his playing days were over.

Clarence (Happy) Day: A sound, steady defenseman for 10 years with the Toronto Maple Leafs and later with the New York Americans. Was also an NHL referee, coach and general manager of the Maple Leafs. *Elected 1961.*

Alex Delvecchio: Red Wings' iron-man center who missed just 43 games in 22 seasons with club. Scored 456 goals in 1,549 games and won Lady Byng Trophy for clean play three times. *Elected 1977.*

Cyril (Cy) Denneny: A relatively slow-skating left wing, but he possessed one of the most accurate shots among players of his era. Played 11 years with Ottawa, starting in 1917, and had one season at Boston. *Elected 1959.*

Marcel Dionne: Was a leading center for 19 years (Detroit, Los Angeles, New York Rangers), winning the scoring title in 1979–80 with the Kings and the Lady Byng Trophy twice. Made the All-Star team four times. Retired with 1,771 points in third place on the all-time scoring list. *Elected 1992.*

Gordon Drillon: Averaged 22 goals a season when 20-goal scorers were rare. Played six years with Maple Leafs in the 1930s and led team in scoring three straight seasons. *Elected 1975.*

Charles Graham Drinkwater: Starred as an amateur player late in the 19th century. Played on championship teams at McGill University in Montreal and for the Montreal Victorias. *Elected 1950.*

Ken Dryden: Backbone of six Stanley Cup champions with Montreal in the 1970s. Won Smythe, Calder and Vezina Trophies and recorded miniscule 2.24 goals-against average in 397 NHL games. *Elected 1983.*

Woody Dumart: A tenacious two-way left wing with the Boston Bruins from 1935–36 through 1953–54, he teamed with Milt Schmidt and Bobby Bauer on the Bruins' famed "Kraut Line" (Later the "Kitchener Line"). Was a key figure in the Bruins' Stanley Cup crowns in 1939 and 1941. *Elected 1992.*

Thomas Dunderdale: First Australian-born player to achieve Hall of Fame status. Played 12 years in the PCHA and scored more goals than any player in the league. *Elected 1974.*

William Ronald (Bill) Durnan: Captured the Vezina Trophy six times, including four in succession, while playing for the Montreal Canadiens. Named five times as NHL's first All-Star team goalie. *Elected 1964.*

Mervyn (Red) Dutton: Starred as defenseman for Calgary of the Western Canadian League, then for the Montreal Maroons and New York Americans of NHL. Was also coach of Americans and served as league president from 1943 to 1945. *Elected 1958.*

Cecil (Babe) Dye: Greatest goal scorer of the 1920s. Playing for the Toronto St. Pats, he scored 163 goals in 149 games over six seasons. Finished career with 200 goals in 255 games. *Elected 1970.*

Phil Esposito: First player to break 100-point barrier (1968–69). Unmovable center won five scoring titles, finishing 18-year career with Chicago, Boston and New York Rangers with 717 goals and 1,590 points. *Elected 1984.*

Tony Esposito: Five-time All-Star with Chicago played 873 games over 15 seasons. Won or shared Vezina Trophy three times, including rookie year. *Elected 1988.*

Arthur Farrell: A team-oriented forward, he was a key figure when the Montreal Shamrocks won the Stanley Cup twice in a row (1899, 1900). *Elected 1965.*

Ferdinand Charles (Fernie) Flaman: Standout 17-year defenseman for the Bruins and Leafs. Played on 1951 Toronto Stanley Cup winner. Coached AHL, WHL and CHL teams to titles. U.S. College Coach of Year at Northeastern in 1982. *Elected 1990.*

Frank Foyston: Standout center in Western Canadian League from 1916 to 1926 while with Seattle and Victoria, compiling 186 goals. Later, played two years for the Detroit Cougars. *Elected 1958.*

Frank Fredrickson: An outstanding amateur player and a star in the Pacific Coast, Western Canadian and National Hockey Leagues. As a center, he played in the NHL for Detroit, Boston and Pittsburgh, also coaching and managing Pittsburgh in 1930–31. *Elected 1958.*

Bill Gadsby: Overcame polio to become one of NHL's best defensemen for 20 seasons. Played

Bernie (Boom Boom) Geoffrion got his nickname because of his crushing slapshots.

The Rangers' record book is dominated by Rod Gilbert.

for the Black Hawks, Rangers and Red Wings and was named first-team All-Star three times. *Elected 1970.*

Bob Gainey: A checking left winger during a 16-year career, all with the Montreal Canadiens, he played on five Stanley Cup championship teams. Won the Selke Trophy four times as the league's top defensive forward. *Elected 1992.*

Charles (Chuck) Gardiner: A brilliant goalie for the Chicago Black Hawks for seven consecutive seasons, starting in 1928. Twice winner of the Vezina Trophy. Also made first All-Star team twice. *Elected 1945.*

Herbert Martin (Herb) Gardiner: Turned pro at 31 years of age with Calgary of the Western Canadian League. Defenseman joined the Montreal Canadiens four years later and was named the league's Most Valuable Player. *Elected 1958.*

James Henry (Jimmy) Gardner: Left wing played for the Montreal Shamrocks, Montreal Wanderers and Montreal Canadiens. Also

coached the Hamilton, Ont., team of the NHL in 1924–25. *Elected 1962.*

Bernie Geoffrion: Nicknamed "Boom Boom" for the sound his slapshot made as it crashed against the boards. Produced 393 goals in 16 seasons with the New York Rangers and Montreal. Coached Rangers for half a season, later coached Atlanta and did short stint at Montreal. *Elected 1972.*

Eddie Gerard: As a defenseman and captain, he led the Ottawa Senators to three Stanley Cup titles. Coached the Montreal Maroons in 1926 and was manager of the New York Americans in 1931. *Elected 1945.*

Eddie Giacomin: A 10-year goaltender with the New York Rangers, he topped the NHL in victories for three straight seasons, starting in 1966–67. Wound up career in Detroit with overall 289-206-97 record and 2.82 GAA. *Elected 1987.*

Rod Gilbert: Right wing set or equaled 20 team scoring records during brilliant 16-year career with the New York Rangers. Totaled 1,021 points in 1,065 games despite playing with a bad back. *Elected 1982.*

Hamilton Livingstone (Billy) Gilmour: Played for the Ottawa Silver Seven, winners of three straight Stanley Cup crowns, starting in 1902–03. *Elected 1962.*

Frank (Moose) Goheen: A defenseman born in White Bear, Minn., he played for St. Paul in the U.S. Amateur Association and was a member of the 1920 American Olympic team. *Elected 1952.*

Ebenezer R. (Ebbie) Goodfellow: Started out as a center, but was moved to defense by the Detroit Red Wings. Was named the NHL's Most Valuable Player in 1939–40. *Elected 1963.*

Michael (Mike) Grant: Joined the Montreal Victorias in 1894 when they won the Stanley Cup. Later organized exhibition games in the United States. *Elected 1950.*

Wilfred (Shorty) Green: Right wing played in senior league in northern Ontario until he turned pro with the Hamilton Tigers of the NHL in 1923. Later played for the New York Americans. *Elected 1962.*

Silas (Si) Griffis: A defenseman known for his speed, he turned pro with the Kenora Thistles in 1907 when they defeated the Montreal Wanderers for the Stanley Cup. He captained the Vancouver Millionaires, who won the Stanley Cup in 1915. *Elected 1950.*

George Hainsworth: Recorded 22 shutouts during 44-game NHL schedule while with the Montreal Canadiens in 1928–29. Won Vezina Trophy three straight years and later was traded to Toronto. *Elected 1961.*

Glenn Hall: An All-Star goalie for 11 of his 18 years with Detroit, Chicago and St. Louis. Set record for most consecutive games by a goaltender (502) and ended career with 2.51 goals-against average. *Elected 1975.*

Joseph Henry (Joe) Hall: Noted as a slam-bang defenseman. Played for Kenora Thistles, Montreal Shamrocks, Quebec Bulldogs and Montreal Canadiens, through 1918–19. *Elected 1961.*

Doug Harvey: Seven-time winner of the James Norris Trophy as NHL's leading defenseman. Named to All-Star team 11 times in 17 seasons. Played the point on Montreal's awesome power play during the 1950s. *Elected 1973.*

George Hay: Was forward in western Canada with Winnipeg, Regina and Portland until he joined the Chicago Black Hawks in 1926. Later played for Detroit Cougars and Red Wings. *Elected 1958.*

William Milton (Riley) Hern: Mostly a goalie, but played some as a forward. Starred for the Montreal Wanderers when they won the Stanley Cup in 1907, 1908 and 1910. *Elected 1962.*

Bryan Hextall: Scored 20 or more goals in seven of 12 seasons with the Rangers in the 1930s and 1940s. Three-time All-Star right wing who led NHL in scoring in 1941–42 with 56 points. *Elected 1969.*

Harry (Hap) Holmes: Starred in five professional leagues over a 15-year goaltending career. Played on four Stanley Cup champions. Memory is perpetuated by trophy carrying his name awarded to leading goalie in American Hockey League each season. *Elected 1972.*

Charles Thomas (Tom) Hooper: Played as forward for Kenora Thistles, starting in 1901. Was on Kenora team which won Stanley Cup by defeating the Montreal Wanderers in 1907. *Elected 1962.*

G. Reginald (Red) Horner: A rough defenseman, he accumulated 1,254 penalty minutes during 12 years with the Toronto Maple Leafs, starting in 1928. *Elected 1965.*

Miles Gilbert (Tim) Horton: Inspirational leader of great Maple Leaf teams of the 1960s. Strong defenseman who played 18 years before tragic auto accident claimed his life in 1974. *Elected 1977.*

Gordie Howe: Record-setting right wing. Played for 25 years with Detroit Red Wings and was named to the All-Star team in 21 of those years. Six-time scoring champion and six-time winner of the Hart Trophy as MVP. Made remarkable comeback, playing six more seasons in the WHA, then one more in the NHL before he retired at the age of 52. *Elected 1972.*

Dick Irvin played for Chicago before becoming a successful coach in the NHL.

Sydney Harris (Syd) Howe: A forward, he shares the modern record of six goals in a game made with the Detroit Red Wings in 1944. Spent 16 seasons in the NHL. *Elected 1965.*

Harry Howell: Appeared in more games (1,581) than any defenseman in the history of major-league hockey. Had 24-year career in NHL and WHA and was Norris Trophy winner in 1966–67 while with Rangers. *Elected 1979.*

Robert Marvin (Bobby) Hull: Left wing who scored over 900 goals in brilliant 23-year career in NHL and WHA. Most dominant scorer of the 1960s, cracking 50-goal barrier five times with Chicago. Career total of 610 NHL goals is fifth on all-time list. *Elected 1983.*

John Bower (Bouse) Hutton: Goalie for the Ottawa Silver Seven Cup champions of 1903 and 1904. Also was star goalie in lacrosse. *Elected 1962.*

Harry Hyland: A right winger, he turned pro with the Montreal Shamrocks in 1908–09. Joined the Montreal Wanderers the next year and remained with them until 1918 when he became member of Ottawa Senators. *Elected 1962.*

James Dickenson (Dick) Irvin: Played for Regina and Portland of Western Canadian League and for Chicago Black Hawks of NHL as a forward. Also coached Black Hawks, Toronto and Montreal Canadiens, winning four Stanley Cup titles. *Elected 1958.*

Harvey (Busher) Jackson: Gained fame on Toronto's ''Kid Line'' with Charlie Conacher and Joe Primeau in 1930s. Led Leafs to three NHL titles. Named to five All-Star teams and won scoring title in 1932–33. Finished career with New York Americans and Boston Bruins. *Elected 1961.*

Ivan (Ching) Johnson: Was one of the original New York Rangers in 1926–27. A defenseman who relished delivering hard bodychecks, he played in the NHL for 12 years, the last with the New York Americans. *Elected 1958.*

Ernie (Moose) Johnson: Played for Montreal Wanderers until 1910 when moved to New Westminster of Pacific Coast League. Was defenseman throughout most of career, but also played forward. *Elected 1952.*

Scoring champ Guy Lafleur was a point machine on four championship Canadien teams.

Thomas Christian Johnson: Played on six Stanley Cup winners during 15-year career as defenseman for Montreal and Boston in the 1950s and 1960s. Norris Trophy winner in 1958–59. *Elected 1970.*

Aurel Joliat: A 140-pound left wing, he played on a line with the great Howie Morenz for the Montreal Canadiens. Was exceptionally fast and clever. Started 16-year career with Canadiens in 1922. *Elected 1947.*

Gordon (Duke) Keats: A forward, he was a long-time star in the Western Canadian League, mostly with Edmonton. Later played for Boston, Detroit and Chicago of NHL. *Elected 1958.*

Leonard (Red) Kelly: Broke into NHL in 1947 and played 20 seasons as top defenseman for Detroit and center for Toronto. Won Lady Byng Trophy four times and played on eight Stanley Cup winners. *Elected 1969.*

Theodore (Ted) Kennedy: As a center, he sparked the Toronto Maple Leafs to five Stanley Cup championships. Was team captain from 1948 until retirement in 1955. *Elected 1966.*

David Michael Keon: Checking center played 22 pro seasons. Won Calder Trophy with Toronto in 1960–61 and Conn Smythe in 1967. Picked up just 151 penalty minutes in 1,725 games. *Elected 1986.*

Elmer James Lach: Was center on line with Maurice Richard in 1944–45 when the Rocket scored a record 50 goals in 50 games. Played for Montreal Canadiens for 14 years, three times being voted to league's first All-Star team. *Elected 1966.*

Guy Damien Lafleur: Dazzling Montreal center was three-time scoring champion, MVP twice and six-time All-Star. Helped Habs to four straight Cups from 1976 to 1979. Played for Rangers and Quebec after four-year retirement. *Elected 1988.*

Edouard (Newsy) Lalonde: Started pro career with Cornwall in 1905 and was one of finest

Montreal's Jacques Lemaire was on a Cup winner eight times.

Canadiens from 1909 to 1918. He had outstanding speed. Played on a line with Newsy Lalonde. *Elected 1962.*

Hughie Lehman: A professional goalie for 19 years. Standout in Pacific Coast Hockey Association for New Westminster and Vancouver. Played for Chicago Black Hawks in 1926–27, their first season in NHL. *Elected 1958.*

Jacques Gerard Lemaire: Montreal center took Stanley Cup victory lap eight times in 11 years with 139 points in 145 playoff games. Scored 366 goals and 835 points in 853 regular-season games. *Elected 1984.*

Percy LeSueur: Goalie for the Ottawa Senators from 1906 to 1913. Played for Toronto in 1914 and later coached Hamilton team of the NHL. *Elected 1961.*

Herbert Lewis: Known as "The Duke of Duluth" for his great years with Duluth in the American Hockey League, flashy, high-speed left wing played 11 years with the Detroit Cougars, Falcons and Red Wings. Was on two Stanley Cup championship teams and started in the first All-Star Game in 1934. *Elected 1989.*

Theodore (Ted) Lindsay: Aggressive, combative, productive left wing for Detroit Red Wings. One of the highest career scorers at his position. Emerged from four-year retirement as player in 1964–65 and helped Wings win league title. *Elected 1966.*

Harry Lumley: Signed by Detroit when he was only 16, he became one of NHL's greatest goaltenders in 16-year career. Recorded 71 shutouts in regular season and seven more in playoffs. *Elected 1980.*

Duncan (Mickey) MacKay: Played forward for the Vancouver Millionaires from 1914 to 1926. He joined the Chicago Black Hawks in 1926–27 and later played for Pittsburgh and Boston of the NHL. *Elected 1952.*

Frank Mahovlich: A star from first season, when he was Rookie of Year. Left wing played on six Stanley Cup winners with Montreal and Toronto and finished career with 533 goals and 1,103 points. *Elected 1981.*

Joe Malone: Scored 44 goals during 22-game schedule in 1917–18, his first NHL season with the Montreal Canadiens. Holds NHL record of

scorers and roughest players of his era. Played with Montreal Canadiens of NHL and with other teams in the National Hockey Association and Pacific Coast Hockey Association. *Elected 1950.*

Jacques Laperriere: Strong and mobile backliner anchored defense on Montreal teams that won six Cups during his 12-year career. Won Calder Trophy in 1962–63. *Elected 1987.*

Jean Baptiste (Jack) Laviolette: Played both as a forward and a defenseman for the Montreal

Blackhawk playmaker Stan Mikita won the scoring crown four times.

seven goals in a Stanley Cup game. *Elected 1950.*

Sylvio Mantha: Played defense for the Montreal Canadiens for 13 years, starting in 1923–24. Team finished in first place nine times during that period. Was player-coach for Boston Bruins in 1936. *Elected 1960.*

Jack Marshall: Played center for the Montreal Wanderers when they won the Stanley Cup in 1906, 1908 and 1910. Was captain of Toronto team which won Cup in 1914. *Elected 1965.*

Fred G. (Steamer) Maxwell: A star amateur who never became a professional, his position was that of rover when each team consisted of seven players. Played senior hockey in Winnipeg, starting in 1909. Later became a coach of amateur and professional teams. *Elected 1962.*

Lanny McDonald: Had a 16-year NHL career that began in Toronto in 1973 and was capped when he captained the Calgary Flames to their first Stanley Cup championship in 1989. Right wing made four All-Star Game appearances and represented Team NHL at the 1979 Challenge Cup. *Elected 1992.*

Frank McGee: A center for the Ottawa Silver Seven. In a Stanley Cup game against Dawson City in 1905, he scored 14 goals, including eight in succession during a span of eight minutes and 20 seconds. *Elected 1945.*

William George (Billy) McGimsie: Was a center for 10 years for the Kenora Thistles. Played in several Stanley Cup series against the Montreal Wanderers and Ottawa Silver Seven, the first in 1903. *Elected 1962.*

George McNamara: Helped the Toronto team win the Stanley Cup in 1914 while playing defense. Before that he was with the Montreal Wanderers and with Waterloo of the Trolley League. *Elected 1958.*

Stanley (Stan) Mikita: One of the greatest playmaking centers in NHL history, he chalked up 926 assists in 22 years with the Chicago Black Hawks. Led league in scoring four times and twice won Hart and Lady Byng Trophies. *Elected 1983.*

Richard Dickie Moore: Twice led NHL in scoring despite assortment of serious injuries. Left wing helped Canadiens win six Stanley Cups in

his 12 years there, starting in 1951. Scored 608 points in 719 NHL games. *Elected 1974.*

Patrick Joseph (Paddy) Moran: A standup goalie who used his stick to good advantage, he turned pro with the Quebec Bulldogs in 1902. Played for Haileybury in 1911, but returned to Quebec and helped the Bulldogs win the Stanley Cup in 1912 and 1913. *Elected 1958.*

Howie Morenz: A flashy, dynamic center, he starred for 14 years in the NHL, mostly with the Montreal Canadiens. Montreal traded him to Chicago in 1934 and he moved to the New York Rangers in 1935 before returning to the Canadiens for the 1936–37 campaign. *Elected 1945.*

William (Bill) Mosienko: Best remembered for scoring three goals in a record 21 seconds while playing for Chicago against the New York Rangers on March 23, 1952. Was right wing on line with Bentley brothers, Max and Doug. *Elected 1965.*

Frank Nighbor: A center, he played pro hockey in leagues in Eastern and Western Canada from 1915 to 1929. Starred for Vancouver Millionaires and Ottawa Senators. Scored 41 goals in 20 games in 1916–17. *Elected 1947.*

Reginald (Reg) Noble: Primarily a left wing, but played some defense for Toronto Arenas, Toronto St. Pats, Montreal Maroons and Detroit Cougars. Helped Maroons with Stanley Cup in 1925–26. *Elected 1962.*

Herbert William (Buddy) O'Connor: Center had just 34 penalty minutes in 10-year career with Montreal and New York Rangers. Scored 60 points in 60 games for Rangers to win MVP and Lady Byng honors in 1947–48. *Elected 1988.*

Harold (Harry) Oliver: Played as a forward for 11 NHL seasons for the Boston Bruins and New York Americans. Weighed only 155 pounds and rarely was penalized. Helped Bruins win two Stanley Cup crowns. *Elected 1967.*

Murray Bert Olmstead: Tough left wing played on four Stanley Cup Winners at Montreal in the 1950s before helping Toronto take the title in 1962. Amassed 421 points and 884 penalty minutes in 848 games. *Elected 1985.*

Bobby Orr: Six knee operations cut brilliant NHL career to nine years with Boston and Chicago. The only defenseman ever to win a scoring championship (he did it twice), Orr scored 915 points in 657 games. Won Norris Trophy as best defenseman eight consecutive years through 1974–75 season. *Elected 1979.*

Bernard Marcel (Bernie) Parent: Backstopped Flyers to consecutive Stanley Cup titles in 1974 and 1975, winning Conn Smythe both years. In 608 regular-season games, posted 55 shutouts and 2.55 GAA. *Elected 1984.*

Douglas Bradford (Brad) Park: High-scoring defenseman was seven-time All-Star for the Rangers, Bruins and Red Wings in 17-year career. Scored 213 goals and 896 points in 1,113 games. Played in 161 postseason games. *Elected 1988.*

Lester Patrick: Patriarch of famous hockey family, he was an outstanding player for the Montreal Wanderers and Renfrew Millionaires. He helped form the Pacific Coast Hockey Association and, in 1926, came east to coach and manage the New York Rangers in their first NHL season. Remained with Rangers until 1946. *Elected 1947.*

Lynn Patrick: Fearing charges of nepotism, his father, Lester, wouldn't put Lynn on the New York Rangers until another club threatened to claim him. In his decade with the team, Lynn led Rangers in scoring twice and scored 335 points in 455 games. *Elected 1980.*

Gilbert Perreault: Superb skater and puckhandler scored 512 goals and 1,326 points in 1,191 games over 17 years with Buffalo. Calder Trophy winner in 1971 and Lady Byng recipient in 1972. *Elected 1990.*

Tommy Phillips: Was a hard-shooting, slick, stickhandling forward for the Kenora Thistles. In 1906, he scored seven goals in a two-game Stanley Cup series against the Montreal Wanderers. *Elected 1945.*

Pierre Pilote: Defenseman broke in with Chicago in 1956 and did not miss a game his first five seasons. Three-time Norris Trophy winner had 498 points in 890 regular-season games. *Elected 1975.*

Didier (Pit) Pitre: Joined the Montreal Canadiens in 1909 and was noted for his blistering shot. A 200-pound forward, he played for the Canadiens until 1923, when he retired. *Elected 1962.*

Jacques Plante: The first goalie to popularize the mask, Plante had an outstanding 2.34 goals-against average in 837 games and recorded 82 shutouts. Played on six of Montreal's Stanley Cup champions. *Elected 1978.*

Denis Charles Potvin: Seven-time All-Star set NHL career records for goals, assists and points for defensemen during 15 seasons with Islanders. Won Norris Trophy three times, Calder in 1974. Captained four Cup winners. *Elected 1991.*

Walter (Babe) Pratt: A defenseman, he began pro career with New York Rangers in January 1936, and was traded to Toronto in November 1942. A standout offensive player for a rearguard. *Elected 1966.*

A. Joseph (Joe) Primeau: Center for famous Kid Line that included Charlie Conacher and Harvey Jackson. A clever stickhandler and playmaker and an excellent penalty-killer for the Toronto Maple Leafs. *Elected 1963.*

Marcel Pronovost: Twenty-year veteran of NHL play who played integral role on five Stanley Cup winners. Broke in with Detroit in 1950 and played there 15 years before trade to Toronto. Solid defender scored 345 points in 1,206 games. *Elected 1978.*

Bob Pulford: Resolute left wing played on four Cup winners in Toronto. Played 16 seasons, final two with Kings, scoring 281 goals and 643 points in 1,079 games. *Elected 1991.*

Harvey Pulford: Played defense for the Ottawa Silver Seven from 1893 to 1908. Was one of the most effective bodycheckers of his era and had reputation for being a clean player. *Elected 1945.*

Bill Quackenbush: The cleanest defenseman in NHL history, he collected only 95 minutes of penalties in 13 seasons. A five-time All-Star with Detroit and Boston, he was Lady Byng winner in 1949. *Elected 1976.*

Frank Rankin: Played rover position when each team played with seven men. Starred for teams in Stratford, Ont., and Toronto, beginning in 1906–07 season. *Elected 1961.*

Jean Ratelle: Smooth-skating center scored 491 goals and 1,267 points in 1,281 games with Rangers and Bruins from 1960 to 1981. Won

Marcel Pronovost patrolled NHL blue lines for 20 years and played on five Cup winners.

Henri Richard of the Canadiens (left) and Alex Delvecchio of the Red Wings were rewarded for their brilliant play with election to the Hall of Fame.

Lady Byng twice, spending just 276 minutes in penalty box. *Elected 1985.*

Claude Earl (Chuck) Rayner: Played 10 seasons in the NHL, all of them in New York. Had 25 career shutouts and was named to the All-Star team three times. Named winner of the Hart Trophy as Most Valuable Player in 1949–50, the second goalie to win that award. *Elected 1973.*

Kenneth (Ken) Reardon: A rugged, fearless defenseman for the Montreal Canadiens, starting in 1940–41. Voted to the NHL All-Star team four times. Later, was a front-office executive for the Canadiens. *Elected 1966.*

Henri Richard: Younger brother of Rocket Richard played on 11 All-Star champions in Montreal. Center twice led the league in assists and

❰❰ *Jean Ratelle had a 21-season career with the Rangers and Bruins.*

finished with 1,046 points in 1,256 games. *Elected 1979.*

Maurice (Rocket) Richard: Famed Montreal Canadiens' right wing had record 544 career goals until Detroit's Gordie Howe surpassed it. Played 18 NHL seasons before retiring after the 1959–60 campaign and was voted into the Hall of Fame nine months later. *Elected 1960.*

George Richardson: Never a professional, but an outstanding amateur from Kingston, Ont. Was with Queen's University team which won the Allan Cup in 1909. *Elected 1950.*

Gordon Roberts: Played for Montreal Wanderers while attending McGill University and studying medicine. When he graduated, he moved west to practice but continued playing hockey. Set an all-time scoring record in Pacific Coast Hockey Association with 43 goals in 23 games. *Elected 1971.*

Bullet Joe Simpson was a New York Americans' defenseman after pre-NHL career with Winnipeg and Edmonton.

Arthur Howey (Art) Ross: Turned pro with the Kenora Thistles in 1906. Also played for Hailey-bury and the Montreal Wanderers. Later was coach and general manager of the Boston Bruins. *Elected 1945.*

Blair Russell: A left-wing amateur star for the Montreal Victorias in the early 1900s. On February 23, 1905, he scored six goals in one game. *Elected 1965.*

Ernie Russell: Top scorer for the Montreal Wanderers, for whom he scored 32 goals during a 12-game regular-season schedule in 1910. *Elected 1965.*

J. D. (Jack) Ruttan: A leading amateur player starting in 1905–06 with the Armstrong's Point team of Winnipeg. Also played in the Manitoba University League and the Winnipeg Senior League. *Elected 1962.*

Serge Aubrey Savard: Was key defensive stalwart on seven Montreal Cup winners over 14 seasons. Joined Winnipeg in 1981–82, helping Jets to biggest single-season improvement in NHL history. *Elected 1986.*

Terry Sawchuk: Considered one of greatest goalies in history. Played more seasons, more games and had more shutouts than any other netminder. Finished career with 103 shutouts, only goalie ever to reach the century mark. *Elected 1971.*

Fred Scanlan: A forward for the Montreal Shamrocks, winners of the Stanley Cup in 1898–99 and 1899–1900. Known for his clever play and accurate shot. *Elected 1965.*

Milton Conrad (Milt) Schmidt: A strong skater, smart stickhandler and prolific scorer, he centered Boston's famous Kraut Line that also included Bobby Bauer and Woody Dumart. *Elected 1961.*

David (Sweeney) Schriner: A left winger, he starred for the New York Americans and Toronto Maple Leafs. Twice won the NHL's scoring title, in 1935–36 and 1936–37. *Elected 1962.*

Earl Walter Seibert: Was noted for his ability as a rushing defenseman for the New York Rangers, Chicago Black Hawks and Detroit Red Wings. Voted to circuit's first All-Star team four times. *Elected 1963.*

Oliver Levi Seibert: Earl Siebert's father. Was member of the Berlin Rangers, winners of the Western Ontario Association title from 1900 to 1906. Was a forward during most of his career. *Elected 1961.*

Edward (Eddie) Shore: Generally regarded as the greatest defenseman of all time. Played for the Boston Bruins for 13 1/2 years, then was

Serge Savard's defense led to seven Cups for Montreal. **»**

traded to the New York Americans, for whom he played a half season. *Elected 1947.*

Albert (Babe) Siebert: Was outstanding left wing for Montreal Maroons. Switched to defense in the mid-1930s and continued to star with the New York Rangers, Boston Bruins and Montreal Canadiens. *Elected 1964.*

Harold (Bullet Joe) Simpson: A fast-skating defenseman, he played for teams in Winnipeg and Edmonton before joining the New York Americans in 1925. Was general manager of the Americans from 1932 to 1935. *Elected 1962.*

Darryl Glen Sittler: Prolific center amassed 1,121 career points in 15 seasons, including record 10 points (six goals, four assists) in one game for Leafs in February, 1976. Scored goal in overtime that won 1976 Canada Cup. *Elected 1989.*

Alfred E. (Alf) Smith: Was captain of the Ottawa Silver Seven in 1903, 1904 and 1905. Also captained the Pittsburgh Athletic Club in 1909, his final year as a player. *Elected 1962.*

Clinton James (Snuffy) Smith: Two-time Lady Byng winner committed just 12 minor penalties in 10-year career centering for the New York Rangers and Chicago. Set then-NHL mark with 49 assists in 50-game season for the Hawks in 1943–44. *Elected 1991.*

Reginald (Hooley) Smith: Combined with Nels Stewart and Babe Siebert to form the Montreal Maroons' great "S" line in the 1930s. Scored 200 goals in 17 seasons as right wing and part-time defenseman. *Elected 1972.*

Thomas Smith: An early star, he played center for three Stanley Cup championship teams before formation of National Hockey League. Won three scoring titles and twice scored nine goals in a single game. Also had an eight-goal game, a six-goal game and five times scored five goals in a game. *Elected 1973.*

Allan Stanley: Durable defenseman played in 1,244 games over 21-year NHL career. Helped Toronto win four Stanley Cups in early 1960s and played in eight All-Star games. *Elected 1981.*

Russell (Barney) Stanley: A forward for the Stanley Cup-winning Vancouver Millionaires in the 1914–15 season. Was named general manager-coach of the Chicago Black Hawks in 1927. *Elected 1962.*

John (Black Jack) Stewart: A defensive star for the Detroit Red Wings for 10 years, starting in 1938–39. Named to the league's first All-Star team three times. *Elected 1964.*

Nelson (Nels) Stewart: A forward, he held the career scoring record of 324 goals until it was broken by Maurice Richard. Starred for the Montreal Maroons, Boston Bruins and New York Americans. *Elected 1962.*

Bruce Stuart: A center, he played for the Portage Lakes team of Houghton, Mich., in the early 1900s. Later played for the Montreal Wanderers and the Ottawa Silver Seven. *Elected 1961.*

William (Hod) Stuart: A brother of Bruce Stuart, he also played in Houghton, Mich., and for the Montreal Wanderers. Was a defenseman. *Elected 1945.*

Fred (Cyclone) Taylor: A high-scoring forward for teams in Houghton, Mich., Ottawa, Renfrew and Vancouver. He was a whirlwind on the ice and is reported to have scored a goal once while skating backwards. *Elected 1947.*

Cecil (Tiny) Thompson: Was a goalie in the NHL for 12 seasons, 10 for the Boston Bruins and two for the Detroit Red Wings. Twice was voted to the league's first All-Star team. *Elected 1959.*

Vladislav Tretiak: Goaltender led Soviets to 10 world titles and three Olympic gold medals from 1970–85. Registered 1.78 GAA in 98 World Championship games. First Soviet player in Hall of Fame. *Elected 1989.*

Harry Trihey: Was a rover who starred for McGill University and as captain of the Montreal Shamrocks when they won two Stanley Cup titles. *Elected 1950.*

Norm Ullman: Scored 20 or more goals in 16 of his 20 seasons in NHL. Centering for Detroit and Toronto, he scored a total of 1,229 points. He led the NHL with 42 goals in 1964–65. *Elected 1982.*

Georges Vezina: Turned pro as a goalie with the Montreal Canadiens in 1910 and played with them until November 1925. Died of tuberculosis the following year. Trophy for the goalies is awarded annually in his memory. *Elected 1945.*

John Phillip (Jack) Walker: Credited with having originated the hook check. Starred mostly on the West Coast for teams in Seattle and Victoria. Also played for Detroit in 1926–27 and 1927–28. *Elected 1960.*

Martin (Marty) Walsh: Played for Ottawa in the Eastern Canada Amateur Association, starting in 1908. Was leading scorer of the National Hockey Association for three seasons. *Elected 1962.*

Harry Watson: Played all three forward positions on crack amateur teams, including the Toronto Granites. Was with the Granites in 1924 when they represented Canada and won the Olympic title. *Elected 1962.*

Ralph (Cooney) Weiland: Center played 11 seasons in NHL. Twice a member of Stanley Cup champions, he coached Boston to the Cup in 1940–41. After leaving pros, he launched a

successful coaching career at Harvard University. *Elected 1971.*

Harry Westwick: Was a rover for the Ottawa Silver Seven when they won three consecutive Stanley Cup titles in the early 1900s. *Elected 1962.*

Fred Whitcroft: A prolific scorer, he played for the Kenora Thistles and Peterborough Colts. Later played for Edmonton, where he scored 49 goals in 1908. *Elected 1962.*

Gordon Allan (Phat) Wilson: Ranked among the all-time great amateur players. Was one of the stars of teams in Port Arthur, Ont., from 1918 to 1933. *Elected 1962.*

Lorne (Gump) Worsley: A two-time Vezina Trophy winner and member of four Stanley Cup winners, Worsley had 43 shutouts and a 2.93 goals-against average in 24 seasons. Played for three NHL teams and had greatest success at Montreal in the late 1960s. *Elected 1980.*

Roy Worters: Only 5-foot-3 and 130 pounds, he starred in the NHL for 12 seasons, mostly with the New York Americans. Compiled 2.36 goals-against average in 488 games and won both the Hart and Vezina Trophies. *Elected 1969.*

REFEREES, LINESMEN

Neil P. Armstrong: Began as a part-time linesman in NHL in 1957–58. Four seasons later, became a referee, never missing an assignment in 16 seasons. Officiated 1,733 regular-season games, 208 playoff games, and 10 All-Star games. *Elected 1991.*

John Ashley: Worked 605 games over 12 NHL seasons and was regarded as league's best when he retired in 1972. *Elected 1981.*

William L. (Bill) Chadwick: A native New Yorker, he officiated NHL games for 16 years. Introduced hand signals to explain penalties such as holding and tripping. *Elected 1964.*

Chaucer Elliott: Started refereeing in 1903 and worked in the Ontario Hockey Association for 10 seasons. *Elected 1961.*

George Hayes: Became first official to work in more than 1,000 games, ending 19-season career as a linesman in 1965 with 1,544 regular-season games. Officiated in 149 post-season contests and 11 All-Star games. *Elected 1988.*

Robert W. (Bobby) Hewitson: An NHL referee for almost 10 years until 1934. Later he became secretary and curator of the Hockey Hall of Fame. *Elected 1963.*

Fred J. (Mickey) Ion: Was a leading official in amateur leagues and in the Pacific Coast League and National Hockey League until 1943. *Elected 1961.*

Matt Pavelich: First linesman to be inducted into the Hall of Fame. Colorful, steady and respected, he set a mark for officiating most playoff games. Worked 1,727 regular-season games through April 1979. *Elected 1987.*

Michael J. (Mike) Rodden: Refereed 1,187 NHL games and was also known as a successful football coach in Canada. *Elected 1962.*

J. Cooper Smeaton: Was referee-in-chief of the NHL until 1937. Also officiated in amateur leagues and in the National Hockey Association. *Elected 1961.*

Roy A. (Red) Storey: An NHL referee from 1951 until he resigned on April 11, 1959. Worked more than 2,000 games in various circuits. *Elected 1967.*

Frank Udvari: Missed only two games in a 15-year NHL career that began in 1951. Later served as supervisor of officials. Previously refereed in the American Hockey League, where he served as referee-in-chief. *Elected 1973.*

BUILDERS

Charles F. Adams: Organizer of the Boston Bruins in 1924, first American team in the National Hockey League. Also negotiated for the erection of the Boston Garden. *Elected 1960.*

Weston W. Adams, Sr.: Longtime president and chairman of the board of both the Boston Bruins and Boston Garden. Was a goalie at Harvard when his father, Charles F. Adams, was awarded Boston franchise, first NHL franchise in United States. *Elected 1972*

Frank Ahearn: A director, president and owner of the Ottawa Senators. Became president in 1922 and held that position until 1934, when

the franchise was transferred to St. Louis. *Elected 1962.*

J. F. (Bunny) Ahearne: Served as president of the International Ice Hockey Federation from 1957 through 1975, organizing European, Olympic and other international hockey events. *Elected 1977.*

Sir Montagu Allan: A Montreal financier and sportsman, he presented the Allan Cup for competition in 1908. The trophy is emblematic of the Senior Amateur Championship of Canada. *Elected 1945.*

Keith Allen: Made his contribution over a quarter of a century as coach and executive with the Philadelphia Flyers. Molded an expansion team that twice won the Stanley Cup (under coach Fred Shero) and was unbeaten for 35 games in 1979-80. *Elected 1992.*

Harold E. Ballard: Spent much of his life building amateur and professional hockey in his native Toronto. Was principal owner of the Maple Leafs and a major force in the NHL. *Elected 1977.*

Father David Bauer, C.S.B.: Ordained Basilian priest whose hockey background included playing left wing on the Oshawa Generals' 1944 Memorial Cup winner. Conceived, developed and coached first Canadian National Hockey Team. *Elected 1989.*

J. P. Bickell: First president, and then chairman of the board, of Maple Leaf Gardens. Award named after him is given to outstanding Toronto player each season. *Elected 1968.*

Scott Bowman: Winningest coach in NHL regular-season history. Guided Montreal to five Stanley Cup titles and expansion St. Louis to three final-round appearances. Coached Team Canada to 1976 Canada Cup victory. *Elected 1991.*

George V. Brown: A pioneer of hockey in the United States. Organized the Boston Athletic Association hockey team and was the manager of the Boston Arena and Boston Garden. *Elected 1961.*

Walter A. Brown: Was president of the Boston Bruins and general manager of Boston Garden. Also coached the Boston Olympics to five U.S. national titles between 1930 and 1940. *Elected 1962.*

Frank Buckland: Coached and organized junior hockey around Toronto for 40 years and served the Ontario Hockey Association as both president and treasurer. *Elected 1985.*

J. A. (Jack) Butterfield: Largely credited with keeping minor-league hockey alive when the NHL expanded in 1967. Served as president of the American Hockey League, starting in 1966. *Elected 1980.*

Frank Calder: First president of the National Hockey League. Served from 1917 until his death in February 1943. Trophy in his memory is awarded annually to the outstanding rookie player. *Elected 1947.*

Angus Daniel Campbell: Played an important part in the development of amateur hockey in Cobalt, Ont., area. Was the first president of the Northern Ontario Association, which was formed in 1919. *Elected 1964.*

Clarence S. Campbell: President of the National Hockey League from September 1946 through 1976–77. Earlier was an NHL referee. *Elected 1966.*

Joseph Cattarinich: One of the original owners of the Canadiens in 1921, he was partly responsible for Montreal's proud NHL heritage. *Elected 1977.*

Joseph (Leo) Dandurand: Was among three persons who purchased the Montreal Canadiens in November 1921. He later coached the Canadiens. Was a delegate to the organizing meeting in 1914 of the Canadian Amateur Hockey Association. *Elected 1963.*

Frank Dilio: A president and secretary of the Junior Amateur Hockey Association. Later served as registrar and secretary of the Quebec Amateur Hockey Association until 1962. *Elected 1964.*

George Dudley: Was president of the Canadian Amateur Hockey Association, the Ontario Hockey Association and the International Ice Hockey Federation. Headed the hockey section of the 1960 Olympic Games. *Elected 1968.*

Jimmie Dunn: A leading administrator and executive of junior teams and leagues in Western Canada. *Elected 1968.*

Robert Alan Eagleson: Executive Director of the NHL Players' Association helped bring hockey salaries in line with other pro sports. Led

negotiations to create Canada Cup series. *Elected 1989.*

Emile (The Cat) Francis: A staunch supporter of amateur hockey in the United States since the 1960s, he is a former NHL goalie who became a coach and then executive with the New York Rangers, St. Louis Blues and Hartford Whalers. *Elected 1982.*

J. L. (Jack) Gibson: Organizer of the first hockey league in the world—the International League—in 1904–05. *Elected 1976.*

Thomas Patrick Gorman: Among the founders of the National Hockey League. Coached or managed seven Stanley Cup-winning teams while with the Montreal Canadiens and Maroons, Ottawa Senators and Chicago Black Hawks. *Elected 1963.*

William (Bill) Hanley: Known as "Mr. OHA." Former timekeeper at Leafs' games, he became secretary-manager of the Ontario Hockey Association for 27 years until his retirement in 1974. *Elected 1986.*

Charles Hay: Oil-company executive coordinated negotiations for the 1972 series between Canada and Soviet Union. Organized Team Canada that participated in historic eight-game series. *Elected 1974.*

Jim Hendy: President of the United States League and later general manager of the Cleveland Barons of the American League. Published the *Hockey Guide,* a leading statistical compendium in the early 1930s. *Elected 1968.*

Foster William Hewitt: A hockey broadcaster for 50 years. Renowned for his exciting descriptions of games involving the Toronto Maple Leafs. *Elected 1965.*

William Abraham Hewitt: A secretary of the Ontario Hockey Association and a secretary and registrar for the Canadian Amateur Association. Was a sports editor of the *Toronto Star. Elected 1947.*

Fred J. Hume: A leading amateur hockey executive in Western Canada. Later, helped develop the New Westminster professional team and the Western Hockey League. *Elected 1962.*

George (Punch) Imlach: Legendary Toronto coach and GM from 1958 through 1968–69. Guided Leafs to 10 playoff berths and four

Stanley Cup titles. Became Buffalo coach and GM in 1970, rejoining Leafs in 1979 for three seasons. *Elected 1984.*

Tommy Ivan: Coached Red Wings to three Stanley Cup crowns in the early 1950s and then moved on to rebuild a struggling Chicago franchise. One of the game's greatest coaches and executives. *Elected 1974.*

W. M. (Bill) Jennings: One of the principal architects of NHL expansion in 1967. Served as president of the New York Rangers and a governor of the league for nearly 20 years. *Elected 1975.*

Bob Johnson: A Minneapolis-born star at the University of Minnesota, he went on to become a legendary coach at the University of Wisconsin before becoming coach of the Calgary Flames. After serving as executive director of USA Hockey, he coached the Pittsburgh Penguins to the Stanley Cup championship in 1990-1991. He died of cancer on November 19, 1991. *Elected 1992.*

Gordon Juckes: Served the Canadian Amateur Hockey Association in executive positions from 1960 through 1978. *Elected 1979.*

General John Reed Kilpatrick: President of the New York Rangers and Madison Square Garden for 22 years. Also served on the Board of Governors of the NHL. *Elected 1960.*

G. A. (Al) Leader: President of the Western Hockey League for 25 years until his retirement in 1969. *Elected 1969.*

Robert LeBel: Former president of three amateur hockey groups and a life member of both the Quebec and Canadian Amateur Hockey Associations. *Elected 1970.*

Thomas F. Lockhart: Organizer and president of the Amateur Hockey Association of the United States and the Eastern Hockey League. Was also a business manager of the New York Rangers. *Elected 1965.*

Paul Loicq: A native of Belgium, he was a president of the International Ice Hockey Federation. Credited with having helped influence the Winter Olympic Games Committee to include hockey on the program. *Elected 1961.*

John Mariucci: Developed American high-school hockey programs in Minnesota. Former Black

Hawk defenseman coached U.S. team to Olympic silver medal in 1956. North Stars' executive won the Lester Patrick Award. *Elected 1985.*

Frank Mathers: A product of Winnipeg, he became a top defenseman in the American Hockey League, subsequently coaching the Hershey Bears and later becoming their president and general manager. Known as the AHL's top ambassador, he retired following the 1990-91 season and was fittingly honored by the Bears with a "Frank Mathers" night. *Elected 1992.*

Major Frederic McLaughlin: Pioneered professional hockey in Chicago. Was an owner and the first president of the Black Hawks and nicknamed the team in honor of the Black Hawk division he commanded during World War I. *Elected 1963.*

John Calverley (Jake) Milford: Discerning judge of talent coached 14 seasons in Ranger system before assuming GM positions in Los Angeles and Vancouver. Built Vancouver Canucks' club that made the 1982 Stanley Cup finals. *Elected 1984.*

Sen. Harland de Montarville Molson: Former owner of the Montreal Canadiens. *Elected 1973.*

Francis Nelson: A vice-president of the Ontario Hockey Association and an OHA Governor to the Amateur Athletic Union of Canada. *Elected 1947.*

Bruce A. Norris: Became one of the youngest owners in pro sport in 1955 when he took over the Detroit Red Wings at age 31. Ran the Detroit franchise until 1982. *Elected 1969.*

James Norris: He purchased Detroit's NHL franchise in 1933 and changed the name of the team from the Falcons to the Red Wings. He was also an owner of the Detroit Olympia and Chicago Stadium. *Elected 1958.*

James D. Norris: Became a co-owner of the Chicago Black Hawks in 1946 after helping his father, James Norris, with the administrative duties of the Detroit Red Wings. *Elected 1962.*

William M. Northey: President of the Montreal Amateur Athletic Association and a managing director of the Montreal Forum. Was the first trustee of the Allan Cup when it was presented for amateur competition. *Elected 1947.*

John Ambrose O'Brien: Helped with the formation of the National Hockey Association in December 1909, a five-team league which included the Montreal Canadiens and the Montreal Wanderers. *Elected 1962.*

Frank Patrick: With his brother, Lester Patrick, he played for the famed Renfrew Millionaires. The two later organized the Pacific Coast Hockey Association. Frank also coached the Boston Bruins and was a general manager of the Montreal Canadiens. *Elected 1958.*

Allan W. Pickard: An executive for several teams and leagues in Western Canada. He was a president of the Saskatchewan Amateur Association and the Canadian Amateur Association. *Elected 1958.*

Rudy Pilous: At age 28 in 1942, he established the junior club in St. Catharines, making the playoffs next three seasons. Coached Chicago's 1961 Stanley Cup winner, Denver's WHL champs in 1964 and managed Winnipeg to two WHA titles. *Elected 1985.*

Norman Robert (Bud) Poile: Served hockey for a half century as an All-Star NHL center, minor-league coach, GM at Philadelphia and Vancouver, WHA vice president and long-term commissioner of the CHL and IHL. *Elected 1990.*

Sam Pollock: Director of personnel for the Canadiens from 1950 through 1964, during which time the team won six Stanley Cup titles. Assembled Team Canada '76, winners of the Canada Cup. *Elected 1978.*

Senator Donat Raymond: A president of the Montreal Maroons and the Montreal Canadiens, he headed the Canadian Arena Company which financed the construction of the Montreal Forum in 1924. *Elected 1958.*

John Ross Robertson: A member of the Canadian Parliament, he donated trophies to the winners of the senior, intermediate and junior divisions of the Ontario Hockey Association. *Elected 1947.*

Claude C. Robinson: Was the first secretary of the Canadian Amateur Association and managed the Canadian team in the 1932 Olympic Games. *Elected 1947.*

Philip D. Ross: Named by Lord Stanley one of the trustees of the Stanley Cup in 1893 and served in that role for 56 years. *Elected 1976.*

Frank J. Selke: Worked as coach, manager and front-office executive for almost 60 years. Was with the Toronto Maple Leafs in various capacities before becoming managing director of the Montreal Canadiens in 1946. *Elected 1960.*

Harry Sinden: Never played in the NHL, but made his mark as coach and general manager of the Boston Bruins. Coached team to first championship in 29 years in 1970 and was GM of the Bruins' Cup-winning team two years later. *Elected 1983.*

Frank D. Smith: A founder in 1911 and later secretary-treasurer of the Beaches Hockey League, which became the Toronto Hockey League. *Elected 1962.*

Conn Smythe: Long-time, fiery president of the Toronto Maple Leafs. Was instrumental in the building of Maple Leaf Gardens, which was opened in November 1931. *Elected 1958.*

Ed Snider: Lobbied to bring NHL hockey to Philadelphia in the 1967 expansion. Part of group that arranged construction of The Spectrum as home for Flyers. Built organization that won the Stanley Cup in its seventh year. *Elected 1988.*

Captain James T. Sutherland: An organizer of teams and leagues in the Kingston, Ont., area, he coached the Kingston Junior team and served as president of the Ontario Hockey Association and the Canadian Amateur Hockey Association. *Elected 1947.*

Lord Stanley of Preston: As Governor General of Canada in 1893, he donated the Stanley Cup to the championship hockey club of the Dominion. *Elected 1945.*

Anatoli V. Tarasov: Generally regarded as the architect of hockey in the Soviet Union. Coached Soviets to nine amateur titles and three Olympic gold metals before retiring in 1972. *Elected 1974.*

Lloyd Turner: Helped organize the Western Canadian League in 1918. Coached and managed the Fort William, Ont., team and was a founder of teams and leagues in Calgary, Alta. *Elected 1958.*

W. Thayer Tutt: Instrumental in the progress of amateur hockey in the United States. Helped start NCAA tournament and later served as International Ice Hockey Federation president. *Elected 1978.*

Carl P. Voss: Named first referee-in-chief of NHL in 1950 and made enormous contributions in the scouting of referees and linesmen. *Elected 1974.*

Fred Waghorne: A native of England, he was among the founders of the Toronto Hockey League. As a referee, he was responsible for introducing a whistle for stopping play during a game. A bell had been used previously. *Elected 1961.*

Arthur M. Wirtz: Got into the hockey business in 1931 when, in partnership with James Norris, he bought the Detroit Red Wings. Switched holdings to native Chicago in 1954, where he rebuilt Black Hawks into one of NHL's most prosperous franchises. *Elected 1971.*

William Wirtz: Joined Chicago Black Hawks in 1952 and served two terms as chairman of the NHL Board of Governors. Helped formulate expansion plans and was largely responsible for their success. *Elected 1976.*

John A. Ziegler: Became the fourth NHL president and CEO since 1917 in September 1977. Negotiated settlement with the WHA in 1979, ending costly talent war. During tenure, oversaw other expansions in 1991 and 1992. *Elected 1987.*

ELMER FERGUSON MEMORIAL AWARD WINNERS

In recognition of members of the newspaper profession whose words have brought honor to journalism and hockey.

Barton, Charlie, *Buffalo Courier Express*

Beauchamp, Jacques, *Montreal Matin/Journal de Montreal*

Brennan, Red, *Toronto Star*

Burchard, Jim, *New York World-Telegram*

Burnett, Red, *Toronto Star*

Carroll, Dink, *Montreal Gazette*

Coleman, Jim, *Southam Newspapers*

Darnata, Ted, *Chicago Daily News*

Delano, Hugh, *New York Post*

Desjardins, Marcel, *Montreal La Presse*

Dulmage, Jack, *Windsor Star*

Dunnell, Milt, *Toronto Star*

Ferguson, Elmer, *Montreal Newspapers*

Fisher, Red, *Montreal Star/Gazette*

Fitzgerald, Tom, *Boston Globe*

Frayne, Trent, *Toronto Telegram/Globe and Mail/Sun*

Gross, George, *Toronto Telegram*

Johnston, Dick, *Buffalo News*

Laney, Al, *New York Herald-Tribune*

Larochelle, Claude, *Le Soleil*

L'Esperance, Zotique, *le Journal de Montreal*

Mayer, Charles, *le Journal de Montreal*

MacLeod, Rex, *Toronto Globe and Mail*

Monahan, Leo, *Boston Herald*

Moriarty, Tim, *UPI/Newsday*

Nichols, Joe, *The New York Times*

O'Brien, Andy, *Weekend Magazine*

Orr, Frank, *Toronto Star*

Olan, Ben, *Associated Press (N.Y.)*

O'Meara, Basil, *Montreal Star*

Proudfoot, Jim, *Toronto Star*

Raymond, Bertrand, *le Journal de Montreal*

Rosa, Fran, *Boston Globe*

Vipond, Jim, *Toronto Globe and Mail*

Lewis, Walter, *Detroit Times*

Young, Scott, *Toronto Globe and Mail/Telegram*

FOSTER HEWITT MEMORIAL AWARD WINNERS

In recognition of broadcasters who made outstanding contributions to their profession and hockey.

Cusick, Fred, *Boston*

Gallivan, Danny, *Montreal*

Hewitt, Foster, *Toronto*

Irvin, Dick, *Montreal*

Kelly, Dan, *St. Louis*

Lecavelier, Rene, *Montreal*

Lynch, Budd, *Detroit*

Martyn, Bruce, *Detroit*

McDonald, Jiggs, *New York Islanders*

McKnight, Wes, *Toronto*

Petit, Lloyd, *Chicago*

Smith, Doug, *Montreal*

Wilson, Bob, *Boston*

UNITED STATES HOCKEY HALL OF FAME

The United States Hockey Hall of Fame is located in Eveleth, Minn., which bills itself as "The Hockey Capital of the U.S.A." This midwestern mining community has sent more than a dozen players to the NHL, including goalie Frank (Mr. Zero) Brimsek, a legendary performer with the Boston Bruins. One of its natives, Mark Pavelich, starred on the 1980 U.S. gold-medal Olympic hockey team.

Opened in 1973, the Hall of Fame honors notable American players and their feats, and it tributes the game's innovators. Its "Evolution of Hockey Time Tunnel" traces the course of the sport on every level—youth, college, international, professional.

Enshrinees, in addition to players, include coaches, administrators, and a referee, Bill Chadwick, who is among a number of others in Toronto's Hall of Fame as well. Enshrinees are selected annually.

PLAYERS

Abel, Clarence (Taffy)

Baker, Hobart (Hobey)

Bartholome, Earl

Bessone, Peter

Blake, Robert

Brimsek, Frank

Chaisson, Ray

Chase, John

Christian, Roger

Christian, William

Cleary, Robert

Cleary, William

Conroy, Anthony

Dahlstrom, Carl (Cully)

DesJardins, Victor

Desmond, Richard

Dill, Robert

Everett, Doug

Ftorek, Robbie

Garrison, John

Garrity, Jack

Goheen, Frank (Moose)

Harding, Austin

Iglehart, Stewart

Johnson, Virgil

Karakas, Mike

Kirrane, Jack

Lane, Myles

Linder, Joseph

LoPresti, Sam

Mariucci, John

Matchefts, John

Mayasich, John

McCartan, Jack

Moe, William

Moseley, Fred

Murray, Hugh (Muzz)

Nelson, Hubert (Hub)

Olson, Eddie

Owen, George

Palmer, Winthrop

Paradise, Robert

Purpur, Clifford (Fido)

Riley, William

Romnes, Elwin (Doc)

Rondeau, Richard

Williams, Thomas

Winters, Frank (Coddy)

Yackel, Ken

COACHES

Almquist, Oscar

Brooks, Herb

Gordon, Malcolm

Heyliger, Victor

Ikola, Willard

Jeremiah, Edward

Johnson, Bob

Kelley, John (Snooks)

Pleban, John (Connie)

Riley, Jack

Ross, Larry

Thompson, Clifford

Stewart, William

Winsor, Alfred (Ralph)

ADMINISTRATORS

Brown, George

Brown, Walter

Bush, Walter

Clark, Donald

Gibson, J.C. (Doc)

Jennings, William

Kahler, Nick

Lockhart, Thomas

Marvin, Cal

Ridder, Robert

Trumble, Harold

Tutt, William

Wirtz, William

Wright, Lyle

REFEREE

Chadwick, Bill

14

NHL RECORDS

INDIVIDUAL

Most seasons played—26, Gordie Howe, Detroit, 1946–47 through 1970–71; Hartford, 1979–80.

Most games played—1,767, Gordie Howe, Detroit and Hartford.

Most goals—801, Gordie Howe, Detroit and Hartford.

Most assists—1,514, Wayne Gretzky, Edmonton and Los Angeles.

Most points—2,263, Wayne Gretzky, Edmonton and Los Angeles.

Most goals by a center, career—741, Wayne Gretzky, Edmonton and Los Angeles.

Most assists by a center, career—1,514, Wayne Gretzky, Edmonton and Los Angeles.

Most points by a center, career—2,263, Wayne Gretzky, Edmonton and Los Angeles.

Most goals by a left wing, career—610, Bobby Hull, Chicago, Winnipeg and Hartford.

Most assists by a left wing, career—813, John Bucyk, Detroit and Boston.

Most points by a left wing, career—1,369, John Bucyk, Detroit and Boston.

Most goals by a right wing, career—Gordie Howe, Detroit and Hartford.

《 *Quebec's Peter Stastny set a record with 109 points in his rookie season (1980–81).*

Most assists by a right wing, career—1,049, Gordie Howe, Detroit and Hartford.

Most goals by a defenseman, career—318, Paul Coffey, Edmonton, Pittsburgh and Los Angeles.

Most assists by a defenseman, career—796, Paul Coffey, Edmonton, Pittsburgh and Los Angeles.

Most points by a defenseman, career—1,114, Paul Coffey, Edmonton, Pittsburgh and Los Angeles.

Most penalty minutes, career—3,966, Dave Williams, Toronto, Vancouver, Detroit, Los Angeles and Hartford, 1974–75 through 1987-88.

Most consecutive games—964, Doug Jarvis, Montreal, Washington and Hartford, from Oct. 8, 1975 to Oct. 10, 1987.

Most games appeared in by a goaltender, career—971, Terry Sawchuk, Detroit, Boston, Toronto, Los Angeles and New York Rangers, 1949–50 through 1969–70.

Most consecutive complete games by a goaltender—502, Glenn Hall, Detroit and Chicago, from 1955–56 to 1962–63.

Most shutouts by a goaltender, career—103, Terry Sawchuk, Detroit, Boston, Toronto, Los Angeles and New York Rangers.

Most times scoring three or more goals, game—49, Wayne Gretzky, Edmonton and Los Angeles.

Most 40-or-more-goal seasons—12, Wayne Gretzky, Edmonton and Los Angeles.

Most 50-or-more goal seasons—9, Mike Bossy, New York Islanders; Wayne Gretzky, Edmonton and Los Angeles.

Most 60-or-more goals seasons—5, Mike Bossy, New York Islanders; Wayne Gretzky, Edmonton and Los Angeles.

Most 100-or-more point seasons—13, Wayne Gretzky, Edmonton and Los Angeles.

Most goals, season—92, Wayne Gretzky, Edmonton, 1981–82.

Most assists, season—163, Wayne Gretzky, Edmonton, 1985–86.

Most points, season—215, Wayne Gretzky, Edmonton, 1985–86.

Most goals, one season, including playoffs—100, Wayne Gretzky, Edmonton, 1983–84.

Most assists, one season, including playoffs—174, Wayne Gretzky, Edmonton, 1985–86.

Most points, one season, including playoffs—255, Wayne Gretzky, Edmonton, 1984–85.

Most goals, season, by a defenseman—48, Paul Coffey, Edmonton, 1985–86.

Most assists, season, by a defenseman—102, Bobby Orr, Boston, 1970–71.

Most points, season, by a defenseman—139, Bobby Orr, Boston, 1970–71.

Most goals, season, by a rookie—53, Mike Bossy, New York Islanders, 1977–78.

Most assists, season, by a rookie—70, Peter Stastny, Quebec, 1980–81.

Most points, season, by a rookie—109, Peter Stastny, Quebec, 1980–81.

Most power-play goals, one season—34, Tim Kerr, Philadelphia, 1985–86.

Most shorthanded goals, season—13, Mario Lemieux, Pittsburgh, 1988-89.

Most penalty minutes, season—472, Dave Schultz, Philadelphia, 1974–75.

Most shutouts by a goalie, season—22, George Hainsworth, Montreal, 1928–29; modern record: 15, Tony Esposito, Chicago, 1969–70.

Longest undefeated streak, goaltender—32, Gerry Cheevers, Boston, 1971–72 (24 wins, 8 ties).

Most games, goalie, season—75, Grant Fuhr, Edmonton, 1987–88.

Most wins, goalie, season—47, Bernie Parent, Philadelphia, 1973–74.

Longest consecutive point-scoring streak—51 Games, Wayne Gretzky, Edmonton, 1983–84.

Longest consecutive point-scoring streak, defenseman—28 games, Paul Coffey, Edmonton, 1985–86.

Longest consecutive goal-scoring streak—16 games, Punch Broadbent, Ottawa, 1921–22; modern record, 13 games, Charlie Simmer, Los Angeles, 1979–80.

Longest consecutive assist-scoring streak—23 games, Wayne Gretzky, Los Angeles, 1990–91.

Longest consecutive shutout streak, goalie—461 minutes, 29 seconds, Alex Connell, Ottawa, 1927–28; modern record: 309 minutes, 21 seconds, Bill Durnan, Montreal, 1948–49.

Most goals, one season, by a center—92, Wayne Gretzky, Edmonton, 1981–82.

Most goals, season, by a right wing—86, Brett Hull, St. Louis, 1990–91.

Most goals, season, by a left wing—60, Steve Shutt, Montreal, 1976–77.

Most assists, season, by a center—163, Wayne Gretzky, Edmonton, 1985–86.

Most assists, season, by a right wing—83, Mike Bossy, New York Islanders, 1981–82.

Most assists, season, by a left wing—69, Kevin Stevens, Pittsburgh, 1991–92.

Most goals, season, by a rookie defenseman—23, Brian Leetch, New York Rangers, 1988–89.

Most assists, season, by a rookie defenseman—60, Larry Murphy, Los Angeles, 1980–81.

Most points, season, by a center—215, Wayne Gretzky, Edmonton, 1985–86.

Most points, season, by a right wing—147, Mike Bossy, New York Islanders, 1981–82.

Most points, season, by a left wing—123, Kevin Stevens, Pittsburgh, 1991-92.

Most points, season, by a rookie defenseman—76, Larry Murphy, Los Angeles, 1980–81.

Most points, season, by a goaltender—14, Grant Fuhr, Edmonton, 1983–84.

Most goals, one game—7, Joe Malone, Quebec, vs. Toronto, Jan. 31, 1920.

Most assists, one game—7, Billy Taylor, Detroit, at Chicago, March 16, 1947; Wayne Gretzky, Edmonton, vs. Washington, Feb. 15, 1980; Wayne Gretzky, Edmonton, at Chicago, Dec. 11, 1985; Wayne Gretzky, Edmonton, vs. Quebec, Feb. 14, 1986.

Most points, one game—10, Darryl Sittler, Toronto, vs. Boston, Feb. 7, 1976 (6 goals, 4 assists).

Most goals, one game, by a defenseman—5, Ian Turnbull, Toronto, vs. Detroit, Feb. 2, 1977.

Most assists, one game, by a defenseman—6, Babe Pratt, Toronto, vs. Boston, Jan. 8, 1944; Pat Stapleton, Chicago, vs. Detroit, Mar. 30, 1969; Bobby Orr, Boston, at Vancouver, Jan. 1, 1973; Ron Stackhouse, Pittsburgh, vs. Philadelphia, Mar. 8, 1975; Paul Coffey, Edmonton, vs. Detroit, Mar. 14, 1986; Gary Suter, Calgary, vs. Edmonton, Apr. 4, 1986.

Most points, one game, by a defenseman—8, Tom Bladon, Philadelphia, vs. Cleveland, Dec. 11, 1977; Paul Coffey, Edmonton, vs. Detroit, Mar. 14, 1986.

Most penalties, one game—10, Chris Nilan, Boston, vs. Hartford, Mar. 31, 1991.

Most penalty minutes, one game—67, Randy Holt, Los Angeles, at Philadelphia, Mar. 11, 1979.

Most goals, one period—4, Busher Jackson, Toronto, at St. Louis, Nov. 20, 1934; Max Bentley, Chicago, vs. New York Rangers, Jan. 28, 1943; Clint Smith, Chicago, vs. Montreal, Mar. 4, 1945; Red Berenson, St. Louis, at Philadelphia, Nov. 7, 1968; Wayne Gretzky, Edmonton, vs. St. Louis, Feb. 18, 1981; Grant Mulvey, Chicago, vs. St. Louis, Feb. 3, 1982; Bryan Trottier, New York Islanders, vs. Philadelphia, Feb. 13, 1982; Al Secord, Chicago, vs. Toronto, Jan. 7, 1987; Joe Nieuwendyk, Calgary, vs. Winnipeg, Jan. 11, 1989.

Most assists, one period—5, Dale Hawerchuk, Winnipeg, at Los Angeles, Mar. 6, 1984.

Most points, one period—6, Bryan Trottier, New York Islanders, vs. New York Rangers, Dec. 23, 1978.

Fastest goal from start of game—5 seconds, Doug Smail, Winnipeg, vs. St. Louis, Dec. 20, 1981; Bryan Trottier, New York Islanders, at Boston, Mar. 22, 1984; Alexander Mogilny, Buffalo, at Toronto, Dec. 21, 1991.

Fastest goal from start of period—4 seconds, Claude Provost, Montreal, vs. Boston, Nov. 9, 1957; Denis Savard, Chicago, vs. Hartford, Jan. 12, 1986.

Fastest two goals—4 seconds, Nels Stewart, Montreal Maroons, vs. Boston, Jan. 3, 1931.

Fastest three goals—21 seconds, Bill Mosienko, Chicago, at New York Rangers, Mar. 23, 1952.

TEAM

Most points, season—132, Montreal Canadiens, 1976-77.

Fewest points, season—8, Quebec Bulldogs, 1919-20; modern: 21, Washington Capitals, 1974-75.

Most victories, season—60, Montreal Canadiens, 1976-77.

Fewest victories, season—4, Quebec Bulldogs, 1919-20, and Philadelphia Quakers, 1930-31; modern: 8, Washington Capitals, 1974-75.

Most losses, season—67, Washington Capitals, 1974-75.

Fewest losses, season—5, Ottawa Senators, 1919-20, Boston Bruins, 1929-30, and Montreal Canadiens, 1943-44; modern: 8, Montreal Canadiens, 1976-77.

Most ties, season—24, Philadelphia Flyers, 1969-70.

Most home victories, season—36, Philadelphia Flyers, 1975-76.

Most road victories, season—27, Montreal Canadiens, 1976-77 and 1977-78.

Most home losses, season—29, Pittsburgh Penguins, 1983-84.

Most road losses, season—39, Washington Capitals, 1974-75.

Fewest home victories, season—2, Chicago Blackhawks, 1927-28; modern: 6, Chicago Blackhawks, 1954-55 and Washington Capitals, 1975-76.

Fewest road victories, season—0, Toronto Arenas, 1918-19, Quebec Bulldogs, 1919-20, Pittsburgh Pirates, 1929-30; modern: 1, Washington Capitals, 1974-75.

Fewest home losses, season—0, Ottawa Senators, 1922-23, Montreal Canadiens, 1943-44; modern: 1, Montreal Canadiens, 1976-77.

Fewest road losses, season—3, Montreal Canadiens, 1928-29; modern: Montreal Canadiens, 1972-73, 1974-75 and 1977-78.

Longest winning streak—15 games, New York Islanders, Jan. 21, 1982 through Feb. 20, 1982.

Longest undefeated streak—35 games, Philadelphia Flyers, Oct. 14, 1979 through Jan. 6, 1980 (25 wins, 10 ties).

Longest home undefeated streak—34 games, Montreal Canadiens, Nov. 1, 1976 through Apr. 2, 1977 (28 wins, 6 ties).

Longest winning streak, home—20 games, Boston Bruins, Dec. 3, 1929 through Mar. 18, 1930; Philadelphia Flyers, Jan. 4, 1976 through Apr. 3, 1976.

Longest winning streak, road—10, Buffalo Sabres, Dec. 10, 1983 through Jan. 23, 1984.

Longest undefeated streak, road—23 games, Montreal Canadiens, Nov. 27, 1974 through Mar. 12, 1975.

Longest losing streak—17 games, Washington Capitals, Feb. 18, 1975 through Mar. 26, 1975.

Longest losing streak from start of season—11 games, New York Rangers, 1943-44.

Longest home losing streak—11 games, Boston Bruins, Dec. 8, 1924 through Feb. 17, 1925; Washington Capitals, Feb. 18, 1975 through Mar. 30, 1975.

Longest road losing streak—37 games, Washington Capitals, Oct. 9, 1974 through Mar. 26, 1975.

Longest winless streak—30 games, Winnipeg Jets, Oct. 19, 1980 through Dec. 20, 1980 (23 losses, 7 ties).

Longest winless streak from start of season—15 games, New York Rangers, 1943-44 (14 losses, 1 tie).

Longest home winless streak—15 games, Chicago Blackhawks, Dec. 16, 1928 through Feb. 28, 1929; Montreal Canadiens, Dec. 16, 1939 through Mar. 7, 1940.

Longest road winless streak—37 games, Washington Capitals, Oct. 9, 1974 through Mar. 26, 1975.

Longest non-shutout streak—264 games, Los Angeles Kings, Mar. 15, 1986 through Apr. 6, 1989.

Most consecutive shutout losses—8, Chicago Blackhawks, 1928-29.

Most shutouts, season—22, Montreal Canadiens, 1928-29; modern: 15, Chicago Blackhawks, 1969-70.

Most goals, season—446, Edmonton Oilers, 1983-84.

Fewest goals, season—33, Chicago Blackhawks, 1928-29; modern: 133, Chicago Blackhawks, 1953-54.

Most goals allowed, season—446, Washington Capitals, 1974-75.

Fewest goals allowed, season—42, Ottawa Senators, 1925-26; modern: 131, Toronto Maple Leafs, 1953-54 and Montreal Canadiens, 1955-56.

Most power-play goals, season—120, Pittsburgh Penguins, 1988-89.

Most power-play goals allowed, season—122, Chicago Blackhawks, 1988-89.

Most shorthanded goals, season—36, Edmonton Oilers, 1983-84.

Most shorthanded goals allowed, season—22, Pittsburgh Penguins, 1984-85; Minnesota North Stars, 1991-92.

Most penalty minutes, season—2,713, Buffalo Sabres, 1991-92.

Most goals, one team, game—16, Montreal Canadiens, at Quebec, Mar. 3, 1920.

Most goals, both teams, game—21, Montreal Canadiens (14) vs. Toronto St. Patricks (7), at Montreal, Jan. 10, 1920; Edmonton Oilers (12) at Chicago Blackhawks (9), Dec. 11, 1985.

Most consecutive goals, one team, game—15, Detroit Red Wings, vs. New York Rangers, Jan. 23, 1944.

Most points, one team, game—40, Buffalo Sabres, vs. Washington Capitals, Dec. 21, 1975 (14 goals, 26 assists).

Most points, both teams, game—62, Edmonton Oilers (12 goals, 24 assists) at Chicago Blackhawks (9 goals, 17 assists), Dec. 11, 1985.

Most shots, one team, game—83, Boston Bruins, vs. Chicago, Mar. 4, 1941.

Most shots, both teams, game—141, New York Americans (73) vs. Pittsburgh Pirates (68), Dec. 26, 1925.

Most penalties, one team, game—44, Edmonton Oilers, at Los Angeles, Feb. 28, 1990.

Most penalties, both teams, game—85, Edmonton Oilers (44) at Los Angeles Kings (41), Feb. 28, 1990.

Most penalty minutes, one team, game—211, Minnesota North Stars, at Boston, Feb. 26, 1981.

Most penalty minutes, both teams, game—406, Minnesota North Stars (211) at Boston Bruins (195), Feb. 26, 1981.

Most goals, one team, period—9, Buffalo Sabres, vs. Toronto, Mar. 19, 1981.

Most goals, both teams, one period—12, Buffalo Sabres (9) vs. Toronto Maple Leafs (3), Mar. 19, 1981; Edmonton Oilers (6) at Chicago Blackhawks (6), Dec. 11, 1985.

Most points, one team, one period—23, New York Rangers, vs. California, Nov. 21, 1971; Buffalo Sabres, vs. Washington, Dec. 21, 1975; Buffalo Sabres, vs. Toronto, Mar. 19, 1981.

Most shots, one team, one period—33, Boston Bruins, vs. Chicago, Mar. 4, 1941.

Most penalties, both teams, one period—67, Minnesota North Stars (34) at Boston Bruins (33), Feb. 26, 1981.

Most penalty minutes, both teams, one period—372, Philadelphia Flyers (188) vs. Los Angeles Kings (184), Mar. 11, 1979.

Most penalty minutes, one team, one period—188, Philadelphia Flyers, vs. Los Angeles, Mar. 11, 1979.

Fastest six goals, both teams—3 minutes, 15 seconds, Montreal (4) vs. Chicago (2), Jan. 4, 1944.

Fastest five goals, both teams—1 minute, 24 seconds, Chicago (3) at Toronto (2), Oct. 15, 1983.

Fastest five goals, one team—2 minutes, 7 seconds, Pittsburgh Penguins, vs. St. Louis, Nov. 22, 1972.

Fastest four goals, both teams—53 seconds, Chicago (3) at Toronto (1), Oct. 15, 1983.

Fastest four goals, one team—1 minute, 20 seconds—Boston Bruins, vs. New York Rangers, Jan. 21, 1945.

Fastest three goals, both teams—15 seconds, New York Rangers (2) at Minnesota North Stars (1), Feb. 10, 1983.

Fastest three goals, one team—20 seconds, Boston Bruins, vs. Vancouver, Feb. 25, 1971.

Fastest two goals, both teams—2 seconds, St. Louis Blues (1) at Boston Bruins (1), Dec. 19, 1987.

Fastest two goals, one team—4 seconds, Montreal Maroons, vs. Boston, Jan. 3, 1931; Buffalo Sabres, vs. California, Oct. 17, 1974; Toronto Maple Leafs, at Quebec, Dec. 29, 1988; Calgary Flames, at Quebec, Oct, 17, 1989.

Fastest two goals from start of period, both teams—14 seconds, New York Rangers (1) at Quebec Nordiques (1), Nov. 5, 1983.

Fastest two goals from start of game, one team—24 seconds, Edmonton Oilers, at Los Angeles, Mar. 28, 1982.

Fastest two goals from start of period, one team—21 seconds, Chicago Blackhawks, at Minnesota, Nov. 5, 1983.

THE TROPHIES

HART MEMORIAL TROPHY

Awarded to the player "most valuable to his team." Selected in a vote of hockey writers and broadcasters. The award was presented by the National Hockey League in 1960 after the original Hart Trophy was retired to the Hockey Hall of Fame. The original Hart Trophy was donated in 1923 by Dr. David A. Hart, father of Cecil Hart, former manager-coach of the Montreal Canadiens.

1923–24	Frank Nighbor, Ottawa
1924–25	Billy Burch, Hamilton
1925–26	Nels Stewart, Montreal M.
1926–27	Herb Gardiner, Montreal C.
1927–28	Howie Morenz, Montreal C.
1928–29	Roy Worters, New York A.
1929–30	Nels Stewart, Montreal M.
1930–31	Howie Morenz, Montreal C.
1931–32	Howie Morenz, Montreal C.
1932–33	Eddie Shore, Boston

1933–34	Aurel Joliat, Montreal C.
1934–35	Eddie Shore, Boston
1935–36	Eddie Shore, Boston
1936–37	Babe Siebert, Montreal C.
1937–38	Eddie Shore, Boston
1938–39	Toe Blake, Montreal C.
1939–40	Ebbie Goodfellow, Detroit
1940–41	Bill Cowley, Boston
1941–42	Tommy Anderson, New York A.
1942–43	Bill Cowley, Boston
1943–44	Babe Pratt, Toronto
1944–45	Elmer Lach, Montreal C.
1945–46	Max Bentley, Chicago
1946–47	Maurice Richard, Montreal
1947–48	Buddy O'Connor, New York
1948–49	Sid Abel, Detroit
1949–50	Charlie Rayner, New York
1950–51	Milt Schmidt, Boston
1951–52	Gordie Howe, Detroit
1952–53	Gordie Howe, Detroit
1953–54	Al Rollins, Chicago
1954–55	Ted Kennedy, Toronto
1955–56	Jean Beliveau, Montreal
1956–57	Gordie Howe, Detroit
1957–58	Gordie Howe, Detroit
1958–59	Andy Bathgate, New York
1959–60	Gordie Howe, Detroit
1960–61	Bernie Geoffrion, Montreal
1961–62	Jacques Plante, Montreal
1962–63	Gordie Howe, Detroit
1963–64	Jean Beliveau, Montreal
1964–65	Bobby Hull, Chicago

1965–66	Bobby Hull, Chicago
1966–67	Stan Mikita, Chicago
1967–68	Stan Mikita, Chicago
1968–69	Phil Esposito, Boston
1969–70	Bobby Orr, Boston
1970–71	Bobby Orr, Boston
1971–72	Bobby Orr, Boston
1972–73	Bobby Clarke, Philadelphia
1973–74	Phil Esposito, Boston
1974–75	Bobby Clarke, Philadelphia
1975–76	Bobby Clarke, Philadelphia
1976–77	Guy Lafleur, Montreal
1977–78	Guy Lafleur, Montreal
1978–79	Bryan Trottier, New York I.
1979–80	Wayne Gretzky, Edmonton
1980–81	Wayne Gretzky, Edmonton
1981–82	Wayne Gretzky, Edmonton
1982–83	Wayne Gretzky, Edmonton
1983–84	Wayne Gretzky, Edmonton
1984–85	Wayne Gretzky, Edmonton
1985–86	Wayne Gretzky, Edmonton
1986–87	Wayne Gretzky, Edmonton
1987–88	Mario Lemieux, Pittsburgh
1988–89	Wayne Gretsky, Edmonton
1989–90	Mark Messier, Edmonton
1990–91	Brett Hull, St. Louis
1991–92	Mark Messier, New York R.

ART ROSS TROPHY

Awarded to the player who compiles the highest number of scoring points during the regular season.

If players are tied for the lead, the trophy is awarded to the one with the most goals. If still tied, it is given to the player with the fewer number of games played. If these do not break the deadlock, the trophy is presented to the player who scored his first goal of the season at the earliest date.

The trophy was presented by Art Ross, the former manager-coach of the Boston Bruins, to the NHL in 1947.

Season	Player and Club	Games Played	Goals	Assists	Points
1917–18	Joe Malone, Mont. C	20	44	—	44
1918–19	Newsy Lalonde, Mont. C	17	23	9	32
1919–20	Joe Malone, Quebec	24	39	9	48
1920–21	Newsy Lalonde, Mont. C	24	33	8	41
1921–22	Punch Broadbent, Ottawa	24	32	14	46
1922–23	Babe Dye, Toronto	22	26	11	37
1923–24	Cy Denneny, Ottawa	21	22	1	23
1924–25	Babe Dye, Toronto	29	38	6	44
1925–26	Nels Stewart, Montreal	36	34	8	42
1926–27	Bill Cook, N.Y. Rangers	44	33	4	37
1927–28	Howie Morenz, Mont. C	43	33	18	51
1928–29	Ace Bailey, Toronto	44	22	10	32
1929–30	Cooney Weiland, Boston	44	43	30	73
1930–31	Howie Morenz, Mont. C	39	28	23	51
1931–32	Harvey Jackson, Toronto	48	28	25	53
1932–33	Bill Cook, N.Y. Rangers	48	28	22	50
1933–34	Charlie Conacher, Toronto	42	32	20	52
1934–35	Charlie Conacher, Toronto	48	36	21	57
1935–36	Dave Schriner, NYA	48	19	26	45
1936–37	Dave Schriner, NYA	48	21	25	46
1937–38	Gordie Drillon, Toronto	48	26	26	52
1938–39	Toe Blake, Mont. C	48	24	23	47
1939–40	Milt Schmidt, Boston	48	22	30	52
1940–41	Bill Cowley, Boston	46	17	45	62
1941–42	Bryan Hextall, New York R	48	24	32	56
1942–43	Doug Bentley, Chicago	50	33	40	73
1943–44	Herbie Cain, Boston	48	36	46	82
1944–45	Elmer Lach, Montreal	50	26	54	80
1945–46	Max Bentley, Chicago	47	31	30	61
1946–47	Max Bentley, Chicago	60	29	43	72
1947–48	Elmer Lach, Montreal	60	30	31	61
1948–49	Roy Conacher, Chicago	60	26	42	68
1949–50	Ted Lindsay, Detroit	69	23	55	78
1950–51	Gordie Howe, Detroit	70	43	43	86
1951–52	Gordie Howe, Detroit	70	47	39	86
1952–53	Gordie Howe, Detroit	70	49	46	95
1953–54	Gordie Howe, Detroit	70	33	48	81
1954–55	Bernie Geoffrion, Montreal	70	38	37	75
1955–56	Jean Beliveau, Montreal	70	47	41	88
1956–57	Gordie Howe, Detroit	70	44	45	89
1957–58	Dickie Moore, Montreal	70	36	48	84
1958–59	Dickie Moore, Montreal	70	41	55	96
1959–60	Bobby Hull, Chicago	70	39	42	81

Season	Player and Club	Games Played	Goals	Assists	Points
1960–61	Bernie Geoffrion, Montreal	64	50	45	95
1961–62	Bobby Hull, Chicago	70	50	34	84
1962–63	Gordie Howe, Detroit	70	38	48	86
1963–64	Stan Mikita, Chicago	70	39	50	89
1964–65	Stan Mikita, Chicago	70	28	59	87
1965–66	Bobby Hull, Chicago	65	54	43	97
1966–67	Stan Mikita, Chicago	70	35	62	97
1967–68	Stan Mikita, Chicago	72	40	47	87
1968–69	Phil Esposito, Boston	74	49	77	126
1969–70	Bobby Orr, Boston	76	33	87	120
1970–71	Phil Esposito, Boston	78	76	76	152
1971–72	Phil Esposito, Boston	76	66	67	133
1972–73	Phil Esposito, Boston	78	55	75	130
1973–74	Phil Esposito, Boston	78	68	77	145
1974–75	Bobby Orr, Boston	80	46	89	135
1975–76	Guy Lafleur, Montreal	80	56	69	125
1976–77	Guy Lafleur, Montreal	80	56	80	136
1977–78	Guy Lafleur, Montreal	78	60	72	132
1978–79	Bryan Trottier, New York I.	76	47	87	134
1979–80	Marcel Dionne, L.A.	80	53	84	137
1980–81	Wayne Gretzky, Edmonton	80	55	109	164
1981–82	Wayne Gretzky, Edmonton	80	92	120	212
1982–83	Wayne Gretzky, Edmonton	80	71	125	196
1983–84	Wayne Gretzky, Edmonton	74	87	118	205
1984–85	Wayne Gretzky, Edmonton	80	73	135	208
1985–86	Wayne Gretzky, Edmonton	80	52	163	215
1986–87	Wayne Gretzky, Edmonton	79	62	121	183
1987–88	Mario Lemieux, Pittsburgh	77	70	98	168
1988–89	Mario Lemieux, Pittsburgh	76	85	114	199
1989–90	Wayne Gretzky, L.A.	73	40	102	142
1990–91	Wayne Gretzky, L.A.	78	41	122	163
1991–92	Mario Lemieux, Pittsburgh	64	44	87	131

VEZINA TROPHY

Awarded to the goalie voted most valuable by the hockey writers and broadcasters. Up until the 1981–82 season, the trophy was awarded to the goalie or goalies for the team which gave up the fewest goals during the regular season.

The trophy was presented to the NHL in 1926–27 by the owners of the Montreal Canadiens in memory of Georges Vezina, former Canadien goalie.

1926–27	George Hainsworth, Montreal C.
1927–28	George Hainsworth, Montreal C.
1928–29	George Hainsworth, Montreal C.
1929–30	Tiny Thompson, Boston
1930–31	Roy Worters, New York A.
1931–32	Charlie Gardiner, Chicago
1932–33	Tiny Thompson, Boston
1933–34	Charlie Gardiner, Chicago
1934–35	Lorne Chabot, Chicago
1935–36	Tiny Thompson, Boston
1936–37	Normie Smith, Detroit
1937–38	Tiny Thompson, Boston
1938–39	Frank Brimsek, Boston
1939–40	Davey Kerr, New York

1940–41	Turk Broda, Toronto
1941–42	Frank Brimsek, Boston
1942–43	Johnny Mowers, Detroit
1943–44	Bill Durnan, Montreal
1944–45	Bill Durnan, Montreal
1945–46	Bill Durnan, Montreal
1946–47	Bill Durnan, Montreal
1947–48	Turk Broda, Toronto
1948–49	Bill Durnan, Montreal
1949–50	Bill Durnan, Montreal
1950–51	Al Rollins, Toronto
1951–52	Terry Sawchuk, Detroit
1952–53	Terry Sawchuk, Detroit
1953–54	Harry Lumley, Toronto
1954–55	Terry Sawchuk, Detroit
1955–56	Jacques Plante, Montreal
1956–57	Jacques Plante, Montreal
1957–58	Jacques Plante, Montreal
1958–59	Jacques Plante, Montreal
1959–60	Jacques Plante, Montreal
1960–61	Johnny Bower, Toronto
1961–62	Jacques Plante, Montreal
1962–63	Glenn Hall, Chicago
1963–64	Charlie Hodge, Montreal
1964–65	Terry Sawchuk, Toronto
	Johnny Bower, Toronto
1965–66	Lorne Worsley, Montreal
	Charlie Hodge, Montreal
1966–67	Glenn Hall, Chicago
	Denis DeJordy, Chicago
1967–68	Lorne Worsley, Montreal
	Rogatien Vachon, Montreal

1968–69	Glenn Hall, St. Louis
	Jacques Plante, St. Louis
1969–70	Tony Esposito, Chicago
1970–71	Ed Giacomin, New York
	Gilles Villemure, New York
1971–72	Tony Esposito, Chicago
	Gary Smith, Chicago
1972–73	Ken Dryden, Montreal
1973–74	Bernie Parent, Philadelphia
	Tony Esposito, Chicago
1974–75	Bernie Parent, Philadelphia
1975–76	Ken Dryden, Montreal
1976–77	Ken Dryden, Montreal
	Michel Larocque, Montreal
1977–78	Ken Dryden, Montreal
	Michel Larocque, Montreal
1978–79	Ken Dryden, Montreal
	Michel Larocque, Montreal
1979–80	Bob Sauve, Buffalo
	Don Edwards, Buffalo
1980–81	Richard Sevigny, Montreal
	Denis Herron, Montreal
	Michel Larocque, Montreal
1981–82	Bill Smith, New York I.
1982–83	Pete Peeters, Boston
1983–84	Tom Barrasso, Buffalo
1984–85	Pelle Lindbergh, Philadelphia
1985–86	John Vanbiesbrouck, New York R.
1986–87	Ron Hextall, Philadelphia
1987–88	Grant Fuhr, Edmonton
1988–89	Patrick Roy, Montreal
1989–90	Patrick Roy, Montreal
1990–91	Ed Belfour, Chicago
1991–92	Patrick Roy, Montreal

FRANK J. SELKE TROPHY

Awarded to the forward "who best excels in the defensive aspects of the game." Selection is by the hockey writers and broadcasters.

The trophy was presented to the NHL in 1977 in honor of Frank J. Selke, who spent more than 60 years in the game as coach, manager and front-office executive.

1977–78	Bob Gainey, Montreal
1978–79	Bob Gainey, Montreal
1979–80	Bob Gainey, Montreal
1980–81	Bob Gainey, Montreal
1981–82	Steve Kasper, Boston
1982–83	Bobby Clarke, Philadelphia
1983–84	Doug Jarvis, Washington
1984–85	Craig Ramsay, Buffalo
1985–86	Troy Murray, Chicago
1986–87	Dave Poulin, Philadelphia
1987–88	Guy Carbonneau, Montreal
1988–89	Guy Carbonneau, Montreal
1989–90	Rick Meagher, St. Louis
1990–91	Dirk Graham, Chicago
1991–92	Guy Carbonneau, Montreal

JAMES NORRIS MEMORIAL TROPHY

Awarded to the league's best defenseman. Selected by a vote of hockey writers and broadcasters.

It was presented in 1953 by the four children of the late James Norris Sr., in memory of the former owner-president of the Detroit Red Wings.

1953–54	Red Kelly, Detroit
1954–55	Doug Harvey, Montreal
1955–56	Doug Harvey, Montreal
1956–57	Doug Harvey, Montreal
1957–58	Doug Harvey, Montreal
1958–59	Tom Johnson, Montreal
1959–60	Doug Harvey, Montreal
1960–61	Doug Harvey, Montreal
1961–62	Doug Harvey, New York
1962–63	Pierre Pilote, Chicago
1963–64	Pierre Pilote, Chicago
1964–65	Pierre Pilote, Chicago
1965–66	Jacques Laperriere, Montreal
1966–67	Harry Howell, New York R.
1967–68	Bobby Orr, Boston
1968–69	Bobby Orr, Boston
1969–70	Bobby Orr, Boston
1970–71	Bobby Orr, Boston

To be eligible to receive the trophy, a player cannot have participated in more than 20 games in any preceding season or in six or more games in each of any two preceding seasons.

From 1932–33 to 1936–37 the top rookies were named but no trophy was presented.

1932–33	Carl Voss, Detroit
1933–34	Russ Blinco, Montreal M.
1934–35	Dave Schriner, New York A.
1935–36	Mike Karakas, Chicago
1936–37	Syl Apps, Toronto
1937–38	Cully Dahlstrom, Chicago
1938–39	Frank Brimsek, Boston
1939–40	Kilby MacDonald, New York R.
1940–41	Johnny Quilty, Montreal C.
1941–42	Grant Warwick, New York R.
1942–43	Gaye Stewart, Toronto
1943–44	Gus Bodnar, Toronto
1944–45	Frank McCool, Toronto
1945–46	Edgar Laprade, New York R.
1946–47	Howie Meeker, Toronto
1947–48	Jim McFadden, Detroit
1948–49	Pentti Lund, New York R.
1949–50	Jack Gelineau, Boston
1950–51	Terry Sawchuk, Detroit
1951–52	Bernie Geoffrion, Montreal
1952–53	Lorne Worsley, New York R.

1971–72	Bobby Orr, Boston
1972–73	Bobby Orr, Boston
1973–74	Bobby Orr, Boston
1974–75	Bobby Orr, Boston
1975–76	Denis Potvin, New York I.
1976–77	Larry Robinson, Montreal
1977–78	Denis Potvin, New York I.
1978–79	Denis Potvin, New York I.
1979–80	Larry Robinson, Montreal
1980–81	Randy Carlyle, Pittsburgh
1981–82	Doug Wilson, Chicago
1982–83	Rod Langway, Washington
1983–84	Rod Langway, Washington
1984–85	Paul Coffey, Edmonton
1985–86	Paul Coffey, Edmonton
1986–87	Ray Bourque, Boston
1987–88	Ray Bourque, Boston
1988–89	Chris Chelios, Montreal
1989–90	Ray Bourque, Boston
1990–91	Ray Bourque, Boston
1991–92	Brian Leetch, New York R.

CALDER MEMORIAL TROPHY

Awarded to the league's outstanding rookie. Selected by a vote of hockey writers and broadcasters. It was originated in 1937 by Frank Calder, first president of the NHL. After his death in 1943, the league presented the Calder Memorial Trophy in his memory.

1953–54	Camille Henry, New York R.
1954–55	Ed Litzenberger, Chicago
1955–56	Glenn Hall, Detroit
1956–57	Larry Regan, Boston
1957–58	Frank Mahovlich, Toronto
1958–59	Ralph Backstrom, Montreal
1959–60	Bill Hay, Chicago
1960–61	Dave Keon, Toronto
1961–62	Bobby Rousseau, Montreal
1962–63	Kent Douglas, Toronto
1963–64	Jacques Laperriere, Montreal
1964–65	Roger Crozier, Detroit
1965–66	Brit Selby, Toronto
1966–67	Bobby Orr, Boston
1967–68	Derek Sanderson, Boston
1968–69	Danny Grant, Minnesota
1969–70	Tony Esposito, Chicago
1970–71	Gil Perreault, Buffalo
1971–72	Ken Dryden, Montreal
1972–73	Steve Vickers, New York R.
1973–74	Denis Potvin, New York I.
1974–75	Eric Vail, Atlanta
1975–76	Bryan Trottier, New York I.
1976–77	Willi Plett, Atlanta
1977–78	Mike Bossy, New York I.
1978–79	Bobby Smith, Minnesota
1979–80	Ray Bourque, Boston
1980–81	Peter Stastny, Quebec
1981–82	Dale Hawerchuk, Winnipeg
1982–83	Steve Larmer, Chicago
1983–84	Tom Barrasso, Buffalo
1984–85	Mario Lemieux, Pittsburgh
1985–86	Gary Suter, Calgary
1986–87	Luc Robitaille, Los Angeles
1987–88	Joe Nieuwendyk, Calgary
1988–89	Brian Leetch, New York R.
1989–90	Sergei Makarov, Calgary
1990–91	Ed Belfour, Chicago
1991–92	Pavel Bure, Vancouver

CONN SMYTHE TROPHY

Awarded to the Most Valuable Player in the Stanley Cup playoffs. Selected in a vote of the NHL Governors.

The trophy was presented by Maple Leaf Gardens Ltd. in 1964 to honor the former coach, manager, president and owner of the Toronto Maple Leafs.

1964–65	Jean Beliveau, Montreal
1965–66	Roger Crozier, Detroit
1966–67	Dave Keon, Toronto
1967–68	Glenn Hall, St. Louis
1968–69	Serge Savard, Montreal
1969–70	Bobby Orr, Boston
1970–71	Ken Dryden, Montreal
1971–72	Bobby Orr, Boston
1972–73	Yvan Cournoyer, Montreal
1973–74	Bernie Parent, Philadelphia
1974–75	Bernie Parent, Philadelphia
1975–76	Reggie Leach, Philadelphia
1976–77	Guy Lafleur, Montreal

1977–78	Larry Robinson, Montreal
1978–79	Bob Gainey, Montreal
1979–80	Bryan Trottier, New York I.
1980–81	Butch Goring, New York I.
1981–82	Mike Bossy, New York I.
1982–83	Billy Smith, New York I.
1983–84	Mark Messier, Edmonton
1984–85	Wayne Gretzky, Edmonton
1985–86	Patrick Roy, Montreal
1986–87	Ron Hextall, Philadelphia
1987–88	Wayne Gretzky, Edmonton
1988–89	Al MacInnis, Calgary
1989–90	Bill Ranford, Edmonton
1990–91	Mario Lemieux, Pittsburgh
1991–92	Mario Lemieux, Pittsburgh

WILLIAM M. JENNINGS AWARD

Awarded to the goalie or goalies on the team which gives up the fewest goals during the regular season. To be eligible, a goalie must play at least 25 games.

The trophy was presented to the NHL in 1982 in memory of William M. Jennings, an architect of the league's expansion from six teams to the present 21.

1981–82	Denis Herron, Montreal
	Rick Wamsley, Montreal

1924–25	Frank Nighbor, Ottawa
1925–26	Frank Nighbor, Ottawa
1926–27	Billy Burch, New York A.
1927–28	Frank Boucher, New York R.
1928–29	Frank Boucher, New York R.
1929–30	Frank Boucher, New York R.
1930–31	Frank Boucher, New York R.
1931–32	Joe Primeau, Toronto
1932–33	Frank Boucher, New York R.
1933–34	Frank Boucher, New York R.
1934–35	Frank Boucher, New York R.
1935–36	Doc Romnes, Chicago
1936–37	Marty Barry, Detroit
1937–38	Gordie Drillon, Toronto
1938–39	Clint Smith, New York R.
1939–40	Bobby Bauer, Boston
1940–41	Bobby Bauer, Boston
1941–42	Syl Apps, Toronto
1942–43	Max Bentley, Chicago
1943–44	Clint Smith, Chicago
1944–45	Bill Mosienko, Chicago
1945–46	Toe Blake, Montreal
1946–47	Bobby Bauer, Boston
1947–48	Buddy O'Connor, New York R.
1948–49	Bill Quackenbush, Detroit
1949–50	Edgar Laprade, New York R.
1950–51	Red Kelly, Detroit
1951–52	Sid Smith, Toronto
1952–53	Red Kelly, Detroit
1953–54	Red Kelly, Detroit
1954–55	Sid Smith, Toronto
1955–56	Earl Reibel, Detroit

1982–83	Billy Smith, New York I.
	Roland Melanson, New York I.
1983–84	Al Jensen, Washington
	Pat Riggin, Washington
1984–85	Tom Barrasso, Buffalo
	Bob Sauve, Buffalo
1985–86	Bob Froese, Philadelphia
	Darren Jensen, Philadelphia
1986–87	Patrick Roy, Montreal
	Brian Hayward, Montreal
1987–88	Patrick Roy, Montreal
	Brian Hayward, Montreal
1988–89	Patrick Roy, Montreal
	Brian Hayward, Montreal
1989–90	Andy Moog, Boston
	Rejean Lemelin, Boston
1990–91	Ed Belfour, Chicago
1991–92	Patrick Roy, Montreal

LADY BYNG TROPHY

Awarded to the player combining the highest type of sportsmanship and gentlemanly conduct plus a high standard of playing ability. Selected by a vote of hockey writers and broadcasters.

Lady Byng, the wife of the Governor-General of Canada in 1925, presented the trophy to the NHL during that year.

1956–57	Andy Hebenton, New York R.
1957–58	Camille Henry, New York R.
1958–59	Alex Delvecchio, Detroit
1959–60	Don McKenney, Boston
1960–61	Red Kelly, Toronto
1961–62	Dave Keon, Toronto
1962–63	Dave Keon, Toronto
1963–64	Ken Wharram, Chicago
1964–65	Bobby Hull, Chicago
1965–66	Alex Delvecchio, Detroit
1966–67	Stan Mikita, Chicago
1967–68	Stan Mikita, Chicago
1968–69	Alex Delvecchio, Detroit
1969–70	Phil Goyette, St. Louis
1970–71	Johnny Bucyk, Boston
1971–72	Jean Ratelle, New York R.
1972–73	Gil Perreault, Buffalo
1973–74	John Bucyk, Boston
1974–75	Marcel Dionne, Detroit
1975–76	Jean Ratelle, NYR-Boston
1976–77	Marcel Dionne, Los Angeles
1977–78	Butch Goring, Los Angeles
1978–79	Bob MacMillan, Atlanta
1979–80	Wayne Gretzky, Edmonton
1980–81	Rick Kehoe, Pittsburgh
1981–82	Rick Middleton, Boston
1982–83	Mike Bossy, New York I.
1983–84	Mike Bossy, New York I.
1984–85	Jari Kurri, Edmonton
1985–86	Mike Bossy, New York I.
1986–87	Joe Mullen, Calgary
1987–88	Mats Naslund, Montreal
1988–89	Joe Mullen, Calgary
1989–90	Brett Hull, St. Louis
1990–91	Wayne Gretzky, Los Angeles
1991–92	Wayne Gretsky, Los Angeles

BILL MASTERTON TROPHY

Awarded by the Professional Hockey Writers' Association to "the NHL player who exemplifies the qualities of perseverance, sportsmanship and dedication to hockey." Named for the late Minnesota North Star player.

1967–68	Claude Provost, Montreal
1968–69	Ted Hampson, Oakland
1969–70	Pit Martin, Chicago
1970–71	Jean Ratelle, New York R.
1971–72	Bobby Clarke, Philadelphia
1972–73	Lowell MacDonald, Pittsburgh
1973–74	Henri Richard, Montreal
1974–75	Don Luce, Buffalo
1975–76	Rod Gilbert, New York R.
1976–77	Ed Westfall, New York I.
1977–78	Butch Goring, Los Angeles
1978–79	Serge Savard, Montreal
1979–80	Al MacAdam, Minnesota
1980–81	Blake Dunlop, St. Louis
1981–82	Glenn Resch, Colorado
1982–83	Lanny McDonald, Calgary
1983–84	Brad Park, Detroit
1984–85	Anders Hedberg, New York R.

1985–86	Charlie Simmer, Boston
1986–87	Doug Jarvis, Hartford
1987–88	Bob Bourne, Los Angeles
1988–89	Tim Kerr, Philadelphia
1989–90	Gord Kluzak, Boston
1990–91	Dave Taylor, Los Angeles
1991–92	Mark Fitzpatrick, New York I.

JACK ADAMS AWARD

Awarded by the National Hockey League Broadcasters' Association to the "NHL coach adjudged to have contributed the most to his team's success." It is presented in memory of the late Jack Adams, longtime coach and general manager of the Detroit Red Wings.

1973–74	Fred Shero, Philadelphia
1974–75	Bob Pulford, Los Angeles
1975–76	Don Cherry, Boston
1976–77	Scotty Bowman, Montreal
1977–78	Bobby Kromm, Detroit
1978–79	Al Arbour, New York I.
1979–80	Pat Quinn, Philadelphia
1980–81	Red Berenson, St. Louis
1981–82	Tom Watt, Winnipeg
1982–83	Orval Tessier, Chicago
1983–84	Bryan Murray, Washington
1984–85	Mike Keenan, Philadelphia

players, officials, coaches, executives and referees.

Selected by a six-man committee consisting of the President of the NHL, an NHL Governor, a hockey writer for a U.S. national news service, a nationally syndicated sports columnist, an ex-player in the Hockey Hall of Fame and a sports director of a U.S. national radio-television network.

Presented by the New York Rangers in 1966 to honor the memory of the long-time general manager and coach of the New York Rangers.

1965–66	Jack Adams
1966–67	Gordie Howe
	Charles Adams
	James Norris, Sr.
1967–68	Tom Lockhart
	Walter Brown
	John R. Kilpatrick
1968–69	Bobby Hull
	Edward Jeremiah
1969–70	Eddie Shore
	Jim Hendy
1970–71	Bill Jennings
	John Sollenberger
	Terry Sawchuk

1985–86	Glen Sather, Edmonton
1986–87	Jacques Demers, Detroit
1987–88	Jacques Demers, Detroit
1988–89	Pat Burns, Montreal
1989–90	Bob Murdoch, Winnipeg
1990–91	Brian Sutter, St. Louis
1991–92	Pat Quinn, Vancouver

KING CLANCY MEMORIAL TROPHY

Awarded the player who best exemplifies leadership qualities on and off the ice and has made a noteworthy humanitarian contribution to his community. The award is in honor of the Hall of Fame defenseman.

1987–88	Lanny McDonald, Calgary
1988–89	Bryan Trottier, New York I.
1989–90	Kevin Lowe, Edmonton
1990–91	Dave Taylor, Los Angeles
1991–92	Ray Bourque, Boston

LESTER PATRICK TROPHY

Awarded for outstanding service to hockey in the United States. Eligible recipients are

1971–72	Clarence Campbell
	John Kelly
	Cooney Weiland
	James D. Norris
1972–73	Walter Bush, Jr.
1973–74	Alex Delvecchio
	Murray Murdoch
1974–75	Donald Clark
	Bill Chadwick
	Tommy Ivan
1975–76	Stan Mikita
	George Leader
	Bruce Norris
1976–77	John Bucyk
	Murray Armstrong
	John Mariucci
1977–78	Phil Esposito
	Tom Fitzgerald
	Bill Tutt
	William Wirtz
1978–79	Bobby Orr
1979–80	Robert Clarke
	Edward Snider
	Fred Shero
	U.S. Olympic hockey team
1980–81	Charles Schulz
1981–82	Emile Francis
1982–83	Bill Torrey
1983–84	John A. Ziegler, Jr.
	Arthur Howie Ross
1984–85	Jack Butterfield
	Arthur M. Wirtz
1985–86	John MacInnes
	Jack Riley
1986–87	Hobey Baker
	Frank Mathers
1987–88	Keith Allen
	Fred Cusick
	Bob Johnson
1988–89	Dan Kelly
	Lou Nanne
	Lynn Patrick
	Bud Poile
1989–90	Len Ceglarski
1990–91	Rod Gilberg
	Mike Illitch
1991–92	Al Arbour
	Lou Lamoriello
	Art Berglund

LESTER B. PEARSON AWARD

Presented to the NHL's outstanding player as selected by members of the NHL Players' Association. Lester B. Pearson was Prime Minister of Canada.

1970–71	Phil Esposito, Boston
1971–72	Jean Ratelle, New York R.
1972–73	Bobby Clarke, Philadelphia
1973–74	Phil Esposito, Boston
1974–75	Bobby Orr, Boston
1975–76	Guy Lafleur, Montreal
1976–77	Guy Lafleur, Montreal
1977–78	Guy Lafleur, Montreal

1978–79	Marcel Dionne, Los Angeles
1979–80	Marcel Dionne, Los Angeles
1980–81	Mike Liut, St. Louis
1981–82	Wayne Gretzky, Edmonton
1982–83	Wayne Gretzky, Edmonton
1983–84	Wayne Gretzky, Edmonton
1984–85	Wayne Gretzky, Edmonton
1985–86	Mario Lemieux, Pittsburgh
1986–87	Wayne Gretzky, Edmonton
1987–88	Mario Lemieux, Pittsburgh
1988–89	Steve Yzerman, Detroit
1989–90	Mark Messier, Edmonton
1990–91	Brett Hull, St. Louis
1991–92	Mark Messier, New York R.

The Lester B. Pearson Award

PRESIDENTS' TROPHY

Awarded the club finishing the regular season with the best overall record. The winner receives $200,000, half to the club and the other half to be split among the players.

1985–86	Edmonton 56-17-7
1986–87	Edmonton 50-24-6
1987–88	Calgary 48-23-9
1988–89	Calgary 54-17-9
1989–90	Boston 46-25-9
1990–91	Chicago 49-23-8
1991–92	New York R. 50-25-5

PRINCE OF WALES TROPHY

The Prince of Wales donated the trophy to the NHL in 1924. From 1927–28 to 1937–38, it was presented to the team finishing first in the American Division of the NHL. From 1938–39 through 1966–67, it was given to the first-place team in the one-division league. It was subsequently awarded to the first-place finisher in the East Division. Beginning with 1981–82, the trophy has gone to the team advancing to the Stanley Cup finals as the winner of the Wales Conference.

1924–25	Montreal C.
1925–26	Montreal M.
1926–27	Ottawa
1927–28	Boston
1928–29	Boston
1929–30	Boston
1930–31	Boston
1931–32	New York R.
1932–33	Boston
1933–34	Detroit
1934–35	Boston

1935–36	Detroit
1936–37	Detroit
1937–38	Boston
1938–39	Boston
1939–40	Boston
1940–41	Boston
1941–42	New York R.
1942–43	Detroit
1943–44	Montreal
1944–45	Montreal
1945–46	Montreal
1946–47	Montreal
1947–48	Toronto
1948–49	Detroit
1949–50	Detroit
1950–51	Detroit
1951–52	Detroit
1952–53	Detroit
1953–54	Detroit
1954–55	Detroit
1955–56	Montreal
1956–57	Detroit
1957–58	Montreal
1958–59	Montreal
1959–60	Montreal
1960–61	Montreal
1961–62	Montreal
1962–63	Montreal
1963–64	Montreal
1964–65	Detroit
1965–66	Montreal
1966–67	Chicago
1967–68	Montreal
1968–69	Montreal
1969–70	Chicago
1970–71	Boston
1971–72	Boston
1972–73	Montreal
1973–74	Boston
1974–75	Buffalo
1975–76	Montreal
1976–77	Montreal
1977–78	Montreal
1978–79	Montreal
1979–80	Buffalo
1980–81	Montreal
1981–82	New York I.
1982–83	New York I.
1983–84	New York I.
1984–85	Philadelphia
1985–86	Montreal
1986–87	Philadelphia
1987–88	Boston
1988–89	Montreal
1989–90	Boston
1990–91	Pittsburgh
1991–92	Pittsburgh

CLARENCE S. CAMPBELL BOWL

Named for the former president of the NHL, the award originally was given to the champions of the West Division. Since 1981–82, it has gone to the team advancing to the Stanley

Cup finals as the winner of the Campbell Conference.

1967–68	Philadelphia
1968–69	St. Louis
1969–70	St. Louis
1970–71	Chicago
1971–72	Chicago
1972–73	Chicago
1973–74	Philadelphia
1974–75	Philadelphia
1975–76	Philadelphia
1976–77	Philadelphia
1977–78	New York I.
1978–79	New York I.
1979–80	Philadelphia
1980–81	New York I.
1981–82	Vancouver
1982–83	Edmonton
1983–84	Edmonton
1984–85	Edmonton
1985–86	Calgary
1986–87	Edmonton
1987–88	Edmonton
1988–89	Calgary
1989–90	Edmonton
1990–91	Minnesota
1991–92	Chicago

THE ALL-STAR TEAMS

Selected by a vote of hockey writers and broadcasters in each NHL city at the end of the season. The balloting originated with the 1930–31 campaign.

1930–31
First
		Second
Gardiner, Chicago	Goal	Thompson, Boston
Shore, Boston	Defense	Mantha, Montreal C.
Clancy, Toronto	Defense	Johnson, New York R.
Morenz, Montreal C.	Center	Boucher, New York R.
Bill Cook, New York R.	Right Wing	Clapper, Boston
Joliat, Montreal C.	Left Wing	Bun Cook, New York R.

1931–32
Gardiner, Chicago	Goal	Worters, New York A.
Shore, Boston	Defense	Mantha, Montreal C.
Johnson, New York R.	Defense	Clancy, Toronto
Morenz, Montreal C.	Center	Smith, Mont. M
Bill Cook, New York R.	Right Wing	C. Conacher, Toronto
Jackson, Toronto	Left Wing	Joliat, Montreal C.

1932–33
Roach, Detroit	Goal	Gardiner, Chicago
Shore, Boston	Defense	Clancy, Toronto
Johnson, New York R.	Defense	L. Conacher, Mont. M
Boucher, New York R.	Center	Morenz, Montreal C.
Bill Cook, New York R.	Right Wing	C. Conacher, Toronto
Northcott, Mont. M	Left Wing	Jackson, Toronto

1933–34
Gardiner, Chicago	Goal	Worters, New York A.
Clancy, Toronto	Defense	Shore, Boston
L. Conacher, Chicago	Defense	Johnson, New York R.
Boucher, New York R.	Center	Primeau, Toronto
C. Conacher, Toronto	Right Wing	Bill Cook, New York R.
Jackson, Toronto	Left Wing	Joliat, Montreal C.

1934–35
Chabot, Chicago	Goal	Thompson, Boston
Shore, Boston	Defense	Wentworth, Mont. M
Seibert, New York R.	Defense	Coulter, Chicago
Boucher, New York R.	Center	Weiland, Detroit
C. Conacher, Toronto	Right Wing	Clapper, Boston
Jackson, Toronto	Left Wing	Joliat, Montreal C.

1935–36
Thompson, Boston	Goal	Cude, Montreal C.
Shore, Boston	Defense	Siebert, Chicago
Seibert, Boston R.	Defense	Goodfellow, Detroit
Smith, Mont. M	Center	Thoms, Toronto
C. Conacher, Toronto	Right Wing	Dillon, New York R.
Schriner, New York A.	Left Wing	Thompson, Chicago

1936–37
Smith, Detroit	Goal	Cude, Montreal C.
Seibert, Montreal C.	Defense	Siebert, Chicago
Goodfellow, Detroit	Defense	C. Conacher, Mont. M
Barry, Detroit	Center	Chapman, New York A.
Aurie, Detroit	Right Wing	Dillon, New York R.
Jackson, Toronto	Left Wing	Schriner, New York A.

1937–38

Thompson, Boston	Goal	Kerr, New York R.
Shore, Boston	Defense	Coulter, New York R.
Siebert, Montreal C.	Defense	Seibert, Chicago
Cowley, Boston	Center	Apps, Toronto
*Dillon, New York R.	Right Wing	*Drillon, Toronto
Thompson, Chicago	Left Wing	Blake, Montreal C.

*Dillon and Drillon tied for first place in the voting and shared positions on the first and second teams.

1938–39

Brimsek, Boston	Goal	Robertson, New York A.
Shore, Boston	Defense	Seibert, Chicago
Clapper, Boston	Defense	Coulter, New York R.
Apps, Toronto	Center	N. Colville, New York R.
Drillon, Toronto	Right Wing	Bauer, Boston
Blake, Montreal C.	Left Wing	Gottselig, Chicago

1939–40

Kerr, New York R.	Goal	Brimsek, Boston
Clapper, Boston	Defense	Coulter, New York R.
Goodfellow, Detroit	Defense	Seibert, Chicago
Schmidt, Boston	Center	N. Colville, New York R.
Hextall, New York R.	Right Wing	Bauer, Boston
Blake, Montreal C.	Left Wing	Dumart, Boston

1940–41

Broda, Toronto	Goal	Brimsek, Boston
Clapper, Boston	Defense	Seibert, Chicago
Stanowski, Toronto	Defense	Heller, New York R.
Cowley, Boston	Center	Apps, Toronto
Hextall, New York R.	Right Wing	Bauer, Boston
Schriner, Toronto	Left Wing	Dumart, Boston

1941–42

Brimsek, Boston	Goal	Broda, Toronto
Seibert, Chicago	Defense	Egan, New York A.
Anderson, New York A.	Defense	McDonald, Toronto
Apps, Toronto	Center	Watson, New York R.
Hextall, New York R.	Right Wing	Drillon, Toronto
L. Patrick, New York R.	Left Wing	Abel, Detroit

1942–43

Mowers, Detroit	Goal	Brimsek, Boston
Seibert, Chicago	Defense	Crawford, Boston
Stewart, Detroit	Defense	Hollett, Boston
Cowley, Boston	Center	Apps, Toronto
Carr, Toronto	Right Wing	Hextall, New York R.
D. Bentley, Chicago	Left Wing	L. Patrick, New York R.

1943–44

Durnan, Montreal	Goal	Bibeault, Toronto
Seibert, Chicago	Defense	Bouchard, Montreal
Pratt, Toronto	Defense	Clapper, Boston
Cowley, Boston	Center	Lach, Montreal
Carr, Toronto	Right Wing	Richard, Montreal
D. Bentley, Chicago	Left Wing	Cain, Boston

1944–45

Durnan, Montreal	Goal	Karakas, Chicago
Bouchard, Montreal	Defense	Harmon, Montreal
Hollett, Detroit	Defense	Pratt, Toronto
Lach, Montreal	Center	Cowley, Boston
Richard, Montreal	Right Wing	Mosienko, Chicago
Blake, Montreal	Left Wing	S. Howe, Detroit

1945–46

Durnan, Montreal	Goal	Brimsek, Boston
Crawford, Boston	Defense	Reardon, Montreal
Bouchard, Montreal	Defense	Stewart, Detroit
M. Bentley, Chicago	Center	Lach, Montreal
Richard, Montreal	Right Wing	Mosienko, Chicago
Stewart, Toronto	Left Wing	Blake, Montreal

1946–47

Durnan, Montreal	Goal	Brimsek, Boston
Reardon, Montreal	Defense	Stewart, Detroit
Bouchard, Montreal	Defense	Quackenbush, Detroit
Schmidt, Boston	Center	M. Bentley, Chicago
Richard, Montreal	Right Wing	Bauer, Boston
D. Bentley, Chicago	Left Wing	Dumart, Boston

1947–48

Broda, Toronto	Goal	Brimsek, Boston
Quackenbush, Detroit	Defense	Reardon, Montreal
Stewart, Detroit	Defense	N. Colville, New York
Lach, Montreal	Center	O'Connor, New York
Richard, Montreal	Right Wing	Poile, Chicago
Lindsay, Detroit	Left Wing	Stewart, Chicago

1948–49

Durnan, Montreal	Goal	Rayner, New York
Quackenbush, Detroit	Defense	Harmon, Montreal
Stewart, Detroit	Defense	Reardon, Montreal
Abel, Detroit	Center	D. Bentley, Chicago
Richard, Montreal	Right Wing	Howe, Detroit
Conacher, Chicago	Left Wing	Lindsay, Detroit

1949–50

Durnan, Montreal	Goal	Rayner, New York
Mortson, Toronto	Defense	Reise, Detroit
Reardon, Montreal	Defense	Kelly, Detroit
Abel, Detroit	Center	Kennedy, Toronto
Richard, Montreal	Right Wing	Howe, Detroit
Lindsay, Detroit	Left Wing	Leswick, New York

1950–51

Sawchuk, Detroit	Goal	Rayner, New York
Kelly, Detroit	Defense	Thomson, Toronto
Quackenbush, Boston	Defense	Reise, Detroit
Schmidt, Boston	Center	Abel, Detroit
		Kennedy, Toronto
Howe, Detroit	Right Wing	Richard, Montreal
Lindsay, Detroit	Left Wing	Smith, Toronto

1951–52

Sawchuk, Detroit	Goal	Henry, Boston
Kelly, Detroit	Defense	Buller, New York
Harvey, Montreal	Defense	Thomson, Toronto
Lach, Montreal	Center	Schmidt, Boston
Howe, Detroit	Right Wing	Richard, Montreal
Lindsay, Detroit	Left Wing	Smith, Toronto

1952–53

Sawchuk, Detroit	Goal	McNeil, Montreal
Kelly, Detroit	Defense	Quackenbush, Boston
Harvey, Montreal	Defense	Gadsby, Chicago
Mackell, Boston	Center	Delvecchio, Detroit
Howe, Detroit	Right Wing	Richard, Montreal
Lindsay, Detroit	Left Wing	Olmstead, Montreal

1953–54

Lumley, Toronto	Goal	Sawchuk, Detroit
Kelly, Detroit	Defense	Gadsby, Chicago
Harvey, Montreal	Defense	Horton, Toronto
Mosdell, Montreal	Center	Kennedy, Toronto
Howe, Detroit	Right Wing	Richard, Montreal
Lindsay, Detroit	Left Wing	Sandford, Boston

1954–55

Lumley, Toronto	Goal	Sawchuk, Detroit
Harvey, Montreal	Defense	Goldham, Detroit
Kelly, Detroit	Defense	Flaman, Boston
Beliveau, Montreal	Center	Mosdell, Montreal
Richard, Montreal	Right Wing	Geoffrion, Montreal
Smith, Toronto	Left Wing	Lewicki, New York

1955–56

Plante, Montreal	Goal	Hall, Detroit
Harvey, Montreal	Defense	Kelly, Detroit
Gadsby, New York	Defense	Johnson, Montreal
Beliveau, Montreal	Center	Sloan, Toronto
M. Richard, Montreal	Right Wing	Howe, Detroit
Lindsay, Detroit	Left Wing	Olmstead, Montreal

1956–57

Hall, Detroit	Goal	Plante, Montreal
Harvey, Montreal	Defense	Flaman, Boston
Kelly, Detroit	Defense	Gadsby, New York
Beliveau, Montreal	Center	Litzenberger, Chicago
Howe, Detroit	Right Wing	M. Richard, Montreal
Lindsay, Detroit	Left Wing	Chevrefils, Boston

1957–58

Hall, Chicago	Goal	Plante, Montreal
Harvey, Montreal	Defense	Flaman, Boston
Gadsby, New York	Defense	Pronovost, Detroit
H. Richard, Montreal	Center	Beliveau, Montreal
Howe, Detroit	Right Wing	Bathgate, New York
Moore, Montreal	Left Wing	Henry, New York

1958–59

Plante, Montreal	Goal	Sawchuk, Detroit
Johnson, Montreal	Defense	Pronovost, Detroit
Gadsby, New York	Defense	Harvey, Montreal
Beliveau, Montreal	Center	H. Richard, Montreal
Bathgate, New York	Right Wing	Howe, Detroit
Moore, Montreal	Left Wing	Delvecchio, Detroit

1959–60

Hall, Chicago	Goal	Plante, Montreal
Harvey, Montreal	Defense	Stanley, Toronto
Pronovost, Detroit	Defense	Pilote, Chicago
Beliveau, Montreal	Center	Horvath, Boston
Howe, Detroit	Right Wing	Geoffrion, Montreal
Hull, Chicago	Left Wing	Prentice, New York

1960–61

Bower, Toronto	Goal	Hall, Chicago
Harvey, Montreal	Defense	Stanley, Toronto
Pronovost, Detroit	Defense	Pilote, Chicago
Beliveau, Montreal	Center	H. Richard, Montreal
Geoffrion, Montreal	Right Wing	Howe, Detroit
Mahovlich, Toronto	Left Wing	Moore, Montreal

1961–62

Plante, Montreal	Goal	Hall, Chicago
Harvey, New York	Defense	Brewer, Toronto
Talbot, Montreal	Defense	Pilote, Chicago
Mikita, Chicago	Center	Keon, Toronto
Bathgate, New York	Right Wing	Howe, Detroit
Hull, Chicago	Left Wing	Mahovlich, Toronto

1962–63

Hall, Chicago	Goal	Sawchuk, Detroit
Pilote, Chicago	Defense	Horton, Toronto
Brewer, Toronto	Defense	Vasko, Chicago
Mikita, Chicago	Center	Richard, Montreal
Howe, Detroit	Right Wing	Bathgate, New York
Mahovlich, Toronto	Left Wing	Hull, Chicago

1963–64

Hall, Chicago	Goal	Hodge, Montreal
Pilote, Chicago	Defense	Vasko, Chicago
Horton, Toronto	Defense	Laperriere, Montreal
Mikita, Chicago	Center	Beliveau, Montreal
Wharram, Chicago	Right Wing	Howe, Detroit
Hull, Chicago	Left Wing	Mahovlich, Toronto

1964–65

Crozier, Detroit	Goal	Hodge, Montreal
Pilote, Chicago	Defense	Gadsby, Detroit
Laperriere, Montreal	Defense	Brewer, Toronto
Ullman, Detroit	Center	Mikita, Chicago
Provost, Montreal	Right Wing	Howe, Detroit
B. Hull, Chicago	Left Wing	Mahovlich, Toronto

1965–66

Hall, Chicago	Goal	Worsley, Montreal
Laperriere, Montreal	Defense	Stanley, Toronto
Pilote, Chicago	Defense	Stapleton, Chicago
Mikita, Chicago	Center	Beliveau, Montreal
Howe, Detroit	Right Wing	Rousseau, Montreal
B. Hull, Chicago	Left Wing	Mahovlich, Toronto

1966–67

Giacomin, New York	Goal	Hall, Chicago
Pilote, Chicago	Defense	Horton, Toronto
Howell, New York	Defense	Orr, Boston
Mikita, Chicago	Center	Ullman, Detroit
Wharram, Chicago	Right Wing	Howe, Detroit
B. Hull, Chicago	Left Wing	Marshall, New York

1967–68

Worsley, Montreal	Goal	Giacomin, New York
Orr, Boston	Defense	J. C. Tremblay, Mont.
Horton, Toronto	Defense	Neilson, New York
Mikita, Chicago	Center	Esposito, Boston
Howe, Detroit	Right Wing	Gilbert, New York
B. Hull, Chicago	Left Wing	Bucyk, Boston

1968–69

Hall, St. Louis	Goal	Giacomin, New York
Orr, Boston	Defense	Green, Boston
Horton, Toronto	Defense	Harris, Montreal
Esposito, Boston	Center	Beliveau, Montreal
Howe, Detroit	Right Wing	Cournoyer, Montreal
B. Hull, Chicago	Left Wing	F. Mahovlich, Detroit

1969–70

Esposito, Chicago	Goal	Giacomin, New York
Orr, Boston	Defense	Brewer, Detroit
Park, New York	Defense	Laperriere, Montreal
Esposito, Boston	Center	Mikita, Chicago
Howe, Detroit	Right Wing	McKenzie, Boston
B. Hull, Chicago	Left Wing	F. Mahovlich, Detroit

1970–71

Giacomin, New York	Goal	Plante, Toronto
Orr, Boston	Defense	Park, New York
Tremblay, Montreal	Defense	Stapleton, Chicago
Esposito, Boston	Center	Keon, Toronto
Hodge, Boston	Right Wing	Cournoyer, Montreal
Bucyk, Boston	Left Wing	B. Hull, Chicago

1971–72

Esposito, Chicago	Goal	Dryden, Montreal
Orr, Boston	Defense	White, Chicago
Park, New York	Defense	Stapleton, Chicago
Esposito, Boston	Center	Ratelle, New York
Gilbert, New York	Right Wing	Cournoyer, Montreal
B. Hull, Chicago	Left Wing	Hadfield, New York

1972–73

Dryden, Montreal	Goal	Esposito, Chicago
Orr, Boston	Defense	Park, New York R.
Lapointe, Montreal	Defense	White, Chicago
Esposito, Boston	Center	Clarke, Philadelphia
Redmond, Detroit	Right Wing	Cournoyer, Montreal
F. Mahovlich, Montreal	Left Wing	D. Hull, Chicago

1973–74

Parent, Philadelphia	Goal	Esposito, Chicago
Orr, Boston	Defense	White, Chicago
Park, New York R.	Defense	Ashbee, Philadelphia
Esposito, Boston	Center	Clarke, Philadelphia
Hodge, Boston	Right Wing	Redmond, Detroit
Martin, Buffalo	Left Wing	Cashman, Boston

1974–75

Parent, Philadelphia	Goal	Vachon, Los Angeles
Orr, Boston	Defense	Lapointe, Montreal
D. Potvin, New York I.	Defense	Salming, Toronto
Clarke, Philadelphia	Center	Esposito, Boston
Lafleur, Montreal	Right Wing	Robert, Buffalo
Martin, Buffalo	Left Wing	Vickers, New York R.

1975–76

Dryden, Montreal	Goal	Resch, New York I.
D. Potvin, New York I.	Defense	Salming, Toronto
Park, Boston	Defense	Lapointe, Montreal
Clarke, Philadelphia	Center	Perreault, Buffalo
Lafleur, Montreal	Right Wing	Leach, Philadelphia
Barber, Philadelphia	Left Wing	Martin, Buffalo

1976–77

Dryden, Montreal	Goal	Vachon, Los Angeles
Robinson, Montreal	Defense	D. Potvin, New York I.
Salming, Toronto	Defense	Lapointe, Montreal
Dionne, Los Angeles	Center	Perreault, Buffalo
Lafleur, Montreal	Right Wing	McDonald, Toronto
Shutt, Montreal	Left Wing	Martin, Buffalo

1977–78

Dryden, Montreal	Goal	Edwards, Buffalo
D. Potvin, New York I.	Defense	Robinson, Montreal
Park, Boston	Defense	Salming, Toronto
Trottier, New York I.	Center	Sittler, Toronto
Lafleur, Montreal	Right Wing	Bossy, New York I.
Gillies, New York I.	Left Wing	Shutt, Montreal

1978–79

Dryden, Montreal	Goal	Resch, New York I.
D. Potvin, New York I.	Defense	Salming, Toronto
Robinson, Montreal	Defense	Savard, Montreal
Trottier, New York I.	Center	Dionne, Los Angeles
Lafleur, Montreal	Right Wing	Bossy, New York I.
Gillies, New York I.	Left Wing	Barber, Philadelphia

1979–80

Esposito, Chicago	Goal	Edwards, Buffalo
Robinson, Montreal	Defense	Salming, Toronto
Bourque, Boston	Defense	Schoenfeld, Buffalo
Dionne, Los Angeles	Center	Gretzky, Edmonton
Lafleur, Montreal	Right Wing	Gare, Buffalo
Simmer, Los Angeles	Left Wing	Shutt, Montreal

1980–81

Liut, St. Louis	Goal	Lessard, Los Angeles
Potvin, New York I.	Defense	Robinson, Montreal
Carlyle, Pittsburgh	Defense	Bourque, Boston
Gretzky, Edmonton,	Center	Dionne, Los Angeles
Bossy, New York I.	Right Wing	Taylor, Los Angeles
Simmer, Los Angeles	Left Wing	Barber, Philadelphia

1981–82

Smith, New York I.	Goal	Fuhr, Edmonton
Wilson, Chicago	Defense	Coffey, Edmonton
Bourque, Boston	Defense	Engblom, Montreal
Gretzky, Edmonton	Center	Trottier, New York I.
Bossy, New York I.	Right Wing	Middleton, Boston
Messier, Edmonton	Left Wing	Tonelli, New York I.

1982–83

Peeters, Boston	Goal	Melanson, New York I.
Howe, Philadelphia	Defense	Bourque, Boston
Langway, Washington	Defense	Coffey, Edmonton
Gretzky, Edmonton	Center	Savard, Chicago
Bossy, New York I.	Right Wing	McDonald, Calgary
Messier, Edmonton	Left Wing	Goulet, Quebec

1983–84

Barrasso, Buffalo	Goal	Riggin, Washington
Langway, Washington	Defense	Coffey, Edmonton
Bourque, Boston	Defense	Potvin, New York I.
Gretzky, Edmonton	Center	Trottier, New York I.
Bossy, New York I.	Right Wing	Kurri, Edmonton
Goulet, Quebec	Left Wing	Messier, Edmonton

1984–85

Lindbergh, Philadelphia	Goal	Barrasso, Buffalo
Coffey, Edmonton	Defense	Langway, Washington
Bourque, Boston	Defense	Wilson, Chicago
Gretzky, Edmonton	Center	Hawerchuk, Winnipeg
Kurri, Edmonton	Right Wing	Bossy, New York I.
Ogrodnick, Detroit	Left Wing	Tonelli, New York I.

1985–86

Vanbiesbrouck, NYR	Goal	Froese, Philadelphia
Coffey, Edmonton	Defense	Robinson, Montreal
Howe, Philadelphia	Defense	Bourque, Boston
Gretzky, Edmonton	Center	Lemieux, Pittsburgh
Bossy, New York I.	Right Wing	Kurri, Edmonton
Goulet, Quebec	Left Wing	Naslund, Montreal

1986–87

Hextall, Philadelphia	Goal	Liut, Hartford
Bourque, Boston	Defense	Murphy, Washington
Howe, Philadelphia	Defense	MacInnis, Calgary
Gretzky, Edmonton	Center	Lemieux, Pittsburgh
Kurri, Edmonton	Right Wing	Kerr, Philadelphia
Goulet, Quebec	Left Wing	Robitaille, Los Angeles

1987–88

Fuhr, Edmonton	Goal	Roy, Montreal
Bourque, Boston	Defense	Suter, Calgary
Stevens, Washington	Defense	McCrimmon, Calgary
Lemieux, Pittsburgh	Center	Gretzky, Edmonton
Loob, Calgary	Right Wing	Neely, Boston
Robitaille, Los Angeles	Left Wing	Goulet, Quebec

1988–89

Roy, Montreal	Goal	Vernon, Calgary
Chelios, Montreal	Defense	MacInnis, Calgary
Coffey, Pittsburgh	Defense	Bourque, Boston
Lemieux, Pittsburgh	Center	Gretzky, Los Angeles
J. Mullen, Calgary	Right Wing	Kurri, Edmonton
Robitaille, Los Angeles	Left Wing	Gallant, Detroit

1989–90

Roy, Montreal	Goal	Puppa, Buffalo
Bourque, Boston	Defense	Coffey, Pittsburgh
MacInnis, Calgary	Defense	Wilson, Chicago
Messier, Edmonton	Center	Gretzky, Los Angeles
Hull, St. Louis	Right Wing	Neely, Boston
Robitaille, Los Angeles	Left Wing	Bellows, Minnesota

1990–91

Belfour, Chicago	Goal	Roy, Montreal
Bourque, Boston	Defense	Chelios, Chicago
MacInnis, Calgary	Defense	Leetch, New York R.
Gretzky, Los Angeles	Center	Oates, St. Louis
Hull, St. Louis	Right Wing	Neely, Boston
Robitaille, Los Angeles	Left Wing	K. Stevens, Pittsburgh

1991–92
Roy, Montreal   Goal   McLean, Vancouver
Leetch, New York R.   Defense   Housley, Winnipeg
Bourque, Boston   Defense   S. Stevens, New Jersey
Messier, New York R.   Center   Lemieux, Pittsburgh
Hull, St. Louis   Right Wing   Recchi, Philadelphia
K. Stevens, Pittsburgh   Left Wing   Robitaille, Los Angeles

NHL ENTRY DRAFT

1969

First Round

1. Montreal—Rejean Houle, Montreal Jr. Canadiens; 2. Montreal—Marc Tardif, Montreal Jr. Canadiens; 3. Boston—Don Tannahill, Niagara Falls; 4. Boston—Frank Spring, Edmonton Oil Kings; 5. Minnesota—Dick Redmond, St. Catharines; 6. Philadelphia—Bob Currier, Cornwall; 7. Oakland—Tony Featherstone, Peterborough; 8. New York R.—Andre Dupont, Montreal Jr. Canadiens; 9. Toronto—Ernie Moser, Estevan; 10. Detroit—Jim Rutherford, Hamilton; 11. Boston—Ivan Boldirev, Oshawa; 12. New York R.—Pierre Jarry, Ottawa; 13. Chicago—J.P. Bordileau, Montreal Jr. Canadiens; 14. Minnesota—Dennis O'Brien, St. Catharines.

Second Round

15. Pittsburgh—Rick Kessell, Oshawa; 16. Los Angeles—Dale Hoganson, Estevan; 17. Philadelphia—Bobby Clarke, Flin Flon; 18. Oakland—Ron Stackhouse, Peterborough; 19. St. Louis—Mike Lowe, Loyola College; 20. Toronto—Doug Brindley, Niagara Falls; 21. Detroit—Ron Garwasiuk, Regina; 22. Boston—Art Quoquochi, Montreal Jr. Canadiens; 23. New York R.—Bert Wilson, London; 24. Chicago—Larry Romanchych, Flin Flon; 25. Minnesota—Gilles Gilbert, London; 26. Pittsburgh—Michel Briere, Shawinigan Falls; 27. Los Angeles—Greg Boddy, Edmonton Oil Kings; 28. Philadelphia—Bill Brossart, Estevan.

1970

First Round

1. Buffalo—Gilbert Perreault, Montreal Jr. Canadiens; 2. Vancouver—Dale Tallon, Toronto Marlboros; 3. Boston—Reg Leach, Flin Flon; 4. Boston—Rick MacLeish, Peterborough; 5. Montreal—Ray Martiniuk, Flin Flon; 6. Montreal—Chuck Lefley, Canadian Nationals; 7. Pittsburgh—Greg Polis, Estevan; 8. Toronto—Darryl Sittler, London; 9. Boston—Ron Plumb, Peterborough; 10. Oakland—Chris Oddleifson, Winnipeg Jets; 11. New York R.—Norm Gratton, Montreal Jr. Canadiens; 12. Detroit—Serge Lajeunesse, Montreal Jr. Canadiens; 13. Boston—Bob Stewart, Oshawa; 14. Chicago—Dan Maloney, London.

Second Round

15. Buffalo—Butch Deadmarsh, Brandon; 16. Vancouver—Jim Hargreaves, Winnipeg Jets; 17. Minnesota—Fred Harvey, Hamilton; 18. Philadelphia—Bill Clement, Ottawa; 19. Oakland—Pete Laframboise, Ottawa; 20. Minnesota—Fred Barrett, Toronto Marlboros; 21. Pittsburgh—John Stewart, Flin Flon; 22. Toronto—Errol Thompson, Charlottetown; 23. St. Louis—Murray Keogan, U. of Minnesota; 24. Los Angeles—Al McDonough, St. Catharines; 25. New York R.—Mike Murphy, Toronto Marlboros; 26. Detroit—Bobby Guindon, Montreal Jr. Canadiens; 27. Boston—Dan Bouchard, London; 28. Chicago—Mike Archambault, Drummondville.

1971

First Round

1. Montreal—Guy Lafleur, Quebec Remparts; 2. Detroit—Marcel Dionne, St. Catharines; 3. Vancouver—Jocelyn Guevremont, Montreal Jr. Canadiens; 4. St. Louis—Gene Carr, Flin Flon; 5. Buffalo—Rick Martin, Montreal Jr. Canadiens; 6. Boston—Ron Jones, Edmonton Oil Kings; 7. Montreal—Chuck Arnason, Flin Flon; 8. Philadelphia—Larry Wright, Regina; 9. Philadelphia—Pierre Plante, Drummondville; 10. New York R.—Steve Vickers, Toronto Marlboros; 11. Montreal—Murray Wilson, Ottawa; 12. Chicago—Dan Spring, Edmonton Oil Kings; 13. New York R.—Steve Durbano, Toronto Marlboros; 14. Boston—Terry O'Reilly, Oshawa.

Second Round

15. California—Ken Baird, Flin Flon; 16. Detroit—Henry Boucha, U.S. Nationals; 17. Vancouver—Bobby Lalonde, Montreal Jr. Canadiens; 18. Pittsburgh—Brian MaKenzie, St. Catherines; 19. Buffalo—Craig Ramsay, Peterborough; 20. Montreal—Larry Robinson, Kitchener; 21. Minnesota—Rod Norrish, Regina; 22. Toronto—Rick Kehoe, Hamilton; 23. Toronto—Dave Fortier, St. Catherines; 24. Montreal—Michel Deguise, Sorel; 25. Montreal—Terry French, Ottawa; 26. Chicago—Dave Kryskow, Edmonton Oil Kings; 27. New York R.—Tom Williams, Hamilton; 28. Boston—Curt Ridley, Portage.

1972

First Round

1. New York I.—Billy Harris, Toronto Marlboros; 2. Atlanta—Jacques Richard, Quebec Remparts; 3. Vancouver—Don Lever, Niagara Falls; 4. Montreal—Steve Shutt, Toronto Marlboros; 5. Buffalo—Jim Schoenfeld, Niagara Falls; 6. Montreal—Michel Larocque, Ottawa; 7. Philadelphia—Bill Barber, Kitchener; 8. Montreal—Dave Gardner, Toronto Marlboros; 9. St. Louis—Wayne Merrick, Ottawa; 10. New York—Albert Blanchard, Kitchener; 11. Toronto—George Ferguson, Toronto Marlboros; 12. Minnesota—Jerry Byers, Kitchener; 13. Chicago—Phil Russell, Edmonton Oil Kings; 14. Montreal—John Van Boxmeer, Edmonton Oil Kings; 15. New York R.—Bobby MacMillan, St. Catharines; 16. Boston—Mike Bloom, St. Catharines.

Second Round

17. New York I.—Lorne Henning, New Westminster; 18. Atlanta—Dwight Bialowas, Regina; 19. Vancouver—Brian McSheffrey, Ottawa; 20. Los Angeles—Don Kozak, Edmonton Oil Kings; 21. New York R.—Larry Sacharuk, Saskatoon; 22. California—Tom Cassidy, Kitchener; 23. Philadelphia—Tom Bladon, Edmonton Oil Kings; 24. Pittsburgh—Jack Lynch, Oshawa; 25. Buffalo–Larry Carriere, Loyola College; 26. Detroit—Pierre Guite, St. Catharines; 27. Toronto—Randy Osburn, Lon-

don; 28. California—Stan Weir, Medicine Hat; 29. Pittsburgh—Bernie Lukowich, New Westminster; 30. New York R.—Rene Villemure, Shawinigan; 31. Boston—Wayne Elder, London.

1973

First Round

1. New York I.—Denis Potvin, Ottawa; 2. Atlanta—Tom Lysiak, Medicine Hat; 3. Vancouver—Dennis Ververgaert, London; 4. Toronto—Lanny McDonald, Medicine Hat; 5. St. Louis—John Davidson, Calgary Centennials; 6. Boston—Andre Savard, Quebec Remparts; 7. Pittsburgh—Blaine Stoughton, Flin Flon; 8. Montreal—Bob Gainey, Peterborough; 9. Vancouver—Bob Dailey, Toronto Marlboros; 10. Toronto—Bob Neeley, Peterborough; 11. Detroit—Terry Richardson, New Westminster; 12. Buffalo—Morris Titanic, Sudbury; 13. Chicago—Darcy Rota, Edmonton Oil Kings; 14. New York R.—Rick Middleton, Oshawa; 15. Toronto—Ian Turnbull, Ottawa; 16. Atlanta—Vic Mercredi, New Westminster.

Second Round

17. Montreal—Glen Goldup, Toronto Marlboros; 18. Minnesota—Blake Dunlop, Ottawa; 19. Vancouver—Paulin Bordeleau, Toronto Marlboros; 20. Philadelphia—Larry Goodenough, London; 21. Atlanta—Eric Vail, Sudbury; 22. Montreal—Peter Marrin, Toronto Marlboros; 23. Pittsburgh—Wayne Bianchin, Flin Flon; 24. St. Louis—George Pesut, Saskatoon; 25. Minnesota—John Rogers, Edmonton Oil Kings; 26. Philadelphia—Brent Levins, Swift Current; 27. Pittsburgh—Colin Campbell, Peterborough; 28. Buffalo—Jean Landry, Quebec Remparts; 29. Chicago—Reg Thomas, London; 30. New York R.—Pat Hickey, Hamilton; 31. Boston—Jim Jones, Peterborough; 32. Montreal—Ron Andruff, Flin Flon.

1974

First Round

1. Washington—Greg Joly, Regina; 2. Kansas City—Wilf Paiement, St. Catharines; 3.

California—Rick Hampton, St. Catharines; 4. New York I.—Clark Gillies, Regina; 5. Montreal—Cam Connor, Flin Flon; 6. Minnesota—Doug Hicks, Flin Flon; 7. Montreal—Doug Risebrough, Kitchener; 8. Pittsburgh—Pierre Larouche, Sorel; 9. Detroit—Bill Lochead, Oshawa; 10. Montreal—Rick Chartraw, Kitchener; 11. Buffalo—Lee Fogolin, Oshawa; 12. Montreal—Mario Tremblay, Montreal Jrs.; 13. Toronto—Jack Valiquette, Sault; 14. New York R.—Dave Maloney, Kitchener; 15. Montreal—Gord McTavish, Sudbury; 16. Chicago—Grant Mulvey, Calgary Centennials; 17. California—Ron Chipperfield, Brandon; 18. Boston—Dan Larway, Swift Current.

Second Round

19. Washington—Mike Marson, Sudbury; 20. Kansas City—Glen Burdon, Regina; 21. California—Bruce Affleck, U. of Denver; 22. New York I.—Bryan Trottier, Swift Current; 23. Vancouver—Ron Sedlbauer, Kitchener; 24. Minnesota—Rick Nantais, Quebec Remparts; 25. Boston—Mark Howe, Toronto Marlboros; 26. St. Louis—Bob Hess, New Westminster; 27. Pittsburgh—Jacques Cossette, Sorel; 28. Atlanta—Guy Chouinard, Quebec Remparts; 29. Buffalo—Danny Gare, Calgary Centennials; 30. Montreal—Gary McGregor, Cornwall; 31. Toronto—Dave Williams, Swift Current; 32. New York R.—Ron Greschner, Swift Current; 33. Montreal—Gilles Lupien, Montreal Jrs.; 34. Chicago—Alain Daigle, Trois Rivieres; 35. Philadelphia—Don McLean, Sudbury; 36. Boston—Peter Sturgeon, Kitchener.

1975

First Round

1. Philadelphia—Mel Bridgman, Victoria; 2. Kansas City—Barry Dean, Medicine Hat; 3. California—Ralph Klassen, Saskatoon; 4. Minnesota—Bryan Maxwell, Medicine Hat; 5. Detroit—Rick Lapointe, Victoria; 6. Toronto—Don Ashby, Calgary Centennials; 7. Chicago—Greg Vaydik, Medicine Hat; 8. Atlanta—Richard Mulhern, Sherbrooke; 9. Montreal—Robin Sadler, Edmonton Oil Kings; 10.

Vancouver—Rick Blight, Brandon; 11. New York I.—Pat Price, Brandon; 12. New York R.—Wayne Dillon, Toronto Marlboros; 13. Pittsburgh—Gord Laxton, New Westminster; 14. Boston—Doug Halward, Peterborough; 15. Montreal—Pierre Mondou, Montreal Jrs.; 16. Los Angeles—Tim Young, Ottawa; 17. Buffalo—Bob Sauve, Laval; 18. Washington—Alex Forsyth, Kingston.

Second Round

19. Washington—Peter Scamurra, Peterborough; 20. Kansas City—Don Cairns, Victoria; 21. California—Dennis Maruk, London; 22. Montreal—Brian Engblom, U. of Wisconsin; 23. Detroit—Jerry Rollins, Winnipeg Jr. Jets; 24. Toronto—Doug Jarvis, Peterborough; 25. Chicago—Daniel Arndt, Saskatoon; 26. Atlanta—Rick Bowness, Montreal Jrs.; 27. St. Louis—Ed Staniowski, Regina; 28. Vancouver—Brad Gassoff, Kamloops; 29. New York I.—David Salvian, St. Catharines; 30. New York R.—Doug Soetaert, Edmonton Oil Kings; 31. Pittsburgh—Russ Anderson, U. of Minnesota; 32. Boston—Barry Smith, New Westminster; 33. Los Angeles—Terry Bucyk, Lethbridge; 34. Montreal—Kelvin Greenbank, Winnipeg Jr. Jets; 35. Buffalo—Ken Breitenbach, St. Catharines; 36. St. Louis—Jamie Masters, Ottawa.

1976

First Round

1. Washington—Rick Green, London; 2. Pittsburgh—Blair Chapman, Saskatoon; 3. Minnesota—Glen Sharpley, Hull; 4. Detroit—Fred Williams, Saskatoon; 5. California—Bjorn Johansson, Sweden; 6. New York R.—Don Murdoch, Medicine Hat; 7. St. Louis—Bernie Federko, Saskatoon; 8. Atlanta—Dave Shand, Peterborough; 9. Chicago—Real Cloutier, Quebec Remparts; 10. Atlanta—Harold Phillipoff, New Westminster; 11. Kansas City—Paul Gardner, Oshawa; 12. Montreal—Peter Lee, Ottawa; 13. Montreal—Rod Schutt, Sudbury; 14. New York I.—Alex McKendry, Sudbury; 15. Washington—Greg Carroll, Medicine Hat; 16. Boston—Clayton Pachal, New Westmin-

ster; 17. Philadelphia—Mark Suzor, Kingston; 18. Montreal—Bruce Baker, Ottawa.

Second Round

19. Pittsburgh—Greg Malone, Oshawa; 20. St. Louis—Brian Sutter, Lethbridge; 21. Los Angeles—Steve Clippingdale, New Westminster; 22. Detroit—Reed Larson, U. of Minnesota; 23. California—Vern Stenlund, London; 24. New York R.—Dave Farrish, Sudbury; 25. St. Louis—John Smrke, Toronto Marlboros; 26. Vancouver—Bob Manno, St. Catharines; 27. Chicago—Jeff McDill, Victoria; 28. Atlanta—Bobby Simpson, Sherbrooke; 29. Pittsburgh—Peter Marsh, Sherbrooke; 30. Toronto—Randy Carlyle, Sudbury; 31. Minnesota—Jim Roberts, Ottawa; 32. New York I.—Mike Kaszycki, Sault; 33. Buffalo—Joe Kowal, Hamilton; 34. Boston—Larry Gloeckner, Victoria; 35. Philadelphia—Drew Callander, Regina; 36. Montreal—Barry Melrose, Kamloops.

1977

First Round

1. Detroit—Dale McCourt, St. Catharines; 2. Colorado—Barry Beck, New Westminster; 3. Washington—Robert Picard, Montreal Jrs.; 4. Vancouver—Jere Gillis, Sherbrooke; 5. Cleveland—Mike Crombeen, Kingston; 6. Chicago—Doug Wilson, Ottawa; 7. Minnesota—Brad Maxwell, New Westminster; 8. New York R.—Lucien DeBlois, Sorel; 9. St. Louis—Scott Campbell, London; 10. Montreal—Mark Napier, Toronto Marlboros; 11. Toronto—John Anderson, Toronto Marlboros; 12. Toronto—Trevor Johanson, Toronto Marlboros; 13. New York R.—Ron Duguay, Sudbury; 14. Buffalo—Ric Seiling, St. Catharines; 15. New York I.—Mike Bossy, Laval; 16. Boston—Dwight Foster, Kitchener; 17. Philadelphia—Kevin McCarthy, Winnipeg Monarchs; 18. Montreal—Norm Dupont, Montreal Jrs.

Second Round

19. Chicago—Jean Savard, Quebec Remparts; 20. Atlanta—Miles Zaharko, New Westminster; 21. Washington—Mark Lofthouse, New Westminster; 22. Vancouver—Jeff Bandura, Portland; 23. Cleveland—Daniel Chicoine, Sherbrooke; 24. Toronto—Bob Gladney, Oshawa; 25. Minnesota—Dave Semenko, Brandon; 26. New York R.—Mike Keating, St. Catharines; 27. St. Louis—Neil Labatte, Toronto Marlboros; 28. Atlanta—Don Laurence, Kitchener; 29. Toronto—Rocky Saganiuk, Lethbridge; 30. Pittsburgh—Jim Hamilton, London; 31. Atlanta—Brian Hill, Medicine Hat; 32. Buffalo—Ron Areshenkoff, Medicine Hat; 33. New York I.—John Tonelli, Toronto Marlboros; 34. Boston—Dave Parro, Saskatoon; 35. Philadelphia—Tom Gorence, U. of Minnesota; 36. Montreal—Rod Langway, U. of New Hampshire.

1978

First Round

1. Minnesota—Bobby Smith, Ottawa; 2. Washington—Ryan Walter, Seattle; 3. St. Louis—Wayne Babych, Portland; 4. Vancouver—Bill Derlago, Brandon; 5. Colorado—Mike Gillis, Kingston; 6. Philadelphia—Behn Wilson, Kingston; 7. Philadelphia—Ken Linseman, Kingston; 8. Montreal—Danny Geoffrion, Cornwall; 9. Detroit—Willie Huber, Hamilton; 10. Chicago—Tim Higgins, Ottawa; 11. Atlanta—Brad Marsh, London; 12. Detroit—Brent Peterson, Portland; 13. Buffalo—Larry Playfair, Portland; 14. Philadelphia—Danny Lucas, Sault; 15. New York I.—Steve Tambellini, Lethbridge; 16. Boston—Al Secord, Hamilton; 17. Montreal—Dave Hunter, Sudbury; 18. Washington—Tim Coulis, Hamilton.

Second Round

19. Minnesota—Steve Payne, Ottawa; 20. Washington—Paul Mulvey, Portland; 21. Toronto—Joel Quenneville, Windsor; 22. Vancouver—Curt Fraser, Victoria; 23. Washington—Paul MacKinnon, Peterborough; 24. Minnesota—Steve Christoff, U. of Minnesota; 25. Pittsburgh—Mike Meeker, Peterborough; 26. New York R.—Don Maloney, Kitchener; 27. Colorado—Merlin Malinowski, Medicine Hat; 28. Detroit—Glenn Hicks, Flin Flon; 29.

Chicago—Doug Lecuyer, Portland; 30. Montreal—Dale Yakiwchuk, Portland; 31. Detroit—Al Jensen, Hamilton; 32. Buffalo—Tony McKegney, Kingston; 33. Philadelphia—Mike Simurda, Kingston; 34. New York I.—Randy Johnston, Peterborough; 35. Boston—Graeme Nicolson, Cornwall; 36. Montreal—Ron Carter, Sherbrooke.

1979

First Round

1. Colorado—Rob Ramage, London; 2. St. Louis—Perry Turnbull, Portland; 3. Detroit—Mike Foligno, Sudbury; 4. Washington—Mike Gartner, Niagara Falls; 5. Vancouver—Rick Vaive, Sherbrooke; 6. Minnesota—Craig Hartsburg, Sault; 7. Chicago—Keith Brown, Portland; 8. Boston—Ray Bourque, Verdun; 9. Toronto—Laurie Boschman, Brandon; 10. Minnesota—Tom McCarthy, Oshawa; 11. Buffalo—Mike Ramsey, U. of Minnesota; 12. Atlanta—Paul Reinhart, Kitchener; 13. New York R.—Doug Sulliman, Kitchener; 14. Philadelphia—Brian Propp, Brandon; 15. Boston—Brad McCrimmon, Brandon; 16. Los Angeles—Jay Wells, Kingston; 17. New York I.—Duane Sutter, Lethbridge; 18. Hartford—Ray Allison, Brandon; 19. Winnipeg—Jimmy Mann, Sherbrooke; 20. Quebec—Michel Goulet, Quebec Remparts; 21. Edmonton—Kevin Lowe, Quebec Remparts.

Second Round

22. Philadelphia—Blake Wesley, Portland; 23. Atlanta—Mike Perovich, Brandon; 24. Washington—Errol Rausse, Seattle; 25. New York I.—Tomas Jonsson, Sweden; 26. Vancouver—Brent Ashton, Saskatoon; 27. Montreal—Gaston Gingras, Hamilton; 28. Chicago—Tim Trimper, Peterborough; 29. Los Angeles—Dean Hopkins, London; 30. Los Angeles—Mark Hardy, Montreal Jrs.; 31. Pittsburgh—Paul Marshall, Brantford; 32. Buffalo—Lindy Ruff, Lethbridge; 33. Atlanta—Pat Riggin, London; 34. New York R.—Ed Hospodar, Ottawa; 35. Philadelphia—Pelle Lindbergh, Sweden; 36. Boston—Doug Morrison, Lethbridge; 37. Montreal—Mats Naslund, Sweden;

38. New York I.—Billy Carroll, London; 39. Hartford—Stuart Smith, Peterborough; 40. Winnipeg—Dave Christian, U. of North Dakota; 41. Quebec—Dale Hunter, Sudbury; 42. Minnesota—Neal Broten, U. of Minnesota.

1980

First Round

1. Montreal—Doug Wickenheiser, Regina; 2. Winnipeg—Dave Babych, Portland; 3. Chicago—Denis Savard, Montreal Jrs.; 4. Los Angeles—Larry Murphy, Peterborough; 5. Washington—Darren Veitch, Regina; 6. Edmonton—Paul Coffey, Kitchener; 7. Vancouver—Rick Lanz, Oshawa; 8. Hartford—Fred Arthur, Cornwall; 9. Pittsburgh—Mike Bullard, Brantford; 10. Los Angeles—Jimmy Fox, Ottawa; 11. Detroit—Mike Blaisdell, Regina; 12. St. Louis—Rik Wilson, Kingston; 13. Calgary—Denis Cyr, Montreal Jrs.; 14. New York R.—Jim Malone, Toronto Marlboros; 15. Chicago—Jerome Dupont, Toronto Marlboros; 16. Minnesota—Brad Palmer, Victoria; 17. New York I.—Brent Sutter, Red Deer; 18. Boston—Barry Pederson, Victoria; 19. Colorado—Paul Gagne, Windsor; 20. Buffalo—Steve Patrick, Brandon; 21. Philadelphia—Mike Stothers, Kingston.

Second Round

22. Colorado—Joe Ward, Seattle; 23. Winnipeg—Moe Mantha, Toronto Marlboros; 24. Quebec—Normand Rochefort, Quebec Remparts; 25. Toronto—Craig Muni, Kingston; 26. Toronto—Bob McGill, Victoria; 27. Montreal—Ric Nattress, Brantford; 28. Chicago—Steve Ludzik, Niagara Falls; 29. Hartford—Michel Galarneau, Hull; 30. Chicago—Ken Solheim, Medicine Hat; 31. Calgary—Tony Curtale; Brantford; 32. Calgary—Kevin LaVallee, Brantford; 33. Los Angeles—Greg Terrion, Brantford; 34. Los Angeles—Dave Morrison, Peterborough; 35. New York R.—Mike Allison, Sudbury; 36. Chicago—Len Dawes, Victoria; 37. Minnesota—Don Beaupre, Sudbury; 38. New York I.—Kelly Hrudey, Medicine Hat; 39. Calgary—Steve Konroyd, Oshawa; 40. Montreal—John Chabot, Hull; 41.

Buffalo—Mike Moller, Lethbridge; 42. Philadelphia—Jay Fraser, Ottawa.

1981

First Round

1. Winnipeg—Dale Hawerchuk, Cornwall; 2. Los Angeles—Doug Smith, Ottawa; 3. Washington—Bobby Carpenter, St. John's H.S.; 4. Hartford—Ron Francis, Sault; 5. Colorado—Joe Cirella, Oshawa; 6. Toronto—Jim Benning, Portland; 7. Montreal—Mark Hunter, Brantford; 8. Edmonton—Grant Fuhr, Victoria; 9. New York R.—James Patrick, U. of North Dakota; 10. Vancouver—Garth Butcher, Regina; 11. Quebec—Randy Moller, Lethbridge; 12. Chicago—Tony Tanti, Oshawa; 13. Minnesota—Ron Meighan, Niagara Falls; 14. Boston—Normand Leveille, Chicoutimi; 15. Calgary—Al MacInnis, Kitchener; 16. Philadelphia—Steve Smith, Sault; 17. Buffalo—Jiri Dudacek, Kladno; 18. Montreal—Gilbert Delorme, Chicoutimi; 19. Montreal—Jan Ingman, Sweden; 20. St. Louis—Marty Ruff, Lethbridge; 21. New York I.—Paul Boutilier, Sherbrooke.

Second Round

22. Winnipeg—Scott Arniel, Cornwall; 23. Detroit—Claude Loiselle, Windsor; 24. Toronto—Gary Yaremchuk, Portland; 25. Chicago—Kevin Griffin, Portland; 26. Colorado—Rick Chernomaz, Victoria; 27. Minnesota—Dave Donnelly, St. Albert; 28. Pittsburgh—Steve Gatzos, Sault; 29. Edmonton—Todd Strueby, Regina; 30. New York R.—Jan Erixon, Skelleftea; 31. Minnesota—Mike Sands, Sudbury; 32. Montreal—Lars Eriksson, Brynas; 33. Minnesota—Tom Hirsch, Patrick Henry H.S.; 34. Minnesota—Dave Preuss, St. Thomas Academy; 35. Boston—Luc Dufour, Chicoutimi; 36. St. Louis—Hakan Nordin, Sweden; 37. Philadelphia—Rich Costello, Natick H.S.; 38. Buffalo—Hannu Virta, TPS Finland; 39. Los Angeles—Dean Kennedy, Brandon; 40. Montreal—Chris Chelios, Moose Jaw; 41. Minnesota—Jali Wahlsten, TPS Finland; 42. New York I.—Gord Dineen, Sault.

1982

First Round

1. Boston—Gord Kluzak, Nanaimo; 2. Minnesota—Brian Bellows, Kitchener; 3. Toronto—Gary Nylund, Portland; 4. Philadelphia—Ron Sutter, Lethbridge; 5. Washington—Scott Stevens, Kitchener; 6. Buffalo—Phil Housley, South St. Paul H.S.; 7. Chicago—Ken Yaremchuk, Portland; 8. New Jersey—Rocky Trottier, Nanaimo; 9. Buffalo—Paul Cyr, Victoria; 10. Pittsburgh—Rich Sutter, Lethbridge; 11. Vancouver—Michel Petit, Sherbrooke; 12. Winnipeg—Jim Kyte, Cornwall; 13. Quebec—David Shaw, Kitchener; 14. Hartford—Paul Lawless, Windsor; 15. New York R.—Chris Kontos, Toronto Marlboros; 16. Buffalo—Dave Andreychuk, Oshawa; 17. Detroit—Murray Craven, Medicine Hat; 18. New Jersey—Ken Daneyko, Seattle; 19. Montreal—Alain Heroux, Chicoutimi; 20. Edmonton—Jim Playfair, Portland; 21. New York I.—Patrick Flatley, U. of Wisconsin.

Second Round

22. Boston—Brian Curran, Portland; 23. Detroit—Yves Courteau, Laval; 24. Toronto—Gary Leeman, Regina; 25. Toronto—Peter Ihnacak, Czech. National Team; 26. Buffalo—Mike Anderson, N. St. Paul H.S.; 27. Los Angeles—Mike Heidt, Calgary Wranglers; 28. Chicago—Rene Badeau, Quebec Remparts; 29. Calgary—Dave Reierson, Prince Albert; 30. Buffalo—Jens Johansson, Sweden; 31. Montreal—Jocelyn Gauvreau, Granby; 32. Montreal—Kent Carlson, St. Lawrence U.; 33. Montreal—David Maley, Edina H.S.; 34. Quebec—Paul Gillis, Niagara Falls; 35. Hartford—Mark Paterson, Ottawa; 36. New York R.—Tomas Sandstrom, Sweden; 37. Calgary—Richard Kromm, Portland; 38. Pittsburgh—Tim Hrynewich, Sudbury; 39. Boston—Lyndon Byers, Regina; 40. Montreal—Scott Sandelin, Hibbing H.S.; 41. Edmonton—Steve Graves, Sault; 42. New York I.—Vern Smith, Lethbridge.

1983

First Round

1. Minnesota—Brian Lawton, Mt. St. Charles H.S.; 2. Hartford—Sylvain Turgeon, Hull; 3. New York I.—Pat LaFontaine, Verdun; 4. Detroit—Steve Yzerman, Peterborough; 5. Buffalo—Tom Barrasso, Acton-Boxboro H.S.; 6. New Jersey—John MacLean, Oshawa; 7. Toronto—Russ Courtnall, Victoria; 8. Winnipeg—Andrew McBain, North Bay; 9. Vancouver—Cam Neely, Portland; 10. Buffalo—Normand Lacombe, U. of New Hampshire; 11. Buffalo—Adam Creighton, Ottawa; 12. New York R.—Dave Gagner, Brantford; 13. Calgary—Dan Quinn, Belleville; 14. Winnipeg—Bobby Dollas, Laval; 15. Pittsburgh—Bob Errey, Peterborough; 16. New York I.—Gerald Diduck, Lethbridge; 17. Montreal—Alfie Turcotte, Porland; 18. Chicago—Bruce Cassidy, Ottawa; 19. Edmonton—Jeff Beukeboom, Sault; 20. Hartford—David Jensen, Lawrence Academy; 21. Boston—Nevin Markwart, Regina.

Second Round

22. Pittsburgh—Todd Charlesworth, Oshawa; 23. Hartford—Ville Siren, Ilves (Finland); 24. New Jersey—Shawn Evans, Peterborough; 25. Detroit—Lane Lambert, Saskatoon; 26. Montreal—Claude Lemieux, Trois Rivieres; 27. Montreal—Sergio Momesso, Shawinigan; 28. Toronto—Jeff Jackson, Brantford; 29. Winnipeg—Brad Berry, St. Albert; 30. Vancouver—David Bruce, Kitchener; 31. Buffalo—John Tucker, Kitchener; 32. Quebec—Yves Heroux, Chicoutimi; 33. New York R.—Randy Heath, Portland; 34. Buffalo—Richard Hajdu, Kamloops; 35. Montreal—Todd Francis, Brantford; 36. Minnesota—Malcolm Parks, St. Albert; 37. New York I.—Grant McKechney, Kitchener; 38. Minnesota—Frantisek Musil, Czech. National Team; 39. Chicago—Wayne Presley, Kitchener; 40. Edmonton—Mike Golden, Reading H.S.; 41. Philadelphia—Peter Zezel, Toronto Marlboros; 42. Boston—Greg Johnston, Toronto Marlboros.

1984

First Round

1. Pittsburgh—Mario Lemieux, Laval; 2. New Jersey—Kirk Muller, Guelph; 3. Chicago—Ed Olczyk, Team USA; 4. Toronto—Al Iafrate, Belleville; 5. Montreal—Petr Svoboda, Czech. Jrs.; 6. Los Angeles—Craig Redmond, Team Canada; 7. Detroit—Shawn Burr, Kitchener; 8. Montreal—Shayne Corson, Brantford; 9. Pittsburgh—Doug Bodger, Kamloops; 10. Vancouver—J.J. Daigneault, Longueuil; 11. Hartford—Sylvain Cote, Quebec Remparts; 12. Calgary—Gary Roberts, Ottawa; 13. Minnesota—David Quinn, Kent H.S.; 14. New York R.—Terry Carkner, Peterborough; 15. Quebec—Trevor Stienburg, Guelph; 16. Pittsburgh—Roger Belanger, Kingston; 17. Washington—Kevin Hatcher, North Bay; 18. Buffalo—Bo Mikael Andersson, Sweden; 19. Boston—Dave Pasin, Prince Albert; 20. New York I.—Duncan MacPherson, Saskatoon; 21. Edmonton—Selmar Odelein, Regina.

Second Round

22. Philadelphia—Greg Smyth, London; 23. New Jersey—Craig Billington, Belleville; 24. Los Angeles—Brian Wilks, Kitchener; 25. Toronto—Todd Gill, Windsor; 26. St. Louis—Brian Benning, Portland; 27. Philadelphia—Scott Mellanby, Henry Carr; 28. Detroit—Doug Houda, Calgary Wranglers; 29. Montreal—Stephane Richer, Granby; 30. Winnipeg—Peter Douris, U. of New Hampshire; 31. Vancouver—Jeff Rohlicek, Portland; 32. St. Louis—Anthony Hrkac, Orillia; 33. Calgary—Ken Sabourin, Sault; 34. Washington—Stephen Leach, Matignon H.S.; 35. New York R.—Raimo Helminen, Ilves (Finland); 36. Quebec—Jeff Brown, Sudbury; 37. Philadelphia—Jeff Chychrun, Kingston; 38. Calgary—Paul Ranheim, Edina H.S.; 39. Buffalo—Doug Trapp, Regina; 40. Boston—Ray Podloski, Portland; 41. New York I.—Bruce Melanson, Oshawa; 42. Edmonton—Daryl Reaugh, Kamloops.

1985

First Round

1. Toronto—Wendel Clark, Saskatoon; 2. Pittsburgh—Craig Simpson, Michigan State; 3. New Jersey—Craig Wolanin, Kitchener; 4. Vancouver—Jim Sandlak, London; 5. Hartford—Dana Murzyn, Calgary Wranglers; 6. New York I.—Brad Dalgarno, Hamilton; 7. New York R.—Ulf Dahlen, Ostersund; 8. Detroit—Brent Fedyk, Regina; 9. Los Angeles—Craig Duncanson, Sudbury; 10. Los Angeles—Dan Gratton, Oshawa; 11. Chicago—David Manson, Prince Albert; 12. Montreal—Jose Charbonneau, Drummondville; 13. New York I.—Derek King, Sault; 14. Buffalo—Carl Johansson, Sweden; 15. Quebec—Dave Latta, Kitchener; 16. Montreal—Tom Chorske, Minneapolis H.S.; 17. Calgary—Chris Biotti, Belmont Hill H.S.; 18. Winnipeg—Ryan Stewart, Kamloops; 19. Washington—Yvon Corriveau, Toronto Marlboros; 20. Edmonton—Scott Metcalfe, Kingston; 21. Philadelphia—Glen Seabrooke, Peterborough.

Second Round

22. Toronto—Ken Soangler, Calgary Wranglers; 23. Pittsburgh—Lee Giffin, Oshawa; 24. New Jersey—Sean Burke, Toronto Marlboros; 25. Vancouver—Troy Gamble, Medicine Hat; 26. Hartford—Kay Whitmore, Peterborough; 27. Calgary—Joe Nieuwendyk, Cornell; 28. New York R.—Mike Richter, Northwood Prep; 29. Detroit—Jeff Sharples, Kelowna; 30. Los Angeles—Par Edlund, Sweden; 31. Boston—Alain Cote, Quebec Remparts; 32. New Jersey—Eric Weinrich, North Yarmouth; 33. Montreal—Todd Richard, Armstrong H.S.; 34. New York I.—Brad Lauer, Regina; 35. Buffalo—Benoit Hogue, St. Jean; 36. Quebec—Jason Lafreniere, Hamilton; 37. St. Louis—Herb Raglan, Kingston; 38. Calgary—Jeff Wenaas, Medicine Hat; 39. Winnipeg—Roger Ohman, Sweden; 40. Washington—John Druce, Peterborough; 41. Edmonton—Todd Carnelly, Kamloops; 42. Philadelphia—Bruce Rendall, Chatham.

1986

First Round

1. Detroit—Joe Murphy, Michigan State; 2. Los Angeles—Jimmy Carson, Verdun; 3. New Jersey—Neil Brady, Medicine Hat; 4. Pittsburgh—Zarley Zalapski, Team Canada; 5. Buffalo—Shawn Anderson, Team Canada; 6. Toronto—Vincent Damphousse, Laval; 7. Vancouver—Dan Woodley, Portland; 8. Winnipeg—Pat Elynuik, Prince Albert; 9. New York R.—Brian Leetch, Avon Old Farms H.S.; 10. St. Louis—Jocelyn Lemieux, Laval; 11. Hartford—Scott Young, Boston U.; 12. Minnesota—Warren Babe, Lethbridge; 13. Boston—Craig Janney, Boston College; 14. Chicago—Everett Sanipass, Verdun; 15. Montreal—Mark Pederson, Medicine Hat; 16. Calgary—George Pelawa, Bemidji H.S.; 17. New York I.—Tom Fitzgerald, Austin Prep; 18. Quebec—Tom McRae, Sudbury; 19. Washington—Jeff Greenlaw, Team Canada; 20. Philadelphia—Kerry Huffman, Guelph; 21. Edmonton—Kim Issel, Prince Albert.

Second Round

22. Detroit—Adam Graves, Windsor; 23. Philadelphia—Jukka Seppo, Finland; 24. New Jersey—Todd Copeland, Belmont Hill H.S.; 25. Pittsburgh—Dave Capuano, Mt. St. Charles H.S.; 26. Buffalo—Greg Brown, St. Mark's; 27. Montreal—Benoit Brunet, Hull; 28. Philadelphia—Kent Hawley, Ottawa; 29. Winnipeg—Teppo Numminen, Tappara (Finland); 30. Minnesota—Neil Wilkinson, Selkirk; 31. St. Louis—Mike Posma, Buffalo Jrs.; 32. Hartford—Marc LaForge, Kingston; 33. Minnesota—Dean Kolstad, Prince Albert; 34. Boston—Pekka Tirkkonen, Sapko (Finland); 35. Chicago—Mark Kurzawski, Windsor; 36. Toronto—Darryl Shannon, Windsor; 37. Calgary—Brian Glynn, Saskatoon; 38. New York I.—Dennis Vaske, Armstrong H.S.; 39. Quebec—Jean M. Routhier, Hull; 40. Washington—Steve Seftel, Kingston; 41. Quebec—Stephane Guerard, Shawinigan; 42. Edmonton—Jamie Nichols, Portland.

1987

First Round

1. Buffalo—Pierre Turgeon, Granby; 2. New Jersey—Brendan Shanahan, London; 3. Boston—Glen Wesley, Portland; 4. Los Angeles—Wayne McBean, Medicine Hat; 5. Pittsburgh—Chris Joseph, Seattle; 6. Minnesota—David Archibald, Portland; 7. Toronto—Luke Richardson, Peterborough; 8. Chicago—Jimmy Waite, Chicoutimi; 9. Quebec—Bryan Fogarty, Kingston; 10. New York R.—Jayson More, New Westminster; 11. Detroit—Yves Racine, Longueuil; 12. St. Louis—Keith Osborne, North Bay; 13. New York I.—Dean Chynoweth, Medicine Hat; 14. Boston—Stephane Quintal, Granby; 15. Quebec—Joe Sakic, Swift Current; 16. Winnipeg—Bryan Marchment, Belleville; 17. Montreal—Andrew Cassels, Ottawa; 18. Hartford—Jody Hull, Peterborough; 19. Calgary—Bryan Deasley, U. of Michigan; 20. Philadelphia—Darren Rumble, Kitchener; 21. Edmonton—Peter Soberlak, Swift Current.

Second Round

22. Buffalo—Brad Miller, Regina; 23. New Jersey—Rickard Persson, Ostersund; 24. Vancouver—Rob Murphy, Laval; 25. Calgary—Stephane Matteau, Hull; 26. Pittsburgh—Richard Tabaracci, Cornwall; 27. Los Angeles—Mark Fitzpatrick, Medicine Hat; 28. Toronto—Daniel Marois, Chicoutimi; 29. Chicago—Ryan McGill, Swift Current; 30. Philadelphia—Jeff Harding, St. Michael's; 31. New York R.—Daniel Lacroix, Granby; 32. Detroit—Gordon Kruppke, Prince Albert; 33. Montreal—John Leclair, Bellows Academy; 34. New York I.—Jeff Hackett, Oshawa; 35. Minnesota—Scott McCrady, Medicine Hat; 36. Washington—Jeff Ballantyne, Ottawa; 37. Winnipeg—Patrik Eriksson, Brynas; 38. Montreal—Eric Desjardins, Granby; 39. Hartford—Adam Burt, North Bay; 40. Calgary—Kevin Grant, Kitchener; 41. Detroit—Bob Wilkie, Swift Current; 42. Edmonton—Brad Werenka, Northern Michigan.

1988

First Round

1. Minnesota—Mike Modano, Prince Albert; 2. Vancouver—Trevor Linden, Medicine Hat; 3. Quebec—Curtis Leschyshyn, Saskatoon; 4. Pittsburgh—Darrin Shannon, Windsor; 5. Quebec—Daniel Dore, Drummondville; 6. Toronto—Scott Pearson, Kingston; 7. Los Angeles—Martin Gelinas, Hull; 8. Chicago—Jeremy Roenick, Thayer Academy; 9. St. Louis—Rod Brind'Amour, Notre Dame; 10. Winnipeg—Teemu Selanne, Jokerit (Finland); 11. Hartford—Chris Govedaris, Toronto Marlboros; 12. New Jersey—Corey Foster, Peterborough; 13. Buffalo—Joel Savage, Victoria; 14. Philadelphia—Claude Boivin, Drummondville; 15. Washington—Reginald Savage, Victoriaville; 16. New York I.—Kevin Cheveldayoff, Brandon; 17. Detroit—Kory Kocur, Saskatoon; 18. Boston—Robert Cimetta, Toronto Marlboros; 19. Edmonton—Francois Leroux, St. Jean; 20. Montreal—Eric Charron, Trois-Rivieres; 21. Calgary—Jason Muzzatti, Michigan State.

Second Round

22. New York R.—Troy Mallette, Sault; 23. New Jersey—Jeff Christian, London; 24. Quebec—Stephane Fiset, Victoriaville; 25. Pittsburgh—Mark Major, North Bay; 26. New York R.—Murray Duval, Spokane; 27. Toronto—Tie Domi, Peterborough; 28. Los Angeles—Paul Holden, London; 29. New York I.—Wayne Doucet, Hamilton; 30. St. Louis—Adrien Plavsic, U. of New Hampshire; 31. Winnipeg—Russ Romaniuk, St. Boniface; 32. Hartford—Barry Richter, Culver Academy; 33. Vancouver—Leif Rohlin, VIK (Sweden); 34. Montreal—Martin St. Amour, Verdun; 35. Philadelphia—Pat Murray, Michigan State; 36. Washington—Tim Taylor, London; 37. New York I.—Sean LeBrun, New Westminster; 38. Detroit—Serge Anglehart, Drummondville; 39. Edmonton—Petro Koivunen, K-Espoo (Finland); 40. Minnesota—Link Gaetz, Spokane; 41. Washington—Wade Bartley, Dauphin; 42. Calgary—Todd Harkins, Miami of Ohio.

1989

First Round

1. Quebec—Mats Sundin, Nacka (Sweden); 2. New York I.—Dave Chyzowski, Kamloops; 3. Toronto—Scott Thornton, Belleville; 4. Winnipeg—Stu Barnes, Tri-Cities; 5. New Jersey—Bill Guerin, Springfield; 6. Chicago—Adam Bennett, Sudbury; 7. Minnesota—Doug Zmolek, John Marshall; 8. Vancouver—Jason Herter, U. of North Dakota; 9. St. Louis—Jason Marshall, Vernon; 10. Hartford—Bobby Holik, Jihlava (Czech.); 11. Detroit—Mike Sillinger, Regina; 12. Toronto—Rob Pearson, Belleville; 13. Montreal—Lindsay Vallis, Seattle; 14. Buffalo—Kevin Haller, Regina; 15. Edmonton—Jason Soules, Niagara Falls; 16. Pittsburgh—Jamie Heward, Regina; 17. Boston—Shayne Stevenson, Kitchener; 18. New Jersey—Jason Miller, Medicine Hat; 19. Washington—Olaf Kolzig, Tri-Cities; 20. New York R.—Steven Rice, Kitchener; 21. Toronto—Steve Bancroft, Belleville.

Second Round

22. Quebec—Adam Foote, Sault St. Marie; 23. New York I.—Travis Green, Spokane; 24. Calgary—Kent Manderville, Notre Dame; 25. Winnipeg—Dan Ratushny, Cornell; 26. New Jersey—Jarrod Skalde, Oshawa; 27. Chicago—Michael Speer, Guelph; 28. Minnesota—Mike Craig, Oshawa; 29. Vancouver—Robert Woodward, Deerfield; 30. Montreal—Patrice Brisebois, Laval; 31. St. Louis—Rick Corriveau, London; 32. Detroit—Bob Boughner, Sault; 33. Philadelphia—Greg Johnson, Thunder Bay; 34. Philadelphia—Patrik Juhlin, Sweden; 35. Washington—Byron Dafoe, Portland; 36. Edmonton—Richard Borgo, Kitchener; 37. Pittsburgh—Paul Laus, Niagara Falls; 38. Boston—Mike Parson, Guelph; 39. Los Angeles—Brent Thompson, Medicine Hat; 40. New York R.—Jason Prosofsky, Medicine Hat; 41. Montreal—Steve Larouche, Trois-Rivieres; 42. Calgary—Ted Drury, Fairfield Prep.

1990

First Round

1. Quebec—Owen Nolan, Cornwall; 2. Vancouver—Petr Nedved, Seattle; 3. Detroit—Keith Primeau, Niagara Falls; 4. Philadelphia—Mike Ricci, Peterborough; 5. Pittsburgh—Jaromir Jagr, Kladno (Cezch.); 6. New York I.—Scott Scissons, Saskatoon; 7. Los Angeles—Darryl Sydor, Kamloops; 8. Minnesota—Derian Hatcher, North Bay; 9. Washington—John Slaney, Cornwall; 10. Toronto—Drake Berehowsky, Kingston; 11. Calgary—Trevor Kidd, Brandon; 12. Montreal—Turner Stevenson, Seattle; 13. New York R.—Michael Stewart, Michigan State; 14. Buffalo—Brad May, Niagara Falls; 15. Hartford—Mark Greig, Lethbridge; 16. Chicago—Karl Dykhuis, Hull; 17. Edmonton—Scott Allison, Prince Albert; 18. Vancouver—Shawn Antoski, North Bay; 19. Winnipeg—Keith Tkaczuk, Malden Catholic; 20. New Jersey—Martin Brodeur, St. Hyacinthe; 21. Boston—Bryan Smolinski, Michigan State.

Second Round

22. Quebec—Ryan Hughes, Cornell; 23. Vancouver—Jiri Slegr, Litvinov (Czech.); 24. New Jersey—David Harlock, U. of Michigan; 25. Philadelphia—Chris Simon, Ottawa; 26. Calgary—Nicolas Perreault, Hawkesbury; 27. New York I.—Chris Taylor, London; 28. Los Angeles—Brandy Semchuk, Canadian Olympic; 29. New Jersey—Chris Gotziaman, Roseau; 30. Washington—Rod Pasma, Cornwall; 31. Toronto—Felix Potvin, Chicoutimi; 32. Calgary—Vesa Viitakoski, Saipa; 33. St. Louis—Craig Johnson, Hill-Murray H.S.; 34. New York R.—Doug Weight, Lake Superior; 35. Winnipeg—Mike Muller, Wayzata; 36. Hartford—Geoff Sanderson, Swift Current; 37. Chicago—Ivan Droppa, L. Mikulas (Czech.); 38. Edmonton—Alexandre Legault, Boston U.; 39. Montreal—Ryan Kuwabara, Ottawa; 40. Philadelphia—Mikael Renberg, Pitea (Sweden); 41. Calgary—Etienne Belzile, Cornell; 42. Philadelphia—Terran Sandwith, Tri-Cities.

1991

First Round

1. Quebec—Eric Lindros, Oshawa; 2. San Jose—Pat Falloon, Spokane; 3. New Jersey—

Scott Niedermayer, Kamloops; 4. New York I.—Scott Lachance, Boston U.; 5. Winnipeg—Aaron Ward, U. of Michigan; 6. Philadelphia—Peter Forsberg, Modo; 7. Vancouver—Alex Stojanov, Hamilton; 8. Minnesota—Richard Matvichuk, Saskatoon; 9. Hartford—Patrick Poulin, St. Hyacinthe; 10. Detroit—Martin Lapointe, Laval; 11. New Jersey—Brian Rolston, Detroit; 12. Edmonton—Tyler Wright, Swift Current; 13. Buffalo—Phillippe Boucher, Granby; 14. Washington—Pat Peake, Detroit; 15. New York R.—Alexei Kovalev, Dynamo Moscow; 16. Pittsburgh—Markus Naslund, Modo; 17. Montreal—Brent Bilodeau, Seattle; 18. Boston—Glen Murray, Sudbury; 19. Calgary—Niklas Sundblad, AIK Sweden; 20. Edmonton—Martin Rucinsky, Litvinov (Czech.); 21. Washington—Trevor Halverson, North Bay; 22. Chicago—Dean McAmmond, Prince Albert.

Second Round

23. San Jose—Ray Whitney, Spokane; 24. Quebec—Rene Corbet, Drummondville; 25. Washington—Eric Lavigne, Hull; 26. New York I.—Zigmund Palffy, Nitra (Czech.); 27. St. Louis—Steve Staios, Niagara Falls; 28. Montreal—Jim Campbell, Northwood Prep; 29. Vancouver—Jassen Cullimore, Peterborough; 30. San Jose—Sandis Ozolnich, Dyanamo Riga; 31. Hartford—Martin Hamrlik, TJ Zlin (Czech.); 32. Detroit—Jamie Pushor, Lethbridge; 33. New Jersey—Donevan Hextall, Prince Albert; 34. Edmonton—Andrew Verner, Peterborough; 35. Buffalo—Jason Dawe, Peterborough; 36. Washington—Jeff Nelson, Prince Albert; 37. New York R.—Darcy Werenka, Lethbridge; 38. Pittsburgh—Rusty Fitzgerald, Duluth East H.S.; 39. Chicago—Michael Pomichter, Springfield; 40. Boston—Josef Stumpel, Nitra (Czech.); 41. Calgary—Francois Groleau, Shawinigan; 42. Los Angeles—Guy Leveque, Cornwall; 43. Montreal—Craig Darby, Albany Academy; 44. Chicago—Jamie Matthews, Sudbury.

1992

First Round

1. Tampa Bay—Roman Hamrlik, ZLIN; 2. Alexei Yashin, Ottawa, Dynamo Moscow; 3.

San Jose—Mike Rathje, Medicine Hat; 4. Quebec—Todd Warriner, Windsor; 5. New York I.—Darius Kasparaitis, Dynamo Moscow; 6. Calgary—Cory Stillman, Windsor; 7. Philadelphia—Ryan Sittler, Nichols; 8. Toronto—Brandon Covery; 9. Hartford—Robert Petrovicky, Dukla Trencin; 10. San Jose—Andrei Nazarov, Dynamo Moscow; 11. Buffalo—David Cooper, Medicine Hat; 12. Chicago—Sergei Krivokrasov, CSKA; 13. Edmonton—Joe Hulbig, St. Sebastian's; 14. Washington—Sergei Gonchar, Chelybinsk; 15. Philadelphia—Jason Bowen, Tri-City; 16. Boston—Dmitri Kvartalnov, San Diego; 17. Winnipeg—Sergei Bautin, Dynamo Moscow; 18. New Jersey—Jason Smith, Regina; 19. Pittsburgh—Martin Straka, Plzen; 20. Montreal—David Wilkie, Kamloops; 21. Vancouver—Libor Polasek, Vitkovice; 22. Detroit—Curtis Bowen, Ottawa; 23. Toronto—Grant Marshall, Ottawa; 24. New York R.—Peter Ferraro, Waterloo Jr. A.

Second Round

25. Ottawa—Chad Penney, North Bay; 26. Tampa Bay—Drew Bannister, Sault Ste. Marie; 27. Winnipeg—Boris Mironev, CSKA; 28. Quebec—Paul Brousseau, Hull; 29. Quebec—Tuomas Gronman, Tacoma; 30. Calgary—Chris O'Sullivan, Catholic Memorial; 31. Philadelphia—Denis Metlyuk, Lada Togliatti; 32. Washington—Jim Carey, Catholic Memorial; 33. Montreal—Valeri Buri, Spokane; 34. Minnesota—Jarkko Varvio, HPK; 35. Buffalo—Josef Cierny, Zvolen; 36. Chicago—Jeff Shantz, Regina; 37. Edmonton—Martin Reichel, Freiburg; 38. St. Louis—Igor Korolev, Dynamo Moscow; 39. Los Angeles—Justin Hocking, Spokane; 40. Vancouver—Mike Peca, Ottawa; 41. Chicago—Sergei Klimovich, Dynamo Moscow; 42. New Jersey, Sergei Brylin, CSKA; 43. Pittsburgh—Marc Hussey, Moose Jaw; 44. Montreal—Keli Corpse, Kingston; 45. Vancouver—Mike Fountain, Oshawa; 46. Detroit—Darren McCarty, Belleville; 47. Hartford—Andrei Nikolishin, Dynamo Moscow; 48. New York R.—Mattias Norstrom, AIK.

WHA PROPERTIES, LTD.

ROBERT MARVIN HULL $1,000,000.00

One Million

WORLD HOCKEY
ASSOCIATION

The World Hockey Association was an enigma. Loved by some but hated by others, the WHA led a turbulent seven years (1972–79) of existence that rocked hockey institutions.

Many would say the WHA was nothing more than a carpet-bagging league, constantly on the prowl searching for gullible owners in new cities populated by naive fans.

But others would argue long into the night, extolling the merits of the league, not the least of which was bargaining power for players and the emergence of major-league hockey in areas that would have been forever overlooked by the National Hockey League.

At one time or another, the league embraced 32 teams in 24 cities, 20 of which were eventually abandoned.

Reliable estimates say the owners of those 32 teams lost $50 million while the 803 players who performed in the WHA earned $120 million. The agents—virtually unheard of until the new league came along—collected 10 percent of their bounty.

《 *Bobby Hull and wife Joanne said ''Thanks a million'' after Hull jumped to the WHA in 1972.*

Almost every player in professional hockey benefited in some way from the WHA. Owners of NHL teams scrambled to keep their organizations intact, even if it meant doubling or tripling the salaries of minor leaguers.

Born of enterprising Californians, buoyed by the creation of the American Basketball Association, their original brainchild, the WHA was founded by Gary Davidson and Dennis Murphy.

Not steeped in hockey, both would be gone before the league would reach its third anniversary.

Two players, each a legend in his time, made the WHA go. Bobby Hull, a personable, 33-year-old superstar with the Chicago Black Hawks, left the NHL and its followers aghast when he signed a $2.75-million contract to coach and play for the Winnipeg Jets.

Possessed of a pioneer spirit and the notion that he was improving the lot of all players, Hull joined the league on June 27, 1972. Enticing him, too, was $1 million up front.

Other established players followed him to the new league. Among them were Gerry Cheevers, Dave Keon, Johnny McKenzie, Frank Mahovlich and J.C. Tremblay.

But no signing had the impact Gordie Howe's did. In a historic event, the 46-year-old NHL immortal and his teenage sons, Mark and Marty, joined the Houston Aeros in June 1973.

It was more than a publicity stunt. Not only did he play 419 games, collecting 508 points, but he was a two-time All-Star on right wing and won MVP honors once.

Fittingly, the league championship trophy was sponsored by a finance company, Avco.

The Avco Cup was won by Winnipeg on three occasions as the Jets blended Europeans and Canadians into a championship team. Perhaps the finest line in professional hockey at the time was the combination of Hull and two young Swedes, Ulf Nilsson and Anders Hedberg.

Houston, led by the Howes, won the Avco Cup twice while the Quebec Nordiques and New England Whalers were champions once.

Although the league died in June 1979, it left a legacy. Four of its original teams—the Edmonton Oilers, Hartford (New England) Whalers, Quebec Nordiques and Winnipeg Jets—were admitted to the NHL. They had proven themselves.

1972–73

The WHA thought big. Twelve teams drafted 1,081 persons, not all of them players. One would-be general manager, Scotty Munro of the Calgary Broncos, picked Soviet Premier Alexei Kosygin.

Unable to post $100,000 performance bonds, two franchises—Miami and Calgary—pulled out before the season began. Cleveland and Chicago took their places.

The first player signed was left winger Steve Sutherland, swiped off the Port Huron Wings International League roster by the Los Angeles Sharks.

《 Derek Sanderson played only eight games in the WHA (with the Philadelphia Blazers) before bolting back to Boston and the NHL in 1972–73.

By August, most than 300 players were under contract. Among them was a center, Derek Sanderson, who signed a 10-year pact with the Philadelphia Blazers for a reported $2.325 million. He played only eight games and was bought out for $1 million.

An Alberta right winger, Ron Anderson, scored the WHA's first goal on October 11 in Ottawa. The Oilers won, 7–4.

The New England Whalers did the best job of recruiting and reaped their just reward—winning the first WHA championship.

Based in Boston, where they divided their time between the Arena and the Garden, the Whalers were led by a stout defense manned by such stalwarts as Rick Ley and Brad Selwood, plucked off the roster of the Toronto Maple Leafs; Jim Dorey, from the New York Rangers, and Ted Green, the former Bruin who would show he could bounce back from a serious head injury. Their coach was Jack Kelley, a respected tactician from Boston University.

New England (46–30–2) won the Eastern Division while the Western was won by Winnipeg (43–31–4). They met in a best-of-seven league final, with the Whalers winning in five games.

Center Andre Lacroix of Philadelphia won the first scoring championship with 50 goals and 74 assists.

1972–73

FINAL STANDINGS

Eastern Division

	W	L	T	PTS	GF	GA
New England	46	30	2	94	318	263
Cleveland	43	32	3	89	287	239
Philadelphia	38	40	0	76	288	305
Ottawa	35	39	4	74	279	301
Quebec	33	40	5	71	276	313
New York	33	43	2	68	303	334

Western Division

	W	L	T	PTS	GF	GA
Winnipeg	43	31	4	90	285	249
Houston	39	35	4	82	284	269
Los Angeles	37	35	6	80	259	250
Alberta	38	37	3	79	269	256
Minnesota	38	37	3	79	250	269
Chicago	26	50	2	54	245	295

The Howe family—father Gordie and sons Marty and Mark—take the ice for their first WHA game together on September 25, 1973.

LEADING SCORERS	G	A	PTS
Lacroix, Philadelphia	50	74	124
Ward, New York	51	67	118
Lawson, Philadelphia	61	45	106
Webster, New England	53	50	103
Hull, Winnipeg	51	52	103
Beaudin, Winnipeg	38	65	103
Bordeleau, Winnipeg	47	54	101
Caffery, New England	39	61	100
Labossiere, Houston	36	60	93
Carleton, Ottawa	42	49	91

1973–74

The Houston Aeros were older than most teams. Many of their players had been stars in the old Western Hockey League.

However, their coach, Bill Dineen, had his eye on two youngsters. Mark and Marty Howe were showing signs of becoming excellent hockey players with a junior team, the Toronto Marlies.

Bill Dineen knew he couldn't sign any Canadian youngsters before their 19th birthday. But the Howe boys were Americans.

Not one to take advantage of his friend, Dineen thought he should call Gordie to seek his permission. Howe, idle and disgruntled in his self-described role as vice-president in charge of paper clips for the Detroit Red Wings, asked Dineen if he would like to make it a threesome—Gordie to return to active play, joined by his sons.

The caper was pulled off and the Aeros finished in first place (48–25–5) in the Western Division, then roared through the playoffs, sweeping the Chicago Cougars in four straight games for the championship.

It was a season in which the Ottawa Nationals became the Toronto Toros, Philadelphia

moved to Vancouver and the New York Raiders became the Golden Blades and then the Jersey Knights when bill collectors chased them out of New York to Cherry Hill, New Jersey, a suburb of Philadelphia.

Mike (Shakey) Walton of the Minnesota Fighting Saints won the league scoring championship with 57 goals and 60 assists. But the league's Most Valuable Player was none other than Gordie Howe, a 47-year-old phenomenon.

1973–74

FINAL STANDINGS

Eastern Division

	W	L	T	PTS	GF	GA
New England	43	31	4	90	291	260
Toronto	41	33	4	86	304	272
Cleveland	37	32	9	83	266	264
Chicago	38	35	5	81	271	273
Quebec	38	36	4	80	306	280
New Jersey	32	42	4	68	268	313

Western Division

	W	L	T	PTS	GF	GA
Houston	48	25	5	101	318	219
Minnesota	44	32	2	90	332	275
Edmonton	38	37	3	79	268	269
Winnipeg	34	39	5	73	264	296
Vancouver	27	50	1	55	278	345
Los Angeles	25	53	0	50	239	339

LEADING SCORERS

	G	A	PTS
Walton, Minnesota	57	60	117
Lacroix, New Jersey	31	80	111
G. Howe, Houston	31	69	100
Hull, Winnipeg	53	42	95
Connelly, Minnesota	42	53	95
Carleton, Toronto	37	55	92
Lawson, Vancouver	50	38	88
Campbell, Vancouver	27	61	88
Bernier, Quebec	37	49	86
Lund, Houston	33	53	86

1974–75

Interest in the WHA was at an all-time high. An All-Star team represented Canada in an eight-game series with the Soviet National team. Although it was able to win only one game, the WHA did receive considerable publicity for itself and its players.

The Indianapolis Racers and Phoenix Roadrunners were accepted as expansion franchises. The New Jersey Knights finally found a home, moving to San Diego, where they became the Mariners, and the New England Whalers, lured by a new convention center, left Boston for Hartford, Conn.

The Los Angeles Sharks were on the move, too. They headed for Detroit and became the Michigan Stags, then the Baltimore Blades. Slowly, they were going down the tubes.

The 14-team league was divided into three divisions—the Canadian, Western and Eastern. The head office was moved from Newport Beach, Cal., to Toronto. And the league bank was located in Winnipeg, where Ben Hatskin sat as chairman of the Board.

League attendance jumped from 2.7 million to 4.1 with the Howes and Houston leading the way.

Bobby Hull was creating a stir, too, frolicking beside his new Swedish linemates, Anders Hedberg and Ulf Nilsson, in Winnipeg.

Hull scored 77 goals in 78 games. But the scoring championship went to Andre Lacroix of San Diego with 41 goals and 106 assists on a line with Wayne Rivers and Rick Sentes. Rivers had 54 goals.

Sparked by Ron Grahame's three shutouts and Mark Howe's 22 points, Houston breezed through the playoffs, suffering only one loss. The Quebec Nordiques were no match for the Aeros in the final as Houston won in four straight games.

1974–75

FINAL STANDINGS

Canadian Division

	W	L	T	PTS	GF	GA
Quebec	46	32	0	92	331	299
Toronto	43	33	2	88	349	304
Winnipeg	38	35	5	81	322	293
Vancouver	37	39	2	76	256	270
Edmonton	36	38	4	76	279	279

Eastern Division

	W	L	T	PTS	GF	GA
New England	43	30	5	91	274	279
Cleveland	35	40	3	73	236	258
Chicago	30	47	1	61	261	312
Indianapolis	18	57	3	39	216	338

Western Division

	W	L	T	PTS	GF	GA
Houston	53	25	0	106	369	247
San Diego	43	31	4	90	326	268
Minnesota	42	33	3	87	308	279
Phoenix	39	31	8	86	300	265
Baltimore	21	53	4	46	205	341

LEADING SCORERS	G	A	PTS
Lacroix, San Diego	41	106	147
Hull, Winnipeg	77	65	142
Bernier, Quebec	54	68	122
Nilsson, Winnipeg	26	94	120
Lund, Houston	33	75	108
Rivers, San Diego	54	53	107
Hedberg, Winnipeg	53	47	100
G. Howe, Houston	34	65	99
Dillon, Toronto	29	66	95
Walton, Minnesota	48	45	93

1975–76

The Winnipeg Jets were a unique hockey club. They were owned by no one. More than 5,000 citizens had put up amounts ranging from $25 to $25,000 to keep the team viable. Shares were non-redeemable.

Some donors actually put their shares in the name of their pets. But the Jets weren't going to the dogs.

Their lineup included nine Europeans—two Finns and seven Swedes. They trained in Finland and Sweden and even stopped off in Prague, Czechoslovakia, for two exhibition games against the National team.

Returning the favor, the Czechs flew the Jets home to Canada free of charge.

Then, at Christmas, they traveled to Moscow for the Izvestia Cup. They became a better hockey club, perfecting a whirling style of play that frustrated their opponents.

Fourteen teams started the season but only 12 finished. The Minnesota Fighting Saints and Denver Spurs went by the wayside. The Spurs, a new entry owned by Ivan Mullenix of St. Louis, lasted only 41 games. The Vancouver Blazers moved to Calgary, where they became the Cowboys. The Cincinnati Stingers joined up and the Chicago Cougars dropped out.

The Indianapolis Racers (35–39–6), Houston Aeros (53–27–0) and Winnipeg (52–27–2) won divisional titles, and the Jets emerged as league champions. They swept the defending champions from Houston in the Avco Cup final.

The Quebec Nordiques gained some consolation when left winger Marc Tardif won the

« *San Diego's Andre Lacroix led the WHA with 147 points in 1974–75.*

scoring championship with 71 goals and 77 assists for 148 points, a league record.

1975–76

FINAL STANDINGS

Canadian Division

	W	L	T	PTS	GF	GA
Winnipeg	52	27	2	106	345	254
Quebec	50	27	4	104	371	316
Calgary	41	35	4	86	307	282
Edmonton	27	49	5	59	268	345
Toronto	24	52	5	53	335	398

Eastern Division

	W	L	T	PTS	GF	GA
Indianapolis	35	39	6	76	245	247
Cleveland	35	40	5	75	273	279
New England	33	40	7	73	255	290
Cincinnati	35	44	1	71	285	340

Western Division

	W	L	T	PTS	GF	GA
Houston	53	27	0	106	341	263
Phoenix	39	35	6	84	302	287
San Diego	36	38	6	78	303	290
Minnesota	30	25	4	64	211	212
Ottawa	14	26	1	29	134	172

LEADING SCORERS	G	A	PTS
Tardif, Quebec	71	77	148
Hull, Winnipeg	53	70	123
Cloutier, Quebec	60	54	114
Nilsson, Winnipeg	38	76	114
Ftorek, Phoenix	41	72	113
Bordeleau, Quebec	37	72	109
Hedberg, Winnipeg	50	55	105
Houle, Quebec	51	52	103
Bernier, Quebec	34	68	102
G. Howe, Houston	32	70	102

1976–77

The WHA, upon completing its fourth season, had survived longer than anyone had thought. Its teams had gradually grown stronger, and challenges were sought.

Even the warlords of the NHL had begun to mellow. Passively, they agreed to a 21-game exhibition series in September. The benefits would be twofold. The games would not only serve as preseason conditioners, but the competition between leagues would serve as a built-in rivalry.

When the series was over, the WHA teams had won 13 games, tied two others and lost six.

"Game in and game out, our teams can play with their teams," said Howard Baldwin, the WHA president. "We proved it indisputably."

Political points, to be sure.

Internally, the new league continued to lose teams and gain cities. A second edition of the Minnesota Fighting Saints lasted only 42

Quebec's Real Cloutier captured the WHA's 1976–77 scoring title.

games. The Toronto Toros moved to Birmingham, Ala., and became the Bulls.

But the big newsmakers were the Quebec Nordiques, Robbie Ftorek, the Howes and Anders Hedberg, the Swedish Express of the Winnipeg Jets.

Suffering from a case of "Bolinitis"—a malady named after the difficult Houston Aero owner, George Bolin—the Howes left Texas for New England. Ftorek, a small but dynamic center with the lowly Phoenix Roadrunners, became the first American-born athlete to win MVP honors in major professional hockey.

Hedberg, a 25-year-old right winger, broke one of hockey's most prestigious records, scoring 51 goals in 49 games, breaking the "50 in 50" mark previously set in the NHL by Maurice (The Rocket) Richard.

« *Mike Walton soared, but the Minnesota Fighting Saints fell by the wayside in 1975–76.*

The Nordiques won their first Avco Cup by beating Winnipeg in a final series that went the full seven games. Veteran center Serge Bernier was a terror in the playoffs, collecting 14 goals and 22 assists in 17 games. The scoring champion was his teammate, Real (Buddy) Cloutier, with 66 goals, 75 assists for 141 points.

1976–77

FINAL STANDINGS

Eastern Division	W	L	T	PTS	GF	GA
Quebec	47	31	3	97	353	295
Cincinnati	39	37	5	83	354	303
Indianapolis	36	37	8	80	276	305
New England	35	40	6	76	275	290
Birmingham	31	46	4	66	289	309
Minnesota	19	18	5	43	136	129

Western Division	W	L	T	PTS	GF	GA
Houston	50	24	6	106	320	241
Winnipeg	46	32	2	94	366	291
San Diego	40	37	4	84	284	283
Edmonton	34	43	4	72	243	304
Calgary	31	43	7	69	252	296
Phoenix	28	48	4	60	281	383

*Anders Hedberg and Ulf Nilsson enabled Winnipeg to win the
Avco Cup in 1978, then skated off to the NHL.*

LEADING SCORERS	G	A	PTS
Cloutier, Quebec	66	75	141
Hedberg, Winnipeg	70	61	131
Nilsson, Winnipeg	39	85	124
Ftorek, Phoenix	46	71	117
Lacroix, San Diego	32	82	114
Tardif, Quebec	49	60	109
Leduc, Cincinnati	52	55	107
Bordeleau, Quebec	32	75	107
Stoughton, Cincinnati	52	52	104
Napier, Birmingham	60	36	96
Sobchuk, Cincinnati	44	52	96
Bernier, Quebec	43	53	96

1977-78

Howard Baldwin was in tears as he stood in the lobby of the Auberge des Gouverneurs in Quebec City the morning after the WHA's sixth All-Star Game. His bags were packed and he was on his way home to Hartford to inspect the damage. At 4 A.M., he had received a call informing him that the roof of the Hartford Civic Center had collapsed under the weight of snow.

Baldwin, the Whalers' trustee and president of the WHA, could barely speak. The hopes and dreams of his franchise hinged on the building that injected new life into downtown Hartford. However, nearby Springfield, in Massachusetts, came to the rescue by making the arena available to the Whalers.

It was the second piece of bad news the WHA had received. The other haymaker landed earlier in the boardrooms where men representing the Winnipeg Jets announced details of an offer two of their top players had received from the New York Rangers. Anders Hedberg and Ulf Nilsson would eventually go for $2.4 million.

Now, the National Hockey League was raiding the WHA.

Only eight teams surfaced for the sixth season. Ray Kroc (McDonald's hamburger king) decided he had wasted enough money

on the San Diego Mariners. The Phoenix Roadrunners lost their backers, too, and so did the Calgary Cowboys.

The survivors were lumped into one division. As a novelty, All-Star teams from the Soviet Union and Czechoslovakia played eight-game schedules in the WHA.

Scoring champ and MVP was Marc Tardif, the Quebec left winger who shattered his own record with 65 goals and 89 assists for 154 points.

The Birmingham Bulls, coached by Glen Sonmor, were the rogues of the league. Before each game a Baptist minister would read the invocation. Then the brawling would start. After the games, Sonmor would lead the fans in song at The Bar Across The Street.

The Jets, however, were the class of the league. Reeling off 50 wins in the regular season, they gathered momentum in the playoffs to eliminate Birmingham in five and New England in four to win their second Avco Cup.

1977-78

FINAL STANDINGS

	W	L	T	PTS	GF	GA
Winnipeg	50	28	2	102	381	270
New England	44	31	5	93	335	269
Houston	42	34	4	88	296	302
Quebec	40	37	3	83	349	347
Edmonton	38	39	3	79	309	307
Birmingham	36	41	3	75	287	314
Cincinnati	35	42	3	73	298	332
Indianapolis	24	51	5	53	267	353
Soviet All-Stars	3	4	1	7	27	36
Czechoslovakia	1	6	1	3	21	40

LEADING SCORERS

	G	A	PTS
Tardif, Quebec	65	89	154
Cloutier, Quebec	56	73	129
U. Nilsson, Winnipeg	37	89	126
Hedberg, Winnipeg	63	59	122
Hull, Winnipeg	46	71	117
Lacroix, Houston	36	77	113
Ftorek, Cincinnati	59	50	109
K. Nilsson, Winnipeg	42	65	107
G. Howe, New England	34	62	96
M. Howe, New England	30	61	91

1978-79

No one really believed the WHA's seventh season would be its last. Hopes had been built up before. As early as April 1973, the WHA and NHL had met to discuss a possible merger.

Gradually, the number of teams was dwindling. What had once been a 14-team league was now reduced to six. The league was running out of cities. But there was a movement afoot to incorporate a division in Europe.

The WHA was alive and kicking as evidenced by two shrewd moves. Nelson Skalbania, the flamboyant Vancouver businessman, had robbed the cradle of Canadian hockey. Acting on behalf of his team, the Indianapolis Racers, Skalbania signed Wayne Gretzky, a 17-year-old sensation, to a personal services contract.

Indianapolis fans, who had never heard of him before, showed only a casual interest in the skinny, blond kid. With only a few season tickets sold, Skalbania started looking for a buyer. He found two prospects in Winnipeg's Michael Gobuty and Edmonton's Peter Pocklington.

Boarding a plane in Indianapolis, Gretzky didn't know where it would land. Pocklington sweetened his offer. The pilot was instructed to proceed to Edmonton. Days later, the Racers folded.

The Jets had already spent a bundle, buying 12 contracts from the folding Houston Aeros.

Real (Buddy) Cloutier of Quebec won his second scoring championship with 75 goals, 54 assists for a total of 129 points.

Edmonton, led by Gretzky's 110 points, finished on top with a 48-30-2 record. But the Oilers couldn't capture their first and the last Avco Cup.

Sparked by the Houston acquisitions, most notably Terry Ruskowski, Rich Preston and Morris Lukowich, the Jets whipped Edmonton in five games in the league final.

The last Avco Cup was theirs. And still is.

1978-79

FINAL STANDINGS

	W	L	T	PTS	GF	GA
Edmonton	48	30	2	98	340	266
Quebec	41	34	5	87	288	271
Winnipeg	39	35	6	84	307	306
New England	37	34	9	83	298	287
Cincinnati	33	41	6	72	274	284
Birmingham	32	42	6	70	286	311

LEADING SCORERS

	G	A	PTS
Cloutier, Quebec	75	54	129
Ftorek, Cincinnati	39	77	116
Gretzky, Edmonton	46	64	110
M. Howe, New England	42	65	107
K. Nilsson, Winnipeg	39	68	107
Lukowich, Winnipeg	65	34	99
Tardif, Quebec	41	55	96
Lacroix, New England	32	56	88
Sullivan, Winnipeg	46	40	86
Ruskowski, Winnipeg	20	66	86

« *Wayne Gretzky made sure he'd be an Edmonton Oiler for a while when he signed a 20-year contract in 1979.*

390 THE COMPLETE ENCYCLOPEDIA OF HOCKEY

16

ANOTHER PART OF THE ICE

The world of hockey is by no means limited to the National Hockey League. It has an extensive minor-league network as well as flourishing amateur and collegiate programs in the United States and Canada. And, of course, there are the European countries that produce significant exports to the NHL.

An increasing number of players have graduated from the collegiate and Olympic ranks into the NHL. They date back to Red Berenson, the super center of the NHL's expansion West Division in the late 1960s who led all collegiate scorers when he was at Michigan in 1961–62, and Tony Esposito, an All-American goalie at Michigan Tech.

Forward Tommy Williams, who played for eight years with the Boston Bruins in the 1960s, was a member of the U.S. championship Olympic team in 1960. The 1980 gold-medal U.S. squad was the NHL springboard for such others as Ken Morrow, Mike Ramsey, Neil Broten and Dave Christian. Pat LaFontaine, Chris Chelios, Al Iafrate and Ed Olczyk are among the graduates of the 1984 U.S. Olympic

« Members of the victorious U.S. Olympic hockey team sing the national anthem at the awards ceremony in Lake Placid in 1980.

team and the 1988 contingent produced Brian Leetch, Craig Janney and Kevin Stevens.

COLLEGE HOCKEY

From somewhat modest beginnings, collegiate hockey in the United States has grown tremendously since the National Collegiate Athletic Association started its annual championship hockey tournament in 1948.

U.S. colleges recruit players from Canada as well as the U.S., and the program has become almost as extensive as the one the schools follow in tracking down talented football players. Most collegiate rosters are stacked with Canadian imports, but in recent years more and more American-born youths are playing hockey in college.

The U.S. triumph in the 1980 Olympic Games provided incentive for home-grown talent to pursue their sport. The number of those moving into the professional ranks is increasing as more youngsters recognize the value of a college education before trying pro hockey.

A list of NCAA champions and runners-up follows:

Brad Shelstad of the University of Minnesota stops Michigan Tech's George Lyle in the 1974 NCAA championship game won by Minnesota.

Division I

1948
1. Michigan
2. Dartmouth

1949
1. Boston College
2. Dartmouth

1950
1. Colorado College
2. Boston University

1951
1. Michigan
2. Brown

1952
1. Michigan
2. Colorado College

1953
1. Michigan
2. Minnesota

1954
1. Rensselaer
2. Minnesota

1955
1. Michigan
2. Colorado College

1956
1. Michigan
2. Michigan Tech

1957
1. Colorado College
2. Michigan

1958
1. Denver University
2. North Dakota

1959
1. North Dakota
2. Michigan State

1960
1. Denver University
2. Michigan Tech

1961
1. Denver University
2. St. Lawrence

1962
1. Michigan Tech
2. Clarkson

1963
1. North Dakota
2. Denver University

1964
1. Michigan
2. Denver University

1965
1. Michigan Tech
2. Boston College

1966
1. Michigan State
2. Clarkson

1967
1. Cornell
2. Boston University

1968
1. Denver University
2. North Dakota

1969
1. Denver University
2. Cornell

1970
1. Cornell
2. Clarkson

1971
1. Boston University
2. Minnesota

Action at the 1932 Winter Olympics in Lake Placid, as Germany (dark uniforms) opposes Canada. The defending champion Canadians wound up winning their fourth gold medal in a row.

1972
1. Boston University
2. Cornell

1973
1. Wisconsin
2. Denver University

1974
1. Minnesota
2. Michigan Tech

1975
1. Michigan Tech
2. Minnesota

1976
1. Minnesota
2. Michigan Tech

1977
1. Wisconsin
2. Michigan

1978
1. Boston University
2. Boston College

1979
1. Minnesota
2. North Dakota

1980
1. North Dakota
2. Northern Michigan

1981
1. Wisconsin
2. Minnesota

1982
1. North Dakota
2. Wisconsin

1983
1. Wisconsin
2. Harvard

1984
1. Bowling Green
2. Minnesota (Duluth)

1985
1. Rensselaer
2. Providence

1986
1. Michigan State
2. Harvard

1987
1. North Dakota
2. Harvard

1988
1. Lake Superior State
2. St. Lawrence

1989
1. Harvard
2. Minnesota

1990
1. Wisconsin
2. Colgate

1991
1. Northern Michigan
2. Boston University

1992
1. Lake Superior State
2. Wisconsin

OLYMPIC GAMES

When the Winter Olympics began in 1924, hockey was one of the sports on the schedule. It had been added to the Olympic program in 1920, when there was a single competition instead of separate winter and summer Games. Canada dominated at first, winning the championship in each of the first four Olympic competitions. The Canadians won two more titles following World War II before the Soviet Union started a domination which led to eight championships in the next ten Olympics through 1992. The two times the Russians missed were in 1960 and 1980, and in both cases it was the United States that pulled major upsets.

The Americans were given little chance to win in 1960, but were determined to score an upset. "We knew with a couple of breaks we could upset the odds," recalled goaltender Jack McCartan. The U.S. team had one thing

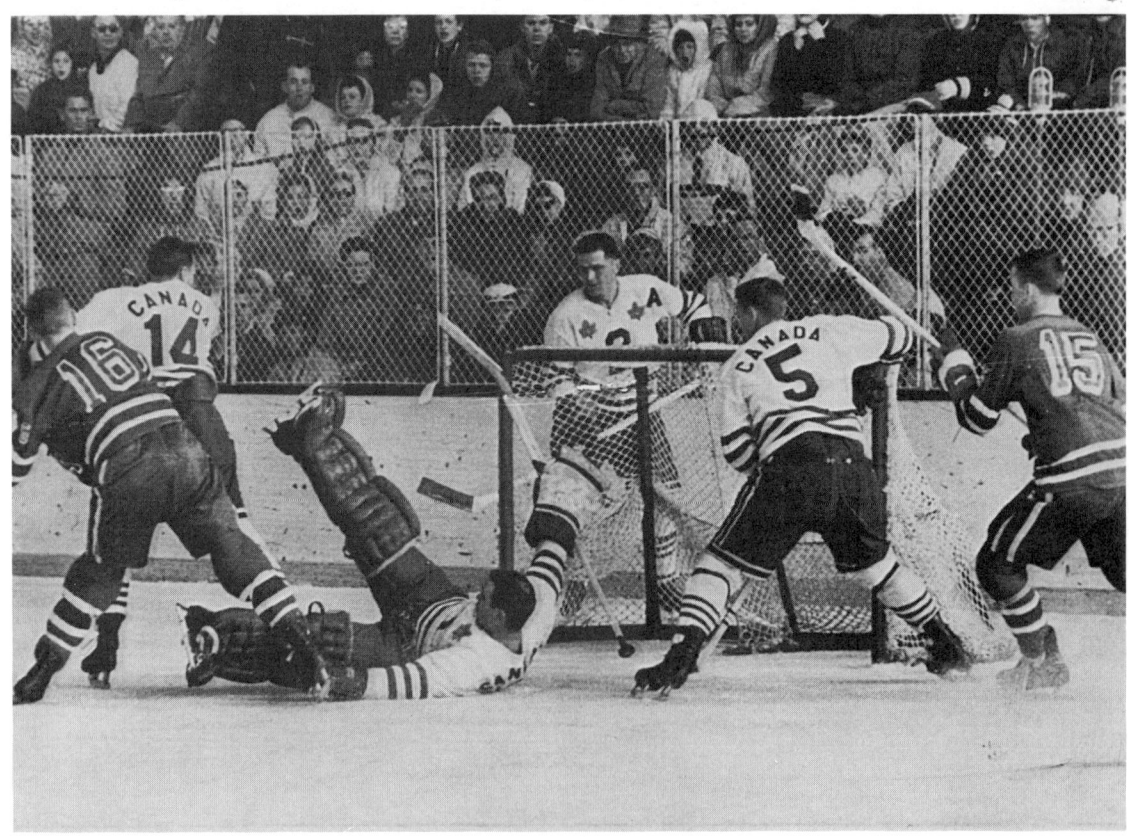

Paul Johnson (15) has just scored the winning goal for the U.S. in its 2–1 decision over Canada in the 1960 Olympic semifinals at Squaw Valley, Cal.

Rob McClanahan beats Finnish goalie Jorma Valtonen to break a tie and clinch the gold medal for the U.S. at the 1980 Winter Olympics.

going for them: the Games were held at Squaw Valley, California.

After winning four games in the preliminaries, the Americans passed a big test by edging Canada, 2–1, as McCartan made 39 saves. The U.S. squad then rallied to stun the Russians, 3–2, setting up the championship game against Czechoslovakia. Again the Americans rallied, scoring six times in the final period to win, 9–4, and take the gold.

Twenty years later, another group of young Americans game their country an even bigger thrill as they came from nowhere to skate off with the Olympic gold.

The 1980 Games were again held in the United States—at Lake Placid, New York— and once more the U.S. team was a heavy underdog. Just a few days before the Games began, the Americans lost, 11–3, to the Russians in an exhibition game. U.S. coach Herb

Brooks was hoping his team could get a silver or bronze medal.

They didn't; they came home with the gold. After tying Sweden with a last-minute goal in their opening game, the Americans raced to four straight wins to advance to the semifinals. Awaiting them there were the vaunted Soviets. Before the game, Brooks told his players, "You were born to be hockey players. You were meant to be here. This moment is yours."

And the game was theirs, too, as Mike Eruzione snapped a tie with ten minutes left and the U.S. held on for a stunning 4–3 victory. That sent the Americans into the finals against Finland in a game that would settle it all.

The U.S. squad, which averaged just 20 years of age, spotted the Finns a 2–1 lead going into the last period but then roared back for three goals. When the game ended, thou-

Czechoslovakia's Ladislav Lubina upends U.S. goalic Ray LeBlanc in the 1992 Olympic semifinals at Meribel, France. The Czechs won the game, 6–1, and the bronze medal.

players (Pat LaFontaine, David A. Jensen and Ed Olczyk) and they had some big moments, including a 3–3 tie with Norway and a 7–3 rout of Austria. But the team wound up seventh in the final standings.

The Soviet Union won all seven of its games to take the gold medal ahead of Czechoslovakia, Sweden and Canada.

In 1988, the Americans unleased a high-scoring team that scored goals by the half-dozen, but they also yielded them by the half-dozen. Nobody had beaten the Soviet Union since the U.S. did it in 1980 and the Americans came within a ricocheted slapshot of tying the Russians after being behind by four goals. The Soviet Union won the game, 7–5, and went on to capture the title.

The Soviets no longer carried CCCP on their jerseys at the 1992 Olympics. Reflecting the new independence of nations in the Soviet sphere, they were called the Unified Team in the hockey competition at Meribel, France. But nothing changed in the superior quality of their game as the Unified Team took the gold again, defeating Canada, 3–1, in the final.

Both the silver-winning Canada and the United States made bold challenges, with the Canadians featuring Eric Lindros, the celebrated NHL holdout, high-scoring Joe Juneau and goalie Sean Burke.

The U.S. squad, with minor leaguer Ray LeBlanc starring in goal, raised hopes of another "Miracle on Ice" when it went unbeaten going into the final round. But losses to the Unified Team (5–2) and bronze-winning Czechoslovakia (6–1) resulted in a fourth-place finish and no medal for the U.S.

The list of Olympic medal winners follows:

sands of fans started singing "God Bless America" and waving American flags. The Soviet streak of four consecutive Olympic gold medals had been stopped. The U.S. had its gold and the Russians had to settle for silver.

There would be no repeat performance in the 1984 Olympics at Sarajevo, Yugoslavia. The U.S. featured what was described as a "Diaper Line" consisting of three high-school

1920
1. Canada
2. USA
3. Czechoslovakia

1924
1. Canada
2. USA
3. Great Britain

1928
1. Canada
2. Sweden
3. Switzerland

1932
1. Canada
2. USA
3. Germany

1936
1. Great Britain
2. Canada
3. USA
   No Olympics in 1940 or
   1944

1948
1. Canada
1. Czechoslovakia
3. Switzerland

1952
1. Canada
2. USA
3. Sweden

1956
1. Soviet Union
2. USA
3. Canada

Canada's Eric Lindros (left), Kent Manderville (center) and Gordon Ross Hynes are the picture of defeat after the Unified Team won the Olympics' championship game, 3–1, in 1992.

1960
1. USA
2. Canada
3. Soviet Union

1964
1. Soviet Union
2. Sweden
3. Czechoslovakia

1968
1. Soviet Union
2. Czechoslovakia
3. Canada

1972
1. Soviet Union
2. USA
3. Czechoslovakia

1976
1. Soviet Union
2. Czechoslovakia
3. West Germany

1980
1. USA
2. Soviet Union
3. Sweden

1984
1. Soviet Union
2. Czechoslovakia
3. Sweden

1988
1. Soviet Union
2. Finland
3. Sweden

1992
1. Unified Team
2. Canada
3. Czechoslovakia

WORLD CHAMPIONSHIPS

Except for the Olympic years of 1984 and 1988—and time out for World War II—hockey has staged World Championships annually since 1924. The Soviet Union has monopolized the competition, winning the crown nine straight years from 1963 through 1971 and in 22 years overall.

The Russians are clearly acknowledged as the best "amateur" players in the world, especially remarkable when one considers that they didn't even take up hockey until the late 1940s.

But the Soviet Union has played as a unit virtually year-round and it shows in world competition, when they are frequently playing

teams, such as the U.S., that get together for a relatively short period before the competition. The list of World Championship results follows:

1924
1. Canada
2. USA
3. Great Britain

1928
1. Canada
2. Sweden
3. Switzerland

1930
1. Canada
2. Germany
3. Switzerland

1931
1. Canada
2. USA
3. Austria

1932
1. Canada
2. USA
3. Germany

1933
1. USA
2. Canada
3. Czechoslovakia

1934
1. Canada
2. USA
3. Germany

1935
1. Canada
2. Switzerland
3. Great Britain

1936
1. Great Britain
2. Canada
3. USA

1937
1. Canada
2. Great Britain
3. Switzerland

1938
1. Canada
2. Great Britain
3. Czechoslovakia

1939
1. Canada
2. USA
3. Switzerland

1947
1. Czechoslovakia
2. Sweden
3. Austria

1948
1. Canada
2. Czechoslovakia
3. Switzerland

1949
1. Czechoslovakia
2. Canada
3. USA

1950
1. Canada
2. USA
3. Switzerland

1951
1. Canada
2. Sweden
3. Switzerland

1952
1. Canada
2. USA
3. Sweden

1953
1. Sweden
2. German Federal
   Republic
3. Switzerland

1954
1. Soviet Union
2. Canada
3. Sweden

1955
1. Canada
2. Soviet Union
3. Czechoslovakia

1956
1. Soviet Union
2. USA
3. Canada

1957
1. Sweden
2. Soviet Union
3. Czechoslovakia

1958
1. Canada
2. Soviet Union
3. Sweden

1959
1. Canada
2. Soviet Union
3. Czechoslovakia

1960
1. USA
2. Canada
3. Soviet Union

1961
1. Canada
2. Czechoslovakia
3. Soviet Union

1962
1. Sweden
2. Canada
3. USA

1963
1. Soviet Union
2. Sweden
3. Czechoslovakia

1964
1. Soviet Union
2. Sweden
3. Czechoslovakia

1965
1. Soviet Union
2. Czechoslovakia
3. Sweden

1966
1. Soviet Union
2. Czechoslovakia
3. Canada

1967
1. Soviet Union
2. Sweden
3. Canada

1968
1. Soviet Union
2. Czechoslovakia
3. Canada

1969
1. Soviet Union
2. Sweden
3. Czechoslovakia

1970
1. Soviet Union
2. Sweden
3. Czechoslovakia

1971
1. Soviet Union
2. Czechoslovakia
3. Sweden

1972
1. Czechoslovakia
2. Soviet Union
3. Sweden

1973
1. Soviet Union
2. Sweden
3. Czechoslovakia

1974
1. Soviet Union
2. Czechoslovakia
3. Sweden

1975
1. Soviet Union
2. Czechoslovakia
3. Sweden

1976
1. Czechoslovakia
2. Soviet Union
3. Sweden

1977
1. Czechoslovakia
2. Sweden
3. Soviet Union

1978
1. Soviet Union
2. Czechoslovakia
3. Canada

1979
1. Soviet Union
2. Czechoslovakia
3. Sweden

1980
1. USA
2. Soviet Union
3. Sweden

1981
1. Soviet Union
2. Sweden
3. Czechoslovakia

1982
1. Soviet Union
2. Czechoslovakia
3. Canada

1983
1. Soviet Union
2. Czechoslovakia
3. Canada

1985
1. Czechoslovakia
2. Canada
3. Soviet Union

1986
1. Soviet Union
2. Sweden
3. Canada

1987
1. Sweden
2. Soviet Union
3. Czechoslovakia

1989
1. Soviet Union
2. Canada
3. Czechoslovakia

1990
1. Soviet Union
2. Sweden
3. Czechoslovakia

1991
1. Sweden
2. Canada
3. Soviet Union

1992
1. Sweden
2. Finland
3. Czechoslovakia

INTERNATIONAL CHALLENGES

The Soviet Union's dominance of the Olympics and other world competitions led to the inevitable argument over who was better: the Russians or the National Hockey League professionals. One way to settle it was head-to-head on ice.

The first confrontation came in 1972, when the NHL All-Stars played the Russians in an eight-game series. The NHL team won, but just barely, when Paul Henderson scored in the last minute of the final game, to give his squad a 4–3–1 edge in games.

In 1976, the NHL stars of Team Canada defeated Czechoslovakia on an overtime goal by Darryl Sittler that enabled Canada to capture the Canada Cup tournament.

The NHL All-Stars met the Soviets in a three-game Challenge Cup series at New York's Madison Square Garden in February 1979 and the Russians rallied after dropping the first game to take the set, two games to one. The USSR continued its winning ways in the 1981 Canada Cup. The Soviets walloped the Canadians, 8–1, in the final game to take home the Cup.

Over the years since then, Soviet teams have played various Canadian and U.S. units—NHL All-Stars, Team Canada, Team USA and a range of NHL clubs. From 1972 through 1991, the Russians have won 83 of 140 games.

For the NHL, its greatest success came in a tour of Leningrad, Moscow, Kiev and Riga in September 1989. Playing against Dynamo Moscow, Dynamo Riga, the Red Army and the Soviet Wings, the Washington Capitals and Calgary Flames each won three games and lost one in the eight-game series.

ALL-TIME
NHL PLAYER REGISTER

The following sections (the first covering forwards and defensemen; the second, goalies) include the record of every player who has ever appeared in an NHL game. In addition, NHL players who performed in the World Hockey Association also have their WHA records listed.

Where information is missing, it was unavailable.

The following are the abbreviations used for the various teams, Canadian provinces and column headings:

Alb (WHA)	Alberta Oilers	Mont	Montreal Canadiens	Van (WHA)	Vancouver Blazers
Atl	Atlanta Flames	Mont M	Montreal Maroons	Wash	Washington Capitals
Balt (WHA)	Baltimore Blades	Mont W	Montreal Wanderers	Winn or	
Birm (WHA)	Birmingham Bulls	NE (WHA)	New England Whalers	Winn (WHA)	Winnipeg Jets
Bos	Boston Bruins	NJ	New Jersey Devils		
Brk	Brooklyn Americans	NJ (WHA)	New Jersey Knights		
Buf	Buffalo Sabres	NYA	New York Americans		

CANADIAN PROVINCES

Cal	California Golden Seals	NYI	New York Islanders	Alta.	Alberta
Calg	Calgary Flames	NYR	New York Rangers	B.C.	British Columbia
Calg (WHA)	Calgary Cowboys	NY (WHA)	New York Golden Blades,	Man.	Manitoba
Chi	Chicago Blackhawks		Raiders	N.B.	New Brunswick
Chi (WHA)	Chicago Cougars	Oak	Oakland Seals	Nfld.	Newfoundland
Cin (WHA)	Cincinnati Stingers	Ott	Ottawa Senators	N.S.	Nova Scotia
Clev	Cleveland Barons	Ott (WHA)	Ottawa Nationals	Ont.	Ontario
Clev (WHA)	Cleveland Crusaders	Phil	Philadelphia Flyers	P.E.I.	Prince Edward Island
Col	Colorado Rockies	Phil Q	Philadelphia Quakers	Que.	Quebec
Den (WHA)	Denver Spurs	Phil (WHA)	Philadelphia Blazers	Sask.	Saskachewan
Det	Detroit Cougars,	Phoe (WHA)	Phoenix Roadrunners	Yuk.	The Yukon
	Falcons, Red Wings	Pitt	Pittsburgh Penguins	N.W.T.	Northwest Territory
Edm or		Pitt Pi	Pittsburgh Pirates		
Edm (WHA)	Edmonton Oilers	Que	Quebec Bulldogs,		
Ham	Hamilton Tigers		Nordiques	**COLUMN HEADINGS**	
Hart or		Que (WHA)	Quebec Nordiques		
Hart (WHA)	Hartford Whalers	SD (WHA)	San Diego Mariners	**A**	Assists
Hou (WHA)	Houston Aeros	SJ	San Jose Sharks	**Avg.**	Average
Ind (WHA)	Indianapolis Racers	StL	St. Louis Blues	**G**	Goals
KC	Kansas City Scouts	StL E	St. Louis Eagles	**GA**	Goals against
LA	Los Angeles Kings	Tor	Toronto Arenas,	**GP**	Games played
LA (WHA)	Los Angeles Sharks		Maple Leafs,	**Min.**	Minutes played
Mich (WHA)	Michigan Stags		St. Pats	**NHL**	National Hockey League
Minn	Minnesota North Stars	Tor (WHA)	Toronto Toros	**PIM**	Penalties in minutes
Minn (WHA)	Minnesota Fighting Saints	Van	Vancouver Canucks	**Pts.**	Points
				SO	Shutouts
				WHA	World Hockey Association

FORWARDS and DEFENSEMEN

Season	Team	GP	G	A	Pts.	PIM
ABBOTT, Reginald	*5-10 155 C*					
B. Winnipeg, Man., Feb. 4, 1930						
52-53	Mont	3	0	0	0	0
ABEL, Clarence John (Taffy)		*6-1 225 D*				
B. Sault Ste. Marie, Mich., May 28, 1900						
26-27	NYR	44	8	4	12	78
27-28	NYR	22	0	1	1	28
28-29	NYR	33	2	1	3	41
29-30	Chi	38	3	3	6	42
30-31	Chi	43	0	1	1	45
31-32	Chi	48	3	3	6	34
32-33	Chi	47	0	4	4	63
33-34	Chi	46	2	1	3	28
Totals		321	18	18	36	359
Playoff Totals		38	1	1	2	58
ABEL, Gerald Scott	*6-2 168 LW*					
B. Detroit, Mich., Dec. 25, 1944						
66-67	Det	1	0	0	0	0
ABEL, Sidney Gerald	*5-11 190 C*					
B. Melville, Sask., Feb. 22, 1918						
38-39	Det	15	1	1	2	0
39-40	Det	24	1	5	6	4
40-41	Det	47	11	22	33	29
41-42	Det	48	18	31	49	45
42-43	Det	49	18	24	42	33
45-46	Det	7	0	2	2	0
46-47	Det	60	19	29	48	29
47-48	Det	60	14	30	44	69
48-49	Det	60	28	26	54	49
49-50	Det	70	34	35	69	46
50-51	Det	69	23	38	61	30
51-52	Det	62	17	36	53	32
52-53	Chi	39	5	4	9	6
53-54	Chi	3	0	0	0	4
Totals		613	189	283	472	376
Playoff Totals		96	28	30	58	77
ABGRALL, Dennis Harvey	*6-1 180 RW*					
B. Mooseomin, Sask., Apr. 24, 1953						
75-76	LA	13	0	2	2	4
76-77	Cin (WHA)	80	23	39	62	22
77-78	Cin (WHA)	65	13	11	24	13
NHL Totals		13	0	2	2	4
WHA Totals		145	36	50	86	35
WHA Playoff Totals		4	2	0	2	5
ABRAHAMSSON, Thommy	*6-2 190 D*					
B. Ulmea, Sweden, Apr. 12, 1947						
74-75	NE (WHA)	76	8	22	30	46
75-76	NE (WHA)	63	14	21	35	47
76-77	NE (WHA)	64	6	24	30	33
80-81	Hart	32	6	11	17	16
NHL Totals		32	6	11	17	16
WHA Totals		203	28	67	95	126
WHA Playoff Totals		22	2	7	9	15
ACHTYMICHUK, Eugene Edward						
	5-11 170 C					
B. Lamont, Alta., Sept. 7, 1932						
51-52	Mont	1	0	0	0	0
56-57	Mont	3	0	0	0	0
57-58	Mont	16	3	5	8	2
58-59	Det	12	0	0	0	0
Totals		32	3	5	8	2
ACOMB, Douglas Raymond	*5-10 165 C*					
B. Toronto, Ont., May 15, 1949						
69-70	Tor	2	0	1	1	0
ACTON, Keith Edward	*5-8 167 C*					
B. Newmarket, Ont., Apr. 15, 1958						
79-80	Mont	2	0	1	1	0
80-81	Mont	61	15	24	39	74
81-82	Mont	78	36	52	88	88

Season	Team	GP	G	A	Pts.	PIM
ACTON, Keith Edward *(Continued)*						
82-83	Mont	78	24	26	50	63
83-84	Mont-Minn	71	20	45	65	64
84-85	Minn	78	20	38	58	90
85-86	Minn	79	26	32	58	100
86-87	Minn	78	16	29	45	56
87-88	Minn-Edm	72	11	17	28	95
88-89	Edm-Phil	71	14	25	39	111
89-90	Phil	69	13	14	27	80
90-91	Phil	76	14	23	37	131
91-92	Phil	50	7	9	16	98
Totals		863	216	335	551	1050
Playoff Totals		62	12	21	33	80
ADAM, Douglas Patrick	*5-10 165 LW*					
B. Toronto, Ont., Sept. 7, 1923						
49-50	NYR	4	0	1	1	0
ADAM, Russell Norm	*5-10 185 C*					
B. Windsor, Ont., May 5, 1961						
82-83	Tor	8	1	2	3	11
ADAMS, Greg	*6-3 185 C*					
B. Nelson, B.C., Aug. 1, 1963						
84-85	NJ	36	12	9	21	14
85-86	NJ	78	35	42	77	30
86-87	NJ	72	20	27	47	19
87-88	Van	80	36	40	76	30
88-89	Van	61	19	14	33	24
89-90	Van	65	30	20	50	18
90-91	Van	55	21	24	45	10
91-92	Van	76	30	27	57	26
Totals		523	203	203	406	171
Playoff Totals		18	2	5	7	8
ADAMS, Gregory Charles	*6-1 190 LW*					
B. Duncan, B.C., May 31, 1960						
80-81	Phil	6	3	0	3	8
81-82	Phil	33	4	15	19	105
82-83	Hart	79	10	13	23	216
83-84	Wash	57	2	6	8	133
84-85	Wash	51	6	12	18	72
85-86	Wash	78	18	38	56	152
86-87	Wash	67	14	30	44	184
87-88	Wash	78	15	12	27	153
88-89	Edm-Van	61	8	7	15	117
89-90	Que-Det	35	4	10	14	33
Totals		545	84	143	227	1173
Playoff Totals		43	2	11	13	153
ADAMS, John Ellis (Jack)	*5-10 163 LW*					
B. Calgary, Alta., May 5, 1920						
40-41	Mont	42	6	12	18	11
Playoff Totals		3	0	0	0	0
ADAMS, John James (Jack)	*C*					
B. Ft. William, Ont., June 14, 1895						
17-18	Tor	8	0	0	0	15
18-19	Tor	17	3	3	6	17
22-23	Tor	23	19	9	28	42
23-24	Tor	22	13	3	16	49
24-25	Tor	27	21	8	29	66
25-26	Tor	36	21	5	26	52
26-27	Ott	40	5	1	6	66
Totals		173	82	29	111	307
Playoff Totals		10	3	0	3	12
ADAMS, Stewart	*LW*					
B. 1904						
29-30	Chi	24	4	6	10	16
30-31	Chi	37	5	13	18	18
31-32	Chi	26	0	5	5	20
32-33	Tor	19	0	2	2	0
Totals		106	9	26	35	60
Playoff Totals		11	3	3	6	14

Season	Team	GP	G	A	Pts.	PIM
ADDUONO, Rick	*5-11 182 C*					
B. Thunder Bay, Ont., Dec. 5, 1955						
75-76	Bos	1	0	0	0	0
78-79	Birm	80	20	33	53	67
	(WHA)					
79-80	Atl	3	0	0	0	2
NHL Totals		4	0	0	0	2
WHA Totals		80	20	33	53	67
AFFLECK, Robert (Bruce)	*6-0 205 D*					
B. Salmon Arm, B.C., May 5, 1954						
74-75	StL	13	0	2	2	4
75-76	StL	80	4	26	30	20
76-77	StL	80	5	20	25	24
77-78	StL	75	4	14	18	26
78-79	StL	26	1	3	4	12
79-80	Van	5	0	1	1	0
83-84	NYI	1	0	0	0	0
Totals		280	14	66	80	86
Playoff Totals		8	0	0	0	0
AGNEW, Jim	*6-1 190 D*					
B. Hartney, Man., Mar. 21, 1966						
86-87	Van	4	0	0	0	0
87-88	Van	10	0	1	1	16
89-90	Van	7	0	0	0	36
90-91	Van	20	0	0	0	81
91-92	Van	24	0	0	0	56
Totals		65	0	1	1	189
Playoff Totals		4	0	0	0	6
AHERN, Frederick Vincent Jr.						
	6-0 180 RW					
B. Boston, Mass., Feb. 12, 1952						
74-75	Cal	3	2	1	3	0
75-76	Cal	44	17	8	25	43
76-77	Clev	25	4	4	8	20
77-78	Clev-Col	74	8	17	25	67
Totals		146	31	30	61	130
Playoff Totals		2	0	1	1	2
AHLIN	*F*					
37-38	Chi	1	0	0	0	0
AHOLA, Peter	*6-3 205 D*					
B. Espoo, Finland, May 14, 1968						
91-92	LA	71	7	12	19	101
Playoff Totals		6	0	0	0	2
AHRENS, Chris Alfred	*5-10 162 D*					
B. San Bernardino, Calif., July 31, 1952						
73-74	Minn	3	0	1	1	0
74-75	Minn	44	0	2	2	7
75-76	Minn	2	0	0	0	2
76-77	Minn	2	0	0	0	5
77-78	Minn	1	0	0	0	0
77-78	Edm	4	0	0	0	15
	(WHA)					
NHL Totals		52	0	3	3	14
WHA Totals		4	0	0	0	15
NHL Playoff Totals		1	0	0	0	0
AILSBY, Lloyd Harold	*5-11 194 D*					
B. Lac Pelletier, Sask., May 11, 1917						
51-52	NYR	3	0	0	0	2
AITKEN, Brad	*6-3 200 LW*					
B. Scarborough, Ont., Oct. 30, 1967						
87-88	Pitt	5	1	1	2	0
90-91	Pitt-Edm	9	0	2	2	25
Totals		14	1	3	4	25
ALBELIN, Tommy	*6-1 190 D*					
B. Stockholm, Sweden, May 21, 1964						
87-88	Que	60	3	23	26	47
88-89	Que-NJ	60	9	28	37	67
89-90	NJ	68	6	23	29	63

Season	Team	GP	G	A	Pts.	PIM
ALBELIN, Tommy (Continued)						
90-91	NJ	47	2	12	14	44
91-92	NJ	19	0	4	4	4
Totals		254	20	90	110	225
Playoff Totals		4	1	2	3	2
ALBRIGHT, Clinton Howard 6-2 180 C						
B. Winnipeg, Man., Feb. 28, 1926						
48-49	NYR	59	14	5	19	19
ALDCORN, Gary William 5-11 180 F						
B. Shaunavon, Sask., Mar. 7, 1935						
56-57	Tor	22	5	1	6	4
57-58	Tor	59	10	14	24	12
58-59	Tor	5	0	3	3	2
59-60	Det	70	22	29	51	32
60-61	Det-Bos	70	4	9	13	28
Totals		226	41	56	97	78
Playoff Totals		6	1	2	3	4
ALEXANDER, Claire Arthur 6-1 175 D						
B. Collingwood, Ont., June 16, 1945						
74-75	Tor	42	7	11	18	12
75-76	Tor	33	2	6	8	6
76-77	Tor	48	1	12	13	12
77-78	Van	32	8	18	26	6
78-79	Edm (WHA)	54	8	23	31	16
NHL Totals		155	18	47	65	36
WHA Totals		54	8	23	31	16
NHL Playoff Totals		16	2	4	6	4
ALEXANDRE, Arthur F						
31-32	Mont	10	0	2	2	8
32-33	Mon	1	0	0	0	0
Totals		11	0	2	2	8
Playoff Totals		4	0	0	0	0
ALLEN, Courtney Keith (Keith and Bingo) 5-11 190 D						
B. Saskatoon, Sask., Aug. 21, 1923						
53-54	Det	10	0	4	4	2
54-55	Det	18	0	0	0	6
Totals		28	0	4	4	8
Playoff Totals		5	0	0	0	0
ALLEN, George Trenholme 5-10 162 D						
B. Bayfield, N.B., July 27, 1914						
38-39	NYR	19	6	6	12	10
39-40	Chi	48	10	12	22	26
40-41	Chi	44	14	17	31	22
41-42	Chi	43	7	13	20	31
42-43	Chi	47	10	14	24	26
43-44	Chi	45	17	24	41	36
45-46	Chi	44	11	15	26	16
46-47	Mont	49	7	14	21	12
Totals		339	82	115	197	179
Playoff Totals		41	9	10	19	32
ALLEN, Jeffrey D						
B. Hull, Que., May 17, 1957						
77-78	Cin (WHA)	2	0	0	0	0
77-78	Clev	4	0	0	0	2
ALLEN, Vivan Mariner (Squee) 5-6 140 RW						
B. Bayfield, N.B., Sept. 9, 1916						
40-41	NYA	6	0	1	1	0
ALLEY, Steve 6-0 185 LW						
B. Anoka, Minn., Dec. 29, 1953						
77-78	Birm (WHA)	27	8	12	20	11
78-79	Birm (WHA)	78	17	24	41	36
79-80	Hart	7	1	1	2	0
80-81	Hart	8	2	2	4	11
NHL Totals		15	3	3	6	11
WHA Totals		105	25	36	61	47
NHL Playoff Totals		3	0	1	1	0
WHA Playoff Totals		5	1	0	1	5
ALLISON, David Bryan 6-1 200 D						
B. Fort Frances, Ont., Apr. 14, 1959						
83-84	Mont	3	0	0	0	12
ALLISON, Michael Earnest 6-0 200 LW						
B. Fort Frances, Ont., Mar. 28, 1961						
80-81	NYR	75	26	38	64	83
81-82	NYR	48	7	15	22	74
82-83	NYR	39	11	9	20	37
83-84	NYR	45	8	12	20	64
84-85	NYR	31	9	15	24	17
85-86	NYR	28	2	13	15	22
86-87	Tor	71	7	16	23	66
87-88	Tor-LA	52	16	15	31	67

Season	Team	GP	G	A	Pts.	PIM
ALLISON, Michael Earnest (Continued)						
88-89	LA	55	14	22	36	122
89-90	LA	55	2	11	13	78
Totals		499	102	166	268	630
Playoff Totals		82	9	17	26	135
ALLISON, Raymond Peter 5-10 195 RW						
B. Cranbrook, B.C., Mar. 4, 1959						
79-80	Hart	64	16	12	28	13
80-81	Hart	6	1	0	1	0
81-82	Phil	51	17	37	54	104
82-83	Phil	67	21	30	51	57
83-84	Phil	37	8	13	21	47
84-85	Phil	11	1	1	2	2
86-87	Phil	2	0	0	0	0
Totals		238	64	93	157	223
Playoff Totals		12	2	3	5	20
ALLUM, William James Douglas 5-11 194 D						
B. Winnipeg, Man., Oct. 9, 1916						
40-41	NYR	1	0	1	1	0
AMADIO, David A. 6-1 205 D						
B. Glace Bay, N.S., Apr. 23, 1939						
57-58	Det	2	0	0	0	2
67-68	LA	58	4	6	10	101
68-69	LA	65	1	5	6	60
Totals		125	5	11	16	163
Playoff Totals		16	1	2	3	18
AMODEO, Michael 5-10 190 D						
B. Toronto, Ont., June 22, 1952						
72-73	Ott (WHA)	61	1	14	15	77
73-74	Tor (WHA)	77	0	11	11	82
74-75	Tor (WHA)	64	1	13	14	50
75-76	Tor (WHA)	31	4	8	12	35
77-78	Winn (WHA)	3	1	1	2	0
78-79	Winn (WHA)	64	4	18	22	29
79-80	Winn	19	0	0	0	2
NHL Totals		19	0	0	0	2
WHA Totals		300	11	65	76	273
WHA Playoff Totals		27	1	7	8	59
AMONTE, Anthony (Tony) 6-0 180 RW						
B. Hingham, Mass., Aug. 2, 1970						
90-91	NYR	0	0	0	0	0
91-92	NYR	79	35	34	69	55
Totals		79	35	34	69	55
Playoff Totals		15	3	8	11	4
ANDERSON, Dale Norman 6-3 190 D						
B. Regina, Sask., Mar. 5, 1932						
56-57	Det	13	0	0	0	6
Playoff Totals		2	0	0	0	0
ANDERSON, Douglas 5-7 157 C						
B. Edmonton, Alta., Oct. 20, 1927						
52-53	Mont	0	0	0	0	0
Playoff Totals		2	0	0	0	0
ANDERSON, Earl Orlin 6-0 185 RW						
B. Roseau, Minn., Feb. 24, 1951						
74-75	Det-Bos	64	9	7	16	16
75-76	Bos	5	0	1	1	2
76-77	Bos	40	10	11	21	4
Totals		109	19	19	38	22
Playoff Totals		5	0	1	1	0
ANDERSON, Glenn Chris 5-11 175 LW						
B. Vancouver, B.C., Oct. 2, 1960						
80-81	Edm	58	30	23	53	24
81-82	Edm	80	38	67	105	71
82-83	Edm	72	48	56	104	70
83-84	Edm	80	54	45	99	65
84-85	Edm	80	42	39	81	69
85-86	Edm	72	54	48	102	90
86-87	Edm	80	35	38	73	65
87-88	Edm	80	38	50	88	58
88-89	Edm	79	16	48	64	93
89-90	Edm	73	34	38	72	107
90-91	Edm	74	24	31	55	59
91-92	Tor	72	24	33	57	100
Totals		900	437	516	953	871
Playoff Totals		164	81	102	183	314
ANDERSON, James William 5-9 170 LW						
B. Pembroke, Ont., Dec. 1, 1930						
67-68	LA	7	1	2	3	2
Playoff Totals		4	0	0	0	2
ANDERSON, John Murray 5-11 190 RW						
B. Toronto, Ont., Mar. 28, 1957						
77-78	Tor	17	1	2	3	2

Season	Team	GP	G	A	Pts.	PIM
ANDERSON, John Murray (Continued)						
78-79	Tor	71	15	11	26	10
79-80	Tor	74	25	28	53	22
80-81	Tor	75	17	26	43	31
81-82	Tor	69	31	26	57	30
82-83	Tor	80	31	49	80	24
83-84	Tor	73	37	31	68	22
84-85	Tor	75	32	31	63	27
85-86	Que-Hart	79	29	45	74	28
86-87	Hart	76	31	44	75	19
87-88	Hart	63	17	32	49	20
88-89	Hart	62	16	24	40	28
Totals		814	282	349	631	263
Playoff Totals		37	9	18	27	2
ANDERSON, Murray Craig 5-10 175 D						
B. Dauphin, Man., Aug. 28, 1949						
74-75	Wash	40	0	1	1	68
ANDERSON, Perry Lynn 6-0 195 LW						
B. Barrie, Ont., Oct. 14, 1961						
81-82	StL	5	1	2	3	0
82-83	StL	18	5	2	7	14
83-84	StL	50	7	5	12	195
84-85	StL	71	9	9	18	146
85-86	NJ	51	7	12	19	91
86-87	NJ	57	10	9	19	107
87-88	NJ	60	4	6	10	222
88-89	NJ	39	3	6	9	128
90-91	NJ	1	0	0	0	5
91-92	SJ	48	4	8	12	141
Totals		400	50	59	109	1049
Playoff Totals		36	2	1	3	161
ANDERSON, Ronald Chester (Goings) 6-0 180 RW						
B. Red Deer, Alta., July 29, 1945						
67-68	Det	18	2	0	2	13
68-69	Det-LA	63	3	5	8	34
69-70	StL	59	9	9	18	36
70-71	Buf	74	14	12	26	44
71-72	Buf	37	0	4	4	19
72-73	Alb (WHA)	73	14	15	29	43
73-74	Edm (WHA)	19	5	2	7	6
NHL Totals		251	28	30	58	146
WHA Totals		92	19	17	36	49
NHL Playoff Totals		5	0	0	4	5
ANDERSON, Ronald Henry 5-10 165 RW						
B. Moncton, N.B., Jan. 21, 1950						
74-75	Wash	28	9	7	16	8
ANDERSON, Russell Vincent 6-3 210 D						
B. Des Moines, Iowa, Feb. 12, 1955						
76-77	Pitt	66	2	11	13	81
77-78	Pitt	74	2	16	18	150
78-79	Pitt	72	3	13	16	93
79-80	Pitt	76	5	22	27	150
80-81	Pitt	34	3	14	17	112
81-82	Pitt-Hart	56	1	4	5	183
82-83	Hart	57	0	6	6	171
83-84	LA	70	5	12	17	126
84-85	LA	14	1	1	2	20
Totals		519	22	99	121	1086
Playoff Totals		10	0	3	3	28
ANDERSON, Shawn 6-1 180 D						
B. Montreal, Que., Feb. 7, 1968						
86-87	Buf	41	2	11	13	23
87-88	Buf	23	1	2	3	17
88-89	Buf	33	2	10	12	18
89-90	Buf	16	1	3	4	8
90-91	Que	31	3	10	13	21
Totals		144	9	36	45	87
Playoff Totals		5	0	1	1	4
ANDERSON, Thomas Linton (Cowboy) 5-10 180 LW						
B. Edinburgh, Scotland, July 9, 1911						
34-35	Det	27	5	2	7	16
35-36	Det	24	3	2	5	20
36-37	NYA	45	10	15	25	24
37-38	NYA	45	4	21	25	22
38-39	NYA	47	13	27	40	14
39-40	NYA	48	12	19	31	22
40-41	NYA	35	3	12	15	8
41-42	NYA	48	12	29	41	64
Totals		319	62	127	189	190
Playoff Totals		16	2	7	9	62
ANDERSON, William D						
B. Tilsonberg, Ont., Dec. 13, 1912						
42-43	Bos	0	0	0	0	0
Playoff Totals		1	0	0	0	0

ANDERSSON, Bo Mikael *5-11 185 LW*

B. Malmo, Sweden, May 10, 1966

Season	Team	GP	G	A	Pts.	PIM
85-86	Buf	32	1	9	10	4
86-87	Buf	16	0	3	3	0
87-88	Buf	37	3	20	23	10
88-89	Buf	14	0	1	1	4
89-90	Hart	50	13	24	37	6
90-91	Hart	41	4	7	11	8
91-92	Hart	74	18	29	47	14
Totals		264	39	93	132	46
Playoff Totals		13	1	5	6	8

ANDERSSON, Kent-Erik *6-2 185 RW*

B. Orebro, Sweden, May 24, 1951

Season	Team	GP	G	A	Pts.	PIM
77-78	Minn	73	15	18	33	4
78-79	Minn	41	9	4	13	4
79-80	Minn	61	9	10	19	8
80-81	Minn	77	17	24	41	22
81-82	Minn	70	9	12	21	18
82-83	NYR	71	8	20	28	14
83-84	NYR	63	5	15	20	8
Totals		456	72	103	175	78
Playoff Totals		50	4	11	15	4

ANDERSSON, Peter *6-2 200 D*

B. Ferdertaive, Sweden, Mar. 2, 1962

Season	Team	GP	G	A	Pts.	PIM
83-84	Wash	42	3	7	10	20
84-85	Wash	57	0	10	10	20
85-86	Wash-Que	73	7	24	31	40
Totals		172	10	41	51	80
Playoff Totals		7	0	2	2	2

ANDRASCIK, Steve George *5-11 200 RW*

B. Sherridon, Man., Nov. 6, 1948

Season	Team	GP	G	A	Pts.	PIM
71-72	NYR	0	0	0	0	0
74-75	Ind (WHA)	77	6	11	17	58
75-76	Cin (WHA)	20	3	2	5	21
NHL Playoff Totals		1	0	0	0	0
WHA Totals		97	9	13	22	79

ANDREA, Paul Lawrence *5-10 174 RW*

B. North Sydney, N.S., July 31, 1941

Season	Team	GP	G	A	Pts.	PIM
65-66	NYR	4	1	1	2	0
67-68	Pitt	65	11	21	32	2
68-69	Pitt	25	7	6	13	2
70-71	Cal-Buf	56	12	21	33	8
72-73	Clev (WHA)	66	21	30	51	12
73-74	Clev (WHA)	69	15	18	33	14
NHL Totals		150	31	49	80	12
WHA Totals		135	36	48	84	26
WHA Playoff Totals		14	3	8	11	2

ANDREWS, Lloyd *F*

Season	Team	GP	G	A	Pts.	PIM
21-22	Tor	11	0	0	0	0
22-23	Tor	23	5	4	9	10
23-24	Tor	12	2	1	3	0
24-25	Tor	7	1	0	1	0
Totals		53	8	5	13	10
Playoff Totals		7	2	0	2	5

ANDREYCHUK, David *6-3 195 C*

B. Hamilton, Ont., Sept. 29, 1963

Season	Team	GP	G	A	Pts.	PIM
82-83	Buf	43	14	23	37	16
83-84	Buf	78	38	42	80	42
84-85	Buf	64	31	30	61	54
85-86	Buf	80	36	51	87	61
86-87	Buf	77	25	48	73	46
87-88	Buf	80	30	48	78	112
88-89	Buf	56	28	24	52	40
89-90	Buf	73	40	42	82	42
90-91	Buf	80	36	33	69	32
91-92	Buf	80	41	50	91	71
Totals		711	319	391	710	516
Playoff Totals		41	12	20	32	32

ANDRUFF, Ronald Nicholas *6-0 185 C*

B. Chemainus, B.C., July 10, 1953

Season	Team	GP	G	A	Pts.	PIM
74-75	Mont	5	0	0	0	2
75-76	Mont	1	0	0	0	0
76-77	Col	66	4	18	22	21
77-78	Col	78	15	18	33	31
78-79	Col	3	0	0	0	0
Totals		153	19	36	55	54
Playoff Totals		2	0	0	0	0

ANGOTTI, Louis Frederick *5-8 170 C*

B. Toronto, Ont., Jan. 16, 1938

Season	Team	GP	G	A	Pts.	PIM
64-65	NYR	70	9	8	17	20
65-66	NYR=Chi	51	6	12	18	14
66-67	Chi	63	6	12	18	21
67-68	Phil	70	12	37	49	35
68-69	Pitt	71	17	20	37	36
69-70	Chi	70	12	26	38	25
70-71	Chi	65	9	16	25	19
71-72	Chi	65	5	10	15	23
72-73	Chi	77	15	22	37	26

ANGOTTI, Louis Frederick *(Continued)*

Season	Team	GP	G	A	Pts.	PIM
73-74	StL	51	12	23	35	9
74-75	Chi	26	2	5	7	9
NHL Totals		653	103	186	289	228
WHA Totals		26	2	5	7	9
NHL Playoff Totals		65	8	8	16	17

ANHOLT, Darrel *6-2 230 D*

B. Hardisty, Alta., Nov. 23, 1962

Season	Team	GP	G	A	Pts.	PIM
83-84	Chi	1	0	0	0	0

ANSLOW, Hubert Wallace (Hub) *5-11 173 LW*

B. Pembroke, Ont., Mar. 23, 1926

Season	Team	GP	G	A	Pts.	PIM
47-48	NYR	2	0	0	0	0

ANTONOVICH, Michael J. *5-6 155 C*

B. Calumet, Minn., Oct. 18, 1951

Season	Team	GP	G	A	Pts.	PIM
72-73	Minn (WHA)	75	20	19	39	46
73-74	Minn (WHA)	68	21	29	50	4
74-75	Minn (WHA)	67	24	26	50	20
75-76	Minn (WHA)	57	25	21	46	18
75-76	Minn	12	0	2	2	8
76-77	Minn-Edm-NE (WHA)	75	40	31	71	38
77-78	NE (WHA)	75	32	35	67	32
78-79	NE (WHA)	69	20	27	47	35
79-80	Hart	5	0	1	1	2
81-82	Minn	2	0	0	0	0
82-83	NJ	30	7	7	14	11
83-84	NJ	38	3	5	8	16
NHL Totals		87	10	15	25	37
WHA Totals		486	182	188	370	193
WHA Playoff Totals		57	21	20	41	28

ANTOSKI, Shawn *6-4 235 LW*

B. Brantford, Ont., Mar. 25, 1970

Season	Team	GP	G	A	Pts.	PIM
90-91	Van	2	0	0	0	0
91-92	Van	4	0	0	0	29
Totals		6	0	0	0	29

APPS, Charles Joseph Sylvanus (Syl) *6-0 173 C*

B. Paris, Ont., Jan. 18, 1915

Season	Team	GP	G	A	Pts.	PIM
36-37	Tor	48	16	29	45	10
37-38	Tor	47	21	29	50	9
38-39	Tor	44	15	25	40	4
39-40	Tor	27	13	17	30	5
40-41	Tor	41	20	24	44	6
41-42	Tor	38	18	23	41	0
42-43	Tor	29	23	17	40	2
45-46	Tor	40	24	16	40	2
46-47	Tor	54	25	24	49	6
47-48	Tor	55	26	27	53	12
Totals		423	201	231	432	56
Playoff Totals		69	25	28	53	16

APPS, Sylvanus Marshall (Syl) *6-0 195 C*

B. Toronto, Ont., Aug. 1, 1947

Season	Team	GP	G	A	Pts.	PIM
70-71	NYR-Pitt	62	10	18	28	32
71-72	Pitt	72	15	44	59	78
72-73	Pitt	77	29	56	85	18
73-74	Pitt	75	24	61	85	37
74-75	Pitt	79	24	55	79	43
75-76	Pitt	80	32	67	99	24
76-77	Pitt	72	18	43	61	20
77-78	Pitt-LA	79	19	33	52	18
78-79	LA	80	7	30	37	29
79-80	LA	51	5	16	21	12
Totals		727	183	423	606	311
Playoff Totals		23	5	5	10	23

ARBOUR, Alger Joseph (Al) *6-1 180 D*

B. Sudbury, Ont., Nov. 1, 1932

Season	Team	GP	G	A	Pts.	PIM
53-54	Det	36	0	1	1	18
56-57	Det	44	1	6	7	38
57-58	Det	69	1	6	7	104
58-59	Chi	70	2	10	12	86
59-60	Chi	57	1	5	6	66
60-61	Chi	53	3	2	5	40
61-62	Tor	52	1	5	6	68
62-63	Tor	4	1	0	1	4
63-64	Tor	6	0	1	1	0
65-66	Tor	4	0	1	1	2
67-68	StL	74	1	10	11	50
68-69	StL	67	1	6	7	50
69-70	StL	68	0	3	3	85
70-71	StL	22	0	2	2	6
Totals		626	12	58	70	617
Playoff Totals		86	1	8	9	92

ARBOUR, Amos *F*

Season	Team	GP	G	A	Pts.	PIM
18-19	Mont	1	0	0	0	0

ARBOUR, Amos *(Continued)*

Season	Team	GP	G	A	Pts.	PIM
19-20	Mont	20	22	4	26	10
20-21	Mont	22	14	3	17	40
21-22	Ham	23	8	3	11	6
22-23	Ham	23	6	1	7	6
23-24	Tor	20	1	2	3	4
Totals		109	51	13	64	66

ARBOUR, Ernest (Ty) *F*

Season	Team	GP	G	A	Pts.	PIM
26-27	Pitt Pi	41	7	8	15	10
27-28	Pitt Pi-Chi	39	5	5	10	32
28-29	Chi	44	3	4	7	32
29-30	Chi	42	10	8	18	26
30-31	Chi	41	3	3	6	12
Totals		207	28	28	56	112
Playoff Totals		11	2	0	2	6

ARBOUR, John A. (Jack) *F*

Season	Team	GP	G	A	Pts.	PIM
26-27	Det	37	4	1	5	46
28-29	Tor	10	1	0	1	10
Totals		47	5	1	6	56

ARBOUR, John Gilbert (Jack) *5-11 195 D*

B. Niagara Falls, Ont., Sept. 28, 1945

Season	Team	GP	G	A	Pts.	PIM
65-66	Bos	2	0	0	0	0
67-68	Bos	4	0	1	1	11
68-69	Pitt	17	0	2	2	35
70-71	Van-StL	66	1	6	7	93
71-72	Stl	17	0	0	0	10
72-73	Minn (WHA)	76	6	27	33	188
73-74	Minn (WHA)	77	6	43	49	192
74-75	Minn (WHA)	70	11	43	54	67
75-76	Den-Minn (WHA)	42	2	17	19	63
76-77	Minn-Calg (WHA)	70	4	34	38	60
NHL Totals		106	1	9	10	149
WHA Totals		335	29	164	193	570
NHL Playoff Totals		5	0	0	0	0
WHA Playoff Totals		28	3	13	16	62

ARCHAMBAULT, Michel Joseph *5-8 160 LW*

B. St. Hyacinthe, Que., Sept. 27, 1950

Season	Team	GP	G	A	Pts.	PIM
72-73	Que (WHA)	57	12	25	37	36
76-77	Chi	3	0	0	0	0

ARCHIBALD, David *6-1 190 C*

B. Chilliwack, B.C., Apr. 14, 1969

Season	Team	GP	G	A	Pts.	PIM
87-88	Minn	78	13	20	33	26
88-89	Minn	72	14	19	33	14
89-90	Minn-NYR	31	3	8	11	12
Totals		181	30	47	77	52
Playoff Totals		5	0	1	1	0

ARCHIBALD, James *5-11 175 RW*

B. Craik, Sask., June 6, 1961

Season	Team	GP	G	A	Pts.	PIM
84-85	Minn	4	1	2	3	11
85-86	Minn	11	0	0	0	32
86-87	Minn	1	0	0	0	2
Totals		16	1	2	3	45

ARESHENKOFF, Ronald *6-0 175 C*

B. Grand Forks, B.C., June 13, 1957

Season	Team	GP	G	A	Pts.	PIM
79-80	Edm	4	0	0	0	0

ARMSTRONG, George Edward (Chief) *6-1 194 RW*

B. Skead, Ont., July 6, 1930

Season	Team	GP	G	A	Pts.	PIM
49-50	Tor	2	0	0	0	0
51-52	Tor	20	3	3	6	30
52-53	Tor	52	14	11	25	54
53-54	Tor	63	17	15	32	60
54-55	Tor	66	10	18	28	80
55-56	Tor	67	16	32	48	97
56-57	Tor	54	18	26	44	37
57-58	Tor	59	17	25	42	93
58-59	Tor	59	20	16	36	37
59-60	Tor	70	23	28	51	60
60-61	Tor	47	14	19	33	21
61-62	Tor	70	21	32	53	27
62-63	Tor	70	19	24	43	27
63-64	Tor	66	20	17	37	14
64-65	Tor	59	15	22	37	14
65-66	Tor	70	16	35	51	12
66-67	Tor	70	9	24	33	26
67-68	Tor	62	13	21	34	4
68-69	Tor	53	11	16	27	10
69-70	Tor	49	13	15	28	12
70-71	Tor	59	7	18	25	6
Totals		1187	296	417	713	721
Playoff Totals		110	26	34	60	52

ARMSTRONG, Murray Alexander
5-10 170 C
B. Manor, Sask., Jan. 1, 1916

Season	Team	GP	G	A	Pts.	PIM
37-38	Tor	9	0	0	0	0
38-39	Tor	3	0	1	1	0
39-40	NYA	48	16	20	36	12
40-41	NYA	47	10	14	24	6
41-42	NYA	45	6	22	28	15
43-44	Det	28	12	22	34	4
44-45	Det	50	15	24	39	31
45-46	Det	40	8	18	26	4
Totals		270	67	121	188	72
Playoff Totals		30	4	6	10	2

ARMSTRONG, Norman Gerrard (Red)
5-11 205 D
B. Owen Sound, Ont., Oct. 17, 1938

Season	Team	GP	G	A	Pts.	PIM
62-63	Tor	7	1	1	2	2

ARMSTRONG, Robert Richard   6-1 180 D
B. Toronto, Ont., Apr. 17, 1931

Season	Team	GP	G	A	Pts.	PIM
50-51	Bos	2	0	0	0	2
52-53	Bos	55	0	8	8	45
53-54	Bos	64	2	10	12	81
54-55	Bos	57	1	3	4	38
55-56	Bos	68	0	12	12	122
56-57	Bos	57	1	15	16	79
57-58	Bos	47	1	4	5	66
58-59	Bos	60	1	9	10	50
59-60	Bos	69	5	14	19	96
60-61	Bos	54	0	10	10	72
61-62	Bos	9	2	1	3	20
Totals		542	13	86	99	671
Playoff Totals		42	1	7	8	28

ARMSTRONG, Tim   5-11 170 C
B. Toronto, Ont., May 12, 1967

Season	Team	GP	G	A	Pts.	PIM
88-89	Tor	11	1	0	1	6

ARMSTRONG, William   6-2 195 C
B. London, Ont., June 25, 1966

Season	Team	GP	G	A	Pts.	PIM
90-91	Phil	1	0	1	1	1

ARNASON, Ernest Charles (Chuck)
5-10 185 RW
B. Dauphin, Man., July 15, 1951

Season	Team	GP	G	A	Pts.	PIM
71-72	Mont	17	3	0	3	4
72-73	Mont	19	1	1	2	2
73-74	Atl-Pitt	74	20	11	31	17
74-75	Pitt	78	26	32	58	32
75-76	Pitt-KC	69	21	13	34	35
76-77	Col	61	13	10	23	10
77-78	Col-Clev	69	25	21	46	18
78-79	Minn-Wash	14	0	2	2	4
Totals		401	109	90	199	122
Playoff Totals		9	2	4	6	4

ARNIEL, Scott   6-1 170 C
B. Cornwall, Ont., Sept. 17, 1962

Season	Team	GP	G	A	Pts.	PIM
81-82	Winn	17	1	8	9	14
82-83	Winn	75	13	5	18	46
83-84	Winn	80	21	35	56	68
84-85	Winn	79	22	22	44	81
85-86	Winn	80	18	25	43	40
86-87	Buf	63	11	14	25	59
87-88	Buf	73	17	23	40	61
88-89	Buf	80	18	23	41	46
89-90	Buf	79	18	14	32	77
90-91	Winn	75	5	17	22	87
91-92	Bos	29	5	3	8	20
Totals		730	149	189	338	599
Playoff Totals		34	3	3	6	39

ARTHUR, Frederick Edward   6-5 210 D
B. Toronto, Ont., Mar. 6, 1961

Season	Team	GP	G	A	Pts.	PIM
80-81	Hart	3	0	0	0	0
81-82	Phil	74	1	7	8	47
82-83	Phil	3	0	1	1	2
Totals		80	1	8	9	49
Playoff Totals		4	0	0	0	2

ARUNDEL, John O'Gorman   5-11 181 D
B. Winnipeg, Man., Nov. 4, 1927

Season	Team	GP	G	A	Pts.	PIM
49-50	Tor	3	0	0	0	0

ASHBEE, William Barry (Barry)
5-10 180 D
B. Weston, Ont., July 28, 1939

Season	Team	GP	G	A	Pts.	PIM
65-66	Bos	14	0	3	3	14
70-71	Phil	64	4	23	27	44
71-72	Phil	73	6	14	20	75
72-73	Phil	64	1	17	18	106
73-74	Phil	69	4	13	17	52
Totals		284	15	70	85	291
Playoff Totals		17	0	4	4	22

ASHBY, Donald Alan (Ash)   6-1 185 C
B. Kamloops, B.C., Mar. 8, 1955

Season	Team	GP	G	A	Pts.	PIM
75-76	Tor	50	6	15	21	10
76-77	Tor	76	19	23	42	24
77-78	Tor	12	1	2	3	0
78-79	Tor-Col	15	2	3	5	0
79-80	Col-Edm	29	10	10	20	4
80-81	Col	6	2	3	5	2
Totals		188	40	56	96	40
Playoff Totals		12	1	0	1	4

ASHTON, Brent Kenneth   6-1 210 LW
B. Saskatoon, Sask., May 18, 1960

Season	Team	GP	G	A	Pts.	PIM
79-80	Van	47	5	14	19	11
80-81	Van	77	18	11	29	57
81-82	Col	80	24	36	60	26
82-83	NJ	76	14	19	33	47
83-84	Minn	68	7	10	17	54
84-85	Minn-Que	78	31	31	62	53
85-86	Que	77	26	32	58	64
86-87	Que-Det	81	40	35	75	39
87-88	Det	73	26	27	53	50
88-89	Winn	75	31	37	68	36
89-90	Winn	79	22	34	56	37
90-91	Winn	61	12	24	36	58
91-92	Winn-Bos	68	18	22	40	51
Totals		940	274	332	606	583
Playoff Totals		79	24	22	46	68

ASHWORTH, Frank   5-9 165 C
B. Moose Jaw, Sask., Oct. 16, 1927

Season	Team	GP	G	A	Pts.	PIM
46-47	Chi	18	5	4	9	2

ASMUNDSON, Oscar   5-11 170 C
B. Red Deer, Alta., Nov. 17, 1908

Season	Team	GP	G	A	Pts.	PIM
32-33	NYR	48	5	10	15	20
33-34	NYR	46	2	6	8	8
34-35	Det-StLE	14	4	7	11	2
36-37	NYA	2	0	0	0	0
37-38	Mont	2	0	0	0	0
Totals		112	11	23	34	30
Playoff Totals		9	0	2	2	4

ATANAS, Walter (Ants)   5-8 168 RW
B. Hamilton, Ont., Dec. 22, 1922

Season	Team	GP	G	A	Pts.	PIM
44-45	NYR	49	13	8	21	40

ATKINSON, Steven John   5-11 170 RW
B. Toronto, Ont., Oct. 16, 1948

Season	Team	GP	G	A	Pts.	PIM
68-69	Bos	1	0	0	0	0
70-71	Buf	57	20	18	38	12
71-72	Buf	67	14	10	24	26
72-73	Buf	61	9	9	18	36
73-74	Buf	70	6	10	16	22
74-75	Wash	46	11	4	15	8
75-76	Tor (WHA)	52	2	6	8	22
NHL Totals		302	60	51	111	104
WHA Totals		52	2	6	8	22
NHL Playoff Totals		1	0	0	0	0

ATTWELL, Robert Allan   6-0 192 RW
B. Spokane, Wash., Dec. 26, 1959

Season	Team	GP	G	A	Pts.	PIM
79-80	Col	7	1	1	2	0
80-81	Col	15	0	4	4	0
Totals		22	1	5	6	0

ATTWELL, Ronald Allan   6-2 208 C
B. Humber Summit, Ont., Feb. 9, 1935

Season	Team	GP	G	A	Pts.	PIM
67-68	StL-NYR	21	1	7	8	8

AUBIN, Normand   6-0 185 C
B. St.-Leonard, Que., July 26, 1960

Season	Team	GP	G	A	Pts.	PIM
81-82	Tor	43	14	12	26	22
82-83	Tor	26	4	1	5	8
Totals		69	18	13	31	30
Playoff Totals		1	0	0	0	0

AUBRY, Pierre   5-10 175 LW
B. Cap-de-la-Madeleine, Que., Apr. 15, 1960

Season	Team	GP	G	A	Pts.	PIM
80-81	Que	1	0	0	0	0
81-82	Que	62	10	13	23	27
82-83	Que	77	7	9	16	48
83-84	Que-Det	37	5	2	7	25
84-85	Det	25	2	2	4	33
Totals		202	24	26	50	133
Playoff Totals		20	1	1	2	32

AUBUCHON, Oscar (Ossie)   5-10 175 LW
B. St. Hyacinthe, Que., Jan. 1, 1917

Season	Team	GP	G	A	Pts.	PIM
42-43	Bos	3	3	0	3	0
43-44	Bos-NYR	47	16	12	28	4
Totals		50	19	12	31	4
Playoff Totals		6	1	0	1	0

AUDETTE, Donald   5-8 180 RW
B. Laval, Que., Sept. 23, 1969

Season	Team	GP	G	A	Pts.	PIM
90-91	Buf	8	4	3	7	4
91-92	Buf	63	31	17	48	75
Totals		71	35	20	55	79
Playoff Totals		2	0	0	0	0

AUGE, Les   6-1 190 D
B. St. Paul, Minn., May 16, 1953

Season	Team	GP	G	A	Pts.	PIM
80-81	Col	6	0	3	3	4

AURIE, Harry Lawrence (Larry)
5-6 148 RW
B. Sudbury, Ont., Feb. 8, 1905

Season	Team	GP	G	A	Pts.	PIM
27-28	Det	44	13	3	16	43
28-29	Det	35	1	1	2	26
29-30	Det	43	14	5	19	28
30-31	Det	41	12	6	18	23
31-32	Det	48	12	8	20	18
32-33	Det	45	12	11	23	25
33-34	Det	48	16	19	35	36
34-35	Det	48	17	29	46	24
35-36	Det	44	16	18	34	17
36-37	Det	45	23	20	43	20
37-38	Det	47	10	9	19	19
38-39	Det	1	1	0	1	0
Totals		489	147	129	276	279
Playoff Totals		24	6	9	15	10

AWREY, Donald William   6-0 195 D
B. Kitchener, Ont., July 18, 1943

Season	Team	GP	G	A	Pts.	PIM
63-64	Bos	16	1	0	1	4
64-65	Bos	47	2	3	5	41
65-66	Bos	70	4	3	7	74
66-67	Bos	4	1	0	1	6
67-68	Bos	74	3	12	15	150
68-69	Bos	73	0	13	13	149
69-70	Bos	73	3	10	13	120
70-71	Bos	74	4	21	25	141
71-72	Bos	34	1	8	9	52
72-73	Bos	78	2	17	19	90
73-74	Bos	75	5	16	21	51
74-75	StL-Mont	76	1	19	20	62
75-76	Mont	72	0	12	12	29
76-77	Pitt	79	1	12	13	40
77-78	NYR	78	2	8	10	38
78-79	Col	56	1	4	5	18
Totals		979	31	158	189	1065
Playoff Totals		71	0	18	18	150

AYERS, Thomas Vernon (Vern)
6-2 220 D
B. Toronto, Ont., Apr. 27, 1909

Season	Team	GP	G	A	Pts.	PIM
30-31	NYA	26	2	1	3	54
31-32	NYA	45	2	4	6	82
32-33	NYA	48	0	3	3	97
33-34	Mont M	17	0	0	0	19
34-35	StLE	47	2	2	4	60
35-36	NYR	28	0	4	4	38
Totals		211	6	14	20	350

BABANDO, Peter Joseph   5-9 187 LW
B. Braeburn, Pa., May 10, 1925

Season	Team	GP	G	A	Pts.	PIM
47-48	Bos	60	23	11	34	52
48-49	Bos	58	19	14	33	34
49-50	Det	56	6	6	12	25
50-51	Chi	70	18	19	37	36
51-52	Chi	49	11	14	25	29
52-53	Chi-NYR	58	9	9	18	18
Totals		351	86	73	159	194
Playoff Totals		17	3	3	6	6

BABCOCK, Bob   6-1 225 D
B. Agincourt, Ont., Aug. 3, 1968

Season	Team	GP	G	A	Pts.	PIM
90-91	Wash	1	0	0	0	0

BABE, Warren   6-3 200 LW
B. Medicine Hat, Alta., Sept. 7, 1968

Season	Team	GP	G	A	Pts.	PIM
87-88	Minn	6	0	1	1	4
88-89	Minn	14	2	3	5	19
90-91	Minn	1	0	1	1	0
Totals		21	2	5	7	23
Playoff Totals		2	0	0	0	0

BABIN, Mitch   6-2 195 C
B. Kapuskasing, Ont., Dec. 1, 1954

Season	Team	GP	G	A	Pts.	PIM
75-76	StL	8	0	0	0	0

BABY, John George   6-0 195 D
B. Sudbury, Ont., May 18, 1957

Season	Team	GP	G	A	Pts.	PIM
77-78	Clev	24	2	7	9	26
78-79	Minn	2	0	1	1	0
Totals		26	2	8	10	26

Season	Team	GP	G	A	Pts.	PIM
BABYCH, David Michael	6-2 205 D					
B. Edmonton, Alta., May 23, 1961						
80-81	Winn	69	6	38	44	90
81-82	Winn	79	19	49	68	92
82-83	Winn	79	13	61	74	56
83-84	Winn	66	18	39	57	62
84-85	Winn	78	13	49	62	78
85-86	Winn-Hart	81	14	55	69	50
86-87	Hart	66	8	33	41	44
87-88	Hart	71	14	36	50	54
88-89	Hart	70	6	41	47	54
89-90	Hart	72	6	37	43	62
90-91	Hart	8	0	6	6	4
91-92	Van	75	5	24	29	63
Totals		814	122	468	590	709
Playoff Totals		62	13	29	42	77
BABYCH, Wayne Joseph	5-11 191 RW					
B. Edmonton, Alta., June 6, 1958						
78-79	Stl	67	27	36	63	75
79-80	StL	59	26	35	61	49
80-81	StL	78	54	42	96	93
81-82	StL	51	19	25	44	51
82-83	StL	71	16	23	39	62
83-84	StL	70	13	29	42	52
84-85	Pitt	65	20	34	54	35
85-86	Pitt-Que-Hart	54	17	22	39	77
86-87	Hart	4	0	0	0	4
Totals		519	192	246	438	498
Playoff Totals		41	7	9	16	24
BACA, Jergus	6-2 210 D					
B. Kosice, Czechoslovakia, Jan. 4, 1965						
90-91	Hart	9	0	2	2	14
91-92	Hart	1	0	0	0	0
Totals		10	0	2	2	14
BACKMAN, Michael Charles	5-10 175 RW					
B. Halifax, N.S., Feb. 2, 1955						
81-82	NYR	3	0	2	2	4
82-83	NYR	7	1	3	4	6
83-84	NYR	8	0	1	1	8
Totals		18	1	6	7	18
Playoff Totals		10	2	2	4	2
BACKOR, Peter	6-0 185 D					
B. Ft. William, Ont., Apr. 29, 1919						
44-45	Tor	36	4	5	9	6
BACKSTROM, Ralph Gerald	5-10 170 C					
B. Kirkland Lake, Ont., Sept. 18, 1937						
56-57	Mont	3	0	0	0	0
57-58	Mont	2	0	1	1	0
58-59	Mont	64	18	22	40	19
59-60	Mont	64	13	15	28	24
60-61	Mont	69	12	20	32	44
61-62	Mont	66	27	38	65	29
62-63	Mont	70	23	12	35	51
63-64	Mont	70	8	21	29	41
64-65	Mont	70	25	30	55	41
65-66	Mont	67	22	20	42	10
66-67	Mont	69	14	27	41	39
67-68	Mont	70	20	25	45	14
68-69	Mont	72	13	28	41	16
69-70	Mont	72	19	24	43	20
70-71	Mont-LA	49	15	17	32	8
71-72	LA	76	23	29	52	22
72-73	LA-Chi	79	26	32	58	8
73-74	Chi (WHA)	78	33	50	83	26
74-75	Chi (WHA)	70	15	24	39	28
75-76	Ott-NE(WHA)	79	35	48	83	20
76-77	NE(WHA)	77	17	31	48	30
NHL Totals		1032	278	361	639	386
WHA Totals		304	100	153	253	104
NHL Playoff Totals		116	27	32	59	68
WHA Playoff Totals		38	10	18	28	12
BAILEY, Garnet Edward (Ace)						
5-11 192 LW						
B. Lloydminster, Sask., June 13, 1948						
68-69	Bos	8	3	3	6	10
69-70	Bos	58	11	11	22	82
70-71	Bos	36	0	6	6	44
71-72	Bos	73	9	13	22	64
72-73	Bos-Det	70	10	24	34	105
73-74	Det-StL	67	16	17	33	53
74-75	StL-Wash	71	19	39	58	121
75-76	Wash	67	13	19	32	75
76-77	Wash	78	19	27	46	51
77-78	Wash	40	7	12	19	28
78-79	Edm (WHA)	38	5	4	9	22
NHL Totals		568	107	171	278	633
WHA Totals		38	5	4	9	22

Season	Team	GP	G	A	Pts.	PIM
BAILEY, Garnet Edward (Ace)						
(Continued)						
NHL Playoff Totals		15	2	4	6	28
WHA Playoff Totals		2	0	0	0	4
BAILEY, Irvine Wallace (Ace)						
5-10 160 RW						
B. Bracebridge, Ont., July 3, 1903						
26-27	Tor	42	15	13	28	82
27-28	Tor	43	9	3	12	72
28-29	Tor	44	22	10	32	78
29-30	Tor	43	22	21	43	69
30-31	Tor	40	23	19	42	46
31-32	Tor	41	8	5	13	62
32-33	Tor	47	10	8	18	52
33-34	Tor	13	2	3	5	11
Totals		313	111	82	193	472
Playoff Totals		21	3	4	7	12
BAILEY, Reid	6-2 200 D					
B. Toronto, Ont., May 28, 1956						
80-81	Phil	17	1	3	4	55
81-82	Phil	10	0	0	0	23
82-83	Tor	1	0	0	0	2
83-84	Hart	12	0	0	0	25
Totals		40	1	3	4	105
Playoff Totals		16	0	2	2	25
BAILEY, Robert Allan	6-0 197 RW					
B. Kenora, Ont., May 29, 1931						
53-54	Tor	48	2	7	9	70
54-55	Tor	32	4	2	6	52
55-56	Tor	6	0	0	0	6
57-58	Chi-Det	64	9	12	21	79
Totals		150	15	21	36	207
Playoff Totals		10	0	4	4	22
BAILLARGEON, Joel	6-1 205 LW					
B. Quebec City, Que., Oct. 6, 1964						
86-87	Winn	11	0	1	1	15
87-88	Winn	4	0	1	1	12
88-89	Que	5	0	0	0	4
Totals		20	0	2	2	31
BAIRD, Kenneth Stewart	6-0 190 D					
B. Flin Flon, Man., Feb. 1, 1951						
71-72	Cal	10	0	2	2	15
72-73	Alb (WHA)	75	14	15	29	112
73-74	Edm (WHA)	68	17	19	36	115
74-75	Edm (WHA)	77	30	28	58	151
75-76	Edm (WHA)	48	13	24	37	87
76-77	Edm-Calg (WHA)	9	1	2	3	2
77-78	Winn (WHA)	55	16	11	27	31
NHL Totals		10	0	2	2	15
WHA Totals		332	91	99	190	498
WHA Playoff Totals		16	4	6	10	30
BAKER, Jamie	6-0 190 C					
B. Ottawa, Ont., Aug. 31, 1966						
89-90	Que	1	0	0	0	0
90-91	Que	18	2	0	2	8
91-92	Que	52	7	10	17	32
Totals		71	9	10	19	40
BAKER, William Robert	6-1 195 D					
B. Grand Rapids, Mich., Nov. 29, 1956						
80-81	Mont-Col	24	0	3	3	44
81-82	Col-StL	49	3	8	11	67
82-83	NYR	70	4	14	18	64
Totals		143	7	25	32	175
Playoff Totals		6	0	0	0	0
BAKOVIC, Peter George	6-2 200 RW					
B. Thunder Bay, Ont., Jan. 31, 1965						
87-88	Van	10	2	0	2	48
BALDERIS, Helmut	5-11 190 RW					
B. Riga, Latvia, June 30, 1952						
89-90	Minn	26	3	6	9	2
BALDWIN, Douglas	6-0 175 D					
B. Winnipeg, Man., Nov. 2, 1922						
45-46	Tor	15	0	1	1	6
46-47	Det	4	0	0	0	0
47-48	Chi	5	0	0	0	2
Totals		24	0	1	1	8
BALFOUR, Earl Frederick	6-1 180 LW					
B. Toronto, Ont., Jan. 4, 1933						
51-52	Tor	3	0	0	0	2
53-54	Tor	17	0	1	1	6

Season	Team	GP	G	A	Pts.	PIM
BALFOUR, Earl Frederick	(Continued)					
55-56	Tor	59	14	5	19	40
57-58	Tor	1	0	0	0	0
58-59	Chi	70	10	8	18	10
59-60	Chi	70	3	5	8	16
60-61	Chi	68	3	3	6	4
Totals		288	30	22	52	78
Playoff Totals		26	0	3	3	4
BALFOUR, Murray	5-9 178 RW					
B. Regina, Sask., Aug. 24, 1936						
56-57	Mont	2	0	0	0	2
57-58	Mont	3	1	1	2	4
59-60	Chi	61	18	12	30	55
60-61	Chi	70	21	27	48	123
61-62	Chi	49	15	15	30	72
62-63	Chi	65	10	23	33	35
63-64	Chi	41	2	10	12	36
64-65	Bos	15	0	2	2	26
Totals		306	67	90	157	353
Playoff Totals		40	9	10	19	45
BALL, Terry James	5-8 165 D					
B. Selkirk, Man., Nov. 29, 1944						
67-68	Phil	1	0	0	0	0
69-70	Phil	61	7	18	25	20
70-71	Buf	2	0	0	0	0
71-72	Buf	10	0	1	1	6
72-73	Minn (WHA)	76	6	34	40	66
73-74	Minn (WHA)	71	8	28	36	34
74-75	Minn (WHA)	76	8	37	45	36
75-76	Clev-Cin (WHA)	59	5	29	34	30
76-77	Birm (WHA)	23	1	6	7	8
NHL Totals		74	7	19	26	26
WHA Totals		305	28	134	162	174
WHA Playoff Totals		28	5	8	13	14
BALON, David Alexander	5-10 172 LW					
B. Wakaw, Sask., Aug. 2, 1937						
59-60	NYR	3	0	0	0	0
60-61	NYR	13	1	2	3	8
61-62	NYR	30	4	11	15	11
62-63	NYR	70	11	13	24	72
63-64	Mont	70	24	18	42	80
64-65	Mont	63	18	23	41	61
65-66	Mont	45	3	7	10	24
66-67	Mont	48	11	8	19	31
67-68	Minn	73	15	32	47	84
68-69	NYR	75	10	21	31	57
69-70	NYR	76	33	37	70	100
70-71	NYR	78	36	24	60	34
71-72	NYR-Van	75	23	24	47	23
72-73	Van	57	3	2	5	22
73-74	Que (WHA)	9	0	0	0	2
NHL Totals		776	192	222	414	607
WHA Totals		9	0	0	0	2
NHL Playoff Totals		78	14	21	35	109
BALTIMORE, Byron Don	6-2 200 D					
B. Whitehorse, Yuk., Aug. 26, 1952						
74-75	Chi (WHA)	77	8	12	20	110
75-76	Ott-Ind (WHA)	78	2	18	20	62
76-77	Ind (WHA)	55	0	15	15	63
77-78	Ind-Cin (WHA)	50	3	16	19	70
78-79	Ind-Cin (WHA)	71	5	11	16	85
79-80	Edm	2	0	0	0	4
NHL Totals		2	0	0	0	4
WHA Totals		331	18	72	90	390
WHA Playoff Totals		19	0	1	1	11
BALUIK, Stanley	5-8 160 C					
B. Port Arthur, Ont., Oct. 5, 1935						
59-60	Bos	7	0	0	0	2
BANDURA, Jeffrey Mitchell Joseph	6-1 195 D					
B. White Rock, B.C., Apr. 4, 1957						
80-81	NYR	2	0	1	1	0
BARAHONA, Ralph J.	5-10 180 C					
B. Long Beach, Cal., Nov. 16, 1965						
90-91	Bos	3	2	1	3	0
91-92	Bos	3	0	1	1	0
Totals		6	2	2	4	0
BARBE, Andre Joseph (Andy)	6-0 175 RW					
B. Coniston, Ont., July 27, 1923						
50-51	Tor	1	0	0	0	2

406

BARBER, Donald *6-1 205 LW*
B. Victoria, B.C., Dec. 2, 1964

Season	Team	GP	G	A	Pts.	PIM
88-89	Minn	23	8	5	13	8
89-90	Minn	44	15	19	34	32
90-91	Minn-Winn	23	1	2	3	18
91-92	Winn-Que-SJ	25	1	6	7	6
Totals		115	25	32	57	64
Playoff Totals		11	4	4	8	10

BARBER, William Charles *6-0 190 LW*
B. Callander, Ont., July 11, 1952

Season	Team	GP	G	A	Pts.	PIM
72-73	Phil	69	30	34	64	46
73-74	Phil	75	34	35	69	54
74-75	Phil	79	34	37	71	66
75-76	Phil	80	50	62	112	104
76-77	Phil	73	20	35	55	62
77-78	Phil	80	41	31	72	34
78-79	Phil	79	34	46	80	22
79-80	Phil	79	40	32	72	17
80-81	Phil	80	43	42	85	69
81-82	Phil	80	45	44	89	85
82-83	Phil	66	27	33	60	28
83-84	Phil	63	22	32	54	36
Totals		903	420	463	883	623
Playoff Totals		129	53	55	108	109

BARILKO, William *5-11 184 D*
B. Timmins, Ont., Mar. 25, 1927

Season	Team	GP	G	A	Pts.	PIM
46-47	Tor	18	3	7	10	33
47-48	Tor	57	5	9	14	147
48-49	Tor	60	5	4	9	95
49-50	Tor	59	7	10	17	85
50-51	Tor	58	6	6	12	96
Totals		252	26	36	62	456
Playoff Totals		47	5	7	12	104

BARKLEY, Douglas *6-2 185 D*
B. Lethbridge, Alta., Jan. 6, 1937

Season	Team	GP	G	A	Pts.	PIM
57-58	Chi	3	0	0	0	0
59-60	Chi	3	0	0	0	2
62-63	Det	70	3	24	27	78
63-64	Det	67	11	21	32	115
64-65	Det	67	5	20	25	122
65-66	Det	43	5	15	20	65
Totals		253	24	80	104	382
Playoff Totals		30	0	9	9	63

BARLOW, Robert George *5-10 175 F*
B. Hamilton, Ont., June 17, 1935

Season	Team	GP	G	A	Pts.	PIM
69-70	Minn	70	16	17	33	10
70-71	Minn	7	0	0	0	0
74-75	Phoe (WHA)	51	6	20	26	8
NHL Totals		77	16	17	33	10
WHA Totals		51	6	20	26	8
NHL Playoff Totals		6	2	2	4	6

BARNES, Blair *5-11 190 RW*
B. Windsor, Ont., Sept. 21, 1960

Season	Team	GP	G	A	Pts.	PIM
82-83	LA	1	0	0	0	0

BARNES, Norman Leonard Charles
6-0 190 D
B. Toronto, Ont., Aug. 24, 1953

Season	Team	GP	G	A	Pts.	PIM
76-77	Phil	1	0	0	0	0
79-80	Phil	59	4	21	25	59
80-81	Phil-Hart	76	1	13	14	100
81-82	Hart	20	1	4	5	19
Totals		156	6	38	44	178
Playoff Totals		12	0	0	0	8

BARNES, Stu *5-10 175 C*
B. Edmonton, Alta., Dec. 25, 1970

Season	Team	GP	G	A	Pts.	PIM
91-92	Winn	46	8	9	17	26

BARON, Murray *6-3 215 D*
B. Prince George, B.C., June 1, 1967

Season	Team	GP	G	A	Pts.	PIM
89-90	Phil	16	2	2	4	12
90-91	Phil	67	8	8	16	74
91-92	StL	67	3	8	11	94
Totals		150	13	18	31	180
Playoff Totals		2	0	0	0	2

BARON, Normand *6-0 205 LW*
B. Verdun, Que., Dec. 15, 1957

Season	Team	GP	G	A	Pts.	PIM
83-84	Mont	4	0	0	0	12
85-86	StL	23	2	0	2	39
Totals		27	2	0	2	51
Playoff Totals		3	0	0	0	22

BARR, David *6-1 185 RW*
B. Toronto, Ont., Nov. 30, 1960

Season	Team	GP	G	A	Pts.	PIM
81-82	Bos	2	0	0	0	0
82-83	Bos	10	1	1	2	7
83-84	NYR-StL	7	0	0	0	2

BARR, David *(Continued)*

Season	Team	GP	G	A	Pts.	PIM
84-85	StL	75	16	18	34	32
85-86	StL	72	13	38	51	70
86-87	StL-Hart-Det	69	15	17	32	68
87-88	Det	51	14	26	40	58
88-89	Det	73	27	32	59	69
89-90	Det	62	10	25	35	45
90-91	Det	70	18	22	40	55
91-92	NJ	41	6	12	18	42
Totals		532	120	191	311	448
Playoff Totals		63	11	9	20	60

BARRETT, Frederick William *6-0 194 D*
B. Ottawa, Ont., Dec. 6, 1950

Season	Team	GP	G	A	Pts.	PIM
70-71	Minn	57	0	13	13	75
72-73	Minn	46	2	4	6	21
73-74	Minn	40	0	7	7	12
74-75	Minn	62	3	18	21	82
75-76	Minn	79	2	9	11	66
76-77	Minn	60	1	8	9	46
77-78	Minn	79	0	15	15	59
78-79	Minn	45	1	9	10	48
79-80	Minn	80	8	14	22	71
80-81	Minn	62	4	8	12	72
81-82	Minn	69	1	15	16	89
82-83	Minn	51	1	3	4	22
83-84	LA	15	2	0	2	8
Totals		745	25	123	148	671
Playoff Totals		44	0	2	2	60

BARRETT, John David *6-1 210 D*
B. Ottawa, Ont., July 1, 1958

Season	Team	GP	G	A	Pts.	PIM
80-81	Det	56	3	10	13	60
81-82	Det	69	1	12	13	93
82-83	Det	79	4	10	14	74
83-84	Det	78	2	8	10	78
84-85	Det	71	6	19	25	117
85-86	Det-Wash	79	2	15	17	137
86-87	Wash	55	2	2	4	43
87-88	Minn	1	0	1	1	2
Totals		488	20	77	97	604
Playoff Totals		16	2	2	4	50

BARRIE, Douglas Robert *5-9 175 D*
B. Edmonton, Alta., Oct. 2, 1946

Season	Team	GP	G	A	Pts.	PIM
68-69	Pitt	8	1	1	2	8
70-71	Buf	75	4	23	27	168
71-72	Buf-LA	75	5	18	23	92
72-73	Alb (WHA)	54	9	22	31	111
73-74	Edm (WHA)	69	4	27	31	214
74-75	Edm (WHA)	78	12	33	45	122
75-76	Edm (WHA)	79	4	21	25	81
76-77	Edm (WHA)	70	8	19	27	92
NHL Totals		158	10	42	52	268
WHA Totals		350	37	122	159	620
WHA Playoff Totals		12	1	1	2	22

BARRIE, Len *5-11 190 C*
B. Kelowna, B.C., June 4, 1969

Season	Team	GP	G	A	Pts.	PIM
89-90	Phil	1	0	0	0	0

BARRY, Edward Thomas *5-10 180 LW*
B. Wellesley, Mass., Oct. 9, 1919

Season	Team	GP	G	A	Pts.	PIM
46-47	Bos	19	1	3	4	2

BARRY, Martin J. *5-11 175 C*
B. Quebec City, Que., Dec. 8, 1905

Season	Team	GP	G	A	Pts.	PIM
27-28	NYA	7	1	0	1	2
29-30	Bos	44	18	15	33	8
30-31	Bos	44	20	11	31	26
31-32	Bos	48	21	17	38	22
32-33	Bos	48	24	13	37	40
33-34	Bos	48	27	12	39	12
34-35	Bos	48	20	20	40	33
35-36	Bos	48	21	19	40	16
36-37	Det	48	17	27	44	6
37-38	Det	48	9	20	29	34
38-39	Det	48	13	28	41	4
39-40	Mont	30	4	10	14	2
Totals		509	195	192	387	205
Playoff Totals		43	15	18	33	34

BARRY, William Raymond (Ray)
5-11 170 C
B. Boston, Mass., Oct. 4, 1928

Season	Team	GP	G	A	Pts.	PIM
51-52	Bos	18	1	2	3	6

BARTEL, Robin Dale *6-0 200 D*
B. Drake, Sask., May 16, 1961

Season	Team	GP	G	A	Pts.	PIM
85-86	Calg	1	0	0	0	0
86-87	Vanc	40	0	1	1	14
Totals		41	0	1	1	14

BARTEL, Robin Dale *(Continued)*

Season	Team	GP	G	A	Pts.	PIM
Playoff Totals		6	0	0	0	16

BARTLETT, James Baker (Rocky)
5-9 165 LW
B. Verdun, Que., May 27, 1932

Season	Team	GP	G	A	Pts.	PIM
54-55	Mont	2	0	0	0	4
55-56	NYR	12	0	1	1	8
58-59	NYR	70	11	9	20	118
59-60	NYR	44	8	4	12	48
60-61	Bos	63	15	9	24	95
Totals		191	34	23	57	273
Playoff Totals		2	0	0	0	0

BARTON, Clifford John *5-7 155 RW*
B. Sault Ste. Marie, Mich., Sept. 3, 1907

Season	Team	GP	G	A	Pts.	PIM
29-30	Pitt Pi	39	4	2	6	4
30-31	PhilQ	43	6	7	13	18
39-40	NYR	3	0	0	0	0
Totals		85	10	9	19	22

BASSEN, Bob *5-10 180 C*
B. Calgary, Alta., May 6, 1965

Season	Team	GP	G	A	Pts.	PIM
85-86	NYI	11	2	1	3	6
86-87	NYI	77	7	10	17	89
87-88	NYI	77	6	16	22	99
88-89	NYI-Chi	68	5	16	21	83
89-90	Chi	6	1	1	2	8
90-91	StL	79	16	18	34	183
91-92	StL	79	7	25	32	167
Totals		397	44	87	131	635
Playoff Totals		52	3	10	13	106

BATHE, Francis Lenard *6-1 190 D*
B. Oshawa, Ont., Sept. 27, 1954

Season	Team	GP	G	A	Pts.	PIM
74-75	Det	19	0	3	3	31
75-76	Det	7	0	1	1	9
77-78	Phil	1	0	0	0	0
78-79	Phil	21	1	3	4	76
79-80	Phil	47	0	7	7	111
80-81	Phil	44	0	3	3	175
81-82	Phil	28	1	3	4	68
82-83	Phil	57	1	8	9	72
Totals		224	3	28	31	542
Playoff Totals		27	1	3	4	42

BATHGATE, Andrew James *6-0 180 RW*
B. Winnipeg, Man., Aug. 28, 1932

Season	Team	GP	G	A	Pts.	PIM
52-53	NYR	18	0	1	1	6
53-54	NYR	20	2	2	4	18
54-55	NYR	70	20	20	40	37
55-56	NYR	70	19	47	66	59
56-57	NYR	70	27	50	77	60
57-58	NYR	65	30	48	78	42
58-59	NYR	70	40	48	88	48
59-60	NYR	70	26	48	74	28
60-61	NYR	70	29	48	77	22
61-62	NYR	70	28	56	84	44
62-63	NYR	70	35	46	81	54
63-64	NYR-Tor	71	19	58	77	34
64-65	Tor	55	16	29	45	34
65-66	Det	70	15	32	47	25
66-67	Det	60	8	23	31	24
67-68	Pitt	74	20	39	59	55
70-71	Pitt	76	15	29	44	34
74-75	Van (WHA)	11	1	6	7	2
NHL Totals		1069	349	624	973	624
WHA Totals		11	1	6	7	2
NHL Playoff Totals		54	21	14	35	76

BATHGATE, Frank Douglas *5-10 162 C*
B. Winnipeg, Man., Feb. 14, 1930

Season	Team	GP	G	A	Pts.	PIM
52-53	NYR	2	0	0	0	2

BAUER, Robert Theodore *5-6 150 RW*
B. Waterloo, Ont., Feb. 16, 1915

Season	Team	GP	G	A	Pts.	PIM
35-36	Bos	1	0	0	0	0
36-37	Bos	1	1	0	1	0
37-38	Bos	48	20	14	34	9
38-39	Bos	48	13	18	31	4
39-40	Bos	48	17	26	43	2
40-41	Bos	48	17	22	39	2
41-42	Bos	36	13	22	35	11
45-46	Bos	39	11	10	21	4
46-47	Bos	58	30	24	54	4
51-52	Bos	1	1	1	2	0
Totals		328	123	137	260	36
Playoff Totals		48	11	8	19	6

BAUMGARTNER, Ken *6-1 200 D*
B. Flin Flon, Man., Mar. 11, 1966

Season	Team	GP	G	A	Pts.	PIM
87-88	LA	30	2	3	5	189
88-89	LA	49	1	3	4	288
89-90	LA-NYI	65	1	5	6	222
90-90	NYI	78	1	6	7	282
91-92	NYI-Tor	55	0	1	1	225
Totals		277	5	18	23	1206

BAUMGARTNER, Ken *(Continued)*

Season	Team	GP	G	A	Pts.	PIM
Playoff Totals		14	0	1	1	63

BAUMGARTNER, Michael Edward
6-1 195 D
B. Roseau, Minn., Jan. 30, 1949

Season	Team	GP	G	A	Pts.	PIM
74-75	KC	17	0	0	0	0

BAUN, Robert Neil *5-9 182 D*
B. Lanigan, Sask., Sept, 9, 1936

Season	Team	GP	G	A	Pts.	PIM
56-57	Tor	20	0	5	5	37
57-58	Tor	67	1	9	10	91
58-59	Tor	51	1	8	9	87
59-60	Tor	61	8	9	17	59
60-61	Tor	70	1	14	15	70
61-62	Tor	65	4	11	15	94
62-63	Tor	48	4	8	12	65
63-64	Tor	52	4	14	18	113
64-65	Tor	70	0	18	18	160
65-66	Tor	44	0	6	6	68
66-67	Tor	54	2	8	10	83
67-68	Oak	67	3	10	13	81
68-69	Det	76	4	16	20	121
69-70	Det	71	1	18	19	112
70-71	Det-Tor	69	1	20	21	147
71-72	Tor	74	2	12	14	101
72-73	Tor	5	1	1	2	4
Totals		964	37	187	224	1493
Playoff Totals		96	3	12	15	171

BAWA, Robin *6-2 214 RW*
B. Chemainus, B.C., Mar. 26, 1966

Season	Team	GP	G	A	Pts.	PIM
89-90	Wash	5	1	0	1	6
91-92	Van	2	0	0	0	0
Totals		7	1	0	1	6
Playoffs Totals		1	0	0	0	0

BAXTER, Paul Gordon *5-11 200 D*
B. Winnipeg, Man., Oct. 25, 1955

Season	Team	GP	G	A	Pts.	PIM
74-75	Clev (WHA)	5	0	0	0	37
75-76	Clev (WHA)	67	3	7	10	201
76-77	Que (WHA)	66	6	17	23	244
77-78	Que (WHA)	76	6	29	35	240
78-79	Que (WHA)	76	10	36	46	240
79-80	Que	61	7	13	20	145
80-81	Pitt	51	5	14	19	204
81-82	Pitt	76	9	34	43	409
82-83	Pitt	75	11	21	32	238
83-84	Calg	74	7	20	27	182
84-85	Calg	70	5	14	19	126
85-86	Calg	47	4	3	7	194
86-87	Calg	18	0	2	2	66
NHL Totals		472	48	121	169	1564
WHA Totals		290	25	89	114	962
NHL Playoff Totals		40	0	5	5	162
WHA Playoff Totals		30	6	11	17	94

BEADLE, Sandy James *6-2 185 LW*
B. Regina, Sask., July 12, 1960

Season	Team	GP	G	A	Pts.	PIM
80-81	Winn	6	1	0	1	2

BEATON, Alexander Francis (Frank, Seldom)
5-10 200 LW
B. Antigonish, N.S., Apr. 28, 1953

Season	Team	GP	G	A	Pts.	PIM
75-76	Cin (WHA)	29	2	3	5	61
76-77	Edm (WHA)	68	4	9	13	274
77-78	Birm (WHA)	56	6	9	15	279
78-79	NYR	2	0	0	0	0
79-80	NYR	23	1	1	2	43
NHL Totals		25	1	1	2	43
WHA Totals		153	12	21	33	614
WHA Playoff Totals		10	2	2	4	31

BEATTIE, John (Red) *5-9 170 LW*
B. Ibstock, England, Oct. 7, 1907

Season	Team	GP	G	A	Pts.	PIM
30-31	Bos	32	10	11	21	25
31-32	Bos	2	0	0	0	0
32-33	Bos	48	8	12	20	12
33-34	Bos	48	9	13	22	26
34-35	Bos	48	9	18	27	27
35-36	Bos	48	14	18	32	27
36-37	Bos	48	8	7	15	10
37-38	Bos-Det-NYA	44	4	6	10	5
38-39	NYA	17	0	0	0	5
Totals		335	62	85	147	137
Playoff Totals		22	4	2	6	6

BEAUDIN, Norman Joseph Andrew
5-8 170 RW
B. Montmartre, Sask., Nov. 28, 1941

Season	Team	GP	G	A	Pts.	PIM
67-68	StL	13	1	1	2	4
70-71	Minn	12	0	1	1	0
72-73	Winn (WHA)	78	38	65	103	15

BEAUDIN, Norman Joseph Andrew
(Continued)

Season	Team	GP	G	A	Pts.	PIM
73-74	Winn (WHA)	74	27	28	55	8
74-75	Winn (WHA)	77	16	31	47	8
75-76	Winn (WHA)	80	16	31	47	38
NHL Totals		25	1	2	3	4
WHA Totals		309	97	155	252	69
WHA Playoff Totals		31	18	19	37	14

BEAUDOIN, Serge *6-2 215 D*
B. Montreal, Que., Nov. 30, 1952

Season	Team	GP	G	A	Pts.	PIM
73-74	Van (WHA)	26	1	11	12	37
74-75	Van (WHA)	4	0	0	0	2
75-76	Phoe (WHA)	76	0	21	21	102
76-77	Phoe (WHA)	77	6	24	30	136
77-78	Birm (WHA)	77	8	26	34	115
78-79	Birm (WHA)	72	5	21	26	127
79-80	Atl	3	0	0	0	0
NHL Totals		3	0	0	0	0
WHA Totals		332	20	103	123	519
WHA Playoff Totals		10	2	0	2	56

BEAUDOIN, Yves *5-11 180 D*
B. Pointe-aux-Trembles, Que., Jan. 7, 1965

Season	Team	GP	G	A	Pts.	PIM
85-86	Wash	4	0	0	0	0
86-87	Wash	6	0	0	0	5
87-88	Wash	1	0	0	0	0
Totals		11	0	0	0	5

BEAUPRE, Donald William *5-8 150*
B. Waterloo, Ont., Sept. 19, 1961

Season	Team	GP	G	A	Pts.	PIM
80-81	Minn	0	0	0	0	0
Playoff Totals		6	0	0	0	0

BECK, Barry David *6-3 215 D*
B. Vancouver, B.C., June 3, 1957

Season	Team	GP	G	A	Pts.	PIM
77-78	Col	75	22	38	60	89
78-79	Col	63	14	28	42	91
79-80	Col-NYR	71	15	50	65	106
80-81	NYR	75	11	23	34	231
81-82	NYR	60	9	29	38	111
82-83	NYR	66	12	22	34	112
83-84	NYR	72	9	27	36	134
84-85	NYR	56	7	19	26	65
85-86	NYR	25	4	8	12	24
89-90	LA	52	1	7	8	53
Totals		615	104	251	355	1016
Playoff Totals		51	10	23	33	77

BECKETT, Robert Owen *6-0 185 C*
B. Unionville, Ont., Apr. 8, 1936

Season	Team	GP	G	A	Pts.	PIM
56-57	Bos	18	0	3	3	2
57-58	Bos	9	0	0	0	2
61-62	Bos	34	7	2	9	14
63-64	Bos	7	0	1	1	0
Totals		68	7	6	13	18

BEDARD, James Arthur *5-10 181*
B. Niagara Falls, Ont., Nov. 14, 1956

Season	Team	GP	G	A	Pts.	PIM
77-78	Wash	43	0	2	2	4

BEDARD, James Leo *6-0 180 D*
B. Admiral, Sask., Nov. 19, 1927

Season	Team	GP	G	A	Pts.	PIM
49-50	Chi	5	0	0	0	2
50-51	Chi	17	1	1	2	6
Totals		22	1	1	2	8

BEDNARSKI, John Severn *5-10 195 D*
B. Thunder Bay, Ont., July 4, 1952

Season	Team	GP	G	A	Pts.	PIM
74-75	NYR	35	1	10	11	37
75-76	NYR	59	1	8	9	77
76-77	NYR	5	0	0	0	0
79-50	Edm	1	0	0	0	0
Totals		100	2	18	20	114
Playoff Totals		1	0	0	0	0

BEERS, Bob *6-2 200 D*
B. Cheektowaga, N.Y., May 20, 1967

Season	Team	GP	G	A	Pts.	PIM
89-90	Bos	3	0	1	1	6
90-91	Bos	16	0	1	1	10
91-92	Bos	31	0	5	5	29
Totals		50	0	7	7	45
Playoff Totals		21	1	1	2	22

BEERS, Edward Joseph *6-2 200 LW*
B. Merritt, B.C., Oct. 12, 1959

Season	Team	GP	G	A	Pts.	PIM
81-82	Calg	5	1	1	2	21
82-83	Calg	41	11	15	26	21

BEERS, Edward Joseph *(Continued)*

Season	Team	GP	G	A	Pts.	PIM
83-84	Calg	73	36	39	75	88
84-85	Calg	74	28	40	68	94
85-86	Calg-StL	57	18	21	39	32
Totals		250	94	116	210	256
Playoff Totals		41	7	10	17	47

BEHLING, Richard Clarence *D*
B. Kitchener, Ont., Mar. 16, 1916

Season	Team	GP	G	A	Pts.	PIM
40-41	Det	3	0	0	0	0
42-43	Det	2	1	0	1	2
Totals		5	1	0	1	2

BEISLER, Frank *D*
B. New Haven, Conn.

Season	Team	GP	G	A	Pts.	PIM
36-37	NYA	1	0	0	0	0
39-40	NYA	1	0	0	0	0
Totals		2	0	0	0	0

BELANGER, Alain *6-1 190 RW*
B. St. Janvier, Que., Jan. 18, 1956

Season	Team	GP	G	A	Pts.	PIM
77-78	Tor	9	0	1	1	6

BELANGER, Jesse *6-0 170 C*
B. St. Georges de Beauce, Que., June 15, 1969

Season	Team	GP	G	A	Pts.	PIM
91-92	Mont	4	0	0	0	0

BELANGER, Roger *6-0 190 C*
B. St. Catharines, Ont., Dec. 1, 1965

Season	Team	GP	G	A	Pts.	PIM
84-85	Pitt	44	3	5	8	32

BELISLE, Daniel George *5-10 175 Rw*
B. South Porcupine, Ont., May 9, 1937

Season	Team	GP	G	A	Pts.	PIM
60-61	NYR	4	2	0	2	0

BELIVEAU, Jean Arthur *6-3 205 C*
B. Trois Rivieres, Que., Aug. 31, 1931

Season	Team	GP	G	A	Pts.	PIM
50-51	Mont	2	1	1	2	0
52-53	Mont	3	5	0	5	0
53-54	Mont	44	13	21	34	22
54-55	Mont	70	37	36	73	58
55-56	Mont	70	47	41	88	143
56-57	Mont	69	33	51	84	105
57-58	Mont	55	27	32	59	93
58-59	Mont	64	45	46	91	67
59-60	Mont	60	34	40	74	57
60-61	Mont	69	32	58	90	57
61-62	Mont	43	18	23	41	36
62-63	Mont	69	18	49	67	68
63-64	Mont	68	28	50	78	42
64-65	Mont	58	20	23	43	76
65-66	Mont	67	29	48	77	50
66-67	Mont	53	12	26	38	22
67-68	Mont	59	31	37	68	28
68-69	Mont	69	33	49	82	55
69-70	Mont	63	19	30	49	10
70-71	Mont	70	25	51	76	40
Totals		1125	507	712	1219	1029
Playoff Totals		162	79	97	176	211

BELL, Bruce *6-0 190 D*
B. Toronto, Ont., Feb. 15, 1965

Season	Team	GP	G	A	Pts.	PIM
84-85	Que	75	6	31	37	44
85-86	StL	75	2	18	20	43
86-87	StL	45	3	13	16	18
87-88	NYR	13	1	2	3	8
89-90	Edm	1	0	0	0	0
Totals		209	12	64	76	113
Playoff Totals		34	3	5	8	41

BELL, Harry *5-8 180 D*
B. Regina, Sask., Oct. 31, 1925

Season	Team	GP	G	A	Pts.	PIM
46-47	NYR	1	0	1	1	0

BELL, Joseph Alexander *5-10 170 LW*
B. Portage la Prairie, Man., Nov. 27, 1923

Season	Team	GP	G	A	Pts.	PIM
42-43	NYR	15	2	5	7	6
46-47	NYR	47	6	4	10	12
Totals		62	8	9	17	18

BELL, William *C/D*
B. Lachine, Que., June 10, 1891

Season	Team	GP	G	A	Pts.	PIM
17-18	Mont W-Mont	8	1	0	1	3
18-19	Mont	1	0	0	0	0
20-21	Mont	4	0	0	0	0
21-22	Mont-Ott	23	2	1	3	4
22-23	Mont	15	0	0	0	0
23-24	Mont	10	0	0	0	0
Totals		61	3	1	4	7
Playoff Totals		9	0	0	0	0

BELLAND, Neil 5-11 175 D
B. Parry Sound, Ont., Apr. 3, 1961

Season	Team	GP	G	A	Pts.	PIM
81-82	Van	28	3	6	9	16
82-23	Van	14	2	4	6	4
83-84	Van	44	7	13	20	24
84-85	Van	13	0	6	6	6
85-86	Van	7	1	2	3	4
86-87	Pitt	3	0	1	1	0
Totals		109	13	32	45	54
Playoff Totals		21	2	9	11	23

BELLEFEUILLE, Peter RW

Season	Team	GP	G	A	Pts.	PIM
25-26	Tor	36	14	2	16	22
26-27	Tor-Det	31	6	0	6	26
28-29	Det	1	1	0	1	0
29-30	Det	24	5	2	7	10
Totals		92	26	4	30	58

BELLEMER, Andrew D
B. Penetang, Ont., July 3, 1904

Season	Team	GP	G	A	Pts.	PIM
32-33	Mont M	15	0	0	0	0

BELLOWS, Brian 5-11 200 RW
B. St. Catharines, Ont., Sept. 1, 1964

Season	Team	GP	G	A	Pts.	PIM
82-83	Minn	78	35	30	65	27
83-84	Minn	78	41	42	83	66
84-85	Minn	78	26	36	62	72
85-86	Minn	77	31	48	79	46
86-87	Minn	65	26	27	53	34
87-88	Minn	77	40	41	81	81
88-89	Minn	60	23	27	50	55
89-90	Minn	80	55	44	99	72
90-91	Minn	80	35	40	75	43
91-92	Minn	80	30	45	75	41
Totals		753	342	380	722	537
Playoff Totals		81	34	49	83	111

BEND, John Linthwaite (Lin) 5-9 165 C
B. Poplar Point, Man., Dec. 20, 1922

Season	Team	GP	G	A	Pts.	PIM
42-43	NYR	8	3	1	4	2

BENNETT, Adam 6-4 206 D
B. Georgetown, Ont., Mar. 30, 1971

Season	Team	GP	G	A	Pts.	PIM
91-92	Chi	5	0	0	0	12

BENNETT, Curt Alexander 6-3 195 C
B. Regina, Sask., Mar. 27, 1948

Season	Team	GP	G	A	Pts.	PIM
70-71	StL	4	2	0	2	0
71-72	StL	31	3	5	8	30
72-73	NYR-Atl	68	18	18	36	20
73-74	Atl	71	17	24	41	34
74-75	Atl	80	31	33	64	40
75-76	Atl	80	34	31	65	61
76-77	Atl	76	22	25	47	36
77-78	Atl-StL	75	10	24	34	64
78-79	StL	74	14	19	33	62
79-80	Atl	21	1	3	4	0
Totals		580	152	182	334	347
Playoff Totals		21	1	1	2	57

BENNETT, Eric (Ric) 6-3 200 LW
B. Springfield, Mass., July 24, 1967

Season	Team	GP	G	A	Pts.	PIM
89-90	NYR	6	1	0	1	5
90-91	NYR	6	0	0	0	6
91-92	NYR	3	0	1	1	2
Totals		15	1	1	2	13

BENNETT, Frank F
B. Toronto, Ont.

Season	Team	GP	G	A	Pts.	PIM
43-44	Det	7	0	1	1	2

BENNETT, Harvey A., Jr. 6-4 215 C
B. Cranston, R.I., Aug. 9, 1952

Season	Team	GP	G	A	Pts.	PIM
74-75	Pitt	7	0	0	0	0
75-76	Pitt-Wash	74	15	13	28	92
76-77	Wash-Phil	69	14	14	28	94
77-78	Phil-Minn	66	12	10	22	91
78-79	StL	52	3	9	12	63
Totals		268	44	46	90	340
Playoff Totals		4	0	0	0	0

BENNETT, Maxwell RW
B. Cobalt, Ont., Nov. 4, 1912

Season	Team	GP	G	A	Pts.	PIM
35-36	Mont	1	0	0	0	0

BENNETT, William 6-5 235 LW
B. Warwick, R.I., May 31, 1953

Season	Team	GP	G	A	Pts.	PIM
78-79	Bos	7	1	4	5	2
79-80	Hart	24	3	3	6	63
Totals		31	4	7	11	65

BENNING, Brian 6-0 195 D
B. Edmonton, Alta., June 10, 1966

Season	Team	GP	G	A	Pts.	PIM
84-85	StL	4	0	2	2	0
86-87	StL	78	13	36	49	110
87-88	StL	77	8	29	37	107
88-89	StL	66	8	26	34	102

BENNING, Brian (Continued)

Season	Team	GP	G	A	Pts.	PIM
89-90	StL-LA	55	6	19	25	106
90-91	LA	61	7	24	31	127
91-92	LA-Phil	75	4	42	46	134
Totals		416	46	178	224	686
Playoff Totals		48	3	20	23	74

BENNING, James 6-0 183 D
B. Edmonton, Alta., Apr. 29, 1963

Season	Team	GP	G	A	Pts.	PIM
81-82	Tor	74	7	24	31	46
82-83	Tor	74	5	17	22	47
83-84	Tor	79	12	39	51	66
84-85	Tor	80	9	35	44	55
85-86	Tor	52	4	21	25	71
86-87	Tor-Van	59	2	11	13	44
87-88	Van	77	7	26	33	58
88-89	Van	65	3	9	12	48
89-90	Van	45	3	9	12	26
Totals		605	52	191	243	461
Playoff Totals		7	1	1	2	2

BENOIT, Joseph 5-9 160 RW
B. St. Albert, Alta., Feb. 27, 1916

Season	Team	GP	G	A	Pts.	PIM
40-41	Mont	45	16	16	32	32
41-42	Mont	46	20	16	36	27
42-43	Mont	49	30	27	57	23
45-46	Mont	39	9	10	19	8
46-47	Mont	6	0	0	0	4
Totals		185	75	69	144	94
Playoff Totals		11	6	3	9	11

BENSON, Robert D
B. Buffalo, N.Y.

Season	Team	GP	G	A	Pts.	PIM
24-25	Bos	8	0	1	1	4

BENSON, William Lloyd 5-11 165 C
B. Winnipeg, Man., July 29, 1920

Season	Team	GP	G	A	Pts.	PIM
40-41	NYA	22	3	4	7	4
41-42	NYA	45	8	21	29	31
Totals		67	11	25	36	35

BENTLEY, Douglas Wagner 5-8 145 LW
B. Delisle, Sask., Sept. 3, 1916

Season	Team	GP	G	A	Pts.	PIM
39-40	Chi	39	12	7	19	12
40-41	Chi	47	8	20	28	12
41-42	Chi	38	12	14	26	11
42-43	Chi	50	33	40	73	18
43-44	Chi	50	38	39	77	22
45-46	Chi	36	19	21	40	16
46-47	Chi	52	21	34	55	18
47-48	Chi	60	20	37	57	16
48-49	Chi	58	23	43	66	38
49-50	Chi	64	20	33	53	28
50-51	Chi	44	9	23	32	20
51-52	Chi	8	2	3	5	4
53-54	NYR	20	2	10	12	2
Totals		566	219	324	543	217
Playoff Totals		23	9	8	17	8

BENTLEY, Maxwell Herbert Lloyd 5-8 158 C
B. Delisle, Sask., Mar. 1, 1920

Season	Team	GP	G	A	Pts.	PIM
40-41	Chi	36	7	10	17	6
41-42	Chi	39	13	17	30	19
42-43	Chi	47	26	44	70	2
45-46	Chi	47	31	30	61	6
46-47	Chi	60	29	43	72	12
47-48	Chi-Tor	59	26	28	54	10
48-49	Tor	60	19	22	41	18
49-50	Tor	69	23	18	41	14
50-51	Tor	67	21	41	62	34
51-52	Tor	69	24	17	41	40
52-53	Tor	36	12	11	23	16
53-54	NYR	57	14	18	32	15
Totals		646	245	299	544	192
Playoff Totals		52	18	27	45	14

BENTLEY, Reginald RW
B. Delisle, Sask., May 3, 1914

Season	Team	GP	G	A	Pts.	PIM
42-43	Chi	11	1	2	3	2

BERALDO, Paul 5-11 175 RW
B. Hamilton, Ont., Oct. 5, 1967

Season	Team	GP	G	A	Pts.	PIM
87-88	Bos	3	0	0	0	0
88-89	Bos	7	0	0	0	4
Totals		10	0	0	0	4

BERANEK, Josef 6-0 180 RW
B. Litvinov, Czechoslovakia, Oct. 25, 1969

Season	Team	GP	G	A	Pts.	PIM
91-92	Edm	58	12	16	28	18
Playoff Totals		12	2	1	3	0

BEREHOWSKY, Drake 6-1 210 D
B. Toronto, Ont., Jan. 3, 1972

Season	Team	GP	G	A	Pts.	PIM
90-91	Tor	8	0	1	1	25
91-92	Tor	1	0	0	0	0
Totals		9	0	1	1	25

BERENSON, Gordon Arthur (Red) 6-0 195 C
B. Regina, Sask., Dec. 8, 1939

Season	Team	GP	G	A	Pts.	PIM
61-62	Mont	4	1	2	3	4
62-63	Mont	37	2	6	8	15
63-64	Mont	69	7	9	16	12
64-65	Mont	3	1	2	3	0
65-66	Mont	23	3	4	7	12
66-67	NYR	30	0	5	5	2
67-68	NYR-StL	74	24	30	54	24
68-69	StL	76	35	47	82	43
69-70	StL	67	33	39	72	38
70-71	StL-Det	69	21	38	59	16
71-72	Det	78	28	41	69	16
72-73	Det	78	13	30	43	8
73-74	Det	76	24	42	66	28
74-75	Det-StL	71	15	22	37	20
75-76	StL	72	20	27	47	47
76-77	StL	80	21	28	49	8
77-78	StL	80	13	25	38	12
Totals		987	261	397	658	305
Playoff Totals		85	23	14	37	49

BEREZAN, Perry Edmund 6-2 190 C
B. Edmonton, Alta., Dec. 5, 1964

Season	Team	GP	G	A	Pts.	PIM
84-85	Calg	9	3	2	5	4
85-86	Calg	55	12	21	33	39
86-87	Calg	24	5	3	8	24
87-88	Calg	29	7	12	19	66
88-89	Calg-Minn	51	5	8	13	27
89-90	Minn	64	3	12	15	31
90-91	Minn	52	11	6	17	30
91-92	SJ	66	12	7	19	30
Totals		350	58	71	129	251
Playoff Totals		31	4	7	11	34

BERG, Bill 6-1 190 D
B. St. Catharines, Ont., Oct. 21, 1967

Season	Team	GP	G	A	Pts.	PIM
88-89	NYI	7	1	2	3	10
90-91	NYI	78	9	14	23	67
91-92	NYI	47	5	9	14	28
Totals		132	15	25	40	105

BERGDINON, Fred F
B. Quebec City, Que.

Season	Team	GP	G	A	Pts.	PIM
25-26	Bos	2	0	0	0	0

BERGEN, Todd 6-3 185 C
B. Prince Albert, Sask., July 11, 1963

Season	Team	GP	G	A	Pts.	PIM
84-85	Phil	14	11	5	16	4
Playoff Totals		17	4	9	13	8

BERGER, Michael 6-0 200 D
B. Edmonton, Alta., June 2, 1967

Season	Team	GP	G	A	Pts.	PIM
87-88	Minn	29	3	1	4	65
88-89	Minn	1	0	0	0	2
Totals		30	3	1	4	67

BERGERON, Michel 5-10 170 RW
B. Chicoutimi, Que., Nov. 11, 1954

Season	Team	GP	G	A	Pts.	PIM
74-75	Det	25	10	7	17	10
75-76	Det	72	32	27	59	48
76-77	Det	74	21	12	33	98
77-78	Det-NYI	28	10	6	16	2
78-79	Wash	30	7	6	13	7
Totals		229	80	58	138	165

BERGERON, Yves 5-9 165 RW
B. Malartic, Que., Jan. 11, 1952

Season	Team	GP	G	A	Pts.	PIM
72-73	Que (WHA)	65	14	19	33	32
74-75	Pitt	2	0	0	0	0
76-77	Pitt	1	0	0	0	0
NHL Totals		3	0	0	0	0
WHA Totals		65	14	19	33	32

BERGEVIN, Marc 6-0 185 D
B. Montreal, Que., Aug. 11, 1965

Season	Team	GP	G	A	Pts.	PIM
84-85	Chi	60	0	6	6	54
85-86	Chi	71	7	7	14	60
86-87	Chi	66	4	10	14	66
87-88	Chi	58	1	6	7	85
88-89	Chi-NYI	69	2	13	15	80
89-90	NYI	18	0	4	4	30
90-91	Hart	4	0	0	0	4
91-92	Hart	75	7	17	24	64
Totals		421	21	63	84	443
Playoff Totals		17	1	3	4	6

Season	Team	GP	G	A	Pts.	PIM

BERGLAND, Tim *6-3 180 C*
B. Crookston, Minn., Jan. 11, 1965

Season	Team	GP	G	A	Pts.	PIM
89-90	Wash	32	2	5	7	31
90-91	Wash	47	5	9	14	21
91-92	Wash	22	1	4	5	2
Totals		101	8	18	26	54
Playoff Totals		26	2	2	4	22

BERGLOFF, Robert Kane *6-1 185 D*
B. Dickinson, N.D., July 26, 1958

Season	Team	GP	G	A	Pts.	PIM
82-83	Minn	2	0	0	0	5

BERGLUND, Bo *5-10 175 RW*
B. Sjalevad, Sweden, Apr. 6, 1955

Season	Team	GP	G	A	Pts.	PIM
83-84	Que	75	16	27	43	20
84-85	Que-Minn	45	10	10	20	14
85-86	Minn-Phil	10	2	2	4	6
Totals		130	28	39	67	40
Playoff Totals		9	2	0	2	6

BERGMAN, Gary Gunnar *5-11 185 D*
B. Kenora, Ont., Oct. 7, 1938

Season	Team	GP	G	A	Pts.	PIM
64-65	Det	58	4	7	11	85
65-66	Det	61	3	16	19	96
66-67	Det	70	5	30	35	129
67-68	Det	74	13	28	41	109
68-69	Det	76	7	30	37	80
69-70	Det	69	6	17	23	122
70-71	Det	68	8	25	33	149
71-72	Det	75	6	31	37	138
72-73	Det	68	3	28	31	71
73-74	Det-Minn	68	3	29	32	84
74-75	Det	76	5	25	30	104
75-76	KC	75	5	33	38	82
Totals		838	68	299	367	1249
Playoff Totals		21	0	5	5	20

BERGMAN, Thommie Lars Rudolph
6-2 200 D
B. Munkfors, Sweden, Dec. 10, 1947

Season	Team	GP	G	A	Pts.	PIM
72-73	Det	75	9	12	21	70
73-74	Det	43	0	3	3	21
74-75	Det	18	0	1	1	27
74-75	Winn (WHA)	49	4	15	19	70
75-76	Winn (WHA)	81	11	30	41	111
76-77	Winn (WHA)	42	2	24	26	37
77-78	Winn (WHA)	65	5	28	33	43
77-78	Det	14	1	6	7	16
78-79	Det	68	10	17	27	64
79-80	Det	28	1	5	6	45
NHL Totals		246	21	44	65	243
WHA Totals		237	22	97	119	261
NHL Playoff Totals		7	0	2	2	2
WHA Playoff Tot.		13	3	10	13	6

BERGQVIST, Jonas *6-0 185 RW*
B. Hassleholm, Sweden, Sept. 26, 1962

Season	Team	GP	G	A	Pts.	PIM
89-90	Calg	22	2	5	7	10

BERLINQUETTE, Louis *LW*

Season	Team	GP	G	A	Pts.	PIM
17-18	Mont	20	2	0	2	9
18-19	Mont	18	5	3	8	9
19-20	Mont	24	7	7	14	36
20-21	Mont	24	12	9	21	24
21-22	Mont	24	12	5	17	8
22-23	Mont	24	2	3	5	4
24-25	Mont M	29	4	2	6	22
25-26	Pitt Pi	30	0	0	0	8
Totals		193	44	29	73	120
Playoff Totals		16	1	1	2	0

BERNIER, Serge Joseph *6-1 190 C*
B. Padoue, Que., Apr. 29, 1947

Season	Team	GP	G	A	Pts.	PIM
68-69	Phil	1	0	0	0	2
69-70	Phil	1	0	1	1	0
70-71	Phil	77	23	28	51	77
71-72	Phil-LA	70	23	22	45	63
72-73	LA	75	22	46	68	43
73-74	Que (WHA)	74	37	49	86	107
74-45	Que (WHA)	76	54	68	122	75
75-76	Que (WHA)	70	34	68	102	91
76-77	Que (WHA)	74	43	53	96	94
77-78	Que (WHA)	58	26	52	78	48
78-79	Que (WHA)	65	36	46	82	71
79-80	Que	32	8	14	22	31
80-81	Que	46	2	8	10	18
NHL Totals		302	78	119	197	234
WHA Totals		417	230	336	566	486
NHL Playoff Totals		5	1	1	2	0
WHA Playoff Totals		50	28	46	74	41

BERRY, Brad *6-2 190 D*
B. Bashaw, Alta., Apr. 1, 1965

Season	Team	GP	G	A	Pts.	PIM
85-86	Winn	13	1	0	1	10
86-87	Winn	52	2	8	10	60
87-88	Winn	48	0	6	6	75
88-89	Winn	38	0	9	9	45
89-90	Winn	12	1	2	3	6
91-92	Minn	7	0	0	0	6
Totals		170	4	25	29	202
Playoff Totals		13	0	1	1	16

BERRY, Douglas Alan *6-1 190 C*
B. New Westminster, B.C., June 3, 1957

Season	Team	GP	G	A	Pts.	PIM
78-79	Edm (WHA)	29	6	3	9	4
79-80	Col	75	7	23	30	16
80-81	Col	46	3	10	13	8
NHL Totals		121	10	33	43	24
WHA Totals		29	6	3	9	4

BERRY, Frederick Allan *5-9 175 C*
B. Stoney Plains, Alta., Mar. 26, 1956

Season	Team	GP	G	A	Pts.	PIM
76-77	Det	3	0	0	0	0

BERRY, Kenneth E. *5-8 175 LW*
B. Burnaby, B.C., June 21, 1960

Season	Team	GP	G	A	Pts.	PIM
81-82	Edm	15	2	3	5	9
83-84	Edm	13	2	3	5	10
87-88	Van	14	2	3	5	6
88-89	Van	13	2	1	3	5
Totals		55	8	10	18	30

BERRY, Robert Victor *6-0 190 LW*
B. Montreal, Que., Nov. 29, 1943

Season	Team	GP	G	A	Pts.	PIM
68-69	Mont	2	0	0	0	0
70-71	LA	77	25	38	63	52
71-72	LA	78	17	22	39	44
72-73	LA	78	36	28	64	75
73-74	LA	77	23	33	56	56
74-75	LA	80	25	23	48	60
75-76	LA	80	20	22	42	37
76-77	LA	69	13	25	38	20
Totals		541	159	191	350	344
Playoff Totals		26	2	6	8	6

BERUBE, Craig *6-2 205 LW*
B. Calihoo, Alta., Dec. 17, 1965

Season	Team	GP	G	A	Pts.	PIM
86-87	Phil	7	0	0	0	57
87-88	Phil	27	3	2	5	108
88-89	Phil	53	1	1	2	199
09-90	Phil	74	4	14	18	291
90-91	Phil	74	8	9	17	293
91-92	Tor-Calg	76	6	11	17	264
Totals		311	22	37	59	1212
Playoff Totals		21	0	0	0	73

BESLER, Phillip Rudolph *RW*
B. Melville, Sask., Dec. 9, 1913

Season	Team	GP	G	A	Pts.	PIM
35-36	Bos	8	0	0	0	0
38-39	Chi-Det	22	1	4	5	18
Totals		30	1	4	5	18

BESSONE, Peter *5-10 200 D*
B. New Bedford, Mass., Jan. 13, 1913

Season	Team	GP	G	A	Pts.	PIM
37-38	Det	6	0	1	1	6

BETHEL, John Charles *5-11 185 LW*
B. Montreal, Que., Apr. 15, 1957

Season	Team	GP	G	A	Pts.	PIM
79-80	Winn	17	0	2	2	4

BETTIO, Silvio Angelo (Sam) *5-8 175 LW*
B. Copper Cliff, Ont., Dec. 1, 1928

Season	Team	GP	G	A	Pts.	PIM
49-50	Bos	44	9	12	21	32

BEUKEBOOM, Jeff *6-4 215 D*
B. Ajax, Ont., Mar. 28, 1965

Season	Team	GP	G	A	Pts.	PIM
86-87	Edm	44	3	8	11	124
87-88	Edm	73	5	20	25	201
88-89	Edm	36	0	5	5	94
89-90	Edm	46	1	12	13	86
90-91	Edm	67	3	7	10	150
91-92	Edm-NYR	74	1	15	16	200
Totals		340	13	67	80	855
Playoff Totals		42	3	6	9	97

BEVERLEY, Nicholas Gerald (Nick)
6-2 185 D
B. Toronto, Ont., Apr. 21, 1947

Season	Team	GP	G	A	Pts.	PIM
66-67	Bos	2	0	0	0	0
69-40	Bos	2	0	0	0	2
71-72	Bos	1	0	0	0	0
72-73	Bos	76	1	10	11	26
73-74	Bos-Pitt	77	2	14	16	21
74-75	NYR	54	3	15	18	19
75-76	NYR	63	1	8	9	46
76-77	NYR-Minn	61	2	17	19	8

BEVERLEY, Nicholas Gerald (Nick)
(Continued)

Season	Team	GP	G	A	Pts.	PIM
77-78	Minn	57	7	14	21	18
78-79	LA-Col	59	2	7	9	6
79-80	Col	46	0	9	9	10
Totals		498	18	94	112	156
Playoff Totals		7	0	1	1	0

BIALOWAS, Dwight Joseph *6-0 185 D*
B. Regina, Sask., Sept. 8, 1952

Season	Team	GP	G	A	Pts.	PIM
73-74	Atl	11	0	0	0	2
74-75	Atl-Minn	77	5	19	24	22
75-76	Minn	58	5	18	23	22
76-77	Minn	18	1	9	10	0
Totals		164	11	46	57	46

BIANCHIN, Wayne Richard *5-10 180 LW*
B. Nanaimo, B.C., Sept. 6, 1953

Season	Team	GP	G	A	Pts.	PIM
73-74	Pitt	69	12	13	25	38
74-75	Pitt	2	0	0	0	0
75-76	Pitt	14	1	5	6	4
76-77	Pitt	79	28	6	34	28
77-78	Pitt	61	20	13	33	40
78-79	Pitt	40	7	4	11	20
79-80	Edm	11	0	0	0	7
Totals		276	68	41	109	137
Playoff Totals		3	0	1	1	6

BIDNER, Richard Todd (Todd) *6-2 205 LW*
B. Petrolia, Ont., July 4, 1961

Season	Team	GP	G	A	Pts.	PIM
81-82	Wash	12	2	1	3	7

BIGGS, Don *5-8 175 C*
B. Mississauga, Ont., Apr. 7, 1965

Season	Team	GP	G	A	Pts.	PIM
84-85	Minn	1	0	0	0	0
89-90	Phil	11	2	0	2	8
Totals		12	2	0	2	8

BIGNELL, Larry Irvin *6-0 170 D*
B. Edmonton, Alta., Jan. 7, 1950

Season	Team	GP	G	A	Pts.	PIM
73-74	Pitt	20	0	3	3	2
75-76	Ott (WHA)	41	5	5	10	43
NHL Playoff Totals		3	0	0	0	2

BILODEAU, Gilles *6-1 220 LW*
B. St. Prime, Que., July 31, 1955

Season	Team	GP	G	A	Pts.	PIM
75-76	Tor (WHA)	14	0	1	1	38
76-77	Brim (WHA)	34	2	6	8	133
77-78	Birm (WHA)	59	2	2	4	258
78-79	Que (WHA)	36	3	6	9	141
79-80	Que	9	0	1	1	25
NHL Totals		9	0	1	1	25
WHA Totals		143	7	15	22	570
WHA Playoff Totals		6	0	0	0	52

BIONDA, Jack Arthur *6-0 175 D*
B. Huntsville, Ont., Sept. 18, 1933

Season	Team	GP	G	A	Pts.	PIM
55-56	Tor	13	0	1	1	18
56-57	Bos	35	2	3	5	43
57-58	Bos	42	1	4	5	50
58-59	Bos	3	0	1	1	2
Totals		93	3	9	12	113
Playoff Totals		11	0	1	1	14

BISSETT, Thomas *6-0 180 C*
B. Seattle, Wash., Mar. 13, 1966

Season	Team	GP	G	A	Pts.	PIM
90-91	Det	5	0	0	0	0

BJUGSTAD, Scott *6-1 185 RW*
B. St. Paul, Minn., June 2, 1961

Season	Team	GP	G	A	Pts.	PIM
83-84	Minn	5	0	0	0	2
84-85	Minn	72	11	4	15	32
85-86	Minn	80	43	33	76	24
86-87	Minn	39	4	9	13	43
87-88	Minn	33	10	12	22	15
88-89	Pitt	24	3	0	3	4
89-90	LA	11	1	2	3	2
90-91	LA	31	2	4	6	12
91-92	LA	22	2	4	6	10
Totals		317	76	68	144	144
Playoff Totals		9	0	1	1	2

BLACK, James *5-11 185 C*
B. Regina, Sask., Aug. 15, 1969

Season	Team	GP	G	A	Pts.	PIM
89-90	Hart	1	0	0	0	0
90-91	Hart	1	0	0	0	0
91-92	Hart	30	4	6	10	14
Totals		32	4	6	10	14

BLACK, Stephen *6-0 185 LW*
B. Fort William, Ont., Mar. 31, 1927

Season	Team	GP	G	A	Pts.	PIM
49-50	Det	69	7	14	21	53
50-51	Det-Chi	44	4	6	10	24
Totals		113	11	20	31	77
Playoff Totals		13	0	0	0	13

BLACKBURN, John Donald (Don) *6-0 190 LW*
B. Kirkland Lake, Ont., May 14, 1938

Season	Team	GP	G	A	Pts.	PIM
62-63	Bos	6	0	5	5	4
67-68	Phil	67	9	20	29	23
68-69	Phil	48	7	9	16	36
69-70	NYR	3	0	0	0	0
70-71	NYR	1	0	0	0	0
72-73	NYI-Minn	60	7	10	17	24
73-74	NE (WHA)	75	20	39	59	18
74-75	NE (WHA)	50	18	32	50	10
75-76	NE (WHA)	21	2	3	5	6
NHL Totals		185	23	44	67	87
WHA Totals		146	40	74	114	34
NHL Playoff Totals		12	3	0	3	10
WHA Playoff Totals		12	3	6	9	6

BLACKBURN, Robert John *5-11 198 D*
B. Rouyn, Que., Feb. 1, 1938

Season	Team	GP	G	A	Pts.	PIM
68-69	NYR	11	0	0	0	0
69-70	Pitt	60	4	7	11	51
70-71	Pitt	64	4	5	9	54
Totals		135	8	12	20	105
Playoff Totals		6	0	0	0	4

BLADE, Henry Gordon (Hank) *6-0 182 C*
B. Peterborough, Ont., Apr. 28, 1921

Season	Team	GP	G	A	Pts.	PIM
46-47	Chi	18	1	3	4	2
47-48	Chi	6	1	0	1	0
Totals		24	2	3	5	2

BLADON, Thomas George (Bomber) *6-1 195 D*
B. Edmonton, Alta., Dec. 29, 1952

Season	Team	GP	G	A	Pts.	PIM
72-73	Phil	78	11	31	42	26
73-74	Phil	70	12	22	34	37
74-75	Phil	76	9	20	29	54
75-76	Phil	80	14	23	37	68
76-77	Phil	80	10	43	53	39
77-78	Phil	79	11	24	35	57
78-79	Pitt	78	4	23	27	64
79-80	Pitt	57	2	6	8	35
80-81	Edm-Winn-Det	12	0	5	5	12
Totals		610	73	197	270	392
Playoff Totals		86	8	29	37	70

BLAINE, Gary James *5-11 190 D*
B. St. Boniface, Man., Feb. 27, 1908

Season	Team	GP	G	A	Pts.	PIM
54-55	Mont	1	0	0	0	0

BLAIR, Andrew Dryden *6-1 180 C*
B. Winnipeg, Man., Feb. 27,1908

Season	Team	GP	G	A	Pts.	PIM
28-29	Tor	44	12	15	27	41
29-30	Tor	42	11	10	21	27
30-31	Tor	44	11	8	19	32
31-32	Tor	48	9	14	23	35
32-33	Tor	43	6	9	15	38
33-34	Tor	47	14	9	23	35
34-35	Tor	45	6	14	20	22
35-36	Tor	45	5	4	9	60
36-37	Chi	44	0	3	3	33
Totals		402	74	86	160	323
Playoff Totals		38	6	6	12	32

BLAIR, Charles (Chuck) *5-10 175 RW*
B. Edinburgh, Scotland, July 23, 1928

Season	Team	GP	G	A	Pts.	PIM
48-49	Tor	1	0	0	0	0
50-51	Tor	2	0	0	0	0
Totals		3	0	0	0	0

BLAIR, George (Dusty) *5-8 160 C*
B. South Porcupine, Ont., Sept. 15, 1929

Season	Team	GP	G	A	Pts.	PIM
50-51	Tor	2	0	0	0	0

BLAISDELL, Michael Walter *6-1 195 RW*
B. Moose Jaw, Sask., Jan. 18, 1960

Season	Team	GP	G	A	Pts.	PIM
80-81	Det	32	3	6	9	10
81-82	Det	80	23	32	55	48
82-83	Det	80	18	23	41	22
83-84	NYR	36	5	6	11	31
84-85	NYR	12	1	0	1	11
85-86	Pitt	66	15	14	29	36
86-87	Pitt	10	1	1	2	2
87-88	Tor	18	3	2	5	2
88-89	Tor	9	1	0	1	4
Totals		343	70	84	154	166
Playoff Totals		6	1	2	3	10

BLAKE, Francis Joseph (Mickey) *5-10 186 D*
B. Barriefield, Ont., Oct. 31, 1912

Season	Team	GP	G	A	Pts.	PIM
34-35	StL E	8	1	1	2	2
35-36	Bos-Tor	8	0	0	0	2
Totals		16	1	1	2	4

BLAKE, Hector (Toe) *5-9 165 LW*
B. Victoria Mines, Ont., Aug. 21, 1912

Season	Team	GP	G	A	Pts.	PIM
32-33	Mont M	1	0	0	0	0
34-35	Mont M	8	0	0	0	0
35-36	Mont	11	1	2	3	28
36-37	Mont	43	10	12	22	12
37-38	Mont	43	17	16	33	33
38-39	Mont	48	24	23	47	10
39-40	Mont	48	17	19	36	48
40-41	Mont	48	12	20	32	49
41-42	Mont	48	17	28	45	19
42-43	Mont	48	23	36	59	26
43-44	Mont	41	26	33	59	10
44-45	Mont	49	29	38	67	25
45-46	Mont	50	29	21	50	2
46-47	Mont	60	21	29	50	6
47-48	Mont	32	9	15	24	4
Totals		578	235	292	527	272
Playoff Totals		57	25	37	62	23

BLAKE, Robert (Rob) *6-3 200 D*
B. Simcoe, Ont., Dec. 10, 1969

Season	Team	GP	G	A	Pts.	PIM
89-90	LA	4	0	0	0	4
90-91	LA	75	12	34	46	125
91-92	LA	57	7	13	20	102
Totals		136	19	47	66	231
Playoff Totals		26	4	8	12	42

BLIGHT, Richard Derek *6-2 195 RW*
B. Portage La Prairie, Man., Oct. 17, 1955

Season	Team	GP	G	A	Pts.	PIM
75-76	Van	74	25	31	56	29
76-77	Van	78	28	40	68	32
77-78	Van	80	25	38	63	33
78-79	Van	56	5	10	15	16
79-80	Van	33	12	6	18	54
80-81	Van	3	1	0	1	4
82-83	LA	2	0	0	0	2
Totals		326	96	125	221	170
Playoff Totals		5	0	5	5	2

BLINCO, Russell Percival (Beaver) *5-10 171 C*
B. Grand Mere, Que., Mar. 12, 1908

Season	Team	GP	G	A	Pts.	PIM
33-34	Mont M	31	14	9	23	2
34-35	Mont M	48	13	14	27	4
35-36	Mont M	46	13	10	23	10
36-37	Mont M	48	6	12	18	2
37-38	Mont M	47	10	9	19	4
38-39	Chi	48	3	12	15	2
Totals		268	59	66	125	24
Playoff Totals		19	3	3	6	4

BLOCK, Kenneth Richard *5-10 184 D*
B. Grunthal, Man., Mar. 18, 1944

Season	Team	GP	G	A	Pts.	PIM
70-71	Van	1	0	0	0	0
72-73	NY (WHA)	78	5	53	58	43
73-74	NY-NJ (WHA)	74	3	43	46	22
74-75	SD-Ind (WHA)	73	1	28	29	30
75-76	Ind (WHA)	79	1	25	26	28
76-77	Ind (WHA)	52	3	10	13	25
77-78	Ind (WHA)	77	1	25	26	34
78-79	Ind (WHA)	22	2	3	5	10
NHL Totals		1	0	0	0	0
WHA Totals		455	16	187	203	192
WHA Playoff Totals		9	0	2	2	6

BLOEMBERG, Jeff *6-1 205 D*
B. Listowel, Ont., Jan. 31, 1968

Season	Team	GP	G	A	Pts.	PIM
88-89	NYR	9	0	0	0	0
89-90	NYR	28	3	3	6	25
90-91	NYR	3	0	2	2	0
91-92	NYR	3	0	1	1	0
Totals		43	3	6	9	25
Playoff Totals		7	0	3	3	5

BLOOM, Michael Carroll *6-3 205 LW*
B. Ottawa, Ont., Apr. 12, 1952

Season	Team	GP	G	A	Pts.	PIM
73-74	SD (WHA)	76	25	44	69	-
74-75	Wash-Det	80	11	27	38	94
75-76	Det	76	13	17	30	99
76-77	Det	45	6	3	9	22
NHL Totals		201	30	47	77	215
WHA Totals		76	25	44	69	—

BLOMQVIST, Timo *6-0 198 D*
B. Helsinki, Finland, Jan. 23, 1961

Season	Team	GP	G	A	Pts.	PIM
81-82	Wash	44	1	11	12	62
82-83	Wash	61	1	17	18	67
83-84	Wash	65	1	19	20	84
84-85	Wash	53	1	4	5	51
86-87	NJ	20	0	2	2	29
Totals		243	4	53	57	293
Playoff Totals		13	0	0	0	24

BLUM, John Joseph *6-3 205 D*
B. Detroit, Mich., Oct. 8, 1959

Season	Team	GP	G	A	Pts.	PIM
82-83	Edm	5	0	3	3	24
83-84	Edm-Bos	16	1	2	3	32
84-85	Bos	75	3	13	16	263
85-86	Bos	61	1	7	8	80
86-87	Wash	66	2	8	10	133
87-88	Bos	19	0	1	1	70
88-89	Det	6	0	0	0	8
89-90	Bos	2	0	0	0	0
Totals		250	7	34	41	610
Playoff Totals		20	0	2	2	27

BODAK, Robert Peter *6-2 195 LW*
B. Thunder Bay, Ont., May 28, 1961

Season	Team	GP	G	A	Pts.	PIM
87-88	Calg	3	0	0	0	22
89-90	Hart	1	0	0	0	7
Totals		4	0	0	0	29

BODDY, Gregg Allen *6-2 200 D*
B. Ponoka, Alta., Mar. 19, 1949

Season	Team	GP	G	A	Pts.	PIM
71-72	Van	40	2	5	7	45
72-73	Van	74	3	11	14	50
73-74	Van	53	2	10	12	59
74-75	Van	72	11	12	23	56
75-76	Van	34	5	6	11	33
76-77	SD-Edm (WHA)	64	2	19	21	60
NHL Totals		273	23	44	67	243
WHA Totals		64	2	19	21	60
NHL Playoff Totals		3	0	0	0	0
WHA Playoff Totals		4	1	2	3	14

BODGER, Doug *6-2 210 D*
B. Chemainus, B.C., June 18, 1966

Season	Team	GP	G	A	Pts.	PIM
84-85	Pitt	65	5	26	31	67
85-86	Pitt	79	4	33	37	63
86-87	Pitt	76	11	38	49	52
87-88	Pitt	69	14	31	45	103
88-89	Pitt-Buf	71	8	44	52	59
89-90	Buf	71	12	36	48	64
90-91	Buf	58	5	23	28	54
91-92	Buf	73	11	35	46	108
Totals		562	70	266	336	570
Playoff Totals		22	4	8	12	19

BODNAR, August (Gus) *5-10 160 C*
B. Fort William, Ont., Aug. 24, 1925

Season	Team	GP	G	A	Pts.	PIM
43-44	Tor	50	22	40	62	18
44-45	Tor	49	8	36	44	18
45-46	Tor	49	14	23	37	14
46-47	Tor	39	4	6	10	10
47-48	Chi	46	13	22	35	23
48-49	Chi	59	19	26	45	14
49-50	Chi	70	11	28	39	6
50-51	Chi	44	8	12	20	8
51-52	Chi	69	14	26	40	26
52-53	Chi	66	16	13	29	26
53-54	Chi-Bos	59	9	18	27	30
54-55	Bos	67	4	4	8	14
Totals		667	142	254	396	207
Playoff Totals		32	4	3	7	10

BOEHM, Ronald John *5-7 160 LW*
B. Saskatoon, Sask., Aug. 14, 1943

Season	Team	GP	G	A	Pts.	PIM
67-68	Oak	16	2	1	3	10

BOESCH, Garth Vernon *6-0 180 D*
B. Milestone, Sask., Oct. 7, 1920

Season	Team	GP	G	A	Pts.	PIM
46-47	Tor	35	4	5	9	47
47-48	Tor	45	2	7	9	52
48-49	Tor	59	1	10	11	43
49-50	Tor	58	2	6	8	63
Totals		197	9	28	37	205
Playoff Totals		34	2	5	7	18

BOH, Rick *5-10 185 C*
B. Kamloops, B.C., May 18, 1964

Season	Team	GP	G	A	Pts.	PIM
87-88	Minn	8	2	1	3	4

BOILEAU, Marc Claude *5-11 170 C*
B. Pointe Claire, Que., Sept. 3, 1932

Season	Team	GP	G	A	Pts.	PIM
61-62	Det	54	5	6	11	8

BOILEAU, Rene *F*

Season	Team	GP	G	A	Pts.	PIM
25-26	NYA	7	0	0	0	0

BOIMISTRUCK, Frederick *5-11 191 D*
B. Sudbury, Ont., Nov. 4, 1962

Season	Team	GP	G	A	Pts.	PIM
81-82	Tor	57	2	11	13	32
82-83	Tor	26	2	3	5	13
Totals		83	4	14	18	45

BOISVERT, Serge *5-9 172 RW*
B. Drummondville, Ont., June 1, 1959

Season	Team	GP	G	A	Pts.	PIM
82-83	Tor	17	0	2	2	4
84-85	Mont	14	2	2	4	0
85-86	Mont	9	2	2	4	2
86-87	Mont	1	0	0	0	0
87-88	Mont	5	1	1	2	2
Totals		46	5	7	12	8
Playoff Totals		23	3	7	10	4

BOIVIN, Claude *6-2 200 LW*
B. Ste. Foy, Que., Mar. 1, 1970

Season	Team	GP	G	A	Pts.	PIM
91-92	Phil	58	5	13	18	187

BOIVIN, Leo Joseph *5-7 190 D*
B. Prescott, Ont., Aug. 2, 1932

Season	Team	GP	G	A	Pts.	PIM
51-52	Tor	2	0	1	1	4
52-53	Tor	70	2	13	15	97
53-54	Tor	58	1	6	7	81
54-55	Tor-Bos	66	6	11	17	113
55-56	Bos	68	4	16	20	80
56-57	Bos	55	2	8	10	55
57-58	Bos	33	0	4	4	54
58-59	Bos	70	5	16	21	94
59-60	Bos	70	4	21	25	66
60-61	Bos	57	6	17	23	50
61-62	Bos	65	5	18	23	89
62-63	Bos	62	2	24	26	48
63-64	Bos	65	10	14	24	42
64-65	Bos	67	3	10	13	68
65-66	Bos-Det	62	0	10	10	50
66-67	Det	69	4	17	21	55
67-68	Pitt	73	9	13	22	74
68-69	Pitt-Minn	69	6	19	25	42
69-70	Minn	69	3	12	15	30
Totals		1150	72	250	322	1192
Playoff Totals		54	3	10	13	59

BOLAND, Michael Anthony *5-10 185 RW*
B. Montreal, Que., Dec. 16, 1949

Season	Team	GP	G	A	Pts.	PIM
72-73	Ott (WHA)	41	1	15	16	44
74-75	Phil	2	0	0	0	0
WHA Playoff Totals		1	0	0	0	12

BOLAND, Michael John *6-0 190 D*
B. London, Ont., Oct. 29, 1954

Season	Team	GP	G	A	Pts.	PIM
74-75	KC	1	0	0	0	0
78-79	Buf	22	1	2	3	29
Totals		23	1	2	3	29
Playoff Totals		3	1	0	1	2

BOLDIREV, Ivan *6-0 190 C*
B. Zranjanin, Yugoslavia, Aug. 15, 1949

Season	Team	GP	G	A	Pts.	PIM
70-71	Bos	2	0	0	0	0
71-72	Bos-Cal	68	16	25	41	60
72-73	Cal	56	11	23	34	58
73-74	Cal	78	25	31	56	22
74-75	Chi	80	24	43	67	54
75-76	Chi	78	28	34	62	33
76-77	Chi	80	24	38	62	40
77-78	Chi	80	35	45	80	34
78-79	Chi-Atl	79	35	43	78	31
79-80	Atl-Van	79	32	35	67	34
80-81	Van	72	26	33	59	34
81-82	Van	78	33	40	73	45
82-83	Van-Det	72	18	37	55	26
83-84	Det	75	35	48	83	20
84-85	Det	75	19	30	49	16
Totals		1052	361	505	866	507
Playoff Totals		48	13	20	33	14

BOLDUC, Daniel George *5-9 180 LW*
B. Waterville, Maine, Apr. 6, 1953

Season	Team	GP	G	A	Pts.	PIM
75-76	NE (WHA)	14	2	5	7	14
76-77	NE (WHA)	33	8	3	11	15
77-78	NE (WHA)	41	5	5	10	22
78-79	Det	56	16	13	29	14
79-80	Det	44	6	5	11	19
83-84	Calg	2	0	1	1	0
NHL Totals		102	22	19	41	33
WHA Totals		88	15	13	28	51
NHL Playoff Totals		1	0	0	0	0
WHA Playoff Totals		30	3	10	13	8

BOLDUC, Michel *6-2 210 D*
B. Angegardien, Que., Mar. 13, 1961

Season	Team	GP	G	A	Pts.	PIM
81-82	Que	3	0	0	0	0
82-83	Que	7	0	0	0	6
Totals		10	0	0	0	6

BOLL, Frank Thurman (Buzz)
5-10 166 LW
B. Filmore, Sask., Mar. 6, 1911

Season	Team	GP	G	A	Pts.	PIM
33-34	Tor	42	12	8	20	21
34-35	Tor	47	14	4	18	4
35-36	Tor	44	15	13	28	14
36-37	Tor	25	6	3	9	12
37-38	Tor	44	14	11	25	18
38-39	Tor	11	0	0	0	0
39-40	NYA	47	5	10	15	18
40-41	NYA	46	12	14	26	16
41-42	NYA	48	11	15	26	23
42-43	Bos	43	25	27	52	20
43-44	Bos	39	19	25	44	2
Totals		436	133	130	263	148
Playoff Totals		29	7	3	10	13

BOLONCHUK, Larry Kenneth Mitchell
5-10 190 D
B. Winnipeg, Man., Feb. 26, 1952

Season	Team	GP	G	A	Pts.	PIM
72-73	Van	15	0	0	0	6
75-76	Wash	1	0	1	1	0
76-77	Wash	9	0	0	0	12
77-78	Wash	49	3	8	11	79
Totals		74	3	9	12	97

BOLTON, Hugh Edward *6-3 190 D*
B. Toronto, Ont., Apr. 15, 1929

Season	Team	GP	G	A	Pts.	PIM
49-50	Tor	2	0	0	0	2
50-51	Tor	13	1	3	4	2
51-52	Tor	60	3	13	16	73
52-53	Tor	9	0	0	0	10
53-54	Tor	9	0	0	0	10
54-55	Tor	69	2	19	21	55
55-56	Tor	67	4	16	20	65
56-57	Tor	6	0	0	0	0
Totals		235	10	51	61	217
Playoff Totals		17	0	5	5	14

BONAR, Daniel *5-9 175 C*
B. Brandon, Man., Sept. 23, 1956

Season	Team	GP	G	A	Pts.	PIM
80-81	LA	71	11	15	26	57
81-82	LA	79	13	23	36	111
82-83	LA	20	1	1	2	40
Totals		170	25	39	64	208
Playoff Totals		14	3	4	7	22

BONDRA, Peter *5-11 180 RW*
B. Luck, Soviet Union, Feb. 7, 1966

Season	Team	GP	G	A	Pts.	PIM
90-91	Wash	54	12	16	28	47
91-92	Wash	71	28	28	56	42
Totals		115	40	44	84	89
Playoff Totals		11	6	3	9	6

BONIN, Marcel *5-9 175 LW*
B. Montreal, Que., Sept. 12, 1932

Season	Team	GP	G	A	Pts.	PIM
52-53	Det	37	4	9	13	14
53-54	Det	1	0	0	0	0
54-55	Det	69	16	20	36	53
55-56	Bos	67	9	9	18	49
57-58	Mont	66	15	24	39	37
58-59	Mont	57	13	30	43	38
59-60	Mont	59	17	34	51	59
60-61	Mont	65	16	35	51	45
61-62	Mont	33	7	14	21	41
Totals		454	97	175	272	336
Playoff Totals		50	11	14	25	51

BOO, James McQuaid *6-1 200 D*
B. Rolla, Mo., Nov. 12, 1954

Season	Team	GP	G	A	Pts.	PIM
77-78	Minn	6	0	0	0	22

BOONE, Carl George (Buddy)
5-7 158 RW
B. Kirkland Lake, Ont., Sept. 11, 1932

Season	Team	GP	G	A	Pts.	PIM
57-58	Bos	34	5	3	8	28
Playoff Totals		22	2	1	3	25

BOOTHMAN, George Edward *6-2 175 D*
B. Calgary, Alta., Sept. 25, 1916

Season	Team	GP	G	A	Pts.	PIM
42-43	Tor	9	1	1	2	4
43-44	Tor	49	16	18	34	14
Totals		58	17	19	36	18
Playoff Totals		5	2	1	3	2

BORDELEAU, Christian Gerard *5-8 172 C*
B. Noranda, Que., Sept. 23, 1947

Season	Team	GP	G	A	Pts.	PIM
68-69	Mont	13	1	3	4	4
69-40	Mont	48	2	13	15	18
70-71	StL	78	21	32	53	48
71-72	StL-Chi	66	14	17	31	12
72-73	Winn (WHA)	78	47	54	101	12
73-74	Winn (WHA)	75	26	49	75	22

BORDELEAU, Christian Gerard *(Continued)*

Season	Team	GP	G	A	Pts.	PIM
74-75	Winn-Que (WHA)	71	23	41	64	24
75-76	Que (WHA)	74	37	72	109	42
76-77	Que (WHA)	72	32	75	107	34
77-78	Que (WHA)	26	9	22	31	28
78-79	Que (WHA)	16	5	12	17	0
NHL Totals		205	38	65	103	82
WHA Totals		412	179	325	504	162
WHA Playoff Totals		19	4	7	11	17
WHA Playoff Totals		53	16	34	50	16

BORDELEAU, Jean-Pierre (J.P.)
6-0 170 RW
B. Noranda, Que., June 13, 1949

Season	Team	GP	G	A	Pts.	PIM
71-72	Chi	3	0	2	2	2
72-73	Chi	73	15	15	30	6
73-74	Chi	64	11	9	20	11
74-75	Chi	59	7	8	15	4
75-76	Chi	76	12	18	30	6
76-77	Chi	60	15	14	29	20
77-78	Chi	76	15	25	40	32
78-79	Chi	63	15	21	36	34
79-80	Chi	45	7	14	21	28
Totals		519	97	126	223	143
Playoff Totals		48	3	6	9	12

BORDELEAU, Paulin Joseph (Paul)
5-9 162 RW
B. Noranda, Que., Jan. 29, 1953

Season	Team	GP	G	A	Pts.	PIM
73-74	Van	68	11	13	24	20
74-75	Van	67	17	31	48	21
75-76	Van	48	5	12	17	6
76-77	Que (WHA)	80	42	41	83	52
77-78	Que (WHA)	77	42	23	65	29
78-79	Que (WHA)	77	17	12	29	44
NHL Totals		183	33	56	89	47
WHA Totals		234	101	76	177	125
NHL Playoff Totals		5	2	1	3	0
WHA Playoff Totals		31	17	15	32	14

BOROTSIK, John Nicholas (Jack)
5-9 178 C
B. Brandon, Man., Nov. 26, 1949

Season	Team	GP	G	A	Pts.	PIM
74-75	StL	1	0	0	0	0

BORSATO, Luciano *5-10 165 C*
B. Richmond Hill, Ont., Jan. 7, 1966

Season	Team	GP	G	A	Pts.	PIM
90-91	Winn	1	0	1	1	2
91-92	Winn	56	15	21	36	45
Totals		57	15	22	37	47
Playoff Totals		1	0	0	0	0

BOSCHMAN, Laurie Joseph *6-0 185 C*
B. Major, Sask., June 4, 1960

Season	Team	GP	G	A	Pts.	PIM
79-80	Tor	80	16	32	48	78
80-81	Tor	53	14	19	33	178
81-82	Tor-Edm	65	11	22	33	187
82-83	Edm-Winn	74	11	17	28	219
83-84	Winn	61	28	46	74	234
84-85	Winn	80	32	44	76	180
85-86	Winn	77	27	42	69	241
86-87	Winn	80	17	24	41	152
87-88	Winn	80	25	23	48	229
88-89	Winn	70	10	26	36	163
89-90	Winn	66	10	17	27	103
90-91	NJ	78	11	9	20	79
91-92	NJ	75	8	20	28	121
Totals		939	220	341	561	2164
Playoff Totals		57	8	13	21	140

BOSSY, Michel (Mike) *6-0 186 RW*
B. Montreal, Que., Jan. 22, 1957

Season	Team	GP	G	A	Pts.	PIM
77-78	NYI	73	53	38	91	6
78-79	NYI	80	69	57	126	25
79-80	NYI	75	51	41	92	12
80-81	NYI	79	68	51	119	32
81-82	NYI	80	64	83	147	22
82-83	NYI	79	60	58	118	20
83-84	NYI	67	51	67	118	8
84-85	NYI	76	58	59	117	38
85-86	NYI	80	61	62	123	14
86-87	NYI	63	38	37	75	33
Totals		752	573	553	1126	210
Playoff Totals		129	85	75	160	38

BOSTROM, Helge *5-7 185 D*
B. Winnipeg, Man., Jan. 9, 1894

Season	Team	GP	G	A	Pts.	PIM
29-30	Chi	20	0	1	1	8
30-31	Chi	42	2	2	4	32
31-32	Chi	14	0	0	0	4
32-33	Chi	20	1	0	1	14
Totals		96	3	3	6	58
Playoff Totals		13	0	0	0	16

BOTELL, Mark *6-4 212 D*
B. Scarborough, Ont., Aug. 27, 1961

Season	Team	GP	G	A	Pts.	PIM
81-82	Phil	32	4	10	14	31

BOTHWELL, Timothy *6-3 190 D*
B. Vancouver, B.C., May 6, 1955

Season	Team	GP	G	A	Pts.	PIM
78-79	NYR	1	0	0	0	2
79-80	NYR	45	4	6	10	20
80-81	NYR	3	0	1	1	0
81-82	NYR	13	0	3	3	10
82-83	StL	61	4	11	15	34
83-84	StL	62	2	13	15	65
84-85	StL	79	4	22	26	62
85-86	Hart	62	2	8	10	53
86-87	Hart-StL	76	6	16	22	46
87-88	StL	78	6	13	19	76
88-89	StL	22	0	0	0	14
Totals		502	28	93	121	382
Playoff Totals		49	0	3	3	56

BOTTING, Cameron Allen (Cam)
6-2 205 RW
B. Kingston, Ont., Mar. 10, 1954

Season	Team	GP	G	A	Pts.	PIM
75-76	Atl	2	0	1	1	0

BOUCHA, Henry Charles *6-0 185 C*
B. Warroad, Minn., June 1, 1951

Season	Team	GP	G	A	Pts.	PIM
71-72	Det	16	1	0	1	2
72-43	Det	73	14	14	28	82
73-74	Det	70	19	12	31	32
74-75	Minn	51	15	14	29	23
75-76	KC	28	4	7	11	14
75-76	Minn (WHA)	36	15	20	35	47
76-77	Col	9	0	2	2	4
Totals		247	53	49	102	157
Playoff Totals		36	15	20	35	47

BOUCHARD, Edmond *F*
B. Trois Rivieres, Que.

Season	Team	GP	G	A	Pts.	PIM
21-22	Mont	18	1	4	5	4
22-23	Ham	24	5	12	17	32
23-24	Ham-Mont	24	5	0	5	2
24-25	Ham	29	2	2	4	14
25-26	NYA	34	3	1	4	10
26-27	NYA	38	2	1	3	12
27-28	NYA	39	1	0	1	27
28-29	NYA-Pitt	17	0	0	0	4
Totals		223	19	20	39	105

BOUCHARD, Emile Joseph (Butch)
6-2 205 D
B. Montreal, Que., Sept. 11, 1920

Season	Team	GP	G	A	Pts.	PIM
41-42	Mont	44	0	6	6	38
42-43	Mont	45	2	16	18	47
43-44	Mont	39	5	14	19	52
44-45	Mont	50	11	23	34	34
45-46	Mont	45	7	10	17	52
46-47	Mont	60	5	7	12	60
47-48	Mont	60	4	6	10	78
48-49	Mont	27	3	3	6	42
49-50	Mont	69	1	7	8	88
50-51	Mont	52	3	10	13	80
51-52	Mont	60	3	9	12	45
52-53	Mont	58	2	8	10	55
53-54	Mont	70	1	10	11	89
54-55	Mont	70	2	15	17	81
55-56	Mont	36	0	0	0	22
Totals		785	49	144	193	863
Playoff Totals		113	11	21	32	121

BOUCHARD, Pierre *6-2 205 D*
B. Longueuil, Que., Feb. 20, 1948

Season	Team	GP	G	A	Pts.	PIM
70-71	Mont	51	0	3	3	50
71-72	Mont	60	3	5	8	39
72-73	Mont	41	0	7	7	69
73-74	Mont	60	1	14	15	25
74-75	Mont	79	3	9	12	65
75-76	Mont	66	1	11	12	50
76-77	Mont	73	4	11	15	52
77-78	Mont	59	4	6	10	29
78-79	Wash	1	0	0	0	0
79-80	Wash	54	5	9	14	16
80-81	Wash	50	3	7	10	28
81-82	Wash	1	0	0	0	10
Totals		595	24	82	106	433
Playoff Totals		76	3	10	13	56

BOUCHARD, Richard Joseph (Dick)
5-8 155 RW
B. Lettelier, Man., Dec. 2, 1934

Season	Team	GP	G	A	Pts.	PIM
54-55	NYR	1	0	0	0	0

BOUCHER, Francois X. (Frank, Raffles)
5-8 185 RW
B. Ottawa, Ont., Oct. 7, 1901

Season	Team	GP	G	A	Pts.	PIM
21-22	Ott	24	9	1	10	4

BOUCHER, Francois X. (Frank, Raffles)
(Continued)

Season	Team	GP	G	A	Pts.	PIM
26-27	NYR	44	13	15	28	17
27-28	NYR	44	23	12	35	14
28-29	NYR	44	10	16	26	8
29-30	NYR	42	26	36	62	16
30-31	NYR	44	12	27	39	20
31-32	NYR	48	12	23	35	18
32-33	NYR	46	7	28	35	4
33-34	NYR	48	14	30	44	4
34-35	NYR	48	13	32	45	2
35-36	NYR	48	11	18	29	2
36-37	NYR	44	7	13	20	5
37-38	NYR	18	0	1	1	2
43-44	NYR	15	4	10	14	2
Totals		557	161	262	423	118
Playoff Totals		56	16	18	34	12

BOUCHER, George (Buck) *F*
B. Ottawa, Ont., 1896

Season	Team	GP	G	A	Pts.	PIM
17-18	Ott	22	9	0	9	27
18-19	Ott	17	5	2	7	21
19-20	Ott	22	10	4	14	34
20-21	Ott	23	12	5	17	43
21-22	Ott	23	12	8	20	10
22-23	Ott	23	15	9	24	44
23-24	Ott	21	14	5	19	28
24-25	Ott	28	15	4	19	80
25-26	Ott	36	8	4	12	64
26-27	Ott	44	8	3	11	115
27-28	Ott	44	7	5	12	78
28-29	Ott-Mont M	41	4	2	6	70
29-30	Mont M	39	2	6	8	50
30-31	Mont M	31	0	0	0	25
31-32	Chi	43	1	5	6	50
Totals		457	122	62	184	739
Playoff Totals		44	11	4	15	84

BOUCHER, Robert *F*
B. Ottawa, Ont.

Season	Team	GP	G	A	Pts.	PIM
23-24	Mont	12	0	0	0	0

BOUCHER, William *RW*
B. Ottawa, Ont.

Season	Team	GP	G	A	Pts.	PIM
21-22	Mont	24	17	5	22	18
22-23	Mont	24	23	4	27	52
23-24	Mont	23	16	6	22	33
24-25	Mont	30	18	13	31	92
25-26	Mont	34	8	5	13	112
26-27	Mont-Bos	35	6	0	6	26
27-28	NYA	43	5	2	7	58
Totals		213	93	35	128	391
Playoff Totals		21	9	3	12	35

BOUDREAU, Bruce Allan *5-9 175 C*
B. Toronto, Ont., Jan. 9, 1955

Season	Team	GP	G	A	Pts.	PIM
76-77	Tor	15	2	5	7	4
77-78	Tor	40	11	18	29	12
78-79	Tor	26	4	3	7	2
79-80	Tor	2	0	0	0	2
80-81	Tor	39	10	14	24	18
81-82	Tor	12	0	2	2	6
85-86	Chi	7	1	0	1	2
Totals		141	28	42	70	46
Playoff Totals		9	2	0	2	0

BOUDRIAS, Andre G. *5-8 165 LW*
B. Montreal, Que., Sept. 19, 1943

Season	Team	GP	G	A	Pts.	PIM
63-44	Mont	4	1	4	5	2
64-65	Mont	1	0	0	0	2
66-67	Mont	2	0	1	1	0
67-68	Minn	74	18	35	53	42
68-69	Minn-Chi	73	8	19	27	10
69-70	StL	50	3	14	17	20
70-71	Van	77	25	41	66	16
71-72	Van	78	27	34	61	26
72-73	Van	77	30	40	70	24
73-74	Van	78	16	59	75	18
74-75	Van	77	16	62	78	46
75-76	Van	71	7	31	38	10
76-77	Que (WHA)	74	12	31	43	12
77-78	Que (WHA)	66	10	17	27	22
NHL Totals		662	151	340	491	216
WHA Totals		140	22	48	70	34
NHL Playoff Totals		34	6	10	16	12
WHA Playoff Totals		28	3	14	17	10

BOUGHNER, Barry Michael *5-10 180 LW*
B. Delhi, Ont., Jan. 29, 1948

Season	Team	GP	G	A	Pts.	PIM
69-70	Oak	4	0	0	0	2
70-71	Cal	16	0	0	0	9
Totals		20	0	0	0	11

BOURBONNAIS, Dan *5-10 181 LW*
B. Winnipeg, Man., Mar. 3, 1962

Season	Team	GP	G	A	Pts.	PIM
81-82	Hart	24	3	9	12	11
83-84	Hart	35	0	16	16	0
Totals		59	3	25	28	11

BOURBONNAIS, Rick *6-0 186 RW*
B. Toronto, Ont., Apr. 20, 1955

Season	Team	GP	G	A	Pts.	PIM
75-76	StL	7	0	0	0	8
76-77	StL	33	6	8	14	10
77-78	StL	31	3	7	10	11
Totals		71	9	15	24	29
Playoff Totals		4	0	1	1	0

BOURCIER, Conrad *5-7 145 C*
B. Montreal, Que., May 28, 1916

Season	Team	GP	G	A	Pts.	PIM
35-36	Mont	6	0	0	0	0

BOURCIER, Jean-Louis *5-11 175 LW*
B. Montreal, Que., Jan. 3, 1912

Season	Team	GP	G	A	Pts.	PIM
35-36	Mont	9	0	1	1	0

BOURGEAULT, Leo A. *5-6 165 D*
B. Sturgeon Falls, Ont., Jan. 17, 1903

Season	Team	GP	G	A	Pts.	PIM
26-27	Tor-NYR	42	2	1	3	72
27-28	NYR	37	7	0	7	7
28-29	NYR	44	2	3	5	59
29-30	NYR	44	7	6	13	54
30-31	NYR-Ott	38	0	5	5	40
32-33	Ott-Mont	50	2	2	4	27
33-34	Mont	48	4	3	7	10
34-35	Mont	4	0	0	0	0
Totals		307	24	20	44	269
Playoff Totals		24	1	1	2	18

BOURGEOIS, Charles Marc *6-4 205 D*
B. Moncton, N.B., Nov. 11, 1959

Season	Team	GP	G	A	Pts.	PIM
81-82	Calg	54	2	13	15	112
82-83	Calg	15	2	3	5	21
83-84	Calg	17	1	3	4	35
84-85	Calg	47	2	10	12	134
85-86	Calg-StL	60	7	12	19	244
86-87	StL	66	2	12	14	164
87-88	StL-Hart	31	0	1	1	78
Totals		290	16	54	70	788
Playoff Totals		40	2	3	5	194

BOURNE, Robert Glen *6-3 200 C*
B. Kindersley, Sask., June 21, 1954

Season	Team	GP	G	A	Pts.	PIM
74-75	NYI	77	16	23	39	12
75-76	NYI	14	2	3	5	13
76-77	NYI	75	16	19	35	30
77-78	NYI	80	30	33	63	31
78-79	NYI	80	30	31	61	48
79-80	NYI	73	15	25	40	52
80-81	NYI	78	35	41	76	62
81-82	NYI	76	27	26	53	77
82-83	NYI	77	20	42	62	55
83-84	NYI	78	22	34	56	75
84-85	NYI	44	8	12	20	51
85-86	NYI	62	17	15	32	36
86-87	LA	78	13	9	22	35
87-88	LA	72	7	11	18	28
Totals		964	258	324	582	605
Playoff Totals		139	40	56	96	108

BOURQUE, Phillippe Richard *6-1 200 LW*
B. Chelmsford, Mass., June 8, 1962

Season	Team	GP	G	A	Pts.	PIM
83-84	Pitt	5	0	1	1	12
85-86	Pitt	4	0	0	0	2
86-87	Pitt	22	2	3	5	32
87-88	Pitt	21	4	12	16	20
88-89	Pitt	80	17	26	43	97
89-90	Pitt	76	22	17	39	108
90-91	Pitt	78	20	14	34	106
91-92	Pitt	58	10	16	26	58
Totals		344	75	89	164	435
Playoff Totals		56	13	12	25	107

BOURQUE, Raymond Jean *5-11 197 D*
B. Montreal, Que., Dec. 28, 1960

Season	Team	GP	G	A	Pts.	PIM
79-80	Bos	80	17	48	65	73
80-81	Bos	67	27	29	56	96
81-82	Bos	65	17	49	66	51
82-83	Bos	65	22	51	73	20
83-84	Bos	78	31	65	96	57
84-85	Bos	73	20	66	86	53
85-86	Bos	74	19	58	77	68
86-87	Bos	78	23	72	95	36
87-88	Bos	78	17	64	81	72
88-89	Bos	60	18	43	61	52
89-90	Bos	76	19	65	84	50
90-91	Bos	76	21	73	94	75
91-92	Bos	80	21	60	81	56
Totals		950	272	743	1015	759
Playoff Totals		135	30	95	125	131

BOUTETTE, Patrick Michael *5-8 175 RW*
B. Windsor, Ont., Mar. 1, 1952

Season	Team	GP	G	A	Pts.	PIM
75-76	Tor	77	10	22	32	140
76-77	Tor	80	18	18	36	107
77-78	Tor	80	17	19	36	120
78-79	Tor	80	14	19	33	136
79-80	Tor	79	13	35	48	92
80-81	Hart	80	28	52	80	160
81-82	Pitt	80	23	51	74	230
82-83	Pitt	80	27	29	56	152
83-84	Pitt	73	14	26	40	142
84-85	Pitt-Hart	47	7	11	18	75
Totals		756	171	282	453	1354
Playoff Totals		46	10	14	24	109

BOUTILIER, Paul Andre *5-11 188 D*
B. Sydney, N.S., May 3, 1963

Season	Team	GP	G	A	Pts.	PIM
81-82	NYI	1	0	0	0	0
82-83	NYI	29	4	5	9	24
83-84	NYI	28	0	11	11	36
84-85	NYI	78	12	23	35	90
85-86	NYI	77	4	30	34	100
86-87	Bos-Minn	62	7	13	20	92
87-88	NYR-Winn	10	0	1	1	12
88-89	Winn	3	0	0	0	4
Totals		288	27	83	110	358
Playoff Totals		41	1	9	10	45

BOWCHER, Clarence *D*
B. Sudbury, Ont.

Season	Team	GP	G	A	Pts.	PIM
26-27	NYA	11	0	1	1	4
27-28	NYA	36	2	1	3	106
Totals		47	2	2	4	110

BOWMAN, Ralph B. (Scotty) *5-11 190 D*
B. Winnipeg, Man., June 20, 1911

Season	Team	GP	G	A	Pts.	PIM
33-34	Ott	46	0	2	2	64
34-35	StL E-Det	44	3	5	8	72
35-36	Det	48	3	2	5	44
36-37	Det	37	0	1	1	24
37-38	Det	45	0	2	2	26
38-39	Det	43	2	3	5	26
39-40	Det	11	0	2	2	4
Totals		274	8	17	25	260
Playoff Totals		22	2	2	4	6

BOWMAN, Robert (Kirk) *5-9 178 LW*
B. Leamington, Ont., Sept. 30, 1952

Season	Team	GP	G	A	Pts.	PIM
73-74	LA (WHA)	10	0	2	2	0
76-77	Chi	55	10	13	23	6
77-78	Chi	33	1	4	5	13
NHL Totals		88	11	17	28	19
WHA Totals		10	0	2	2	0
NHL Playoff Totals		7	1	0	1	0

BOWNASS, John (Jack) *6-1 200 D*
B. Winnipeg, Man., July 27, 1930

Season	Team	GP	G	A	Pts.	PIM
57-58	Mont	4	0	1	1	0
58-89	NYR	35	1	2	3	20
59-60	NYR	37	2	5	7	34
61-62	NYR	4	0	0	0	4
Totals		80	3	8	11	58

BOWNESS, Richard Gary (Rick)
6-1 185 RW
B. Moncton, N.B., Jan. 25, 1955

Season	Team	GP	G	A	Pts.	PIM
75-76	Atl	5	0	0	0	0
76-77	Atl	28	0	4	4	29
77-78	Det	61	8	11	19	76
78-79	StL	24	1	3	4	30
79-80	StL	10	1	2	3	11
80-81	Winn	45	8	17	25	45
Totals		173	18	37	55	191
Playoff Totals		5	0	0	0	2

BOYD, Irwin (Yank) *5-10 152 RW*
B. Ardmore, Pa., Nov. 13, 1908

Season	Team	GP	G	A	Pts.	PIM
31-32	Bos	30	10	10	20	31
34-35	Det	42	2	3	5	14
42-43	Bos	20	6	5	11	6
43-44	Bos	5	0	1	1	0
Totals		97	18	19	37	51
Playoff Totals		15	0	1	1	4

BOYD, Randy Keith *5-11 192 D*
B. Coniston, Ont., Jan. 23, 1962

Season	Team	GP	G	A	Pts.	PIM
81-82	Pitt	23	0	2	2	49
82-83	Pitt	56	4	14	18	71
83-84	Pitt-Chi	28	0	5	5	22
84-85	Chi	3	0	0	0	6
85-86	NYI	55	2	12	14	79
86-87	NYI	30	7	17	24	37
87-88	Van	60	7	16	23	64
88-89	Van	2	0	1	1	0
Totals		257	20	67	87	328
Playoff Totals		13	0	2	2	26

BOYD, William G. *5-10 185 RW*
B. Belleville, Ont., May 15, 1898

Season	Team	GP	G	A	Pts.	PIM
26-27	NYR	41	4	1	5	40
27-28	NYR	43	4	0	4	11
28-29	NYR	11	0	0	0	5
29-30	NYA	43	7	6	13	16
Totals		138	15	7	22	72
Playoff Totals		9	0	0	0	2

BOYER, Walter (Wally) *5-8 165 C*
B. Cowan, Man., Sept, 27, 1937

Season	Team	GP	G	A	Pts.	PIM
65-66	Tor	46	4	17	21	23
66-67	Chi	42	5	6	11	15
67-68	Oak	74	13	20	33	44
68-69	Pitt	62	10	19	29	17
69-70	Pitt	72	11	12	23	34
70-71	Pitt	68	11	30	41	30
71-72	Pitt	1	0	1	1	0
72-73	Winn (WHA)	69	6	28	34	27
NHL Totals		365	54	105	159	163
WHA Totals		69	6	28	34	27
NHL Playoff Totals		15	1	3	4	0
WHA Playoff Totals		14	4	2	6	4

BOYKO, Darren *5-9 170 C*
B. Winnipeg, Man., Jan. 16, 1964

Season	Team	GP	G	A	Pts.	PIM
88-89	Winn	1	0	0	0	0

BOZEK, Steven Michael *5-11 170 C*
B. Kelowna, B.C., Nov. 26, 1960

Season	Team	GP	G	A	Pts.	PIM
81-82	LA	71	33	23	56	68
82-83	LA	53	13	13	26	14
83-84	Calg	46	10	10	20	16
84-85	Calg	54	13	22	35	6
85-86	Calg	64	21	22	43	24
86-87	Calg	71	17	18	35	22
87-88	Calg-StL	33	3	7	10	14
88-89	Van	71	17	18	35	64
89-90	Van	58	14	9	23	32
90-91	Van	62	15	17	32	22
91-92	SJ	58	8	8	16	27
Totals		641	164	167	331	309
Playoff Totals		58	12	11	23	69

BOZON, Philippe *5-10 175 LW*
B. Charmonix, France, Nov. 30, 1966

Season	Team	GP	G	A	Pts.	PIM
91-92	StL	9	1	3	4	4
Playoff Totals		6	1	0	1	27

BRACKENBOROUGH, John *C*

Season	Team	GP	G	A	Pts.	PIM
25-26	Bos	7	0	0	0	0

BRACKENBURY, John Curtis (Curt)
5-10 197 RW
B. Kapuskasing, Ont., Jan. 31, 1952

Season	Team	GP	G	A	Pts.	PIM
73-74	Chi (WHA)	4	0	1	1	11
74-75	Minn (WHA)	7	0	0	0	22
75-76	Minn-Que (WHA)	74	8	14	22	365
76-77	Que (WHA)	77	16	13	29	146
77-78	Que (WHA)	33	4	9	13	54
78-79	Que (WHA)	70	13	13	26	155
79-80	Que	63	6	8	14	55
80-81	Edm	58	2	7	9	153
81-82	Edm	14	0	2	2	12
82-83	StL	6	1	0	1	6
NHL Totals		141	9	17	26	226
WHA Totals		265	41	50	91	753
NHL Playoff Totals		2	0	0	0	0
WHA Playoff Totals		48	5	9	14	161

BRADLEY, Barton William *5-7 150 C*
B. Ft. William, Ont., July 29, 1930

Season	Team	GP	G	A	Pts.	PIM
49-50	Bos	1	0	0	0	0

BRADLEY, Brian Walter Richard
5-10 170 C
B. Kitchener, Ont., Jan. 21, 1965

Season	Team	GP	G	A	Pts.	PIM
85-86	Calg	5	0	1	1	0
86-87	Calg	40	10	18	28	16
87-88	Van	11	3	5	8	6
88-89	Van	71	18	27	45	42
89-90	Van	67	19	29	48	48
90-91	Van-Tor	70	11	31	42	62
91-92	Tor	59	10	21	31	48
Totals		323	71	132	203	222
Playoff Totals		8	3	4	7	10

BRADLEY, Walter Lyle *5-9 160 C*
B. Lloydminster, Sask., July 31, 1943

Season	Team	GP	G	A	Pts.	PIM
73-74	Cal	4	1	0	1	2
76-77	Clev	2	0	0	0	0
Totals		6	1	0	1	2

BRADY, Neil *6-2 200 C*
B. Montreal, Que., Apr. 12, 1968

Season	Team	GP	G	A	Pts.	PIM
89-90	NJ	19	1	4	5	13
90-91	NJ	3	0	0	0	0
91-92	NJ	7	1	0	1	4
Totals		29	2	4	6	17

BRAGNALO, Richard James (Rick)
5-8 160 C
B. Thunder Bay, Ont., Dec. 1, 1951

Season	Team	GP	G	A	Pts.	PIM
75-76	Wash	19	2	10	12	8
76-77	Wash	80	11	12	23	16
77-78	Wash	44	2	13	15	22
78-79	Wash	2	0	0	0	0
Totals		145	15	35	50	46

BRANNIGAN, Andrew John *5-11 190 D*
B. Winnipeg, Man., Apr. 11, 1922

Season	Team	GP	G	A	Pts.	PIM
40-41	NYA	6	1	0	1	5
41-42	NYA	20	0	2	2	26
Totals		26	1	2	3	31

BRASAR, Per-Olov *5-10 180 LW*
B. Falun, Sweden, Sept. 30, 1950

Season	Team	GP	G	A	Pts.	PIM
77-78	Minn	77	20	37	57	6
78-79	Minn	68	6	28	34	6
79-80	Minn-Van	70	10	24	34	7
80-81	Van	80	22	41	63	8
81-82	Van	53	6	12	18	6
Totals		348	64	142	206	33
Playoff Totals		13	1	2	3	0

BRAYSHAW, Russell Ambrose
5-10 170 LW
B. Saskatoon, Sask., Jan. 17, 1918

Season	Team	GP	G	A	Pts.	PIM
44-45	Chi	43	5	9	14	24

BREAULT, Frank *5-11 185 RW*
B. Acton Vale, Que., May 11, 1967

Season	Team	GP	G	A	Pts.	PIM
90-91	LA	17	1	4	5	6
91-92	LA	6	1	0	1	30
Totals		23	2	4	6	36

BREITENBACH, Ken *6-1 190 D*
B. Welland, Ont., Jan. 9, 1955

Season	Team	GP	G	A	Pts.	PIM
75-76	Buf	7	0	0	0	6
76-77	Buf	31	0	5	5	18
78-79	Buf	30	1	8	9	25
Totals		68	1	13	14	49
Playoff Totals		8	0	1	1	4

BRENNAN, Daniel *6-3 210 LW*
B. Dawson Creek, B.C., Oct. 1, 1962

Season	Team	GP	G	A	Pts.	PIM
83-84	LA	2	0	0	0	0
85-86	LA	6	0	1	1	9
Totals		8	0	1	1	9

BRENNAN, Douglas R. *5-10 180 D*
B. Peterborough, Ont., Jan. 10, 1905

Season	Team	GP	G	A	Pts.	PIM
31-32	NYR	38	4	3	7	40
32-33	NYR	48	5	4	9	94
33-34	NYR	37	0	0	0	18
Totals		123	9	7	16	152
Playoff Totals		16	1	0	1	21

BRENNAN, Thomas E. *5-8 155 RW*
B. Philadelphia, Pa., Jan. 22, 1922

Season	Team	GP	G	A	Pts.	PIM
43-44	Bos	21	2	1	3	2
44-45	Bos	1	0	1	1	0
Totals		22	2	2	4	2

BRENNEMAN, John Gary *5-10 175 LW*
B. Fort Erie, Ont., Jan. 5, 1943

Season	Team	GP	G	A	Pts.	PIM
64-65	Chi-NYR	39	4	3	7	8
65-66	NYR	11	0	0	0	14
66-67	Tor	41	6	4	10	4
67-68	Det-Oak	40	10	10	20	14
68-69	Oak	21	1	2	3	6
Totals		152	21	19	40	46

BRETTO, Joseph *6-1 248 D*
B. Hibbing, Minn., Nov. 29, 1912

Season	Team	GP	G	A	Pts.	PIM
44-45	Chi	3	0	0	0	4

BREWER, Carl Thomas *5-10 180 D*
B. Toronto, Ont., Oct. 21, 1938

Season	Team	GP	G	A	Pts.	PIM
57-58	Tor	2	0	0	0	0
58-59	Tor	69	3	21	24	125
59-60	Tor	67	4	19	23	150
60-61	Tor	51	1	14	15	92
61-62	Tor	67	1	22	23	89
62-63	Tor	70	2	23	25	168
63-64	Tor	57	4	9	13	114
64-65	Tor	70	4	23	27	177
69-70	Det	70	2	37	39	51

BREWER, Carl Thomas *(Continued)*

Season Team	GP	G	A	Pts.	PIM
70-71 StL	19	2	9	11	29
71-72 StL	42	2	16	18	40
73-74 Tor (WHA)	77	2	23	25	42
79-80 Tor	20	0	5	5	2
NHL Totals	604	25	198	223	1037
WHA Totals	77	2	23	25	42
NHL Playoff Totals	72	3	17	20	146
WHA Playoff Totals	12	0	4	4	11

BRICKLEY, Andy *6-0 195 C*
B. Melrose, Mass., Aug. 9, 1961

82-83 Phil	3	1	1	2	0
83-84 Pitt	50	18	20	38	9
84-85 Pitt	45	7	15	22	10
86-87 NJ	51	11	12	23	8
87-88 NJ	45	8	14	22	14
88-89 Bos	71	13	22	35	20
89-90 Bos	43	12	28	40	8
90-91 Bos	40	2	9	11	8
91-92 Bos	23	10	17	27	2
Totals	371	82	138	220	79
Playoff Totals	16	0	3	3	4

BRIDEN, E. Archibald (Archie) *F*

26-27 Det	42	5	2	7	36
29-30 Pitt Pi	30	4	3	7	20
Totals	72	9	5	14	56

BRIDGMAN, Melvin John *6-0 190 C*
B. Trenton, Ont., Apr. 28, 1955

75-76 Phil	80	23	27	50	86
76-77 Phil	70	19	38	57	120
77-78 Phil	76	16	32	48	203
78-79 Phil	76	24	35	59	184
79-80 Phil	74	16	31	47	136
80-81 Phil	77	14	37	51	195
81-82 Phil-Calg	72	33	54	87	141
82-83 Calg	79	19	31	50	103
83-84 NJ	79	23	38	61	121
84-85 NJ	80	22	39	61	105
85-86 NJ	78	23	40	63	80
86-87 NJ-Det	64	10	33	43	99
87-88 Det	57	6	11	17	42
88-89 Van	15	4	3	7	10
Totals	977	252	449	701	1625
Playoff Totals	125	28	39	67	298

BRIERE, Michel Edouard *5-10 165 C*
B. Malartic, Que., Oct. 21, 1949

69-70 Pitt	76	12	32	44	20
Playoff Totals	10	5	3	8	17

BRIND'AMOUR, Rod *6-1 200 LW/C*
B. Ottawa, Ont., Aug. 9, 1970

89-90 StL	79	26	35	61	46
90-91 StL	78	17	32	49	93
91-92 Phil	80	33	44	77	100
Totals	237	76	111	187	239
Playoff Totals	30	9	13	22	20

BRINDLEY, Douglas Allen *6-1 175 C*
B. Walkerton, Ont., June 8, 1949

70-71 Tor	3	0	0	0	0
72-73 Clev (WHA)	73	15	11	26	6
73-74 Clev (WHA)	30	13	9	22	13
NHL Totals	3	0	0	0	0
WHA Totals	103	28	20	48	19
WHA Playoff Totals	5	0	1	1	2

BRINK, Milton *F*

36-37 Chi	5	0	0	0	0

BRISEBOIS, Patrice *6-1 175 D*
B. Montreal, Que., Jan. 27, 1971

90-91 Mont	10	0	2	2	4
91-92 Mont	26	2	6	8	20
Totals	36	2	8	10	24
Playoff Totals	11	2	4	6	6

BRISSON, Gerald (Gerry) *5-9 155 RW*
B. St. Boniface, Man., Sept. 3, 1937

62-63 Mont	4	0	2	2	4

BRITZ, Greg *6-0 190 RW*
B. Buffalo, N.Y., Jan. 3, 1961

83-84 Tor	6	0	0	0	2
84-85 Tor	1	0	0	0	2
86-87 Hart	1	0	0	0	0
Totals	8	0	0	0	4

BROADBENT, Harry L. (Punch) *RW*
B. Ottawa, Ont., July 13, 1892

18-19 Ott	8	4	2	6	12
19-20 Ott	20	19	4	23	39
20-21 Ott	9	4	1	5	6

BROADBENT, Harry L. (Punch) *(Continued)*

Season Team	GP	G	A	Pts.	PIM
21-22 Ott	24	32	14	46	24
22-23 Ott	24	14	0	14	32
23-24 Ott	22	9	4	13	44
24-25 Mont M	30	15	4	19	75
25-26 Mont M	36	12	5	17	112
26-27 Mont M	42	9	5	14	42
27-28 Ott	43	3	2	5	62
28-29 NYA	44	1	4	5	59
Totals	302	122	45	167	507
Playoff Totals	41	13	3	16	69

BROCHU, Stephane *6-1 185 D*
B. Sherbrooke, Que., Aug. 15, 1967

88-89 NYR	1	0	0	0	0

BRODEN, Connell (Connie) *5-8 160 C*
B. Montreal, Que., Apr. 6, 1932

55-56 Mont	3	0	0	0	2
57-58 Mont	3	2	1	3	0
Totals	6	2	1	3	2
Playoff Totals	7	0	1	1	0

BROOKE, Robert W. *6-1 200 C*
B. Melrose, Mass., Dec. 18, 1960

83-84 NYR	9	1	2	3	4
84-85 NYR	72	7	9	16	79
85-86 NYR	79	24	20	44	111
86-87 NYR-Minn	80	13	23	36	98
87-88 Minn	77	5	20	25	108
88-89 Minn	57	7	9	16	57
89-90 Minn-NJ	73	12	14	26	63
Totals	447	69	97	166	520
Playoff Totals	34	9	9	18	59

BROOKS, Gordon John (Gord)
5-8 168 RW
B. Cobourg, Ont., Sept. 11, 1950

71-72 StL	2	0	0	0	0
73-74 StL	30	6	8	14	12
74-75 Wash	38	1	10	11	25
Totals	70	7	18	25	37

BROPHY, Bernard *F*
B. Collingwood, Ont.

25-26 Mont M	10	0	0	0	0
28-29 Det	37	2	4	6	23
29-30 Det	15	2	0	2	2
Totals	62	4	4	8	25
Playoff Totals	2	0	0	0	2

BROSSART, William (Willie) *6-0 190 D*
B. Allan, Sask., May 29, 1949

70-71 Phil	1	0	0	0	0
71-72 Phil	42	0	4	4	12
72-73 Phil	4	0	1	1	0
73-74 Tor	17	0	1	1	20
74-75 Tor-Wash	16	1	0	1	16
75-76 Wash	49	0	8	8	40
Totals	129	1	14	15	88
Playoff Totals	1	0	0	0	0

BROTEN, Aaron *5-10 175 LW*
B. Roseau, Minn., Nov. 14, 1960

80-81 Col	2	0	0	0	0
81-82 Col	58	15	24	39	6
82-83 NJ	73	16	39	55	28
83-84 NJ	80	13	23	36	36
84-85 NJ	80	22	37	57	38
85-86 NJ	66	18	25	43	26
86-87 NJ	80	26	53	79	36
87-88 NJ	80	26	57	83	80
88-89 NJ	80	16	43	59	81
89-90 NJ-Minn	77	18	18	36	58
90-91 Que-Tor	47	11	8	19	38
91-92 Winn	25	4	5	9	14
Totals	748	185	330	515	441
Playoff Totals	34	7	18	25	40

BROTEN, Neal Lemoy *5-9 160 C*
B. Roseau, Minn., Nov. 29, 1959

80-81 Minn	3	2	0	2	12
81-82 Minn	73	38	60	98	42
82-83 Minn	79	32	45	77	43
83-84 Minn	76	28	61	89	43
84-85 Minn	80	19	37	56	39
85-86 Minn	80	29	76	105	47
86-87 Minn	46	18	35	53	33
87-88 Minn	54	9	30	39	32
88-89 Minn	68	18	38	56	57
89-90 Minn	80	23	62	85	45
90-91 Minn	79	13	56	69	26
91-92 Minn	76	8	26	34	16
Totals	794	237	526	763	435
Playoff Totals	104	26	49	75	65

BROTEN, Paul *5-11 170 C*
B. Roseau, Minn., Oct. 27, 1965

89-90 NYR	32	5	3	8	26
90-91 NYR	28	4	6	10	18
91-92 NYR	74	13	15	28	102
Totals	134	22	24	46	146
Playoff Totals	24	2	3	5	14

BROWN, Adam *5-10 175 LW*
B. Johnstone, Scotland, Feb. 4, 1920

41-42 Det	28	6	9	15	15
43-44 Det	50	24	18	42	56
45-46 Det	48	20	11	31	27
46-47 Det-Chi	64	19	30	49	87
47-48 Chi	32	7	10	17	41
48-49 Chi	58	8	12	20	69
49-50 Chi	25	2	2	4	16
50-51 Chi	53	10	12	22	16
51-52 Bos	33	8	9	17	6
Totals	391	104	113	217	333
Playoff Totals	26	2	4	6	14

BROWN, Cam *6-1 205 LW*
B. Saskatoon, Sask., May 15, 1969

90-91 Van	1	0	0	0	7

BROWN, David *6-5 205 RW*
B. Saskatoon, Sask., Oct. 12, 1962

82-83 Phil	2	0	0	0	5
83-84 Phil	19	1	5	6	98
84-85 Phil	57	3	6	9	165
85-86 Phil	76	10	7	17	277
86-87 Phil	62	7	3	10	274
87-88 Phil	47	12	5	17	114
88-89 Phil-Edm	72	0	5	5	156
89-90 Edm	60	0	6	6	145
90-91 Edm	58	3	4	7	160
91-92 Phil	70	4	2	6	81
Totals	523	40	43	83	1475
Playoff Totals	77	2	3	5	209

BROWN, Doug *5-10 180 RW*
B. Southboro, Mass., July 12, 1964

86-87 NJ	4	0	1	1	0
87-88 NJ	70	14	11	25	20
88-89 NJ	63	15	10	25	15
89-90 NJ	69	14	20	34	16
90-91 NJ	58	14	16	30	4
91-92 NJ	71	11	17	28	27
Totals	334	68	75	143	82
Playoff Totals	32	7	4	11	10

BROWN, Frederick *F*
B. Kingston, Ont.

27-28 Mont M	19	1	0	1	0
Playoff Totals	9	0	0	0	0

BROWN, George Allan *5-11 185 C*
B. Winnipeg, Man., May 17, 1912

36-37 Mont	27	4	6	10	10
37-38 Mont	34	1	7	8	14
38-39 Mont	18	1	9	10	10
Totals	79	6	22	28	34
Playoff Totals	7	0	0	0	2

BROWN, Gerald William Joseph (Gerry)
5-10 176 LW
B. Edmonton, Alta., July 7, 1917

41-42 Det	13	4	4	8	0
45-46 Det	10	0	1	1	2
Totals	23	4	5	9	2
Playoff Totals	12	2	1	3	4

BROWN, Greg *6-0 180 D*
B. Hartford, Conn., Mar. 7, 1968

90-91 Buf	39	1	2	3	35

BROWN, Harold Fraser *5-10 160 RW*
B. Brandon, Man., Sept. 14, 1920

45-46 NYR	13	2	1	3	2

BROWN, Jeff *6-1 202 D*
B. Ottawa, Ont., Apr. 30, 1966

85-86 Que	8	3	2	5	6
86-87 Que	44	7	22	29	16
87-88 Que	78	16	36	52	64
88-89 Que	78	21	47	68	62
89-90 Que-StL	77	16	38	54	55
90-91 StL	67	12	47	59	39
91-92 StL	80	20	39	59	38
Totals	432	95	230	325	280
Playoff Totals	45	10	23	33	14

BROWN, Jim *6-4 210 D*
B. Phoenix, Ariz., Mar. 1, 1960

82-83 LA	3	0	1	1	5

Season	Team	GP	G	A	Pts.	PIM
BROWN, Keith Jeffrey 6-1 195 D						
B. Corner Brook, Nfld., May 6, 1960						
79-80	Chi	76	2	18	20	27
80-81	Chi	80	9	34	43	80
81-82	Chi	33	4	20	24	26
82-83	Chi	50	4	27	31	20
83-84	Chi	74	10	25	35	94
84-85	Chi	56	1	22	23	55
85-86	Chi	70	11	29	40	87
86-87	Chi	73	4	23	27	86
87-88	Chi	24	3	6	9	45
88-89	Chi	74	2	16	18	84
89-90	Chi	67	5	20	25	87
90-91	Chi	45	1	10	11	55
91-92	Chi	57	6	10	16	69
Totals		779	62	260	322	815
Playoff Totals		99	4	31	35	182
BROWN, Larry Wayne 6-2 210 D						
B. Brandon, Man., Apr. 14, 1947						
69-70	NYR	15	0	3	3	8
70-71	Det-NYR	64	2	5	7	18
71-72	Phil	12	0	0	0	2
72-73	LA	55	0	7	7	46
73-74	LA	45	0	4	4	14
74-75	LA	78	1	15	16	50
75-76	LA	74	2	5	7	33
76-77	LA	55	1	6	7	24
77-78	LA	57	1	8	9	23
Totals		455	7	53	60	218
Playoff Totals		35	0	4	4	10
BROWN, Patrick Cornelius (Connie) 5-7 168 C						
B. Van Kleek Hill, Ont., Jan. 11, 1917						
38-39	Det	20	1	0	1	0
39-40	Det	36	8	3	11	2
40-41	Det	3	1	2	3	0
41-42	Det	9	0	3	3	4
42-43	Det	23	5	16	21	6
Totals		91	15	24	39	12
Playoff Totals		14	2	3	5	0
BROWN, Rob 5-11 185 RW						
B. Kingston, Ont., Apr. 10, 1968						
87-88	Pitt	51	24	20	44	56
88-89	Pitt	68	49	66	115	118
89-90	Pitt	80	33	47	80	102
90-91	Pitt-Hart	69	24	34	58	132
91-92	Hart-Chi	67	21	26	47	71
Totals		335	151	193	344	479
Playoff Totals		24	8	7	15	33
BROWN, Stanley 5-9 150 F						
B. North Bay, Ont., May 9, 1898						
26-27	NYR	24	6	2	8	14
27-28	Det	24	2	0	2	4
Totals		48	8	2	10	18
Playoff Totals		2	0	0	0	0
BROWN, Stewart Arnold (Arnie) 5-11 185 D						
B. Apsley, Ont., Jan. 28, 1942						
61-62	Tor	2	0	0	0	0
63-64	Tor	4	0	0	0	6
64-65	NYR	58	1	11	12	145
65-66	NYR	64	1	7	8	106
66-67	NYR	69	2	10	12	61
67-68	NYR	74	1	25	26	83
68-69	NYR	74	10	12	22	48
69-70	NYR	73	15	21	36	78
70-71	NYR-Det	75	5	18	23	54
71-72	Det	77	2	23	25	84
72-73	NYI-Atl	63	5	8	13	44
73-74	Atl	48	2	6	8	29
74-75	Mich-Van (WHA)	60	3	5	8	40
NHL Totals		681	44	141	185	738
WHA Totals		60	3	5	8	40
NHL Playoff Totals		22	0	6	6	23
BROWN, Wayne Hewetson 5-8 150 RW						
B. Deloro, Ont., Nov. 16, 1930						
53 54	Bos	0	0	0	0	0
Playoff Totals		4	0	0	0	2
BROWNE, Cecil LW						
27-28	CHI	13	2	0	2	4
BROWNSCHIDLE, Jeffrey Paul 6 2 205 D						
B. Buffalo, N.Y., Mar. 1, 1959						
81-82	Hart	3	0	1	1	2
82-83	Hart	4	0	0	0	0
Totals		7	0	1	1	2

Season	Team	GP	G	A	Pts.	PIM
BROWNSCHIDLE, John J. (Jack) 6-2 195 D						
B. Buffalo, N.Y., Oct. 2, 1955						
77-78	StL	40	2	15	17	23
78-79	StL	64	10	24	34	14
79-80	StL	77	12	32	44	8
80-81	StL	71	5	23	28	12
81-82	StL	80	5	33	38	26
82-83	StL	72	1	22	23	30
83-84	StL-Hart	64	3	9	12	29
84-85	Hart	17	1	4	5	5
85-86	Hart	9	0	0	0	4
Totals		494	39	162	201	151
Playoff Totals		26	0	5	5	18
BRUBAKER, Jeffery J. 6-2 210 LW						
B. Hagerstown, Md., Feb. 24, 1958						
78-79	NE (WHA)	12	0	0	0	19
79-80	Hart	3	0	1	1	2
80-81	Hart	43	5	3	8	93
81-82	Mont	3	0	1	1	32
83-84	Calg	4	0	0	0	19
84-85	Tor	68	8	4	12	209
85-86	Tor-Edm	25	1	0	1	79
87-88	NYR	31	2	0	2	78
88-89	Det	1	0	0	0	0
Totals		178	16	9	25	512
Playoff Totals		2	0	0	0	27
BRUCE, Arthur Gordon (Gordie) 5-11 195 LW						
B. Ottawa, Ont., May 9, 1919						
40-41	Bos	8	0	1	1	2
41-42	Bos	15	4	8	12	11
45-46	Bos	5	0	0	0	0
Totals		28	4	9	13	13
Playoff Totals		7	2	3	5	4
BRUCE, David 5-11 187 RW						
B. Thunder Bay, Ont., Oct. 7, 1964						
85-86	Van	12	0	1	1	14
86-87	Van	50	9	7	16	109
87-88	Van	28	7	3	10	57
88-89	Van	53	7	7	14	65
90-91	StL	12	1	2	3	14
91-92	SJ	60	22	16	38	46
Totals		215	46	36	82	305
Playoff Totals		3	0	0	0	2
BRUCE, Morley D						
17-18	Ott	7	0	0	0	0
19-20	Ott	21	1	0	1	2
20-21	Ott	21	3	1	4	23
21-22	Ott	23	4	0	4	2
Totals		72	8	1	9	27
Playoff Totals		12	0	0	0	3
BRUMWELL, James (Murray) 6-2 190 D						
B. Calgary, Alta., Mar. 31, 1960						
80-81	Minn	0	0	0	0	0
81-82	Minn	21	0	3	3	18
82-83	NJ	59	5	14	19	34
83-84	NJ	42	7	13	20	14
85-86	NJ	1	0	0	0	0
86-87	NJ	1	0	0	0	2
87-88	NJ	3	0	1	1	2
Totals		128	12	31	43	70
Playoff Totals		2	0	0	0	2
BRUNET, Benoit 5-11 184 LW						
B. Ste.-Anne de Bellevue, Que., Aug. 24, 1968						
88-89	Mont	2	0	1	1	0
90-91	Mont	17	1	3	4	0
91-92	Mont	18	4	6	10	14
Totals		37	5	10	15	14
BRUNETEAU, Edward Ernest Henry 5-9 172 RW						
B. St. Boniface, Man., Aug. 1, 1919						
40-41	Det	12	1	1	2	2
43-44	Det	2	0	1	1	0
44-45	Det	42	12	13	25	6
45-46	Det	46	17	12	29	11
46-47	Det	60	9	14	23	14
47-48	Det	18	1	1	2	2
48-49	Det	1	0	0	0	0
Totals		181	40	42	82	35
Playoff Totals		26	7	6	13	0
BRUNETEAU, Modere (Mud) 5-11 185 RW						
B. St. Boniface, Man., Nov. 28, 1914						
35-36	Det	24	2	0	2	2
36-37	Det	42	9	7	16	18
37-38	Det	24	3	6	9	16

Season	Team	GP	G	A	Pts.	PIM
BRUNETEAU, Modere (Mud) *(Continued)*						
38-39	Det	20	3	7	10	0
39-40	Det	48	10	14	24	10
40-41	Det	45	11	17	28	12
41-42	Det	48	14	19	33	8
42-43	Det	50	23	22	45	2
43-44	Det	39	35	18	53	4
44-45	Det	43	23	24	47	6
45-46	Det	28	6	4	10	2
Totals		411	139	138	277	80
Playoff Totals		77	23	14	37	22
BRYDGE, William H. 5-9 195 D						
B. Renfrew, Ont., 1901						
26-27	Tor	41	6	3	9	76
28-29	Det	31	2	2	4	59
29-30	NYA	41	2	6	8	64
30-31	NYA	43	2	5	7	70
31-32	NYA	48	2	8	10	77
32-33	NYA	48	4	15	19	60
33-34	NYA	48	6	7	13	44
34-35	NYA	47	2	6	8	29
35-36	NYA	21	0	0	0	27
Totals		368	26	52	78	506
Playoff Totals		2	0	0	0	4
BRYDGES, Paul 5-11 180 C						
B. Guelph, Ont., June 21, 1965						
86-87	Buf	15	2	2	4	6
BRYDSON, Glenn 5-9 170 RW						
B. Swansea, Ont., Nov. 7, 1910						
30-31	Mont M	14	0	0	0	4
31-32	Mont M	47	12	13	25	44
32-33	Mont M	48	11	17	28	26
33-34	Mont M	37	4	5	9	19
34-35	StL E	48	11	18	29	45
35-36	NYR-Chi	52	10	16	26	39
36-37	Chi	34	7	7	14	20
37-38	Chi	19	1	3	4	6
Totals		299	56	79	135	203
Playoff Totals		11	0	0	0	8
BRYDSON, Gordon (Gord) F						
B. Toronto, Ont.						
29-30	Tor	8	2	0	2	8
BUBLA, Jiri 5-11 200 D						
B. Usti Nad Labem, Czechoslovakia, Jan. 27, 1950						
81-82	Van	23	1	1	2	16
82-83	Van	72	2	28	30	59
83-84	Van	62	6	33	39	43
84-85	Van	56	2	15	17	54
85-86	Van	43	6	24	30	30
Totals		256	17	101	118	202
Playoff Totals		6	0	0	0	7
BUCHANAN, Allaster William (Al) 5-8 160 LW						
B. Winnipeg, Man., May 17, 1927						
48-49	Tor	3	0	1	1	2
49-50	Tor	1	0	0	0	0
Totals		4	0	1	1	2
BUCHANAN, Michael Murray 6-1 185 D						
B. Sault Ste. Marie, Ont., Mar. 1, 1932						
51-52	Chi	1	0	0	0	0
BUCHANAN, Ralph Leonard (Bucky) 5-8 172 C						
B. Montreal, Que., Dec. 28, 1922						
48-49	NYR	2	0	0	0	0
BUCHANAN, Ronald Leonard 6-3 178 C						
B. Montreal, Que., Nov. 15, 1944						
66-67	Bos	3	0	0	0	0
69-70	StL	2	0	0	0	0
72-73	Clev (WHA)	75	37	44	81	20
73-74	Clev (WHA)	49	18	27	45	2
74-75	Clev-Edm-Ind (WHA)	58	24	24	48	22
75-76	Ind (WHA)	23	4	7	11	4
NHL Totals		5	0	0	0	0
WHA Totals		205	83	102	185	48
WHA Playoff Totals		14	7	3	10	2
BUCHBERGER, Kelly 6-2 210 LW						
B. Langenburg, Sask., Dec. 2, 1966						
87-88	Edm	19	1	0	1	81
88-89	Edm	66	5	9	14	234
89-90	Edm	55	2	6	8	168
90-91	Edm	64	3	1	4	160
91-92	Edm	79	20	24	44	157
Totals		283	31	40	71	800

Season	Team	GP	G	A	Pts.	PIM
BUCHBERGER, Kelly *(Continued)*						
Playoff Totals		50	3	11	14	75
BUCYK, John Paul (Chief)	*6-0 215 LW*					
B. Edmonton, Alta., May 12, 1935						
55-56	Det	38	1	8	9	20
56-57	Det	66	10	11	21	41
57-58	Bos	68	21	31	52	57
58-59	Bos	69	24	36	60	36
59-60	Bos	56	16	36	52	26
60-61	Bos	70	19	20	39	48
61-62	Bos	67	20	40	60	32
62-63	Bos	69	27	39	66	36
63-64	Bos	62	18	36	54	36
64-65	Bos	68	26	29	55	24
65-66	Bos	63	27	30	57	12
66-67	Bos	59	18	30	48	12
67-68	Bos	72	30	39	69	8
68-69	Bos	70	24	42	66	18
69-70	Bos	76	31	38	69	13
70-71	Bos	78	51	65	116	8
71-72	Bos	78	32	51	83	4
72-73	Bos	78	40	53	93	12
73-74	Bos	76	31	44	75	8
74-75	Bos	78	29	52	81	10
75-76	Bos	77	36	47	83	20
76-77	Bos	49	20	23	43	12
77-78	Bos	53	5	13	18	4
Totals		1540	556	813	1369	497
Playoff Totals		124	41	62	103	42
BUCYK, Randy	*5-11 185 C*					
B. Edmonton, Alta., Nov. 9, 1962						
85-86	Mont	17	4	2	6	8
87-88	Calg	2	0	0	0	0
Totals		19	4	2	6	8
Playoff Totals		2	0	0	0	0
BUHR, Douglas Leonard	*6-3 215 LW*					
B. Vancouver, B.C., June 29, 1949						
74-75	KC	6	0	2	2	4
BUKOVICH, Anthony John (Tony)						
	5-11 160 C					
B. Painesdale, Mich., Aug. 30, 1918						
43-44	Det	30	0	1	1	0
44-45	Det	14	7	2	9	6
Totals		44	7	3	10	6
Playoff Totals		6	0	1	1	0
BULLARD, Michael Brian	*5-10 185 C*					
B. Ottawa, Ont., Mar. 10, 1961						
80-81	Pitt	15	1	2	3	19
81-82	Pitt	75	36	27	63	91
82-83	Pitt	57	22	22	44	60
83-84	Pitt	76	51	41	92	57
84-85	Pitt	68	32	31	63	75
85-86	Pitt	77	41	42	83	69
86-87	Pitt-Calg	71	30	36	66	51
87-88	Calg	79	48	55	103	68
88-89	StL-Phil	74	27	38	65	106
89-90	Phil	70	27	37	64	67
91-92	Tor	65	14	14	28	42
Totals		727	329	345	674	705
Playoff Totals		40	11	18	29	44
BULLER, Hyman (Hy)	*5-11 185 D*					
B. Montreal, Que., Mar. 15, 1926						
43-44	Det	7	0	3	3	4
44-45	Det	2	0	0	0	2
51-52	NYR	68	12	23	35	96
52-53	NYR	70	7	18	25	73
53-54	NYR	41	3	14	17	40
Totals		188	22	58	80	215
BULLEY, Edward H. (Ted)	*6-1 192 LW*					
B. Windsor, Ont., Mar. 25, 1955						
76-77	Chi	2	0	0	0	0
77-78	Chi	79	23	28	51	141
78-79	Chi	75	27	23	50	153
79-80	Chi	66	14	17	31	136
80-81	Chi	68	18	16	34	95
81-82	Chi	59	12	18	30	120
82-83	Chi	39	4	9	13	47
83-84	Pitt	26	3	2	5	12
Totals		414	101	113	214	704
Playoff Totals		29	5	5	10	24
BURCH, William	*6-0 200 C*					
B. Yonkers, N.Y., Nov. 20, 1900						
22-23	Ham	10	6	2	8	2
23-24	Ham	24	16	2	18	4
24-25	Ham	27	20	4	24	10
25-26	NYA	36	22	3	25	33
26-27	NYA	43	19	8	27	40
27-28	NYA	32	10	2	12	34
28-29	NYA	44	11	5	16	45

Season	Team	GP	G	A	Pts.	PIM
BURCH, William *(Continued)*						
29-30	NYA	35	7	3	10	22
30-31	NYA	44	14	8	22	35
31-32	NYA	48	7	15	22	71
32-33	Bos-Chi	47	5	1	6	6
Totals		390	137	53	190	302
Playoff Totals		2	0	0	0	0
BURCHELL, Frederick (Skippy)	*5-6 145*					
C						
B. Montreal, Que., Jan. 9, 1931						
50-51	Mont	2	0	0	0	0
53-54	Mont	2	0	0	0	2
Totals		4	0	0	0	2
BURDON, Glen William	*6-2 178 C*					
B. Regina, Sask., Aug. 4, 1954						
74-75	KC	11	0	2	2	0
BURE, Pavel	*5-11 176 RW/LW*					
B. Moscow, USSR, Mar. 31, 1971						
91-92	Van	65	34	26	60	30
Playoff Totals		13	6	4	10	14
BUREAU, Marc	*6-0 190 C*					
B. Trois-Rivieres, Que., May 19, 1966						
89-90	Calg	5	0	0	0	4
90-91	Calg-Minn	14	0	6	6	6
91-92	Minn	46	6	4	10	50
Totals		65	6	10	16	60
Playoff Totals		28	3	2	5	34
BUREGA, William	*6-1 200 D*					
B. Winnipeg, Man., Mar. 13, 1932						
55-56	Bos	4	0	1	1	4
BURKE, Edward A.	*F*					
B. Toronto, Ont., June 3, 1907						
31-32	Bos	16	3	0	3	12
32-33	NYA	15	2	0	2	4
33-34	NYA	46	20	10	30	24
34-35	NYA	29	4	10	14	15
Totals		106	29	20	49	55
BURKE, Martin Alphonsus						
	5-7 160 D					
B. Toronto, Ont., Jan. 28, 1903						
27-28	Mont-Pitt Pi	46	2	1	3	61
28-29	Mont	44	4	2	6	68
29-30	Mont	44	2	11	13	71
30-31	Mont	44	2	5	7	91
31-32	Mont	48	3	6	9	50
32-33	Mont-Ott	45	2	5	7	46
33-34	Mont	45	1	4	5	28
34-35	Chi	47	2	2	4	29
35-36	Chi	40	0	3	3	49
36-37	Chi	41	1	3	4	28
37-38	Chi-Mont	50	0	5	5	39
Totals		494	19	47	66	560
Playoff Totals		31	2	4	6	44
BURMEISTER, Roy	*5-10 155 LW*					
B. Collingwood, Ont., 1909						
29-30	NYA	40	1	1	2	0
30-31	NYA	11	0	0	0	0
31-32	NYA	16	3	2	5	2
Totals		67	4	3	7	2
BURNETT, James Kelvin (Kelly)						
	5-10 160 C					
B. Lachine, Que., June 16, 1926						
52-53	NYR	3	1	0	1	0
BURNS, Charles Frederick	*5-11 170 C*					
B. Detroit, Mich., Feb. 14, 1936						
58-59	Det	70	9	11	20	32
59-60	Bos	62	10	17	27	46
60-61	Bos	62	15	26	41	16
61-62	Bos	70	11	17	28	43
62-63	Bos	68	12	10	22	13
67-68	Oak	73	9	26	35	20
68-69	Pitt	76	13	38	51	22
69-70	Minn	50	3	13	16	10
70-71	Minn	76	9	19	28	13
71-72	Minn	77	11	14	25	24
72-73	Minn	65	4	7	11	13
Totals		749	106	198	304	252
Playoff Totals		31	5	4	9	4
BURNS, Gary	*6-1 190 C*					
B. Cambridge, Mass., Jan. 16, 1955						
80-81	NYR	11	2	2	4	18
Playoff Totals		5	0	0	0	6

Season	Team	GP	G	A	Pts.	PIM
BURNS, Norman	*6-0 195 C*					
B. Youngstown, Alta., Feb. 20, 1918						
41-42	NYR	11	0	4	4	2
BURNS, Robert	*5-9 155 LW*					
B. Gore Bay, Ont., Apr. 4, 1905						
27-28	Chi	1	0	0	0	0
28-29	Chi	7	0	0	0	6
29-30	Chi	12	1	0	1	2
Totals		20	1	0	1	8
BURNS, Robert Arthur (Robin)						
	6-0 195 LW					
B. Montreal, Que., Aug. 27, 1946						
70-71	Pitt	10	0	3	3	4
71-72	Pitt	5	0	0	0	8
72-73	Pitt	26	0	2	2	20
74-75	KC	71	18	15	33	70
75-76	KC	78	13	18	31	37
Totals		190	31	38	69	139
BURR, Shawn	*6-1 195 LW/C*					
B. Sarnia, Ont., July 1, 1966						
84-85	Det	9	0	0	0	2
85-86	Det	5	1	0	1	4
86-87	Det	80	22	25	47	107
87-88	Det	78	17	23	40	97
88-89	Det	79	19	27	46	78
89-90	Det	76	24	32	56	82
90-91	Det	80	20	30	50	112
91-92	Det	79	19	32	51	118
Totals		486	122	169	291	600
Playoff Totals		49	12	14	26	65
BURRIDGE, Randy	*5-9 180 LW*					
B. Fort Erie, Ont., Jan. 7, 1966						
85-86	Bos	52	17	25	42	28
86-87	Bos	23	1	4	5	16
87-88	Bos	79	27	28	55	105
88-89	Bos	80	31	30	61	39
89-90	Bos	63	17	15	32	47
90-91	Bos	62	15	13	28	40
91-92	Wash	66	23	44	67	50
Totals		425	131	159	290	325
Playoff Totals		80	12	31	43	89
BURROWS, David James	*6-1 190 D*					
B. Toronto, Ont., Jan. 11, 1949						
71-72	Pitt	77	2	10	12	48
72-73	Pitt	78	3	24	27	46
73-74	Pitt	71	3	14	17	30
74-75	Pitt	72	2	15	17	49
75-76	Pitt	80	7	22	29	51
76-77	Pitt	69	3	6	9	29
77-78	Pitt	67	4	15	19	24
78-79	Tor	65	2	11	13	28
79-80	Tor	80	3	16	19	42
80-81	Tor-Pitt	59	0	2	2	30
Totals		724	29	135	164	377
Playoff Totals		29	1	5	6	25
BURRY, Berthold (Bert)	*D*					
32-33	Ott	4	0	0	0	0
BURT, Adam	*6-0 195 D*					
B. Detroit, Mich., Jan. 15, 1969						
88-89	Hart	5	0	0	0	6
89-90	Hart	63	4	8	12	105
90-91	Hart	42	2	7	9	63
91-92	Hart	66	9	15	24	93
Totals		176	15	30	45	267
Playoff Totals		4	0	0	0	0
BURTON, Cumming Scott (Cummy)						
	5-10 175 RW					
B. Sudbury, Ont., May 12, 1936						
55-56	Det	3	0	0	0	0
57-58	Det	26	0	1	1	12
58-59	Det	14	0	1	1	9
Totals		43	0	2	2	21
Playoff Totals		3	0	0	0	0
BURTON, Nelson Keith	*6-0 205 LW*					
B. Sydney, N.S., Nov. 6, 1957						
77-78	Wash	5	1	0	1	8
78-79	Wash	3	0	0	0	13
Totals		8	1	0	1	21
BUSH, Edward Webster	*6-1 195 D*					
B. Collingwood, Ont., July 11, 1918						
38-39	Det	9	0	0	0	0
41-42	Det	18	4	6	10	50
Totals		27	4	6	10	50
Playoff Totals		12	1	6	7	23

Season	Team	GP	G	A	Pts.	PIM
BUSKAS, Rod	*6-1 197 D*					
B. Wetaskiwin, Alta., Jan. 7, 1961						
82-83	Pitt	41	2	2	4	102
83-84	Pitt	47	2	4	6	60
84-85	Pitt	69	2	7	9	191
85-86	Pitt	72	2	7	9	159
86-87	Pitt	68	3	15	18	123
87-88	Pitt	76	4	8	12	206
88-89	Pitt	52	1	5	6	105
89-90	Van-Pitt	23	0	3	3	49
90-91	LA	57	3	8	11	182
91-92	LA-Chi	47	0	4	4	91
Totals		552	19	63	82	1268
Playoff Totals		18	0	3	3	45
BUSNIUK, Michael	*6-3 200 D*					
B. Thunder Bay, Ont., Dec. 13, 1951						
79-80	Phil	71	2	18	20	93
80-81	Phil	72	1	5	6	204
Totals		143	3	23	26	297
Playoff Totals		25	2	5	7	34
BUSNIUK, Ronald Edward	*5-11 180 RW*					
B. Fort William, Ont. Aug. 13, 1948						
72-73	Buf	1	0	0	0	0
73-74	Buf	5	0	3	3	4
74-75	Minn (WHA)	73	2	21	23	176
75-76	Minn-NE (WHA)	71	2	14	16	205
76-77	Edm (WHA)	84	3	11	14	224
77-78	Edm (WHA)	59	2	18	20	157
NHL Totals		6	0	3	3	4
WHA Totals		287	9	64	73	762
WHA Playoff Totals		39	2	5	7	132
BUSWELL, Walter Gerard	*5-11 170 D*					
B. Montreal, Que., Nov. 6, 1907						
32-33	Det	46	2	4	6	16
33-34	Det	47	1	2	3	8
34-35	Det	47	1	3	4	32
35-36	Mont	44	0	2	2	34
36-37	Mont	44	0	4	4	30
37-38	Mont	48	2	15	17	24
38-39	Mont	46	3	7	10	10
39-40	Mont	46	1	3	4	10
Totals		368	10	40	50	164
Playoff Totals		24	2	1	3	10
BUTCHER, Garth	*6-0 200 D*					
B. Regina, Sask., Jan. 8, 1963						
81-82	Van	5	0	0	0	9
82-83	Van	55	1	13	14	104
83-84	Van	28	2	0	2	34
84-85	Van	75	3	9	12	152
85-86	Van	70	4	7	11	188
86-87	Van	70	5	15	20	207
87-88	Van	80	6	17	23	285
88-89	Van	78	0	20	20	227
89-90	Van	80	6	14	20	205
90-91	Van-StL	82	6	16	22	289
91-92	StL	68	5	15	20	189
Totals		691	38	126	164	1889
Playoff Totals		32	5	4	9	92
BUTLER, Jerome Patrick	*6-0 180 RW*					
B. Sarnia, Ont., Feb. 27, 1951						
72-73	NYR	8	1	0	1	4
73-74	NYR	26	6	10	16	24
74-75	NYR	78	17	16	33	102
75-76	StL	66	17	24	41	75
76-77	StL	80	12	20	32	65
77-78	StL-Tor	82	9	9	18	54
78-79	Tor	76	8	7	15	52
79-80	Tor-Van	78	11	12	23	50
80-81	Van	80	12	15	27	60
81-82	Van	25	3	1	4	15
82-83	Winn	42	3	6	9	14
Totals		641	99	120	219	515
Playoff Totals		48	3	3	6	79
BUTLER, John Richard (Dick)	*5-7 175 RW*					
B. Delisle, Sask., June 2, 1926						
47-48	Chi	7	2	0	2	0
BUTTERS, William Joseph	*5-9 192 D*					
B. St. Paul Minn., Jan. 10, 1951						
74-75	Minn (WHA)	24	2	2	4	58
75-76	Minn-Hou (WHA)	73	0	19	19	138
76-77	Minn-Edm-NE (WHA)	75	1	17	18	215
77-78	NE (WHA)	45	1	13	14	69

Season	Team	GP	G	A	Pts.	PIM
BUTTERS, William Joseph	*(Continued)*					
77-78	Minn	23	1	0	1	30
78-79	Minn	49	0	4	4	47
NHL Totals		72	1	4	5	77
WHA Totals		217	4	51	55	480
WHA Playoff Totals		34	1	4	5	87
BUTTREY, Gordon (Gord)	*5-7 167 F*					
B. Regina, Sask., Mar. 17, 1926						
43-44	Chi	10	0	0	0	0
Playoff Totals		10	0	0	0	0
BUYNAK, Gordon	*6-1 180 D*					
B. Detroit, Mich., Mar. 19, 1954						
74-75	StL	4	0	0	0	2
BYCE, John	*6-1 180 RW*					
B. Madison, Wisc., Aug. 9, 1967						
90-91	Bos	18	1	3	4	6
91-92	Bos	3	1	0	1	0
Totals		21	2	3	5	6
Playoff Totals		8	2	0	2	2
BYERS, Gordon Charles (Gord)	*5-9 182 D*					
B. Eganville, Ont., Mar. 11, 1930						
49-50	Bos	1	0	1	1	0
BYERS, Jerry William	*5-11 170 LW*					
B. Kentville, N.S., Mar. 29, 1952						
72-73	Minn	14	0	2	2	6
73-74	Minn	10	0	0	0	0
74-75	Atl	12	1	1	2	4
77-78	NYR	7	2	1	3	0
Totals		43	3	4	7	10
BYERS, Lyndon	*6-1 200 RW*					
B. Nipawin, Sask., Feb. 29, 1964						
83-84	Bos	10	2	4	6	32
84-85	Bos	33	3	8	11	41
85-86	Bos	5	0	2	2	9
86-87	Bos	18	2	3	5	53
87-88	Bos	53	10	14	24	236
88-89	Bos	49	0	4	4	218
89-90	Bos	43	4	4	8	159
90-91	Bos	19	2	2	4	82
91-92	Bos	31	1	1	2	129
Totals		261	24	42	66	370
Playoff Totals		37	2	2	4	96
BYERS, Michael Arthur	*5-10 185 RW*					
B. Toronto, Ont., Sept. 11, 1946						
67-68	Tor	10	2	2	4	0
68-69	Tor-Phil	10	0	2	2	2
70-71	LA	72	27	18	45	14
71-72	LA-Buf	74	13	12	25	23
72-73	LA-NE (WHA)	75	25	21	46	24
73-74	NE (WHA)	78	29	21	50	6
74-75	NE (WHA)	72	22	26	48	10
75-76	NE-Cin (WHA)	41	7	6	13	0
NHL Totals		166	42	34	76	39
WHA Totals		266	83	74	157	40
NHL Playoff Totals		4	0	1	1	0
WHA Playoff Totals		25	10	11	21	20
BYRAM, Shawn	*6-2 204 LW*					
B. Neepawa, Man., Sept. 12, 1968						
90-91	NYI	4	0	0	0	14
91-92	Chi	1	0	0	0	0
Totals		5	0	0	0	14
CAFFERY, John (Jack)	*6-0 175 C*					
B. Kingston, Ont., June 30, 1934						
54-55	Tor	3	0	0	0	0
56-57	Bos	47	2	2	4	20
57-58	Bos	7	1	0	1	2
Totals		57	3	2	5	22
Playoff Totals		10	1	0	1	4
CAFFERY, Terrance Michael	*5-9 165 C*					
B. Toronto, Ont., Apr. 1, 1949						
69-70	Chi	6	0	0	0	0
70-71	Minn	8	0	0	0	0
72-73	NE (WHA)	74	39	61	100	14
74-75	NE (WHA)	67	15	37	52	12
75-76	NE-Calg (WHA)	23	5	13	18	4
NHL Totals		14	0	0	0	0
WHA Totals		164	59	111	170	30
NHL Playoff Totals		1	0	0	0	0
WHA Playoff Totals		8	3	7	10	0

Season	Team	GP	G	A	Pts.	PIM
CAHAN, Lawrence Louis	*6-0 195 D*					
B. Ft. William, Ont., Dec. 25, 1933						
54-55	Tor	58	0	6	6	64
55-56	Tor	21	0	2	2	46
56-57	NYR	61	5	4	9	65
57-58	NYR	34	1	1	2	20
58-59	NYR	16	1	0	1	8
61-62	NYR	57	2	7	9	85
62-63	NYR	56	6	14	20	47
63-64	NYR	53	4	8	12	80
64-65	NYR	26	0	5	5	32
67-68	Oak	74	9	15	24	80
68-69	LA	72	3	11	14	76
69-70	LA	70	4	8	12	50
70-71	LA	67	3	11	14	44
72-73	Chi (WHA)	75	1	10	11	44
73-74	Chi (WHA)	3	0	0	0	2
NHL Totals		665	38	92	130	698
WHA Totals		78	1	10	11	46
NHL Playoff Totals		29	1	1	2	38
CAHILL, Charles (Chuck)	*F*					
25-26	Bos	31	0	1	1	4
26-27	Bos	1	0	0	0	0
Totals		32	0	1	1	4
CAIN, Herbert	*5-11 180 LW*					
B. Newmarket, Ont., Dec. 24, 1913						
33-34	Mont M	31	4	5	9	14
34-35	Mont M	44	20	7	27	13
35-36	Mont M	47	5	13	18	16
36-37	Mont M	43	13	17	30	18
37-38	Mont M	47	11	19	30	10
38-39	Mont	45	13	14	27	26
39-40	Bos	48	21	10	31	30
40-41	Bos	40	8	10	18	6
41-42	Bos	35	8	10	18	2
42-43	Bos	45	18	18	36	19
43-44	Bos	48	36	46	82	4
44-45	Bos	50	32	13	45	16
45-46	Bos	48	17	12	29	4
Totals		571	206	194	400	178
Playoff Totals		64	16	13	29	13
CAIN, James F. (Dutch)	*D*					
B. Newmarket, Ont.						
24-25	Mont M	28	4	0	4	27
25-26	Mont M-Tor	33	0	0	0	8
Totals		61	4	0	4	35
CAIRNS, Donald	*6-1 195 LW*					
B. Calgary, Alta., Oct. 8, 1955						
75-76	KC	7	0	0	0	0
76-77	Col	2	0	1	1	2
Totals		9	0	1	1	2
CALDER, Eric	*6-1 180 D*					
B. Kitchener, Ont., July 26, 1963						
81-82	Wash	1	0	0	0	0
82-83	Wash	1	0	0	0	0
Totals		2	0	0	0	0
CALLADINE, Norman	*5-9 155 C*					
B. Peterborough, Ont., 1916						
42-43	Bos	3	0	1	1	0
43-44	Bos	49	16	27	43	8
44-45	Bos	11	3	1	4	0
Totals		63	19	29	48	8
CALLANDER, John (Jock)	*6-1 185 RW*					
B. Regina, Sask., Apr. 23, 1961						
87-88	Pitt	41	11	16	27	45
88-89	Pitt	30	6	5	11	20
89-90	Pitt	30	4	7	11	49
91-92	Pitt	0	0	0	0	0
Totals		101	21	28	49	114
Playoff Totals		22	3	11	14	12
CALLANDER, Leonard Drew	*6-2 188 C*					
B. Regina, Sask., Aug. 17, 1956						
76-77	Phil	2	1	0	1	0
77-78	Phil	1	0	0	0	0
78-79	Phil-Van	32	4	1	5	7
79-80	Van	4	1	1	2	0
Totals		39	6	2	8	7
CALLIGHEN, Brett	*5-11 182 C*					
B. Toronto, Ont., May 15, 1953						
76-77	NE-Edm (WHA)	62	15	26	41	89
77-78	Edm (WHA)	80	20	30	50	112
78-79	Edm (WHA)	71	31	39	70	79
79-80	Edm	59	23	35	58	72

CALLIGHEN, Brett *(Continued)*

Season	Team	GP	G	A	Pts.	PIM
80-81	Edm	55	25	35	60	32
81-82	Edm	46	8	19	27	28
NHL Totals		160	56	89	145	132
WHA Totals		213	66	95	161	280
NHL Playoff Totals		14	4	6	10	8
WHA Playoff Totals		23	9	13	22	38

CALLIGHEN, Francis Charles Winslow (Patsy) *5-6 175 LW*
B. Toronto, Ont., Feb. 13, 1906

Season	Team	GP	G	A	Pts.	PIM
27-28	NYR	36	0	0	0	32
Playoff Totals		9	0	0	0	0

CAMAZZOLA, Anthony Bert (Tony) *6-2 210 D*
B. Vancouver, B.C., Sept. 11, 1962

Season	Team	GP	G	A	Pts.	PIM
81-82	Wash	3	0	0	0	0

CAMAZZOLA, James *5-11 190 LW*
B. Vancouver, B.C., Jan. 5, 1964

Season	Team	GP	G	A	Pts.	PIM
83-84	Chi	1	0	0	0	0
86-87	Chi	2	0	0	0	0
Totals		3	0	0	0	0

CAMERON, Alan Richard *6-0 205 D*
B. Edmonton, Alta., Oct. 21, 1955

Season	Team	GP	G	A	Pts.	PIM
75-76	Det	38	2	8	10	49
76-77	Det	80	3	13	16	112
77-78	Det	63	2	7	9	94
78-79	Det	9	0	3	3	8
79-80	Winn	63	3	11	14	72
80-81	Winn	29	1	2	3	21
Totals		282	11	44	55	356
Playoff Totals		7	0	1	1	2

CAMERON, Angus (Scotty) *6-1 175 C*
B. Prince Albert, Sask., Nov. 5, 1921

Season	Team	GP	G	A	Pts.	PIM
42-43	NYR	35	8	11	19	0

CAMERON, Craig Lauder *6-0 200 RW*
B. Edmonton, Alta., July 19, 1945

Season	Team	GP	G	A	Pts.	PIM
66-67	Det	1	0	0	0	0
67-68	StL	32	7	2	9	8
68-69	StL	72	11	5	16	40
70-71	StL	78	14	6	20	32
71-72	Minn	64	2	1	3	11
72-73	NYI	72	19	14	33	27
73-74	NYI	78	15	14	29	28
74-75	NYI-Minn	77	11	13	24	22
75-76	Minn	78	8	10	18	34
Totals		552	87	65	152	202
Playoff Totals		27	3	1	4	17

CAMERON, David William *6-0 185 C*
B. Charlottetown, P.E.I., July 29, 1958

Season	Team	GP	G	A	Pts.	PIM
81-82	Col	66	11	12	23	103
82-83	NJ	35	5	4	9	50
83-84	NJ	67	9	12	21	85
Totals		168	25	28	53	238

CAMERON, Harold Hugh (Harry) *D*
B. Pembroke, Ont., Feb. 6, 1890

Season	Team	GP	G	A	Pts.	PIM
17-18	Tor	20	17	0	17	17
18-19	Tor-Ott	14	11	3	14	35
19-20	Tor-Mont	23	16	1	17	11
20-21	Tor	24	18	9	27	55
21-22	Tor	24	19	8	27	18
22-23	Tor	22	9	6	15	18
Totals		127	90	27	117	154
Playoff Totals		20	7	3	10	29

CAMERON, William *RW*
B. Timmins, Ont., 1904

Season	Team	GP	G	A	Pts.	PIM
23-24	Mont	18	0	0	0	2
25-26	NYA	21	0	0	0	0
Totals		39	0	0	0	2
Playoff Totals		6	0	0	0	0

CAMPBELL, Bryan Albert *6-0 175 C*
B. Sudbury, Ont., Mar. 27, 1944

Season	Team	GP	G	A	Pts.	PIM
67-68	LA	44	6	15	21	16
68-69	LA	18	2	1	3	4
69-70	LA-Chi	45	5	5	10	6
70-71	Chi	78	17	37	54	26
71-72	Chi	75	5	13	18	22
72-73	Phil (WHA)	75	25	48	73	85
73-74	Van (WHA)	76	27	62	89	50
74-75	Van (WHA)	78	29	34	63	24
75-76	Cin (WHA)	77	22	50	72	24
76-77	Ind-Edm (WHA)	74	13	46	59	24
77-78	Edm (WHA)	53	7	13	20	12
NHL Totals		260	35	71	106	74
WHA Totals		433	123	253	376	219

CAMPBELL, Bryan Albert *(Continued)*

Season	Team	GP	G	A	Pts.	PIM
NHL Playoff Totals		22	3	4	7	2
WHA Playoff Totals		8	3	2	5	8

CAMPBELL, Colin John *5-9 190 D*
B. London, Ont., Jan. 28, 1953

Season	Team	GP	G	A	Pts.	PIM
73-74	Vanc (WHA)	78	3	20	23	191
74-75	Pitt	59	4	15	19	172
75-76	Pitt	64	7	10	17	105
76-77	Col	54	3	8	11	67
77-78	Pitt	55	1	9	10	103
78-79	Pitt	65	2	18	20	137
79-80	Edm	72	2	11	13	196
80-81	Van	42	1	8	9	75
81-82	Van	47	0	8	8	131
82-83	Det	53	1	7	8	74
83-84	Det	68	3	4	7	108
84-85	Det	57	1	5	6	124
NHL Totals		636	25	103	128	1292
WHA Totals		78	3	20	23	191
NHL Playoff Tot.		45	4	10	14	181

CAMPBELL, David *D*
B. Lachute, Que., Apr. 27, 1896

Season	Team	GP	G	A	Pts.	PIM
20-21	Mont	3	0	0	0	0

CAMPBELL, Donald William *F*
B. Drumheller, Alta., July 12, 1925

Season	Team	GP	G	A	Pts.	PIM
43-44	Chi	17	1	3	4	8

CAMPBELL, Earl (Spiff) *F*

Season	Team	GP	G	A	Pts.	PIM
23-24	Ott	18	4	1	5	6
24-25	Ott	30	0	0	0	0
25-26	NYA	29	1	0	1	6
Totals		77	5	1	6	12
Playoff Totals		2	0	0	0	0

CAMPBELL, Scott *6-3 205 D*
B. Toronto, Ont., June 22, 1957

Season	Team	GP	G	A	Pts.	PIM
77-78	Hou (WHA)	75	8	29	37	116
78-79	Winn (WHA)	74	3	15	18	248
79-80	Winn	63	3	17	20	136
80-81	Winn	14	1	4	5	55
81-82	StL	3	0	0	0	52
NHL Totals		80	4	21	25	243
WHA Totals		149	11	44	55	364
WHA Playoff Totals		16	1	3	4	33

CAMPBELL, Wade Allan *6-4 220 D*
B. Peace River, Alta., Jan. 2, 1961

Season	Team	GP	G	A	Pts.	PIM
82-83	Winn	42	1	2	3	50
83-84	Winn	79	7	14	21	147
84-85	Winn	40	1	6	7	21
85-86	Winn-Bos	32	0	1	1	42
86-87	Bos	14	0	3	3	24
87-88	Bos	6	0	1	1	21
Totals		213	9	27	36	305
Playoff Totals		10	0	0	0	20

CAMPEAU, Jean Claude (Tod) *5-11 175 C*
B. St. Jerome, Que., June 4, 1923

Season	Team	GP	G	A	Pts.	PIM
43-44	Mont	2	0	0	0	0
47-48	Mont	14	2	2	4	4
48-49	Mont	26	3	7	10	12
Totals		42	5	9	14	16
Playoff Totals		1	0	0	0	0

CAMPEDELLI, Dom *6-1 185 D*
B. Cohasset, Mass., Apr. 3, 1964

Season	Team	GP	G	A	Pts.	PIM
85-86	Mont	2	0	0	0	0

CAPUANO, David *6-2 190 C*
B. Warwick, R.I., July 27, 1968

Season	Team	GP	G	A	Pts.	PIM
89-90	Pitt-Van	33	3	5	8	12
90-91	Van	61	13	31	44	42
Totals		94	16	36	52	54

CAPUANO, Jack *6-2 210 D*
B. Cranston, R.I., July 7, 1966

Season	Team	GP	G	A	Pts.	PIM
89-90	Tor	1	0	0	0	0
90-91	Van	3	0	0	0	0
91-92	Bos	2	0	0	0	0
Totals		6	0	0	0	0

CARBONNEAU, Guy *5-11 180 C*
B. Sept Iles, Que., Mar. 18, 1960

Season	Team	GP	G	A	Pts.	PIM
80-81	Mont	2	0	1	1	0
82-83	Mont	77	18	29	47	68
83-84	Mont	78	24	30	54	75
84-85	Mont	79	23	34	57	43
85-86	Mont	80	20	36	56	57
86-87	Mont	79	18	27	45	68
87-88	Mont	80	17	21	38	61
88-89	Mont	79	26	30	56	44

CARBONNEAU, Guy *(Continued)*

Season	Team	GP	G	A	Pts.	PIM
89-90	Mont	68	19	36	55	37
90-91	Mont	78	20	24	44	63
91-92	Mont	72	18	21	39	39
Totals		772	203	289	492	555
Playoff Tot.		134	26	37	63	111

CARBOL, Leo *5-10 170 D*
B. Ottawa, Ont., June 5, 1912

Season	Team	GP	G	A	Pts.	PIM
42-43	Chi	6	0	1	1	4

CARDIN, Claude *5-7 160 LW*
B. Sorel, Que., May 28, 1943

Season	Team	GP	G	A	Pts.	PIM
67-68	StL	1	0	0	0	0

CARDWELL, Stephen Michael *5-11 190 LW*
B. Toronto, Ont., Aug. 13, 1950

Season	Team	GP	G	A	Pts.	PIM
70-71	Pitt	5	0	1	1	15
71-72	Pitt	28	7	8	15	18
72-73	Pitt	20	2	2	4	2
73-74	Minn (WHA)	77	23	23	46	100
74-75	Clev (WHA)	75	9	13	22	127
NHL Totals		53	9	11	20	35
WHA Totals		152	32	36	68	227
NHL Playoff Totals		4	0	0	0	2
WHA Playoff Totals		15	0	1	1	34

CAREY, George *RW*

Season	Team	GP	G	A	Pts.	PIM
19-20	Que	20	11	5	16	4
20-21	Ham	20	7	1	8	8
21-22	Ham	23	3	2	5	2
22-23	Ham	5	1	0	1	0
23-24	Tor	4	0	0	0	0
Totals		72	22	8	30	14

CARKNER, Terry *6-3 210 D*
B. Smiths Falls, Ont., Mar. 7, 1966

Season	Team	GP	G	A	Pts.	PIM
86-87	NYR	52	2	13	15	118
87-88	Que	63	3	24	27	159
88-89	Phil	78	11	32	43	149
89-90	Phil	63	4	18	22	169
90-91	Phil	79	7	25	32	204
91-92	Phil	73	4	12	16	195
Totals		408	31	124	155	994
Playoff Totals		20	1	5	6	28

CARLETON, Kenneth Wayne *6-2 215 LW*
B. Sudbury, Ont., Aug. 4, 1946

Season	Team	GP	G	A	Pts.	PIM
65-66	Tor	2	0	1	1	0
66-67	Tor	5	1	0	1	14
67-68	Tor	65	8	11	19	34
68-69	Tor	12	1	3	4	6
69-70	Tor-Bos	49	6	20	26	29
70-71	Bos	69	22	24	46	44
71-72	Cal	76	17	14	31	45
72-73	Ott (WHA)	75	42	49	91	42
73-74	Tor (WHA)	78	37	55	92	31
74-75	NE (WHA)	73	35	39	74	50
75-76	NE-Edm (WHA)	61	17	37	54	12
76-77	Birm (WHA)	3	1	0	1	0
NHL Totals		278	55	73	128	172
WHA Totals		290	132	180	312	135
NHL Playoff Totals		18	2	4	6	14
WHA Playoff Totals		25	8	21	29	24

CARLIN, Brian John *5-10 175 LW*
B. Calgary, Alta., June 13, 1950

Season	Team	GP	G	A	Pts.	PIM
71-72	LA	5	1	0	1	0
72-73	Alb (WHA)	65	12	22	34	6
73-74	Edm (WHA)	5	1	0	1	0
NHL Totals		5	1	0	1	0
WHA Totals		70	13	22	35	6

CARLSON, Jack Anthony *6-3 205 LW*
B. Virginia, Minn., Aug. 23, 1954

Season	Team	GP	G	A	Pts.	PIM
74-75	Minn (WHA)	32	5	5	10	85
75-76	Minn-Edm (WHA)	68	9	11	20	220
76-77	Minn-Edm (WHA)	71	11	8	19	136
77-78	NE (WHA)	34	2	7	9	61
78-79	NE (WHA)	67	9	20	29	192
78-79	Minn	16	3	0	3	40
80-81	Minn	43	7	2	9	108
81-82	Minn	57	8	4	12	103
82-83	StL	54	6	1	7	58
83-84	StL	58	6	8	14	95
86-87	Minn	8	0	0	0	13
NHL Totals		236	30	15	45	417
WHA Totals		272	36	51	87	694
NHL Playoff Totals		25	1	2	3	72

CARLSON, Jack Anthony (Continued)

Season Team	GP	G	A	Pts.	PIM
WHA Playoff Totals	28	3	4	7	68

CARLSON, Kent 6-3 200 D
B. Concord, N.H., Jan. 11, 1962

Season Team	GP	G	A	Pts.	PIM
83-84 Mont	65	3	7	10	73
84-85 Mont	18	1	1	2	33
85-86 Mont-StL	28	2	3	5	42
88-89 Wash	2	1	0	1	0
Totals	113	7	11	18	148
Playoff Totals	8	0	0	0	13

CARLSON, Steven Edward 6-3 180 C
B. Virginia, Minn., Aug. 26, 1955

Season Team	GP	G	A	Pts.	PIM
75-76 Minn (WHA)	10	0	1	1	23
76-77 Minn-NE (WHA)	52	9	17	26	48
77-78 NE (WHA)	38	6	7	13	11
78-79 Edm (WHA)	73	18	22	40	50
79-80 LA	52	9	12	21	23
NHL Totals	52	9	12	21	23
WHA Totals	173	33	47	80	132
NHL Playoff Totals	4	1	1	2	7
WHA Playoff Totals	29	3	8	11	23

CARLSSON, Anders 5-11 185 C
B. Gavie, Sweden, Nov. 25, 1960

Season Team	GP	G	A	Pts.	PIM
86-87 NJ	48	2	18	20	14
87-88 NJ	9	1	0	1	0
88-89 NJ	47	4	8	12	20
Totals	104	7	26	33	34
Playoff Totals	3	1	0	1	2

CARLYLE, Randy Robert 5-10 200 D
B. Sudbury, Ont., Apr. 19, 1956

Season Team	GP	G	A	Pts.	PIM
76-77 Tor	45	0	5	5	51
77-78 Tor	49	2	11	13	31
78-79 Pitt	70	13	34	47	78
79-80 Pitt	67	8	28	36	45
80-81 Pitt	76	16	67	83	136
81-82 Pitt	73	11	64	75	131
82-83 Pitt	61	15	41	56	110
83-84 Pitt-Winn	55	3	26	29	84
84-85 Winn	71	13	38	51	98
85-86 Winn	68	16	33	49	93
86-87 Winn	71	16	26	42	93
87-88 Winn	78	15	44	59	210
88-89 Winn	78	6	38	44	78
89-90 Winn	53	3	15	18	50
90-91 Winn	52	9	19	28	44
91-92 Winn	66	1	9	10	54
Totals	1033	147	498	645	1386
Playoff Totals	69	9	24	33	120

CARNEY, Keith E. 6-1 199 D
B. Pawtucket, R.I., Feb. 3, 1970

Season Team	GP	G	A	Pts.	PIM
91-92 Buf	14	1	2	3	18
Playoff Totals	7	0	3	3	0

CARON, Alain Luc (Boom Boom) 5-10 175 RW
B. Dolbeau, Que., Apr. 27, 1938

Season Team	GP	G	A	Pts.	PIM
67-68 Oak	58	9	13	22	18
68-69 Mont	2	0	0	0	0
72-73 Que (WHA)	68	36	27	63	14
73-74 Que (WHA)	59	31	15	46	10
74-75 Que-Balt (WHA)	68	15	8	23	6
NHL Totals	60	9	13	22	18
WHA Totals	195	82	50	132	30

CARPENTER, Everard Lorne (Eddie) D
B. Hartford, Mich.

Season Team	GP	G	A	Pts.	PIM
19-20 Que	24	8	3	11	19
20-21 Ham	20	2	1	3	4
Totals	44	10	4	14	23

CARPENTER, Robert 6-0 190 C/LW
B. Beverly, Mass., July 13, 1963

Season Team	GP	G	A	Pts.	PIM
81-82 Wash	80	32	35	67	69
82-83 Wash	80	32	37	69	64
83-84 Wash	80	28	40	68	51
84-85 Wash	80	53	42	95	87
85-86 Wash	80	27	29	56	105
86-87 Wash-NYR-LA	60	9	18	27	47
87-88 LA	71	19	33	52	84
88-89 LA-Bos	57	16	24	40	26
89-90 Bos	80	25	31	56	97
90-91 Bos	29	8	8	16	22
91-92 Bos	60	25	23	48	46
Totals	757	274	320	594	698
Playoff Totals	74	16	21	37	100

CARR, Alfred George Robert (Red) 5-8 178 LW
B. Winnipeg, Man.

Season Team	GP	G	A	Pts.	PIM
43-44 Tor	5	0	1	1	4

CARR, Eugene William (Gene) 5-11 185 C
B. Nanaimo, B.C., Sept. 17, 1951

Season Team	GP	G	A	Pts.	PIM
71-72 StL-NYR	74	11	10	21	34
72-73 NYR	50	9	10	19	50
73-74 NYR-LA	50	7	16	23	51
74-75 LA	80	7	32	39	103
75-76 LA	38	8	11	19	16
76-77 LA	68	15	12	27	25
77-78 LA-Pitt	75	19	37	56	80
78-79 Atl	30	3	8	11	6
Totals	465	79	136	215	365
Playoff Totals	35	5	8	13	66

CARR, Lorne Bell 5-8 161 RW
B. Stoughton, Sask., July 2, 1910

Season Team	GP	G	A	Pts.	PIM
33-34 NYR	14	0	0	0	0
34-35 NYA	48	17	14	31	14
35-36 NYA	44	8	10	18	4
36-37 NYA	47	18	16	34	22
37-38 NYA	48	16	7	23	12
38-39 NYA	47	19	18	37	16
39-40 NYA	48	8	17	25	17
40-41 NYA	48	13	19	32	10
41-42 Tor	47	16	17	33	4
42-43 Tor	50	27	33	60	15
43-44 Tor	50	36	38	74	9
44-45 Tor	47	11	25	36	7
45-46 Tor	42	5	8	13	2
Totals	580	194	222	416	132
Playoff Totals	53	10	9	19	13

CARRIERE, Larry 6-1 190 D
B. Montreal, Que., Jan. 30, 1952

Season Team	GP	G	A	Pts.	PIM
72-73 Buf	40	2	8	10	52
73-74 Buf	77	6	24	30	103
74-75 Buf	80	1	11	12	111
75-76 Atl	75	4	15	19	96
76-77 Atl-Van	74	3	12	15	71
77-78 Van-LA-Buf	18	0	3	3	30
79-80 Tor	2	0	1	1	0
Totals	366	16	74	90	463
Playoff Totals	27	0	3	3	42

CARRIGAN, Eugene (Gene) 6-1 200 C
B. Edmonton, Alta., July 5, 1907

Season Team	GP	G	A	Pts.	PIM
30-31 NYR	33	2	0	2	13
34-35 StL E	4	0	1	0	0
Totals	37	2	1	3	13
Playoff Totals	4	0	0	0	0

CARROLL, George D

Season Team	GP	G	A	Pts.	PIM
24-25 Mont M-Bos	15	0	0	0	9

CARROLL, Gregory John 6-0 185 C
B. Gimli, Man., Nov. 10, 1956

Season Team	GP	G	A	Pts.	PIM
76-77 Cin (WHA)	77	15	39	54	53
77-78 NE-Cin (WHA)	74	15	27	42	63
78-79 Wash-Det	60	7	15	22	20
79-80 Hart	71	13	19	32	24
NHL Totals	131	20	34	54	44
WHA Totals	151	30	66	96	116
WHA Playoff Totals	4	1	2	3	0

CARROLL, William Allan 5-10 190 C
B. Toronto, Ont., Jan. 19, 1959

Season Team	GP	G	A	Pts.	PIM
80-81 NYI	18	4	4	8	6
81-82 NYI	72	9	20	29	32
82-83 NYI	71	1	11	12	24
83-84 NYI	39	5	2	7	12
84-85 Edm	65	8	9	17	22
85-86 Edm-Det	26	2	6	8	11
86-87 Det	31	1	2	3	6
Totals	322	30	54	84	113
Playoff Totals	71	6	12	18	18

CARRUTHERS, Gordon (Dwight) 5-9 185 D
B. Lashburn, Sask., Nov. 7, 1944

Season Team	GP	G	A	Pts.	PIM
65-66 Det	1	0	0	0	0
67-68 Phil	1	0	0	0	0
Totals	2	0	0	0	0

CARSE, Robert Allison 5-9 170 LW
B. Edmonton, Alta., July 19, 1919

Season Team	GP	G	A	Pts.	PIM
39-40 Chi	22	3	5	8	11
40-41 Chi	43	9	9	18	9
41-42 Chi	33	7	16	23	10

CARSE, Robert Allison (Continued)

Season Team	GP	G	A	Pts.	PIM
42-43 Chi	47	10	22	32	6
47-48 Mont	22	3	3	6	16
Totals	167	32	55	87	52
Playoff Totals	10	0	2	2	2

CARSE, William Alexander 5-8 165 C
B. Edmonton, Alta., May 29, 1914

Season Team	GP	G	A	Pts.	PIM
38-39 NYR	1	0	1	1	0
39-40 Chi	48	10	13	23	10
40-41 Chi	32	5	15	20	12
41-42 Chi	43	13	14	27	16
Totals	124	28	43	71	38
Playoff Totals		3	2	5	0

CARSON, Frank R. 5-7 165 RW
B. Parry Sound, Ont., Jan. 12, 1902

Season Team	GP	G	A	Pts.	PIM
25-26 Mont M	16	2	1	3	6
26-27 Mont M	44	2	3	5	12
27-28 Mont M	21	0	1	1	10
30-31 NYA	44	6	7	13	36
31-32 Det	31	10	14	24	31
32-33 Det	45	12	13	25	35
33-34 Det	47	10	9	19	36
Totals	248	42	48	90	166
Playoff Totals	22	0	2	2	9

CARSON, Gerald (Stub) 5-10 175 D
B. Parry Sound, Ont., Oct. 10, 1905

Season Team	GP	G	A	Pts.	PIM
28-29 Mont-NYR	40	0	0	0	9
29-30 Mont	35	1	0	1	8
32-33 Mont	48	5	2	7	53
33-34 Mont	48	5	1	6	51
34-35 Mont	48	0	5	5	56
36-37 Mont M	42	1	3	4	28
Totals	261	12	11	23	205
Playoff Totals	22	0	0	0	12

CARSON, Jimmy 6-0 200 C
B. Southfield, Mich., July 20, 1968

Season Team	GP	G	A	Pts.	PIM
86-87 LA	80	37	42	79	22
87-88 LA	80	55	52	107	45
88-89 Edm	80	49	51	100	36
89-90 Edm-Det	48	21	18	39	8
90-91 Det	64	21	25	46	28
91-92 Det	80	34	35	69	30
Totals	432	217	223	440	169
Playoff Totals	35	12	10	22	20

CARSON, Lindsay Warren 6-2 195 C
B. Oxbow, Sask., Nov. 21, 1960

Season Team	GP	G	A	Pts.	PIM
81-82 Phil	18	0	1	1	32
82-83 Phil	78	18	19	37	67
83-84 Phil	16	1	3	4	10
84-85 Phil	77	20	19	39	123
85-86 Phil	50	9	12	21	84
86-87 Phil	71	11	15	26	141
87-88 Phil-Hart	63	7	11	18	67
Totals	373	66	80	146	524
Playoff Totals	49	4	10	14	56

CARSON, William Joseph F
B. Bracebridge, Ont., Nov. 25, 1900

Season Team	GP	G	A	Pts.	PIM
26-27 Tor	40	16	6	22	41
27-28 Tor	32	20	6	26	36
28-29 Tor-Bos	43	11	8	19	55
29-30 Bos	44	7	4	11	24
Totals	159	54	24	78	156
Playoff Totals	11	3	0	3	14

CARTER, John 5-10 175 LW
B. Winchester, Mass., May 3, 1963

Season Team	GP	G	A	Pts.	PIM
85-86 Bos	3	0	0	0	0
86-87 Bos	8	0	1	1	0
87-88 Bos	4	0	1	1	2
88-89 Bos	44	12	10	22	24
89-90 Bos	76	17	22	39	26
90-91 Bos	50	4	7	11	68
91-92 SJ	4	0	0	0	0
Totals	189	33	41	74	120
Playoff Totals	31	7	5	12	51

CARTER, Lyle Dwight 6-1 185 F
B. Truro, N.S., Apr. 29, 1945

Season Team	GP	G	A	Pts.	PIM
71-72 Cal	15	0	0	0	2

CARTER, Ronald 6-1 205 RW
B. Montreal, Que., Mar. 14, 1958

Season Team	GP	G	A	Pts.	PIM
79-80 Edm	2	0	0	0	0

CARTER, William 5-11 155 C
B. Cornwall, Ont., Dec. 2, 1937

Season Team	GP	G	A	Pts.	PIM
57-58 Mont	1	0	0	0	0
60-61 Bos	8	0	0	0	2
61-62 Mont	7	0	0	0	4
Totals	16	0	0	0	6

CARVETH, Joseph Gordon 5-10 180 RW
B. Regina, Sask., Mar. 21, 1918

Season	Team	GP	G	A	Pts.	PIM
40-41	Det	19	2	1	3	2
41-42	Det	29	6	11	17	2
42-43	Det	43	18	18	36	6
43-44	Det	46	21	35	56	6
44-45	Det	50	26	28	54	10
45-46	Det	48	17	18	35	18
46-47	Bos	51	21	15	36	10
47-48	Bos-Mont	57	9	19	28	8
48-49	Mont	60	15	22	37	8
49-50	Mont-Det	71	14	18	32	15
50-51	Det	30	1	4	5	0
Totals		504	150	189	339	85
Playoff Totals		69	21	16	37	28

CASHMAN, Wayne John 6-1 208 LW
B. Kingston, Ont., June 24, 1945

Season	Team	GP	G	A	Pts.	PIM
64-65	Bos	1	0	0	0	0
67-68	Bos	12	0	4	4	2
68-69	Bos	51	8	23	31	49
69-70	Bos	70	9	26	35	79
70-71	Bos	77	21	58	79	100
71-72	Bos	74	23	29	52	103
72-73	Bos	76	29	39	68	100
73-74	Bos	78	30	59	89	111
74-75	Bos	42	11	22	33	24
75-76	Bos	80	28	43	71	87
76-77	Bos	65	15	37	52	76
77-78	Bos	76	24	38	62	69
78-79	Bos	75	27	40	67	63
79-80	Bos	44	11	21	32	19
80-81	Bos	77	25	35	60	80
81-82	Bos	64	12	31	43	59
82-83	Bos	65	4	11	15	20
Totals		1027	277	516	793	1041
Playoff Totals		145	31	57	88	250

CASSELS, Andrew 6-0 192 C
B. Bramalea, Ont., July 23, 1969

Season	Team	GP	G	A	Pts.	PIM
89-90	Mont	6	2	0	2	2
90-91	Mont	54	6	19	25	20
91-92	Hart	67	11	30	41	18
Totals		127	19	49	68	40
Playoff Totals		15	2	6	8	8

CASSIDY, Bruce 5-11 175 D
B. Ottawa, Ont., May 20, 1965

Season	Team	GP	G	A	Pts.	PIM
83-84	Chi	1	0	0	0	0
85-86	Chi	1	0	0	0	0
86-87	Chi	2	0	0	0	0
87-88	Chi	21	3	10	13	6
88-89	Chi	9	0	2	2	4
89-90	Chi	2	1	1	2	0
Totals		36	4	13	17	10
Playoff Totals		1	0	0	0	0

CASSIDY, Thomas E. J. 5-11 180 C
B. Blind River, Ont., Mar. 15, 1952

Season	Team	GP	G	A	Pts.	PIM
77-78	Pitt	26	3	4	7	15

CASSOLATO, Anthony Gerald
5-11 183 RW
B. Guelph, Ont., May 7, 1956

Season	Team	GP	G	A	Pts.	PIM
76-77	SD (WHA)	43	13	12	25	26
77-78	Birm (WHA)	77	18	25	43	59
78-79	Birm (WHA)	64	13	7	20	62
79-80	Wash	9	0	2	2	0
80-81	Wash	2	0	0	0	0
81-82	Wash	12	1	4	5	4
NHL Totals		23	1	6	7	4
WHA Totals		184	44	44	88	147
WHA Playoff Totals		7	0	0	0	8

CAUFIELD, Jay 6-4 230 RW
B. Philadelphia, Pa., July 17, 1960

Season	Team	GP	G	A	Pts.	PIM
86-87	NYR	13	2	1	3	45
87-88	Minn	1	0	0	0	0
88-89	Pitt	58	1	4	5	285
89-90	Pitt	37	1	2	3	123
90-91	Pitt	23	1	1	2	71
91-92	Pitt	52	0	0	0	183
Totals		184	5	8	13	707
Playoff Totals		17	0	0	0	42

CAVALLINI, Gino John 6-1 215 LW
B. Toronto, Ont., Nov. 24, 1962

Season	Team	GP	G	A	Pts.	PIM
84-85	Calg	27	6	10	16	14
85-86	Calg-StL	57	13	12	25	62
86-87	StL	80	18	26	44	54
87-88	StL	64	15	17	32	62
88-89	StL	74	20	23	43	79
89-90	StL	80	15	15	30	77

CAVALLINI, Gino John (Continued)

Season	Team	GP	G	A	Pts.	PIM
90-91	StL	78	8	27	35	81
91-92	StL-Que	66	10	14	24	44
Totals		526	105	144	249	473
Playoff Totals		70	14	19	33	66

CAVALLINI, Paul 6-1 210 D
B. Toronto, Ont., Oct. 13, 1965

Season	Team	GP	G	A	Pts.	PIM
86-87	Wash	6	0	2	2	8
87-88	Wash-StL	72	6	10	16	152
88-89	StL	65	4	20	24	128
89-90	StL	80	8	39	47	106
90-91	StL	67	10	25	35	89
91-92	StL	66	10	25	35	95
Totals		356	38	121	159	578
Playoff Totals		49	7	15	22	86

CERESINO, Raymond 5-8 160 RW
B. Port Arthur, Ont., Apr. 24, 1929

Season	Team	GP	G	A	Pts.	PIM
48-49	Tor	12	1	1	2	2

CERNIK, Frantisek 5-10 189 LW/RW
B. Novy Jicin, Czechoslovakia, June 3, 1953

Season	Team	GP	G	A	Pts.	PIM
84-85	Det	49	5	4	9	13

CHABOT, John David 6-2 200 C
B. Summerside, P.E.I., May 18, 1962

Season	Team	GP	G	A	Pts.	PIM
83-84	Mont	56	18	25	43	13
84-85	Mont-Pitt	77	9	51	60	14
85-86	Pitt	77	14	31	45	6
86-87	Pitt	72	14	22	36	8
87-88	Det	78	13	44	57	10
88-89	Det	52	2	10	12	6
89-90	Det	69	9	40	49	24
90-91	Det	27	5	5	10	4
Totals		508	84	228	312	85
Playoff Totals		33	6	20	26	2

CHAD, John 5-10 167 RW
B. Provost, Alta., Sept. 16, 1919

Season	Team	GP	G	A	Pts.	PIM
39-40	Chi	22	8	3	11	11
40-41	Chi	45	7	18	25	16
45-46	Chi	13	0	1	1	2
Totals		80	15	22	37	29
Playoff Totals		10	0	1	1	2

CHALMERS, William (Chick) 6-0 180 C
B. Stratford, Ont., Jan. 24, 1934

Season	Team	GP	G	A	Pts.	PIM
53-54	NYR	1	0	0	0	0

CHALUPA, Milan 5-10 183 D
B. Oudolen, Czechoslovakia, July 4, 1953

Season	Team	GP	G	A	Pts.	PIM
84-85	Det	14	0	5	5	6

CHAMBERS, Shawn 6-2 210 D
B. Sterling Heights, Mich., Oct. 11, 1966

Season	Team	GP	G	A	Pts.	PIM
87-88	Minn	19	1	7	8	21
88-89	Minn	72	5	19	24	80
89-90	Minn	78	8	18	26	81
90-91	Minn	29	1	3	4	24
91-92	Wash	2	0	0	0	2
Totals		200	15	47	62	208
Playoff Totals		33	2	10	12	26

CHAMBERLAIN, Erwin Groves (Murph)
5-11 172 C
B. Shawville, Que., Feb. 14, 1915

Season	Team	GP	G	A	Pts.	PIM
37-38	Tor	43	4	12	16	51
38-39	Tor	48	10	16	26	32
39-40	Tor	40	5	17	22	63
40-41	Mont	45	10	15	25	75
41-42	Mont-NYA	37	12	12	24	46
42-43	Bos	45	9	24	33	67
43-44	Mont	47	15	32	47	85
44-45	Mont	32	2	12	14	38
45-46	Mont	40	12	14	26	42
46-47	Mont	49	10	10	20	97
47-48	Mont	30	6	3	9	62
48-49	Mont	54	5	8	13	111
Totals		510	100	175	275	769
Playoff Totals		66	14	17	31	96

CHAMPAGNE, Andre Joseph Orius
6-0 190 LW
B. Eastview, Ont., Sept. 19, 1943

Season	Team	GP	G	A	Pts.	PIM
62-63	Tor	2	0	0	0	0

CHAPDELAINE, Rene 6-1 195 D
B. Weyburn, Sask., Sept. 27, 1966

Season	Team	GP	G	A	Pts.	PIM
90-91	LA	3	0	1	1	10
91-92	LA	16	0	1	1	10
Totals		19	0	2	2	20

CHAPMAN, Arthur V. 5-10 170 C
B. Winnipeg, Man., May 29, 1906

Season	Team	GP	G	A	Pts.	PIM
30-31	Bos	44	7	7	14	22
31-32	Bos	48	11	14	25	18
32-33	Bos	46	3	6	9	19
33-34	Bos-NYA	46	5	10	15	15
34-35	NYA	47	9	34	43	4
35-36	NYA	48	10	28	38	14
36-37	NYA	43	8	23	31	36
37-38	NYA	45	2	27	29	8
38-39	NYA	45	3	19	22	2
39-40	NYA	26	4	6	10	2
Totals		438	62	174	236	140
Playoff Totals		25	1	5	6	9

CHAPMAN, Blair Douglas 6-1 190 RW
B. Lloydminster, Sask., June 13, 1956

Season	Team	GP	G	A	Pts.	PIM
76-77	Pitt	80	14	23	37	16
77-78	Pitt	75	24	20	44	37
78-79	Pitt	71	10	8	18	18
79-80	Pitt-StL	64	25	26	51	28
80-81	StL	55	20	26	46	41
81-82	StL	18	6	11	17	8
82-83	StL	39	7	11	18	10
Totals		402	106	125	231	158
Playoff Totals		25	4	6	10	15

CHAPMAN, Brian 6-0 195 D
B. Brockville, Ont., Feb. 10, 1968

Season	Team	GP	G	A	Pts.	PIM
90-91	Hart	3	0	0	0	29

CHARBONNEAU, Jose (Joe) 6-0 195 RW
B. Ferme-Neuve, Que., Nov. 21, 1966

Season	Team	GP	G	A	Pts.	PIM
87-88	Mont	16	0	2	2	6
88-89	Mont-Van	22	1	4	5	12
Totals		38	1	6	7	18
Playoff Totals		8	0	0	0	4

CHARBONNEAU, Stephane 6-0 195 RW
B. Ste-Adele, Que., June 27, 1970

Season	Team	GP	G	A	Pts.	PIM
91-92	Que	2	0	0	0	0

CHARLEBOIS, Robert Richard (Chuck)
6-0 175 LW
B. Cornwall, Ont., May 27, 1944

Season	Team	GP	G	A	Pts.	PIM
67-68	Minn	7	1	0	1	0
72-73	Ott (WHA)	78	24	40	64	28
73-74	NE (WHA)	74	4	7	11	6
74-75	NE (WHA)	8	1	0	1	0
75-76	NE (WHA)	28	3	3	6	0
NHL Totals		7	1	0	1	0
WHA Totals		188	32	50	82	34
WHA Playoff Tot.		16	2	1	3	8

CHARLESWORTH, Todd 6-1 190 D
B. Calgary, Alta., Mar. 22, 1965

Season	Team	GP	G	A	Pts.	PIM
83-84	Pitt	10	0	0	0	8
84-85	Pitt	67	1	8	9	31
85-86	Pitt	2	0	1	1	0
86-87	Pitt	1	0	0	0	0
87-88	Pitt	6	2	0	2	2
89-90	NYR	7	0	0	0	6
Totals		93	3	9	12	47

CHARRON, Guy Joseph Jean 5-10 180 C
B. Verdun, Que., Jan. 24, 1949

Season	Team	GP	G	A	Pts.	PIM
69-70	Mont	5	0	0	0	0
70-71	Mont-Det	39	10	6	16	8
71-72	Det	64	9	16	25	12
72-73	Det	75	18	18	36	23
73-74	Det	76	25	30	55	10
74-75	Det-KC	77	14	39	53	27
75-76	KC	78	27	44	71	12
76-77	Wash	80	36	46	82	10
77-78	Wash	80	38	35	73	12
78-79	Wash	80	28	42	70	24
79-80	Wash	33	11	20	31	6
80-81	Wash	47	5	13	18	2
Totals		734	221	309	530	146

CHARTIER, David 5-9 170 C
B. St. Lazare, Man., Feb. 15, 1961

Season	Team	GP	G	A	Pts.	PIM
80-81	Winn	1	0	0	0	0

CHARTRAW, Raymond Richard (Rick)
6-2 210 D
B. Caracas, Venezuela, July 13, 1954

Season	Team	GP	G	A	Pts.	PIM
74-75	Mont	12	0	0	0	6
75-76	Mont	16	1	3	·4	25
76-77	Mont	43	3	4	7	59
77-78	Mont	68	4	12	16	64
78-79	Mont	62	5	11	16	29
79-80	Mont	66	5	7	12	35
80-81	Mont-LA	35	1	6	7	32
81-82	LA	33	2	8	10	56

CHARTRAW, Raymond Richard (Rick) *(Continued)*

Season	Team	GP	G	A	Pts.	PIM
82-83	LA-NYR	57	5	7	12	68
83-84	NYR-Edm	28	2	6	8	25
Totals		420	28	64	92	399
Playoff Totals		75	7	9	16	80

CHASE, Kelly Wayne *5-11 192 RW*
B. Porcupine Plain, Sask., Oct. 25, 1967

Season	Team	GP	G	A	Pts.	PIM
89-90	StL	43	1	3	4	244
90-91	StL	2	1	0	1	15
91-92	StL	46	1	2	3	264
Totals		91	3	5	8	523
Playoff Totals		16	1	0	1	33

CHECK, Ludic (Lude) *154 F*
B. Brandon, Man., May 22, 1919

Season	Team	GP	G	A	Pts.	PIM
43-44	Det	1	0	0	0	0
44-45	Chi	26	6	2	8	4
Totals		27	6	2	8	4

CHELIOS, Chris *6-1 186 D*
B. Chicago, Ill., Jan. 25, 1962

Season	Team	GP	G	A	Pts.	PIM
83-84	Mont	12	0	2	2	12
84-85	Mont	74	9	55	64	87
85-86	Mont	41	8	26	34	67
86-87	Mont	71	11	33	44	124
87-88	Mont	71	20	41	61	172
88-89	Mont	80	15	58	73	185
89-90	Mont	53	9	22	31	136
90-91	Chi	77	12	52	64	192
91-92	Chi	80	9	47	56	245
Totals		579	93	336	429	1220
Playoff Totals		122	23	74	97	269

CHERNOFF, Michael Terence *5-9 175 LW*
B. Yorkton, Sask., May 13, 1946

Season	Team	GP	G	A	Pts.	PIM
68-69	Minn	1	0	0	0	0
73-74	Van (WHA)	36	11	10	21	4
74-75	Van (WHA)	3	0	0	0	0
NHL Totals		1	0	0	0	0
WHA Totals		39	11	10	21	4

CHERNOMAZ, Richard *5-8 185 RW*
B. Selkirk, Man., Sept. 1, 1963

Season	Team	GP	G	A	Pts.	PIM
81-82	Col	2	0	0	0	0
83-84	NJ	7	2	1	3	2
84-85	NJ	3	0	2	2	2
86-87	NJ	25	6	4	10	8
87-88	Calg	2	1	0	1	0
88-89	Calg	1	0	0	0	0
91-92	Calg	11	0	0	0	6
Totals		51	9	7	16	18

CHERRY, Richard John (Dick) *6-0 200 D*
B. Kingston, Ont., Mar. 18, 1937

Season	Team	GP	G	A	Pts.	PIM
56-57	Bos	6	0	0	0	4
68-69	Phil	71	9	6	15	18
69-70	Phil	68	3	4	7	23
Totals		145	12	10	22	45
Playoff Totals		4	1	0	1	4

CHERRY, Donald Stewart (Grapes) *5-11 180 D*
B. Kingston, Ont., Feb. 5, 1934

Season	Team	GP	G	A	Pts.	PIM
54-55	Bos	0	0	0	0	0
Playoff Totals		1	0	0	0	0

CHEVREFILS, Real *5-10 175 LW*
B. Timmins, Ont., May 2, 1932

Season	Team	GP	G	A	Pts.	PIM
51-52	Bos	33	8	17	25	8
52-53	Bos	69	19	14	33	44
53-54	Bos	14	4	1	5	2
54-55	Bos	64	18	22	40	30
55-56	Det-Bos	63	14	12	26	34
56-57	Bos	70	31	17	48	38
57-58	Bos	44	9	9	18	21
58-69	Bos	30	1	5	6	8
Totals		387	104	97	201	185
Playoff Totals		30	5	4	9	20

CHIASSON, Steve *6-0 205 D*
B. Barrie, Ont., Apr. 14, 1967

Season	Team	GP	G	A	Pts.	PIM
86-87	Det	45	1	4	5	73
87-88	Det	29	2	9	11	57
88-89	Det	65	12	35	47	149
89-90	Det	67	14	28	42	114
90-91	Det	42	3	17	20	80
91-92	Det	62	10	24	34	136
Totals		310	42	117	159	609
Playoff Totals		32	8	9	17	87

CHICOINE, Daniel *5-11 192 RW*
B. Sherbrooke, Que., Nov. 30, 1957

Season	Team	GP	G	A	Pts.	PIM
77-78	Clev	6	0	0	0	0
78-79	Minn	1	0	0	0	0
79-80	Minn	24	1	2	3	12
Totals		31	1	2	3	12
Playoff Totals		1	0	0	0	0

CHINNICK, Richard Vaughn (Rick) *5-11 180 RW*
B. Chatham, Ont., Aug. 15, 1953

Season	Team	GP	G	A	Pts.	PIM
73-74	Minn	1	0	1	1	0
74-75	Minn	3	0	1	1	0
Totals		4	0	2	2	0

CHIPPERFIELD, Ronald James *5-11 180 C*
B. Brandon, Man., Mar. 28, 1954

Season	Team	GP	G	A	Pts.	PIM
74-75	Van (WHA)	78	19	20	39	30
75-76	Calg (WHA)	75	42	41	83	32
76-77	Calg (WHA)	81	27	27	54	32
77-78	Edm (WHA)	80	33	52	85	48
78-79	Edm (WHA)	55	32	37	69	47
79-80	Edm-Que	79	22	23	45	32
80-81	Que	4	0	1	1	2
NHL Totals		83	22	24	46	34
WHA Totals		369	153	177	330	189
WHA Playoff Totals		28	15	15	30	14

CHISHOLM, Alexander (Lex) *C*
B. Galt, Ont., Apr. 1, 1915

Season	Team	GP	G	A	Pts.	PIM
39-40	Tor	28	6	8	14	11
40-41	Tor	26	4	0	4	8
Totals		54	10	8	18	19
Playoff Totals		3	1	0	1	0

CHISHOLM, Arthur *C*

Season	Team	GP	G	A	Pts.	PIM
60-61	Bos	3	0	0	0	0

CHISHOLM, Colin *6-2 185 D*
B. Edmonton, Alta., Feb. 25, 1963

Season	Team	GP	G	A	Pts.	PIM
86-87	Minn	1	0	0	0	0

CHORNEY, Marc *6-0 200 D*
B. Sudbury, Ont., Nov. 8, 1959

Season	Team	GP	G	A	Pts.	PIM
80-81	Pitt	8	1	6	7	14
81-82	Pitt	60	1	6	7	63
82-83	Pitt	67	3	5	8	66
83-84	Pitt-LA	75	3	10	13	66
Totals		210	8	27	35	209
Playoff Totals		7	0	1	1	2

CHORSKE, Tom *6-1 204 RW*
B. Minneapolis, Minn., Sept. 18, 1966

Season	Team	GP	G	A	Pts.	PIM
89-90	Mont	14	3	1	4	2
90-91	Mont	57	9	11	20	32
91-92	NJ	76	19	17	36	32
Totals		147	31	29	60	66
Playoff Totals		7	0	3	3	4

CHOUINARD, Eugene (Gene) *D*

Season	Team	GP	G	A	Pts.	PIM
27-28	Ott	8	0	0	0	0

CHOUINARD, Guy Camil *5-11 180 C*
B. Quebec City, Que., Oct. 20, 1956

Season	Team	GP	G	A	Pts.	PIM
74-75	Atl	5	0	0	0	2
75-76	Atl	4	0	2	2	2
76-77	Atl	80	17	33	50	8
77-78	Atl	73	28	30	58	8
78-79	Atl	80	50	57	107	14
79-80	Atl	76	31	46	77	22
80-81	Calg	52	31	52	83	24
81-82	Calg	64	23	57	80	12
82-83	Calg	80	13	59	72	18
83-84	StL	64	12	34	46	10
Totals		578	205	370	575	120
Playoff Totals		46	9	28	37	12

CHRISTIAN, David *6-0 175 RW*
B. Warroad, Minn., May 12, 1959

Season	Team	GP	G	A	Pts.	PIM
79-80	Winn	15	8	10	18	2
80-81	Winn	80	28	43	71	22
81-82	Winn	80	25	51	76	28
82-83	Winn	55	18	26	44	23
83-84	Wash	80	29	52	81	28
84-85	Wash	80	26	43	69	14
85-86	Wash	80	41	42	83	15
86-87	Wash	76	23	27	50	8
87-88	Wash	80	37	21	58	26
88-89	Wash	80	34	31	65	12
89-90	Wash-Bos	78	15	25	40	12

CHRISTIAN, David *(Continued)*

Season	Team	GP	G	A	Pts.	PIM
90-91	Bos	78	32	21	53	41
91-92	StL	78	20	24	44	41
Totals		940	336	416	752	272
Playoff Totals		100	32	25	57	27

CHRISTIAN, Jeff *6-1 195 LW*
B. Burlington, Ont., July 3, 1970

Season	Team	GP	G	A	Pts.	PIM
91-92	NJ	2	0	0	0	2

CHRISTIE, Michael Hunt *6-0 190 D*
B. Big Spring, Tex., Dec. 20, 1949

Season	Team	GP	G	A	Pts.	PIM
74-75	Cal	34	0	14	14	76
75-76	Cal	78	3	18	21	152
76-77	Clev	79	6	27	33	79
77-78	Clev-Col	69	3	14	17	77
78-79	Col	68	1	10	11	88
79-80	Col	74	1	17	18	78
80-81	Col-Van	10	1	1	2	0
Totals		412	15	101	116	550
Playoff Totals		2	0	0	0	0

CHRISTOFF, Steve *6-1 180 C*
B. Richfield, Minn., Jan. 23, 1958

Season	Team	GP	G	A	Pts.	PIM
79-80	Minn	20	8	7	15	19
80-81	Minn	56	26	13	39	58
81-82	Minn	69	26	29	55	14
82-83	Calg	45	9	8	17	4
83-84	LA	58	8	7	15	13
Totals		248	77	64	141	108
Playoff Totals		35	16	12	28	25

CHRYSTAL, Robert Harry *6-0 180 D*
B. Winnipeg, Man., Apr. 30, 1930

Season	Team	GP	G	A	Pts.	PIM
53-54	NYR	64	5	5	10	44
54-55	NYR	68	6	9	15	68
Totals		132	11	14	25	112

CHURCH, John (Jack) *5-11 180 D*
B. Kamsack, Sask., May 24, 1915

Season	Team	GP	G	A	Pts.	PIM
38-39	Tor	3	0	2	2	2
39-40	Tor	31	1	4	5	62
40-41	Tor	11	0	1	1	22
41-42	Tor-NYA	42	1	6	7	40
42-43	NYA	15	1	3	4	10
45-46	Bos	43	2	6	8	28
Totals		145	5	22	27	164
Playoff Totals		25	1	1	2	18

CHURLA, Shane *6-1 200 RW*
B. Fernie, B.C., June 24, 1965

Season	Team	GP	G	A	Pts.	PIM
86-87	Hart	20	0	1	1	78
87-88	Hart-Calg	31	1	5	6	146
88-89	Calg-Minn	18	1	0	1	79
89-90	Minn	53	2	3	5	292
90-91	Minn	40	2	2	4	286
91-92	Minn	57	4	1	5	278
Totals		219	10	12	22	1159
Playoff Totals		38	2	2	4	193

CHYCHRUN, Jeff *6-4 215 D*
B. LaSalle, Que., May 3, 1966

Season	Team	GP	G	A	Pts.	PIM
86-87	Phil	1	0	0	0	4
87-88	Phil	3	0	0	0	4
88-89	Phil	80	1	4	5	245
89-90	Phil	79	2	7	9	248
90-91	Phil	36	0	6	6	105
91-92	LA-Pitt	43	0	4	4	103
Totals		242	3	21	24	709
Playoff Totals		19	0	2	2	65

CHYNOWETH, Dean *6-2 190 D*
B. Calgard, Alta., Oct. 30, 1968

Season	Team	GP	G	A	Pts.	PIM
88-89	NYI	6	0	0	0	48
89-90	NYI	20	2	2	2	39
90-91	NYI	25	1	1	2	59
91-92	NYI	11	1	0	1	23
Totals		62	2	3	5	169

CHYZOWSKI, David *6-2 190 LW*
B. Edmonton, Alta., July 11, 1971

Season	Team	GP	G	A	Pts.	PIM
89-90	NYI	34	8	6	14	45
90-91	NYI	56	5	9	14	61
91-92	NYI	12	1	1	2	17
Totals		102	14	16	30	123

CIAVAGLIA, Peter *5-10 175 C*
B. Albany, N.Y., July 15, 1969

Season	Team	GP	G	A	Pts.	PIM
91-92	Buf	2	0	0	0	0

CICCARELLI, Dino *5-10 175 RW*
B. Sarnia, Ont., Feb. 8, 1960

Season	Team	GP	G	A	Pts.	PIM
80-81	Minn	32	18	12	30	29
81-82	Minn	76	55	51	106	138
82-83	Minn	77	37	38	75	94
83-84	Minn	79	38	33	71	58

CICCARELLI, Dino *(Continued)*

Season	Team	GP	G	A	Pts.	PIM
84-85	Minn	51	15	17	32	41
85-86	Minn	75	44	45	89	51
86-87	Minn	80	52	51	103	88
87-88	Minn	67	41	45	86	79
88-89	Minn-Wash	76	44	30	74	76
89-90	Wash	80	41	38	79	122
90-91	Wash	54	21	18	39	66
91-92	Wash	78	38	38	76	78
Totals		825	444	416	860	920
Playoff Totals		94	49	37	86	133

CICCONE, Enrico *6-4 200 D*

B. Montreal, Que., Apr. 10, 1970

Season	Team	GP	G	A	Pts.	PIM
91-92	Minn	11	0	0	0	48

CICHOCKI, Chris *5-11 185 RW*

B. Detroit, Mich., Sept. 17, 1963

Season	Team	GP	G	A	Pts.	PIM
85-86	Det	59	10	11	21	21
86-87	Det	2	0	0	0	2
87-88	NJ	5	1	0	1	2
88-89	NJ	2	0	1	1	2
Totals		68	11	12	23	27

CIESLA, Henry Edward (Hank) *6-2 190 C*

B. St. Catharines, Ont., Oct. 15, 1934

Season	Team	GP	G	A	Pts.	PIM
55-56	Chi	70	8	23	31	22
56-57	Chi	70	10	8	18	28
57-58	NYR	60	2	6	8	16
58-59	NYR	69	6	14	20	21
Totals		269	26	51	77	87
Playoff Totals		6	0	2	2	0

CIGER, Zdeno *6-2 190 LW*

B. Martin, Czechoslovakia, Oct. 19, 1969

Season	Team	GP	G	A	Pts.	PIM
90-91	NJ	45	8	17	25	8
91-92	NJ	20	6	5	11	10
Totals		65	14	22	36	18
Playoff Totals		13	2	6	8	4

CIMETTA, Robert *6-0 190 LW*

B. Toronto, Ont., Feb. 15, 1970

Season	Team	GP	G	A	Pts.	PIM
88-89	Bos	7	2	0	2	0
89-90	Bos	47	8	9	17	33
90-91	Tor	25	2	4	6	21
91-92	Tor	24	4	3	7	12
Totals		103	16	16	32	66
Playoff Totals		1	0	0	0	15

CIRELLA, Joe *6-3 210 D*

B. Hamilton, Ont., May 9, 1963

Season	Team	GP	G	A	Pts.	PIM
81-82	Col	65	7	12	19	52
82-83	NJ	2	0	1	1	4
83-84	NJ	79	11	33	44	137
84-85	NJ	66	6	18	24	141
85-86	NJ	66	6	23	29	147
86-87	NJ	65	9	22	31	111
87-88	NJ	80	8	31	39	191
88-89	NJ	80	3	19	22	155
89-90	Que	56	4	14	18	67
90-91	Que-NYR	58	3	10	13	111
91-92	NYR	67	3	12	15	121
Totals		684	60	195	255	1237
Playoff Totals		38	0	13	13	98

CIRONE, Jason *5-9 185 C*

B. Toronto, Ont., Feb. 21, 1971

Season	Team	GP	G	A	Pts.	PIM
91-92	Winn	3	0	0	0	2

CLACKSON, Kimble Gerald (Kim) *5-11 195 D*

B. Saskatoon, Sask., Feb. 13, 1955

Season	Team	GP	G	A	Pts.	PIM
75-76	Ind (WHA)	77	1	12	13	351
76-77	Ind (WHA)	71	3	8	11	168
77-78	Winn (WHA)	52	2	7	9	203
78-79	Winn (WHA)	71	0	12	12	210
79-80	Pitt	45	0	3	3	166
80-81	Que	61	0	5	5	204
NHL Totals		106	0	8	8	370
WHA Totals		271	6	39	45	932
NHL Playoff Totals		8	0	0	0	70
WHA Playoff Totals		33	0	7	7	138

CLANCY, Francis Michael (King) *5-9 184 D*

B. Ottawa, Ont., Feb. 25, 1903

Season	Team	GP	G	A	Pts.	PIM
21-22	Ott	24	4	5	9	19
22-23	Ott	24	3	1	4	20
23-24	Ott	24	9	8	17	18
24-25	Ott	29	14	5	19	61
25-26	Ott	35	8	4	12	80
26-27	Ott	43	9	10	19	78
27-28	Ott	39	8	7	15	73
28-29	Ott	44	13	2	15	89
29-30	Ott	44	17	23	40	83

CLANCY, Francis Michael (King) *(Continued)*

Season	Team	GP	G	A	Pts.	PIM
30-31	Tor	44	7	14	21	63
31-32	Tor	48	10	9	19	61
32-33	Tor	48	13	12	25	79
33-34	Tor	46	11	17	28	62
34-35	Tor	47	5	16	21	53
35-36	Tor	47	5	10	15	61
36-37	Tor	6	1	0	1	4
Totals		592	137	143	280	904
Playoff Totals		61	9	8	17	92

CLANCY, Terrance John *6-0 195 RW*

B. Ottawa, Ont., Apr. 2, 1943

Season	Team	GP	G	A	Pts.	PIM
67-68	Oak	7	0	0	0	2
68-69	Tor	2	0	0	0	0
69-70	Tor	52	6	5	11	31
72-73	Tor	32	0	1	1	6
Totals		93	6	6	12	39

CLAPPER, Aubrey Victor (Dit) *6-2 195 RW*

B. Newmarket, Ont., Feb. 9, 1907

Season	Team	GP	G	A	Pts.	PIM
27-28	Bos	40	4	1	5	20
28-29	Bos	40	9	2	11	48
29-30	Bos	44	41	20	61	48
30-31	Bos	43	22	8	30	50
31-32	Bos	48	17	22	39	21
32-33	Bos	48	14	14	28	42
33-34	Bos	48	10	12	22	6
34-35	Bos	48	21	16	37	21
35-36	Bos	44	12	13	25	14
36-37	Bos	48	17	8	25	25
37-38	Bos	46	6	9	15	24
38-39	Bos	42	13	13	26	22
39-40	Bos	44	10	18	28	25
40-41	Bos	48	8	18	26	24
41-42	Bos	32	3	12	15	31
42-43	Bos	38	5	18	23	12
43-44	Bos	50	6	25	31	13
44-45	Bos	46	8	14	22	16
45-46	Bos	30	2	3	5	0
46-47	Bos	6	0	0	0	0
Totals		833	228	246	474	462
Playoff Totals		86	13	17	30	50

CLARK, Andrew *D*

Season	Team	GP	G	A	Pts.	PIM
27-28	Bos	5	0	0	0	0

CLARK, Daniel *6-1 195 D*

B. Toronto, Ont., Nov. 3, 1957

Season	Team	GP	G	A	Pts.	PIM
78-79	NYR	4	0	1	1	6

CLARK, Dean *6-1 180 D*

B. Edmonton, Alta., Jan. 10, 1964

Season	Team	GP	G	A	Pts.	PIM
83-84	Edm	1	0	0	0	0

CLARK, Gordon Corson (Gordie) *5-10 180 RW*

B. Glasgow, Scotland, May 31, 1952

Season	Team	GP	G	A	Pts.	PIM
74-75	Bos	1	0	0	0	0
75-76	Bos	7	0	1	1	0
78-79	Cin (WHA)	21	3	3	6	2
NHL Totals		8	0	1	1	0
WHA Totals		21	3	3	6	2
NHL Playoff Totals		1	0	0	0	0

CLARK, Wendel *5-11 194 LW*

B. Kelvington, Sask., Oct. 25, 1966

Season	Team	GP	G	A	Pts.	PIM
85-86	Tor	66	34	11	45	227
86-87	Tor	80	37	23	60	271
87-88	Tor	28	12	11	23	80
88-89	Tor	15	7	4	11	66
89-90	Tor	38	18	8	26	116
90-91	Tor	63	18	16	34	152
91-92	Tor	43	19	21	40	123
Totals		333	145	94	239	1035
Playoff Totals		28	12	7	19	104

CLARKE, Robert Earle (Bobby) *5-10 185 C*

B. Flin Flon, Man., Aug. 13, 1949

Season	Team	GP	G	A	Pts.	PIM
69-70	Phil	76	15	31	46	68
70-71	Phil	77	27	36	63	78
71-72	Phil	78	35	46	81	87
72-73	Phil	78	37	67	104	80
73-74	Phil	77	35	52	87	113
74-75	Phil	80	27	89	116	125
75-76	Phil	76	30	89	119	136
76-77	Phil	80	27	63	90	71
77-78	Phil	71	21	68	89	83
78-79	Phil	80	16	57	73	68
79-80	Phil	76	12	57	69	65
80-81	Phil	80	19	46	65	140
81-82	Phil	62	17	46	63	154

CLARKE, Robert Earle (Bobby) *(Continued)*

Season	Team	GP	G	A	Pts.	PIM
82-83	Phil	80	23	62	85	115
83-84	Phil	73	17	43	60	70
Totals		1144	358	852	1210	1453
Playoff Tot.		136	42	77	119	152

CLEGHORN, Ogilvie (Odie) *RW*

B. Montreal, Que., 1891

Season	Team	GP	G	A	Pts.	PIM
18-19	Mont	17	23	6	29	22
19-20	Mont	21	19	3	22	30
20-21	Mont	21	5	4	9	8
21-22	Mont	23	21	3	24	26
22-23	Mont	24	19	7	26	14
23-24	Mont	22	3	3	6	14
24-25	Mont	30	3	2	5	14
25-26	Pitt Pi	17	3	1	4	4
26-27	Pitt Pi	3	0	0	0	0
27-28	Pitt Pi	2	0	0	0	0
Totals		180	96	29	125	132
Playoff Totals		23	9	2	11	2

CLEGHORN, Sprague *D*

B. Montreal, Que., 1890

Season	Team	GP	G	A	Pts.	PIM
18-19	Ott	18	6	6	12	27
19-20	Ott	21	16	5	21	62
20-21	Ott-Tor	16	5	5	10	35
21-22	Mont	24	17	7	24	63
22-23	Mont	24	9	4	13	34
23-24	Mont	23	8	3	11	39
24-25	Mont	27	8	1	9	82
25-26	Bos	28	6	5	11	49
26-27	Bos	44	7	1	8	84
27-28	Bos	37	2	2	4	14
Totals		262	84	39	123	489
Playoff Totals		37	7	8	15	48

CLEMENT, William H. *6-1 194 C*

B. Buckingham, Que., Dec. 20, 1950

Season	Team	GP	G	A	Pts.	PIM
71-72	Phil	49	9	14	23	39
72-73	Phil	73	14	14	28	51
73-74	Phil	39	9	8	17	34
74-75	Phil	68	21	16	37	42
75-76	Wash-Atl	77	23	31	54	49
76-77	Atl	67	17	26	43	27
77-78	Atl	70	20	30	50	34
78-79	Atl	65	12	23	35	14
79-80	Atl	64	7	14	21	32
80-81	Calg	78	12	20	32	33
81-82	Calg	69	4	12	16	28
Totals		719	148	208	356	383
Playoff Totals		50	5	3	8	26

CLINE, Bruce *5-7 137 RW*

B. Massawippi, Que., Nov. 14, 1931

Season	Team	GP	G	A	Pts.	PIM
56-57	NYR	30	2	3	5	10

CLIPPINGDALE, Steve *6-2 195 LW*

B. Vancouver, B.C., Apr. 29, 1956

Season	Team	GP	G	A	Pts.	PIM
76-77	LA	16	1	2	3	9
79-80	Wash	3	0	0	0	0
Totals		19	1	2	3	9
Playoff Totals		1	0	0	0	0

CLOUTIER, Real *5-10 185 RW*

B. St. Emile, Que., July 30, 1956

Season	Team	GP	G	A	Pts.	PIM
74-75	Que (WHA)	63	26	27	53	36
75-76	Que (WHA)	80	60	54	114	27
76-77	Que (WHA)	76	66	75	141	39
77-78	Que (WHA)	73	56	73	129	19
78-79	Que (WHA)	77	75	54	129	48
79-80	Que	67	42	47	89	12
80-81	Que	34	15	16	31	18
81-82	Que	67	37	60	97	34
82-83	Que	68	28	39	67	30
83-84	Buf	77	24	36	60	25
84-85	Buf	4	0	0	0	0
NHL Totals		317	146	198	344	119
WHA Totals		369	283	283	566	169
NHL Playoff Tot.		25	7	5	12	20
WHA Playoff Tot.		48	33	30	63	31

CLOUTIER, Rejean *6-0 180 D*

B. Windsor, Ont., Feb. 15, 1960

Season	Team	GP	G	A	Pts.	PIM
79-80	Det	3	0	1	1	0
81-82	Det	2	0	1	1	2
Totals		5	0	2	2	2

CLOUTIER, Roland *5-8 157 C*

B. Rouyn-Noranda, Que., Oct. 6, 1957

Season	Team	GP	G	A	Pts.	PIM
77-78	Det	1	0	0	0	0
78-79	Det	19	6	6	12	2
79-80	Que	14	2	3	5	0
Totals		34	8	9	17	2

Season	Team	GP	G	A	Pts.	PIM
CLUNE, Walter James (Wally)	*5-9 150 D*					
B. Toronto, Ont., Feb. 29, 1930						
55-56	Mont	5	0	0	0	6
COALTER, Gary Merritt Charles						
5-10 185 RW						
B. Toronto, Ont., July 8, 1950						
73-74	Cal	4	0	0	0	0
74-75	KC	30	2	4	6	2
Totals		34	2	4	6	2
COATES, Stephen John	*5-9 172 RW*					
B. Toronto, Ont., July 2, 1950						
76-77	Det	5	1	0	1	24
COCHRANE, Glen Macleod	*6-2 205 D*					
B. Cranbrook, B.C., Jan. 29, 1958						
78-79	Phil	1	0	0	0	0
80-81	Phil	31	1	8	9	219
81-82	Phil	63	6	12	18	329
82-83	Phil	77	2	22	24	237
83-84	Phil	67	7	16	23	225
84-85	Phil	18	0	3	3	100
85-86	Van	49	0	3	3	125
86-87	Van	14	0	0	0	52
87-88	Chi	73	1	8	9	204
88-89	Chi-Edm	18	0	0	0	65
Totals		411	17	72	89	1556
Playoff Totals		5	1	1	2	31
COFFEY, Paul Douglas	*6-1 200 D*					
B. Weston, Ont., June 1, 1961						
80-81	Edm	74	9	23	32	130
81-82	Edm	80	29	60	89	106
82-83	Edm	80	29	67	96	87
83-84	Edm	80	40	86	126	104
84-85	Edm	80	37	84	121	97
85-86	Edm	79	48	90	138	120
86-87	Edm	59	17	50	67	49
87-88	Pitt	46	15	52	67	93
88-89	Pitt	75	30	83	113	195
89-90	Pitt	80	29	74	103	95
90-91	Pitt	76	24	69	93	128
91-92	Pitt-LA	64	11	58	69	87
Totals		873	318	796	1114	1291
Playoff Totals		123	44	92	136	206
COFLIN, Hugh Alexander	*6-0 190 D*					
B. Blaine Lake, Sask., Dec. 15, 1928						
50-51	Chi	31	0	3	3	33
COLE, Danton	*5-11 189 RW*					
B. Pontiac, Mich., Jan. 10, 1967						
89-90	Winn	2	1	1	2	0
90-91	Winn	66	13	11	24	24
91-92	Winn	52	7	5	12	32
Totals		120	21	17	38	56
COLLEY, Thomas	*5-9 162 C*					
B. Toronto, Ont., Aug. 21, 1953						
74-75	Minn	1	0	0	0	2
COLLINGS, Norman (Dodger)	*F*					
B. Bradford, Ont.						
34-35	Mont	1	0	1	1	0
COLLINS, Ranleigh (Gary)	*5-11 190 C*					
B. Toronto, Ont., Sept. 27, 1935						
58-59	Tor	0	0	0	0	0
Playoff Totals		2	0	0	0	0
COLLINS, William Earl	*6-0 178 RW*					
B. Ottawa, Ont., July 13, 1943						
67-68	Minn	71	9	11	20	41
68-69	Minn	75	9	10	19	24
69-70	Minn	74	29	9	38	48
70-71	Mont-Det	76	11	18	29	49
71-72	Det	71	15	25	40	38
72-73	Det	78	21	21	42	44
73-74	Det-StL	66	15	17	32	51
74-75	StL	70	22	15	37	34
75-76	NYR	50	4	4	8	38
76-77	Phil-Wash	63	12	15	27	30
77-78	Wash	74	10	9	19	18
Totals		768	157	154	311	415
Playoff Totals		18	3	5	8	12
COLLYARD, Robert Leander	*5-9 170 C*					
B. Hibbing, Minn., Oct. 16, 1949						
73-74	StL	10	1	3	4	4
COLMAN, Mike	*6-3 218 D*					
B. Stoneham, Mass., Aug. 4, 1968						
91-92	SJ	15	0	1	1	32
COLVILLE, Matthew Lamont (Mac)						
5-8 175 RW						
B. Edmonton, Alta., Jan. 8, 1916						
35-36	NYR	18	1	4	5	6
36-37	NYR	46	7	12	19	10
37-38	NYR	48	14	14	28	18
38-39	NYR	48	7	21	28	26
39-40	NYR	47	7	14	21	12
40-41	NYR	47	14	17	31	18
41-42	NYR	46	14	16	30	26
45-46	NYR	39	7	6	13	8
46-47	NYR	14	0	0	0	8
Totals		353	71	104	175	132
Playoff Totals		40	9	10	19	14
COLVILLE, Neil McNeil	*6-0 175 C*					
B. Edmonton, Alta., Aug. 4, 1914						
35-36	NYR	1	0	0	0	0
36-37	NYR	45	10	18	28	33
37-38	NYR	45	17	19	36	11
38-39	NYR	47	18	19	37	12
39-40	NYR	48	19	19	38	22
40-41	NYR	48	14	28	42	28
41-42	NYR	48	8	25	33	37
44-45	NYR	4	0	1	1	2
45-46	NYR	49	5	4	9	25
46-47	NYR	60	4	16	20	16
47-48	NYR	55	4	12	16	25
48-49	NYR	14	0	5	5	2
Totals		464	99	166	265	213
Playoff Totals		46	7	19	26	33
COLWILL, Leslie John	*5-11 170 RW*					
B. Divide, Sask., Jan. 1, 1935						
58-59	NYR	69	7	6	13	16
COMEAU, Reynald Xavier (Rey)						
5-8 173 C						
B. Montreal, Que., Oct. 25, 1948						
71-72	Mont	4	0	0	0	0
72-73	Atl	77	21	21	42	19
73-74	Atl	78	11	23	34	16
74-75	Atl	75	14	20	34	40
75-76	Atl	79	17	22	39	42
76-77	Atl	80	15	18	33	16
77-78	Atl	79	10	22	32	20
78-79	Col	70	8	10	18	16
79-80	Col	22	2	5	7	6
Totals		564	98	141	239	175
Playoff Totals		9	2	1	3	8
CONACHER, Brian Kennedy	*6-3 197 LW*					
B. Toronto, Ont., Aug. 31, 1941						
61-62	Tor	1	0	0	0	0
65-66	Tor	2	0	0	0	2
66-67	Tor	66	14	13	27	47
67-68	Tor	64	11	14	25	31
71-72	Det	22	3	1	4	4
72-73	Ott (WHA)	69	8	19	27	32
NHL Totals		155	28	28	56	84
WHA Totals		69	8	19	27	32
NHL Playoff Totals		12	3	2	5	21
WHA Playoff Totals		5	1	3	4	4
CONACHER, Charles William, Jr. (Pete)						
5-10 165 LW						
B. Toronto, Ont., July 29, 1932						
51-52	Chi	2	0	1	1	0
52-53	Chi	41	5	6	11	7
53-54	Chi	70	19	9	28	23
54-55	Chi-NYR	70	12	11	23	12
55-56	NYR	41	11	11	22	10
57-58	Tor	5	0	1	1	5
Totals		229	47	39	86	57
Playoff Totals		7	0	0	0	0
CONACHER, Charles William (The Bomber)						
6-1 195 RW						
B. Toronto, Ont., Dec. 20, 1910						
29-30	Tor	38	20	9	29	48
30-31	Tor	37	31	12	43	78
31-32	Tor	44	34	14	48	66
32-33	Tor	40	14	19	33	64
33-34	Tor	42	32	20	52	38
34-35	Tor	47	36	21	57	24
35-36	Tor	44	23	15	38	74
36-37	Tor	15	3	5	8	16
37-38	Tor	19	7	9	16	6
38-39	Det	40	8	15	23	29
39-40	NYA	48	10	18	28	41
40-41	NYA	16	4	7	11	32
Totals		460	225	173	398	516
Playoff Totals		49	17	18	35	53
CONACHER, James	*5-10 155 C*					
B. Motherwell, Scotland, May 5, 1921						
45-46	Det	20	1	5	6	6
46-47	Det	33	16	13	29	2
47-48	Det	60	17	23	40	2
48-49	Det-Chi	59	26	23	49	43
49-50	Chi	66	13	20	33	14
50-51	Chi	52	10	27	37	16
51-52	Chi-NYR	21	1	2	3	2
52-53	NYR	17	1	4	5	2
Totals		328	85	117	202	87
Playoff Totals		19	5	2	7	4
CONACHER, Lionel Pretoria (Big Train)						
6-1 195 D						
B. Toronto, Ont., May 24, 1901						
25-26	Pitt Pi	33	9	4	13	64
26-27	Pitt Pi-NYA	40	8	9	17	93
27-28	NYA	36	11	6	17	82
28-29	NYA	44	5	2	7	132
29-30	NYA	39	4	6	10	73
30-31	Mont	35	4	3	7	57
31-32	Mont M	46	7	9	16	60
32-33	Mont M	47	7	21	28	61
33-34	Chi	48	10	13	23	87
34-35	Mont M	40	2	6	8	44
35-36	Mont M	47	7	7	14	65
36-37	Mont M	45	6	19	25	64
Totals		500	80	105	185	882
Playoff Totals		32	2	2	4	34
CONACHER, Patrick John	*5-8 190 LW*					
B. Edmonton, Alta., May 1, 1959						
79-80	NYR	17	0	5	5	4
82-83	NYR	5	0	1	1	4
83-84	Edm	45	2	8	10	31
85-86	NJ	2	0	2	2	2
87-88	NJ	24	2	5	7	12
88-89	NJ	55	7	5	12	14
89-90	NJ	19	3	3	6	4
90-91	NJ	49	5	11	16	27
91-92	NJ	43	7	3	10	16
Totals		259	26	43	69	114
Playoff Totals		42	5	6	11	34
CONACHER, Roy Gordon	*6-1 175 LW*					
B. Toronto, Ont., Oct. 5, 1916						
38-39	Bos	47	26	11	37	12
39-40	Bos	31	18	12	30	9
40-41	Bos	41	24	14	38	7
41-42	Bos	43	24	13	37	12
45-46	Bos	4	2	1	3	0
46-47	Det	60	30	24	54	6
47-48	Chi	52	22	27	49	4
48-49	Chi	60	26	42	68	8
49-50	Chi	70	25	31	56	16
50-51	Chi	70	26	24	50	16
51-52	Chi	12	3	1	4	0
Totals		490	226	200	426	90
Playoff Totals		42	15	15	30	14
CONN, Hugh Maitland (Red)	*170 F*					
B. Hartley, Man., Oct. 25, 1908						
33-34	NYA	48	4	17	21	12
34-35	NYA	48	5	11	16	10
Totals		96	9	28	37	22
CONN, Rob	*6-2 200 LW/RW*					
B. Calgary, Alb., Sept. 3, 1968						
91-92	Chi	2	0	0	0	2
CONNELLY, Wayne Francis	*5-10 170*					
RW						
B. Rouyn, Que., Dec. 16, 1939						
60-61	Mont	3	0	0	0	0
61-62	Bos	61	8	12	20	34
62-63	Bos	18	2	6	8	2
63-64	Bos	26	2	3	5	12
66-67	Bos	64	13	17	30	12
67-68	Minn	74	35	21	56	40
68-69	Minn-Det	74	18	25	43	11
69-70	Det	76	23	36	59	10
70-71	Det-StL	79	13	29	42	21
71-72	StL-Van	68	19	25	44	14
72-73	Minn (WHA)	78	40	30	70	16
73-74	Minn (WHA)	78	42	53	95	16
74-75	Minn (WHA)	76	38	33	71	16
75-76	Minn-Clev (WHA)	71	29	25	54	23
76-77	Calg-Edm (WHA)	63	18	21	39	22
NHL Totals		543	133	174	307	156
WHA Totals		366	167	162	329	93
NHL Playoff Tot.		24	11	7	18	4

CONNELLY, Wayne Francis *(Continued)*

Season	Team	GP	G	A	Pts.	PIM
WHA Playoff Tot.		36	16	15	31	16

CONNOLLY, Albert Patrick (Bert) *5-11 174 LW*
B. Montreal, Que., Apr. 22, 1909

Season	Team	GP	G	A	Pts.	PIM
34-35	NYR	47	10	11	21	23
35-36	NYR	25	2	2	4	10
37-38	Chi	15	1	2	3	4
Totals		87	13	15	28	37
Playoff Totals		14	1	0	1	0

CONNOR, Cameron Duncan *6-2 200 RW*
B. Winnipeg, Man., Aug. 10, 1954

Season	Team	GP	G	A	Pts.	PIM
74-75	Phoe (WHA)	57	9	19	28	168
75-76	Phoe (WHA)	73	18	21	39	295
76-77	Hou (WHA)	76	35	32	67	224
77-78	Hou (WHA)	68	21	16	37	217
78-79	Mont	23	1	3	4	39
79-80	Edm-NYR	50	7	16	23	173
80-81	NYR	15	1	3	4	44
82-83	NYR	1	0	0	0	0
NHL Totals		89	9	22	31	256
WHA Totals		274	83	88	171	904
NHL Playoff Totals		20	5	0	5	6
WHA Playoff Totals		23	5	4	9	92

CONNOR, Harold (Harry) *F*
B. Ottawa, Ont.

Season	Team	GP	G	A	Pts.	PIM
27-28	Bos	42	9	1	10	26
28-29	NYA	43	6	2	8	83
29-30	Ott-Bos	38	1	2	3	26
30-31	Ott	11	0	0	0	4
Totals		134	16	5	21	139
Playoff Totals		10	0	0	0	2

CONNORS, Robert *D*

Season	Team	GP	G	A	Pts.	PIM
26-27	NYA	6	1	0	1	0
28-29	Det	41	13	3	16	68
29-30	Det	31	3	7	10	42
Totals		78	17	10	27	110
Playoff Totals		2	0	0	0	0

CONROY, Allan *5-8 170 C*
B. Calgary, Alta., Jan. 17, 1966

Season	Team	GP	G	A	Pts.	PIM
91-92	Phil	31	2	9	11	74

CONTINI, Joseph Mario *5-10 178 C*
B. Galt, Ont., Jan. 29, 1957

Season	Team	GP	G	A	Pts.	PIM
77-78	Col	37	12	9	21	28
78-79	Col	30	5	12	17	6
80-81	Minn	1	0	0	0	0
Totals		68	17	21	38	34
Playoff Totals		2	0	0	0	0

CONVEY, Edward *F*
B. Toronto, Ont.

Season	Team	GP	G	A	Pts.	PIM
30-31	NYA	2	0	0	0	0
31-32	NYA	21	1	0	1	21
32-33	NYA	13	0	1	1	12
Totals		36	1	1	2	33

COOK, Alexander Leone Lally (Bud) *5-9 160 C*
B. Kingston, Ont., Nov. 15, 1907

Season	Team	GP	G	A	Pts.	PIM
31-32	Bos	28	4	4	8	14
33-34	Ott	19	1	0	1	8
34-35	StL	4	0	0	0	0
Totals		51	5	4	9	22

COOK, Frederick Joseph (Bun) *5-11 180 LW*
B. Kingston, Ont., Sept. 18, 1903

Season	Team	GP	G	A	Pts.	PIM
26-27	NYR	44	14	9	23	42
27-28	NYR	44	14	14	28	28
28-29	NYR	43	13	5	18	70
29-30	NYR	43	24	18	42	55
30-31	NYR	44	18	17	35	72
31-32	NYR	45	14	20	34	43
32-33	NYR	48	22	15	37	35
33-34	NYR	48	18	15	33	36
34-35	NYR	48	13	21	34	26
35-36	NYR	26	4	5	9	12
36-37	Bos	40	4	5	9	8
Totals		473	158	144	302	427
Playoff Totals		46	15	3	18	57

COOK, Lloyd *D*

Season	Team	GP	G	A	Pts.	PIM
24-25	Bos	4	1	0	1	0

COOK, Robert Arthur *6-0 190 RW*
B. Sudbury, Ont., Jan. 6, 1946

Season	Team	GP	G	A	Pts.	PIM
70-71	Van	2	0	0	0	0
72-73	Det-NYI	46	11	7	18	18

COOK, Robert Arthur *(Continued)*

Season	Team	GP	G	A	Pts.	PIM
73-74	NYI	22	2	1	3	4
74-75	Minn	2	0	1	1	0
Totals		72	13	9	22	22

COOK, Thomas John *5-7 140 C*
B. Ft. William, Ont., May 7, 1907

Season	Team	GP	G	A	Pts.	PIM
29-30	Chi	41	14	16	30	16
30-31	Chi	44	15	14	29	34
31-32	Chi	48	12	13	25	36
32-33	Chi	47	12	14	26	30
34-35	Chi	47	13	18	31	33
35-36	Chi	47	4	8	12	20
36-37	Chi	17	0	2	2	0
37-38	Mont M	20	2	4	6	0
Totals		311	72	89	161	169
Playoff Totals		24	2	4	6	17

COOK, William Osser *5-10 170 RW*
B. Brantford, Ont., Oct. 9, 1896

Season	Team	GP	G	A	Pts.	PIM
26-27	NYR	44	33	4	37	58
27-28	NYR	43	18	6	24	42
28-29	NYR	43	15	8	23	41
29-30	NYR	44	29	30	59	56
30-31	NYR	44	30	12	42	39
31-32	NYR	48	34	14	48	33
32-33	NYR	48	28	22	50	51
33-34	NYR	48	13	13	26	21
34-35	NYR	48	21	15	36	23
35-36	NYR	21	1	4	5	16
36-37	NYR	21	1	4	5	6
Totals		452	223	132	355	386
Playoff Totals		46	13	12	25	66

COOPER, Carson E. *F*
B. Cornwall, Ont.

Season	Team	GP	G	A	Pts.	PIM
24-25	Bos	12	5	3	8	4
25-26	Bos	36	28	3	31	10
26-27	Bos-Mont	24	9	3	12	16
27-28	Det	43	15	2	17	32
28-29	Det	44	18	9	27	14
29-30	Det	44	18	18	36	14
30-31	Det	43	14	14	28	10
31-32	Det	48	3	5	8	11
Totals		294	110	57	167	111
Playoff Totals		4	0	0	0	2

COOPER, Edward William *5-10 188 LW*
B. Loon Lake, Sask., Aug. 28, 1960

Season	Team	GP	G	A	Pts.	PIM
80-81	Col	47	7	7	14	46
81-82	Col	2	1	0	1	0
Totals		49	8	7	15	46

COOPER, Harold Wallace (Hal) *5-5 155 RW*
B. New Liskeard, Ont., Aug. 29, 1915

Season	Team	GP	G	A	Pts.	PIM
44-45	NYR	8	0	0	0	2

COOPER, Joseph *6-1 200 D*
B. Winnipeg, Man., Dec. 14, 1914

Season	Team	GP	G	A	Pts.	PIM
35-36	NYR	1	0	0	0	0
36-37	NYR	48	0	3	3	42
37-38	NYR	46	3	2	5	56
38-39	Chi	17	3	3	6	10
39-40	Chi	44	4	7	11	59
40-41	Chi	45	5	5	10	66
41-42	Chi	47	6	14	20	58
43-44	Chi	13	1	0	1	17
44-45	Chi	50	4	17	21	50
45-46	Chi	50	2	7	9	46
46-47	NYR	59	2	8	10	38
Totals		420	30	66	96	442
Playoff Totals		32	3	5	8	60

COPP, Robert Alonzo *5-11 180 D*
B. Port Elgin, N.B., Nov. 15, 1918

Season	Team	GP	G	A	Pts.	PIM
42-43	Tor	38	3	9	12	24
50-51	Tor	2	0	0	0	2
Totals		40	3	9	12	26

CORBEAU, Albert (Bert) *D*

Season	Team	GP	G	A	Pts.	PIM
17-18	Mont	20	8	0	8	22
18-19	Mont	16	2	1	3	51
19-20	Mont	23	11	5	16	59
20-21	Mont	24	12	1	13	86
21-22	Mont	22	4	7	11	26
22-23	Ham	21	10	3	13	36
23-24	Tor	24	8	6	14	55
24-25	Tor	30	4	3	7	67
25-26	Tor	36	5	5	10	121
26-27	Tor	41	1	2	3	88
Totals		257	65	33	98	611
Playoff Totals		14	2	0	2	10

CORBETT, Michael Charles *6-2 200 RW*
B. Toronto, Ont., Oct. 4, 1942

Season	Team	GP	G	A	Pts.	PIM
67-68	LA	2	0	0	0	0
Playoff Totals		2	0	1	1	2

CORCORAN, Norman *6-0 165 C*
B. Toronto, Ont., Aug. 15, 1931

Season	Team	GP	G	A	Pts.	PIM
49-50	Bos	1	0	0	0	0
52-53	Bos	1	0	0	0	0
54-55	Bos	2	0	0	0	2
55-56	Det-Chi	25	1	3	4	19
Totals		29	1	3	4	21
Playoff Totals		4	0	0	0	6

CORKUM, Bob *6-2 215 RW*
B. Salisbury, Mass., Dec. 18, 1967

Season	Team	GP	G	A	Pts.	PIM
89-90	Buf	8	2	0	2	2
91-92	Buf	20	2	4	6	21
Totals		28	4	4	8	23
Playoff Totals		12	1	3	4	4

CORMIER, Roger *F*

Season	Team	GP	G	A	Pts.	PIM
25-26	Mont	1	0	0	0	0

CORRIGAN, Charles Hubert Patrick (Chuck) *6-1 192 RW*
B. Moosomin, Sask., May 22, 1916

Season	Team	GP	G	A	Pts.	PIM
37-38	Tor	3	0	0	0	0
40-41	NYA	16	2	2	4	2
Totals		19	2	2	4	2

CORRIGAN, Michael Douglas *5-10 175 LW*
B. Ottawa, Ont., Jan. 11, 1946

Season	Team	GP	G	A	Pts.	PIM
67-68	LA	5	0	0	0	2
69-70	LA	36	6	4	10	30
70-71	Van	76	21	28	49	103
71-72	Van-LA	75	15	26	41	120
72-73	LA	78	37	30	67	146
73-74	LA	75	16	26	42	119
74-75	LA	80	13	21	34	61
75-76	LA	71	22	21	43	71
76-77	Pitt	73	14	27	41	36
77-78	Pitt	25	8	12	20	10
Totals		594	152	195	347	698
Playoff Totals		17	2	3	5	20

CORRIVEAU, Fred Andre (Andre) *5-8 135 RW*
B. Grand Mere, Que., May 15, 1928

Season	Team	GP	G	A	Pts.	PIM
53-54	Mont	3	0	1	1	0

CORRIVEAU, Yvon *6-2 205 LW*
B. Welland, Ont., Feb. 8, 1967

Season	Team	GP	G	A	Pts.	PIM
85-86	Wash	2	0	0	0	0
86-87	Wash	17	1	1	2	24
87-88	Wash	44	10	9	19	84
88-89	Wash	33	3	2	5	62
89-90	Wash-Hart	63	13	7	20	72
90-91	Hart	23	1	1	2	18
91-92	Hart	38	12	8	20	36
Totals		220	40	28	68	296
Playoff Totals		29	5	7	12	50

CORSON, Shayne *6-0 201 C*
B. Barrie, Ont., Aug. 13, 1966

Season	Team	GP	G	A	Pts.	PIM
85-86	Mont	3	0	0	0	2
86-87	Mont	55	12	11	23	144
87-88	Mont	71	12	27	39	152
88-89	Mont	80	26	24	50	193
89-90	Mont	76	31	44	75	144
90-91	Mont	71	23	24	47	138
91-92	Mont	64	17	36	53	118
Totals		420	121	166	287	891
Playoff Totals		75	24	29	53	179

CORY, Keith Ross *6-2 195 D*
B. Calgary, Alta., Feb. 4, 1957

Season	Team	GP	G	A	Pts.	PIM
79-80	Winn	46	2	9	11	32
80-81	Winn	5	0	1	1	9
Totals		51	2	10	12	41

COSSETE, Jacques *5-9 185 RW*
B. Rouyn-Noranda, Que., June 20, 1954

Season	Team	GP	G	A	Pts.	PIM
75-76	Pitt	7	0	2	2	9
77-78	Pitt	19	1	2	3	4
78-79	Pitt	38	7	2	9	16
Totals		64	8	6	14	29
Playoff Totals		3	0	1	1.	4

COSTELLO, Lester John Thomas *5-8 158 LW*
B. South Porcupine, Ont., Feb. 16, 1928

Season	Team	GP	G	A	Pts.	PIM
48-49	Tor	15	2	3	5	11
Playoff Totals		6	2	2	4	2

Season	Team	GP	G	A	Pts.	PIM

COSTELLO, Murray *6-3 190 C*
B. South Porcupine, Ont., Feb. 24, 1934

53-54	Chi	40	3	2	5	6
54-55	Bos	54	4	11	15	25
55-56	Bos-Det	65	6	6	12	23
56-57	Det	3	0	0	0	0
Totals		162	13	19	32	54
Playoff Totals		5	0	0	0	2

COSTELLO, Richard *6-0 175 C*
B. Farmington, Mass., June 27, 1963

83-84	Tor	10	2	1	3	2
85-86	Tor	2	0	1	1	0
Totals		12	2	2	4	2

COTCH, Charles *F*

24-25	Ham	11	1	0	1	0

COTE, Alain *5-10 205 LW*
B. Matane, Que., May 3, 1957

77-78	Que (WHA)	27	3	5	8	8
78-79	Que (WHA)	79	14	13	27	23
79-80	Que	41	5	11	16	13
80-81	Que	51	8	18	26	64
81-82	Que	79	15	16	31	82
82-83	Que	79	12	28	40	45
83-84	Que	77	19	24	43	41
84-85	Que	80	13	22	35	31
85-86	Que	78	13	21	34	29
86-87	Que	80	12	24	36	38
87-88	Que	76	4	18	22	26
88-89	Que	55	2	8	10	14
NHL Totals		696	103	190	293	383
WHA Totals		106	17	18	35	31
NHL Playoff Totals		67	9	15	24	44
WHA Playoff Totals		15	1	2	3	2

COTE, Alain Gabriel *6-0 200 D*
B. Montmagny, Que., Apr. 14, 1967

85-86	Bos	32	0	6	6	14
86-87	Bos	3	0	0	0	0
87-88	Bos	2	0	0	0	0
88-89	Bos	31	2	3	5	51
89-90	Wash	2	0	0	0	2
90-91	Mont	28	0	6	6	26
91-92	Mont	13	0	3	3	22
Totals		111	2	18	20	115
Playoff Totals		11	0	2	2	26

COTE, Raymond *5-11 170 C*
B. Pincher Creek, Alta., May 31, 1961

83-84	Edm	13	0	0	0	2
84-85	Edm	2	0	0	0	2
Totals		15	0	0	0	4
Playoff Totals		14	3	2	5	0

COTE, Sylvain *5-11 185 D*
B. Quebec City, Que., Jan. 19, 1966

84-85	Hart	67	3	9	12	17
85-86	Hart	2	0	0	0	0
86-87	Hart	67	2	8	10	20
87-88	Hart	67	7	21	28	30
88-89	Hart	78	8	9	17	49
89-90	Hart	28	4	2	6	14
90-91	Hart	73	7	12	19	17
91-92	Wash	78	11	29	40	31
Totals		360	42	90	132	178
Playoff Totals		24	2	8	10	16

COTTON, Harold (Baldy) *5-10 155 LW*
B. Nanticoke, Ont., Nov. 5, 1902

25-26	Pitt Pi	33	7	1	8	22
26-27	Pitt Pi	35	5	0	5	17
27-28	Pitt Pi	42	9	3	12	40
28-29	Pitt Pi-Tor	43	4	4	8	46
29-30	Tor	41	21	17	38	47
30-31	Tor	43	12	17	29	45
31-32	Tor	47	5	13	18	41
[illegible]	[illegible]	[illegible]	[illegible]	11	[illegible]	[illegible]
33-34	Tor	47	8	14	22	46
34-35	Tor	47	11	14	25	36
35-36	NYA	45	7	9	16	23
36-37	NYA	29	2	0	2	23
Totals		500	101	103	204	415
Playoff Totals		43	4	9	13	46

COUGHLIN, James (Jack) *F*

17-18	Tor	6	2	0	2	0
19-20	Que-Mont	11	0	0	0	0
20-21	Ham	2	0	0	0	0
Totals		19	2	0	2	0

COULIS, Tim *6-0 200 LW*
B. Kenora, Ont., Feb. 24, 1958

79-80	Wash	19	1	2	3	27
83-84	Minn	2	0	0	0	4

Season	Team	GP	G	A	Pts.	PIM

COULIS, Tim *(Continued)*

84-85	Minn	7	1	1	2	34
85-86	Minn	19	2	2	4	73
Totals		47	4	5	9	138
Playoff Totals		3	1	0	1	2

COULSON, D'Arcy *D*

30-31	Phil Q	28	0	0	0	103

COULTER, Arthur Edmond *5-11 185 D*
B. Winnipeg, Man., May 31, 1909

31-32	Chi	13	0	1	1	23
32-33	Chi	46	3	2	5	53
33-34	Chi	46	5	2	7	59
34-35	Chi	48	4	8	12	68
35-36	Chi-NYR	48	1	7	8	44
36-37	NYR	47	1	5	6	27
37-38	NYR	43	5	10	15	90
38-39	NYR	44	4	8	12	58
39-40	NYR	48	1	9	10	68
40-41	NYR	35	5	14	19	42
41-42	NYR	47	1	16	17	31
Totals		465	30	82	112	563
Playoff Totals		49	4	5	9	61

COULTER, Neal *6-2 180 RW*
B. London, Ont., Jan. 2, 1963

85-86	NYI	16	3	4	7	4
86-87	NYI	9	2	1	3	7
87-88	NYI	1	0	0	0	0
Totals		26	5	5	10	11
Playoff Totals		1	0	0	0	0

COULTER, Thomas *F*

33-34	Chi	2	0	0	0	0

COURNOYER, Yvan Serge (Roadrunner)
5-7 178 RW
B. Drummondville, Que., Nov. 22, 1943

63-64	Mont	5	4	0	4	0
64-65	Mont	55	7	10	17	10
65-66	Mont	65	18	11	29	8
66-67	Mont	69	25	15	40	14
67-68	Mont	64	28	32	60	23
68-69	Mont	76	43	44	87	31
69-70	Mont	72	27	36	63	23
70-71	Mont	65	37	36	73	21
71-72	Mont	73	47	36	83	15
72-73	Mont	67	40	39	79	18
73-74	Mont	67	40	33	73	18
74-75	Mont	76	29	45	74	32
75-76	Mont	71	32	36	68	20
76-77	Mont	60	25	28	53	8
77-78	Mont	68	24	29	53	12
78-79	Mont	15	2	5	7	2
Totals		968	428	435	863	255
Playoff Totals		147	64	63	127	47

COUTURE, Gerald Joseph Wilfred Arthur (Doc) *6-2 185 C*
B. Saskatoon, Sask., Aug. 6, 1925

45-46	Det	43	3	7	10	18
46-47	Det	30	5	10	15	0
47-48	Det	19	3	6	9	2
48-49	Det	51	19	10	29	6
49-50	Det	70	24	7	31	21
50-51	Det	53	7	6	13	2
51-52	Mont	10	0	1	1	4
52-53	Chi	70	19	18	37	22
53-54	Chi	40	6	5	11	14
Totals		386	86	70	156	89
Playoff Totals		45	9	7	16	4

COUTURE, Rosario (Rosie, Lolo)
5-11 164 RW
B. St. Boniface, Man., July 24, 1905

28-29	Chi	43	1	3	4	22
29-30	Chi	43	8	8	16	63
30-31	Chi	44	8	11	19	30
[illegible]	[illegible]	[illegible]	[illegible]	[illegible]	[illegible]	[illegible]
32-33	Chi	46	10	7	17	26
33-34	Chi	48	5	8	13	21
34-35	Chi	27	7	9	16	14
35-36	Mont	10	0	1	1	0
Totals		309	48	56	104	184
Playoff Totals		23	1	5	6	15

COUTURE, Wilfred (Billy, Coutu)
B. Sault Ste. Marie, Ont.

17-18	Mont	19	2	0	2	30
18-19	Mont	15	1	1	2	18
19-20	Mont	17	4	0	4	30
20-21	Ham	24	8	4	12	74
21-22	Mont	23	4	3	7	4
22-23	Mont	24	5	2	7	37
23-24	Mont	16	3	1	4	8
24-25	Mont	28	3	2	5	49

Season	Team	GP	G	A	Pts.	PIM

COUTURE, Wilfred (Billy, Coutu) *(Continued)*

25-26	Mont	33	2	4	6	95
26-27	Bos	40	1	1	2	25
Totals		239	33	18	51	370
Playoff Totals		32	2	0	2	42

COURTEAU, Yves *5-10 185 RW*
B. Montreal, Que., Apr. 25, 1964

84-85	Calg	14	1	4	5	4
85-86	Calg	4	1	1	2	0
86-87	Hart	4	0	0	0	0
Totals		22	2	5	7	4
Playoff Totals		1	0	0	0	0

COURTENAY, Edward *6-4 200 RW*
B. Verdun, Que., Feb. 2, 1968

91-92	SJ	5	0	0	0	0

COURTNALL, Geoff *6-1 190 LW*
B. Victoria, B.C., Aug. 18, 1962

83-84	Bos	4	0	0	0	0
84-85	Bos	64	12	16	28	82
85-86	Bos	64	21	16	37	61
86-87	Bos	65	13	23	36	117
87-88	Bos-Edm	74	36	30	66	123
88-89	Wash	79	42	38	80	112
89-90	Wash	80	35	39	74	104
90-91	StL-Van	77	33	32	65	64
91-92	Van	70	23	34	57	118
Totals		577	215	228	443	779
Playoff Totals		67	15	32	47	100

COURTNALL, Russell *5-11 183 C/RW*
B. Duncan, B.C., June 2, 1965

83-84	Tor	14	3	9	12	6
84-85	Tor	69	12	10	22	44
85-86	Tor	73	22	38	60	52
86-87	Tor	79	29	44	73	90
87-88	Tor	65	23	26	49	47
88-89	Tor-Mont	73	23	18	41	19
89-90	Mont	80	27	32	59	27
90-91	Mont	79	26	50	76	29
91-92	Mont	27	7	14	21	6
Totals		559	172	241	413	320
Playoff Totals		84	30	21	51	58

COURTURIER, Sylvain *6-2 205 C*
B. Greenfield Park, Que., Apr. 23, 1968

88-89	LA	16	1	3	4	2
90-91	LA	3	0	1	1	0
91-92	LA	14	3	1	4	2
Totals		33	4	5	9	4

COWAN, Thomas *D*

30-31	Phil	1	0	0	0	0

COWICK, Robert Bruce (Bruce)
6-1 200 LW
B. Victoria, B.C., Aug. 18, 1951

74-75	Wash	65	5	6	11	41
75-76	StL	5	0	0	0	2
Totals		70	5	6	11	43
Playoff Totals		8	0	0	0	9

COWLEY, William Mailes *5-10 165 C*
B. Bristol, Que., June 12, 1912

34-35	StLE	41	5	7	12	10
35-36	Bos	48	11	10	21	17
36-37	Bos	46	13	22	35	35
37-38	Bos	48	17	22	39	8
38-39	Bos	34	8	34	42	2
39-40	Bos	48	13	27	40	24
40-41	Bos	46	17	45	62	16
41-42	Bos	28	4	23	27	6
42-43	Bos	48	27	45	72	10
43-44	Bos	36	30	41	71	12
44-45	Bos	49	25	40	65	12
45-46	Bos	26	12	12	24	6
[illegible]	[illegible]	[illegible]	[illegible]	[illegible]	[illegible]	[illegible]
Totals		549	195	353	548	174
Playoff Totals		64	13	33	46	22

COX, Daniel Smith *5-10 180 LW*
B. Little Current, Ont., Oct. 12, 1903

26-27	Tor	14	0	1	1	4
27-28	Tor	41	9	6	15	27
28-29	Tor	42	12	7	19	14
29-30	Tor-Ott	42	4	6	10	20
30-31	Ott	44	9	12	21	12
31-32	Det	47	4	6	10	23
32-33	Ott	47	4	7	11	8
33-34	Ott-NYR	42	5	4	9	2
34-35	StLE	10	0	0	0	0
Totals		329	47	49	96	110
Playoff Totals		10	0	1	1	6

Season	Team	GP	G	A	Pts.	PIM
COXE, Craig *6-4 200 C*						
B. Chula Vista, Cal., Jan. 21, 1964						
84-85	Van	9	0	0	0	49
85-86	Van	57	3	5	8	176
86-87	Van	15	1	0	1	31
87-88	Van-Calg	71	7	15	22	218
88-89	StL	41	0	7	7	127
89-90	Van	25	1	4	5	66
90-91	Van	7	0	0	0	27
91-92	SJ	10	2	0	2	19
Totals		265	14	31	45	713
Playoff Totals		5	1	0	1	18
CRAIG, Mike *6-0 180 RW*						
B. London, Ont., June 6, 1971						
90-91	Minn	39	8	4	12	32
91-92	Minn	67	15	16	31	155
Totals		106	23	20	43	187
Playoff Totals		14	2	1	3	27
CRAIGWELL, Dale *5-10 178 C*						
B. Toronto, Ont., Apr. 24, 1971						
91-92	SJ	32	5	11	16	8
CRASHLEY, William Barton (Bart) *6-0 180 D*						
B. Toronto, Ont., June 15, 1946						
65-66	Det	1	0	0	0	0
66-67	Det	2	0	0	0	2
67-68	Det	57	2	14	16	18
68-69	Det	1	0	0	0	0
72-73	LA (WHA)	70	18	27	45	10
73-74	LA (WHA)	78	4	26	30	16
74-75	KC-Det	75	5	21	26	24
75-76	LA	4	0	1	1	6
NHL Totals		140	7	36	43	50
WHA Totals		148	22	53	75	26
WHA Playoff Totals		6	0	2	2	2
CRAVEN, Murray *6-3 190 LW*						
B. Medicine Hat, Alta., July 20, 1964						
82-83	Det	31	4	7	11	6
83-84	Det	15	0	4	4	6
84-85	Phil	80	26	35	61	30
85-86	Phil	78	21	33	54	34
86-87	Phil	77	19	30	49	38
87-88	PHil	72	30	46	76	58
88-89	Phil	51	9	28	37	52
89-90	Phil	76	25	50	75	42
90-91	Phil	77	19	47	66	53
91-92	Phil-Hart	73	27	33	60	46
Totals		630	180	313	493	365
Playoff Totals		51	12	18	30	34
CRAWFORD, Jack Shea (John) *5-11 200 D*						
B. Dublin, Ont., Oct. 26, 1916						
37-38	Bos	2	0	0	0	0
38-39	Bos	38	4	8	12	12
39-40	Bos	36	1	4	5	26
40-41	Bos	45	2	8	10	27
41-42	Bos	43	2	9	11	37
42-43	Bos	49	5	18	23	24
43-44	Bos	34	4	16	20	8
44-45	Bos	40	5	19	24	10
45-46	Bos	48	7	9	16	10
46-47	Bos	58	1	17	18	16
47-48	Bos	45	3	11	14	10
48-49	Bos	55	2	13	15	14
49-50	Bos	46	2	8	10	8
Totals		539	38	140	178	202
Playoff Totals		66	4	13	17	36
CRAWFORD, Louis *6-0 185 LW*						
B. Belleville, Ont., Nov. 5, 1962						
89-90	Bos	7	0	0	0	20
91-92	Bos	19	2	1	3	9
Totals		26	2	1	3	29
CRAWFORD, Marc Joseph *5-11 185 LW*						
B. Belleville, Ont., Feb. 13, 1961						
81-82	Van	40	4	8	12	29
82-83	Van	41	4	5	9	28
83-84	Van	19	0	1	1	9
84-85	Van	1	0	0	0	4
85-86	Van	54	11	14	25	92
86-87	Van	21	0	3	3	67
Totals		176	19	31	50	229
Playoff Totals		20	1	2	3	44
CRAWFORD, Robert (Bobby) *5-8 180 RW*						
B. Long Island, N.Y., May 27, 1960						
80-81	Col	15	1	3	4	6
82-83	Det	1	0	0	0	0
Totals		16	1	3	4	6

Season	Team	GP	G	A	Pts.	PIM
CRAWFORD, Robert Remi (Bob) *5-11 180 RW*						
B. Belleville, Ont., Apr. 6, 1959						
79-80	StL	8	1	0	1	2
81-82	StL	3	0	1	1	0
82-83	StL	27	5	9	14	2
83-84	Hart	80	36	25	61	32
84-85	Hart	45	14	14	28	8
85-86	Hart-NYR	68	15	22	37	26
86-87	NYR-Wash	15	0	0	0	2
Totals		246	71	71	142	72
Playoff Totals		11	0	1	1	8
CRAWFORD, Samuel Russell (Rusty) *LW*						
B. Cardinal, Ont., Nov. 7, 1884						
17-18	Ott-Tor	20	3	0	3	33
18-19	Tor	18	7	3	10	18
Totals		38	10	3	13	51
Playoff Totals		2	2	1	3	0
CREIGHTON, Adam *6-5 214 C*						
B. Burlington, Ont., June 2, 1965						
83-84	Buf	7	2	2	4	4
84-85	Buf	30	2	8	10	33
85-86	Buf	19	1	1	2	2
86-87	Buf	56	18	22	40	26
87-88	Buf	36	10	17	27	87
88-89	Buf-Chi	67	22	24	46	136
89-90	Chi	80	34	36	70	224
90-91	Chi	72	22	29	51	135
91-92	Chi-NYI	77	21	15	36	118
Totals		444	132	154	286	765
Playoff Totals		41	8	13	21	113
CREIGHTON, David Theodore *6-1 181 C*						
B. Port Arthur, Ont., June 24, 1930						
48-49	Bos	12	1	3	4	0
49-50	Bos	64	18	13	31	13
50-51	Bos	56	5	4	9	4
51-52	Bos	49	20	17	37	18
52-53	Bos	45	8	8	16	14
53-54	Bos	69	20	20	40	27
54-55	Tor-Chi	63	9	8	17	14
55-56	NYR	70	20	31	51	43
56-57	NYR	70	18	21	39	42
57-58	NYR	70	17	35	52	40
58-59	Tor	34	3	9	12	4
59-60	Tor	14	1	5	6	4
Totals		616	140	174	314	223
Playoff Totals		51	11	13	24	20
CREIGHTON, James *F*						
30-31	Det	11	1	0	1	2
CRESSMAN, David Gregory *6-1 180 LW*						
B. Kitchener, Ont., Jan. 2, 1950						
74-75	Minn	5	2	0	2	4
75-76	Minn	80	4	8	12	33
Totals		85	6	8	14	37
CRESSMAN, Glen *5-8 155 C*						
B. Peterborough, Ont., Aug. 29, 1934						
56-57	Mont	4	0	0	0	2
CRISP, Terrance Arthur (Terry) *5-10 180 C*						
B. Parry Sound, Ont., May 28, 1943						
65-66	Bos	3	0	0	0	0
67-68	StL	73	9	20	29	10
68-69	StL	57	6	9	15	14
69-70	StL	26	5	6	11	2
70-71	StL	54	5	11	16	13
71-72	StL	75	13	18	31	12
72-73	NYI-Phil	66	5	21	26	8
73-74	Phil	71	10	21	31	28
74-75	Phil	71	8	19	27	20
75-76	Phil	38	6	9	15	28
76-77	Phil	2	0	0	0	0
Totals		536	67	134	201	135
Playoff Totals		110	15	28	43	40
CRISTOFOLI, Ed *6-2 205 C*						
B. Trail, B.C., May 14, 1967						
89-90	Mont	9	0	1	1	4
CROGHEN, Maurice *F*						
B. Montreal, Que., Nov. 19, 1914						
37-38	Mont M	16	0	0	0	4
CROMBEEN, Michael Joseph *5-11 190 RW*						
B. Sarnia, Ont., Apr. 16, 1957						
77-78	Clev	48	3	4	7	13
78-79	StL	37	3	8	11	34
79-80	StL	71	10	12	22	20
80-81	StL	66	9	14	23	58
81-82	StL	71	19	8	27	32

Season	Team	GP	G	A	Pts.	PIM
CROMBEEN, Michael Joseph						
(Continued)						
82-83	StL	80	6	11	17	20
83-84	Hart	56	1	4	5	25
84-85	Hart	46	4	7	11	16
Totals		475	55	68	123	218
Playoff Totals		27	6	2	8	32
CRONIN, Shawn *6-2 210 D*						
B. Flushing, Mich., Aug. 20, 1963						
88-89	Wash	1	0	0	0	0
89-90	Winn	61	0	4	4	243
90-91	Winn	67	1	5	6	189
91-92	Winn	65	0	4	4	271
Totals		194	1	13	14	703
Playoff Totals		9	0	0	0	13
CROSSETT, Stanley *F*						
30-31	Phil Q	21	0	0	0	10
CROSSMAN, Douglas *6-2 190 D*						
B. Peterborough, Ont., June 30, 1960						
80-81	Chi	9	0	2	2	2
81-82	Chi	70	12	28	40	24
82-83	Chi	80	13	40	53	46
83-84	Phil	78	7	28	35	63
84-85	Phil	80	4	33	37	65
85-86	Phil	80	6	37	43	55
86-87	Phil	78	9	31	40	29
87-88	Phil	76	9	29	38	43
88-89	LA	74	10	15	25	53
89-90	NYI	80	15	44	59	54
90-91	NYI-Hart-Det	74	8	29	37	48
91-92	Det	26	0	8	8	14
Totals		805	93	324	417	496
Playoff Totals		97	12	39	51	105
CROTEAU, Gary Paul *6-0 202 LW*						
B. Sudbury, Ont., June 20, 1946						
68-69	LA	11	5	1	6	6
69-70	LA-Det	13	0	2	2	2
70-71	Cal	74	15	28	43	12
71-72	Cal	73	12	12	24	11
72-73	Cal	47	6	15	21	8
73-74	Cal	76	14	21	35	16
74-75	KC	77	8	11	19	16
75-76	KC	79	19	14	33	12
76-77	Col	78	24	27	51	14
77-78	Col	62	17	22	39	24
78-79	Col	79	23	18	41	18
79-80	Col	15	1	4	5	4
Totals		684	144	175	319	143
Playoff Totals		11	3	2	5	8
CROWDER, Bruce *6-0 180 RW*						
B. Essex, Ont., Mar. 25, 1957						
81-82	Bos	63	16	11	27	31
82-83	Bos	80	21	19	40	58
83-84	Bos	74	6	14	20	44
84-85	Pitt	26	4	7	11	23
Totals		243	47	51	98	156
Playoff Totals		31	8	4	12	41
CROWDER, Keith Scott *6-0 190 RW*						
B. Windsor, Ont., Jan. 6, 1959						
78-79	Birm (WHA)	5	1	0	1	17
80-81	Bos	47	13	12	25	172
81-82	Bos	71	23	21	44	101
82-83	Bos	74	35	39	74	105
83-84	Bos	63	24	28	52	128
84-85	Bos	79	32	38	70	142
85-86	Bos	78	38	46	84	177
86-87	Bos	58	22	30	52	106
87-88	Bos	68	17	26	43	173
88-89	Bos	69	15	18	33	147
89-90	LA	55	4	13	17	93
NHL Totals		662	223	271	494	1346
WHA Totals		5	1	0	1	17
NHL Playoff Totals		85	14	22	36	218
CROWDER, Troy *6-4 215 RW*						
B. Sudbury, Ont., May 3, 1968						
89-90	NJ	10	0	0	0	23
90-91	NJ	59	6	3	9	182
91-92	Det	7	0	0	0	35
Totals		76	6	3	9	240
Playoff Totals		4	0	0	0	22
CROZIER, Joseph Richard *6-0 180 D*						
B. Winnipeg, Man., Feb. 19, 1929						
59-60	Tor	5	0	3	3	2

CRUTCHFIELD, Nelson (Nels) *6-1 175 C*
B. Knowlton, Que., July 12, 1911

Season	Team	GP	G	A	Pts.	PIM
34-35	Mont	41	5	5	10	20
Playoff Totals		2	0	1	1	22

CULHANE, Jim *6-0 195 D*
B. Halleybury, Ont., Mar. 13, 1965

Season	Team	GP	G	A	Pts.	PIM
89-90	Hart	6	0	1	1	4

CULLEN, Brian Joseph *5-10 164 C*
B. Ottawa, Ont., Nov. 11, 1933

Season	Team	GP	G	A	Pts.	PIM
54-55	Tor	27	3	5	8	6
55-56	Tor	21	2	6	8	8
56-57	Tor	46	8	12	20	27
57-58	Tor	67	20	23	43	29
58-59	Tor	59	4	14	18	10
59-60	NYR	64	8	21	29	6
60-61	NYR	42	11	19	30	6
Totals		326	56	100	156	92
Playoff Totals		19	3	0	3	2

CULLEN, Charles Francis (Barry)
6-0 175 RW
B. Ottawa, Ont., June 16, 1935

Season	Team	GP	G	A	Pts.	PIM
55-56	Tor	3	0	0	0	4
56-57	Tor	51	6	10	16	30
57-58	Tor	70	16	25	41	37
58-59	Tor	40	6	8	14	17
59-60	Det	55	4	9	13	23
Totals		219	32	52	84	111
Playoff Totals		6	0	0	0	2

CULLEN, John *5-10 185 C*
B. Puslinch, Ont., Aug. 2, 1964

Season	Team	GP	G	A	Pts.	PIM
88-89	Pitt	79	12	37	49	112
89-90	Pitt	72	32	60	92	138
90-91	Pitt-Hart	78	39	71	110	101
91-92	Hart	77	26	51	77	141
Totals		306	109	219	328	492
Playoff Totals		24	7	14	21	50

CULLEN, Raymond Murray *5-11 180 C*
B. Ottawa, Ont., Sept. 20, 1941

Season	Team	GP	G	A	Pts.	PIM
65-66	NYR	8	1	3	4	0
66-67	Det	27	8	8	16	8
67-68	Minn	67	28	25	53	18
68-69	Minn	67	26	38	64	44
69-70	Minn	74	17	28	45	8
70-71	Van	70	12	21	33	42
Totals		313	92	123	215	120
Playoff Totals		20	3	10	13	2

CUMMINS, Barry Kenneth *5-9 175 D*
B. Regina, Sask., Jan. 25, 1949

Season	Team	GP	G	A	Pts.	PIM
73-74	Cal	36	1	2	3	39

CUMMINS, Jim *6-2 203 RW*
B. Dearborn, Mich., May 17, 1970

Season	Team	GP	G	A	Pts.	PIM
91-92	Det	1	0	0	0	7

CUNNEYWORTH, Randy William
6-0 190 LW
B. Etobicoke, Ont., May 10, 1961

Season	Team	GP	G	A	Pts.	PIM
80-81	Buf	1	0	0	0	2
81-82	Buf	20	2	4	6	47
85-86	Pitt	75	15	30	45	74
86-87	Pitt	79	26	27	53	142
87-88	Pitt	71	35	39	74	141
88-89	Pitt	70	25	19	44	156
89-90	Winn-Hart	71	14	15	29	75
90-91	Hart	32	9	5	14	49
91-92	Hart	39	7	10	17	71
Totals		458	133	149	282	757
Playoff Totals		23	6	5	11	37

CUNNNINGHAM, James *5-11 185 LW*
B. St. Paul, Minn., Aug. [illegible], [illegible]

Season	Team	GP	G	A	Pts.	PIM
77-78	Phil	1	0	0	0	4

CUNNINGHAM, Leslie Roy *5-8 165 C*
B. Calgary, Alta., Oct. 4, 1913

Season	Team	GP	G	A	Pts.	PIM
36-37	NYA	23	1	8	9	19
39-40	Chi	37	6	11	17	2
Totals		60	7	19	26	21
Playoff Totals		1	0	0	0	2

CUNNINGHAM, Robert Gordon
5-11 168 C
B. Wolland, Ont., Feb. 26, 1941

Season	Team	GP	G	A	Pts.	PIM
60-61	NYR	3	0	1	1	0
61-62	NYR	1	0	0	0	0
NHL Totals		4	0	1	1	0
WHA Playoff Totals		5	1	1	2	2

CUPOLO, William Donald *5-8 170 RW*
B. Niagara Falls, Ont., Jan. 8, 1924

Season	Team	GP	G	A	Pts.	PIM
44-45	Bos	47	11	13	24	10
Playoff Totals		7	1	2	3	0

CURRAN, Brian *6-5 215 D*
B. Toronto, Ont., Nov. 5, 1963

Season	Team	GP	G	A	Pts.	PIM
83-84	Bos	16	1	1	2	57
84-85	Bos	56	0	1	1	158
85-86	Bos	43	2	5	7	192
86-87	NYI	68	0	10	10	356
87-88	NYI-Tor	29	0	2	2	87
88-89	Tor	47	1	4	5	185
89-90	Tor	72	2	9	11	301
90-91	Tor-Buf	21	0	1	1	50
91-92	Buf	3	0	0	0	14
Totals		355	6	33	39	1400
Playoff Totals		24	0	1	1	122

CURRIE, Dan *6-2 198 LW*
B. Burlington, Ont., Mar. 15, 1968

Season	Team	GP	G	A	Pts.	PIM
90-91	Edm	5	0	0	0	0
91-92	Edm	7	1	0	1	0
Totals		12	1	0	1	0

CURRIE, Glen *6-2 180 C*
B. Montreal, Que., July 18, 1958

Season	Team	GP	G	A	Pts.	PIM
79-80	Wash	32	2	0	2	2
80-81	Wash	40	5	13	18	16
81-82	Wash	43	7	7	14	14
82-83	Wash	68	11	28	39	20
83-84	Wash	80	12	24	36	20
84-85	Wash	44	1	5	6	19
85-86	LA	12	1	2	3	9
87-88	LA	7	0	0	0	0
Totals		326	39	79	118	100
Playoff Totals		12	1	3	4	4

CURRIE, Hugh Roy *6-0 190 D*
B. Saskatoon, Sask., Oct. 22, 1925

Season	Team	GP	G	A	Pts.	PIM
50-51	Mont	1	0	0	0	0

CURRIE, Tony *5-11 165 RW*
B. Sydney Mines, N.S., Nov. 12, 1957

Season	Team	GP	G	A	Pts.	PIM
77-78	StL	22	4	5	9	4
78-79	StL	36	4	15	19	0
79-80	StL	40	19	14	33	4
80-81	StL	61	23	32	55	38
81-82	StL-Van	60	23	25	48	19
82-83	Van	8	1	1	2	0
83-84	Van-Hart	50	15	19	34	6
84-85	Hart	13	3	8	11	12
Totals		290	92	119	211	83
Playoff Totals		16	4	12	16	14

CURRY, Floyd James (Busher)
5-11 175 RW
B. Chapleau, Ont., Aug. 11, 1925

Season	Team	GP	G	A	Pts.	PIM
47-48	Mont	31	1	5	6	0
49-50	Mont	49	8	8	16	8
50-51	Mont	69	13	14	27	23
51-52	Mont	64	20	18	38	10
52-53	Mont	68	16	6	22	10
53-54	Mont	70	13	8	21	22
54-55	Mont	68	11	10	21	36
55-56	Mont	70	14	18	32	10
56-57	Mont	70	7	9	16	20
57-58	Mont	42	2	3	5	8
Totals		601	105	99	204	147
Playoff Totals		91	23	17	40	38

CURTALE, Tony *6-0 183 D*
B. Detroit, Mich., Jan. 29, 1962

Season	Team	GP	G	A	Pts.	PIM
80-81	Calg	2	0	0	0	0

CURTIS, Paul Edwin *6-0 185 D*
B. Peterborough, Ont., Sept. 29, 1947

Season	Team	GP	G	A	Pts.	PIM
69-70	Mont	1	0	0	0	0
70-71	LA	64	1	13	14	82
71-72	LA	64	1	12	13	57
72-73	LA-StL	56	1	9	10	22
74-75	Balt (WHA)	76	4	15	19	32
NHL Totals		185	3	34	37	161
WHA Totals		76	4	15	19	32
NHL Playoff Totals		5	0	0	0	2

CUSHENAN, Ian Robertson *6-1 195 D*
B. Hamilton, Ont., Nov. 29, 1933

Season	Team	GP	G	A	Pts.	PIM
56-57	Chi	11	0	0	0	13
57-58	Chi	61	2	8	10	67
58-59	Mont	35	1	2	3	28
59-60	NYR	17	0	1	1	12
63-64	Det	5	0	0	0	4
Totals		129	3	11	14	124

CUSSON, Jean *5-10 175 LW*
B. Verdon, Que., Oct. 5, 1942

Season	Team	GP	G	A	Pts.	PIM
67-68	Oak	2	0	0	0	0

CYR, Denis *5-10 180 RW*
B. Verdun, Que., Feb. 4, 1961

Season	Team	GP	G	A	Pts.	PIM
80-81	Calg	10	1	4	5	0
81-82	Calg	45	12	10	22	13
82-83	Calg-Chi	52	8	9	17	2
83-84	Chi	46	12	13	25	19
84-85	StL	9	5	3	8	0
85-86	StL	31	3	4	7	2
Totals		193	41	43	84	36
Playoff Totals		4	0	0	0	0

CYR, Paul *5-10 185 LW*
B. Port Alberni, B.C., Oct. 31, 1963

Season	Team	GP	G	A	Pts.	PIM
82-83	Buf	36	15	12	27	59
83-84	Buf	71	16	27	43	52
84-85	Buf	71	22	24	46	63
85-86	Buf	71	20	31	51	120
86-87	Buf	73	11	16	27	122
87-88	Buf-NYR	60	5	14	19	79
88-89	NYR	1	0	0	0	2
90-91	Hart	70	12	13	25	107
91-92	Hart	17	0	3	3	19
Totals		470	101	140	241	623
Playoff Totals		24	4	6	10	31

DAHLEN, Ulf *6-2 195 LW/RW*
B. Ostersund, Sweden, Jan. 12, 1967

Season	Team	GP	G	A	Pts.	PIM
87-88	NYR	70	29	23	52	26
88-89	NYR	56	24	19	43	50
89-90	NYR-Minn	76	20	22	42	30
90-91	Minn	66	21	18	39	6
91-92	Minn	79	36	30	66	10
Totals		347	130	112	242	122
Playoff Totals		33	3	13	16	8

DAHLIN, Kjell *6-0 175 RW*
B. Timra, Sweden, Mar. 2, 1963

Season	Team	GP	G	A	Pts.	PIM
85-86	Mont	77	32	39	71	4
86-87	Mont	41	12	8	20	0
87-88	Mont	48	13	12	25	6
Totals		166	57	59	116	0
Playoff Totals		35	6	11	17	6

DAHLQUIST, Chris *6-1 190 D*
B. Fridley, Minn., Dec. 14, 1962

Season	Team	GP	G	A	Pts.	PIM
85-86	Pitt	5	1	2	3	2
86-87	Pitt	19	0	1	1	20
87-88	Pitt	44	3	6	9	69
88-89	Pitt	43	1	5	6	42
89-90	Pitt	62	4	10	14	56
90-91	Pitt-Minn	64	3	8	11	63
91-92	Minn	74	1	13	14	68
Totals		311	13	45	58	320
Playoff Totals		32	1	6	7	26

DAHLSTROM, Carl S. (Cully) *5-1 175 C*
B. Minneapolis, Minn., July 3, 1913

Season	Team	GP	G	A	Pts.	PIM
37-38	Chi	48	10	9	19	11
38-39	Chi	48	6	14	20	2
39-40	Chi	45	11	19	30	15
40-41	Chi	40	11	14	25	6
41-42	Chi	33	13	14	27	6
42-43	Chi	38	11	13	24	10
43-44	Chi	50	20	22	42	8
44-45	Chi	40	6	13	19	0
Totals		342	88	118	206	58
Playoff Totals		29	6	8	14	4

DAIGLE, Roland Alain (Alain)
5-10 180 RW
B. Cap-de-la-Madeleine, Que., Aug. 24, 1954

Season	Team	GP	G	A	Pts.	PIM
74-75	Chi	52	5	4	9	6
75-76	Chi	71	15	9	24	15
76-77	Chi	73	12	8	20	11
77-78	Chi	53	6	6	12	95
78-79	Chi	74	11	14	25	55
79-80	Chi	66	7	9	16	22
Totals		389	56	50	106	204
Playoff Totals		17	0	1	1	0

DAIGNEAULT, Jean-Jacques *5-11 185 D*
B. Montreal, Que., Oct. 12, 1965

Season	Team	GP	G	A	Pts.	PIM
84-85	Van	67	4	23	27	69
85-86	Van	64	5	23	28	45
86-87	Phil	77	6	16	22	56
87-88	Phil	28	2	2	4	12
89-90	Mont	36	2	10	12	14
90-91	Mont	51	3	16	19	31
91-92	Mont	79	4	14	18	36
Totals		402	26	104	130	263
Playoff Totals		37	1	6	7	6

DAILEY, Robert Scott 6-5 220 D
B. Kingston, Ont., May 3, 1953

Season	Team	GP	G	A	Pts.	PIM
73-74	Van	76	7	17	24	143
74-75	Van	70	12	36	48	103
75-76	Van	67	15	24	39	119
76-77	Van-Phil	76	9	30	39	90
77-78	Phil	76	21	36	57	62
78-79	Phil	70	9	30	39	63
79-80	Phil	61	13	26	39	71
80-81	Phil	53	7	27	34	141
81-82	Phil	12	1	5	6	22
Totals		561	94	231	325	814
Playoff Totals		63	12	34	46	106

DALEY, Franklin D

Season	Team	GP	G	A	Pts.	PIM
28-29	Det	5	0	0	0	0
Playoff Totals		2	0	0	0	0

DALEY, Patrick Lloyd 6-1 176 LW
B. Marieville, France, Mar. 27, 1959

Season	Team	GP	G	A	Pts.	PIM
79-80	Winn	5	1	0	1	4
80-81	Winn	7	0	0	0	9
Totals		12	1	0	1	13

DALGARNO, Brad 6-3 215 RW
B. Vancouver, B.C., Aug. 11, 1967

Season	Team	GP	G	A	Pts.	PIM
85-86	NYI	2	1	0	1	0
87-88	NYI	38	2	8	10	58
88-89	NYI	55	11	10	21	86
90-91	NYI	41	3	12	15	24
91-92	NYI	15	2	1	3	12
Totals		151	19	31	50	180
Playoff Totals		5	0	1	1	19

DALLMAN, Marty 5-10 180 C
B. Niagara Falls, Ont., Feb. 15, 1963

Season	Team	GP	G	A	Pts.	PIM
87-88	Tor	2	0	1	1	0
88-89	Tor	4	0	0	0	0
Totals		6	0	1	1	0

DALLMAN, Rod 5-11 185 LW
B. Quesnel, B.C., Jan. 26, 1967

Season	Team	GP	G	A	Pts.	PIM
87-88	NYI	3	1	0	1	6
88-89	NYI	1	0	0	0	15
91-92	Phil	2	0	0	0	5
Totals		6	1	0	1	26
Playoff Totals		1	0	1	1	0

DAME, Aurelia N. (Bunny) LW
B. Edmonton, Alta.

Season	Team	GP	G	A	Pts.	PIM
41-42	Mont	34	2	5	7	4

DAMPHOUSSE, Vincent 6-1 190 LW
B. Montreal, Que., Dec. 17, 1967

Season	Team	GP	G	A	Pts.	PIM
86-87	Tor	80	21	25	46	26
87-88	Tor	75	12	36	48	40
88-89	Tor	80	26	42	68	75
89-90	Tor	80	33	61	94	56
90-91	Tor	79	26	47	73	65
91-92	Edm	80	38	51	89	53
Totals		474	156	262	418	315
Playoff Totals		39	7	16	23	28

DAMORE, Henry John (Hank, Lou Costello) 5-5 200 C
B. Niagara Falls, Ont., July 17, 1919

Season	Team	GP	G	A	Pts.	PIM
43-44	NYR	4	1	0	1	2

DANEYKO, Kenneth 6-0 210 D
B. Windsor, Ont., Apr. 17, 1964

Season	Team	GP	G	A	Pts.	PIM
83-84	NJ	11	1	4	5	17
84-85	NJ	1	0	0	0	10
85-86	NJ	44	0	10	10	100
86-87	NJ	79	2	12	14	183
87-88	NJ	80	5	7	12	239
88-89	NJ	80	5	5	10	283
89-90	NJ	74	6	15	21	216
90-91	NJ	80	4	16	20	249
91-92	NJ	80	1	7	8	170
Totals		529	24	76	100	1467
Playoff Totals		40	3	10	13	130

DANIELS, Jeff 6-1 195 LW
B. Oshawa, Ont., June 24, 1968

Season	Team	GP	G	A	Pts.	PIM
90-91	Pitt	11	0	2	2	2
91-92	Pitt	2	0	0	0	0
Totals		13	0	2	2	2

DANIELS, Kimbi 5-11 175 C
B. Brandon, Man., Jan. 19, 1972

Season	Team	GP	G	A	Pts.	PIM
90-91	Phil	2	0	1	1	0
91-92	Phil	25	1	1	2	4
Totals		27	1	2	3	4

DAOUST, Daniel 5-11 170 C
B. Montreal, Que., Feb. 29, 1960

Season	Team	GP	G	A	Pts.	PIM
82-83	Mont-Tor	52	18	34	52	35
83-84	Tor	78	18	56	74	88
84-85	Tor	79	17	37	54	98
85-86	Tor	80	7	13	20	88
86-87	Tor	33	4	3	7	35
87-88	Tor	67	9	8	17	57
88-89	Tor	68	7	5	12	54
89-90	Tor	65	7	11	18	89
Totals		522	87	167	254	544
Playoff Totals		32	7	5	12	83

DARK, Michael 6-3 210 D
B. Sarnia, Ont., Sept. 17, 1963

Season	Team	GP	G	A	Pts.	PIM
86-87	StL	13	2	0	2	2
87-88	StL	30	3	6	9	12
Totals		43	5	6	11	14

DARRAGH, Harold Edward (Harry and Howl) 5-1 145 F
B. Ottawa, Ont., Sept. 13, 1902

Season	Team	GP	G	A	Pts.	PIM
25-26	Pitt Pi	35	10	7	17	6
26-27	Pitt Pi	42	12	3	15	4
27-28	Pitt Pi	44	13	2	15	16
28-29	Pitt Pi	43	9	3	12	6
29-30	Pitt Pi	42	15	17	32	6
30-31	Phil Q-Bos	35	3	5	8	6
31-32	Tor	48	5	10	15	6
32-33	Tor	19	1	2	3	0
Totals		308	68	49	117	50
Playoff Totals		16	1	3	4	4

DARRAGH, John Proctor (Jack) RW
B. Ottawa, Ont., Dec. 4, 1890

Season	Team	GP	G	A	Pts.	PIM
17-18	Ott	18	14	0	14	3
18-19	Ott	14	12	1	13	27
19-20	Ott	22	22	5	27	22
20-21	Ott	24	11	8	19	20
22-23	Ott	24	7	7	14	14
23-24	Ott	18	2	0	2	2
Totals		120	68	21	89	88
Playoff Totals		21	14	2	16	17

DAVID, Richard 6-0 195 LW
B. Notre Dame de la Salette, Que., Apr. 8, 1958

Season	Team	GP	G	A	Pts.	PIM
78-79	Que (WHA)	14	0	4	4	4
79-80	Que	10	0	0	0	2
81-82	Que	5	1	1	2	4
82-83	Que	16	3	3	6	4
NHL Totals		31	4	4	8	10
WHA Totals		14	0	4	4	4
NHL Playoff Totals		1	0	0	0	0

DAVIDSON, Gordon John (Gord) 5-11 188 D
B. Stratton, Ont., Aug. 5, 1918

Season	Team	GP	G	A	Pts.	PIM
42-43	NYR	35	2	3	5	4
43-44	NYR	16	1	3	4	4
Totals		51	3	6	9	8

DAVIDSON, Robert E. 5-11 185 F
B. Toronto, Ont., Feb. 10, 1912

Season	Team	GP	G	A	Pts.	PIM
34-35	Tor	5	0	0	0	6
35-36	Tor	35	4	4	8	32
36-37	Tor	46	8	7	15	43
37-38	Tor	48	3	17	20	52
38-39	Tor	47	4	10	14	29
39-40	Tor	48	8	18	26	56
40-41	Tor	37	3	6	9	39
41-42	Tor	37	6	20	26	39
42-43	Tor	50	13	23	36	20
43-44	Tor	47	19	28	47	21
44-45	Tor	50	17	18	35	49
45-46	Tor	41	9	9	18	12
Totals		491	94	160	254	398
Playoff Totals		82	5	17	22	79

DAVIE, Robert Howard (Pinkie) 6-0 170 D
B. Beausejour, Man., Sept. 12, 1912

Season	Team	GP	G	A	Pts.	PIM
33-34	Bos	9	0	0	0	6
34-35	Bos	30	0	1	1	17
35-36	Bos	2	0	0	0	2
Totals		41	0	1	1	25

DAVIES, Kenneth George (Buck) 5-6 160 C
B. Bowmanville, Ont., Aug. 10, 1922

Season	Team	GP	G	A	Pts.	PIM
47-48	NYR	0	0	0	0	0
Playoff Totals		1	0	0	0	0

DAVIS, Kim 5-11 170 C
B. Flin Flon, Man., Oct. 31, 1957

Season	Team	GP	G	A	Pts.	PIM
77-78	Pitt	1	0	0	0	0
78-79	Pitt	1	1	0	1	0
79-80	Pitt	24	3	7	10	4
80-81	Pitt-Tor	10	1	0	1	8
Totals		36	5	7	12	12
Playoff Totals		4	0	0	0	0

DAVIS, Lorne Austin 5-11 190 RW
B. Regina, Sask., July 20, 1930

Season	Team	GP	G	A	Pts.	PIM
51-52	Mont	3	1	1	2	2
53-54	Mont	37	6	4	10	2
54-55	Chi-Det	30	0	5	5	6
55-56	Bos	15	0	1	1	0
59-60	Bos	10	1	1	2	10
Totals		95	8	12	20	20
Playoff Totals		18	3	1	4	10

DAVIS, Malcolm Sterling 5-11 180 LW
B. Lockeport, N.S., Oct. 10, 1956

Season	Team	GP	G	A	Pts.	PIM
80-81	Det	5	2	0	2	0
82-83	Buf	24	8	12	20	0
83-34	Buf	11	2	1	3	4
84-85	Buf	47	17	9	26	26
85-86	Buf	7	2	0	2	4
Totals		100	31	22	53	34
Playoff Totals		7	1	0	1	0

DAVIS, Robert F
B. Lachine, Que.

Season	Team	GP	G	A	Pts.	PIM
32-33	Det	3	0	0	0	0

DAVISON, Murray 6-2 190 D
B. Brantford, Ont., June 10, 1938

Season	Team	GP	G	A	Pts.	PIM
65-66	Bos	1	0	0	0	0

DAVYDOV, Evgeny 6-0 183 LW
B. Chelyabinsk, Soviet Union, May 27, 1967

Season	Team	GP	G	A	Pts.	PIM
91-92	Winn	12	4	3	7	8
Playoff Totals		7	2	2	4	2

DAWES, Robert James 6-1 170 D
B. Saskatoon, Sask., Nov. 29, 1924

Season	Team	GP	G	A	Pts.	PIM
46-47	Tor	1	0	0	0	0
48-49	Tor	5	1	0	1	0
49-50	Tor	11	1	2	3	2
50-51	Mont	15	0	5	5	4
Totals		32	2	7	9	6
Playoff Totals		10	0	0	0	2

DAY, Clarence Henry (Hap) 5-11 175 LW
B. Owen Sound, Ont., June 14, 1901

Season	Team	GP	G	A	Pts.	PIM
24-25	Tor	26	10	12	22	33
25-26	Tor	36	14	2	16	26
26-27	Tor	44	11	5	16	50
27-28	Tor	22	9	8	17	48
28-29	Tor	44	6	6	12	84
29-30	Tor	43	7	14	21	77
30-31	Tor	44	1	13	14	56
31-32	Tor	47	7	8	15	33
32-33	Tor	47	6	14	20	46
33-34	Tor	48	9	10	19	35
34-35	Tor	45	2	4	6	38
35-36	Tor	44	1	13	14	41
36-37	Tor	48	3	4	7	20
37-38	NYA	43	0	3	3	14
Totals		581	86	116	202	601
Playoff Totals		53	4	7	11	56

DAY, Joseph 5-11 180 LW
B. Chicago, Ill., May 11, 1968

Season	Team	GP	G	A	Pts.	PIM
91-92	Hart	24	0	3	3	10

DEA, William Fraser 5-8 175 LW
B. Edmonton, Alta., Apr. 3, 1933

Season	Team	GP	G	A	Pts.	PIM
53-54	NYR	14	1	1	2	2
56-57	Det	69	15	15	30	14
57-58	Det-Chi	63	9	12	21	10
67-68	Pitt	73	16	12	28	6
68-69	Pitt	66	10	8	18	4
69-70	Det	70	10	3	13	6
70-71	Det	42	6	3	9	2
Totals		397	67	54	121	44
Playoff Totals		11	2	0	2	6

DEACON, Donald John 5-9 190 LW
B. Regina, Sask., June 2, 1913

Season	Team	GP	G	A	Pts.	PIM
36-37	Det	4	0	0	0	2
38-39	Det	8	1	3	4	2
39-40	Det	18	5	1	6	2
Totals		30	6	4	10	6
Playoff Totals		2	2	1	3	0

DEADMARSH, Ernest Charles (Butch) *5-10 185 LW*
B. Trail, B.C., Apr. 5, 1950

Season	Team	GP	G	A	Pts.	PIM
70-71	Buf	10	0	0	0	9
71-72	Buf	12	1	1	2	4
72-73	Buf-Atl	53	2	1	3	34
73-74	Atl	42	6	1	7	89
74-75	KC	20	3	2	5	19
74-75	Van (WHA)	38	7	8	15	128
75-76	Calg (WHA)	79	26	28	54	196
76-77	Minn-Calg (WHA)	73	22	21	43	128
77-78	Cin (WHA)	65	8	9	17	118
NHL Totals		137	12	5	17	155
WHA Totals		255	63	66	129	570
NHL Playoff Totals		4	0	0	0	17
WHA Playoff Totals		8	0	1	1	14

DEAN, Barry James *6-1 195 LW*
B. Maple Creek, Sask., Feb. 26, 1955

Season	Team	GP	G	A	Pts.	PIM
75-76	Phoe (WHA)	71	9	25	34	110
76-77	Col	79	14	25	39	92
77-78	Phil	56	7	18	25	34
78-79	Phil	30	4	13	17	20
NHL Totals		165	25	56	81	146
WHA Totals		71	9	25	34	110

DEBENEDET, Nelson Flavio *6-1 195 LW*
B. Cardenona, Italy, Dec. 31, 1947

Season	Team	GP	G	A	Pts.	PIM
73-74	Det	15	4	1	5	2
74-75	Pitt	31	6	3	9	11
Totals		46	10	4	14	13

DeBLOIS, Lucien *5-11 200 LW*
B. Joliette, Que., June 21, 1957

Season	Team	GP	G	A	Pts.	PIM
77-78	NYR	71	22	8	30	27
78-79	NYR	62	11	17	28	26
79-80	NYR-Col	76	27	20	47	43
80-81	Col	74	26	16	42	78
81-82	Winn	65	25	27	52	87
82-83	Winn	79	27	27	54	69
83-84	Winn	80	34	45	79	50
84-85	Mont	51	12	11	23	20
85-86	Mont	61	14	17	31	48
86-87	NYR	40	3	8	11	27
87-88	NYR	74	9	21	30	103
88-89	NYR	73	9	24	33	107
89-90	Que	70	9	8	17	45
90-91	Que-Tor	52	12	14	26	43
91-92	Tor Winn	65	9	13	22	41
Totals		993	249	276	525	814
Playoff Totals		52	7	6	13	38

DEBOL, David *5-11 175 C*
B. Clair Shores, Mich., Mar. 27, 1956

Season	Team	GP	G	A	Pts.	PIM
77-78	Cin (WHA)	9	3	2	5	2
78-79	Cin (WHA)	59	10	27	37	9
79-80	Hart	48	12	14	26	4
80-81	Hart	44	14	12	26	0
NHL Totals		92	26	26	52	4
WHA Totals		68	13	29	42	11
NHL Playoff Totals		3	0	0	0	0

DeBRUSK, Louis *6-1 225 LW*
B. Dunnville, Ont., June 13, 1968

Season	Team	GP	G	A	Pts.	PIM
91-92	Edm	25	2	1	3	124

DEFAZIO, Dean *5-11 185 LW*
B. Ottawa, Ont., Apr. 16, 1963

Season	Team	GP	G	A	Pts.	PIM
83-84	Pitt	22	0	2	2	28

DEGRAY, Dale Edward *6-0 200 D*
B. Oshawa, Ont., Sept. 1, 1963

Season	Team	GP	G	A	Pts.	PIM
85-86	Caig	1	0	0	0	0
86-87	Calg	27	6	7	13	29
87-88	Tor	56	6	18	24	63
88-89	LA	63	6	22	28	97
89-90	Buf	6	0	0	0	6
Totals		153	18	47	65	195
Playoff Totals		13	1	3	4	28

DELMONTE, Armond Romeo (Dutch) *5-10 190 C*
B. Timmins, Ont., Jan. 4, 1925

Season	Team	GP	G	A	Pts.	PIM
45-46	Bos	1	0	0	0	0

DELORME, Gilbert *6-1 205 D*
B. Boucherville, Que., Nov. 25, 1962

Season	Team	GP	G	A	Pts.	PIM
81-82	Mont	60	3	8	11	55
82-83	Mont	78	12	21	33	89
83-84	Mont-StL	71	2	12	14	49
84-85	StL	74	2	12	14	53
85-86	Que	64	2	18	20	51
86-87	Que-Det	43	2	5	7	47
87-88	Det	55	2	8	10	81

DELORME, Gilbert *(Continued)*

Season	Team	GP	G	A	Pts.	PIM
88-89	Det	42	1	3	4	51
89-90	Pitt	54	3	7	10	44
Totals		541	31	92	123	520
Playoff Totals		56	1	9	10	56

DELORME, Ronald Elmer *6-2 185 C*
B. North Battleford, Sask., Sept. 3, 1955

Season	Team	GP	G	A	Pts.	PIM
75-76	Den (WHA)	22	1	3	4	28
76-77	Col	29	6	4	10	23
77-78	Col	68	10	11	21	47
78-79	Col	77	20	8	28	68
79-80	Col	75	19	24	43	76
80-81	Col	65	11	16	27	70
81-82	Van	59	9	8	17	177
82-83	Van	56	5	8	13	87
83-84	Van	64	2	2	4	68
84-85	Van	31	1	2	3	51
NHL Totals		524	83	83	166	667
WHA Totals		22	1	3	4	28
NHL Playoff Totals		25	1	2	3	59

DELORY, Valentine Arthur *5-10 160 LW*
B. Toronto, Ont., Feb. 14, 1927

Season	Team	GP	G	A	Pts.	PIM
48-49	NYR	1	0	0	0	0

DePALMA, Larry *6-0 195 LW*
B. Trenton, Mich., Oct. 27, 1965

Season	Team	GP	G	A	Pts.	PIM
85-86	Minn	1	0	0	0	0
86-87	Minn	56	9	6	15	219
87-88	Minn	7	1	1	2	15
88-89	Minn	43	5	7	12	102
90-91	Minn	14	3	0	3	26
Totals		121	18	14	32	362
Playoff Totals		2	0	0	0	6

DELPARTE, Guy Philipp *5-9 178 LW*
B. Prince Albert, Sask., Aug. 30, 1949

Season	Team	GP	G	A	Pts.	PIM
76-77	Col	48	1	8	9	18

DERLAGO, William Anthony *5-10 195 C*
B. Birtle, Man., Aug. 25, 1958

Season	Team	GP	G	A	Pts.	PIM
78-79	Van	9	4	4	8	2
79-80	Van-Tor	77	16	27	43	40
80-81	Tor	80	35	39	74	26
81-82	Tor	75	34	50	84	42
82-83	Tor	58	13	24	37	27
83-84	Tor	79	40	20	60	50
84-85	Tor	62	31	31	62	21
85-86	Tor-Bos-Winn	67	10	21	31	21
86-87	Winn-Que	48	6	11	17	18
Totals		555	189	227	416	247
Playoff Totals		13	5	0	5	8

DELVECCHIO, Alexander Peter (Alex) *6-0 195 C*
B. Ft. William, Ont., Dec. 4, 1931

Season	Team	GP	G	A	Pts.	PIM
50-51	Det	1	0	0	0	0
51-52	Det	65	15	22	37	22
52-53	Det	70	16	43	59	28
53-54	Det	69	11	18	29	34
54-55	Det	69	17	31	48	37
55-56	Det	70	25	26	51	24
56-57	Det	48	16	25	41	8
57-58	Det	70	21	38	59	22
58-59	Det	70	19	35	54	6
59-60	Det	70	19	28	47	8
60-61	Det	70	27	35	62	26
61-62	Det	70	26	43	69	18
62-63	Det	70	20	44	64	8
63-64	Det	70	23	30	53	11
64-65	Det	68	25	42	67	16
65-66	Det	70	31	38	69	16
66-67	Det	70	17	38	55	10
67-68	Det	74	22	48	70	14
68-69	Det	72	25	58	83	8
69-70	Det	73	21	47	68	24
70-71	Det	77	21	34	55	6
71-72	Det	75	20	45	65	22
72-73	Det	77	18	53	71	13
73-74	Det	11	1	4	5	2
Totals		1549	456	825	1281	383
Playoff Totals		121	35	69	104	29

DEMARCO, Albert George (Ab) *6-0 168 C*
B. North Bay, Ont., May 10,1916

Season	Team	GP	G	A	Pts.	PIM
38-39	Chi	2	1	0	1	0
39-40	Chi	17	0	5	5	17
42-43	Tor-Bos	7	4	2	6	0
43-44	Bos-NYR	39	14	19	33	2
44-45	NYR	50	24	30	54	10
45-46	NYR	50	20	27	47	20
46-47	NYR	44	9	10	19	4
Totals		209	72	93	165	53
Playoff Totals		11	3	0	3	2

DEMARCO, Albert Thomas (Ab) *6-0 170 D*
B. North Bay, Ont., Feb. 27, 1949

Season	Team	GP	G	A	Pts.	PIM
69-70	NYR	3	0	0	0	0
70-71	NYR	2	0	1	1	0
71-72	NYR	48	4	7	11	4
72-73	NYR-StL	65	8	22	30	17
73-74	StL-Pitt	57	10	21	31	15
74-75	Pitt-Van	69	12	15	27	25
75-76	Van-LA	64	7	11	18	8
76-77	LA	33	3	3	6	6
77-78	Edm (WHA)	47	6	8	14	20
78-79	Bos	3	0	0	0	0
NHL Totals		344	44	80	124	75
WHA Totals		47	6	8	14	20
NHL Playoff Totals		25	1	2	3	17
WHA Playoff Totals		1	0	0	0	0

DEMERES, Antonio (Tony) *5-9 180 RW*
B. Chambly Basin, Que., July 22,1917

Season	Team	GP	G	A	Pts.	PIM
37-38	Mont	6	0	0	0	0
39-40	Mont	14	2	3	5	2
40-41	Mont	46	13	10	23	17
41-42	Mont	7	3	4	7	4
42-43	Mont	9	2	5	7	0
43-44	NYR	1	0	0	0	0
Totals		83	20	22	42	23
Playoff Totals		3	0	0	0	0

DENIS, Jean Paul (Johnny) *5-8 170 RW*
B. Montreal, Que., Feb. 28, 1924

Season	Team	GP	G	A	Pts.	PIM
46-47	NYR	6	0	1	1	0
49-50	NYR	4	0	1	1	2
Totals		10	0	2	2	2

DENIS, Louis Gilbert (Lulu) *5-8 140 RW*
B. Vonda, Sask., June 7, 1928

Season	Team	GP	G	A	Pts.	PIM
49-50	Mont	2	0	1	1	0
50-51	Mont	1	0	0	0	0
Totals		3	0	1	1	0

DENNENY, Corbett *LW*
B. Cornwall, Ont., 1894

Season	Team	GP	G	A	Pts.	PIM
17-18	Tor	21	20	0	20	8
18-19	Tor	16	7	3	10	15
19-20	Tor	23	23	12	35	18
20-21	Tor	20	17	6	23	27
21-22	Tor	24	19	7	26	28
22-23	Tor	1	1	0	1	0
23-34	Ham	23	0	0	0	6
26-27	Tor	29	7	1	8	24
27-28	Chi	18	5	0	5	12
Totals		175	99	29	128	138
Playoff Totals		15	7	4	11	6

DENNENY, Cyril Joseph (Cy) *LW*
B. Farran's Point, Ont., Dec. 23, 1897

Season	Team	GP	G	A	Pts.	PIM
17-18	Ott	22	36	0	36	34
18-19	Ott	18	18	4	22	43
19-20	Ott	22	16	2	18	21
20-21	Ott	24	34	5	39	0
21-22	Ott	22	27	12	39	18
22-23	Ott	24	21	10	31	20
23-24	Ott	21	22	1	23	10
24-25	Ott	28	27	15	42	16
25-26	Ott	36	24	12	36	18
26-27	Ott	42	17	6	23	16
27-28	Ott	44	3	0	3	12
28-29	Bos	23	1	2	3	2
Totals		326	246	69	315	210
Playoff Totals		37	18	3	21	31

DENNIS, Norman Marshall *5-10 175 C*
B. Aurora, Ont., Dec. 10, 1942

Season	Team	GP	G	A	Pts.	PIM
68-69	StL	2	0	0	0	2
69-70	StL	5	3	0	3	5
70-71	StL	4	0	0	0	0
71-72	StL	1	0	0	0	4
Totals		12	3	0	3	11
Playoff Totals		5	0	0	0	2

DENOIRD, Gerald (Gerry) *F*

Season	Team	GP	G	A	Pts.	PIM
22-23	Tor	15	0	0	0	0

DESAULNIERS, Gerard *5-11 152 C*
B. Shawinigan Falls, Quebec, Dec 31, 1928

Season	Team	GP	G	A	Pts.	PIM
50-51	Mont	3	0	1	1	2
52-53	Mont	2	0	1	1	2
53-54	Mont	3	0	0	0	0
Totals		8	0	2	2	4

DESILETS, Joffre Wilfred *5-10 170 RW*
B. Capreal, Ont., Apr. 16, 1915

Season	Team	GP	G	A	Pts.	PIM
35-36	Mont	38	7	6	13	0

DESILETS, Joffre Wilfred *(Continued)*

Season	Team	GP	G	A	Pts.	PIM
36-37	Mont	48	7	12	19	17
37-38	Mont	32	6	7	13	6
38-39	Chi	48	11	13	24	28
39-40	Chi	26	6	7	13	6
Totals		192	37	45	82	57
Playoff Totals		7	1	0	1	7

DESJARDINS, Eric *6-11 200 D*
B. Rouyn, Que., June 14, 1969

Season	Team	GP	G	A	Pts.	PIM
88-89	Mont	36	2	12	14	26
89-90	Mont	55	3	13	16	51
90-91	Mont	62	7	18	25	27
91-92	Mont	77	6	32	38	50
Totals		230	18	75	93	154
Playoff Totals		44	5	8	13	28

DESJARDINS, Martin *5-11 179 C*
B. Ste.-Rose, Que., Jan. 28, 1967

Season	Team	GP	G	A	Pts.	PIM
89-90	Mont	8	0	2	2	2

DESJARDINS, Victor Arthur *5-9 160 C*
B. Sault Ste. Marie, Mich., July 4, 1900

Season	Team	GP	G	A	Pts.	PIM
30-31	Chi	39	3	12	15	11
31-32	NYR	48	3	3	6	16
Totals		87	6	15	21	27
Playoff Totals		16	0	0	0	0

DESLAURIERS, Jacques *6-0 170 D*
B. Montreal, Que., Sept. 3, 1928

Season	Team	GP	G	A	Pts.	PIM
55-56	Mont	2	0	0	0	0

DEVINE, Kevin *5-8 165 LW*
B. Toronto, Ont., Dec. 9, 1954

Season	Team	GP	G	A	Pts.	PIM
82-83	NYI	2	0	1	1	8

DEWAR, Thomas *D*
B. Frobisher, Sask., June 10, 1913

Season	Team	GP	G	A	Pts.	PIM
43-44	NYR	9	0	2	2	4

DEWSBURY, Albert Percy *6-2 202 D*
B. Goderich, Ont., Apr. 12, 1926

Season	Team	GP	G	A	Pts.	PIM
46-47	Det	23	2	1	3	12
49-50	Det	11	2	2	4	2
50-51	Chi	67	5	14	19	79
51-52	Chi	69	7	17	24	99
52-53	Chi	69	5	16	21	97
53-54	Chi	69	6	15	21	44
54-55	Chi	2	0	1	1	10
55-56	Chi	37	3	12	15	22
Totals		347	30	78	108	365
Playoff Totals		14	1	5	6	16

DEZIEL, Michael *5-11 180 D*
B. Sorel, Que., Jan. 13, 1954

Season	Team	GP	G	A	Pts.	PIM
74-75	Buf	0	0	0	0	0
Playoff Totals		1	0	0	0	0

DHEERE, Marcel Albert (Ching)
5-7 175 LW
B. St. Boniface, Man., Dec. 19, 1920

Season	Team	GP	G	A	Pts.	PIM
42-43	Mont	11	1	2	3	2
Playoff Totals		5	0	0	0	6

DIACHUK, Edward *6-1 195 LW*
B. Vergreville, Alta., Aug. 16, 1936

Season	Team	GP	G	A	Pts.	PIM
60-61	Det	12	0	0	0	19

DICK, Harry *5-11 210 D*
B. Port Colborne, Ont., Nov. 22, 1922

Season	Team	GP	G	A	Pts.	PIM
46-47	Chi	12	0	1	1	12

DICKENS, Ernest Leslie *6-10 175 D*
B. Winnipeg, Man., June 25, 1921

Season	Team	GP	G	A	Pts.	PIM
41-42	Tor	10	2	2	4	6
45-46	Tor	15	1	3	4	6
47-48	Chi	54	5	15	20	30
48-49	Chi	59	2	3	5	14
49-50	Chi	70	0	13	13	22
50-51	Chi	70	2	8	10	20
Totals		278	12	44	56	98
Playoff Totals		13	0	0	0	4

DICKENSON, John Herbert (Herb)
5-11 175 LW
B. Mount Hope, Ont., June 11, 1931

Season	Team	GP	G	A	Pts.	PIM
51-52	NYR	37	14	13	27	8
52-53	NYR	11	4	4	8	2
Totals		48	18	17	35	10

DIDUCK, Gerald *6-2 207 D*
B. Edmonton, Alta., Apr. 6, 1965

Season	Team	GP	G	A	Pts.	PIM
84-85	NYI	65	2	8	10	80
85-86	NYI	10	1	2	3	2
86-87	NYI	30	2	3	5	67
87-88	NYI	68	7	12	19	113

DIDUCK, Gerald *(Continued)*

Season	Team	GP	G	A	Pts.	PIM
88-89	NYI	65	11	21	32	155
89-90	NYI	76	3	17	20	163
90-91	Mont-Van	63	4	9	13	105
91-92	Van	77	6	21	27	224
Totals		454	36	93	129	909
Playoff Totals		36	2	1	3	110

DIETRICH, Don Armond *6-1 195 D*
B. Deloraine, Man., Apr. 5, 1961

Season	Team	GP	G	A	Pts.	PIM
83-84	Chi	17	0	5	5	0
85-86	NJ	11	0	2	2	10
Totals		28	0	7	7	10

DILL, Robert Edward *5-8 185 D*
B. St. Paul, Minn., Apr. 25, 1920

Season	Team	GP	G	A	Pts.	PIM
43-44	NYR	28	6	10	16	66
44-45	NYR	48	9	5	14	69
Totals		76	15	15	30	135

DILLABOUGH, Robert Wellington
5-10 180 C
B. Belleville, Ont., Apr. 14, 1941

Season	Team	GP	G	A	Pts.	PIM
61-62	Det	5	0	0	0	2
64-65	Det	4	0	0	0	2
65-66	Bos	53	7	13	20	18
66-67	Bos	60	6	12	18	14
67-68	Pitt	47	7	12	19	18
68-69	Pitt-Oak	62	7	12	19	6
69-70	Oak	52	5	5	10	16
72-73	Clev(WHA)	72	8	8	16	8
NHL Totals		283	32	54	86	76
WHA Totals		72	8	8	16	8
NHL Playoff Totals		17	3	0	3	0
WHA Playoff Totals		9	1	0	1	0

DILLON, Cecil Graham (Ceece)
5-10 173 F
B. Toledo, Ohio, Apr. 26, 1908

Season	Team	GP	G	A	Pts.	PIM
30-31	NYR	25	7	3	10	8
31-32	NYR	48	23	15	38	22
32-33	NYR	48	21	10	31	12
33-34	NYR	48	13	26	39	10
34-35	NYR	48	25	9	34	4
35-36	NYR	48	18	14	32	12
36-37	NYR	48	20	11	31	13
37-38	NYR	48	21	18	39	6
38-39	NYR	48	12	15	27	6
39-40	Det	44	7	10	17	12
Totals		453	167	131	298	105
Playoff Totals		43	14	9	23	14

DILLON, Gary Kevin *5-10 173 C*
B. Toronto, Ont., Feb. 28, 1959

Season	Team	GP	G	A	Pts.	PIM
80-81	Col	13	1	1	2	29

DILLON, Gerald Wayne (Wayne)
6-0 185 C
B. Toronto, Ont., May 25, 1955

Season	Team	GP	G	A	Pts.	PIM
73-74	Tor (WHA)	71	30	35	65	13
74-75	Tor (WHA)	77	29	66	95	22
75-76	NYR	79	21	24	45	10
76-77	NYR	78	17	29	46	33
77-78	NYR	59	5	13	18	15
78-79	Birm (WHA)	64	12	27	39	43
79-80	Winn	13	0	0	0	2
NHL Totals		229	43	66	109	60
WHA Totals		212	71	128	199	78
NHL Playoff Totals		3	0	1	1	0
WHA Playoff Totals		18	9	10	19	13

DiMAIO, Robert (Rob) *5-8 175 C*
B. Calgary, Alta., Feb. 19, 1968

Season	Team	GP	G	A	Pts.	PIM
88-89	NYI	16	1	0	1	30
89-90	NYI	7	0	0	0	2
90-91	NYI	1	0	0	0	0
91-92	NYI	50	5	2	7	43
Totals		74	6	2	8	75
Playoff Totals		1	1	0	1	4

DINEEN, Gary Daniel Patrick *5-10 175 C*
B. Montreal, Que., Dec. 24, 1943

Season	Team	GP	G	A	Pts.	PIM
68-69	Minn	4	0	1	1	0

DINEEN, Gordon *6-0 195 D*
B. Quebec City, Que., Sept. 21, 1962

Season	Team	GP	G	A	Pts.	PIM
82-83	NYI	2	0	0	0	4
83-84	NYI	43	1	11	12	32
84-85	NYI	48	1	12	13	89
85-86	NYI	57	1	8	9	81
86-87	NYI	71	4	10	14	110
87-88	NYI-Minn	70	5	13	18	83
88-89	Minn-Pitt	40	1	3	4	44
89-90	Pitt	69	1	8	9	125

DINEEN, Gordon *(Continued)*

Season	Team	GP	G	A	Pts.	PIM
90-91	Pitt	9	0	0	0	4
91-92	Pitt	1	0	0	0	0
Totals		410	14	65	79	572
Playoff Totals		40	1	7	8	68

DINEEN, Kevin *5-11 195 RW*
B. Quebec City, Que., Oct. 28, 1963

Season	Team	GP	G	A	Pts.	PIM
84-85	Hart	57	25	16	41	120
85-86	Hart	57	33	35	68	124
86-87	Hart	78	40	39	79	110
87-88	Hart	74	25	25	50	217
88-89	Hart	79	45	44	89	167
89-90	Hart	67	25	41	66	164
90-91	Hart	61	17	30	47	104
91-92	Hart-Phil	80	30	32	62	143
Totals		553	240	262	502	1149
Playoff Totals		38	17	14	31	101

DINEEN, Peter Kevin *5-11 190 D*
B. Kingston, Ont., Nov. 19, 1960

Season	Team	GP	G	A	Pts.	PIM
86-87	LA	11	0	2	2	8
89-90	Det	2	0	0	0	5
Totals		13	0	2	2	13

DINEEN, William Patrick *5-11 180 RW*
B. Arvida, Que., Sept. 18, 1932

Season	Team	GP	G	A	Pts.	PIM
53-54	Det	70	17	8	25	34
54-55	Det	69	10	9	19	36
55-56	Det	70	12	7	19	30
56-57	Det	51	6	7	13	12
57-58	Det-Chi	63	6	13	19	12
Totals		323	51	44	95	124
Playoff Totals		37	1	1	2	18

DINSMORE, Charles A. (Chuck, Dinny) *F*
B. Toronto, Ont., July 23, 1903

Season	Team	GP	G	A	Pts.	PIM
24-25	Mont M	30	2	1	3	26
25-26	Mont M	33	3	1	4	18
26-27	Mont M	28	1	0	1	6
29-30	Mont M	9	0	0	0	0
Totals		100	6	2	8	50
Playoff Totals		12	1	0	1	16

DIONNE, Gilbert *6-0 194 LW*
B. Drummondville, Que., Sept. 19, 1970

Season	Team	GP	G	A	Pts.	PIM
90-91	Mont	2	0	0	0	0
91-92	Mont	39	21	13	34	10
Totals		41	21	13	34	10
Playoff Totals		11	3	4	7	10

DIONNE, Marcel Elphege *5-8 185 C*
B. Drummondville, Que., Aug. 3, 1951

Season	Team	GP	G	A	Pts.	PIM
71-72	Det	78	28	49	77	14
72-73	Det	77	40	50	90	21
73-74	Det	74	24	54	78	10
74-75	Det	80	47	74	121	14
75-76	LA	80	40	54	94	38
76-77	LA	80	53	69	122	12
77-78	LA	70	36	43	79	37
78-79	LA	80	59	71	130	30
79-80	LA	80	53	84	137	32
80-81	LA	80	58	77	135	70
81-82	LA	78	50	67	117	50
82-83	LA	80	56	51	107	22
83-84	LA	66	39	53	92	28
84-85	LA	80	46	80	126	46
85-86	LA	80	36	58	94	42
86-87	LA-NYR	81	28	56	84	60
87-88	NYR	67	31	34	65	54
88-89	NYR	37	7	16	23	20
Totals		1348	731	1040	1771	600
Playoff Totals		49	21	24	45	17

DI PIETRO, Paul *5-9 181 C*
B. Sault Ste. Marie, Ont., Sept 8, 1970

Season	Team	GP	G	A	Pts.	PIM
91-92	Mont	33	4	6	10	25

DIRK, Robert *6-4 205 D*
B. Regina, Sask., Aug. 20, 1966

Season	Team	GP	G	A	Pts.	PIM
87-88	StL	7	0	1	1	16
88-89	StL	9	0	1	1	11
89-90	StL	37	1	1	2	128
90-91	StL-Van	52	2	3	5	120
91-92	Van	72	2	7	9	126
Totals		177	5	13	18	401
Playoff Totals		28	0	1	1	35

DJOOS, Per *5-11 170 D*
B. Mora, Sweden, May 11, 1968

Season	Team	GP	G	A	Pts.	PIM
90-91	Det	26	0	12	12	16
91-92	NYR	50	1	18	19	40
Totals		76	1	30	31	56

DOAK, Gary Walter 5-11 191 D
B. Goderich, Ont., Feb. 26, 1946

Season	Team	GP	G	A	Pts.	PIM
65-66	Det-Bos	24	0	8	8	40
66-67	Bos	29	0	1	1	50
67-68	Bos	59	2	10	12	100
68-69	Bos	22	3	3	6	37
69-70	Bos	44	1	7	8	63
70-71	Van	77	2	10	12	112
71-72	Van-NYR	55	1	11	12	46
72-73	Det-Bos	49	0	5	5	53
73-74	Bos	69	0	4	4	44
74-75	Bos	40	0	0	0	30
75-76	Bos	58	1	6	7	60
76-77	Bos	76	3	13	16	107
77-78	Bos	61	4	13	17	50
78-79	Bos	63	6	11	17	28
79-80	Bos	52	0	5	5	45
80-81	Bos	11	0	0	0	12
Totals		789	23	107	130	877
Playoff Totals		78	2	4	6	121

DOBBIN, Brian 5-11 205 RW
B. Petrolia, Ont., Aug. 18, 1966

Season	Team	GP	G	A	Pts.	PIM
86-87	Phil	12	2	1	3	14
87-88	Phil	21	3	5	8	6
88-89	Phil	14	0	1	1	8
89-90	Phil	9	1	1	2	11
91-92	Bos	7	1	0	1	22
Totals		63	7	8	15	61
Playoff Totals		2	0	0	0	17

DOBSON, James 6-1 176 RW
B. Winnipeg, Man., Feb. 29, 1960

Season	Team	GP	G	A	Pts.	PIM
79-80	Minn	1	0	0	0	0
80-81	Minn	1	0	0	0	0
81-82	Minn-Col	9	0	0	0	6
Totals		11	0	0	0	6

DOHERTY, Fredrick F

Season	Team	GP	G	A	Pts.	PIM
18-19	Mont M	3	0	0	0	0

DOLLAS, Bobby 6-2 212 D
B. Montreal, Que., Jan. 31, 1965

Season	Team	GP	G	A	Pts.	PIM
83-84	Winn	1	0	0	0	0
84-85	Winn	9	0	0	0	0
85-86	Winn	46	0	5	5	66
87-88	Que	9	0	0	0	2
88-89	Que	16	0	3	3	16
90-91	Det	56	3	5	8	20
91-92	Det	27	3	1	4	20
Totals		164	6	14	20	124
Playoff Totals		12	1	1	2	15

DOMI, Tahir (Tie) 5-10 200 RW
B. Windsor, Ont., Nov. 1 1969

Season	Team	GP	G	A	Pts.	PIM
89-90	Tor	2	0	0	0	42
90-91	NYR	28	1	0	1	185
91-92	NYR	46	2	4	6	246
Totals		76	3	4	7	473

DONALDSON, Robert Gary (Gary) F
B. Trail, B.C., July 15, 1952

Season	Team	GP	G	A	Pts.	PIM
73-74	Chi	1	0	0	0	0
76-77	Hou (WHA)	5	0	0	0	6

DONATELLI, Clark 5-10 190 LW
B. Providence, R.I., Nov. 22, 1965

Season	Team	GP	G	A	Pts.	PIM
89-90	Minn	25	3	3	6	17
91-92	Bos	10	0	1	1	22
Totals		35	3	4	7	39
Playoff Totals		2	0	0	0	0

DONATO, Ted 5-10 170 C
B. Dedham, Mass., Apr. 18, 1968

Season	Team	GP	G	A	Pts.	PIM
91-92	Bos	10	1	2	3	8
Playoff Totals		15	3	4	7	4

DONNELLY, Babe D
B. Sault Ste. Marie, Ont., Dec. ??, 1906

Season	Team	GP	G	A	Pts.	PIM
26-27	Mont M	34	0	1	1	14
Playoff Totals		2	0	0	0	0

DONNELLY, David 5-11 185 C
B. Edmonton, Alta., Feb. 2, 1962

Season	Team	GP	G	A	Pts.	PIM
83-84	Bos	16	3	4	7	2
84-85	Bos	38	6	8	14	46
85-86	Bos	8	0	0	0	17
86-87	Chi	71	6	12	18	81
87-88	Edm	4	0	0	0	4
Totals		137	15	24	39	150
Playoff Totals		5	0	0	0	0

DONNELLY, Gordon 6-1 202 RW
B. Montreal, Que., Apr. 5, 1962

Season	Team	GP	G	A	Pts.	PIM
83-84	Que	38	0	5	5	60
84-85	Que	22	0	0	0	33

DONNELLY, Gordon (Continued)

Season	Team	GP	G	A	Pts.	PIM
85-86	Que	36	2	2	4	85
86-87	Que	38	0	2	2	143
87-88	Que	63	4	3	7	301
88-89	Que-Winn	73	10	10	20	274
89-90	Winn	55	3	3	6	222
90-91	Winn	57	3	4	7	265
91-92	Winn-Buf	71	2	3	5	316
Totals		453	24	32	56	1699
Playoff Totals		26	0	2	2	61

DONNELLY, Mike 5-11 185 LW
B. Detroit, Mich., Oct. 10, 1963

Season	Team	GP	G	A	Pts.	PIM
86-87	NYR	5	1	1	2	0
87-88	NYR-Buf	57	8	10	18	52
88-89	Buf	22	4	6	10	10
89-90	Buf	12	1	2	3	8
90-91	LA	53	7	5	12	41
91-92	LA	80	29	16	45	20
Totals		229	50	40	90	131
Playoff Totals		18	6	4	10	10

DORAN, John Michael (Red) 6-0 195 D
B. Belleville, Ont., May 24, 1911

Season	Team	GP	G	A	Pts.	PIM
33-34	NYA	39	1	4	5	40
35-36	NYA	25	4	2	6	44
36-37	NYA	21	0	1	1	10
37-38	Det	7	0	0	0	10
39-40	Mont	6	0	3	3	6
Totals		98	5	10	15	110
Playoff Totals		3	0	0	0	0

DORAN, Lloyd George (Red) 6-0 175 C
B. South Porcupine, Ont., Jan. 10, 1921

Season	Team	GP	G	A	Pts.	PIM
46-47	Det	24	3	2	5	10

DORATY, Kenneth Edward 5-7 133 F
B. Stittsville, Ont., June 23, 1906

Season	Team	GP	G	A	Pts.	PIM
26-27	Chi	18	0	0	0	0
32-33	Tor	38	5	11	16	16
33-34	Tor	34	9	10	19	6
34-35	Tor	11	1	4	5	0
37-38	Det	2	0	1	1	2
Totals		103	15	26	41	24
Playoff Totals		15	7	2	9	2

DORE, Andre Hector 6-2 200 D
B. Montreal, Que., Feb. 11, 1958

Season	Team	GP	G	A	Pts.	PIM
78-79	NYR	2	0	0	0	0
79-80	NYR	2	0	0	0	0
80-81	NYR	15	1	3	4	15
81 82	NYR	56	4	16	20	64
82-83	NYR-StL	77	5	27	32	64
83-84	StL-Que	80	4	28	32	83
84-85	NYR	25	0	7	7	35
Totals		257	14	81	95	261
Playoff Totals		23	1	2	3	32

DORE, Daniel 6-3 202 RW
B. Ferme-Neuve, Que., Apr. 9, 1970

Season	Team	GP	G	A	Pts.	PIM
89-90	Que	16	2	3	5	59
90-91	Que	1	0	0	0	0
Totals		17	2	3	5	59

DOREY, Robert James (Jim) 6-1 190 D
B. Kingston, Ont., Aug. 17, 1947

Season	Team	GP	G	A	Pts.	PIM
68-69	Tor	61	8	22	30	200
69-70	Tor	46	6	11	17	99
70-71	Tor	74	7	22	29	198
71-72	Tor-NYR	51	4	19	23	56
72-73	NE (WHA)	75	7	56	63	95
73-74	NE (WHA)	77	6	40	46	134
74-75	NE-Tor (WHA)	74	16	40	56	112
75-76	Tor (WHA)	74	9	51	60	134
76-77	Que (WHA)	73	13	34	47	102
77-78	Que (WHA)	26	1	9	10	23
78-79	Que (WHA)	32	0	2	2	17
NHL Totals		232	25	74	99	553
WHA Totals		431	52	232	284	617
NHL Playoff Totals		11	0	2	2	40
WHA Playoff Totals		51	5	33	38	131

DORION, Dan 5-9 180 C
B. Astoria, N.Y., Mar. 2, 1963

Season	Team	GP	G	A	Pts.	PIM
85-86	NJ	3	1	1	2	0
87-88	NJ	1	0	0	0	2
Totals		4	1	1	2	2

DORNHOEFER, Gerhardt Otto (Gary) 6-1 190 RW
B. Kitchener, Ont., Feb. 2, 1943

Season	Team	GP	G	A	Pts.	PIM
63-64	Bos	32	12	10	22	20
64-65	Bos	20	0	1	1	13
65-66	Bos	10	0	1	1	2
67-68	Phil	65	13	30	43	134

DORNHOEFER, Gerhardt Otto (Gary) (Continued)

Season	Team	GP	G	A	Pts.	PIM
68-69	Phil	60	8	16	24	80
69-70	Phil	65	26	29	55	96
70-71	Phil	57	20	20	40	93
71-72	Phil	75	17	32	49	183
72-73	Phil	77	30	49	79	168
73-74	Phil	57	11	39	50	125
74-75	Phil	69	17	27	44	102
75-76	Phil	74	28	35	63	128
76-77	Phil	79	25	34	59	85
77-78	Phil	47	7	5	12	62
Totals		787	214	328	542	1291
Playoff Totals		80	17	19	36	203

DOROHOY, Edward 5-9 150 C
B. Medicine Hat, Alta., Mar. 13, 1929

Season	Team	GP	G	A	Pts.	PIM
48-49	Mont	16	0	0	0	6

DOUGLAS, Jordy Paul 6-0 200 LW
B. Winnipeg, Man., Jan. 20, 1958

Season	Team	GP	G	A	Pts.	PIM
78-79	NE(WHA)	51	6	10	16	15
79-80	Hart	77	33	24	57	39
80-81	Hart	55	13	9	22	29
81-82	Hart	30	10	7	17	44
82-83	Minn	68	13	14	27	30
83-84	Minn-Winn	31	7	6	13	18
84-85	Winn	7	0	2	2	0
NHL Totals		268	76	62	138	160
WHA Totals		51	6	10	16	15
NHL Playoff Totals		6	0	0	0	4

DOUGLAS, Kent Gemmell 5-10 189 D
B. Cobalt, Ont., Feb 6, 1936

Season	Team	GP	G	A	Pts.	PIM
62-63	Tor	70	7	15	22	105
63-64	Tor	43	0	1	1	29
64-65	Tor	67	5	23	28	129
65-66	Tor	64	6	14	20	97
66-67	Tor	39	2	12	14	48
67-68	Oak-Det	76	11	21	32	126
68-69	Det	69	2	29	31	97
72-73	NY (WHA)	60	3	15	18	74
NHL Totals		428	33	115	148	631
WHA Totals		60	3	15	18	74
NHL Playoff Totals		19	1	3	4	33

DOUGLAS, Leslie Gordon (Les) 5-9 165 C
B. Perth, Ont., Dec. 5, 1918

Season	Team	GP	G	A	Pts.	PIM
40-41	Det	18	1	2	3	2
42-43	Det	21	5	8	13	4
45-46	Det	1	0	0	0	0
46-47	Det	12	0	2	2	2
Totals		52	6	12	18	8
Playoff Totals		10	3	2	5	0

DOURIS, Peter 6-1 195 RW
B. Toronto, Ont., Feb. 19, 1966

Season	Team	GP	G	A	Pts.	PIM
85-86	Winn	11	0	0	0	0
86-87	Winn	6	0	0	0	0
87-88	Winn	4	0	2	2	0
89-90	Bos	36	5	6	11	15
90-91	Bos	39	5	2	7	9
91-92	Bos	54	10	13	23	10
Totals		150	20	23	43	34
Playoff Totals		23	2	5	7	16

DOWD, James 6-1 185 RW
B. Brick, N.J., Dec. 25, 1968

Season	Team	GP	G	A	Pts.	PIM
91-92	NJ	1	0	0	0	0

DOWNIE, David M. 5-7 168 C
B. Burke's Falls, Ont., Mar. 11, 1909

Season	Team	GP	G	A	Pts.	PIM
32-33	Tor	11	0	1	1	2

DOYON, Mario 6-0 174 D
B. Quebec City, Que., Aug. 27, 1968

Season	Team	GP	G	A	Pts.	PIM
88-89	Chi	7	1	1	2	6
89-90	Que	9	2	3	5	6
91-92	Chi	12	0	0	0	4
Totals		28	3	4	7	16

DRAPER, Bruce 5-10 157 F
B. Toronto, Ont., Oct. 2, 1940

Season	Team	GP	G	A	Pts.	PIM
62-63	Tor	1	0	0	0	0

DRAPER, Kris 5-11 190 C
B. Toronto, Ont., May 24, 1971

Season	Team	GP	G	A	Pts.	PIM
90-91	Winn	3	1	0	1	5
91-92	Winn	10	2	0	2	2
Totals		13	3	0	3	7
Playoff Totals		2	0	0	0	0

DRILLON, Gordon Arthur 6-2 178 LW
B. Moncton, N.B., Oct. 23, 1914

Season	Team	GP	G	A	Pts.	PIM
36-37	Tor	41	16	17	33	2

DRILLON, Gordon Arthur *(Continued)*

Season	Team	GP	G	A	Pts.	PIM
37-38	Tor	48	26	26	52	4
38-39	Tor	40	18	16	34	15
39-40	Tor	43	21	19	40	13
40-41	Tor	42	23	21	44	2
41-42	Tor	48	23	18	41	6
42-43	Mont	49	28	22	50	14
Totals		311	155	139	294	56
Playoff Totals		50	26	15	41	10

DRISCOLL, Peter John (Drisk) *6-0 190 LW*
B. Kingston, Ont., Oct 27, 1954

Season	Team	GP	G	A	Pts.	PIM
74-75	Van(WHA)	21	3	2	5	40
75-76	Calg(WHA)	75	16	18	34	127
76-77	Calg(WHA)	76	23	29	52	120
77-78	Que-Ind(WHA)	77	28	28	56	158
78-79	Ind-Edm(WHA)	77	20	24	44	132
79-80	Edm	39	1	5	6	54
80-81	Edm	21	2	3	5	43
NHL Totals		60	3	8	11	97
WHA Totals		326	90	101	191	577
NHL Playoff Totals		3	0	0	0	0
WHA Playoff Totals		23	3	11	14	49

DRIVER, Bruce *6-0 185 D*
B. Toronto, Ont., Apr. 29, 1962

Season	Team	GP	G	A	Pts.	PIM
83-84	NJ	4	0	2	2	0
84-85	NJ	67	9	23	32	36
85-86	NJ	40	3	15	18	32
86-87	NJ	74	6	28	34	36
87-88	NJ	74	15	40	55	68
88-89	NJ	27	1	15	16	24
89-90	NJ	75	7	46	53	63
90-91	NJ	73	9	36	45	62
91-92	NJ	78	7	35	42	66
Totals		512	57	240	297	387
Playoff Totals		40	5	18	23	34

DROLET, Rene Georges *5-7 155 RW*
B. Quebec City, Que., Nov. 13, 1944

Season	Team	GP	G	A	Pts.	PIM
71-72	Phil	1	0	0	0	0
74-75	Det	1	0	0	0	0
Totals		2	0	0	0	0

DROUILLARD, Clarence Joseph (Clare) *5-7 150 C*
B. Windsor, Ont., Mar. 2, 1914

Season	Team	GP	G	A	Pts.	PIM
37-38	Det	10	0	1	1	0

DROUIN, Jude *5-9 165 C*
B. Mont-Louis, Que., Oct. 28, 1948

Season	Team	GP	G	A	Pts.	PIM
68-69	Mont	9	0	1	1	0
69-70	Mont	3	0	0	0	2
70-71	Minn	75	16	52	68	49
71-72	Minn	63	13	43	56	31
72-73	Minn	78	27	46	73	61
73-74	Minn	65	19	24	43	30
74-75	Minn-NYI	78	18	36	54	22
75-76	NYI	76	21	41	62	58
76-77	NYI	78	24	29	53	27
77-78	NYI	56	5	17	22	12
79-80	Winn	78	8	16	24	50
80-81	Winn	7	0	0	0	4
Totals		666	151	305	456	346
Playoff Totals		72	27	41	68	33

DROUIN, Emile Paul (Polly) *5-7 160 LW*
B. Verdun, Que., Jan. 1916

Season	Team	GP	G	A	Pts.	PIM
35-36	Mont	30	1	8	9	19
36-37	Mont	4	0	0	0	0
37-38	Mont	31	7	13	20	8
38-39	Mont	28	7	11	18	2
39-40	Mont	42	4	11	15	51
40-41	Mont	21	4	7	11	0
Totals		156	23	50	73	80
Playoff Totals		5	0	1	1	5

DRUCE, John *6-2 200 RW*
B. Peterbrough, Ont., Feb. 23, 1966

Season	Team	GP	G	A	Pts.	PIM
88-89	Wash	48	8	7	15	62
89-90	Wash	45	8	3	11	52
90-91	Wash	80	22	36	58	46
91-92	Wash	57	19	18	37	39
Totals		240	57	64	121	199
Playoff Totals		34	16	4	20	32

DRUMMOND, John S. *D*
B. Toronto, Ont., Oct. 20, 1918

Season	Team	GP	G	A	Pts.	PIM
44-45	NYR	2	0	0	0	0

DRURY, Herbert *5-7 165 F*
B. 1895

Season	Team	GP	G	A	Pts.	PIM
25-26	Pitt Pi	33	6	2	8	40
26-27	Pitt Pi	42	5	1	6	48

DRURY, Herbert *(Continued)*

Season	Team	GP	G	A	Pts.	PIM
27-28	Pitt Pi	43	6	4	10	44
28-29	Pitt Pi	44	5	4	9	49
29-30	Pitt Pi	27	2	0	2	12
30-31	Phil Q	24	0	2	2	10
Totals		213	24	13	37	203
Playoff Totals		4	1	1	2	0

DUBE, Joseph Gilles (Gilles) *5-10 165 LW*
B. Sherbrooke, Que., June 2, 1927

Season	Team	GP	G	A	Pts.	PIM
49-50	Mont	12	1	2	3	2
Playoff Totals		2	0	0	0	0

DUBE, Normand G. (Norm) *5-11 185 LW*
B. Sherbrooke, Que., Sept. 12, 1951

Season	Team	GP	G	A	Pts.	PIM
74-75	KC	56	8	10	18	54
75-76	KC	1	0	0	0	0
76-77	Que(WHA)	39	15	18	33	8
77-78	Que(WHA)	73	16	31	47	17
78-79	Que(WHA)	36	2	13	15	4
NHL Totals		57	8	10	18	54
WHA Totals		148	33	62	95	29
WHA Playoff Totals		24	5	14	19	17

DUCHESNE, Gaetan *5-11 197 LW*
B. Quebec City, Que., July 11, 1962

Season	Team	GP	G	A	Pts.	PIM
81-82	Wash	74	9	14	23	46
82-83	Wash	77	18	19	37	52
83-84	Wash	79	17	19	36	29
84-85	Wash	67	15	23	38	32
85-86	Wash	80	11	28	39	39
86-87	Wash	74	17	35	52	53
87-88	Que	80	24	23	47	83
88-89	Que	70	8	21	29	56
89-90	Minn	72	12	8	20	33
90-91	Minn	68	9	9	18	18
91-92	Minn	73	8	15	23	102
Totals		814	148	214	362	543
Playoff Totals		70	13	9	22	85

DUCHESNE, Steve *5-11 195 D*
B. Sept-Iles, Que., June 30, 1965

Season	Team	GP	G	A	Pts.	PIM
86-87	LA	75	13	25	38	74
87-88	LA	71	16	39	55	109
88-89	LA	79	25	50	75	92
89-90	LA	79	20	42	62	36
90-91	LA	78	21	41	62	66
91-92	Phil	78	18	38	56	86
Totals		460	113	235	348	463
Playoff Totals		43	13	26	39	44

DUDLEY, Richard Clarence (Rick And Duds) *6-0 190 LW*
B. Toronto, Ont., Jan. 31, 1949

Season	Team	GP	G	A	Pts.	PIM
72-73	Buf	6	0	1	1	7
73-74	Buf	67	13	13	26	71
74-75	Buf	78	31	39	70	116
75-76	Cin (WHA)	74	43	38	81	156
76-77	Cin (WHA)	77	41	47	88	102
77-78	Cin (WHA)	72	30	41	71	156
78-79	Cin (WHA)	47	17	20	37	102
78-79	Buf	24	5	6	11	2
79-80	Buf	66	11	22	33	58
80-81	Buf-Winn	68	15	18	33	38
NHL Totals		309	75	99	174	292
WHA Totals		270	131	146	277	516
NHL Playoff Totals		25	7	2	9	69
WHA Playoff Totals		4	0	1	1	7

DUFF, Terrance Richard (Dick) *5-9 166 LW*
B. Kirkland Lake, Ont., Feb. 18, 1936

Season	Team	GP	G	A	Pts.	PIM
54-55	Tor	3	0	0	0	2
55-56	Tor	69	18	19	37	74
56-57	Tor	70	26	14	40	50
57-58	Tor	65	26	23	49	79
58-59	Tor	69	29	24	53	73
59-60	Tor	67	19	22	41	51
60-61	Tor	67	16	17	33	54
61-62	Tor	51	17	20	37	37
62-63	Tor	69	16	19	35	56
63-64	Tor-NYR	66	11	14	25	61
64-65	NYR-Mont	69	12	16	28	36
65-66	Mont	63	21	24	45	78
66-67	Mont	51	12	11	23	23
67-68	Mont	66	25	21	46	21
68-69	Mont	68	19	21	40	55
69-70	Mont-LA	49	6	9	15	12
70-71	LA-Buf	60	8	13	21	12
71-72	Buf	8	2	2	4	0
Totals		1030	283	289	572	774
Playoff Totals		114	30	49	79	78

DUFOUR, Luc *5-11 180 LW*
B. Chicoutimi, Que., Feb. 13, 1963

Season	Team	GP	G	A	Pts.	PIM
82-83	Bos	73	14	11	25	107
83-84	Bos	41	6	4	10	47
84-85	Que-StL	53	3	6	9	45
Totals		167	23	21	44	199
Playoff Totals		18	1	0	1	32

DUFOUR, Marc *6-0 175 RW*
B. Trois Rivieres, Que., Sept. 11, 1941

Season	Team	GP	G	A	Pts.	PIM
63-64	NYR	10	1	0	1	2
64-65	NYR	2	0	0	0	0
68-69	LA	2	0	0	0	0
Totals		14	1	0	1	2

DUFRESNE, Donald *6-1 206 D*
B. Rimouski, Que., Apr. 10, 1967

Season	Team	GP	G	A	Pts.	PIM
88-89	Mont	13	0	1	1	43
89-90	Mont	18	0	4	4	23
90-91	Mont	53	2	13	15	55
91-92	Mont	3	0	0	0	2
Totals		87	2	18	20	123
Playoff Totals		26	1	3	4	43

DUGGAN, James (Jack) *D*

Season	Team	GP	G	A	Pts.	PIM
25-26	Ott	27	0	0	0	0
Playoff Totals		2	0	0	0	0

DUGGAN, Ken *6-3 210 D*
B. Toronto, Ont., Feb. 21, 1963

Season	Team	GP	G	A	Pts.	PIM
87-88	Minn	1	0	0	0	0

DUGUAY, Ronald *6-2 210 C*
B. Sudbury, Ont., July 6, 1957

Season	Team	GP	G	A	Pts.	PIM
77-78	NYR	71	20	20	40	43
78-79	NYR	79	27	36	63	35
79-80	NYR	73	28	22	50	37
80-81	NYR	50	17	21	38	83
81-82	NYR	72	40	36	76	82
82-83	NYR	72	19	25	44	58
83-84	Det	80	33	47	80	34
84-85	Det	80	38	51	89	51
85-86	Det-Pitt	80	24	36	61	32
86-87	Pitt-NYR	74	14	25	39	39
87-88	NYR-LA	63	6	10	16	40
88-89	LA	70	7	17	24	48
Totals		864	274	346	620	582
Playoff Totals		89	31	22	53	118

DUGUID, Lorne Wallace *5-11 185 LW*
B. Bolton, Ont., Apr. 4, 1910

Season	Team	GP	G	A	Pts.	PIM
31-32	Mont M	13	0	0	0	6
32-33	Mont M	48	4	7	11	38
33-34	Mont M	5	0	1	1	0
34-35	Det	34	3	3	6	9
35-36	Det-Bos	34	1	4	5	2
36-37	Bos	1	1	0	1	2
Totals		135	9	15	24	57
Playoff Totals		2	0	0	0	4

DUMART, Woodrow Wilson Clarence (Woody, Porky) *6-1 200 LW*
B. Kitchener, Ont., Dec. 23, 1916

Season	Team	GP	G	A	Pts.	PIM
35-36	Bos	1	0	0	0	0
36-37	Bos	17	4	4	8	2
37-38	Bos	48	13	14	27	6
38-39	Bos	45	14	15	29	2
39-40	Bos	48	22	21	43	16
40-41	Bos	40	18	15	33	2
41-42	Bos	35	14	15	29	8
45-46	Bos	50	22	12	34	2
46-47	Bos	60	24	28	52	12
47-48	Bos	59	21	16	37	14
48-49	Bos	59	11	12	23	6
49-50	Bos	69	14	25	39	14
50-51	Bos	70	20	21	41	7
51-52	Bos	39	5	8	13	0
52-53	Bos	62	5	9	14	2
53-54	Bos	69	4	3	7	6
Totals		771	211	218	429	99
Playoff Totals		88	12	15	27	23

DUNBAR, Dale *6-0 200 D*
B. Winthrop, Mass., Oct. 14, 1961

Season	Team	GP	G	A	Pts.	PIM
85-86	Van	1	0	0	0	2
88-89	Bos	1	0	0	0	0
Totals		2	0	0	0	2

DUNCAN, Arthur *D*

Season	Team	GP	G	A	Pts.	PIM
26-27	Det	34	3	2	5	26
27-28	Tor	43	7	5	12	97
28-29	Tor	39	4	4	8	53
29-30	Tor	38	4	5	9	49
30-31	Tor	2	0	0	0	0
Totals		156	18	16	34	225
Playoff Totals		5	0	0	0	4

DUNCAN, Iain *6-1 200 LW*

B. Weston, Ont., Aug. 4, 1963

Season	Team	GP	G	A	Pts.	PIM
86-87	Winn	6	1	2	3	0
87-88	Winn	62	19	23	42	73
88-89	Winn	57	14	30	44	74
90-91	Winn	2	0	0	0	2
Totals		127	34	55	89	149
Playoff Totals		11	0	3	3	6

DUNCANSON, Craig *6-0 190 LW*

B. Sudbury, Ont., Mar. 17, 1967

Season	Team	GP	G	A	Pts.	PIM
85-86	LA	2	0	1	1	0
86-87	LA	2	0	0	0	24
87-88	LA	9	0	0	0	12
88-89	LA	5	0	0	0	0
89-90	LA	10	3	2	5	9
90-91	Winn	7	2	0	2	16
Totals		35	5	3	8	61

DUNDAS, Rocky *6-0 195 RW*

B. Regina, Sask., Jan. 30, 1967

Season	Team	GP	G	A	Pts.	PIM
89-90	Tor	5	0	0	0	14

DUNLOP, Blake Robert *5-10 170 C*

B. Hamilton, Ont., Apr. 4, 1953

Season	Team	GP	G	A	Pts.	PIM
73-74	Minn	12	0	0	0	2
74-75	Minn	52	9	18	27	8
75-76	Minn	33	9	11	20	8
76-77	Minn	3	0	1	1	0
77-78	Phil	3	0	1	1	0
78-79	Phil	66	20	28	48	16
79-80	StL	72	18	27	45	28
80-81	StL	80	20	67	87	40
81-82	StL	77	25	53	78	32
82-83	StL	78	22	44	66	14
83-84	StL-Det	74	7	24	31	24
Totals		550	130	274	404	172
Playoff Totals		40	4	10	14	18

DUNLOP, Frank *F*

Season	Team	GP	G	A	Pts.	PIM
43-44	Tor	15	0	1	1	2

DUNN, David George *6-2 200 D*

B. Wapella, Sask., Aug. 19, 1948

Season	Team	GP	G	A	Pts.	PIM
73-74	Van	68	11	22	33	76
74-75	Van-Tor	73	3	11	14	153
75-76	Tor	43	0	8	8	84
76-77	Winn(WHA)	40	3	11	14	129
77-78	Winn(WHA)	66	6	20	26	79
NHL Totals		184	14	41	55	313
WHA Totals		106	9	31	40	208
NHL Playoff Totals		10	1	1	2	41
WHA Playoff Totals		29	5	6	11	23

DUNN, Richard L. *6-0 200 D*

B. Boston, Mass., May 12, 1957

Season	Team	GP	G	A	Pts.	PIM
77-78	Buf	25	0	3	3	16
78-79	Buf	24	0	3	3	14
79-80	Buf	80	7	31	38	61
80-81	Buf	79	7	42	49	34
81-82	Buf	72	7	19	26	73
82-83	Calg	80	3	11	14	47
83-84	Hart	63	5	20	25	30
84-85	Hart	13	1	4	5	2
85-86	Buf	29	4	5	9	25
86-87	Buf	2	0	1	1	2
87-88	Buf	12	2	0	2	8
88-89	Buf	4	0	1	1	2
Totals		483	36	140	176	314
Playoff Totals		36	3	15	18	24

DUPERE, Denis Gilles *6-1 200 LW*

B. Jonquiere, Que., June 21, 1948

Season	Team	GP	G	A	Pts.	PIM
70-71	Tor	20	1	2	3	4
71-72	Tor	77	7	10	17	4
72-73	Tor	61	13	23	36	10
73-74	Tor	34	8	9	17	8
74-75	Wash-StL	75	23	21	44	16
75-76	KC	43	6	8	14	16
76-77	Col	57	7	11	18	4
77-78	Col	54	15	15	30	4
Totals		421	80	99	179	66
Playoff Totals		16	1	0	1	0

DUPONT, Andre (Moose) *6-0 200 D*

B. Trois-Rivieres, Que., July 27, 1949

Season	Team	GP	G	A	Pts.	PIM
70-71	NYR	7	1	2	3	21
71-72	StL	60	3	10	13	147
72-73	StL-Phil	71	4	26	30	215
73-74	Phil	75	3	20	23	216
74-75	Phil	80	11	21	32	276
75-76	Phil	75	9	27	36	214
76-77	Phil	69	10	19	29	168
77-78	Phil	69	2	12	14	225
78-79	Phil	77	3	9	12	135
79-80	Phil	58	1	7	8	107
80-81	Que	63	5	8	13	93

DUPONT, Andre (Moose) *(Continued)*

Season	Team	GP	G	A	Pts.	PIM
81-82	Que	60	4	12	16	100
82-83	Que	46	3	12	15	69
Totals		810	59	185	244	1986
Playoff Totals		140	14	18	32	352

DUPONT, Jerome *6-3 190 D*

B. Ottawa, Ont., Feb. 21, 1962

Season	Team	GP	G	A	Pts.	PIM
81-82	Chi	34	0	4	4	51
82-83	Chi	1	0	0	0	0
83-84	Chi	36	2	2	4	116
84-85	Chi	55	3	10	13	105
85-86	Chi	75	2	13	15	173
86-87	Tor	13	0	0	0	23
Totals		214	7	29	36	468
Playoff Totals		20	0	2	2	56

DUPONT, Normand *5-10 185 LW*

B. Montreal, Que., Feb. 5, 1957

Season	Team	GP	G	A	Pts.	PIM
79-80	Mont	35	1	3	4	4
80-81	Winn	80	27	26	53	8
81-82	Winn	62	13	25	38	22
82-83	Winn	39	7	16	23	6
83-84	Hart	40	7	15	22	12
Totals		256	55	85	140	52
Playoff Totals		13	4	2	6	0

DUPRE, Yanic *6-0 189 LW*

B. Montreal, Que., Nov. 20, 1972

Season	Team	GP	G	A	Pts.	PIM
91-92	Phil	1	0	0	0	0

DURBANO, Harry Steven (Steve) *6-1 210 D*

B. Toronto, Ont., Dec. 12, 1951

Season	Team	GP	G	A	Pts.	PIM
72-73	StL	49	3	18	21	231
73-74	StL-Pitt	69	8	19	27	284
74-75	Pitt	1	0	1	1	10
75-76	Pitt-KC	69	1	19	20	370
76-77	Col	19	0	2	2	129
77-78	Birm (WHA)	45	6	4	10	284
78-79	StL	13	1	1	2	103
NHL Totals		220	13	60	73	1127
WHA Totals		45	6	4	10	284
NHL Playoff Totals		5	0	2	2	8
WHA Playoff Totals		4	0	2	2	16

DURIS, Vitezslav *6-1 185 D*

B. Pizen, Czechoslovakia, Jan. 5, 1954

Season	Team	GP	G	A	Pts.	PIM
80-81	Tor	57	1	12	13	50
82-83	Tor	32	2	8	10	12
Totals		89	3	20	23	62
Playoff Totals		3	0	1	1	2

DUSSAULT, Joseph Normand (Norm) *5-7 165 C*

B. Springfield, Mass., Sept. 26, 1925

Season	Team	GP	G	A	Pts.	PIM
47-48	Mont	28	5	10	15	4
48-49	Mont	47	9	8	17	6
49-50	Mont	67	13	24	37	22
50-51	Mont	64	4	20	24	15
Totals		206	31	62	93	47
Playoff Totals		7	3	1	4	0

DUTKOWSKI, Laudas Joseph (Duke) *5-10 185 D*

B. Regina, Sask., Aug. 30, 1902

Season	Team	GP	G	A	Pts.	PIM
26-27	Chi	28	3	2	5	16
29-30	Chi	44	7	10	17	42
30-31	Chi-NYA	37	2	4	6	40
32-33	NYA	48	4	7	11	43
33-34	NYA-Chi-NYR	43	0	7	7	31
Totals		200	16	30	46	172
Playoff Totals		6	0	0	0	6

DUTTON, Mervyn A. (Red) *6-0 185 D*

B. Russell, Man., July 23, 1898

Season	Team	GP	G	A	Pts.	PIM
26-27	Mont M	44	4	4	8	108
27-28	Mont M	42	7	6	13	94
28-29	Mont M	44	1	3	4	139
29-30	Mont M	43	3	13	16	98
30-31	NYA	44	1	11	12	71
31-32	NYA	47	3	5	8	107
32-33	NYA	43	0	2	2	74
33-34	NYA	48	2	8	10	65
34-35	NYA	48	3	7	10	46
35-36	NYA	46	5	8	13	69
Totals		449	29	67	96	871
Playoff Totals		18	1	0	1	33

DVORAK, Miroslav *5-10 195 D*

B. Htuboka nad Vitavou, Czech., Oct. 11, 1951

Season	Team	GP	G	A	Pts.	PIM
82-83	Phil	80	4	33	37	20

DVORAK, Miroslav *(Continued)*

Season	Team	GP	G	A	Pts.	PIM
83-84	Phil	66	4	27	31	27
84-85	Phil	47	3	14	17	4
Totals		193	11	74	85	51
Playoff Totals		18	0	2	2	6

DYKHUIS, Karl *6-2 184 D*

B. Sept-Iles, Que., July 8, 1972

Season	Team	GP	G	A	Pts.	PIM
91-92	Chi	6	1	3	4	4

DWYER, Michael *5-11 172 LW*

B. Brampton, Ont., Sept. 16, 1957

Season	Team	GP	G	A	Pts.	PIM
78-79	Col	12	2	3	5	2
79-80	Col	10	0	0	0	19
80-81	Calg	4	0	1	1	4
81-82	Calg	5	0	2	2	0
Totals		31	2	6	8	25
Playoff Totals		1	1	0	1	0

DYCK, Henry Richard *5-7 155 C*

B. Saskatoon, Sask., Sept. 5, 1911

Season	Team	GP	G	A	Pts.	PIM
43-44	NYR	1	0	0	0	0

DYE, Cecil Henry (Babe) *RW*

B. Hamilton, Ont., May 13, 1898

Season	Team	GP	G	A	Pts.	PIM
19-20	Tor	21	12	3	15	0
20-21	Ham-Tor	24	35	2	37	32
21-22	Tor	24	30	7	37	18
22-23	Tor	22	26	11	37	19
23-24	Tor	19	17	2	19	23
24-25	Tor	29	38	6	44	41
25-26	Tor	31	18	5	23	26
26-27	Chi	41	25	5	30	14
27-28	Chi	11	0	0	0	0
28-29	NYA	42	1	0	1	17
30-31	Tor	6	0	0	0	0
Totals		270	202	41	243	190
Playoff Totals		15	11	2	13	11

DYKSTRA, Steven *6-2 210 D*

B. Edmonton, Alta., Dec. 1, 1962

Season	Team	GP	G	A	Pts.	PIM
85-86	Buf	64	4	21	25	108
86-87	Buf	37	0	1	1	179
87-88	Buf-Edm	42	3	4	7	130
88-89	Pitt	65	1	6	7	126
89-90	Hart	9	0	0	0	2
Totals		217	8	32	40	545
Playoff Totals		1	0	0	0	2

DYTE, John Leonard (Jack) *6-0 D*

B. Kingston, Ont., Oct. 13, 1918

Season	Team	GP	G	A	Pts.	PIM
43-44	Chi	27	1	0	1	31

EAGLES, Michael *5-10 180 C*

B. Sussex, N.B., Mar. 7, 1963

Season	Team	GP	G	A	Pts.	PIM
82-83	Que	2	0	0	0	2
85-86	Que	73	11	12	23	49
86-87	Que	73	13	19	32	55
87-88	Que	76	10	10	20	74
88-89	Chi	47	5	11	16	44
89-90	Chi	23	1	2	3	34
90-91	Winn	44	0	9	9	79
91-92	Winn	65	7	10	17	118
Totals		403	47	73	120	455
Playoff Totals		14	1	0	1	20

EAKIN, Bruce Glen *5-11 190 C*

B. Winnipeg, Man., Sept. 18, 1962

Season	Team	GP	G	A	Pts.	PIM
81-82	Calg	1	0	0	0	0
83-84	Calg	7	2	1	3	4
84-85	Calg	1	0	0	0	0
85-86	Det	4	0	1	1	0
Totals		13	2	2	4	4

EATOUGH, Jeff *5-9 168 RW*

B. Toronto, Ont., June 2, 1963

Season	Team	GP	G	A	Pts.	PIM
81-82	Buf	1	0	0	0	0

EASTWOOD, Michael *6-2 190 C*

B. Ottawa, Ont., July 1, 1967

Season	Team	GP	G	A	Pts.	PIM
91-92	Tor	9	0	2	2	4

EAVES, Michael Gordon *5-10 180 C*

B. Denver, Colo., June 10, 1956

Season	Team	GP	G	A	Pts.	PIM
78-79	Minn	3	0	0	0	0
79-80	Minn	56	18	28	46	11
80-81	Minn	48	10	24	34	18
81-82	Minn	25	11	10	21	0
82-83	Minn	75	16	16	32	21
83-84	Calg	61	14	36	50	20
84-85	Calg	56	14	29	43	10
Totals		324	83	143	226	80
Playoff Totals		43	7	10	17	14

EAVES, Murray *5-10 185 C*

B. Calgary, Alta., May 10, 1960

Season	Team	GP	G	A	Pts.	PIM
80-81	Winn	12	1	2	3	5

EAVES, Murray *(Continued)*

Season	Team	GP	G	A	Pts.	PIM
81-82	Winn	2	0	0	0	0
82-83	Winn	26	2	7	9	2
83-84	Winn	2	0	0	0	0
84-85	Winn	3	0	3	3	0
85-86	Winn	4	1	0	1	0
87-88	Det	7	0	1	1	2
89-90	Det	1	0	0	0	0
Totals		57	4	13	17	9
Playoff Totals		4	0	1	1	2

ECCLESTONE, Timothy James *5-10 195 RW*
B. Toronto, Ont., Sept. 24, 1947

Season	Team	GP	G	A	Pts.	PIM
67-68	StL	50	6	8	14	36
68-69	StL	68	11	23	34	31
69-70	StL	65	16	21	37	59
70-71	StL-Det	74	19	34	53	47
71-72	Det	72	18	35	53	33
72-73	Det	78	18	30	48	28
73-74	Det-Tor	60	9	19	28	38
74-75	Tor-Atl	67	14	22	36	34
75-76	Atl	69	6	21	27	30
76-77	Atl	78	9	18	27	26
77-78	Atl	11	0	2	2	2
Totals		692	126	233	359	364
Playoff Totals		48	6	11	17	76

EDBERG, Rolf Arne *5-10 175 C*
B. Stockholm, Sweden, Sept. 29, 1950

Season	Team	GP	G	A	Pts.	PIM
78-79	Wash	76	14	27	41	6
79-80	Wash	63	23	56	46	12
80-81	Wash	45	8	8	16	6
Totals		184	45	58	103	24

EDDOLLS, Frank Herbert *5-8 180 D*
B. Lachine, Que., July 5, 1921

Season	Team	GP	G	A	Pts.	PIM
44-45	Mont	43	5	8	13	20
45-46	Mont	8	0	1	1	6
46-47	Mont	6	0	0	0	0
47-48	NYR	58	6	13	19	16
48-49	NYR	34	4	2	6	10
49-50	NYR	58	2	6	8	20
50-51	NYR	68	3	8	11	24
51-52	NYR	42	3	5	8	18
Totals		317	23	43	66	114
Playoff Totals		30	0	2	2	10

EDESTRAND, Darryl *5-11 185 D*
B. Strathroy, Ont., Nov. 6, 1945

Season	Team	GP	G	A	Pts.	PIM
67-68	StL	12	0	0	0	2
69-70	Phil	2	0	0	0	6
71-72	Pitt	77	10	23	33	52
72-73	Pitt	78	15	24	39	88
73-74	Pitt-Bos	55	3	8	11	20
74-75	Bos	68	1	9	10	56
75-76	Bos	77	4	17	21	103
76-77	Bos	17	0	3	3	16
77-78	Bos-LA	14	0	2	2	21
78-79	LA	55	1	4	5	46
Totals		455	34	90	124	410
Playoff Totals		42	3	9	12	57

EDMUNDSON, Garry Frank *6-0 173 LW*
B. Sexsmith, Alta., May 6, 1932

Season	Team	GP	G	A	Pts.	PIM
51-52	Mont	1	0	0	0	0
59-60	Tor	39	4	6	10	47
60-61	Tor	3	0	0	0	0
Totals		43	4	6	10	47
Totals		11	0	1	1	8

EDUR, Thomas *6-1 185 D*
B. Toronto, Ont., Nov. 18, 1954

Season	Team	GP	G	A	Pts.	PIM
73-74	Clev (WHA)	76	7	31	38	26
74-75	Clev (WHA)	61	3	20	23	28
75-76	Clev (WHA)	80	7	28	35	62
76-77	Col	80	7	25	32	39
77-78	Col-Pitt	78	10	45	55	28
NHL Totals		158	17	70	87	67
WHA Totals		217	17	79	96	116
WHA Playoff Totals		13	3	5	8	0

EGAN, Martin Joseph (Pat) *5-10 190 D*
B. Blackie, Alta., Apr. 25, 1918

Season	Team	GP	G	A	Pts.	PIM
39-40	NYA	10	4	3	7	6
40-41	NYA	39	4	9	13	51
41-42	NYA	48	8	20	28	124
42-43	Det-Bos	48	15	28	43	95
44-45	Bos	48	7	15	22	86
45-46	Bos	41	8	10	18	32
46-47	Bos	60	7	18	25	89
47-48	Bos	60	8	11	19	81
48-49	Bos	60	6	18	24	92
49-50	NYR	70	5	11	16	50
50-51	NYR	70	5	10	15	70
Totals		554	77	153	230	776

EGAN, Martin Joseph (Pat) *(Continued)*

Season	Team	GP	G	A	Pts.	PIM
Playoff Totals		44	9	4	13	44

EGERS, John Richard (Jack) *6-1 175 RW*
B. Sudbury, Ont., Jan. 28, 1949

Season	Team	GP	G	A	Pts.	PIM
69-70	NYR	6	3	0	3	2
70-71	NYR	60	7	10	17	50
71-72	NYR-StL	80	23	26	49	48
72-73	StL	78	24	24	48	26
73-74	StL-NYR	34	1	4	5	12
74-75	Wash	14	3	2	5	8
75-76	Wash	12	3	3	6	8
Totals		284	64	69	133	154
Playoff Totals		32	5	6	11	32

EHMAN, Gerald Joseph *6-0 190 RW*
B. Cudworth, Sask., Nov. 3, 1932

Season	Team	GP	G	A	Pts.	PIM
57-58	Bos	1	1	0	1	0
58-59	Det-Tor	44	12	14	26	16
59-60	Tor	69	12	16	28	26
60-61	Tor	14	1	1	2	2
63-64	Tor	4	1	1	2	0
67-68	Oak	73	19	25	44	20
68-69	Oak	70	21	24	45	12
69-70	Oak	76	11	19	30	8
70-71	Cal	78	18	18	36	16
Totals		429	96	118	214	100
Playoff Totals		41	10	10	20	12

EKLUND, Per-Erik (Pelle) *5-10 175 C*
B. Stockholm, Sweden, Mar. 22, 1963

Season	Team	GP	G	A	Pts.	PIM
85-86	Phil	70	15	51	66	12
86-87	Phil	72	14	41	55	2
87-88	Phil	71	10	32	42	12
88-89	Phil	79	18	51	69	23
89-90	Phil	70	23	39	62	16
90-91	Phil	73	19	50	69	14
91-92	Phil	51	7	16	23	4
Totals		486	106	280	386	83
Playoff Totals		57	10	33	43	4

ELDEBRINK, Anders *5-11 190 D*
B. Kalix, Sweden, Dec. 11, 1960

Season	Team	GP	G	A	Pts.	PIM
81-82	Van	38	1	8	9	21
82-83	Van-Que	17	2	3	5	8
Totals		55	3	11	14	29
Playoff Totals		14	0	0	0	10

ELIK, Boris (Bo) *5-10 190 LW*
B. Geraldton, Ont., Oct. 17, 1929

Season	Team	GP	G	A	Pts.	PIM
62-63	Det	3	0	0	0	0

ELIK, Todd *6-2 190 C*
B. Brampton, Ont., Apr. 15, 1966

Season	Team	GP	G	A	Pts.	PIM
89-90	LA	48	10	23	33	4
90-91	LA	74	21	37	58	58
91-92	Minn	62	15	31	46	125
Totals		184	46	91	137	187
Playoff Totals		27	6	17	23	18

ELLETT, David *6-1 200 D*
B. Cleveland, Ohio, Mar. 30, 1964

Season	Team	GP	G	A	Pts.	PIM
84-85	Winn	80	11	27	38	85
85-86	Winn	80	15	31	46	96
86-87	Winn	78	13	31	44	53
87-88	Winn	68	13	45	58	106
88-89	Winn	75	22	34	56	62
89-90	Winn	77	17	29	46	96
90-91	Winn-Tor	77	12	37	49	75
91-92	Tor	79	18	33	51	95
Totals		614	121	267	388	668
Playoff Totals		33	4	16	20	22

ELLIOT, Fred H. *F*

Season	Team	GP	G	A	Pts.	PIM
28-29	Ott	43	2	0	2	6

ELLIS, Ronald John Edward *5-9 195 RW*
B. Lindsay, Ont., Jan. 8, 1945

Season	Team	GP	G	A	Pts.	PIM
63-64	Tor	1	0	0	0	0
64-65	Tor	62	23	16	39	14
65-66	Tor	70	19	23	42	24
66-67	Tor	67	22	23	45	14
67-68	Tor	74	28	20	48	8
68-69	Tor	72	25	21	46	12
69-70	Tor	76	35	19	54	14
70-71	Tor	78	24	29	53	10
71-72	Tor	78	23	24	47	17
72-73	Tor	78	22	29	51	22
73-74	Tor	70	23	25	48	12
74-75	Tor	79	32	29	61	25
77-78	Tor	80	26	24	50	17
78-79	Tor	63	16	12	28	10
79-80	Tor	59	12	11	23	6
80-81	Tor	27	2	3	5	2
Totals		1034	332	308	640	207
Playoff Totals		70	18	8	26	20

ELORANTA, Karl *6-2 200 D*
B. Lahti, Finland, Feb. 29, 1956

Season	Team	GP	G	A	Pts.	PIM
81-82	Calg-StL	31	1	12	13	20
82-83	Calg	80	4	40	44	43
83-84	Calg	78	5	34	39	44
84-85	Calg	65	2	11	13	39
86-87	Calg	13	1	6	7	9
Totals		267	13	103	116	155
Playoff Totals		26	1	7	8	19

ELYNUIK, Pat *6-0 185 RW*
B. Foam Lake, Sask., Oct. 30, 1967

Season	Team	GP	G	A	Pts.	PIM
87-88	Winn	13	1	3	4	12
88-89	Winn	56	26	25	51	29
89-90	Winn	80	32	42	74	83
90-91	Winn	80	31	34	65	73
91-92	Winn	60	25	25	50	65
Totals		289	115	129	254	259
Playoff Totals		14	4	6	10	6

EMBERG, Edward *F*
B. Montreal, Que., Nov. 18, 1921

Season	Team	GP	G	A	Pts.	PIM
44-45	Mont	0	0	0	0	0
Playoff Totals		2	1	0	1	0

EMERSON, Nelson *5-11 165 C*
B. Hamilton, Ont., Aug. 17, 1967

Season	Team	GP	G	A	Pts.	PIM
90-91	StL	4	0	3	3	2
91-92	StL	79	23	36	59	66
Totals		83	23	39	62	68
Playoff Totals		6	3	3	6	21

EMMS, Leighton (Hap) *6-0 190 LW*
B. Barrie, Ont., Jan. 12, 1905

Season	Team	GP	G	A	Pts.	PIM
26-27	Mont M	8	0	0	0	0
27-28	Mont M	8	0	1	1	10
30-31	NYA	44	5	4	9	56
31-32	NYA-Det	33	7	9	16	38
32-33	Det	41	9	13	22	63
33-34	Det	47	7	7	14	51
34-35	Bos-NYA	39	3	3	6	27
35-36	NYA	31	1	5	6	12
36-37	NYA	47	4	8	12	48
37-38	NYA	22	1	3	4	6
Totals		320	37	53	90	311
Playoff Totals		14	0	0	0	12

ENDEAN, Craig *5-11 170 LW*
B. Kamloops, B.C., Apr. 13, 1968

Season	Team	GP	G	A	Pts.	PIM
86-87	Winn	2	0	1	1	0

ENGBLOM, Brian Paul *6-2 190 D*
B. Winnipeg, Man., Jan. 27, 1955

Season	Team	GP	G	A	Pts.	PIM
77-78	Mont	28	1	2	3	23
78-79	Mont	62	3	11	14	60
79-80	Mont	70	3	20	23	43
80-81	Mont	80	3	25	28	96
81-82	Mont	76	4	29	33	76
82-83	Wash	73	5	22	27	59
83-84	Wash-LA	80	2	28	30	67
84-85	LA	79	4	19	23	70
85-86	LA-Buf	79	4	17	21	77
86-87	Calg	32	0	4	4	28
Totals		659	29	177	206	599
Playoff Totals		48	3	9	12	43

ENGELE, Jerome Wilfred (Jerry) *6-0 197 D*
B. Humboldt, Sask., Nov. 26, 1950

Season	Team	GP	G	A	Pts.	PIM
75-76	Minn	17	0	1	1	16
76-77	Minn	31	1	7	8	41
77-78	Minn	52	1	5	6	105
Totals		100	2	13	15	162
Playoff Totals		2	0	1	1	0

ENGLISH, John *6-2 190 D*
B. Toronto, Ont., May 13, 1966

Season	Team	GP	G	A	Pts.	PIM
87-88	LA	3	1	3	4	4

ENNIS, Jim *6-0 200 D*
B. Sherwood Park, Alta., July 10, 1967

Season	Team	GP	G	A	Pts.	PIM
87-88	Edm	5	1	0	1	10

ERICKSON, Autry Raymond (Aut) *6-0 188 D*
B. Lethbridge, Alta., Jan. 25, 1938

Season	Team	GP	G	A	Pts.	PIM
59-60	Bos	58	1	6	7	29
60-61	Bos	68	2	6	8	65
62-63	Chi	3	0	0	0	8
63-64	Chi	31	0	1	1	34
67-68	Oak	66	4	11	15	46
69-70	Oak	1	0	0	0	0
Totals		227	7	24	31	182
Playoff Totals		7	0	0	0	2

ERICKSON, Bryan 5-9 170 RW
B. Roseau, Minn., Mar. 7, 1960

Season	Team	GP	G	A	Pts.	PIM
83-84	Wash	45	12	17	29	16
84-85	Wash	57	15	13	28	23
85-86	LA	55	20	23	43	36
86-87	LA	68	20	30	50	26
87-88	LA-Pitt	53	7	19	26	20
90-91	Winn	6	0	7	7	0
91-92	Winn	10	2	4	6	0
Totals		294	76	113	189	121
Playoff Totals		11	3	4	7	7

ERICKSON, Grant Charles 5-9 165 LW
B. Pierceland, Sask., Apr. 28, 1947

Season	Team	GP	G	A	Pts.	PIM
68-69	Bos	2	1	0	1	0
69-70	Minn	4	0	0	0	4
72-73	Clev(WHA)	77	15	29	44	23
73-74	Clev(WHA)	78	23	27	50	26
74-75	Clev(WHA)	78	12	15	27	24
75-76	Phoe(WHA)	33	4	4	8	6
NHL Totals		6	1	0	1	4
WHA Totals		266	54	75	129	79
WHA Playoff Totals		19	2	5	7	2

ERIKSSON, Bengt Roland (Rolie) 6-3 190 C
B. Storatuna, Sweden, Mar. 1, 1954

Season	Team	GP	G	A	Pts.	PIM
76-77	Minn	80	25	44	69	10
77-78	Minn	78	21	39	60	12
78-79	Van	35	2	12	14	4
78-79	Winn (WHA)	33	5	10	15	2
NHL Totals		193	48	95	143	26
WHA Totals		33	5	10	15	2
NHL Playoff Totals		2	1	0	1	0
WHA Playoff Totals		10	1	4	5	0

ERIKSSON, Peter 6-4 224 LW
B. Kramfors, Sweden, July 12, 1965

Season	Team	GP	G	A	Pts.	PIM
89-90	Edm	20	3	3	6	24

ERIKSSON, Thomas 6-2 180 D
B. Stockholm, Sweden, Oct. 16, 1959

Season	Team	GP	G	A	Pts.	PIM
80-81	Phil	24	1	10	11	14
81-82	Phil	1	0	0	0	4
83-84	Phil	68	11	33	44	37
84-85	Phil	72	10	29	39	36
85-86	Phil	43	0	4	4	16
Totals		208	22	76	98	107
Playoff Totals		19	0	3	3	6

ERIXON, Jan 6-0 190 RW
B. Skelleftea, Sweden, July 8, 1962

Season	Team	GP	G	A	Pts.	PIM
83-84	NYR	75	5	25	30	16
84-85	NYR	66	7	22	29	33
85-86	NYR	31	2	17	19	4
86-87	NYR	68	8	18	26	24
87-88	NYR	70	7	19	26	33
88-89	NYR	44	4	11	15	27
89-90	NYR	58	4	9	13	8
90-91	NYR	53	7	18	25	8
91-92	NYR	46	8	9	17	4
Totals		511	52	148	200	157
Playoff Totals		58	7	7	14	16

ERREY, Bob 5-10 180 LW
B. Montreal, Que., Sept. 21, 1964

Season	Team	GP	G	A	Pts.	PIM
83-84	Pitt	65	9	13	22	29
84-85	Pitt	16	0	2	2	7
85-86	Pitt	37	11	6	17	8
86-87	Pitt	72	16	18	34	46
87-88	Pitt	17	3	6	9	18
88-89	Pitt	76	26	32	58	124
89-90	Pitt	78	20	19	39	109
90-91	Pitt	79	20	22	42	115
91-92	Pitt	78	19	16	35	119
Totals		518	124	134	258	573
Playoff Totals		49	9	4	13	51

ESAU, Leonard 6-3 190 D
B. Meadow Lake, Sask., June 3, 1968

Season	Team	GP	G	A	Pts.	PIM
91-92	Tor	2	0	0	0	0

ESPOSITO, Phillip Anthony (Espo) 6-1 205 C
B. Sault Ste. Marie, Ont., Feb. 20, 1942

Season	Team	GP	G	A	Pts.	PIM
63-64	Chi	27	3	2	5	2
64-65	Chi	70	23	32	55	44
65-66	Chi	69	27	26	53	49
66-67	Chi	69	21	40	61	40
67-68	Bos	74	35	49	84	21
68-69	Bos	74	49	77	126	79
69-70	Bos	76	43	56	99	50
70-71	Bos	78	76	76	152	71
71-72	Bos	76	66	67	133	76
72-73	Bos	78	55	75	130	87
73-74	Bos	78	68	77	145	58

ESPOSITO, Phillip Anthony (Espo)
(Continued)

Season	Team	GP	G	A	Pts.	PIM
74-75	Bos	79	61	66	127	62
75-76	Bos-NYR	74	35	48	83	36
76-77	NYR	80	34	46	80	52
77-78	NYR	79	38	43	81	53
78-79	NYR	80	42	36	78	14
79-80	NYR	80	34	44	78	73
80-81	NYR	41	7	13	20	20
Totals		1282	717	873	1590	887
Playoff Totals		130	61	76	137	137

EVANS, Christopher Bruce 5-9 180 D
B. Toronto, Ont., Sept. 14, 1946

Season	Team	GP	G	A	Pts.	PIM
69-70	Tor	2	0	0	0	0
71-72	Buf-StL	63	6	18	24	98
72-73	StL	77	9	12	21	31
73-74	StL-Det	77	4	9	13	10
74-75	KC-StL	22	0	3	3	4
75-76	Calg(WHA)	75	3	20	23	50
76-77	Calg(WHA)	81	7	27	34	60
77-78	Que(WHA)	48	1	4	5	26
NHL Totals		241	19	42	61	143
WHA Totals		204	11	51	62	136
NHL Playoff Totals		12	1	1	2	8
WHA Playoff Totals		10	5	5	10	4

EVANS, Daryl Thomas 5-8 185 LW
B. Toronto, Ont., Jan. 12, 1961

Season	Team	GP	G	A	Pts.	PIM
81-82	LA	14	2	6	8	2
82-83	LA	80	18	22	40	21
83-84	LA	4	0	1	1	0
84-85	LA	7	1	0	1	2
85-86	Wash	6	0	1	1	0
86-87	TOr	2	1	0	1	0
Totals		113	22	30	52	25
Playoff Totals		11	5	8	13	12

EVANS, Doug 5-9 170 LW
B. Peterborough, Ont., June 2, 1963

Season	Team	GP	G	A	Pts.	PIM
85-86	StL	13	1	0	1	2
86-87	StL	53	3	13	16	91
87-88	StL	41	5	7	12	49
88-89	StL	53	7	12	19	81
89-90	StL-Winn	30	10	8	18	33
90-91	Winn	70	7	27	34	108
91-92	Winn	30	7	7	14	68
Totals		290	40	74	114	432
Playoff Totals		22	3	4	7	38

EVANS, John (Paul) 5-9 185 C
B. Toronto, Ont., May 2, 1954

Season	Team	GP	G	A	Pts.	PIM
78-79	Phil	44	6	5	11	12
80-81	Phil	1	0	0	0	2
82-83	Phil	58	8	20	28	20
Totals		103	14	25	39	34
Playoff Totals		1	0	0	0	0

EVANS, Kevin Robert 5-9 185 LW
B. Peterborough, Ont., July 10, 1965

Season	Team	GP	G	A	Pts.	PIM
90-91	Minn	4	0	0	0	19
91-92	SJ	5	0	1	1	25
Totals		9	0	1	1	44

EVANS, Paul Edward Vincent 5-11 175 C
B. Peterborough, Ont., Feb. 24, 1955

Season	Team	GP	G	A	Pts.	PIM
76-77	Tor	7	1	1	2	19
77-78	Tor	4	0	0	0	2
Totals		11	1	1	2	21
Playoff Totals		2	0	0	0	0

EVANS, Shawn 6-3 195 D
B. Kingston, Ont., Sept. 7, 1965

Season	Team	GP	G	A	Pts.	PIM
85-86	StL	7	0	0	0	2
89-90	NYI	2	1	0	1	0
Totals		9	1	0	1	2

EVANS, Stewart (Stu) 5-10 170 D
B. Ottawa, Ont., June 19, 1908

Season	Team	GP	G	A	Pts.	PIM
30-31	Det	43	1	4	5	14
32-33	Det	48	2	6	8	74
33-34	Det-Mont M	44	4	2	6	55
34-35	Mont M	46	5	7	12	54
35-36	Mont M	47	3	5	8	57
36-37	Mont M	48	6	7	13	54
37-38	Mont M	48	5	11	16	59
38-39	Mont	43	2	7	9	58
Totals		367	28	49	77	425
Playoff Totals		26	0	0	0	20

EVANS, William John (Jack, Tex) 6-1 194 D
B. Garnant, South Wales, Apr. 21, 1928

Season	Team	GP	G	A	Pts.	PIM
48-49	NYR	3	0	0	0	4

EVANS, William John (Jack, Tex)
(Continued)

Season	Team	GP	G	A	Pts.	PIM
49-50	NYR	2	0	0	0	2
50-51	NYR	49	1	0	1	95
51-52	NYR	52	1	6	7	83
53-54	NYR	44	4	4	8	73
54-55	NYR	47	0	5	5	91
55-56	NYR	70	2	9	11	104
56-57	NYR	70	3	6	9	110
57-58	NYR	70	4	8	12	108
58-59	Chi	70	1	8	9	75
59-60	Chi	68	0	4	4	60
60-61	Chi	69	0	8	8	58
61-62	Chi	70	3	14	17	80
62-63	Chi	68	0	8	8	46
Totals		752	19	80	99	989
Playoff Totals		56	2	2	4	97

EVASON, Dean 5-10 180 C
B. Flin Flon, Man., Aug. 22, 1964

Season	Team	GP	G	A	Pts.	PIM
83-84	Wash	2	0	0	0	2
84-85	Wash-Hart	17	3	4	7	2
85-86	Hart	55	20	28	48	65
86-87	Hart	80	22	37	59	67
87-88	Hart	77	10	18	28	115
88-89	Hart	67	11	17	28	60
89-90	Hart	78	18	25	43	138
90-91	Hart	75	6	23	29	170
91-92	SJ	74	11	15	26	94
Totals		525	101	167	268	713
Playoff Totals		38	8	15	23	108

EWEN, Todd 6-2 220 RW
B. Saskatoon, Sask., Mar. 22, 1966

Season	Team	GP	G	A	Pts.	PIM
86-87	StL	23	2	0	2	84
87-88	StL	64	4	2	6	227
88-89	StL	34	4	5	9	171
89-90	StL-Mont	44	4	6	10	169
90-91	Mont	28	3	2	5	128
91-92	Mont	46	1	2	3	130
Totals		239	18	17	35	909
Playoff Totals		40	0	0	0	87

EZINICKI, William (Wild Bill) 5-10 170 RW
B. Winnipeg, Man., Mar. 11, 1924

Season	Team	GP	G	A	Pts.	PIM
44-45	Tor	8	1	4	5	17
45-46	Tor	24	4	8	12	29
46-47	Tor	60	17	20	37	93
47-48	Tor	60	11	20	31	97
48-49	Tor	52	13	15	28	145
49-50	Tor	67	10	12	22	144
50-51	Bos	53	16	19	35	119
51-52	Bos	28	5	5	10	47
54-55	NYR	16	2	2	4	22
Totals		368	79	105	184	713
Playoff Totals		40	5	8	13	87

FAHEY, John (Trevor) 6-0 180 LW
B. New Waterford, N.S., Jan. 4, 1944

Season	Team	GP	G	A	Pts.	PIM
64-65	NYR	1	0	0	0	0

FAIRBAIRN, William John 5-10 195 RW
B. Brandon, Man., Jan. 7, 1947

Season	Team	GP	G	A	Pts.	PIM
68-69	NYR	1	0	0	0	0
69-70	NYR	76	23	33	56	23
70-71	NYR	56	7	23	30	32
71-72	NYR	78	22	37	59	53
72-73	NYR	78	30	33	63	23
73-74	NYR	78	18	44	62	12
74-75	NYR	80	24	37	61	10
75-76	NYR	80	13	15	28	8
76-77	NYR-Minn	60	10	22	32	2
77-78	Minn-StL	66	14	17	31	10
78-79	StL	5	1	0	1	0
Totals		658	162	261	423	173
Playoff Totals		54	13	22	35	42

FALLOON, Pat 5-10 180 RW
B. Birtle, Man., Sept. 22, 1972

Season	Team	GP	G	A	Pts.	PIM
91-92	SJ	79	25	34	59	16

FALKENBERG, Robert Arthur (Steady) 6-0 205 D
B. Stettler, Alta., Jan. 1, 1946

Season	Team	GP	G	A	Pts.	PIM
66-67	Det	16	1	1	2	10
67-68	Det	20	0	3	3	10
68-69	Det	5	0	0	0	0
70-71	Det	9	0	1	1	6
71-72	Det	4	0	0	0	0
72-73	Alb (WHA)	76	6	23	29	44
73-74	Edm (WHA)	78	3	14	17	32
74-75	SD (WHA)	78	2	18	20	42
75-76	SD (WHA)	79	3	13	16	31
76-77	SD (WHA)	64	0	6	6	34

FALKENBERG, Robert Arthur (Steady) (Continued)

Season	Team	GP	G	A	Pts.	PIM
77-78	Edm (WHA)	2	0	0	0	0
NHL Totals		54	1	5	6	26
WHA Totals		377	14	74	88	183
WHA Playoff Totals		28	1	5	6	24

FARRANT, Walter Leslie (Whitey)
5-10 155 RW
B. Toronto, Ont., Aug. 12, 1912

Season	Team	GP	G	A	Pts.	PIM
43-44	Chi	1	0	0	0	0

FARRISH, David Allan 6-1 195 D
B. Wingham, Ont., Aug. 1, 1956

Season	Team	GP	G	A	Pts.	PIM
76-77	NYR	80	2	17	19	102
77-78	NYR	66	3	5	8	62
78-79	NYR	71	1	19	20	61
79-80	Que-Tor	24	1	8	9	30
80-81	Tor	74	2	18	20	90
82-83	Tor	56	4	24	28	38
83-84	Tor	59	4	19	23	57
Totals		430	17	110	127	440
Playoff Totals		14	0	2	2	24

FASHOWAY, Gordon 5-11 180 F
B. Portage La Prairie, Man., June 16, 1926

Season	Team	GP	G	A	Pts.	PIM
50-51	Chi	13	3	2	5	14

FAUBERT, Mario 6-1 175 D
B. Valleyfield, Que., Dec. 2, 1954

Season	Team	GP	G	A	Pts.	PIM
74-75	Pitt	10	1	0	1	0
75-76	Pitt	21	1	8	9	10
76-77	Pitt	47	2	11	13	32
77-78	Pitt	18	0	6	6	11
79-80	Pitt	49	5	13	18	31
80-81	Pitt	72	8	44	52	118
81-82	Pitt	14	4	8	12	14
Totals		231	21	90	111	216
Playoff Totals		10	2	2	4	6

FAULKNER, Alexander Selm 5-8 165 C
B. Bishops Falls, Nfld., May 21, 1936

Season	Team	GP	G	A	Pts.	PIM
61-62	Tor	1	0	0	0	0
62-63	Det	70	10	10	20	6
63-64	Det	30	5	7	12	9
Totals		101	15	17	32	15
Playoff Totals		12	5	0	5	2

FAUSS, Ted 6-2 205 D
B. Clark Mills, N.Y., June 30, 1961

Season	Team	GP	G	A	Pts.	PIM
86-87	Tor	15	0	1	1	11
87-88	Tor	13	0	1	1	4
Totals		28	0	2	2	15

FEAMSTER, David Allan 5-11 180 D
B. Detroit, Mich., Sept. 10, 1958

Season	Team	GP	G	A	Pts.	PIM
81-82	Chi	29	0	2	2	29
82-83	Chi	78	6	12	18	69
83-84	Chi	46	6	7	13	42
84-85	Chi	16	1	3	4	14
Totals		169	13	24	37	155
Playoff Totals		33	3	5	8	61

FEATHERSTONE, Anthony James (Tony)
5-11 187 RW
B. Toronto, Ont., July 31, 1949

Season	Team	GP	G	A	Pts.	PIM
69-70	Oak	9	0	1	1	17
70-71	Cal	67	8	8	16	44
73-74	Minn	54	9	12	21	4
74-75	Tor (WHA)	76	25	38	63	26
75-76	Tor (WHA)	32	4	7	11	5
NHL Totals		130	17	21	38	65
WHA Totals		108	29	45	74	31
NHL Playoff Totals		2	0	0	0	0
WHA Playoff Totals		6	2	1	3	2

FEATHERSTONE, Glen 6-4 216 D
B. Toronto, Ont., July 8, 1968

Season	Team	GP	G	A	Pts.	PIM
88-89	StL	18	0	2	2	22
89-90	StL	58	0	12	12	145
90-91	StL	68	5	15	20	204
91-92	Bos	8	1	0	1	20
Totals		152	6	29	35	391
Playoff Totals		27	0	2	2	78

FEDERKO, Bernard Allan 6-0 190 C
B. Foam Lake, Sask., May 12, 1956

Season	Team	GP	G	A	Pts.	PIM
76-77	StL	31	14	9	23	15
77-78	StL	72	17	24	41	27
78-79	StL	74	31	64	95	14
79-80	StL	79	38	56	94	24
80-81	StL	78	31	73	104	47
81-82	StL	74	30	62	92	70
82-83	StL	75	24	60	84	24

FEDERKO, Bernard Allan (Continued)

Season	Team	GP	G	A	Pts.	PIM
83-84	StL	79	41	66	107	43
84-85	StL	76	30	73	103	27
85-86	StL	80	34	68	102	34
86-87	StL	64	20	52	72	32
87-88	StL	79	20	69	89	52
88-89	StL	66	22	45	67	54
89-90	StL	73	17	40	57	24
Totals		1000	369	761	1130	487
Playoff Totals		91	35	66	101	83

FEDEROV, Sergei 6-1 190 C
B. Moscow, USSR, Dec. 13, 1969

Season	Team	GP	G	A	Pts.	PIM
90-91	Det	77	31	48	79	66
91-92	Det	80	32	54	86	72
Totals		157	63	102	165	138
Playoff Totals		18	6	10	16	12

FEDYK, Brent 6-0 195 RW
B. Yorkton, Sask., Mar. 8, 1967

Season	Team	GP	G	A	Pts.	PIM
87-88	Det	2	0	1	1	2
88-89	Det	5	2	0	2	0
89-90	Det	27	1	4	5	24
90-91	Det	67	16	19	35	38
91-92	Det	61	5	8	13	42
Totals		162	24	32	56	106
Playoff Totals		7	1	0	1	4

FELIX, Chris 5-10 191 D
B. Bramalea, Ont., May 27, 1964

Season	Team	GP	G	A	Pts.	PIM
88-89	Wash	21	0	8	8	8
89-90	Wash	6	1	0	1	2
90-91	Wash	8	0	4	4	0
Totals		35	1	12	13	10
Playoff Totals		2	0	1	1	0

FELSNER, Denny 6-0 185 LW
B. Warren, Mich., Apr. 29, 1970

Season	Team	GP	G	A	Pts.	PIM
91-92	StL	3	0	1	1	0
Playoff Totals		1	0	0	0	0

FELTRIN, Anthony Louis (Tony)
5-11 185 D
B. Ladysmith, B.C., Dec. 6, 1961

Season	Team	GP	G	A	Pts.	PIM
80-81	Pitt	2	0	0	0	0
81-82	Pitt	4	0	0	0	4
82-83	Pitt	32	3	3	6	40
85-86	NYR	10	0	0	0	21
Totals		48	3	3	6	65

FENTON, Paul John 5-11 180 LW
B. Springfield, Mass., Dec. 22, 1959

Season	Team	GP	G	A	Pts.	PIM
84-85	Hart	33	7	5	12	10
85-86	Hart	1	0	0	0	0
86-87	NYR	8	0	0	0	2
87-88	LA	71	20	23	43	46
88-89	LA-Winn	80	16	12	28	39
89-90	Winn	80	32	18	50	40
90-91	Winn-Tor-Calg	78	14	21	35	28
91-92	SJ	60	11	4	15	33
Totals		411	100	83	183	198
Playoff Totals		17	4	1	5	27

FENYVES, David 5-11 195 D
B. Dunnville, Ont., Apr. 29, 1960

Season	Team	GP	G	A	Pts.	PIM
82-83	Buf	24	0	8	8	14
83-84	Buf	10	0	4	4	9
84-85	Buf	60	1	8	9	27
85-86	Buf	47	0	7	7	37
86-87	Buf	7	1	0	1	0
87-88	Phil	5	0	0	0	0
88-89	Phil	1	0	1	1	0
89-90	Phil	12	0	0	0	4
90-91	Phil	40	1	4	5	28
Totals		206	3	32	35	119
Playoff Totals		11	0	0	0	9

FERGUS, Thomas Joseph 6-3 210 C
B. Chicago, Ill., June 16, 1962

Season	Team	GP	G	A	Pts.	PIM
81-82	Bos	61	15	24	39	12
82-83	Bos	80	28	35	63	39
83-84	Bos	69	25	36	61	12
84-85	Bos	79	30	43	73	75
85-86	Tor	78	31	42	73	64
86-87	Tor	57	21	28	49	57
87-88	Tor	63	19	31	50	81
88-89	Tor	80	22	45	67	48
89-90	Tor	54	19	26	45	62
90-91	Tor	14	5	4	9	8
91-92	Tor-Van	55	15	23	38	21
Totals		690	230	337	567	479
Playoff Totals		65	21	17	38	48

FERGUSON F

Season	Team	GP	G	A	Pts.	PIM
39-40	Chi	1	0	0	0	0

FERGUSON, George Stephen 6-0 195 C
B. Trenton, Ont., Aug. 22, 1952

Season	Team	GP	G	A	Pts.	PIM
72-73	Tor	72	10	13	23	34
73-74	Tor	16	0	4	4	4
74-75	Tor	69	19	30	49	61
75-76	Tor	79	12	32	44	76
76-77	Tor	50	9	15	24	24
77-78	Tor	73	7	16	23	37
78-79	Pitt	80	21	29	50	37
79-80	Pitt	73	21	28	49	36
80-81	Pitt	79	25	18	43	42
81-82	Pitt	71	22	31	53	45
82-83	Pitt-Minn	72	8	12	20	16
83-84	Minn	63	6	10	16	19
Totals		797	160	238	398	431
Playoff Totals		86	14	23	37	44

FERGUSON, John Bowie (Fergie)
5-11 190 LW
B. Vancouver, B.C., Sept. 5, 1938

Season	Team	GP	G	A	Pts.	PIM
63-64	Mont	59	18	27	45	125
64-65	Mont	69	17	27	44	156
65-66	Mont	65	11	14	25	153
66-67	Mont	67	20	22	42	177
67-68	Mont	61	15	18	33	117
68-69	Mont	71	29	23	52	45
69-70	Mont	48	19	13	32	139
70-71	Mont	60	16	14	30	32
Totals		500	145	158	303	944
Playoff Totals		85	20	18	38	260

FERGUSON, Lorne Robert (Fergie)
6-0 185 LW
B. Palmerston, Ont., May 26, 1930

Season	Team	GP	G	A	Pts.	PIM
49-50	Bos	3	1	1	2	0
50-51	Bos	70	16	17	33	31
51-52	Bos	27	3	4	7	14
54-55	Bos	69	20	14	34	24
55-56	Bos-Det	63	15	12	27	30
56-57	Det	70	13	10	23	26
57-58	Det-Chi	53	7	12	19	24
58-59	Chi	67	7	10	17	44
Totals		422	82	80	162	193
Playoff Totals		31	6	3	9	24

FERGUSON, Norman Gerard 5-8 165 RW
B. Sydney, N.S., Oct. 16, 1945

Season	Team	GP	G	A	Pts.	PIM
68-69	Oak	76	34	20	54	31
69-70	Oak	72	11	9	20	19
70-71	Cal	54	14	17	31	9
71-72	Cal	77	14	20	34	13
72-73	NY (WHA)	56	28	40	68	8
73-74	NY-NJ (WHA)	75	15	21	36	12
74-75	SD (WHA)	78	36	33	69	6
75-76	SD (WHA)	79	37	37	74	12
76-77	SD (WHA)	77	39	32	71	5
77-78	Edm (WHA)	71	26	21	47	2
NHL Totals		279	73	66	139	72
WHA Totals		436	181	184	365	45
NHL Playoff Totals		10	1	4	5	7
WHA Playoff Totals		26	10	9	19	9

FERNER, Mark 6-0 193 D
B. Regina, Sask., Sept. 5, 1965

Season	Team	GP	G	A	Pts.	PIM
86-87	Buf	13	0	3	3	9
88-89	Buf	2	0	0	0	2
89-90	Wash	2	0	0	0	0
90-91	Wash	7	0	1	1	4
Totals		24	0	4	4	15

FERRARO, Ray 5-10 185 C
B. Trail, B.C., Aug. 23, 1964

Season	Team	GP	G	A	Pts.	PIM
84-85	Hart	44	11	17	28	40
85-86	Hart	76	30	47	77	57
86-87	Hart	80	27	32	59	42
87-88	Hart	68	21	29	50	81
88-89	Hart	80	41	35	76	86
89-90	Hart	79	25	29	54	109
90-91	Hart-NYI	76	21	21	42	70
91-92	NYI	80	40	40	80	92
Totals		583	216	250	466	577
Playoff Totals		33	7	11	18	24

FETISOV, Viacheslav 6-1 220 D
B. Moscow, USSR, May 20, 1958

Season	Team	GP	G	A	Pts.	PIM
89-90	NJ	72	8	34	42	52
90-91	NJ	67	3	16	19	62
91-92	NJ	70	3	23	26	108
Totals		209	14	73	87	222
Playoff Totals		19	0	5	5	33

FIDLER, Michael Edward 5-11 195 LW
B. Everett, Mass., Aug. 19, 1956

Season	Team	GP	G	A	Pts.	PIM
76-77	Clev	46	17	16	33	17

FIDLER, Michael Edward *(Continued)*

Season	Team	GP	G	A	Pts.	PIM
77-78	Clev	78	23	28	51	38
78-79	Minn	59	23	26	49	42
79-80	Minn	24	5	4	9	13
80-81	Minn-Hart	58	14	21	35	10
81-82	Hart	2	0	1	1	0
82-83	Chi	4	2	1	3	4
Totals		271	84	97	181	124

FIELD, Wilfred Spence *5-11 185 D*

B. Winnipeg, Man., Apr. 29, 1915

Season	Team	GP	G	A	Pts.	PIM
36-37	NYA	1	0	0	0	0
38-39	NYA	43	1	3	4	37
39-40	NYA	45	1	3	4	28
40-41	NYA	36	5	6	11	31
41-42	Brk	41	6	9	15	23
44-45	Mont-Chi	48	4	4	8	32
Totals		214	17	25	42	151
Playoff Totals		5	0	0	0	2

FIELDER, Guyle Abner (Guy) *5-9 165 C*

B. Potlatch, Idaho, Nov. 21, 1930

Season	Team	GP	G	A	Pts.	PIM
50-51	Chi	30	0	0	0	0
57-58	Det	6	0	0	0	2
Totals		36	0	0	0	2
Playoff Totals		6	0	0	0	2

FILLION, Louis Robert (Bob) *5-9 170 LW*

B. Thetford Mines, Que., July 12, 1921

Season	Team	GP	G	A	Pts.	PIM
43-44	Mont	41	7	23	30	14
44-45	Mont	31	6	8	14	12
45-46	Mont	50	10	6	16	12
46-47	Mont	57	6	3	9	16
47-48	Mont	32	4	9	13	8
48-49	Mont	59	3	9	12	14
49-50	Mont	57	1	3	4	8
Totals		327	37	61	98	84
Playoff Totals		33	7	4	11	10

FILLION, Marcel *5-7 175 LW*

B. Thetford Mines, Que., May 28, 1923

Season	Team	GP	G	A	Pts.	PIM
44-45	Bos	1	0	0	0	0

FILMORE, Thomas *5-11 189 RW*

B. Thamesford, Ont., 1906

Season	Team	GP	G	A	Pts.	PIM
30-31	Det	40	6	2	8	10
31-32	Det-NYA	40	8	6	14	14
32-33	NYA	33	1	4	5	9
33-34	Bos	3	0	0	0	0
Totals		116	15	12	27	33

FINKBEINER, Lloyd *F*

B. Guelph, Ont., Mar. 12, 1920

Season	Team	GP	G	A	Pts.	PIM
40-41	NYA	1	0	0	0	0

FINLEY, Jeff *6-2 185 D*

B. Edmonton, Alta., Apr. 14. 1967

Season	Team	GP	G	A	Pts.	PIM
87-88	NYI	10	0	5	5	15
88-89	NYI	4	0	0	0	6
89-90	NYI	11	0	1	1	0
90-91	NYI	11	0	0	0	4
91-92	NYI	51	1	10	11	26
Totals		87	1	16	17	51
Playoff Totals		6	0	2	2	4

FINN, Steven *6-0 198 D*

B. Laval, Que., Aug. 20, 1966

Season	Team	GP	G	A	Pts.	PIM
85-86	Que	17	0	1	1	28
86-87	Que	36	2	5	7	40
87-88	Que	75	3	7	10	198
88-89	Que	77	2	6	8	235
89-90	Que	64	3	9	12	208
90-91	Que	71	6	13	19	228
91-92	Que	65	4	7	11	192
Totals		405	20	48	68	1129
Playoff Totals		13	0	2	2	29

FINNEY, Joseph Sidney (Sid) *5-10 160 C*

B. Banbridge, Ireland, May 1, 1929

Season	Team	GP	G	A	Pts.	PIM
51-52	Chi	35	6	5	11	0
52-53	Chi	18	4	2	6	4
53-54	Chi	6	0	0	0	0
Totals		59	10	7	17	4
Playoff Totals		7	0	0	0	2

FINNIGAN, Edward *F*

B. Shawville, Que.

Season	Team	GP	G	A	Pts.	PIM
35-36	Bos	3	0	0	0	0

FINNIGAN, Frank *5-9 165 RW*

B. Shawville, Que., July 9, 1903

Season	Team	GP	G	A	Pts.	PIM
23-24	Ott	4	0	0	0	0
24-25	Ott	29	0	0	0	20
25-26	Ott	36	2	0	2	24
26-27	Ott	36	15	1	16	52
27-28	Ott	38	20	5	25	34

FINNIGAN, Frank *(Continued)*

Season	Team	GP	G	A	Pts.	PIM
28-29	Ott	44	15	4	19	71
29-30	Ott	43	21	15	36	46
30-31	Ott	44	9	8	17	40
31-32	Tor	47	8	13	21	45
32-33	Ott	45	4	14	18	37
33-34	Ott	48	10	10	20	10
34-35	StLE-Tor	45	7	5	12	12
35-36	Tor	48	2	6	8	10
36-37	Tor	48	2	7	9	4
Totals		555	115	88	203	405
Playoff Totals		39	6	9	15	22

FIORENTINO, Peter *6-1 200 D*

B. Niagara Falls, Ont., Dec. 22, 1968

Season	Team	GP	G	A	Pts.	PIM
91-92	NYR	1	0	0	0	0

FISCHER, Ronald Alexander *6-2 195 D*

B. Merritt, B.C., Apr. 12, 1959

Season	Team	GP	G	A	Pts.	PIM
81-82	Buf	15	0	7	7	6
82-83	Buf	3	0	0	0	0
Totals		18	0	7	7	6

FISHER, Alvin *F*

Season	Team	GP	G	A	Pts.	PIM
24-25	Tor	9	1	0	1	4

FISHER, Craig *6-3 185 C*

B. Oshawa, Ont., June 30, 1970

Season	Team	GP	G	A	Pts.	PIM
89-90	Phil	2	0	0	0	0
90-91	Phil	2	0	0	0	0
Totals		4	0	0	0	0

FISHER, Duncan Robert (Dunc)
5-8 165 RW

B. Regina, Sask., Aug. 30, 1927

Season	Team	GP	G	A	Pts.	PIM
48-49	NYR	60	9	16	25	40
49-50	NYR	70	12	21	33	42
50-51	NYR-Bos	65	9	20	29	20
51-52	Bos	65	15	12	27	2
52-53	Bos	7	0	1	1	0
58-59	Det	8	0	0	0	0
Totals		275	45	70	115	104
Playoff Totals		21	4	4	8	14

FISHER, Joseph H. *6-0 175 RW*

B. Medicine Hat, Alta., July 4, 1916

Season	Team	GP	G	A	Pts.	PIM
39-40	Det	34	2	4	6	2
40-41	Det	28	5	8	13	11
41-42	Det	3	0	0	0	0
42-43	Det	1	1	0	1	0
Totals		66	8	12	20	13
Playoff Totals		15	2	1	3	6

FITCHNER, Robert Douglas *6-0 190 C*

B. Sudbury, Ont., Dec. 22, 1950

Season	Team	GP	G	A	Pts.	PIM
73-74	Edm (WHA)	31	1	2	3	21
74-75	Ind (WHA)	78	11	19	30	96
75-76	Ind-Que (WHA)	73	22	25	47	134
76-77	Que (WHA)	81	9	30	39	105
77-78	Que (WHA)	72	15	28	43	76
78-79	Que (WHA)	79	10	35	45	69
79-80	Que	70	11	20	31	59
80-81	Que	8	1	0	1	0
NHL Totals		78	12	20	32	59
WHA Totals		414	68	139	207	501
NHL Playoff Totals		3	0	0	0	10
WHA Playoff Totals		37	6	12	18	34

FITZPATRICK, Alexander Stewart (Sandy)
6-1 195 C

B. Paisley, Scotland, Dec. 22, 1944

Season	Team	GP	G	A	Pts.	PIM
64-65	NYR	4	0	0	0	2
67-68	Minn	18	3	6	9	6
Totals		22	3	6	9	8
Playoff Totals		12	0	0	0	0

FITZGERALD, Tom *6-1 195 C*

B. Melrose, Mass., Aug. 28, 1968

Season	Team	GP	G	A	Pts.	PIM
88-89	NYI	23	3	5	8	10
89-90	NYI	19	2	5	7	4
90-91	NYI	41	5	5	10	24
91-92	NYI	45	6	11	17	28
Totals		128	16	26	42	66
Playoff Totals		4	1	0	1	4

FITZPATRICK, Ross *6-0 190 C*

B. Penticton, B.C., Oct. 7, 1960

Season	Team	GP	G	A	Pts.	PIM
82-83	Phil	1	0	0	0	0
83-84	Phil	12	4	2	6	0
84-85	Phil	5	1	0	1	0
85-86	Phil	2	0	0	0	0
Totals		20	5	2	7	0

FLAMIN, Ferdinand Charles (Fernie)
5-10 190 D

B. Dysart, Sask., Jan. 25, 1927

Season	Team	GP	G	A	Pts.	PIM
44-45	Bos	1	0	0	0	0
45-46	Bos	1	0	0	0	0
46-47	Bos	23	1	4	5	41
47-48	Bos	56	4	6	10	69
48-49	Bos	60	4	12	16	62
49-50	Bos	69	2	5	7	122
50-51	Bos-Tor	53	3	7	10	101
51-52	Tor	61	0	7	7	110
52-53	Tor	66	2	6	8	110
53-54	Tor	62	0	8	8	84
54-55	Bos	70	4	14	18	150
55-56	Bos	62	4	17	21	70
56-57	Bos	68	6	25	31	108
57-58	Bos	66	0	15	15	71
58-59	Bos	70	0	21	21	101
59-60	Bos	60	2	18	20	112
60-61	Bos	62	2	9	11	59
Totals		910	34	174	208	1370
Playoff Totals		63	4	8	12	93

FLATLEY, Patrick *6-2 197 RW*

B. Toronto, Ont., Oct. 3, 1963

Season	Team	GP	G	A	Pts.	PIM
83-84	NYI	16	2	7	9	6
84-85	NYI	78	20	31	51	106
85-86	NYI	73	18	34	52	66
86-87	NYI	63	16	35	51	81
87-88	NYI	40	9	15	24	28
88-89	NYI	41	10	15	25	31
89-90	NYI	62	17	32	49	101
90-91	NYI	56	20	25	45	74
91-92	NYI	38	8	28	36	14
Totals		467	120	222	342	507
Playoff Totals		44	16	8	24	49

FLEMING, Reginald Stephen (Reggie)
5-10 185 LW

B. Montreal, Que., Apr. 21, 1936

Season	Team	GP	G	A	Pts.	PIM
59-60	Mont	3	0	0	0	2
60-61	Chi	66	4	4	8	145
61-62	Chi	70	7	9	16	71
62-63	Chi	64	7	7	14	99
63-64	Chi	61	3	6	9	140
64-65	Bos	67	18	23	41	136
65-66	Bos-NYR	69	14	20	34	166
66-67	NYR	61	15	16	31	146
67-68	NYR	73	17	7	24	132
68-69	NYR	72	8	12	20	138
69-70	Phil	65	9	18	27	134
70-71	Buf	78	6	10	16	159
72-73	Chi (WHA)	74	23	45	68	93
73-74	Chi (WHA)	45	2	12	14	49
NHL Totals		749	108	132	240	1468
WHA Totals		119	25	57	82	142
NHL Playoff Totals		50	3	6	9	106
WHA Playoff Totals		12	0	4	4	12

FLESCH *F*

Season	Team	GP	G	A	Pts.	PIM
20-21	Ham	1	0	0	0	0

FLESCH, John Patrick *6-2 200 LW*

B. Sudbury, Ont., July 15, 1953

Season	Team	GP	G	A	Pts.	PIM
74-75	Minn	57	8	15	23	47
75-76	Minn	33	3	2	5	47
77-78	Pitt	29	7	5	12	19
79-80	Col	5	0	1	1	4
Totals		124	18	23	41	117

FLETCHER, Steven *6-3 205 LW*

B. Montreal, Que., Mar. 31, 1962

Season	Team	GP	G	A	Pts.	PIM
88-89	Winn	3	0	0	0	5
Playoff Totals		1	0	0	0	5

FLETT, William Myer (Cowboy)
6-1 205 RW

B. Vermillion, Alta., July 21, 1943

Season	Team	GP	G	A	Pts.	PIM
67-68	LA	73	26	20	46	97
68-69	LA	72	24	25	49	53
69-70	LA	69	14	18	32	70
70-71	LA	64	13	24	37	57
71-72	LA-Phil	76	18	22	40	44
72-73	Phil	69	43	31	74	53
73-74	Phil	67	17	27	44	51
74-75	Tor	77	15	25	40	38
75-76	Atl	78	23	17	40	30
76-77	Atl	24	4	4	8	6
76-77	Edm (WHA)	48	34	20	54	20
77-78	Edm (WHA)	74	41	28	69	34
78-79	Edm (WHA)	73	28	36	64	14
79-80	Edm	20	5	2	7	2
NHL Totals		689	202	215	417	501
WHA Totals		195	103	84	187	68

FLETT, William Myer (Cowboy)   5-6 160 C
(Continued)

Season Team	GP	G	A	Pts.	PIM
NHL Playoff Totals	52	7	16	23	42
WHA Playoff Totals	15	5	4	9	4

FLEURY, Theoren   5-6 160 C
B. Oxbow, Sask., June 29, 1968

88-89	Calg	36	14	20	34	46
89-90	Calg	80	31	35	66	157
90-91	Calg	79	51	53	104	136
91-92	Calg	80	33	40	73	133
Totals		275	129	148	277	472
Playoff Totals		35	9	14	23	48

FLICHEL, Todd   6-3 195 D
B. Osgoode, Ont., Sept. 14, 1964

87-88	Winn	2	0	0	0	2
88-89	Winn	1	0	0	0	0
89-90	Winn	3	0	1	1	2
Totals		6	0	1	1	4

FLOCKHART, Robert Walter (Rob)
6-0 185 RW
B. Sicamous, B.C., Feb. 6, 1956

76-77	Van	5	0	0	0	0
77-78	Van	24	0	1	1	9
78-79	Van	14	1	1	2	0
79-80	Minn	10	1	3	4	2
80-81	Minn	2	0	0	0	0
Totals		55	2	5	7	11
Playoff Totals		1	1	0	1	2

FLOCKHART, Ronald   5-11 185 C
B. Smithers, B.C., Oct. 10, 1960

80-81	Phil	14	3	7	10	11
81-82	Phil	72	33	39	72	44
82-83	Phil	73	29	31	60	49
83-84	Phil-Pitt	76	27	21	48	44
84-85	Pitt-Mont	54	10	17	27	18
85-86	StL	79	22	45	67	26
86-87	StL	60	16	19	35	12
87-88	StL	21	5	4	9	4
88-89	Bos	4	0	0	0	0
Totals		453	145	183	328	208
Playoff Totals		29	11	18	29	16

FLOYD, Larry David   5-8 180 C
B. Peterborough, Ont., May 1, 1961

82-83	NJ	5	1	0	1	2
83-84	NJ	7	1	3	4	7
Totals		12	2	3	5	9

FOGARTY, Bryan   6-2 198 D
B. Brantford, Ont., June 11, 1969

89-90	Que	45	4	10	14	31
90-91	Que	45	9	22	31	24
91-92	Que	20	3	12	15	16
Totals		110	16	44	60	71

FOGOLIN, Lee Joseph   6-0 205 D
B. Chicago, Ill., Feb. 7, 1955

74-75	Buf	50	2	2	4	59
75-76	Buf	58	0	9	9	64
76-77	Buf	71	3	15	18	100
77-78	Buf	76	0	23	23	98
78-79	Buf	74	3	19	22	103
79-80	Edm	80	5	10	15	104
80-81	Edm	80	13	17	30	139
81-82	Edm	80	4	25	29	154
82-83	Edm	72	0	18	18	92
83-84	Edm	80	5	16	21	125
84-85	Edm	79	4	14	18	126
85-86	Edm	80	4	22	26	129
86-87	Edm-Buf	44	1	5	6	25
Totals		924	44	195	239	1318
Playoff Totals		108	5	19	24	173

FOGOLIN, Lidio John (Lee)   5-11 200 D
B. Fort William, Ont., Feb. 27, 1926

48-49	Det	43	1	2	3	59
49-50	Det	64	4	8	12	63
50-51	Det-Chi	54	3	11	14	79
51-52	Chi	69	0	9	9	96
52-53	Chi	70	2	8	10	79
53-54	Chi	68	0	1	1	95
54-55	Chi	9	0	1	1	16
55-56	Chi	51	0	8	8	88
Totals		428	10	48	58	575
Playoff Totals		28	0	2	2	30

FOLCO, Peter Kevin   6-0 185 D
B. Montreal, Que., Aug. 13, 1953

73-74	Van	2	0	0	0	0
75-76	Tor (WHA)	19	1	8	9	15

FOLCO, Peter Kevin *(Continued)*

76-77	Birm	2	0	0	0	0
	(WHA)					
NHL Totals		2	0	0	0	0
WHA Totals		21	1	8	9	15

FOLEY, Gerald James   6-0 172 RW
B. Ware, Mass., Sept. 22, 1932

54-55	Tor	4	0	0	0	8
56-57	NYR	69	7	9	16	48
57-58	NYR	68	2	5	7	43
68-69	LA	1	0	0	0	0
Totals		142	9	14	23	99
Playoff Totals		9	0	1	1	2

FOLEY, Gilbert Anthony (Rick)   6-4 225 D
B. Niagara Falls, Ont., Sept. 22, 1945

70-71	Chi	2	0	1	1	8
71-72	Phil	58	11	25	36	168
73-74	Det	7	0	0	0	4
75-76	Tor (WHA)	11	1	2	3	6
NHL Totals		67	11	26	37	180
WHA Totals		11	1	2	3	6
NHL Playoff Totals		4	0	1	1	4

FOLIGNO, Mike Anthony   6-2 195 RW
B. Sudbury, Ont., Jan. 29, 1959

79-80	Det	80	36	35	71	109
80-81	Det	80	28	35	63	210
81-82	Det-Buf	82	33	44	77	177
82-83	Buf	66	22	25	47	135
83-84	Buf	70	32	31	63	151
84-85	Buf	77	27	29	56	154
85-86	Buf	79	41	39	80	168
86-87	Buf	75	30	29	59	176
87-88	Buf	74	29	28	57	220
88-89	Buf	75	27	22	49	156
89-90	Buf	61	15	25	40	99
90-91	Buf-Tor	68	12	12	24	107
91-92	Tor	33	6	8	14	50
Totals		920	338	362	700	1912
Playoff Totals		39	13	11	24	143

FOLK, William Joseph   6-0 190 D
B. Regina, Sask., July 11, 1927

51-52	Det	8	0	0	0	2
52-53	Det	4	0	0	0	2
Totals		12	0	0	4	

FONTAINE, Leonard Joseph   5-7 165 RW
B. Quebec City, Que., Feb. 25, 1948

72-73	Det	39	8	10	18	6
73-74	Det	7	0	1	1	4
74-75	Mich	21	1	8	9	6
	(WHA)					
NHL Totals		46	8	11	19	10
WHA Totals		21	1	8	9	6

FONTAS, Jon   5-10 185 C
B. Arlington, Mass., Apr. 16, 1955

79-80	Minn	1	0	0	0	0
80-81	Minn	1	0	0	0	0
Totals		2	0	0	0	0

FONTEYNE, Valere Ronald (Val)
5-9 155 LW
B. Wetaskiwin, Alta., Dec. 2, 1933

59-60	Det	69	4	7	11	2
60-61	Det	66	6	11	17	4
61-62	Det	70	5	5	10	4
62-63	Det	67	6	14	20	4
63-64	NYR	69	7	18	25	4
64-65	NYR-Det	43	2	6	8	8
65-66	Det	59	5	10	15	0
66-67	Det	28	1	1	2	0
67-68	Pitt	69	6	28	34	0
68-69	Pitt	74	12	17	29	2
69-70	Pitt	68	11	15	26	2
70-71	Pitt	70	4	9	13	0
71-72	Pitt	68	6	13	19	0
72-73	Alb (WHA)	77	7	32	39	2
73-74	Edm	72	9	13	22	2
	(WHA)					
NHL Totals		820	75	154	229	28
WHA Totals		149	16	45	61	4
NHL Playoff Totals		59	3	10	13	8
WHA Playoff Totals		5	1	0	1	0

FONTINATO, Louis (Louie, The Leaper)
6-1 195 D
B. Guelph, Ont., Jan. 20, 1932

54-55	NYR	27	2	2	4	60
55-56	NYR	70	3	15	18	202
56-57	NYR	70	3	12	15	139
57-58	NYR	70	3	8	11	152
58-59	NYR	64	7	6	13	149

FONTINATO, Louis (Louie, The Leaper)
(Continued)

59-60	NYR	64	2	11	13	137
60-61	NYR	53	2	3	5	100
61-62	Mont	54	2	13	15	167
62-63	Mont	63	2	8	10	141
Totals		535	26	78	104	1247
Playoff Totals		21	0	2	2	42

FOOTE, Adam   6-1 180 D
B. Toronto, Ont., July 10, 1971

91-92	Que	46	2	5	7	44

FORBES, David Stephen   5-10 180 LW
B. Montreal, Que., Nov. 16, 1948

73-74	Bos	63	10	16	26	41
74-75	Bos	69	18	12	30	80
75-76	Bos	79	16	13	29	52
76-77	Bos	73	9	11	20	47
77-78	Wash	77	11	11	22	119
78-79	Wash	2	0	1	1	2
78-79	Cin (WHA)	73	6	5	11	83
NHL Totals		363	64	64	128	341
WHA Totals		73	6	5	11	83
NHL Playoff Totals		45	1	4	5	13
WHA Playoff Totals		3	0	1	1	7

FORBES, Michael D.   6-2 200 D
B. Brampton, Ont., Sept. 20, 1957

77-78	Bos	32	0	4	4	15
79-80	Edm	2	0	0	0	0
81-82	Edm	16	1	7	8	26
Totals		50	1	11	12	41

FOREY, Conley Michael (Connie)
6-2 185 LW
B. Montreal, Que., Oct. 18, 1950

73-74	StL	4	0	0	0	2

FORSEY, John (Jack)   F

42-43	Tor	19	7	9	16	10
Playoff Totals		3	0	1	1	0

FORSLUND, Gustav (Gus)   150 F
B. Sweden, Apr. 25, 1908

32-33	Ott	48	4	9	13	2

FORSLUND, Thomas   5-11 200 RW
B. Falun, Sweden, Nov. 24, 1968

91-92	Calg	38	5	9	14	12

FORSYTH, Alex   6-2 195 C
B. Galt, Ont., Jan. 6, 1955

76-77	Wash	1	0	0	0	0

FORTIER, Charles   F

23-24	Mont	1	0	0	0	0

FORTIER, David Edward   5-11 190 D
B. Sudbury, Ont., June 17, 1951

72-73	Tor	23	4	5	63	
74-75	NYI	65	6	12	18	79
75-76	NYI	59	0	2	68	
76-77	Van	58	1	3	4	125
77-78	Ind (WHA)	54	1	15	16	86
NHL Totals		205	8	21	29	335
WHA Totals		54	1	15	16	86
NHL Playoff Totals		20	0	2	2	33

FORTIER, Marc   6-0 192 C
B. Windsor, Que., Feb. 26, 1966

87-88	Que	27	4	10	14	12
88-89	Que	57	20	19	39	45
89-90	Que	59	13	17	30	28
90-91	Que	14	0	4	4	6
91-92	Que	39	5	9	14	33
Totals		196	42	59	101	124

FORTIN, Raymond Henri   5-8 180 D
B. Brummondville, Que., Mar. 11, 1941

67-68	StL	24	0	2	4	8
68-69	StL	11	1	0	1	6
69-70	StL	57	1	4	5	19
Totals		92	2	6	8	33
Playoff Totals		6	0	0	0	8

FOSTER, Corey   6-3 200 D
B. Ottawa, Ont., Oct. 27, 1969

88-89	NJ	2	0	0	0	0
91-92	Phil	25	3	4	7	20
Totals		27	3	4	7	20

FOSTER, Dwight Alexander   5-11 195 C
B. Toronto, Ont., Apr. 2, 1957

77-78	Bos	14	2	1	3	6
78-79	Bos	44	11	13	24	14

FOSTER, Dwight Alexander (Continued)

Season	Team	GP	G	A	Pts.	PIM
79-80	Bos	57	10	28	38	42
80-81	Bos	77	24	28	52	62
81-82	Col	70	12	19	31	41
82-83	NJ-Det	62	17	22	39	60
83-84	Det	52	9	12	21	50
84-85	Det	50	16	16	32	56
85-86	Det-Bos	68	6	12	18	52
86-87	Bos	47	4	12	16	37
Totals		541	111	163	274	420
Playoff Totals		35	5	12	17	4

FOSTER, Harold C. (Harry, Yip) 198 D
B. Guelph, Ont., Nov. 25, 1907

Season	Team	GP	G	A	Pts.	PIM
29-30	NYR	31	0	0	0	10
31-32	Bos	34	1	2	3	12
33-34	Det	6	0	0	0	2
34-35	Det	12	2	0	2	8
Totals		83	3	2	5	32

FOSTER, Herbert Stanley 5-9 168 LW
B. Brockville, Ont., Aug. 9, 1913

Season	Team	GP	G	A	Pts.	PIM
40-41	NYR	4	1	0	1	5
47-48	NYR	1	0	0	0	0
Totals		5	1	0	1	5

FOTIU, Nicholas Evlampios 6-2 210 LW
B. Staten Island, N.Y., May 25, 1952

Season	Team	GP	G	A	Pts.	PIM
76-77	NYR	70	4	8	12	174
77-78	NYR	59	2	7	9	105
78-79	NYR	71	3	5	8	190
79-80	Hart	74	10	8	18	107
80-81	Hart-NYR	69	9	9	18	170
81-82	NYR	70	8	10	18	151
82-83	NYR	72	8	13	21	90
83-84	NYR	40	7	6	13	115
84-85	NYR	46	4	7	11	54
85-86	Calg	9	0	1	1	21
86-87	Calg	42	5	3	8	145
87-88	Phil	23	0	0	0	40
88-89	Edm	1	0	0	0	0
Totals		646	60	77	137	1362
Playoff Totals		38	0	4	4	67

FOWLER, James William 5-11 168 D
B. Toronto, Ont., Apr. 6, 1915

Season	Team	GP	G	A	Pts.	PIM
36-37	Tor	48	7	11	18	22
37-38	Tor	48	10	12	22	8
38-39	Tor	39	1	6	7	9
Totals		135	18	29	47	39
Playoff Totals		18	0	3	3	2

FOWLER, Thomas 5-11 165 C
B. Winnipeg, Man., May 18, 1924

Season	Team	GP	G	A	Pts.	PIM
46-47	Chi	24	0	1	1	18

FOX, Gregory Brent 6-2 190 D
B. Port McNeil, B.C., Aug. 12, 1953

Season	Team	GP	G	A	Pts.	PIM
77-78	Atl	16	1	2	3	25
78-79	Atl-Chi	78	0	17	17	86
79-80	Chi	71	4	11	15	73
80-81	Chi	75	3	16	19	112
81-82	Chi	79	2	19	21	137
82-83	Chi	76	0	12	12	81
83-84	Chi-Pitt	73	2	10	12	97
84-85	Pitt	26	2	5	7	26
Totals		494	14	92	106	637
Playoff Totals		44	1	9	10	67

FOX, James Charles 5-8 185 RW
B. Coniston, Ont., May 18, 1960

Season	Team	GP	G	A	Pts.	PIM
80-81	LA	71	18	25	43	8
81-82	LA	77	30	38	68	23
82-83	LA	77	28	40	68	8
83-84	LA	80	30	42	72	26
84-85	LA	79	30	53	83	10
85-86	LA	39	14	17	31	2
86-87	LA	76	19	42	61	48
87-88	LA	68	16	35	51	18
89-90	LA	11	1	1	2	0
Totals		578	186	293	479	143
Playoff Totals		22	4	8	12	0

FOYSTON, Frank C. C
B. Minesing, Ont., Feb. 2, 1891

Season	Team	GP	G	A	Pts.	PIM
26-27	Det	41	10	5	15	16
27-28	Det	23	7	2	9	16
Totals		64	17	7	24	32

FRAMPTON, Robert Percy James 5-10 175 LW
B. Toronto, Ont., Jan. 20, 1929

Season	Team	GP	G	A	Pts.	PIM
49-50	Mont	2	0	0	0	0
Playoff Totals		3	0	0	0	0

FRANCESCHETTI, Lou 6-0 190 LW
B. Toronto, Ont., Mar. 28, 1958

Season	Team	GP	G	A	Pts.	PIM
81-82	Wash	30	2	10	12	23
83-84	Wash	2	0	0	0	0
84-85	Wash	22	4	7	11	45
85-86	Wash	76	7	14	21	131
86-87	Wash	75	12	9	21	127
87-88	Wash	59	4	8	12	113
88-89	Wash	63	7	10	17	123
89-90	Tor	80	21	15	36	127
90-91	Tor-Buf	51	2	8	10	58
91-92	Buf	1	0	0	0	0
Totals		459	59	81	140	747
Playoff Totals		44	3	2	5	111

FRANCIS, Robert (Bobby) 5-9 175 C
B. North Battleford, Sask., Dec. 5, 1958

Season	Team	GP	G	A	Pts.	PIM
82-83	Det	14	2	0	2	0

FRANCIS, Ronald 6-2 200 C
B. Sault Ste. Marie, Ont., Mar. 1, 1963

Season	Team	GP	G	A	Pts.	PIM
81-82	Hart	59	25	43	68	51
82-83	Hart	79	31	59	90	60
83-84	Hart	72	23	60	83	45
84-85	Hart	80	24	57	81	66
85-86	Hart	53	24	53	77	24
86-87	Hart	75	30	63	93	45
87-88	Hart	80	25	50	75	87
88-89	Hart	69	29	48	77	36
89-90	Hart	80	32	69	101	73
90-91	Hart-Pitt	81	23	64	87	72
91-92	Pitt	70	21	33	54	30
Totals		798	287	599	886	589
Playoff Totals		78	23	43	66	50

FRASER, Archibald McKay (Archie) F
B. Souris, Man., Feb. 9, 1914

Season	Team	GP	G	A	Pts.	PIM
43-44	NYR	3	0	1	1	0

FRASER, Curt M. 6-1 200 LW
B. Cincinnati, Ohio, Jan. 12, 1958

Season	Team	GP	G	A	Pts.	PIM
78-79	Van	78	16	19	35	116
79-80	Van	78	17	25	42	143
80-81	Van	77	25	24	49	118
81-82	Van	79	28	39	67	175
82-83	Van-Chi	74	12	20	32	176
83-84	Chi	29	5	12	17	28
84-85	Chi	73	25	25	50	109
85-86	Chi	61	29	39	68	84
86-87	Chi	75	25	25	50	182
87-88	Chi-Minn	37	5	7	12	77
88-89	Minn	35	5	5	10	70
89-90	Minn	8	1	0	1	22
Totals		704	193	240	433	1306
Playoff Totals		65	15	18	33	198

FRASER, Gordon (Gord) D
B. Pembroke, Ont.

Season	Team	GP	G	A	Pts.	PIM
26-27	Chi	43	14	6	20	89
27-28	Chi-Det	41	4	2	6	60
28-29	Det	13	0	0	0	12
29-30	Mont-Pitt Pi	40	6	4	10	41
30-31	Phil Q	7	0	0	0	22
Totals		144	24	12	36	224
Playoff Totals		2	1	0	1	6

FRASER, Jack F

Season	Team	GP	G	A	Pts.	PIM
23-24	Ham	1	0	0	0	0

FRASER, James Harvey (Harry) 5-10 168 C
B. Souris, Man., Oct. 14, 1918

Season	Team	GP	G	A	Pts.	PIM
44-45	Chi	21	5	4	9	0

FRAWLEY, William Daniel (Dan) 6-1 190 RW
B. Sturgeon Falls, Ont., June 2, 1962

Season	Team	GP	G	A	Pts.	PIM
83-84	Chi	0	0	0	0	0
84-85	Chi	30	4	3	7	64
85-86	Pitt	69	10	11	21	174
86-87	Pitt	78	14	14	28	218
87-88	Pitt	47	6	8	14	152
88-89	Pitt	46	3	4	7	66
Totals		273	37	40	77	674
Playoff Totals		1	0	0	0	0

FREDERICKSON, Frank 5-11 175 C
B. Winnipeg, Man., 1895

Season	Team	GP	G	A	Pts.	PIM
26-27	Det-Bos	44	18	13	31	45
27-28	Bos	44	10	4	14	83
28-29	Bos-Pitt Pi	43	6	8	14	52
29-30	Pitt Pi	9	4	7	11	20
30-31	Det	25	1	2	3	6
Totals		165	39	34	73	206
Playoff Totals		10	2	5	7	26

FREER, Mark 5-10 180 C
B. Peterborough, Ont., July 14, 1968

Season	Team	GP	G	A	Pts.	PIM
86-87	Phil	1	0	1	1	0
87-88	Phil	1	0	0	1	0
88-89	Phil	5	0	1	1	0
89-90	Phil	2	0	0	0	0
91-92	Phil	50	6	7	13	18
Totals		59	6	9	15	18

FREW, Irvine (Irv) 5-9 180 D
B. Kilsyth, Scotland, Aug. 16, 1907

Season	Team	GP	G	A	Pts.	PIM
33-34	Mont M	30	2	1	3	41
34-35	StLE	47	0	2	2	89
35-36	Mont	18	0	2	2	16
Totals		95	2	5	7	146
Playoff Totals		4	0	0	0	6

FRIDAY, Tim 6-0 190 D
B. Burbank, Cal., Mar. 5, 1961

Season	Team	GP	G	A	Pts.	PIM
85-86	Det	23	0	3	3	6

FRIDGEN, Dan 5-11 175 LW
B. Arnprior, Ont., May 18, 1959

Season	Team	GP	G	A	Pts.	PIM
81-82	Hart	2	0	1	1	0
82-83	Hart	11	2	2	4	2
Totals		13	2	3	5	2

FRIEST, Ronald 5-11 185 LW
B. Windsor, Ont., Nov. 4, 1958

Season	Team	GP	G	A	Pts.	PIM
80-81	Minn	4	1	0	1	10
81-82	Minn	10	0	0	0	31
82-83	Minn	50	6	7	13	150
Totals		64	7	7	14	191
Playoff Totals		6	1	0	1	7

FRIG, Leonard Elroy (Len) 5-11 190 D
B. Lethbridge, Alta., Oct. 23, 1950

Season	Team	GP	G	A	Pts.	PIM
73-74	Cal	66	4	10	14	35
74-75	Cal	80	3	17	20	127
75-76	Cal	62	3	12	15	55
76-77	Clev	66	2	7	9	213
77-78	StL	30	1	3	4	45
79-80	StL	7	0	2	2	2
Totals		311	13	51	64	477
Playoff Totals		14	2	1	3	0

FROST, Harold (Harry) 5-11 165 RW
B. Kerr Lake, Ont., Aug. 17, 1914

Season	Team	GP	G	A	Pts.	PIM
38-39	Bos	3	0	0	0	0
Playoff Totals		1	0	0	0	0

FRYCER, Miroslav 6-0 200 RW
B. Ostrava, Czechoslovakia, Sept. 27, 1959

Season	Team	GP	G	A	Pts.	PIM
81-82	Que-Tor	59	24	23	47	78
82-83	Tor	67	25	30	55	90
83-84	Tor	47	10	16	26	55
84-85	Tor	65	25	30	55	55
85-86	Tor	73	32	43	75	74
86-87	Tor	29	7	8	15	28
87-88	Tor	38	12	20	32	41
88-89	Det-Edm	37	12	13	25	65
Totals		415	147	183	330	486
Playoff Totals		17	3	8	11	16

FRYDAY, Robert George 5-10 155 RW
B. Toronto, Ont., Dec. 5, 1928

Season	Team	GP	G	A	Pts.	PIM
49-50	Mont	2	1	0	1	0
51-52	Mont	3	0	0	0	0
Totals		5	1	0	1	0

FTOREK, Robert Brian 5-10 155 C
B. Needham, Mass., Jan. 2, 1952

Season	Team	GP	G	A	Pts.	PIM
72-73	Det	3	0	0	0	0
73-74	Det	12	2	5	7	4
74-75	Phoe (WHA)	63	31	37	68	29
75-76	Phoe (WHA)	80	41	72	113	109
76-77	Phoe (WHA)	80	46	71	117	86
77-78	Cin (WHA)	80	59	50	109	54
78-79	Cin (WHA)	80	39	77	116	87
79-80	Que	52	18	33	51	28
80-81	Que	78	24	49	73	104
81-82	Que-NYR	49	9	32	41	28
82-83	NYR	61	12	19	31	41
83-84	NYR	31	3	2	5	22
84-85	NYR	40	9	10	19	35
NHL Totals		334	77	150	227	262
WHA Totals		373	216	307	523	365
NHL Playoff Totals		19	9	6	15	28
WHA Playoff Totals		13	6	10	16	10

FULLAN, Lawrence *5-11 185 LW*
B. Toronto, Ont., Aug. 11, 1949

Season	Team	GP	G	A	Pts.	PIM
74-75	Wash	4	1	0	1	0

FUSCO, Mark *5-9 175 D*
B. Burlington, Mass., Mar. 12, 1961

Season	Team	GP	G	A	Pts.	PIM
83-84	Hart	17	0	4	4	2
84-85	Hart	63	3	8	11	40
Totals		80	3	12	15	42

GADSBY, William Alexander *6-0 185 D*
B. Calgary, Alta., Aug. 8, 1927

Season	Team	GP	G	A	Pts.	PIM
46-47	Chi	48	8	10	18	31
47-48	Chi	60	6	10	16	66
48-49	Chi	50	3	10	13	85
49-50	Chi	70	10	24	34	138
50-51	Chi	25	3	7	10	32
51-52	Chi	59	7	15	22	87
52-53	Chi	68	2	20	22	84
53-54	Chi	70	12	29	41	108
54-55	Chi-NYR	70	11	13	24	61
55-56	NYR	70	9	42	51	84
56-57	NYR	70	4	37	41	72
57-58	NYR	65	14	32	46	48
58-59	NYR	70	5	46	51	56
59-60	NYR	65	9	22	31	60
60-61	NYR	65	9	26	35	49
61-62	Det	70	7	30	37	88
62-63	Det	70	4	24	28	116
63-64	Det	64	2	16	18	80
64-65	Det	61	0	12	12	122
65-66	Det	58	5	12	17	72
Totals		1248	130	437	567	1539
Playoff Totals		67	4	23	27	92

GAETZ, Link *6-4 210 D*
B. Vancouver, B.C., Oct. 2, 1968

Season	Team	GP	G	A	Pts.	PIM
88-89	Minn	12	0	2	2	53
89-90	Minn	5	0	0	0	33
91-92	SJ	48	6	6	12	324
Totals		65	6	8	14	410

GAGE, Joseph William (Jody)
6-0 190 RW
B. Toronto, Ont., Nov. 29, 1959

Season	Team	GP	G	A	Pts.	PIM
80-81	Det	16	2	2	4	22
81-82	Det	31	9	10	19	2
83-84	Det	3	0	0	0	0
85-86	Buf	7	3	2	5	0
87-88	Buf	2	0	0	0	0
91-92	Buf	9	0	1	1	2
Totals		68	14	15	29	26

GAGNE, Arthur E. *RW*

Season	Team	GP	G	A	Pts.	PIM
26-27	Mont	44	14	3	17	42
27-28	Mont	44	20	10	30	75
28-29	Mont	44	7	3	10	52
29-30	Bos-Ott	39	6	5	11	38
30-31	Ott	44	19	11	30	50
31-32	Det	13	1	1	2	0
Totals		228	67	33	100	257
Playoff Totals		11	2	1	3	20

GAGNE, Paul *5-10 180 LW*
B. Iroquois Falls, Ont., Feb. 6, 1962

Season	Team	GP	G	A	Pts.	PIM
80-81	Col	61	25	16	41	12
81-82	Col	59	10	12	22	17
82-83	NJ	63	14	15	29	13
83-84	NJ	66	14	18	32	33
84-85	NJ	79	24	19	43	28
85-86	NJ	47	19	19	38	14
88-89	Tor	16	3	2	5	6
89-90	NYI	9	1	0	1	4
Totals		400	110	101	211	127

GAGNE, Pierre Reynald *6-0 180 LW*
B. North Bay, Ont., June 5, 1940

Season	Team	GP	G	A	Pts.	PIM
59-60	Bos	2	0	0	0	0

GAGNER, Dave *5-10 180 C*
B. Chatham, Ont., Dec. 11, 1964

Season	Team	GP	G	A	Pts.	PIM
84-85	NYR	38	6	6	12	16
85-86	NYR	32	4	6	10	19
86-87	NYR	10	1	4	5	12
87-88	Minn	51	8	11	19	55
88-89	Minn	75	35	43	78	104
89-90	Minn	79	40	38	78	54
90-91	Minn	73	40	42	82	114
91-92	Minn	78	31	40	71	107
Totals		436	165	190	355	481
Playoff Totals		37	16	22	38	52

GAINEY, Robert Michael *6-2 200 LW*
B. Peterborough, Ont., Dec. 13, 1953

Season	Team	GP	G	A	Pts.	PIM
73-74	Mont	66	3	7	10	34
74-75	Mont	80	17	20	37	49
75-76	Mont	78	15	13	28	57

GAINEY, Robert Michael *(Continued)*

Season	Team	GP	G	A	Pts.	PIM
76-77	Mont	80	14	19	33	41
77-78	Mont	66	15	16	31	57
78-79	Mont	79	20	18	38	44
79-80	Mont	64	14	19	33	32
80-81	Mont	78	23	24	47	36
81-82	Mont	79	21	24	45	24
82-83	Mont	80	12	18	30	43
83-84	Mont	77	17	22	39	41
84-85	Mont	79	19	13	32	40
85-86	Mont	80	20	23	43	20
86-87	Mont	47	8	8	16	19
87-88	Mont	78	11	11	22	14
88-89	Mont	49	10	7	17	34
Totals		1160	239	262	501	585
Playoff Totals		182	25	48	73	151

GAGNON, Germain *6-0 172 LW*
B. Chicoutimi, Que., Dec. 9, 1942

Season	Team	GP	G	A	Pts.	PIM
71-72	Mont	4	0	0	0	0
72-73	NYI	63	12	29	41	31
73-74	NYI-Chi	76	11	28	39	12
74-75	Chi	80	16	35	51	21
75-76	Chi-KC	36	1	9	10	8
Totals		259	40	101	141	72
Playoff Totals		19	2	3	5	2

GAGNON, Johnny (Black Cat)
5-5 140 RW
B. Chicoutimi, Que., June 8, 1905

Season	Team	GP	G	A	Pts.	PIM
30-31	Mont	41	18	7	25	43
31-32	Mont	48	19	18	37	40
32-33	Mont	48	12	23	35	64
33-34	Mont	48	9	15	24	25
34-35	Bos-Mont	47	2	6	8	11
35-36	Mont	48	7	9	16	42
36-37	Mont	48	20	16	36	38
37-38	Mont	47	13	17	30	9
38-39	Mont	45	12	22	34	23
39-40	Mont-NYA	34	8	8	16	0
Totals		454	120	141	261	295
Playoff Totals		32	12	12	24	37

GAINOR, Norman (Dutch) *6-1 170 C*
B. Calgary, Alta., Apr. 10, 1904

Season	Team	GP	G	A	Pts.	PIM
27-28	Bos	41	8	4	12	35
28-29	Bos	39	14	5	19	30
29-30	Bos	43	18	31	49	39
30-31	Bos	32	8	3	11	14
31-32	NYR	46	3	9	12	9
32-33	Ott	2	0	0	0	0
34-35	Mont M	40	0	4	4	2
Totals		243	51	56	107	129
Playoff Totals		25	2	1	3	14

GALARNEAU, Michel *6-2 180 C*
B. Montreal, Que., Mar. 1, 1961

Season	Team	GP	G	A	Pts.	PIM
80-81	Hart	30	2	6	8	9
81-82	Hart	10	0	0	0	4
82-83	Hart	38	5	4	9	21
Totals		78	7	10	17	34

GALBRAITH, Percival (Perk) *5-10 162 LW*
B. Toronto, Ont., 1899

Season	Team	GP	G	A	Pts.	PIM
26-27	Bos	42	9	8	17	26
27-28	Bos	42	6	5	11	26
28-29	Bos	38	2	1	3	44
29-30	Bos	44	7	9	16	38
30-31	Bos	43	2	3	5	28
31-32	Bos	47	2	1	3	28
32-33	Bos	47	1	2	3	28
33-34	Ott-Bos	44	0	2	2	5
Totals		347	29	31	60	223
Playoff Totals		31	4	7	11	24

GALLAGHER, John James Patrick
5-11 188 D
B. Kenora, Ont., Jan. 19, 1909

Season	Team	GP	G	A	Pts.	PIM
30-31	Mont M	35	4	2	6	35
31-32	Mont M	19	1	0	1	18
32-33	Mont M-Det	41	4	6	10	48
33-34	Det	1	0	0	0	0
36-37	NYA-Det	20	1	0	1	12
37-38	NYA	47	3	6	9	18
38-39	NYA	41	1	5	6	22
Totals		204	14	19	33	153
Playoff Totals		22	2	3	5	27

GALLANT, Gerard *5-10 185 LW*
B. Summerside, P.E.I., Sept. 2, 1963

Season	Team	GP	G	A	Pts.	PIM
84-85	Det	32	6	12	18	66
85-86	Det	52	20	19	39	106
86-87	Det	80	38	34	72	216
87-88	Det	73	34	39	73	242

GALLANT, Gerard *(Continued)*

Season	Team	GP	G	A	Pts.	PIM
88-89	Det	76	39	54	93	230
89-90	Det	69	36	44	80	254
90-91	Det	45	10	16	26	111
91-92	Det	69	14	22	36	187
Totals		496	197	240	437	1412
Playoff Totals		52	17	19	36	174

GALLEY, Garry *6-0 190 D*
B. Montreal, Que., Apr. 16, 1963

Season	Team	GP	G	A	Pts.	PIM
84-85	LA	78	8	30	38	82
85-86	LA	49	9	13	22	46
86-87	LA-Wash	48	6	21	27	67
87-88	Wash	58	7	23	30	44
88-89	Bos	78	8	21	29	80
89-90	Bos	71	8	27	35	75
90-91	Bos	70	6	21	27	84
91-92	Bos-Phil	77	5	27	32	117
Totals		529	57	183	240	595
Playoff Totals		64	7	13	20	109

GALLIMORE, James (Jamie) *6-0 180 RW*
B. Edmonton, Alta., Nov. 28, 1957

Season	Team	GP	G	A	Pts.	PIM
77-78	Minn	2	0	0	0	0

GALLINGER, Donald C. *6-0 170 C*
B. Port Colborne, Ont., Apr. 10, 1925

Season	Team	GP	G	A	Pts.	PIM
42-43	Bos	48	14	20	34	16
43-44	Bos	23	13	5	18	6
45-46	Bos	50	17	23	40	18
46-47	Bos	47	11	19	30	12
47-48	Bos	54	10	21	31	37
Totals		222	65	88	153	89
Playoff Totals		23	5	5	10	19

GAMBLE, Richard Frank (Dick)
6-0 178 LW
B. Moncton, N.B., Nov. 16, 1928

Season	Team	GP	G	A	Pts.	PIM
50-51	Mont	1	0	0	0	0
51-52	Mont	64	23	17	40	8
52-53	Mont	69	11	13	24	26
53-54	Mont	32	4	8	12	18
54-55	Chi	14	2	0	2	6
55-56	Mont	12	0	3	3	8
65-66	Tor	2	1	0	1	0
66-67	Tor	1	0	0	0	0
Totals		195	41	41	82	66
Playoff Totals		14	1	2	3	4

GAMBUCCI, Gary Allan *5-9 175 C*
B. Hibbing, Minn., Sept. 27, 1946

Season	Team	GP	G	A	Pts.	PIM
71-72	Minn	9	1	0	1	0
73-74	Minn	42	1	7	8	9
74-75	Minn (WHA)	67	19	18	37	19
75-76	Minn (WHA)	45	10	6	16	14
NHL Totals		51	2	7	9	9
WHA Totals		112	29	24	53	33
WHA Playoff Totals		12	4	0	4	6

GANCHAR, Perry *5-9 180 RW*
B. Saskatoon, Sask., Oct. 28, 1963

Season	Team	GP	G	A	Pts.	PIM
83-84	StL	1	0	0	0	0
84-85	StL	7	0	2	2	0
87-88	Mont-Pitt	31	3	5	8	36
88-89	Pitt	3	0	0	0	0
Totals		42	3	7	10	36
Playoff Totals		7	3	1	4	0

GANS, David *5-10 180 C*
B. Brantford, Ont., June 6, 1964

Season	Team	GP	G	A	Pts.	PIM
82-83	LA	3	0	0	0	0
85-86	LA	3	0	0	0	2
Totals		6	0	0	0	2

GARDINER, Herbert Martin *D*
B. Winnipeg, Man., May 8, 1891

Season	Team	GP	G	A	Pts.	PIM
26-27	Mont	44	6	6	12	26
27-28	Mont	44	4	3	7	26
28-29	Chi-Mont	13	0	0	0	0
Totals		101	10	9	19	52
Playoff Totals		7	0	1	1	14

GARDNER, Calvin Pearly (Finger)
6-1 175 C
B. Transcona, Man., Oct. 30, 1924

Season	Team	GP	G	A	Pts.	PIM
45-46	NYR	16	8	2	10	2
46-47	NYR	52	13	16	29	30
47-48	NYR	58	7	18	25	71
48-49	Tor	53	13	22	35	35
49-50	Tor	30	7	19	26	12
50-51	Tor	66	23	28	51	42
51-52	Tor	70	15	26	41	40
52-53	Chi	70	11	24	35	60
53-54	Bos	70	14	20	34	62

GARDNER, Calvin Pearly (Finger)
(Continued)

Season	Team	GP	G	A	Pts.	PIM
54-55	Bos	70	16	22	38	40
55-56	Bos	70	15	21	36	57
56-57	Bos	70	12	20	32	66
Totals		695	154	238	392	517
Playoff Totals		61	7	10	17	20

GARDNER, David Calvin *6-0 183 C*
B. Toronto, Ont., Aug. 23, 1952

Season	Team	GP	G	A	Pts.	PIM
72-73	Mont	5	1	1	2	0
73-74	Mont-StL	46	6	12	18	8
74-75	StL-Cal	72	16	22	38	6
75-76	Cal	74	16	32	48	8
76-77	Clev	76	16	22	38	9
77-78	Clev	75	19	25	44	10
79-80	Phil	2	1	1	2	0
Totals		350	75	115	190	41

GARDNER, Paul Malone *6-0 195 C*
B. Fort Erie, Ont., Mar. 5. 1956

Season	Team	GP	G	A	Pts.	PIM
76-77	Col	60	30	29	59	25
77-78	Col	46	30	22	52	29
78-79	Col-Tor	75	30	28	58	32
79-80	Tor	45	11	13	24	10
80-81	Pitt	62	34	40	74	59
81-82	Pitt	59	36	33	69	28
82-83	Pitt	70	28	27	55	12
83-84	Pitt	16	0	5	5	6
84-85	Wash	12	2	4	6	6
85-86	Buf	2	0	0	0	0
Totals		447	201	201	402	207
Playoff Totals		16	2	6	8	14

GARDNER, William Scott *5-10 180 C*
B. Toronto, Ont., Mar. 18, 1960

Season	Team	GP	G	A	Pts.	PIM
80-81	Chi	1	0	0	0	0
81-82	Chi	69	8	15	23	20
82-83	Chi	77	15	25	40	12
83-84	Chi	79	27	21	48	12
84-85	Chi	74	17	34	51	12
85-86	Chi-Hart	64	4	18	22	10
86-87	Hart	8	0	1	1	0
87-88	Chi	2	1	0	1	2
88-89	Chi	6	1	1	2	0
Totals		380	73	115	188	68
Playoff Totals		45	3	8	11	17

GARE, Daniel Mirl *5-9 175 RW*
B. Nelson, B.C., May 14, 1954

Season	Team	GP	G	A	Pts.	PIM
74-75	Buf	78	31	31	62	75
75-76	Buf	79	50	23	73	129
76-77	Buf	35	11	15	26	73
77-78	Buf	69	39	38	77	95
78-79	Buf	71	27	40	67	90
79-80	Buf	76	56	33	89	90
80-81	Buf	73	46	39	85	109
81-82	Buf-Det	58	20	23	43	99
82-83	Det	79	26	35	61	107
83-84	Det	63	13	13	26	147
84-85	Det	71	27	29	56	163
85-86	Det	57	7	9	16	102
86-87	Edm	18	1	3	4	6
Totals		827	354	331	685	1285
Playoff Totals		64	25	21	46	195

GARIEPY, Raymond *5-8 180 D*
B. Toronto, Ont., Sept. 4, 1928

Season	Team	GP	G	A	Pts.	PIM
53-54	Bos	35	1	6	7	39
55-56	Tor	1	0	0	0	4
Totals		36	1	6	7	43

GARLAND, Stephen (Scott) *6-1 185 C*
B. Regina, Sask., May 16, 1952

Season	Team	GP	G	A	Pts.	PIM
75-76	Tor	16	4	3	7	8
76-77	Tor	69	9	20	29	83
78-79	LA	6	0	1	1	24
Totals		91	13	24	37	115
Playoff Totals		7	1	2	3	35

GARNER, Robert William *5-11 180 C*
B. Weston, Ont., Aug. 17, 1958

Season	Team	GP	G	A	Pts.	PIM
82-83	Pitt	1	0	0	0	0

GARPENLOV, Johan *5-11 183 LW*
B. Stockholm, Sweden, Mar. 21, 1968

Season	Team	GP	G	A	Pts.	PIM
90-91	Det	71	18	22	40	18
91-92	Det-SJ	28	6	7	13	8
Totals		99	24	29	53	26
Playoff Totals		6	0	1	1	4

GARRETT, Dudley (Red) *5-11 190 D*
B. Toronto, Ont., July 24, 1924

Season	Team	GP	G	A	Pts.	PIM
42-43	NYR	23	1	1	2	18

GARTNER, Michael Alfred *6-0 190 RW*
B. Ottawa, Ont., Oct. 29, 1959

Season	Team	GP	G	A	Pts.	PIM
78-79	Cin (WHA)	78	27	25	52	123
79-80	Wash	77	36	32	68	66
80-81	Wash	80	48	46	94	100
81-82	Wash	80	35	45	80	121
82-83	Wash	73	38	38	76	54
83-84	Wash	80	40	45	85	90
84-85	Wash	80	50	52	102	71
85-86	Wash	74	35	40	75	63
86-87	Wash	78	41	32	73	61
87-88	Wash	80	48	33	81	73
88-89	Wash-Minn	69	33	36	69	73
89-90	Minn-NYR	79	45	41	86	38
90-91	NYR	79	49	20	69	53
91-92	NYR	76	40	41	81	55
NHL Totals		1005	538	501	1039	918
WHA Totals		78	27	25	52	123
NHL Playoff Totals		81	30	39	69	83
WHA Playoff Totals		3	0	2	2	2

GASSOFF, Robert Allen *5-10 195 D*
B. Quesnel, B.C., Apr. 17, 1953

Season	Team	GP	G	A	Pts.	PIM
73-74	StL	28	0	3	3	84
74-75	StL	60	4	14	18	222
75-76	StL	80	1	12	13	306
76-77	StL	77	6	18	24	254
Totals		245	11	47	58	866
Playoff Totals		9	0	1	1	16

GASSOFF, Howard Bradley (Brad)
5-11 195 LW
B. Quesnel, B.C., Nov. 13, 1955

Season	Team	GP	G	A	Pts.	PIM
75-76	Van	4	0	0	0	5
76-77	Van	37	6	4	10	35
77-78	Van	47	9	6	15	70
78-79	Van	34	4	7	11	53
Totals		122	19	17	36	163
Playoff Totals		3	0	0	0	0

GATZOS, Steve *5-11 185 RW*
B. Toronto, Ont., June 22, 1961

Season	Team	GP	G	A	Pts.	PIM
81-82	Pitt	16	6	8	14	14
82-83	Pitt	44	6	7	13	52
83-84	Pitt	23	3	3	6	15
84-85	Pitt	6	0	2	2	2
Totals		89	15	20	35	83
Playoff Totals		1	0	0	0	0

GAUDREAULT, Armand Gerard
5-9 155 LW
B. Lac St. Jean, Que., July 14, 1921

Season	Team	GP	G	A	Pts.	PIM
44-45	Bos	44	15	9	24	27
Playoff Totals		7	0	2	2	8

GAUDREAULT, Leonard (Leo)
5-9 152 LW
B. Chicoutimi, Que.

Season	Team	GP	G	A	Pts.	PIM
27-28	Mont	32	6	2	8	24
28-29	Mont	11	0	0	0	4
32-33	Mont	24	2	2	4	2
Totals		67	8	4	12	30

GAULIN, Jean-Marc *5-10 180 RW*
B. Balve, Germany, Mar. 3, 1962

Season	Team	GP	G	A	Pts.	PIM
82-83	Que	1	0	0	0	0
83-84	Que	2	0	0	0	0
84-85	Que	22	3	3	6	8
85-86	Que	1	1	0	1	0
Totals		26	4	3	7	8
Playoff Totals		1	0	0	0	0

GAUME, Dallas *5-10 185 C*
B. Innisfal, Alta., Aug. 27, 1963

Season	Team	GP	G	A	Pts.	PIM
88-89	Hart	4	1	1	2	0

GAUTHIER, Arthur *F*

Season	Team	GP	G	A	Pts.	PIM
26-27	Mont	13	0	0	0	0
Playoff Totals		1	0	0	0	0

GAUTHIER, Jean Philippe *6-1 200 D*
B. Montreal, Que., Mar. 29, 1937

Season	Team	GP	G	A	Pts.	PIM
60-61	Mont	4	0	1	1	8
61-62	Mont	12	0	1	1	10
62-63	Mont	65	1	17	18	46
63-64	Mont	1	0	0	0	2
65-66	Mont	2	0	0	0	0
66-67	Mont	2	0	0	0	2
67-68	Phil	65	5	7	12	74
68-69	Bos	11	0	2	2	8
69-70	Mont	4	0	1	1	0
72-73	NY (WHA)	31	2	1	3	21
NHL Totals		166	6	29	35	150
WHA Totals		31	2	1	3	21
NHL Playoff Totals		14	1	3	4	22

GAUTHIER, Luc *5-9 205 D*
B. Longueuil, Que., Apr. 19, 1964

Season	Team	GP	G	A	Pts.	PIM
90-91	Mont	3	0	0	0	2

GAUTHIER, Rene Fernand (Fern)
5-11 175 RW
B. Chicoutimi, Que., Aug. 31, 1919

Season	Team	GP	G	A	Pts.	PIM
43-44	NYR	33	14	10	24	0
44-45	Mont	50	18	13	31	23
45-46	Det	30	9	8	17	6
46-47	Det	40	1	12	13	2
47-48	Det	35	1	5	6	2
48-49	Det	41	3	2	5	2
Totals		229	46	50	96	35
Playoff Totals		22	5	1	6	7

GAUVREAU, Jocelyn *5-11 180 D*
B. Masham, Que., Mar. 4, 1964

Season	Team	GP	G	A	Pts.	PIM
83-84	Mont	2	0	0	0	0

GAVIN, Robert (Stewart) *6-0 190 LW/RW*
B. Ottawa, Ont., Mar. 15, 1960

Season	Team	GP	G	A	Pts.	PIM
80-81	Tor	14	1	2	3	13
81-82	Tor	38	5	6	11	29
82-83	Tor	63	6	5	11	44
83-84	Tor	80	10	22	32	90
84-85	Tor	73	12	13	25	38
85-86	Hart	76	26	29	55	51
86-87	Hart	79	20	21	41	28
87-88	Hart	56	11	10	21	59
88-89	Minn	73	8	18	26	34
89-90	Minn	80	12	13	25	76
90-91	Minn	38	4	4	8	36
91-92	Minn	35	5	4	9	27
Totals		705	120	147	267	525
Playoff Totals		66	14	20	34	75

GEALE, Robert Charles *5-11 175 C*
B. Edmonton, Alta., Apr. 17, 1962

Season	Team	GP	G	A	Pts.	PIM
84-85	Pitt	1	0	0	0	2

GEE, George *5-11 180 C*
B. Stratford, Ont., June 28, 1922

Season	Team	GP	G	A	Pts.	PIM
45-46	Chi	35	14	15	29	12
46-47	Chi	60	20	20	40	26
47-48	Chi	60	14	25	39	18
48-49	Chi-Det	51	7	14	21	31
49-50	Det	69	17	21	38	42
50-51	Det	70	17	20	37	19
51-52	Chi	70	18	31	49	39
52-53	Chi	67	18	21	39	99
53-54	Chi	69	10	16	26	59
Totals		551	135	183	318	345
Playoff Totals		41	6	13	19	32

GELDART, Gary Daniel *5-8 155 D*
B. Moncton, N.B., June 14, 1950

Season	Team	GP	G	A	Pts.	PIM
70-71	Minn	4	0	0	0	5

GELINAS, Martin *5-11 195 LW*
B. Shawinigan, Que., June 5, 1970

Season	Team	GP	G	A	Pts.	PIM
88-89	Edm	6	1	2	3	0
89-90	Edm	46	17	8	25	30
90-91	Edm	73	20	20	40	34
91-92	Edm	68	11	18	29	62
Totals		193	49	48	97	126
Playoff Totals		53	6	12	18	41

GENDRON, Jean Guy (Smitty)
5-9 165 LW
B. Montreal, Que., Aug. 30, 1934

Season	Team	GP	G	A	Pts.	PIM
55-56	NYR	63	5	7	12	38
56-57	NYR	70	9	6	15	40
57-58	NYR	70	10	17	27	68
58-59	Bos	60	15	9	24	57
59-60	Bos	67	24	11	35	64
60-61	Bos-Mont	66	10	19	29	75
61-62	NYR	69	14	11	25	71
62-63	Bos	66	21	22	43	42
63-64	Bos	54	5	13	18	43
67-68	Phil	1	0	1	1	2
68-69	Phil	74	20	35	55	65
69-70	Phil	71	23	21	44	54
70-71	Phil	76	20	16	36	46
71-72	Phil	56	6	13	19	36
72-73	Que (WHA)	63	17	33	50	113
73-74	Que (WHA)	64	11	8	19	42
NHL Totals		863	182	201	383	701
WHA Totals		127	28	41	69	155
NHL Playoff Totals		42	7	4	11	47

GEOFFRION, Bernard Joseph Andre (Boom Boom) *5-11 185 RW*
B. Montreal, Que., Feb. 16, 1931

Season	Team	GP	G	A	Pts.	PIM
50-51	Mont	18	8	6	14	9
51-52	Mont	67	30	24	54	66
52-53	Mont	65	22	17	39	37

GEOFFRION, Bernard Joseph Andre (Boom Boom) *(Continued)*

Season	Team	GP	G	A	Pts.	PIM
53-54	Mont	54	29	25	54	87
54-55	Mont	70	38	37	75	57
55-56	Mont	59	29	33	62	66
56-57	Mont	41	19	21	40	18
57-58	Mont	42	27	23	50	51
58-59	Mont	59	22	44	66	30
59-60	Mont	59	30	41	71	36
60-61	Mont	64	50	45	95	29
61-62	Mont	62	23	36	59	36
62-63	Mont	51	23	18	41	73
63-64	Mont	55	21	18	39	41
66-67	NYR	58	17	25	42	42
67-68	NYR	59	5	16	21	11
Totals		883	393	429	822	689
Playoff Totals		132	58	60	118	88

GEOFFRION, Daniel *5-10 185 RW*
B. Montreal, Que., Jan. 24, 1958

Season	Team	GP	G	A	Pts.	PIM
78-79	Que (WHA)	77	12	14	26	74
79-80	Mont	32	0	6	6	12
80-81	Winn	78	20	26	46	82
81-82	Winn	1	0	0	0	5
NHL Totals		111	20	32	52	99
WHA Totals		77	12	14	26	74
NHL Playoff Totals		2	0	0	0	7
WHA Playoff Totals		4	1	2	3	2

GERAN, Gerald Pierce *F*
B. Holyoke, Mass., Aug. 3, 1896

Season	Team	GP	G	A	Pts.	PIM
17-18	Mont W	4	0	0	0	0
25-26	Bos	33	5	1	6	6
Totals		37	5	1	6	6

GERARD, Edward George *F*
B. Ottawa, Ont., Feb. 22, 1890

Season	Team	GP	G	A	Pts.	PIM
17-18	Ott	21	13	0	13	12
18-19	Ott	18	4	6	10	17
19-20	Ott	21	9	3	12	19
20-21	Ott	24	11	4	15	18
21-22	Ott	21	7	9	16	16
22-23	Ott	23	6	8	14	24
Totals		128	50	30	80	106
Playoff Totals		26	7	3	10	51

GERMAIN, Eric *6-1 195 D*
B. Quebec City, Que., June 26, 1966

Season	Team	GP	G	A	Pts.	PIM
87-88	LA	4	0	1	1	13

GETLIFFE, Raymond *5-11 175 C*
B. Galt, Ont., Apr. 3, 1914

Season	Team	GP	G	A	Pts.	PIM
35-36	Bos	1	0	0	0	2
36-37	Bos	48	16	15	31	28
37-38	Bos	36	11	13	24	16
38-39	Bos	43	10	12	22	11
39-40	Mont	46	11	12	23	29
40-41	Mont	39	15	10	25	25
41-42	Mont	45	11	15	26	35
42-43	Mont	50	18	28	46	56
43-44	Mont	44	28	25	53	44
44-45	Mont	41	16	7	23	34
Totals		393	136	137	273	280
Playoff Totals		45	9	10	19	30

GIALLONARDO, Mario *5-11 201 D*
B. Toronto, Ont., Sept. 27, 1957

Season	Team	GP	G	A	Pts.	PIM
79-80	Col	8	0	1	1	2
80-81	Col	15	0	2	2	4
Totals		23	0	3	3	6

GIBBS, Barry Paul *5-11 195 D*
B. Lloydminster, Sask., Sept. 28, 1948

Season	Team	GP	G	A	Pts.	PIM
67-68	Bos	16	0	0	0	2
68-69	Bos	8	0	0	0	2
69-70	Minn	56	3	13	16	182
70-71	Minn	68	5	15	20	132
71-72	Minn	75	4	20	24	128
72-73	Minn	63	10	24	34	54
73-74	Minn	76	9	29	38	82
74-75	Minn-Atl	76	7	33	40	61
75-76	Atl	76	8	21	29	92
76-77	Atl	66	1	16	17	63
77-78	Atl-StL	78	7	17	24	69
78-79	StL	76	2	27	29	46
79-80	LA	63	2	9	11	32
Totals		797	58	224	282	945
Playoff Totals		36	4	2	6	67

GIBSON, Don *6-1 210 D*
B. Deloraine, Man., Dec. 29, 1967

Season	Team	GP	G	A	Pts.	PIM
90-91	Van	14	0	3	3	20

GIBSON, Douglas John *5-10 175 C*
B. Peterborough, Ont., Sept. 28, 1953

Season	Team	GP	G	A	Pts.	PIM
73-74	Bos	2	0	0	0	0

GIBSON, Douglas John *(Continued)*

Season	Team	GP	G	A	Pts.	PIM
75-76	Bos	50	7	18	25	0
77-78	Wash	11	2	1	3	0
Totals		63	9	19	28	0
Playoff Totals		1	0	0	0	0

GIBSON, John William *6-3 210 D*
B. St. Catharines, Ont., June 2, 1959

Season	Team	GP	G	A	Pts.	PIM
78-79	Winn (WHA)	9	0	1	1	5
80-81	LA	4	0	0	0	21
81-82	LA-Tor	33	0	2	2	85
83-84	Winn	11	0	0	0	14
NHL Totals		48	0	2	2	120
WHA Totals		9	0	1	1	5

GIESEBRECHT, Roy (Gus) *6-0 177 C*
B. Pembroke, Ont., Sept. 16, 1918

Season	Team	GP	G	A	Pts.	PIM
38-39	Det	28	10	10	20	2
39-40	Det	30	4	7	11	2
40-41	Det	43	7	18	25	7
41-42	Det	34	6	16	22	2
Totals		135	27	51	71	13
Playoff Totals		17	2	3	5	0

GIFFIN, Lee *6-0 188 RW*
B. Chatham, Ont., Apr. 1, 1967

Season	Team	GP	G	A	Pts.	PIM
86-87	Pitt	8	1	1	2	0
87-88	Pitt	19	0	2	2	9
Totals		27	1	3	4	9

GILBERT, Edward Ferguson *6-0 185 C*
B. Hamilton, Ont., Mar. 12, 1952

Season	Team	GP	G	A	Pts.	PIM
74-75	KC	80	16	22	38	14
75-76	KC-Pitt	79	5	9	14	8
76-77	Pitt	7	0	0	0	0
78-79	Cin (WHA)	29	3	3	6	40
NHL Totals		166	21	31	52	22
WHA Totals		29	3	3	6	40

GILBERT, Gregory Scott *6-1 191 LW*
B. Mississauga, Ont., Jan. 22, 1962

Season	Team	GP	G	A	Pts.	PIM
81-82	NYI	1	1	0	1	0
82-83	NYI	45	8	11	19	30
83-84	NYI	79	31	35	66	59
84-85	NYI	58	13	25	38	36
85-86	NYI	60	9	19	28	82
86-87	NYI	51	6	7	13	26
87-88	NYI	76	17	28	45	46
88-89	NYI-Chi	59	8	13	21	45
89-90	Chi	70	12	25	37	54
90-91	Chi	72	10	15	25	58
91-92	Chi	50	7	5	12	35
Totals		621	122	183	305	471
Playoff Totals		100	16	27	43	148

GILBERT, Jeannot Elmourt (Jean) *5-9 170 C*
B. Port Alfred, Que., Dec. 29, 1940

Season	Team	GP	G	A	Pts.	PIM
62-63	Bos	5	0	0	0	4
64-65	Bos	4	0	0	0	0
73-74	Que (WHA)	75	17	39	56	20
74-75	Que (WHA)	58	7	21	28	12
NHL Totals		9	0	0	0	4
WHA Totals		133	24	60	84	32
WHA Playoff Totals		11	3	6	9	2

GILBERT, Rodrique Gabriel (Rod) *5-9 180 RW*
B. Montreal, Que., July 1, 1941

Season	Team	GP	G	A	Pts.	PIM
60-61	NYR	1	0	1	1	2
61-62	NYR	1	0	0	0	0
62-63	NYR	70	11	20	31	20
63-64	NYR	70	24	40	64	62
64-65	NYR	70	25	36	61	52
65-66	NYR	34	10	15	25	20
66-67	NYR	64	28	18	46	12
67-68	NYR	73	29	48	77	12
68-69	NYR	66	28	49	77	22
69-70	NYR	72	16	37	53	22
70-71	NYR	78	30	31	61	65
71-72	NYR	73	43	54	97	64
72-73	NYR	76	25	59	84	25
73-74	NYR	75	36	41	77	20
74-75	NYR	76	36	61	97	22
75-76	NYR	70	36	50	86	32
76-77	NYR	77	27	48	75	50
77-78	NYR	19	2	7	9	6
Totals		1065	406	615	1021	508
Playoff Totals		79	34	33	67	43

GILBERTSON, Stanley Frank *6-0 175 LW*
B. Duluth, Minn., Oct. 29, 1944

Season	Team	GP	G	A	Pts.	PIM
71-72	Cal	78	16	16	32	47
72-73	Cal	66	6	15	21	19
73-74	Cal	76	18	12	30	39

GILBERTSON, Stanley Frank *(Continued)*

Season	Team	GP	G	A	Pts.	PIM
74-75	Cal-StL-Wash	62	13	15	28	18
75-76	Wash-Pitt	79	26	22	48	12
76-77	Pitt	67	6	9	15	13
Totals		428	85	89	174	148
Playoff Totals		3	1	1	2	2

GILCHRIST, Brent *5-11 181 LW*
B. Moose Jaw, Sask., Apr. 3, 1967

Season	Team	GP	G	A	Pts.	PIM
88-89	Mont	49	8	16	24	16
89-90	Mont	57	9	15	24	28
90-91	Mont	51	6	9	15	10
91-92	Mont	79	23	27	50	57
Totals		236	46	67	113	111
Playoff Totals		41	10	8	18	24

GILES, Curt *5-8 175 D*
B. The Pas, Man., Nov. 30, 1958

Season	Team	GP	G	A	Pts.	PIM
79-80	Minn	37	2	7	9	31
80-81	Minn	67	5	22	27	56
81-82	Minn	74	3	12	15	87
82-83	Minn	76	2	21	23	70
83-84	Minn	70	6	22	28	59
84-85	Minn	77	5	25	30	49
85-86	Minn	69	6	21	27	30
86-87	Minn-NYR	72	2	20	22	54
87-88	NYR-Minn	72	1	12	13	76
88-89	Minn	76	5	10	15	77
89-90	Minn	74	1	12	13	48
90-91	Minn	70	4	10	14	48
91-92	StL	13	1	1	2	8
Totals		947	43	195	238	693
Playoff Totals		100	6	16	22	116

GILHEN, Randy *6-0 190 C*
B. Zweibrucken, West Germany, June 13, 1963

Season	Team	GP	G	A	Pts.	PIM
82-83	Hart	2	0	1	1	0
86-87	Winn	2	0	0	0	0
87-88	Winn	13	3	2	5	15
88-89	Winn	64	5	3	8	38
89-90	Pitt	61	5	11	16	54
90-91	Pitt	72	15	10	25	51
91-92	LA-NYR	73	10	13	23	28
Totals		317	38	40	78	186
Playoff Totals		33	3	2	5	26

GILL, Todd *6-0 185 D*
B. Brockville, Ont., Nov. 9, 1965

Season	Team	GP	G	A	Pts.	PIM
84-85	Tor	10	1	0	1	13
85-86	Tor	15	1	2	3	28
86-87	Tor	61	4	27	31	92
87-88	Tor	65	8	17	25	131
88-89	Tor	59	11	14	25	72
89-90	Tor	48	1	14	15	92
90-91	Tor	72	2	22	24	113
91-92	Tor	74	2	15	17	91
Totals		404	30	113	143	632
Playoff Totals		25	3	8	11	78

GILLEN, Donald *6-3 222 RW*
B. Dodsland, Sask., Dec. 24, 1960

Season	Team	GP	G	A	Pts.	PIM
79-80	Phil	1	1	0	1	0
81-82	Hart	34	1	4	5	22
Totals		35	2	4	6	22

GILLIE, Ferrand *F*
B. Cornwall, Ont.

Season	Team	GP	G	A	Pts.	PIM
28-29	Det	1	0	0	0	0

GILLIES, Clark *6-3 215 LW*
B. Moose Jaw, Sask., Apr. 7, 1954

Season	Team	GP	G	A	Pts.	PIM
74-75	NYI	80	25	22	47	66
75-76	NYI	80	34	27	61	96
76-77	NYI	70	33	22	55	93
77-78	NYI	80	35	50	85	76
78-79	NYI	75	35	56	91	68
79-80	NYI	73	19	35	54	49
80-81	NYI	80	33	45	78	99
81-82	NYI	79	38	39	77	75
82-83	NYI	70	21	20	41	76
83-84	NYI	76	12	16	28	65
84-85	NYI	54	15	17	32	73
85-86	NYI	55	4	10	14	55
86-87	Buf	61	10	17	27	81
87-88	Buf	25	5	2	7	51
Totals		958	319	378	697	1023
Playoff Totals		164	47	47	94	284

GILLIS, Jere Alan *6-0 190 LW*
B. Bend, Ore., Jan. 18, 1957

Season	Team	GP	G	A	Pts.	PIM
77-78	Van	79	23	18	41	35
78-79	Van	78	13	12	25	33
79-80	Van	67	13	17	30	108
80-81	Van-NYR	46	10	14	24	8
81-82	NYR-Que	38	5	10	15	16

GILLIS, Jere Alan *(Continued)*

Season	Team	GP	G	A	Pts.	PIM
82-83	Buf	3	0	0	0	0
83-84	Van	37	9	13	22	7
84-85	Van	37	5	11	16	23
86-87	Phil	1	0	0	0	0
Totals		386	78	95	173	230
Playoff Totals		19	4	7	11	9

GILLIS, Michael David *6-1 195 LW*
B. Sudbury, Ont., Dec. 1, 1958

Season	Team	GP	G	A	Pts.	PIM
78-79	Col	30	1	7	8	6
79-80	Col	40	4	5	9	22
80-81	Col-Bos	68	13	11	24	69
81-82	Bos	53	9	8	17	54
82-83	Bos	5	0	1	1	0
83-84	Bos	50	6	11	17	35
Totals		246	33	43	76	186
Playoff Totals		27	2	5	7	10

GILLIS, Paul *5-11 198 C*
B. Toronto, Ont., Dec. 31, 1963

Season	Team	GP	G	A	Pts.	PIM
82-83	Que	7	0	2	2	2
83-84	Que	57	8	9	17	59
84-85	Que	77	14	28	42	168
85-86	Que	80	19	24	43	203
86-87	Que	76	13	26	39	267
87-88	Que	80	7	10	17	164
88-89	Que	79	15	25	40	163
89-90	Que	71	8	14	22	234
90-91	Que-Chi	62	3	13	16	144
91-92	Chi-Hart	14	0	2	2	54
Totals		603	87	153	240	1458
Playoff Totals		42	3	14	17	156

GILMOUR, Douglas *5-11 170 C*
B. Kingston, Ont., June 25, 1963

Season	Team	GP	G	A	Pts.	PIM
83-84	StL	80	25	28	53	57
84-85	StL	78	21	36	57	49
85-86	StL	74	25	28	53	41
86-87	StL	80	42	63	105	58
87-88	StL	72	36	50	86	59
88-89	Calg	72	26	59	85	44
89-90	Calg	78	24	67	91	54
90-91	Calg	78	20	61	81	144
91-92	Calg-Tor	78	26	61	87	78
Totals		690	245	453	698	584
Playoff Totals		86	32	51	83	99

GINGRAS, Gaston Reginald *6-0 190 D*
B. Temiscamingue, Que., Feb. 13, 1959

Season	Team	GP	G	A	Pts.	PIM
78-79	Birm (WHA)	60	13	21	34	35
79-80	Mont	34	3	7	10	18
80-81	Mont	55	5	16	21	22
81-82	Mont	34	6	18	24	28
82-83	Mont-Tor	67	11	26	37	18
83-84	Tor	59	7	20	27	16
84-85	Tor	5	0	2	2	0
85-86	Mont	34	8	18	26	12
86-87	Mont	66	11	34	45	21
87-88	Mont- StL	70	7	23	30	20
88-89	StL	52	3	10	13	6
NHL Totals		476	61	174	235	161
WHA Totals		60	13	21	34	35
NHL Playoff Totals		52	6	18	24	20

GIRARD, Kenneth *6-0 184 RW*
B. Toronto, Ont., Dec. 8, 1936

Season	Team	GP	G	A	Pts.	PIM
56-57	Tor	3	0	1	1	2
57-58	Tor	3	0	0	0	0
59-60	Tor	1	0	0	0	0
Totals		7	0	1	1	2

GIRARD, Robert *6-0 180 LW*
B. Montreal, Que., Apr. 12, 1949

Season	Team	GP	G	A	Pts.	PIM
75-76	Cal	80	16	26	42	54
76-77	Clev	68	11	10	21	33
77-78	Clev-Wash	77	9	18	27	17
78-79	Wash	79	9	15	24	36
79-80	Wash	1	0	0	0	0
Totals		305	45	69	114	140

GIROUX, Arthur Joseph *5-1 165 RW*
B. Strathmore, Alta., June 6, 1907

Season	Team	GP	G	A	Pts.	PIM
32-33	Mont	40	5	2	7	14
34-35	Bos	10	1	0	1	0
35-36	Det	4	0	2	2	0
Totals		54	6	4	10	14
Playoff Totals		2	0	0	0	0

GIROUX, Larry Douglas *6-0 190 D*
B. Weyburn, Sask., Aug. 28, 1951

Season	Team	GP	G	A	Pts.	PIM
73-74	StL	74	5	17	22	59
74-75	KC-Det	60	2	26	28	84
75-76	Det	10	1	1	2	25
76-77	Det	2	0	0	0	2
77-78	Det	5	0	3	3	4

GIROUX, Larry Douglas *(Continued)*

Season	Team	GP	G	A	Pts.	PIM
78-79	StL	73	5	22	27	111
79-80	StL-Hart	50	2	5	7	48
Totals		274	15	74	89	333
Playoff Totals		5	0	0	0	4

GIROUX, Pierre Yves Richard
5-11 185 C
B. Brownsburg, Que., Nov. 17, 1955

Season	Team	GP	G	A	Pts.	PIM
82-83	LA	6	1	0	1	17

GLADNEY, Robert Lawrence *5-11 185 D*
B. Come-by-Chance, Nfld., Aug. 27, 1957

Season	Team	GP	G	A	Pts.	PIM
82-83	LA	1	0	0	0	2
83-84	Pitt	13	1	5	6	2
Totals		14	1	5	6	4

GLADU, Joseph Jean Paul *5-10 180 LW*
B. St. Hyacinthe, Que., June 20, 1921

Season	Team	GP	G	A	Pts.	PIM
44-45	Bos	40	6	14	20	2
Playoff Totals		7	2	2	4	0

GLENNIE, Brian Alexander *6-1 200 D*
B. Toronto, Ont., Aug. 29, 1946

Season	Team	GP	G	A	Pts.	PIM
69-70	Tor	52	1	14	15	50
70-71	Tor	54	0	8	8	31
71-72	Tor	61	2	8	10	44
72-73	Tor	44	1	10	11	54
73-74	Tor	65	4	18	22	100
74-75	Tor	63	1	7	8	110
75-76	Tor	69	0	8	8	75
76-77	Tor	69	1	10	11	73
77-78	Tor	77	2	15	17	62
78-79	LA	18	2	2	4	22
Totals		572	14	100	114	621
Playoff Totals		32	0	1	1	66

GLENNON, Matthew *6-0 185 LW*
B. Hull, Mass., Sept. 20, 1968

Season	Team	GP	G	A	Pts.	PIM
91-92	Bos	3	0	0	0	2

GLOECKNER, Lorry *6-2 210 D*
B. Kindersley, Sask., Jan. 25, 1956

Season	Team	GP	G	A	Pts.	PIM
78-79	Det	13	0	2	2	6

GLOOR, Daniel Harold *5-9 170 C*
B. Stratford, Ont., Dec. 4, 1952

Season	Team	GP	G	A	Pts.	PIM
73-74	Van	2	0	0	0	0

GLOVER, Frederick Austin *5-9 175 RW*
B. Toronto, Ont., Jan. 5, 1928

Season	Team	GP	G	A	Pts.	PIM
49-50	Det	7	0	0	0	0
51-52	Det	54	9	9	18	25
52-53	Chi	31	4	2	6	37
Totals		92	13	11	24	62
Playoff Totals		3	0	0	0	0

GLOVER, Howard Edward *5-11 195 RW*
B. Toronto, Ont., Feb. 14, 1935

Season	Team	GP	G	A	Pts.	PIM
58-59	Chi	13	0	1	1	2
60-61	Det	66	21	8	29	46
61-62	Det	39	7	8	15	44
63-64	NYR	25	1	0	1	9
68-69	Mont	1	0	0	0	0
Totals		144	29	17	46	101
Playoff Totals		11	1	2	3	2

GLYNN, Brian *6-4 215 D*
B. Iserlohn, West Germany, Nov. 23, 1967

Season	Team	GP	G	A	Pts.	PIM
87-88	Calg	67	5	14	19	87
88-89	Calg	9	0	1	1	19
89-90	Calg	1	0	0	0	0
90-91	Minn	66	8	11	19	83
91-92	Minn-Edm	62	4	18	22	30
Totals		205	17	44	61	219
Playoff Totals		40	6	7	13	30

GODDEN, Ernie Alfred *5-7 154 C*
B. Keswick, Ont., Mar. 13, 1961

Season	Team	GP	G	A	Pts.	PIM
81-82	Tor	5	1	1	2	6

GODFREY, Warren Edward (Rocky)
6-1 190 D
B. Toronto, Ont., Mar. 23, 1931

Season	Team	GP	G	A	Pts.	PIM
52-53	Bos	60	1	13	14	40
53-54	Bos	70	5	9	14	71
54-55	Bos	62	1	17	18	58
55-56	Det	67	2	6	8	86
56-57	Det	69	1	8	9	103
57-58	Det	67	2	16	18	56
58-59	Det	69	6	4	10	44
59-60	Det	69	5	9	14	60
60-61	Det	63	3	16	19	62
61-62	Det	69	4	13	17	84
62-63	Bos	66	2	9	11	56

GODFREY, Warren Edward (Rocky)
(Continued)

Season	Team	GP	G	A	Pts.	PIM
63-64	Det	4	0	0	0	2
64-65	Det	11	0	0	0	8
65-66	Det	26	0	4	4	22
66-67	Det	2	0	0	0	0
67-68	Det	12	0	1	1	0
Totals		786	32	125	157	752
Playoff Totals		52	1	4	5	42

GODIN, Hogomer Gabriel (Sammy)
5-9 156 RW
B. Rockland, Ont., Sept. 20, 1909

Season	Team	GP	G	A	Pts.	PIM
27-28	Ott	24	0	0	0	0
28-29	Ott	23	2	1	3	21
33-34	Mont	36	2	2	4	15
Totals		83	4	3	7	36

GODIN, Joseph Alain (Eddy)
5-10 187 RW
B. Donnacona, Que., Mar. 29, 1957

Season	Team	GP	G	A	Pts.	PIM
77-78	Wash	18	3	3	6	6
78-79	Wash	9	0	3	3	6
Totals		27	3	6	9	12

GODYNYUK, Alexander *6-0 207 D*
B. Kiev, Soviet Union, Jan. 27, 1970

Season	Team	GP	G	A	Pts.	PIM
90-91	Tor	18	0	3	3	16
91-92	Tor-Calg	37	3	7	10	63
Totals		55	3	10	13	79

GOEGAN, Peter John *6-1 200 D*
B. Fort William, Ont., Mar. 6, 1934

Season	Team	GP	G	A	Pts.	PIM
57-58	Det	14	0	2	2	28
58-59	Det	67	1	11	12	109
59-60	Det	21	3	0	3	6
60-61	Det	67	5	29	34	48
61-62	Det-NYR	46	5	7	12	30
62-63	Det	62	1	8	9	48
63-64	Det	12	0	0	0	8
64-65	Det	4	1	0	1	2
65-66	Det	13	0	2	2	14
66-67	Det	31	2	6	8	12
67-68	Minn	46	1	2	3	30
Totals		383	19	67	86	335
Playoff Totals		33	1	3	4	61

GOERTZ, Dave *5-11 199 D*
B. Edmonton, Alta., Mar. 28, 1965

Season	Team	GP	G	A	Pts.	PIM
87-88	Pitt	2	0	0	0	2

GOLDHAM, Robert John *6-1 195 D*
B. Georgetown, Ont., May 12, 1922

Season	Team	GP	G	A	Pts.	PIM
41-42	Tor	19	4	7	11	25
45-46	Tor	49	7	14	21	44
46-47	Tor	11	1	1	2	10
47-48	Chi	38	2	9	11	38
48-49	Chi	60	1	10	11	43
49-50	Chi	67	2	10	12	57
50-51	Det	61	5	18	23	31
51-52	Det	69	0	14	14	24
52-53	Det	70	1	13	14	32
53-54	Det	69	1	15	16	50
54-55	Det	69	1	16	17	14
55-56	Det	68	3	16	19	32
Totals		650	28	143	171	400
Playoff Totals		66	3	14	17	53

GOLDSWORTHY, Leroy D. *6-0 190 RW*
B. Two Harbors, Minn., Oct. 18, 1908

Season	Team	GP	G	A	Pts.	PIM
29-30	NYR	44	4	1	5	16
30-31	Det	13	1	0	1	2
32-33	Det	26	3	6	9	6
33-34	Chi	28	3	3	6	0
34-35	Chi-Mont	40	20	9	29	15
35-36	Mont	47	15	11	26	8
36-37	Bos	47	8	6	14	8
37-38	Bos	45	9	10	19	14
38-39	NYA	47	3	11	14	10
Totals		337	66	57	123	79
Playoff Totals		22	1	0	1	4

GOLDSWORTHY, William Alfred
6-0 190 RW
B. Kitchener, Ont., Aug. 24, 1944

Season	Team	GP	G	A	Pts.	PIM
64-65	Bos	2	0	0	0	0
65-66	Bos	13	3	1	4	6
66-67	Bos	18	3	5	8	21
67-68	Minn	68	14	19	33	68
68-69	Minn	68	14	10	24	110
69-70	Minn	75	36	29	65	89
70-71	Minn	77	34	31	65	85
71-72	Minn	78	31	31	62	59
72-73	Minn	75	27	33	60	97
73-74	Minn	74	48	26	74	73
74-75	Minn	71	37	35	72	77

GOLDSWORTHY, William Alfred *(Continued)*

Season	Team	GP	G	A	Pts.	PIM
75-76	Minn	68	24	22	46	47
76-77	Minn-NYR	77	12	15	27	49
77-78	NYR	7	0	1	1	12
77-78	Ind (WHA)	32	8	10	18	10
78-79	Edm (WHA)	17	4	2	6	14
NHL Totals		771	283	258	541	793
WHA Totals		49	12	12	24	24
NHL Playoff Totals		40	18	19	37	30
WHA Playoff Totals		4	1	1	2	11

GOLDUP, Glenn Michael *6-0 190 RW*
B. St. Catharines, Ont., Apr. 26, 1953

Season	Team	GP	G	A	Pts.	PIM
73-74	Mont	6	0	0	0	0
74-75	Mont	9	0	1	1	2
75-76	Mont	3	0	0	0	2
76-77	LA	28	7	6	13	29
77-78	LA	66	14	18	32	66
78-79	LA	73	15	22	37	89
79-80	LA	55	10	11	21	78
80-81	LA	49	6	9	15	35
81-82	LA	2	0	0	0	0
Totals		291	52	67	119	301
Playoff Totals		16	4	3	7	22

GOLDUP, Henry G. (Hank) *5-11 175 LW*
B. Kingston, Ont., Oct. 29, 1918

Season	Team	GP	G	A	Pts.	PIM
40-41	Tor	26	10	5	15	9
41-42	Tor	44	12	18	30	13
42-43	Tor-NYR	44	12	27	39	37
44-45	NYR	48	17	25	42	25
45-46	NYR	19	6	1	7	11
Totals		181	57	76	133	95
Playoff Totals		26	5	1	6	6

GOODEN, William Francis Charles
5-9 175 LW
B. Winnipeg, Man., Sept. 8, 1924

Season	Team	GP	G	A	Pts.	PIM
42-43	NYR	12	0	3	3	0
43-44	NYR	41	9	8	17	15
Totals		53	9	11	20	15

GOODENOUGH, Larry J. *6-0 195 D*
B. Toronto, Ont., Jan. 19, 1953

Season	Team	GP	G	A	Pts.	PIM
74-75	Phil	20	3	9	12	0
75-76	Phil	77	8	34	42	83
76-77	Phil-Van	62	6	17	23	48
77-78	Van	42	1	6	7	28
78-79	Van	36	4	9	13	18
79-80	Van	5	0	2	2	2
Totals		242	22	77	99	179
Playoff Totals		22	3	15	18	10

GOODFELLOW, Ebenezer Ralston (Ebbie)
6-0 180 C
B. Ottawa, Ont., Apr. 9, 1907

Season	Team	GP	G	A	Pts.	PIM
29-30	Det	44	17	17	34	54
30-31	Det	44	25	23	48	32
31-32	Det	48	14	16	30	56
32-33	Det	40	12	8	20	47
33-34	Det	48	13	13	26	45
34-35	Det	48	12	24	36	44
35-36	Det	48	5	18	23	69
36-37	Det	48	9	16	25	43
37-38	Det	29	0	7	7	18
38-39	Det	48	8	8	16	36
39-40	Det	43	11	17	28	31
40-41	Det	47	5	17	22	35
41-42	Det	8	2	2	4	2
42-43	Det	11	1	4	5	4
Totals		554	134	190	324	516
Playoff Totals		45	8	8	16	65

GORDON, Frederick *F*

Season	Team	GP	G	A	Pts.	PIM
26-27	Det	36	5	5	10	28
27-28	Bos	41	3	2	5	40
Totals		77	8	7	15	68
Playoff Totals		1	0	0	0	0

GORDON, John (Jackie) *5-8 154 C*
B. Winnipeg, Man., Mar. 3, 1928

Season	Team	GP	G	A	Pts.	PIM
48-49	NYR	31	3	9	12	0
49-50	NYR	1	0	0	0	0
50-51	NYR	4	0	1	1	0
Totals		36	3	10	13	0
Playoff Totals		9	1	1	2	7

GORENCE, Thomas *6-0 190 RW*
B. St. Paul, Minn., Mar. 11, 1957

Season	Team	GP	G	A	Pts.	PIM
78-79	Phil	42	13	6	19	10
79-80	Phil	51	8	13	21	15
80-81	Phil	79	24	18	42	46
81-82	Phil	66	5	8	13	8

GORENCE, Thomas *(Continued)*

Season	Team	GP	G	A	Pts.	PIM
82-83	Phil	53	7	7	14	10
83-84	Edm	12	1	1	2	0
Totals		303	58	53	111	89
Playoff Totals		37	9	6	15	47

GORING, Robert Thomas (Butch)
5-9 170 C
B. St. Boniface, Man., Oct. 22, 1949

Season	Team	GP	G	A	Pts.	PIM
69-70	LA	59	13	23	36	8
70-71	LA	19	2	5	7	2
71-72	LA	74	21	29	50	2
72-73	LA	67	28	31	59	2
73-74	LA	70	28	33	61	2
74-75	LA	60	27	33	60	6
75-76	LA	80	33	40	73	8
76-77	LA	78	30	55	85	6
77-78	LA	80	37	36	73	2
78-79	LA	80	36	51	87	16
79-80	LA-NYI	81	26	53	79	14
80-81	NYI	78	23	37	60	0
81-82	NYI	67	15	17	32	10
82-83	NYI	75	19	20	39	8
83-84	NYI	71	22	24	46	8
84-85	NYI-Bos	68	15	26	41	8
Totals		1107	375	513	888	102
Playoff Totals		134	38	50	88	32

GORMAN, David Peter *5-11 185 RW*
B. Oshawa, Ont., Apr. 8, 1955

Season	Team	GP	G	A	Pts.	PIM
74-75	Phoe (WHA)	13	3	5	8	10
75-76	Phoe (WHA)	67	11	20	31	28
76-77	Phoe-Birm (WHA)	57	9	13	22	38
77-78	Birm (WHA)	63	19	21	40	93
78-79	Birm (WHA)	60	14	24	38	18
79-80	Atl	3	0	0	0	0
NHL Totals		3	0	0	0	0
WHA Totals		260	56	83	139	187
WHA Playoff Totals		9	1	3	4	24

GORMAN, Edwin *D*

Season	Team	GP	G	A	Pts.	PIM
24-25	Ott	30	11	3	14	49
25-26	Ott	23	2	1	3	12
26-27	Ott	39	1	0	1	17
27-28	Tor	19	0	1	1	30
Totals		111	14	5	19	108
Playoff Totals		8	0	0	0	2

GOSSELIN, Benoit *5-11 190 LW*
B. Montreal, Que., July 19, 1957

Season	Team	GP	G	A	Pts.	PIM
77-78	NYR	7	0	0	0	33

GOSSELIN, Guy *5-10 185 D*
B. Rochester, Minn., Jan. 6, 1964

Season	Team	GP	G	A	Pts.	PIM
87-88	Winn	5	0	0	0	6

GOTAAS, Steve *5-10 180 C*
B. Camrose, Alta., May 10, 1967

Season	Team	GP	G	A	Pts.	PIM
87-88	Pitt	36	5	6	11	45
88-89	Minn	12	1	3	4	6
90-91	Minn	1	0	0	0	2
Totals		49	6	9	15	53
Playoff Totals		3	0	1	1	5

GOTTSELIG, John P. *5-11 158 LW*
B. Odessa, Russia, June 24, 1905

Season	Team	GP	G	A	Pts.	PIM
28-29	Chi	42	5	3	8	26
29-30	Chi	39	21	4	25	28
30-31	Chi	42	20	12	32	14
31-32	Chi	43	14	15	29	50
32-33	Chi	42	11	11	22	6
33-34	Chi	48	16	14	30	4
34-35	Chi	48	19	18	37	16
35-36	Chi	40	14	15	29	4
36-37	Chi	47	9	21	30	10
37-38	Chi	48	13	19	32	22
38-39	Chi	48	16	23	39	15
39-40	Chi	38	8	15	23	7
40-41	Chi	8	1	4	5	5
42-43	Chi	10	2	6	8	12
43-44	Chi	45	8	15	23	6
44-45	Chi	1	0	0	0	0
Totals		589	177	195	372	225
Playoff Totals		43	13	13	26	20

GOULD, John Milton *5-11 197 RW*
B. Beeton, Ont., Apr. 11, 1949

Season	Team	GP	G	A	Pts.	PIM
71-72	Buf	2	1	0	1	0
72-73	Buf	8	0	1	1	0
73-74	Buf-Van	75	13	12	25	10
74-75	Van	78	34	31	65	27
75-76	Van	70	32	27	59	16

GOULD, John Milton *(Continued)*

Season	Team	GP	G	A	Pts.	PIM
76-77	Van-Atl	79	15	23	38	10
77-78	Atl	79	19	28	47	21
78-79	Atl	61	8	7	15	18
79-80	Buf	52	9	9	18	11
Totals		504	131	138	269	113
Playoff Totals		14	3	2	5	4

GOULD, Robert (Bobby) *6-0 195 RW*
B. Petrolia, Ont., Sept. 2, 1957

Season	Team	GP	G	A	Pts.	PIM
79-80	Atl	1	0	0	0	0
80-81	Calg	3	0	0	0	0
81-82	Calg-Wash	76	21	13	34	73
82-83	Wash	80	22	18	40	43
83-84	Wash	78	21	19	40	74
84-85	Wash	78	14	19	33	69
85-86	Wash	79	19	19	38	26
86-87	Wash	78	23	27	50	74
87-88	Wash	72	12	14	26	56
88-89	Wash	75	5	13	18	65
89-90	Bos	77	8	17	25	92
Totals		697	145	159	304	572
Playoff Totals		78	15	13	28	58

GOULD, Larry Stephen *5-9 170 LW*
B. Alliston, Ont., Aug. 16, 1952

Season	Team	GP	G	A	Pts.	PIM
73-74	Van	2	0	0	0	0

GOULET, Michel *6-1 195 LW*
B. Peribonka, Que., Apr. 21, 1960

Season	Team	GP	G	A	Pts.	PIM
78-79	Birm (WHA)	78	28	30	58	65
79-80	Que	77	22	32	54	48
80-81	Que	76	32	39	71	45
81-82	Que	80	42	42	84	48
82-83	Que	80	57	48	105	51
83-84	Que	75	56	65	121	76
84-85	Que	69	55	40	95	55
85-86	Que	75	53	51	104	64
86-87	Que	75	49	47	96	61
87-88	Que	80	48	58	106	56
88-89	Que	69	26	38	64	67
89-90	Que-Chi	65	20	30	50	51
90-91	Chi	74	27	38	65	65
91-92	Chi	75	22	41	63	69
NHL Totals		970	509	569	1078	756
WHA Totals		78	28	30	58	65
NHL Playoff Totals		89	39	38	77	110

GOUPILLE, Clifford (Red) *6-0 190 D*
B. Trois Rivieres, Que., Sept. 2, 1915

Season	Team	GP	G	A	Pts.	PIM
35-36	Mont	4	0	0	0	0
36-37	Mont	4	0	0	0	0
37-38	Mont	47	4	5	9	44
38-39	Mont	18	0	2	2	24
39-40	Mont	48	2	10	12	48
40-41	Mont	48	3	6	9	81
41-42	Mont	47	1	5	6	51
42-43	Mont	6	2	0	2	8
Totals		222	12	28	40	256
Playoff Totals		8	2	0	2	6

GOVEDARIS, Chris *6-0 200 LW*
B. Toronto, Ont., Feb. 2, 1970

Season	Team	GP	G	A	Pts.	PIM
89-90	Hart	12	0	1	1	6
90-91	Hart	14	1	3	4	4
Totals		26	1	4	5	10
Playoff Totals		2	0	0	0	2

GOYER, Gerald Francis *6-1 196 C*
B. Belleville, Ont., Oct. 20, 1936

Season	Team	GP	G	A	Pts.	PIM
67-68	Chi	40	1	2	3	4
Playoff Totals		3	0	0	0	2

GOYETTE, Joseph Georges Philipe (Phil)
5-11 170 C
B. Lachine, Que., Oct. 31, 1933

Season	Team	GP	G	A	Pts.	PIM
56-57	Mont	14	3	4	7	0
57-58	Mont	70	9	37	46	8
58-59	Mont	63	10	18	28	8
59-60	Mont	65	21	22	43	4
60-61	Mont	62	7	4	11	4
61-62	Mont	69	7	27	34	18
62-63	Mont	32	5	8	13	2
63-64	NYR	67	24	41	65	15
64-65	NYR	52	12	34	46	6
65-66	NYR	60	11	31	42	6
66-67	NYR	70	12	49	61	6
67-68	NYR	73	25	40	65	10
68-69	NYR	67	13	32	45	8
69-70	StL	72	29	49	78	16
70-71	Buf	60	15	46	61	6
71-72	Buf-NYR	45	4	25	29	14
Totals		941	207	467	674	131
Playoff Totals		94	17	29	46	26

GRABOSKI, Anthony Rudel (Tony)
5-10 170 F
B. Timmins, Ont., May 9, 1916

Season	Team	GP	G	A	Pts.	PIM
40-41	Mont	34	4	3	7	6
41-42	Mont	23	2	5	7	8
42-43	Mont	9	0	2	2	4
Totals		66	6	10	16	18
Playoff Totals		2	0	0	0	0

GRACIE, Robert J. 5-8 155 LW
B. North Bay, Ont., Nov. 8, 1910

Season	Team	GP	G	A	Pts.	PIM
30-31	Tor	8	4	2	6	4
31-32	Tor	48	13	8	21	29
32-33	Tor	48	9	13	22	27
33-34	Bos-NYA	48	6	12	18	20
34-35	NYA-Mont M	46	12	9	21	15
35-36	Mont M	46	11	14	25	31
36-37	Mont M	48	11	25	36	18
37-38	Mont M	48	12	19	31	32
38-39	Mont-Chi	38	4	7	11	31
Totals		378	82	109	191	207
Playoff Totals		33	4	7	11	4

GRADIN, Thomas 5-11 170 C
B. Solleftea, Sweden, Feb. 18, 1956

Season	Team	GP	G	A	Pts.	PIM
78-79	Van	76	20	31	51	22
79-80	Van	80	30	45	75	22
80-81	Van	79	21	48	69	34
81-82	Van	76	37	49	86	32
82-83	Van	80	32	54	86	61
83-84	Van	75	21	57	78	32
84-85	Van	76	22	42	64	43
85-86	Van	71	14	27	41	34
86-87	Bos	64	12	31	43	18
Totals		677	209	384	593	298
Playoff Totals		42	17	25	42	20

GRAHAM, Dirk Milton 5-11 198 LW/RW
B. Regina, Sask., July 29, 1959

Season	Team	GP	G	A	Pts.	PIM
83-84	Minn	6	1	1	2	0
84-85	Minn	36	12	11	23	23
85-86	Minn	80	22	33	55	87
86-87	Minn	76	25	29	54	142
87-88	Minn-Chi	70	24	24	48	71
88-89	Chi	80	33	45	78	89
89-90	Chi	73	22	32	54	102
90-91	Chi	80	24	21	45	88
91-92	Chi	80	17	30	47	89
Totals		581	180	226	406	691
Playoff Totals		64	15	23	38	80

GRAHAM, Edward Dixon (Ted)
5-10 173 D
B. Owen Sound, Ont., June 30, 1906

Season	Team	GP	G	A	Pts.	PIM
27-28	Chi	16	1	0	1	8
29-30	Chi	26	1	2	3	23
30-31	Chi	42	0	7	7	38
31-32	Chi	48	0	3	3	40
32-33	Chi	47	3	8	11	57
33-34	Mont M-Det	47	3	1	4	39
34-35	Det-StL E	37	0	2	2	28
35-36	Bos	48	4	1	5	37
36-37	Bos-NYA	32	2	1	3	30
Totals		343	14	25	39	300
Playoff Totals		23	3	1	4	34

GRAHAM, Leth LW
B. 1894

Season	Team	GP	G	A	Pts.	PIM
20-21	Ott	13	0	0	0	0
21-22	Ott	2	2	0	2	0
22-23	Ham	4	1	0	1	0
23-24	Ott	3	0	0	0	0
24-25	Ott	3	0	0	0	0
25-26	Ott	1	0	0	0	0
Totals		26	3	0	3	0
Playoff Totals		1	0	0	0	0

GRAHAM, Patrick Thomas 6-1 190 LW
B. Toronto, Ont., May 25, 1961

Season	Team	GP	G	A	Pts.	PIM
81-82	Pitt	42	6	8	14	55
82-83	Pitt	20	1	5	6	16
83-84	Tor	41	4	4	8	65
Totals		103	11	17	28	136
Playoff Totals		4	0	0	0	2

GRAHAM, Rodney Douglas (Rod)
5-11 185 LW
B. London, Ont., Aug. 19, 1946

Season	Team	GP	G	A	Pts.	PIM
74-75	Bos	14	2	1	3	7

GRANATO, Tony 5-10 185 LW
B. Downers Grove, Ill., July 25, 1964

Season	Team	GP	G	A	Pts.	PIM
88-89	NYR	78	36	27	63	140
89-90	NYR-LA	56	12	24	36	122

GRANATO, Tony (Continued)

Season	Team	GP	G	A	Pts.	PIM
90-91	LA	68	30	34	64	154
91-92	LA	80	39	29	68	187
Totals		282	117	114	231	603
Playoff Totals		36	8	14	22	71

GRANT, Daniel Frederick 5-10 188 LW
B. Fredericton, N.B., Feb. 21, 1946

Season	Team	GP	G	A	Pts.	PIM
65-66	Mont	1	0	0	0	0
67-68	Mont	22	3	4	7	10
68-69	Minn	75	34	31	65	46
69-70	Minn	76	29	28	57	23
70-71	Minn	78	34	23	57	46
71-72	Minn	78	18	25	43	18
72-73	Minn	78	32	35	67	12
73-74	Minn	78	29	35	64	16
74-75	Det	80	50	37	87	28
75-76	Det	39	10	13	23	20
76-77	Det	42	2	10	12	4
77-78	Det-LA	54	12	21	33	2
78-79	LA	35	10	11	21	8
Totals		736	263	273	536	233
Playoff Totals		43	10	14	24	19

GRATTON, Dan 6-0 185 C
B. Brantford, Ont., Dec. 7, 1966

Season	Team	GP	G	A	Pts.	PIM
87-88	LA	7	1	0	1	5

GRATTON, Normand Lionel (Norm)
5-11 165 LW
B. LaSalle, Que., Dec. 22, 1950

Season	Team	GP	G	A	Pts.	PIM
71-72	NYR	3	0	1	1	0
72-73	Atl-Buf	50	9	11	20	24
73-74	Buf	57	6	11	17	16
74-75	Buf-Minn	59	17	18	35	10
75-76	Minn	32	7	3	10	14
Totals		201	39	44	83	64
Playoff Totals		6	0	1	1	2

GRAVES, Adam 5-11 185 C
B. Toronto, Ont., Apr. 12, 1968

Season	Team	GP	G	A	Pts.	PIM
87-88	Det	9	0	1	1	8
88-89	Det	56	7	5	12	60
89-90	Det-Edm	76	9	13	22	136
90-91	Edm	76	7	18	25	127
91-92	NYR	80	26	33	59	139
Totals		297	49	70	119	470
Playoff Totals		55	12	13	25	65

GRAVES, Steve 5-10 175 LW
B. Trenton, Ont., Apr. 7, 1964

Season	Team	GP	G	A	Pts.	PIM
83-84	Edm	2	0	0	0	0
86-87	Edm	12	2	0	2	0
87-88	Edm	21	3	4	7	10
Totals		35	5	4	9	10

GRAVELLE, Joseph Gerard (Leo, The Gazelle) 5-8 158 RW
B. Aylmer, Que., June 10, 1925

Season	Team	GP	G	A	Pts.	PIM
46-47	Mont	53	16	14	30	12
47-48	Mont	15	0	0	0	0
48-49	Mont	36	4	6	10	6
49-50	Mont	70	19	10	29	18
50-51	Mont-Det	49	5	4	9	6
Totals		223	44	34	78	42
Playoff Totals		17	4	1	5	2

GRAVES, Hilliard Donald 5-11 175 RW
B. Saint John, N.B., Oct. 18, 1950

Season	Team	GP	G	A	Pts.	PIM
70-71	Cal	14	0	0	0	0
72-73	Cal	75	27	25	52	34
73-74	Cal	64	11	18	29	48
74-75	Atl	67	10	19	29	30
75-76	Atl	80	19	30	49	16
76-77	Atl-Van	79	18	25	43	34
77-78	Van	80	21	26	47	18
78-79	Van	62	11	15	26	14
79-80	Winn	05	1	5	6	15
Totals		556	118	163	281	209
Playoff Totals		2	0	0	0	0

GRAY, Alexander 5-10 170 RW
B. Glasgow, Scotland, June 21, 1899

Season	Team	GP	G	A	Pts.	PIM
27-28	NYR	43	7	0	7	28
28-29	Tor	7	0	0	0	2
Totals		50	7	0	7	30
Playoff Totals		13	1	0	1	0

GRAY, Terrence Stanley (Terry)
6-0 175 RW
B. Montreal, Que., Mar. 21, 1938

Season	Team	GP	G	A	Pts.	PIM
61-62	Bos	42	8	7	15	15
63-64	Mont	4	0	0	0	6
67-68	LA	65	12	16	28	22

GRAY, Terrence Stanley (Terry)
(Continued)

Season	Team	GP	G	A	Pts.	PIM
68-69	StL	8	4	0	4	4
69-70	StL	28	2	5	7	17
Totals		147	26	28	54	64
Playoff Totals		35	5	5	10	22

GREEN LW

Season	Team	GP	G	A	Pts.	PIM
28-29	Det	2	0	0	0	0

GREEN, Edward Joseph (Ted)
5-10 200 D
B. Eriksdale, Man., Mar. 23, 1940

Season	Team	GP	G	A	Pts.	PIM
60-61	Bos	1	0	0	0	2
61-62	Bos	66	3	8	11	116
62-63	Bos	70	1	11	12	117
63-64	Bos	70	4	10	14	145
64-65	Bos	70	8	27	35	156
65-66	Bos	27	5	13	18	113
66-67	Bos	47	6	10	16	67
67-68	Bos	72	7	36	43	133
68-69	Bos	65	8	38	46	99
70-71	Bos	78	5	37	42	60
71-72	Bos	54	1	16	17	21
72-73	NE (WHA)	78	16	30	46	47
73-74	NE (WHA)	75	7	26	33	42
74-75	NE (WHA)	57	6	14	20	29
75-76	Winn (WHA)	79	5	23	28	73
76-77	Winn (WHA)	70	4	21	25	45
77-78	Winn (WHA)	73	4	22	26	52
78-79	Winn (WHA)	20	0	2	2	16
NHL Totals		620	48	206	254	1029
WHA Totals		452	42	138	180	304
NHL Playoff Totals		31	4	8	12	54
WHA Playoff Totals		58	2	16	18	62

GREEN, Redvers (Red) LW
B. Sudbury, Ont.

Season	Team	GP	G	A	Pts.	PIM
23-24	Ham	23	11	0	11	20
24-25	Ham	30	19	4	23	63
25-26	NYA	35	13	4	17	42
26-27	NYA	44	10	4	14	53
27-28	NYA	40	6	1	7	67
28-29	Bos	25	0	0	0	16
Totals		197	59	13	72	261

GREEN, Richard Douglas (Rick)
6-3 220 D
B. Belleville, Ont., Feb. 20, 1956

Season	Team	GP	G	A	Pts.	PIM
76-77	Wash	45	3	12	15	16
77-78	Wash	60	5	14	19	67
78-79	Wash	71	8	33	41	62
79-80	Wash	71	4	20	24	52
80-81	Wash	65	8	23	31	91
81-82	Wash	65	3	25	28	93
82-83	Mont	66	2	24	26	58
83-84	Mont	7	0	1	1	7
84-85	Mont	77	1	18	19	30
85-86	Mont	46	3	2	5	20
86-87	Mont	72	1	9	10	10
87-88	Mont	59	2	11	13	33
88-89	Mont	72	1	14	15	25
90-91	Det	65	2	14	16	24
91-92	NYI	4	0	0	0	0
Totals		845	43	220	263	588
Playoff Tot.		100	3	16	19	73

GREEN, Wilfred Thomas (Wilf, Shorty) RW
B. Sudbury, Ont., July 17, 1896

Season	Team	GP	G	A	Pts.	PIM
23-24	Ham	22	7	2	9	19
24-25	Ham	28	18	1	19	75
25-26	NYA	32	6	4	10	40
26-27	NYA	21	2	1	3	17
Totals		103	33	8	41	151

GREENLAW, Jeff 6-1 230 LW
B. Toronto, Ont., Feb. 28, 1968

Season	Team	GP	G	A	Pts.	PIM
86-87	Wash	22	0	3	3	44
90-91	Wash	10	2	0	2	10
91-92	Wash	5	0	1	1	34
Totals		37	2	4	6	88
Playoff Totals		2	0	0	0	21

GREGG, Randall John 6-4 215 D
B. Edmonton, Alta., Feb. 19, 1956

Season	Team	GP	G	A	Pts.	PIM
82-83	Edm	80	6	22	28	54
83-84	Edm	80	13	27	40	56
84-85	Edm	57	3	20	23	32
85-86	Edm	64	2	26	28	47
86-87	Edm	52	8	16	24	42
87-88	Edm	15	1	2	3	8
88-89	Edm	57	3	15	18	28

Season	Team	GP	G	A	Pts.	PIM

GREGG, Randall John (Continued)

Season	Team	GP	G	A	Pts.	PIM
89-90	Edm	48	4	20	24	42
91-92	Van	21	1	4	5	24
Totals		474	41	152	193	333
Playoff Totals		137	13	38	51	127

GREIG, Bruce 6-2 220 LW
B. High River, Alta., May 9, 1953

73-74	Cal	1	0	0	0	4
74-75	Cal	8	0	1	1	42
76-77	Calg (WHA)	7	1	1	2	10
77-78	Cin (WHA)	32	3	1	4	57
78-79	Ind (WHA)	21	3	7	10	64
NHL Totals		9	1	2	3	46
WHA Totals		60	7	9	16	131

GREIG, Mark 5-11 190 RW
B. High River, Alta., Jan. 25, 1970

90-91	Hart	4	0	0	0	0
91-92	Hart	17	0	5	5	6
Totals		21	0	5	5	6

GRENIER, Lucien S. J. 5-10 163 RW
B. Malartic, Que., Nov. 3, 1946

69-70	Mont	23	2	3	5	2
70-71	LA	68	9	7	16	12
71-72	LA	60	3	4	7	4
Totals		151	14	14	28	18
Playoff Totals		2	0	0	0	0

GRENIER, Richard 5-11 170 C
B. Montreal, Que., Sept. 18, 1952

| 72-73 | NYI | 10 | 1 | 1 | 2 | 2 |
| 76-77 | Que (WHA) | 34 | 11 | 9 | 20 | 4 |

GRESCHNER, Ronald John 6-2 185 D
B. Goodsoil, Sask., Dec. 22, 1954

74-75	NYR	70	8	37	45	93
75-76	NYR	77	6	21	27	93
76-77	NYR	80	11	36	47	89
77-78	NYR	78	24	48	72	100
78-79	NYR	60	17	36	53	66
79-80	NYR	76	21	37	58	103
80-81	NYR	74	27	41	68	112
81-82	NYR	29	5	11	16	16
82-83	NYR	10	3	5	8	0
83-84	NYR	77	12	44	56	117
84-85	NYR	48	16	29	45	42
85-86	NYR	78	20	28	48	104
86-87	NYR	61	6	34	40	62
87-88	NYR	51	1	5	6	82
88-89	NYR	58	1	10	11	94
89-90	NYR	55	1	9	10	53
Totals		982	179	431	610	1226
Playoff Totals		84	17	32	49	106

GRETZKY, Wayne (The Great) 6-0 175 C
B. Brantford, Ont., Jan. 26, 1961

78-79	Ind-Edm (WHA)	80	46	64	110	19
79-80	Edm	79	51	86	137	21
80-81	Edm	80	55	109	164	28
81-82	Edm	80	92	120	212	26
82-83	Edm	80	71	125	196	59
83-84	Edm	74	87	118	205	39
84-85	Edm	80	73	135	208	52
85-86	Edm	80	52	163	215	46
86-87	Edm	79	62	121	183	28
87-88	Edm	64	40	109	149	24
88-89	LA	78	54	114	168	26
89-90	LA	73	40	102	142	42
90-91	LA	78	41	122	163	16
91-92	LA	74	31	90	121	34
NHL Totals		999	749	1514	2263	441
WHA Totals		80	46	64	110	19
NHL Playoff Totals		156	95	211	306	60
WHA Playoff Totals		13	10	10	20	2

GRIGOR, George (Shorty) F
B. Edinburgh, Scotland

| 43-44 | Chi | 2 | 1 | 0 | 1 | 0 |
| **Playoff Totals** | | 1 | 0 | 0 | 0 | 0 |

GRIMSON, Stu 6-5 220 LW
B. Kamloops, B.C., May 20, 1965

88-89	Calg	1	0	0	0	5
89-90	Calg	3	0	0	0	17
90-91	Chi	35	0	1	1	183
91-92	Chi	54	2	2	4	234
Totals		93	2	3	5	439
Playoff Totals		19	0	1	1	56

GRISDALE, John Russell 6-0 195 D
B. Geraldton, Ont., Aug. 23, 1948

| 72-73 | Tor | 49 | 1 | 7 | 8 | 76 |
| 74-75 | Tor-Van | 60 | 1 | 12 | 13 | 95 |

Season	Team	GP	G	A	Pts.	PIM

GRISDALE, John Russell (Continued)

75-76	Van	38	2	6	8	54
76-77	Van	20	0	2	2	20
77-78	Van	42	0	9	9	47
78-79	Van	41	0	3	3	54
Totals		250	4	39	43	346
Playoff Totals		10	0	1	1	15

GRONSDAHL, Lloyd Gilford (Gabby) 5-9 170 RW
B. Norquay, Sask., May 10, 1921

| 41-42 | Bos | 10 | 1 | 2 | 3 | 0 |

GRONSTRAND, Jari 6-3 195 D
B. Tampere, Finland, Nov. 14, 1962

86-87	Minn	47	1	6	7	27
87-88	NYR	62	3	11	14	63
88-89	Que	25	1	3	4	14
89-90	Que-NYI	48	3	5	8	29
90-91	NYI	3	0	1	1	2
Totals		185	8	26	34	135
Playoff Totals		3	0	0	0	4

GROSS, Lloyd George 5-8 175 LW
B. Kitchener, Ont., Oct. 15, 1907

26-27	Tor	16	1	1	2	0
33-34	NYA-Bos-Det	40	9	4	13	18
34-35	Det	6	1	0	1	2
Totals		62	11	5	16	20
Playoff Totals		1	0	0	0	0

GROSSO, Donald (Count) 5-11 170 LW
B. Sault Ste. Marie, Ont., Apr. 12, 1915

39-40	Det	28	2	3	5	11
40-41	Det	45	8	7	15	14
41-42	Det	48	23	30	53	13
42-43	Det	50	15	17	32	10
43-44	Det	42	16	31	47	13
44-45	Det-Chi	41	15	16	31	10
45-46	Chi	47	7	10	17	17
46-47	Bos	33	0	2	2	2
Totals		334	86	116	202	90
Playoff Totals		50	14	12	26	46

GROSVENAR, Leonard (Len) F
B. Ottawa, Ont.

27-28	Ott	41	1	2	3	18
28-29	Ott	42	3	2	5	16
29-30	Ott	14	0	3	3	19
30-31	Ott	34	5	4	9	25
31-32	NYA	12	0	0	0	0
32-33	Mont	4	0	0	0	0
Totals		147	9	11	20	78
Playoff Totals		4	0	0	0	2

GROULX, Wayne 6-1 185 C
B. Welland, Ont., Feb. 2, 1965

| 84-85 | Que | 1 | 0 | 0 | 0 | 0 |

GRUEN, Daniel Patrick 5-11 190 LW
B. Thunder Bay, Ont., June 26, 1952

72-73	Det	2	0	0	0	0
73-74	Det	18	1	3	4	7
74-75	Mich-Winn (WHA)	66	19	28	47	94
75-76	Clev (WHA)	80	26	24	50	72
76-77	Minn-Calg (WHA)	35	11	9	20	19
76-77	Col	29	8	10	18	12
NHL Totals		49	9	13	22	19
WHA Totals		181	56	61	117	185
WHA Playoff Totals		3	0	1	1	0

GRUHL, Scott Kenneth 5-11 185 LW
B. Port Colborne, Ont., Sept. 13, 1959

81-82	LA	7	2	1	3	2
82-83	LA	7	0	2	2	4
87-88	Pitt	6	1	0	1	0
Totals		20	3	3	6	6

GRYP, Robert Douglas 6-1 190 LW
B. Chatham, Ont., May 6, 1950

73-74	Bos	1	0	0	0	0
74-75	Wash	27	5	8	13	21
75-76	Wash	46	6	5	11	12
Totals		74	11	13	24	33

GUAY, Francois 6-0 190 C
B. Gatineau, Que., June 8, 1968

| 89-90 | Buf | 1 | 0 | 0 | 0 | 0 |

GUAY, Paul 5-11 185 RW
B. Providence, R.I., Sept. 2, 1963

| 83-84 | Phil | 14 | 2 | 6 | 8 | 14 |
| 84-85 | Phil | 2 | 0 | 1 | 1 | 0 |

Season	Team	GP	G	A	Pts.	PIM

GUAY, Paul (Continued)

85-86	LA	23	3	3	6	18
86-87	LA	35	2	5	7	16
87-88	LA	33	4	4	8	40
88-89	LA-Bos	7	0	2	2	2
90-91	NYI	3	0	2	2	2
Totals		117	11	23	34	92
Playoff Totals		9	0	1	1	12

GUERARD, Stephane 6-2 198 D
B. Ste. Elizabeth, Que., Apr. 12, 1968

87-88	Que	30	0	0	0	34
88-89	Que	4	0	0	0	6
Totals		34	0	0	0	40

GUERIN, Bill 6-2 190 C/RW
B. Wilbraham, Mass., Nov. 9, 1970

| 91-92 | NJ | 5 | 0 | 1 | 1 | 9 |
| **Playoff Totals** | | 6 | 3 | 0 | 3 | 4 |

GUEVREMONT, Jocelyn Marcel Josh 6-2 200 D
B. Montreal, Que., Mar. 1, 1951

71-72	Van	75	13	38	51	44
72-73	Van	78	16	26	42	46
73-74	Van	72	15	24	39	34
74-75	Van-Buf	66	7	25	32	32
75-76	Buf	80	12	40	52	57
76-77	Buf	80	9	29	38	46
77-78	Buf	66	7	28	35	46
78-79	Buf	34	3	8	11	8
79-80	NYR	20	2	5	7	6
Totals		571	84	223	307	319
Playoff Totals		40	4	17	21	18

GUIDOLIN, Aldo Reno 6-0 180 D
B. Forks of Credit, Ont., June 6, 1932

52-53	NYR	30	4	4	8	24
53-54	NYR	68	2	6	8	51
54-55	NYR	70	2	5	7	34
55-56	NYR	14	1	0	1	8
Totals		182	9	15	24	117

GUIDOLIN, Armand (Bep) 5-8 175 LW
B. Thorold, Ont., Dec. 9, 1925

42-43	Bos	42	7	15	22	43
43-44	Bos	47	17	25	42	58
45-46	Bos	50	15	17	32	62
46-47	Bos	56	10	13	23	73
47-48	Det	58	12	10	22	78
48-49	Det-Chi	60	4	17	21	116
49-50	Chi	70	17	34	51	42
50-51	Chi	69	12	22	34	56
51-52	Chi	67	13	18	31	78
Totals		519	107	171	278	606
Playoff Totals		24	5	7	12	35

GUINDON, Robert Pierre 5-9 175 LW
B. Labelle, Que., Nov. 19, 1950

72-73	Que (WHA)	71	28	28	56	31
73-74	Que (WHA)	77	31	39	70	30
74-75	Que (WHA)	69	12	18	30	23
75-76	Winn (WHA)	39	3	3	6	14
76-77	Winn (WHA)	69	10	17	27	19
77-78	Winn (WHA)	77	20	22	42	18
78-79	Winn (WHA)	71	8	18	26	21
79-80	Winn	6	0	1	1	0
NHL Totals		6	0	1	1	0
WHA Totals		473	112	145	257	156
WHA Playoff Totals		64	24	19	43	33

GUSAROV, Alexei 6-2 183 D
B. Leningrad, Soviet Union, July 8, 1964

90-91	Que	36	3	9	12	12
91-92	Que	68	5	18	23	22
Totals		104	8	27	35	34

GUSTAFSSON, Bengt-Ake 5-11 198 C
B. Kariskoga, Sweden, Mar. 23, 1958

79-80	Wash	80	22	38	60	17
80-81	Wash	72	21	34	55	26
81-82	Wash	70	26	34	60	40
82-83	Wash	67	22	42	64	16
83-84	Wash	69	32	43	75	16
84-85	Wash	51	14	29	43	8
85-86	Wash	70	23	52	75	26
87-88	Wash	78	18	36	54	29
88-89	Wash	72	18	51	69	18
Totals		629	196	359	555	196
Playoff Totals		32	9	19	28	16

Season	Team	GP	G	A	Pts.	PIM
GUSTAVSSON, Peter	*6-1 188 LW*					
B. Bollebydg, Sweden, Mar. 30, 1958						
81-82	Col	2	0	0	0	0
GUY, Kevan	*6 3 202 D*					
B. Edmonton, Alta., July 16, 1965						
86-87	Calg	24	0	4	4	19
87-88	Calg	11	0	3	3	8
88-89	Van	45	2	2	4	34
89-90	Van	30	2	5	7	32
90-91	Van-Calg	43	1	6	7	43
91-92	Calg	3	0	0	0	2
Totals		156	5	20	25	138
Playoff Totals		5	0	1	1	23
HAANPAA, Ari	*6-1 190 RW*					
B. Nokia, Finland, Nov. 29, 1965						
85-86	NYI	18	0	7	7	20
86-87	NYI	41	6	4	10	17
87-88	NYI	1	0	0	0	0
Totals		60	6	11	17	37
Playoff Totals		6	0	0	0	10
HAAS, David	*6-2 196 LW*					
B. Toronto, Ont., June 23, 1968						
90-91	Edm	5	1	0	1	0
HABSCHEID, Marc Joseph	*6-0 185 RW/C*					
B. Swift Current, Sask., Mar. 1, 1963						
81-82	Edm	7	1	3	4	2
82-83	Edm	32	3	10	13	14
83-84	Edm	9	1	0	1	6
84-85	Edm	26	5	3	8	4
85-86	Minn	6	2	3	5	0
86-87	Minn	15	2	0	2	2
87-88	Minn	16	4	11	15	6
88-89	Minn	76	23	31	54	40
89-90	Det	66	15	11	26	33
90-91	Det	46	9	8	17	22
91-92	Calg	46	7	11	18	42
Totals		345	72	91	163	171
Playoff Totals		12	1	3	4	13
HACHBORN, Leonard	*5-10 175 C*					
B. Brantford, Ont., Sept. 4, 1961						
83-84	Phil	38	11	21	32	4
84-85	Phil	40	5	17	22	23
85-86	LA	24	4	1	5	2
Totals		102	20	39	59	25
Playoff Totals		7	0	3	3	7
HADDON, Lloyd Ward	*6 0 195 D*					
B. Sarnia, Ont., Aug. 10, 1938						
59-60	Det	8	0	0	0	2
Playoff Totals		1	0	0	0	0
HADFIELD, Victor Edward	*6-0 190 LW*					
B. Oakville, Ont., Oct. 4, 1940						
61-62	NYR	44	3	1	4	22
62-63	NYR	36	5	6	11	32
63-64	NYR	69	14	11	25	151
64-65	NYR	70	18	20	38	102
65-66	NYR	67	16	19	35	112
66-67	NYR	69	13	20	33	80
67-68	NYR	59	20	19	39	45
68-69	NYR	73	26	40	66	108
69-70	NYR	71	20	34	54	69
70-71	NYR	63	22	22	44	38
71-72	NYR	78	50	56	106	142
72-73	NYR	63	28	34	62	60
73-74	NYR	77	27	28	55	75
74-75	Pitt	78	31	42	73	72
75-76	Pitt	76	30	35	65	46
76-77	Pitt	9	0	2	2	0
Totals		1002	323	389	712	1154
Playoff Totals		73	27	21	48	117
HAGGARTY, James	*5-11 167 LW*					
B. Port Arthur, Ont., Apr. 14, 1914						
41-42	Mont	5	1	1	2	0
Playoff Totals		3	2	1	3	0
HAGGLUND, Roger	*6-1 175 D*					
B. Umea, Sweden, July 2, 1961						
84-85	Que	3	0	0	0	0
HAGMAN, Matti Risto Tapio (Hakki)						
6-1 184 C						
B. Helsinki, Finland, Sept. 21, 1955						
76-77	Bos	75	11	17	28	0
77-78	Bos	15	4	1	5	6
77-78	Que (WHA)	53	25	31	56	16
80-81	Edm	75	20	33	53	16
81-82	Edm	72	21	38	59	18
NHL Totals		237	56	89	145	40
WHA Totals		53	25	31	56	16
HAGMAN, Matti Risto Tapio (Hakki)						
(Continued)						
NHL Playoff Totals		20	5	2	7	6
HAIDY, Gordon Adam (Adam)						
5-10 185 RW						
B. Winnipeg, Man., Apr. 11, 1928						
49-50	Det	0	0	0	0	0
Playoff Totals		1	0	0	0	0
HAJDU, Richard	*6-1 185 LW*					
B. Victoria, B.C., May 10, 1965						
85-86	Buf	3	0	0	0	4
86-87	Buf	2	0	0	0	0
Totals		5	0	0	0	4
HAJT, William Albert	*6-3 205 D*					
B. Borden, Sask., Nov. 18, 1951						
73-74	Buf	6	0	2	2	0
74-75	Buf	76	3	26	29	68
75-76	Buf	80	6	21	27	48
76-77	Buf	79	6	20	26	56
77-78	Buf	76	4	18	22	30
78-79	Buf	40	3	8	11	20
79-80	Buf	75	4	12	16	24
80-81	Buf	68	2	19	21	42
81-82	Buf	65	2	9	11	44
82-83	Buf	72	3	12	15	26
83-84	Buf	79	3	24	27	32
84-85	Buf	57	5	13	18	14
85-86	Buf	58	1	16	17	25
86-87	Buf	23	0	2	2	4
Totals		854	42	202	244	433
Playoff Totals		80	2	16	18	70
HAKANSSON, Anders	*6-2 190 LW*					
B. Munkfors, Sweden, Apr. 27, 1956						
81-82	Minn	72	12	4	16	29
82-83	Minn-Pitt	67	9	12	21	35
83-84	LA	80	15	17	32	41
84-85	LA	73	12	12	24	28
85-86	LA	38	4	1	5	8
Totals		330	52	46	98	141
Playoff Totals		6	0	0	0	2
HALDERSON, Harold (Slim)	*6-3 200 D*					
B. Winnipeg, Man., Jan. 6, 1900						
26-27	Det-Tor	44	3	2	5	65
HALE, Larry James	*6-1 180 D*					
B. Summerland, B.C., Oct. 9, 1941						
68-69	Phil	67	3	16	19	28
69-70	Phil	53	1	9	10	28
70-71	Phil	70	1	11	12	34
71-72	Phil	6	0	1	1	0
72-73	Hou (WHA)	68	4	26	30	65
73-74	Hou (WHA)	69	2	14	16	39
74-75	Hou (WHA)	76	2	18	20	40
75-76	Hou (WHA)	77	2	12	14	30
76-77	Hou (WHA)	67	0	14	14	18
77-78	Hou (WHA)	56	2	11	13	22
NHL Totals		196	5	37	42	90
WHA Totals		413	12	95	107	214
NHL Playoff Totals		8	0	0	0	12
WHA Playoff Totals		65	4	15	19	22
HALEY, Leonard Frank (Len)						
5-7 168 RW						
B. Edmonton, Alta., Sept. 15, 1931						
59-60	Det	27	1	2	3	12
60-61	Det	3	1	0	1	2
Totals		30	2	2	4	14
Playoff Totals		6	1	3	4	6
HALKIDIS, Bob	*5-11 200 D*					
B. Toronto, Ont., Mar. 5, 1966						
85-86	Buf	37	1	9	10	115
86-87	Buf	6	1	1	2	10
87-88	Buf	30	0	3	3	115
88-89	Buf	16	0	1	1	66
89-90	LA	20	0	4	4	56
90-91	LA	34	1	3	4	133
91-92	Tor	46	3	3	6	145
Totals		179	6	24	30	649
Playoff Totals		11	0	0	0	41
HALL, Del Allison	*5-10 170 C*					
B. Peterborough, Ont., May 7, 1949						
71-72	Cal	1	0	0	0	0
72-73	Cal	6	0	0	0	0
73-74	Cal	2	0	2	2	2
75-76	Phoe (WHA)	80	47	44	91	10
76-77	Phoe (WHA)	80	38	41	79	30
HALL, Del Allison *(Continued)*						
77-78	Edm (WHA)	26	4	3	7	4
NHL Totals		9	2	0	2	2
WHA Totals		186	89	88	177	44
WHA Playoff Totals		5	2	3	5	0
HALL, Gary Wayne	*5-8 170 LW*					
B. Melita, Man., May 22, 1939						
60-61	NYR	4	0	0	0	0
HALL, Joseph Henry (Bad Joe)	*F*					
B. Stratfordshire, England, May 3, 1882						
17-18	Mont	20	8	0	8	60
18-19	Mont	17	7	1	8	85
Totals		37	15	1	16	145
Playoff Totals		12	0	2	2	31
HALL, Murray Winston	*6-0 175 C*					
B. Kirkland Lake, Ont., Nov. 24, 1940						
61-62	Chi	2	0	0	0	0
63-64	Chi	23	2	0	2	4
65-66	Det	1	0	0	0	0
66-67	Det	12	4	3	7	4
67-68	Minn	17	2	1	3	10
70-71	Van	77	21	38	59	22
71-72	Van	32	6	6	12	6
72-73	Hou (WHA)	76	28	42	70	84
73-74	Hou (WHA)	78	30	28	58	25
74-75	Hou (WHA)	78	18	29	47	28
75-76	Hou (WHA)	80	20	26	46	18
NHL Totals		164	35	48	83	46
WHA Totals		312	96	125	221	155
NHL Playoff Totals		6	0	0	0	0
WHA Playoff Totals		54	21	17	38	32
HALL, Robert	*F*					
25-26	NYA	8	0	0	0	0
HALL, Taylor	*5-11 180 LW*					
B. Regina, Sask., Feb. 20, 1964						
83-84	Van	4	1	0	1	0
84-85	Van	7	1	4	5	19
85-86	Van	19	5	5	10	6
86-87	Van	4	0	0	0	0
87-88	Bos	7	0	0	0	4
Totals		41	7	9	16	29
HALLER, Kevin	*6-2 183 D*					
B. Trochu, Alta., Dec. 5, 1970						
89-90	Buf	2	0	0	0	0
90-91	Buf	21	1	8	9	20
91-92	Buf-Mont	66	8	17	25	92
Totals		89	9	25	34	112
Playoff Totals		15	1	4	5	16
HALLIDAY, Milton	*F-D*					
B. Ottawa, Ont.						
26-27	Ott	38	1	0	1	4
27-28	Ott	13	0	0	0	2
28-29	Ott	16	0	0	0	0
Totals		67	1	0	1	6
Playoff Totals		6	0	0	0	0
HALLIN, Mats	*6-2 200 LW*					
B. Eskilstuna, Sweden, Mar. 9, 1958						
82-83	NYI	30	7	7	14	26
83-84	NYI	40	2	5	7	27
84-85	NYI	38	5	0	5	50
85-86	Minn	38	3	2	5	86
86-87	Minn	6	0	0	0	4
Totals		152	17	14	31	193
Playoff Totals		15	1	0	1	13
HALWARD, Douglas Robert	*6-1 200 D*					
B. Toronto, Ont., Nov. 1, 1955						
75-76	Bos	22	1	5	6	6
76-77	Bos	18	2	2	4	6
77-78	Bos	25	0	2	2	2
78-79	LA	27	1	5	6	13
79-80	LA	63	11	45	56	52
80-81	LA-Van	58	4	16	20	100
81-82	Van	37	4	13	17	40
82-83	Van	75	19	33	52	83
83-84	Van	54	7	16	23	35
84-85	Van	71	7	27	34	82
85-86	Van	70	8	25	33	111
86-87	Van-Det	21	0	6	6	53
87-88	Det	70	5	21	26	130
88-89	Det-Edm	42	0	8	8	61
Totals		653	69	224	293	774
Playoff Totals		47	7	10	17	113
HAMEL, Gilles	*6-0 185 LW*					
B. Asbestos, Que., Mar. 18, 1960						
80-81	Buf	51	10	9	19	53
81-82	Buf	16	2	7	9	2

Season	Team	GP	G	A	Pts.	PIM

HAMEL, Gilles *(Continued)*

Season	Team	GP	G	A	Pts.	PIM
82-83	Buf	66	22	20	42	26
83-84	Buf	75	21	23	44	37
84-85	Buf	80	18	30	48	36
85-86	Buf	77	19	25	44	61
86-87	Winn	79	27	21	48	24
87-88	Winn	63	8	11	19	35
88-89	Winn-LA	12	0	1	1	2
Totals		519	127	147	274	276
Playoff Totals		27	4	5	9	10

HAMEL, Herbert (Hap) *F*

Season	Team	GP	G	A	Pts.	PIM
30-39	Tor	2	0	0	0	14

HAMEL, Jean *5-11 195 D*
B. Asbestos, Que., June 6, 1952

Season	Team	GP	G	A	Pts.	PIM
72-73	StL	55	2	7	9	24
73-74	StL-DET	45	1	4	5	46
74-75	Det	80	5	19	24	136
74-76	Det	77	3	9	12	129
76-77	Det	71	1	10	11	63
77-78	Det	32	2	6	8	34
78-79	Det	52	2	4	6	72
79-80	Det	49	1	4	5	43
80-81	Det	68	5	7	12	57
81-82	Que	40	1	6	7	32
82-83	Que	51	2	7	9	38
83-84	Mont	79	1	12	13	92
Totals		699	26	95	121	766
Playoff Totals		33	0	2	2	44

HAMILL, Robert George (Red)
5-11 180 LW
B. Toronto, Ont., 11, 1917

Season	Team	GP	G	A	Pts.	PIM
37-38	Bos	6	0	1	1	2
38-39	Bos	7	0	1	1	0
39-40	Bos	28	10	8	18	16
40-41	Bos	8	0	1	1	0
41-42	Bos-Chi	43	24	12	36	23
42-43	Chi	50	28	16	44	44
45-46	Chi	38	20	17	37	23
46-47	Chi	60	21	19	40	12
47-48	Chi	60	11	13	24	18
48-49	Chi	57	8	4	12	16
49-50	Chi	59	6	2	8	6
50-51	Chi	2	0	0	0	0
Totals		418	128	94	222	160
Playoff Totals		23	2	1	3	20

HAMILTON, Allan Guy *6-1 195 D*
B. Flin Flon, Man., Aug. 20, 1946

Season	Team	GP	G	A	Pts.	PIM
65-66	NYR	4	0	0	0	0
67-68	NYR	2	0	0	0	0
68-69	NYR	16	0	0	0	0
69-70	NYR	59	0	5	5	54
70-71	Buf	69	2	28	30	71
71-72	Buf	76	4	30	34	105
72-73	Alb(WHA)	78	11	50	61	124
73-74	Edm(WHA)	77	14	45	59	104
74-75	Edm(WHA)	25	1	13	14	42
75-76	Edm(WHA)	54	2	32	34	78
76-77	Edm(WHA)	81	8	37	45	60
77-78	Edm(WHA)	59	11	43	54	46
78-79	Edm(WHA)	80	6	38	44	38
79-80	EDm	31	4	15	19	20
NHL Totals		257	10	78	88	250
WHA Totals		454	53	258	311	492
NHL Playoff Totals		7	0	0	0	2
WHA Playoff Totals		26	5	11	16	29

HAMILTON, Charles (Chuck)
5-11 175 LW
B. Kirkland Lake, Ont., Jan. 18, 1939

Season	Team	GP	G	A	Pts.	PIM
61-62	Mont	1	0	0	0	0
72-73	StL	3	0	2	2	2
Totals		4	0	2	2	2

HAMILTON, James *6-0 180 RW*
B. Barrie, Ont., Jan. 18, 1957

Season	Team	GP	G	A	Pts.	PIM
77-78	Pitt	25	2	4	6	2
78-79	Pitt	2	0	0	0	0
79-80	Pitt	10	2	0	2	0
80-81	Pitt	20	1	6	7	18
81-82	Pitt	11	5	3	8	2
82-83	Pitt	5	0	2	2	2
83-84	Pitt	11	2	2	4	4
84-85	Pitt	11	2	1	3	0
Totals		95	14	18	32	28
Playoff Totals		6	3	0	3	0

HAMILTON, John McIvor (Jack)
5-7 170 C
B. Trenton, Ont., June 2, 1925

Season	Team	GP	G	A	Pts.	PIM
42-43	Tor	49	4	22	26	60
43-44	Tor	49	20	17	37	4
45-46	Tor	40	7	9	16	12
Totals		138	31	48	79	76

HAMILTON, John McIvor (Jack)
(Continued)

Season	Team	GP	G	A	Pts.	PIM
Playoff Totals		11	2	1	3	0

HAMMOND, Ken *6-1 190 D*
B. Port Credit, Ont., Aug. 22, 1963

Season	Team	GP	G	A	Pts.	PIM
84-85	LA	3	1	0	1	0
85-86	LA	3	0	1	1	2
86-87	LA	10	0	2	2	11
87-88	LA	46	7	9	16	69
88-89	Edm-NYR-Tor	22	0	3	3	20
90-91	Bos	1	1	0	1	2
91-92	SJ-Van	46	5	10	15	82
Totals		131	14	25	39	186
Playoff Totals		15	0	0	0	24

HAMILTON, Reginald (Reg) *5-11 180 D*
B. Toronto, Ont., Apr. 29, 1914

Season	Team	GP	G	A	Pts.	PIM
35-36	Tor	7	0	0	0	0
36-37	Tor	39	3	7	10	32
37-38	Tor	45	1	4	5	43
38-39	Tor	48	0	7	7	54
39-40	Tor	23	2	2	4	23
40-41	Tor	45	3	12	15	59
41-42	Tor	22	0	4	4	27
42-43	Tor	11	1	1	2	68
43-44	Tor	39	4	12	16	32
44-45	Tor	50	3	12	15	41
45-46	Chi	48	1	7	8	31
46-47	Chi	10	0	3	3	2
Totals		387	18	71	89	412
Playoff Totals		64	6	6	12	54

HAMMARSTROM, Hans Inge *6-0 180 LW*
B. Sundsvall, Sweden, Jan. 20, 1948

Season	Team	GP	G	A	Pts.	PIM
73-74	Tor	66	20	23	43	14
74-75	Tor	69	21	20	41	23
75-76	Tor	76	19	21	40	21
76-77	Tor	78	24	17	41	16
77-78	Tor-StL	73	20	20	40	10
78-79	StL	65	12	22	34	8
Totals		427	116	123	239	92
Playoff Totals		13	2	3	5	4

HAMPSON, Edward George (Ted)
5-8 173 C
B. Togo, Sask., Dec. 11, 1936

Season	Team	GP	G	A	Pts.	PIM
59-60	Tor	41	2	8	10	17
60-61	NYR	69	6	14	20	4
61-62	NYR	68	4	24	28	10
62-63	NYR	46	4	2	6	2
63-64	Det	7	0	1	1	0
64-65	Det	1	0	0	0	0
66-67	Det	65	13	35	48	4
67-68	Det-Oak	71	17	37	54	14
68-69	Oak	76	26	49	75	6
69-70	Oak	76	17	35	52	10
70-71	Cal-Minn	78	14	26	40	18
71-72	Minn	78	5	14	19	6
72-73	Minn(WHA)	77	17	45	62	20
73-74	Minn(WHA)	77	18	38	55	9
74-75	Minn(WHA)	78	17	36	53	6
75-76	Minn-Que(WHA)	73	9	25	34	16
NHL Totals		676	108	245	353	91
WHA Totals		305	60	144	204	51
NHL Playoff Totals		35	7	10	17	4
WHA Playoff Totals		33	8	14	22	18

HAMPSON, Gordon *6-3 210 LW*
B. Vancouver, B.C., Feb. 13, 1959

Season	Team	GP	G	A	Pts.	PIM
82-83	Calg	4	0	0	0	5

HAMPTON, Richard Charles (Rick)
6-0 190 D
B. King, Ont., June 14, 1956

Season	Team	GP	G	A	Pts.	PIM
74-75	Cal	78	8	17	25	59
75-76	Cal	73	14	37	51	54
76-77	Clev	57	16	24	40	13
77-78	Clev	77	18	18	36	19
78-79	LA	49	3	17	20	22
79-80	LA	3	0	0	0	0
Totals		337	59	113	172	167
Playoff Totals		1	0	0	0	0

HAMWAY, Mark *6-0 190 RW*
B. Detroit, Mich., Aug. 9, 1961

Season	Team	GP	G	A	Pts.	PIM
84-85	NYI	2	0	0	0	0
85-86	NYI	49	5	12	17	9
86-87	NYI	2	0	1	1	0
Totals		53	5	13	18	9
Playoff Totals		1	0	0	0	0

HANDY, Ronald *5-11 175 LW*
B. Toronto, Ont., Jan. 5, 1963

Season	Team	GP	G	A	Pts.	PIM
85-85	NYI	10	0	2	2	0
87-88	StL	4	0	1	1	0
Totals		14	0	3	3	0

HANGSLEBEN, Alan (Hank) *6-1 195 D*
B. Warroad, Minn., Feb. 22, 1953

Season	Team	GP	G	A	Pts.	PIM
74-75	NE(WHA)	26	0	4	4	8
75-76	NE(WHA)	78	2	23	25	62
76-77	NE(WHA)	74	13	9	22	79
77-78	NE(WHA)	79	11	18	29	140
78-79	NE(WHA)	77	10	19	29	148
79-80	Hart-Wash	74	13	22	35	114
80-81	Wash	76	5	19	24	198
81-82	Wash-LA	35	3	7	10	84
NHL Totals		185	21	48	69	396
WHA Totals		334	36	73	109	437
WHA Playoff Totals		47	4	12	16	97

HANNA, John *6-0 195 D*
B. Sydney, N. S., Apr. 5, 1935

Season	Team	GP	G	A	Pts.	PIM
58-59	NYR	70	1	10	11	83
59-60	NYR	61	4	8	12	87
60-61	NYR	46	1	8	9	34
63-64	Mont	6	0	0	0	2
67-68	Phil	15	0	0	0	0
72-73	Clev(WHA)	66	6	20	26	68
NHL Totals		198	6	26	32	206
WHA Totals		66	6	20	26	68

HANNAN, David *5-10 185 C*
B. Sudbury, Ont., Nov. 26, 1961

Season	Team	GP	G	A	Pts.	PIM
81-82	Pitt	1	0	0	0	0
82-83	Pitt	74	11	22	33	127
83-84	Pitt	24	2	3	5	33
84-85	Pitt	30	6	7	13	43
85-86	Pitt	75	17	18	35	91
86-87	Pitt	58	10	15	25	56
87-88	Pitt-Edm	72	13	14	27	66
88-89	Pitt	72	10	20	30	157
89-90	Tor	39	6	9	15	55
90-91	Tor	74	11	23	34	82
91-92	Tor-Buf	47	4	6	10	64
Totals		566	90	137	227	774
Playoff Totals		30	4	2	6	18

HANNIGAN, John Gordon (Gord)
5-7 163 C
B. Schumacher, Ont., Jan. 19, 1929

Season	Team	GP	G	A	Pts.	PIM
52-53	Tor	65	17	18	35	51
53-54	Tor	35	4	4	8	18
54-55	Tor	13	0	2	2	8
55-56	Tor	48	8	7	15	40
Totals		161	29	31	60	117
Playoff Totals		9	2	0	2	8

HANNIGAN, Patrick Edward *5-10 190 RW*
B. Timmins, Ont., Mar. 5, 1936

Season	Team	GP	G	A	Pts.	PIM
59-60	Tor	1	0	0	0	0
60-61	NYR	53	11	9	20	24
61-62	NYR	56	8	14	22	34
67-68	Phil	65	11	15	26	36
68-69	Phil	7	0	1	1	22
Totals		182	30	39	69	116
Playoff Totals		11	1	2	3	11

HANNIGAN, Raymond James *F*
B. Schumacher, Ont., July 14, 1927

Season	Team	GP	G	A	Pts.	PIM
48-49	Tor	3	0	0	0	2

HANSEN, Richard John *5-10 197 C*
B. Bronx, N.Y., Oct. 30, 1955

Season	Team	GP	G	A	Pts.	PIM
76-77	NYI	4	1	0	1	0
77-78	NYI	2	0	0	0	0
78-79	NYI	12	1	6	7	4
81-82	StL	2	0	2	2	2
Totals		20	2	8	10	6

HANSON, David *6-0 190 D*
B. Cumberland, Wis., Apr. 12, 1954

Season	Team	GP	G	A	Pts.	PIM
76-77	Minn-NE(WHA)	8	0	2	2	44
77-78	Birm(WHA)	42	7	16	23	241
78-79	Birm(WHA)	53	6	22	28	212
78-79	Det	11	0	0	0	26
79-80	Minn	22	1	1	2	39
NHL Totals		33	1	1	2	65
WHA Totals		103	13	40	53	497
WHA Playoff Totals		6	0	1	1	48

HANSON, Emil *5-10 180 D*
B. Centerville, S.D., Nov. 18, 1907

Season	Team	GP	G	A	Pts.	PIM
32-33	Det	7	0	0	0	6

Season	Team	GP	G	A	Pts.	PIM
HANSON, Keith	6-5 210 D					
B. Ada, Minn., Apr. 26, 1957						
83-84	Calg	25	0	2	2	77
HANSON, Oscar (Ossie)	D					
B. U.S.A.						
37-38	Chi	7	0	0	0	0
HARBARUK, Mikolaj Nickolas (Nick)						
6-0 195 RW						
B. Drohiczyn, Poland, Aug. 16, 1943						
69-70	Pitt	74	5	17	22	56
70-71	Pitt	78	13	12	25	108
71-72	Pitt	78	12	17	29	46
72-73	Pitt	78	10	15	25	47
73-74	StL	56	5	14	19	16
74-75	Ind(WHA)	78	20	23	43	52
75-76	Ind(WHA)	76	23	19	42	24
76-77	Ind(WHA)	27	2	2	4	2
NHL Totals		364	45	75	120	273
WHA Totals		181	45	44	89	78
NHL Playoff Totals		14	3	1	4	20
WHA Playoff Totals		13	3	1	4	10
HARDING, Jeff	6-3 200 RW					
B. Toronto, Ont., Apr. 6, 1969						
88-89	Phil	6	0	0	0	29
89-90	Phil	9	0	0	0	18
Totals		15	0	0	0	47
HARDY, Jocelyn Joseph (Joe)	6-0 175 C					
B. Kenogami, Que., Dec. 5, 1945						
69-70	Oak	23	5	4	9	20
70-71	Cal	40	4	10	14	31
72-73	Clev(WHA)	72	17	33	50	80
73-74	Chi(WHA)	77	24	35	59	55
74-75	Chi-SD(WHA)	61	5	26	31	66
NHL Totals		63	9	14	23	51
WHA Totals		210	46	94	140	201
NHL Playoff Totals		4	0	0	0	0
WHA Playoff Totals		24	4	10	14	13
HARDY, Mark Lea	5-11 195 D					
B. Semaden, Switzerland, Feb. 1, 1959						
79-80	LA	15	0	1	1	10
80-81	LA	77	5	20	25	77
81-82	LA	77	6	39	45	130
82-83	LA	74	5	34	39	101
83-84	LA	79	8	41	49	122
84-85	LA	78	14	39	53	97
85-86	LA	55	6	21	27	71
86-87	LA	73	3	27	30	120
87-88	LA-NYR	80	8	24	32	130
88-89	Minn-NYR	60	4	16	20	71
89-90	NYR	54	0	15	15	94
90-91	NYR	70	1	5	6	89
91-92	NYR	52	1	8	9	65
Totals		844	61	290	351	1177
Playoff Totals		52	4	14	18	128
HARGREAVES, James Albert (Cement Head)						
5-11 185 D						
B. Winnipeg, Man., May 2, 1950						
70-71	Van	7	0	1	1	33
72-73	Van	59	1	6	7	72
73-74	Winn(WHA)	53	1	4	5	50
74-75	Ind-SD(WHA)	78	10	15	25	75
75-76	SD(WHA)	43	1	1	2	26
NHL Totals		66	1	7	8	105
WHA Totals		174	12	20	32	151
WHA Playoff Totals		15	1	0	1	8
HARKINS, Todd	6-3 210 C					
B. Cleveland, Ohio, Oct. 8, 1968						
91-92	Calg	5	0	0	0	7
HARLOW, Scott	6-1 185 LW					
B. East Bridgewater, Mass., Oct. 11, 1963						
87-88	StL	1	0	1	1	0
HARMON, David Glen (Glen)	5-8 165 D					
B. Holland, Man., Jan. 2, 1921						
42-43	Mont	27	5	9	14	25
43-44	Mont	43	5	16	21	36
44-45	Mont	45	5	8	13	41
45-46	Mont	49	7	10	17	28
46-47	Mont	57	5	9	14	53
47-48	Mont	56	10	4	14	52
48-49	Mont	59	8	12	20	44
49-50	Mont	62	3	16	19	28
50-51	Mont	57	2	12	14	27
Totals		452	50	96	146	334
Playoff Totals		53	5	10	15	37

Season	Team	GP	G	A	Pts.	PIM
HARMS, John	5-8 160 RW					
B. Saskatoon, Sask., Apr. 29, 1925						
43-44	Chi	1	0	0	0	0
44-45	Chi	43	5	5	10	21
Totals		44	5	5	10	21
Playoff Totals		3	3	0	3	2
HARNOTT, Walter Herbert (Happy)						
5-7 170 F						
B. Montreal, Que., Sept. 24, 1909						
33-34	Bos	6	0	0	0	6
HARPER, Terrance Victor (Terry)						
6-1 197 D						
B. Regina, Sask., Jan. 27, 1940						
62-63	Mont	14	1	1	2	10
63-64	Mont	70	2	15	17	149
64-65	Mont	62	0	7	7	93
65-66	Mont	69	1	11	12	91
66-67	Mont	56	0	16	16	99
67-68	Mont	57	3	8	11	66
68-69	Mont	21	0	3	3	37
69-70	Mont	75	4	18	22	109
70-71	Mont	78	1	21	22	116
71-72	Mont	52	2	12	14	35
72-73	LA	77	1	8	9	74
73-74	LA	77	0	17	17	119
74-75	LA	80	5	21	26	120
75-76	Det	69	8	25	33	59
76-77	Det	52	4	8	12	28
77-78	Det	80	2	17	19	85
78-79	Det	51	0	6	6	58
79-80	StL	11	1	5	6	6
80-81	Col	15	0	2	2	8
Totals		1066	35	221	256	1362
Playoff Totals		112	4	13	17	140
HARRER, Tim	6-0 185 RW					
B. Bloomington, Minn., May 10, 1957						
82-83	Calg	3	0	0	0	2
HARRINGTON, Leland K. (Hago)						
5-8 163 LW						
B. Melrose, Mass.						
25-26	Bos	26	7	2	9	6
27-28	Bos	22	1	0	1	7
32-33	Mont	24	1	1	2	2
Totals		72	9	3	12	15
Playoff Totals		4	1	0	1	2
HARRIS, Edward Alexander (Ted)						
6-2 183 D						
B. Winnipeg, Man., July 18, 1936						
63-64	Mont	4	0	1	1	0
64-65	Mont	68	1	14	15	107
65-66	Mont	53	0	13	13	81
66-67	Mont	65	2	16	18	86
67-68	Mont	67	5	16	21	78
68-69	Mont	76	7	18	25	102
69-70	Mont	74	3	17	20	116
70-71	Minn	78	2	13	15	130
71-72	Minn	78	2	15	17	77
72-73	Minn	78	7	23	30	89
73-74	Minn-Det-StL	77	0	16	16	86
74-75	Phil	70	1	6	7	48
Totals		788	30	168	198	1000
Playoff Totals		100	1	22	23	230
HARRIS, Frederick Henry (Smokey)	lW					
24-25	Bos	6	3	1	4	8
30-31	Bos	34	2	4	6	20
Totals		40	5	5	10	28
Playoff Totals		2	0	0	0	0
HARRIS, George Francis (Duke)						
6-0 204 RW						
B. Sarnia, Ont., Feb. 25, 1942						
67-68	Minn-Tor	26	1	4	5	4
72-73	Hou(WHA)	75	30	12	42	14
73-74	Chi(WHA)	64	14	16	30	20
74-75	Chi(WHA)	54	9	19	28	18
NHL Totals		26	1	4	5	4
WHA Totals		193	53	47	100	52
WHA Playoff Totals		28	7	7	14	6
HARRIS, Hugh Thomas	6-1 195 C					
B. Toronto, Ont., June 7, 1948						
72-73	Buf	60	12	26	38	17
73-74	NE(WHA)	75	24	28	52	78
74-75	Phoe-Van(WHA)	80	33	44	77	34
75-76	Calg-Ind(WHA)	71	17	36	53	42
76-77	Ind(WHA)	46	21	35	56	21

Season	Team	GP	G	A	Pts.	PIM
HARRIS, Hugh Thomas (Continued)						
77-78	Ind-Cin(WHA)	64	12	30	42	36
NHL Totals		60	12	26	38	17
WHA Totals		336	107	173	280	211
NHL Playoff Totals		3	0	0	0	0
WHA Playoff Totals		16	2	9	11	19
HARRIS, Ronald Thomas	5-9 190 D					
B. Verdun, Que., June 30, 1942						
62-63	Det	1	0	1	1	0
63-64	Det	3	0	0	0	7
67-68	Oak	54	4	6	10	60
68-69	Det	73	3	13	16	91
69-70	Det	72	2	19	21	99
70-71	Det	42	2	8	10	65
71-72	Det	61	1	10	11	80
72-73	Atl-NYR	70	5	14	19	25
73-74	NYR	63	2	12	14	25
74-75	NYR	34	1	7	8	22
75-76	NYR	3	0	1	1	0
Totals		476	20	91	111	474
Playoff Totals		28	4	3	7	33
HARRIS, William Edward	6-0 165 C					
B. Toronto, Ont., July 29, 1935						
55-56	Tor	70	9	13	22	8
56-57	Tor	23	4	6	10	6
57-58	Tor	68	16	28	44	32
58-59	Tor	70	22	30	52	29
59-60	Tor	70	13	25	38	29
60-61	Tor	66	12	27	39	30
61-62	Tor	67	15	10	25	14
62-63	Tor	65	8	24	32	22
63-64	Tor	63	6	12	18	17
64-65	Tor	48	1	6	7	0
65-66	Det	24	1	4	5	6
67-68	Oak	62	12	17	29	2
68-69	Oak-Pitt	73	7	17	24	10
Totals		769	126	219	345	205
Playoff Totals		62	8	10	18	30
HARRIS, William Edward	6-2 195 RW					
B. Toronto, Ont., Jan. 29, 1952						
72-73	NYI	78	28	22	50	35
73-74	NYI	78	23	27	50	34
74-75	NYI	80	25	37	62	34
75-76	NYI	80	32	38	70	54
76-77	NYI	80	24	43	67	44
77-78	NYI	80	22	38	60	40
78-79	NYI	80	15	39	54	18
79-80	NYI-LA	78	19	18	37	43
80-81	LA	80	20	29	49	36
81-82	LA-Tor	36	3	3	6	10
82-83	Tor	76	11	19	30	26
83-84	Tor-LA	71	9	14	23	20
Totals		897	231	327	558	394
Playoff Totals		71	19	19	38	48
HARRISON, Edward Francis (Fran)						
6-0 170 LW						
B. Mimico, Ont., July 25, 1927						
47-48	Bos	52	6	7	13	8
48-49	Bos	59	5	5	10	20
49-50	Bos	70	14	12	26	23
50-51	Bos-NYR	13	2	0	2	2
Totals		194	27	24	51	53
Playoff Totals		9	1	0	1	2
HARRISON, James David	5-11 185 C					
B. Bonnyville, Alta., July 9, 1947						
68-69	Bos	16	1	2	3	21
69-70	Bos-Tor	54	10	11	21	52
70-71	Tor	78	13	20	33	108
71-72	Tor	66	19	17	36	104
72-73	Alb(WHA)	66	39	47	86	93
73-74	Edm(WHA)	46	24	45	69	99
74-75	Clev(WHA)	60	20	22	42	106
75-76	Clev(WHA)	59	34	38	72	62
76-77	Chi	60	18	23	41	97
77-78	Chi	26	2	8	10	13
78-79	Chi	21	4	5	9	22
79-80	Edm	3	0	0	0	0
NHL Totals		324	67	86	153	417
WHA Totals		231	117	152	269	360
NHL Playoff Totals		13	1	1	2	43
WHA Playoff Totals		8	1	3	4	13
HART, Gerald William	5-9 190 D					
B. Flin Flon, Man., Jan. 1, 1948						
68-69	Det	1	0	0	0	2
69-70	Det	3	0	0	0	2
70-71	Det	64	2	7	9	148
71-72	Det	3	0	0	0	0
72-73	NYI	47	1	11	12	158
73-74	NYI	70	1	10	11	61
74-75	NYI	71	4	14	18	143

HART, Gerald William *(Continued)*

Season	Team	GP	G	A	Pts.	PIM
75-76	NYI	80	6	18	24	151
76-77	NYI	80	4	18	22	98
77-78	NYI	78	2	23	25	94
78-79	NYI	50	2	14	16	78
79-80	Que	71	3	23	26	59
80-81	Que-StL	69	4	11	15	142
81-82	StL	35	0	1	1	102
82-83	StL	8	0	0	0	2
Totals		730	29	150	179	1240
Playoff Totals		78	3	12	15	175

HART, Wilfred Harold (Gizzy) *5-9 171 LW*
B. Weyburn, Sask., June 1, 1903

Season	Team	GP	G	A	Pts.	PIM
26-27	Det-Mont	38	3	3	6	8
27-28	Mont	44	3	2	5	4
32-33	Mont	18	0	3	3	0
Totals		100	6	8	14	12
Playoff Totals		8	0	1	1	0

HARTMAN, Mike *6-0 190 LW*
B. Detroit, Mich., Feb. 7, 1967

Season	Team	GP	G	A	Pts.	PIM
86-87	Buf	17	3	3	6	69
87-88	Buf	18	3	1	4	90
88-89	Buf	70	8	9	17	316
89-90	Buf	60	11	10	21	211
90-91	Buf	60	9	3	12	204
91-92	Winn	75	4	4	8	264
Totals		300	38	30	68	1154
Playoff Totals		21	0	0	0	106

HARTSBURG, Craig *6-1 200 D*
B. Stratford, Ont., June 29, 1959

Season	Team	GP	G	A	Pts.	PIM
79-80	Minn	79	14	30	44	81
80-81	Minn	74	13	30	43	124
81-82	Minn	76	17	60	77	117
82-83	Minn	78	12	50	62	109
83-84	Minn	26	7	7	14	37
84-85	Minn	32	7	11	18	54
85-86	Minn	75	10	47	57	127
86-87	Minn	73	11	50	61	93
87-88	Minn	27	3	16	19	29
88-89	Minn	30	4	14	18	47
Totals		570	98	315	413	818
Playoff Totals		61	15	27	42	70

HARVEY, Douglas Norman *5-11 180 D*
B. Montreal, Que., Dec. 19, 1924

Season	Team	GP	G	A	Pts.	PIM
47-48	Mont	35	4	4	8	32
48-49	Mont	55	3	13	16	87
49-50	Mont	70	4	20	24	76
50-51	Mont	70	5	24	29	93
51-52	Mont	68	6	23	29	82
52-53	Mont	69	4	30	34	67
53-54	Mont	68	8	29	37	110
54-55	Mont	70	6	43	49	58
55-56	Mont	62	5	39	44	60
56-57	Mont	70	6	44	50	92
57-58	Mont	68	9	32	41	131
58-59	Mont	61	4	16	20	61
59-60	Mont	66	6	21	27	45
60-61	Mont	58	6	33	39	48
61-62	NYR	69	6	24	30	42
62-63	NYR	68	4	35	39	92
63-64	NYR	14	0	2	2	10
66-67	Det	2	0	0	0	0
68-69	StL	70	2	20	22	30
Totals		1113	88	452	540	1216
Playoff Totals		137	8	64	72	152

HARVEY, Frederic John Charles (Buster) *6-0 185 RW*
B. Fredericton, N.B., Apr. 2, 1950

Season	Team	GP	G	A	Pts.	PIM
70-71	Minn	59	12	8	20	36
72-73	Minn	68	21	34	55	16
73-74	Minn	72	16	17	33	14
74-75	Atl	79	17	27	44	16
75-76	Atl-KC-Det	75	13	21	34	31
76-77	Det	54	11	11	22	18
Totals		407	90	118	208	131
Playoff Totals		14	0	2	2	8

HARVEY, Lionel Hugh *6-0 175 LW*
B. Kingston, Ont., June 25, 1949

Season	Team	GP	G	A	Pts.	PIM
74-75	KC	8	0	0	0	2
75-76	KC	10	1	1	2	2
Totals		18	1	1	2	4

HASSARD, Robert Harry *6-0 165 C*
B. Lloydminster, Sask., Mar. 26, 1929

Season	Team	GP	G	A	Pts.	PIM
49-50	Tor	1	0	0	0	0
50-51	Tor	12	0	1	1	0
52-53	Tor	70	8	23	31	14

HASSARD, Robert Harry *(Continued)*

Season	Team	GP	G	A	Pts.	PIM
53-54	Tor	26	1	4	5	4
54-55	Chi	17	0	0	0	4
Totals		126	9	28	37	22

HATCHER, Derian *6-5 205 D*
B. Sterling Heights, Mich., June 4, 1972

Season	Team	GP	G	A	Pts.	PIM
91-92	Minn	43	7	5	12	88
Playoff Totals		5	0	2	2	8

HATCHER, Kevin *6-4 225 D*
B. Detroit, Mich., Sept. 9, 1966

Season	Team	GP	G	A	Pts.	PIM
84-85	Wash	2	1	0	1	0
85-86	Wash	79	9	10	19	119
86-87	Wash	78	8	16	24	144
87-88	Wash	71	14	27	41	137
88-89	Wash	62	13	27	40	101
89-90	Wash	80	13	41	54	102
90-91	Wash	79	24	50	74	69
91-92	Wash	79	17	37	54	105
Totals		530	99	208	307	777
Playoff Totals		66	13	27	40	173

HATOUM, Edward *5-10 185 RW*
B. Beirut, Lebanon, Dec. 7, 1947

Season	Team	GP	G	A	Pts.	PIM
68-69	Det	16	2	1	3	2
69-70	Det	5	0	2	2	2
70-71	Van	26	1	3	4	21
72-73	Chi(WHA)	15	1	1	2	2
73-74	Van(WHA)	37	3	12	15	8
NHL Totals		47	3	6	9	25
WHA Totals		52	4	13	17	10

HAWERCHUK, Dale *5-11 185 C*
B. Toronto, Ont., Apr. 4, 1963

Season	Team	GP	G	A	Pts.	PIM
81-82	Winn	80	45	58	103	47
82-83	Winn	79	40	51	91	31
83-84	Winn	80	37	65	102	73
84-85	Winn	80	53	77	130	74
85-86	Winn	80	46	59	105	44
86-87	Winn	80	47	53	100	52
87-88	Winn	80	44	77	121	59
88-89	Winn	75	41	55	96	28
89-90	Winn	79	26	55	81	60
90-91	Buf	80	31	58	89	32
91-92	Buf	77	23	75	98	27
Totals		870	433	683	1116	527
Playoff Totals		51	20	42	62	49

HAWGOOD, Greg *5-8 175 LW/D*
B. Edmonton, Alta., Aug. 10, 1968

Season	Team	GP	G	A	Pts.	PIM
87-88	Bos	1	0	0	0	0
88-89	Bos	56	16	24	40	84
89-90	Bos	77	11	27	38	76
90-91	Bos	6	0	1	1	6
91-92	Edm	20	2	11	13	22
Totals		160	29	63	92	188
Playoff Totals		41	2	8	10	39

HAWKINS, Todd *6-1 195 LW/RW*
B. Kingston, Ont., Aug. 2, 1966

Season	Team	GP	G	A	Pts.	PIM
88-89	Van	4	0	0	0	9
89-90	Van	4	0	0	0	6
91-92	Tor	2	0	0	0	0
Totals		10	0	0	0	15

HAWORTH, Alan Joseph *5-10 190 C*
B. Drummondville, Ont., Sept. 1, 1960

Season	Team	GP	G	A	Pts.	PIM
80-81	Buf	49	16	20	36	34
81-82	Buf	57	21	18	39	30
82-83	Wash	74	23	27	50	34
83-84	Wash	75	24	31	55	52
84-85	Wash	76	23	26	49	48
85-86	Wash	71	34	39	73	72
86-87	Wash	50	25	16	41	43
87-88	Que	72	23	34	57	112
Totals		524	189	211	400	425
Playoff Totals		42	12	16	28	0

HAWORTH. Gordon Joseph *5-10 165 C*
B. Drummondville, Que., Feb. 20, 1932

Season	Team	GP	G	A	Pts.	PIM
52-53	NYR	2	0	1	1	0

HAWRYLIW, Neil *5-11 185 RW*
B. Fielding, Sask., Nov. 9, 1955

Season	Team	GP	G	A	Pts.	PIM
81-82	NYI	1	0	0	0	0

HAY, George William *LW*
B. Listowel, Ont., Jan. 10, 1898

Season	Team	GP	G	A	Pts.	PIM
26-27	Chi	37	14	8	22	12
27-28	Det	42	22	13	35	20
28-29	Det	42	11	8	19	14
29-80	Det	42	18	15	33	8
30-31	Det	44	8	10	18	24

HAY, George William *(Continued)*

Season	Team	GP	G	A	Pts.	PIM
32-33	Det	34	1	6	7	6
33-34	Det	1	0	0	0	0
Totals		242	74	60	134	84
Playoff Totals		8	2	3	5	14

HAY, James Alexander (Red Eye) *5-11 185 D*
B. Saskatoon, Sask., May 15, 1931

Season	Team	GP	G	A	Pts.	PIM
52-53	Det	42	1	4	5	2
53-54	Det	12	0	0	0	0
54-55	Det	21	0	1	1	20
Totals		75	1	5	6	22
Playoff Totals		9	1	0	1	2

HAY, William Charles (Red) *6-3 197 C*
B. Saskatoon, Sask., Dec. 8, 1935

Season	Team	GP	G	A	Pts.	PIM
59-60	Chi	70	18	37	55	31
60-61	Chi	69	11	48	59	45
61-62	Chi	60	11	52	63	34
62-63	Chi	64	12	33	45	36
63-64	Chi	70	23	33	56	30
64-65	Chi	69	11	26	37	36
65-66	Chi	68	20	31	51	20
66-67	Chi	36	7	13	20	33
Totals		506	113	273	386	265
Playoff Totals		67	15	21	36	62

HAYEK, Peter *5-10 198 D*
B. Minneapolis, Minn., Nov. 16, 1957

Season	Team	GP	G	A	Pts.	PIM
81-82	Minn	1	0	0	0	0

HAYES, Christopher Joseph *5-10 180 LW*
B. Rouyn, Que., Aug. 24, 1946

Season	Team	GP	G	A	Pts.	PIM
71-72	Bos	0	0	0	0	0
Playoff Totals		1	0	0	0	0

HAYNES, Paul *5-10 160 C*
B. Montreal, Que., Mar. 1, 1910

Season	Team	GP	G	A	Pts.	PIM
30-31	Mont M	19	1	0	1	0
31-32	Mont M	11	1	0	1	0
32-33	Mont M	47	16	25	41	18
33-34	Mont M	45	5	4	9	18
34-35	Mont M-Bos	48	5	5	10	8
35-36	Mont	48	5	19	24	24
36-37	Mont	47	8	18	26	24
37-38	Mont	48	13	22	35	25
38-39	Mont	47	5	33	38	27
39-40	Mont	23	2	8	10	8
40-41	Mont	7	0	0	0	12
Totals		390	61	134	195	164
Playoff Totals		25	2	8	10	13

HAYWARD, Rick *6-0 180 D*
B. Toledo, Ohio, Feb. 25, 1966

Season	Team	GP	G	A	Pts.	PIM
90-91	LA	4	0	0	0	5

HAZLETT, Steven *5-9 170 LW*
B. Sarnia, Ont., Dec. 12, 1957

Season	Team	GP	G	A	Pts.	PIM
79-80	Van	1	0	0	0	0

HEAD, Galen Russell *5-10 170 RW*
B. Grand Prairie, Alta., Apr. 6, 1947

Season	Team	GP	G	A	Pts.	PIM
67-68	Det	1	0	0	0	0

HEADLEY, Fern James (Curley) *5-11 175 D*
B. Christie. N.D., Mar. 2, 1901

Season	Team	GP	G	A	Pts.	PIM
24-25	Bos-Mont	27	1	1	2	6
Playoff Totals		5	0	0	0	0

HEALEY, Richard Thomas (Dick) *5-10 170 D*
B. Vancouver, B.C., Mar. 12, 1938

Season	Team	GP	G	A	Pts.	PIM
60-61	Det	1	0	0	0	2

HEASLIP, Mark Patrick *5-10 190 RW*
B. Duluth, Minn., Dec. 26, 1951

Season	Team	GP	G	A	Pts.	PIM
76-77	NYR	19	1	0	1	31
77-78	NYR	29	5	10	15	34
78-79	LA	69	4	9	13	45
Totals		117	10	19	29	110
Playoff Totals		5	0	0	0	2

HEATH, Randy *5-8 160 LW*
B. Vancouver, B.C., Nov. 11, 1964

Season	Team	GP	G	A	Pts.	PIM
84-85	NYR	12	2	3	5	15
85-86	NYR	1	0	1	1	0
Totals		13	2	4	6	15

HEBENTON, Andrew Alexander *5-9 182 RW*
B. Winnipeg, Man., Oct, 3, 1929

Season	Team	GP	G	A	Pts.	PIM
55-56	NYR	70	24	14	38	8

HEBENTON, Andrew Alexander *(Continued)*

Season	Team	GP	G	A	Pts.	PIM
56-57	NYR	70	21	23	44	10
57-58	NYR	70	21	24	45	17
58-59	NYR	70	33	29	62	8
59-60	NYR	70	19	27	46	4
60-61	NYR	70	26	28	54	10
61-62	NYR	70	18	24	42	10
62-63	NYR	70	15	22	37	8
63-64	Bos	70	12	11	23	8
Totals		630	189	202	391	83
Playoff Totals		22	6	5	11	8

HEDBERG, Anders *5-11 175 RW*
B. Ornskoldsvik, Sweden, Feb. 25, 1951

Season	Team	GP	G	A	Pts.	PIM
74-75	Winn(WHA)	65	53	47	100	45
75-76	Winn(WHA)	76	50	55	105	48
76-77	Winn(WHA)	68	70	61	131	48
77-78	Winn(WHA)	77	63	59	122	60
78-79	NYR	80	33	45	78	33
79-80	NYR	80	32	39	71	21
80-81	NYR	80	30	40	70	52
81-82	NYR	4	0	1	1	0
82-83	NYR	78	25	34	59	12
83-84	NYR	79	32	35	67	16
84-85	NYR	64	20	31	51	10
NHL Totals		465	172	225	397	144
WHA Totals		286	236	222	458	201
NHL Playoff Totals		58	22	24	46	31
WHA Playoff Totals		42	35	28	63	30

HEDICAN, Brett *6-2 188 LW*
B. St. Paul, Minn., Aug. 10, 1970

Season	Team	GP	G	A	Pts.	PIM
91-92	StL	4	1	0	1	0
Playoff Totals		5	0	0	0	0

HEFFERNAN, Frank *F*

Season	Team	GP	G	A	Pts.	PIM
19-20	Tor	17	0	0	0	4

HEFFERNAN, Gerald J. *5-9 160 RW*
B. Montreal, Que., July 24, 1916

Season	Team	GP	G	A	Pts.	PIM
41-42	Mont	40	5	15	20	15
43-44	Mont	43	28	20	48	12
Totals		83	33	35	68	27
Playoff Totals		11	3	3	6	8

HEIDT, Michael *6-1 190 D*
B. Calgary, Alta., Nov. 4, 1963

Season	Team	GP	G	A	Pts.	PIM
83-84	LA	6	0	1	1	7

HEINDL, William Wayne *5-10 175 LW*
B. Sherbrooke, Que., May 13, 1946

Season	Team	GP	G	A	Pts.	PIM
70-71	Minn	12	1	1	2	0
71-72	Minn	2	0	0	0	0
72-73	NYR	4	1	0	1	0
73-74	Clev(WHA)	67	4	14	18	4
NHL Totals		18	2	1	3	0
WHA Totals		67	4	14	18	4
WHA Playoff Totals		5	0	1	1	2

HEINRICH, Lionel Grant *5-10 180 LW*
B. Churchbridge, Sask., Apr. 20, 1934

Season	Team	GP	G	A	Pts.	PIM
55-56	Bos	35	1	1	2	33

HEINZE, Stephen *5-11 180 C*
B. Lawrence, Mass., Jan. 30, 1970

Season	Team	GP	G	A	Pts.	PIM
91-92	Bos	14	3	4	7	6
Playoff Totals		7	0	3	3	17

HEISKALA, Earl Waldemar *6-0 185 LW*
B. Kirkland lake, Ont., Nov. 30, 1942

Season	Team	GP	G	A	Pts.	PIM
68-69	Phil	21	3	3	6	51
69-70	Phil	65	8	7	15	171
70-71	Phil	41	2	1	3	72
72-73	LA(WHA)	70	12	17	29	150
73-74	LA(WHA)	24	2	6	8	45
NHL Totals		127	13	11	24	294
WHA Totals		94	14	23	37	195
WHA Playoff Totals		5	1	1	2	4

HELANDER, Peter *6-1 185 D*
B. Stockholm, Sweden, Dec. 4, 1951

Season	Team	GP	G	A	Pts.	PIM
82-83	LA	7	0	1	1	0

HELLER, Ehrhardt Henry (Ott) *6-0 195 D*
B. Kitchener, Ont., June 2, 1910

Season	Team	GP	G	A	Pts.	PIM
31-32	NYR	21	2	2	4	9
32-33	NYR	40	5	7	12	31
33-34	NYR	48	2	5	7	29
34-35	NYR	47	3	11	14	31
35-36	NYR	43	2	11	13	40
36-37	NYR	48	5	12	17	42
37-38	NYR	48	2	14	16	68
38-39	NYR	48	0	23	23	42
39-40	NYR	47	5	14	19	26
40-41	NYR	48	2	16	18	42
41-42	NYR	35	6	5	11	22

HELLER, Ehrhardt Henry (Ott) *(Continued)*

Season	Team	GP	G	A	Pts.	PIM
42-43	NYR	45	4	14	18	14
43-44	NYR	50	8	27	35	29
44-45	NYR	45	7	12	19	26
45-46	NYR	34	2	3	5	14
Totals		647	55	176	231	465
Playoff Totals		61	6	8	14	61

HELMAN, Harold (Harry) *D*

Season	Team	GP	G	A	Pts.	PIM
22-23	Ott	24	0	0	0	5
23-24	Ott	17	1	0	1	2
24-26	Ott	1	0	0	0	0
Totals		42	1	0	1	7
Playoff Totals		5	0	0	0	0

HELMINEN, Raimo Ilmari *6-0 183 C*
B. Tampere, Finland, Mar. 11, 1964

Season	Team	GP	G	A	Pts.	PIM
85-86	NYR	66	10	30	40	10
86-87	NYR-Minn	27	2	5	7	2
88-89	NYI	24	1	11	12	4
Totals		117	13	46	59	16
Playoff Totals		2	0	0	0	0

HEMMERLING, Elmer Charles (Tony) *5-11 178 LW*
B. Landis, Sask., May 11, 1913

Season	Team	GP	G	A	Pts.	PIM
35-36	NYA	6	0	0	0	0
36-37	NYA	18	3	3	6	4
Totals		24	3	3	6	4

HENDERSON, Archie *6-6 220 RW*
B. Calgary, Alta., Feb. 17, 1957

Season	Team	GP	G	A	Pts.	PIM
80-81	Wash	7	1	0	1	28
81-82	Minn	1	0	0	0	0
82-83	Hart	15	2	1	3	64
Totals		23	3	1	4	92

HENDERSON, John Murray (Murray, Moe) *6-0 180 D*
B. Toronto, Ont., Sept. 5, 1921

Season	Team	GP	G	A	Pts.	PIM
44-45	Bos	5	0	1	1	4
45-46	Bos	48	4	11	15	30
46-47	Bos	57	5	12	17	63
47-48	Bos	49	6	8	14	50
48-49	Bos	60	2	9	11	28
49-50	Bos	64	3	8	11	42
50-51	Bos	66	4	7	11	37
51-52	Bos	56	0	6	6	51
Totals		405	24	62	86	305
Playoff Totals		41	2	3	5	23

HENDERSON, Paul Garnet *5-11 180 LW*
B. Kincardine, Ont., Jan. 28, 1943

Season	Team	GP	G	A	Pts.	PIM
62-63	Det	2	0	0	0	9
63-64	Det	32	3	3	6	6
64-65	Det	70	8	13	21	30
65-66	Det	69	22	24	46	34
66-67	Det	46	21	19	40	10
67-68	Det-Tor	63	18	26	44	43
68-69	Tor	74	27	32	59	16
69-70	Tor	67	20	22	42	18
70-71	Tor	72	30	30	60	34
71-72	Tor	73	38	19	57	32
72-73	Tor	40	18	16	34	18
73-74	Tor	69	24	31	55	40
74-75	Tor(WHA)	58	30	33	63	18
75-76	Tor(WHA)	65	26	29	55	22
76-77	Birm(WHA)	81	23	25	48	30
77-78	Birm(WHA)	80	37	29	66	22
78-79	Birm(WHA)	76	24	27	51	20
79-80	Atl	30	7	6	13	6
NHL Totals		707	236	241	477	296
WHA Totals		360	140	143	283	112
NHL Playoff Totals		56	11	14	25	28
WHA Playoff Totals		5	1	1	2	0

HENDRICKSON, John Gunnard *5-11 175 D*
B. Kingston, Ont., Dec. 5, 1936

Season	Team	GP	G	A	Pts.	PIM
57-58	Det	1	0	0	0	0
58-59	Det	3	0	0	0	2
61-62	Det	1	0	0	0	2
Totals		5	0	0	0	4

HENNING, Lorne Edward *5-11 185 C*
B. Melfort, Sask., Feb. 22, 1952

Season	Team	GP	G	A	Pts.	PIM
72-73	NYI	63	7	19	26	14
73-74	NYI	60	12	15	27	6
74-75	NYI	61	5	6	11	6
75-76	NYI	80	7	10	17	16
76-77	NYI	80	13	18	31	10
77-78	NYI	79	12	15	27	16
78-79	NYI	73	13	20	33	14
79-80	NYI	39	3	6	9	6
80-81	NYI	9	1	2	3	14
Totals		544	73	111	184	102

HENNING, Lorne Edward *(Continued)*

Season	Team	GP	G	A	Pts.	PIM
Playoff Totals		81	7	7	14	8

HENRY, Camille Joseph Wilfred (Eel) *5-8 152 C*
B. Quebec City, Que., Jan. 31,1933

Season	Team	GP	G	A	Pts.	PIM
53-54	NYR	66	24	15	39	10
54-55	NYR	21	5	2	7	4
56-57	NYR	36	14	15	29	2
57-58	NYR	70	32	24	56	2
58-59	NYR	70	23	35	58	2
59-60	NYR	49	12	15	27	6
60-61	NYR	53	28	25	53	8
61-62	NYR	60	23	15	38	8
62-63	NYR	60	37	23	60	8
63-64	NYR	68	29	26	55	8
64-65	NYR-Chi	70	26	18	44	22
67-68	NYR	36	8	12	20	0
68-69	StL	64	17	22	39	8
69-70	StL	4	1	2	3	0
Totals		727	279	249	528	88
Playoff Totals		47	6	12	18	7

HENRY, Dale *6-0 205 LW*
B. Prince Albert, Sask., Sept. 24, 1964

Season	Team	GP	G	A	Pts.	PIM
84-85	NYI	16	2	1	3	19
85-86	NYI	7	1	3	4	15
86-87	NYI	19	3	3	6	46
87-88	NYI	48	5	15	20	115
88-89	NYI	22	2	2	4	66
89-90	NYI	20	0	2	2	2
Totals		132	13	26	39	263
Playoff Totals		14	1	0	1	19

HEPPLE, Alan *5-9 200 D*
B. Blaydon-on-Tyne, England, Aug. 16, 1963

Season	Team	GP	G	A	Pts.	PIM
83-84	NJ	1	0	0	0	7
84-85	NJ	1	0	0	0	0
85-86	NJ	1	0	0	0	0
Totals		3	0	0	0	7

HERBERTS, James *F*
B. Collingwood, Ont., 1897

Season	Team	GP	G	A	Pts.	PIM
24-25	Bos	30	17	5	22	50
25-26	Bos	36	26	5	31	47
26-27	Bos	34	15	7	22	51
27-28	Tor	43	15	4	19	64
28-29	Det	40	9	5	14	34
29-30	Det	23	1	3	4	4
Totals		206	83	29	112	250
Playoff Totals		9	3	0	3	35

HERCHENRATTER, Arthur *6-0 185 LW*
B. Kitchener, Ont., Nov. 24, 1917

Season	Team	GP	G	A	Pts.	PIM
40-41	Det	10	1	2	3	2

HERGERTS, Frederick *6-0 190 C*
B. Calgary, Alta., Jan. 29, 1913

Season	Team	GP	G	A	Pts.	PIM
34-35	NYA	18	2	4	6	2
35-36	NYA	1	0	0	0	0
Totals		19	2	4	6	2

HERGESHEIMER, Phillip *5-10 175 RW*
B. Winnipeg, Man., July 9, 1914

Season	Team	GP	G	A	Pts.	PIM
39-40	Chi	41	9	11	20	6
40-41	Chi	47	8	16	24	9
41-42	Chi-Bos	26	3	11	14	4
42-43	Chi	9	1	3	4	0
Totals		123	21	41	62	19
Playoff Totals		7	0	0	0	2

HERGESHEIMER, Walter Edgar (Wally, Hergie) *5-8 155 RW*
B. Winnipeg, Man., Jan. 8, 1927

Season	Team	GP	G	A	Pts.	PIM
51-52	NYR	68	26	12	38	6
52-53	NYR	70	30	29	59	10
53-54	NYR	66	27	16	43	42
54-55	NYR	14	4	2	6	4
55-56	NYR	70	22	18	40	26
56-57	Chi	41	2	8	10	12
58-59	NYR	22	3	0	3	6
Totals		351	114	85	199	106
Playoff Totals		5	1	0	1	0

HERON, Robert Geatrex (Red) *5-11 170 C*
B. Tornoto, Ont., Dec. 31, 1917

Season	Team	GP	G	A	Pts.	PIM
38-39	Tor	6	0	0	0	0
39-40	Tor	42	11	12	23	12
40-41	Tor	35	9	5	14	12
41-42	NYA-Mont	23	1	2	3	14
Totals		106	21	19	40	38
Playoff Totals		16	2	2	4	55

Season	Team	GP	G	A	Pts.	PIM
HEROUX, Yves	*5-11 185 RW*					
B. Terrebonne, Que., Apr. 27, 1965						
86-87	Que	1	0	0	0	0
HERVEY, Matt	*5-11 205 D*					
B. Whittier, Cal., May 16, 1966						
88-89	Winn	2	0	0	0	4
91-92	Bos	16	0	1	1	55
Totals		18	0	1	1	59
Playoff Totals		5	0	0	0	6
HESS, Robert George	*5-11 180 D*					
B. Middleton, N.S., May 19, 1955						
74-75	StL	79	9	30	39	58
75-76	StL	78	9	23	32	58
76-77	StL	53	4	18	22	14
77-78	StL	55	2	12	14	16
78-79	StL	27	3	4	7	14
80-81	StL-Buf	4	0	0	0	4
81-82	Buf	33	0	8	8	14
83-84	Hart	3	0	0	0	0
Totals		329	27	95	122	178
Playoff Totals		4	1	1	2	2
HEXIMER, Orville Russell (Obs)	*5-7 159 LW*					
B. Niagara Falls, Ont., Feb. 16, 1910						
29-30	NYR	19	1	0	1	4
32-33	Bos	48	7	5	12	24
34-35	NYA	18	5	2	7	0
Totals		85	13	7	20	28
Playoff Totals		5	0	0	0	2
HEXTALL, Bryan Aldwyn	*5-10 180 RW*					
B. Grenfell, Sask., July 31, 1913						
36-37	NYR	1	0	1	1	0
37-38	NYR	48	17	4	21	6
38-39	NYR	48	20	15	35	18
39-40	NYR	48	24	15	39	52
40-41	NYR	48	26	18	44	16
41-42	NYR	48	24	32	56	30
42-43	NYR	50	27	32	59	28
43-44	NYR	50	21	33	54	41
45-46	NYR	3	0	1	1	0
46-47	NYR	60	21	10	31	12
47-48	NYR	43	8	14	22	18
Totals		447	188	175	363	221
Playoff Totals		37	8	9	17	19
HEXTALL, Bryan Lee	*5-11 185 C*					
B. Winnipeg, Man., May 23, 1941						
62-63	NYR	21	0	2	2	10
69-70	Pitt	66	12	19	31	87
70-71	Pitt	76	16	32	48	133
71-72	Pitt	78	20	24	44	126
72-73	Pitt	78	21	33	54	113
73-74	Pitt-Atl	77	4	11	15	94
74-75	Atl	74	18	16	34	62
75-76	Det-Minn	79	8	24	32	113
Totals		549	99	161	260	738
Playoff Totals		18	0	4	4	59
HEXTALL, Dennis Harold	*5-11 175 C*					
B. Winnipeg, Man., Apr. 17, 1943						
68-69	NYR	13	1	4	5	25
69-70	LA	28	5	7	12	40
70-71	Cal	78	21	31	52	217
71-72	Minn	33	6	10	16	49
72-73	Minn	78	30	52	82	140
73-74	Minn	78	20	62	82	138
74-75	Minn	80	17	57	74	147
75-76	Minn-Det	76	16	44	60	164
76-77	Det	78	14	32	46	158
77-78	Det	78	16	33	49	195
78-79	Det-Wash	46	8	17	23	76
79-80	Wash	15	1	1	2	49
Totals		681	153	350	503	1398
Playoff Totals		22	3	3	6	45
HEYLIGER, Victor	*5-8 175 C*					
B. Boston, Mass., Sept. 26, 1919						
37-38	Chi	8	0	0	0	0
43-44	Chi	26	2	3	5	2
Totals		34	2	3	5	2
HICKE, Ernest Allan	*5-11 180 LW*					
B. Regina, Sask., Nov. 7, 1947						
70-71	Cal	78	22	25	47	62
71-72	Cal	68	11	12	23	55
72-73	Atl-NYI	59	14	23	37	37
73-74	NYI	55	6	7	13	26
74-75	NYI-Minn	62	17	19	36	91
75-76	Minn	80	23	19	42	77
76-77	Minn	77	30	20	50	41
77-78	LA	41	9	15	24	18
Totals		520	132	140	272	407

Season	Team	GP	G	A	Pts.	PIM
HICKE, Ernest Allan *(Continued)*						
Playoff Totals		2	1	0	1	0
HICKE, William Lawrence	*5-8 170 RW*					
B. Regina, Sask., Mar. 31, 1938						
59-60	Mont	43	3	10	13	17
60-61	Mont	70	18	27	45	31
61-62	Mont	70	20	31	51	42
62-63	Mont	70	17	22	39	39
63-64	Mont	48	11	9	20	41
64-65	Mont-NYR	57	6	12	18	32
65-66	NYR	49	9	18	27	21
66-67	NYR	48	3	4	7	11
67-68	Oak	52	21	19	40	32
68-69	Oak	67	25	36	61	68
69-70	Oak	69	15	29	44	14
70-71	Cal	74	18	17	35	41
71-72	Pitt	12	2	0	2	6
72-73	Alb(WHA)	73	14	24	38	20
NHL Totals		729	168	234	402	395
WHA Totals		73	14	24	38	20
NHL Playoff Totals		42	3	10	13	41
HICKEY, Greg	*5-10 160 LW*					
B. Toronto, Ont., Mar. 8, 1955						
77-78	NYR	1	0	0	0	0
HICKEY, Patrick Joseph	*6-1 190 LW*					
B. Brantford, Ont., May 15, 1953						
73-74	Tor(WHA)	78	26	29	55	52
74-75	Tor(WHA)	74	34	34	68	50
75-76	NYR	70	14	22	36	36
76-77	NYR	80	23	17	40	35
77-78	NYR	80	40	33	73	47
78-79	NYR	80	34	41	75	56
79-80	NYR-Col-Tor	76	31	27	58	36
80-81	Tor	72	16	33	49	49
81-82	Tor-NYR-Que	61	15	15	30	36
82-83	StL	1	0	0	0	0
83-84	StL	69	9	11	20	24
84-85	StL	57	10	13	23	32
NHL Totals		646	192	212	404	351
WHA Totals		152	60	63	123	102
NHL Playoff Totals		55	5	11	16	37
WHA Playoff Totals		17	3	4	7	16
HICKS, Douglas Allan	*6-0 185 D*					
B. Cold Lake, Alta., May 28, 1955						
74-75	Minn	80	6	12	18	51
75-76	Minn	80	5	13	18	54
76-77	Minn	79	5	14	19	68
77-78	Minn-Chi	74	3	16	19	53
78-79	Chi	44	1	8	9	15
79-80	Edm	78	9	31	40	52
80-81	Edm	59	5	16	21	76
81-82	Edm-Wash	61	3	21	24	66
82-83	Wash	6	0	0	0	7
Totals		561	37	131	168	442
Playoff Totals		18	2	1	3	15
HICKS, Glenn	*5-10 177 LW*					
B. Red Deer, Alta., Aug. 28, 1958						
78-79	Winn(WHA)	69	6	10	16	48
79-80	Det	50	1	2	3	43
80-81	Det	58	5	10	15	84
NHL Totals		108	6	12	18	127
WHA Totals		69	6	10	16	48
WHA Playoff Totals		7	1	1	2	4
HICKS, Harold H. (Hal)	*D*					
B. Ottawa, Ont., Dec. 10, 1900						
28-29	Mont M	44	2	0	2	27
29-80	Det	44	3	2	5	35
30-31	Det	22	2	0	2	10
Totals		110	7	2	9	72
HICKS, Wayne Wilson	*5-10 190 RW*					
B. Aberdeen, Wash., Apr. 9, 1937						
60-61	Chi	1	0	0	0	0
62-63	Bos	65	7	9	16	14
63-64	Mont	2	0	0	0	0
67-68	Phil-Pitt	47	6	14	20	8
Totals		115	13	23	36	22
Playoff Totals		2	0	1	1	2
HIDI, Andre Lawrence	*6-2 205 LW*					
B. Toronto, Ont., June 5, 1960						
83-84	Wash	1	0	0	0	0
84-85	Wash	6	2	1	3	9
Totals		7	2	1	3	9
Playoff Totals		2	0	0	0	0
HIEMER, Ullrich (Uli)	*6-1 190 D*					
B. Fussen, W. Germany, Sept. 21, 1962						
84-85	NJ	53	5	24	29	70

Season	Team	GP	G	A	Pts.	PIM
HIEMER, Ullrich (Uli) *(Continued)*						
85-86	NJ	50	8	16	24	61
86-87	NJ	40	6	14	20	45
Totals		143	19	54	73	176
HIGGINS, Paul	*6-1 195 RW*					
B. St. John, N.B., Jan. 13, 1962						
81-82	Tor	3	0	0	0	17
82-83	Tor	22	0	0	0	135
Totals		25	0	0	0	152
Playoff Totals		1	0	0	0	0
HIGGINS, Tim Ray	*6-1 185 RW*					
B. Ottawa, Ont., Feb. 7, 1958						
78-79	Chi	36	7	16	23	30
79-80	Chi	74	13	12	25	50
80-81	Chi	78	24	35	59	86
81-82	Chi	74	20	30	50	85
82-83	Chi	64	14	9	23	63
83-84	Chi-NJ	69	19	14	33	48
84-85	NJ	71	19	29	48	30
85-86	NJ	59	9	17	26	47
86-87	Det	77	12	14	26	124
87-88	Det	62	12	13	25	94
88-89	Det	42	5	9	14	62
Totals		706	154	198	352	719
Playoff Totals		65	5	8	13	77
HILDEBRAND, Isaac Bruce (Ike)	*5-8 155 RW*					
B. Winnipeg, Man., May 27, 1927						
53-54	NYR-Chi	38	7	11	18	16
54-55	Chi	3	0	0	0	0
Totals		41	7	11	18	16
HILL, Alan Douglas	*6-1 175 LW/C*					
B. Nanaimo, B.C., Apr. 22, 1955						
76-77	Phil	9	2	4	6	27
77-78	Phil	3	0	0	0	0
78-79	Phil	31	5	11	16	28
79-80	Phil	61	16	10	26	53
80-81	Phil	57	10	15	25	45
81-82	Phil	41	6	13	19	58
86-87	Phil	7	0	2	2	4
87-88	Phil	12	1	0	1	10
Totals		221	40	55	95	227
Playoff Totals		51	8	11	19	43
HILL, Brian Nelson	*6-0 175 RW*					
B. Regina, Sask., Jan. 12, 1957						
79-80	Hart	19	1	1	2	4
HILL, John Melvin (Mel, Sudden Death)	*5-10 175 RW*					
B. Glenboro, Man., Feb. 15, 1914						
37-38	Bos	8	2	0	2	2
38-39	Bos	44	10	10	20	16
39-40	Bos	37	9	11	20	19
40-41	Bos	41	5	4	9	4
41-42	Brk	47	14	23	37	10
42-43	Tor	49	17	27	44	47
43-44	Tor	17	9	10	19	6
44-45	Tor	45	18	17	35	14
45-46	Tor	35	5	7	12	10
Totals		323	89	109	198	128
Playoff Totals		43	12	7	19	18
HILL, Sean	*6-0 195 D*					
B. Duluth, Minn., Feb. 14, 1970						
90-91	Mont	0	0	0	0	0
91-92	Mont	0	0	0	0	0
Playoff Totals		5	1	0	1	2
HILLER, Wilbert Carl (Dutch)	*5-8 170 LW*					
B. Kitchener, Ont., May 11, 1915						
37-38	NYR	9	1	1	2	
38-39	NYR	48	10	19	29	22
39-40	NYR	48	13	18	31	57
40-41	NYR	45	8	10	18	20
41-42	Det-Bos	50	7	10	17	19
42-43	Mont	42	8	6	14	4
43-44	NYR	50	18	22	40	15
44-45	Mont	48	16	36	52	20
45-46	Mont	45	7	11	18	4
Totals		385	91	113	204	163
Playoff Totals		48	9	8	17	21
HILLIER, Randy George	*6-1 192 D*					
B. Toronto, Ont., Mar. 30, 1960						
81-82	Bos	25	0	8	8	29
82-83	Bos	70	0	10	10	99
83-84	Bos	69	3	12	15	125
84-85	Pitt	45	2	19	21	54
85-86	Pitt	28	0	3	3	53
86-87	Pitt	55	4	8	12	97
87-88	Pitt	55	1	12	13	144

HILLIER, Randy George *(Continued)*

Season	Team	GP	G	A	Pts.	PIM
88-89	Pitt	68	1	23	24	141
89-90	Pitt	61	3	12	15	71
90-91	Pitt	31	2	2	4	32
91-92	NYI-Buf	36	0	1	1	59
Totals		543	16	110	126	906
Playoff Totals		28	0	2	2	93

HILLMAN, Floyd Arthur *5-11 170 D*

B. Ruthven, Ont., Nov. 19, 1933

Season	Team	GP	G	A	Pts.	PIM
56-57	Bos	6	0	0	0	10

HILLMAN, Larry Morley *6-0 181 D*

B. Kirkland Lake, Ont., Feb. 5, 1937

Season	Team	GP	G	A	Pts.	PIM
54-55	Det	6	0	0	0	2
55-56	Det	47	0	3	3	53
56-57	Det	16	1	2	3	4
57-58	Bos	70	3	19	22	60
58-59	Bos	55	3	10	13	19
59-60	Bos	2	0	1	1	2
60-61	Tor	62	3	10	13	59
61-62	Tor	5	0	0	0	4
62-63	Tor	5	0	0	0	2
63-64	Tor	33	0	4	4	31
64-65	Tor	2	0	0	0	2
65-66	Tor	48	3	25	28	34
66-67	Tor	55	4	19	23	40
67-68	Tor	55	3	17	20	13
68-69	Minn-Mont	37	1	10	11	17
69-70	Phil	76	5	26	31	73
70-71	Phil	73	3	13	16	39
71-72	LA-Buf	65	2	13	15	69
72-73	Buf	78	5	24	29	56
73-74	Clev(WHA)	44	5	21	26	37
74-75	Clev(WHA)	77	0	16	16	83
75-76	Winn(WHA)	71	1	12	13	62
NHL Totals		790	36	196	232	579
WHA Totals		192	6	49	55	182
NHL Playoff Totals		74	2	9	11	30
WHA Playoff Totals		17	1	5	6	40

HILLMAN, Wayne James *6-1 205 D*

B. Kirkland Lake, Ont., Nov. 13, 1938

Season	Team	GP	G	A	Pts.	PIM
61-62	Chi	19	0	2	2	14
62-63	Chi	67	3	5	8	74
63-64	Chi	59	1	4	5	31
64-65	Chi-NYR	41	1	8	9	34
65-66	NYR	68	3	17	20	70
66-67	NYR	67	2	12	14	43
67-68	NYR	62	0	5	5	46
68-69	Minn	50	0	8	8	32
69-70	Phil	68	3	5	8	69
70-71	Phil	69	5	7	12	47
71-72	Phil	47	0	3	3	21
72-73	Phil	74	0	10	10	33
73-74	Clev(WHA)	66	1	7	8	51
74-75	Clev(WHA)	60	2	9	11	37
NHL Totals		691	18	86	104	514
WHA Totals		126	3	16	19	88
NHL Playoff Totals		28	0	3	3	19
WHA Playoff Totals		10	0	2	2	18

HILWORTH, John *6-4 205 D*

B. Jasper, Alta., May 23, 1957

Season	Team	GP	G	A	Pts.	PIM
77-78	Det	5	0	0	0	12
78-79	Det	37	1	1	2	66
79-80	Det	15	0	0	0	11
Totals		57	1	1	2	89

HIMES, Norman *5-9 145 F*

B. Galt, Ont., Apr. 13, 1903

Season	Team	GP	G	A	Pts.	PIM
26-27	NYA	42	9	2	11	14
27-28	NYA	44	14	5	19	22
28-29	NYA	44	10	0	10	25
29-30	NYA	44	28	22	50	15
30-31	NYA	44	15	9	24	18
31-32	NYA	48	7	21	28	9
32-33	NYA	48	9	25	34	12
33-34	NYA	48	9	16	25	10
34-35	NYA	40	5	13	18	2
Totals		402	106	113	219	127
Playoff Totals		2	0	0	0	0

HINDMARCH, David *5-11 180 RW*

B. Vancouver, B.C., Oct. 15, 1958

Season	Team	GP	G	A	Pts.	PIM
80-81	Calg	1	1	0	1	0
81-82	Calg	9	3	0	3	0
82-83	Calg	60	11	12	23	23
83-84	Calg	29	6	5	11	2
Totals		99	21	17	38	25
Playoff Totals		10	0	0	0	6

HINSE, Andre Joseph Charles *5-9 172 LW*

B. Trois Rivieres, Que., Apr. 19, 1945

Season	Team	GP	G	A	Pts.	PIM
67-68	Tor	4	0	0	0	0
73-74	Hou(WHA)	69	24	56	80	39

HINSE, Andre Joseph Charles *(Continued)*

Season	Team	GP	G	A	Pts.	PIM
74-75	Hou(WHA)	75	39	47	86	12
75-76	Hou(WHA)	70	35	38	73	6
76-77	Phoe(WHA)	42	4	10	14	12
NHL Totals		4	0	0	0	0
WHA Totals		256	102	151	253	69
WHA Playoff Totals		42	15	16	31	28

HINTON, Daniel Anthony *6-1 175 LW*

B. Toronto, Ont., May 24, 1953

Season	Team	GP	G	A	Pts.	PIM
76-77	Chi	14	0	0	0	16

HIRSCH, Tom *6-4 210 D*

B. Minneapolis, Minn., Jan 27, 1963

Season	Team	GP	G	A	Pts.	PIM
83-84	Minn	15	1	3	4	20
84-85	Minn	15	0	4	4	10
87-88	Minn	1	0	0	0	0
Totals		31	1	7	8	30
Playoff Totals		12	0	0	0	6

HIRSCHFELD, John Albert (Bert) *5-10 165 LW*

B. Halifax, N.S., Mar. 1, 1929

Season	Team	GP	G	A	Pts.	PIM
49-50	Mont	13	1	2	3	2
50-51	Mont	20	0	2	2	0
Totals		33	1	4	5	2
Playoff Totals		5	1	0	1	0

HITCHMAN, Lionel *6-0 167 D*

B. Toronto, Ont., 1903

Season	Team	GP	G	A	Pts.	PIM
22-23	Ott	3	0	1	1	12
23-24	Ott	24	2	6	8	24
24-25	Ott-Bos	30	3	0	3	24
25-26	Bos	36	7	4	11	70
26-27	Bos	40	3	6	9	70
27-28	Bos	43	5	3	8	87
28-29	Bos	37	1	0	1	64
29-30	Bos	39	2	7	9	39
30-31	Bos	43	0	2	2	40
31-32	Bos	48	4	3	7	36
32-33	Bos	41	0	1	1	34
33-34	Bos	29	1	0	1	4
Totals		413	28	33	61	504
Playoff Totals		40	4	1	5	77

HISLOP, James Donald (Jamie) *5-10 180 RW*

B. Sarnia, Ont., Jan. 20, 1954

Season	Team	GP	G	A	Pts.	PIM
76-77	Cin(WHA)	46	7	9	26	6
77-78	Cin(WHA)	80	24	43	67	17
78-79	Chi(WHA)	80	30	40	70	45
79-80	Que	80	19	20	39	6
80-81	Que-Calg	79	25	31	56	26
81-82	Calg	80	16	25	41	35
82-83	Calg	79	14	19	33	17
83-84	Calg	27	1	8	9	2
NHL Totals		345	75	103	178	86
WHA Totals		206	61	102	163	68
NHL Playoff Totals		28	3	2	5	11
WHA Playoff Totals		7	2	5	7	4

HLINKA, Ivan *6-2 220 C*

B. Most, Czechoslovakia, Jan. 26, 1950

Season	Team	GP	G	A	Pts.	PIM
81-82	Van	72	23	37	60	16
82-83	Van	65	19	44	63	12
Totals		137	42	81	123	28
Playoff Totals		16	3	10	13	8

HODGE, Kenneth Jr. *6-1 200 C/RW*

B. Windsor, Ont., Apr. 13, 1966

Season	Team	GP	G	A	Pts.	PIM
88-89	Minn	5	1	1	2	0
90-91	Bos	70	30	29	59	20
91-92	Bos	42	6	11	17	10
Totals		117	37	41	78	30
Playoff Totals		15	4	6	10	6

HODGE, Kenneth Raymond *6-2 210 RW*

B. Birmingham, England, June 25, 1944

Season	Team	GP	G	A	Pts.	PIM
64-65	Chi	1	0	0	0	2
65-66	Chi	63	6	17	23	47
66-67	Chi	69	10	25	35	59
67-68	Bos	74	25	31	56	31
68-69	Bos	75	45	45	90	75
69-70	Bos	72	25	29	54	87
70-71	Bos	78	43	62	105	113
71-72	Bos	60	16	40	56	81
72-73	Bos	73	37	44	81	58
73-74	Bos	76	50	55	105	43
74-75	Bos	72	23	43	66	90
75-76	Bos	72	25	36	61	42
76-77	NYR	78	21	41	62	43
77-78	NYR	18	2	4	6	8
Totals		881	328	472	800	779
Playoff Totals		97	34	47	81	120

HODGSON, Daniel *5-10 165 C*

B. Fort Vermillion, Alta., Aug. 29, 1965

Season	Team	GP	G	A	Pts.	PIM
85-86	Tor	40	13	12	25	12
86-87	Van	43	9	13	22	25
87-88	Van	8	3	7	10	2
88-89	Van	23	4	13	17	25
Totals		114	29	45	74	64

HODGSON, Edward James (Ted) *5-11 175 RW*

B. Hobbema, Alta., June 30, 1945

Season	Team	GP	G	A	Pts.	PIM
66-67	Bos	4	0	0	0	0
72-73	Clev(WHA)	74	15	23	38	93
73-74	Clev-LA(WHA)	33	3	11	14	28
NHL Totals		4	0	0	0	0
WHA Totals		107	18	34	52	121
WHA Playoff Totals		9	1	3	4	13

HODGSON, Richard (Rick) *6-0 175 RW*

B. Medicine Hat, Alta., May 23, 1956

Season	Team	GP	G	A	Pts.	PIM
79-80	Hart	6	0	0	0	6
Playoff Totals		1	0	0	0	0

HOEKSTRA, Cecil Thomas *6-1 175 C*

B. Winnipeg, Man., Apr. 2, 1935

Season	Team	GP	G	A	Pts.	PIM
59-60	Mont	4	0	0	0	0

HOEKSTRA, Edward Adrian *5-11 170 C*

B. Winnipeg, Man., Nov. 4, 1937

Season	Team	GP	G	A	Pts.	PIM
67-68	Phil	70	15	21	36	6
72-73	Hou(WHA)	78	11	28	39	12
73-74	Hou(WHA)	19	2	0	2	0
NHL Totals		70	15	21	36	6
WHA Totals		97	13	28	41	12
NHL Playoff Totals		7	0	1	1	0
WHA Playoff Totals		9	1	2	3	0

HOENE, Phil George *5-9 175 LW*

B. Duluth, Minn., Mar. 15, 1949

Season	Team	GP	G	A	Pts.	PIM
72-73	LA	4	0	1	1	0
73-74	LA	31	2	3	5	22
74-75	LA	2	0	0	0	0
Totals		37	2	4	6	22

HOFFINGER, Victor *D*

Season	Team	GP	G	A	Pts.	PIM
27-28	Chi	18	0	1	1	18
28-29	Chi	10	0	0	0	12
Totals		28	0	1	1	30

HOFFMAN, Micheal *5-11 180 LW*

B. Barrie, Ont., Feb. 26, 1963

Season	Team	GP	G	A	Pts.	PIM
82-83	Hart	2	0	1	1	0
84-85	Hart	1	0	0	0	0
85-86	Hart	6	1	2	3	2
Totals		9	1	3	4	2

HOFFMEYER, Robert Frank *6-0 180 D*

B. Dodsland, Sask., July 27, 1955

Season	Team	GP	G	A	Pts.	PIM
77-78	Chi	5	0	1	1	12
78-79	Chi	6	0	2	2	5
81-82	Phil	57	7	20	27	142
82-83	Phil	35	2	11	13	40
83-84	NJ	58	4	12	16	61
84-85	NJ	37	1	6	7	65
Totals		198	14	52	66	325
Playoff Totals		3	0	1	1	25

HOFFORD, James *6-0 190 D*

B. Sudbury, Ont., Oct. 4, 1964

Season	Team	GP	G	A	Pts.	PIM
85-86	Buf	5	0	0	0	5
86-87	Buf	12	0	0	0	40
88-89	LA	1	0	0	0	2
Totals		18	0	0	0	47

HOGABOAM, William Harold *5-11 170 C*

B. Swift Current, Sask., Sept. 5, 1949

Season	Team	GP	G	A	Pts.	PIM
72-73	Atl-Det	6	1	0	1	2
73-74	Det	47	18	23	41	12
74-75	Det	60	14	27	41	16
75-76	Det-Minn	68	28	23	51	36
76-77	Minn	73	10	15	25	16
77-78	Minn	8	1	2	3	4
78-79	Minn-Det	28	5	7	12	4
79-80	Det	42	3	12	15	10
Totals		332	80	109	189	100
Playoff Totals		2	0	0	0	0

HOGANSON, Dale Gordon (Red) *5-10 190 D*

B. North Battleford, Sask., July 8, 1949

Season	Team	GP	G	A	Pts.	PIM
69-70	LA	49	1	7	8	37
70-71	LA	70	4	10	14	52
71-72	LA-Mont	31	1	2	3	16
72-73	Mont	25	0	2	2	2

HOGANSON, Dale Gordon (Red)
(Continued)

Season	Team	GP	G	A	Pts.	PIM
73-74	Que(WHA)	62	8	33	41	27
74-75	Que(WHA)	78	9	35	44	47
75-76	Que(WHA)	45	3	14	17	18
76-77	Birm(WHA)	81	7	48	55	48
77-78	Birm(WHA)	43	1	12	13	29
78-79	Que(WHA)	69	2	19	21	17
79-80	Que	77	4	36	40	31
80-81	Que	61	3	14	17	32
81-82	Que	30	0	6	6	16
NHL Totals		343	13	77	90	186
WHA Totals		378	30	161	191	186
NHL Playoff Totals		11	0	3	3	12
WHA Playoff Tot.		27	2	6	8	15

HOGUE, Benoit 5-10 190 C
B. Repentigny, Que., Oct. 28, 1966

Season	Team	GP	G	A	Pts.	PIM
87-88	Buf	3	1	1	2	0
88-89	Buf	69	14	30	44	120
89-90	Buf	45	11	7	18	79
90-91	Buf	76	19	28	47	76
91-92	Buf-NYI	75	30	46	76	67
Totals		268	75	112	187	342
Playoff Totals		13	3	1	4	37

HOLBROOK, Terry Eugene 6-0 185 RW
B. Petrolia, Ont., July 11, 1950

Season	Team	GP	G	A	Pts.	PIM
72-73	Minn	21	2	3	5	0
73-74	Minn	22	1	3	4	4
74-75	Clev(WHA)	78	10	13	23	7
75-76	Clev(WHA)	15	1	2	3	6
NHL Totals		43	3	6	9	4
WHA Totals		93	11	15	26	13
NHL Playoff Totals		6	0	0	0	0
WHA Playoff Totals		8	0	1	1	0

HOLIK, Robert (Bobby) 6-3 210 LW
B. Jihlava, Czechoslovakia, Jan. 1, 1971

Season	Team	GP	G	A	Pts.	PIM
90-91	Hart	78	21	22	43	113
91-92	Hart	76	21	24	45	44
Totals		154	42	46	88	157
Playoff Totals		13	0	1	1	13

HOLLAND, Jerry Allan 5-10 190 LW
B. Bearverlodge, Alta., Aug. 25, 1954

Season	Team	GP	G	A	Pts.	PIM
74-75	NYR	1	1	0	1	0
75-76	NYR	36	7	4	11	6
77-78	Edm(WHA)	22	2	1	3	14
NHL Totals		37	8	4	12	6
WHA Totals		22	2	1	3	14

HOLLETT, Frank William (Flash)
6-0 180 D
B. North Sydney, N.S., Apr. 13, 1912

Season	Team	GP	G	A	Pts.	PIM
33-34	Tor-Ott	34	7	4	11	25
34-35	Tor	48	10	16	26	38
35-36	Tor-Bos	17	2	6	8	10
36-37	Bos	47	3	7	10	22
37-38	Bos	48	4	10	14	54
38-39	Bos	47	10	17	27	35
39-40	Bos	44	10	18	28	18
40-41	Bos	42	9	15	24	23
41-42	Bos	48	19	14	33	41
42-43	Bos	50	19	25	44	19
43-44	Bos-Det	52	15	19	34	38
44-45	Det	50	20	21	41	39
45-46	Det	38	4	9	13	16
Totals		565	132	181	313	378
Playoff Totals		79	8	26	34	38

HOLLINGWORTH, Gordon (Bucky)
5-11 185 D
B. Verdun, Que., July 24, 1933

Season	Team	GP	G	A	Pts.	PIM
54-55	Chi	70	3	9	12	135
55-56	Det	41	0	2	2	28
56-57	Det	25	0	1	1	16
57-58	Det	27	1	2	3	22
Totals		163	4	14	18	201
Playoff Totals		3	0	0	0	2

HOLLOWAY, Bruce 6-0 200 D
B. Revelstoke, B.C., June 27, 1963

Season	Team	GP	G	A	Pts.	PIM
84-85	Van	2	0	0	0	0

HOLMES, Charles Frank (Chuck)
6-0 185 RW
B. Edmonton, Alta., Sept. 21, 1934

Season	Team	GP	G	A	Pts.	PIM
58-59	Det	15	0	3	3	6
61-62	Det	8	1	0	1	4
Totals		23	1	3	4	10

HOLMES, Louis 150 F
B. England, Jan. 29, 1911

Season	Team	GP	G	A	Pts.	PIM
31-32	Chi	41	1	4	5	6
32-33	Chi	18	0	0	0	0
Totals		59	1	4	5	6
Playoff Totals		2	0	0	0	2

HOLMES, Warren 6-1 195 C
B. Beeton, Ont., Feb. 18, 1957

Season	Team	GP	G	A	Pts.	PIM
81-82	LA	3	0	2	2	0
82-83	LA	39	8	16	24	7
83-84	LA	3	0	0	0	0
Totals		45	8	18	26	7

HOLMES, William F
B. Weyburn, Sask., 1899

Season	Team	GP	G	A	Pts.	PIM
25-26	Mont	9	1	0	1	2
26-27	NYA	1	0	0	0	0
29-30	NYA	42	5	4	9	33
Totals		52	6	4	10	35

HOLMGREN, Paul Howard 6-3 210 RW
B. St. Paul, Minn., Dec. 22, 1955

Season	Team	GP	G	A	Pts.	PIM
75-76	Minn(WHA)	51	14	16	30	121
75-76	Phil	1	0	0	0	2
76-77	Phil	59	14	12	26	201
77-78	Phil	62	16	18	34	190
78-79	Phil	57	19	10	29	168
79-80	Phil	74	30	35	65	267
80-81	Phil	77	22	37	59	306
81-82	Phil	41	9	22	31	183
82-83	Phil	77	19	24	43	178
83-84	Phil-Minn	63	11	18	29	151
84-85	Minn	16	4	3	7	38
NHL Totals		527	144	179	323	1684
WHA Totals		51	14	16	30	121
NHL Playoff Totals		82	19	32	51	195

HOLOTA, John Paul 5-6 160 C
B. Hamilton, Ont., Feb. 25, 1921

Season	Team	GP	G	A	Pts.	PIM
42-43	Det	12	2	0	2	0
45-46	Det	3	0	0	0	0
Totals		15	2	0	2	0

HOLST, Greg 5-10 170 C
B. Montreal, Que., Feb. 21, 1954

Season	Team	GP	G	A	Pts.	PIM
75-76	NYR	2	0	0	0	0
76-77	NYR	5	0	0	0	0
77-78	NYR	4	0	0	0	0
Totals		11	0	0	0	0

HOLT, Gareth Ray (Gary) 5-9 175 LW
B. Sarnia, Ont., Nov. 1, 1952

Season	Team	GP	G	A	Pts.	PIM
73-74	Cal	1	0	0	0	0
74-75	Cal	1	0	1	1	0
75-76	Cal	48	6	5	11	50
76-77	Clev	2	0	1	1	2
77-78	StL	49	7	4	11	81
Totals		101	13	11	24	133

HOLT, Stewart Randall (Randy)
5-11 185 D
B. Pembroke, Ont., Jan. 15, 1953

Season	Team	GP	G	A	Pts.	PIM
74-75	Chi	12	0	1	1	13
75-76	Chi	12	0	0	0	13
76-77	Chi	12	0	3	3	14
77-78	Chi-Clev	54	1	4	5	249
78-79	Van-LA	58	1	9	10	282
79-80	LA	42	0	1	1	94
80-81	Calg	48	0	5	5	165
81-82	Calg-Wash	61	2	6	8	259
82-83	Wash	70	0	8	8	275
83-84	Phil	26	0	0	0	74
Totals		395	4	37	41	1438
Playoff Totals		21	2	3	5	83

HOLWAY, Albert Robert (Toots)
6-1 190 D
B. Toronto, Ont., Sept. 24, 1902

Season	Team	GP	G	A	Pts.	PIM
23-24	Tor	6	1	0	1	0
24-25	Tor	25	2	2	4	20
25-26	Tor-Mont M	29	0	0	0	6
26-27	Mont M	13	0	0	0	10
28-29	Pitt Pi	44	4	0	4	20
Totals		117	7	2	9	56
Playoff Totals		8	0	0	0	2

HOMENUKE, Ronald Wayne
5-10 180 RW
B. Hazelton, B.C., Jan. 5, 1952

Season	Team	GP	G	A	Pts.	PIM
72-73	Van	1	0	0	0	0

HOOVER, Ron 6-1 185 C/LW
B. Oakville, Ont., Oct. 28, 1966

Season	Team	GP	G	A	Pts.	PIM
89-90	Bos	2	0	0	0	0

HOOVER, Ron (Continued)

Season	Team	GP	G	A	Pts.	PIM
90-91	Bos	15	4	0	4	31
91-92	StL	1	0	0	0	0
Totals		18	4	0	4	31
Playoff Totals		8	0	0	0	18

HOPKINS, Dean Robert 6-1 210 RW
B. Cobourg, Ont., June 6, 1959

Season	Team	GP	G	A	Pts.	PIM
79-80	LA	60	8	6	14	39
80-81	LA	67	8	18	26	118
81-82	LA	41	2	13	15	102
82-83	LA	49	5	12	17	43
85-86	Edm	1	0	0	0	0
88-89	Que	5	0	2	2	4
Totals		223	23	51	74	306
Playoff Totals		18	1	5	6	29

HOPKINS, Larry Harold 6-1 215 LW
B. Oshawa, Ont., Mar. 17, 1954

Season	Team	GP	G	A	Pts.	PIM
77-78	Tor	2	0	0	0	0
79-80	Winn	5	0	0	0	0
81-82	Winn	41	10	15	25	22
82-83	Winn	12	3	1	4	4
Totals		60	13	16	29	26
Playoff Totals		6	0	0	0	2

HORACEK, Tony 6-4 210 LW
B. Vancouver, B.C., Feb. 3, 1967

Season	Team	GP	G	A	Pts.	PIM
89-90	Phil	48	5	5	10	117
90-91	Phil	34	3	6	9	49
91-92	Phil-Chi	46	2	7	9	72
Totals		128	10	18	28	238
Playoff Totals		2	1	0	1	2

HORAVA, Miloslav 6-0 193 D
B. Kladno, Czechoslovakia, Aug. 14, 1961

Season	Team	GP	G	A	Pts.	PIM
88-89	NYR	6	0	1	1	0
89-90	NYR	45	4	10	14	26
90-91	NYR	29	1	6	7	12
Totals		80	5	17	22	38
Playoff Totals		2	0	1	1	0

HORBUL, Douglas George 5-9 170 LW
B. Nokomis, Sask., July 27, 1952

Season	Team	GP	G	A	Pts.	PIM
74-75	KC	4	1	0	1	2

HORDY, Michael 5-10 180 D
B. Thunder Bay, Ont., Oct. 10, 1956

Season	Team	GP	G	A	Pts.	PIM
78-79	NYI	2	0	0	0	0
79-80	NYI	9	0	0	0	7
Totals		11	0	0	0	7

HORECK, Peter 5-9 160 RW
B. Massey, Ont., June 15, 1923

Season	Team	GP	G	A	Pts.	PIM
44-45	Chi	50	20	16	36	44
45-46	Chi	50	20	21	41	34
46-47	Chi-Det	56	16	19	35	61
47-48	Det	50	12	17	29	44
48-49	Det	60	14	16	30	46
49-50	Bos	34	5	5	10	22
50-51	Bos	66	10	13	23	57
51-52	Chi	60	9	11	20	22
Totals		426	106	118	224	330
Playoff Totals		34	6	8	14	43

HORNE, George (Shorty) F

Season	Team	GP	G	A	Pts.	PIM
25-26	Mont M	13	0	0	0	2
26-27	Mont M	2	0	0	0	0
28-29	Tor	39	9	3	12	32
Totals		54	9	3	12	34
Playoff Totals		4	0	0	0	4

HORNER, George Reginald (Red)
6-0 190 D
B. Lynden, Ont., May 29, 1909

Season	Team	GP	G	A	Pts.	PIM
28-29	Tor	22	0	0	0	30
29-30	Tor	33	2	7	9	96
30-31	Tor	42	1	11	12	71
31-32	Tor	42	7	9	16	97
32-33	Tor	48	3	8	11	144
33-34	Tor	40	11	10	21	146
34-35	Tor	46	4	8	12	125
35-36	Tor	43	2	9	11	167
36-37	Tor	48	3	9	12	124
37-38	Tor	47	4	20	24	92
38-39	Tor	48	4	10	14	85
39-40	Tor	31	1	9	10	87
Totals		490	42	110	152	1264
Playoff Totals		71	7	10	17	166

HORNUNG, Lawrence John 6-0 190 D
B. Gravelburg, Sask., Oct. 10, 1945

Season	Team	GP	G	A	Pts.	PIM
70-71	StL	1	0	0	0	0
71-72	StL	47	2	9	11	10
72-73	Winn(WHA)	77	13	45	58	28

HORNUNG, Lawrence John *(Continued)*

Season	Team	GP	G	A	Pts.	PIM
73-74	Winn(WHA)	51	4	19	23	18
74-75	Winn(WHA)	69	7	25	32	21
75-76	Winn(WHA)	76	3	18	21	26
76-77	Edm-SD(WHA)	79	6	10	16	8
77-78	Winn(WHA)	19	1	4	5	2
NHL Totals		48	2	9	11	10
WHA Totals		371	34	121	155	103
NHL Playoff Totals		11	0	2	2	2
WHA Playoff Totals		37	2	12	14	6

HORTON, Miles Gilbert (Tim) *5-10 180 D*
B. Cochrane, Ont., Jan. 12, 1930

Season	Team	GP	G	A	Pts.	PIM
49-50	Tor	1	0	0	0	2
51-52	Tor	4	0	0	0	8
52-53	Tor	70	2	14	16	85
53-54	Tor	70	7	24	31	94
54-55	Tor	67	5	9	14	84
55-56	Tor	35	0	5	5	36
56-57	Tor	66	6	19	25	72
57-58	Tor	53	6	20	26	39
58-59	Tor	70	5	21	26	76
59-60	Tor	70	3	29	32	69
60-61	Tor	57	6	15	21	75
61-62	Tor	70	10	28	38	88
62-63	Tor	70	6	19	25	69
63-64	Tor	70	9	20	29	71
64-65	Tor	70	12	16	28	95
65-66	Tor	70	6	22	28	76
66-67	Tor	70	8	17	25	70
67-68	Tor	69	4	23	27	82
68-69	Tor	74	11	29	40	107
69-70	Tor-NYR	74	4	24	28	107
70-71	NYR	78	2	18	20	57
71-72	Pitt	44	2	9	11	40
72-73	Buf	69	1	16	17	56
73-74	Buf	55	0	6	6	53
Totals		1446	115	403	518	1611
Playoff Totals		126	11	39	50	183

HORVATH, Bronco Joseph *5-10 185 C*
B. Port Colborne, Ont., Mar. 12, 1930

Season	Team	GP	G	A	Pts.	PIM
55-56	NYR	66	12	17	29	40
56-57	NYR-Mont	8	1	2	3	4
57-58	Bos	67	30	36	66	71
58-59	Bos	45	19	20	39	58
59-60	Bos	68	39	41	80	60
60-61	Bos	47	15	15	30	15
61-62	Chi	69	17	29	46	21
62-63	NYR-Tor	50	7	19	26	46
67-68	Minn	14	1	6	7	4
Totals		434	141	185	326	319
Playoff Totals		36	12	9	21	18

HOSPODAR, Edward David *6-2 210 D*
B. Bowling Green, Ohio, Feb. 9, 1959

Season	Team	GP	G	A	Pts.	PIM
79-80	NYR	20	0	1	1	76
80-81	NYR	61	5	14	19	214
81-82	NYR	41	3	8	11	152
82-83	Hart	72	1	9	10	199
83-84	Hart	59	0	9	9	163
84-85	Phil	50	3	4	7	130
85-86	Phil-Minn	60	3	3	6	146
86-87	Phil	45	2	2	4	136
87-88	Buf	42	0	1	1	98
Totals		450	17	51	68	1314
Playoff Totals		44	4	1	5	206

HOSTAK, Martin *6-3 198 C*
B. Hradec Kralove, Czech., Nov. 11, 1967

Season	Team	GP	G	A	Pts.	PIM
90-91	Phil	50	3	10	13	22
91-92	Phil	5	0	1	1	2
Totals		55	3	11	14	24

HOTHAM, Gregory *5-11 185 D*
B. London, Ont., Mar. 7, 1956

Season	Team	GP	G	A	Pts.	PIM
79-80	Tor	46	3	10	13	10
80-81	Tor	11	1	1	2	11
81-82	Tor-Pitt	28	4	6	10	16
82-83	Pitt	58	2	30	32	39
83-84	Pitt	76	5	25	30	59
84-85	Pitt	11	0	2	2	4
Totals		230	15	74	89	139
Playoff Totals		5	0	3	3	6

HOUCK, Paul *5-11 185 RW*
B. North Vancouvor, B.C., Aug. 12, 1963

Season	Team	GP	G	A	Pts.	PIM
85-86	Minn	3	1	0	1	0
86-87	Minn	12	0	2	2	2
87-88	Minn	1	0	0	0	0
Totals		16	1	2	3	2

HOUDA, Doug *6-2 190 D*
B. Blairmore, Alta., June 3, 1966

Season	Team	GP	G	A	Pts.	PIM
85-86	Det	6	0	0	0	4

HOUDA, Doug *(Continued)*

Season	Team	GP	G	A	Pts.	PIM
87-88	Det	11	1	1	2	10
88-89	Det	57	2	11	13	67
89-90	Det	73	2	9	11	127
90-91	Det-Hart	41	1	6	7	84
91-92	Hart	56	3	6	9	125
Totals		244	9	33	42	417
Playoff Totals		18	0	3	3	21

HOUDE, Claude Daniel *6-1 190 D*
B. Drummondville, Que., Nov. 8, 1947

Season	Team	GP	G	A	Pts.	PIM
74-75	KC	34	3	4	7	20
75-76	KC	25	0	2	2	20
Totals		59	3	6	9	40

HOUGH, Mike *6-1 192 LW*
B. Montreal, Que., Feb. 6, 1963

Season	Team	GP	G	A	Pts.	PIM
86-87	Que	56	6	8	14	79
87-88	Que	17	3	2	5	2
88-89	Que	46	9	10	19	39
89-90	Que	43	13	13	26	84
90-91	Que	63	13	20	33	111
91-92	Que	61	16	22	38	77
Totals		286	60	75	135	392
Playoff Totals		9	0	3	3	26

HOULDER, Bill *6-2 212 D*
B. Thunder Bay, Ont., Mar. 11, 1967

Season	Team	GP	G	A	Pts.	PIM
87-88	Wash	30	1	2	3	10
88-89	Wash	8	0	3	3	4
89-90	Wash	41	1	11	12	28
90-91	Buf	7	0	2	2	4
91-92	Buf	10	1	0	1	8
Totals		96	3	18	21	54

HOULE, Rejean *5-11 170 LW/RW*
B. Rouyn, Que., Oct. 25, 1949

Season	Team	GP	G	A	Pts.	PIM
69-70	Mont	9	0	1	1	0
70-71	Mont	66	10	9	19	28
71-72	Mont	77	11	17	28	21
72-73	Mont	72	13	35	48	36
73-74	Que(WHA)	69	27	35	62	17
74-75	Que(WHA)	64	40	52	92	37
75-76	Que(WHA)	81	51	52	103	61
76-77	Mont	65	22	30	52	24
77-78	Mont	76	30	28	58	50
78-79	Mont	66	17	34	51	43
79-80	Mont	60	18	27	45	68
80-81	Mont	77	27	31	58	83
81-82	Mont	51	11	32	43	34
82-83	Mont	16	2	3	5	8
NHL Totals		635	161	247	408	395
WHA Totals		214	118	139	257	115
NHL Playoff Totals		90	14	34	48	66
WHA Playoff Totals		20	12	6	18	10

HOUSLEY, Phil *5-10 179 D*
B. St. Paul, Minn., Mar. 9, 1964

Season	Team	GP	G	A	Pts.	PIM
82-83	Buf	77	19	47	66	39
83-84	Buf	75	31	46	77	33
84-85	Buf	73	16	53	69	28
85-86	Buf	79	15	47	62	54
86-87	Buf	78	21	46	67	57
87-88	Buf	74	29	37	66	96
88-89	Buf	72	26	44	70	47
89-90	Buf	80	21	60	81	32
90-91	Winn	78	23	53	76	24
91-92	Winn	74	23	63	86	92
Totals		760	224	496	720	502
Playoff Totals		42	11	21	32	22

HOUSTON, Kenneth Lyle *6-2 210 RW*
B. Desden, Ont., Sept. 15, 1953

Season	Team	GP	G	A	Pts.	PIM
75-76	Atl	38	5	6	11	11
76-77	Atl	78	20	24	44	35
77-78	Atl	74	22	16	38	51
78-79	Atl	80	21	31	52	135
79-80	Atl	80	23	31	54	100
80-81	Calg	42	15	15	30	93
81-82	Calg	70	22	22	44	91
82-83	Wash	71	25	14	39	93
83-84	Wash-LA	37	8	8	16	15
Totals		570	161	167	328	624
Playoff Totals		35	10	9	19	66

HOWARD, Jack Francis (Frank) *D*
B. London, Ont., Oct. 15, 1915

Season	Team	GP	G	A	Pts.	PIM
36-37	Tor	2	0	0	0	0

HOWATT, Garry Robert Charles
5-9 175 LW
B. Grand Center, Alta., Sept. 26, 1952

Season	Team	GP	G	A	Pts.	PIM
72-73	NYI	8	0	1	1	18
73-74	NYI	78	6	11	17	204
74-75	NYI	77	18	30	48	121
75-76	NYI	80	21	13	34	197
76-77	NYI	70	13	15	28	182

HOWATT, Garry Robert Charles *(Continued)*

Season	Team	GP	G	A	Pts.	PIM
77-78	NYI	61	7	12	19	146
78-79	NYI	75	16	12	28	205
79-80	NYI	77	8	11	19	219
80-81	NYI	70	4	15	19	174
81-82	Hart	80	18	32	50	242
82-83	NJ	38	1	4	5	114
83-84	NJ	6	0	0	0	14
Totals		720	112	156	268	1836
Playoff Totals		87	12	14	26	289

HOWE, Gordon (Gordie) *6-0 205 RW*
B. Floral, Sask., Mar. 31, 1928

Season	Team	GP	G	A	Pts.	PIM
46-47	Det	58	7	15	22	52
47-48	Det	60	16	28	44	63
48-49	Det	40	12	25	37	57
49-50	Det	70	35	33	68	69
50-51	Det	70	43	43	86	74
51-52	Det	70	47	39	86	78
52-53	Det	70	49	46	95	57
53-54	Det	70	33	48	81	109
54-55	Det	64	29	33	62	68
55-56	Det	70	38	41	79	100
56-57	Det	70	44	45	89	72
57-58	Det	64	33	44	77	40
58-59	Det	70	32	46	78	57
59-60	Det	70	28	45	73	46
60-61	Det	64	23	49	72	30
61-62	Det	70	33	44	77	54
62-63	Det	70	38	48	86	100
63-64	Det	69	26	47	73	70
64-65	Det	70	29	47	76	104
65-66	Det	70	29	46	75	83
66-67	Det	69	25	40	65	53
67-68	Det	74	39	43	82	53
68-69	Det	76	44	59	103	58
69-70	Det	76	31	40	71	58
70-71	Det	63	23	29	52	38
73-74	Hou(WHA)	70	31	69	100	46
74-75	Hou(WHA)	75	34	65	99	84
75-76	Hou(WHA)	78	32	70	102	76
76-77	Hou(WHA)	62	24	44	68	57
77-78	NE(WHA)	76	34	62	96	85
78-79	NE(WHA)	58	19	24	43	51
79-80	Hart	80	15	26	41	42
NHL Totals		1767	801	1049	1850	1685
WHA Totals		419	174	334	508	399
NHL Playoff Totals		157	68	92	160	220
WHA Playoff Totals		78	28	43	71	115

HOWE, Mark Steven *5-11 185 D*
B. Detroit, Mich., May 28, 1955

Season	Team	GP	G	A	Pts.	PIM
73-74	Hou(WHA)	76	38	41	79	20
74-75	Hou(WHA)	74	36	40	76	30
75-75	Hou(WHA)	72	39	37	76	38
76-77	Hou(WHA)	57	23	52	75	46
77-78	NE(WHA)	70	30	61	91	32
78-79	NE(WHA)	77	42	65	107	32
79-80	Hart	74	24	56	80	20
80-81	Hart	63	19	46	65	54
81-82	Hart	76	8	45	53	18
82-83	Phil	76	20	47	67	18
83-84	Phil	71	19	34	53	44
84-85	Phil	73	18	39	57	31
85-86	Phil	77	24	58	82	36
86-87	Phil	69	15	43	58	37
87-88	Phil	75	19	43	62	62
88-89	Phil	52	9	29	38	45
89-90	Phil	40	7	21	28	24
90-91	Phil	19	0	10	10	8
91-92	Phil	42	7	18	25	18
NHL Totals		807	189	489	678	415
WHA Totals		426	208	296	504	198
NHL Playoff Totals		85	9	47	56	32
WHA Playoff Totals		74	41	51	92	48

HOWE, Marty Gordon *6-1 195 D*
B. Detroit, Mich., Feb. 18, 1954

Season	Team	GP	G	A	Pts.	PIM
73-74	Hou(WHA)	73	4	20	24	90
74-75	Hou(WHA)	75	13	21	34	89
75-76	Hou(WHA)	80	14	23	37	81
76-77	Hou(WHA)	80	17	28	45	103
77-78	NE(WHA)	75	10	10	20	66
78-79	NE(WHA)	66	9	15	24	31
79-80	Hart	6	0	1	1	4
80-81	Hart	12	0	1	1	25
81-82	Hart	13	0	4	4	2
82-83	Bos	78	1	11	12	24
83-84	Hart	69	0	11	11	34
84-85	Hart	19	1	1	2	10
NHL Totals		197	2	29	31	99
WHA Totals		449	67	117	184	460
NHL Playoff Totals		15	1	2	3	9
WHA Playoff Totals		75	9	14	23	85

HOWE, Sydney Harris *5-9 165 C*
B. Ottawa, Ont., Sept. 18, 1911

Season	Team	GP	G	A	Pts.	PIM
29-30	Ott	14	1	1	2	2
30-31	Phil Q	44	9	11	20	20
31-32	Tor	3	0	0	0	0
32-33	Ott	48	12	12	24	17
33-34	Ott	41	13	7	20	18
34-35	StLE-Det	50	22	25	47	34
35-36	Det	48	16	14	30	26
36-37	Det	42	17	10	27	10
37-38	Det	47	8	19	27	14
38-39	Det	48	16	20	36	11
39-40	Det	48	14	23	37	17
40-41	Det	48	20	24	44	8
41-42	Det	48	16	19	35	6
42-43	Det	50	20	35	55	10
43-44	Det	40	32	28	60	6
44-45	Det	46	17	36	53	6
45-46	Det	26	4	7	11	9
Totals		691	237	291	528	214
Playoff Totals		70	17	27	44	10

HOWE, Victor Stanley *6-0 172 RW*
B. Saskatoon, Sask., Nov. 2, 1929

Season	Team	GP	G	A	Pts.	PIM
50-51	NYR	3	1	0	1	0
53-54	NYR	1	0	0	0	0
54-55	NYR	29	2	4	6	10
Totals		33	3	4	7	10

HOWELL, Henry Vernon (Harry)
6-1 200 D
B. Hamilton, Ont., Dec. 28, 1932

Season	Team	GP	G	A	Pts.	PIM
52-53	NYR	67	3	8	11	46
53-54	NYR	67	7	9	16	58
54-55	NYR	70	2	14	16	87
55-56	NYR	70	3	15	18	77
56-57	NYR	65	2	10	12	70
57-58	NYR	70	4	7	11	62
58-59	NYR	70	4	10	14	101
59-60	NYR	67	7	6	13	58
60-61	NYR	70	7	10	17	62
61-62	NYR	66	6	15	21	89
62-63	NYR	70	5	20	25	55
63-64	NYR	70	5	31	36	75
64-65	NYR	68	2	20	22	63
65-66	NYR	70	4	29	33	92
66-67	NYR	70	12	28	40	54
67-68	NYR	74	5	24	29	62
68-69	NYR	56	4	7	11	36
69-70	Oak	55	4	16	20	52
70-71	Cal-LA	46	3	17	20	18
71-72	LA	77	1	17	18	53
72-73	LA	73	4	11	15	28
73-74	NY-NJ(WHA)	65	3	23	26	24
74-75	SD(WHA)	74	4	10	14	28
75-76	Calg(WHA)	31	0	3	3	6
NHL Totals		1411	94	324	418	1298
WHA Totals		170	7	36	43	58
NHL Playoff Totals		38	3	3	6	32
WHA Playoff Totals		7	1	0	1	12

HOWELL, Ronald *D*
B. Hamilton, Ont., Dec. 4, 1935

Season	Team	GP	G	A	Pts.	PIM
54-55	NYR	3	0	0	0	4
55-56	NYR	1	0	0	0	0
Totals		4	0	0	0	4

HOWSE, Donald Gordon *6-0 182 LW*
B. Grand Falls, Nfld., July 28, 1952

Season	Team	GP	G	A	Pts.	PIM
79-80	LA	33	2	5	7	6
Playoff Totals		2	0	0	0	0

HOWSON, Donald (Scott) *5-11 160 C*
B. Toronto, Ont., Apr. 9, 1960

Season	Team	GP	G	A	Pts.	PIM
84-85	NYI	8	4	1	5	2
85-86	NYI	10	1	2	3	2
Totals		18	5	3	8	4

HOYDA, David Allan *6-0 206 LW*
B. Edmonton, Alta., May 20, 1957

Season	Team	GP	G	A	Pts.	PIM
77-78	Phil	41	1	3	4	119
78-79	Phil	67	3	13	16	138
79-80	Winn	15	1	1	2	35
80-81	Winn	9	1	0	1	7
Totals		132	6	17	23	299
Playoff Totals		12	0	0	0	17

HRDINA, Jiri *6-0 195 C*
B. Prague, Czechoslovakia, Jan. 5, 1958

Season	Team	GP	G	A	Pts.	PIM
87-88	Calg	9	2	5	7	2
88-89	Calg	70	22	32	54	26
89-90	Calg	64	12	18	30	31
90-91	Calg-Pitt	51	6	17	23	17
91-92	Pitt	56	3	13	16	16
Totals		250	45	85	130	92

HRDINA, Jiri *(Continued)*

Season	Team	GP	G	A	Pts.	PIM
Playoff Totals		46	2	5	7	24

HRECHKOSY, David John *6-2 216 LW*
B. Winnipeg, Man., Nov. 1, 1951

Season	Team	GP	G	A	Pts.	PIM
73-74	Cal	2	0	0	0	0
74-75	Cal	72	29	14	43	25
75-76	Cal-StL	51	12	8	20	14
76-77	StL	15	1	2	3	2
Totals		140	42	24	66	41
Playoff Totals		3	1	0	1	2

HRKAC, Anthony *5-11 170 C*
B. Thunder Bay, Ont., July 7, 1966

Season	Team	GP	G	A	Pts.	PIM
87-88	StL/67	11	37	48	22	
88-89	ST L	70	17	28	45	8
89-90	StL-Que	50	9	20	29	10
90-91	Que	70	16	32	48	16
91-92	SJ-Chi	40	3	12	15	10
Totals		297	56	129	185	66
Playoff Totals		17	7	2	9	6

HRYNEWICH, Tim *5-11 190 LW*
B. Leamington, Ont., Oct. 2, 1963

Season	Team	GP	G	A	Pts.	PIM
82-83	Pitt	30	2	3	5	48
83-84	Pitt	25	4	5	9	34
Totals		55	6	8	14	82

HRYCUIK, James Peter *5-10 178 C*
B. Rosthern, Sask., Oct. 7, 1949

Season	Team	GP	G	A	Pts.	PIM
74-75	Wash	21	5	5	10	12

HRYMNAK, Stefan (Steve) *5-10 178 D*
B. Port Arthur, Ont., Mar. 3, 1926

Season	Team	GP	G	A	Pts.	PIM
51-52	Chi	18	2	1	3	4
Playoff Totals		2	0	0	0	0

HUARD, Roland (Rolly) *F*

Season	Team	GP	G	A	Pts.	PIM
30-31	Tor	1	1	0	1	0

HUBER, Wilhelm Heinrich (Willie)
6-5 230 D
B. Strasskirchen, W. Germany, Jan. 15, 1958

Season	Team	GP	G	A	Pts.	PIM
78-79	Det	68	7	24	31	114
79-80	Det	76	17	23	40	164
80-81	Det	80	15	34	49	130
81-82	Det	74	15	30	45	98
82-83	Det	74	14	29	43	106
83-84	NYR	42	9	14	23	60
84-85	NYR	49	3	11	14	55
85-86	NYR	70	7	8	15	85
86-87	NYR	66	8	22	30	68
87-88	NYR-Van-Phil	56	9	22	31	70
Totals		655	104	217	321	950
Playoff Totals		33	5	5	10	35

HUBICK, Gregory Wayne *5-11 183 D*
B. Strasbourg, Sask., Nov. 12, 1951

Season	Team	GP	G	A	Pts.	PIM
75-76	Tor	72	6	8	14	10
79-80	Van	5	0	1	1	0
Totals		77	6	9	15	10

HUCK, Anthony Francis (Fran) *5-7 165 C*
B. Regina, Sask., Dec. 4, 1945

Season	Team	GP	G	A	Pts.	PIM
69-70	Mont	2	0	0	0	0
70-71	Mont-StL	34	8	10	18	18
72-73	StL	58	16	20	36	20
73-74	Winn (WHA)	74	26	48	74	68
74-75	Minn (WHA)	78	22	45	67	26
75-76	Minn (WHA)	59	17	32	49	27
76-77	Winn (WHA)	12	2	2	4	10
77-78	Winn (WHA)	5	0	0	0	2
NHL Totals		94	24	30	54	38
WHA Totals		228	67	127	194	133
NHL Playoff Totals		11	3	4	7	2
WHA Playoff Totals		23	3	15	18	14

HUCUL, Frederick Albert *5-11 188 D*
B. Tubrose, Sask., Dec. 5, 1931

Season	Team	GP	G	A	Pts.	PIM
50-51	Chi	3	1	0	1	2
51-52	Chi	34	3	7	10	37
52-53	Chi	57	5	7	12	25
53-54	Chi	27	0	3	3	19
67-68	StL	43	2	13	15	30
Totals		164	11	30	41	113
Playoff Totals		6	1	0	1	10

HUDDY, Charles William *6-0 210 D*
B. Oshawa, Ont., June 2, 1959

Season	Team	GP	G	A	Pts.	PIM
80-81	Edm	12	2	5	7	6
81-82	Edm	41	4	11	15	46
82-83	Edm	76	20	37	57	58
83-84	Edm	75	8	34	42	43
84-85	Edm	80	7	44	51	46
85-86	Edm	76	6	35	41	55
86-87	Edm	58	4	15	19	35
87-88	Edm	77	13	28	41	71
88-89	Edm	76	11	33	44	52
89-90	Edm	70	1	23	24	56
90-91	Edm	53	5	22	27	32
91-92	LA	56	4	19	23	43
Totals		750	85	306	391	543
Playoff Tot.		144	17	62	69	115

HUDSON, Alexander (Lex) *6-3 184 D*
B. Winnipeg, Man., Dec. 31, 1955

Season	Team	GP	G	A	Pts.	PIM
78-79	Pitt	2	0	0	0	0
Playoff Totals		2	0	0	0	0

HUDSON, David Richard *6-0 175 C*
B. St. Thomas, Ont., Dec. 28, 1949

Season	Team	GP	G	A	Pts.	PIM
72-73	NYI	69	12	19	31	17
73-74	NYI	63	2	10	12	7
74-75	KC	70	9	32	41	27
75-76	KC	74	11	20	31	12
76-77	Col	73	15	21	36	14
77-78	Col	60	10	22	32	12
Totals		409	59	124	183	89
Playoff Totals		2	1	1	2	0

HUDSON, Mike *6-1 201 C/LW*
B. Guelph, Ont., Feb. 6, 1967

Season	Team	GP	G	A	Pts.	PIM
88-89	Chi	41	7	16	23	20
89-90	Chi	49	9	12	21	56
90-91	Chi	55	7	9	16	62
91-92	Chi	76	14	15	29	92
Totals		221	37	52	89	330
Playoff Totals		36	4	9	13	54

HUDSON, Ronald *5-10 175 RW*
B. Timmins, Ont., Apr. 18, 1914

Season	Team	GP	G	A	Pts.	PIM
37-38	Det	33	5	2	7	2
39-40	Det	1	0	0	0	0
Totals		34	5	2	7	2

HUFFMAN, Kerry *6-2 200 D*
B. Peterborough, Ont., Jan. 3, 1968

Season	Team	GP	G	A	Pts.	PIM
86-87	Phil	9	0	0	0	2
87-88	Phil	52	6	17	23	34
88-89	Phil	29	0	11	11	31
89-90	Phil	43	1	12	13	34
90-91	Phil	10	1	2	3	10
91-92	Phil	60	14	18	32	41
Totals		203	22	60	82	152
Playoff Totals		2	0	0	0	0

HUGGINS, Allan *F*
B. Toronto, Ont.

Season	Team	GP	G	A	Pts.	PIM
30-31	Mont M	20	1	1	2	2

HUGHES, Albert *F*
B. Collingwood, Ont.

Season	Team	GP	G	A	Pts.	PIM
30-31	NYA	42	5	7	12	14
31-32	NYA	18	1	1	2	8
Totals		60	6	8	14	22

HUGHES, Brent Allen *5-11 185 LW*
B. New Westminster, B.C., Apr. 5, 1966

Season	Team	GP	G	A	Pts.	PIM
88-89	Winn	28	3	2	5	82
89-90	Winn	11	1	2	3	33
91-92	Bos	8	1	1	2	38
Totals		47	5	5	10	153
Playoff Totals		10	2	0	2	20

HUGHES, Brenton Alexander (Brent)
6-0 205 D
B. Bowmanville, Ont., June 17, 1943

Season	Team	GP	G	A	Pts.	PIM
67-68	LA	44	4	10	14	36
68-69	LA	72	2	19	21	73
69-70	LA	52	1	7	8	108
70-71	Phil	30	1	10	11	21
71-72	Phil	63	2	20	22	35
72-73	Phil-StL	37	3	12	15	32
73-74	StL-Det	71	1	21	22	92
74-75	KC	66	1	18	19	43
75-76	SD (WHA)	78	7	28	35	63
76-77	SD (WHA)	62	4	13	17	48
77-78	Birm (WHA)	80	9	35	44	48
78-79	Birm (WHA)	48	3	3	6	21
NHL Totals		435	15	117	132	440
WHA Totals		268	23	79	102	180

HUGHES, Brenton Alexander (Brent)
(Continued)

Season Team	GP	G	A	Pts.	PIM
NHL Playoff Totals	23	1	3	4	53
WHA Playoff Totals	22	2	9	11	18

HUGHES, Frank *5-10 180 LW*
B. Fernie, B.C., Oct. 1, 1949

Season Team	GP	G	A	Pts.	PIM
71-72 Cal	5	0	0	0	0
72-73 Hou (WHA)	76	22	19	41	41
73-74 Hou (WHA)	73	42	42	84	47
74-75 Hou (WHA)	76	48	35	83	35
75-76 Hou (WHA)	80	31	45	76	26
76-77 Hou-Phoe (WHA)	75	27	37	64	22
77-78 Hou (WHA)	11	3	2	5	2
NHL Totals	5	0	0	0	0
WHA Totals	391	173	180	353	173
WHA Playoff Totals	54	24	16	40	33

HUGHES, Howard Duncan *5-9 180 RW*
B. St. Boniface, Man., Apr. 4, 1939

Season Team	GP	G	A	Pts.	PIM
67-68 LA	74	9	14	23	20
68-69 LA	73	16	14	30	10
69-70 LA	21	0	4	4	0
Totals	168	25	32	57	30
Playoff Totals	14	2	0	2	2

HUGHES, J. Rusty *D*

Season Team	GP	G	A	Pts.	PIM
29-30 Det	40	0	1	1	48

HUGHES, John F. (Jack) *6-1 205 D*
B. Somerville, Mass., July 20, 1957

Season Team	GP	G	A	Pts.	PIM
80-81 Col	38	2	5	7	91
81-82 Col	8	0	0	0	13
Totals	46	2	5	7	104

HUGHES, John Spencer *5-11 200 D*
B. Charlottetown, P.E.I., Mar. 18, 1954

Season Team	GP	G	A	Pts.	PIM
74-75 Phoe (WHA)	72	4	25	29	201
75-76 Cin (WHA)	79	3	34	37	204
76-77 Cin (WHA)	79	3	27	30	113
77-78 Hou (WHA)	79	3	25	28	130
78-79 Ind-Edm (WHA)	63	5	19	24	130
79-80 Van	52	2	11	13	181
80-81 Edm	18	0	3	3	30
NHL Totals	70	2	14	16	211
WHA Totals	372	18	130	148	778
NHL Playoff Totals	7	0	1	1	16
WHA Playoff Totals	23	2	1	3	49

HUGHES, Patrick *6-1 180 RW*
B. Calgary, Alta., Mar. 25, 1955

Season Team	GP	G	A	Pts.	PIM
77-78 Mont	3	0	0	0	2
78-79 Mont	41	9	8	17	22
79-80 Pitt	76	18	14	32	78
80-81 Pitt-Edm	60	10	9	19	161
81-82 Edm	68	24	22	46	99
82-83 Edm	80	25	20	45	85
83-84 Edm	77	27	28	55	61
84-85 Edm	73	12	13	25	85
85-86 Buf	50	4	9	13	25
86-87 StL-Hart	45	1	5	6	28
Totals	573	130	128	258	653
Playoff Totals	71	8	25	33	77

HULL, Brett *5-10 201 RW*
B. Belleville, Ont., Aug. 9, 1964

Season Team	GP	G	A	Pts.	PIM
86-87 Calg	5	1	0	1	0
87-88 Calg-StL	65	32	32	64	16
88-89 StL	78	41	43	84	33
89-90 StL	80	72	41	113	24
90-91 StL	78	86	45	131	22
91-92 StL	73	70	39	109	48
Totals	379	302	200	502	143
Playoff Totals	57	42	28	70	35

HULL, Dennis William *5-11 195 LW*
B. Pointe Anne, Ont., Nov. 19, 1944

Season Team	GP	G	A	Pts.	PIM
64-65 Chi	55	10	4	14	18
65-66 Chi	25	1	5	6	6
66-67 Chi	70	25	17	42	33
67-68 Chi	74	18	15	33	34
68-69 Chi	72	30	34	64	25
69-70 Chi	76	17	35	52	31
70-71 Chi	78	40	26	66	16
71-72 Chi	78	30	39	69	10
72-73 Chi	78	39	51	90	27
73-74 Chi	74	29	39	68	15
74-75 Chi	69	16	21	37	10
75-76 Chi	80	27	39	66	28
76-77 Chi	75	16	17	33	2
77-78 Det	55	5	9	14	6
Totals	959	303	351	654	261
Playoff Totals	104	33	34	67	30

HULL, Jody *6-2 200 RW*
B. Cambridge, Ont., Feb. 2, 1969

Season Team	GP	G	A	Pts.	PIM
88-89 Hart	60	16	18	34	10
89-90 Hart	38	7	10	17	21
90-91 NYR	47	5	8	13	10
91-92 NYR	3	0	0	0	2
Totals	148	28	36	64	43
Playoff Totals	6	0	1	1	4

HULL, Robert Marvin (Golden Jet)
5-10 193 LW
B. Pointe Anne, Ont., Jan. 3, 1939

Season Team	GP	G	A	Pts.	PIM
57-58 Chi	70	13	34	47	62
58-59 Chi	70	18	32	50	50
59-60 Chi	70	39	42	81	68
60-61 Chi	67	31	25	56	43
61-62 Chi	70	50	34	84	35
62-63 Chi	65	31	31	62	27
63-64 Chi	70	43	44	87	50
64-65 Chi	61	39	32	71	32
65-66 Chi	65	54	43	97	70
66-67 Chi	66	52	28	80	52
67-68 Chi	71	44	31	75	39
68-69 Chi	74	58	49	107	48
69-70 Chi	61	38	29	67	8
70-71 Chi	78	44	52	96	32
71-72 Chi	78	50	43	93	24
72-73 Winn (WHA)	63	51	52	103	37
73-74 Winn (WHA)	75	53	42	95	38
74-75 Winn (WHA)	78	77	65	142	41
75-76 Winn (WHA)	80	53	70	123	30
76-77 Winn (WHA)	34	21	32	53	14
77-78 Winn (WHA)	77	46	71	117	23
78-79 Winn (WHA)	4	2	3	5	0
79-80 Winn-Hart	27	6	11	17	0
NHL Totals	1063	610	560	1170	640
WHA Totals	411	303	335	638	183
NHL Playoff Totals	119	62	67	129	102
WHA Playoff Totals	60	43	37	80	38

HUNT, Fredrick Tennyson (Fritz)
5-8 160 RW
B. Brantford, Ont., Jan. 17, 1918

Season Team	GP	G	A	Pts.	PIM
40-41 NYA	15	2	5	7	0
44-45 NYR	44	13	9	22	6
Totals	59	15	14	29	6

HUNTER, Dale Robert *5-10 198 C*
B. Petrolia, Ont., July 31, 1960

Season Team	GP	G	A	Pts.	PIM
80-81 Que	80	19	44	63	226
81-82 Que	80	22	50	72	272
82-83 Que	80	17	46	63	206
83-84 Que	77	24	55	79	232
84-85 Que	80	20	52	72	209
85-86 Que	80	28	42	70	265
86-87 Que	46	10	29	39	135
87-88 Wash	79	22	37	59	240
88-89 Wash	80	20	37	57	219
89-90 Wash	80	23	39	62	233
90-91 Wash	76	16	30	46	234
91-92 Wash	80	28	50	78	205
Totals	918	249	511	760	2676
Playoff Totals	120	29	56	85	563

HUNTER, David *5-11 195 LW*
B. Petrolia, Ont., Jan. 1, 1958

Season Team	GP	G	A	Pts.	PIM
78-79 Edm (WHA)	72	7	25	32	134
79-80 Edm	80	12	31	43	103
80-81 Edm	78	12	16	28	98
81-82 Edm	63	16	22	38	63
82-83 Edm	80	13	18	31	120
83-84 Edm	80	22	26	48	90
84-85 Edm	80	17	19	36	122
85-86 Edm	62	15	22	37	77
86-87 Edm	77	6	9	15	79
87-88 Edm-Pitt	80	14	21	35	83
88-89 Winn-Edm	66	6	6	12	83
NHL Totals	746	133	190	323	918
WHA Totals	72	7	25	32	134
NHL Playoff Tot.	105	16	24	40	211
WHA Playoff Tot.	13	2	3	5	42

HUNTER, Mark *6-0 200 RW*
B. Petrolia, Ont., Nov. 12, 1962

Season Team	GP	G	A	Pts.	PIM
81-82 Mont	71	14	11	29	143
82-83 Mont	31	8	8	16	73
83-84 Mont	22	6	4	10	42
84-85 Mont	72	21	12	33	123
85-86 StL	78	44	30	74	171

HUNTER, Mark *(Continued)*

Season Team	GP	G	A	Pts.	PIM
86-87 StL	74	36	33	69	167
87-88 StL	66	32	31	63	136
88-89 Calg	66	22	8	30	194
89-90 Calg	10	2	3	5	39
90-91 Calg-Hart	68	14	18	32	165
91-92 Hart	63	10	13	23	159
Totals	621	213	171	384	1412
Playoff Totals	79	18	20	38	230

HUNTER, Timothy Robert *6-2 202 RW*
B. Calgary, Alta., Sept. 10, 1960

Season Team	GP	G	A	Pts.	PIM
81-82 Calg	2	0	0	0	9
82-83 Calg	16	1	0	1	54
83-84 Calg	43	4	4	8	130
84-85 Calg	71	11	11	22	259
85-86 Calg	66	8	7	15	291
86-87 Calg	73	6	15	21	361
87-88 Calg	68	8	5	13	337
88-89 Calg	75	3	9	12	375
89-90 Calg	67	2	3	5	279
90-91 Calg	34	5	2	7	143
91-92 Calg	30	1	3	4	167
Totals	545	49	59	108	2405
Playoff Totals	86	5	7	12	352

HURAS, Larry Robert *6-2 200 D*
B. Listowel, Ont., July 8, 1955

Season Team	GP	G	A	Pts.	PIM
76-77 NYR	1	0	0	0	0

HURLBURT, Robert George *5-11 185 LW*
B. Toronto, Ont., May 1, 1950

Season Team	GP	G	A	Pts.	PIM
74-75 Van	1	0	0	0	2

HURLEY, Paul Michael *5-11 185 D*
B. Melrose, Mass., July 12, 1946

Season Team	GP	G	A	Pts.	PIM
68-69 Bos	1	0	1	1	0
72-73 NE (WHA)	78	3	15	18	58
73-74 NE (WHA)	52	3	11	14	21
74-75 NE (WHA)	75	3	26	29	36
75-76 NE-Edm (WHA)	72	1	18	19	34
76-77 Calg (WHA)	34	0	6	6	32
NHL Totals	1	0	1	1	0
WHA Totals	311	10	76	86	181
WHA Playoff Totals	25	0	8	8	18

HURST, Ronald *5-9 175 RW*
B. Toronto, Ont., May 18, 1931

Season Team	GP	G	A	Pts.	PIM
55-56 Tor	50	7	5	12	62
56-57 Tor	14	2	2	4	8
Totals	64	9	7	16	70
Playoff Totals	3	0	2	2	4

HUSCROFT, Jamie *6-2 200 D*
B. Creston, B.C., Jan. 9, 1967

Season Team	GP	G	A	Pts.	PIM
88-89 NJ	15	0	2	2	51
89-90 NJ	42	2	3	5	149
90-91 NJ	8	0	1	1	27
Totals	65	2	6	8	227
Playoff Totals	8	0	0	0	22

HUSTON, Ronald Earle *5-9 170 C*
B. Manitou, Man., Apr. 8, 1945

Season Team	GP	G	A	Pts.	PIM
73-74 Cal	23	3	10	13	0
74-75 Cal	56	12	21	33	8
75-76 Phoe (WHA)	79	22	44	66	4
76-77 Phoe (WHA)	80	20	39	59	10
NHL Totals	79	15	31	46	8
WHA Totals	159	42	83	125	14
WHA Playoff Totals	5	1	1	2	0

HUTCHINSON, Ronald Wayne *5-10 175 C*
B. Flin Flon, Man., Oct. 24, 1936

Season Team	GP	G	A	Pts.	PIM
60-61 NYR	9	0	0	0	0

HUTCHISON, David Joseph *6-3 205 D*
B. London, Ont., May 2, 1952

Season Team	GP	G	A	Pts.	PIM
72-73 Phil (WHA)	28	0	2	2	34
73-74 Van (WHA)	69	0	13	13	151
74-75 LA	68	0	6	6	133
75-76 LA	50	0	10	10	181
76-77 LA	70	6	11	17	220
77-78 LA	44	0	10	10	71
78-79 Tor	79	4	15	19	235
79-80 Tor-Chi	69	1	11	12	101
80-81 Chi	59	2	9	11	124
81-82 Chi	66	5	18	23	246
82-83 NJ	32	1	4	5	102
83-84 Tor	47	0	3	3	137
NHL Totals	584	19	97	116	1550
WHA Totals	97	0	15	15	185
NHL Playoff Totals	48	2	12	14	149
WHA Playoff Totals	3	0	0	0	2

HUTTON, William David 5-10 165 D
B. Calgary, Alta., Jan. 28, 1910

Season	Team	GP	G	A	Pts.	PIM
29-30	Bos-Ott	34	2	1	3	2
30-31	Bos-Phil Q	30	1	1	2	6
Totals		64	3	2	5	8
Playoff Totals		0	0	0	0	0

HYLAND, Harold M. (Harry) RW
B. Montreal, Que., Jan. 2, 1889

17-18	Mont W-Ott	16	14	0	14	9

HYNES, David E. 5-9 182 LW
B. Cambridge, Mass., Apr. 17, 1951

73-74	Bos	3	0	0	0	0
74-75	Bos	19	4	0	4	2
76-77	NE (WHA)	22	5	4	9	4
NHL Totals		22	4	0	4	2
WHA Totals		22	5	4	9	4

HYNES, Gord 6-1 170 D
B. Montreal, Que., July 22, 1966

91-92	Bos	15	0	5	5	6
Playoff Totals		12	1	2	3	6

IAFRATE, Al 6-3 220 D
B. Dearborn, Mich., Mar. 21, 1966

84-85	Tor	68	5	16	21	51
85-86	Tor	65	8	25	33	40
86-87	Tor	80	9	21	30	55
87-88	Tor	77	22	30	52	80
88-89	Tor	65	13	20	33	72
89-90	Tor	75	21	42	63	135
90-91	Tor-Wash	72	9	23	32	237
91-92	Wash	78	17	34	51	180
Totals		580	104	211	315	850
Playoff Totals		46	9	15	24	57

IHNACAK, Miroslav 5-11 175 LW
B. Poprad, Czechoslovakia, Nov. 19, 1962

85-86	Tor	21	2	4	6	27
86-87	Tor	34	6	5	11	12
88-89	Det	1	0	0	0	0
Totals		56	8	9	17	39
Playoff Totals		1	0	0	0	0

IHNACAK, Peter 5-11 180 C
B. Poprad, Czechoslovakia, May 3, 1957

82-83	Tor	80	28	38	66	44
83-84	Tor	47	10	13	23	24
84-85	Tor	70	22	22	44	24
85-86	Tor	63	18	27	45	16
86-87	Tor	58	12	27	39	16
87-88	Tor	68	10	20	30	41
88-89	Tor	26	2	16	18	10
89-90	Tor	5	0	2	2	0
Totals		417	102	165	267	175
Playoff Totals		28	4	10	14	25

IMLACH, Brent F
B. Toronto, Ont., Nov. 16, 1946

65-66	Tor	2	0	0	0	2
66-67	Tor	1	0	0	0	0
Totals		3	0	0	0	2

INGARFIELD, Earl Thompson 5-11 185 C
B. Lethbridge, Alta., Oct. 25, 1934

58-59	NYR	35	1	2	3	10
59-60	NYR	20	1	2	3	2
60-61	NYR	66	13	21	34	18
61-62	NYR	70	26	31	57	18
62-63	NYR	69	19	24	43	40
63-64	NYR	63	15	11	26	26
64-65	NYR	69	15	13	28	40
65-66	NYR	68	20	16	36	35
66-67	NYR	67	12	22	34	12
67-68	Pitt	50	15	22	37	12
68-69	Pitt-Oak	66	16	30	46	12
69-70	Oak	54	21	24	45	10
70-71	Cal	49	5	8	13	4
Totals		746	179	226	405	239
Playoff Totals		21	9	8	17	10

INGARFIELD, Earl Thompson, Jr.
5-10 175 C
B. Manhasset, N.Y., Jan. 30, 1959

79-80	Atl	1	0	0	0	0
80-81	Calg-Det	38	4	4	8	22
Totals		39	4	4	8	22
Playoff Totals		2	0	1	1	0

INGLIS, William John 5-9 160 C
B. Ottawa, Ont., May 11, 1943

67-68	LA	12	1	1	2	0

INGLIS, William John (Continued)

68-69	LA	10	0	1	1	0
70-71	Buf	14	0	1	1	4
Totals		36	1	3	4	4
Playoff Totals		11	1	2	3	4

INGOLDSBY, John Gordon (Jack, Ding)
6-2 210 RW
B. Toronto, Ont., June 21, 1924

42-43	Tor	8	0	1	1	0
43-44	Tor	21	5	0	5	15
Totals		29	5	1	6	15

INGRAM, Frank 5-7 185 RW
B. Graven, Sask., Sept. 17, 1907

24-25	Bos	1	0	0	0	0
29-30	Chi	37	6	10	16	28
30-31	Chi	43	17	4	21	37
31-32	Chi	21	1	2	3	4
Totals		102	24	16	40	69
Playoff Totals		11	0	1	1	2

INGRAM, Ronald Walter 5-11 185 D
B. Toronto, Ont., July 5, 1933

56-57	Chi	45	1	6	7	21
63-64	Det-NYR	66	4	9	13	58
64-65	NYR	3	0	0	0	2
Totals		114	5	15	20	81
Playoff Totals		2	0	0	0	0

IRVIN, James Dickinson (Dick) F
B. Limestone Ridge, Ont., July 19, 1892

26-27	Chi	44	18	18	36	34
27-28	Chi	14	5	4	9	12
28-29	Chi	36	6	1	7	30
Totals		94	29	23	52	76
Playoff Totals		2	2	0	2	4

IRVINE, Edward Amos (Ted) 6-2 195 LW
B. Winnipeg, Man., Dec. 8, 1944

63-64	Bos	1	0	0	0	0
67-68	LA	73	18	22	40	26
68-69	LA	76	15	24	39	47
69-70	LA-NYR	75	11	16	27	38
70-71	NYR	76	20	18	38	137
71-72	NYR	78	15	21	36	66
72-73	NYR	53	8	12	20	54
73-74	NYR	75	26	20	46	105
74-75	NYR	79	17	17	34	66
75-76	StL	69	10	13	23	80
76-77	StL	69	14	14	28	38
Totals		724	154	177	331	657
Playoff Totals		83	16	24	40	115

IRWIN, Ivan Duane (Ivan the Terrible)
6-2 185 D
B. Chicago, Ill., Mar. 13, 1927

52-53	Mont	4	0	1	1	0
53-54	NYR	56	2	12	14	109
54-55	NYR	60	0	13	13	85
55-56	NYR	34	0	1	1	20
57-58	NYR	1	0	0	0	0
Totals		155	2	27	29	214
Playoff Totals		5	0	0	0	8

ISAKSSON, Ulf 6-1 185 LW
B. Norfunda, Sweden, Mar. 19, 1954

82-83	LA	50	7	15	22	10

ISSEL, Kim 6-4 196 RW
B. Regina, Sask., Sept. 25, 1967

88-89	Edm	4	0	0	0	0

JACKSON, Arthur M. 5-7 165 C
B. Toronto, Ont., Dec. 15, 1915

34-35	Tor	20	1	3	4	4
35-36	Tor	48	5	15	20	14
36-37	Tor	14	0	2	2	2
37-38	Bos	48	9	3	12	24
38-39	NYA	48	12	13	25	15
39-40	Bos	45	7	18	25	6
40-41	Bos	47	17	15	32	10
41-42	Bos	47	6	18	24	25
42-43	Bos	50	22	31	53	20
43-44	Bos	49	21	38	59	8
44-45	Bos-Tor	50	14	21	35	16
Totals		466	116	175	291	144
Playoff Totals		51	8	12	20	27

JACKSON, Donald Clinton 6-3 210 D
B. Minneapolis, Minn., Sept. 2, 1956

77-78	Minn	2	0	0	0	2
78-79	Minn	5	0	0	0	2
79-80	Minn	10	0	4	4	18
80-81	Minn	10	0	3	3	19
81-82	Edm	8	0	0	0	18

JACKSON, Donald Clinton (Continued)

82-83	Edm	71	2	8	10	136
83-84	Edm	60	8	12	20	120
84-85	Edm	78	3	17	20	141
85-86	Edm	45	2	8	10	93
86-87	NYR	22	1	0	1	91
Totals		311	16	52	68	640
Playoff Totals		53	4	5	9	147

JACKSON, Harold Russell (Hal)
5-11 175 D
B. Cedar Springs, Ont., Aug. 1, 1917

36-37	Chi	40	1	3	4	6
37-38	Chi	4	0	0	0	0
40-41	Det	1	0	0	0	0
42-43	Det	4	0	4	4	6
43-44	Det	50	7	12	19	76
44-45	Det	50	5	6	11	45
45-46	Det	36	3	4	7	36
46-47	Det	37	1	5	6	39
Totals		222	17	34	51	208
Playoff Totals		31	1	2	3	33

JACKSON, James Kenneth 5-9 190 LW
B. Oshawa, Ont., Feb. 1, 1960

82-83	Calg	48	8	12	20	7
83-84	Calg	49	6	14	20	13
84-85	Calg	10	1	4	5	0
87-88	Buf	5	2	0	2	0
Totals		112	17	30	47	20
Playoff Totals		14	3	2	5	6

JACKSON, Jeff 6-1 195 LW
B. Dresden, Ont., Apr. 24, 1965

84-85	Tor	17	0	1	1	24
85-86	Tor	5	1	2	3	2
86-87	Tor-NYR	64	13	8	21	79
87-88	Que	68	9	18	27	103
88-89	Que	33	4	6	10	28
89-90	Que	65	8	12	20	71
90-91	Que	10	3	1	4	4
91-92	Chi	1	0	0	0	2
Totals		263	38	48	86	313
Playoff Totals		6	1	1	2	16

JACKSON, John Alexander 5-10 185 D
B. Windsor, Ont., May 3, 1925

46-47	Chi	48	2	5	7	38

JACKSON, Lloyd Edgar 5-9 150 C
B. Ottawa, Ont., Jan. 7, 1912

36-37	NYA	14	1	1	2	0

JACKSON, Ralph Harvey (Busher)
5-11 195 F
B. Toronto, Ont., Jan. 19, 1911

29-30	Tor	32	12	6	18	29
30-31	Tor	43	18	13	31	81
31-32	Tor	48	28	25	53	63
32-33	Tor	48	27	17	44	43
33-34	Tor	38	20	18	38	38
34-35	Tor	42	22	22	44	27
35-36	Tor	47	11	11	22	19
36-37	Tor	46	21	19	40	12
37-38	Tor	48	17	17	34	18
38-39	Tor	42	10	17	27	12
39-40	NYA	43	12	8	20	10
40-41	NYA	46	8	18	26	4
41-42	Bos	27	5	7	12	18
42-43	Bos	44	19	15	34	38
43-44	Bos	42	11	21	32	25
Totals		636	241	234	475	437
Playoff Totals		71	18	12	30	53

JACKSON, Stanton (Stan) LW

21-22	Tor	1	0	0	0	0
23-24	Tor	21	1	1	2	6
24-25	Tor-Bos	27	5	0	5	36
25-26	Bos	28	3	3	6	30
26-27	Ott	7	0	0	0	2
Totals		84	9	4	13	74

JACKSON, Walter (Red) 160 F
B. Instock, England, June 3, 1908

32-33	NYA	35	10	2	12	6
33-34	NYA	46	6	9	15	12
34-35	NYA	1	0	0	0	0
Totals		82	16	11	27	18

JACOBS, Paul F

18-19	Tor	1	0	0	0	0

JACOBS, Timothy James 5-10 180 D
B. Espanola, Ont., Mar. 28, 1952

75-76	Cal	46	0	10	10	35

Season	Team	GP	G	A	Pts.	PIM
JAGR, Jaromir	*6-2 208 RW*					
B. Kladno, Czechoslovakia, Feb. 15, 1972						
90-91	Pitt	80	27	30	57	42
91-92	Pitt	70	32	37	69	34
Totals		150	59	67	126	76
Playoff Totals		45	14	23	37	12
JALO, Risto	*5-11 185 C*					
B. Tampere, Finland, July 18, 1962						
85-86	Edm	3	0	3	3	0
JALONEN, Kari	*6-3 190 C*					
B. Oulu, Finland, Jan. 6, 1960						
82-83	Calg	25	9	3	12	4
83-84	Calg-Edm	12	0	3	3	0
Totals		37	9	6	15	4
Playoff Totals		5	1	0	1	0
JAMES, Gerald Edwin (Gerry)	*5-11 191 RW*					
B. Regina, Sask., Oct. 22, 1934						
54-55	Tor	1	0	0	0	0
55-56	Tor	46	3	3	6	50
56-57	Tor	53	4	12	16	90
57-58	Tor	15	3	2	5	61
59-60	Tor	34	4	9	13	56
Totals		149	14	26	40	257
Playoff Totals		15	1	0	1	8
JAMES, Valmore (Val)	*6-2 205 LW*					
B. Ocala, Fla., Feb. 14, 1957						
81-82	Buf	7	0	0	0	16
86-87	Tor	4	0	0	0	14
Totals		11	0	0	0	30
JAMIESON, James	*5-8 170 D*					
B. Brantford, Ont., Mar. 21, 1922						
43-44	NYR	1	0	1	1	0
JANKOWSKI, Louis Casimer	*6-0 184 LW*					
B. Regina, Sask., June 27, 1931						
50-51	Det	1	0	1	1	0
52-53	Det	22	1	2	3	0
53-54	Chi	68	15	13	28	7
54-55	Chi	36	3	2	5	8
Totals		127	19	18	37	15
Playoff Totals		1	0	0	0	0
JANNEY, Craig	*6-1 190 C*					
B. Hartford, Conn., Sept. 26, 1967						
87-88	Bos	15	7	9	16	0
88-89	Bos	62	16	46	62	12
89-90	Bos	55	24	38	62	4
90-91	Bos	77	26	66	92	8
91-92	Bos-StL	78	18	69	87	22
Totals		287	91	228	319	46
Playoff Totals		75	17	62	79	45
JANSSENS, Mark	*6-3 216 C*					
B. Surrey, B.C., May 19, 1968						
87-88	NYR	1	0	0	0	0
88-89	NYR	5	0	0	0	0
89-90	NYR	80	5	8	13	161
90-91	NYR	67	9	7	16	172
91-92	NYR-Minn	7	0	0	0	5
Totals		160	14	15	29	338
Playoff Totals		15	5	1	6	16
JARRETT, Douglas William	*6-1 205 D*					
B. London, Ont., Apr. 22, 1944						
64-65	Chi	46	2	15	17	34
65-66	Chi	66	4	12	16	71
66-67	Chi	70	5	21	26	76
67-68	Chi	74	4	19	23	48
68-69	Chi	69	0	13	13	58
69-70	Chi	72	4	20	24	78
70-71	Chi	51	1	12	13	46
71-72	Chi	78	6	23	29	68
72-73	Chi	49	2	11	13	18
73-74	Chi	67	5	11	16	45
74-75	Chi	79	5	21	26	66
75-76	NYR	45	0	4	4	19
76-77	NYR	9	0	0	0	4
Totals		775	38	182	220	631
Playoff Totals		99	7	16	23	82
JARRETT, Gary Walter	*5-8 170 LW*					
B. Toronto, Ont., Sept. 3, 1942						
60-61	Tor	1	0	0	0	0
66-67	Det	4	0	0	0	0
67-68	Det	68	18	21	39	20
68-69	Oak	63	22	23	45	22
69-70	Oak	75	12	19	31	31
70-71	Cal	75	15	19	34	40
71-72	Cal	55	5	10	15	18
72-73	Clev (WHA)	77	40	39	79	79

Season	Team	GP	G	A	Pts.	PIM
JARRETT, Gary Walter	*(Continued)*					
73-74	Clev (WHA)	75	31	39	70	68
74-75	Clev (WHA)	77	17	24	41	70
75-76	Clev (WHA)	69	16	17	33	22
NHL Totals		341	72	92	164	131
WHA Totals		298	104	119	223	239
NHL Playoff Totals		11	3	1	4	9
WHA Playoff Totals		22	9	8	17	34
JARRY, Pierre Joseph Reynald	*5-11 182 LW*					
B. Montreal, Que., Mar. 30, 1949						
71-72	NYR-Tor	52	6	7	13	33
72-73	Tor	74	19	18	37	42
73-74	Tor-Det	64	17	31	48	27
74-75	Det	39	8	13	21	4
75-76	Minn	59	21	18	39	32
76-77	Minn	21	8	13	21	2
77-78	Minn	35	9	17	26	2
77-78	Edm (WHA)	18	4	10	14	4
NHL Totals		344	88	117	205	142
WHA Totals		18	4	10	14	4
NHL Playoff Totals		5	0	1	1	0
WHA Playoff Totals		5	1	0	1	4
JARVENPAA, Hannu	*6-0 194 RW*					
B. Ii, Finland, May 19, 1963						
86-87	Winn	20	1	8	9	8
87-88	Winn	41	6	11	17	34
88-89	Winn	53	4	7	11	41
Totals		114	11	26	37	83
JARVI, Iiro	*6-1 198 LW*					
B. Helsinki, Finland, Mar. 23, 1965						
88-89	Que	75	11	30	41	40
89-90	Que	41	7	13	20	18
Totals		116	18	43	61	58
JARVIS, Douglas	*5-9 170 C*					
B. Brantford, Ont., Mar. 24, 1955						
75-76	Mont	80	5	30	35	16
76-77	Mont	80	16	22	38	14
77-78	Mont	80	11	28	39	23
78-79	Mont	80	10	13	23	16
79-80	Mont	80	13	11	24	28
80-81	Mont	80	16	22	38	34
81-82	Mont	80	20	28	48	20
82-83	Wash	80	8	22	30	10
83-84	Wash	80	13	29	42	12
84-85	Wash	80	9	28	37	32
85-86	Wash-Hart	82	9	18	27	36
86-87	Hart	80	9	13	22	20
87-88	Hart	2	0	0	0	2
Totals		964	139	264	403	263
Playoff Tot.		105	14	27	41	42
JARVIS, James (Bud)	*5-6 165 LW*					
B. Fort William, Ont., Dec. 7, 1907						
29-30	Pitt Pi	41	11	8	19	32
30-31	Phil Q	43	5	7	12	30
36-37	Tor	24	1	0	1	0
Totals		108	17	15	32	62
JARVIS, Wesley Herbert	*5-11 185 C*					
B. Toronto, Ont., May 30, 1958						
79-80	Wash	63	11	15	26	8
80-81	Wash	55	9	14	23	20
81-82	Wash	26	1	12	13	18
82-83	Minn	3	0	0	0	2
83-84	LA	61	9	13	22	36
84-85	Tor	26	0	1	1	2
85-86	Tor	2	1	0	1	2
87-88	Tor	1	0	0	0	0
Totals		237	31	55	86	98
Playoff Totals		2	0	0	0	2
JAVANAINEN, Arto	*6-0 185 LW*					
B. Pori, Finland, Apr. 8, 1959						
84-85	Pitt	14	4	1	5	2
JEFFREY, Lawrence Joseph	*5-11 189 LW*					
B. Zurich, Ont., Oct. 12, 1940						
61-62	Det	18	5	3	8	20
62-63	Det	53	5	11	16	62
63-64	Det	58	10	18	28	87
64-65	Det	41	4	2	6	48
65-66	Tor	20	1	1	2	22
66-67	Tor	56	11	17	28	27
67-68	NYR	47	2	4	6	15
68-69	NYR	75	1	6	7	12
Totals		368	39	62	101	293
Playoff Totals		38	4	10	14	42

Season	Team	GP	G	A	Pts.	PIM
JENKINS, Dean	*6-0 190 RW*					
B. Billerica, Mass., Nov. 21, 1959						
83-84	LA	5	0	0	0	2
JENKINS, Roger	*5-11 173 D*					
B. Appleton, Wis., Nov. 18, 1911						
30-31	Tor-Chi	31	0	1	1	14
32-33	Chi	45	3	10	13	42
33-34	Chi	48	2	2	4	63
34-35	Mont	45	4	6	10	63
35-36	Bos	42	2	6	8	51
36-37	Mont-Mont M-NYA	37	1	4	5	14
37-38	Chi	39	1	8	9	26
38-39	Chi-NYA	41	2	2	4	6
Totals		328	15	39	54	279
Playoff Totals		25	1	7	8	12
JENNINGS, Grant	*6-3 200 D*					
B. Hudson Bay, Sask., May 5, 1965						
88-89	Hart	55	3	10	13	159
89-90	Hart	64	3	6	9	171
90-91	Hart-Pitt	57	2	7	9	108
91-92	Pitt	53	4	5	9	104
Totals		229	12	28	40	542
Playoff Totals		35	2	1	3	58
JENNINGS, Joseph William (Bill)	*5-9 165 RW*					
B. Toronto, Ont., June 28, 1917						
40-41	Det	12	1	5	6	2
41-42	Det	16	2	1	3	6
42-43	Det	8	3	3	6	2
43-44	Det	33	6	11	17	10
44-45	Bos	39	20	13	33	25
Totals		108	32	33	65	45
Playoff Totals		20	4	4	8	6
JENSEN, Chris	*5-11 170 RW*					
B. Fort St. John, B.C., Oct. 28, 1963						
85-86	NYR	9	1	3	4	0
86-87	NYR	37	6	7	13	21
87-88	NYR	7	0	1	1	2
89-90	Phil	1	0	0	0	0
90-91	Phil	18	2	1	3	2
91-92	Phil	2	0	0	0	0
Totals		74	9	12	21	25
JENSEN, David A.	*6-1 195 C*					
B. Newton, Mass., Aug. 19, 1965						
84-85	Hart	13	0	4	4	6
85-86	Wash	5	1	0	1	0
86-87	Wash	46	8	8	16	12
87-88	Wash	5	0	1	1	4
Totals		69	9	13	22	22
Playoff Totals		11	0	0	0	2
JENSEN, David Henry	*6-1 185 D*					
B. Minneapolis, Minn., May 3, 1961						
83-84	Minn	8	0	1	1	0
84-85	Minn	5	0	1	1	4
85-86	Minn	5	0	0	0	7
Totals		18	0	2	2	11
JENSEN, Steven Allan	*6-2 190 LW*					
B. Minneapolis, Minn., Apr. 14, 1955						
75-76	Minn	19	7	6	13	6
76-77	Minn	78	22	23	45	62
77-78	Minn	74	13	17	30	73
78-79	LA	72	23	8	31	57
79-80	LA	76	21	15	36	13
80-81	LA	74	19	19	38	88
81-82	LA	45	8	19	27	19
Totals		438	113	107	220	318
Playoff Totals		12	0	3	3	9
JEREMIAH, Edward J.	*D*					
B. Worcester, Mass., Nov. 4, 1905						
31-32	NYA-Bos	15	0	1	1	0
JERRARD, Paul	*5-10 185 RW*					
B. Winnipeg, Man., Apr. 20, 1965						
88-89	Minn	5	0	0	0	4
JERWA, Frank	*6-1 179 LW*					
B. Bankhead, Alta., Feb. 28, 1910						
31-32	Bos	29	4	5	9	14
32-33	Bos	34	3	4	7	23
33-34	Bos	7	0	0	0	2
34-35	Bos-StL E	21	4	7	11	14
Totals		91	11	16	27	53
JERWA, Joseph	*5-2 185 D*					
B. Bankhead, Alta., Jan. 22, 1909						
30-31	NYR	33	4	7	11	72
31-32	Bos	6	0	0	0	8

JERWA, Joseph *(Continued)*

Season	Team	GP	G	A	Pts.	PIM
33-34	Bos	3	0	0	0	8
35-36	NYA	48	9	12	21	65
36-37	Bos-NYA	48	9	13	22	57
37-38	NYA	47	3	14	17	53
38-39	NYA	48	4	12	16	52
Totals		233	29	58	87	315
Playoff Totals		17	2	3	5	20

JIRIK, Jaroslav *5-11 170 RW*
B. Vojnuv Mestac, Czechoslovakia, Dec. 10, 1939

Season	Team	GP	G	A	Pts.	PIM
69-70	StL	3	0	0	0	0

JOANETTE, Rosario (Kit) *5-11 168 C*
B. Valleyfield, Que., July 27, 1919

Season	Team	GP	G	A	Pts.	PIM
44-45	Mont	2	0	1	1	4

JODZIO, Richard Joseph (Rick) *6-1 190 LW*
B. Edmonton, Alta., June 3, 1954

Season	Team	GP	G	A	Pts.	PIM
74-75	Van (WHA)	44	1	3	4	159
75-76	Calg (WHA)	47	10	7	17	137
76-77	Calg (WHA)	46	4	6	10	61
77-78	Col-Clev	70	2	8	10	71
NHL Totals		70	2	8	10	71
WHA Totals		137	15	16	31	357
WHA Playoff Totals		2	0	0	0	14

JOHANNESEN, Glen *6-2 220 D*
B. Lac Laronge, Sask., Feb. 15, 1962

Season	Team	GP	G	A	Pts.	PIM
85-86	NYI	2	0	0	0	0

JOHANNSON, John *6-1 175 C*
B. Rochester, Minn., Oct. 18, 1961

Season	Team	GP	G	A	Pts.	PIM
83-84	NJ	5	0	0	0	0

JOHANSEN, Trevor Daniel *5-9 200 D*
B. Thunder Bay, Ont., Mar. 30, 1957

Season	Team	GP	G	A	Pts.	PIM
77-78	Tor	79	2	14	16	82
78-79	Tor-Col	51	2	7	9	64
79-80	Col	62	3	8	11	45
80-81	Col	35	0	7	7	18
81-82	LA-Tor	59	4	10	14	73
Totals		286	11	46	57	282
Playoff Totals		13	0	3	3	21

JOHANSSON, Bjorn *6-0 195 D*
B. Orebro, Sweden, Jan. 15, 1956

Season	Team	GP	G	A	Pts.	PIM
76-77	Clev	10	1	1	2	4
77-78	Clev	5	0	0	0	6
Totals		15	1	1	2	10

JOHANSSON, Calle *5-11 205 D*
B. Goteburg, Sweden, Feb. 14, 1967

Season	Team	GP	G	A	Pts.	PIM
87-88	Buf	71	4	38	42	37
88-89	Buf-Wash	59	3	18	21	37
89-90	Wash	70	8	31	39	25
90-91	Wash	80	11	41	52	23
91-92	Wash	80	14	42	56	49
Totals		360	40	170	210	171
Playoff Totals		44	4	21	25	16

JOHANSSON, Roger *6-1 185 D*
B. Ljungby, Sweden, Apr. 17, 1967

Season	Team	GP	G	A	Pts.	PIM
89-90	Calg	35	0	5	5	48
90-91	Calg	38	4	13	17	47
Totals		73	4	18	22	95

JOHNS, Donald Ernest *5-11 190 D*
B. Brantford, Ont., Dec. 13, 1937

Season	Team	GP	G	A	Pts.	PIM
60-61	NYR	63	1	7	8	34
62-63	NYR	6	0	4	4	6
63-64	NYR	57	1	9	10	26
64-65	NYR	22	0	1	1	4
65-66	Mont	1	0	0	0	0
67-68	Minn	4	0	0	0	6
Totals		153	2	21	23	76

JOHNSON, Allan Edmund *5-11 185 RW*
B. Winnipeg, Man., Mar. 30, 1935

Season	Team	GP	G	A	Pts.	PIM
56-57	Mont	2	0	1	1	2
60-61	Det	70	16	21	37	14
61-62	Det	31	5	6	11	14
62-63	Det	2	0	0	0	0
Totals		105	21	28	49	30
Playoff Totals		11	2	2	4	6

JOHNSON, Brian *6-1 185 RW*
B. Montreal, Que., Apr. 1, 1960

Season	Team	GP	G	A	Pts.	PIM
83-84	Det	3	0	0	0	5

JOHNSON, Daniel Douglas *5-11 170 C*
B. Winnipegosis, Man., Oct. 1, 1944

Season	Team	GP	G	A	Pts.	PIM
69-70	Tor	1	0	0	0	0
70-71	Van	66	15	11	26	16
71-72	Van-Det	54	3	8	11	8
72-73	Winn (WHA)	76	19	23	42	17
73-74	Winn (WHA)	78	16	21	37	20
74-75	Winn (WHA)	78	18	14	32	25
NHL Totals		121	18	19	37	24
WHA Totals		232	53	58	111	62
WHA Playoff Totals		18	5	1	6	5

JOHNSON, Earl O. *6-0 185 C*
B. Fort Francis, Ont., June 28, 1931

Season	Team	GP	G	A	Pts.	PIM
53-54	Det	1	0	0	0	0

JOHNSON, Ivan Wilfred (Ching) *5-11 210 D*
B. Winnipeg, Man., Dec. 7, 1897

Season	Team	GP	G	A	Pts.	PIM
26-27	NYR	27	3	2	5	66
27-28	NYR	43	10	6	16	146
28-29	NYR	9	0	0	0	14
29-30	NYR	30	3	3	6	82
30-31	NYR	44	2	6	8	77
31-32	NYR	47	3	10	13	106
32-33	NYR	48	8	9	17	127
33-34	NYR	48	2	6	8	86
34-35	NYR	26	2	3	5	34
35-36	NYR	47	5	3	8	58
36-37	NYR	34	0	0	0	2
37-38	NYA	32	0	0	0	10
Totals		435	38	48	86	808
Playoff Totals		60	5	2	7	161

JOHNSON, Jim *6-1 190 D*
B. New Hope, Minn., Aug. 9, 1962

Season	Team	GP	G	A	Pts.	PIM
85-86	Pitt	80	3	26	29	115
86-87	Pitt	80	5	25	30	116
87-88	Pitt	55	1	12	13	87
88-89	Pitt	76	2	14	16	163
89-90	Pitt	75	3	13	16	154
90-91	Pitt-Minn	68	1	14	15	123
91-92	Minn	71	4	10	14	102
Totals		505	19	114	133	860
Playoff Totals		32	1	9	10	114

JOHNSON, Mark *5-9 170 C*
B. Madison, Wisc., Sept. 22, 1957

Season	Team	GP	G	A	Pts.	PIM
79-80	Pitt	17	3	5	8	4
80-81	Pitt	73	10	23	33	50
81-82	Pitt-Minn	56	12	13	25	40
82-83	Hart	73	31	38	69	28
83-84	Hart	79	35	52	87	27
84-85	Hart-StL	66	23	34	57	23
85-86	NJ	80	21	41	62	16
86-87	NJ	68	25	26	51	22
87-88	NJ	54	14	19	33	14
88-89	NJ	40	13	25	38	24
89-90	NJ	63	16	29	45	12
Totals		669	203	305	508	260
Playoff Totals		37	16	12	28	10

JOHNSON, Norman B. *F*
B. Moose Jaw, Sask., Nov. 27, 1932

Season	Team	GP	G	A	Pts.	PIM
57-58	Bos	15	2	3	5	8
58-59	Bos-Chi	46	3	17	20	33
Totals		61	5	20	25	41
Playoff Totals		14	4	0	4	6

JOHNSON, Norman James (Jim, J.J.) *5-9 190 C*
B. Winnipeg, Man., Nov. 7, 1942

Season	Team	GP	G	A	Pts.	PIM
64-65	NYR	1	0	0	0	0
65-66	NYR	5	1	0	1	0
66-67	NYR	2	0	0	0	0
67-68	Phil	13	2	1	3	2
68-69	Phil	69	17	27	44	20
69-70	Phil	72	18	30	48	17
70-71	Phil	66	16	29	45	16
71-72	Phil-LA	74	21	24	45	18
72-73	Minn (WHA)	33	9	14	23	12
73-74	Minn (WHA)	71	15	39	54	30
74-75	Minn-Ind (WHA)	53	8	18	26	12
NHL Totals		302	75	111	186	73
WHA Totals		157	32	71	103	54
NHL Playoff Totals		7	0	2	2	2
WHA Playoff Totals		16	3	5	8	6

JOHNSON, Terrance *6-3 210 D*
B. Calgary, Alta., Nov. 28, 1958

Season	Team	GP	G	A	Pts.	PIM
79-80	Que	3	0	0	0	2

JOHNSON, Terrance *(Continued)*

Season	Team	GP	G	A	Pts.	PIM
80-81	Que	13	0	1	1	46
81-82	Que	6	0	1	1	5
82-83	Que	3	0	0	0	2
83-84	StL	65	2	6	8	143
84-85	StL	74	0	7	7	120
85-86	StL-Calg	73	1	8	9	158
86-87	Tor	48	0	1	1	104
Totals		285	3	24	27	580
Playoff Totals		38	0	4	4	118

JOHNSON, Thomas Christian *6-0 180 D*
B. Baldur, Man., Feb. 18, 1928

Season	Team	GP	G	A	Pts.	PIM
47-48	Mont	1	0	0	0	0
50-51	Mont	70	2	8	10	128
51-52	Mont	67	0	7	7	76
52-53	Mont	70	3	8	11	63
53-54	Mont	70	7	11	18	85
54-55	Mont	70	6	19	25	74
55-56	Mont	64	3	10	13	75
56-57	Mont	70	4	11	15	59
57-58	Mont	66	3	18	21	75
58-59	Mont	70	10	29	39	76
59-60	Mont	64	4	25	29	59
60-61	Mont	70	1	15	16	54
61-62	Mont	62	1	17	18	45
62-63	Mont	43	3	5	8	28
63-64	Bos	70	4	21	25	33
64-65	Bos	51	0	9	9	30
Totals		978	51	213	264	960
Playoff Totals		111	8	15	23	109

JOHNSON, Virgil *5-8 165 D*
B. Minneapolis, Minn., Mar. 4, 1912

Season	Team	GP	G	A	Pts.	PIM
37-38	Chi	25	1	0	1	2
43-44	Chi	48	1	8	9	23
44-45	Chi	2	0	1	1	2
Totals		75	2	9	11	27
Playoff Totals		19	0	3	3	4

JOHNSON, William Odd *6-0 163 C*
B. Port Aurthur, Ont., July 27, 1928

Season	Team	GP	G	A	Pts.	PIM
49-50	Tor	1	0	0	0	0

JOHNSTON, Bernard *5-11 185 C*
B. Toronto, Ont., Sept. 15, 1956

Season	Team	GP	G	A	Pts.	PIM
79-80	Hart	32	8	13	21	8
80-81	Hart	25	4	11	15	8
Totals		57	12	24	36	16
Playoff Totals		3	0	1	1	0

JOHNSTON, George Joseph (Wingy) *5-8 160 RW*
B. St. Charles, Man., July 30, 1920

Season	Team	GP	G	A	Pts.	PIM
41-42	Chi	2	2	0	2	0
42-43	Chi	30	10	7	17	0
45-46	Chi	16	5	4	9	2
46-47	Chi	10	3	1	4	0
Totals		58	20	12	32	2

JOHNSTON, Greg *6-1 205 RW*
B. Barrie, Ont., Jan. 14, 1965

Season	Team	GP	G	A	Pts.	PIM
83-84	Bos	15	2	1	3	2
84-85	Bos	6	0	0	0	0
85-86	Bos	20	0	2	2	0
86-87	Bos	76	12	15	27	79
88-89	Bos	57	11	10	21	32
89-90	Bos	9	1	1	2	6
90-91	Tor	1	0	0	0	0
91-92	Tor	3	0	1	1	5
Totals		187	26	30	56	124
Playoff Totals		22	2	1	3	12

JOHNSTON, John (Jay) *5-11 180 D*
B. Hamilton, Ont., Feb. 28, 1958

Season	Team	GP	G	A	Pts.	PIM
80-81	Wash	2	0	0	0	9
81-82	Wash	6	0	0	0	0
Totals		8	0	0	0	9

JOHNSTON, Joseph John (Joey) *5-10 180 LW*
B. Peterborough, Ont., Mar. 3, 1949

Season	Team	GP	G	A	Pts.	PIM
68-69	Minn	12	1	0	1	6
71-72	Cal	77	15	17	32	107
72-73	Cal	71	28	21	49	62
73-74	Cal	78	27	40	67	67
74-75	Cal	62	14	23	37	72
75-76	Chi	32	0	5	5	6
Totals		332	85	106	191	320

JOHNSTON, Lawrence Marshall (Marsh) *5-11 175 D*
B. Birch Hills, Sask., June 6, 1941

Season	Team	GP	G	A	Pts.	PIM
67-68	Minn	7	0	0	0	6
68-69	Minn	13	0	0	0	2
69-70	Minn	28	0	5	5	14

JOHNSTON, Lawrence Marshall (Marsh)
(Continued)

Season	Team	GP	G	A	Pts.	PIM
70-71	Minn	1	0	0	0	0
71-72	Cal	74	2	11	13	4
72-73	Cal	78	10	20	30	14
73-74	Cal	50	2	16	18	24
Totals		251	14	52	66	64
Playoff Totals		6	0	0	0	2

JOHNSTON, Lawrence Roy *5-11 195 D*
B. Kitchener, Ont., July 20, 1943

Season	Team	GP	G	A	Pts.	PIM
67-68	LA	4	0	0	0	4
71-72	Det	65	4	20	24	111
72-73	Det	73	1	12	13	169
73-74	Det	65	2	12	14	139
74-75	Mich (WHA)	49	0	9	9	93
74-75	KC	16	0	7	7	10
75-76	KC	72	2	10	12	112
76-77	Col	25	0	3	3	35
NHL Totals		320	9	64	73	580
WHA Totals		49	0	9	9	93

JOHNSTON, Randy John *6-0 190 D*
B. Brampton, Ont., June 2, 1958

Season	Team	GP	G	A	Pts.	PIM
79-80	NYI	4	0	0	0	4

JOHNSTONE, Edward Lavern
5-9 175 RW
B. Brandon, Man., Mar. 2, 1954

Season	Team	GP	G	A	Pts.	PIM
74-75	Mich (WHA)	23	4	4	8	43
75-76	NYR	10	2	1	3	4
77-78	NYR	53	13	13	26	44
78-79	NYR	30	5	3	8	27
79-80	NYR	78	14	21	35	60
80-81	NYR	80	30	38	68	100
81-82	NYR	68	30	28	58	57
82-83	NYR	52	15	21	36	27
83-84	Det	46	12	11	23	54
85-86	Det	3	1	0	1	2
86-87	Det	6	0	0	0	0
NHL Totals		426	122	136	258	375
WHA Totals		23	4	4	8	43
NHL Playoff Totals		55	13	10	23	83

JOHNSTONE, Robert Ross (Ross)
6-0 185 D
B. Montreal, Que., Apr. 7, 1926

Season	Team	GP	G	A	Pts.	PIM
43-44	Tor	18	2	0	2	6
44-45	Tor	24	3	4	7	8
Totals		42	5	4	9	14
Playoff Totals		3	0	0	0	0

JOLIAT, Aurel Emile *5-6 136 LW*
B. Ottawa, Ont., Aug. 29, 1901

Season	Team	GP	G	A	Pts.	PIM
22-23	Mont	24	13	9	22	31
23-24	Mont	24	15	5	20	19
24-25	Mont	24	29	11	40	85
25-26	Mont	35	17	9	26	52
26-27	Mont	43	14	4	18	79
27-28	Mont	44	28	11	39	105
28-29	Mont	44	12	5	17	59
29-30	Mont	42	19	12	31	40
30-31	Mont	43	13	22	35	73
31-32	Mont	48	15	24	39	46
32-33	Mont	48	18	21	39	53
33-34	Mont	48	22	15	37	27
34-35	Mont	48	17	12	29	18
35-36	Mont	48	15	8	23	16
36-37	Mont	47	17	15	32	30
37-38	Mont	44	6	7	13	24
Totals		654	270	190	460	757
Playoff Totals		54	14	19	33	89

JOLIAT, Rene (Bobby) *F*

Season	Team	GP	G	A	Pts.	PIM
24-25	Mont	1	0	0	0	0

JOLY, Gregory James *6-1 190 D*
B. Calgary, Alta., May 30, 1954

Season	Team	GP	G	A	Pts.	PIM
74-75	Wash	44	1	7	8	44
75-76	Wash	54	8	17	25	28
76-77	Det	53	1	11	12	14
77-78	Det	79	7	20	27	73
78-79	Det	20	0	4	4	6
79-80	Det	59	3	10	13	45
80-81	Det	17	0	2	2	10
81-82	Det	37	1	5	6	30
82-83	Det	2	0	0	0	0
Totals		365	21	76	97	250
Playoff Totals		5	0	0	0	8

JOLY, Yvan Rene *5-11 175 RW*
B. Hawkesbury, Ont., Feb. 6, 1960

Season	Team	GP	G	A	Pts.	PIM
80-81	Mont	1	0	0	0	0
82-83	Mont	1	0	0	0	0
Totals		2	0	0	0	0

JOLY, Yvan Rene *(Continued)*

Season	Team	GP	G	A	Pts.	PIM
Playoff Totals		10	0	0	0	0

JONATHAN, Stanley Carl *5-8 175 LW*
B. Oshweken, Ont., Sept. 5, 1955

Season	Team	GP	G	A	Pts.	PIM
75-76	Bos	1	0	0	0	0
76-77	Bos	69	17	13	30	69
77-78	Bos	68	27	25	52	116
78-79	Bos	33	6	9	15	96
79-80	Bos	79	21	19	40	208
80-81	Bos	74	14	24	38	192
81-82	Bos	67	6	17	23	57
82-83	Bos-Pitt	20	0	3	3	13
Totals		411	91	110	201	751
Playoff Totals		63	8	4	12	137

JONES, Alvin Bernard (Buck) *6-0 180 D*
B. Owen Sound, Ont., Aug. 17, 1918

Season	Team	GP	G	A	Pts.	PIM
38-39	Det	11	0	1	1	6
39-40	Det	2	0	0	0	0
41-42	Det	21	2	1	3	8
42-43	Tor	16	0	0	0	22
Totals		50	2	2	4	36
Playoff Totals		12	0	1	1	18

JONES, Brad *6-0 195 LW*
B. Sterling Heights, Mich., June 26, 1965

Season	Team	GP	G	A	Pts.	PIM
86-87	Winn	4	1	0	1	0
87-88	Winn	19	2	5	7	15
88-89	Winn	22	6	5	11	6
89-90	Winn	2	0	0	0	0
90-91	LA	53	9	11	20	57
91-92	Phil	48	7	10	17	44
Totals		148	25	31	56	122
Playoff Totals		9	1	1	2	2

JONES, James Harrison *5-9 177 C*
B. Woodbridge, Ont., Jan. 2, 1953

Season	Team	GP	G	A	Pts.	PIM
73-74	Van (WHA)	18	3	2	5	23
74-75	Van (WHA)	63	11	7	18	39
77-78	Tor	78	4	9	13	23
78-79	Tor	69	9	9	18	45
79-80	Tor	1	0	0	0	0
NHL Totals		148	13	18	31	68
WHA Totals		81	14	9	23	62
NHL Playoff Totals		19	1	5	6	11

JONES, James William *5-10 185 D*
B. Espanola, Ont., July 27, 1949

Season	Team	GP	G	A	Pts.	PIM
71-72	Cal	2	0	0	0	0
73-74	Chi (WHA)	1	0	0	0	0

JONES, Robert Charles *6-1 192 LW*
B. Espanola, Ont., Nov. 27, 1945

Season	Team	GP	G	A	Pts.	PIM
68-69	NYR	2	0	0	0	0
72-73	LA-NY (WHA)	76	13	19	32	32
73-74	NJ (WHA)	78	17	28	45	20
74-75	Balt (WHA)	5	0	1	1	8
75-76	Ind (WHA)	2	0	0	0	0
NHL Totals		2	0	0	0	0
WHA Totals		161	30	48	78	60

JONES, Ronald Perry *6-1 190 D*
B. Vermillion, Alta., Apr. 11, 1951

Season	Team	GP	G	A	Pts.	PIM
71-72	Bos	1	0	0	0	0
72-73	Bos	7	0	0	0	2
73-74	Pitt	25	0	3	3	15
74-75	Wash	19	1	1	2	16
75-76	Wash	2	0	0	0	0
Totals		54	1	4	5	33

JONSSON, Tomas *5-11 183 D*
B. Falun, Sweden, Apr. 12, 1960

Season	Team	GP	G	A	Pts.	PIM
81-82	NYI	70	9	25	34	51
82-83	NYI	72	13	35	48	50
83-84	NYI	72	11	36	47	54
84-85	NYI	69	16	34	50	58
85-86	NYI	77	14	30	44	62
86-87	NYI	47	6	25	31	36
87-88	NYI	72	6	41	47	115
88-89	NYI-Edm	73	10	33	43	56
Totals		552	85	259	344	482
Playoff Totals		80	11	26	37	97

JOSEPH, Anthony *6-4 203 RW*
B. Cornwall, Ont., Mar. 1, 1969

Season	Team	GP	G	A	Pts.	PIM
88-89	Winn	2	1	0	1	0

JOSEPH, Chris *6-2 210 D*
B. Burnaby, B.C., Sept. 10, 1969

Season	Team	GP	G	A	Pts.	PIM
87-88	Pitt-Edm	24	0	8	8	18
88-89	Edm	44	4	5	9	54
89-90	Edm	4	0	2	2	2
90-91	Edm	49	5	17	22	59
91-92	Edm	7	0	0	0	8
Totals		128	9	32	41	141

JOSEPH, Chris *(Continued)*

Season	Team	GP	G	A	Pts.	PIM
Playoff Totals		5	1	3	4	2

JOYAL, Edward Abel *6-0 180 C*
B. Edmonton, Alta., May 8, 1940

Season	Team	GP	G	A	Pts.	PIM
62-63	Det	14	2	8	10	0
63-64	Det	47	10	7	17	17
64-65	Det	46	8	14	22	4
65-66	Tor	14	0	2	2	2
67-68	LA	74	23	34	57	20
68-69	LA	73	33	19	52	24
69-70	LA	59	18	22	40	8
70-71	LA	69	20	21	41	14
71-72	LA-Phil	70	14	7	21	35
72-73	Alb (WHA)	71	22	16	38	16
73-74	Edm (WHA)	45	8	10	18	2
74-75	Edm (WHA)	78	22	25	47	2
75-76	Edm (WHA)	45	5	4	9	6
NHL Totals		466	128	134	262	124
WHA Totals		239	57	55	112	26
NHL Playoff Totals		50	11	8	19	18
WHA Playoff Totals		5	2	0	2	4

JOYCE, Robert Thomas *6-1 195 LW*
B. St. John, N.B., July 11, 1966

Season	Team	GP	G	A	Pts.	PIM
87-88	Bos	15	7	5	12	10
88-89	Bos	77	18	31	49	46
89-90	Bos-Wash	47	6	10	16	26
90-91	Wash	17	3	3	6	8
91-92	Winn	1	0	0	0	0
Totals		157	34	49	83	90
Playoff Totals		46	15	9	24	29

JUCKES, Winston Bryan (Bing)
5-10 165 LW
B. Hamiota, Man., June 14, 1926

Season	Team	GP	G	A	Pts.	PIM
47-48	NYR	2	0	0	0	0
49-50	NYR	14	2	1	3	6
Totals		16	2	1	3	6

JULIEN, Claude *6-0 198 D*
B. Blind River, Ont., Apr. 23, 1960

Season	Team	GP	G	A	Pts.	PIM
84-85	Que	1	0	0	0	0
85-86	Que	13	0	1	1	25
Totals		14	0	1	1	25

JUNEAU, Joseph *6-0 175 C*
B. Pont-Rouge, Que., Jan. 5, 1968

Season	Team	GP	G	A	Pts.	PIM
91-92	Bos	14	5	14	19	4
Playoff Totals		15	4	8	12	21

JUTILA, Timo *5-7 175 D*
B. Finland, Dec. 24, 1963

Season	Team	GP	G	A	Pts.	PIM
84-85	Buf	10	1	5	6	13

JUZDA, William (Fireman, Beast)
5-8 203 D
B. Winnipeg, Man., Oct. 29, 1920

Season	Team	GP	G	A	Pts.	PIM
40-41	NYR	5	0	0	0	2
41-42	NYR	45	4	8	12	29
45-46	NYR	32	1	3	4	17
46-47	NYR	45	3	5	8	60
47-48	NYR	60	3	9	12	70
48-49	Tor	38	1	2	3	23
49-50	Tor	62	1	14	15	23
50-51	Tor	65	0	9	9	64
51-52	Tor	46	1	4	5	65
Totals		398	14	54	68	353
Playoff Totals		42	0	3	3	46

KABEL, Robert Gerald *6-0 183 C*
B. Dauphin, Minn., Dec. 11, 1934

Season	Team	GP	G	A	Pts.	PIM
59-60	NYR	44	5	11	16	32
60-61	NYR	4	0	2	2	2
Totals		48	5	13	18	34

KACHOWSKI, Mark Edward *5-11 200 LW*
B. Edmonton, Alta., Feb. 20, 1965

Season	Team	GP	G	A	Pts.	PIM
87-88	Pitt	38	5	3	8	126
88-89	Pitt	12	1	1	2	43
89-90	Pitt	14	0	1	1	40
Totals		64	6	5	11	209

KACHUR, Edward Charles *5-8 170 RW*
B. Fort William, Ont., Apr. 22, 1934

Season	Team	GP	G	A	Pts.	PIM
56-57	Chi	34	5	7	12	21
57-58	Chi	62	5	7	12	14
Totals		96	10	14	24	35

KAESE, Trent *5-11 205 RW*
B. Nanaimo, B.C., Sept. 9, 1967

Season	Team	GP	G	A	Pts.	PIM
88-89	Buf	1	0	0	0	0

KAISER, Vernon Charles *6-0 180 LW*
B. Preston, Ont., Sept. 28, 1925

Season	Team	GP	G	A	Pts.	PIM
50-51	Mont	50	7	5	12	33
Playoff Totals		2	0	0	0	0

KALBFLEISH, Walter Morris (Jeff) *5-10 175 D*
B. New Hamburg, Ont., Dec. 18, 1911

Season	Team	GP	G	A	Pts.	PIM
33-34	Ott	22	0	4	4	20
34-35	StL E	3	0	0	0	6
35-36	NYA	4	0	0	0	2
36-37	NYA-Bos	7	0	0	0	4
Totals		36	0	4	4	32
Playoff Totals		5	0	0	0	2

KALETA, Alexander (Killer) *5-11 175 LW*
B. Canmore, Alta., Nov. 29, 1919

Season	Team	GP	G	A	Pts.	PIM
41-42	Chi	48	7	21	28	24
45-46	Chi	49	19	27	46	17
46-47	Chi	57	24	20	44	37
47-48	Chi	52	10	16	26	40
48-49	NYR	56	12	19	31	18
49-50	NYR	67	17	14	31	40
50-51	NYR	58	3	4	7	26
Totals		387	92	121	213	202
Playoff Totals		17	1	6	7	2

KALLUR, Anders *5-11 185 RW*
B. Ludvika, Sweden, July 6, 1952

Season	Team	GP	G	A	Pts.	PIM
79-80	NYI	76	22	30	52	18
80-81	NYI	78	36	28	64	32
81-82	NYI	58	18	22	40	18
82-83	NYI	55	6	8	14	33
83-84	NYI	65	9	14	23	24
84-85	NYI	51	10	8	18	26
Totals		383	101	110	211	149
Playoff Totals		78	12	23	35	32

KAMENSKY, Valeri *6-2 198 LW*
B. Voskrensk, Soviet Union, Apr. 18, 1966

Season	Team	GP	G	A	Pts.	PIM
91-92	Que	23	7	14	21	14

KAMINSKI, Kevin *5-9 170 C*
B. Churchbridge, Sask., Mar. 13, 1969

Season	Team	GP	G	A	Pts.	PIM
88-89	Minn	1	0	0	0	0
89-90	Que	1	0	0	0	0
91-92	Que	5	0	0	0	45
Totals		7	0	0	0	45

KAMINSKY, Max *5-10 160 C*
B. Niagara Falls, Ont., Apr. 19, 1913

Season	Team	GP	G	A	Pts.	PIM
33-34	Ott	38	9	17	26	14
34-35	StL E-Bos	49	12	15	27	4
35-36	Bos	37	1	2	3	20
36-37	Mont M	6	0	0	0	0
Totals		130	22	34	56	38
Playoff Totals		4	0	0	0	0

KAMPMAN, Rudolph (Bingo) *5-9 187 D*
B. Kitchener, Ont., Mar. 12, 1914

Season	Team	GP	G	A	Pts.	PIM
37-38	Tor	32	1	2	3	56
38-39	Tor	41	2	8	10	52
39-40	Tor	39	6	9	15	59
40-41	Tor	39	1	4	5	53
41-42	Tor	38	4	7	11	67
Totals		189	14	30	44	287
Playoff Totals		47	1	4	5	38

KANE, Francis Joseph (Red) *5-11 190 D*
B. Stratford, Ont., Jan. 19, 1923

Season	Team	GP	G	A	Pts.	PIM
43-44	Det	2	0	0	0	0

KANNEGIESSER, Gordon Cameron *6-0 190 D*
B. North Bay, Ont., Dec. 21, 1945

Season	Team	GP	G	A	Pts.	PIM
67-68	StL	19	0	1	1	13
71-72	StL	4	0	0	0	2
72-73	Hou (WHA)	45	0	10	10	32
73-74	Hou (WHA)	78	0	20	20	26
74-75	Ind (WHA)	4	1	4	5	4
NHL Totals		23	0	1	1	15
WHA Totals		127	1	34	35	62
WHA Playoff Totals		12	0	3	3	13

KANNEGIESSER, Sheldon Bruce *6-0 198 D*
B. North Bay, Ont., Aug. 15, 1947

Season	Team	GP	G	A	Pts.	PIM
70-71	Pitt	18	0	2	2	29
71-72	Pitt	54	2	4	6	47
72-73	Pitt-NYR	6	0	1	1	0
73-74	NYR-LA	63	4	20	24	55
74-75	LA	74	2	23	25	57
75-76	LA	70	4	9	13	36

KANNEGIESSER, Sheldon Bruce
(Continued)

Season	Team	GP	G	A	Pts.	PIM
76-77	LA	39	1	1	2	28
77-78	Van	42	1	7	8	36
Totals		366	14	67	81	288
Playoff Totals		18	0	2	2	10

KARJALAINEN, Kyosti *6-1 190 RW*
B. Gavle, Sweden, June 19, 1967

Season	Team	GP	G	A	Pts.	PIM
91-92	LA	28	1	8	9	12
Playoff Totals		3	0	1	1	2

KARLANDER, Allan David *5-8 170 C*
B. Lac la Hache, B.C., Nov. 5, 1946

Season	Team	GP	G	A	Pts.	PIM
69-70	Det	41	5	10	15	6
70-71	Det	23	1	4	5	10
71-72	Det	71	15	20	35	29
72-73	Det	77	15	22	37	25
73-74	NE (WHA)	77	20	41	61	46
74-75	NE (WHA)	48	7	14	21	2
75-76	Ind (WHA)	79	19	26	45	36
76-77	Ind (WHA)	65	17	28	45	23
NHL Totals		212	36	56	92	70
WHA Totals		269	63	109	172	107
NHL Playoff Totals		4	0	1	1	0
WHA Playoff Totals		21	3	7	10	6

KARPA, David *6-1 190 D*
B. Regina, Sask., May 7, 1971

Season	Team	GP	G	A	Pts.	PIM
91-92	Que	4	0	0	0	14

KASATONOV, Alexei *6-1 215 D*
B. Leningrad, Soviet Union, Oct. 14, 1959

Season	Team	GP	G	A	Pts.	PIM
89-90	NJ	39	6	15	21	16
90-91	NJ	78	10	31	41	76
91-92	NJ	76	12	28	40	70
Totals		193	28	74	102	162
Playoff Totals		20	2	7	9	36

KASPER, Stephen Neil *5-8 160 C*
B. Montreal, Que., Sept. 28, 1961

Season	Team	GP	G	A	Pts.	PIM
80-81	Bos	76	21	35	56	94
81-82	Bos	73	20	31	51	72
82-83	Bos	24	2	6	8	24
83-84	Bos	27	3	11	14	19
84-85	Bos	77	16	24	40	33
85-86	Bos	80	17	23	40	73
86-87	Bos	79	20	30	50	51
87-88	Bos	79	26	44	70	35
88-89	Bos-LA	78	19	31	50	63
89-90	LA	77	17	28	45	27
90-91	LA	67	9	19	28	33
91-92	Phil	16	3	2	5	10
Totals		753	173	284	457	534
Playoff Totals		94	20	28	48	82

KASTELIC, Edward *6-2 200 RW*
B. Toronto, Ont., Jan. 29, 1964

Season	Team	GP	G	A	Pts.	PIM
85-86	Wash	15	0	0	0	73
86-87	Wash	23	1	1	2	83
87-88	Wash	35	1	0	1	78
88-89	Hart	10	0	2	2	15
89-90	Hart	67	6	2	8	198
90-91	Hart	45	2	2	4	211
91-92	Hart	25	1	3	4	61
Totals		220	11	10	21	719
Playoff Totals		8	1	0	1	32

KASZYCKI, Michael *5-9 190 C*
B. Milton, Ont., Feb. 27, 1956

Season	Team	GP	G	A	Pts.	PIM
77-78	NYI	58	13	29	42	24
78-79	NYI	71	16	18	34	37
79-80	NYI-Wash-Tor	69	12	18	30	35
80-81	Tor	6	0	2	2	2
82-83	Tor	22	1	13	14	10
Totals		226	42	80	122	108
Playoff Totals		19	2	6	8	10

KEA, Adrian Joseph (Ed) *6-3 200 D*
B. Weesp, Holland, Jan. 19, 1948

Season	Team	GP	G	A	Pts.	PIM
73-74	Atl	3	0	2	2	0
74-75	Atl	50	1	9	10	39
75-76	Atl	78	8	19	27	101
76-77	Atl	72	4	21	25	63
77-78	Atl	60	3	23	26	40
78-79	Atl	53	6	18	24	40
79-80	StL	69	3	16	19	79
80-81	StL	74	3	18	21	60
81-82	StL	78	2	14	16	62
82-83	StL	46	0	5	5	24
Totals		583	30	145	175	508
Playoff Totals		32	2	4	6	39

KEANE, Mike *5-10 178 RW*
B. Winnipeg, Man., May 29, 1967

Season	Team	GP	G	A	Pts.	PIM
88-89	Mont	69	16	19	35	69
89-90	Mont	74	9	15	24	78
90-91	Mont	73	13	23	36	50
91-92	Mont	67	11	30	41	64
Totals		283	49	87	136	261
Playoff Totals		52	8	7	15	47

KEANS, Douglas Frederick *5-7 174*
B. Pembroke, Ont., Jan. 7, 1958

Season	Team	GP	G	A	Pts.	PIM
79-80	LA	0	0	0	0	0
Playoff Totals		1	0	0	0	0

KEARNES, Dennis McAleer *5-9 185 D*
B. Kingston, Ont., Sept. 27, 1945

Season	Team	GP	G	A	Pts.	PIM
71-72	Van	73	3	26	29	59
72-73	Van	72	4	33	37	51
73-74	Van	52	4	13	17	30
74-75	Van	49	1	11	12	31
75-76	Van	80	5	46	51	48
76-77	Van	80	5	55	60	60
77-78	Van	80	4	43	47	27
78-79	Van	78	3	31	34	28
79-80	Van	67	1	18	19	24
80-81	Van	46	1	14	15	28
Totals		677	31	290	321	386
Playoff Totals		11	1	2	3	8

KEATING, John R. (Jack) *F*
B. St. John, N.B.

Season	Team	GP	G	A	Pts.	PIM
31-32	NYA	22	5	3	8	6
32-33	NYA	13	0	2	2	11
Totals		35	5	5	10	17

KEATING, John Thomas (Red) *6-0 180 LW*
B. Kitchener, Ont., Oct. 9, 1916

Season	Team	GP	G	A	Pts.	PIM
38-39	Det	1	0	1	1	2
39-40	Det	10	2	0	2	2
Totals		11	2	1	3	4

KEATING, Michael Joseph *6-0 185 LW*
B. Toronto, Ont., Jan. 21, 1957

Season	Team	GP	G	A	Pts.	PIM
77-78	NYR	1	0	0	0	0

KEATS, Gordon Blanchard (Duke) *C*
B. Montreal, Que., Mar. 1, 1895

Season	Team	GP	G	A	Pts.	PIM
26-27	Det	40	16	8	24	52
27-28	Det-Chi	37	14	10	24	61
28-29	Chi	3	0	1	1	0
Totals		80	30	19	49	113

KECZMER, Dan *6-1 190 D*
B. Mt. Clemens, Mich., May 25, 1968

Season	Team	GP	G	A	Pts.	PIM
90-91	Minn	9	0	1	1	6
91-92	Hart	1	0	0	0	0
Totals		10	0	1	1	6

KEELING, Melville Sidney (Butch) *6-0 180 LW*
B. Owen Sound, Ont., Aug. 10, 1905

Season	Team	GP	G	A	Pts.	PIM
26-27	Tor	30	11	2	13	29
27-28	Tor	43	10	6	16	52
28-29	NYR	43	6	3	9	35
29-30	NYR	44	19	7	26	34
30-31	NYR	44	13	9	22	35
31-32	NYR	48	17	3	20	38
32-33	NYR	47	8	6	14	22
33-34	NYR	48	15	5	20	20
34-35	NYR	47	15	4	19	14
35-36	NYR	47	13	5	18	22
36-37	NYR	48	22	4	26	18
37-38	NYR	39	8	9	17	12
Totals		528	157	63	220	331
Playoff Totals		47	11	11	22	32

KEENAN, Lawrence Christopher *5-10 177 LW*
B. North Bay, Ont., Oct. 1, 1940

Season	Team	GP	G	A	Pts.	PIM
61-62	Tor	2	0	0	0	0
67-68	StL	40	12	8	20	4
68-69	StL	47	5	9	14	6
69-70	StL	56	10	23	33	8
70-71	StL-Buf	60	8	23	31	6
71-72	Buf-Phil	29	3	1	4	4
Totals		234	38	64	102	28
Playoff Totals		47	15	16	31	12

KEHOE, Rick Thomas *5-11 180 RW*
B. Windsor, Ont., July 15, 1951

Season	Team	GP	G	A	Pts.	PIM
71-72	Tor	38	8	8	16	4
72-73	Tor	77	33	42	75	20
73-74	Tor	69	18	22	40	8
74-75	Pitt	76	32	31	63	22
75-76	Pitt	71	29	47	76	6

Season	Team	GP	G	A	Pts.	PIM
KEHOE, Rick Thomas *(Continued)*						
76-77	Pitt	80	30	27	57	10
77-78	Pitt	70	29	21	50	10
78-79	Pitt	57	27	18	45	2
79-80	Pitt	79	30	30	60	4
80-81	Pitt	80	55	33	88	6
81-82	Pitt	71	33	52	85	8
82-83	Pitt	75	29	36	65	12
83-84	Pitt	57	18	27	45	8
84-85	Pitt	6	0	2	2	0
Totals		906	371	396	767	120
Playoff Totals		39	4	17	21	4
KEKALAINEN, Jarmo 6-0 190 LW						
B. Tampere, Finland, July 3, 1966						
89-90	Bos	11	2	2	4	8
90-91	Bos	16	2	1	3	6
Totals		27	4	3	7	14
KELLER, Ralph 5-9 175 D						
B. Wilkie, Sask., Feb. 6, 1936						
62-63	NYR	3	1	0	1	6
KELLGREN, Christer 6-0 173 RW						
B. Goteborg, Sweden, Aug. 15, 1958						
81-82	Col	5	0	0	0	0
KELLY, David Leslie 6-2 205 RW						
B. Chatham, Ont., Sept. 20, 1952						
76-77	Det	16	2	0	2	4
KELLY, John Paul 6-1 215 LW						
B. Edmonton, Alta., Nov. 15, 1959						
79-80	LA	40	2	5	7	28
80-81	LA	19	3	6	9	8
81-82	LA	70	12	11	23	100
82-83	LA	65	16	15	31	52
83-84	LA	72	7	14	21	73
84-85	LA	73	8	10	18	55
85-86	LA	61	6	9	15	50
Totals		400	54	70	124	366
Playoff Totals		18	1	1	2	41
KELLY, John Robert (Battleship) 6-2 195 LW						
B. Fort William, Ont., June 6, 1946						
73-74	StL-Pitt	67	16	18	34	123
74-75	Pitt	69	27	24	51	120
75-76	Pitt	77	25	30	55	149
76-77	Pitt	74	10	21	31	115
77-78	Chi	75	7	11	18	95
78-79	Chi	63	2	5	7	85
Totals		425	87	109	196	687
Playoff Totals		23	6	3	9	40
KELLY, Leonard Patrick (Red) 6-0 195 C						
B. Simcoe, Ont., July 9, 1927						
47-48	Det	60	6	14	20	13
48-49	Det	59	5	11	16	10
49-50	Det	70	15	25	40	9
50-51	Det	70	17	37	54	24
51-52	Det	67	16	31	47	16
52-53	Det	70	19	27	46	8
53-54	Det	62	16	33	49	18
54-55	Det	70	15	30	45	28
55-56	Det	70	16	34	50	39
56-57	Det	70	10	25	35	18
57-58	Det	61	13	18	31	26
58-59	Det	67	8	13	21	34
59-60	Det-Tor	68	12	17	29	18
60-61	Tor	64	20	50	70	12
61-62	Tor	58	22	27	49	6
62-63	Tor	66	20	40	60	8
63-64	Tor	70	11	34	45	16
64-65	Tor	70	18	28	46	8
65-66	Tor	63	8	24	32	12
66-67	Tor	61	14	24	38	4
Totals		1316	281	542	823	327
Playoff Totals		164	33	59	92	51
KELLY Peter Cameron 5-10 170 RW						
B. St. Vital, Man., May 22, 1913						
34-35	StL E	25	3	10	13	14
35-36	Det	48	6	8	14	30
36-37	Det	48	5	4	9	12
37-38	Det	9	0	1	1	2
38-39	Det	32	4	9	13	4
40-41	NYA	10	3	5	8	2
41-42	Brk	8	0	1	1	4
Totals		180	21	38	59	68
Playoff Totals		19	3	1	4	8
KELLY, Regis J. (Pep) 5-6 152 F						
B. North Bay, Ont., Jan. 9, 1914						
34-35	Tor	47	11	8	19	14
35 36	Tor	42	11	8	19	24
36-37	Tor-Chi	45	15	4	19	8

Season	Team	GP	G	A	Pts.	PIM
KELLY, Regis J. (Pep) *(Continued)*						
37-38	Tor	43	9	10	19	25
38-39	Tor	48	11	11	22	12
39-40	Tor	34	11	9	20	15
40-41	Chi	22	5	3	8	7
41-42	Brk	8	1	0	1	0
Totals		289	74	53	127	105
Playoff Totals		39	7	6	13	10
KELLY, Robert James (Hound) 5-10 200 LW						
B. Oakville, Ont., Nov. 25, 1950						
70-71	Phil	76	14	18	32	70
71-72	Phil	78	14	15	29	157
72-73	Phil	77	10	11	21	238
73-74	Phil	65	4	10	14	130
74-75	Phil	67	11	18	29	99
75-76	Phil	79	12	8	20	125
76-77	Phil	73	22	24	46	117
77-78	Phil	74	19	13	32	95
78-79	Phil	77	7	31	38	132
79-80	Phil	75	15	20	35	122
80-81	Wash	80	26	36	62	157
81-82	Wash	16	0	4	4	12
Totals		837	154	208	362	1454
Playoff Totals		101	9	14	23	172
KEMP, Kevin Glen 6-0 188 D						
B. Ottawa, Ont., May 3, 1954						
80-81	Hart	3	0	0	0	4
KEMP, Stanley 5-9 165 D						
B. Hamilton, Ont., Mar. 2, 1924						
48-49	Tor	1	0	0	0	2
KENDALL, William 5-8 168 F						
B. Winnipeg, Man., Apr. 1, 1910						
33-34	Chi	20	3	0	3	0
34-35	Chi	47	6	4	10	16
35-36	Chi	23	2	1	3	0
36-37	Chi-Tor	32	5	4	9	10
37-38	Chi	10	0	1	1	2
Totals		132	16	10	26	28
Playoff Totals		0	0	0	0	0
KENNEDY, Edward (Dean) 6-2 205 D						
B. Redver, Sask., Jan. 18, 1963						
82-83	LA	55	0	12	12	97
83-84	LA	37	1	5	6	50
85-86	LA	78	2	10	12	132
86-87	LA	66	6	14	20	91
87-88	LA	58	1	11	12	158
88-89	NYR-LA	67	3	11	14	103
89-90	Buf	80	2	12	14	53
90-91	Buf	64	4	8	12	119
91-92	Winn	18	2	4	6	21
Totals		523	21	87	108	824
Playoff Totals		30	1	7	8	57
KENNEDY, Forbes Taylor 5-8 185 C						
B. Dorchester, N.B., Aug. 18, 1935						
56-57	Chi	69	8	13	21	102
57-58	Det	70	11	16	27	135
58-59	Det	67	1	4	5	49
59-60	Det	17	1	2	3	8
61-62	Det	14	1	0	1	8
62-63	Bos	49	12	18	30	46
63-64	Bos	70	8	17	25	95
64-65	Bos	52	6	4	10	41
65-66	Bos	50	4	6	10	55
67-68	Phil	73	10	18	28	130
68-69	Phil-Tor	72	8	10	18	219
Totals		603	70	108	178	888
Playoff Totals		12	2	4	6	64
KENNEDY, Sheldon 5-11 170 RW						
B. Brandon, Man., June 15, 1969						
89-90	Det	20	2	7	9	10
90-91	Det	7	1	0	1	12
91-92	Det	27	3	8	11	24
Totals		54	6	15	21	46
KENNEDY, Theodore (Teeder) 5-11 180 C						
B. Humberstone, Ont., Dec. 12, 1925						
42-43	Tor	2	0	1	1	0
43-44	Tor	49	26	23	49	2
44-45	Tor	49	29	25	54	14
45-46	Tor	21	3	2	5	4
46-47	Tor	60	28	32	60	27
47-48	Tor	60	25	21	46	32
48-49	Tor	59	18	21	39	25
49-50	Tor	53	20	24	44	34
50-51	Tor	63	18	43	61	32
51-52	Tor	70	19	33	52	33
52-53	Tor	43	14	23	37	42
53-54	Tor	67	15	23	38	78

Season	Team	GP	G	A	Pts.	PIM
KENNEDY, Theodore (Teeder)						
(Continued)						
54-55	Tor	70	10	42	52	74
56-57	Tor	30	6	16	22	35
Totals		696	231	329	560	432
Playoff Totals		78	29	31	60	32
KENNY, William Ernest (Eddie) 6-2 195 D						
B. Vermillion, Alta., Aug. 20, 1907						
30-31	NYR	6	0	0	0	0
34-35	Chi	5	0	0	0	18
Totals		11	0	0	0	18
KEON, David Michael 5-9 167 C						
B. Noranda, Que., Mar. 22, 1940						
60-61	Tor	70	20	25	45	6
61-62	Tor	64	26	35	61	2
62-63	Tor	68	28	28	56	2
63-64	Tor	70	23	37	60	6
64-65	Tor	65	21	29	50	10
65-66	Tor	69	24	30	54	4
66-67	Tor	66	19	33	52	2
67-68	Tor	67	11	37	48	4
68-69	Tor	75	27	34	61	12
69-70	Tor	72	32	30	62	6
70-71	Tor	76	38	38	76	4
71-72	Tor	72	18	30	48	4
72-73	Tor	76	37	36	73	2
73-74	Tor	74	25	28	53	7
74-75	Tor	78	16	43	59	4
75-76	Minn-Ind (WHA)	69	29	45	74	6
76-77	Minn-NE (WHA)	76	27	63	90	10
77-78	NE (WHA)	77	24	38	62	2
78-79	NE (WHA)	79	22	43	65	2
79-80	Hart	76	10	52	62	10
80-81	Hart	80	13	34	47	26
81-82	Hart	78	8	11	19	6
NHL Totals		1296	396	590	986	117
WHA Totals		301	102	189	291	20
NHL Playoff Totals		92	32	36	68	6
WHA Playoff Totals		36	13	23	36	8
KERR, Alan 5-11 195 RW						
B. Hazelton, B.C., Mar. 28, 1964						
84-85	NYI	19	3	1	4	24
85-86	NYI	7	0	1	1	16
86-87	NYI	72	7	10	17	175
87-88	NYI	80	24	34	58	198
88-89	NYI	71	20	18	38	144
89-90	NYI	75	15	21	36	129
90-91	NYI	2	0	0	0	5
91-92	Det	58	3	8	11	133
Totals		384	72	93	165	824
Playoff Totals		38	5	4	9	70
KERR, Reginald John (Reg) 5-10 180 LW/C						
B. Oxbow, Sask., Oct. 16, 1957						
77-78	Clev-Chi	9	0	4	4	7
78-79	Chi	73	16	24	40	50
79-80	Chi	49	9	8	17	17
80-81	Chi	70	30	30	60	56
81-82	Chi	59	11	28	39	39
83-84	Edm	3	0	0	0	0
Totals		263	66	94	160	169
Playoff Totals		7	1	0	1	7
KERR, Tim 6-3 225 C						
B. Windsor, Ont., Jan. 5, 1960						
80-81	Phil	68	22	23	45	84
81-82	Phil	61	21	30	51	138
82-83	Phil	24	11	8	19	6
83-84	Phil	79	54	39	93	29
84-85	Phil	74	54	44	98	57
85-86	Phil	76	58	26	84	79
86-87	Phil	75	58	37	95	57
87-88	Phil	8	3	2	5	12
88-89	Phil	69	48	40	88	73
89-90	Phil	40	24	24	48	34
90-91	Phil	27	10	14	24	8
91-92	NYR	32	7	11	18	12
Totals		633	370	298	668	589
Playoff Totals		81	40	31	71	58
KESSELL, Richard John (Rick) 5-10 175 C						
B. Toronto, Ont., July 27, 1949						
69-70	Pitt	8	1	2	3	2
70-71	Pitt	6	0	2	2	2
71-72	Pitt	3	0	1	1	0
72-73	Pitt	67	1	13	14	0
73-74	Cal	51	2	6	8	4
Totals		135	4	24	28	8

Season	Team	GP	G	A	Pts.	PIM
KETOLA, Veli-Pekka	6-3 220 C					
B. Pori, Finland, Mar. 28, 1948						
74-75	Winn (WHA)	74	23	28	51	25
75-76	Winn (WHA)	80	32	36	68	32
76-77	Winn-Calg (WHA)	81	29	35	64	61
81-82	Col	44	9	5	14	4
NHL Totals		44	9	5	14	4
WHA Totals		235	84	99	183	118
WHA Playoff Totals		13	7	5	12	2
KETTER, Kerry Kenneth	6-1 202 D					
B. Prince George, B.C., Sept. 20, 1947						
72-73	Atl	41	0	2	2	58
75-76	Edm (WHA)	48	1	9	10	20
NHL Totals		41	0	2	2	58
WHA Totals		48	1	9	10	20
KHARIN, Sergei	5-11 180 RW					
B. Odintsovo, Soviet Union, Feb. 20, 1963						
90-91	Winn	7	2	3	5	2
KHRISTICH, Dmitri	6-1 187 LW/C					
B. Kiev, Soviet Union, July 23, 1969						
90-91	Wash	40	13	14	27	21
91-92	Wash	80	36	37	73	35
Totals		120	49	51	100	56
Playoff Totals		18	4	5	9	21
KIDD, Ian	5-11 195 D					
B. Gresham, Ore., May 11, 1964						
87-88	Van	19	4	7	11	25
88-89	Van	1	0	0	0	0
Totals		20	4	7	11	25
KIESSLING, Udo	5-10 180 D					
B. Crimmitschau, Germany, May 21, 1955						
81-82	Minn	1	0	0	0	2
KILREA, Brian Blair	5-11 182 C					
B. Ottawa, Ont., Oct. 21, 1934						
57-58	Det	1	0	0	0	0
67-68	LA	25	3	5	8	12
Totals		26	3	5	8	12
KILREA, Hector J. (Hec)	5-7 175 LW					
B. Blackburn, Ont., June 11, 1907						
25-26	Ott	35	5	0	5	12
26-27	Ott	42	11	7	18	48
27-28	Ott	43	19	4	23	66
28-29	Ott	38	5	7	12	36
29-30	Ott	44	36	22	58	72
30-31	Ott	44	14	8	22	44
31-32	Det	47	13	3	16	28
32-33	Ott	47	14	8	22	26
33-34	Tor	43	10	13	23	15
34-35	Tor	46	11	13	24	16
35-36	Det	48	6	17	23	37
36-37	Det	48	6	9	15	20
37-38	Det	48	9	9	18	10
38-39	Det	48	8	9	17	8
39-40	Det	12	0	0	0	0
Totals		633	167	129	296	438
Playoff Totals		48	8	7	15	18
KILREA, Kenneth Armstrong	6-0 170 LW					
D. Ottawa, Ont., Jan. 16, 1919						
38-39	Det	1	0	0	0	0
39-40	Det	40	10	8	18	4
40-41	Det	12	2	0	2	0
41-42	Det	21	3	12	15	4
43-44	Det	14	1	3	4	0
Totals		88	16	23	39	8
Playoff Totals		10	2	2	4	4
KILREA, Walter Charles (Wally)	5-7 150 F					
B. Ottawa, Ont., Feb. 18, 1909						
29-30	Ott	42	4	2	6	4
30-31	Phil Q	44	8	12	20	22
31-32	NYA	48	3	8	11	18
32-33	Ott-Mont M	38	5	12	17	16
33-34	Mont M	44	3	1	4	7
34-35	Det	2	0	0	0	0
35-36	Det	44	4	10	14	10
36-37	Det	48	8	13	21	6
37-38	Det	5	0	0	0	4
Totals		315	35	58	93	87
Playoff Totals		25	2	4	6	6

Season	Team	GP	G	A	Pts.	PIM
KIMBLE, Darin	6-2 205 RW					
B. Lucky Lake, Sask., Nov. 22, 1968						
88-89	Que	26	3	1	4	154
89-90	Que	44	5	5	10	185
90-91	Que-StL	61	3	6	9	242
91-92	StL	46	1	3	4	166
Totals		177	12	15	27	747
Playoff Totals		18	0	0	0	45
KINDRACHUK, Orest	5-10 175 C					
B. Nanton, Alta., Sept. 14, 1950						
72-73	Phil	2	0	0	0	0
73-74	Phil	71	11	30	41	85
74-75	Phil	60	10	21	31	72
75-76	Phil	76	26	49	75	101
76-77	Phil	78	15	36	51	79
77-78	Phil	73	17	45	62	128
78-79	Pitt	79	18	42	60	84
79-80	Pitt	52	17	29	46	63
80-81	Pitt	13	3	9	12	34
81-82	Wash	4	1	0	1	2
Totals		508	118	261	379	648
Playoff Totals		76	20	40	60	53
KING, Derek	6-1 203 LW					
B. Hamilton, Ont., Feb. 11, 1967						
86-87	NYI	2	0	0	0	0
87-88	NYI	55	12	24	36	30
88-89	NYI	60	14	29	43	14
89-90	NYI	46	13	27	40	20
90-91	NYI	66	19	26	45	44
91-92	NYI	80	40	38	78	46
Totals		309	98	144	242	154
Playoff Totals		9	0	2	2	6
KING, Frank Edward	5-11 185 C					
B. Toronto, Ont., Mar. 7, 1929						
50-51	Mont	10	1	0	1	2
KING, Kris	5-11 210 LW					
B. Bracebridge, Ont., Feb. 18, 1966						
87-88	Det	3	1	0	1	2
88-89	Det	55	2	3	5	168
89-90	NYR	68	6	7	13	286
90-91	NYR	72	11	14	25	154
91-92	NYR	79	10	9	19	224
Totals		277	30	33	63	834
Playoff Totals		31	6	2	8	90
KING, Wayne Gordon	5-10 185 C					
B. Midland, Ont., Sept. 4, 1951						
73-74	Cal	2	0	0	0	0
74-75	Cal	25	4	7	11	8
75-76	Cal	46	1	11	12	26
Totals		73	5	18	23	34
KINSELLA, Brian Edward	5-11 180 C					
B. Barrie, Ont., Feb. 11, 1954						
75-76	Wash	4	0	1	1	0
76-77	Wash	6	0	0	0	0
Totals		10	0	1	1	0
KINSELLA, Thomas Raymond (Ray)	F					
B. Ottawa, Ont., Jan. 27, 1911						
30-31	Ott	14	0	0	0	0
KIRK, Robert Hunter	5-9 180 RW					
B. Belfast, Ireland, Aug. 8, 1910						
37-38	NYR	39	4	8	12	14
KIRKPATRICK, Robert Drynan	5-10 165 C					
B. Regina, Sask., Dec. 1, 1915						
42-43	NYR	49	12	12	24	6
KIRTON, Mark Robert	5-10 170 C					
B. Regina, Sask., Feb. 3, 1958						
79-80	Tor	2	1	0	1	2
80-81	Tor-Det	61	18	13	31	24
81-82	Det	74	14	28	42	62
82-83	Det-Van	41	5	7	12	10
83-84	Van	26	2	3	5	2
84-85	Van	62	17	5	22	21
Totals		266	57	56	113	121
Playoff Totals		4	1	2	3	7
KISIO, Kelly W.	5-9 170 C					
B. Peace River, Alta. Sept. 18, 1959						
82-83	Det	15	4	3	7	0
83-84	Det	70	23	37	60	34
84-85	Det	75	20	41	61	56
85-86	Det	76	21	48	69	85
86-87	NYR	70	24	40	64	73
87-88	NYR	77	23	55	78	88
88-89	NYR	70	26	36	62	91
89-90	NYR	68	22	44	66	105

Season	Team	GP	G	A	Pts.	PIM
KISIO, Kelly W. (Continued)						
90-91	NYR	51	15	20	35	58
91-92	SJ	48	11	26	37	54
Totals		620	189	350	539	644
Playoff Totals		25	3	11	14	25
KITCHEN, Chapman Hobie (Hobie)	D					
B. Toronto. Ont.						
25-26	Mont M	30	5	2	7	16
26-27	Det	17	0	2	2	42
Totals		47	5	4	9	58
KITCHEN, Michael Elwin	5-10 180 D					
B. Newmarket, Ont., Feb. 1, 1956						
76-77	Col	60	1	8	9	36
77-78	Col	61	2	17	19	45
78-79	Col	53	1	4	5	28
79-80	Col	42	1	6	7	25
80-81	Col	75	1	7	8	100
81-82	Col	63	1	8	9	60
82-83	NJ	77	4	8	12	52
83-84	NJ	43	1	4	5	24
Totals		474	12	62	74	370
Playoff Totals		2	0	0	0	2
KITCHEN, William	6-1 200 D					
B. Schomburg, Ont., Oct. 2, 1960						
81-82	Mont	1	0	0	0	7
82-83	Mont	8	0	0	0	4
83-84	Mont	3	0	0	0	2
84-85	Tor	29	1	4	5	27
Totals		41	1	4	5	40
Playoff Totals		3	0	1	1	0
KLATT, Trent	6-1 208 C					
B. Robbinsdale, Minn., Jan. 30, 1971						
91-92	Minn	1	0	0	0	0
Playoff Totals		6	0	0	0	2
KLEIN, James Lloyd (Dede)	6-0 185 LW					
B. Saskatoon, Sask., Jan. 13, 1910						
28-29	Bos	14	1	0	1	5
31-32	Bos	6	1	0	1	0
32-33	NYA	15	2	2	4	4
33-34	NYA	48	13	9	22	34
34-35	NYA	30	7	3	10	9
35-36	NYA	42	4	8	12	14
36-37	NYA	11	2	1	3	2
37-38	NYA	3	0	1	1	0
Totals		169	30	24	54	68
Playoff Totals		5	0	0	0	2
KLEMM, Jon	6-3 200 D					
B. Cranbrook, B.C., Jan. 8, 1970						
91-92	Que	4	0	1	1	0
KLIMA, Petr	6-0 190 LW					
B. Chomutov, Czechoslovakia, Dec. 23, 1964						
85-86	Det	74	32	24	56	16
86-87	Det	77	30	23	53	42
87-88	Det	78	37	25	62	46
88-89	Det	51	25	16	41	44
89-90	Det-Edm	76	30	33	63	72
90-91	Edm	70	40	28	68	113
91-92	Edm	57	21	13	34	52
Totals		483	215	162	377	385
Playoff Totals		85	26	24	50	65
KLINGBELL, Ernest (Ike)	F					
36-37	Chi	5	1	2	3	2
KLUKAY, Joseph Francis (Duke of Paducah)	6-0 175 LW					
B. Sault Ste. Marie, Ont., Nov. 6, 1922						
46-47	Tor	55	9	20	29	12
47-48	Tor	59	15	15	30	28
48-49	Tor	45	11	10	21	11
49-50	Tor	70	15	16	31	11
50-51	Tor	70	14	16	30	16
51-52	Tor	43	4	8	12	6
52-53	Bos	70	13	16	29	20
53-54	Bos	70	20	17	37	27
54-55	Bos-Tor	66	8	8	16	48
55-56	Tor	18	0	1	1	2
Totals		566	109	127	236	181
Playoff Totals		71	13	10	23	23
KLUZAK, Gordon	6-4 215 D					
B. Climax, Sask., Mar. 4, 1964						
82-83	Bos	70	1	6	7	105
83-84	Bos	80	10	27	37	135
85-86	Bos	70	8	31	39	155
87-88	Bos	66	6	31	37	135
88-89	Bos	3	0	1	1	2

Season	Team	GP	G	A	Pts.	PIM
KLUZAK, Gordon *(Continued)*						
89-90	Bos	8	0	2	2	11
90-91	Bos	2	0	0	0	0
Totals		299	25	98	123	543
Playoff Totals		46	6	13	19	129
KNIBBS, William Arthur	6-1 180 C					
B. Toronto, Ont., Jan. 24, 1942						
64-65	Bos	53	7	10	17	4
KNOTT, William Earl (Nick)	6-1 200 D					
B. Kingston, Ont., July 23, 1920						
41-42	Brk	14	3	1	4	9
KNOX, Paul William (Bill)	RW					
54-55	Tor	1	0	0	0	0
KOCUR, Joe	6-0 195 RW					
B. Calgary, Alta., Dec. 21, 1964						
84-85	Det	17	1	0	1	64
85-86	Det	59	9	6	15	377
86-87	Det	77	9	9	18	276
87-88	Det	63	7	7	14	263
88-89	Det	60	9	9	18	213
89-90	Det	71	16	20	36	268
90-91	Det-NYR	57	5	4	9	289
91-92	NYR	51	7	4	11	121
Totals		455	63	59	122	1871
Playoff Totals		50	4	8	12	154
KOLSTAD, Dean	6-6 210 D					
B. Edmonton, Alta., June 16, 1968						
88-89	Minn	25	1	5	6	42
90-91	Minn	5	0	0	0	15
Totals		30	1	5	6	57
KOMADOSKI, Neil George	6-0 200 D					
B. Winnipeg, Man., Nov. 5, 1951						
72-73	LA	62	1	8	9	67
73-74	LA	68	2	4	6	43
74-75	LA	75	4	12	16	69
75-76	LA	80	3	15	18	165
76-77	LA	68	3	9	12	109
77-78	LA-StL	58	2	14	16	97
78-79	StL	42	1	2	3	30
79-80	StL	49	0	12	12	52
Totals		502	16	76	92	632
Playoff Totals		23	0	2	2	47
KONIK, George Samuel	5-10 200 LW					
B. Flin Flon, Man., May 4, 1938						
67-68	Pitt	52	7	8	15	26
72-73	Minn (WHA)	54	4	12	16	34
KONOWALCHUK, Steve	6-0 175 C					
B. Salt Lake City, Utah, Nov. 11, 1972						
91-92	Wash	1	0	0	0	0
KONROYD, Stephen Mark	6-1 195 D					
B. Scarborough, Ont., Feb. 10, 1961						
80-81	Calg	4	0	0	0	4
81-82	Calg	63	3	14	17	78
82-83	Calg	79	4	13	17	73
83-84	Calg	80	1	13	14	94
84-85	Calg	64	3	23	26	73
85-86	Calg-NYI	73	7	25	32	80
86-87	NYI	72	5	16	21	70
87-88	NYI	62	2	15	17	99
88-89	NYI-Chi	78	6	12	18	42
89-90	Chi	75	3	14	17	34
90-91	Chi	70	0	12	12	40
91-92	Chi-Hart	82	4	24	28	97
Totals		802	38	181	219	784
Playoff Totals		96	10	15	25	99
KONSTANTINOV, Vladimir	5-11 176 D					
B. Murmansk, Soviet Union, Mar. 19, 1967						
91-92	Det	79	8	25	33	172
Playoff Totals		11	0	1	1	16
KONTOS, Christopher	6-1 195 LW/C					
B. Toronto, Ont., Dec. 10, 1963						
82-83	NYR	44	8	7	15	33
83-84	NYR	6	0	1	1	8
84-85	NYR	28	4	8	12	24
86-87	Pitt	31	8	9	17	6
87-88	Pitt-LA	42	3	17	20	14
88-89	LA	7	2	1	3	2
89-90	LA	6	2	2	4	4
Totals		164	27	45	72	91
Playoff Totals		20	11	0	11	12
KOPAK, Russell	5-10 158 C					
B. Edmonton, Alta., Apr. 26, 1924						
43-44	Bos	24	7	9	16	0

Season	Team	GP	G	A	Pts.	PIM
KORDIC, Dan	6-5 220 D					
B. Edmonton, Alta., Apr. 18, 1971						
91-92	Phil	46	1	3	4	126
KORDIC, John	6-2 210 RW					
B. Edmonton, Alta., Mar. 22, 1965						
85-86	Mont	5	0	1	1	12
86-87	Mont	44	5	3	8	151
87-88	Mont	60	2	6	8	159
88-89	Mont-Tor	52	1	2	3	198
89-90	Tor	55	9	4	13	252
90-91	Tor-Wash	10	0	0	0	110
91-92	Que	19	0	2	2	115
Totals		245	17	18	35	997
Playoff Totals		41	4	3	7	131
KORNEY, Michael Wayne	6-3 195 RW					
B. Dauphin, Man., Sept. 15, 1953						
73-74	Det	2	0	0	0	0
74-75	Det	30	8	2	10	18
75-76	Det	27	1	7	8	23
78-79	NYR	18	0	1	1	18
Totals		77	9	10	19	59
KOROLL, Clifford Eugene	6-0 195 RW					
B. Canora, Sask., Oct. 1, 1946						
69-70	Chi	73	18	19	37	44
70-71	Chi	72	16	34	50	85
71-72	Chi	76	22	23	45	51
72-73	Chi	77	33	24	57	38
73-74	Chi	78	21	25	46	32
74-75	Chi	80	27	32	59	27
75-76	Chi	80	25	33	58	29
76-77	Chi	80	15	26	41	8
77-78	Chi	73	16	15	31	19
78-79	Chi	78	12	19	31	20
79-80	Chi	47	3	4	7	6
Totals		814	208	254	462	359
Playoff Totals		85	19	29	48	67
KOTANEN, Elno Richard (Dick)	5-11 190 D					
B. Strathmore, Alta., Nov. 18, 1925						
48-49	Det	1	0	1	1	0
50-51	NYR	1	0	0	0	0
Totals		2	0	1	1	0
KOWAL, Joseph Douglas	6-5 212 LW					
B. Toronto, Ont., Feb. 3, 1956						
76-77	Buf	16	0	5	5	6
77-78	Buf	6	0	0	0	7
Totals		22	0	5	5	13
Playoff Totals		2	0	0	0	0
KOZAK, Donald	5-9 184 RW					
B. Saskatoon, Sask., Feb. 2, 1952						
72-73	LA	72	14	6	20	104
73-74	LA	76	21	14	35	54
74-75	LA	77	16	15	31	64
75-76	LA	62	20	24	44	94
76-77	LA	79	15	17	32	89
77-78	LA	43	8	5	13	45
78-79	Van	28	2	5	7	30
Totals		437	96	86	182	480
Playoff Totals		29	7	2	9	69
KOZAK, Leslie Paul	6-0 185 F					
B. Yorkton, Sask., Oct. 28, 1940						
61-62	Tor	12	1	0	1	2
KOZLOV, Viacheslav	5-10 172 C					
B. Voskresensk, Soviet Union, May 3, 1972						
91-92	Det	7	0	2	2	2
KRAFTCHECK, Stephen	5-10 185 D					
B. Tinturn, Ont., Mar. 3, 1929						
50-51	Bos	22	0	0	0	8
51-52	NYR	58	8	9	17	30
52-53	NYR	69	2	9	11	45
58-59	Tor	8	1	0	1	0
Totals		157	11	18	29	83
Playoff Totals		6	0	0	0	7
KRAKE, Philip Gordon (Skip)	5-11 170 C					
B. North Battleford, Sask., Oct. 14, 1943						
63-64	Bos	2	0	0	0	0
65-66	Bos	2	0	0	0	0
66-67	Bos	15	6	2	8	4
67-68	Bos	68	5	7	12	13
68-69	LA	30	3	9	12	11
69-70	LA	58	5	17	22	86
70-71	Buf	74	4	5	9	68
72-73	Clev (WHA)	26	9	10	19	61
73-74	Clev (WHA)	69	20	36	56	94
74-75	Clev (WHA)	71	15	23	38	108

Season	Team	GP	G	A	Pts.	PIM
KRAKE, Philip Gordon (Skip) *(Continued)*						
75-76	Edm (WHA)	41	8	8	16	55
NHL Totals		249	23	40	63	182
WHA Totals		207	52	77	129	318
NHL Playoff Totals		10	1	0	1	17
WHA Playoff Totals		19	2	4	6	66
KRAVCHUK, Igor	6-1 200 D					
B. Ufa, Soviet Union, Sept. 13, 1966						
91-92	Chi	18	1	8	9	4
Playoff Totals		18	2	6	8	8
KRAVETS, Mikhail	5-10 176 LW					
B. Leningrad, Soviet Union, Nov. 11, 1963						
91-92	SJ	1	0	0	0	0
KRENTZ, Dale	5-11 190 LW					
B. Steinbach, Man., Dec. 19, 1961						
86-87	Det	8	0	0	0	0
87-88	Det	6	2	0	2	5
88-89	Det	16	3	3	6	4
Totals		30	5	3	8	9
Playoff Totals		2	0	0	0	0
KROL, Joseph	5-11 173 LW					
B. Winnipeg, Man., Aug. 13, 1915						
36-37	NYR	1	0	0	0	0
38-39	NYR	1	1	1	2	0
41-42	Brk	24	9	3	12	8
Totals		26	10	4	14	8
KROMM, Richard Gordon (Rich)	5-11 180 LW					
B. Trail, B.C., Mar. 29, 1964						
83-84	Calg	53	11	12	23	27
84-85	Calg	73	20	32	52	32
85-86	Calg-NYI	77	19	24	43	35
86-87	NYI	70	12	17	29	20
87-88	NYI	71	5	10	15	20
88-89	NYI	20	1	6	7	4
90-91	NYI	6	1	0	1	0
91-92	NYI	1	0	0	0	0
Totals		371	69	101	170	138
Playoff Totals		36	2	6	8	22
KRON, Robert	5-10 174 LW					
B. Brno, Czechoslovakia, Feb. 27, 1967						
90-91	Van	76	12	20	32	21
91-92	Van	36	2	2	4	2
Totals		112	14	22	36	23
Playoff Totals		11	1	2	3	2
KROOK, Kevin Bradley	5-11 187 D					
B. Cold Lake, Alta., Apr. 5, 1958						
78-79	Col	3	0	0	0	2
KRULICKI, James John	5-11 180 LW					
B. Kitchener, Ont., Mar. 9, 1948						
70-71	NYR-Det	41	0	3	3	6
KRUPP, Uwe	6-6 235 D					
B. Cologne, W. Germany, June 24, 1965						
86-87	Buf	26	1	4	5	23
87-88	Buf	75	2	9	11	151
88-89	Buf	70	5	13	18	55
89-90	Buf	74	3	20	23	85
90-91	Buf	74	12	32	44	66
91-92	Buf-NYI	67	8	29	37	49
Totals		386	31	107	138	429
Playoff Totals		23	1	2	3	29
KRUPPKE, Gord	6-1 200 D					
B. Slave Lake, Alta., Apr. 2, 1969						
90-91	Det	4	0	0	0	0
KRUSE, Paul	6-0 202 LW					
B. Merritt, B.C., Mar. 15, 1970						
90-91	Calg	1	0	0	0	7
91-92	Calg	16	3	1	4	65
Totals		17	3	1	4	72
KRUSHELNYSKI, Michael	6-2 200 LW/C					
B. Montreal, Que., Apr. 27, 1960						
81-82	Bos	17	3	3	6	2
82-83	Bos	79	23	42	65	43
83-84	Bos	66	25	20	45	55
84-85	Edm	80	43	45	88	60
85-86	Edm	54	16	24	40	22
86-87	Edm	80	16	35	51	67
87-88	Edm	76	20	27	47	64
88-89	LA	78	26	36	62	110
89-90	LA	63	16	25	41	50

Season Team	GP	G	A	Pts.	PIM
KRUSHELNYSKI, Michael *(Continued)*					
90-91 LA-Tor	74	18	27	45	58
91-92 Tor	72	9	15	24	72
Totals	739	215	299	514	603
Playoff Totals	109	26	36	62	98
KRYGIER, Todd *5-11 180 LW*					
D. Northville, Mich., Oct. 12, 1966					
89-90 Hart	58	18	12	30	52
90-91 Hart	72	13	17	30	95
91-92 Wash	67	13	17	30	107
Totals	197	44	46	90	254
Playoff Totals	18	4	4	8	8
KRYSKOW, David Roy *5-10 175 LW*					
B. Edmonton, Alta., Dec. 25, 1951					
72-73 Chi	11	1	0	1	0
73-74 Chi	72	7	12	19	22
74-75 Wash-Det	69	10	19	29	87
75-76 Atl	79	15	25	40	65
76-77 Calg (WHA)	45	16	17	33	47
77-78 Winn (WHA)	71	20	21	41	16
NHL Totals	231	33	56	89	174
WHA Totals	116	36	38	74	63
NHL Playoff Totals	12	2	0	2	4
WHA Playoff Totals	9	4	4	8	2
KRYZANOWSKI, Edward Lloyd *5-10 178 D*					
B. Fort Francis, Ont., Nov. 14, 1925					
48-49 Bos	36	1	3	4	10
49-50 Bos	59	6	10	16	12
50-51 Bos	69	3	6	9	10
51-52 Bos	70	5	3	8	33
52-53 Chi	5	0	0	0	0
Totals	239	15	22	37	65
Playoff Totals	18	0	1	1	4
KUCERA, Frantisek *6-2 205 D*					
B. Prague, Czechoslovakia, Feb. 3, 1968					
90-91 Chi	40	2	12	14	32
91-92 Chi	61	3	10	13	36
Totals	101	5	22	27	68
Playoff Totals	6	0	0	0	0
KUDELSKI, Bob *6-1 200 RW*					
B. Springfield, Mass., Mar. 3, 1964					
87-88 LA	26	0	1	1	8
88-89 LA	14	1	3	4	17
89-90 LA	62	22	13	36	49
90-91 LA	72	22	13	36	46
91-92 LA	80	22	21	43	42
Totals	254	69	51	120	162
Playoff Totals	22	4	4	8	4
KUHN, Gordon (Doggie) *F*					
B. Truro, N.S.					
32-33 NYA	12	1	1	2	4
KUKULOWICZ, Adolph Frank (Aggie) *6-2 175 C*					
B. Winnipeg, Man., Apr. 2, 1933					
52-53 NYR	3	1	0	1	0
53-54 NYR	1	0	0	0	0
Totals	4	1	0	1	0
KULAK, Stuart *5-10 180 RW*					
B. Edmonton, Alta., Mar. 10, 1963					
82-83 Van	4	1	1	2	0
86-87 Van-Edm-NYR	54	4	2	6	78
87-88 Que	14	1	1	2	28
88-89 Winn	18	2	0	2	24
Totals	90	8	4	12	130
Playoff Totals	3	0	0	0	2
KULLMAN, Arnold Edwin *5-6 175 C*					
B. Winnipeg, Man., Oct. 9, 1927					
47-48 Bos	1	0	0	0	0
49-50 Bos	12	0	1	1	11
Totals	13	0	1	1	11
KULLMAN, Edward George *5-7 170 RW*					
B. Winnipeg, Man., Dec. 12, 1923					
47-48 NYR	51	15	17	32	32
48-49 NYR	18	4	5	9	14
50-51 NYR	70	14	18	32	88
51-52 NYR	64	11	10	21	59
52-53 NYR	70	8	10	18	61
53-54 NYR	70	4	10	14	44
Totals	343	56	70	126	298
Playoff Totals	6	1	0	1	2
KUMPEL, Mark *6-0 190 RW*					
B. Wakefield, Mass., Mar. 7, 1961					
84-85 Que	42	8	7	15	26
85-86 Que	47	10	12	22	17
86-87 Que-Det	45	1	9	10	16
87-88 Det-Winn	45	4	6	10	23
89-90 Winn	56	8	9	17	21
90-91 Winn	53	7	3	10	10
Totals	288	38	46	84	113
Playoff Totals	39	6	4	10	14
KUNTZ, Alan Robert *5-11 165 LW*					
B. Toronto, Ont., June 4, 1919					
41-42 NYR	31	10	11	21	10
45-46 NYR	14	0	1	1	2
Totals	45	10	12	22	12
Playoff Totals	6	1	0	1	2
KUNTZ, Murray Robert *5-10 180 LW*					
B. Ottawa, Ont., Dec. 19, 1945					
74-75 StL	7	1	2	3	0
KURRI, Jari *6-1 195 RW*					
B. Helsinki, Finland, May 18, 1960					
80-81 Edm	75	32	43	75	40
81-82 Edm	71	32	54	86	32
82-83 Edm	80	45	59	104	22
83-84 Edm	64	52	61	113	14
84-85 Edm	73	71	64	135	30
85-86 Edm	78	68	63	131	22
86-87 Edm	79	54	54	108	41
87-88 Edm	80	43	53	96	30
88-89 Edm	76	44	58	102	69
89-90 Edm	78	33	60	93	48
91-92 LA	73	23	37	60	24
Totals	827	497	606	1103	372
Playoff Totals	150	93	112	205	105
KURTENBACH, Orland John *6-2 195 C*					
B. Cudworth, Sask., Sept. 7, 1936					
60-61 NYR	10	0	6	6	2
61-62 Bos	8	0	0	0	6
63-64 Bos	70	12	25	37	91
64-65 Bos	64	6	20	26	86
65-66 Tor	70	9	6	15	54
66-67 NYR	60	11	25	36	58
67-68 NYR	73	15	20	35	82
68-69 NYR	2	0	0	0	2
69-70 NYR	53	4	10	14	47
70-71 Van	52	21	32	53	84
71-72 Van	78	24	37	61	48
72-73 Van	47	9	19	28	38
73-74 Van	52	8	13	21	30
Totals	639	119	213	332	628
Playoff Totals	19	2	4	6	70
KURVERS, Tom *6-2 195 D*					
B. Minneapolis, Minn., Sept. 14, 1962					
84-85 Mont	75	10	35	45	30
85-86 Mont	62	7	23	30	36
86-87 Mont-Buf	56	6	17	23	22
87-88 NJ	56	5	29	34	46
88-89 NJ	74	16	50	66	38
89-90 NJ-Tor	71	15	37	52	29
90-91 Tor-Van	51	4	26	30	28
91-92 NYI	74	9	47	56	30
Totals	519	72	264	336	259
Playoff Totals	42	8	20	28	60
KURYLUK, Mervin *5-11 185 LW*					
B. Yorkton, Sask., Aug. 10, 1937					
61-62 Chi	0	0	0	0	0
Playoff Totals	2	0	0	0	0
KUSHNER, Dale *6-1 195 LW*					
B. Terrace, B.C., June 13, 1966					
89-90 NYI	2	0	0	0	2
90-91 Phil	63	7	11	18	195
91-92 Phil	19	3	2	5	18
Totals	84	10	13	23	215
KUZYK, Kenneth Michael *6-1 195 RW*					
B. Toronto, Ont., Aug. 11, 1953					
76-77 Clev	13	0	5	5	2
77-78 Clev	28	5	4	9	6
Totals	41	5	9	14	8
KWONG, Lawrence (King) *5-6 150 RW*					
B. Vernon, B.C., June 17, 1923					
47-48 NYR	1	0	0	0	0
KYLE, Walter Lawrence (Gus) *6-1 202 D*					
B. Dysart, Sask., Sept. 11, 1923					
49-50 NYR	70	3	5	8	143
KYLE, Walter Lawrence (Gus) *(Continued)*					
50-51 NYR	64	2	3	5	92
51-52 Bos	69	1	12	13	127
Totals	203	6	20	26	362
Playoff Totals	14	1	2	3	34
KYLE, William Miller *6-1 175 C*					
B. Dysart, Sask., Dec. 23, 1924					
49-50 NYR	2	0	0	0	0
50-51 NYR	1	0	3	3	0
Totals	3	0	3	3	0
KYLLONEN, Markku *5-11 187 LW*					
B. Joensuu, Finland, Feb. 15, 1962					
88-89 Winn	9	0	2	2	2
KYPREOS, Nicholas *6-0 195 LW*					
B. Toronto, Ont., June 4, 1966					
89-90 Wash	31	5	4	9	82
90-91 Wash	79	9	9	18	196
91-92 Wash	65	4	6	10	206
Totals	175	18	19	37	484
Playoff Totals	16	1	1	2	53
KYTE, James (Jim) *6-5 210 D*					
B. Ottawa, Ont., Mar. 21, 1964					
82-83 Winn	2	0	0	0	0
83-84 Winn	58	1	2	3	55
84-85 Winn	71	0	3	3	111
85-86 Winn	71	1	3	4	126
86-87 Winn	72	5	5	10	162
87-88 Winn	51	1	3	4	128
88-89 Winn	74	3	9	12	190
89-90 Pitt	56	3	1	4	125
90-91 Pitt-Calg	43	0	9	9	155
91-92 Calg	21	0	1	1	107
Totals	519	14	36	50	1159
Playoff Totals	31	0	0	0	80
LABADIE, Joseph Michel (Mike) *5-11 170 RW*					
B. St. Francis Assisi, Que., Aug. 17, 1932					
52-53 NYR	3	0	0	0	0
LABATTE, Neil Joseph Henry *6-2 178 D*					
B. Toronto, Ont., Apr. 24, 1957					
78-79 StL	22	0	2	2	13
81-82 StL	4	0	0	0	6
Totals	26	0	2	2	19
L'ABBE, Maurice Joseph (Moe) *5-9 170 RW*					
B. Montreal, Que., Aug. 12, 1947					
72-73 Chi	5	0	1	1	0
LABINE, Leo Gerald *5-10 178 RW*					
B. Haileybury, Ont., July 22, 1931					
51-52 Bos	15	2	4	6	9
52-53 Bos	51	8	15	23	69
53-54 Bos	68	16	19	35	57
54-55 Bos	67	24	18	42	75
55-56 Bos	68	16	18	34	104
56-57 Bos	67	18	29	47	128
57-58 Bos	62	7	14	21	60
58-59 Bos	70	9	23	32	74
59-60 Bos	63	16	28	44	58
60-61 Bos-Det	64	9	21	30	66
61-62 Det	48	3	4	7	30
Totals	643	128	193	321	730
Playoff Totals	60	11	12	23	82
LABOSSIERRE, Gordon William *6-1 180 C*					
B. St. Boniface, Man., Jan. 2, 1940					
63-64 NYR	15	0	0	0	12
64-65 NYR	1	0	0	0	0
67-68 LA	68	13	27	40	31
68-69 LA	48	10	18	28	12
70-71 LA-Minn	74	19	14	33	20
71-72 Minn	9	2	3	5	0
72-73 Hou (WHA)	77	36	60	96	56
73-74 Hou (WHA)	67	19	36	55	30
74-75 Hou (WHA)	76	23	34	57	40
75-76 Hou (WHA)	80	24	32	56	18
NHL Totals	215	44	62	106	75
WHA Totals	300	102	162	264	144
NHL Playoff Totals	10	2	3	5	28
WHA Playoff Totals	50	16	28	44	44
LABOVITCH, Maxwell *5-10 165 RW*					
B. Winnipeg, Man., Jan. 18, 1924					
43-44 NYR	5	0	0	0	4

Season	Team	GP	G	A	Pts.	PIM
LABRAATEN, Daniel	*6-0 190 LW*					
B. Leksland, Sweden, June 9, 1951						
76-77	Winn(WHA)	64	24	27	51	21
77-78	Winn(WHA)	47	18	16	34	30
78-79	Det	78	19	19	38	8
79-80	Det	76	30	27	57	8
80-81	Det-Calg	71	12	15	27	25
81-82	Calg	43	10	12	22	6
NHL Totals		268	71	73	144	47
WHA Totals		111	42	43	85	51
NHL Playoff Totals		5	1	0	1	4
WHA Playoff Totals		24	8	18	26	23
LABRE, Yvon Jules	*5-10 190 D*					
B. Sudbury, Ont., Nov. 29, 1949						
70-71	Pitt	21	1	1	2	19
73-74	Pitt	16	1	2	3	13
74-75	Wash	76	4	23	27	182
75-76	Wash	80	2	20	22	146
76-77	Wash	62	3	11	14	169
77-78	Wash	22	0	8	8	41
78-79	Wash	51	1	13	14	80
79-80	Wash	18	0	5	5	38
80-81	Wash	25	2	4	6	100
Totals		371	14	87	101	788
LABRIE, Guy	*6-0 185 D*					
B. St. Charles Bellechase, Que., Aug. 11, 1920						
43-44	Bos	15	2	7	9	2
44-45	NYR	27	2	2	4	14
Totals		42	4	9	13	16
LACH, Elmer James	*5-10 170 C*					
B. Nokomis, Sask., Jan. 22, 1918						
40-41	Mont	43	7	14	21	16
41-42	Mont	1	0	1	1	0
42-43	Mont	45	18	40	58	14
43-44	Mont	48	24	48	72	23
44-45	Mont	50	26	54	80	37
45-46	Mont	50	13	34	47	34
46-47	Mont	31	14	16	30	22
47-48	Mont	60	30	31	61	72
48-49	Mont	36	11	18	29	59
49-50	Mont	64	15	33	48	33
50-51	Mont	65	21	24	45	45
51-52	Mont	70	15	50	65	36
52-53	Mont	53	16	25	41	56
53-54	Mont	48	5	20	25	28
Totals		664	215	406	623	475
Playoff Totals		76	19	45	64	36
LACHANCE, Earl	*F*					
26-27	Mont	1	0	0	0	0
LACHANCE, Michel	*6-0 190 D*					
B. Quebec City, Que., Apr. 11, 1955						
78-79	Col	21	0	4	4	22
LACHANCE, Scott	*6-1 197 D*					
B. Charlottesville, Va., Oct. 22, 1972						
91-92	NYI	17	1	4	5	9
LACOMBE, Francois	*5-10 175 D*					
B. Lachine, Que., Feb. 24, 1948						
68-69	Oak	72	2	16	18	50
69-70	Oak	2	0	0	0	0
70-71	Buf	1	0	1	1	2
72-73	Que (WHA)	61	10	18	28	123
73-74	Que (WHA)	71	9	26	35	41
74-75	Que (WHA)	55	7	17	24	54
75-76	Calg (WHA)	71	3	28	31	62
76-77	Que (WHA)	81	5	22	27	86
77-78	Que (WHA)	22	1	7	8	12
78-79	Que (WHA)	78	3	21	24	44
79-80	Que	3	0	0	0	2
NHL Totals		78	2	17	19	54
WHA Totals		439	38	139	177	422
NHL Playoff Totals		3	1	0	1	0
WHA Playoff Totals		54	5	10	15	36
LACOMBE, Normand	*6-0 210 RW*					
B. Pierrefonds, Que., Oct. 18, 1964						
84-85	Buf	30	2	4	6	25
85-86	Buf	25	6	7	13	13
86-87	Buf-Edm	40	4	7	11	10
87-88	Edm	53	8	9	17	36
88-89	Edm	64	17	11	28	57
89-90	Edm-Phil	33	5	4	9	28
90-91	Phil	74	11	20	31	27
Totals		319	53	62	115	196
Playoff Totals		26	5	1	6	49
LACROIX, Andre Joseph	*5-8 175 C*					
B. Lauzon, Que., June 5, 1945						
67-68	Phil	18	6	8	14	6
LACROIX, Andre Joseph *(Continued)*						
68-69	Phil	75	24	32	56	4
69-70	Phil	74	22	36	58	14
70-71	Phil	78	20	22	42	12
71-72	Chi	51	4	7	11	6
72-73	Phil (WHA)	78	50	74	124	83
73-74	NY-NJ (WHA)	78	31	80	111	54
74-75	SD (WHA)	78	41	106	147	63
75-76	SD (WHA)	80	29	72	101	42
76-77	SD (WHA)	81	32	82	114	79
77-78	Hou (WHA)	78	36	77	113	57
78-79	NE (WHA)	78	32	56	88	34
79-80	Hart	29	3	14	17	2
NHL Totals		325	79	119	198	44
WHA Totals		551	251	547	798	412
NHL Playoff Totals		16	2	5	7	0
WHA Playoff Totals		48	14	29	43	30
LACROIX, Pierre	*5-11 185 D*					
B. Quebec City, Que., Apr. 11, 1959						
79-80	Que	76	9	21	30	45
80-81	Que	61	5	34	39	54
81-82	Que	68	4	23	27	74
82-83	Que-Hart	69	6	30	36	24
Totals		274	24	108	132	197
Playoff Totals		8	0	2	2	10
LADOUCEUR, Randy	*6-2 220 D*					
B. Brockville, Ont., June 30, 1960						
82-83	Det	27	0	4	4	16
83-84	Det	71	3	17	20	58
84-85	Det	80	3	27	30	108
85-86	Det	78	5	13	18	196
86-87	Det-Hart	70	5	9	14	121
87-88	Hart	67	1	7	8	91
88-89	Hart	75	2	5	7	95
89-90	Hart	71	3	12	15	126
90-91	Hart	67	1	3	4	118
91-92	Hart	74	1	9	10	127
Totals		680	24	106	130	1056
Playoff Totals		40	5	8	13	159
LAFLEUR, Guy Damien	*6-0 185 RW*					
B. Thurso, Que., Sept. 20, 1951						
71-72	Mont	73	29	35	64	48
72-73	Mont	69	28	27	55	51
73-74	Mont	73	21	35	56	29
74-75	Mont	70	53	66	119	37
75-76	Mont	80	56	69	125	36
76-77	Mont	80	56	80	136	20
77-78	Mont	78	60	72	132	26
78-79	Mont	80	52	77	129	28
79-80	Mont	74	50	75	125	12
80-81	Mont	51	27	43	70	29
81-82	Mont	66	27	57	84	24
82-83	Mont	68	27	49	76	12
83-84	Mont	80	30	40	70	19
84-85	Mont	19	2	3	5	10
88-89	NYR	67	18	27	45	12
89-90	Que	39	12	22	34	4
90-91	Que	59	12	16	28	2
Totals		1126	560	793	1353	399
Playoff Totals		128	58	76	134	67
LAFLEUR, Rene	*F*					
24-25	Mont	1	0	0	0	0
LaFONTAINE, Pat	*5-9 170 C*					
B. St. Louis, Mo., Feb. 22, 1965						
83-84	NYI	15	13	6	19	6
84-85	NYI	67	19	35	54	32
85-86	NYI	65	30	23	53	43
86-87	NYI	80	38	32	70	70
87-88	NYI	75	47	45	92	52
88-89	NYI	79	45	43	88	26
89-90	NYI	74	54	51	105	38
90-91	NYI	75	41	44	85	42
91-92	Buf	57	46	47	93	98
Totals		587	333	326	659	407
Playoff Totals		57	22	24	46	34
LAFORCE, Ernest	*D*					
B. Montreal, Que., June 23, 1916						
42-43	Mont	1	0	0	0	0
LaFOREST, Robert	*5-10 195 RW*					
B. Sault Ste. Marie, Ont., May 19, 1963						
83-84	LA	5	1	0	1	2
LAFORGE, Claude Roger	*5-9 172 LW*					
B. Sorel, Que., July 1, 1936						
57-58	Mont	4	0	0	0	0
58-59	Det	57	2	5	7	18
60-61	Det	10	1	0	1	2
61-62	Det	38	10	9	19	20
63-64	Det	17	2	3	5	4
64-65	Det	1	0	0	0	0
LAFORGE, Claude Roger *(Continued)*						
67-68	Phil	63	9	16	25	36
68-69	Phil	2	0	0	0	0
Totals		192	24	33	57	82
Playoff Totals		5	1	2	3	15
LAFORGE, Marc	*6-3 210 LW*					
B. Sudbury, Ont., Jan. 3, 1968						
89-90	Hart	9	0	0	0	43
LAFRAMBOISE, Peter Alfred	*6-2 185 C*					
B. Ottawa, Ont., Jan. 18, 1950						
71-72	Cal	5	0	0	0	0
72-73	Cal	77	16	25	41	26
73-74	Cal	65	7	7	14	14
74-75	Wash-Pitt	80	10	23	33	30
76-77	Edm (WHA)	17	0	5	5	12
NHL Totals		227	33	55	88	70
WHA Totals		17	0	5	5	12
NHL Playoff Totals		9	1	0	1	0
LAFRANCE, Adelard (Adie)	*F*					
B. Chapleau, Ont., Jan. 13, 1912						
33-34	Mont	3	0	0	0	2
Playoff Totals		2	0	0	0	0
LAFRANCE, Leo	*F*					
26-27	Mont	4	0	0	0	0
27-28	Mont-Chi	29	2	0	2	6
Totals		33	2	0	2	6
LAFRENIERE, Jason	*5-11 185 C*					
B. St. Catharines, Ont., Dec. 6, 1966						
86-87	Que	56	13	15	28	8
87-88	Que	40	10	19	29	4
88-89	NYR	38	8	16	24	6
Totals		134	31	50	81	18
Playoff Totals		15	1	5	6	19
LAFRENIERE, Roger Joseph	*6-0 190 LW*					
B. Montreal, Que., July 24, 1942						
62-63	Det	3	0	0	0	4
72-73	StL	10	0	0	0	0
Totals		13	0	0	0	4
LAGACE, Jean-Guy	*5-10 185 D*					
B. L'Abord a Plouffe, Que., Feb. 5, 1945						
68-69	Pitt	13	0	1	1	14
70-71	Buf	3	0	0	0	2
72-73	Pitt	31	1	5	6	32
73-74	Pitt	31	2	6	8	34
74-75	Pitt-KC	40	3	17	20	61
75-76	KC	69	3	10	13	108
Totals		187	9	39	48	251
LAGACE, Michel	*F*					
68-69	Pitt	17	0	1	1	14
LAIDLAW, Thomas	*6-1 205 D*					
B. Brampton, Ont., Apr. 15, 1958						
80-81	NYR	80	6	23	29	100
81-82	NYR	79	3	18	21	104
82-83	NYR	80	0	10	10	75
83-84	NYR	79	3	15	18	62
84-85	NYR	61	1	11	12	52
85-86	NYR	68	6	12	18	103
86-87	NYR-LA	74	1	13	14	69
87-88	LA	57	1	12	13	47
88-89	LA	70	3	17	20	63
89-90	LA	57	1	8	9	42
Totals		705	25	139	164	717
Playoff Totals		69	4	17	21	78
LAIRD, Robbie	*5-9 165 LW*					
B. Regina, Sask., Dec. 29, 1954						
79-80	Minn	1	0	0	0	0
LAJEUNESSE, Serge	*5-10 185 RW*					
B. Montreal, Que., June 11, 1950						
70-71	Det	62	1	3	4	55
71-72	Det	7	0	0	0	20
72-73	Det	28	0	1	1	26
73-74	Phil	1	0	0	0	0
74-75	Phil	5	0	0	0	2
Totals		103	1	4	5	103
Playoff Totals		7	1	2	3	4
LALANDE, Hector	*5-9 157 C*					
B. North Bay, Ont., Nov. 24, 1934						
53-54	Chi	2	0	0	0	2
55-56	Chi	65	8	18	26	70
56-57	Chi	50	11	17	28	38
57-58	Chl-Det	34	2	4	6	12
Totals		151	21	39	60	122

LALONDE, Edouard C. (Newsy) *C*
B. Cornwall, Ont., Oct. 31, 1887

Season	Team	GP	G	A	Pts.	PIM
17-18	Mont	14	23	0	23	16
18-19	Mont	17	23	9	32	40
19-20	Mont	23	36	6	42	33
20-21	Mont	24	33	8	41	36
21-22	Mont	20	9	4	13	11
26-27	NYA	1	0	0	0	2
Totals		99	124	27	151	138
Playoff Totals		12	22	1	23	19

LALONDE, Robert Patrick *5-5 155 C*
B. Montreal, Que., Mar. 27, 1951

Season	Team	GP	G	A	Pts.	PIM
71-72	Van	27	1	5	6	2
72-73	Van	77	20	27	47	32
73-74	Van	36	3	4	7	18
74-75	Van	74	17	30	47	48
75-76	Van	71	14	36	50	46
76-77	Van	68	17	15	32	39
77-78	Atl	73	14	23	37	28
78-79	Atl	78	24	32	56	24
79-80	Atl-Bos	74	10	26	36	30
80-81	Bos	62	4	12	16	31
81-82	Calg	1	0	0	0	0
Totals		641	124	210	334	298
Playoff Totals		16	4	2	6	6

LALONDE, Ronald Leo *5-10 170 C*
B. Toronto, Ont., Oct. 30, 1952

Season	Team	GP	G	A	Pts.	PIM
72-73	Pitt	9	0	0	0	2
73-74	Pitt	73	10	17	27	14
74-75	Pitt-Wash	74	12	17	29	27
75-76	Wash	80	9	19	28	19
76-77	Wash	76	12	17	29	24
77-78	Wash	67	1	5	6	16
78-79	Wash	18	1	3	4	4
Totals		397	45	78	123	106

LALOR, Mike *6-0 200 D*
B. Buffalo, N.Y., Mar. 8, 1963

Season	Team	GP	G	A	Pts.	PIM
85-86	Mont	62	3	5	8	56
86-87	Mont	57	0	10	10	47
87-88	Mont	66	1	10	11	113
88-89	Mont-StL	48	2	18	20	69
89-90	StL	78	0	16	16	81
90-91	Wash	68	1	5	6	61
91-92	Wash-Winn	79	7	10	17	78
Totals		458	14	74	88	505
Playoff Totals		80	5	8	13	155

LAMB, Joseph Gordon *5-9 170 RW*
B. Sussex, N.B., June 18, 1906

Season	Team	GP	G	A	Pts.	PIM
27-28	Mont M	21	8	5	13	39
28-29	Mont M-Ott	35	4	1	5	52
29-30	Ott	44	29	20	49	119
30-31	Ott	44	11	14	25	91
31-32	NYA	48	14	11	25	71
32-33	Bos	42	11	8	19	68
33-34	Bos	48	10	15	25	47
34-35	Mont-StLE	38	14	14	28	23
35-36	Mont M	35	0	3	3	12
36-37	NYA	48	3	9	12	53
37-38	NYA-Det	41	4	1	5	26
Totals		444	108	101	209	601
Playoff Totals		18	1	1	2	51

LAMB, Mark *5-9 180 C*
B. Ponteix, Sask., Aug. 3, 1964

Season	Team	GP	G	A	Pts.	PIM
85-86	Calg	1	0	0	0	0
86-87	Det	22	2	1	3	8
87-88	Edm	2	0	0	0	0
88-89	Edm	20	2	8	10	14
89-90	Edm	58	12	16	28	42
90-91	Edm	37	4	8	12	25
91-92	Edm	59	6	22	28	46
Totals		199	26	55	81	135
Playoff Totals		70	7	19	26	51

LAMBERT, Dan *5-8 177 D*
B. St. Boniface, Man., Jan. 12, 1970

Season	Team	GP	G	A	Pts.	PIM
90-91	Que	1	0	0	0	0
91-92	Que	28	6	9	15	22
Totals		29	6	9	15	22

LAMBERT, Lane *6-0 185 RW*
B. Melfort, Sask., Nov. 18, 1964

Season	Team	GP	G	A	Pts.	PIM
83-84	Det	73	20	15	35	115
84-85	Det	69	14	11	25	104
85-86	Det	34	2	3	5	130
86-87	NYR-Que	33	7	7	14	51
87-88	Que	61	13	28	41	98
88-89	Que	13	2	2	4	23
Totals		283	58	66	124	521
Playoff Totals		17	2	4	6	40

LAMBERT, Yvon Pierre *6-0 195 LW*
B. Drummondville, Que., May 20, 1950

Season	Team	GP	G	A	Pts.	PIM
72-73	Mont	1	0	0	0	0
73-74	Mont	60	6	10	16	42
74-75	Mont	80	32	35	67	74
75-76	Mont	80	32	35	67	28
76-77	Mont	79	24	28	52	50
77-78	Mont	77	18	22	40	20
78-79	Mont	79	26	40	66	26
79-80	Mont	77	21	32	53	23
80-81	Mont	73	22	32	54	39
81-82	Buf	77	25	39	64	38
Totals		683	206	273	479	340
Playoff Totals		90	27	22	49	67

LAMBY, Richard A. (Dick) *6-1 200 D*
B. Auburn, Mass., May 3, 1955

Season	Team	GP	G	A	Pts.	PIM
78-79	StL	9	0	4	4	12
79-80	StL	12	0	1	1	10
80-81	StL	1	0	0	0	0
Totals		22	0	5	5	22

LAMIRANDE, Jean-Paul *5-8 170 D*
B. Shawinigan Falls, Que., Aug. 21, 1923

Season	Team	GP	G	A	Pts.	PIM
46-47	NYR	14	1	1	2	14
47-48	NYR	18	0	1	1	6
49-50	NYR	16	4	3	7	6
54-55	Mont	1	0	0	0	0
Totals		49	5	5	10	26
Playoff Totals		8	0	0	0	4

LAMOUREUX, Leo Peter *5-11 175 D*
B. Espanola, Ont., Oct. 1, 1906

Season	Team	GP	G	A	Pts.	PIM
41-42	Mont	1	0	0	0	0
42-43	Mont	46	2	16	18	43
43-44	Mont	44	8	23	31	32
44-45	Mont	49	2	22	24	38
45-46	Mont	45	5	7	12	18
46-47	Mont	50	2	11	13	14
Totals		235	19	79	98	145
Playoff Totals		28	1	6	7	16

LAMOUREUX, Mitch *5-6 175 C*
B. Ottawa, Ont., Aug. 22, 1962

Season	Team	GP	G	A	Pts.	PIM
83-84	Pitt	8	1	1	2	6
84-85	Pitt	62	10	8	18	53
87-88	Phil	3	0	0	0	0
Totals		73	11	9	20	59

LAMPMAN, Michael David *6-2 195 LW*
B. Hamilton, Ont., Apr. 20, 1950

Season	Team	GP	G	A	Pts.	PIM
72-73	StL	18	2	3	5	2
73-74	StL-Van	29	2	0	2	0
75-76	Wash	27	7	12	19	28
76-77	Wash	22	6	5	11	4
Totals		96	17	20	37	34

LANCIEN, John Gordon (Jack) *6-0 188 D*
B. Regina, Sask., June 14, 1923

Season	Team	GP	G	A	Pts.	PIM
46-47	NYR	1	0	0	0	0
49-50	NYR	43	1	4	5	27
50-51	NYR	19	0	1	1	8
Totals		63	1	5	6	35
Playoff Totals		6	0	1	1	2

LANDON, Larry *6-0 191 RW*
B. Niagara Falls, Ont., May 4, 1958

Season	Team	GP	G	A	Pts.	PIM
83-84	Mont	2	0	0	0	0
84-85	Tor	7	0	0	0	2
Totals		9	0	0	0	2

LANE, Gordon *6-1 190 D*
B. Brandon, Man., Mar. 31, 1953

Season	Team	GP	G	A	Pts.	PIM
75-76	Wash	3	1	0	1	12
76-77	Wash	80	2	15	17	207
77-78	Wash	69	2	9	11	195
78-79	Wash	64	3	15	18	147
79-80	Wash-NYI	74	4	18	22	205
80-81	NYI	60	3	9	12	124
81-82	NYI	51	0	13	13	98
82-83	NYI	44	3	4	7	87
83-84	NYI	37	0	3	3	70
84-85	NYI	57	1	8	9	83
Totals		539	19	94	113	1228
Playoff Totals		75	3	14	17	214

LANE, Myles J. *6-0 180 D*
B. Melrose, Mass., Oct. 2, 1905

Season	Team	GP	G	A	Pts.	PIM
28-29	NYR-Bos	29	2	0	2	24
29-30	Bos	3	0	0	0	0
33-34	Bos	28	2	1	3	17
Totals		60	4	1	5	41
Playoff Totals		10	0	0	0	0

LANGDON, Stephen Murray *5-11 175 LW*
B. Toronto, Ont., Dec. 23, 1953

Season	Team	GP	G	A	Pts.	PIM
74-75	Bos	1	0	1	1	0
75-76	Bos	4	0	0	0	2
77-78	Bos	2	0	0	0	0
Totals		7	0	1	1	2
Playoff Totals		4	0	0	0	0

LANGELLE, Peter *5-10 170 C*
B. Winnipeg, Man., Nov. 4, 1917

Season	Team	GP	G	A	Pts.	PIM
38-39	Tor	2	1	0	1	0
39-40	Tor	39	7	14	21	2
40-41	Tor	48	4	15	19	0
41-42	Tor	48	10	22	32	9
Totals		137	22	51	73	11
Playoff Totals		41	5	9	14	4

LANGEVIN, Chris *6-0 190 LW*
B. Montreal, Que., Nov. 27, 1959

Season	Team	GP	G	A	Pts.	PIM
83-85	Buf	6	1	0	1	2
85-86	Buf	16	2	1	3	20
Totals		22	3	1	4	22

LANGEVIN, David *6-2 200 D*
B. St. Paul, Minn., May 15, 1954

Season	Team	GP	G	A	Pts.	PIM
76-77	Edm (WHA)	77	7	16	23	94
77-78	Edm (WHA)	62	6	22	28	90
78-79	Edm (WHA)	77	6	21	27	76
79-80	NYI	76	3	13	16	109
80-81	NYI	75	1	16	17	122
81-82	NYI	73	1	20	21	82
82-83	NYI	73	4	17	21	64
83-84	NYI	69	3	16	19	53
84-85	NYI	56	0	13	13	35
85-86	Minn	80	0	8	8	58
86-87	LA	11	0	4	4	7
NHL Totals		513	12	107	119	530
WHA Totals		216	19	59	78	260
NHL Playoff Totals		87	2	15	17	106
WHA Playoff Totals		23	2	4	6	44

LANGLAIS, Joseph Alfred Alain (Alain) *5-10 175 LW*
B. Chicoutimi, Que., Oct. 9, 1950

Season	Team	GP	G	A	Pts.	PIM
73-74	Minn	14	3	3	6	8
74-75	Minn	11	1	1	2	2
Totals		25	4	4	8	10

LANGLOIS, Albert (Junior) *6-0 205 D*
B. Magog, Que., Nov. 6, 1934

Season	Team	GP	G	A	Pts.	PIM
57-58	Mont	1	0	0	0	0
58-59	Mont	48	0	3	3	26
59-60	Mont	67	1	14	15	48
60-61	Mont	61	1	12	13	56
61-62	NYR	69	7	18	25	90
62-63	NYR	60	2	14	16	62
63-64	NYR-Det	61	5	8	13	45
64-65	Det	65	1	12	13	107
65-66	Bos	65	4	10	14	54
Totals		497	21	91	112	488
Playoff Totals		53	1	5	6	50

LANGLOIS, Charles *D*
B. Latbiniere, Que., Aug. 25, 1894

Season	Team	GP	G	A	Pts.	PIM
24-25	Ham	30	6	1	7	59
25-26	NYA	36	9	1	10	76
26-27	NYA-Pitt Pi	45	7	1	8	44
27-28	Pitt Pi-Mont	40	0	0	0	22
Totals		151	22	3	25	201
Playoff Totals		2	0	0	0	0

LANGWAY, Rod Corry *6-3 218 D*
B. Formosa, Taiwan, May 3, 1957

Season	Team	GP	G	A	Pts.	PIM
77-78	Birm (WHA)	52	3	18	21	52
78-79	Mont	45	3	4	7	30
79-80	Mont	77	7	29	36	81
80-81	Mont	80	11	34	45	120
81-82	Mont	66	5	34	39	116
82-83	Wash	80	3	29	32	75
83-84	Wash	80	9	24	33	61
84-85	Wash	79	4	22	26	54
85-86	Wash	71	1	17	18	61
86-87	Wash	78	2	25	27	53
87-88	Wash	63	3	13	16	28
88-89	Wash	76	2	19	21	65
89-90	Wash	58	0	8	8	39
90-91	Wash	56	1	7	8	24
91-92	Wash	64	0	13	13	22
NHL Totals		963	51	278	329	829
WHA Totals		52	3	18	21	52
NHL Playoff Totals		104	5	22	27	96

LANGWAY, Rod Corry *(Continued)*

Season	Team	GP	G	A	Pts.	PIM
WHA Playoff Totals		4	0	0	0	9

LANTHIER, Jean-Marc *6-2 195 RW*
B. Montreal, Que., Mar. 27, 1963

Season	Team	GP	G	A	Pts.	PIM
83-84	Van	11	2	1	3	2
84-85	Van	27	6	4	10	13
85-86	Van	62	7	10	17	12
87-88	Van	5	1	1	2	2
Totals		105	16	16	32	29

LANYON, Edward George (Ted) *5-11 170 D*
B. Winnipeg, Man., June 11, 1939

Season	Team	GP	G	A	Pts.	PIM
67-68	Pitt	5	0	0	0	4

LANZ, Rick Roman *6-2 203 D*
B. Karlouy Vary, Czech., Sept. 16, 1961

Season	Team	GP	G	A	Pts.	PIM
80-81	Van	76	7	22	29	40
81-82	Van	39	3	11	14	48
82-83	Van	74	10	38	48	46
83-84	Van	79	18	39	57	45
84-85	Van	57	2	17	19	69
85-86	Van	75	15	38	53	73
86-87	Van-Tor	61	3	25	28	42
87-88	Tor	75	6	22	28	65
88-89	Tor	32	1	9	10	18
91-92	Chi	1	0	0	0	2
Totals		569	65	221	286	448
Playoff Totals		28	3	8	11	35

LAPERRIERE, Joseph Jacques Hughes (Jacques) *6-2 190 D*
B. Rouyn, Que., Nov. 22, 1941

Season	Team	GP	G	A	Pts.	PIM
62-63	Mont	6	0	2	2	2
63-64	Mont	65	2	28	30	102
64-65	Mont	67	5	22	27	92
65-66	Mont	57	6	25	31	85
66-67	Mont	61	0	20	20	48
67-68	Mont	72	4	21	25	84
68-69	Mont	69	5	26	31	45
69-70	Mont	73	6	31	37	98
70-71	Mont	49	0	16	16	20
71-72	Mont	73	3	25	28	50
72-73	Mont	57	7	16	23	34
73-74	Mont	42	2	10	12	14
Totals		691	40	242	282	674
Playoff Totals		88	9	22	31	101

LAPOINTE, Claude *5-9 173 C*
B. Lachine, Que., Oct. 11, 1968

Season	Team	GP	G	A	Pts.	PIM
90-91	Que	13	2	2	4	4
91-92	Que	78	13	20	33	86
Totals		91	15	22	37	90

LAPOINTE, Guy Gerard *6-0 205 D*
B. Montreal, Que., Mar. 18, 1948

Season	Team	GP	G	A	Pts.	PIM
68-69	Mont	1	0	0	0	2
69-70	Mont	5	0	0	0	4
70-71	Mont	78	15	29	44	107
71-72	Mont	69	11	38	49	58
72-73	Mont	76	19	35	54	117
73-74	Mont	71	13	40	53	63
74-75	Mont	80	28	47	75	88
75-76	Mont	77	21	47	68	78
76-77	Mont	77	25	51	76	53
77-78	Mont	49	13	29	42	19
78-79	Mont	69	13	42	55	43
79-80	Mont	45	6	20	26	29
80-81	Mont	33	1	9	10	79
81-82	Mont-StL	55	1	25	26	76
82-83	StL	54	3	23	26	43
83-84	Bos	45	2	16	18	34
Totals		884	171	451	622	893
Playoff Totals		123	26	44	70	138

LAPOINTE, Martin *5-11 197 RW*
B. Lachine, Que., Sept. 12, 1973

Season	Team	GP	G	A	Pts.	PIM
91-92	Det	4	0	1	1	5
Playoff Totals		3	0	1	1	4

LAPOINTE, Richard Paul *6-2 200 D*
B. Victoria, B.C., Aug. 2, 1955

Season	Team	GP	G	A	Pts.	PIM
75-76	Det	80	10	23	33	95
76-77	Det-Phil	71	3	19	22	119
77-78	Phil	47	4	16	20	91
78-79	Phil	77	3	18	21	53
79-80	StL	80	6	19	25	87
80-81	StL	80	8	25	33	124
81-82	StL	71	2	20	22	127
82-83	Que	43	2	9	11	59
83-84	Que	22	2	10	12	12
84-85	LA	73	4	13	17	46
85-86	LA	20	0	4	4	18
Totals		664	44	176	220	831
Playoff Totals		46	2	7	9	64

LAPPIN, Peter *5-11 180 RW*
B. St. Charles, Ill., Dec. 31, 1965

Season	Team	GP	G	A	Pts.	PIM
89-90	Minn	6	0	0	0	2
91-92	SJ	1	0	0	0	0
Totals		7	0	0	0	2

LAPRADE, Edgar Louis *5-8 157 C*
B. Mine Center, Ont., Oct. 10, 1919

Season	Team	GP	G	A	Pts.	PIM
45-46	NYR	49	15	19	34	0
46-47	NYR	58	15	25	40	9
47-48	NYR	59	13	34	47	7
48-49	NYR	56	18	12	30	12
49-50	NYR	60	22	22	44	2
50-51	NYR	42	10	13	23	0
51-52	NYR	70	9	29	38	8
52-53	NYR	11	2	1	3	2
53-54	NYR	35	1	6	7	2
54-55	NYR	60	3	11	14	0
Totals		500	108	172	280	42
Playoff Totals		18	4	9	13	4

LaPRAIRIE, Benjamin (Bun) *D*

Season	Team	GP	G	A	Pts.	PIM
36-37	Chi	7	0	0	0	0

LARIONOV, Igor *5-9 165 C*
B. Voskresensk, Soviet Union, Dec. 3, 1960

Season	Team	GP	G	A	Pts.	PIM
89-90	Van	74	17	27	44	20
90-91	Van	64	13	21	34	14
91-92	Van	72	21	44	65	56
Totals		210	51	92	143	90
Playoff Totals		19	4	7	11	10

LARIVIERE, Garry Joseph *6-0 190 D*
B. St. Catharines, Ont., Dec. 6, 1954

Season	Team	GP	G	A	Pts.	PIM
74-75	Phoe (WHA)	4	0	1	1	28
75-76	Phoe (WHA)	79	7	17	24	100
76-77	Phoe-Que (WHA)	76	7	26	33	56
77-78	Que (WHA)	80	7	49	56	78
78-79	Que (WHA)	50	5	33	38	54
79-80	Que	75	2	19	21	56
80-81	Que-Edm	65	3	15	18	56
81-82	Edm	62	1	21	22	41
82-83	Edm	17	0	2	2	14
NHL Totals		219	6	57	63	167
WHA Totals		289	26	126	152	316
NHL Playoff Totals		14	0	5	5	8
WHA Playoff Totals		38	3	15	18	18

LARMER, Jeff *5-10 175 LW*
B. Peterborough, Ont., Nov. 10, 1962

Season	Team	GP	G	A	Pts.	PIM
81-82	Col	8	1	1	2	8
82-83	NJ	65	21	24	45	21
83-84	NJ-Chi	76	15	26	41	28
84-85	Chi	7	0	0	0	0
85-86	Chi	2	0	0	0	0
Totals		158	37	51	88	57
Playoff Totals		5	1	0	1	2

LARMER, Steve Donald *5-11 189 RW*
B. Peterborough, Ont., June 16, 1961

Season	Team	GP	G	A	Pts.	PIM
80-81	Chi	4	0	1	1	0
81-82	Chi	3	0	0	0	0
82-83	Chi	80	43	47	90	28
83-84	Chi	80	35	40	75	34
84-85	Chi	80	46	40	86	16
85-86	Chi	80	31	45	76	47
86-87	Chi	80	28	56	84	22
87-88	Chi	80	41	48	89	42
88-89	Chi	80	43	44	87	54
89-90	Chi	80	31	59	90	40
90-91	Chi	80	44	57	101	79
91-92	Chi	80	29	45	74	65
Totals		807	371	482	853	427
Playoff Totals		103	45	63	108	69

LAROCHELLE, Wildor *5-8 158 F*
B. Sorel, Que., Oct. 23, 1906

Season	Team	GP	G	A	Pts.	PIM
25-26	Mont	33	2	1	3	10
26-27	Mont	41	0	1	1	6
27-28	Mont	40	3	1	4	30
28-29	Mont	2	0	0	0	0
29-30	Mont	44	14	11	25	28
30-31	Mont	40	8	5	13	35
31-32	Mont	48	18	8	26	16
32-33	Mont	47	11	4	15	27
33-34	Mont	48	16	11	27	27
34-35	Mont	48	9	19	28	12
35-36	Mont-Chi	40	2	3	5	14
36-37	Chi	43	9	10	19	6
Totals		474	92	74	166	211
Playoff Totals		34	6	4	10	24

LAROCQUE, Denis *6-1 205 D*
B. Hawkesbury, Ont., Oct. 5, 1967

Season	Team	GP	G	A	Pts.	PIM
87-88	LA	8	0	1	1	18

LAROSE, Charles Bonner *F*

Season	Team	GP	G	A	Pts.	PIM
25-26	Bos	6	0	0	0	0

LAROSE, Claude *5-10 170 LW*
B. St. Jean, Que., May 17, 1955

Season	Team	GP	G	A	Pts.	PIM
75-76	Cin (WHA)	79	28	24	52	19
76-77	Cin (WHA)	81	30	46	76	8
77-78	Cin-Ind (WHA)	79	25	36	61	18
78-79	Ind (WHA)	13	5	8	13	0
79-80	NYR	25	4	7	11	2
NHL Totals		25	4	7	11	2
WHA Totals		252	88	114	202	45
NHL Playoff Totals		2	0	0	0	0
WHA Playoff Totals		4	2	1	3	0

LAROSE, Claude David *6-0 170 RW*
B. Hearst, Ont., Mar. 2, 1942

Season	Team	GP	G	A	Pts.	PIM
62-63	Mont	4	0	0	0	0
63-64	Mont	21	1	1	2	43
64-65	Mont	68	21	16	37	82
65-66	Mont	64	15	18	33	67
66-67	Mont	69	19	16	35	82
67-68	Mont	42	2	9	11	28
68-69	Minn	67	25	37	62	106
69-70	Minn	75	24	23	47	109
70-71	Mont	64	10	13	23	90
71-72	Mont	77	20	18	38	64
72-73	Mont	73	11	23	34	30
73-74	Mont	39	17	7	24	52
74-75	Mont-StL	64	11	19	30	44
75-76	StL	67	13	25	38	48
76-77	StL	80	29	19	48	22
77-78	StL	69	8	13	21	20
Totals		943	226	257	483	887
Playoff Totals		97	14	18	32	143

LAROSE, Guy *5-9 175 C*
B. Hull, Que., Aug. 31, 1967

Season	Team	GP	G	A	Pts.	PIM
88-89	Winn	3	0	1	1	6
90-91	Winn	7	0	0	0	8
91-92	Tor	34	9	5	14	27
Totals		44	9	6	15	41

LAROUCHE, Pierre *5-11 175 C*
B. Taschereau, Que., Nov. 16, 1955

Season	Team	GP	G	A	Pts.	PIM
74-75	Pitt	79	31	37	68	52
75-76	Pitt	76	53	58	111	33
76-77	Pitt	65	29	34	63	14
77-78	Pitt-Mont	64	23	37	60	11
78-79	Mont	36	9	13	22	4
79-80	Mont	73	50	41	91	16
80-81	Mont	61	25	28	53	28
81-82	Mont-Hart	67	34	37	71	12
82-83	Hart	38	18	22	40	8
83-84	NYR	77	48	33	81	22
84-85	NYR	65	24	36	60	8
85-86	NYR	28	20	7	27	4
86-87	NYR	73	28	35	63	12
87-88	NYR	10	3	9	12	13
Totals		812	395	427	822	237
Playoff Totals		64	20	34	54	16

LARSON, Norman Lyle *6-0 175 RW*
B. Moose Jaw, Sask., Oct. 13, 1920

Season	Team	GP	G	A	Pts.	PIM
40-41	NYA	48	9	9	18	6
41-42	NYA	40	16	9	25	6
46-47	NYR	1	0	0	0	0
Totals		89	25	18	43	12

LARSON, Reed David *6-0 195 D*
B. Minneapolis, Minn., July 30, 1956

Season	Team	GP	G	A	Pts.	PIM
76-77	Det	14	0	1	1	23
77-78	Det	75	19	41	60	95
78-79	Det	79	18	49	67	169
79-80	Det	80	22	44	66	101
80-81	Det	78	27	31	58	153
81-82	Det	80	21	39	60	112
82-83	Det	80	22	52	74	104
83-84	Det	78	23	39	62	122
84-85	Det	77	17	45	62	139
85-86	Det-Bos	80	22	45	67	117
86-87	Bos	66	12	24	36	95
87-88	Bos	62	10	24	34	93
88-89	Edm-NYI-Minn	54	9	29	38	68
89-90	Buf	1	0	0	0	0
Totals		904	222	463	685	1391
Playoff Totals		32	4	7	11	63

LARTER, Tyler *5-10 185 C*
B. Charlottetown, P.E.I., Mar. 12, 1968

Season	Team	GP	G	A	Pts.	PIM
89-90	Wash	1	0	0	0	0

LATAL, Jiri *6-0 190 D*
B. Olomouc, Czechoslovakia, Feb. 2, 1967

Season Team	GP	G	A	Pts.	PIM
89-90 Phil	32	6	13	19	6
90-91 Phil	50	5	21	26	14
91-92 Phil	10	1	2	3	4
Totals	92	12	36	48	24

LATOS, James *6-1 200 RW*
B. Wakaw, Sask., Jan. 4, 1966

Season Team	GP	G	A	Pts.	PIM
88-89 NYR	1	0	0	0	0

LATREILLE, Philippe J. (Phil) *F*
B. Montreal, Que., Apr. 20, 1938

Season Team	GP	G	A	Pts.	PIM
60-61 NYR	4	0	0	0	2

LATTA, David *6-1 190 LW*
B. Thunder Bay, Ont., Jan. 3, 1967

Season Team	GP	G	A	Pts.	PIM
85-86 Que	1	0	0	0	0
87-88 Que	10	0	0	0	0
88-89 Que	24	4	8	12	4
90-91 Que	1	0	0	0	0
Totals	36	4	8	12	4

LAUDER, Martin *D*

Season Team	GP	G	A	Pts.	PIM
27-28 Bos	3	0	0	0	2

LAUEN, Michael Arthur *6-1 185 RW*
B. Edina, Minn., Feb. 9, 1961

Season Team	GP	G	A	Pts.	PIM
83-84 Winn	3	0	1	1	0

LAUER, Brad *6-0 195 LW*
B. Humboldt, Sask., Oct. 27, 1966

Season Team	GP	G	A	Pts.	PIM
86-87 NYI	61	7	14	21	65
87-88 NYI	69	17	18	35	67
88-89 NYI	14	3	2	5	2
89-90 NYI	63	6	18	24	19
90-91 NYI	44	4	8	12	45
91-92 NYI-Chi	14	1	0	1	6
Totals	265	38	60	98	204
Playoff Totals	22	6	4	10	20

LAUGHLIN, Craig *6-0 190 RW*
B. Toronto, Ont., Sept. 19, 1957

Season Team	GP	G	A	Pts.	PIM
81-82 Mont	36	12	11	23	33
82-83 Wash	75	17	27	44	41
83-84 Wash	80	20	32	52	69
84-85 Wash	78	16	34	50	38
85-86 Wash	75	30	45	75	43
86-87 Wash	80	22	30	52	67
87-88 Wash-LA	59	9	13	22	32
88-89 Tor	66	10	13	23	41
Totals	549	136	205	341	364
Playoff Totals	33	6	6	12	20

LAUGHTON, Michael Frederic *6-2 185 C*
B. Nelson, B.C., Feb. 21, 1944

Season Team	GP	G	A	Pts.	PIM
67-68 Oak	35	2	6	8	38
68-69 Oak	53	20	23	43	12
69-70 Oak	76	16	19	35	39
70-71 Cal	25	1	0	1	2
72-73 NY (WHA)	67	16	20	36	44
73-74 NY-NJ (WHA)	71	20	18	38	34
74-75 SD (WHA)	65	7	9	16	22
NHL Totals	189	39	48	87	91
WHA Totals	203	43	47	90	100
NHL Playoff Totals	11	2	4	6	0
WHA Playoff Totals	10	4	1	5	0

LAURENCE, Donald (Red) *5-9 173 C*
B. Galt, Ont., June 27, 1957

Season Team	GP	G	A	Pts.	PIM
78-79 Atl	59	14	20	34	6
79-80 StL	20	1	2	3	8
Totals	79	15	22	37	14

LaVALLEE, Kevin A. *5-8 180 LW*
B. Sudbury, Ont., Sept. 16, 1961

Season Team	GP	G	A	Pts.	PIM
80-81 Calg	77	15	20	35	16
81-82 Calg	75	32	29	61	30
82-83 Calg	60	19	16	35	17
83-84 LA	19	3	3	6	2
84-85 StL	38	15	17	32	8
85-86 StL	64	18	20	38	8
86-87 Pitt	33	8	20	28	4
Totals	366	110	125	235	85
Playoff Totals	32	5	8	13	24

LaVARRE, Mark *5-11 170 RW*
B. Evanston, Ill., Feb. 21, 1965

Season Team	GP	G	A	Pts.	PIM
85-86 Chi	2	0	0	0	0
86-87 Chi	58	8	15	23	33
87-88 Chi	18	1	1	2	25
Totals	78	9	16	25	58
Playoff Totals	1	0	0	0	2

LAVENDER, Brian James *6-0 180 LW*
B. Edmonton, Alta., Apr. 20, 1947

Season Team	GP	G	A	Pts.	PIM
71-72 StL	46	5	11	16	54
72-73 NYI-Det	69	8	8	16	61
73-74 Det	4	0	0	0	11
74-75 Cal	65	3	7	10	48
75-76 Den (WHA)	37	2	0	2	7
NHL Totals	184	16	26	42	174
WHA Totals	37	2	0	2	7
NHL Playoff Totals	3	0	0	0	0

LAVIOLETTE, Jean-Baptiste (Jack) *D*
B. Belleville, Ont., July 27, 1879

Season Team	GP	G	A	Pts.	PIM
17-18 Mont	18	2	0	2	0
Playoff Totals	2	0	0	0	0

LAVIOLETTE, Peter *6-2 200 D*
B. Norwood, Mass., Dec. 7, 1964

Season Team	GP	G	A	Pts.	PIM
88-89 NYR	12	0	0	0	6

LAVOIE, Dominic *6-2 205 D*
B. Montreal, Que., Nov. 21, 1967

Season Team	GP	G	A	Pts.	PIM
88-89 StL	1	0	0	0	0
89-90 StL	13	1	1	2	16
90-91 StL	6	1	2	3	2
91-92 StL	6	0	1	1	10
Totals	26	2	4	6	28

LAWLESS, Paul *5-11 185 LW*
B. Scarborough, Ont., July 2, 1964

Season Team	GP	G	A	Pts.	PIM
82-83 Hart	47	6	9	15	4
83-84 Hart	6	0	3	3	0
85-86 Hart	64	17	21	38	20
86-87 Hart	60	22	32	54	14
87-88 Hart-Phil-Van	49	4	11	15	16
88-89 Tor	7	0	0	0	0
89-90 Tor	6	0	1	1	0
Totals	239	49	77	126	54
Playoff Totals	3	0	2	2	2

LAWSON, Daniel Michael *5-11 180 RW*
B. Toronto, Ont., Oct. 30, 1947

Season Team	GP	G	A	Pts.	PIM
67-68 Det	1	0	0	0	0
68-69 Det-Minn	62	8	10	18	25
69-70 Minn	45	9	8	17	19
70-71 Minn	33	1	5	6	2
71-72 Buf	78	10	6	16	15
72-73 Phil (WHA)	78	61	45	106	35
73-74 Van (WHA)	78	55	33	88	14
74-75 Van (WHA)	78	33	43	76	19
75-76 Calg (WHA)	80	44	52	96	46
76-77 Calg-Winn (WHA)	78	30	26	56	28
NHL Totals	219	28	29	57	61
WHA Totals	392	223	199	422	142
NHL Playoff Totals	16	0	1	1	2
WHA Playoff Totals	26	6	9	15	25

LAWTON, Brian *6-0 190 LW*
B. New Brunswick, N.J., June 29, 1965

Season Team	GP	G	A	Pts.	PIM
83-84 Minn	58	10	21	31	33
84-85 Minn	40	5	6	11	24
85-86 Minn	65	18	17	35	36
86-87 Minn	66	21	23	44	86
87-88 Minn	74	17	24	41	71
88-89 NYR-Hart	65	17	26	43	67
89-90 Hart-Que-Bos	35	7	7	14	30
91-92 SJ	59	15	22	37	42
Totals	462	110	146	256	389
Playoff Totals	11	1	1	2	12

LAXDAL, Derek *6-1 175 RW*
B. St. Boniface, Man., Feb. 21, 1966

Season Team	GP	G	A	Pts.	PIM
84-85 Tor	3	0	0	0	6
86-87 Tor	2	0	0	0	7
87-88 Tor	5	0	0	0	4
88-89 Tor	41	9	6	15	65
89-90 NYI	12	3	1	4	6
90-91 NYI	4	0	0	0	0
Totals	67	12	7	19	90
Playoff Totals	1	0	2	2	2

LAYCOE, Harold Richardson (Hal) *6-1 175 D*
B. Sutherland, Sask., June 23, 1922

Season Team	GP	G	A	Pts.	PIM
45-46 NYR	17	0	2	2	6
46-47 NYR	58	1	12	13	25
47-48 Mont	14	1	2	3	4
48-49 Mont	51	3	5	8	31
49-50 Mont	30	0	2	2	21
50-51 Mont-Bos	44	1	3	4	29
51-52 Bos	70	5	7	12	61
52-53 Bos	54	2	10	12	36
53-54 Bos	58	3	16	19	29

LAYCOE, Harold Richardson (Hal)
(Continued)

Season Team	GP	G	A	Pts.	PIM
54-55 Bos	70	4	13	17	34
55-56 Bos	65	5	5	10	16
Totals	531	25	77	102	292
Playoff Totals	40	2	5	7	39

LAZARO, Jeff *5-10 180 LW*
B. Waltham, Mass., Mar. 21, 1968

Season Team	GP	G	A	Pts.	PIM
90-91 Bos	49	5	13	18	67
91-92 Bos	27	3	6	9	31
Totals	76	8	19	27	98
Playoff Totals	28	3	3	6	32

LEACH, Jamie *6-1 198 RW*
B. Winnipeg, Man., Aug. 25, 1969

Season Team	GP	G	A	Pts.	PIM
89-90 Pitt	10	0	3	3	0
90-91 Pitt	7	2	0	2	0
91-92 Pitt	38	5	4	9	8
Totals	55	7	7	14	8

LEACH, Lawrence Raymond *6-2 180 C*
B. Lloydminster, Sask., June 18, 1936

Season Team	GP	G	A	Pts.	PIM
58-59 Bos	29	4	12	16	26
59-60 Bos	69	7	12	19	47
61-62 Bos	28	2	5	7	18
Totals	126	13	29	42	91
Playoff Totals	7	1	1	2	8

LEACH, Reginald Joseph *6-0 180 RW*
B. Riverton, Man., Apr. 23, 1950

Season Team	GP	G	A	Pts.	PIM
70-71 Bos	23	2	4	6	0
71-72 Bos-Cal	73	13	20	33	19
72-73 Cal	76	23	12	35	45
73-74 Cal	78	22	24	46	34
74-75 Phil	80	45	33	78	63
75-76 Phil	80	61	30	91	41
76-77 Phil	77	32	14	46	23
77-78 Phil	72	24	28	52	24
78-79 Phil	76	34	20	54	20
79-80 Phil	76	50	26	76	28
80-81 Phil	79	34	36	70	59
81-82 Phil	66	26	21	47	18
82-83 Det	78	15	17	32	13
Totals	934	381	285	666	387
Playoff Totals	94	47	22	69	22

LEACH, Stephen *5-11 180 RW*
B. Cambridge, Mass., Jan. 16, 1966

Season Team	GP	G	A	Pts.	PIM
85-86 Wash	11	1	1	2	2
86-87 Wash	15	1	0	1	6
87-88 Wash	8	1	1	2	17
88-89 Wash	74	11	19	30	94
89-90 Wash	70	18	14	32	104
90-91 Wash	68	11	19	30	99
91-92 Bos	78	31	29	60	147
Totals	324	74	83	157	469
Playoff Totals	59	10	6	16	38

LEAVINS, Jim *5-11 185 D*
B. Dinsmore, Sask., July 28, 1960

Season Team	GP	G	A	Pts.	PIM
85-86 Det	37	2	11	13	26
86-87 NYR	4	0	1	1	4
Totals	41	2	12	14	30

LEBEAU, Patrick *5-10 172 LW*
B. St. Jerome, Que., Mar. 17, 1970

Season Team	GP	G	A	Pts.	PIM
90-91 Mont	2	1	1	2	0

LEBEAU, Stephan *5-10 172 C*
B. St. Jerome, Que., Feb. 28, 1968

Season Team	GP	G	A	Pts.	PIM
88-89 Mont	1	0	1	1	2
89-90 Mont	57	15	20	35	11
90-91 Mont	73	22	31	53	24
91-92 Mont	77	27	31	58	14
Totals	208	64	83	147	51
Playoff Totals	14	4	6	10	6

LeBLANC, Fernand (Fern) *5-9 170 C*
B. Gaspesie, Que., Jan. 12, 1956

Season Team	GP	G	A	Pts.	PIM
76-77 Det	3	0	0	0	0
77-78 Det	2	0	0	0	0
78-79 Det	29	5	6	11	0
Totals	34	5	6	11	0

LeBLANC, Jean-Paul (J.P.) *5-10 175 C*
B. South Durham, Que., Oct. 20, 1946

Season Team	GP	G	A	Pts.	PIM
68-69 Chi	6	1	2	3	0
72-73 LA (WHA)	77	19	50	69	49
73-74 LA (WHA)	78	20	46	66	58
74-75 Balt (WHA)	78	16	33	49	100
75-76 Denver (WHA)	15	1	5	6	25
75-76 Det	46	4	9	13	39
76-77 Det	74	11	18	29	40

LeBLANC, Jean-Paul (J.P.) *(Continued)*

Season	Team	GP	G	A	Pts.	PIM
77-78	Det	3	0	2	2	4
78-79	Det	24	2	6	8	4
NHL Totals		153	14	30	44	87
WHA Totals		248	56	134	190	232
NHL Playoff Totals		2	0	0	0	0
WHA Playoff Totals		6	0	5	5	2

LeBLANC, John Glenn *6-1 190 LW*
B. Campbellton, N.B., Jan. 21, 1964

Season	Team	GP	G	A	Pts.	PIM
86-87	Van	2	1	0	1	0
87-88	Van	41	12	10	22	18
88-89	Edm	2	1	0	1	0
91-92	Winn	16	6	1	7	6
Totals		61	20	11	31	24
Playoff Totals		1	0	0	0	0

LeBRUN, Albert Ivan *6-0 195 D*
B. Timmins, Ont., Dec. 1, 1940

Season	Team	GP	G	A	Pts.	PIM
60-61	NYR	4	0	2	2	4
65-66	NYR	2	0	0	0	0
Totals		6	0	2	2	4

LECAINE, William Joseph *6-0 172 LW*
B. Moose Jaw, Sask., Mar. 11, 1940

Season	Team	GP	G	A	Pts.	PIM
68-69	Pitt	4	0	0	0	0

LeCLAIR, John *6-2 215 LW*
B. St. Albans, Vt., July 5, 1969

Season	Team	GP	G	A	Pts.	PIM
90-91	Mont	10	2	5	7	2
91-92	Mont	59	8	11	19	14
Totals		69	10	16	27	16
Playoff Totals		11	1	1	2	6

LECLAIR, John Louis (Jackie) *5-10 175 C*
B. Quebec City, Que., May 30, 1929

Season	Team	GP	G	A	Pts.	PIM
54-55	Mont	59	11	22	33	12
55-56	Mont	54	6	8	14	30
56-57	Mont	47	3	10	13	14
Totals		160	20	40	60	56
Playoff Totals		20	6	1	7	6

LECLERC, Renald (Rene) *5-11 165 RW*
B. Ville-de-Vanier, Que., Nov. 12, 1947

Season	Team	GP	G	A	Pts.	PIM
68-69	Det	43	2	3	5	62
70-71	Det	44	8	8	16	30
72-73	Que (WHA)	60	24	28	52	111
73-74	Que (WHA)	58	17	27	44	84
74-75	Que (WHA)	73	18	32	50	85
75-76	Que-Ind (WHA)	82	33	38	71	87
76-77	Ind (WHA)	68	25	30	55	43
77-78	Ind (WHA)	60	12	15	27	31
78-79	Ind-Que (WHA)	45	5	7	12	20
NHL Totals		87	10	11	21	92
WHA Totals		446	134	177	311	461
WHA Playoff Totals		34	10	13	23	52

LECUYER, Douglas J. *5-9 180 LW*
B. Wainwright, Alta., Mar. 10, 1958

Season	Team	GP	G	A	Pts.	PIM
78-79	Chi	2	1	0	1	0
79-80	Chi	53	3	10	13	59
80-81	Chi-Winn	59	6	17	23	107
82-83	Pitt	12	1	4	5	12
Totals		126	11	31	42	178

LEDINGHAM, Walter Norman *5-11 180 LW*
B. Weyburn, Sask., Oct. 26, 1950

Season	Team	GP	G	A	Pts.	PIM
72-73	Chi	9	0	1	1	4
74-75	NYI	2	0	1	1	0
76-77	NYI	4	0	0	0	0
Totals		15	0	2	2	4

LeDUC, Albert (Battleship) *5-9 180 D*
B. Valleyfield, Que., Nov. 22, 1902

Season	Team	GP	G	A	Pts.	PIM
25-26	Mont	32	10	3	13	62
26-27	Mont	43	5	2	7	62
27-28	Mont	43	8	5	13	73
28-29	Mont	43	9	2	11	79
29-30	Mont	44	6	8	14	90
30-31	Mont	44	8	6	14	82
31-32	Mont	41	5	3	8	60
32-33	Mont	48	5	3	8	62
33-34	Ott-NYR	42	1	3	4	40
34-35	Mont	4	0	0	0	4
Totals		384	57	35	92	614
Playoff Totals		31	5	6	11	32

LeDUC, Richard Henri *5-11 170 C*
B. Ile Perrot, Que., Aug. 24, 1951

Season	Team	GP	G	A	Pts.	PIM
72-73	Bos	5	1	1	2	2
73-74	Bos	28	3	3	6	12
74-75	Clev (WHA)	78	34	31	65	122

LeDUC, Richard Henri *(Continued)*

Season	Team	GP	G	A	Pts.	PIM
75-76	Clev (WHA)	79	36	22	58	76
76-77	Cin (WHA)	81	52	55	107	75
77-78	Cin-Ind (WHA)	82	37	46	83	82
78-79	Ind-Que (WHA)	74	35	41	76	44
79-80	Que	75	21	27	48	49
80-81	Que	22	3	7	10	6
NHL Totals		130	28	38	66	69
WHA Totals		394	194	195	389	399
NHL Playoff Totals		5	0	0	0	9
WHA Playoff Totals		16	3	8	11	20

LEDYARD, Grant *6-2 200 D*
B. Winnipeg, Man., Nov. 19, 1961

Season	Team	GP	G	A	Pts.	PIM
84-85	NYR	42	8	12	20	53
85-86	NYR-LA	79	9	27	36	98
86-87	LA	67	14	23	37	93
87-88	LA-Wash	44	5	10	16	66
88-89	Wash-Buf	74	4	16	20	51
89-90	Buf	67	2	13	15	37
90-91	Buf	60	8	23	31	46
91-92	Buf	50	5	16	21	45
Totals		483	55	140	195	489
Playoff Totals		33	5	7	12	56

LEE, Edward *6-2 180 RW*
B. Rochester, N.Y., Dec. 17, 1961

Season	Team	GP	G	A	Pts.	PIM
84-85	Que	2	0	0	0	5

LEE, Peter John *5-9 180 RW*
B. Ellesmere, England, Jan. 2, 1956

Season	Team	GP	G	A	Pts.	PIM
77-78	Pitt	60	5	13	18	19
78-79	Pitt	80	32	26	58	24
79-80	Pitt	74	16	29	45	20
80-81	Pitt	80	30	34	64	86
81-82	Pitt	74	18	16	34	98
82-83	Pitt	63	13	13	26	10
Totals		431	114	131	245	257
Playoff Totals		19	0	8	8	4

LEE, Robert *D*

Season	Team	GP	G	A	Pts.	PIM
42-43	Mont	1	0	0	0	0

LEEMAN, Gary *5-11 175 RW*
B. Toronto, Ont., Feb. 19, 1964

Season	Team	GP	G	A	Pts.	PIM
83-84	Tor	52	4	8	12	31
84-85	Tor	53	5	26	31	72
85-86	Tor	53	9	23	32	20
86-87	Tor	80	21	31	52	66
87-88	Tor	80	30	31	61	62
88-89	Tor	61	32	43	75	66
89-90	Tor	80	51	44	95	63
90-91	Tor	52	17	12	29	39
91-92	Tor-Calg	63	9	19	28	81
Totals		574	178	237	415	500
Playoff Totals		24	7	14	21	34

LEETCH, Brian *5-11 185 D*
B. Corpus Christi, Tex., Mar. 3, 1968

Season	Team	GP	G	A	Pts.	PIM
87-88	NYR	17	2	12	14	0
88-89	NYR	68	23	48	71	50
89-90	NYR	72	11	45	56	26
80-91	NYR	80	16	72	88	42
91-92	NYR	80	22	80	102	26
Totals		317	74	257	331	144
Playoff Totals		23	8	16	24	6

LEFEVBRE, Sylvain *6-2 204 D*
B. Richmond, Que., Oct. 14, 1967

Season	Team	GP	G	A	Pts.	PIM
89-90	Mont	68	3	10	13	61
90-91	Mont	63	5	18	23	30
91-92	Mont	69	3	14	17	91
Totals		200	11	42	53	182
Playoff Totals		19	1	0	1	10

LEFLEY, Bryan Andrew *6-0 184 D*
B. Grosse Isle, Man., Oct. 18, 1948

Season	Team	GP	G	A	Pts.	PIM
72-73	NYI	63	3	7	10	56
73-74	NYI	7	0	0	0	0
74-75	KC	29	0	3	3	6
76-77	Col	58	0	6	6	27
77-78	Col	71	4	13	17	12
Totals		228	7	29	36	101
Playoff Totals		2	0	0	0	0

LEFLEY, Charles Thomas (Chuck) *6-2 185 LW*
B. Winnipeg, Man., Jan. 20, 1950

Season	Team	GP	G	A	Pts.	PIM
70-71	Mont	1	0	0	0	0
71-72	Mont	16	0	2	2	0
72-73	Mont	65	21	25	46	22
73-74	Mont	74	23	31	54	34
74-75	Mont-StL	75	24	28	52	28
75-76	StL	75	43	42	85	41
76-77	StL	71	11	30	41	12

LEFLEY, Charles Thomas (Chuck) *(Continued)*

Season	Team	GP	G	A	Pts.	PIM
79-80	StL	28	6	6	12	0
80-81	StL	2	0	0	0	0
Totals		407	128	164	292	137
Playoff Totals		29	5	8	13	10

LEGER, Roger *5-11 210 D*
B. L'Annonciation, Que., Mar. 26, 1919

Season	Team	GP	G	A	Pts.	PIM
43-44	NYR	7	1	2	3	2
46-47	Mont	49	4	18	22	12
47-48	Mont	48	4	14	18	26
48-49	Mont	28	6	7	13	10
49-50	Mont	55	3	12	15	21
Totals		187	18	53	71	71
Playoff Totals		20	0	7	7	14

LEGGE, Barry Graham *6-0 186 D*
B. Winnipeg, Man., Oct. 22, 1954

Season	Team	GP	G	A	Pts.	PIM
74-75	Balt (WHA)	36	3	18	21	20
75-76	Ott-Clev (WHA)	75	6	15	21	37
76-77	Minn-Cin (WHA)	76	7	22	29	39
77-78	Cin (WHA)	78	7	17	24	114
78-79	Cin (WHA)	80	3	8	11	131
79-80	Que	31	0	3	3	18
80-81	Winn	38	0	6	6	69
81-82	Winn	38	1	2	3	57
NHL Totals		107	1	11	12	144
WHA Totals		345	26	80	106	341
WHA Playoff Totals		10	0	5	5	12

LEGGE, Norman Randall (Randy) *5-11 184 D*
B. Newmarket, Ont., Dec. 16, 1945

Season	Team	GP	G	A	Pts.	PIM
72-73	NYR	12	0	2	2	2
74-75	Balt (WHA)	78	1	14	15	69
75-76	Winn-Clev (WHA)	45	1	8	9	28
76-77	SD (WHA)	69	1	9	10	69
NHL Totals		12	0	2	2	2
WHA Totals		192	3	31	34	166
WHA Playoff Totals		10	0	0	0	18

LEHMANN, Tommy *6-1 185 C*
B. Solna, Sweden, Feb. 3, 1964

Season	Team	GP	G	A	Pts.	PIM
87-88	Bos	9	1	3	4	6
88-89	Bos	26	4	2	6	10
89-90	Edm	1	0	0	0	0
Totals		36	5	5	10	16

LEHTO, Petteri *5-11 195 D*
B. Turku, Finland, Mar. 23, 1961

Season	Team	GP	G	A	Pts.	PIM
84-85	Pitt	6	0	0	0	4

LEHTONEN, Antero *6-0 185 LW*
B. Tampere, Finland, Apr. 12, 1954

Season	Team	GP	G	A	Pts.	PIM
79-80	Wash	65	9	12	21	14

LEHVONEN, Henri *6-0 185 D*
B. Sarnia, Ont., Aug. 26, 1950

Season	Team	GP	G	A	Pts.	PIM
74-75	KC	4	0	0	0	0

LEIER, Edward *5-11 165 C*
B. Poland, Nov. 3, 1927

Season	Team	GP	G	A	Pts.	PIM
49-50	Chi	5	0	1	1	0
50-51	Chi	11	2	0	2	2
Totals		16	2	1	3	2

LEINONEN, Mikko *6-0 175 C*
B. Tampere, Finland, July 15, 1955

Season	Team	GP	G	A	Pts.	PIM
81-82	NYR	53	11	20	31	18
82-83	NYR	78	17	34	51	23
83-84	NYR	28	3	23	26	28
84-85	Wash	3	0	1	1	2
Totals		162	31	78	109	71
Playoff Totals		20	2	11	13	28

LEITER, Ken *6-1 195 D*
B. Detroit, Mich., Apr. 19, 1961

Season	Team	GP	G	A	Pts.	PIM
84-85	NYI	5	0	2	2	2
85-86	NYI	9	1	1	2	6
86-87	NYI	74	9	20	29	30
87-88	NYI	51	4	13	17	24
89-90	Minn	4	0	0	0	0
Totals		143	14	36	50	62
Playoff Totals		15	0	6	6	8

LEITER, Robert Edward *5-9 164 C*
B. Winnipeg, Man., Mar. 22, 1941

Season	Team	GP	G	A	Pts.	PIM
62-63	Bos	51	9	13	22	34
63-64	Bos	56	6	13	19	43
64-65	Bos	18	3	1	4	6
65-66	Bos	9	2	1	3	2
68-69	Bos	1	0	0	0	0

Season Team	GP	G	A	Pts.	PIM
LEITER, Robert Edward *(Continued)*					
71-72 Pitt	78	14	17	31	18
72-73 Atl	78	26	34	60	19
73-74 Atl	78	26	26	52	10
74-75 Atl	52	10	18	28	8
75-76 Atl	26	2	3	5	4
75-76 Calg (WHA)	51	17	17	34	8
NHL Totals	447	98	126	224	144
WHA Totals	51	17	17	34	8
NHL Playoff Totals	8	3	0	3	2
WHA Playoff Totals	3	2	0	2	0

LEMAIRE, Jacques Gerard *5-10 180 C*
B. LaSalle, Que., Sept. 7, 1945

Season Team	GP	G	A	Pts.	PIM
67-68 Mont	69	22	20	42	16
68-69 Mont	75	29	34	63	29
69-70 Mont	69	32	28	60	16
70-71 Mont	78	28	28	56	18
71-72 Mont	77	32	49	81	26
72-73 Mont	77	44	51	95	16
73-74 Mont	66	29	38	67	10
74-75 Mont	80	36	56	92	20
75-76 Mont	61	20	32	52	20
76-77 Mont	75	34	41	75	22
77-78 Mont	76	36	61	97	14
78-79 Mont	50	24	31	55	10
Totals	853	366	469	835	217
Playoff Totals	145	61	78	139	63

LEMAY, Maurice (Moe) *5-11 185 LW*
B. Saskatoon, Sask., Feb. 18, 1962

Season Team	GP	G	A	Pts.	PIM
81-82 Van	5	1	2	3	0
82-83 Van	44	11	9	20	41
83-84 Van	56	12	18	30	38
84-85 Van	74	21	31	52	68
85-86 Van	48	16	15	31	92
86-87 Van-Edm	62	10	19	29	164
87-88 Edm-Bos	6	0	0	0	2
88-89 Bos-Winn	22	1	0	1	37
Totals	317	72	94	166	442
Playoff Totals	28	6	3	9	55

LEMELIN, Rejean *5-11 160*
B. Sherbrooke, Que., Nov. 19, 1954

Season Team	GP	G	A	Pts.	PIM
80-81 Calg	6	0	0	0	0

LEMELIN, Roger Marcel *6-3 215 D*
B. Iroquois Falls, Ont., Feb. 6, 1954

Season Team	GP	G	A	Pts.	PIM
74-75 KC	8	0	1	1	6
75-76 KC	11	0	0	0	0
Totals	19	0	1	1	6

LEMIEUX, Alain *6-0 185 C*
B. Montreal, Que., May 24, 1961

Season Team	GP	G	A	Pts.	PIM
81-82 StL	3	0	1	1	0
82-83 StL	42	9	25	34	18
83-84 StL	17	4	5	9	6
84-85 StL-Que	49	15	13	28	12
85-86 Que	7	0	0	0	2
86-87 Pitt	1	0	0	0	0
Totals	119	28	44	72	38
Playoff Totals	19	4	6	10	0

LEMIEUX, Claude *6-1 215 RW*
B. Buckingham, Que., July 16, 1965

Season Team	GP	G	A	Pts.	PIM
83-84 Mont	8	1	1	2	12
84-85 Mont	1	0	1	1	7
85-86 Mont	10	1	2	3	22
86-87 Mont	76	27	26	53	156
87-88 Mont	78	31	30	61	137
88-89 Mont	69	29	22	51	136
89-90 Mont	39	8	10	18	106
90-91 NJ	78	30	17	47	105
91-92 NJ	74	41	27	68	109
Totals	433	168	136	304	790
Playoff Totals	91	30	26	56	285

LEMIEUX, Jacques *6-2 185 F*
B. Matane, Que., Apr. 8, 1943

Season Team	GP	G	A	Pts.	PIM
67-68 LA	16	0	3	3	8
69-70 LA	3	0	1	1	0
Totals	19	0	4	4	8
Playoff Totals	1	0	0	0	0

LEMIEUX, Jean Louis *6-1 180 D*
B. Noranda, Que., May 31, 1952

Season Team	GP	G	A	Pts.	PIM
73-74 Atl	32	3	5	8	6
74-75 Atl	75	3	24	27	19
75-76 Atl-Wash	66	10	23	33	12
76-77 Wash	15	4	4	8	2
77-78 Wash	16	3	7	10	0
Totals	204	23	63	86	39
Playoff Totals	3	1	1	2	0

LEMIEUX, Jocelyn *5-10 200 RW*
B. Mont-Laurier, Que., Nov. 18, 1967

Season Team	GP	G	A	Pts.	PIM
86-87 StL	53	10	8	18	94
87-88 StL	23	1	0	1	42
88-89 Mont	1	0	1	1	0
89-90 Mont-Chi	73	14	13	27	108
90-91 Chi	67	6	7	13	119
91-92 Chi	78	6	10	16	80
Totals	295	37	39	76	443
Playoff Totals	50	4	10	14	82

LEMIEUX, Mario *6-4 210 C*
B. Montreal, Que., Oct. 5, 1965

Season Team	GP	G	A	Pts.	PIM
84-85 Pitt	73	43	57	100	54
85-86 Pitt	79	48	93	141	43
86-87 Pitt	63	54	53	107	57
87-88 Pitt	77	70	98	168	92
88-89 Pitt	76	85	114	199	100
89-90 Pitt	59	45	78	123	78
90-91 Pitt	26	19	26	45	30
91-92 Pitt	64	44	87	131	94
Totals	517	408	606	1014	548
Playoff Totals	49	44	53	97	34

LEMIEUX, Real Gaston *5-11 180 LW*
B. Victoriaville, Que., Jan. 3, 1945

Season Team	GP	G	A	Pts.	PIM
66-67 Det	1	0	0	0	0
67-68 LA	74	12	23	35	60
68-69 LA	75	11	29	40	78
69-70 NYR-LA	73	6	10	16	51
70-71 LA	43	3	6	9	22
71-72 LA	78	13	25	38	28
72-73 LA	74	5	10	15	19
73-74 LA-NYR-Buf	38	1	1	2	4
Totals	456	51	104	155	262
Playoff Totals	18	2	4	6	10

LEMIEUX, Richard Bernard (Dick) *5-8 160 C*
B. Temiscamingue So., Que., Apr. 19, 1951

Season Team	GP	G	A	Pts.	PIM
71-72 StL	42	7	9	16	4
72-73 Van	78	17	35	52	41
73-74 Van	72	5	17	22	23
74-75 KC	79	10	20	30	64
75-76 KC-Atl	3	0	1	1	0
76-77 Calg (WHA)	33	6	11	17	9
NHL Totals	274	39	82	121	132
WHA Totals	33	6	11	17	9
NHL Playoff Totals	2	0	0	0	0

LEMIEUX, Robert *D*
B. Montreal, Que., Dec. 16, 1944

Season Team	GP	G	A	Pts.	PIM
67-68 Oak	19	0	1	1	12

LENARDON, Tim *6-2 185 C/LW*
B. Trail, B.C., May 11, 1962

Season Team	GP	G	A	Pts.	PIM
86-87 NJ	7	1	1	2	0
89-90 Van	8	1	0	1	4
Totals	15	2	1	3	4

LEPINE, Alfred (Pit) *C*
B. St. Anne de Bellevue, Que., July 31, 1901

Season Team	GP	G	A	Pts.	PIM
25-26 Mont	27	9	1	10	18
26-27 Mont	44	16	1	17	20
27-28 Mont	20	4	1	5	6
28-29 Mont	44	6	1	7	48
29-30 Mont	44	24	9	33	47
30-31 Mont	44	17	7	24	63
31-32 Mont	48	19	11	30	32
32-33 Mont	46	8	8	16	45
33-34 Mont	48	10	8	18	44
34-35 Mont	48	12	19	31	16
35-36 Mont	32	6	10	16	4
36-37 Mont	34	7	8	15	15
37-38 Mont	47	5	14	19	24
Totals	526	143	98	241	382
Playoff Totals	41	7	5	12	26

LEPINE, Hector (Hec) *F*

Season Team	GP	G	A	Pts.	PIM
25-26 Mont	33	5	2	7	2

LEROUX, Francois *6-6 221 D*
B. Ste.-Adele, Que., Apr. 18, 1970

Season Team	GP	G	A	Pts.	PIM
88-89 Edm	2	0	0	0	0
89-90 Edm	3	0	1	1	0
90-91 Edm	1	0	2	2	0
91-92 Edm	4	0	0	0	7
Totals	10	0	3	3	7

LEROUX, Gaston *F*

Season Team	GP	G	A	Pts.	PIM
35-36 Mont	2	0	0	0	0

LESCHYSHYN, Curtis *6-1 205 D*
B. Thompson, Man., Sept. 21, 1969

Season Team	GP	G	A	Pts.	PIM
88-89 Que	71	4	9	13	71
89-90 Que	68	2	6	8	44
90-91 Que	55	3	7	10	49
91-92 Que	42	5	12	17	42
Totals	236	14	34	48	206

LESIEUR, Arthur *5-10 191 D*
B. Fall River, Mass., Sept. 13, 1907

Season Team	GP	G	A	Pts.	PIM
28-29 Mont-Chi	17	0	0	0	0
30-31 Mont	21	2	0	2	14
31-32 Mont	24	1	2	3	12
35-36 Mont	38	1	0	1	24
Totals	100	4	2	6	50
Playoff Totals	14	0	0	0	4

LESSARD, Rick *6-2 200 D*
B. Timmins, Ont., Jan. 9, 1968

Season Team	GP	G	A	Pts.	PIM
88-89 Calg	6	0	1	1	2
90-91 Calg	1	0	1	1	0
91-92 SJ	8	0	2	2	16
Totals	15	0	4	4	18

LESUK, William Anton *5-9 187 LW*
B. Moose Jaw, Sask., Nov. 1, 1946

Season Team	GP	G	A	Pts.	PIM
68-69 Bos	5	0	1	1	0
69-70 Bos	3	0	0	0	0
70-71 Phil	78	17	19	36	81
71-72 Phil-LA	72	11	16	27	45
72-73 LA	67	6	14	20	90
73-74 LA	35	2	1	3	32
74-75 Wash	79	8	11	19	77
75-76 Winn (WHA)	81	15	21	36	92
76-77 Winn (WHA)	78	14	27	41	85
77-78 Winn (WHA)	80	9	18	27	48
78-79 Winn (WHA)	79	17	15	32	44
79-80 Winn	49	0	1	1	43
NHL Totals	388	44	63	107	368
WHA Totals	318	55	81	136	269
NHL Playoff Totals	9	1	0	1	12
WHA Playoff Totals	50	7	11	18	48

LESWICK, Anthony Joseph (Tough Tony) *5-6 160 LW*
B. Humboldt, Sask., Mar. 17, 1923

Season Team	GP	G	A	Pts.	PIM
45-46 NYR	50	15	9	24	9
46-47 NYR	59	27	14	41	51
47-48 NYR	60	24	16	40	76
48-49 NYR	60	13	14	27	70
49-50 NYR	69	19	25	44	70
50-51 NYR	70	15	11	26	112
51-52 Det	70	9	10	19	93
52-53 Det	70	15	12	27	87
53-54 Det	70	6	18	24	90
54-55 Det	70	10	17	27	137
55-56 Chi	70	11	11	22	71
57-58 Det	22	1	2	3	2
Totals	740	165	159	324	868
Playoff Totals	59	13	10	23	91

LESWICK, Jack *F*

Season Team	GP	G	A	Pts.	PIM
33-34 Chi	47	1	7	8	16

LESWICK, Peter John *5-6 145 RW*
B. Saskatoon, Sask., July 12, 1918

Season Team	GP	G	A	Pts.	PIM
36-37 NYA	1	1	0	1	0
44-45 Bos	2	0	0	0	0
Totals	3	1	0	1	0

LEVANDOSKI, Joseph Thomas *5-10 185 RW*
B. Cobalt, Ont., Mar. 17, 1921

Season Team	GP	G	A	Pts.	PIM
46-47 NYR	8	1	1	2	0

LEVEILLE, Normand *5-10 175 LW*
B. Montreal, Que., Jan. 10, 1963

Season Team	GP	G	A	Pts.	PIM
81-82 Bos	66	14	19	33	49
82-83 Bos	9	3	6	9	0
Totals	75	17	25	42	49

LEVER, Donald Richard *5-11 185 C*
B. South Porcupine, Ont., Nov. 14, 1952

Season Team	GP	G	A	Pts.	PIM
72-73 Van	78	10	26	38	49
73-74 Van	78	23	25	48	28
74-75 Van	80	38	30	68	49
75-76 Van	80	25	40	65	93
76-77 Van	80	27	30	57	28
77-78 Van	75	17	32	49	58
78-79 Van	71	23	21	44	17
79-80 Van-Atl	79	35	33	68	36
80-81 Calg	62	26	31	57	56
81-82 Calg-Col	82	30	39	69	26

LEVER, Donald Richard *(Continued)*

Season	Team	GP	G	A	Pts.	PIM
82-83	NJ	79	23	30	53	68
83-84	NJ	70	14	19	33	44
84-85	NJ	67	10	8	18	31
85-86	Buf	29	7	1	8	6
86-87	Buf	10	3	2	5	4
Totals		1020	313	367	680	593
Playoff Totals		30	7	10	17	26

LEVIE, Craig Dean *5-11 190 D*
B. Calgary, Alta., Aug. 17, 1959

Season	Team	GP	G	A	Pts.	PIM
81-82	Winn	40	4	9	13	48
82-83	Winn	22	4	5	9	31
83-84	Minn	37	6	13	19	44
84-85	StL	61	6	23	29	33
85-86	Minn	14	2	2	4	8
86-87	Van	9	0	1	1	13
Totals		183	22	53	75	177
Playoff Totals		16	2	3	5	32

LEVINSKY, Alexander (Mine Boy) *5-10 184 D*
B. Syracuse, N.Y., Feb. 2, 1910

Season	Team	GP	G	A	Pts.	PIM
30-31	Tor	8	0	1	1	2
31-32	Tor	47	5	5	10	29
32-33	Tor	48	5	11	16	61
33-34	Tor	47	5	11	16	38
34-35	NYR-Chi	44	3	8	11	22
35-36	Chi	48	1	7	8	69
36-37	Chi	48	0	8	8	32
37-38	Chi	48	3	2	5	18
38-39	Chi	29	1	3	4	16
Totals		367	23	56	79	287
Playoff Totals		34	2	1	3	20

LEVO, Tapio *6-2 200 D*
B. Pori, Finland, Sept. 24, 1955

Season	Team	GP	G	A	Pts.	PIM
81-82	Col	34	9	13	22	14
82-83	NJ	73	7	40	47	22
Totals		107	16	53	69	36

LEWICKI, Daniel *5-9 165 LW*
B. Fort William, Ont., Mar. 12, 1931

Season	Team	GP	G	A	Pts.	PIM
50-51	Tor	61	16	18	34	26
51-52	Tor	51	4	9	13	26
52-53	Tor	4	1	3	4	2
53-54	Tor	7	0	1	1	12
54-55	NYR	70	29	24	53	8
55-56	NYR	70	18	27	45	26
56-57	NYR	70	18	20	38	47
57-58	NYR	70	11	19	30	26
58-59	Chi	58	8	14	22	4
Totals		461	105	135	240	177
Playoff Totals		28	0	4	4	8

LEWIS, David Rodney *6-2 205 D*
B. Kindersley, Sask., July 3, 1953

Season	Team	GP	G	A	Pts.	PIM
73-74	NYI	66	2	15	17	58
74-75	NYI	78	5	14	19	98
75-76	NYI	73	0	19	19	54
76-77	NYI	79	4	24	28	44
77-78	NYI	77	3	11	14	58
78-79	NYI	79	5	18	23	43
79-80	NYI-LA	73	6	17	23	66
80-81	LA	67	1	12	13	98
81-82	LA	64	1	13	14	75
82-83	LA	79	2	10	12	53
83-84	NJ	66	2	5	7	63
84-85	NJ	74	3	9	12	78
85-86	NJ	69	0	15	15	81
86-87	Det	58	2	5	7	66
87-88	Det	6	0	0	0	18
Totals		1008	36	187	223	953
Playoff Totals		91	1	20	21	143

LEWIS, Douglas *5-8 155 LW*
B. Winnipeg, Man., Mar. 3, 1921

Season	Team	GP	G	A	Pts.	PIM
46-47	Mont	3	0	0	0	0

LEWIS, Herbert A. *5-9 160 LW*
B. Calgary, Alta., Apr. 17, 1907

Season	Team	GP	G	A	Pts.	PIM
28-29	Det	37	9	5	14	33
29-30	Det	44	20	11	31	36
30-31	Det	44	15	6	21	38
31-32	Det	48	5	14	19	21
32-33	Det	48	20	14	34	20
33-34	Det	43	16	15	31	15
34-35	Det	48	16	27	43	26
35-36	Det	45	14	23	37	25
36-37	Det	45	14	18	32	14
37-38	Det	42	13	18	31	12
38-39	Det	39	6	10	16	8
Totals		483	148	161	309	248
Playoff Totals		38	13	10	23	6

LEWIS, Robert Dale *6-0 190 LW*
B. Edmonton, Alta., July 28, 1952

Season	Team	GP	G	A	Pts.	PIM
75-76	NYR	8	0	0	0	0

LEY, Richard Norman (Rick) *5-9 185 D*
B. Orillia, Ont., Nov. 2, 1948

Season	Team	GP	G	A	Pts.	PIM
68-69	Tor	38	1	11	12	39
69-70	Tor	48	2	13	15	102
70-71	Tor	76	4	16	20	151
71-72	Tor	67	1	14	15	124
72-73	NE (WHA)	76	3	27	30	108
73-74	NE (WHA)	72	6	35	41	148
74-75	NE (WHA)	62	6	36	42	50
75-76	NE (WHA)	67	8	30	38	78
76-77	NE (WHA)	55	2	21	23	102
77-78	NE (WHA)	73	3	41	44	95
78-79	NE (WHA)	73	7	20	27	135
79-80	Hart	65	4	16	20	92
80-81	Hart	16	0	2	2	20
NHL Totals		310	12	72	84	528
WHA Totals		478	35	210	245	716
NHL Playoff Totals		14	0	2	2	20
WHA Playoff Totals		73	7	33	40	142

LIBA, Igor *6-0 192 LW*
B. Kosice, Czechoslovakia, Nov. 4, 1960

Season	Team	GP	G	A	Pts.	PIM
88-89	NYR-LA	37	7	18	25	36
Playoff Totals		2	0	0	0	2

LIBETT, Lynn Nicholas (Nick) *6-1 195 LW*
B. Stratford, Ont., Dec. 9, 1945

Season	Team	GP	G	A	Pts.	PIM
67-68	Det	22	2	1	3	12
68-69	Det	75	10	14	24	34
69-70	Det	76	20	20	40	39
70-71	Det	78	16	13	29	25
71-72	Det	77	31	22	53	50
72-73	Det	78	19	34	53	56
73-74	Det	67	24	24	48	37
74-75	Det	80	23	28	51	39
75-76	KC	80	20	26	46	71
76-77	Det	80	14	27	41	25
77-78	Det	80	23	22	45	46
78-79	Det	68	15	19	34	20
79-80	Pitt	78	14	12	26	14
80-81	Pitt	43	6	6	12	4
Totals		982	237	268	505	472
Playoff Totals		16	6	2	8	2

LICARI, Anthony *5-7 147 RW*
B. Ottawa, Ont., Apr. 9, 1921

Season	Team	GP	G	A	Pts.	PIM
46-47	Det	9	0	1	1	0

LIDDINGTON, Robert Allen *6-0 175 LW*
B. Calgary, Alta., Sept. 15, 1948

Season	Team	GP	G	A	Pts.	PIM
1970-71	Tor	11	0	1	1	2
72-73	Chi (WHA)	78	20	11	31	24
73-74	Chi (WHA)	73	26	21	47	20
74-75	Chi (WHA)	78	23	18	41	27
75-76	Ott-Hou (WHA)	37	7	8	15	16
76-77	Phoe (WHA)	80	20	24	44	28
NHL Totals		11	0	1	1	2
WHA Totals		346	96	82	178	115
Playoff Totals		18	6	5	11	11

LIDSTER, Doug *6-1 200 D*
B. Kamloops, B.C., Oct. 18, 1960

Season	Team	GP	G	A	Pts.	PIM
83-84	Van	8	0	0	0	4
84-85	Van	78	6	24	30	55
85-86	Van	78	12	16	28	56
86-87	Van	80	12	51	63	40
87-88	Van	64	4	32	36	105
88-89	Van	63	5	17	22	78
89-90	Van	80	8	28	36	36
90-91	Van	78	6	32	38	77
91-92	Van	66	6	23	29	39
Totals		595	59	223	282	490
Playoff Totals		29	2	7	9	28

LIDSTROM, Nicklas *6-1 176 D*
B. Vasteras, Sweden, Apr. 28, 1970

Season	Team	GP	G	A	Pts.	PIM
91-92	Det	80	11	49	60	22
Playoff Totals		11	1	2	3	0

LINDBERG, Chris *6-1 190 LW*
B. Fort Frances, Ont., Apr. 16, 1967

Season	Team	GP	G	A	Pts.	PIM
91-92	Calg	17	2	5	7	17

LINDEN, Trevor *6-4 205 C/RW*
B. Medicine Hat, Alta., Apr. 11, 1970

Season	Team	GP	G	A	Pts.	PIM
88-89	Van	80	30	29	59	41
89-90	Van	73	21	30	51	43
90-91	Van	80	33	37	70	65
91-92	Van	80	31	44	75	99
Totals		313	115	140	225	248

LINDEN, Trevor *(Continued)*

Season	Team	GP	G	A	Pts.	PIM
Playoff Totals		26	7	19	26	16

LINDGREN, Lars *6-1 200 D*
B. Pitea, Sweden, Oct. 12, 1952

Season	Team	GP	G	A	Pts.	PIM
78-79	Van	64	2	19	21	68
79-80	Van	73	5	30	35	66
80-81	Van	52	4	18	22	32
81-82	Van	75	5	16	21	74
82-83	Van	64	6	14	20	48
83-84	Van	66	3	16	19	37
Totals		394	25	113	138	325
Playoff Totals		40	5	6	11	20

LINDHOLM, Mikael *6-1 194 C*
B. Gavle, Sweden, Dec. 19, 1964

Season	Team	GP	G	A	Pts.	PIM
89-90	LA	18	2	2	4	2

LINDSAY, Bill *5-11 185 LW*
B. Big Fork, Man., May 17, 1971

Season	Team	GP	G	A	Pts.	PIM
91-92	Que	23	2	4	6	14

LINDSAY, Robert Blake Theodore (Ted) *5-8 160 LW*
B. Renfrew, Ont., July 29, 1925

Season	Team	GP	G	A	Pts.	PIM
44-45	Det	45	17	6	23	43
45-46	Det	47	7	10	17	14
46-47	Det	59	27	15	42	57
47-48	Det	60	33	19	52	95
48-49	Det	50	26	28	54	97
49-50	Det	69	23	55	78	141
50-51	Det	67	24	35	59	110
51-52	Det	70	30	39	69	123
52-53	Det	70	32	39	71	111
53-54	Det	70	26	36	62	110
54-55	Det	49	19	19	38	85
55-56	Det	67	27	23	50	161
56-57	Det	70	30	55	85	103
57-58	Chi	68	15	24	39	110
58-59	Chi	70	22	36	58	184
59-60	Chi	68	7	19	26	91
64-65	Det	69	14	14	28	173
Totals		1068	379	472	851	1808
Playoff Totals		133	47	49	96	194

LINDSTROM, Bo Morgan (Willy) *6-0 180 RW*
B. Grunns, Sweden, May 5, 1951

Season	Team	GP	G	A	Pts.	PIM
75-76	Winn (WHA)	81	23	36	59	32
76-77	Winn (WHA)	79	44	36	80	37
77-78	Winn (WHA)	77	30	30	60	42
78-79	Winn (WHA)	79	26	36	62	22
79-80	Winn	79	23	26	49	20
80-81	Winn	72	22	13	35	45
81-82	Winn	74	32	27	59	33
82-83	Winn-Edm	73	26	30	56	10
83-84	Edm	73	22	16	38	38
84-85	Edm	80	12	20	32	18
85-86	Pitt	71	14	17	31	30
86-87	Pitt	60	10	13	23	6
NHL Totals		582	161	162	323	200
WHA Totals		316	123	138	261	133
NHL Playoff Totals		57	14	18	32	24
WHA Playoff Totals		51	26	22	48	50

LINSEMAN, Ken *5-11 180 C*
B. Kingston, Ont., Aug. 11, 1958

Season	Team	GP	G	A	Pts.	PIM
77-78	Birm (WHA)	71	38	38	76	126
78-79	Phil	30	5	20	25	23
79-80	Phil	80	22	57	79	107
80-81	Phil	51	17	30	47	150
81-82	Phil	79	24	68	92	275
82-83	Edm	72	33	42	75	181
83-84	Edm	72	18	49	67	119
84-85	Bos	75	24	49	73	126
85-86	Bos	64	23	58	81	97
86-87	Bos	64	15	34	49	126
87-88	Bos	77	29	45	74	167
88-89	Bos	78	27	45	72	164
89-90	Bos-Phil	61	11	25	36	96
90-91	Edm	56	7	29	36	94
91-92	Tor	2	0	0	0	2
NHL Totals		860	256	551	807	1727
WHA Totals		71	38	38	76	126
NHL Playoff Tot.		113	43	77	120	325
WHA Playoff Tot.		5	2	2	4	15

LISCOMBE, Harry Carlyle (Carl) *5-8 170 LW*
B. Perth, Ont., May 17, 1915

Season	Team	GP	G	A	Pts.	PIM
37-38	Det	42	14	10	24	30
38-39	Det	47	8	18	26	13

LISCOMBE, Harry Carlyle (Carl) *(Continued)*

Season	Team	GP	G	A	Pts.	PIM
39-40	Det	30	2	7	9	4
40-41	Det	31	10	10	20	0
41-42	Det	47	13	17	30	30
42-43	Det	50	19	23	42	19
43-44	Det	50	36	37	73	17
44-45	Det	42	23	9	32	18
45-46	Det	44	12	9	21	2
Totals		383	137	140	277	133
Playoff Totals		59	22	19	41	20

LITZENBERGER, Edward C. J. *6-3 194 RW*
B. Neudorf, Sask., July 15, 1932

Season	Team	GP	G	A	Pts.	PIM
52-53	Mont	2	1	0	1	2
53-54	Mont	3	0	0	0	0
54-55	Mont-Chi	73	23	28	51	40
55-56	Chi	70	10	29	39	36
56-57	Chi	70	32	32	64	48
57-58	Chi	70	32	30	62	63
58-59	Chi	70	33	44	77	37
59-60	Chi	52	12	18	30	15
60-61	Chi	62	10	22	32	14
61-62	Det-Tor	69	18	22	40	18
62-63	Tor	58	5	13	18	10
63-64	Tor	19	2	0	2	0
Totals		618	178	238	416	283
Playoff Totals		40	5	13	18	34

LOCAS, Jacques *5-11 175 C*
B. Pointe aux Trembles, Que., Feb. 12, 1926

Season	Team	GP	G	A	Pts.	PIM
47-48	Mont	56	7	8	15	66
48-49	Mont	3	0	0	0	0
Totals		59	7	8	15	66

LOCHEAD, William Alexander *6-1 190 LW*
B. Forest, Ont., Oct. 13, 1954

Season	Team	GP	G	A	Pts.	PIM
74-75	Det	65	16	12	28	34
75-76	Det	53	9	11	20	22
76-77	Det	61	16	14	30	39
77-78	Det	77	20	16	36	47
78-79	Det-Col	67	8	9	17	34
79-80	NYR	7	0	0	0	4
Totals		330	69	62	131	180
Playoff Totals		7	3	0	3	6

LOCKING, Norman Wesley *6-0 165 LW*
B. Owen Sound, Ont., May 24, 1911

Season	Team	GP	G	A	Pts.	PIM
34-35	Chi	35	2	5	7	19
35-36	Chi	13	0	1	1	7
Totals		48	2	6	8	26
Playoff Totals		1	0	0	0	0

LOEWEN, Darcy *5-10 185 LW*
B. Calgary, Alta., Feb. 26, 1969

Season	Team	GP	G	A	Pts.	PIM
89-90	Buf	4	0	0	0	4
90-91	Buf	6	0	0	0	8
91-92	Buf	2	0	0	0	2
Totals		12	0	0	0	14

LOFTHOUSE, Mark *6-2 195 RW/C*
B. New Westminster, B.C., Apr. 21, 1957

Season	Team	GP	G	A	Pts.	PIM
77-78	Wash	18	2	1	3	8
78-79	Wash	52	13	10	23	10
79-80	Wash	68	15	18	33	20
80-81	Wash	3	1	1	2	4
81-82	Det	12	3	4	7	13
82-83	Det	28	8	4	12	18
Totals		181	42	38	80	73

LOGAN, David George *5-10 190 D*
B. Montreal, Que., July 2, 1954

Season	Team	GP	G	A	Pts.	PIM
75-76	Chi	2	0	0	0	0
76-77	Chi	34	0	2	2	61
77-78	Chi	54	1	5	6	77
78-79	Chi	76	1	14	15	176
79-80	Chi-Van	45	3	8	11	143
80-81	Van	7	0	0	0	13
Totals		218	5	29	34	470
Playoff Totals		12	0	0	0	10

LOGAN, Robert *6-0 190 RW*
B. Montreal, Que., Feb. 22, 1964

Season	Team	GP	G	A	Pts.	PIM
86-87	Buf	22	7	3	10	0
87-88	Buf	16	3	2	5	0
88-89	LA	4	0	0	0	0
Totals		42	10	5	15	0

LOISELLE, Claude *5-11 195 C*
B. Ottawa, Ont., May 29, 1963

Season	Team	GP	G	A	Pts.	PIM
81-82	Det	4	1	0	1	2
82-83	Det	18	2	0	2	15
83-84	Det	28	4	6	10	32

LOISELLE, Claude *(Continued)*

Season	Team	GP	G	A	Pts.	PIM
84-85	Det	30	8	1	9	45
85-86	Det	48	7	15	22	142
86-87	NJ	75	16	24	40	137
87-88	NJ	68	17	18	35	121
88-89	NJ	74	7	14	21	209
89-90	Que	72	11	14	25	104
90-91	Que-Tor	66	6	11	17	88
91-92	Tor-NYI	75	7	10	17	115
Totals		558	86	113	199	1010
Playoff Totals		20	4	8	12	50

LOMAKIN, Andrei *5-10 176 LW*
B. Voskresensk, Soviet Union, Apr. 3, 1964

Season	Team	GP	G	A	Pts.	PIM
91-92	Phil	57	14	16	30	26

LONEY, Troy *6-3 209 LW*
B. Bow Island, Alta., Sept. 21, 1963

Season	Team	GP	G	A	Pts.	PIM
83-84	Pitt	13	0	0	0	9
84-85	Pitt	46	10	8	18	59
85-86	Pitt	47	3	9	12	95
86-87	Pitt	23	8	7	15	22
87-88	Pitt	65	5	13	18	151
88-89	Pitt	69	10	6	16	165
89-90	Pitt	67	11	16	27	168
90-91	Pitt	44	7	9	16	85
91-92	Pitt	76	10	16	26	127
Totals		450	64	84	148	881
Playoff Totals		56	7	10	17	97

LONG, Barry Kenneth *6-2 210 D*
B. Brantford, Ont., Jan. 3, 1949

Season	Team	GP	G	A	Pts.	PIM
72-72	LA	70	2	13	15	48
73-74	LA	60	3	19	22	118
74-75	Edm (WHA)	78	20	40	60	116
75-76	Edm (WHA)	78	10	32	42	66
76-77	Edm-Winn (WHA)	73	9	39	48	56
77-78	Winn (WHA)	78	7	24	31	42
78-79	Winn (WHA)	79	5	36	41	42
79-80	Det	80	0	17	17	38
80-81	Winn	65	6	17	23	42
81-82	Winn	5	0	2	2	4
NHL Totals		280	11	68	79	250
WHA Totals		386	51	171	222	322
NHL Playoff Totals		5	0	1	1	18
WHA Playoff Totals		43	3	13	16	20

LONG, Stanley Gordon *5-11 190 D*
B. Owen Sound, Ont., Nov. 6, 1929

Season	Team	GP	G	A	Pts.	PIM
51-52	Mont	0	0	0	0	0
Playoff Totals		3	0	0	0	0

LONSBERRY, David Ross (Ross) *5-11 195 LW*
B. Humboldt, Sask., Feb. 7, 1947

Season	Team	GP	G	A	Pts.	PIM
66-67	Bos	8	0	1	1	2
67-68	Bos	19	2	2	4	12
68-69	Bos	6	0	0	0	2
69-70	LA	76	20	22	42	118
70-71	LA	76	25	28	53	80
71-72	LA-Phil	82	16	21	37	61
72-73	Phil	77	21	29	50	59
73-74	Phil	75	32	19	51	48
74-75	Phil	80	24	25	49	99
75-76	Phil	80	19	28	47	87
76-77	Phil	75	23	32	55	43
77-78	Phil	78	18	30	48	45
78-79	Pitt	80	24	22	46	38
79-80	Pitt	76	15	18	33	36
80-81	Pitt	80	17	33	50	76
Totals		968	256	310	566	806
Playoff Totals		100	21	25	46	87

LOOB, Hakan *5-10 174 RW*
B. Visby, Sweden, July 3, 1960

Season	Team	GP	G	A	Pts.	PIM
83-84	Calg	77	30	25	55	22
84-85	Calg	78	37	35	72	14
85-86	Calg	68	31	36	67	36
86-87	Calg	68	18	26	44	26
87-88	Calg	80	50	56	106	47
88-89	Calg	79	27	58	85	44
Totals		450	193	236	429	189
Playoff Totals		73	26	28	54	16

LOOB, Peter *6-3 190 D*
B. Karlstad, Sweden, July 23, 1957

Season	Team	GP	G	A	Pts.	PIM
84-85	Que	8	1	2	3	0

LORENTZ, James Peter *6-0 180 C*
B. Waterloo, Ont., May 1, 1947

Season	Team	GP	G	A	Pts.	PIM
68-69	Bos	11	1	3	4	6

LORENTZ, James Peter *(Continued)*

Season	Team	GP	G	A	Pts.	PIM
69-70	Bos	68	7	16	23	30
70-71	StL	76	19	21	40	34
71-72	StL-NYR-Buf	52	10	15	25	24
72-73	Buf	78	27	35	62	30
73-74	Buf	78	23	31	54	28
74-75	Buf	72	25	45	70	18
75-76	Buf	75	17	24	41	18
76-77	Buf	79	23	33	56	8
77-78	Buf	70	9	15	24	12
Totals		359	161	238	399	208
Playoff Totals		54	12	10	22	30

LORIMER, Robert Roy *6-1 200 D*
B. Toronto, Ont., Aug. 25, 1953

Season	Team	GP	G	A	Pts.	PIM
76-77	NYI	1	0	1	1	0
77-78	NYI	5	1	0	1	0
78-79	NYI	67	3	18	21	42
79-80	NYI	74	3	16	19	53
80-81	NYI	73	1	12	13	77
81-82	Col	79	5	15	20	68
82-83	NJ	66	3	10	13	42
83-84	NJ	72	2	10	12	62
84-85	NJ	46	2	6	8	35
85-86	NJ	46	2	2	4	52
Totals		529	22	90	112	431
Playoff Totals		49	3	10	13	83

LORRAIN, Rodrique (Rod) *5-5 156 RW*
B. Buckingham, Que., July 1915

Season	Team	GP	G	A	Pts.	PIM
35-36	Mont	1	0	0	0	2
36-37	Mont	47	3	6	9	8
37-38	Mont	48	13	19	32	14
38-39	Mont	38	10	9	19	0
39-40	Mont	41	1	5	6	6
41-42	Mont	4	1	0	1	0
Totals		179	28	39	67	30
Playoff Totals		11	0	3	3	0

LOUGHLIN, Clement (Clem) *6-0 180 D*
B. Carroll, Man., Nov. 15, 1894

Season	Team	GP	G	A	Pts.	PIM
26-27	Det	34	7	3	10	40
27-28	Det	43	1	2	3	21
28-28	Chi	24	0	1	1	16
Totals		101	8	6	14	77

LOUGHLIN, Wilfred *D*

Season	Team	GP	G	A	Pts.	PIM
23-24	Tor	14	0	0	0	2

LOVSIN, Ken *6-0 195 D*
B. Peace River, Alta., Dec. 3, 1966

Season	Team	GP	G	A	Pts.	PIM
90-91	Wash	1	0	0	0	0

LOWDERMILK, Dwayne, Kenneth *6-0 201 D*
B. Burnaby, B.C., Jan. 9, 1958

Season	Team	GP	G	A	Pts.	PIM
80-81	Wash	2	0	1	1	2

LOWE, Darren *5-10 185 RW*
B. Toronto, Ont., Oct. 13, 1960

Season	Team	GP	G	A	Pts.	PIM
83-84	Pitt	8	1	2	3	0

LOWE, Kevin Hugh *6-2 195 D*
B. Lachute, Que., Apr. 15, 1959

Season	Team	GP	G	A	Pts.	PIM
79-80	Edm	64	2	19	21	70
80-81	Edm	79	10	24	34	94
81-82	Edm	80	9	31	40	63
82-83	Edm	80	6	34	40	43
83-84	Edm	80	4	42	46	59
84-85	Edm	80	4	21	25	104
85-86	Edm	74	2	16	18	90
86-87	Edm	77	8	29	37	94
87-88	Edm	70	9	15	24	89
88-89	Edm	76	7	18	25	98
89-90	Edm	78	7	26	33	140
90-91	Edm	73	3	13	16	113
91-92	Edm	55	2	7	9	107
Totals		966	73	295	368	1164
Playoff Totals		170	9	43	52	152

LOWE, Norman E. (Odie) *5-8 140 C*
B. Winnipeg, Man., Apr. 15, 1928

Season	Team	GP	G	A	Pts.	PIM
48-49	NYR	1	0	0	0	0
49-50	NYR	3	1	1	2	0
Totals		4	1	1	2	0

LOWE, Ross Robert *6-1 180 F*
B. Oshawa, Ont., Sept. 21, 1928

Season	Team	GP	G	A	Pts.	PIM
49-50	Bos	3	0	0	0	0
50-51	Bos-Mont	43	5	3	8	40
51-52	Mont	31	1	5	6	42
Totals		77	6	8	14	82

LOWERY, Frederick John (Frock) *D*
B. Ottawa, Ont.

Season	Team	GP	G	A	Pts.	PIM
24-25	Mont M	28	0	0	0	6

LOWERY, Frederick John (Frock) (Continued)

Season	Team	GP	G	A	Pts.	PIM
25-26	Mont M-Pitt Pi	26	1	0	1	4
Totals		54	1	0	1	10
Playoff Totals		2	0	0	0	6

LOWREY, Eddie *F*
B. 1894

17-18	Ott	11	0	0	0	3
18-19	Ott	10	0	0	0	3
20-21	Ham	3	0	0	0	0
Totals		24	0	0	0	6

LOWREY, Gerald *5-8 150 LW*
B. Ottawa, Ont.

27-28	Tor	25	6	5	11	29
28-29	Tor-Pitt Pi	44	5	12	17	30
29-30	Pitt Pi	44	16	14	30	30
30-31	Phil Q	42	13	14	27	27
31-32	Chi	48	8	3	11	32
32-33	Ott	6	0	0	0	0
Totals		209	48	48	96	148
Playoff Totals		2	1	0	1	2

LOWRY, Dave *6-1 195 LW*
B. Sudbury, Ont., Feb. 14, 1965

85-86	Van	73	10	8	18	143
86-87	Van	70	8	10	18	176
87-88	Van	22	1	3	4	38
88-89	StL	21	3	3	6	11
89-90	StL	78	19	6	25	75
90-91	StL	79	19	21	40	168
91-92	StL	75	7	13	20	77
Totals		418	67	64	131	688
Playoff Totals		44	3	11	14	98

LUCAS, Daniel Kenneth *6-1 197 RW*
B. Powell River, B.C., Feb. 28, 1958

78-79	Phil	6	1	0	1	0

LUCAS, David Charles *D*
B. Downeyville, Ont., Mar. 22, 1932

62-63	Det	1	0	0	0	0

LUCE, Donald Harold *6-2 185 C*
B. London, Ont., Oct. 2, 1948

69-70	NYR	12	1	2	3	8
70-71	NYR-Det	67	3	12	15	18
71-72	Buf	78	11	8	19	38
72-73	Buf	78	18	25	43	32
73-74	Buf	75	26	31	57	44
74-75	Buf	80	33	43	76	45
75-76	Buf	77	21	49	70	42
76-77	Buf	80	26	43	69	16
77-78	Buf	78	26	35	61	24
78-79	Buf	79	26	35	61	14
79-90	Buf	80	14	29	43	30
80-91	Buf-LA	71	16	13	29	21
81-82	Tor	39	4	4	8	32
Totals		894	225	329	554	364
Playoff Totals		71	17	22	39	52

LUDVIG, Jan *5-10 190 RW*
B. Liberec, Czechoslovakia, Sept. 17, 1961

82-83	NJ	51	7	10	17	30
83-84	NJ	74	22	32	54	70
84-85	NJ	74	12	19	31	53
85-86	NJ	42	5	9	14	63
86-87	NJ	47	7	9	16	98
87-88	Buf	13	1	6	7	65
88-89	Buf	13	0	2	2	39
Totals		314	54	87	141	418

LUDWIG, Craig Lee *6-3 222 D*
B. Rhinelander, Wisc., Mar. 15, 1961

82-83	Mont	0	0	25	25	59
83-84	Mont	80	7	18	25	52
84-85	Mont	72	5	14	19	90
85-86	Mont	69	2	4	6	63
86-87	Mont	75	4	12	16	105
87-88	Mont	74	4	10	14	69
88-89	Mont	74	3	13	16	73
89-90	Mont	73	1	15	16	108
90-91	NYI	75	1	8	9	77
91-92	Minn	73	2	9	11	54
Totals		745	29	128	157	750
Playoff Totals		117	3	14	17	174

LUDZIK, Steve *5-11 185 C*
B. Toronto, Ont., Apr. 3, 1962

81-82	Chi	8	2	1	3	2
82-83	Chi	66	6	19	25	68
83-84	Chi	80	9	20	29	73
84-85	Chi	79	11	20	31	86
85-86	Chi	49	6	5	11	21
86-87	Chi	52	5	12	17	34

LUDZIK, Steve *(Continued)*

87-88	Chi	73	6	15	21	40
88-89	Chi	6	1	0	1	8
89-90	Buf	11	0	1	1	6
Totals		424	46	93	139	333
Playoff Totals		44	4	8	12	70

LUKOWICH, Bernard Joseph *6-0 190 RW*
B. North Battleford, Sask., Mar. 18, 1952

73-74	Pitt	53	9	10	19	32
74-75	StL	26	4	5	9	2
75-76	Calg (WHA)	15	5	2	7	18
NHL Totals		79	13	15	28	34
WHA Totals		15	5	2	7	18
NHL Playoff Totals		2	0	0	0	0
WHA Playoff Totals		10	4	3	7	8

LUKOWICH, Eugene (Morris) *5-9 170 LW*
B. Speers, Sask., June 1, 1956

76-77	Hou (WHA)	62	27	18	45	67
77-78	Hou (WHA)	80	40	35	75	131
78-79	Winn (WHA)	80	65	34	99	119
79-80	Winn	78	35	39	74	77
80-81	Winn	80	33	34	67	90
81-82	Winn	77	43	49	92	102
82-83	Winn	69	22	21	43	67
83-84	Winn	80	30	25	55	71
84-85	Winn-Bos	69	10	17	27	52
85-86	Bos-LA	69	12	13	25	61
86-87	LA	60	14	21	35	64
NHL Totals		582	199	219	418	584
WHA Totals		222	132	87	219	317
NHL Playoff Totals		11	0	2	2	24
WHA Playoff Totals		27	15	13	28	57

LUKSA, Charles (Chuck) *6-1 197 D*
B. Toronto, Ont., July 15, 1954

78-79	Cin (WHA)	78	8	12	20	116
79-80	Hart	8	0	1	1	4
NHL Totals		8	0	1	1	4
WHA Totals		78	8	12	20	116
WHA Playoff Totals		3	0	0	0	7

LUMLEY, David *6-0 185 RW*
B. Toronto, Ont., Sept. 1, 1954

78-79	Mont	3	0	0	0	0
79-80	Edm	80	20	38	58	138
80-81	Edm	53	7	9	16	74
81-82	Edm	66	32	42	74	96
82-83	Edm	72	13	24	37	158
83-84	Edm	56	6	15	21	68
84-85	Hart-Edm	60	9	23	32	111
85-86	Edm	46	11	9	20	35
86-87	Edm	1	0	0	0	0
Totals		437	98	160	258	680
Playoff Totals		61	6	8	14	131

LUMME, Jyrki *6-1 190 D*
B. Tampere, Finland, July 16, 1966

88-89	Mont	21	1	3	4	10
89-90	Mont-Van	65	4	26	30	49
90-91	Van	80	5	27	32	59
91-92	Van	75	12	32	44	65
Totals		241	22	88	110	183
Playoff Totals		19	4	6	10	4

LUND, Pentti Alexander (Penny) *6-0 185 RW*
B. Helsinki, Finland, Dec. 6, 1925

48-49	NYR	59	14	16	30	16
49-50	NYR	64	18	9	27	16
50-51	NYR	59	4	16	20	6
51-52	Bos	23	0	5	5	0
52-53	Bos	54	8	9	17	2
Totals		259	44	55	99	40
Playoff Totals		18	7	5	12	0

LUNDBERG, Brian Frederick *5-10 190 D*
B. Burnaby, B.C., June 5, 1960

82-83	Pitt	1	0	0	0	2

LUNDE, Leonard Melvin *6-1 194 C*
B. Campbell River, B.C., Nov. 13, 1936

58-59	Det	68	14	12	26	15
59-60	Det	66	6	17	23	10
60-61	Det	53	6	12	18	10
61-62	Det	23	2	9	11	4
62-63	Chi	60	6	22	28	30
65-66	Chi	24	4	7	11	4
67-68	Minn	7	0	1	1	0
70-71	Van	20	1	3	4	2
73-74	Edm (WHA)	71	26	22	48	8
NHL Totals		321	39	83	122	75

LUNDE, Leonard Melvin *(Continued)*

WHA Totals		71	26	22	48	8
NHL Playoff Totals		20	3	2	5	2
WHA Playoff Totals		5	0	1	1	0

LUNDHOLM, Bengt *6-0 180 LW*
B. Falun, Sweden, Aug. 4, 1955

81-82	Winn	66	14	30	44	10
82-83	Winn	58	14	28	42	16
83-84	Winn	57	5	14	19	20
84-85	Winn	78	12	18	30	20
85-86	Winn	16	3	5	8	6
Totals		275	48	95	143	72
Playoff Totals		14	3	4	7	14

LUNDRIGAN, Joseph Roche *5-11 180 D*
B. Corner Brook, Nfld., Sept. 12, 1948

72-73	Tor	49	2	8	10	20
74-75	Wash	3	0	0	0	2
Totals		52	2	8	10	22

LUNDSTROM, Tord *5-11 176 LW*
B. Kiruna, Sweden, Mar. 4, 1945

73-74	Det	11	1	1	2	0

LUNDY, Patrick Anthony *5-10 168 C*
B. Saskatoon, Sask., May 31, 1924

45-46	Det	4	3	2	5	2
46-47	Det	59	17	17	34	10
47-48	Det	11	4	1	5	6
48-49	Det	15	4	3	7	4
50-51	Chi	61	9	9	18	9
Totals		150	37	32	69	31
Playoff Totals		11	2	1	3	0

LUONGO, Christopher *6-0 180 D*
B. Detroit, Mich., Mar. 17, 1967

90-91	Det	4	0	1	1	4

LUPIEN, Gilles *6-6 210 D*
B. Lachute, Que., Apr. 20, 1954

77-78	Mont	46	1	3	4	108
78-79	Mont	72	1	9	10	124
79-80	Mont	56	1	7	8	109
80-81	Pitt-Hart	51	2	5	7	73
81-82	Hart	1	0	1	1	2
Totals		226	5	25	30	416
Playoff Totals		25	0	0	0	21

LUPUL, Gary John *5-8 175 C/LW*
B. Powell River, B.C., Apr. 4, 1959

79-80	Van	51	9	11	20	24
80-81	Van	7	0	2	2	2
81-82	Van	41	10	7	17	26
82-83	Van	40	18	10	28	46
83-84	Van	69	17	27	44	51
84-85	Van	66	12	17	29	82
85-86	Van	19	4	1	5	12
Totals		293	70	75	145	243
Playoff Totals		25	4	7	11	11

LYLE, George *6-2 205 LW*
B. North Vancouver, B.C., Nov. 24, 1953

76-77	NE (WHA)	75	39	33	72	62
77-78	NE (WHA)	68	30	24	54	74
78-79	NE (WHA)	59	17	18	35	54
79-80	Det	27	7	4	11	2
80-81	Det	31	10	14	24	28
81-82	Det-Hart	25	3	14	17	13
82-83	Hart	16	4	6	10	8
NHL Totals		99	24	38	62	51
WHA Totals		202	86	75	161	190
WHA Playoff Totals		26	6	6	12	42

LYNCH, John Alan (Jack) *6-2 180 D*
B. Toronto, Ont., May 25, 1952

72-73	Pitt	47	1	18	19	40
73-74	Pitt-Det	52	3	16	19	48
74-75	Det-Wash	70	3	20	23	62
75-76	Wash	79	9	13	22	78
76-77	Wash	75	5	25	30	90
77-78	Wash	29	1	8	9	4
78-79	Wash	30	2	6	8	14
Totals		382	24	106	130	336

LYNN, Victor Ivan *5-9 185 D*
B. Saskatoon, Sask., Jan. 26, 1925

43-44	Det	3	0	0	0	4
45-46	Mont	2	0	0	0	0
46-47	Tor	31	6	14	20	44
47-48	Tor	60	12	22	34	53
48-49	Tor	52	7	9	16	36
49-50	Tor	70	7	13	20	36
50-51	Bos	56	14	6	20	69
51-52	Bos	12	2	2	4	4

LYNN, Victor Ivan *(Continued)*

Season	Team	GP	G	A	Pts.	PIM
52-53	Chi	29	0	10	10	23
53-54	Chi	11	1	0	1	2
Totals		326	49	76	125	271
Playoff Totals		47	7	10	17	46

LYON, Steven *5-10 169 D*
B. Toronto, Ont., May 16, 1952

Season	Team	GP	G	A	Pts.	PIM
76-77	Pitt	3	0	0	0	2

LYONS, Ronald (Peaches) *LW*

Season	Team	GP	G	A	Pts.	PIM
30-31	Bos-Phil Q	36	2	4	6	29
Playoff Totals		5	0	0	0	0

LYSIAK, Thomas James *6-1 195 C*
B. High Prairie, Alta., Apr. 22, 1953

Season	Team	GP	G	A	Pts.	PIM
73-74	Atl	77	19	45	64	54
74-75	Atl	77	25	52	77	73
75-76	Atl	80	31	51	82	60
76-77	Atl	79	30	51	81	52
77-78	Atl	80	27	42	69	54
78-79	Atl-Chi	66	23	45	68	50
79-80	Chi	77	26	43	69	31
80-81	Chi	72	21	55	76	20
81-82	Chi	71	32	50	82	84
82-83	Chi	61	23	38	61	27
83-84	Chi	54	17	30	47	35
84-85	Chi	74	16	30	46	13
85-86	Chi	51	2	19	21	14
Totals		919	292	551	843	567
Playoff Totals		78	25	38	63	49

MacADAM, Reginald Alan (Al) *6-0 180 RW*
B. Charlottetown, P.E.I., Mar. 16, 1952

Season	Team	GP	G	A	Pts.	PIM
73-74	Phil	5	0	0	0	0
74-75	Cal	80	18	25	43	55
75-76	Cal	80	32	31	63	49
76-77	Clev	80	22	41	63	68
77-78	Clev	80	16	32	48	42
78-79	Minn	69	24	34	58	30
79-80	Minn	80	42	51	93	24
80-81	Minn	78	21	39	60	94
81-82	Minn	79	18	43	61	37
82-83	Minn	73	11	22	33	60
83-84	Minn	80	22	13	35	23
84-85	Van	80	14	20	34	27
Totals		864	240	351	591	509
Playoff Totals		64	20	24	44	21

MacDERMID, Paul *6-1 205 RW*
B. Chesley, Ont., Apr. 14, 1963

Season	Team	GP	G	A	Pts.	PIM
81-82	Hart	3	1	0	1	2
82-83	Hart	7	0	0	0	2
83-84	Hart	3	0	1	1	0
84-85	Hart	31	4	7	11	29
85-86	Hart	74	13	10	23	160
86-87	Hart	72	7	11	18	202
87-88	Hart	80	20	15	35	139
88-89	Hart	74	17	27	44	141
89-90	Hart-Winn	73	13	22	35	169
90-91	Winn	69	15	21	36	128
91-92	Winn-Wash	74	12	16	28	194
Totals		560	102	130	232	1166
Playoff Totals		40	5	11	16	114

MacDONALD, Blair Joseph *5-10 180 RW*
B. Cornwall, Ont., Nov. 17, 1953

Season	Team	GP	G	A	Pts.	PIM
73-74	Edm (WHA)	78	21	24	45	34
74-75	Edm (WHA)	72	22	24	46	14
75-76	Edm-Ind (WHA)	85	27	16	43	22
76-77	Ind (WHA)	81	34	30	64	28
77 78	Edm (WHA)	80	34	34	68	11
78-79	Edm (WHA)	80	34	37	71	44
79-80	Edm	80	46	48	94	6
80-81	Edm-Van	63	24	33	57	37
81-82	Van	59	18	15	33	20
82-83	Van	17	3	4	7	2
NHL Totals		219	91	100	191	65
WHA Totals		476	172	165	337	153
NHL Playoff Totals		11	0	6	6	2
WHA Playoff Totals		43	20	21	41	12

MacDONALD, Brett *6-0 195 D*
B. Bothwell, Ont., Jan. 5, 1966

Season	Team	GP	G	A	Pts.	PIM
87-88	Van	1	0	0	0	0

MacDONALD, Calvin Parker (Parker) *5-11 184 LW*
B. Sydney, N.S., June 14, 1933

Season	Team	GP	G	A	Pts.	PIM
52-53	Tor	1	0	0	0	0
54-55	Tor	62	8	3	11	36

MacDONALD, Calvin Parker (Parker) *(Continued)*

Season	Team	GP	G	A	Pts.	PIM
56-57	NYR	45	7	8	15	24
57-58	NYR	70	8	10	18	30
59-60	NYR	4	0	0	0	0
60-61	Det	70	14	12	26	6
61-62	Det	32	5	7	12	8
62-63	Det	69	33	28	61	32
63-64	Det	68	21	25	46	25
64-65	Det	69	13	33	46	38
65-66	Bos-Det	66	11	16	27	30
66-67	Det	16	3	5	8	2
67-68	Minn	69	19	23	42	22
68-69	Minn	35	2	9	11	0
Totals		676	144	179	323	253
Playoff Totals		75	14	14	28	20

MacDONALD, James Allen Kilby (Kilby) *5-11 178 LW*
B. Ottawa, Ont., Sept. 6, 1914

Season	Team	GP	G	A	Pts.	PIM
39-40	NYR	44	15	13	28	19
40-41	NYR	47	5	6	11	12
43-44	NYR	24	7	9	16	4
44-45	NYR	36	9	6	15	12
Totals		151	36	34	70	47
Playoff Totals		15	1	2	3	4

MacDONALD, Lowell Wilson *5-11 185 RW*
B. New Glasgow, N.S., Aug. 30, 1941

Season	Team	GP	G	A	Pts.	PIM
61-62	Det	1	0	0	0	2
62-63	Det	26	2	1	3	8
63-64	Det	10	1	4	5	0
64-65	Det	9	2	1	3	0
67-68	LA	74	21	24	45	12
68-69	LA	58	14	14	28	10
70-71	Pitt	10	0	1	1	0
72-73	Pitt	78	34	41	75	8
73-74	Pitt	78	43	39	82	14
74-75	Pitt	71	27	33	60	24
75-76	Pitt	69	30	43	73	12
76-77	Pitt	3	1	1	2	0
77-78	Pitt	19	5	8	13	2
Totals		506	180	210	390	92
Playoff Totals		29	11	11	22	12

MacDOUGALL, Kim *5-11 180 D*
B. Regina, Sask., Aug. 29, 1954

Season	Team	GP	G	A	Pts.	PIM
74-75	Minn	1	0	0	0	0

MacEACHERN, Shane *5-11 180 C*
B. Charlottetown, P.E.I., Dec. 14, 1967

Season	Team	GP	G	A	Pts.	PIM
87-88	StL	1	0	0	0	0

MACEY, Hubert (Hub) *5-8 178 C*
B. Big River, Sask., Apr. 13, 1921

Season	Team	GP	G	A	Pts.	PIM
41-42	NYR	9	3	5	8	0
42-43	NYR	9	3	3	6	0
46-47	Mont	12	0	1	1	0
Totals		30	6	9	15	0
Playoff Totals		8	0	0	0	0

MacGREGOR, Bruce Cameron *5-10 180 RW*
B. Edmonton, Alta., Apr. 26, 1941

Season	Team	GP	G	A	Pts.	PIM
60-61	Det	12	0	1	1	0
61-62	Det	65	6	12	18	16
62-63	Det	67	11	11	22	12
63-64	Det	63	11	21	32	15
64-65	Det	66	21	20	41	19
65-66	Det	70	20	14	34	28
66-67	Det	70	28	19	47	14
67-68	Det	71	15	24	39	13
68-69	Det	69	18	23	41	14
69-70	Det	73	15	23	38	24
70-71	Det-NYR	74	18	29	47	22
71-72	NYR	75	19	21	40	22
72-73	NYR	52	14	12	26	12
73-74	NYR	66	17	27	44	6
74-75	Edm (WHA)	72	24	28	52	10
75-76	Edm (WHA)	63	13	10	23	13
NHL Totals		893	213	257	470	217
WHA Totals		135	37	38	75	23
NHL Playoff Totals		107	19	28	47	44

MacGREGOR, Randy Kenneth *5-9 175 RW*
B. Cobourg, Ont., July 9, 1953

Season	Team	GP	G	A	Pts.	PIM
81-82	Hart	2	1	1	2	2

MacGUIGAN, Garth Leslie *6-0 191 C*
B. Charlottetown, P.E.I., Feb. 16, 1956

Season	Team	GP	G	A	Pts.	PIM
79-80	NYI	2	0	0	0	0

MacINNIS, Allan *6-2 196 D*
B. Inverness, N.S., July 11, 1963

Season	Team	GP	G	A	Pts.	PIM
81-82	Calg	2	0	0	0	0
82-83	Calg	14	1	3	4	9
83-84	Calg	51	11	34	45	42
84-85	Calg	67	14	52	66	75
85-86	Calg	77	11	57	68	76
86-87	Calg	79	20	56	76	97
87-88	Calg	80	25	58	83	114
88-89	Calg	79	16	58	74	126
89-90	Calg	79	28	62	90	82
90-91	Calg	78	28	75	103	90
91-92	Calg	72	20	57	77	83
Totals		678	174	512	686	794
Playoff Totals		82	22	65	87	131

MacINTOSH, Ian *F*

Season	Team	GP	G	A	Pts.	PIM
52-53	NYR	4	0	0	0	4

MacIVER, Donald *6-0 200 D*
B. Montreal, Que., May 3, 1955

Season	Team	GP	G	A	Pts.	PIM
79-80	Winn	6	0	0	0	2

MACIVER, Norm *5-11 180 D*
B. Thunder Bay, Ont., Sept. 8, 1964

Season	Team	GP	G	A	Pts.	PIM
86-87	NYR	3	0	1	1	0
87-88	NYR	37	9	15	24	14
88-89	NYR-Hart	63	1	32	33	38
89-90	Edm	1	0	0	0	0
90-91	Edm	21	2	5	7	14
91-92	Edm	57	6	34	40	38
Totals		182	18	87	105	104
Playoff Totals		31	1	6	7	18

MacKASEY, Blair *6-2 200 D*
B. Hamilton, Ont., Dec. 13, 1955

Season	Team	GP	G	A	Pts.	PIM
76-77	Tor	1	0	0	0	2

MacKAY, Calum (Baldy) *5-9 185 LW*
B. Toronto, Ont., Jan. 1, 1927

Season	Team	GP	G	A	Pts.	PIM
46-47	Det	5	0	0	0	0
48-49	Det	1	0	0	0	0
49-50	Mont	52	8	10	18	44
50-51	Mont	70	18	10	28	69
51-52	Mont	12	0	1	1	8
53-54	Mont	47	10	13	23	54
54-55	Mont	50	14	21	35	39
Totals		237	50	55	105	214
Playoff Totals		38	5	13	18	20

MacKAY, David *D*
B. Edmonton, Alta.

Season	Team	GP	G	A	Pts.	PIM
40-41	Chi	29	3	0	3	26
Playoff Totals		5	0	1	1	2

MacKAY, Duncan (Mickey) *C*
B. Chesley, Ont., May 21, 1894

Season	Team	GP	G	A	Pts.	PIM
26-27	Chi	36	14	8	22	23
27-28	Chi	35	17	4	21	23
28-29	Pitt Pi-Bos	40	9	2	11	20
29-30	Bos	40	4	5	9	13
Totals		151	44	19	63	79
Playoff Totals		11	0	0	0	6

MacKAY, Murdo John *5-11 175 C*
B. Fort William, Ont., Aug. 8, 1917

Season	Team	GP	G	A	Pts.	PIM
45-46	Mont	5	0	1	1	0
47-48	Mont	14	0	2	2	0
Totals		19	0	3	3	0
Playoff Totals		15	1	2	3	0

MACKELL, Fleming David *5-8 167 C*
B. Montreal, Que., Apr. 30, 1929

Season	Team	GP	G	A	Pts.	PIM
47-48	Tor	3	0	0	0	2
48-49	Tor	11	1	1	2	0
49-50	Tor	36	7	13	20	0
50-51	Tor	70	12	13	25	40
51-52	Tor-Bos	62	3	16	19	40
52-53	Bos	65	27	17	44	63
53-54	Bos	67	15	32	47	60
54-55	Bos	60	11	24	35	76
55-56	Bos	52	7	9	16	59
56-57	Bos	65	22	17	39	73
57-58	Bos	70	20	40	60	72
58-59	Bos	57	17	23	40	28
59-60	Bos	47	7	15	22	19
Totals		665	149	220	369	532
Playoff Totals		80	22	41	63	75

MacKENZIE, John Barry (Barry) *6-0 190 D*
B. Toronto, Ont., Aug. 16, 1941

Season	Team	GP	G	A	Pts.	PIM
68-69	Minn	6	0	1	1	6

MacKENZIE, William Kenneth *5-11 175 D*
B. Winnipeg, Man., Dec. 12, 1911

Season	Team	GP	G	A	Pts.	PIM
32-33	Chi	35	4	4	8	13

MacKENZIE, William Kenneth *(Continued)*

Season	Team	GP	G	A	Pts.	PIM
33-34	Mont M	48	4	3	7	20
34-35	Mont M-NYR	20	1	0	1	10
36-37	Mont M-Mont	49	4	4	8	38
37-38	Mont-Chi	46	1	2	3	24
38-39	Chi	48	1	0	1	14
39-40	Chi	20	0	1	1	14
Totals		266	15	14	29	133
Playoff Totals		19	1	1	2	11

MACKEY, David *6-4 200 LW*
B. Richmond, B.C., July 24, 1966

Season	Team	GP	G	A	Pts.	PIM
87-88	Chi	23	1	3	4	71
88-89	Chi	23	1	2	3	78
89-90	Minn	16	2	0	2	28
91-92	StL	19	1	0	1	49
Totals		81	5	5	10	226
Playoff Totals		1	0	0	0	0

MACKEY, Reginald *5-7 155 D*
B. Ottawa, Ont., May 7, 1900

Season	Team	GP	G	A	Pts.	PIM
26-27	NYR	34	0	0	0	16
Playoff Totals		1	0	0	0	0

MACKIE, Howard *5-8 175 D*
B. Kitchener, Ont., Aug. 30, 1913

Season	Team	GP	G	A	Pts.	PIM
36-37	Det	13	1	0	1	4
37-38	Det	7	0	0	0	0
Totals		20	1	0	1	4
Playoff Totals		8	0	0	0	0

MacKINNON, Paul *6-0 195 D*
B. Brantford, Ont., Nov. 6, 1958

Season	Team	GP	G	A	Pts.	PIM
78-79	Winn (WHA)	73	2	15	17	70
79-80	Wash	63	1	11	12	22
80-81	Wash	14	0	0	0	22
81-82	Wash	39	2	9	11	35
82-83	Wash	19	2	2	4	8
83-84	Wash	12	0	1	1	4
NHL Totals		147	5	23	28	91
WHA Totals		73	2	15	17	70
WHA Playoff Totals		10	2	5	7	4

MacLEAN, John *6-0 200 RW*
B. Oshawa, Ont., Nov. 20, 1964

Season	Team	GP	G	A	Pts.	PIM
83-84	NJ	23	1	0	1	10
84-85	NJ	61	13	20	33	44
85-86	NJ	74	21	36	57	112
86-87	NJ	80	31	36	67	120
87-88	NJ	76	23	16	39	147
88-89	NJ	74	42	45	87	127
89-90	NJ	80	41	38	79	80
90-91	NJ	78	45	33	78	150
Totals		546	217	224	441	790
Playoff Totals		33	16	15	31	92

MacLEAN, Paul *6-2 218 RW*
B. Grostenquin, France, Mar. 9, 1958

Season	Team	GP	G	A	Pts.	PIM
80-81	StL	1	0	0	0	0
81-82	Winn	74	36	25	61	106
82-83	Winn	80	32	44	76	121
83-84	Winn	76	40	31	71	155
84-85	Winn	79	41	60	101	119
85-86	Winn	69	27	29	56	74
86-87	Winn	72	32	42	74	75
87-88	Winn	77	40	39	79	76
88-89	Det	76	36	35	71	118
89-90	StL	78	34	33	67	100
90-91	StL	37	6	11	17	24
Totals		719	324	349	673	968
Playoff Totals		52	21	14	35	104

MacLEISH, Richard George *5-11 185 C*
B. Lindsay, Ont., Jan. 3, 1950

Season	Team	GP	G	A	Pts.	PIM
70-71	Phil	26	2	4	6	19
71-72	Phil	17	1	2	3	9
72-73	Phil	78	50	50	100	69
73-74	Phil	78	32	45	77	42
74-75	Phil	80	38	41	79	50
75-76	Phil	51	22	23	45	16
76-77	Phil	79	49	48	97	42
77-78	Phil	76	31	39	70	33
78-79	Phil	71	26	32	58	47
79-80	Phil	78	31	35	66	28
80-81	Phil	78	38	36	74	25
81-82	Hart-Pitt	74	19	28	47	44
82-83	Pitt	6	0	5	5	2
83-84	Phil-Det	54	10	22	32	8
Totals		846	349	410	759	434
Playoff Totals		114	54	53	107	38

MacLELLAN, Brian *6-3 215 LW*
B. Guelph, Ont., Oct. 27, 1958

Season	Team	GP	G	A	Pts.	PIM
82-83	LA	8	0	3	3	7

MacLELLAN, Brian *(Continued)*

Season	Team	GP	G	A	Pts.	PIM
83-84	LA	72	25	29	54	45
84-85	LA	80	31	54	85	53
85-86	LA-NYR	78	16	29	45	66
86-87	Minn	76	32	31	63	69
87-88	Minn	75	16	32	48	74
88-89	Minn-Calg	72	18	26	44	118
89-90	Calg	65	20	18	38	26
90-91	Calg	57	13	14	27	55
91-92	Det	23	1	5	6	28
Totals		606	172	241	413	541
Playoff Totals		47	5	9	14	42

MacLEOD, Pat *5-11 190 D*
B. Melfort, Sask., June 15, 1969

Season	Team	GP	G	A	Pts.	PIM
90-91	Minn	1	0	1	1	0
91-92	SJ	37	5	11	16	4
Totals		38	5	12	17	4

MacMILLAN, John *5-9 185 RW*
B. Lethbridge, Alta., Oct. 25, 1935

Season	Team	GP	G	A	Pts.	PIM
60-61	Tor	31	3	5	8	8
61-62	Tor	32	1	0	1	8
62-63	Tor	6	1	1	2	6
63-64	Tor-Det	33	0	3	3	16
64-65	Det	3	0	1	1	0
Totals		105	5	10	15	38
Playoff Totals		12	0	1	1	2

MacMILLAN, Robert Lea *5-11 185 RW*
B. Charlottetown, P.E.I., Dec. 3, 1952

Season	Team	GP	G	A	Pts.	PIM
72-73	Minn (WHA)	75	13	27	40	48
73-74	Minn (WHA)	78	14	34	48	81
74-75	NYR	22	1	2	3	4
75-76	StL	80	20	32	52	41
76-77	StL	80	19	39	58	11
77-78	StL-Atl	80	38	33	71	49
78-79	Atl	79	37	71	108	14
79-80	Atl	77	22	39	61	10
80-81	Calg	77	28	35	63	47
81-82	Calg-Col	80	22	39	61	41
82-83	NJ	71	19	29	48	8
83-84	NJ	71	17	23	40	23
84-85	Chi	36	5	7	12	12
NHL Totals		753	228	349	577	260
WHA Totals		153	27	61	88	129
NHL Playoff Totals		31	8	11	19	16
WHA Playoff Totals		16	2	6	8	4

MacMILLAN, William Stewart *5-10 180 RW*
B. Charlottetown, P.E.I., Mar. 7, 1943

Season	Team	GP	G	A	Pts.	PIM
70-71	Tor	76	22	19	41	42
71-72	Tor	61	10	7	17	39
72-73	Atl	78	10	15	25	52
73-74	NYI	55	4	9	13	16
74-75	NYI	69	13	12	25	12
75-76	NYI	64	9	7	16	10
76-77	NYI	43	6	8	14	13
Totals		446	74	77	151	184
Playoff Totals		53	6	6	12	40

MacNEIL, Allister Wences *5-10 180 D*
B. Sydney, N.S., Sept. 27, 1935

Season	Team	GP	G	A	Pts.	PIM
55-56	Tor	1	0	0	0	2
56-57	Tor	53	4	8	12	84
57-58	Tor	13	0	0	0	9
59-60	Tor	4	0	0	0	2
61-62	Mont	61	1	7	8	74
62-63	Chi	70	2	19	21	100
63-64	Chi	70	5	19	24	91
64-65	Chi	69	3	7	10	119
65-66	Chi	51	0	1	1	34
66-67	NYR	58	0	4	4	44
67-68	Pitt	74	2	10	12	58
Totals		524	17	75	92	617
Playoff Totals		37	0	4	4	67

MacNEIL, Stephen Bernard (Bernie) *5-11 190 LW*
B. Sudbury, Ont., Mar. 7, 1950

Season	Team	GP	G	A	Pts.	PIM
72-73	LA (WHA)	42	4	7	11	48
73-74	StL	4	0	0	0	0
75-76	Cin (WHA)	77	15	12	27	83
NHL Totals		4	0	0	0	0
WHA Totals		119	19	19	38	131

MACOUN, Jamie *6-2 197 D*
B. Newmarket, Ont., Aug. 17, 1961

Season	Team	GP	G	A	Pts.	PIM
82-83	Calg	22	1	4	5	25
83-84	Calg	72	9	23	32	97
84-85	Calg	70	9	30	39	67
85-86	Calg	77	11	21	32	81
86-87	Calg	79	7	33	40	111
88-89	Calg	72	8	19	27	76

MACOUN, Jamie *(Continued)*

Season	Team	GP	G	A	Pts.	PIM
89-90	Calg	78	8	27	35	70
90-91	Calg	79	7	15	22	84
91-92	Calg-Tor	76	5	25	30	71
Totals		625	65	197	262	682
Playoff Totals		84	6	19	25	87

MacPHERSON, James Albert (Bud) *6-3 205 D*
B. Edmonton, Alta., Mar. 21, 1927

Season	Team	GP	G	A	Pts.	PIM
48-49	Mont	3	0	0	0	2
50-51	Mont	62	0	16	16	40
51-52	Mont	54	2	1	3	24
52-53	Mont	59	2	3	5	67
53-54	Mont	41	0	5	5	41
54-55	Mont	30	1	8	9	55
56-57	Mont	10	0	0	0	4
Totals		259	5	33	38	233
Playoff Totals		29	0	3	3	21

MacSWEYN, Donald Ralph *5-11 195 D*
B. Hawkesbury, Ont., Sept. 8, 1942

Season	Team	GP	G	A	Pts.	PIM
67-68	Phil	4	0	0	0	0
68-69	Phil	24	0	4	4	6
69-70	Phil	17	0	0	0	4
71-72	Phil	2	0	1	1	0
72-73	LA (WHA)	78	0	23	23	39
73-74	LA-Van (WHA)	69	2	21	23	58
NHL Totals		47	0	5	5	10
WHA Totals		147	2	44	46	97
NHL Playoff Totals		8	0	0	0	6
WHA Playoff Totals		6	1	2	3	4

MacTAVISH, Craig *6-1 195 C*
B. London, Ont., Aug. 15, 1958

Season	Team	GP	G	A	Pts.	PIM
79-80	Bos	46	11	17	28	8
80-81	Bos	24	3	5	8	13
81-82	Bos	2	0	1	1	0
82-83	Bos	75	10	20	30	18
83-84	Bos	70	20	23	43	35
85-86	Edm	74	23	24	47	70
86-87	Edm	79	20	19	39	55
87-88	Edm	80	15	17	32	47
88-89	Edm	80	21	31	52	55
89-90	Edm	80	21	22	43	89
90-91	Edm	80	17	15	32	76
91-92	Edm	80	12	18	30	98
Totals		770	173	212	385	564
Playoff Totals		141	18	28	46	168

MADIGAN, Cornelius Dennis (Connie) *5-10 185 D*
B. Port Arthur, Ont., Oct. 4, 1934

Season	Team	GP	G	A	Pts.	PIM
72-73	StL	20	0	3	3	25
Playoff Totals		5	0	0	0	4

MADILL, Jeff *5-11 195 RW*
B. Oshawa, Ont., June 21, 1965

Season	Team	GP	G	A	Pts.	PIM
90-91	NJ	14	4	0	4	46

MAGNAN, Marc *5-11 195 LW*
B. Beaumont, Alta., Feb. 17, 1962

Season	Team	GP	G	A	Pts.	PIM
82-83	Tor	4	0	1	1	5

MAGEE Dean *6-2 210 LW*
B. Rocky Mountain House, Alta., Apr. 29, 1955

Season	Team	GP	G	A	Pts.	PIM
77-78	Minn	7	0	0	0	4
78-79	Ind (WHA)	5	0	1	1	10
NHL Totals		7	0	0	0	4
WHA Totals		5	0	1	1	10

MAGGS, Darryl John *6-2 195 D*
B. Victoria, B.C., Apr. 6, 1949

Season	Team	GP	G	A	Pts.	PIM
71-72	Chi	59	7	4	11	4
72-73	Chi-Cal	71	7	15	22	50
73-74	Chi (WHA)	78	8	22	30	148
74-75	Chi (WHA)	77	6	27	33	137
75-76	Ott-Ind (WHA)	78	9	39	48	82
76-77	Ind (WHA)	81	16	55	71	114
77-78	Cin (WHA)	62	8	20	28	37
78-79	Cin (WHA)	27	4	14	18	22
79-80	Tor (WHA)	5	0	0	0	0
NHL Totals		135	14	19	33	54
WHA Totals		403	51	177	228	540
NHL Playoff Totals		4	0	0	0	0
WHA Playoff Totals		34	5	9	14	95

MAGNUSON, Keith Arlen *6-0 185 D*
B. Saskatoon, Sask., Apr. 27, 1947

Season	Team	GP	G	A	Pts.	PIM
69-70	Chi	76	0	24	24	213
70-71	Chi	76	3	20	23	291
71-72	Chi	74	2	19	21	201
72-73	Chi	77	0	19	19	140

Season	Team	GP	G	A	Pts.	PIM

MAGNUSON, Keith Arlen *(Continued)*

Season	Team	GP	G	A	Pts.	PIM
73-74	Chi	57	2	11	13	105
74-75	Chi	48	2	12	14	117
75-76	Chi	48	1	6	7	99
76-77	Chi	37	1	6	7	86
77-78	Chi	67	2	4	6	145
78-79	Chi	26	1	4	5	41
79-80	Chi	3	0	0	0	4
Totals		589	14	125	139	1442
Playoff Totals		68	3	9	12	164

MAGUIRE, Kevin *6-2 200 RW*
B. Toronto, Ont., Jan. 5, 1963

86-87	Tor	17	0	0	0	74
87-88	Buf	46	4	6	10	162
88-89	Buf	60	8	10	18	241
89-90	Buf-Phil	66	6	10	16	121
90-91	Tor	63	9	5	14	180
91-92	Tor	8	1	0	1	4
Totals		260	29	30	59	782
Playoff Totals		11	0	0	0	6

MAHAFFY, John *5-7 165 C*
B. Montreal, Que., July 18, 1919

42-43	Mont	9	2	5	7	4
43-44	NYR	28	9	20	29	0
Totals		37	11	25	36	4
Playoff Totals		1	0	1	1	0

MAHOVLICH, Francis William (Frank)
6-0 205 LW
B. Timmins, Ont., Jan. 10, 1938

56-57	Tor	3	1	0	1	2
57-58	Tor	67	20	16	36	67
58-59	Tor	63	22	27	49	94
59-60	Tor	70	18	21	39	61
60-61	Tor	70	48	36	84	131
61-62	Tor	70	33	38	71	87
62-63	Tor	67	36	37	73	56
63-64	Tor	70	26	29	55	66
64-65	Tor	59	23	28	51	76
65-66	Tor	68	32	24	56	68
66-67	Tor	63	18	28	46	44
67-68	Tor-Det	63	26	26	52	32
68-69	Det	76	49	29	78	38
69-70	Det	74	38	32	70	59
70-71	Det-Mont	73	31	42	73	41
71-72	Mont	76	43	53	96	36
72-73	Mont	78	38	55	93	51
73-74	Mont	71	31	49	80	47
74-75	Tor (WHA)	73	38	44	82	27
75-76	Tor (WHA)	75	34	55	89	14
76-77	Birm (WHA)	17	3	20	23	12
77-78	Birm (WHA)	72	14	24	38	22
NHL Totals		1181	533	570	1103	1056
WHA Totals		237	89	143	232	75
NHL Playoff Totals		137	51	67	118	163
WHA Playoff Totals		9	4	1	5	2

MAHOVLICH, Peter Joseph *6-5 210 C*
B. Timmins, Ont., Oct. 10, 1946

65-66	Det	3	0	1	1	0
66-67	Det	34	1	3	4	16
67-68	Det	15	6	4	10	13
68-69	Det	30	2	2	4	21
69-70	Mont	36	9	8	17	51
70-71	Mont	78	35	26	61	181
71-72	Mont	75	35	32	67	103
72-73	Mont	61	21	38	59	49
73-74	Mont	78	36	37	73	122
74-75	Mont	80	35	82	117	64
75-76	Mont	80	34	71	105	76
76-77	Mont	76	15	47	62	45
77-78	Mon-Pitt	74	28	41	69	41
78-79	Pitt	60	14	39	53	39
79-80	Det	80	16	50	66	69
80-81	Det	24	1	4	5	26
Totals		884	288	485	773	916
Playoff Totals		88	30	42	72	134

MAILHOT, Jacques *6-2 208 LW*
B. Shawinigan, Que., Dec. 5, 1961

88-89	Que	5	0	0	0	33

MAILLEY, Frank *D*

42-43	Mont	1	0	0	0	0

MAIR, James McKay *5-9 170 D*
B. Schumacher, Ont., May 15, 1946

70-71	Phil	2	0	0	0	0
71-72	Phil	2	0	0	0	0
72-73	NYI-Van	64	3	11	14	49
73-74	Van	6	1	3	4	0
74-75	Van	2	0	1	1	0
Totals		76	4	15	19	49

MAIR, James McKay *(Continued)*

Playoff Totals		3	1	2	3	4

MAJEAU, Fernand (Fern) *5-8 155 F*
B. Verdun, Que., May 3, 1916

43-44	Mont	44	20	18	38	39
44-45	Mont	12	2	6	8	4
Totals		56	22	24	46	43
Playoff Totals		1	0	0	0	0

MAJOR, Bruce *6-3 180 C*
B. Vernon, B.C., Jan. 3, 1967

90-91	Que	4	0	0	0	0

MAKAROV, Sergei *5-11 185 RW*
B. Chelyabinsk, Soviet Union, June 19, 1958

89-90	Calg	80	24	62	86	55
90-91	Calg	78	30	49	79	44
91-92	Calg	68	22	48	70	60
Totals		226	76	159	235	159
Playoff Totals		9	1	6	7	0

MAKELA, Mikko *6-2 200 LW*
B. Tampere, Finland, Feb. 28, 1965

85-86	NYI	58	16	20	36	28
86-87	NYI	80	24	33	57	24
87-88	NYI	73	36	40	76	22
88-89	NYI	76	17	28	45	22
89-90	NYI-LA	65	9	17	26	18
90-91	Buf	60	15	7	22	25
Totals		412	117	145	262	139
Playoff Totals		18	3	8	11	14

MAKI, Ronald Patrick (Chico)
5-10 170 RW
B. Sault Ste. Marie, Ont., Aug. 17, 1939

61-62	Chi	16	4	6	10	2
62-63	Chi	65	7	17	24	35
63-64	Chi	68	8	14	22	70
64-65	Chi	65	16	24	40	54
65-66	Chi	68	17	31	48	41
66-67	Chi	56	9	29	38	14
67-68	Chi	60	8	16	24	4
68-69	Chi	66	7	21	28	30
69-70	Chi	75	10	24	34	27
70-71	Chi	72	22	26	48	18
71-72	Chi	62	13	34	47	22
72-73	Chi	77	13	19	32	10
73-74	Chi	69	9	25	34	12
75-76	Chi	22	0	6	6	2
Totals		841	143	292	435	345
Playoff Totals		113	17	36	53	43

MAKI, Wayne *5-11 185 LW*
B. Sault Ste. Marie, Ont., Nov. 10, 1944

67-68	Chi	49	5	5	10	32
68-69	Chi	1	0	0	0	0
69-70	StL	16	2	1	3	4
70-71	Van	78	25	38	63	99
71-72	Van	76	22	25	47	43
72-73	Van	26	3	10	13	6
Totals		246	57	79	136	184
Playoff Totals		2	1	0	1	2

MAKKONEN, Karl *6-0 190 RW*
B. Pori, Finland, Jan. 20, 1955

79-80	Edm	9	2	2	4	0

MALEY, David *6-2 195 LW*
B. Beaver Dam, Wis., Apr. 24, 1963

85-86	Mont	3	0	0	0	0
86-87	Mont	48	6	12	18	55
87-88	NJ	44	4	2	6	65
88-89	NJ	68	5	6	11	249
89-90	NJ	67	8	17	25	160
90-91	NJ	64	8	14	22	151
91-92	NJ-Edm	60	10	17	27	104
Totals		354	41	68	109	784
Playoff Totals		43	5	5	10	111

MALINOWSKI, Merlin Trevis *6-0 190 C*
B. North Battleford, Sask., Sept. 27, 1958

78-79	Col	54	6	17	23	10
79-80	Col	10	2	4	6	2
80-81	Col	69	25	37	62	61
81-82	Col	69	13	28	41	32
82-83	NJ-Hart	80	8	25	33	16
Totals		282	54	111	165	121

MALLETTE, Troy *6-2 210 LW*
B. Sudbury, Ont., Feb. 25, 1970

89-90	NYR	79	13	16	29	305

MALLETTE, Troy *(Continued)*

90-91	NYR	71	12	10	22	252
91-92	Edm-NJ	32	4	7	11	79
Totals		182	29	33	62	636
Playoff Totals		15	2	2	4	99

MALONE, Clifford *5-10 155 RW*
B. Quebec City, Que., Sept. 4, 1925

51-52	Mont	3	0	0	0	0

MALONE, Maurice Joseph (Joe) *F*
B. Sillery, Que., Feb. 28, 1890

17-18	Mont	20	44	0	44	12
18-19	Mont	8	7	1	8	3
19-20	Que	24	39	6	45	12
20-21	Ham	20	30	4	34	2
21-22	Ham	24	25	7	32	4
22-23	Mont	20	1	0	1	2
23-24	Mont	9	0	0	0	0
Totals		125	146	18	164	35
Playoff Totals		9	5	0	5	0

MALONE, William Gregory (Greg)
6-0 190 C
B. Fredicton, N.B., Mar. 8, 1956

76-77	Pitt	66	18	19	37	43
77-78	Pitt	78	18	43	61	80
78-79	Pitt	80	35	30	65	52
79-80	Pitt	51	19	32	51	46
80-81	Pitt	62	21	29	50	68
81-82	Pitt	78	15	24	39	125
82-83	Pitt	80	17	44	61	82
83-84	Hart	78	17	37	54	56
84-85	Hart	76	22	39	61	67
85-86	Hart-Que	49	9	12	21	42
86-87	Que	6	0	1	1	0
Totals		704	191	310	501	661
Playoff Totals		20	3	5	8	32

MALONEY, Daniel Charles *6-2 195 LW*
B. Barrie, Ont., Sept. 24, 1950

70-71	Chi	74	12	14	26	174
72-73	Chi-LA	71	17	24	41	81
73-74	LA	65	15	17	32	113
74-75	LA	80	27	39	66	165
75-76	Det	77	27	39	66	203
76-77	Det	34	13	13	26	64
77-78	Det-Tor	79	19	33	52	176
78-79	Tor	77	17	36	53	157
79-80	Tor	71	17	16	33	102
80-81	Tor	65	20	21	41	183
81-82	Tor	44	8	7	15	71
Totals		737	192	259	451	1489
Playoff Totals		40	4	7	11	35

MALONEY, David Wilfred *6-1 195 D*
B. Kitchener, Ont., July 31, 1956

74-75	NYR	4	0	2	2	0
75-76	NYR	21	1	3	4	66
76-77	NYR	66	3	18	21	100
77-78	NYR	56	2	19	21	63
78-79	NYR	76	11	17	28	151
79-80	NYR	77	12	25	37	186
80-81	NYR	79	11	36	47	132
81-82	NYR	64	13	36	49	105
82-83	NYR	78	8	42	50	132
83-84	NYR	68	7	26	33	168
84-85	NYR-Buf	68	3	22	25	51
Totals		657	71	246	317	1154
Playoff Totals		49	7	17	24	91

MALONEY, Donald Michael *6-1 190 LW*
B. Lindsay, Ont., Sept. 5, 1958

78-79	NYR	28	9	17	26	39
79-80	NYR	79	25	48	73	97
80-81	NYR	61	29	23	52	99
81-82	NYR	54	22	36	58	73
82-83	NYR	78	29	40	69	88
83-84	NYR	79	24	42	66	62
84-85	NYR	37	11	16	27	32
85-86	NYR	68	11	17	28	56
86-87	NYR	72	19	38	57	117
87-88	NYR	66	12	21	33	60
88-89	NYR-Hart	52	7	20	27	39
89-90	NYI	79	16	27	43	47
90-91	NYI	12	0	5	5	6
Totals		765	214	350	564	815
Playoff Totals		94	22	35	57	101

MALONEY, Philip Francis *5-9 170 C*
B. Ottawa, Ont., Oct. 6, 1927

49-50	Bos	70	15	31	46	6
50-51	Bos-Tor	14	3	0	3	2
52-53	Tor	29	2	6	8	2
58-59	Chi	24	2	2	4	6
59-60	Chi	21	6	4	10	0
Totals		158	28	43	71	16

MALONEY, Philip Francis (Continued)
Season	Team	GP	G	A	Pts.	PIM
Playoff Totals		6	0	0	0	0

MALTAIS, Steve *6-2 210 LW*
B. Arvida, Que., Jan. 25, 1969
Season	Team	GP	G	A	Pts.	PIM
89-90	Wash	8	0	0	0	2
90-91	Wash	7	0	0	0	2
91-92	Minn-Que	12	2	1	3	2
Totals		27	2	1	3	6
Playoff Totals		1	0	0	0	0

MALUTA, Raymond William *5-8 173 D*
B. Flin Flon, Man., July 24, 1954
Season	Team	GP	G	A	Pts.	PIM
75-76	Bos	2	0	0	0	2
76-77	Bos	23	2	3	5	4
Totals		25	2	3	5	6
Playoff Totals		2	0	0	0	0

MANASTERSKY, Timothy (Tom) *5-9 185 D*
B. Montreal, Que., Mar. 7, 1929
Season	Team	GP	G	A	Pts.	PIM
50-51	Mont	6	0	0	0	11

MANCUSO, Felix (Gus) *F*
B. Niagara Falls, Ont., Apr. 11, 1914
Season	Team	GP	G	A	Pts.	PIM
37-38	Mont	17	1	1	2	4
38-39	Mont	2	0	0	0	0
39-40	Mont	2	0	0	0	0
42-43	NYR	21	6	8	14	13
Totals		42	7	9	16	17

MANDERVILLE, Kent *6-3 200 LW*
B. Edmonton, Alta., Apr. 12, 1971
Season	Team	GP	G	A	Pts.	PIM
91-92	Tor	15	0	4	4	0

MANDICH, Daniel *6-3 205 D*
B. Brantford, Ont., June 12, 1960
Season	Team	GP	G	A	Pts.	PIM
82-83	Minn	67	3	4	7	169
83-84	Minn	31	2	7	9	77
84-85	Minn	10	0	0	0	32
85-86	Minn	3	0	0	0	25
Totals		111	5	11	16	303
Playoff Totals		7	0	0	0	2

MANERY, Kris Franklin *6-0 185 RW*
B. Leamington, Ont., Sept. 24, 1954
Season	Team	GP	G	A	Pts.	PIM
77-78	Clev	78	22	27	49	14
78-79	Minn	60	17	19	36	16
79-80	Minn-Van-Winn	65	11	9	20	37
80-81	Winn	47	13	9	22	24
Totals		250	63	64	127	91

MANERY, Randy Neal *6-0 185 D*
B. Leamington, Ont., Jan. 10, 1949
Season	Team	GP	G	A	Pts.	PIM
70-71	Det	2	0	0	0	0
71-72	Det	1	0	0	0	0
72-73	Atl	78	5	30	35	44
73-74	Atl	78	8	29	37	75
74-75	Atl	68	5	27	32	48
75-76	Atl	80	7	32	39	42
76-77	Atl	73	5	24	29	33
77-78	LA	79	6	27	33	61
78-79	LA	71	8	27	35	64
79-80	LA	52	6	10	16	48
Totals		582	50	206	256	415
Playoff Totals		13	0	2	2	12

MANN, James Edward *6-0 205 RW*
B. Montreal, Que., Apr. 17, 1959
Season	Team	GP	G	A	Pts.	PIM
79-80	Winn	72	3	5	8	287
80-81	Winn	37	3	3	6	105
81-82	Winn	37	3	2	5	79
82-83	Winn-Que	40	0	1	1	73
83-84	Winn-Que	38	1	2	3	96
84-85	Que	25	0	4	4	54
85-86	Que	35	0	3	3	148
87-88	Pitt	9	0	0	0	53
Totals		293	10	20	30	895
Playoff Totals		22	0	0	0	89

MANN, John Edward Kingsley (Jack) *5-7 180 C*
B. Winnipeg, Man., July 27, 1919
Season	Team	GP	G	A	Pts.	PIM
43-44	NYR	3	0	0	0	0
44-45	NYR	6	3	4	7	0
Totals		9	3	4	7	0

MANN, Kenneth Ross *5-11 200 RW*
B. Hamilton, Ont., Sept. 5, 1953
Season	Team	GP	G	A	Pts.	PIM
75-76	Det	1	0	0	0	0

MANN, Norman Thomas *5-10 155 RW*
B. Bradford, England, Mar. 3, 1914
Season	Team	GP	G	A	Pts.	PIM
38-39	Tor	16	0	0	0	2
40-41	Tor	15	0	3	3	2
Totals		31	0	3	3	4
Playoff Totals		1	0	0	0	0

MANNERS, Rennison (Ren) *F*
Season	Team	GP	G	A	Pts.	PIM
29-30	Pitt Pi	33	3	2	5	14
30-31	Phil Q	4	0	0	0	0
Totals		37	3	2	5	14

MANNO, Robert *6-0 185 D/LW*
B. Niagara Falls, Ont., Oct. 31, 1956
Season	Team	GP	G	A	Pts.	PIM
76-77	Van	2	0	0	0	0
77-78	Van	49	5	14	19	29
78-79	Van	52	5	16	21	42
79-80	Van	40	3	14	17	14
80-81	Van	20	0	11	11	30
81-82	Tor	72	9	41	50	67
83-84	Det	62	9	13	22	60
84-85	Det	74	10	22	32	32
Totals		371	41	131	172	274
Playoff Totals		17	2	4	6	12

MANSON, Dave *6-2 202 D*
B. Prince Albert, Sask., Jan. 27, 1967
Season	Team	GP	G	A	Pts.	PIM
86-87	Chi	63	1	8	9	146
87-88	Chi	54	1	6	7	185
88-89	Chi	79	18	36	54	352
89-90	Chi	59	5	23	28	301
90-91	Chi	75	14	15	29	191
91-92	Edm	79	15	32	47	220
Totals		409	54	120	174	1395
Playoff Totals		66	5	22	27	247

MANSON, Raymond Clifton *5-11 180 LW*
B. St. Boniface, Man., Dec. 3, 1926
Season	Team	GP	G	A	Pts.	PIM
47-48	Bos	1	0	0	0	0
48-49	NYR	1	0	1	1	0
Totals		2	0	1	1	0

MANTHA, Leon-Georges (George) *5-8 162 LW*
B. Lachine, Que., Nov. 29, 1908
Season	Team	GP	G	A	Pts.	PIM
28-29	Mont	31	0	0	0	8
29-30	Mont	44	5	2	7	16
30-31	Mont	44	11	6	17	25
31-32	Mont	48	1	7	8	8
32-33	Mont	43	3	6	9	10
33-34	Mont	44	6	9	15	12
34-35	Mont	42	12	10	22	14
35-36	Mont	35	1	12	13	14
36-37	Mont	47	13	14	27	17
37-38	Mont	47	23	19	42	12
38-39	Mont	25	5	5	10	6
39-30	Mont	42	9	11	20	6
40-41	Mont	6	0	1	1	0
Totals		498	89	102	191	148
Playoff Totals		36	6	2	8	16

MANTHA, Maurice William (Moe) *6-2 210 D*
B. Lakewood, Ohio, Jan. 21, 1961
Season	Team	GP	G	A	Pts.	PIM
80-81	Winn	58	2	23	25	35
81-82	Winn	25	0	12	12	28
82-83	Winn	21	2	7	9	6
83-84	Winn	72	16	38	54	67
84-85	Pitt	71	11	40	51	54
85-86	Pitt	78	15	52	67	102
86-87	Pitt	62	9	31	40	44
87-88	Pitt-Edm-Minn	76	11	27	38	53
88-89	Minn-Phil	46	4	14	18	43
89-90	Winn	73	2	26	28	28
90-91	Winn	57	9	15	24	33
91-92	Winn-Phil	17	0	4	4	8
Totals		656	81	289	370	501
Playoff Totals		17	5	10	15	18

MANTHA, Sylvio *5-10 178 D*
B. Montreal, Que., Apr. 14, 1902
Season	Team	GP	G	A	Pts.	PIM
23-24	Mont	24	1	0	1	9
24-25	Mont	30	2	0	2	16
25-26	Mont	34	2	1	3	66
26-27	Mont	43	10	5	15	77
27-28	Mont	43	4	11	15	61
28-29	Mont	44	9	4	13	56
29-30	Mont	44	13	11	24	108
30-31	Mont	44	4	7	11	75
31-32	Mont	47	5	10	15	62
32-33	Mont	48	4	7	11	50
33-34	Mont	48	4	6	10	24
34-35	Mont	47	3	11	14	36

MANTHA, Sylvio (Continued)
Season	Team	GP	G	A	Pts.	PIM
35-36	Mont	42	2	4	6	25
36-37	Bos	5	0	0	0	2
Totals		543	63	72	135	667
Playoff Totals		46	5	4	9	66

MARACLE, Henry Elmer (Buddy) *F*
B. Ayr, Ont., Sept. 8, 1904
Season	Team	GP	G	A	Pts.	PIM
30-31	NYR	11	1	3	4	4
Playoff Totals		4	0	0	0	0

MARCETTA, Milan (Mike) *6-1 195 C*
B. Cadomin, Alta., Sept. 19, 1936
Season	Team	GP	G	A	Pts.	PIM
67-68	Minn	36	4	12	16	6
68-69	Minn	18	3	2	5	4
Totals		54	7	14	21	10
Playoff Totals		17	7	7	14	4

MARCHMENT, Bryan *6-1 198 D*
B. Scarborough, Ont., May 1, 1969
Season	Team	GP	G	A	Pts.	PIM
88-89	Winn	2	0	0	0	2
89-90	Winn	7	0	2	2	28
90-91	Winn	28	2	4	6	91
91-92	Chi	58	5	10	15	168
Totals		95	7	14	21	289
Playoff Totals		16	1	0	1	36

MARCH, Harold C. (Mush) *5-5 154 RW*
B. Silton, Sask., Oct. 18, 1908
Season	Team	GP	G	A	Pts.	PIM
28-29	Chi	35	3	3	6	6
29-30	Chi	43	8	7	15	48
30-31	Chi	44	11	6	17	36
31-32	Chi	48	12	13	25	36
32-33	Chi	48	9	11	20	38
33-34	Chi	48	4	13	17	26
34-35	Chi	47	13	17	30	48
35-36	Chi	48	16	19	35	48
36-37	Chi	37	11	6	17	31
37-38	Chi	41	11	17	28	16
38-39	Chi	46	10	11	21	29
39-40	Chi	45	9	14	23	49
40-41	Chi	44	8	9	17	16
41-42	Chi	48	6	26	32	22
42-43	Chi	50	7	29	36	46
43-44	Chi	48	10	27	37	16
44-45	Chi	38	5	5	10	12
Totals		758	153	233	386	523
Playoff Totals		48	12	15	27	41

MARCHINKO, Brian Nicholas Wayne *6-0 180 C*
B. Weyburn, Sask., Aug. 2, 1948
Season	Team	GP	G	A	Pts.	PIM
70-71	Tor	2	0	0	0	0
71-72	Tor	3	0	0	0	0
72-73	NYI	36	2	6	8	0
73-74	NYI	6	0	0	0	0
Totals		47	2	6	8	0

MARCINYSHYN, David *6-3 210 D*
B. Edmonton, Alta., Feb. 4, 1967
Season	Team	GP	G	A	Pts.	PIM
90-91	NJ	9	0	1	1	21
91-92	Que	5	0	0	0	26
Totals		14	0	1	1	47

MARCON, Louis Angelo *5-9 178 D*
B. Fort William, Ont., May 28, 1935
Season	Team	GP	G	A	Pts.	PIM
58-59	Det	31	0	1	1	12
59-60	Det	38	0	3	3	30
62-63	Det	1	0	0	0	0
Totals		70	0	4	4	42

MARCOTTE, Donald Michel *5-10 185 LW*
B. Asbestos, Que., Apr. 15, 1947
Season	Team	GP	G	A	Pts.	PIM
65-66	Bos	1	0	0	0	0
68-69	Bos	7	1	0	1	2
69-70	Bos	35	9	3	12	14
70-71	Bos	75	15	13	28	30
71-72	Bos	47	6	4	10	12
72-73	Bos	78	24	31	55	49
73-74	Bos	78	24	26	50	18
74-75	Bos	80	31	33	64	76
75-76	Bos	58	16	20	36	24
76-77	Bos	80	27	18	45	20
77-78	Bos	77	20	34	54	16
78-79	Bos	79	20	27	47	10
79-80	Bos	32	4	11	15	0
80-81	Bos	72	20	13	33	32
81-82	Bos	69	13	21	34	14
Totals		868	230	254	484	317
Playoff Totals		132	34	27	61	81

MARINI, Hector *6-1 200 RW*
B. Timmins, Ont., Jan. 27, 1957
Season	Team	GP	G	A	Pts.	PIM
78-79	NYI	1	0	0	0	2
80-81	NYI	14	4	7	11	39
81-82	NYI	30	4	9	13	53

MARINI, Hector *(Continued)*

Season	Team	GP	G	A	Pts.	PIM
82-83	NJ	77	17	28	45	105
83-84	NJ	32	2	2	4	47
Totals		154	27	46	73	246
Playoff Totals		10	3	6	9	14

MARIO, Frank George *5-8 170 C*

B. Esterhazy, Sask., Feb. 25, 1921

Season	Team	GP	G	A	Pts.	PIM
41-42	Bos	9	1	1	2	0
44-45	Bos	44	8	18	26	24
Totals		53	9	19	28	24

MARIUCCI, John *5-10 200 D*

B. Eveleth, Minn., May 8, 1916

Season	Team	GP	G	A	Pts.	PIM
40-41	Chi	23	0	5	5	33
41-42	Chi	47	5	8	13	44
45-46	Chi	50	3	8	11	58
46-47	Chi	52	2	9	11	110
47-48	Chi	51	1	4	5	63
Totals		223	11	34	45	308
Playoff Totals		8	0	3	3	26

MARK, Gordon *6-4 210 D*

B. Edmonton, Alta., Sept. 10, 1964

Season	Team	GP	G	A	Pts.	PIM
86-87	NJ	36	3	5	8	82
87-88	NJ	19	0	2	2	27
Totals		55	3	7	10	109

MARKELL, John Richard *5-11 185 LW*

B. Cornwall, Ont., Mar. 10, 1956

Season	Team	GP	G	A	Pts.	PIM
79-80	Winn	38	10	7	17	21
80-81	Winn	14	1	3	4	15
Totals		52	11	10	21	36

MARKER, August Solberg (Gus) *F*

B. Wetaskewin, Alta., Aug. 1, 1907

Season	Team	GP	G	A	Pts.	PIM
32-33	Det	15	1	1	2	8
33-34	Det	7	1	0	1	2
34-35	Mont M	42	11	4	15	18
35-36	Mont M	47	7	12	19	10
36-37	Mont M	48	10	12	22	22
37-38	Mont M	48	9	15	24	35
38-39	Tor	43	9	6	15	14
39-40	Tor	42	10	9	19	15
40-41	Tor	27	4	5	9	10
41-42	Brk	17	2	5	7	2
Totals		336	64	69	133	136
Playoff Totals		45	6	8	14	36

MARKHAM, Raymond Joseph *6-3 220 C*

B. Windsor, Ont., Jan. 23, 1958

Season	Team	GP	G	A	Pts.	PIM
79-80	NYR	14	1	1	2	21
Playoff Totals		7	1	0	1	24

MARKLE, John A. (Jack) *F*

B. Thessalon, Ont., 1909

Season	Team	GP	G	A	Pts.	PIM
35-36	Tor	8	0	1	1	0

MARKS, John (Jack) *F*

Season	Team	GP	G	A	Pts.	PIM
17-18	Mont W-Tor	6	0	0	0	0
19-20	Que	1	0	0	0	4
Totals		7	0	0	0	4

MARKS, John Garrison *6-2 200 LW*

B. Hamiota, Man., Mar. 22, 1948

Season	Team	GP	G	A	Pts.	PIM
72-73	Chi	55	3	10	13	21
73-74	Chi	76	13	18	31	22
74-75	Chi	80	17	30	47	56
75-76	Chi	80	21	23	44	43
76-77	Chi	80	7	15	22	41
77-78	Chi	80	15	22	37	26
78-79	Chi	80	21	24	45	35
79-80	Chi	74	6	15	21	51
80-81	Chi	39	8	6	14	28
81-82	Chi	13	1	0	1	7
Totals		657	112	163	275	330
Playoff Totals		57	5	9	14	60

MARKWART, Nevin *5-10 180 LW*

B. Toronto, Ont., Dec. 9, 1964

Season	Team	GP	G	A	Pts.	PIM
83-84	Bos	70	14	16	30	121
84-85	Bos	26	0	4	4	36
85-86	Bos	65	7	15	22	207
86-87	Bos	64	10	9	19	225
87-88	Bos	25	1	12	13	85
89-90	Bos	8	1	2	3	15
90-91	Bos	23	3	3	6	36
91-92	Bos-Calg	28	5	7	12	69
Totals		309	41	68	109	794
Playoff Totals		9	1	0	1	33

MAROIS, Daniel *6-0 190 RW*

B. Montreal, Que., Oct. 3, 1968

Season	Team	GP	G	A	Pts.	PIM
88-89	Tor	76	31	23	54	76
89-90	Tor	68	39	37	76	82

MAROIS, Daniel *(Continued)*

Season	Team	GP	G	A	Pts.	PIM
90-91	Tor	78	21	9	30	112
91-92	Tor-NYI	75	17	16	33	94
Totals		297	108	85	193	364
Playoff Totals		8	3	2	5	12

MAROIS, Mario *5-11 190 D*

B. Quebec City, Que., Dec. 15, 1957

Season	Team	GP	G	A	Pts.	PIM
77-78	NYR	8	1	1	2	15
78-79	NYR	71	5	26	31	153
79-80	NYR	79	8	23	31	142
80-81	NYR-Van-Que	69	5	21	26	181
81-82	Que	71	11	32	43	161
82-83	Que	36	2	12	14	108
83-84	Que	80	13	36	49	151
84-85	Que	76	6	37	43	91
85-86	Que-Winn	76	5	40	45	152
86-87	Winn	79	4	40	44	106
87-88	Winn	79	7	44	51	11
88-89	Winn-Que	49	3	12	15	148
89-90	Que	67	3	15	18	104
90-91	StL	64	2	14	16	81
91-92	StL-Winn	51	1	4	5	72
Totals		955	76	357	433	1746
Playoff Tot.		100	4	34	38	182

MAROTTE, Jean Gilles (Gilles) *5-9 205 D*

B. Montreal, Que., June 7, 1945

Season	Team	GP	G	A	Pts.	PIM
65-66	Bos	51	3	17	20	52
66-67	Bos	67	7	8	15	65
67-68	Chi	73	0	21	21	122
68-69	Chi	68	5	29	34	120
69-70	Chi-LA	72	5	19	24	52
70-71	LA	78	6	27	33	96
71-72	LA	72	10	24	34	83
72-73	LA	78	6	39	45	102
73-74	LA-NYR	68	3	28	31	51
74-75	NYR	77	4	32	36	69
75-76	NYR	57	4	17	21	34
76-77	StL	47	3	4	7	26
77-78	Ind (WHA)	73	3	20	23	76
NHL Totals		808	56	265	321	872
WHA Totals		73	3	20	23	76
NHL Playoff Totals		29	3	3	6	26

MARQUESS, Clarence Emmett (Mark) *5-8 160 RW*

B. Bassano, Alta., Mar. 26, 1925

Season	Team	GP	G	A	Pts.	PIM
46-47	Bos	27	5	4	9	27
Playoff Totals		4	0	0	0	0

MARSH, Charles Bradley (Brad) *6-3 220 D*

B. London, Ont., Mar. 31, 1958

Season	Team	GP	G	A	Pts.	PIM
78-79	Atl	80	0	19	19	101
79-80	Atl	80	2	9	11	119
80-81	Calg	80	1	12	13	87
81-82	Calg-Phil	83	2	23	25	116
82-83	Phil	68	2	11	13	52
83-84	Phil	77	3	14	17	83
84-85	Phil	77	2	18	20	91
85-86	Phil	79	0	13	13	123
86-87	Phil	77	2	9	11	124
87-88	Phil	70	3	9	12	57
88-89	Tor	80	1	15	16	79
89-90	Tor	79	1	13	14	95
90-91	Tor-Det	42	1	3	4	31
91-92	Det	55	3	5	8	53
Totals		1027	23	173	196	1211
Playoff Totals		97	6	18	24	124

MARSH, Gary Arthur *5-9 172 LW*

B. Toronto, Ont., Mar. 9, 1946

Season	Team	GP	G	A	Pts.	PIM
67-68	Det	6	1	3	4	4
68-69	Tor	1	0	0	0	0
Totals		7	1	3	4	4

MARSH, Peter *6-1 180 RW*

B. Halifax, N.S., Dec. 21, 1956

Season	Team	GP	G	A	Pts.	PIM
76-77	Cin (WHA)	76	23	28	51	52
77-78	Cin (WHA)	74	25	25	50	123
78-79	Cin (WHA)	80	43	23	66	95
79-80	Winn	57	18	20	38	59
80-81	Winn-Chi	53	10	13	23	19
81-82	Chi	57	10	18	28	47
82-83	Chi	68	6	14	20	55
83-84	Chi	43	4	6	10	44
NHL Totals		279	48	71	119	224
WHA Totals		230	91	76	167	270
NHL Playoff Totals		26	1	5	6	33
WHA Playoff Totals		7	3	0	3	0

MARSHALL, Albert Leroy (Bert) *6-3 205 D*

B. Kamloops, B.C., Nov. 22, 1943

Season	Team	GP	G	A	Pts.	PIM
65-66	Det	61	0	19	19	45
66-67	Det	57	0	10	10	68
67-68	Det-Oak	57	1	9	10	74
68-69	Oak	68	3	15	18	81
69-70	Oak	72	1	15	16	109
70-71	Cal	32	2	6	8	48
71-72	Cal	66	0	14	14	68
72-73	Cal-NYR	63	2	6	8	85
73-74	NYI	69	1	7	8	84
74-75	NYI	77	2	28	30	58
75-76	NYI	71	0	16	16	72
76-77	NYI	72	4	21	25	61
77-78	NYI	58	0	7	7	44
78-79	NYI	45	1	8	9	29
Totals		868	17	181	198	926
Playoff Totals		72	4	22	26	99

MARSHALL, Donald Robert *5-10 166 LW*

B. Verdun, Que., Mar. 23, 1932

Season	Team	GP	G	A	Pts.	PIM
51-52	Mont	1	0	0	0	0
54-55	Mont	39	5	3	8	9
55-56	Mont	66	4	1	5	10
56-57	Mont	70	12	8	20	6
57-58	Mont	68	22	19	41	14
58-59	Mont	70	10	22	32	12
59-60	Mont	70	16	22	38	4
60-61	Mont	70	14	17	31	8
61-62	Mont	66	18	28	46	12
62-63	Mont	65	13	20	33	6
63-64	NYR	70	11	12	23	8
64-65	NYR	69	20	15	35	2
65-66	NYR	69	26	28	54	6
66-67	NYR	70	24	22	46	4
67-68	NYR	70	19	30	49	2
68-69	NYR	74	20	19	39	12
69-70	NYR	57	9	15	24	6
70-71	Buf	62	20	29	49	6
71-72	Tor	50	2	14	16	0
Totals		1176	265	324	589	127
Playoff Totals		94	8	15	23	14

MARSHALL, Jason *6-2 185 D*

B. Cranbrook, B.C., Feb. 22, 1972

Season	Team	GP	G	A	Pts.	PIM
91-92	StL	2	1	0	1	4

MARSHALL, Paul A. *6-2 180 LW*

B. Toronto, Ont., Sept. 7, 1960

Season	Team	GP	G	A	Pts.	PIM
79-80	Pitt	46	9	12	21	9
80-81	Pitt-Tor	26	3	2	5	6
81-82	Tor	10	2	2	4	2
82-83	Hart	13	1	2	3	0
Totals		95	15	18	33	17
Playoff Totals		1	0	0	0	0

MARSHALL, Willmott Charles (Willie) *5-10 160 C*

B. Kirkland Lake, Ont., Dec. 1, 1931

Season	Team	GP	G	A	Pts.	PIM
52-53	Tor	2	0	0	0	0
54-55	Tor	16	1	14	15	0
55-56	Tor	6	0	0	0	0
58-59	Tor	9	0	1	1	2
Totals		33	1	15	16	2

MARSON, Michael Robert *5-9 200 LW*

B. Scarborough, Ont., July 24, 1955

Season	Team	GP	G	A	Pts.	PIM
74-75	Wash	76	16	12	28	59
75-76	Wash	57	4	7	11	50
76-77	Wash	10	0	1	1	18
77-78	Wash	46	4	4	8	101
78-79	Wash	4	0	0	0	0
79-80	LA	3	0	0	0	5
Totals		196	24	24	48	233

MARTIN, Clare George *5-11 180 D*

B. Waterloo, Ont., Feb. 25, 1922

Season	Team	GP	G	A	Pts.	PIM
41-42	Bos	13	0	1	1	4
46-47	Bos	6	3	0	3	0
47-48	Bos	59	5	13	18	34
49-50	Det	64	2	5	7	14
50-51	Det	50	1	6	7	12
51-52	Chi-NYR	45	1	3	4	14
Totals		237	12	28	40	78
Playoff Totals		22	0	2	2	6

MARTIN, Francis William (Frank) *6-1 194 D*

B. Cayuga, Ont., May 1, 1933

Season	Team	GP	G	A	Pts.	PIM
52-53	Bos	14	0	2	2	6
53-54	Bos	68	3	17	20	38
54-55	Chi	66	4	8	12	35
55-56	Chi	61	3	11	14	21

MARTIN, Francis William (Frank) *(Continued)*

Season	Team	GP	G	A	Pts.	PIM
56-57	Chi	70	1	8	9	12
57-58	Chi	3	0	0	0	10
Totals		282	11	46	57	122
Playoff Totals		10	0	1	1	2

MARTIN, Grant Michael *5-10 190 LW*
B. Smooth Rock Falls, Ont., Mar. 13, 1962

Season	Team	GP	G	A	Pts.	PIM
83-84	Van	12	0	2	2	6
84-85	Van	12	0	1	1	39
85-86	Wash	11	0	1	1	6
86-87	Wash	9	0	0	0	4
Totals		44	0	4	4	55
Playoff Totals		1	1	0	1	2

MARTIN, Hubert Jacques (Pit) *5-9 170 C*
B. Noranda, Que., Dec. 9, 1943

Season	Team	GP	G	A	Pts.	PIM
61-62	Det	1	0	1	1	0
63-64	Det	50	9	12	21	21
64-65	Det	58	8	9	17	32
65-66	Det-Bos	51	17	12	29	10
66-67	Bos	70	20	22	42	40
67-68	Chi	63	16	19	35	36
68-69	Chi	76	23	38	61	73
69-70	Chi	73	30	33	63	61
70-71	Chi	62	22	33	55	40
71-72	Chi	78	24	51	75	56
72-73	Chi	78	29	61	90	30
73-74	Chi	78	30	47	77	43
74-75	Chi	70	19	26	45	34
75-76	Chi	80	32	39	71	44
76-77	Chi	75	17	36	53	22
77-78	Chi-Van	74	16	32	48	48
78-79	Van	64	12	14	26	24
Totals		1101	324	485	809	614
Playoff Totals		100	27	31	58	56

MARTIN, Jack *5-11 184 F*
B. St. Catharines, Ont., Nov. 29, 1940

Season	Team	GP	G	A	Pts.	PIM
60-61	Tor	1	0	0	0	0

MARTIN, Richard Lionel *5-11 179 LW*
B. Verdun, Que., July 26, 1951

Season	Team	GP	G	A	Pts.	PIM
71-72	Buf	73	44	30	74	36
72-73	Buf	75	37	36	73	79
73-74	Buf	78	52	34	86	38
74-75	Buf	68	52	43	95	72
75-76	Buf	80	49	37	86	67
76-77	Buf	66	36	29	65	58
77-78	Buf	65	28	35	63	16
78-79	Buf	73	32	21	53	35
79-80	Buf	80	45	34	79	16
80-81	Buf-LA	24	8	15	23	20
81-82	LA	3	1	3	4	2
Totals		685	384	317	701	439
Playoff Totals		63	24	29	53	74

MARTIN, Ronald D. *130 F*
B. Calgary, Alta., Aug. 22, 1909

Season	Team	GP	G	A	Pts.	PIM
32-33	NYA	47	5	7	12	6
33-34	NYA	47	8	9	17	30
Totals		94	13	16	29	36

MARTIN, Terry George *5-11 195 LW*
B. Barrie, Ont., Oct. 25, 1955

Season	Team	GP	G	A	Pts.	PIM
75-76	Buf	1	0	0	0	0
76-77	Buf	62	11	12	23	8
77-78	Buf	21	3	2	5	9
78-79	Buf	64	6	8	14	33
79-80	Que-Tor	40	6	15	21	2
80-81	Tor	69	23	14	37	32
81-82	Tor	72	25	24	49	39
82-83	Tor	76	14	13	27	28
83-84	Tor	63	15	10	25	51
84-85	Edm-Minn	11	1	3	4	0
Totals		479	104	101	205	202
Playoff Totals		21	4	2	6	26

MARTIN, Thomas Raymond *5-9 170 RW*
B. Toronto, Ont., Oct. 16, 1947

Season	Team	GP	G	A	Pts.	PIM
67-68	Tor	3	1	0	1	0
72-73	Ott (WHA)	75	19	27	46	27
73-74	Tor (WHA)	74	25	32	57	14
74-75	Tor (WHA)	64	14	17	31	18
NHL Totals		3	1	0	1	0
WHA Totals		213	58	76	134	59
WHA Playoff Totals		22	8	13	21	4

MARTIN, Tom *6-2 200 LW*
B. Kelowna, B.C., May 11, 1965

Season	Team	GP	G	A	Pts.	PIM
84-85	Winn	8	1	0	1	42
85-86	Winn	5	0	0	0	0
86-87	Winn	11	1	0	1	49
87-88	Hart	5	1	2	3	14

MARTIN, Tom *(Continued)*

Season	Team	GP	G	A	Pts.	PIM
88-89	Minn-Hart	42	8	7	15	140
89-90	Hart	21	1	2	3	27
Totals		92	12	11	23	249
Playoff Totals		4	0	0	0	6

MARTINEAU, Donald Jean *6-0 190 RW*
B. Kimberley, B.C., Apr. 25, 1952

Season	Team	GP	G	A	Pts.	PIM
73-74	Atl	4	0	0	0	2
74-75	Minn	76	6	9	15	61
75-76	Det	9	0	1	1	0
76-77	Det	1	0	0	0	0
Totals		90	6	10	16	63

MARTINSON, Steven *6-1 205 LW*
B. Minnetonka, Minn., June 21, 1959

Season	Team	GP	G	A	Pts.	PIM
87-88	Det	10	1	1	2	84
88-89	Mont	25	1	0	1	87
89-90	Mont	13	0	0	0	64
91-92	Minn	1	0	0	0	9
Totals		49	2	1	3	244
Playoff Totals		1	0	0	0	10

MARUK, Dennis John *5-8 175 C*
B. Toronto, Ont., Nov. 17, 1955

Season	Team	GP	G	A	Pts.	PIM
75-76	Cal	80	30	32	62	44
76-77	Clev	80	28	50	78	68
77-78	Clev	76	36	35	71	50
78-79	Minn-Wash	78	31	59	90	71
79-80	Wash	27	10	17	27	8
80-81	Wash	80	50	47	97	87
81-82	Wash	80	60	76	136	128
82-83	Wash	80	31	50	81	71
83-84	Minn	71	17	43	60	42
84-85	Minn	71	19	41	60	56
85-86	Minn	70	21	37	58	67
86-87	Minn	67	16	30	46	52
87-88	Minn	22	7	4	11	15
88-89	Minn	6	0	1	1	2
Totals		888	356	522	878	761
Playoff Totals		34	14	22	36	26

MASNICK, Paul Andrew *5-9 165 C*
B. Regina, Sask., Apr. 14, 1931

Season	Team	GP	G	A	Pts.	PIM
50-51	Mont	43	4	1	5	14
51-52	Mont	15	1	2	3	2
52-53	Mont	53	5	7	12	44
53-54	Mont	50	5	21	26	57
54-55	Mont-Chi	30	1	1	2	8
57-58	Tor	41	2	9	11	14
Totals		232	18	41	59	139
Playoff Totals		33	4	5	9	27

MASON, Charles C. (Dutch) *5-10 160 F*
B. Seaforth, Ont., Feb. 1, 1912

Season	Team	GP	G	A	Pts.	PIM
34-35	NYR	46	5	9	14	14
35-36	NYR	28	1	5	6	30
37-38	NYA	2	0	0	0	0
38-39	Det-Chi	19	1	4	5	0
Totals		95	7	18	25	44
Playoff Totals		4	0	1	1	0

MASSECAR, George *LW*
B. Niagara Falls, Ont.

Season	Team	GP	G	A	Pts.	PIM
29-30	NYA	43	7	3	10	18
30-31	NYA	43	4	7	11	16
31-32	NYA	14	1	1	2	12
Totals		100	12	11	23	46

MASTERS, James Edward (Jamie) *6-1 195 D*
B. Toronto, Ont., Apr. 14, 1955

Season	Team	GP	G	A	Pts.	PIM
75-76	StL	7	0	0	0	0
76-77	StL	16	1	7	8	2
78-79	StL	10	0	6	6	0
Totals		33	1	13	14	2
Playoff Totals		2	0	0	0	0

MASTERSON, William (Bat) *6-0 189 C*
B. Winnipeg, Man., Aug. 13, 1938

Season	Team	GP	G	A	Pts.	PIM
67-68	Minn	38	4	8	12	4

MATHERS, Frank Sydney *6-0 182 D*
B. Winnipeg, Man., Mar. 29, 1924

Season	Team	GP	G	A	Pts.	PIM
48-49	Tor	15	1	2	3	2
49-50	Tor	6	0	1	1	2
51-52	Tor	2	0	0	0	0
Totals		23	1	3	4	4

MATHIASON, Dwight *6-1 190 RW*
B. Brandon, Man., May 12, 1963

Season	Team	GP	G	A	Pts.	PIM
85-86	Pitt	4	1	0	1	2
86-87	Pitt	6	0	1	1	2
87-88	Pitt	23	0	6	6	14
Totals		33	1	7	8	18

MATHIESON, Jim *6-1 209 D*
B. Kindersley, Sask., Jan. 24, 1970

Season	Team	GP	G	A	Pts.	PIM
89-90	Wash	2	0	0	0	4

MATTE, Joseph *D*
B. Bourget, Ont., 1893

Season	Team	GP	G	A	Pts.	PIM
19-20	Tor	16	8	2	10	12
20-21	Ham	19	7	9	16	27
21-22	Ham	20	3	3	6	4
25-26	Bos-Mont	9	0	0	0	0
Totals		64	18	14	32	43

MATTE, Joseph *D*
B. Ottawa, Ont., Mar. 3, 1909

Season	Team	GP	G	A	Pts.	PIM
42-43	Chi	12	0	2	2	8

MATTE, Roland *5-10 178 D*
B. Bourget, Ont., Mar. 15, 1909

Season	Team	GP	G	A	Pts.	PIM
29-30	Det	12	0	1	1	0

MATTEAU, Stephane *6-3 195 LW*
B. Rouyn-Noranda, Que., Sept. 2, 1969

Season	Team	GP	G	A	Pts.	PIM
91-92	Calg-Chi	24	6	8	14	64
Playoff Totals		23	4	7	11	24

MATTIUSSI, Richard Arthur (Dick) *5-10 185 D*
B. Smooth Rock Falls, Ont., May 1, 1938

Season	Team	GP	G	A	Pts.	PIM
67-68	Pitt	32	0	2	2	18
68-69	Pitt-Oak	36	1	11	12	30
69-70	Oak	65	4	10	14	38
70-71	Cal	67	3	8	11	38
Totals		200	8	31	39	124
Playoff Totals		8	0	1	1	6

MATZ, Jean (Johnny) *F*

Season	Team	GP	G	A	Pts.	PIM
24-25	Mont	30	3	2	5	0
Playoff Totals		5	0	0	0	2

MAXNER, Wayne Douglas *5-11 170 LW*
B. Halifax, N.S., Sept. 27, 1942

Season	Team	GP	G	A	Pts.	PIM
64-65	Bos	54	7	6	13	42
65-66	Bos	8	1	3	4	6
Totals		62	8	9	17	48

MAXWELL, Brad Robert *6-2 195 D*
B. Brandon, Man., July 8, 1957

Season	Team	GP	G	A	Pts.	PIM
77-78	Minn	75	18	29	47	100
78-79	Minn	70	9	28	37	145
79-80	Minn	58	7	30	37	126
80-81	Minn	27	3	13	16	98
81-82	Minn	51	10	21	31	96
82-83	Minn	77	11	28	39	157
83-84	Minn	78	19	54	73	225
84-85	Minn-Que	68	10	31	41	172
85-86	Tor	52	8	18	26	108
86-87	Van-NYR-Minn	56	3	18	21	43
Totals		612	98	270	368	1270
Playoff Totals		79	12	49	61	178

MAXWELL, Bryan Clifford *6-2 200 D*
B. North Bay, Ont., Sept. 7, 1955

Season	Team	GP	G	A	Pts.	PIM
75-76	Clev (WHA)	73	3	14	17	177
76-77	Cin (WHA)	34	1	8	9	29
77-78	NE (WHA)	17	2	1	3	11
77-78	Minn	18	2	5	7	41
78-79	Minn	25	1	6	7	46
79-80	StL	57	1	11	12	112
80-81	StL	40	3	10	13	137
81-82	Winn	45	1	9	10	110
82-83	Winn	54	7	13	20	131
83-84	Winn	48	3	15	18	111
84-85	Pitt	44	0	8	8	57
NHL Totals		331	18	77	95	745
WHA Totals		124	6	23	29	217
NHL Playoff Totals		15	1	1	2	86
WHA Playoff Totals		6	0	0	0	33

MAXWELL, Kevin *5-9 165 C*
B. Edmonton, Alta., Mar. 30, 1960

Season	Team	GP	G	A	Pts.	PIM
80-81	Minn	6	0	3	3	7
81-82	Minn-Col	46	6	9	15	52
83-84	NJ	14	0	3	3	2
Totals		66	6	15	21	61
Playoff Totals		16	3	4	7	24

MAXWELL, Walter (Wally) *F*
B. Ottawa, Ont., Aug. 24, 1933

Season	Team	GP	G	A	Pts.	PIM
52-53	Tor	2	0	0	0	0

MAY, Alan *6-1 200 RW*
B. Barrhead, Alta., Jan. 14, 1965

Season	Team	GP	G	A	Pts.	PIM
87-88	Bos	3	0	0	0	15
88-89	Edm	3	1	0	1	7
89-90	Wash	77	7	10	17	339

MAY, Alan *(Continued)*

Season	Team	GP	G	A	Pts.	PIM
90-91	Wash	67	4	6	10	264
91-92	Wash	75	6	9	15	221
Totals		225	18	25	43	846
Playoff Totals		33	1	1	2	74

MAY, Brad *6-0 200 LW*
B. Toronto, Ont., Nov. 29, 1971

Season	Team	GP	G	A	Pts.	PIM
91-92	Buf	69	11	6	17	309
Playoff Totals		7	1	4	5	2

MAYER, Patrick *6-3 225 D*
B. Royal Oak, Mich., July 24, 1961

Season	Team	GP	G	A	Pts.	PIM
87-88	Pitt	1	0	0	0	4

MAYER, James Patrick *6-0 190 RW*
B. Capreol, Ont., Oct. 30, 1954

Season	Team	GP	G	A	Pts.	PIM
76-77	Calg (WHA)	21	2	3	5	0
77-78	NE (WHA)	51	11	9	20	21
78-79	Edm (WHA)	2	0	0	0	0
79-80	NYR	4	0	0	0	0
NHL Totals		4	0	0	0	0
WHA Totals		74	13	12	25	21

MAYER, Sheppard E. (Shep) *F*
B. Sturgeon Falls, Ont.

Season	Team	GP	G	A	Pts.	PIM
42-43	Tor	12	1	2	3	4

MAZUR, Edward Joseph (Spider) *6-2 186 LW*
B. Winnipeg, Man., July 25, 1929

Season	Team	GP	G	A	Pts.	PIM
53-54	Mont	67	7	14	21	95
54-55	Mont	25	1	5	6	21
56-57	Chi	15	0	1	1	4
Totals		107	8	20	28	120
Playoff Totals		25	4	5	9	22

MAZUR, Jay *6-2 205 C/RW*
B. Hamilton, Ont., Jan. 22, 1965

Season	Team	GP	G	A	Pts.	PIM
88-89	Van	1	0	0	0	0
89-90	Van	5	0	0	0	4
90-91	Van	36	11	7	18	14
91-92	Van	5	0	0	0	2
Totals		47	11	7	18	20
Playoff Totals		6	0	1	1	8

McADAM, Gary *5-11 175 LW*
B. Smiths Falls, Ont., Dec. 31, 1955

Season	Team	GP	G	A	Pts.	PIM
75-76	Buf	31	1	2	3	2
76-77	Buf	73	13	16	29	17
77-78	Buf	79	19	22	41	44
78-79	Buf-Pitt	68	11	14	25	15
79-80	Pitt	78	19	22	41	63
80-81	Pitt-Det	74	8	23	31	57
81-82	Calg	46	12	15	27	18
82-83	Buf	4	1	0	1	0
83-84	Wash-NJ	62	10	11	21	27
84-85	NJ	4	1	1	2	0
85-86	Tor	15	1	6	7	0
Totals		534	96	132	228	243
Playoff Totals		30	6	5	11	16

McADAM, Samuel *5-8 175 C*
B. Sterling, Scotland, May 31, 1908

Season	Team	GP	G	A	Pts.	PIM
30-31	NYR	5	0	0	0	0

McAMMOND, Dean *5-11 185 C*
B. Grand Cache, B.C., June 15, 1973

Season	Team	GP	G	A	Pts.	PIM
91-92	Chi	5	0	2	2	0
Playoff Totals		3	0	0	0	2

McANDREW, Hazen Bernard *5-9 175 D*
B. Mayo, Que., Aug. 7, 1917

Season	Team	GP	G	A	Pts.	PIM
41-42	Brk	7	0	1	1	6

McANEELEY, Edward Joseph (Ted) *5-9 185 D*
B. Cranbrook, B.C., Nov. 7, 1950

Season	Team	GP	G	A	Pts.	PIM
72-73	Cal	77	4	13	17	75
73-74	Cal	72	4	20	24	62
74-75	Cal	9	0	2	2	4
75-76	Edm (WHA)	79	2	17	19	71
NHL Totals		158	8	35	43	141
WHA Totals		79	2	17	19	71
WHA Playoff Totals		4	0	0	0	0

McATEE, Jerome F. (Jud) *5-9 170 LW*
B. Stratford, Ont., Feb. 5, 1920

Season	Team	GP	G	A	Pts.	PIM
42-43	Det	1	0	0	0	0
43-44	Det	1	0	2	2	0
44-45	Det	44	15	11	26	6
Totals		46	15	13	28	6
Playoff Totals		14	2	1	3	0

McATEE, Norman Jerome *5-8 165 C*
B. Stratford, Ont., June 28, 1921

Season	Team	GP	G	A	Pts.	PIM
46-47	Bos	13	0	1	1	0

McAVOY, George *6-0 190 D*
B. Edmonton, Alta., June 21, 1931

Season	Team	GP	G	A	Pts.	PIM
54-55	Mont	0	0	0	0	0
Playoff Totals		4	0	0	0	0

McBAIN, Andrew *6-1 205 RW*
B. Scarborough, Ont., Jan. 18, 1965

Season	Team	GP	G	A	Pts.	PIM
83-84	Winn	78	11	19	30	37
84-85	Winn	77	7	15	22	45
85-86	Winn	28	3	3	6	17
86-87	Winn	71	11	21	32	106
87-88	Winn	74	32	31	63	145
88-89	Winn	80	37	40	77	71
89-90	Pitt-Van	67	9	14	23	73
90-91	Van	13	0	5	5	32
91-92	Van	1	0	1	1	0
Totals		494	111	148	259	526
Playoff Totals		24	5	7	12	39

McBEAN, Wayne *6-2 190 D*
B. Calgary, Alta., Feb. 21, 1969

Season	Team	GP	G	A	Pts.	PIM
87-88	LA	27	0	1	1	26
88-89	LA-NYI	52	0	6	6	35
89-90	NYI	5	0	1	1	2
90-91	NYI	52	5	14	19	47
91-92	NYI	25	2	4	6	18
Totals		161	7	26	33	128
Playoff Totals		2	1	1	2	0

McBRIDE, Clifford *D*

Season	Team	GP	G	A	Pts.	PIM
28-29	Mont M	1	0	0	0	0
29-30	Tor	1	0	0	0	0
Totals		2	0	0	0	0

McBURNEY, James *F*
B. Sault Ste. Marie, Ont., Jan. 3, 1933

Season	Team	GP	G	A	Pts.	PIM
52-53	Chi	1	0	1	1	0

McCABE, Stanley *D*
B. Ottawa, Ont.

Season	Team	GP	G	A	Pts.	PIM
29-30	Det	25	7	3	10	23
30-31	Det	44	2	1	3	22
32-33	Mont M	1	0	0	0	0
33-34	Mont M	8	0	0	0	4
Totals		78	9	4	13	49

McCAFFREY, Albert (Bert) *D*
B. Listowel, Ont.

Season	Team	GP	G	A	Pts.	PIM
24-25	Tor	30	9	6	15	12
25-26	Tor	36	14	7	21	42
26-27	Tor	43	5	5	10	43
27-28	Tor-Pitt Pi	44	7	4	11	23
28-29	Pitt Pi	42	1	0	1	34
29-30	Pitt Pi-Mont	43	4	7	11	38
30-31	Mont	22	2	1	3	10
Totals		260	42	30	72	202
Playoff Totals		8	2	1	3	12

McCAHILL, John Walter *6-1 215 D*
B. Sarnia, Ont., Dec. 2, 1955

Season	Team	GP	G	A	Pts.	PIM
77-78	Col	1	0	0	0	0

McCAIG, Douglas *6-0 180 D*
B. Guelph, Ont., Feb. 24, 1919

Season	Team	GP	G	A	Pts.	PIM
41-42	Det	9	0	1	1	6
45-46	Det	6	0	1	1	12
46-47	Det	47	2	4	6	64
47-48	Det	29	3	3	6	37
48-49	Det-Chi	56	1	3	4	60
49-50	Chi	64	0	4	4	49
50-51	Chi	53	2	5	7	29
Totals		264	8	21	29	257
Playoff Totals		17	0	1	1	8

McCALLUM, Duncan Selbie *6-1 193 D*
B. Flin Flon, Man., Mar. 29, 1940

Season	Team	GP	G	A	Pts.	PIM
65-66	NYR	2	0	0	0	2
67-68	Pitt	32	0	2	2	36
68-69	Pitt	62	5	13	18	81
69-70	Pitt	14	0	0	0	16
70-71	Pitt	77	9	20	29	95
72-73	Hou (WHA)	69	9	20	29	112
74-75	Chi (WHA)	31	0	10	10	24
NHL Totals		187	14	35	49	230
WHA Totals		100	9	30	39	136
NHL Playoff Totals		10	1	2	3	12
WHA Playoff Totals		10	2	3	5	6

McCALMON, Edward *RW*

Season	Team	GP	G	A	Pts.	PIM
27-28	Chi	23	2	0	2	8
30-31	Phil Q	16	3	0	3	6
Totals		39	5	0	5	14

McCANN, Richard Leo (Rick) *5-9 178 C*
B. Hamilton, Ont., May 27, 1944

Season	Team	GP	G	A	Pts.	PIM
67-68	Det	3	0	0	0	0
68-69	Det	3	0	0	0	0
69-70	Det	18	0	1	1	4
70-71	Det	5	0	0	0	0
71-72	Det	1	0	0	0	0
74-75	Det	13	1	3	4	2
Totals		43	1	4	5	6

McCARTHY, Daniel *5-9 189 C*
B. St. Mary's, Ont., Apr. 7, 1958

Season	Team	GP	G	A	Pts.	PIM
80-81	NYR	5	4	0	4	4

McCARTHY, Kevin *5-11 195 D*
B. Winnipeg, Man., July 14, 1957

Season	Team	GP	G	A	Pts.	PIM
77-78	Phil	62	2	15	17	32
78-79	Phil-Van	23	1	2	3	21
79-80	Van	79	15	30	45	70
80-81	Van	80	16	37	53	85
81-82	Van	71	6	39	45	84
82-83	Van	74	12	28	40	88
83-84	Van-Pitt	78	6	30	36	113
84-85	Pitt	64	9	10	19	30
85-86	Phil	4	0	0	0	4
86-87	Phil	2	0	0	0	0
Totals		537	67	191	258	527
Playoff Totals		21	2	3	5	20

McCARTHY, Thomas *RW*

Season	Team	GP	G	A	Pts.	PIM
19-20	Que	12	11	2	13	0
20-21	Ham	22	8	1	9	10
Totals		34	19	3	22	10

McCARTHY, Thomas Patrick Francis *6-1 190 LW*
B. Toronto, Ont., Sept. 15, 1934

Season	Team	GP	G	A	Pts.	PIM
56-57	Det	3	0	0	0	0
57-58	Det	18	2	1	3	4
58-59	Det	15	2	3	5	4
60-61	Bos	24	4	5	9	0
Totals		60	8	9	17	8

McCARTNEY, Walter *D*

Season	Team	GP	G	A	Pts.	PIM
32-33	Mont	2	0	0	0	0

McCASKILL, Edward Joel (Ted) *6-1 195 C*
B. Kapuskasing, Ont., Oct. 29, 1936

Season	Team	GP	G	A	Pts.	PIM
67-68	Minn	4	0	2	2	0
72-73	LA (WHA)	73	11	11	22	150
73-74	LA (WHA)	18	2	2	4	63
NHL Totals		4	0	2	2	0
WHA Totals		91	13	13	26	213
WHA Playoff Totals		6	2	3	5	12

McCLANAHAN, Rob *5-10 180 C*
B. St. Paul, Minn., Jan. 9, 1958

Season	Team	GP	G	A	Pts.	PIM
79-80	Buf	13	2	5	7	0
80-81	Buf	53	3	12	15	38
81-82	Hart-NYR	39	5	12	17	21
82-83	NYR	78	22	26	48	46
83-84	NYR	41	6	8	14	21
Totals		224	38	63	101	126
Playoff Totals		34	4	12	16	31

McCLELLAND, Kevin William *6-2 205 RW*
B. Oshawa, Ont., July 4, 1962

Season	Team	GP	G	A	Pts.	PIM
81-82	Pitt	10	1	4	5	4
82-83	Pitt	38	5	4	9	73
83-84	Pitt-Edm	76	10	24	34	189
84-85	Edm	62	8	15	23	205
85-86	Edm	79	11	25	36	266
86-87	Edm	72	12	13	25	238
87-88	Edm	74	10	6	16	281
88-89	Edm	79	6	14	20	161
89-90	Edm-Det	71	5	6	11	196
90-91	Det	3	0	0	0	7
91-92	Tor	18	0	1	1	33
Totals		582	68	112	180	1653
Playoff Totals		98	11	18	29	281

McCORD, Dennis Frederick *5-10 190 D*
B. Chatham, Ont., July 28, 1951

Season	Team	GP	G	A	Pts.	PIM
73-74	Van	3	0	0	0	0

McCORD, Robert Lomer *6-1 202 D*
B. Matheson, Ont., Mar. 30, 1934

Season	Team	GP	G	A	Pts.	PIM
63-64	Bos	65	1	9	10	49
64-65	Bos	43	0	6	6	26

McCORD, Robert Lomer *(Continued)*

Season	Team	GP	G	A	Pts.	PIM
65-66	Det	9	0	2	2	16
66-67	Det	14	1	2	3	27
67-68	Det-Minn	73	3	9	12	41
68-69	Minn	69	4	17	21	70
72-73	StL	43	1	13	14	33
Totals		316	10	58	68	262
Playoff Totals		14	2	5	7	10

McCORMACK, John Ronald (Goose) *6-0 185 C*
B. Edmonton, Alta., Aug. 2, 1925

Season	Team	GP	G	A	Pts.	PIM
47-48	Tor	3	0	1	1	0
48-49	Tor	1	0	0	0	0
49-50	Tor	34	6	5	11	0
50-51	Tor	46	6	7	13	2
51-52	Mont	54	2	10	12	4
52-53	Mont	59	1	9	10	9
53-54	Mont	51	5	10	15	12
54-55	Chi	63	5	7	12	8
Totals		311	25	49	74	35
Playoff Totals		22	1	1	2	0

McCOSH, Shawn *6-0 188 C*
B. Oshawa, Ont., June 5, 1969

Season	Team	GP	G	A	Pts.	PIM
91-92	LA	4	0	0	0	4

McCOURT, Dale Allen *5-10 180 C*
B. Falconbridge, Ont., Jan. 26, 1957

Season	Team	GP	G	A	Pts.	PIM
77-78	Det	76	33	39	72	10
78-79	Det	79	28	43	71	14
79-80	Det	80	30	51	81	12
80-81	Det	80	30	56	86	50
81-82	Det-Buf	78	33	36	69	18
82-83	Buf	62	20	32	52	10
83-84	Buf-Tor	77	20	27	47	10
Totals		532	194	284	478	124
Playoff Totals		21	9	7	16	6

McCREARY, Vernon Keith *5-10 180 RW*
B. Sundridge, Ont., June 19, 1940

Season	Team	GP	G	A	Pts.	PIM
64-65	Mont	9	0	3	3	4
67-68	Pitt	70	14	12	26	44
68-69	Pitt	70	25	23	48	42
69-70	Pitt	60	18	8	26	67
70-71	Pitt	59	21	12	33	24
71-72	Pitt	33	4	4	8	22
72-73	Atl	77	20	21	41	21
73-74	Atl	76	18	19	37	62
74-75	Atl	78	11	10	21	8
Totals		532	131	112	243	294
Playoff Totals		16	0	4	4	6

McCREARY, William *6-0 190 RW*
B. Springfield, Mass., Apr. 15, 1960

Season	Team	GP	G	A	Pts.	PIM
80-81	Tor	12	1	0	1	4

McCREARY, William Edward *5-10 172 LW*
B. Sundridge, Ont., Dec. 2, 1934

Season	Team	GP	G	A	Pts.	PIM
53-54	NYR	2	0	0	0	2
54-55	NYR	8	0	2	2	0
57-58	Det	3	1	0	1	2
62-63	Mont	14	2	3	5	0
67-68	StL	70	13	13	26	22
68-69	StL	71	13	17	30	50
69-70	StL	73	15	17	32	16
70-71	StL	68	9	10	19	16
Totals		309	53	62	115	108
Playoff Totals		48	6	16	22	14

McCREEDY, John *5-8 160 RW*
B. Winnipeg, Man., Mar. 23, 1911

Season	Team	GP	G	A	Pts.	PIM
41-42	Tor	47	15	8	23	14
44-45	Tor	17	2	4	6	11
Totals		64	17	12	29	25
Playoff Totals		17	3	2	5	16

McCRIMMON, Byron (Brad) *5-11 197 D*
B. Dodsland, Sask., Mar. 29, 1959

Season	Team	GP	G	A	Pts.	PIM
79-80	Bos	72	5	11	16	94
80-81	Bos	78	11	18	29	148
81-82	Bos	78	1	8	9	83
82-83	Phil	79	4	21	25	61
83-84	Phil	71	0	24	24	76
84-85	Phil	66	8	35	43	81
85-86	Phil	80	13	43	56	85
86-87	Phil	71	10	29	39	52
87-88	Calg	80	7	35	42	98
88-89	Calg	72	5	17	22	96
89-90	Calg	79	4	15	19	78
90-91	Det	64	0	13	13	81
91-92	Det	79	7	22	29	118
Totals		969	75	291	366	1151
Playoff Totals		116	11	18	29	176

McCRIMMON, John James (Jim) *6-1 210 D*
B. Ponoka, Alta., May 29, 1953

Season	Team	GP	G	A	Pts.	PIM
73-74	Edm (WHA)	75	2	3	5	106
74-75	Edm (WHA)	34	1	5	6	50
74-75	StL (WHA)	2	0	0	0	0
75-76	Calg (WHA)	5	0	0	0	2
NHL Totals		2	0	0	0	0
WHA Totals		114	3	8	11	158

McCULLEY, Robert *F*

Season	Team	GP	G	A	Pts.	PIM
34-35	Mont	1	0	0	0	0

McCUTCHEON, Brian Kenneth *5-10 180 LW*
B. Toronto, Ont., Aug. 3, 1949

Season	Team	GP	G	A	Pts.	PIM
74-75	Det	17	3	1	4	2
75-76	Det	8	0	0	0	5
76-77	Det	12	0	0	0	0
Totals		37	3	1	4	7

McCUTCHEON, Darwin *6-4 190 D*
B. Listowel, Ont., Apr. 19, 1962

Season	Team	GP	G	A	Pts.	PIM
81-82	Tor	1	0	0	0	2

McDILL, Jeffrey Donald *5-11 190 RW*
B. Thunder Bay, Ont., Mar. 16, 1956

Season	Team	GP	G	A	Pts.	PIM
76-77	Chi	1	0	0	0	0

McDONAGH, William James *5-9 150 LW*
B. Rouyn, Que., Apr. 30, 1928

Season	Team	GP	G	A	Pts.	PIM
49-50	NYR	4	0	0	0	2

McDONALD, Albert John (John) *5-11 205 RW*
B. Swan River, Man., Nov. 24, 1941

Season	Team	GP	G	A	Pts.	PIM
43-44	NYR	43	10	9	19	6

McDONALD, Alvin Brian (Ab) *6-2 194 LW*
B. Winnipeg, Man., Feb. 18, 1936

Season	Team	GP	G	A	Pts.	PIM
58-59	Mont	69	13	23	36	35
59-60	Mont	68	9	13	22	26
60-61	Chi	61	17	16	33	22
61-62	Chi	65	22	18	40	8
62-63	Chi	69	20	41	61	12
63-64	Chi	70	14	32	46	19
64-65	Bos	60	9	9	18	8
65-66	Det	43	6	16	22	6
66-67	Det	12	0	2	2	7
67-68	Pitt	74	22	21	43	38
68-69	StL	68	21	21	42	12
69-70	StL	64	25	30	55	8
70-71	StL	20	0	5	5	6
71-72	Det	19	2	3	5	0
72-73	Winn (WHA)	77	17	24	41	16
73-74	Winn (WHA)	70	12	17	29	8
NHL Totals		762	182	248	430	200
WHA Totals		147	29	41	70	24
NHL Playoff Totals		84	21	29	50	42
WHA Playoff Totals		18	4	4	8	4

McDONALD, Brian Harold *5-11 190 RW*
B. Toronto, Ont., Mar. 23, 1945

Season	Team	GP	G	A	Pts.	PIM
70-71	Buf	12	0	0	0	29
72-73	Hou (WHA)	71	20	20	40	78
73-74	LA (WHA)	56	22	30	52	54
74-75	Mich-Ind (WHA)	65	17	20	37	34
75-76	Ind (WHA)	62	15	18	33	54
76-77	Ind (WHA)	50	15	13	28	48
NHL Totals		12	0	0	0	29
WHA Totals		304	89	101	190	268
NHL Playoff Totals		8	0	0	0	2
WHA Playoff Totals		26	6	5	11	61

McDONALD, Girard J. (Gerry) *6-3 190 D*
B. Weymouth, Mass., Mar. 18, 1958

Season	Team	GP	G	A	Pts.	PIM
81-82	Hart	3	0	0	0	0

McDONALD, John (Jack) *LW*

Season	Team	GP	G	A	Pts.	PIM
17-18	Mont W-Mont	12	12	0	12	9

McDONALD, John (Jack) *(Continued)*

Season	Team	GP	G	A	Pts.	PIM
18-19	Mont	18	8	4	12	9
19-20	Que	24	7	6	13	4
20-21	Mont-Tor	17	0	1	1	0
21-22	Mont	2	0	0	0	0
Totals		73	27	11	38	22
Playoff Totals		12	0	2	0	

McDONALD, Lanny King *6-0 194 RW*
B. Hanna, Alta., Feb. 16, 1953

Season	Team	GP	G	A	Pts.	PIM
73-74	Tor	70	14	16	30	43
74-75	Tor	64	17	27	44	86
75-76	Tor	75	37	56	93	70
76-77	Tor	80	46	44	90	77
77-78	Tor	74	47	40	87	54
78-79	Tor	79	43	42	85	32
79-80	Tor-Col	81	40	35	75	53
80-81	Col	80	35	46	81	56
81-82	Col-Calg	71	40	42	82	57
82-83	Calg	80	66	32	98	90
83-84	Calg	65	33	33	66	64
84-85	Calg	43	19	18	37	36
85-86	Calg	80	28	43	71	44
86-87	Calg	58	14	12	26	54
87-88	Calg	60	10	13	23	57
88-89	Calg	51	11	7	18	26
Totals		1111	500	506	1006	899
Playoff Totals		117	44	40	84	120

McDONALD, Robert *F*
B. Toronto, Ont., Jan. 4, 1923

Season	Team	GP	G	A	Pts.	PIM
43-44	NYR	1	0	0	0	0

McDONALD, Terry Grant *6-1 180 D*
B. Coquitlam, B.C., June 17, 1955

Season	Team	GP	G	A	Pts.	PIM
75-76	KC	8	0	1	1	6

McDONALD, Wilfred Kennedy (Bucko) *5-9 205 D*
B. Fergus, Ont., Oct. 31, 1911

Season	Team	GP	G	A	Pts.	PIM
34-35	Det	16	1	2	3	8
35-36	Det	48	4	6	10	32
36-37	Det	47	3	5	8	20
37-38	Det	47	3	7	10	14
38-39	Det-Tor	47	3	3	6	22
39-40	Tor	34	2	5	7	13
40-41	Tor	31	6	11	17	12
41-42	Tor	48	2	19	21	24
42-43	Tor	40	2	11	13	39
43-44	Tor-NYR	50	7	10	17	22
44-45	NYR	40	2	9	11	0
Totals		448	35	88	123	206
Playoff Totals		63	6	1	7	24

McDONNELL, Joseph Patrick *6-2 200 D*
B. Kitchener, Ont., May 11, 1961

Season	Team	GP	G	A	Pts.	PIM
81-82	Van	7	0	1	1	12
84-85	Pitt	40	2	9	11	20
85-86	Pitt	3	0	0	0	2
Totals		50	2	10	12	34

McDONNELL, Moylan *D*

Season	Team	GP	G	A	Pts.	PIM
20-21	Ham	20	1	1	2	0

McDONOUGH, Hubie *5-9 180 C*
B. Manchester, N.H., July 8, 1963

Season	Team	GP	G	A	Pts.	PIM
88-89	LA	4	0	1	1	0
89-90	LA-NYI	76	21	15	36	36
90-91	NYI	52	6	6	12	10
91-92	NYI	33	7	2	9	15
Totals		165	34	24	58	61
Playoff Totals		5	1	0	1	4

McDONOUGH, James Allison (Al) *6-1 175 RW*
B. Hamilton, Ont., June 6, 1950

Season	Team	GP	G	A	Pts.	PIM
70-71	LA	6	2	1	3	0
71-72	LA-Pitt	68	10	13	23	16
72-73	Pitt	78	35	41	76	26
73-74	Pitt-Atl	72	24	31	55	27
74-75	Clev (WHA)	78	34	30	64	27
75-76	Clev (WHA)	80	23	22	45	19
76-77	Minn (WHA)	42	9	21	30	6
77-78	Det	13	2	2	4	4
NHL Totals		237	73	88	161	73
WHA Totals		200	66	73	139	52
NHL Playoff Totals		8	0	1	1	2
WHA Playoff Totals		8	3	1	4	2

McDOUGAL, Michael George *6-2 200 RW*
B. Port Huron, Mich., Apr. 30, 1958

Season	Team	GP	G	A	Pts.	PIM
78-79	NYR	1	0	0	0	0
80-81	NYR	2	0	0	0	0

Season	Team	GP	G	A	Pts.	PIM
McDOUGAL, Michael George *(Continued)*						
81-82	Hart	3	0	0	0	0
82-83	Hart	55	8	10	18	43
Totals		61	8	10	18	43
McDOUGALL, William Henry *6-0 185 C*						
B. Mississauga, Ont., Aug. 10, 1966						
90-91	Det	2	0	1	1	0
McEACHERN, Shawn *6-1 180 C*						
B. Waltham, Mass., Feb. 28, 1969						
91-92	Pitt	15	0	4	4	0
Playoff Totals		19	2	7	9	4
McELMURY, James Donald *6-0 190 D*						
B. St. Paul, Minn., Oct. 3, 1949						
72-73	Minn	7	0	1	1	2
74-75	KC	78	5	17	22	25
75-76	KC	38	2	6	8	6
76-77	Col	55	7	23	30	16
77-78	Col	2	0	0	0	0
Totals		180	14	47	61	49
McEWEN, Michael Todd *6-1 185 D*						
B. Hornepayne, Ont., Aug. 10, 1956						
76-77	NYR	80	14	29	43	38
77-78	NYR	57	5	13	18	52
78-79	NYR	80	20	38	58	35
79-80	NYR-Col	76	12	47	59	41
80-81	Col-NYI	78	11	38	49	94
81-82	NYI	73	10	39	49	50
82-83	NYI	42	2	11	13	16
83-84	NYI-LA	62	10	26	36	20
84-85	Wash	56	11	27	38	42
85-86	Det-NYR-Hart	55	5	17	22	30
86-87	Hart	48	8	8	16	32
87-88	Hart	9	0	3	3	10
Totals		716	108	296	404	460
Playoff Totals		78	12	36	48	48
McFADDEN, James Alexander *5-7 178 C*						
B. Belfast, Ireland, Apr. 15, 1920						
47-48	Det	60	24	24	48	12
48-49	Det	55	12	20	32	10
49-50	Det	68	14	16	30	8
50-51	Det	70	14	18	32	10
51-52	Chi	70	10	24	34	14
52-53	Chi	70	23	21	44	29
53-54	Chi	19	3	3	6	6
Totals		412	100	126	226	89
Playoff Totals		49	10	9	19	30
McFADYEN, Donald P. *5-9 163 F*						
B. Grossfield, Alta., Mar. 24, 1907						
32-33	Chi	48	5	9	14	20
33-34	Chi	46	1	3	4	20
34-35	Chi	37	2	5	7	4
35-36	Chi	48	4	16	20	33
Totals		179	12	33	45	77
Playoff Totals		12	2	2	4	5
McFALL, Dan *6-0 180 D*						
B. Kenmore, N.Y., Apr. 8, 1963						
84-85	Winn	2	0	0	0	0
85-86	Winn	7	0	1	1	0
Totals		9	0	1	1	0
McFARLAND, George *D*						
26-27	Chi	2	0	0	0	0
McGEOUGH, James *5-8 170 C*						
B. Regina, Sask., Apr. 13, 1963						
81-82	Wash	4	0	0	0	0
84-85	Wash-Pitt	15	3	4	7	16
85-86	Pitt	17	3	2	5	8
86-87	Pitt	11	1	4	5	8
Totals		57	7	10	17	32
McGIBBON, John Irving *F*						
42-43	Mont	1	0	0	0	2
McGILL, John (Jack) *5-10 150 F*						
B. Ottawa, Ont., Nov. 3, 1910						
34-35	Mont	44	9	1	10	34
35-36	Mont	46	13	7	20	28
36-37	Mont	44	5	2	7	9
Totals		134	27	10	37	71
Playoff Totals		3	2	0	2	0
McGILL, John George (Big Jack) *6-1 180 C*						
B. Edmonton, Alta., Sept. 19, 1921						
41-42	Bos	13	8	11	19	2
44-45	Bos	14	4	2	6	0

Season	Team	GP	G	A	Pts.	PIM
McGILL, John George (Big Jack)						
(Continued)						
45-46	Bos	46	6	14	20	21
46-47	Bos	24	5	9	14	19
Totals		97	23	36	59	42
Playoff Totals		27	7	4	11	17
McGILL, Robert Paul *6-1 193 D*						
B. Edmonton, Alta., Apr. 27, 1962						
81-82	Tor	68	1	10	11	263
82-83	Tor	30	0	0	0	146
83-84	Tor	11	0	2	2	51
84-85	Tor	72	0	5	5	250
85-86	Tor	61	1	4	5	141
86-87	Tor	56	1	4	5	103
87-88	Chi	67	4	7	11	131
88-89	Chi	68	0	4	4	155
89-90	Chi	69	2	10	12	204
90-91	Chi	77	4	5	9	151
91-92	SJ-Det	74	3	1	4	91
Totals		653	16	52	68	1686
Playoff Totals		79	0	0	0	88
McGILL, Ryan *6-2 197 D*						
B. Sherwood Park, Alta., Feb. 28, 1969						
91-92	Chi	9	0	2	2	20
McGREGOR, Donald Alexander (Sandy) *5-11 165 RW*						
B. Toronto, Ont., Mar. 30, 1939						
63-64	NYR	2	0	0	0	2
McGUIRE, Frank S. (Mickey) *F*						
26-27	Pitt Pi	32	3	0	3	6
27-28	Pitt Pi	4	0	0	0	0
Totals		36	3	0	3	6
McHUGH, Michael *5-10 190 LW*						
B. Bowdoin, Mass., Aug. 16, 1965						
88-89	Minn	3	0	0	0	2
89-90	Minn	3	0	0	0	0
90-91	Minn	6	0	0	0	0
91-92	SJ	8	1	0	1	14
Totals		20	1	0	1	16
McILHARGEY, John Cecil (Jack) *6-0 190 D*						
B. Edmonton, Alta., Mar. 7, 1952						
74-75	Phil	2	0	0	0	11
75-76	Phil	57	1	2	3	205
76-77	Phil-Van	61	3	8	11	225
77-78	Van	69	3	5	8	172
78-79	Van	53	2	4	6	129
79-80	Van-Phil	50	0	6	6	136
80-81	Phil-Hart	51	1	6	7	164
81-82	Hart	50	1	5	6	60
Totals		393	11	36	47	1102
Playoff Totals		27	0	3	3	68
McINENLY, Bertram H. *5-9 160 D*						
B. Quebec City, Que., May 6, 1906						
30-31	Det	44	3	5	8	48
31-32	Det-NYA	47	12	7	19	60
32-33	Ott	30	2	2	4	8
33-34	Ott-Bos	9	0	0	0	4
34-35	Bos	33	2	1	3	24
35-36	Bos	3	0	0	0	0
Totals		166	19	15	34	144
Playoff Totals		4	0	0	0	2
McINNIS, Marty *5-11 175 C*						
B. Weymouth, Mass., June 2, 1970						
91-92	NYI	15	3	5	8	0
McINTOSH, Bruce *6-0 178 D*						
B. Minneapolis, Minn., Mar. 17, 1949						
72-73	Minn	2	0	0	0	0
McINTOSH, Paul *5-10 177 D*						
B. Listowel, Ont., Mar. 13, 1954						
74-75	Buf	6	0	1	1	5
75-76	Buf	42	0	1	1	61
Totals		48	0	2	2	66
Playoff Totals		2	0	0	0	7
McINTYRE, John *6-1 180 C*						
B. Ravenswood, Ont., Apr. 29, 1969						
89-90	Tor	59	5	12	17	117
90-91	Tor-LA	69	8	8	16	140
91-92	LA	73	5	19	24	100
Totals		201	18	39	57	357
Playoff Totals		18	0	5	5	38

Season	Team	GP	G	A	Pts.	PIM
McINTYRE, John Archibald (Jack) *5-11 190 LW*						
B. Brussels, Ont., Sept. 8, 1930						
49-50	Bos	5	0	1	1	0
51-52	Bos	52	12	19	31	18
52-53	Bos	70	7	15	22	31
53-54	Chi	23	8	3	11	4
54-55	Chi	65	16	13	29	40
55-56	Chi	46	10	5	15	14
56-57	Chi	70	18	14	32	32
57-58	Chi-Det	68	15	11	26	14
58-59	Det	55	15	14	29	14
59-60	Det	49	8	7	15	6
Totals		499	109	102	211	173
Playoff Totals		29	7	6	13	4
McINTYRE, Lawrence Albert *6-1 190 D*						
B. Moose Jaw, Sask., July 13, 1949						
69-70	Tor	1	0	0	0	0
72-73	Tor	40	0	3	3	26
Totals		41	0	3	3	26
McKAY, Alvin Douglas (Doug) *5-9 165 LW*						
B. Hamilton, Ont., May 28, 1929						
49-50	Det	0	0	0	0	0
Playoff Totals		1	0	0	0	0
McKAY, Randy *6-1 185 RW*						
B. Montreal, Que., Jan. 25, 1967						
88-89	Det	3	0	0	0	0
89-90	Det	33	3	6	9	51
90-91	Det	47	1	7	8	183
91-92	NJ	80	17	16	33	246
Totals		163	21	29	50	480
Playoff Totals		14	1	4	5	53
McKAY, Raymond Owen *6-4 183 D*						
B. Edmonton, Alta., Aug. 22, 1946						
68-69	Chi	9	0	1	1	12
69-70	Chi	17	0	0	0	23
70-71	Chi	2	0	0	0	0
71-72	Buf	39	0	3	3	18
72-73	Buf	1	0	0	0	0
73-74	Cal	72	2	12	14	49
74-75	Edm (WHA)	69	8	20	28	47
75-76	Clev (WHA)	68	3	10	13	44
76-77	Minn-Birm (WHA)	61	2	10	12	39
77-78	Edm (WHA)	14	1	4	5	4
NHL Totals		140	2	16	18	102
WHA Totals		212	14	44	58	134
NHL Playoff Totals		1	0	0	0	0
WHA Playoff Totals		7	0	1	1	8
McKECHNIE, Walter Thomas John *6-2 200 C*						
B. London, Ont., June 19, 1947						
67-68	Minn	4	0	0	0	0
68-69	Minn	58	5	9	14	22
69-70	Minn	20	1	3	4	21
70-71	Minn	30	3	1	4	34
71-72	Cal	56	11	20	31	40
72-73	Cal	78	16	38	54	58
73-74	Cal	63	23	29	52	54
74-75	Bos-Det	76	9	14	23	14
75-76	Det	80	26	56	82	85
76-77	Det	80	25	34	59	50
77-78	Wash-Clev	69	16	23	39	12
78-79	Tor	79	25	36	61	18
79-80	Tor-Col	71	7	40	47	6
80-81	Col	53	15	23	38	18
81-82	Det	74	18	37	55	35
82-83	Det	64	14	29	43	42
Totals		955	214	392	606	469
Playoff Totals		15	5	12		9
McKEGNEY, Anthony *6-1 200 LW*						
B. Montreal, Que., Feb. 15, 1958						
78-79	Buf	52	8	14	22	10
79-80	Buf	80	23	29	52	24
80-81	Buf	80	37	32	69	24
81-82	Buf	73	23	29	52	41
82-83	Buf	78	36	37	73	18
83-84	Que	75	24	27	51	23
84-85	Que-Minn	57	23	22	45	16
85-86	Minn	70	15	25	40	48
86-87	Minn-NYR	75	31	20	51	72
87-88	StL	80	40	38	78	82
88-89	StL	71	25	17	42	58
89-90	Det-Que	62	18	12	30	53
90-91	Que-Chi	59	17	17	34	48
Totals		912	320	319	639	517
Playoff Totals		79	24	23	47	56

Season	Team	GP	G	A	Pts.	PIM
McKEGNEY, Ian Robert	*5-11 165 D*					
B. Sarnia, Ont., May 7, 1947						
76-77	Chi	3	0	0	0	2
McKELL, Jack	*D*					
19-20	Ott	21	2	0	2	20
20-21	Ott	21	2	1	3	22
Totals		42	4	1	5	42
Playoff Totals		9	0	0	0	0
McKENDRY, Alexander	*6-4 200 LW*					
B. Midland, Ont., Nov. 21, 1956						
77-78	NYI	4	0	0	0	2
78-79	NYI	4	0	0	0	0
79-80	NYI	2	0	0	0	2
80-81	Calg	36	3	6	9	19
Totals		47	3	6	9	23
Playoff Totals		6	2	2	4	0
McKENNA, Sean Michael	*6-0 190 RW*					
B. Asbestos, Que., Mar. 7, 1962						
81-82	Buf	3	0	1	1	2
82-83	Buf	46	10	14	24	4
83-84	Buf	78	20	10	30	45
84-85	Buf	65	20	16	36	41
85-86	Buf-LA	75	10	12	22	35
86-87	LA	69	14	19	33	10
87-88	LA-Tor	70	8	7	15	24
88-89	Tor	3	0	1	1	0
89-90	Tor	5	0	0	0	20
Totals		414	82	80	162	181
Playoff Totals		15	1	2	3	2
McKENNEY, Donald Hamilton	*6-0 175 C*					
B. Smith Falls, Ont., Apr. 30, 1934						
54-55	Bos	69	22	20	42	34
55-56	Bos	65	10	24	34	20
56-57	Bos	69	21	39	60	31
57-58	Bos	70	28	30	58	59
58-59	Bos	70	32	30	62	20
59-60	Bos	70	20	49	69	28
60-61	Bos	68	26	23	49	22
61-62	Bos	70	22	33	55	10
62-63	Bos-NYR	62	22	35	57	6
63-64	NYR-Tor	70	18	23	41	8
64-65	Tor	52	6	13	19	6
65-66	Det	24	1	6	7	0
67-68	StL	39	9	20	29	4
Totals		798	237	345	582	248
Playoff Totals		58	18	29	47	10
McKENNY, James Claude	*6-0 185 D*					
B. Ottawa, Ont., Dec. 1, 1946						
65-66	Tor	2	0	0	0	2
66-67	Tor	6	1	0	1	0
67-68	Tor	5	1	0	1	0
68-69	Tor	7	0	0	0	2
69-70	Tor	73	11	33	44	34
70-71	Tor	68	4	26	30	42
71-72	Tor	76	5	31	36	27
72-73	Tor	77	11	41	52	55
73-74	Tor	77	14	28	42	36
74-75	Tor	66	8	35	43	31
75-76	Tor	46	10	19	29	19
76-77	Tor	76	14	31	45	36
77-78	Tor	15	2	2	4	2
78-79	Tor	10	1	1	2	2
Totals		604	82	247	329	294
Playoff Totals		37	7	9	16	10
McKENZIE, Brian Stewart	*5-10 165 LW*					
B. St. Catherines, Ont., Mar. 16, 1951						
71-72	Pitt	6	1	1	2	4
73-74	Edm (WHA)	78	18	20	38	66
74-75	Ind (WHA)	9	1	0	1	6
NHL Totals		6	1	1	2	4
WHA Totals		87	19	20	39	72
WHA Playoff Totals		5	0	1	1	0
McKENZIE, Jim	*6-3 205 LW/D*					
B. Gull Lake, Sask., Nov. 3, 1969						
89-90	Hart	5	0	0	0	4
90-91	Hart	41	4	3	7	108
91-92	Hart	67	5	1	6	87
Totals		113	9	4	13	199
Playoff Totals		6	0	0	0	8
McKENZIE, John Albert	*5-9 175 RW*					
B. High River, Alta., Dec. 12, 1937						
58-59	Chi	32	3	4	7	22
59-60	Det	59	8	12	20	50
60-61	Det	16	3	1	4	13
63-64	Chi	45	9	9	18	50
64-65	Chi	51	8	10	18	46
65-66	NYR-Bos	71	19	14	33	72
66-67	Bos	69	17	19	36	98

Season	Team	GP	G	A	Pts.	PIM
McKENZIE, John Albert (Continued)						
67-68	Bos	74	28	38	66	107
68-69	Bos	60	29	27	56	99
69-70	Bos	72	29	41	70	114
70-71	Bos	65	31	46	77	120
71-72	Bos	77	22	47	69	126
72-73	Phil (WHA)	60	28	50	78	157
73-74	Van (WHA)	45	14	38	52	71
74-75	Van (WHA)	74	23	37	60	82
75-76	Minn-Cin (WHA)	69	24	36	60	54
76-77	Minn-NE (WHA)	74	28	32	60	77
77-78	NE (WHA)	79	27	29	56	61
78-79	NE (WHA)	76	19	28	47	115
NHL Totals		691	206	268	474	917
WHA Totals		477	163	250	413	617
NHL Playoff Totals		69	15	32	47	133
WHA Playoff Totals		33	14	15	29	42
McKINNON, Alexander	*D*					
B. Sudbury, Ont.						
24-25	Ham	30	8	2	10	45
25-26	NYA	35	5	3	8	34
26-27	NYA	42	2	1	3	29
27-28	NYA	43	3	3	6	71
28-29	Chi	44	1	1	2	56
Totals		194	19	10	29	235
McKINNON, John Douglas	*5-8 170 D*					
B. Guysborough, N.S., July 15, 1902						
25-26	Mont	2	0	0	0	0
26-27	Pitt Pi	44	13	0	13	46
27-28	Pitt Pi	43	3	3	6	46
28-29	Pitt Pi	39	1	0	1	44
29-30	Pitt Pi	41	10	7	17	42
30-31	Phil Q	39	1	1	2	46
Totals		208	28	11	39	224
Playoff Totals		2	0	0	0	4
McKINNON, Robert	*F*					
28-29	Chi	2	0	0	0	0
McLEAN, Fred	*F*					
19-20	Que	7	0	0	0	2
20-21	Ham	2	0	0	0	0
Totals		9	0	0	0	2
McLEAN, Jack	*5-8 165 C*					
B. Winnipeg, Man., Jan. 1, 1923						
42-43	Tor	27	9	8	17	33
43-44	Tor	32	3	15	18	30
44-45	Tor	8	2	1	3	13
Totals		67	14	24	38	76
Playoff Totals		13	2	2	4	8
McLEAN, Robert Donald (Don)	*6-1 200 D*					
B. Niagara Falls, Ont., Jan. 19, 1954						
75-76	Wash	9	0	0	0	6
McLELLAN, Daniel (Scott)	*6-0 170 RW*					
B. Burlington, Ont., Feb. 10, 1963						
82-83	Bos	2	0	0	0	0
McLELLAN, Daniel John (John)	*5-11 150 C*					
B. South Porcupine, Ont., Aug. 6, 1928						
51-52	Tor	2	0	0	0	0
McLELLAN, Todd	*5-11 185 C*					
B. Melville, Sask., Oct. 3, 1967						
87-88	NYI	5	1	1	2	0
McLENAHAN, Roland Joseph (Roly)	*5-7 170 D*					
B. Fredericton, N.B., Oct. 26, 1921						
45-46	Det	9	2	1	3	10
Playoff Totals		2	0	0	0	0
McLEOD, Allan Sidney	*5-11 200 D*					
B. Medicine Hat, Alta., June 17, 1949						
73-74	Det	26	2	2	4	24
74-75	Phoe (WHA)	77	3	16	19	98
75-76	Phoe (WHA)	80	2	17	19	82
76-77	Phoe-Hou (WHA)	80	8	26	34	55
77-78	Hou (WHA)	80	2	22	24	54
78-79	Ind (WHA)	25	0	11	11	22
NHL Totals		26	2	2	4	24
WHA Totals		342	15	92	107	311
WHA Playoff Totals		26	2	9	11	19

Season	Team	GP	G	A	Pts.	PIM
McLEOD, Robert John (Jackie)	*5-8 150 RW*					
B. Regina, Sask., Apr. 30, 1930						
49-50	NYR	38	6	9	15	2
50-51	NYR	41	5	10	15	2
51-52	NYR	13	2	3	5	2
52-53	NYR	3	0	0	0	2
54-55	NYR	11	1	1	2	2
Totals		106	14	23	37	10
Playoff Totals		7	0	0	0	0
McLLWAIN, Dave	*6-0 190 C/RW*					
B. Seaforth, Ont., Jan. 9, 1967						
87-88	Pitt	66	11	8	19	40
88-89	Pitt	24	1	2	3	4
89-90	Winn	80	25	26	51	60
90-91	Winn	60	14	11	25	46
91-92	Winn-Buf-NY-Tor	73	10	18	28	36
Totals		303	61	65	126	186
Playoff Totals		10	0	2	2	2
McMAHON, Michael Clarence	*5-8 215 D*					
B. Brockville, Ont., Feb. 1, 1915						
43-44	Mont	42	7	17	24	98
45-46	Mont-Bos	15	0	1	1	4
Totals		57	7	18	25	102
Playoff Totals		13	1	2	3	30
McMAHON, Michael William	*5-11 175 D*					
B. Quebec City, Que., Aug. 30, 1941						
63-64	NYR	18	0	1	1	16
64-65	NYR	1	0	0	0	0
65-66	NYR	41	0	12	12	34
67-68	Minn	74	14	33	47	71
68-69	Minn-Chi	63	0	19	19	6
69-70	Det-Pitt	14	1	3	4	19
70-71	Buf	12	0	0	0	4
71-72	NYR	1	0	0	0	0
72-73	Minn (WHA)	75	12	39	51	87
73-74	Minn (WHA)	71	10	35	45	82
74-75	Minn (WHA)	54	5	15	20	42
75-76	SD (WHA)	69	2	12	14	38
NHL Totals		224	15	68	83	150
WHA Totals		269	29	101	130	249
NHL Playoff Totals		14	3	7	10	4
WHA Playoff Totals		32	1	14	15	13
McMANAMA, Robert S.	*6-0 180 C*					
B. Belmont, Mass., Oct. 7, 1951						
73-74	Pitt	47	5	14	19	18
74-75	Pitt	40	5	9	14	6
75-76	Pitt	12	1	2	3	4
75-76	NE (WHA)	37	3	10	13	28
NHL Totals		99	11	25	36	28
WHA Totals		37	3	10	13	28
NHL Playoff Totals		8	0	1	1	6
WHA Playoff Totals		4	3	7	4	
McMANUS, A. Samuel (Sammy)	*LW*					
B. Belfast, Ireland, 1909						
34-35	Mont M	25	0	1	1	8
36-37	Bos	1	0	0	0	0
Totals		26	0	1	1	8
Playoff Totals		1	0	0	0	0
McMURCHY, Thomas	*5-9 165 RW*					
B. New Westminster, B.C., Dec. 2, 1963						
83-84	Chi	27	3	1	4	42
84-85	Chi	15	1	2	3	13
85-86	Chi	4	0	0	0	2
87-88	Edm	9	4	1	5	8
Totals		55	8	4	12	65
McNAB, Maxwell Douglas	*6-2 170 C*					
B. Watson, Sask., June 21, 1924						
47-48	Det	12	2	2	4	2
48-49	Det	51	10	13	23	14
49-50	Det	65	4	4	8	8
Totals		128	16	19	35	24
Playoff Totals		25	1	0	1	4
McNAB, Peter Maxwell	*6-3 205 C*					
B. Vancouver, B.C., May 8, 1952						
73-74	Buf	22	3	6	9	2
74-75	Buf	53	22	21	43	8
75-76	Buf	79	24	32	56	16
76-77	Bos	80	38	48	86	11
77-78	Bos	79	41	39	80	4
78-79	Bos	76	35	45	80	10
79-80	Bos	74	40	38	78	10
80-81	Bos	80	37	46	83	24
81-82	Bos	80	36	40	76	19

McNAB, Peter Maxwell *(Continued)*

Season	Team	GP	G	A	Pts.	PIM
82-83	Bos	74	22	52	74	23
83-84	Bos-Van	65	15	22	37	20
84-85	Van	75	23	25	48	10
85-86	NJ	71	19	24	43	14
86-87	NJ	46	8	12	20	8
Totals		954	363	450	813	179
Playoff Totals		107	40	42	82	20

McNABNEY, Sidney *5-7 150 C*
B. Toronto, Ont., Jan. 15, 1929

Season	Team	GP	G	A	Pts.	PIM
50-51	Mont	0	0	0	0	0
Playoff Totals		5	0	1	1	2

McNAMARA, Howard *240 D*

Season	Team	GP	G	A	Pts.	PIM
19-20	Mont	11	1	0	1	2

McNAUGHTON, George *F*

Season	Team	GP	G	A	Pts.	PIM
19-20	Que	1	0	0	0	0

McNEILL, Michael *6-0 195 LW*
B. Winona, Minn., July 22, 1966

Season	Team	GP	G	A	Pts.	PIM
90-91	Chi-Que	37	4	7	11	10
91-92	Que	26	1	4	5	8
Totals		63	5	11	16	18

McNEILL, Stuart (Stu) *F*
B. Port Arthur, Ont., Sept. 25, 1938

Season	Team	GP	G	A	Pts.	PIM
57-58	Det	2	0	0	0	0
58-59	Det	3	1	1	2	2
59-60	Det	5	0	0	0	0
Totals		10	1	1	2	2

McNEILL, William Ronald *5-10 185 RW*
B. Edmonton, Alta., Jan. 26, 1936

Season	Team	GP	G	A	Pts.	PIM
56-57	Det	64	5	10	15	34
57-58	Det	35	5	10	15	29
58-59	Det	54	2	5	7	32
59-60	Det	47	5	13	18	33
62-63	Det	42	3	7	10	12
63-64	Det	15	1	1	2	2
Totals		257	21	46	67	142
Playoff Totals		4	1	1	2	4

McPHEE, George *5-9 170 LW*
B. Guelph, Ont., July 2, 1958

Season	Team	GP	G	A	Pts.	PIM
83-84	NYR	9	1	1	2	11
84-85	NYR	49	12	15	27	139
85-86	NYR	30	4	4	8	63
86-87	NYR	21	4	4	8	34
87-88	NJ	5	3	0	3	8
88-89	NJ	1	0	1	1	2
Totals		115	24	25	49	257
Playoff Totals		29	5	3	8	69

McPHEE, Michael Joseph *6-1 203 LW*
B. Sydney, N.S., July 14, 1960

Season	Team	GP	G	A	Pts.	PIM
83-84	Mont	14	5	2	7	41
84-85	Mont	70	17	22	39	120
85-86	Mont	70	19	21	40	69
86-87	Mont	79	18	21	39	58
87-88	Mont	77	23	20	43	53
88-89	Mont	73	19	22	41	74
89-90	Mont	56	23	18	41	47
90-91	Mont	64	22	21	43	56
91-92	Mont	78	16	15	31	63
Totals		581	162	162	224	581
Playoff Totals		125	26	26	52	191

McRAE, Basil Paul *6-2 205 LW*
B. Beaverton, Ont., Jan. 5, 1961

Season	Team	GP	G	A	Pts.	PIM
81-82	Que	20	4	3	7	69
82-83	Que	22	1	1	2	59
83-84	Tor	3	0	0	0	19
84-85	Tor	1	0	0	0	0
85-86	Det	4	0	0	0	5
86-87	Det-Que	69	11	7	18	342
87-88	Minn	80	5	11	16	382
88-89	Minn	78	12	19	31	365
89-90	Minn	66	9	17	26	351
90-91	Minn	40	1	3	4	224
91-92	Minn	59	5	8	13	245
Totals		442	48	69	117	2061
Playoff Totals		56	6	2	8	309

McRAE, Chris *6-0 200 LW*
B. Beaverton, Ont., Aug. 26, 1965

Season	Team	GP	G	A	Pts.	PIM
87-88	Tor	11	0	0	0	65
88-89	Tor	3	0	0	0	12
89-90	Det	7	1	0	1	45
Totals		21	1	0	1	122

McRAE, Ken *6-1 195 C*
B. Winchester, Ont., Apr. 23, 1968

Season	Team	GP	G	A	Pts.	PIM
87-88	Que	1	0	0	0	0
88-89	Que	37	6	11	17	68

McRAE, Ken *(Continued)*

Season	Team	GP	G	A	Pts.	PIM
89-90	Que	66	7	8	15	191
90-91	Que	12	0	0	0	36
91-92	Que	10	0	1	1	31
Totals		126	13	20	33	326

McREYNOLDS, Brian *6-1 192 C*
B. Penetanguishene, Ont., Jan. 5, 1965

Season	Team	GP	G	A	Pts.	PIM
89-90	Winn	9	0	2	2	4
90-91	NYR	1	0	0	0	0
Totals		10	0	2	2	4

McSHEFFREY, Bryan Gerald *6-2 205 RW*
B. Ottawa, Ont., Sept. 25, 1952

Season	Team	GP	G	A	Pts.	PIM
72-73	Van	33	4	4	8	10
73-74	Van	54	9	3	12	34
74-75	Buf	3	0	0	0	0
Totals		90	13	7	20	44

McSORLEY, Martin J. *6-1 235 D*
B. Hamilton, Ont., May 18, 1963

Season	Team	GP	G	A	Pts.	PIM
83-84	Pitt	72	2	7	9	224
84-85	Pitt	15	0	0	0	15
85-86	Edm	59	11	12	23	265
86-87	Edm	41	2	4	6	159
87-88	Edm	60	9	17	26	223
88-89	LA	66	10	17	27	350
89-90	LA	75	15	21	36	322
90-91	LA	61	7	32	39	221
91-92	LA	71	7	22	29	268
Totals		520	63	132	195	2047
Playoff Totals		84	6	13	19	312

McSWEEN, Don *5-11 195 D*
B. Detroit, Mich., June 9, 1964

Season	Team	GP	G	A	Pts.	PIM
87-88	Buf	5	0	1	1	6
89-90	Buf	4	0	0	0	6
Totals		9	0	1	1	12

McTAGGART, James *5-11 197 D*
B. Weyburn, Sask., Mar. 31, 1960

Season	Team	GP	G	A	Pts.	PIM
80-81	Wash	52	1	6	7	185
81-82	Wash	19	2	4	6	20
Totals		71	3	10	13	205

McTAVISH, Gordon *6-4 200 C*
B. Guelph, Ont., June 3, 1954

Season	Team	GP	G	A	Pts.	PIM
78-79	StL	1	0	0	0	0
79-80	Winn	10	1	3	4	2
Totals		11	1	3	4	2

McVEIGH, Charles (Rabbit) *5-6 145 LW*
B. Kenora, Ont., Mar. 29, 1898

Season	Team	GP	G	A	Pts.	PIM
26-27	Chi	43	12	4	16	23
27-28	Chi	43	6	7	13	10
28-29	NYA	44	6	2	8	16
29-30	NYA	40	14	14	28	32
30-31	NYA	44	5	11	16	23
31-32	NYA	48	12	15	27	16
32-33	NYA	40	7	12	19	10
33-34	NYA	48	15	12	27	4
34-35	NYA	47	7	11	18	4
Totals		397	84	88	172	138
Playoff Totals		4	0	0	0	2

McVICAR, John (Slim) *D*

Season	Team	GP	G	A	Pts.	PIM
30-31	Mont M	40	2	4	6	35
31-32	Mont M	48	0	0	0	28
Totals		88	2	4	6	63
Playoff Totals		2	0	0	0	2

MEAGHER, Richard *5-8 192 C*
B. Belleville, Ont., Nov. 2, 1953

Season	Team	GP	G	A	Pts.	PIM
79-80	Mont	2	0	0	0	0
80-81	Hart	27	7	10	17	19
81-82	Hart	65	24	19	43	51
82-83	Hart-NJ	61	15	14	29	11
83-84	NJ	52	14	14	28	16
84-85	NJ	71	11	20	31	22
85-86	StL	79	11	19	30	28
86-87	StL	80	18	21	39	54
87-88	StL	76	18	16	34	76
88-89	StL	78	15	14	29	53
89-90	StL	76	8	17	25	47
90-91	StL	24	3	1	4	6
Totals		691	144	165	309	383
Playoff Totals		62	8	7	15	41

MEEHAN, Gerald Marcus (Gerry)
6-2 200 C
B. Toronto, Ont., Sept. 3, 1946

Season	Team	GP	G	A	Pts.	PIM
68-69	Tor-Phil	37	0	5	5	6
70-71	Buf	77	24	31	55	8
71-72	Buf	77	19	27	46	12
72-73	Buf	77	31	29	60	21
73-74	Buf	72	20	26	46	17

MEEHAN, Gerald Marcus (Gerry)
(Continued)

Season	Team	GP	G	A	Pts.	PIM
74-75	Buf-Van-Atl	74	14	26	40	6
75-76	Atl-Wash	80	23	35	58	18
76-77	Wash	80	28	36	64	13
77-78	Wash	78	19	24	43	10
78-79	Wash	18	2	4	6	0
78-79	Cin (WHA)	2	0	0	0	0
NHL Totals		670	180	243	423	111
WHA Totals		2	0	0	0	0
NHL Playoff Totals		10	0	1	1	0

MEEKE, Brent Alan *5-11 172 D*
B. Toronto, Ont., Apr. 10, 1952

Season	Team	GP	G	A	Pts.	PIM
72-73	Cal	3	0	0	0	0
73-74	Cal	18	1	9	10	4
74-75	Cal	4	0	0	0	0
75-76	Cal	1	0	0	0	0
76-77	Clev	49	8	13	21	4
Totals		75	9	22	31	8

MEEKER, Howard William *5-8 165 RW*
B. Kitchener, Ont., Nov. 4, 1924

Season	Team	GP	G	A	Pts.	PIM
46-47	Tor	55	27	18	45	76
47-48	Tor	58	14	20	34	62
48-49	Tor	30	7	7	14	56
49-50	Tor	70	18	22	40	35
50-51	Tor	49	6	14	20	24
51-52	Tor	54	9	14	23	50
52-53	Tor	25	1	7	8	26
53-54	Tor	5	1	0	1	0
Totals		346	83	102	185	329
Playoff Totals		42	6	9	15	50

MEEKER, Michael Thomas *5-11 195 RW*
B. Kingston Ont., Feb 23, 1958

Season	Team	GP	G	A	Pts.	PIM
78-79	Pitt	4	0	0	0	5

MEEKING, Harry *LW*
B. Kitchener, Ont., Nov. 4, 1894

Season	Team	GP	G	A	Pts.	PIM
17-18	Tor	20	10	0	10	19
18-19	Tor	14	7	3	10	22
26-27	Det-Bos	29	1	0	1	6
Totals		63	18	3	21	47
Playoff Totals		14	4	2	6	0

MEGER, Paul Carl *5-7 160 LW*
B. Watrous, Sask., Feb. 17, 1929

Season	Team	GP	G	A	Pts.	PIM
50-51	Mont	17	2	4	6	6
51-52	Mont	69	24	18	42	44
52-53	Mont	69	9	17	26	38
53-54	Mont	44	4	9	13	24
54-55	Mont	13	0	4	4	6
Totals		212	39	52	91	118
Playoff Totals		35	3	8	11	16

MEIGHAN, Ron James *6-3 195 D*
B. Montreal, Que., May 26, 1963

Season	Team	GP	G	A	Pts.	PIM
81-82	Minn	7	1	1	2	2
82-83	Pitt	41	2	6	8	16
Totals		48	3	7	10	18

MEISSNER, Barrie Michael *5-9 165 LW*
B. Unity, Sask., July 26, 1946

Season	Team	GP	G	A	Pts.	PIM
67-68	Minn	1	0	0	0	2
68-69	Minn	5	0	1	1	2
Totals		6	0	1	1	4

MEISSNER, Richard Donald (Dick)
5-11 200 RW
B. Kindersley, Sask., Jan. 6, 1940

Season	Team	GP	G	A	Pts.	PIM
59-60	Bos	60	5	6	11	22
60-61	Bos	9	0	1	1	2
61-62	Bos	66	3	3	6	13
63-64	NYR	35	3	5	8	0
64-65	NYR	1	0	0	0	0
Totals		171	11	15	26	37

MELAMETSA, Anssi *6-0 190 LW*
B. Jyvaskyla, Finland, June 21, 1961

Season	Team	GP	G	A	Pts.	PIM
85-86	Winn	27	0	3	3	2

MELIN, Roger Alf *6-4 198 LW*
B. Enkoping, Sweden, Apr. 25, 1956

Season	Team	GP	G	A	Pts.	PIM
80-81	Minn	1	0	0	0	0
81-82	Minn	2	0	0	0	0
Totals		3	0	0	0	0

MELLANBY, Scott *6-1 205 RW*
B. Montreal, Que., June 11, 1966

Season	Team	GP	G	A	Pts.	PIM
85-86	Phil	2	0	0	0	0
86-87	Phil	71	11	21	32	94
87-88	Phil	75	25	26	51	185
88-89	Phil	76	21	29	50	183
89-90	Phil	57	6	17	23	77

MELLANBY, Scott *(Continued)*

Season Team	GP	G	A	Pts.	PIM
90-91 Phil	74	20	21	41	155
91-92 Edm	80	23	27	50	197
Totals	435	106	141	247	891
Playoff Totals	66	11	12	23	119

MELLOR, Thomas Robert *6-1 185 D*
B. Cranston, R.I., Jan. 27, 1950

Season Team	GP	G	A	Pts.	PIM
73-74 Det	25	2	4	6	25
74-75 Det	1	0	0	0	0
Totals	26	2	4	6	25

MELNYK, Larry Joseph *6-0 195 D*
B. Saskatoon, Sask., Feb. 21, 1960

Season Team	GP	G	A	Pts.	PIM
80-81 Bos	26	0	4	4	39
81-82 Bos	48	0	8	8	84
82-83 Bos	1	0	0	0	0
84-85 Edm	28	0	11	11	25
85-86 Edm-NYR	52	3	11	14	76
86-87 NYR	73	3	12	15	182
87-88 NYR-Van	63	2	4	6	107
88-89 Van	74	3	11	14	82
89-90 Van	67	0	2	2	91
Totals	432	11	63	74	686
Playoff Totals	66	2	9	11	127

MELNYK, Michael Gerald (Gerry) *5-10 180 C*
B. Edmonton, Alta., Sept. 16, 1934

Season Team	GP	G	A	Pts.	PIM
59-60 Det	63	10	10	20	12
60-61 Det	70	9	16	25	2
61-62 Chi	63	5	16	21	6
67-68 StL	73	15	35	50	14
Totals	269	39	77	116	34
Playoff Totals	53	6	6	12	6

MELROSE, Barry *6-0 205 D*
B. Kelvington, Sask., July 15, 1956

Season Team	GP	G	A	Pts.	PIM
76-77 Cin (WHA)	29	1	4	5	8
77-78 Cin (WHA)	69	2	9	11	113
78-79 Cin (WHA)	80	2	14	16	222
79-80 Winn	74	4	6	10	124
80-81 Winn-Tor	75	3	6	9	206
81-82 Tor	64	1	5	6	186
82-83 Tor	52	2	5	7	68
83-84 Det	21	0	1	1	74
85-86 Det	14	0	0	0	70
NHL Totals	300	10	23	33	728
WHA Totals	178	5	27	32	343
NHL Playoff Totals	7	0	?	?	38
WHA Playoff Totals	5	0	1	1	8

MENARD, Hillary (Hill) *D*
B. Timmins, Ont., Jan. 15, 1934

Season Team	GP	G	A	Pts.	PIM
53-54 Chi	1	0	0	0	0

MENARD, Howard Hubert *5-8 160 C*
B. Timmins, Ont., Apr. 28, 1942

Season Team	GP	G	A	Pts.	PIM
63-64 Det	3	0	0	0	0
67-68 LA	35	9	15	24	32
68-69 LA	56	10	17	27	31
69-70 Chi-Oak	57	4	10	14	24
Totals	151	23	42	65	87
Playoff Totals	19	3	7	10	36

MERCREDI, Victor Dennis *5-11 185 C*
B. Yellowknife, N.W.T., Mar. 31, 1953

Season Team	GP	G	A	Pts.	PIM
74-75 Atl	2	0	0	0	0
75-76 Calg (WHA)	3	0	0	0	29

MEREDITH, Gregory Paul *6-1 210 RW*
B. Toronto, Ont., Feb. 23, 1958

Season Team	GP	G	A	Pts.	PIM
80-81 Calg	3	1	0	1	0
82-83 Calg	35	5	4	9	8
Totals	38	6	4	10	8
Playoff Totals	5	3	1	4	4

MERKOSKY, Glenn *5-10 175 C*
B. Edmonton, Alta., Apr. 8, 1959

Season Team	GP	G	A	Pts.	PIM
81-82 Hart	7	0	0	0	2
82-83 NJ	34	4	10	14	20
83-84 NJ	5	1	0	1	0
85-86 Det	17	0	2	2	0
89-90 Det	3	0	0	0	0
Totals	66	5	12	17	22

MERONEK, William (Smiley) *F*
B. Stoney Mountain, Man., Apr. 15, 1917

Season Team	GP	G	A	Pts.	PIM
39-40 Mont	7	2	2	4	0
42-43 Mont	12	3	6	9	0
Totals	19	5	8	13	0
Playoff Totals	1	0	0	0	0

MERRICK, Leonard (Wayne) *6-1 195 C*
B. Sarnia, Ont., Apr. 23, 1952

Season Team	GP	G	A	Pts.	PIM
72-73 StL	50	10	11	21	10
73-74 StL	64	20	23	43	32
74-75 StL	76	28	37	65	57
75-76 StL-Cal	75	32	35	67	36
76-77 Clev	80	18	38	56	25
77-78 Clev-NYI	55	12	19	31	16
78-79 NYI	75	20	21	41	24
79-80 NYI	70	13	22	35	16
80-81 NYI	71	16	15	31	30
81-82 NYI	68	12	27	39	20
82-83 NYI	59	4	12	16	27
83-84 NYI	31	6	5	11	10
Totals	774	191	265	456	303
Playoff Totals	102	19	30	49	30

MERRILL, Horace *D*
B. 1885

Season Team	GP	G	A	Pts.	PIM
17-18 Ott	4	0	0	0	0
19-20 Ott	7	0	0	0	0
Totals	11	0	0	0	0

MESSIER, Mark Douglas *6-1 210 C*
B. Edmonton, Alta., Jan. 18, 1961

Season Team	GP	G	A	Pts.	PIM
78-79 Ind-Cin (WHA)	52	1	10	11	58
79-80 Edm	75	12	21	33	120
80-81 Edm	72	23	40	63	102
81-82 Edm	78	50	38	88	119
82-83 Edm	77	48	58	106	72
83-84 Edm	73	37	64	101	165
84-85 Edm	55	23	31	54	57
85-86 Edm	63	35	49	84	68
86-87 Edm	77	37	70	107	73
87-88 Edm	77	37	74	111	103
88-89 Edm	72	33	61	94	130
89-90 Edm	79	45	84	129	79
90-91 Edm	53	12	52	64	34
91-92 NYR	79	35	72	107	76
NHL Totals	930	427	714	1141	1198
WHA Totals	52	1	10	11	58
NHL Playoff Totals	177	87	142	229	181

MESSIER, Mitch *6-2 200 C*
B. Regina, Sask., Aug. 21, 1965

Season Team	GP	G	A	Pts.	PIM
87-88 Minn	13	0	1	1	11
88-89 Minn	3	0	1	1	0
89-90 Minn	2	0	0	0	0
90-91 Minn	2	0	0	0	0
Totals	20	0	2	2	11

MESSIER, Paul Edmond *6-1 184 C*
B. Nottingham, England, Jan. 27, 1958

Season Team	GP	G	A	Pts.	PIM
78-79 Col	9	0	0	0	4

METCLAFE, Scott *6-0 200 LW*
B. Toronto, Ont., Jan. 6, 1967

Season Team	GP	G	A	Pts.	PIM
87-88 Edm-Buf	9	0	1	1	0
88-89 Buf	9	1	1	2	13
89-90 Buf	7	0	0	0	5
Totals	19	1	2	3	18

METZ, Donald Maurice *5-9 165 RW*
B. Wilcox, Sask., Jan. 10, 1916

Season Team	GP	G	A	Pts.	PIM
39-40 Tor	10	1	1	2	4
40-41 Tor	31	4	10	14	6
41-42 Tor	25	2	3	5	8
45-46 Tor	7	1	0	1	0
46-47 Tor	40	4	9	13	10
47-48 Tor	26	4	6	10	2
48-49 Tor	33	4	6	10	12
Totals	172	20	35	55	42
Playoff Totals	47	7	8	15	10

METZ, Nicholas J. (Nick) *5-11 160 LW*
B. Wilcox, Sask., Feb. 16, 1914

Season Team	GP	G	A	Pts.	PIM
34-35 Tor	18	2	2	4	4
35-36 Tor	38	14	6	20	14
36-37 Tor	48	9	11	20	19
37-38 Tor	48	15	7	22	12
38-39 Tor	47	11	10	21	15
39-40 Tor	31	6	5	11	2
40-41 Tor	47	14	21	35	10
41-42 Tor	30	11	9	20	20
44-45 Tor	50	22	13	35	26
45-46 Tor	41	11	11	22	4
46-47 Tor	60	12	16	28	15
47-48 Tor	60	4	8	12	8
Totals	518	131	119	250	149
Playoff Totals	76	19	20	39	31

MICHALUK, Arthur *6-0 182 D*
B. Canmore, Alta., May 4, 1923

Season Team	GP	G	A	Pts.	PIM
47-48 Chi	5	0	0	0	0

MICHALUK, John *5-10 155 F*
B. Canmore, Alta., Nov. 2, 1928

Season Team	GP	G	A	Pts.	PIM
50-51 Chi	1	0	0	0	0

MICHALYUK, David *5-10 189 LW*
B. Wakaw, Sask., May 18, 1962

Season Team	GP	G	A	Pts.	PIM
81-82 Phil	1	0	0	0	0
82-83 Phil	13	2	6	8	8
91-92 Pitt	0	0	0	0	0
Totals	14	2	6	8	8
Playoff Totals	7	1	1	2	0

MICHELETTI, Joseph Robert *6-1 185 D*
B. Hibbing, Minn., Oct. 24, 1954

Season Team	GP	G	A	Pts.	PIM
76-77 Calg (WHA)	14	3	3	6	10
77-78 Edm (WHA)	56	14	34	48	56
78-79 Edm (WHA)	72	14	33	47	85
79-80 StL	54	2	16	18	29
80-81 StL	63	4	27	31	53
81-82 StL-Col	41	5	17	22	32
NHL Totals	158	11	60	71	114
WHA Totals	142	31	70	101	151
NHL Playoff Totals	11	1	11	12	10
WHA Playoff Totals	18	0	11	11	6

MICHELETTI, Patrick *5-9 175 C*
B. Hibbing, Minn., Dec. 11, 1963

Season Team	GP	G	A	Pts.	PIM
87-88 Minn	12	2	0	2	8

MICKEY, Robert Lawrence (Larry) *5-11 180 RW*
B. Lacombe, Alta., Oct. 21, 1943

Season Team	GP	G	A	Pts.	PIM
64-65 Chi	1	0	0	0	0
65-66 NYR	7	0	0	0	2
66-67 NYR	8	0	0	0	0
67-68 NYR	4	0	2	2	0
68-69 Tor	55	8	19	27	43
69-70 Mont	21	4	4	8	4
70-71 LA	65	6	12	18	46
71-72 Phil-Buf	18	1	3	4	8
72-73 Buf	77	15	9	24	47
73-74 Buf	13	3	4	7	8
74-75 Buf	23	2	0	2	2
Totals	292	39	53	92	160
Playoff Totals	9	1	0	1	10

MICKOSKI, Nicholas (Nick) *6-1 193 LW*
B. Winnipeg, Man., Dec. 7, 1927

Season Team	GP	G	A	Pts.	PIM
48-49 NYR	54	13	9	22	20
49-50 NYR	45	10	10	20	10
50-51 NYR	64	20	15	35	12
51-52 NYR	43	7	13	20	20
52-53 NYR	70	19	16	35	39
53-54 NYR	68	19	16	35	22
54-55 NYR-Chi	70	10	33	43	48
55-56 Chi	70	19	20	39	52
56-57 Chi	70	16	20	36	24
57-58 Chi-Det	65	13	18	31	50
58-59 Det	66	11	15	26	20
59-60 Bos	18	1	0	1	2
Totals	703	158	185	343	319
Playoff Totals	18	1	6	7	6

MIDDENDORF, Max *6-4 210 RW*
B. Syracuse, N.Y., Aug. 18, 1967

Season Team	GP	G	A	Pts.	PIM
86-87 Que	6	1	4	5	4
87-88 Que	1	0	0	0	0
89-90 Que	3	0	0	0	0
90-91 Edm	3	1	0	1	2
Totals	13	2	4	6	6

MIDDLETON, Richard David *5-11 180 RW*
B. Toronto, Ont., Dec. 4, 1953

Season Team	GP	G	A	Pts.	PIM
74-75 NYR	47	22	18	40	19
75-76 NYR	77	24	26	50	14
76-77 Bos	72	20	22	42	2
77-78 Bos	79	25	35	60	8
78-79 Bos	71	38	48	86	7
79-80 Bos	80	40	52	92	24
80-81 Bos	80	44	59	103	16
81-82 Bos	75	51	43	94	12
82-83 Bos	80	49	47	96	8
83-84 Bos	80	47	58	105	14
84-85 Bos	80	30	46	76	6
85-86 Bos	49	14	30	44	10
86-87 Bos	76	31	37	68	6
87-88 Bos	59	13	19	32	11
Totals	1005	448	540	988	157
Playoff Totals	114	45	55	100	19

MIGAY, Rudolph Joseph *5-10 175 C*
B. Fort William Ont., Nov. 18, 1928

Season Team	GP	G	A	Pts.	PIM
49-50 Tor	18	1	5	6	8

MIGAY, Rudolph Joseph *(Continued)*

Season	Team	GP	G	A	Pts.	PIM
51-52	Tor	19	2	1	3	12
52-53	Tor	40	5	4	9	22
53-54	Tor	70	8	15	23	60
54-55	Tor	67	8	16	24	66
55-56	Tor	70	12	16	28	52
56-57	Tor	66	15	20	35	51
57-58	Tor	48	7	14	21	18
58-59	Tor	19	1	1	2	4
59-60	Tor	1	0	0	0	0
Totals		418	59	92	151	293
Playoff Totals		15	1	0	1	20

MIKITA, Stanley (Stosh) *5-9 169 C*
B. Skolce, Czechoslovakia, May 20, 1940

Season	Team	GP	G	A	Pts.	PIM
58-59	Chi	3	0	1	1	4
59-60	Chi	67	8	18	26	119
60-61	Chi	66	19	34	53	100
61-62	Chi	70	25	52	77	97
62-63	Chi	65	31	45	76	69
63-64	Chi	70	39	50	89	149
64-65	Chi	70	28	59	87	154
65-66	Chi	68	30	48	78	58
66-67	Chi	70	35	62	97	12
67-68	Chi	72	40	47	87	14
68-69	Chi	74	30	67	97	52
69-70	Chi	76	39	47	86	50
70-71	Chi	74	24	48	72	85
71-72	Chi	74	26	39	65	46
72-73	Chi	57	27	56	83	32
73-74	Chi	76	30	50	80	46
74-75	Chi	79	36	50	86	48
75-76	Chi	48	16	41	57	37
76-77	Chi	57	19	30	49	20
77-78	Chi	76	18	41	59	35
78-79	Chi	65	19	36	55	34
79-80	Chi	17	2	5	7	12
Totals		1394	541	926	1467	1273
Playoff Totals		155	59	91	150	169

MIKKELSON, William Robert *6-0 190 D*
B. Neepawa, Man., May 21, 1948

Season	Team	GP	G	A	Pts.	PIM
71-72	LA	15	0	1	1	6
72-73	NYI	72	1	10	11	45
74-75	Wash	59	3	7	10	52
76-77	Wash	1	0	0	0	2
Totals		147	4	18	22	105

MIKOL, John Stanley (Jim) *6-0 175 D*
B. Kitchener, Ont., June 11, 1938

Season	Team	GP	G	A	Pts.	PIM
62-63	Tor	4	0	1	1	2
64-65	NYR	30	1	3	4	6
Totals		34	1	4	5	8

MILBURY, Michael James *6-1 200 D*
B. Brighton, Mass., June 17, 1952

Season	Team	GP	G	A	Pts.	PIM
75-76	Bos	3	0	0	0	9
76-77	Bos	77	6	18	24	166
77-78	Bos	80	8	30	38	151
78-79	Bos	74	1	34	35	149
79-80	Bos	72	10	13	23	59
80-81	Bos	77	0	18	18	222
81-82	Bos	51	2	10	12	71
82-83	Bos	78	9	15	24	216
83-84	Bos	74	2	17	19	159
84-85	Bos	78	3	13	16	152
85-86	Bos	22	2	5	7	102
86-87	Bos	68	6	16	22	96
Totals		754	49	189	238	1552
Playoff Totals		86	4	24	28	219

MILKS, Herbert (Hib) *5-11 165 LW*
B. Eardley, Ont., Apr. 1, 1902

Season	Team	GP	G	A	Pts.	PIM
25-26	Pitt Pi	36	14	5	19	17
26-27	Pitt Pi	44	16	6	22	18
27-28	Pitt Pi	44	18	3	21	34
28-29	Pitt Pi	44	9	3	12	22
29-30	Pitt Pi	41	13	11	24	36
30-31	Phil Q	44	17	6	23	42
31-32	NYR	45	0	4	4	12
32-33	Ott	16	0	3	3	0
Totals		314	87	41	128	181
Playoff Totals		10	0	0	0	2

MILLAR, Hugh Alexander *5-8 200 D*
B. Edmonton, Alta., Apr. 3, 1921

Season	Team	GP	G	A	Pts.	PIM
46-47	Det	4	0	0	0	0
Playoff Totals		1	0	0	0	0

MILLAR, Mike *5-10 170 RW*
B. St. Catharines, Ont., Apr. 28, 1965

Season	Team	GP	G	A	Pts.	PIM
86-87	Hart	10	2	2	4	0
87-88	Hart	28	7	7	14	6
88-89	Wash	18	6	3	9	4
89-90	Bos	15	1	4	5	0
90-91	Tor	7	2	2	4	2
Totals		78	18	18	36	12

MILLEN, Corey *5-7 168 C*
B. Cloquet, Minn., Apr. 29, 1964

Season	Team	GP	G	A	Pts.	PIM
89-90	NYR	4	0	0	0	2
90-91	NYR	4	3	1	4	0
91-92	NYR-LA	57	21	25	46	66
Totals		65	24	26	50	68
Playoff Totals		12	1	2	4	6

MILLER, Brad *6-4 220 D*
B. Edmonton, Alta., July 23, 1969

Season	Team	GP	G	A	Pts.	PIM
88-89	Buf	7	0	0	0	6
89-90	Buf	1	0	0	0	0
90-91	Buf	13	0	0	0	67
91-92	Buf	42	1	4	5	192
Totals		63	1	4	5	265

MILLER, Earl *F*
B. Regina, Sask.

Season	Team	GP	G	A	Pts.	PIM
27-28	Chi	22	1	1	2	32
28-29	Chi	15	1	1	2	24
29-30	Chi	38	11	5	16	50
30-31	Chi	17	3	4	7	8
31-32	Chi-Tor	24	3	3	6	10
Totals		116	19	14	33	124
Playoff Totals		10	1	0	1	6

MILLER, Jack Leslie *5-8 155 LW*
B. Delisle, Sask., Sept. 16, 1925

Season	Team	GP	G	A	Pts.	PIM
49-50	Chi	6	0	0	0	0
50-51	Chi	11	0	0	0	4
Totals		17	0	0	0	4

MILLER, Jason *6-1 190 C*
B. Edmonton, Alta., Mar. 1, 1971

Season	Team	GP	G	A	Pts.	PIM
90-91	NJ	1	0	0	0	0
91-92	NJ	3	0	0	0	0
Totals		4	0	0	0	0

MILLER, Jay *6-2 210 LW*
B. Wellesley, Mass., July 16, 1960

Season	Team	GP	G	A	Pts.	PIM
85-86	Bos	46	3	0	3	178
86-87	Bos	55	1	4	5	208
87-88	Bos	78	7	12	19	304
88-89	Bos-LA	66	7	7	14	301
89-90	LA	68	10	2	12	224
90-91	LA	66	8	12	20	259
91-92	LA	67	4	7	11	237
Totals		446	40	44	84	1711
Playoff Totals		48	2	3	5	243

MILLER, Kelly *5-11 196 LW*
B. Lansing, Mich., Mar. 3, 1963

Season	Team	GP	G	A	Pts.	PIM
84-85	NYR	5	0	2	2	2
85-86	NYR	74	13	20	33	52
86-87	NYR-Wash	77	16	26	42	48
87-88	Wash	80	9	23	32	35
88-89	Wash	78	19	21	40	45
89-90	Wash	80	18	22	40	49
90-91	Wash	80	24	26	50	29
91-92	Wash	78	14	38	52	49
Totals		552	113	178	291	309
Playoff Totals		79	18	19	37	51

MILLER, Kevin *5-10 191 C*
B. Lansing, Mich., Sept. 9, 1965

Season	Team	GP	G	A	Pts.	PIM
88-89	NYR	24	3	5	8	2
89-90	NYR	16	0	5	5	2
90-91	NYR-Det	74	22	29	51	67
91-92	Det	80	20	26	46	53
Totals		194	45	65	110	124
Playoff Totals		17	3	4	7	24

MILLER, Kip *5-10 160 C*
B. Lansing, Mich., June 11, 1969

Season	Team	GP	G	A	Pts.	PIM
90-91	Que	13	4	3	7	7
91-92	Que-Minn	39	6	12	18	14
Totals		52	10	15	25	21

MILLER, Paul Edward *5-10 170 C*
B. Billerica, Mass., Aug. 21, 1959

Season	Team	GP	G	A	Pts.	PIM
81-82	Col	3	0	3	3	0

MILLER, Perry Elvin *6-1 194 D*
B. Winnipeg, Man., June 24, 1952

Season	Team	GP	G	A	Pts.	PIM
74-75	Winn (WHA)	67	9	19	28	133
75-76	Winn-Minn (WHA)	60	8	10	18	48
76-77	Winn (WHA)	74	14	31	45	124
77-78	Det	62	4	17	21	120
78-79	Det	75	5	23	28	156
79-80	Det	16	0	3	3	41
80-81	Det	64	1	8	9	70
NHL Totals		217	10	51	61	387
WHA Totals		201	31	60	91	305

MILLER, Perry Elvin *(Continued)*

Season	Team	GP	G	A	Pts.	PIM
WHA Playoff Totals		20	4	6	10	27

MILLER, Robert *5-11 180 C*
B. Medford, Mass., Sept. 28, 1956

Season	Team	GP	G	A	Pts.	PIM
77-78	Bos	76	20	20	40	41
78-79	Bos	77	15	33	48	30
79-80	Bos	80	16	25	41	53
80-81	Bos-Col	52	9	5	14	34
81-82	Col	56	11	20	31	27
84-85	LA	63	4	16	20	35
Totals		404	75	119	294	220
Playoff Totals		36	4	7	11	27

MILLER, Thomas William *6-0 187 C*
B. Kitchener, Ont., Mar. 31, 1947

Season	Team	GP	G	A	Pts.	PIM
70-71	Det	29	1	7	8	9
72-73	NYI	69	13	17	30	21
73-74	NYI	19	2	1	3	4
74-75	NYI	1	0	0	0	0
Totals		118	16	25	41	34

MILLER, Warren *6-0 180 RW*
B. South St. Paul, Minn., Jan. 1, 1954

Season	Team	GP	G	A	Pts.	PIM
75-76	Calg (WHA)	3	0	0	0	0
76-77	Calg (WHA)	80	23	32	55	51
77-78	Edm-Que (WHA)	78	16	28	44	68
78-79	NE (WHA)	77	26	23	49	44
79-80	NYR	55	7	6	13	17
80-81	Hart	77	22	22	44	37
81-82	Hart	74	10	12	22	68
82-83	Hart	56	1	10	11	15
NHL Totals		262	40	50	90	137
WHA Totals		238	65	83	148	163
NHL Playoff Totals		6	1	0	1	0
WHA Playoff Totals		34	1	10	11	56

MILLER, William *6-0 160 C*
B. Campbellton, N.B., Aug. 1, 1911

Season	Team	GP	G	A	Pts.	PIM
34-35	Mont M	22	3	0	3	2
35-36	Mont M-Mont	25	1	2	3	2
36-37	Mont	48	3	1	4	12
Totals		95	7	3	10	16
Playoff Totals		12	0	0	0	0

MINER, John *5-10 180 D*
B. Moose Jaw, Sask., Aug. 28, 1965

Season	Team	GP	G	A	Pts.	PIM
87-88	Edm	14	2	3	5	16

MINOR, Gerald *5-8 175 C*
B. Regina, Sask. Oct. 27, 1958

Season	Team	GP	G	A	Pts.	PIM
79-80	Van	5	0	1	1	2
80-81	Van	74	10	14	24	108
81-82	Van	13	0	1	1	6
82-83	Van	39	1	5	6	57
83-84	Van	9	0	0	0	0
Totals		140	11	21	32	173
Playoff Totals		12	1	3	4	25

MIRONOV, Dimitri *6-2 191 D*
B. Moscow, USSR, Dec. 25, 1965

Season	Team	GP	G	A	Pts.	PIM
91-92	Tor	7	1	0	1	0

MISZUK, John Stanley *6-0 200 D*
B. Naliboki, Poland, Sept. 29, 1940

Season	Team	GP	G	A	Pts.	PIM
63-64	Det	42	0	2	2	30
65-66	Chi	2	1	1	2	2
66-67	Chi	3	0	0	0	0
67-68	Phil	74	5	17	22	79
68-69	Phil	66	1	13	14	70
69-70	Minn	50	0	6	6	51
74-75	Balt (WHA)	66	2	19	21	56
75-76	Calg (WHA)	69	2	21	23	66
76-77	Calg (WHA)	79	2	26	28	57
NHL Totals		237	7	39	46	232
WHA Totals		214	6	66	72	179
NHL Playoff Totals		19	0	3	3	19
WHA Playoff Totals		10	0	1	1	10

MITCHELL, Herbert *F*

Season	Team	GP	G	A	Pts.	PIM
24-25	Bos	27	3	0	3	24
25-26	Bos	26	3	0	3	14
Totals		53	6	0	6	38

MITCHELL, William Dickie (Red)
5-10 185 D
B. Port Dalhousie, Ont., Feb. 22, 1930

Season	Team	GP	G	A	Pts.	PIM
41-42	Chi	1	0	0	0	4
42-43	Chi	42	1	1	2	47
44-45	Chi	40	3	4	7	16
Totals		83	4	5	9	67

MITCHELL, William Lawson *5-10 185 D*
B. Toronto, Ont., Sept. 6, 1912

Season	Team	GP	G	A	Pts.	PIM
63-64	Det	1	0	0	0	0

MODANO, Michael *6-3 190 C*
B. Livonia, Mich., June 7, 1970

Season	Team	GP	G	A	Pts.	PIM
89-90	Minn	80	29	46	75	63
90-91	Minn	79	28	36	64	61
91-92	Minn	76	33	44	77	46
Totals		235	90	126	216	170
Playoff Totals		39	12	15	27	32

MOE, William Carl *5-11 185 D*
B. Danvers, Mass., Oct. 2, 1916

Season	Team	GP	G	A	Pts.	PIM
44-45	NYR	35	2	4	6	14
45-46	NYR	48	4	4	8	14
46-47	NYR	59	4	10	14	44
47-48	NYR	59	1	15	16	31
48-49	NYR	60	0	9	9	60
Totals		261	11	42	53	163
Playoff Totals		1	0	0	0	0

MOFFAT, Lyle Gordon *5-10 180 LW*
B. Calgary, Alta., Mar, 19, 1948

Season	Team	GP	G	A	Pts.	PIM
72-73	Tor	1	0	0	0	0
74-75	Tor	22	2	7	9	13
75-76	Clev-Winn (WHA)	75	17	16	33	77
76-77	Winn (WHA)	74	13	11	24	90
77-78	Winn (WHA)	57	9	16	25	39
78-79	Winn (WHA)	70	14	18	32	38
79-80	Winn	74	10	9	19	38
NHL Totals		97	12	16	28	51
WHA Totals		276	53	61	114	244
WHA Playoff Totals		49	13	11	24	46

MOFFATT, Ronald *F*
B. West Hope, N.D.

Season	Team	GP	G	A	Pts.	PIM
32-33	Det	24	1	1	2	6
33-34	Det	5	0	0	0	2
34-35	Det	7	0	0	0	0
Totals		36	1	1	2	8
Playoff Totals		7	0	0	0	0

MOGILNY, Alexander *5-11 195 LW*
B. Khabarovsk, Soviet Union, Feb. 18, 1969

Season	Team	GP	G	A	Pts.	PIM
89-90	Buf	65	15	28	43	16
90-91	Buf	62	30	34	64	16
91-92	Buf	67	39	45	84	73
Totals		194	84	107	191	105
Playoff Totals		12	0	9	9	4

MOHER, Mike *5-10 180 RW*
B. Manitouwadge, Ont., Mar. 26, 1962

Season	Team	GP	G	A	Pts.	PIM
82-83	NJ	9	0	1	1	28

MOHNS, Douglas Allen *6-0 184 D*
B. Capreol, Ont., Dec. 13, 1933

Season	Team	GP	G	A	Pts.	PIM
53-54	Bos	70	13	14	27	27
54-55	Bos	70	14	18	32	82
55-56	Bos	64	10	8	18	48
56-57	Bos	68	6	34	40	89
57-58	Bos	54	5	16	21	28
58-59	Bos	47	6	24	30	40
59-60	Bos	65	20	25	45	62
60-61	Bos	65	12	21	33	63
61-62	Bos	69	16	29	45	74
62-63	Bos	68	7	23	30	63
63-64	Bos	70	9	17	26	95
64-65	Chi	49	13	20	33	84
65-66	Chi	70	22	27	49	63
66-67	Chi	61	25	35	60	58
67-68	Chi	65	24	29	53	33
68-69	Chi	65	22	19	41	47
69-70	Chi	66	6	27	33	46
70-71	Chi-Minn	56	6	11	17	30
71-72	Minn	78	6	30	36	82
72-73	Minn	67	4	13	17	52
73-74	Atl	28	0	3	3	10
74-75	Wash	75	2	19	21	54
Totals		1390	248	462	710	1230
Playoff Totals		94	14	36	50	122

MOHNS, Warren Lloyd *5-9 185 D*
B. Petawawa, Ont., July 31, 1921

Season	Team	GP	G	A	Pts.	PIM
43-44	NYR	1	0	0	0	0

MOKOSAK, Carl *6-1 200 LW*
B. Fort Saskatchewan, Alta., Sept. 22, 1962

Season	Team	GP	G	A	Pts.	PIM
81-82	Calg	1	0	1	1	0
82-83	Calg	41	7	6	13	87
84-85	LA	30	4	8	12	43
85-86	Phil	1	0	0	0	5
86-87	Pitt	3	0	0	0	4
88-89	Bos	7	0	0	0	31
Totals		83	11	15	26	170
Playoff Totals		1	0	0	0	0

MOKOSAK, John *5-11 200 D*
B. Edmonton, Alta., Sept. 7, 1963

Season	Team	GP	G	A	Pts.	PIM
88-89	Det	8	0	1	1	14
89-90	Det	33	0	1	1	82
Totals		41	0	2	2	96

MOLIN, Lars *6-0 180 LW*
B. Ornskoldsvik, Sweden, May 7, 1956

Season	Team	GP	G	A	Pts.	PIM
81-82	Van	72	15	31	46	10
82-83	Van	58	12	27	39	23
83-84	Van	42	6	7	13	4
Totals		172	33	65	98	37
Playoff Totals		19	2	9	11	7

MOLLER, Michael John *6-0 190 RW*
B. Calgary, Alta., June 16, 1962

Season	Team	GP	G	A	Pts.	PIM
80-81	Buf	5	2	2	4	0
81-82	Buf	9	0	0	0	0
82-83	Buf	49	6	12	18	14
83-84	Buf	59	5	11	16	27
84-85	Buf	5	0	2	2	0
85-86	Edm	1	0	0	0	0
86-87	Edm	6	2	1	3	0
Totals		134	15	28	43	41
Playoff Totals		3	0	1	1	0

MOLLER, Randy *6-2 207 D*
B. Red Deer, Alta., Aug. 23, 1963

Season	Team	GP	G	A	Pts.	PIM
82-83	Que	75	2	12	14	145
83-84	Que	74	4	14	18	147
84-85	Que	79	7	22	29	120
85-86	Que	69	5	18	23	141
86-87	Que	71	5	9	14	144
87-88	Que	66	3	22	25	169
88-89	Que	74	7	22	29	136
89-90	NYR	60	1	12	13	139
90-91	NYR	61	4	19	23	161
91-92	NYR-Buf	56	3	9	12	137
Totals		685	41	159	200	1439
Playoff Totals		71	6	14	20	189

MOLLOY, Mitchell Dennis *6-3 212 LW*
B. Red Lake, Ont., Oct. 10, 1966

Season	Team	GP	G	A	Pts.	PIM
89-90	Buf	2	0	0	0	10

MOLYNEAUX, Laurence S. *5-11 208 D*
B. West Sutton, Ont., July 8, 1912

Season	Team	GP	G	A	Pts.	PIM
37-38	NYR	2	0	0	0	2
38-39	NYR	43	0	1	1	18
Totals		45	0	1	1	20
Playoff Totals		3	0	0	0	8

MOMESSO, Sergio *6-3 215 LW*
B. Montreal, Que., Sept. 4, 1965

Season	Team	GP	G	A	Pts.	PIM
83-84	Mont	1	0	0	0	0
85-86	Mont	24	8	7	15	46
86-87	Mont	59	14	17	31	96
87-88	Mont	53	7	14	21	101
88-89	StL	53	9	17	26	139
89-90	StL	79	24	32	56	199
90-91	StL-Van	70	16	20	36	174
91-92	Van	58	20	23	43	198
Totals		397	98	130	228	953
Playoff Totals		58	6	20	26	189

MONAHAN, Garry Michael *6-0 185 LW*
B. Barrie, Ont., Oct. 20, 1946

Season	Team	GP	G	A	Pts.	PIM
67-68	Mont	11	0	0	0	8
68-69	Mont	3	0	0	0	0
69-70	Det-LA	72	3	7	10	37
70-71	Tor	78	15	22	37	79
71-72	Tor	78	14	17	31	47
72-73	Tor	78	13	18	31	53
73-74	Tor	78	9	16	25	70
74-75	Tor-Van	79	14	20	34	51
75-76	Van	66	16	17	33	39
76-77	Van	76	18	26	44	48
77-78	Van	67	10	19	29	28
78-79	Tor	62	4	7	11	25
Totals		748	116	169	285	485
Playoff Totals		22	3	1	4	13

MONAHAN, Hartland Patrick *5-11 197 RW*
B. Montreal, Que., Mar. 29, 1951

Season	Team	GP	G	A	Pts.	PIM
73-74	Cal	1	0	0	0	0
74-75	NYR	6	0	1	1	4
75-76	Wash	80	17	29	46	35
76-77	Wash	79	23	27	50	37
77-78	Pitt-LA	71	12	9	21	45
79-80	StL	72	5	12	17	36
80-81	StL	25	4	2	6	4
Totals		334	61	80	141	161
Playoff Totals		6	0	0	0	4

MONDOU, Armand *5-10 175 LW*
B. Yanaska, Que., June 27, 1905

Season	Team	GP	G	A	Pts.	PIM
28-29	Mont	32	3	4	7	6
29-30	Mont	44	3	5	8	24
30-31	Mont	40	5	4	9	10
31-32	Mont	47	6	12	18	22
32-33	Mont	24	1	3	4	15
33-34	Mont	48	5	3	8	4
34-35	Mont	45	9	15	24	6
35-36	Mont	36	7	11	18	10
36-37	Mont	7	1	1	2	0
37-38	Mont	7	2	4	6	0
38-39	Mont	34	3	7	10	2
39-40	Mont	21	2	2	4	0
Totals		385	47	71	118	99
Playoff Totals		35	3	5	8	12

MONDOU, Pierre *5-10 185 C*
B. Sorel, Que., Nov. 27, 1955

Season	Team	GP	G	A	Pts.	PIM
77-78	Mont	71	19	30	49	8
78-79	Mont	77	31	41	72	26
79-80	Mont	75	30	36	66	12
80-81	Mont	57	17	24	41	16
81-82	Mont	73	35	33	68	57
82-83	Mont	76	29	37	66	31
83-84	Mont	52	15	22	37	8
84-85	Mont	67	18	39	57	21
Totals		548	194	262	456	179
Playoff Totals		69	17	28	45	26

MONGEAU, Michel *5-9 190 C*
B. Nun's Island, Que., Feb. 9, 1965

Season	Team	GP	G	A	Pts.	PIM
89-90	StL	7	1	5	6	2
90-91	StL	7	1	1	2	0
91-92	StL	36	3	12	15	6
Totals		50	5	18	23	8
Playoff Totals		2	0	1	1	0

MONGRAIN, Robert *5-10 165 C*
B. La Sarre, Que., Aug. 31, 1959

Season	Team	GP	G	A	Pts.	PIM
79-80	Buf	34	4	6	10	4
80-81	Buf	4	0	0	0	2
81-82	Buf	24	6	4	10	6
84-85	Buf	8	1	1	2	0
85-86	LA	11	2	3	5	2
Totals		83	13	14	27	14
Playoff Totals		11	1	2	3	2

MONTEITH, Henry George (Hank) *5-10 180 LW*
B. Stratford, Ont., Oct. 2, 1945

Season	Team	GP	G	A	Pts.	PIM
68-69	Det	34	1	9	10	6
69-70	Det	9	0	0	0	4
70-71	Det	34	4	3	7	0
Totals		77	5	12	17	10
Playoff Totals		4	0	0	0	0

MOORE, Richard Winston (Dickie) *5-10 185 RW*
B. Montreal, Que., Jan. 6, 1931

Season	Team	GP	G	A	Pts.	PIM
51-52	Mont	33	18	15	33	44
52-53	Mont	18	2	6	8	19
53-54	Mont	13	1	4	5	12
54-55	Mont	67	16	20	36	32
55-56	Mont	70	11	39	50	55
56-57	Mont	70	29	29	58	56
57-58	Mont	70	36	48	84	65
58-59	Mont	70	41	55	96	61
59-60	Mont	62	22	42	64	54
60-61	Mont	57	35	34	69	62
61-62	Mont	57	19	22	41	54
62-63	Mont	67	24	26	50	61
64-65	Tor	38	2	4	6	68
67-68	StL	27	5	3	8	9
Totals		719	261	347	608	652
Playoff Totals		135	46	64	110	122

MORAN, Ambrose Jason (Amby) *D*

Season	Team	GP	G	A	Pts.	PIM
26-27	Mont	12	0	0	0	10
27-28	Chi	23	1	1	2	14
Totals		35	1	1	2	24

MORE, Jayson 6-1 190 D
B. Souris, Man., Jan. 12, 1969

Season	Team	GP	G	A	Pts.	PIM
88-89	NYR	1	0	0	0	0
89-90	Minn	5	0	0	0	16
91-92	SJ	46	4	13	17	85
Totals		52	4	13	17	101

MORENZ, Howarth William (Howie) 5-9 165 C
B. Mitchell, Ont., June 21, 1902

Season	Team	GP	G	A	Pts.	PIM
23-24	Mont	24	13	3	16	20
24-25	Mont	30	27	7	34	31
25-26	Mont	31	23	3	26	39
26-27	Mont	44	25	7	32	49
27-28	Mont	43	33	18	51	66
28-29	Mont	42	17	10	27	47
29-30	Mont	44	40	10	50	72
30-31	Mont	39	28	23	51	49
31-32	Mont	48	24	25	49	46
32-33	Mont	46	14	21	35	32
33-34	Mont	39	8	13	21	21
34-35	Chi	48	8	26	34	21
35-36	Chi-NYR	42	6	15	21	26
36-37	Mont	30	4	16	20	12
Totals		550	270	197	467	531
Playoff Totals		47	21	11	32	68

MORETTO, Angelo Joseph 6-3 212 C
B. Toronto, Ont., Sept. 18, 1953

Season	Team	GP	G	A	Pts.	PIM
76-77	Clev	5	1	2	3	2
78-79	Ind (WHA)	18	3	1	4	2

MORIN, Pierre (Pete) F
B. Lachine, Que., Dec. 8, 1915

Season	Team	GP	G	A	Pts.	PIM
41-42	Mont	31	10	12	22	7
Playoff Totals		1	0	0	0	0

MORIN, Stephane 6-0 174 C
B. Montreal, Que., Mar. 27, 1969

Season	Team	GP	G	A	Pts.	PIM
89-90	Que	6	0	2	2	2
90-91	Que	48	13	27	40	30
91-92	Que	30	2	8	10	14
Totals		84	15	37	52	46

MORRIS, Bernard D

Season	Team	GP	G	A	Pts.	PIM
24-25	Bos	6	2	0	2	0

MORRIS, Elwin Gordon (Moe) 5-7 185 D
B. Toronto, Ont., Jan. 3, 1921

Season	Team	GP	G	A	Pts.	PIM
43-44	Tor	50	12	21	33	22
44-45	Tor	29	0	2	2	18
45-46	Tor	38	1	5	6	10
48-49	NYR	18	0	1	1	8
Totals		135	13	29	42	58
Playoff Totals		18	4	2	6	16

MORRIS, Jon 6-0 175 C
B. Lowell, Mass., May 6, 1966

Season	Team	GP	G	A	Pts.	PIM
88-89	NJ	4	0	2	2	0
89-90	NJ	20	6	7	13	8
90-91	NJ	53	9	19	28	27
91-92	NJ	7	1	2	3	6
Totals		84	16	30	46	41
Playoff Totals		11	1	7	8	25

MORRISON, David Stuart 6-0 190 RW
B. Toronto, Ont., June 12, 1962

Season	Team	GP	G	A	Pts.	PIM
80-81	LA	3	0	0	0	0
81-82	LA	4	0	0	0	0
82-83	LA	24	3	3	6	4
84-85	Van	8	0	0	0	0
Totals		39	3	3	6	4

MORRISON, Donald MacRae 5-10 165 C
B. Saskatoon, Sask., July 14, 1923

Season	Team	GP	G	A	Pts.	PIM
47-48	Det	40	10	15	25	6
48-49	Det	13	0	1	1	0
50-51	Chi	59	8	12	20	6
Totals		112	18	28	46	12
Playoff Totals		3	0	1	1	0

MORRISON, Douglas 5-11 185 RW
B. Vancouver, B.C., Feb. 1, 1960

Season	Team	GP	G	A	Pts.	PIM
79-80	Bos	1	0	0	0	0
80-81	Bos	18	7	3	10	13
81-82	Bos	6	0	0	0	0
84-85	Bos	1	0	0	0	2
Totals		23	7	3	10	15

MORRISON, Gary 6-2 200 RW
B. Detroit, Mich., Nov. 8, 1955

Season	Team	GP	G	A	Pts.	PIM
79-80	Phil	3	0	2	2	0
80-81	Phil	33	1	13	14	68
81-82	Phil	7	0	0	0	2
Totals		43	1	15	16	70
Playoff Totals		5	0	1	1	2

MORRISON, George Harold 6-1 170 LW
B. Toronto, Ont., Dec. 24, 1948

Season	Team	GP	G	A	Pts.	PIM
70-71	StL	73	15	10	25	6
71-72	StL	42	2	11	13	7
72-73	Minn (WHA)	70	16	24	40	20
73-74	Minn (WHA)	73	40	38	78	37
74-75	Minn (WHA)	76	31	29	60	30
75-76	Calg (WHA)	79	25	32	57	13
76-77	Calg (WHA)	63	11	19	30	10
NHL Totals		115	17	21	38	13
WHA Totals		361	123	142	265	110
NHL Playoff Totals		3	0	0	0	0
WHA Playoff Totals		38	14	17	31	14

MORRISON, James Stuart Hunter 5-10 183 D
B. Montreal, Que., Oct. 11, 1931

Season	Team	GP	G	A	Pts.	PIM
51-52	Bos-Tor	31	0	3	3	6
52-53	Tor	56	1	8	9	36
53-54	Tor	60	9	11	20	51
54-55	Tor	70	5	12	17	84
55-56	Tor	63	2	17	19	77
56-57	Tor	63	3	17	20	44
57-58	Tor	70	3	21	24	62
58-59	Bos	70	8	17	25	42
59-60	Det	70	3	23	26	62
60-61	NYR	19	1	6	7	6
69-70	Pitt	59	5	15	20	40
70-71	Pitt	73	0	10	10	32
Totals		704	40	160	200	542
Playoff Totals		36	0	12	12	38

MORRISON, John W. (Crutchy) F
B. Selkirk, Man.

Season	Team	GP	G	A	Pts.	PIM
25-26	NYA	18	0	0	0	0

MORRISON, Kevin Gregory Joseph 5-11 202 D
B. Sydney, N.S., Oct. 28, 1949

Season	Team	GP	G	A	Pts.	PIM
73-74	NY-NJ (WHA)	78	24	43	67	132
74-75	SD (WHA)	78	20	61	81	143
75-76	SD (WHA)	80	22	43	65	56
76-77	SD (WHA)	75	8	30	38	68
77-78	Ind (WHA)	75	17	40	57	49
78-79	Ind-Que (WHA)	32	2	7	9	14
79-80	Col	41	4	11	15	23
NHL Totals		41	4	11	15	23
WHA Totals		418	93	224	317	462
WHA Playoff Totals		28	2	15	17	22

MORRISON, Henry Lewis (Lew) 6-0 185 RW
B. Gainsborough, Sask., Feb. 11, 1948

Season	Team	GP	G	A	Pts.	PIM
69-70	Phil	66	9	10	19	19
70-71	Phil	78	5	7	12	25
71-72	Phil	58	5	5	10	26
72-73	Atl	78	6	9	15	19
73-74	Atl	52	1	4	5	0
74-75	Wash-Pitt	70	7	9	16	10
75-76	Pitt	78	4	5	9	8
76-77	Pitt	76	2	1	3	0
77-78	Pitt	8	0	2	2	0
Totals		564	39	52	91	107
Playoff Totals		17	0	0	0	2

MORRISON, Mark 5-8 150 C
B. Prince George, B.C., Mar. 11, 1963

Season	Team	GP	G	A	Pts.	PIM
81-82	NYR	9	1	1	2	0
83-84	NYR	1	0	0	0	0
Totals		10	1	1	2	0

MORRISON, Roderick Finlay 5-9 160 RW
B. Saskatoon, Sask., Oct. 7, 1925

Season	Team	GP	G	A	Pts.	PIM
47-48	Det	34	8	7	15	4
Playoff Totals		3	0	0	0	0

MORROW, Ken 6-4 210 D
B. Flint, Mich., Oct. 17, 1956

Season	Team	GP	G	A	Pts.	PIM
79-80	NYI	18	0	3	3	4
80-81	NYI	80	2	11	13	20
81-82	NYI	75	1	18	19	56
82-83	NYI	79	5	11	16	44
83-84	NYI	63	3	11	14	45
84-85	NYI	15	1	7	8	14
85-86	NYI	69	0	12	12	22
86-87	NYI	64	3	8	11	32
87-88	NYI	53	1	4	5	40
88-89	NYI	34	1	3	4	32
Totals		490	17	88	105	309

MORROW, Ken (Continued)

Season	Team	GP	G	A	Pts.	PIM
Playoff Totals		127	11	22	33	97

MORTON, Dean 6-1 196 D
B. Peterborough, Ont., Feb. 27, 1968

Season	Team	GP	G	A	Pts.	PIM
89-90	Det	1	1	0	1	2

MORTSON, James Angus Gerald (Gus) 5-11 190 D
B. New Liskeard, Ont., Jan. 24, 1925

Season	Team	GP	G	A	Pts.	PIM
46-47	Tor	60	5	13	18	133
47-48	Tor	58	7	11	18	118
48-49	Tor	60	2	13	15	85
49-50	Tor	68	3	14	17	85
50-51	Tor	60	3	10	13	142
51-52	Tor	65	1	10	11	106
52-53	Chi	68	5	18	23	88
53-54	Chi	68	5	13	18	132
54-55	Chi	65	2	11	13	133
55-56	Chi	52	5	10	15	87
56-57	Chi	70	5	18	23	147
57-58	Chi	67	3	10	13	62
58-59	Chi	36	0	1	1	22
Totals		797	46	152	198	1340
Playoff Totals		54	5	8	13	68

MOSDELL, Kenneth 6-1 170 C
B. Montreal, Que., July 13, 1922

Season	Team	GP	G	A	Pts.	PIM
41-42	Brk	41	7	9	16	16
44-45	Mont	31	12	6	18	16
45-46	Mont	13	2	1	3	8
46-47	Mont	54	5	10	15	50
47-48	Mont	23	1	0	1	19
48-49	Mont	60	17	9	26	59
49-50	Mont	67	15	12	27	42
50-51	Mont	66	13	18	31	24
51-52	Mont	44	5	11	16	19
52-53	Mont	63	5	14	19	27
53-54	Mont	67	22	24	46	64
54-55	Mont	70	22	32	54	82
55-56	Mont	67	13	17	30	48
56-57	Chi	25	2	4	6	10
57-58	Mont	20	1	1	2	0
Totals		693	141	168	309	484
Playoff Totals		79	16	13	29	48

MOSIENKO, William (Mosi) 5-8 160 RW
B. Winnipeg, Man., Nov. 2, 1921

Season	Team	GP	G	A	Pts.	PIM
41-42	Chi	12	6	8	14	4
42-43	Chi	2	2	0	2	0
43-44	Chi	50	32	38	70	10
44-45	Chi	50	28	26	54	0
45-46	Chi	40	18	30	48	12
46-47	Chi	59	25	27	52	2
47-48	Chi	40	16	9	25	0
48-49	Chi	60	17	25	42	6
49-50	Chi	69	18	28	46	10
50-51	Chi	65	21	15	36	18
51-52	Chi	70	31	22	53	10
52-53	Chi	65	17	20	37	8
53-54	Chi	65	15	19	34	17
54-55	Chi	64	12	15	27	24
Totals		711	258	282	540	121
Playoff Totals		22	10	4	14	15

MOTT, Morris Kenneth 5-10 165 RW
B. Creelman, Sask., May 25, 1946

Season	Team	GP	G	A	Pts.	PIM
72-73	Cal	70	6	7	13	8
73-74	Cal	77	9	17	26	33
74-75	Cal	52	3	8	11	8
76-77	Winn (WHA)	2	0	1	1	5
NHL Totals		199	18	32	50	49
WHA Totals		2	0	1	1	5

MOTTER, Alexander Everett 6-0 175 C
B. Melville, Sask., June 20, 1913

Season	Team	GP	G	A	Pts.	PIM
34-35	Bos	5	0	0	0	0
35-36	Bos	23	1	4	5	4
37-38	Det	33	5	17	22	6
38-39	Det	42	5	11	16	17
39-40	Det	37	7	12	19	28
40-41	Det	47	13	12	25	18
41-42	Det	30	2	4	6	20
42-43	Det	50	6	4	10	42
Totals		267	39	64	103	135
Playoff Totals		40	3	9	12	41

MOXEY, James George 6-1 190 RW
B. Toronto, Ont., May 28, 1953

Season	Team	GP	G	A	Pts.	PIM
74-75	Cal	47	5	4	9	14
75-76	Cal	44	10	16	26	33
76-77	Clev-LA	36	7	7	14	22
Totals		127	22	27	49	69

Season Team	GP	G	A	Pts.	PIM

MULHERN, Richard Sydney *6-1 188 D*
B. Edmonton, Alta., Mar. 1, 1955

Season Team	GP	G	A	Pts.	PIM
75-76 Atl	12	1	0	1	4
76-77 Atl	79	12	32	44	80
77-78 Atl	79	9	23	32	47
78-79 Atl-LA	73	5	21	26	45
79-80 LA-Tor	41	0	13	13	27
80-81 Winn	19	0	4	4	14
Totals	303	27	93	120	217
Playoff Totals	7	0	3	3	5

MULLEN, Brian *5-10 185 RW*
B. New York, N.Y., Mar. 16, 1962

Season Team	GP	G	A	Pts.	PIM
82-83 Winn	80	24	26	50	14
83-84 Winn	75	21	41	62	28
84-85 Winn	69	32	39	71	32
85-86 Winn	79	28	34	62	38
86-87 Winn	69	19	32	51	20
87-88 NYR	74	25	29	54	42
88-89 NYR	78	29	35	64	60
89-90 NYR	76	27	41	68	42
90-91 NYR	79	19	43	62	44
91-92 SJ	72	18	28	46	66
Totals	751	242	348	590	386
Playoff Totals	44	9	14	23	28

MULLEN, Joe *5-9 180 RW*
B. New York, N.Y., Feb. 26, 1957

Season Team	GP	G	A	Pts.	PIM
81-82 StL	45	25	34	59	4
82-83 StL	49	17	30	47	6
83-84 StL	80	41	44	85	19
84-85 StL	79	40	52	92	6
85-86 StL-Calg	77	44	46	90	21
86-87 Calg	79	47	40	87	14
87-88 Calg	80	40	44	84	30
88-89 Calg	79	51	59	110	16
89-90 Calg	78	36	33	69	24
90-91 Pitt	47	17	22	39	6
91-92 Pitt	77	42	45	87	30
Totals	770	400	449	849	176
Playoff Tot.	112	55	41	96	30

MULLER, Kirk *6-0 205 LW*
B. Kingston, Ont., Feb. 8, 1966

Season Team	GP	G	A	Pts.	PIM
84-85 NJ	80	17	37	54	69
85-86 NJ	77	25	41	66	45
86-87 NJ	79	26	50	76	75
87-88 NJ	80	37	57	94	114
88-89 NJ	80	31	43	74	119
89-90 NJ	80	30	56	86	74
90-91 NJ	80	19	51	70	76
91-92 Mont	78	36	41	77	86
Totals	634	221	376	597	658
Playoff Totals	44	9	16	25	89

MULOIN, John Wayne *5-8 176 D*
B. Toronto, Ont., Dec. 24, 1941

Season Team	GP	G	A	Pts.	PIM
63-64 Det	3	0	1	1	2
69-70 Oak	71	3	6	9	53
70-71 Cal-Minn	73	0	14	14	38
72-73 Clev (WHA)	70	2	13	15	62
73-74 Clev (WHA)	76	3	7	10	39
74-75 Clev (WHA)	78	4	17	21	5
75-76 Clev-Edm	37	1	6	7	12
(WHA)					
NHL Totals	147	3	21	24	93
WHA Totals	261	10	43	53	118
NHL Playoff Totals	11	0	0	0	2
WHA Playoff Totals	20	2	4	6	18

MULVENNA, Glenn *5-11 187 C*
B. Calgary, Alta., Feb. 18, 1967

Season Team	GP	G	A	Pts.	PIM
91-92 Pitt	1	0	0	0	2

MULVEY, Grant Michael *6-4 200 RW*
B. Sudbury, Ont., Sept. 17, 1956

Season Team	GP	G	A	Pts.	PIM
74-75 Chi	74	7	4	11	36
75-76 Chi	64	11	17	28	72
76-77 Chi	80	10	14	24	111
77-78 Chi	78	14	24	38	135
78-79 Chi	80	19	15	34	99
79-80 Chi	80	39	26	65	122
80-81 Chi	42	18	14	32	81
81-82 Chi	73	30	19	49	141
82-83 Chi	3	0	0	0	0
83-84 NJ	12	1	2	3	19
Totals	586	149	135	284	816
Playoff Totals	42	10	5	15	70

MULVEY, Paul Joseph *6-4 200 LW*
B. Sudbury, Ont., Sept. 27, 1958

Season Team	GP	G	A	Pts.	PIM
78-79 Wash	55	7	4	11	81
79-80 Wash	77	15	19	34	240
80-81 Wash	55	7	14	21	166
81-82 Pitt-LA	38	1	14	15	126
Totals	225	30	51	81	613

MUMMERY, Harry *245 D*

Season Team	GP	G	A	Pts.	PIM
17-18 Tor	18	3	0	3	24
18-19 Tor	13	2	0	2	27
19-20 Que	24	9	6	15	42
20-21 Mont	24	15	5	20	68
21-22 Ham	20	4	2	6	20
22-23 Ham	7	0	0	0	4
Totals	106	33	13	46	185
Playoff Totals	7	1	4	5	0

MUNI, Craig Douglas *6-3 200 D*
B. Toronto, Ont., July 19, 1962

Season Team	GP	G	A	Pts.	PIM
81-82 Tor	3	0	0	0	2
82-83 Tor	2	0	1	1	0
84-85 Tor	8	0	0	0	0
85-86 Tor	6	0	1	1	4
86-87 Edm	79	7	22	29	85
87-88 Edm	72	4	15	19	77
88-89 Edm	69	5	13	18	71
89-90 Edm	71	5	12	17	81
90-91 Edm	76	1	9	10	77
91-92 Edm	54	2	5	7	34
Totals	440	24	78	102	431
Playoff Totals	83	0	15	15	94

MUNRO, Duncan B. (Dunc) *D*
B. Toronto, Ont.

Season Team	GP	G	A	Pts.	PIM
24-25 Mont M	27	5	1	6	14
25-26 Mont M	33	4	6	10	55
26-27 Mont M	43	6	5	11	42
27-28 Mont M	43	5	2	7	35
28-29 Mont	1	0	0	0	0
29-30 Mont	40	7	2	9	10
30-31 Mont	4	0	1	1	0
31-32 Mont	48	1	1	2	14
Totals	239	28	18	46	170
Playoff Totals	25	3	2	5	24

MUNRO, Gerald (Gerry) *D*
B. Sault Ste. Marie, Ont., Nov. 20, 1897

Season Team	GP	G	A	Pts.	PIM
24-25 Mont M	29	1	0	1	22
25-26 Tor	4	0	0	0	0
Totals	33	1	0	1	22

MURDOCH, Donald Walter (Murder)
5-11 180 RW
B. Cranbrook, B.C., Oct. 25, 1956

Season Team	GP	G	A	Pts.	PIM
76-77 NYR	59	32	24	56	47
77-78 NYR	66	27	28	55	41
78-79 NYR	40	15	22	37	6
79-80 NYR-Edm	66	28	21	49	20
80-81 Edm	40	10	9	19	18
81-82 Det	49	9	13	22	23
Totals	320	121	117	238	155
Playoff Totals	38	18	8	18	16

MURDOCH, John Murray *5-10 180 LW*
B. Lucknow, Ont., May 19, 1904

Season Team	GP	G	A	Pts.	PIM
26-27 NYR	44	6	4	10	12
27-28 NYR	44	7	3	10	14
28-29 NYR	44	8	6	14	18
29-30 NYR	44	13	13	26	22
30-31 NYR	44	7	7	14	8
31-32 NYR	48	5	16	21	32
32-33 NYR	48	5	11	16	23
33-34 NYR	48	17	10	27	29
34-35 NYR	48	14	15	29	14
35-36 NYR	48	2	9	11	9
36-37 NYR	48	0	14	14	16
Totals	508	84	108	192	197
Playoff Totals	55	9	12	21	28

MURDOCH, Robert John *6-0 190 D*
B. Kirkland Lake, Ont., Nov. 20, 1946

Season Team	GP	G	A	Pts.	PIM
70-71 Mont	1	0	2	2	2
71-72 Mont	11	1	1	2	8
72-73 Mont	69	2	22	24	55
73-74 LA	76	8	20	28	85
74-75 LA	80	13	29	42	116
75-76 LA	80	6	29	35	103
76-77 LA	70	9	23	32	79
77-78 LA	76	2	17	19	68
78-79 LA-Atl	67	8	23	31	70
79-80 Atl	80	5	16	21	48
80-81 Calg	74	3	19	22	54
81-82 Calg	73	3	17	20	76
Totals	757	60	218	278	764
Playoff Totals	69	4	18	22	92

MURDOCH, Robert Lovell *5-11 191 RW*
B. Cranbrook, B.C., Jan. 29, 1954

Season Team	GP	G	A	Pts.	PIM
75-76 Cal	78	22	27	49	53
76-77 Clev	57	23	19	42	30
77-78 Clev	71	14	26	40	27
78-79 StL	54	13	13	26	17
Totals	260	72	85	157	127

MURPHY, Brian *6-3 195 C*
B. Toronto, Ont., Aug. 20, 1947

Season Team	GP	G	A	Pts.	PIM
74-75 Det	1	0	0	0	0

MURPHY, Gordon *6-2 195 D*
B. Willowdale, Ont., Mar. 23, 1967

Season Team	GP	G	A	Pts.	PIM
88-89 Phil	75	4	31	35	68
89-90 Phil	75	14	27	41	95
90-91 Phil	80	11	31	42	58
91-92 Phil-Bos	75	5	14	19	84
Totals	303	34	93	127	305
Playoff Totals	34	3	7	10	25

MURPHY, Joe *6-1 190 RW*
B. London, Ont., Oct. 16, 1967

Season Team	GP	G	A	Pts.	PIM
86-87 Det	5	0	1	1	2
87-88 Det	50	10	9	19	37
88-89 Det	26	1	7	8	28
89-90 Det-Edm	71	10	19	29	60
90-91 Edm	80	27	35	62	35
91-92 Edm	80	35	47	82	52
Totals	312	83	118	201	214
Playoff Totals	61	16	30	46	48

MURPHY, Lawrence Thomas (Larry)
6-2 210 D
B. Scarborough, Ont., Mar. 8, 1961

Season Team	GP	G	A	Pts.	PIM
80-81 LA	80	16	60	76	79
81-82 LA	79	22	44	66	95
82-83 LA	77	14	48	62	81
83-84 LA-Wash	78	13	36	49	50
84-85 Wash	79	13	42	55	51
85-86 Wash	78	21	44	65	50
86-87 Wash	80	23	58	81	39
87-88 Wash	79	8	53	61	72
88-89 Wash-Minn	78	11	35	46	82
89-90 Minn	77	10	58	68	44
90-91 Minn-Pitt	75	9	34	43	68
91-92 Pitt	77	21	56	77	50
Totals	937	181	568	749	761
Playoff Tot.	112	26	57	83	187

MURPHY, Michael John *6-0 190 RW*
B. Toronto, Ont., Sept. 12, 1950

Season Team	GP	G	A	Pts.	PIM
71-72 StL	63	20	23	43	19
72-73 StL-NYR	79	22	31	53	53
73-74 NYR-LA	69	15	17	32	38
74-75 LA	78	30	38	68	44
75-76 LA	80	26	42	68	61
76-77 LA	76	25	36	61	58
77-78 LA	72	20	36	56	48
78-79 LA	64	16	29	45	38
79-00 LA	80	27	22	49	29
80-81 LA	68	16	23	39	54
81-82 LA	28	5	10	15	20
82-83 LA	74	16	11	27	52
Totals	831	238	318	556	514
Playoff Totals	66	13	23	36	54

MURPHY, Rob *6-3 205 LW/C*
B. Hull, Que., Apr. 7, 1969

Season Team	GP	G	A	Pts.	PIM
87-88 Van	5	0	0	0	2
88-89 Van	8	0	1	1	2
89-90 Van	12	1	1	2	0
90-91 Van	42	5	1	6	90
91-92 Van	6	0	1	1	6
Totals	73	6	4	10	100
Playoff Totals	4	0	0	0	2

MURPHY, Robert Ronald (Ron)
5-11 185 LW
B. Hamilton, Ont., Apr. 10, 1933

Season Team	GP	G	A	Pts.	PIM
52-53 NYR	15	3	1	4	0
53-54 NYR	27	1	3	4	20
54-55 NYR	66	14	16	30	36
55-56 NYR	66	16	28	44	71
56-57 NYR	33	7	12	19	14
57-58 Chi	69	11	17	28	32
58-59 Chi	59	17	30	47	52
59-60 Chi	63	15	21	36	18
60-61 Chi	70	21	19	40	30
61-62 Chi	60	12	16	28	41
62-63 Chi	68	18	16	34	28
63-64 Chi	70	11	8	19	32
64-65 Det	58	20	19	39	32
65-66 Det-Bos	34	10	8	18	10
66-67 Bos	39	11	16	27	6
67-68 Bos	12	0	1	1	4
68-69 Bos	60	16	38	54	26
69-70 Bos	20	2	5	7	8
Totals	889	205	274	479	460
Playoff Totals	53	7	8	15	26

MURRAY, Allan *5-7 165 D*
B. Stratford, Ont., Nov. 10, 1908

Season Team	GP	G	A	Pts.	PIM
33-34 NYA	48	1	1	2	20
34-35 NYA	43	2	1	3	36

MURRAY, Allan *(Continued)*

Season Team	GP	G	A	Pts.	PIM
35-36 NYA	48	1	0	1	33
36-37 NYA	39	0	2	2	22
37-38 NYA	46	0	1	1	34
38-39 NYA	19	0	0	0	8
39-40 NYA	34	1	4	5	10
Totals	277	5	9	14	163
Playoff Totals	14	0	0	0	8

MURRAY, Glen *6-2 200 RW*
B. Halifax, N.S., Nov. 1, 1972

91-92 Bos	5	3	1	4	0
Playoff Totals	15	4	2	6	10

MURRAY, James Arnold *6-1 165 D*
B. Virden, Man., Nov. 25, 1943

67-68 LA	30	0	2	2	14

MURRAY, Kenneth Richard *6-0 180 D*
B. Toronto, Ont., Jan. 22, 1948

69-70 Tor	1	0	1	1	2
70-71 Tor	4	0	0	0	0
72-73 NYI-Det	70	1	5	6	95
74-75 KC	8	0	2	2	14
75-76 KC	23	0	2	2	24
Totals	106	1	10	11	135

MURRAY, Leonard (Leo) *C*
B. Portage La Prairie, Man., Feb. 15, 1902

32-33 Mont	6	0	0	0	2

MURRAY, Mike *6-0 180 C*
B. Kingston, Ont., Aug. 29, 1966

87-88 Phil	1	0	0	0	0

MURRAY, Pat *6-2 185 LW*
B. Stratford, Ont., Aug. 20, 1969

90-91 Phil	16	2	1	3	15
91-92 Phil	9	1	0	1	0
Totals	25	3	1	4	15

MURRAY, Randall (Randy) *6-1 195 D*
B. Chatham, Ont., Aug. 24, 1945

69-70 Tor	3	0	0	0	2

MURRAY, Rob *6-0 185 C*
B. Toronto, Ont., Apr. 4, 1967

89-90 Wash	41	2	7	9	58
90-91 Wash	17	0	3	3	19
91-92 Winn	9	0	1	1	18
Totals	67	2	11	13	95
Playoff Totals	9	0	0	0	18

MURRAY, Robert John *6-1 195 D*
B. Burlington, Ont., July 16, 1948

73-74 Atl	62	0	3	3	34
74-75 Atl-Van	55	4	8	12	30
75-76 Van	65	2	5	7	28
76-77 Van	12	0	0	0	6
Totals	194	6	16	22	98
Playoff Totals	9	1	1	2	15

MURRAY, Terrence Rodney (Terry)
6-2 190 D
B. Shawville, Que., July 20, 1950

72-73 Cal	23	0	3	3	4
73-74 Cal	58	0	12	12	48
74-75 Cal	9	0	2	2	8
75-76 Phil	3	0	0	0	2
76-77 Phil-Det	59	0	20	20	24
78-79 Phil	5	0	0	0	0
80-81 Phil	71	1	17	18	53
81-82 Wash	74	3	22	25	60
Totals	302	4	76	80	199
Playoff Totals	18	2	2	4	10

MURRAY, Troy Norman *6-1 195 C*
B. Calgary, Alta., July 31, 1962

81-82 Chi	1	0	0	0	0
82-83 Chi	54	8	8	16	27
83-84 Chi	61	15	15	30	45
84-85 Chi	80	26	40	66	82
85-86 Chi	80	45	54	99	94
86-87 Chi	77	28	43	71	59
87-88 Chi	79	22	36	58	96
88-89 Chi	79	21	30	51	113
89-90 Chi	68	17	38	55	86
90-91 Chi	75	14	23	37	74
91-92 Winn	74	17	30	47	69
Totals	728	213	317	530	747
Playoff Totals	89	15	25	40	92

MURZYN, Dana *6-2 200 D*
B. Calgary, Alta., Dec. 9, 1966

85-86 Hart	78	3	23	26	125

MURZYN, Dana *(Continued)*

Season Team	GP	G	A	Pts.	PIM
86-87 Hart	74	9	19	28	95
87-88 Hart-Calg	74	7	11	18	139
88-89 Calg	63	3	19	22	142
89-90 Calg	78	7	13	20	140
90-91 Calg-Van	29	1	2	3	38
91-92 Van	70	3	12	15	145
Totals	466	33	99	132	824
Playoff Totals	49	6	7	13	97

MUSIL, Frantisek *6-3 205 D*
B. Pardubice, Czechoslovakia, Dec. 17, 1964

86-87 Minn	72	2	9	11	148
87-88 Minn	80	9	8	17	213
88-89 Minn	55	1	19	20	54
89-90 Minn	56	2	8	10	109
90-91 Minn-Calg	75	7	16	23	183
91-92 Calg	78	4	8	12	103
Totals	416	25	68	93	810
Playoff Totals	16	1	1	2	28

MYERS, Harold Robert (Hap) *5-11 195 D*
B. Edmonton, Alta., July 28, 1947

70-71 Buf	13	0	0	0	6

MYLES, Victor Robert *6-1 208 D*
B. Fairlight, Sask., Nov. 12, 1915

42-43 NYR	45	6	9	15	57

NACHBAUR, Donald Kenneth *6-2 195 C*
B. Kitimat, B.C., Jan. 30, 1959

80-81 Hart	77	16	17	33	139
81-82 Hart	77	5	21	26	117
82-83 Edm	4	0	0	0	17
85-86 Phil	5	1	1	2	7
86-87 Phil	23	0	2	2	87
87-88 Phil	20	0	4	4	61
88-89 Phil	15	1	0	1	37
89-90 Phil	2	0	1	1	0
Totals	223	23	46	69	465
Playoff Totals	11	1	1	2	24

NAHRGANG, James Herbert *6-0 185 D*
B. Millbank, Ont., Apr. 17, 1951

74-75 Det	1	0	0	0	0
75-76 Det	3	0	1	1	0
76-77 Det	53	5	11	16	34
Totals	57	5	12	17	34

NANNE, Louis Vincent (Lou) *6-0 185 D*
B. Sault Ste. Marie, Ont., June 2, 1941

67-68 Minn	2	0	1	1	0
68-69 Minn	41	2	12	14	47
69-70 Minn	74	3	20	23	75
70-71 Minn	68	5	11	16	22
71-72 Minn	78	21	28	49	27
72-73 Minn	74	15	20	35	39
73-74 Minn	76	11	21	32	46
74-75 Minn	49	6	9	15	35
75-76 Minn	79	3	14	17	45
76-77 Minn	68	2	20	22	12
77-78 Minn	26	0	1	1	8
Totals	635	68	157	225	356
Playoff Totals	32	4	10	14	9

NANTAIS, Richard Francois *5-11 188 LW*
B. Repentigny, Que., Oct. 27, 1954

74-75 Minn	18	4	1	5	9
75-76 Minn	5	0	0	0	17
76-77 Minn	40	1	3	4	53
Totals	63	5	4	9	79

NAPIER, Robert Mark *5-10 183 RW*
B. Toronto, Ont., Jan. 28, 1957

75-76 Tor (WHA)	78	43	50	93	20
76-77 Birm (WHA)	80	60	36	96	24
77-78 Birm (WHA)	79	33	32	65	9
78-79 Mont	54	11	20	31	11
79-80 Mont	76	16	33	49	7
80-81 Mont	79	35	36	71	24
81-82 Mont	80	40	41	81	14
82-83 Mont	73	40	27	67	6
83-84 Mont-Minn	63	16	30	46	17
84-85 Minn-Edm	72	19	44	63	21
85-86 Edm	80	24	32	56	14
86-87 Edm-Buf	77	13	18	31	2
87-88 Buf	47	10	8	18	8
88-89 Buf	66	11	17	28	33
NHL Totals	767	265	306	571	157
WHA Totals	237	136	118	254	53
NHL Playoff Totals	82	18	24	42	11
WHA Playoff Totals	5	0	2	2	14

NASLUND, Mats *5-7 160 LW*
B. Timra, Sweden, Oct. 31, 1959

82-83 Mont	74	26	45	71	10
83-84 Mont	77	29	35	64	4
84-85 Mont	80	42	37	79	14
85-86 Mont	80	43	67	110	16
86-87 Mont	79	25	55	80	16
87-88 Mont	78	24	59	83	14
88-89 Mont	77	33	51	84	14
89-90 Mont	72	21	20	41	19
Totals	617	243	369	612	107
Playoff Totals	97	34	57	91	33

NATTRASS, Ralph William *6-0 200 D*
B. Gainsboro, Sask., May 26, 1925

46-47 Chi	35	4	5	9	34
47-48 Chi	60	5	12	17	79
48-49 Chi	60	4	10	14	99
49-50 Chi	68	5	11	16	96
Totals	223	18	38	56	308

NATTRESS, Eric (Ric) *6-2 210 D*
B. Hamilton, Ont., May 25, 1962

82-83 Mont	40	1	3	4	19
83-84 Mont	34	0	12	12	15
84-85 Mont	5	0	1	1	2
85-86 StL	78	4	20	24	52
86-87 StL	73	6	22	28	24
87-88 Calg	63	2	13	15	37
88-89 Calg	38	1	8	9	47
89-90 Calg	49	1	14	15	26
90-91 Calg	58	5	13	18	63
91-92 Calg-Tor	54	2	19	21	63
Totals	492	22	125	147	348
Playoff Totals	67	5	10	15	60

NATYSHAK, Mike *6-2 201 RW*
B. Belle River, Ont., Nov. 29, 1963

87-88 Que	4	0	0	0	0

NECHAEV, Victor *6-1 183 C*
B. Kuib.-Vost, Siberia, Jan. 28, 1955

82-83 LA	3	1	0	1	0

NEDOMANSKY, Vaclav *6-2 205 RW*
B. Hodonin, Czechoslovakia, Mar. 14, 1944

74-75 Tor (WHA)	78	41	40	81	19
75-76 Tor (WHA)	81	56	42	98	8
76-77 Birm (WHA)	81	36	33	69	10
77-78 Birm (WHA)	12	2	3	5	6
77-78 Det	63	11	17	28	2
78-79 Det	80	38	35	73	19
79-80 Det	79	35	39	74	13
80-81 Det	74	12	20	32	30
81-82 Det	68	12	28	40	22
82-83 StL-NYR	57	14	17	31	2
NHL Totals	421	122	156	278	88
WHA Totals	252	135	118	253	43
NHL Playoff Totals	7	3	5	8	0
WHA Playoff Totals	6	3	1	4	9

NEDVED, Petr *6-3 178 C*
B. Liberec, Czechoslovakia, Dec. 9, 1971

90-91 Van	61	10	6	16	20
91-92 Van	77	15	22	37	36
Totals	138	25	28	53	56
Playoff Totals	11	1	5	6	16

NEEDHAM, Michael *5-10 185 RW*
B. Calgary, Alta., Apr. 4, 1970

91-92 Pitt	0	0	0	0	0
Playoff Totals	5	1	0	1	2

NEELY, Robert Barry *6-1 210 LW*
B. Sarnia, Ont., Nov. 9, 1953

73-74 Tor	54	5	7	12	98
74-75 Tor	57	5	16	21	61
75-76 Tor	69	9	13	22	89
76-77 Tor	70	17	16	33	16
77-78 Tor-Col	33	3	7	10	2
Totals	283	39	59	98	266
Playoff Totals	26	5	7	12	15

NEELY, Cam *6-1 210 RW*
B. Comox, B.C., June 6, 1965

83-84 Van	56	16	15	31	57
84-85 Van	72	21	18	39	137
85-86 Van	73	14	20	34	126
86-87 Bos	75	36	36	72	143
87-88 Bos	69	42	27	69	175
88-89 Bos	74	37	38	75	190
89-90 Bos	76	55	37	92	117

Season Team	GP	G	A	Pts.	PIM
NEELY, Cam *(Continued)*					
90-91 Bos	69	51	40	91	98
91-92 Bos	9	9	3	12	16
Totals	573	281	234	515	1059
Playoff Totals	84	51	31	82	162

NEILSON, James Anthony (Chief) 6-2 205 D
B. Big River, Sask., Nov. 28, 1941

Season Team	GP	G	A	Pts.	PIM
62-63 NYR	69	5	11	16	38
63-64 NYR	69	5	24	29	93
64-65 NYR	62	0	13	13	58
65-66 NYR	65	4	19	23	84
66-67 NYR	61	4	11	15	65
67-68 NYR	67	6	29	35	60
68-69 NYR	76	10	34	44	95
69-70 NYR	62	3	20	23	75
70-71 NYR	77	8	24	32	69
71-72 NYR	78	7	30	37	56
72-73 NYR	52	4	16	20	35
73-74 NYR	72	4	7	11	38
74-75 Cal	72	3	17	20	56
75-76 Cal	26	1	6	7	20
76-77 Clev	47	3	17	20	42
77-78 Clev	68	2	21	23	20
78-79 Edm (WHA)	35	0	5	5	18
NHL Totals	1023	69	299	368	904
WHA Totals	35	0	5	5	18
NHL Playoff Totals	65	1	17	18	61

NELSON, Gordon William 5-7 180 D
B. Kinistino, Sask., May 10, 1947

Season Team	GP	G	A	Pts.	PIM
69-70 Tor	3	0	0	0	11

NELSON, Todd 6-0 201 D
B. Prince Albert, Sask., May 15, 1969

Season Team	GP	G	A	Pts.	PIM
91-92 Pitt	1	0	0	0	0

NEMCHINOV, Sergei 6-0 183 C
B. Moscow, Soviet Union, Jan. 14, 1964

Season Team	GP	G	A	Pts.	PIM
91-92 NYR	73	30	28	58	15
Playoff Totals	13	1	4	5	8

NEMETH, Steve 5-8 170 C
B. Calgary, Alta., Feb. 11, 1967

Season Team	GP	G	A	Pts.	PIM
87-88 NYR	12	2	0	2	2

NESTERENKO, Eric Paul 6-2 197 RW
B. Flin Flon, Man., Oct. 31, 1933

Season Team	GP	G	A	Pts.	PIM
51-52 Tor	1	0	0	0	0
52-53 Tor	35	10	6	16	27
53-54 Tor	68	14	9	23	70
54-55 Tor	62	15	15	30	99
55-56 Tor	40	4	6	10	65
56-57 Chi	24	8	15	23	32
57-58 Chi	70	20	18	38	104
58-59 Chi	70	16	18	34	81
59-60 Chi	61	13	23	36	71
60-61 Chi	68	19	19	38	125
61-62 Chi	68	15	14	29	97
62-63 Chi	67	12	15	27	103
63-64 Chi	70	7	19	26	93
64-65 Chi	56	14	16	30	63
65-66 Chi	67	15	25	40	58
66-67 Chi	68	14	23	37	38
67-68 Chi	71	11	25	36	37
68-69 Chi	72	15	17	32	29
69-70 Chi	67	16	18	34	26
70-71 Chi	76	8	15	23	28
71-72 Chi	38	4	8	12	27
73-74 LA (WHA)	29	2	5	7	8
NHL Totals	1219	250	324	574	1273
WHA Totals	29	2	5	7	8
NHL Playoff Totals	124	13	24	37	127

NETHERY, Lance 6-1 185 C
B. Toronto, Ont., June 28, 1957

Season Team	GP	G	A	Pts.	PIM
80-81 NYR	33	11	12	23	12
81-82 NYR-Edm	8	0	2	2	2
Totals	41	11	14	25	14
Playoff Totals	14	5	3	8	9

NEUFELD, Ray Matthew 6-3 210 RW
B. St. Boniface, Man., Apr. 15, 1959

Season Team	GP	G	A	Pts.	PIM
79-80 Hart	8	1	0	1	0
80-81 Hart	52	5	10	15	44
81-82 Hart	19	4	3	7	4
82-83 Hart	80	26	31	57	86
83-84 Hart	80	27	42	69	97
84-85 Hart	76	27	35	62	129
85-86 Hart-Winn	76	25	38	63	102
86-87 Winn	80	18	18	36	105
87-88 Winn	78	18	18	36	169
88-89 Winn-Bos	45	6	5	11	80
89-90 Bos	1	0	0	0	0
Totals	595	157	200	357	816

NEUFELD, Ray Matthew *(Continued)*

Season Team	GP	G	A	Pts.	PIM
Playoff Totals	28	8	6	14	55

NEVILLE, Michael R. F
B. Toronto, Ont.

Season Team	GP	G	A	Pts.	PIM
17-18 Tor	1	1	0	1	0
24-25 Tor	12	1	0	1	4
25-26 Tor	33	3	3	6	8
30-31 NYA	16	1	0	1	2
Totals	62	6	3	9	14
Playoff Totals	2	0	0	0	0

NEVIN, Robert Frank 6-0 190 RW
B. South Porcupine, Ont., Mar. 18, 1938

Season Team	GP	G	A	Pts.	PIM
57-58 Tor	4	0	0	0	0
58-59 Tor	2	0	0	0	2
60-61 Tor	68	21	37	58	13
61-62 Tor	69	15	30	45	10
62-63 Tor	58	12	21	33	4
63-64 Tor-NYR	63	12	16	28	35
64-65 NYR	64	16	14	30	28
65-66 NYR	69	29	33	62	10
66-67 NYR	67	20	24	44	6
67-68 NYR	74	28	30	58	20
68-69 NYR	71	31	25	56	14
69-70 NYR	68	18	19	37	8
70-71 NYR	78	21	25	46	10
71-72 Minn	72	15	19	34	6
72-73 Minn	66	5	13	18	0
73-74 LA	78	20	30	50	12
74-75 LA	80	31	41	72	19
75-76 LA	77	13	42	55	14
76-77 Edm (WHA)	13	3	2	5	0
NHL Totals	1128	307	419	726	211
WHA Totals	13	3	2	5	0
NHL Playoff Totals	84	16	18	34	24

NEWBERRY, John 6-0 190 C
B. Port Alberni, B.C., Apr. 8, 1962

Season Team	GP	G	A	Pts.	PIM
83-84 Mont	3	0	0	0	0
84-85 Mont	16	0	4	4	6
85-86 Hart	3	0	0	0	0
Totals	22	0	4	4	6
Playoff Totals	2	0	0	0	0

NEWELL, Gordon Richard (Rick) 5-11 180 D
B. Winnipeg, Man., Feb. 18, 1948

Season Team	GP	G	A	Pts.	PIM
72-73 Det	3	0	0	0	0
73-74 Det	4	0	0	0	0
74-75 Phoe (WHA)	25	0	4	4	39
NHL Totals	7	0	0	0	0
WHA Totals	25	0	4	4	39
WHA Playoff Totals	5	0	1	1	2

NEWMAN, Daniel Kenneth 6-1 195 LW
B. Windsor, Ont., Jan. 26, 1952

Season Team	GP	G	A	Pts.	PIM
76-77 NYR	41	9	8	17	37
77-78 NYR	59	5	13	18	22
78-79 Mont	16	0	2	2	4
79-80 Edm	10	3	1	4	0
Totals	126	17	24	41	63
Playoff Totals	3	0	0	0	4

NEWMAN, John D
1930-31 Det 8 1 1 2 0

NICHOLLS, Bernie Irvine 6-0 185 C
B. Haliburton, Ont., June 24, 1961

Season Team	GP	G	A	Pts.	PIM
81-82 LA	22	14	18	32	27
82-83 LA	71	28	22	50	124
83-84 LA	78	41	54	95	83
84-85 LA	80	46	54	100	76
85-86 LA	80	36	61	97	78
86-87 LA	80	33	48	81	101
87-88 LA	65	32	46	78	114
88-89 LA	79	70	80	150	96
89-90 LA-NYR	79	39	73	112	86
90-91 NYR	71	25	48	73	96
91-92 NYR-Edm	50	20	29	49	40
Totals	755	384	533	917	921
Playoff Totals	65	35	40	75	110

NICHOLSON, Allan Douglas 6-1 180 LW
B. Estevan, Sask., Apr. 26, 1936

Season Team	GP	G	A	Pts.	PIM
55-56 Bos	14	0	0	0	4
56-57 Bos	5	0	1	1	0
Totals	19	0	1	1	4

NICHOLSON, Edward George 5-7 171 D
B. Portsmouth, Ont., Sept. 9, 1923

Season Team	GP	G	A	Pts.	PIM
47-48 Det	1	0	0	0	0

NICHOLSON, Graeme Butte 6-0 185 D
B. North Bay, Ont., Jan. 13, 1958

Season Team	GP	G	A	Pts.	PIM
78-79 Bos	1	0	0	0	0
81-82 Col	41	2	7	9	51
82-83 NYR	10	0	0	0	9
Totals	52	2	7	9	60

NICHOLSON, John Ivan 5-9 170 LW
B. Charlottetown, P.E.I., Sept. 9, 1914

Season Team	GP	G	A	Pts.	PIM
37-38 Chi	2	1	0	1	0

NICHOLSON, Neil Andrews 5-11 180 D
B. Saint John, N.B., Sept. 12, 1949

Season Team	GP	G	A	Pts.	PIM
72-73 NYI	30	3	1	4	23
73-74 NYI	8	0	0	0	0
77-78 NYI	1	0	0	0	0
Totals	39	3	1	4	23
Playoff Totals	2	0	0	0	0

NICHOLSON, Paul 6-0 190 LW
B. London, Ont., Feb. 16, 1954

Season Team	GP	G	A	Pts.	PIM
74-75 Wash	39	4	5	9	7
75-76 Wash	14	0	2	2	9
76-77 Wash	9	0	1	1	2
Totals	62	4	8	12	18

NIEDERMAYER, Scott 6-0 195 D
B. Edmonton, Alta., Aug. 31, 1973

Season Team	GP	G	A	Pts.	PIM
91-92 NJ	4	0	1	1	2

NIEKAMP, James Lawrence 6-0 170 D
B. Detroit, Mich., Mar. 11, 1946

Season Team	GP	G	A	Pts.	PIM
70-71 Det	24	0	2	2	27
71-72 Det	5	0	0	0	0
72-73 LA (WHA)	78	7	22	29	155
73-74 LA (WHA)	76	2	19	21	95
74-75 Phoe (WHA)	71	2	26	28	66
75-76 Phoe (WHA)	79	4	14	18	77
76-77 Phoe (WHA)	79	1	15	16	91
NHL Totals	29	0	2	2	27
WHA Totals	383	16	96	112	484
WHA Playoff Totals	11	3	1	4	10

NIENHUIS, Kraig 6-2 205 LW
B. Sarnia, Ont., May 9, 1961

Season Team	GP	G	A	Pts.	PIM
85-86 Bos	70	16	14	30	37
86-87 Bos	16	4	2	6	2
87-88 Bos	1	0	0	0	0
Totals	87	20	16	36	39
Playoff Totals	2	0	0	0	14

NIEUWENDYK, Joe 6-1 195 C
B. Oshawa, Ont., Sept. 10, 1966

Season Team	GP	G	A	Pts.	PIM
86-87 Calg	9	5	1	6	0
87-88 Calg	75	51	41	92	23
88-89 Calg	77	51	31	82	40
89-90 Calg	79	45	50	95	40
90-91 Calg	79	45	40	85	36
91-92 Calg	69	22	34	56	55
Totals	388	219	197	416	194
Playoff Totals	49	23	17	40	25

NIGHBOR, Frank (Dutch) C
B. Pembroke, Ont., Jan. 26, 1893

Season Team	GP	G	A	Pts.	PIM
17-18 Ott	9	11	0	11	3
18-19 Ott	18	18	4	22	27
19-20 Ott	23	26	7	33	18
20-21 Ott	24	18	3	21	10
21-22 Ott	20	7	9	16	16
22-23 Ott	22	11	5	16	16
23-24 Ott	20	10	3	13	14
24-25 Ott	26	5	2	7	18
25-26 Ott	35	12	13	25	40
26-27 Ott	38	6	6	12	26
27-28 Ott	42	8	5	13	46
28-29 Ott	30	1	4	5	22
29-30 Ott-Tor	41	2	0	2	10
Totals	348	135	61	196	266
Playoff Totals	36	11	9	20	27

NIGRO, Frank 5-9 180 C
B. Richmond Hill, Ont., Feb. 11, 1960

Season Team	GP	G	A	Pts.	PIM
82-83 Tor	51	6	15	21	23
83-84 Tor	17	2	3	5	16
Totals	68	8	18	26	39
Playoff Totals	3	0	0	0	2

NILAN, Christopher John 6-0 205 RW
B. Boston, Mass., Feb. 9, 1958

Season Team	GP	G	A	Pts.	PIM
79-80 Mont	15	0	2	2	50
80-81 Mont	57	7	8	15	262
81-82 Mont	49	7	4	11	204
82-83 Mont	66	6	8	14	213

Season Team	GP	G	A	Pts.	PIM
NILAN, Christopher John *(Continued)*					
83-84 Mont	76	16	10	26	338
84-85 Mont	77	21	16	37	358
85-86 Mont	72	19	15	34	274
86-87 Mont	44	4	16	20	266
87-88 Mont-NYR	72	10	10	20	305
88-89 NYR	38	7	7	14	177
89-90 NYR	25	1	2	3	59
90-91 Bos	41	6	9	15	277
91-92 Bos-Mont	56	6	8	14	260
Totals	688	110	115	225	3043
Playoff Tot.	111	8	9	17	541
NILL, James Edward 6-0 185 RW					
B. Hanna, Alta., Apr. 11, 1958					
81-82 StL-Van	69	10	14	24	132
82-83 Van	65	7	15	22	136
83-84 Van-Bos	78	12	8	20	159
84-85 Bos-Winn	69	9	17	26	100
85-86 Winn	61	6	8	14	75
86-87 Winn	36	3	4	7	52
87-88 Winn-Det	60	3	12	15	99
88-89 Det	71	8	7	15	83
89-90 Det	15	0	2	2	18
Totals	524	58	87	145	854
Playoff Totals	59	10	5	15	203
NILSSON, Kent 6-1 195 C					
B. Nynasham, Sweden, Aug. 31, 1956					
77-78 Winn (WHA)	80	42	65	107	8
78-79 Winn (WHA)	78	39	68	107	8
79-80 Atl	80	40	53	93	10
80-81 Calg	80	49	82	131	26
81-82 Calg	41	26	29	55	8
82-83 Calg	80	46	58	104	10
83-84 Calg	67	31	49	80	22
84-85 Calg	77	37	62	99	14
85-86 Minn	61	16	44	60	10
86-87 Minn-Edm	61	18	45	63	16
NHL Totals	547	263	422	685	116
WHA Totals	158	81	133	214	16
NHL Playoff Totals	59	11	41	52	14
WHA Playoff Totals	19	5	19	24	14
NILSSON, Ulf Gosta 5-11 175 C					
B. Nynasham, Sweden, May 11, 1950					
74-75 Winn (WHA)	78	26	94	120	79
75-76 Winn (WHA)	78	38	76	114	84
76-77 Winn (WHA)	71	39	85	124	89
77-78 Winn (WHA)	73	37	89	126	89
78-79 NYR	59	27	39	66	21
79-80 NYR	50	14	44	58	20
80-81 NYR	51	14	25	39	42
82-83 NYR	10	2	4	6	2
NHL Totals	170	57	112	169	85
WHA Totals	300	140	344	484	341
NHL Playoff Totals	25	8	14	22	27
WHA Playoff Totals	42	14	53	67	51
NISTICO, Louis Charles 5-7 170 C					
B. Thunder Bay, Ont., Jan. 25, 1953					
73-74 Tor (WHA)	13	1	3	4	14
74-75 Tor (WHA)	29	11	11	22	75
75-76 Tor (WHA)	65	12	22	34	120
76-77 Birm (WHA)	79	20	36	56	166
77-78 Col	3	0	0	0	0
NHL Totals	3	0	0	0	0
WHA Totals	186	44	72	116	375
WHA Playoff Totals	6	6	1	7	19
NOBLE, Reginald (Reg) 5-8 180 LW					
B. Collingwood, Ont., June 23, 1895					
17-18 Tor	20	28	0	28	23
18-19 Tor	17	11	3	14	35
19-20 Tor	24	24	7	31	51
20-21 Tor	24	20	6	26	54
21-22 Tor	24	17	8	25	10
22-23 Tor	24	12	10	22	41
23-24 Tor	23	12	3	15	23
24-25 Tor-Mont M	30	8	6	14	62
25-26 Mont M	30	9	9	18	36
26-27 Mont M	44	3	3	6	12
27-28 Det	44	6	8	14	63
28-29 Det	44	6	4	10	52
29-30 Det	43	6	4	10	72
30-31 Det	44	2	5	7	42
31-32 Det	48	3	3	6	72

Season Team	GP	G	A	Pts.	PIM
NOBLE, Reginald (Reg) *(Continued)*					
32-33 Det-Mont M	32	0	0	0	22
Totals	515	167	79	246	670
Playoff Totals	32	4	5	9	39
NOEL, Claude 5-11 165 C					
B. Kirkland Lake, Ont., Oct. 31, 1955					
79-80 Wash	7	0	0	0	0
NOLAN, Owen 6-1 194 RW					
B. Belfast, N. Ireland, Feb. 12, 1972					
90-91 Que	59	3	10	13	109
91-92 Que	75	42	31	73	181
Totals	134	45	41	86	290
NOLAN, Patrick F					
21-22 Tor	2	0	0	0	0
NOLAN, Theodore John (Ted) 6-0 185 C					
B. Sault Ste. Marie, Ont., Apr. 7, 1958					
81-82 Det	41	4	13	17	45
83-84 Det	19	1	2	3	26
85-86 Pitt	18	1	1	2	34
Totals	78	6	16	22	105
NOLET, Simon Laurent 5-9 185 RW					
B. St. Odilon, Que., Nov. 23, 1941					
67-68 Phil	4	0	0	0	2
68-69 Phil	35	4	10	14	8
69-70 Phil	56	22	22	44	36
70-71 Phil	74	9	19	28	42
71-72 Phil	67	23	20	43	22
72-73 Phil	70	16	20	36	6
73-74 Phil	52	19	17	36	13
74-75 KC	72	26	32	58	30
75-76 KC-Pitt	80	19	23	42	18
76-77 Col	52	12	19	31	10
Totals	562	150	182	332	187
Playoff Totals	34	6	3	9	8
NOONAN, Brian 6-1 192 RW					
B. Boston, Mass., May 29, 1965					
87-88 Chi	77	10	20	30	44
88-89 Chi	45	4	12	16	28
89-90 Chi	8	0	2	2	6
90-91 Chi	7	0	4	4	2
91-92 Chi	65	19	12	31	81
Totals	202	33	50	83	81
Playoff Totals	22	6	9	15	34
NORDMARK, Robert 6-1 200 D					
B. Lulea, Sweden, Aug. 20, 1962					
87-88 StL	67	3	18	21	60
88-89 Van	80	6	35	41	97
89-90 Van	44	2	11	13	34
90-91 Van	45	2	6	8	63
Totals	236	13	70	83	254
Playoff Totals	7	3	2	5	8
NORIS, Joseph S. 6-0 185 D					
B. Denver, Colo., Oct. 26, 1951					
71-72 Pitt	35	2	5	7	20
72-73 StL	2	0	0	0	0
73-74 Buf	18	0	0	0	2
75-76 SD (WHA)	80	28	40	68	24
76-77 SD (WHA)	73	35	57	92	30
77-78 Birm (WHA)	45	9	19	28	6
NHL Totals	55	2	5	7	22
WHA Totals	198	72	116	188	60
WHA Playoff Totals	18	4	5	9	12
NORRISH, Rod 5-10 185 LW					
B. Saskatoon, Sask., Nov. 27, 1951					
73-74 Minn	9	2	1	3	0
74-75 Minn	12	1	2	3	2
Totals	21	3	3	6	2
NORTHCOTT, Lawrence (Baldy) 6-0 184 LW					
B. Calgary, Alta., Sept. 7, 1908					
28-29 Mont M	6	0	0	0	0
29-30 Mont M	41	10	1	11	6
30-31 Mont M	22	7	3	10	15
31-32 Mont M	47	19	6	25	33
32-33 Mont M	47	22	21	43	30
33-34 Mont M	47	20	13	33	27
34-35 Mont M	47	9	14	23	44
35-36 Mont M	48	15	21	36	41
36-37 Mont M	48	15	14	29	18
37-38 Mont M	47	11	12	23	50
38-39 Chi	46	5	7	12	9
Totals	446	133	112	245	273
Playoff Totals	31	8	5	13	14

Season Team	GP	G	A	Pts.	PIM
NORTON, Jeff 6-2 195 D					
B. Acton, Mass., Nov. 25, 1965					
87-88 NYI	15	1	6	7	14
88-89 NYI	69	1	30	31	74
89-90 NYI	60	4	49	53	65
90-91 NYI	44	3	25	28	16
91-92 NYI	28	1	18	19	18
Totals	216	10	128	138	187
Playoff Totals	7	1	5	6	30
NORWICH, Craig Richard 5-11 175 D					
B. New York, N.Y., Dec. 15, 1955					
77-78 Cin (WHA)	65	7	23	30	48
78-79 Cin (WHA)	80	6	51	57	73
79-80 Winn	70	10	35	45	36
80-81 StL-Col	34	7	23	30	24
NHL Totals	104	17	58	75	60
WHA Totals	145	13	74	87	121
WHA Playoff Totals	3	0	1	1	4
NORWOOD, Lee Charles 6-1 198 D					
B. Oakland, Cal., Feb. 2, 1960					
80-81 Que	11	1	1	2	9
81-82 Que-Wash	28	7	10	17	127
82-83 Wash	8	0	1	1	14
85-86 StL	71	5	24	29	134
86-87 Det	57	6	21	27	163
87-88 Det	51	9	22	31	131
88-89 Det	66	10	32	42	100
89-90 Det	64	8	14	22	95
90-91 Det-NJ	49	6	9	15	137
91-92 Hart-StL	50	3	11	14	110
Totals	455	55	145	200	1020
Playoff Totals	65	6	22	28	171
NOVY, Milan 5-10 196 C					
B. Kladno, Czechoslovakia, Sept. 23, 1951					
82-83 Wash	73	18	30	48	16
Playoff Totals	2	0	0	0	0
NOWAK, Henry Stanley (Hank) 6-1 195 LW					
B. Oshawa, Ont., Nov. 24, 1950					
73-74 Pitt	13	0	0	0	11
74-75 Det-Bos	77	12	21	33	95
75-76 Bos	66	7	3	10	41
76-77 Bos	24	7	5	12	14
Totals	180	26	29	55	161
Playoff Totals	13	1	0	1	8
NUMMINEN, Teppo 6-1 190 D					
B. Tampere, Finland, July 3, 1968					
88-89 Winn	69	1	14	15	36
89-90 Winn	79	11	32	43	20
90-91 Winn	80	8	25	33	28
91-92 Winn	80	5	34	39	32
Totals	308	25	105	130	116
Playoff Totals	14	1	2	3	10
NYKOLUK, Michael 5-11 212 RW					
B. Toronto, Ont., Dec. 11, 1934					
56-57 Tor	32	3	1	4	20
NYLUND, Gary 6-4 210 D					
B. Surrey, B.C., Oct. 28, 1963					
82-83 Tor	16	0	3	3	16
83-84 Tor	47	2	14	16	103
84-85 Tor	76	3	17	20	99
85-86 Tor	79	2	16	18	180
86-87 Chi	80	7	20	27	190
87-88 Chi	76	4	15	19	208
88-89 Chi-NYI	76	7	10	17	137
89-90 NYI	64	4	21	25	144
90-91 NYI	72	2	21	23	105
91-92 NYI	7	0	1	1	10
Totals	586	31	138	169	1192
Playoff Totals	24	0	6	6	63
NYROP, William D. 6-2 205 D					
B. Washington, D.C., July 23, 1952					
75-76 Mont	19	0	3	3	8
76-77 Mont	74	3	19	22	21
77-78 Mont	72	5	21	26	37
81-82 Minn	42	4	8	12	35
Totals	207	12	51	63	101
Playoff Totals	35	1	7	8	22
NYSTROM, Thore Robert (Bobby) 6-1 200 RW					
B. Stockholm, Sweden, Oct. 10, 1952					
72-73 NYI	11	1	1	2	10
73-74 NYI	77	21	20	41	118
74-75 NYI	76	27	28	55	122
75-76 NYI	80	23	25	48	106
76-77 NYI	80	29	27	56	91

Season Team	GP	G	A	Pts.	PIM

NYSTROM, Thore Robert (Bobby)
(Continued)

Season Team	GP	G	A	Pts.	PIM
77-78 NYI	80	30	29	59	94
78-79 NYI	78	19	20	39	113
79-80 NYI	67	21	18	39	94
80-81 NYI	79	14	30	44	145
81-82 NYI	74	22	25	47	103
82-83 NYI	74	10	20	30	98
83-84 NYI	74	15	29	44	80
84-85 NYI	36	2	5	7	58
85-86 NYI	14	1	1	2	16
Totals	900	235	278	513	1248
Playoff Tot.	157	39	44	83	236

OATES, Adam 5-11 189 C
B. Weston, Ont., Aug. 27, 1962

Season Team	GP	G	A	Pts.	PIM
85-86 Det	38	9	11	20	10
86-87 Det	76	15	32	47	21
87-88 Det	63	14	40	54	20
88-89 Det	69	16	62	78	14
89-90 StL	80	23	79	102	30
90-91 StL	61	25	90	115	29
91-92 StL-Bos	80	20	79	99	22
Totals	467	122	393	515	146
Playoff Totals	78	26	66	92	32

OATMAN, Warren Russell 5-10 195 F
B. Tilsonburg, Ont., Feb. 19, 1905

Season Team	GP	G	A	Pts.	PIM
26-27 Det-Mont M	42	11	4	15	42
27-28 Mont M	44	7	4	11	36
28-29 Mont M-NYR	38	2	1	3	22
Totals	124	20	9	29	100
Playoff Totals	17	1	0	1	18

O'BRIEN, Dennis Francis 6-0 195 D
B. Port Hope, Ont., June 10, 1949

Season Team	GP	G	A	Pts.	PIM
70-71 Minn	27	3	2	5	29
71-72 Minn	70	3	6	9	108
72-73 Minn	74	3	11	14	75
73-74 Minn	77	5	12	17	166
74-75 Minn	56	6	10	16	125
75-76 Minn	78	1	14	15	187
76-77 Minn	75	6	18	24	114
77-78 Minn-Col-Clev-Bos	68	2	10	12	77
78-79 Bos	64	2	8	10	107
79-80 Bos	3	0	0	0	2
Totals	592	31	91	122	990
Playoff Totals	34	1	2	3	101

O'BRIEN, Ellard John (Obie) 6-3 183 LW
B. St. Catherines, Ont., May 27, 1930

Season Team	GP	G	A	Pts.	PIM
55-56 Bos	2	0	0	0	0

O'CALLAHAN, Jack 6-1 190 D
B. Charlestown, Mass., July 24, 1957

Season Team	GP	G	A	Pts.	PIM
82-83 Chi	39	0	11	11	46
83-84 Chi	70	4	13	17	67
84-85 Chi	66	6	8	14	105
85-86 Chi	80	4	19	23	116
86-87 Chi	48	1	13	14	59
87-88 NJ	50	7	19	26	97
88-89 NJ	36	5	21	26	51
Totals	389	27	104	131	541
Playoff Totals	32	4	11	15	41

O'CONNELL, Michael Thomas 5-9 180 D
B. Chicago, Ill., Nov. 25, 1955

Season Team	GP	G	A	Pts.	PIM
77-78 Chi	6	1	1	2	2
78-79 Chi	48	4	22	26	20
79-80 Chi	78	8	22	30	52
80-81 Chi-Bos	82	15	38	53	74
81-82 Bos	80	5	34	39	75
82-83 Bos	80	14	39	53	42
83-84 Bos	75	18	42	60	42
84-85 Bos	78	15	40	55	64
85-86 Bos-Det	76	9	28	37	63
86-87 Det	77	5	26	31	70
87-88 Det	48	6	13	19	38
88-89 Det	66	1	15	16	41
89-90 Det	66	4	14	18	22
Totals	860	105	334	439	605
Playoff Totals	82	8	24	32	64

O'CONNOR, Herbert William (Buddy) 5-7 145 F
B. Montreal, Que., June 21, 1916

Season Team	GP	G	A	Pts.	PIM
41-42 Mont	36	9	16	25	4
42-43 Mont	50	15	43	58	2
43-44 Mont	44	12	42	54	6
44-45 Mont	50	21	23	44	2
45-46 Mont	45	11	11	22	2
46-47 Mont	46	10	20	30	6
47-48 NYR	60	24	36	60	8
48-49 NYR	46	11	24	35	0

O'CONNOR, Herbert William (Buddy)
(Continued)

Season Team	GP	G	A	Pts.	PIM
49-50 NYR	66	11	22	33	4
50-51 NYR	66	16	20	36	0
Totals	509	140	257	397	34
Playoff Totals	53	15	21	36	6

O'CONNOR, Myles 5-11 165 D
B. Calgary, Alta., Apr. 2, 1967

Season Team	GP	G	A	Pts.	PIM
90-91 NJ	22	3	1	4	41
91-92 NJ	9	0	2	2	13
Totals	31	3	3	6	54

ODDLEIFSON, Christopher Roy 6-2 185 C
B. Brandon, Man., Sept. 7, 1950

Season Team	GP	G	A	Pts.	PIM
72-73 Bos	6	0	0	0	0
73-74 Bos-Van	70	13	16	29	44
74-75 Van	60	16	35	51	54
75-76 Van	80	16	46	62	88
76-77 Van	80	14	26	40	81
77-78 Van	78	17	22	39	64
78-79 Van	67	11	26	37	51
79-80 Van	75	8	20	28	76
80-81 Van	8	0	0	0	6
Totals	524	95	191	286	464
Playoff Totals	14	1	6	7	8

ODELEIN, Lyle 6-1 206 D
B. Quill Lake, Sask., July 21, 1968

Season Team	GP	G	A	Pts.	PIM
89-90 Mont	8	0	2	2	33
90-91 Mont	52	0	2	2	259
91-92 Mont	71	1	7	8	212
Totals	131	1	11	12	504
Playoff Totals	19	0	0	0	65

ODELEIN, Selmar 6-0 205 D
B. Quill Lake, Sask., Apr. 11, 1966

Season Team	GP	G	A	Pts.	PIM
85-86 Edm	4	0	0	0	0
87-88 Edm	12	0	2	2	33
88-89 Edm	2	0	0	0	2
Totals	18	0	2	2	35

ODGERS, Jeff 6-0 195 LW
B. Spy Hill, Sask., May 31, 1969

Season Team	GP	G	A	Pts.	PIM
91-92 SJ	61	7	4	11	217

ODJICK, Gino 6-2 220 LW
B. Maniwaki, Que., Sept. 7, 1970

Season Team	GP	G	A	Pts.	PIM
90-91 Van	45	7	1	8	296
91-92 Van	65	4	6	10	348
Totals	110	11	7	18	644

O'DONNELL, Frederick James 5-10 175 RW
B. Kingston, Ont., Dec. 6, 1949

Season Team	GP	G	A	Pts.	PIM
72-73 Bos	72	10	4	14	55
73-74 Bos	43	5	7	12	43
74-75 NE (WHA)	76	21	15	36	84
75-76 NE (WHA)	79	11	11	22	81
NHL Totals	115	15	11	26	98
WHA Totals	155	32	26	58	165
NHL Playoff Totals	5	0	1	1	5
WHA Playoff Totals	17	2	5	7	20

O'DONOGHUE, Donald Francis 5-10 180 RW
B. Kingston, Ont., Sept. 27, 1949

Season Team	GP	G	A	Pts.	PIM
69-70 Oak	68	5	6	11	21
70-71 Cal	43	11	9	20	10
71-72 Cal	14	2	2	4	4
72-73 Phil (WHA)	74	16	23	39	43
73-74 Van (WHA)	49	8	6	14	20
74-75 Van (WHA)	4	0	0	0	0
75-76 Cin (WHA)	20	1	8	9	0
NHL Totals	125	18	17	35	35
WHA Totals	147	25	37	62	63
NHL Playoff Totals	3	0	0	0	0
WHA Playoff Totals	4	0	1	1	0

ODROWSKI, Gerald Bernard (Gerry) 5-11 190 D
B. Trout Creek, Ont., Oct. 4, 1938

Season Team	GP	G	A	Pts.	PIM
60-61 Det	68	1	4	5	45
61-62 Det	69	1	6	7	24
62-63 Det	1	0	0	0	0
67-68 Oak	42	4	6	10	10
68-69 Oak	74	5	1	6	24
71-72 StL	55	1	2	3	8
72-73 LA (WHA)	78	6	31	37	89
73-74 LA (WHA)	77	4	32	36	48
74-75 Phoe (WHA)	77	5	38	43	77

ODROWSKI, Gerald Bernard (Gerry)
(Continued)

Season Team	GP	G	A	Pts.	PIM
75-76 Minn-Winn (WHA)	50	1	13	14	16
NHL Totals	309	12	19	31	111
WHA Totals	282	16	114	130	230
NHL Playoff Totals	30	0	1	1	16
WHA Playoff Totals	11	1	4	5	6

O'DWYER, Bill 6-0 190 C
B. Boston, Mass., Jan. 25, 1960

Season Team	GP	G	A	Pts.	PIM
83-84 LA	5	0	0	0	0
84-85 LA	13	1	0	1	15
87-88 Bos	77	7	10	17	83
88-89 Bos	19	1	2	3	8
89-90 Bos	6	0	1	1	7
Totals	126	11	14	25	115
Playoff Totals	10	0	0	0	2

O'FLAHERTY, Gerard Joseph (Gerry) 5-10 182 LW
B. Pittsburgh, Pa., Aug. 31, 1950

Season Team	GP	G	A	Pts.	PIM
71-72 Tor	2	0	0	0	0
72-73 Van	78	13	17	30	29
73-74 Van	78	22	20	42	18
74-75 Van	80	25	17	42	37
75-76 Van	68	20	18	38	47
76-77 Van	72	12	12	24	20
77-78 Van	59	6	11	17	15
78-79 Atl	1	1	0	1	2
Totals	438	99	95	194	168
Playoff Totals	7	2	2	4	6

O'FLAHERTY, John Benedict (Peanuts) 5-7 154 RW
B. Toronto, Ont., Apr. 10, 1918

Season Team	GP	G	A	Pts.	PIM
40-41 NYA	10	4	0	4	0
41-42 Brk	11	1	1	2	0
Totals	21	5	1	6	0

OGLIVIE, Brian Hugh 5-11 186 C
B. Stettler, Alta., Jan. 30, 1952

Season Team	GP	G	A	Pts.	PIM
72-73 Chi	12	1	2	3	18
74-75 StL	20	5	5	10	4
75-76 StL	9	2	1	3	2
76-77 StL	3	0	0	0	0
77-78 StL	32	6	8	14	12
78-79 StL	14	1	5	6	7
Totals	90	15	21	36	43

O'GRADY, George F
Season Team	GP	G	A	Pts.	PIM
17-18 Mont W	4	0	0	0	0

OGRODNICK, John Alexander 6-0 204 LW
B. Ottawa, Ont., June 20, 1959

Season Team	GP	G	A	Pts.	PIM
79-80 Det	41	8	24	32	8
80-81 Det	80	35	35	70	14
81-82 Det	80	28	26	54	28
82-83 Det	80	41	44	85	30
83-84 Det	64	42	36	78	14
84-85 Det	79	55	50	105	30
85-86 Det	76	38	32	70	18
86-87 Det-Que	71	23	44	67	10
87-88 NYR	64	22	32	54	16
88-89 NYR	60	13	29	42	14
89-90 NYR	80	43	31	74	44
90-91 NYR	79	31	23	54	10
91-92 NYR	55	17	13	30	22
Totals	909	396	419	815	258
Playoff Totals	40	18	8	26	6

OJANEN, Janne 6-2 200 C
B. Tampere, Finland, Apr. 9, 1968

Season Team	GP	G	A	Pts.	PIM
88-89 NJ	3	0	1	1	2
89-90 NJ	64	17	13	30	12
91-92 NJ	0	0	0	0	0
Totals	67	17	14	31	14
Playoff Totals	3	0	2	2	0

OKERLUND, Todd 5-11 200 RW
B. Burnsville, Minn., Sept. 6, 1964

Season Team	GP	G	A	Pts.	PIM
87-88 NYI	4	0	0	0	2

OLAUSSON, Fredrik 6-2 200 D
B. Vaxsjo, Sweden, Oct. 5, 1966

Season Team	GP	G	A	Pts.	PIM
86-87 Winn	72	7	29	36	24
87-88 Winn	38	5	10	15	18
88-89 Winn	75	15	47	62	32
89-90 Winn	77	9	46	55	32
90-91 Winn	71	12	29	41	24
91-92 Winn	77	20	42	62	34
Totals	410	68	203	271	164
Playoff Totals	29	4	11	15	10

OLCZYK, Ed *6-1 200 C*

B. Chicago, Ill., Aug. 16, 1966

Season	Team	GP	G	A	Pts.	PIM
84-85	Chi	70	20	30	50	67
85-86	Chi	79	29	50	79	47
86-87	Chi	79	16	35	51	119
87-88	Tor	80	42	33	75	55
88-89	Tor	80	38	52	90	75
89-90	Tor	79	32	56	88	78
90-91	Tor-Winn	79	30	41	71	82
91-92	Winn	64	32	33	65	67
Totals		610	239	330	569	590
Playoff Totals		39	15	13	28	35

OLIVER, Harold (Harry) *5-8 155 RW*

B. Selkirk, Man., Oct. 26, 1898

Season	Team	GP	G	A	Pts.	PIM
26-27	Bos	44	18	6	24	17
27-28	Bos	44	13	5	18	20
28-29	Bos	43	17	6	23	24
29-30	Bos	42	16	5	21	12
30-31	Bos	43	16	14	30	18
31-32	Bos	44	13	7	20	22
32-33	Bos	47	11	7	18	10
33-34	Bos	48	5	9	14	6
34-35	NYA	48	7	9	16	4
35-36	NYA	58	9	16	25	12
36-37	NYA	22	2	1	3	2
Totals		473	127	85	212	147
Playoff Totals		35	10	6	16	22

OLIVER, Murray Clifford *5-9 170 C*

B. Hamilton, Ont., Nov. 14, 1937

Season	Team	GP	G	A	Pts.	PIM
57-58	Det	1	0	1	1	0
59-60	Det	54	20	19	39	6
60-61	Det-Bos	70	17	22	39	16
61-62	Bos	70	17	29	46	21
62-63	Bos	65	22	40	62	38
63-64	Bos	70	24	44	68	41
64-65	Bos	65	20	23	43	76
65-66	Bos	70	18	42	60	30
66-67	Bos	65	9	26	35	16
67-68	Tor	74	16	21	37	18
68-69	Tor	76	14	36	50	16
69-70	Tor	76	14	33	47	16
70-71	Minn	61	9	23	32	8
71-72	Minn	77	27	29	56	16
72-73	Minn	75	11	31	42	10
73-74	Minn	78	17	20	37	4
74-75	Minn	80	19	15	34	24
Totals		1127	274	454	728	356
Playoff Totals		35	9	16	25	10

OLMSTEAD, Murray Bert (Bert) *6-2 183 LW*

B. Scepter, Sask., Sept. 4, 1926

Season	Team	GP	G	A	Pts.	PIM
48-49	Chi	9	0	2	2	4
49-50	Chi	70	20	29	49	40
50-51	Chi-Mont	54	18	23	41	40
51-52	Mont	69	7	28	35	49
52-53	Mont	69	17	28	45	83
53-54	Mont	70	15	37	52	85
54-55	Mont	70	10	48	58	103
55-56	Mont	70	14	56	70	94
56-57	Mont	64	15	33	48	74
57-58	Mont	57	9	28	37	71
58-59	Tor	70	10	31	41	74
59-60	Tor	53	15	21	36	63
60-61	Tor	67	18	34	52	84
61-62	Tor	56	13	23	36	10
Totals		848	181	421	602	874
Playoff Totals		115	16	42	58	101

OLSEN, Darryl *6-0 180 D*

B. Calgary, Alta., Oct. 7, 1966

Season	Team	GP	G	A	Pts.	PIM
91-92	Calg	1	0	0	0	0

OLSON, Dennis *6-0 182 C*

B. Kenora, Ont., Nov. 9, 1934

Season	Team	GP	G	A	Pts.	PIM
57-58	Det	4	0	0	0	0

O'NEIL, Paul Joseph *6-1 177 C*

B. Charlestown, Mass., Aug. 24, 1953

Season	Team	GP	G	A	Pts.	PIM
73-74	Van	5	0	0	0	0
75-76	Bos	1	0	0	0	0
78-79	Birm (WHA)	1	0	0	0	0
NHL Totals		6	0	0	0	0
WHA Totals		1	0	0	0	0

O'NEILL, James Beaton (Peggy) *5-8 160 C*

B. Semans, Sask., Apr. 3, 1913

Season	Team	GP	G	A	Pts.	PIM
33-34	Bos	25	2	2	4	15
34-35	Bos	48	2	11	13	35
35-36	Bos	48	2	11	13	49
36-37	Bos	20	0	2	2	6

O'NEILL, James Beaton (Peggy) *(Continued)*

Season	Team	GP	G	A	Pts.	PIM
40-41	Mont	12	0	3	3	0
41-42	Mont	12	0	1	1	4
Totals		165	6	30	36	109
Playoff Totals		11	1	1	2	13

O'NEILL, Thomas (Windy) *5-10 155 RW*

B. Deseronto, Ont., Sept. 28, 1923

Season	Team	GP	G	A	Pts.	PIM
43-44	Tor	33	8	7	15	29
44-45	Tor	33	2	5	7	24
Totals		66	10	12	22	53
Playoff Totals		4	0	0	0	6

ORBAN, William Terrence *6-0 175 LW*

B. Regina, Sask., Feb. 20, 1944

Season	Team	GP	G	A	Pts.	PIM
67-68	Chi	39	3	2	5	17
68-69	Chi-Minn	66	5	11	16	43
69-70	Minn	9	0	2	2	7
Totals		114	8	15	23	67
Playoff Totals		3	0	0	0	0

O'REE, William Eldon (Willie) *5-10 175 LW*

B. Fredericton, N.B., Oct. 15, 1935

Season	Team	GP	G	A	Pts.	PIM
57-58	Bos	2	0	0	0	0
60-61	Bos	43	4	10	14	26
Totals		45	4	10	14	26

O'REGAN, Thomas Patrick *5-10 180 C*

B. Cambridge, Mass., Dec. 29, 1961

Season	Team	GP	G	A	Pts.	PIM
83-84	Pitt	51	4	10	14	8
84-85	Det	1	0	0	0	0
85-86	Det	9	1	2	3	2
Totals		61	5	12	17	10

O'REILLY, Joseph James Terence (Terry) *6-1 200 RW*

B. Niagara Falls, Ont., June 7, 1951

Season	Team	GP	G	A	Pts.	PIM
71-72	Bos	1	1	0	1	0
72-73	Bos	72	5	22	27	109
73-74	Bos	76	11	24	35	94
74-75	Bos	68	15	20	35	146
75-76	Bos	80	23	27	50	150
76-77	Bos	79	14	41	55	147
77-78	Bos	77	29	61	90	211
78-79	Bos	80	26	51	77	205
79-80	Bos	71	19	42	61	265
80-81	Bos	77	8	35	43	223
81-82	Bos	70	22	30	52	213
82-83	Bos	19	6	14	20	40
83-84	Bos	58	12	18	30	124
84-85	Bos	63	13	17	30	168
Totals		891	204	402	606	2095
Playoff Totals		108	25	42	67	335

ORLANDO, Gaetano (Gates) *5-8 180 C*

B. Montreal, Que., Nov. 13, 1962

Season	Team	GP	G	A	Pts.	PIM
84-85	Buf	11	3	6	9	6
85-86	Buf	60	13	12	25	29
86-87	Buf	27	2	8	10	16
Totals		98	18	26	44	51
Playoff Totals		5	0	4	4	14

ORLANDO, James V. *5-11 185 D*

B. Montreal, Que., Feb. 27, 1916

Season	Team	GP	G	A	Pts.	PIM
36-37	Det	10	0	1	1	8
37-38	Det	6	0	0	0	4
39-40	Det	48	1	3	4	54
40-41	Det	48	1	10	11	99
41-42	Det	48	1	7	8	111
42-43	Det	40	4	3	7	99
Totals		200	7	24	31	375
Playoff Totals		36	0	9	9	105

ORLESKI, David Eugene *6-3 210 LW*

B. Edmonton, Alta., Dec. 26, 1959

Season	Team	GP	G	A	Pts.	PIM
80-81	Mont	1	0	0	0	0
81-82	Mont	1	0	0	0	0
Totals		2	0	0	0	0

ORR, Robert Gordon (Bobby) *6-0 199 D*

B. Parry Sound, Ont., Mar. 20, 1948

Season	Team	GP	G	A	Pts.	PIM
66-67	Bos	61	13	28	41	102
67-68	Bos	46	11	20	31	63
68-69	Bos	67	21	43	64	133
69-70	Bos	76	33	87	120	125
70-71	Bos	78	37	102	139	91
71-72	Bos	76	37	80	117	106
72-73	Bos	63	29	72	101	99
73-74	Bos	74	32	90	122	82
74-75	Bos	80	46	89	135	101
75-76	Bos	10	5	13	18	22

ORR, Robert Gordon (Bobby) *(Continued)*

Season	Team	GP	G	A	Pts.	PIM
76-77	Chi	20	4	19	23	25
78-79	Chi	6	2	2	4	4
Totals		657	270	645	915	953
Playoff Totals		74	26	66	92	107

OSBORNE, Keith *6-1 188 RW*

B. Toronto, Ont., Apr. 2, 1969

Season	Team	GP	G	A	Pts.	PIM
89-90	StL	5	0	2	2	8

OSBORNE, Mark Anatole *6-2 205 LW*

B. Toronto, Ont., Aug. 13, 1961

Season	Team	GP	G	A	Pts.	PIM
81-82	Det	80	26	41	67	61
82-83	Det	80	19	24	43	83
83-84	NYR	73	23	28	51	88
84-85	NYR	23	4	4	8	33
85-86	NYR	62	16	24	40	80
86-87	NYR-Tor	74	22	25	47	113
87-88	Tor	79	23	37	60	102
88-89	Tor	75	16	30	46	112
89-90	Tor	78	23	50	73	91
90-91	Tor-Winn	55	11	11	22	63
91-92	Winn-Tor	54	7	13	20	73
Totals		733	190	287	477	899
Playoff Totals		43	6	13	19	71

OSBURN, Randoulf Allan (Randy) *6-0 190 LW*

B. Collingwood, Ont., Nov. 26, 1952

Season	Team	GP	G	A	Pts.	PIM
72-73	Tor	26	0	2	2	0
74-75	Phil	1	0	0	0	0
Totals		27	0	2	2	0

O'SHEA, Daniel Patrick *6-1 190 C*

B. Toronto, Ont., June 15, 1945

Season	Team	GP	G	A	Pts.	PIM
68-69	Minn	74	15	34	49	57
69-70	Minn	75	10	24	34	82
70-71	Minn-Chi	77	18	19	37	26
71-72	Chi-StL	68	9	12	21	39
72-73	StL	75	12	26	38	30
74-75	Minn (WHA)	76	16	25	41	47
NHL Totals		369	64	115	179	234
WHA Totals		76	16	25	41	47
NHL Playoff Totals		39	3	7	10	62

O'SHEA, Kevin William *6-2 205 RW*

B. Toronto, Ont., May 28, 1947

Season	Team	GP	G	A	Pts.	PIM
70-71	Buf	41	4	4	8	8
71-72	Buf-StL	56	6	9	15	46
72-73	StL	36	3	5	8	31
74-75	Minn (WHA)	68	10	10	20	42
NHL Totals		133	13	18	31	85
WHA Totals		68	10	10	20	42
NHL Playoff Totals		12	2	1	3	10

OSIECKI, Mark *6-2 200 D*

B. St. Paul, Minn., July 23, 1968

Season	Team	GP	G	A	Pts.	PIM
91-92	Calg	50	2	7	9	24

OTTO, Joel Stuart *6-4 220 C*

B. Elk River, Minn., Oct. 29, 1961

Season	Team	GP	G	A	Pts.	PIM
84-85	Calg	17	4	8	12	30
85-86	Calg	79	25	34	59	188
86-87	Calg	68	19	31	50	185
87-88	Calg	62	13	39	52	194
88-89	Calg	72	23	30	53	213
89-90	Calg	75	13	20	33	116
90-91	Calg	76	19	20	39	183
91-92	Calg	78	13	21	34	163
Totals		527	129	203	332	1272
Playoff Totals		71	19	32	51	178

OUELETTE, Adelard Edward (Eddie) *5-8 172 C*

B. Ottawa, Ont., Mar. 11, 1911

Season	Team	GP	G	A	Pts.	PIM
35-36	Chi	43	3	2	5	11
Playoff Totals		1	0	0	0	0

OUELETTE, Gerald Adrian (Gerry) *5-8 170 RW*

B. Grand Falls, N.B., Nov. 1, 1938

Season	Team	GP	G	A	Pts.	PIM
60-61	Bos	34	5	4	9	0

OWCHAR, Dennis *5-11 190 D*

B. Dryden, Ont., Mar. 28, 1953

Season	Team	GP	G	A	Pts.	PIM
74-75	Pitt	46	6	11	17	67
75-76	Pitt	54	5	12	17	19
76-77	Pitt	46	5	18	23	37
77-78	Pitt-Col	82	10	31	41	48
78-79	Col	50	3	13	16	27
79-80	Col	10	1	0	1	2
Totals		288	30	85	115	200
Playoff Totals		10	1	1	2	8

Season	Team	GP	G	A	Pts.	PIM
OWEN, George	5-11 190 D					
B. Hamilton, Ont.						
28-29	Bos	26	5	4	9	48
29-30	Bos	42	9	4	13	31
30-31	Bos	37	12	13	25	33
31-32	Bos	45	12	10	22	29
32-33	Bos	42	6	2	8	10
Totals		192	44	33	77	151
Playoff Totals		21	2	5	7	25
PACHAL, Clayton	5-10 185 LW					
B. Yorkton, Sask., Apr. 21, 1956						
76-77	Bos	1	0	0	0	12
77-78	Bos	10	0	0	0	14
78-79	Col	24	2	3	5	69
Totals		35	2	3	5	95
PADDOCK, Alvin (John)	6-3 190 RW					
B. Brandon, Man., June 9, 1954						
75-76	Wash	8	1	1	2	12
76-77	Phil	5	0	0	0	9
79-80	Phil	32	3	7	10	36
80-81	Que	32	2	5	7	25
82-83	Phil	10	2	1	3	4
Totals		87	8	14	22	86
Playoff Totals		5	2	0	2	0
PAEK, Jim	6-1 194 D					
B. Seoul, Korea, Apr. 7, 1967						
90-91	Pitt	3	0	0	0	9
91-92	Pitt	50	1	7	8	36
Totals		53	1	7	8	45
Playoff Totals		27	1	4	5	8
PAIEMENT, Joseph Wilfred Rosaire (Rosey)	5-11 170 RW					
B. Earlton, Ont., Aug. 12, 1945						
67-68	Phil	7	1	0	1	11
68-69	Phil	27	2	4	6	52
69-70	Phil	9	1	1	2	11
70-71	Van	78	34	28	62	152
71-72	Van	69	10	19	29	117
72-73	Chi (WHA)	78	33	36	69	135
73-74	Chi (WHA)	78	30	43	73	87
74-75	Chi (WHA)	78	26	48	74	97
75-76	NE (WHA)	80	28	43	71	89
76-77	NE-Ind (WHA)	80	23	27	50	103
77-78	Ind (WHA)	61	6	24	30	81
NHL Totals		190	48	52	100	343
WHA Totals		455	146	221	367	592
NHL Playoff Totals		3	3	0	3	0
WHA Playoff Totals		44	13	22	35	72
PAIEMENT, Wilfrid Jr. (Wilf)	6-1 210 RW					
B. Earlton, Ont., Oct. 16, 1955						
74-75	KC	78	26	13	39	101
75-76	KC	57	21	22	43	121
76-77	Col	78	41	40	81	101
77-78	Col	80	31	56	87	114
78-79	Col	65	24	36	60	80
79-80	Col-Tor	75	30	44	74	113
80-81	Tor	77	40	57	97	145
81-82	Tor-Que	77	25	46	71	221
82-83	Que	80	26	38	64	170
83-84	Que	80	39	37	76	121
84-85	Que-NYR	52	8	18	26	158
86-87	Buf	56	20	17	37	108
87-88	Pitt	23	2	6	8	39
Totals		946	356	458	814	1757
Playoff Totals		69	18	17	35	185
PALANGIO, Peter Albert	5-11 175 LW					
B. North Bay, Ont., Oct. 10, 1908						
26-27	Mont	6	0	0	0	0
27-28	Det	14	3	0	3	8
28-29	Mont	2	0	0	0	0
36-37	Chi	30	8	9	17	16
37-38	Chi	19	2	1	3	4
Totals		71	13	10	23	28
Playoff Totals		7	0	0	0	0
PALAZZARI, Aldo	5-7 168 RW					
B. Eveleth, Minn., July 25, 1918						
43-44	Bos-NYR	35	8	3	11	4
PALAZZARI, Douglas John	5-5 170 C					
B. Eveleth, Minn., Nov. 3, 1952						
74-75	StL	73	14	17	31	19
76-77	StL	12	1	0	1	0
77-78	StL	3	1	0	1	0
78-79	StL	20	2	3	5	4
Totals		108	18	20	38	23
Playoff Totals		2	0	0	0	0

Season	Team	GP	G	A	Pts.	PIM
PALMER, Brad Donald	6-0 185 LW					
B. Duncan, B.C., Sept. 14, 1961						
80-81	Minn	23	4	4	8	22
81-82	Minn	72	22	23	45	18
82-83	Bos	73	6	11	17	18
Totals		168	32	38	70	58
Playoff Totals		29	9	5	14	16
PALMER, Robert Hazen	6-0 190 C					
B. Detroit, Mich., Oct. 2, 1952						
73-74	Chi	1	0	0	0	0
74-75	Chi	13	0	2	2	2
75-76	Chi	2	0	1	1	0
Totals		16	0	3	3	2
PALMER, Robert Ross	5-11 190 D					
B. Sarnia, Ont., Sept. 10, 1956						
77-78	LA	48	0	3	3	27
78-79	LA	78	4	41	45	26
79-80	LA	78	4	36	40	18
80-81	LA	13	0	4	4	13
81-82	LA	5	0	2	2	0
82-83	NJ	60	1	10	11	21
83-84	NJ	38	0	5	5	10
Totals		320	9	101	110	115
Playoff Totals		8	1	2	3	6
PANAGABKO, Edwin Arnold	5-8 170 C					
B. Norquay, Sask., May 17, 1934						
55-56	Bos	28	0	3	3	38
56-57	Bos	1	0	0	0	0
Totals		29	0	3	3	38
PAPIKE, Joseph	6-0 175 RW					
B. Eveleth, Minn., Mar. 28, 1915						
40-41	Chi	10	2	2	4	2
41-42	Chi	9	1	0	1	0
44-45	Chi	2	0	1	1	2
Totals		21	3	3	6	4
Playoff Totals		5	0	2	2	0
PAPPIN, James Joseph	6-1 190 RW					
B. Copper Cliff, Ont., Sept. 10, 1939						
63-64	Tor	50	11	8	19	33
64-65	Tor	44	9	9	18	33
65-66	Tor	7	0	3	3	8
66-67	Tor	64	21	11	32	89
67-68	Tor	58	13	15	28	37
68-69	Chi	75	30	40	70	49
69-70	Chi	66	28	25	53	68
70-71	Chi	58	22	23	45	40
71-72	Chi	64	27	21	48	38
72-73	Chi	76	41	51	92	82
73-74	Chi	78	32	41	73	76
74-75	Chi	71	36	27	63	94
75-76	Cal	32	6	13	19	12
76-77	Clev	24	2	8	10	9
Totals		767	278	295	573	667
Playoff Totals		92	33	34	67	101
PARADISE, Robert Harvey	6-1 205 D					
B. St. Paul, Minn., Apr. 22, 1944						
71-72	Minn	4	0	0	0	6
72-73	Atl	71	1	7	8	103
73-74	Atl-Pitt	56	2	8	10	52
74-75	Pitt	78	3	15	18	109
75-76	Pitt-Wash	57	0	8	8	46
76-77	Wash	22	0	5	5	20
77-78	Pitt	64	2	10	12	53
78-79	Pitt	14	0	1	1	4
Totals		368	8	54	62	393
Playoff Totals		12	0	1	1	19
PARGETER, George William	5-7 168 LW					
B. Calgary, Alta., Feb. 24, 1923						
46-47	Mont	4	0	0	0	0
PARISE, Jean Paul (J.P.)	5-9 175 LW					
B. Smooth Rock Falls, Ont., Dec. 11, 1941						
65-66	Bos	3	0	0	0	0
66-67	Bos	18	2	2	4	10
67-68	Tor-Minn	44	11	17	28	27
68-69	Minn	76	22	27	49	53
69-70	Minn	74	24	48	72	72
70-71	Minn	73	11	23	34	60
71-72	Minn	71	19	18	37	70
72-73	Minn	78	27	48	75	96
73-74	Minn	78	18	37	55	42
74-75	Minn-NYI	79	23	32	55	62
75-76	NYI	80	22	35	57	80
76-77	NYI	80	25	31	56	46
77-78	NYI-Clev	79	21	29	50	39
78-79	Minn	57	13	9	22	45
Totals		890	238	356	594	702
Playoff Totals		86	27	31	58	87

Season	Team	GP	G	A	Pts.	PIM
PARIZEAU, Michel Gerard (Mike)	5-10 165 C					
B. Montreal, Que., Apr. 9, 1948						
71-72	StL-Phil	58	3	14	17	18
72-73	Que (WHA)	75	25	48	73	50
73-74	Que (WHA)	78	26	34	60	39
74-75	Que (WHA)	78	28	46	74	69
75-76	Que-Ind (WHA)	81	25	42	67	42
76-77	Ind (WHA)	75	18	37	55	39
77-78	Ind (WHA)	70	13	27	40	47
78-79	Ind-Cin (WHA)	52	7	18	25	32
NHL Totals		58	3	14	17	18
WHA Totals		509	142	252	394	318
WHA Playoff Totals		33	10	14	24	24
PARK, Douglas Bradford (Brad)	6-0 200 D					
B. Toronto, Ont., July 6, 1948						
68-69	NYR	54	3	23	26	70
69-70	NYR	60	11	26	37	98
70-71	NYR	68	7	37	44	114
71-72	NYR	75	24	49	73	130
72-73	NYR	52	10	43	53	51
73-74	NYR	78	25	57	82	148
74-75	NYR	65	13	44	57	104
75-76	NYR-Bos	56	18	41	59	118
76-77	Bos	77	12	55	67	67
77-78	Bos	80	22	57	79	79
78-79	Bos	40	7	32	39	10
79-80	Bos	32	5	16	21	27
80-81	Bos	78	14	52	66	111
81-82	Bos	75	14	42	56	82
82-83	Bos	76	10	26	36	82
83-84	Det	80	5	53	58	85
84-85	Det	67	13	30	43	53
Totals		1113	213	683	896	1429
Playoff Totals		161	35	90	125	217
PARKER, Jeff	6-3 194 RW					
B. St. Paul, Minn., Sept. 7, 1964						
86-87	Buf	15	3	3	6	7
87-88	Buf	4	0	2	2	2
88-89	Buf	57	9	9	18	82
89-90	Buf	61	4	5	9	70
90-91	Hart	4	0	0	0	2
Totals		141	16	19	35	163
Playoff Totals		5	0	0	0	26
PARKES, Ernest	RW					
24-25	Mont M	17	0	0	0	2
PARKS, Greg	5-9 180 C					
B. Edmonton, Alta., Mar. 25, 1967						
90-91	NYI	20	1	2	3	4
91-92	NYI	1	0	0	0	2
Totals		21	1	2	3	6
PARSONS, George Henry	5-11 174 LW					
B. Toronto, Ont., June 28, 1914						
36-37	Tor	5	0	0	0	0
37-38	Tor	30	5	6	11	6
38-39	Tor	29	7	7	14	11
Totals		64	12	13	25	17
Playoff Totals		3	2	5	7	11
PASEK, Dusan	6-1 200 C					
B. Bratislava, Czechoslovakia, Sept. 7, 1960						
88-89	Minn	48	4	10	14	30
Playoff Totals		2	1	0	1	0
PASIN, Dave	6-1 205 RW					
B. Edmonton, Alta., July 8, 1966						
85-86	Bos	71	18	19	37	50
88-89	LA	5	0	0	0	0
Totals		76	18	19	37	50
Playoff Totals		3	0	1	1	0
PASLAWSKI, Gregory Stephen	5-11 190 RW					
B. Kindersley, Sask., Aug. 25, 1961						
83-84	Mont-StL	60	9	10	19	21
84-85	StL	72	22	20	42	21
85-86	StL	56	22	11	33	18
86-87	StL	76	29	35	64	27
87-88	StL	17	2	1	3	4
88-89	StL	75	26	26	52	18
89-90	Winn	71	18	30	48	14
90-91	Winn-Buf	55	11	11	22	14
91-92	Que	80	28	17	45	18
Totals		562	167	161	328	155
Playoff Totals		54	16	13	29	25

PATERSON, Joseph *6-2 207 LW*
B. Toronto, Ont., June 25, 1960

Season	Team	GP	G	A	Pts.	PIM
80-81	Det	38	2	5	7	53
81-82	Det	3	0	0	0	0
82-83	Det	33	2	1	3	14
83-84	Det	41	2	5	7	148
84-85	Phil	6	0	0	0	31
85-86	Phil-LA	52	9	18	27	165
86-87	LA	45	2	1	3	158
87-88	LA-NYR	53	2	6	8	176
88-89	NYR	20	0	1	1	84
Totals		291	19	37	56	829
Playoff Totals		22	3	4	7	77

PATERSON, Mark *5-11 180 D*
B. Ottawa, Ont., Feb. 22, 1964

Season	Team	GP	G	A	Pts.	PIM
82-83	Hart	2	0	0	0	0
83-84	Hart	9	2	0	2	4
84-85	Hart	13	1	3	4	24
85-86	Hart	5	0	0	0	5
Totals		29	3	3	6	33

PATERSON, Richard David *5-9 190 C*
B. Kingston, Ont., Feb. 10, 1958

Season	Team	GP	G	A	Pts.	PIM
79-80	Chi	11	0	2	2	0
80-81	Chi	49	8	2	10	18
81-82	Chi	48	4	7	11	8
82-83	Chi	79	14	9	23	14
83-84	Chi	72	7	6	13	41
84-85	Chi	79	7	12	19	25
85-86	Chi	70	9	3	12	24
86-87	Chi	22	1	2	3	6
Totals		430	50	43	93	136
Playoff Totals		61	7	10	17	51

PATEY, Douglas Edward *5-11 180 RW*
B. Toronto, Ont., Dec. 28, 1956

Season	Team	GP	G	A	Pts.	PIM
76-77	Wash	37	3	1	4	6
77-78	Wash	2	0	1	1	0
78-79	Wash	6	1	0	1	2
Totals		45	4	2	6	8

PATEY, Larry James *6-1 185 C*
B. Toronto, Ont., Mar. 19, 1953

Season	Team	GP	G	A	Pts.	PIM
73-74	Cal	1	0	0	0	0
74-75	Cal	79	25	20	45	68
75-76	Cal-StL	71	12	10	22	49
76-77	StL	80	21	29	50	41
77-78	StL	80	17	17	34	29
78-79	StL	78	15	19	34	60
79-80	StL	78	17	17	34	76
80-81	StL	80	22	23	45	107
81-82	StL	70	14	12	26	97
82-83	StL	67	9	12	21	80
83-84	StL-NYR	26	1	3	4	12
84-85	NYR	7	0	1	1	12
Totals		717	153	163	316	631
Playoff Totals		40	8	10	18	57

PATRICK, Craig *6-0 185 RW*
B. Detroit, Mich., May 20, 1946

Season	Team	GP	G	A	Pts.	PIM
71-72	Cal	59	8	3	11	12
72-73	Cal	71	20	22	42	6
73-74	Cal	59	10	20	30	17
74-75	Cal-StL	57	8	10	18	6
75-76	KC	80	17	18	35	14
76-77	Minn (WHA)	30	6	11	17	6
76-77	Wash	28	7	10	17	2
77-78	Wash	44	1	7	8	4
78-79	Wash	3	1	1	2	0
NHL Totals		401	72	91	163	61
WHA Totals		30	6	11	17	6
NHL Playoff Totals		2	0	1	1	0

PATRICK, Frederick Murray (Muzz)
6-2 200 D
B. Victoria, B.C., June 28, 1915

Season	Team	GP	G	A	Pts.	PIM
37-38	NYR	1	0	2	2	0
38-39	NYR	48	1	10	11	64
39-40	NYR	46	2	4	6	44
40-41	NYR	47	2	8	10	21
45-46	NYR	24	0	2	2	4
Totals		166	5	26	31	133
Playoff Totals		25	4	0	4	34

PATRICK, Glenn Curtiss *6-2 195 D*
B. New York., N.Y., Apr. 26, 1950

Season	Team	GP	G	A	Pts.	PIM
73-74	StL	1	0	0	0	2
74-75	Cal	2	0	0	0	0
76-77	Clev	35	2	3	5	70
76-77	Edm (WHA)	23	0	4	4	62
NHL Totals		38	2	3	5	72
WHA Totals		23	0	4	4	62
WHA Playoff Totals		2	0	0	0	0

PATRICK, James *6-2 204 D*
B. Winnipeg, Man., June 14, 1963

Season	Team	GP	G	A	Pts.	PIM
83-84	NYR	12	1	7	8	2
84-85	NYR	75	8	28	36	71
85-86	NYR	75	14	29	43	88
86-87	NYR	78	10	45	55	62
87-88	NYR	70	17	45	62	52
88-89	NYR	68	11	36	47	41
89-90	NYR	73	14	43	57	50
90-91	NYR	74	10	49	59	58
91-92	NYR	80	14	57	71	54
Totals		605	99	339	438	478
Playoff Totals		63	5	26	31	62

PATRICK, Lester *6-1 180 D*
B. Drummondville, Que., Dec. 30, 1883

Season	Team	GP	G	A	Pts.	PIM
26-27	NYR	1	0	0	0	2

PATRICK, Lynn *6-1 192 LW*
B. Victoria, B.C., Feb. 3, 1912

Season	Team	GP	G	A	Pts.	PIM
34-35	NYR	48	9	13	22	17
35-36	NYR	48	11	14	25	29
36-37	NYR	45	8	16	24	23
37-38	NYR	48	15	19	34	24
38-39	NYR	35	8	21	29	25
39-40	NYR	48	12	16	28	34
40-41	NYR	48	20	24	44	12
41-42	NYR	47	32	22	54	18
42-43	NYR	50	22	39	61	58
45-46	NYR	38	8	6	14	30
Totals		455	145	190	335	270
Playoff Totals		44	10	6	16	22

PATRICK, Stephen Gary *6-4 205 RW*
B. Winnipeg, Man., Feb. 4, 1961

Season	Team	GP	G	A	Pts.	PIM
80-81	Buf	30	1	7	8	25
81-82	Buf	41	8	8	16	64
82-83	Buf	56	9	13	22	26
83-84	Buf	11	1	4	5	6
84-85	Buf-NYR	57	13	20	33	67
85-86	NYR-Que	55	8	16	24	54
Totals		250	40	68	108	242
Playoff Totals		12	0	1	1	12

PATTERSON, Colin *6-2 195 RW/LW*
B. Rexdale, Ont., May 11, 1960

Season	Team	GP	G	A	Pts.	PIM
83-84	Calg	56	13	14	27	15
84-85	Calg	57	22	21	43	5
85-86	Calg	61	14	13	27	22
86-87	Calg	68	13	13	26	41
87-88	Calg	39	7	11	18	28
88-89	Calg	74	14	24	38	56
89-90	Calg	61	5	3	8	20
91-92	Buf	52	4	8	12	30
Totals		468	92	107	199	217
Playoff Totals		77	12	16	28	55

PATTERSON, Dennis G. *5-8 175 D*
B. Peterborough, Ont., Jan. 9, 1950

Season	Team	GP	G	A	Pts.	PIM
74-75	KC	66	1	5	6	39
75-76	KC	69	5	16	21	28
76-77	Edm (WHA)	23	0	2	2	2
79-80	Phil	3	0	1	1	0
NHL Totals		138	6	22	28	67
WHA Totals		23	0	2	2	2

PATTERSON, George F. (Paddy)
6-1 176 RW
B. Kingston, Ont., May 22, 1906

Season	Team	GP	G	A	Pts.	PIM
26-27	Tor	17	4	2	6	17
27-28	Tor-Mont	28	1	1	2	17
28-29	Mont	44	4	5	9	34
29-30	NYA	44	13	4	17	24
30-31	NYA	44	8	6	14	67
31-32	NYA	20	6	0	6	26
32-33	NYA	48	12	7	19	26
33-34	NYA-Bos	23	3	1	4	8
34-35	Det-StL E	21	0	1	1	2
Totals		289	51	27	78	221
Playoff Totals		3	0	0	0	2

PAUL, Arthur Stewart (Butch)
5-11 160 C
B. Rocky Mtn. House, Alta., Sept. 11, 1943

Season	Team	GP	G	A	Pts.	PIM
64-65	Det	3	0	0	0	0

PAULUS, Roland (Rollie) *D*

Season	Team	GP	G	A	Pts.	PIM
25-26	Mont	33	0	0	0	0

PAVELICH, Mark *5-8 170 C*
B. Eveleth, Minn., Feb. 28, 1958

Season	Team	GP	G	A	Pts.	PIM
81-82	NYR	79	33	43	76	67
82-83	NYR	78	37	38	75	52
83-84	NYR	77	29	53	82	96
84-85	NYR	48	14	31	45	29

PAVELICH, Mark *(Continued)*

Season	Team	GP	G	A	Pts.	PIM
85-86	NYR	59	20	20	40	82
86-87	Minn	12	4	6	10	10
91-92	SJ	2	0	1	1	4
Totals		355	137	192	329	340
Playoff Totals		23	7	17	24	14

PAVELICH, Martin Nicholas *5-10 170 LW*
B. Sault Ste. Marie, Ont., Nov. 6, 1927

Season	Team	GP	G	A	Pts.	PIM
47-48	Det	41	4	8	12	10
48-49	Det	60	10	16	26	40
49-50	Det	65	8	15	23	58
50-51	Det	67	9	20	29	41
51-52	Det	68	17	19	36	54
52-53	Det	64	13	20	33	49
53-54	Det	65	9	20	29	57
54-55	Det	70	15	15	30	59
55-56	Det	70	5	13	18	38
56-57	Det	64	3	13	16	48
Totals		634	93	159	252	454
Playoff Totals		91	13	15	28	74

PAVESE, James Peter *6-2 205 D*
B. New York, N.Y., May 8, 1962

Season	Team	GP	G	A	Pts.	PIM
81-82	StL	42	2	9	11	101
82-83	StL	42	0	2	2	45
83-84	StL	4	0	1	1	19
84-85	StL	51	2	5	7	69
85-86	StL	69	4	7	11	116
86-87	StL	69	2	9	11	127
87-88	StL-NYR-Det	25	0	5	5	77
88-89	Det-Hart	44	3	6	9	135
Totals		328	13	44	57	689
Playoff Totals		34	0	6	6	81

PAYER, Evariste P. *F*

Season	Team	GP	G	A	Pts.	PIM
17-18	Mont	1	0	0	0	0

PAYNE, Steven John *6-2 210 LW*
B. Toronto, Ont., Aug. 16, 1958

Season	Team	GP	G	A	Pts.	PIM
78-79	Minn	70	23	17	40	29
79-80	Minn	80	42	43	85	40
80-81	Minn	76	30	28	58	88
81-82	Minn	74	33	45	78	76
82-83	Minn	80	30	39	69	53
83-84	Minn	78	28	31	59	49
84-85	Minn	76	29	22	51	61
85-86	Minn	22	8	4	12	8
86-87	Minn	48	4	6	10	19
87-88	Minn	9	1	3	4	12
Totals		613	228	238	466	435
Playoff Totals		71	35	35	70	60

PAYNTER, Kent *6-0 183 D*
B. Summerside, P.E.I., Apr. 17, 1965

Season	Team	GP	G	A	Pts.	PIM
87-88	Chi	2	0	0	0	2
88-89	Chi	1	0	0	0	2
89-90	Wash	13	1	2	3	18
90-91	Wash	1	0	0	0	15
91-92	Winn	5	0	0	0	4
Totals		22	1	2	3	41
Playoff Totals		4	0	0	0	10

PEARSON, George Alexander Melvin (Mel)
5-10 175 LW
B. Flin Flon, Man., Apr. 29, 1938

Season	Team	GP	G	A	Pts.	PIM
59-60	NYR	23	1	5	6	13
61-62	NYR	3	0	0	0	2
62-63	NYR	5	1	0	1	6
64-65	NYR	5	0	0	0	4
67-68	Pitt	2	0	1	1	0
72-73	Minn (WHA)	70	8	12	20	12
NHL Totals		38	2	6	8	25
WHA Totals		70	8	12	20	12
WHA Playoff Totals		5	2	0	2	0

PEARSON, Rob *6-1 185 RW*
B. Oshawa, Ont., Aug. 3, 1971

Season	Team	GP	G	A	Pts.	PIM
91-92	Tor	47	14	10	24	58

PEARSON, Scott *6-1 205 LW*
B. Cornwall, Ont., Dec. 19, 1969

Season	Team	GP	G	A	Pts.	PIM
88-89	Tor	9	0	1	1	2
89-90	Tor	41	5	10	15	90
90-91	Tor-Que	47	11	4	15	106
91-92	Que	10	1	2	3	14
Totals		107	17	17	34	212
Playoff Totals		2	2	0	2	10

PEDERSEN, Allen *6-3 210 D*
B. Fort Saskatchewan, Alta., Jan. 13, 1965

Season	Team	GP	G	A	Pts.	PIM
86-87	Bos	79	1	11	12	71
87-88	Bos	78	0	6	6	90
88-89	Bos	51	0	6	6	69

PEDERSEN, Allen *(Continued)*

Season	Team	GP	G	A	Pts.	PIM
89-90	Bos	68	1	2	3	71
90-91	Bos	57	2	6	8	107
91-92	Minn	29	0	1	1	10
Totals		362	4	32	36	418
Playoff Totals		64	0	0	0	91

PEDERSON, Barry Alan *5-11 185 C*

B. Big River, Sask., Mar. 13, 1961

Season	Team	GP	G	A	Pts.	PIM
80-81	Bos	9	1	4	5	6
81-82	Bos	80	44	48	92	53
82-83	Bos	77	46	61	107	47
83-84	Bos	80	39	77	116	64
84-85	Bos	22	4	8	12	10
85-86	Bos	79	29	47	76	60
86-87	Van	79	24	52	76	50
87-88	Van	76	19	52	71	92
88-89	Van	62	15	26	41	22
89-90	Van-Pitt	54	6	25	31	39
90-91	Pitt	46	6	8	14	21
91-92	Hart-Bos	37	5	8	13	8
Totals		701	238	416	654	472
Playoff Totals		34	22	30	52	25

PEDERSON, Mark *6-2 196 LW*

B. Prelate, Sask., Jan. 14, 1968

Season	Team	GP	G	A	Pts.	PIM
89-90	Mont	9	0	2	2	2
90-91	Mont-Phil	59	10	16	26	23
91-92	Phil	58	15	25	40	22
Totals		126	25	43	68	47
Playoff Totals		2	0	0	0	0

PEER, Bertram (Bert) *D*

Season	Team	GP	G	A	Pts.	PIM
39-40	Det	1	0	0	0	0

PEIRSON, John Frederick *5-11 170 RW*

B. Winnipeg, Man., July 21, 1925

Season	Team	GP	G	A	Pts.	PIM
46-47	Bos	5	0	0	0	0
47-48	Bos	15	4	2	6	0
48-49	Bos	59	22	21	43	45
49-50	Bos	57	27	25	52	49
50-51	Bos	70	19	19	38	43
51-52	Bos	68	20	30	50	30
52-53	Bos	49	14	15	29	32
53-54	Bos	68	21	19	40	55
55-56	Bos	33	11	14	25	10
56-57	Bos	68	13	26	39	41
57-58	Bos	53	2	2	4	10
Totals		545	153	173	326	315
Playoff Totals		49	9	17	26	26

PELENSKY, Perry *5-11 180 RW*

B. Edmonton, Alta., May 22, 1962

Season	Team	GP	G	A	Pts.	PIM
83-84	Chi	4	0	0	0	5

PELLETIER, Joseph Georges (Roger) *D*

B. Montreal, Que., June 22, 1945

Season	Team	GP	G	A	Pts.	PIM
67-68	Phil	1	0	0	0	0

PELOFFY, Andre Charles *5-8 160 C*

B. Sete, France, Feb. 25, 1951

Season	Team	GP	G	A	Pts.	PIM
74-75	Wash	9	0	0	0	2
77-78	NE (WHA)	10	2	0	2	2
NHL Totals		9	0	0	0	2
WHA Totals		10	2	0	2	2
WHA Playoff Totals		2	0	0	0	0

PELUSO, Mike *6-4 200 LW/D*

B. Pengilly, Minn., Nov. 8, 1965

Season	Team	GP	G	A	Pts.	PIM
89-90	Chi	2	0	0	0	0
90-91	Chi	53	6	1	7	320
91-92	Chi	63	6	3	9	408
Totals		118	12	4	16	728
Playoff Totals		20	1	2	3	10

PELYK, Michael Joseph *6-1 188 D*

B. Toronto, Ont., Sept. 29, 1947

Season	Team	GP	G	A	Pts.	PIM
67-68	Tor	24	0	3	3	55
68-69	Tor	65	3	9	12	146
69-70	Tor	36	1	3	4	37
70-71	Tor	73	5	21	26	54
71-72	Tor	46	1	4	5	44
72-73	Tor	72	3	16	19	118
73-74	Tor	71	12	19	31	94
74-75	Van (WHA)	75	14	26	40	121
75-76	Cin (WHA)	75	10	23	33	117
76-77	Tor	13	0	2	2	4
77-78	Tor	41	1	11	12	14
NHL Totals		441	26	88	114	566
WHA Totals		150	24	49	73	238
NHL Playoff Totals		40	0	3	3	41

PENNINGTON, Clifford *6-0 170 C*

B. Winnipeg, Man., Apr. 18, 1940

Season	Team	GP	G	A	Pts.	PIM
60-61	Mont	4	1	0	1	0

PENNINGTON, Clifford *(Continued)*

Season	Team	GP	G	A	Pts.	PIM
61-62	Bos	70	9	32	41	2
62-63	Bos	27	7	10	17	4
Totals		101	17	42	59	6

PEPLINSKI, James Desmond *6-3 209 RW*

B. Renfrew, Ont., Oct. 24, 1960

Season	Team	GP	G	A	Pts.	PIM
80-81	Calg	80	13	25	38	108
81-82	Calg	74	30	37	67	115
82-83	Calg	80	15	26	41	134
83-84	Calg	74	11	22	33	114
84-85	Calg	80	16	29	45	111
85-86	Calg	77	24	35	59	214
86-87	Calg	80	18	32	50	181
87-88	Calg	75	20	31	51	234
88-89	Calg	79	13	25	38	241
89-90	Calg	6	1	0	1	4
Totals		705	161	262	423	1456
Playoff Totals		99	15	31	46	382

PERLINI, Fred *6-2 175 C*

B. Sault Ste. Marie, Ont., Apr. 12, 1962

Season	Team	GP	G	A	Pts.	PIM
81-82	Tor	7	2	3	5	0
83-84	Tor	1	0	0	0	0
Totals		8	2	3	5	0

PERREAULT, Fernand (Fern) *6-0 180 LW*

B. Chambly Basin, Que., Mar. 31, 1927

Season	Team	GP	G	A	Pts.	PIM
47-48	NYR	2	0	0	0	0
49-50	NYR	1	0	0	0	0
Totals		3	0	0	0	0

PERREAULT, Gilbert (Gil) *6-0 200 C*

B. Victoriaville, Que., Nov. 13, 1950

Season	Team	GP	G	A	Pts.	PIM
70-71	Buf	78	38	34	72	19
71-72	Buf	76	26	48	74	24
72-73	Buf	78	28	60	88	10
73-74	Buf	55	18	33	51	10
74-75	Buf	68	39	57	96	36
75-76	Buf	80	44	69	113	36
76-77	Buf	80	39	56	95	30
77-78	Buf	79	41	48	89	20
78-79	Buf	79	27	58	85	20
79-80	Buf	80	40	66	106	57
80-81	Buf	56	20	39	59	56
81-82	Buf	62	31	42	73	40
82-83	Buf	77	30	46	76	34
83-84	Buf	73	31	59	90	32
84-85	Buf	78	30	53	83	42
85-86	Buf	72	21	39	60	28
86-87	Buf	20	9	7	16	6
Totals		1191	512	814	1326	500
Playoff Totals		90	33	70	103	44

PERRY, Brian Thomas *5-11 180 C*

B. Aldershot, England, Apr. 6, 1944

Season	Team	GP	G	A	Pts.	PIM
68-69	Oak	61	10	21	31	10
69-70	Oak	34	6	8	14	14
70-71	Buf	1	0	0	0	0
72-73	NY (WHA)	74	13	20	33	30
73-74	NY-NJ (WHA)	71	20	11	31	19
NHL Totals		96	16	29	45	24
WHA Totals		145	33	31	64	49
NHL Playoff Totals		8	1	1	2	4
WHA Playoff Totals		6	1	2	3	6

PERSSON, Stefan *6-1 190 D*

B. Umea, Sweden, Dec. 22, 1954

Season	Team	GP	G	A	Pts.	PIM
77-78	NYI	66	6	50	56	54
78-79	NYI	78	10	56	66	57
79-80	NYI	73	4	35	39	76
80-81	NYI	80	9	52	61	82
81-82	NYI	70	6	37	43	99
82-83	NYI	70	4	25	29	71
83-84	NYI	75	9	24	33	65
84-85	NYI	54	3	19	22	30
85-86	NYI	56	1	19	20	40
Totals		622	52	317	369	574
Playoff Totals		102	7	50	57	69

PESUT, George Mathew *6-1 185 D*

B. Saskatoon, Sask., June 17, 1953

Season	Team	GP	G	A	Pts.	PIM
74-75	Cal	47	0	13	13	73
75-76	Cal	45	3	9	12	57
76-77	Calg (WHA)	17	2	0	2	2
NHL Totals		92	3	22	25	130
WHA Totals		17	2	0	2	2

PETERS, Franklin J. (Frank) *D*

B. Rouses Point, N.Y., June 5, 1905

Season	Team	GP	G	A	Pts.	PIM
30-31	NYR	43	0	0	0	59
Playoff Totals		4	0	0	0	2

PETERS, Garry Lorne *5-10 180 C*

B. Regina, Sask., Oct. 9, 1942

Season	Team	GP	G	A	Pts.	PIM
64-65	Mont	13	0	2	2	6
65-66	NYR	63	7	3	10	42
66-67	Mont	4	0	1	1	2
67-68	Phil	31	7	5	12	22
68-69	Phil	66	8	6	14	49
69-70	Phil	59	6	10	16	69
70-71	Phil	73	6	7	13	69
71-72	Bos	2	0	0	0	2
72-73	NY (WHA)	23	2	7	9	24
73-74	NY-NJ (WHA)	34	2	5	7	18
NHL Totals		311	34	34	68	261
WHA Totals		57	4	12	16	42
NHL Playoff Totals		9	2	2	4	31

PETERS, James Meldrum *5-11 165 RW*

B. Verdun, Que., Oct. 2, 1922

Season	Team	GP	G	A	Pts.	PIM
45-46	Mont	47	11	19	30	10
46-47	Mont	60	11	13	24	27
47-48	Mont-Bos	59	13	18	31	44
48-49	Bos	60	16	15	31	8
49-50	Det	70	14	16	30	20
50-51	Det	68	17	21	38	14
51-52	Chi	70	15	21	36	15
52-53	Chi	69	22	19	41	16
53-54	Chi-Det	71	6	8	14	31
Totals		574	125	150	275	185
Playoff Totals		60	5	9	14	22

PETERS, James Stephen, Jr. *6-2 185 C*

B. Montreal, Que., June 20, 1944

Season	Team	GP	G	A	Pts.	PIM
64-65	Det	1	0	0	0	0
65-66	Det	6	1	1	2	2
66-67	Det	2	0	0	0	0
67-68	Det	45	5	6	11	8
68-69	LA	76	10	15	25	28
69-70	LA	74	15	9	24	10
72-73	LA	77	4	5	9	0
73-74	LA	25	2	0	2	0
74-75	LA	3	0	0	0	0
Totals		309	37	36	73	48
Playoff Totals		11	0	2	2	2

PETERS, Steven Alan *5-11 186 C*

B. Peterborough, Ont., Jan. 23, 1960

Season	Team	GP	G	A	Pts.	PIM
79-80	Col	2	0	1	1	0

PETERSON, Brent Ronald *6-0 190 C*

B. Calgary, Alta., Feb. 15, 1958

Season	Team	GP	G	A	Pts.	PIM
79-80	Det	18	1	2	3	2
80-81	Det	53	6	18	24	24
81-82	Det-Buf	61	10	5	15	49
82-83	Buf	75	13	24	37	38
83-84	Buf	70	9	12	21	52
84-85	Buf	74	12	22	34	47
85-86	Van	77	8	23	31	94
86-87	Van	69	7	15	22	77
87-88	Hart	52	2	7	9	40
88-89	Hart	66	4	13	17	61
Totals		620	72	141	213	484
Playoff Totals		31	4	4	8	65

PETIT, Michel *6-1 205 D*

B. St. Malo, Que., Feb. 12, 1964

Season	Team	GP	G	A	Pts.	PIM
82-83	Van	2	0	0	0	0
83-84	Van	44	6	9	15	53
84-85	Van	69	5	26	31	127
85-86	Van	32	1	6	7	27
86-87	Van	69	12	13	25	131
87-88	Van-NYR	74	9	27	36	258
88-89	NYR	69	8	25	33	154
89-90	Que	63	12	24	36	215
90-91	Que-Tor	73	13	26	39	179
91-92	Tor-Calg	70	4	23	27	164
Totals		565	70	179	249	1308
Playoff Totals		5	0	2	2	27

PETTERSSON, Jorgen *6-2 185 LW*

B. Gothenburg, Sweden, July 11, 1956

Season	Team	GP	G	A	Pts.	PIM
80-81	StL	62	37	36	73	24
81-82	StL	77	38	31	69	28
82-83	StL	74	35	38	73	4
83-84	StL	77	28	34	62	29
84-85	StL	75	23	32	55	20
85-86	Hart-Wash	70	13	21	34	12
Totals		435	174	192	366	117
Playoff Totals		44	15	12	27	4

PETTINGER, Eric (Cowboy) *6-0 175 LW*

B. Regina, Sask.

Season	Team	GP	G	A	Pts.	PIM
28-29	Bos-Tor	42	3	3	6	41
29-30	Tor	43	4	9	13	40
30-31	Ott	12	0	0	0	2
Totals		97	7	12	19	83
Playoff Totals		4	1	0	1	8

PETTINGER, Gordon Robinson *6-0 175 C*

B. Regina, Sask., Nov. 17, 1911

Season	Team	GP	G	A	Pts.	PIM
32-33	NYR	35	1	2	3	18
33-34	Det	48	3	14	17	14
34-35	Det	13	2	3	5	2
35-36	Det	33	8	7	15	6
36-37	Det	48	7	15	22	13
37-38	Det-Bos	46	8	13	21	14
38-39	Bos	48	11	14	25	8
39-40	Bos	21	2	6	8	2
Totals		292	42	74	116	77
Playoff Totals		49	4	5	9	11

PHAIR, Lyle *6-1 190 LW*

B. Pilot Mount, Man., Aug. 31, 1961

Season	Team	GP	G	A	Pts.	PIM
85-86	LA	15	0	1	1	2
86-87	LA	5	2	0	2	2
87-88	LA	28	4	6	10	8
Totals		48	6	7	13	12
Playoff Totals		1	0	0	0	0

PHILLIPOFF, Harold *6-3 220 LW*

B. Kamsack, Sask., July 15, 1956

Season	Team	GP	G	A	Pts.	PIM
77-78	Atl	67	17	36	53	128
78-79	Atl-Chi	65	9	21	30	119
79-80	Chi	9	0	0	0	20
Totals		141	26	57	83	267
Playoff Totals		6	0	2	2	9

PHILLIPS, Charles *D*

B. Toronto, Ont., May 10, 1917

Season	Team	GP	G	A	Pts.	PIM
42-43	Mont	17	0	0	0	6

PHILLIPS, Merlyn J. (Bill) *5-7 160 F*

B. Thesselon, Ont., 1896

Season	Team	GP	G	A	Pts.	PIM
25-26	Mont M	12	3	1	4	6
26-27	Mont M	43	15	1	16	45
27-28	Mont M	40	7	5	12	33
28-29	Mont M	42	6	5	11	41
29-30	Mont M	44	13	10	23	38
30-31	Mont M	43	6	1	7	38
31-32	Mont M	46	1	1	2	11
32-33	Mont M-NYA	32	1	7	8	10
Totals		302	52	31	83	222
Playoff Totals		28	6	2	8	19

PHILLIPS, W. J. (Bat) *RW*

B. Carleton Place, Ont.

Season	Team	GP	G	A	Pts.	PIM
29-30	Mont M	27	1	1	2	6
Playoff Totals		4	0	0	0	2

PICARD, Adrien Roger (Roger) *6-0 200 RW*

B. Montreal, Que., Jan. 13, 1935

Season	Team	GP	G	A	Pts.	PIM
67-68	StL	15	2	2	4	21

PICARD, Jean-Noel Yves (Noel) *6-1 185 D*

B. Montreal, Que., Dec. 25, 1938

Season	Team	GP	G	A	Pts.	PIM
64-65	Mont	16	0	7	7	33
67-68	StL	66	1	10	11	142
68-69	StL	67	5	19	24	131
69-70	StL	39	1	4	5	88
70-71	StL	75	3	8	11	119
71-72	StL	15	1	5	6	50
72-73	StL-Atl	57	1	10	11	53
Totals		335	12	63	75	616
Playoff Totals		50	2	11	13	167

PICARD, Michel *5-11 190 LW*

B. Beauport, Que., Nov. 7, 1969

Season	Team	GP	G	A	Pts.	PIM
90-91	Hart	5	1	0	1	2
91-92	Hart	25	3	5	8	6
Totals		30	4	5	9	8

PICARD, Robert Rene Joseph *6-2 207 D*

B. Montreal, Que., May 25, 1957

Season	Team	GP	G	A	Pts.	PIM
77-78	Wash	75	10	27	37	101
78-79	Wash	77	21	44	65	85
79-80	Wash	78	11	43	54	122
80-81	Tor-Mont	67	8	21	29	74
81-82	Mont	62	2	26	28	106
82-83	Mont	64	7	31	38	60
83-84	Mont-Winn	69	6	18	24	34
84-85	Winn	78	12	22	34	107
85-86	Winn-Que	68	9	32	41	53
86-87	Que	78	8	20	28	71
87-88	Que	65	3	13	16	103
88-89	Que	74	7	14	21	61
89-90	Que-Det	44	0	8	8	48
Totals		899	104	319	423	1025
Playoff Totals		36	5	15	20	39

PICHETTE, Dave *6-3 190 D*

B. Grand Falls, Nfld., Feb. 4, 1960

Season	Team	GP	G	A	Pts.	PIM
80-81	Que	46	4	16	20	62
81-82	Que	67	7	30	37	152
82-83	Que	53	3	21	24	49
83-84	Que-StL	46	2	18	20	18
84-85	NJ	71	17	40	57	41
85-86	NJ	33	7	12	19	22
87-88	NYR	6	1	3	4	4
Totals		322	41	140	181	348
Playoff Totals		28	3	7	10	54

PICKETTS, Frederic Harold (Hal) *180 F*

B. Asquith, Sask., Apr. 22, 1909

Season	Team	GP	G	A	Pts.	PIM
33-34	NYA	48	3	1	4	32

PIDHIRNY, Harry *5-11 155 C*

B. Toronto, Ont., Mar. 5, 1928

Season	Team	GP	G	A	Pts.	PIM
57-58	Bos	2	0	0	0	0

PIERCE, Randy Stephen *5-11 185 RW*

B. Arnprior, Ont., Nov. 23, 1957

Season	Team	GP	G	A	Pts.	PIM
77-78	Col	35	9	10	19	15
78-79	Col	70	19	17	36	35
79-80	Col	75	16	23	39	100
80-81	Col	55	9	21	30	52
81-82	Col	5	0	0	0	4
82-83	NJ	3	0	0	0	0
83-84	Hart	17	6	3	9	9
84-85	Hart	17	3	2	5	8
Totals		277	62	76	138	223
Playoff Totals		2	0	0	0	0

PIKE, Alfred G. (Alf) *6-0 187 C*

B. Winnipeg, Man., Sept. 15, 1917

Season	Team	GP	G	A	Pts.	PIM
39-40	NYR	47	8	9	17	38
40-41	NYR	48	6	13	19	23
41-42	NYR	34	8	19	27	16
42-43	NYR	41	6	16	22	48
45-46	NYR	33	7	9	16	18
46-47	NYR	31	7	11	18	2
Totals		234	42	77	119	145
Playoff Totals		21	4	2	6	12

PILON, Richard *6-0 202 D*

B. Saskatoon, Sask., Apr. 30, 1968

Season	Team	GP	G	A	Pts.	PIM
88-89	NYI	62	0	14	14	242
89-90	NYI	14	0	2	2	31
90-91	NYI	60	1	4	5	126
91-92	NYI	65	1	6	7	183
Totals		201	2	26	28	482

PILOTE, Joseph Albert Pierre Paul (Pierre) *5-10 178 D*

B. Kenogami, Que., Dec. 11, 1931

Season	Team	GP	G	A	Pts.	PIM
55-56	Chi	20	3	5	8	34
56-57	Chi	70	3	14	17	117
57-58	Chi	70	6	24	30	91
58-59	Chi	70	7	30	37	79
59-60	Chi	70	7	38	45	100
60-61	Chi	70	6	29	35	165
61-62	Chi	59	7	35	42	97
62-63	Chi	59	8	18	26	57
63-64	Chi	70	7	46	53	84
64-65	Chi	68	14	45	59	162
65-66	Chi	51	2	34	36	60
66-67	Chi	70	6	46	52	90
67-68	Chi	74	1	36	37	69
68-69	Tor	69	3	18	21	46
Totals		890	80	418	498	1251
Playoff Totals		86	8	53	61	102

PINDER, Allen Gerald (Gerry) *5-8 165 LW*

B. Saskatoon, Sask., Sept. 15, 1948

Season	Team	GP	G	A	Pts.	PIM
69-70	Chi	75	19	20	39	41
70-71	Chi	74	13	18	31	35
71-72	Cal	74	23	31	54	59
72-73	Clev (WHA)	78	30	36	66	21
73-74	Clev (WHA)	73	23	33	56	90
74-75	Clev (WHA)	74	13	28	41	71
75-76	Clev (WHA)	79	21	30	51	118
76-77	SD (WHA)	44	6	13	19	36
77-78	Edm (WHA)	5	0	1	1	0
NHL Totals		223	55	69	124	135
WHA Totals		353	93	141	234	336
NHL Playoff Totals		17	0	4	4	6
WHA Playoff Totals		18	5	10	15	40

PIRUS, Joseph Alexander (Alex) *6-1 205 RW*

B. Toronto, Ont., Jan. 12, 1955

Season	Team	GP	G	A	Pts.	PIM
76-77	Minn	79	20	17	37	47
77-78	Minn	61	9	6	15	38

PIRUS, Joseph Alexander (Alex)

(Continued)

Season	Team	GP	G	A	Pts.	PIM
78-79	Minn	15	1	3	4	9
79-80	Det	4	0	2	2	0
Totals		159	30	28	58	94
Playoff Totals		2	0	1	1	2

PITRE, Didier (Cannonball) *200 F*

B. Sault Ste. Marie, Ont., 1884

Season	Team	GP	G	A	Pts.	PIM
17-18	Mont	19	17	0	17	9
18-19	Mont	17	14	4	18	9
19-20	Mont	22	15	7	22	6
20-21	Mont	23	15	1	16	23
21-22	Mont	23	2	3	5	12
22-23	Mont	23	1	2	3	0
Totals		127	64	17	81	59
Playoff Totals		14	2	2	4	0

PIVONKA, Michal *6-2 198 LW*

B. Kladno, Czechoslovakia, Jan. 28, 1966

Season	Team	GP	G	A	Pts.	PIM
86-87	Wash	73	18	25	43	41
87-88	Wash	71	11	23	34	28
88-89	Wash	52	8	19	27	30
89-90	Wash	77	25	39	64	54
90-91	Wash	79	20	50	70	34
91-92	Wash	80	23	57	80	47
Totals		432	105	213	318	234
Playoff Totals		56	11	21	32	43

PLAGER, Barclay Graham *5-11 175 D*

B. Kirkland Lake, Ont., Mar. 26, 1941

Season	Team	GP	G	A	Pts.	PIM
67-68	StL	49	5	15	20	153
68-69	StL	61	4	26	30	120
69-70	StL	75	6	26	32	128
70-71	StL	69	4	20	24	172
71-72	StL	78	7	22	29	176
72-73	StL	68	8	25	33	102
73-74	StL	72	6	20	26	99
74-75	StL	76	4	24	28	96
75-76	StL	64	0	8	8	67
76-77	StL	2	0	1	1	2
Totals		614	44	187	231	1115
Playoff Totals		68	3	20	23	182

PLAGER, Robert Bryan *5-11 195 D*

B. Kirkland Lake, Ont., Mar. 11, 1943

Season	Team	GP	G	A	Pts.	PIM
64-65	NYR	10	0	0	0	18
65-66	NYR	18	0	5	5	5
66-67	NYR	1	0	0	0	0
67-68	StL	53	2	5	7	86
68-69	StL	32	0	7	7	43
69-70	StL	64	3	11	14	113
70-71	StL	70	1	19	20	114
71-72	StL	50	4	7	11	81
72-73	StL	77	2	31	33	107
73-74	StL	61	3	10	13	48
74-75	StL	73	1	14	15	53
75-76	StL	63	3	8	11	90
76-77	StL	54	1	9	10	23
77-78	StL	18	0	0	0	4
Totals		644	20	126	146	802
Playoff Totals		74	2	17	19	195

PLAGER, William Ronald *5-9 175 D*

B. Kirkland Lake, Ont., July 6, 1945

Season	Team	GP	G	A	Pts.	PIM
67-68	Minn	32	0	2	2	30
68-69	StL	2	0	0	0	2
69-70	StL	24	1	4	5	30
70-71	StL	36	0	3	3	45
71-72	StL	65	1	11	12	64
72-73	Atl	76	2	11	13	92
73-74	Minn	1	0	0	0	2
74-75	Minn	7	0	0	0	8
75-76	Minn	20	0	3	3	21
Totals		263	4	34	38	294
Playoff Totals		31	0	2	2	26

PLAMANDON, Gerard Roger (Gerry) *5-7 170 LW*

B. Sherbrooke, Que., Jan. 5, 1925

Season	Team	GP	G	A	Pts.	PIM
45-46	Mont	6	0	2	2	2
47-48	Mont	3	1	1	2	0
48-49	Mont	27	5	5	10	8
49-50	Mont	37	1	5	6	0
50-51	Mont	1	0	0	0	0
Totals		74	7	13	20	10
Playoff Totals		11	5	2	7	2

PLANTE, Cam *6-1 195 D*

B. Brandon, Man., Mar. 12, 1964

Season	Team	GP	G	A	Pts.	PIM
84-85	Tor	2	0	0	0	0

PLANTE, Pierre Renald *6-1 190 RW*

B. Valleyfield, Que., May 14, 1951

Season	Team	GP	G	A	Pts.	PIM
71-72	Phil	24	1	0	1	15
72-73	Phil-StL	51	12	16	28	56
73-74	StL	78	26	28	54	85

PLANTE, Pierre Renald *(Continued)*

Season	Team	GP	G	A	Pts.	PIM
74-75	StL	80	34	32	66	125
75-76	StL	74	14	19	33	77
76-77	StL	76	18	20	38	77
77-78	Chi	77	10	18	28	59
78-79	NYR	70	6	25	31	37
79-80	Que	69	4	14	18	68
Totals		599	125	172	297	599
Playoff Totals		33	2	6	8	51

PLANTERY, Mark P. *6-1 185 D*
B. St. Catherines, Ont., Aug. 14, 1959

Season	Team	GP	G	A	Pts.	PIM
80-81	Winn	25	1	5	6	14

PLAVSIC, Adrien *6-1 190 D*
B. Montreal, Que., Jan. 13, 1970

Season	Team	GP	G	A	Pts.	PIM
89-90	StL-Van	15	3	3	6	10
90-91	Van	48	2	10	12	62
91-92	Van	16	1	9	10	14
Totals		79	6	22	28	86
Playoff Totals		13	1	7	8	4

PLAXTON, Hugh John *184 LW*
B. Barrie, Ont., May 16, 1904

Season	Team	GP	G	A	Pts.	PIM
32-33	Mont M	15	1	2	3	4

PLAYFAIR, James *6-4 220 D*
B. Fort St. James, B.C., May 22, 1964

Season	Team	GP	G	A	Pts.	PIM
83-84	Edm	2	1	1	2	2
87-88	Chi	12	1	3	4	21
88-89	Chi	7	0	0	0	28
Totals		21	2	4	6	51

PLAYFAIR, Larry William *6-4 205 D*
B. Fort St. James, B.C., June 23, 1958

Season	Team	GP	G	A	Pts.	PIM
78-79	Buf	26	0	3	3	60
79-80	Buf	79	2	10	12	145
80-81	Buf	75	3	9	12	169
81-82	Buf	77	6	10	16	258
82-83	Buf	79	4	13	17	180
83-84	Buf	76	5	11	16	211
84-85	Buf	72	3	14	17	157
85-86	Buf-LA	61	1	3	4	126
86-87	LA	37	2	7	9	181
87-88	LA	54	0	7	7	197
88-89	LA-Buf	48	0	6	6	126
89-90	Buf	4	0	1	1	2
Totals		688	26	94	120	1812
Playoff Totals		43	0	6	6	111

PLEAU, Lawrence Winslow *6-1 190 C*
B. Lynn, Mass., June 29, 1947

Season	Team	GP	G	A	Pts.	PIM
69-70	Mont	20	1	0	1	0
70-71	Mont	19	1	5	6	8
71-72	Mont	55	7	10	17	14
72-73	NE (WHA)	78	39	48	87	42
73-74	NE (WHA)	77	26	43	69	35
74-75	NE (WHA)	78	30	34	64	50
75-76	NE (WHA)	75	29	45	74	21
76-77	NE (WHA)	78	11	21	32	22
77-78	NE (WHA)	54	16	18	34	4
78-79	NE (WHA)	28	6	6	12	6
NHL Totals		94	9	15	24	22
WHA Totals		468	157	215	372	180
NHL Playoff Totals		4	0	0	0	0
WHA Playoff Totals		66	29	22	51	37

PLETT, Willi *6-3 205 RW*
B. Paraguay, June 7, 1955

Season	Team	GP	G	A	Pts.	PIM
75-76	Atl	4	0	0	0	0
76-77	Atl	64	33	23	56	123
77-78	Atl	78	22	21	43	171
78-79	Atl	74	23	20	43	213
79-80	Atl	76	13	19	32	231
80-81	Calg	78	38	30	68	239
81-82	Calg	78	21	36	57	288
82-83	Minn	71	25	14	39	170
83-84	Minn	73	15	23	38	316
84-85	Minn	47	14	14	28	157
85-86	Minn	59	10	7	17	231
86-87	Minn	67	6	5	11	263
87-88	Bos	65	2	3	5	170
Totals		834	222	215	437	2572
Playoff Totals		83	24	22	46	466

PLUMB, Robert Edwin (Rob) *5-8 166 LW*
B. Kingston, Ont., Aug. 29, 1957

Season	Team	GP	G	A	Pts.	PIM
77-78	Det	7	2	1	3	0

PLUMB, Ronald William *5-10 175 D*
B. Kingston, Ont., July 17, 1950

Season	Team	GP	G	A	Pts.	PIM
72-73	Phil (WHA)	78	10	41	51	66
73-74	Van (WHA)	75	6	32	38	40
74-75	SD (WHA)	78	10	38	48	56
75-76	Cin (WHA)	80	10	36	46	31
76-77	Cin (WHA)	79	11	58	69	52

PLUMB, Ronald William *(Continued)*

Season	Team	GP	G	A	Pts.	PIM
77-78	Cin-NE (WHA)	81	14	43	57	63
78-79	NE (WHA)	78	4	16	20	33
79-80	Hart	26	3	4	7	14
NHL Totals		26	3	4	7	14
WHA Totals		549	65	264	329	341
WHA Playoff Totals		41	5	15	20	48

POCZA, Harvie D. *6-2 198 LW*
B. Lethbridge, Alta., Sept. 22, 1959

Season	Team	GP	G	A	Pts.	PIM
79-80	Wash	1	0	0	0	0
81-82	Wash	2	0	0	0	0
Totals		3	0	0	0	0

PODDUBNY, Walter Michael *6-1 210 LW*
B. Thunder Bay, Ont., Feb. 14, 1960

Season	Team	GP	G	A	Pts.	PIM
81-82	Edm-Tor	15	3	4	7	8
82-83	Tor	72	28	31	59	71
83-84	Tor	38	11	14	25	48
84-85	Tor	32	5	15	20	26
85-86	Tor	33	12	22	34	25
86-87	NYR	75	40	47	87	49
87-88	NYR	77	38	50	88	76
88-89	Que	72	38	37	75	107
89-90	NJ	33	4	10	14	28
90-91	NJ	14	4	6	10	10
91-92	NJ	7	1	2	3	6
Totals		468	184	238	422	454
Playoff Totals		19	7	2	9	12

PODLOSKI, Ray *6-2 210 C*
B. Edmonton, Alta., Jan. 5, 1966

Season	Team	GP	G	A	Pts.	PIM
88-89	Bos	8	0	1	1	22

PODOLSKY, Nelson (Nellie) *5-10 170 LW*
B. Winnipeg, Man., Dec. 19, 1925

Season	Team	GP	G	A	Pts.	PIM
48-49	Det	1	0	0	0	0
Playoff Totals		7	0	0	0	4

POESCHEK, Rudy *6-2 210 RW/D*
B. Kamloops, B.C., Sept. 29, 1966

Season	Team	GP	G	A	Pts.	PIM
87-88	NYR	1	0	0	0	2
88-89	NYR	52	0	2	2	199
89-90	NYR	15	0	0	0	55
90-91	Winn	1	0	0	0	5
91-92	Winn	4	0	0	0	17
Totals		73	0	2	2	278

POETA, Anthony Joseph *5-5 168 RW*
B. North Bay, Ont., Mar. 4, 1933

Season	Team	GP	G	A	Pts.	PIM
51-52	Chi	1	0	0	0	0

POILE, Donald B. *C*
B. Fort William, Ont., June 1, 1932

Season	Team	GP	G	A	Pts.	PIM
54-55	Det	4	0	0	0	0
57-58	Det	62	7	9	16	12
Totals		66	7	9	16	12
Playoff Totals		4	0	0	0	0

POILE, Norman Robert (Bud) *6-0 185 C*
B. Fort William, Ont., Feb. 10, 1924

Season	Team	GP	G	A	Pts.	PIM
42-43	Tor	48	16	19	35	24
43-44	Tor	11	6	8	14	9
45-46	Tor	9	1	8	9	0
46-47	Tor	59	19	17	36	19
47-48	Tor-Chi	58	25	29	54	14
48-49	Chi-Det	60	21	21	42	8
49-50	NYR-Bos	66	19	20	39	14
Totals		311	107	122	229	88
Playoff Totals		23	4	4	8	8

POIRER, Gordon Arthur *C*
B. Maple Creek, Sask., Oct. 27, 1913

Season	Team	GP	G	A	Pts.	PIM
39-40	Mont	10	0	1	1	0

POLANIC, Thomas Joseph *6-3 205 D*
B. Toronto, Ont., Apr. 2, 1943

Season	Team	GP	G	A	Pts.	PIM
69-70	Minn	16	0	2	2	53
70-71	Minn	3	0	0	0	0
Totals		19	0	2	2	53
Playoff Totals		5	1	1	2	4

POLICH, John *6-1 200 RW*
B. Hibbing, Minn., July 8, 1916

Season	Team	GP	G	A	Pts.	PIM
39-40	NYR	1	0	0	0	0
40-41	NYR	2	0	1	1	0
Totals		3	0	1	1	0

POLICH, Michael D. *5-8 165 LW*
B. Hibbing, Minn., Dec. 19, 1952

Season	Team	GP	G	A	Pts.	PIM
77-78	Mont	1	0	0	0	0
78-79	Minn	73	6	10	16	18
79-80	Minn	78	10	14	24	20
80-81	Minn	74	8	5	13	19
Totals		226	24	29	53	57

POLICH, Michael D. *(Continued)*

Season	Team	GP	G	A	Pts.	PIM
Playoff Totals		23	2	1	3	2

POLIS, Gregory Linn *6-0 195 LW*
B. Westlock, Alta., Aug. 8, 1950

Season	Team	GP	G	A	Pts.	PIM
70-71	Pitt	61	18	15	33	40
71-72	Pitt	76	30	19	49	38
72-73	Pitt	78	26	23	49	36
73-74	Pitt-StL	78	22	25	47	56
74-75	NYR	76	26	15	41	55
75-76	NYR	79	15	21	36	77
76-77	NYR	77	16	23	39	44
77-78	NYR	37	7	16	23	12
78-79	NYR-Wash	25	13	7	20	14
79-80	Wash	28	1	5	6	19
Totals		615	174	169	343	391
Playoff Totals		7	0	2	2	6

POLIZIANI, Daniel *5-11 160 RW*
B. Sydney, N.S., Jan. 8, 1935

Season	Team	GP	G	A	Pts.	PIM
58-59	Bos	1	0	0	0	0
Playoff Totals		3	0	0	0	0

POLONICH, Dennis Daniel *5-6 165 C/RW*
B. Foam Lake, Sask., Dec. 4, 1953

Season	Team	GP	G	A	Pts.	PIM
74-75	Det	4	0	0	0	0
75-76	Det	57	11	12	23	302
76-77	Det	79	18	28	46	274
77-78	Det	79	16	19	35	254
78-79	Det	62	10	12	22	208
79-80	Det	66	2	8	10	127
80-81	Det	32	2	2	4	77
82-83	Det	11	0	1	1	0
Totals		390	59	82	141	1242
Playoff Totals		7	1	0	1	19

POOLEY, Paul *6-0 177 C*
B. Exeter, Ont., Aug. 2, 1960

Season	Team	GP	G	A	Pts.	PIM
84-85	Winn	12	0	2	2	0
85-86	Winn	3	0	1	1	0
Totals		15	0	3	3	0

POPEIN, Lawrence Thomas (Pope)
5-9 165 C
B. Yorkton, Sask., Aug. 11, 1930

Season	Team	GP	G	A	Pts.	PIM
54-55	NYR	70	11	17	28	27
55-56	NYR	64	14	25	39	37
56-57	NYR	67	11	19	30	20
57-58	NYR	70	12	22	34	22
58-59	NYR	61	13	21	34	28
59-60	NYR	66	14	22	36	16
60-61	NYR	4	0	1	1	0
67-68	Oak	47	5	14	19	12
Totals		449	80	141	221	162
Playoff Totals		16	1	4	5	6

POPIEL, Poul Peter (Paul) *5-8 170 D*
B. Sollested, Denmark, Feb. 28, 1943

Season	Team	GP	G	A	Pts.	PIM
65-66	Bos	3	0	1	1	2
67-68	LA	1	0	0	0	0
68-69	Det	62	2	13	15	82
69-70	Det	32	0	4	4	31
70-71	Van	78	10	22	32	61
71-72	Van	38	1	1	2	36
72-73	Hou (WHA)	74	16	48	64	158
73-74	Hou (WHA)	78	7	41	48	126
74-75	Hou (WHA)	78	11	53	64	22
75-76	Hou (WHA)	78	10	36	46	71
76-77	Hou (WHA)	80	12	56	68	87
77-78	Hou (WHA)	80	6	31	37	53
79-80	Edm	10	0	0	0	0
NHL Totals		224	13	41	54	212
WHA Totals		468	62	265	327	517
NHL Playoff Totals		4	1	0	1	4
WHA Playoff Totals		71	7	47	54	118

PORTLAND, John Frederick (Jack)
6-2 185 D
B. Waubaushene, Ont., July 30, 1912

Season	Team	GP	G	A	Pts.	PIM
33-34	Mont	31	0	2	2	10
34-35	Mont-Bos	20	1	1	2	4
35-36	Bos	2	0	0	0	0
36-37	Bos	46	2	4	6	58
37-38	Bos	48	0	5	5	26
38-39	Bos	48	4	5	9	46
39-40	Bos-Chi	44	1	9	10	36
40-41	Chi-Mont	47	2	7	9	38
41-42	Mont	46	2	9	11	53
42-43	Mont	49	3	14	17	52
Totals		381	15	56	71	323
Playoff Totals		33	1	3	4	25

PORVARI, Jukka *5-11 175 RW*
B. Tampere, Finland, Jan. 19, 1954

Season	Team	GP	G	A	Pts.	PIM
81-82	Col	31	2	6	8	0
82-83	NJ	8	1	3	4	4
Totals		39	3	9	12	4

POSA, Victor *6-0 195 LW/D*
B. Bari, Italy, Nov. 5, 1966

Season	Team	GP	G	A	Pts.	PIM
85-86	Chi	2	0	0	0	2

POSAVAD, Mike *5-11 195 D*
B. Brantford, Ont., Jan. 3, 1964

Season	Team	GP	G	A	Pts.	PIM
85-86	StL	6	0	0	0	0
86-87	StL	2	0	0	0	0
Totals		8	0	0	0	0

POTVIN, Denis Charles *6-0 205 D*
B. Ottawa, Ont., Oct. 29, 1953

Season	Team	GP	G	A	Pts.	PIM
73-74	NYI	77	17	37	54	175
74-75	NYI	79	21	55	76	105
75-76	NYI	78	31	67	98	100
76-77	NYI	80	25	55	80	103
77-78	NYI	80	30	64	94	81
78-79	NYI	73	31	70	101	58
79-80	NYI	31	8	33	41	44
80-81	NYI	74	20	56	76	104
81-82	NYI	60	24	37	61	83
82-83	NYI	69	12	54	66	60
83-84	NYI	78	22	63	85	87
84-85	NYI	77	17	51	68	96
85-86	NYI	74	21	38	59	76
86-87	NYI	58	12	30	42	70
87-88	NYI	72	19	32	51	112
Totals		1060	310	742	1052	1354
Playoff Totals		185	56	108	164	253

POTVIN, Jean Rene *5-11 188 D*
B. Ottawa, Ont., Mar. 25, 1949

Season	Team	GP	G	A	Pts.	PIM
70-71	LA	4	1	3	4	2
71-72	LA-Phil	68	5	15	20	41
72-73	Phil-NYI	45	3	12	15	22
73-74	NYI	78	5	23	28	100
74-75	NYI	73	9	24	33	59
75-76	NYI	78	17	55	72	74
76-77	NYI	79	10	36	46	26
77-78	NYI-Clev	74	4	24	28	60
78-79	Minn	64	5	16	21	65
79-80	NYI	32	2	13	15	26
80-81	NYI	18	2	3	5	25
Totals		613	63	224	287	500
Playoff Totals		39	2	9	11	17

POTVIN, Marc *6-1 185 RW*
B. Ottawa, Ont., Jan. 29, 1967

Season	Team	GP	G	A	Pts.	PIM
90-91	Det	9	0	0	0	55
91-92	Det	5	1	0	1	52
Totals		14	1	0	1	107
Playoff Totals		7	0	0	0	32

POUDRIER, Daniel *6-2 175 D*
B. Thetford Mines, Que., Feb. 15, 1964

Season	Team	GP	G	A	Pts.	PIM
85-86	Que	13	1	5	6	10
86-87	Que	6	0	0	0	0
87-88	Que	6	0	0	0	0
Totals		25	1	5	6	10

POULIN, Daniel *5-11 185 D*
B. Robertsville, Que., Sept. 19, 1957

Season	Team	GP	G	A	Pts.	PIM
81-82	Minn	3	1	1	2	2
82-83	Phil	2	2	0	2	2
Totals		5	3	1	4	4

POULIN, David James *5-11 190 C*
B. Timmins, Ont., Dec. 17, 1958

Season	Team	GP	G	A	Pts.	PIM
82-83	Phil	2	2	0	2	2
83-84	Phil	73	31	45	76	47
84-85	Phil	73	30	44	74	59
85-86	Phil	79	27	42	69	49
86-87	Phil	75	25	45	70	53
87-88	Phil	68	19	32	51	32
88-89	Phil	69	18	17	35	49
89-90	Phil-Bos	60	15	27	42	24
90-91	Bos	31	8	12	20	25
91-92	Bos	18	4	4	8	18
Totals		548	179	268	447	358
Playoff Totals		112	28	39	67	103

POULIN, Patrick *6-1 208 LW*
B. Vanier, Que., Apr. 23, 1973

Season	Team	GP	G	A	Pts.	PIM
91-92	Hart	1	0	0	0	2
Playoff Totals		7	2	1	3	0

POUZAR, Jaroslav *5-11 202 LW*
B. Czechoslovakia, Jan. 23, 1952

Season	Team	GP	G	A	Pts.	PIM
82-83	Edm	74	15	18	33	57
83-84	Edm	67	13	19	32	44

POUZAR, Jaroslav *(Continued)*

Season	Team	GP	G	A	Pts.	PIM
84-85	Edm	33	4	8	12	28
86-87	Edm	12	2	3	5	6
Totals		186	34	48	82	135
Playoff Totals		29	6	4	10	16

POWELL, Raymond Henry *6-0 170 C*
B. Timmins, Ont., Nov. 16, 1925

Season	Team	GP	G	A	Pts.	PIM
50-51	Chi	31	7	15	22	2

POWIS, Geoffrey Charles *6-0 179 C*
B. Winnipeg, Man., June 14, 1945

Season	Team	GP	G	A	Pts.	PIM
67-68	Chi	2	0	0	0	0

POWIS, Trevor Lynn (Lynn) *6-0 176 C*
B. Saskatoon, Sask., Apr. 19, 1949

Season	Team	GP	G	A	Pts.	PIM
73-74	Chi	57	8	13	21	6
74-75	KC	73	11	20	31	19
75-76	Calg (WHA)	21	4	10	14	2
76-77	Calg (WHA)	63	30	30	60	40
77-78	Winn (WHA)	69	16	25	41	18
NHL Totals		130	19	33	52	25
WHA Totals		153	50	65	115	60
NHL Playoff Totals		1	0	0	0	0
WHA Playoff Totals		13	7	5	12	9

PRAJSLER, Petr *6-2 200 D*
B. Hradec Kralove, Czech., Sept. 21, 1965

Season	Team	GP	G	A	Pts.	PIM
87-88	LA	7	0	0	0	2
88-89	LA	2	0	3	3	0
89-90	LA	34	3	7	10	47
91-92	Bos	3	0	0	0	2
Totals		46	3	10	13	51
Playoff Totals		4	0	0	0	0

PRATT, John (Jack) *D*
B. Edinburgh, Scotland

Season	Team	GP	G	A	Pts.	PIM
30-31	Bos	32	2	0	2	36
31-32	Bos	5	0	0	0	6
Totals		37	2	0	2	42
Playoff Totals		4	0	0	0	0

PRATT, Kelly Edward *5-9 170 RW*
B. High Prairie, Alta., Feb. 8, 1953

Season	Team	GP	G	A	Pts.	PIM
73-74	Winn (WHA)	46	4	6	10	50
74-75	Pitt	22	0	6	6	15

PRATT, Tracy Arnold *6-2 195 D*
B. New York, N.Y., Mar. 8, 1943

Season	Team	GP	G	A	Pts.	PIM
67-68	Oak	34	0	5	5	90
68-69	Pitt	18	0	5	5	34
69-70	Pitt	65	5	7	12	124
70-71	Buf	76	1	7	8	179
71-72	Buf	27	0	10	10	52
72-73	Buf	74	1	15	16	116
73-74	Buf-Van	78	3	15	18	96
74-75	Van	79	5	17	22	145
75-76	Van	52	1	5	6	72
76-77	Col-Tor	77	1	11	12	118
Totals		580	17	97	114	1026
Playoff Totals		25	0	1	1	62

PRATT, Walter (Babe) *6-3 210 D*
B. Stony Mountain, Man., Jan. 7, 1916

Season	Team	GP	G	A	Pts.	PIM
35-36	NYR	17	1	1	2	16
36-37	NYR	47	8	7	15	23
37-38	NYR	47	5	14	19	56
38-39	NYR	48	2	19	21	20
39-40	NYR	48	4	13	17	61
40-41	NYR	47	3	17	20	52
41-42	NYR	47	4	24	28	45
42-43	NYR-Tor	44	12	27	39	50
43-44	Tor	50	17	40	57	30
44-45	Tor	50	18	23	41	39
45-46	Tor	41	5	20	25	36
46-47	Bos	31	4	4	8	25
Totals		517	83	209	292	453
Playoff Totals		63	12	17	29	90

PRENTICE, Dean Sutherland
5-11 180 LW
B. Schumacher, Ont., Oct. 5, 1932

Season	Team	GP	G	A	Pts.	PIM
52-53	NYR	55	6	3	9	20
53-54	NYR	52	4	13	17	18
54-55	NYR	70	16	15	31	21
55-56	NYR	70	24	18	42	44
56-57	NYR	68	19	23	42	38
57-58	NYR	38	13	9	22	14
58-59	NYR	70	17	33	50	11
59-60	NYR	70	32	34	66	43
60-61	NYR	56	20	25	45	17
61-62	NYR	68	22	38	60	20

PRENTICE, Dean Sutherland
(Continued)

Season	Team	GP	G	A	Pts.	PIM
62-63	NYR-Bos	68	19	34	53	22
63-64	Bos	70	23	16	39	37
64-65	Bos	31	14	9	23	12
65-66	Bos-Det	69	13	31	44	18
66-67	Det	68	23	22	45	18
67-68	Det	69	17	38	55	42
68-69	Det	74	14	20	34	18
69-70	Pitt	75	26	25	51	14
70-71	Pitt	69	21	17	38	18
71-72	Minn	71	20	27	47	14
72-73	Minn	73	26	16	42	22
73-74	Minn	24	2	3	5	4
Totals		1378	391	469	860	485
Playoff Totals		54	13	17	30	38

PRENTICE, Eric Dayton *D*
B. Schumacher, Ont., Aug. 22, 1926

Season	Team	GP	G	A	Pts.	PIM
43-44	Tor	5	0	0	0	4

PRESLEY, Wayne *5-11 180 RW*
B. Detroit, Mich., Mar. 23, 1965

Season	Team	GP	G	A	Pts.	PIM
84-85	Chi	3	0	1	1	0
85-86	Chi	38	7	8	15	38
86-87	Chi	80	32	29	61	114
87-88	Chi	42	12	10	22	52
88-89	Chi	72	21	19	40	100
89-90	Chi	49	6	7	13	69
90-91	Chi	71	15	19	34	122
91-92	SJ-Buf	59	10	16	26	133
Totals		414	103	109	212	628
Playoff Totals		58	20	15	35	112

PRESTON, Richard John *5-11 185 RW*
B. Regina, Sask., May 22, 1952

Season	Team	GP	G	A	Pts.	PIM
74-75	Hou (WHA)	78	20	21	41	10
75-76	Hou (WHA)	77	22	33	55	33
76-77	Hou (WHA)	80	38	41	79	54
77-78	Hou (WHA)	73	25	25	50	52
78-79	Winn (WHA)	80	28	32	60	88
79-80	Chi	80	31	30	61	70
80-81	Chi	47	7	14	21	24
81-82	Chi	75	15	28	43	30
82-83	Chi	79	25	28	53	64
83-84	Chi	75	10	18	28	50
84-85	NJ	75	12	15	27	26
85-86	NJ	76	19	22	41	65
86-87	Chi	73	8	9	17	19
NHL Totals		580	127	164	291	348
WHA Totals		388	133	152	285	237
NHL Playoff Totals		47	4	18	22	56
WHA Playoff Totals		51	16	22	38	39

PRESTON, Yves *5-11 180 LW*
B. Montreal, Que., June 14, 1956

Season	Team	GP	G	A	Pts.	PIM
78-79	Phil	9	3	1	4	0
80-81	Phil	19	4	2	6	4
Totals		28	7	3	10	4

PRIAKHIN, Sergei *6-3 210 RW*
B. Moscow, Soviet Union, Dec. 7, 1963

Season	Team	GP	G	A	Pts.	PIM
88-89	Calg	2	0	0	0	2
89-90	Calg	20	2	2	4	0
90-91	Calg	24	1	6	7	0
Totals		46	3	8	11	2
Playoff Totals		1	0	0	0	0

PRICE, Bob *F*

Season	Team	GP	G	A	Pts.	PIM
19-20	Ott	1	0	0	0	0

PRICE, Garry Noel (Noel) *6-0 185 D*
B. Brockville, Ont., Dec. 9, 1935

Season	Team	GP	G	A	Pts.	PIM
57-58	Tor	1	0	0	0	5
58-59	Tor	28	0	0	0	4
59-60	NYR	6	0	0	0	0
60-61	NYR	1	0	0	0	2
61-62	Det	20	0	1	1	6
65-66	Mont	15	0	6	6	8
66-67	Mont	24	0	3	3	8
67-68	Pitt	70	6	27	33	48
68-69	Pitt	73	2	18	20	79
70-71	LA	62	1	19	20	29
72-73	Atl	54	1	13	14	38
73-74	Atl	62	0	13	13	38
74-75	Atl	80	4	14	18	82
75-76	Atl	3	0	0	0	2
Totals		499	14	114	128	349
Playoff Totals		12	0	1	1	8

PRICE, John Rees (Jack) *5-9 185 D*
B. Goderich, Ont., May 8, 1932

Season	Team	GP	G	A	Pts.	PIM
51-52	Chi	1	0	0	0	0
52-53	Chi	10	0	0	0	2
53-54	Chi	46	4	6	10	22
Totals		57	4	6	10	24

PRICE, John Rees (Jack) *(Continued)*

Season	Team	GP	G	A	Pts.	PIM
Playoff Totals		4	0	0	0	0

PRICE, Shaun Patrick (Pat) *6-2 195 D*
B. Nelson, B.C., Mar. 24, 1955

Season	Team	GP	G	A	Pts.	PIM
74-75	Van (WHA)	68	5	29	34	15
75-76	NYI	4	0	2	2	2
76-77	NYI	71	3	22	25	25
77-78	NYI	52	2	10	12	27
78-79	NYI	55	3	11	14	50
79-80	Edm	75	11	21	32	193
80-81	Edm-Pitt	72	8	34	42	226
81-82	Pitt	77	7	31	38	322
82-83	Pitt-Que	52	2	13	15	132
83-84	Que	72	3	25	28	188
84-85	Que	68	1	26	27	118
85-86	Que	54	3	13	16	82
86-87	Que-NYR	60	0	8	8	130
87-88	Minn	14	0	2	2	20
NHL Totals		726	43	218	261	1456
WHA Totals		68	5	29	34	15
NHL Playoff Totals		74	2	10	12	195

PRICE, Thomas Edward *6-1 190 D*
B. Toronto, Ont., July 12, 1954

Season	Team	GP	G	A	Pts.	PIM
74-75	Cal	3	0	0	0	4
75-76	Cal	5	0	0	0	0
76-77	Clev-Pitt	9	0	2	2	4
77-78	Pitt	10	0	0	0	0
78-79	Pitt	2	0	0	0	4
Totals		29	0	2	2	12

PRIESTLAY, Ken *5-10 190 C*
B. Richmond, B.C., Aug. 24, 1967

Season	Team	GP	G	A	Pts.	PIM
86-87	Buf	34	11	6	17	8
87-88	Buf	33	5	12	17	35
88-89	Buf	15	2	0	2	2
89-90	Buf	35	7	7	14	14
90-91	Pitt	2	0	1	1	0
91-92	Pitt	50	2	8	10	4
Totals		169	27	34	61	63
Playoff Totals		14	0	0	0	21

PRIMEAU, A. Joseph (Joe) *5-11 153 C*
B. Lindsay, Ont., Jan. 29, 1906

Season	Team	GP	G	A	Pts.	PIM
27-28	Tor	2	0	0	0	0
28-29	Tor	6	0	1	1	2
29-30	Tor	43	5	21	26	28
30-31	Tor	38	9	32	41	18
31-32	Tor	46	13	37	50	25
32 33	Tor	48	11	21	32	4
33-34	Tor	45	14	32	46	8
34-35	Tor	37	10	20	30	16
35-36	Tor	45	4	13	17	10
Totals		310	66	177	243	111
Playoff Totals		38	5	18	23	12

PRIMEAU, Keith *6-4 220 C*
B. Toronto, Ont., Nov. 24, 1971

Season	Team	GP	G	A	Pts.	PIM
90-91	Det	58	3	12	15	106
91-92	Det	35	6	10	16	83
Totals		93	9	22	31	189
Playoff Totals		16	1	1	2	39

PRIMEAU, Kevin *RW*

Season	Team	GP	G	A	Pts.	PIM
77-78	Edm (WHA)	7	0	1	1	2
80-81	Van	2	0	0	0	4
NHL Totals		2	0	0	0	4
WHA Totals		7	0	0	0	2
WHA Playoff Totals		2	0	0	0	2

PRINGLE, Ellis (Ellie) *D*
B. Toronto, Ont.

Season	Team	GP	G	A	Pts.	PIM
30-31	NYA	6	0	0	0	0

PROBERT, Bob *6-3 215 LW*
B. Windsor, Ont., June 5, 1965

Season	Team	GP	G	A	Pts.	PIM
85-86	Det	44	8	13	21	186
86-87	Det	63	13	11	24	221
87-88	Det	74	29	33	62	398
88-89	Det	25	4	2	6	106
89-90	Det	4	3	0	3	21
90-91	Det	55	16	23	39	315
91-92	Det	63	20	24	44	276
Totals		328	93	106	199	1523
Playoff Totals		49	13	25	38	192

PRODGERS, George (Goldie) *F*
B. 1892

Season	Team	GP	G	A	Pts.	PIM
19-20	Tor	16	8	6	14	2
20-21	Ham	23	18	8	26	8
21-22	Ham	24	15	4	19	4
22-23	Ham	23	13	3	16	13
23-24	Ham	23	9	1	10	6

PRODGERS, George (Goldie) *(Continued)*

Season	Team	GP	G	A	Pts.	PIM
24-25	Ham	1	0	0	0	0
25-26	Mont	24	0	0	0	0
Totals		134	63	22	85	33

PRONOVOST, Joseph Armand (Andre)
5-9 165 LW
B. Shawinigan Falls, Que., July 9, 1936

Season	Team	GP	G	A	Pts.	PIM
56-57	Mont	64	10	11	21	58
57-58	Mont	66	16	12	28	55
58-59	Mont	70	9	14	23	48
59-60	Mont	69	12	19	31	61
60-61	Mont-Bos	68	12	16	28	34
61-62	Bos	70	15	8	23	70
62-63	Bos-Det	68	13	7	20	24
63-64	Det	70	7	16	23	23
64-65	Det	3	0	1	1	0
67-68	Minn	8	0	0	0	0
Totals		556	94	104	198	373
Playoff Totals		70	11	11	22	58

PRONOVOST, Joseph Jean Dinis (Jean)
5-11 185 RW
B. Shawinigan Falls, Que., Dec. 18, 1945

Season	Team	GP	G	A	Pts.	PIM
68-69	Pitt	76	16	25	41	41
69-70	Pitt	72	20	21	41	45
70-71	Pitt	78	21	24	45	35
71-72	Pitt	68	30	23	53	12
72-73	Pitt	66	21	22	43	16
73-74	Pitt	77	40	32	72	22
74-75	Pitt	78	43	32	75	37
75-76	Pitt	80	52	52	104	24
76-77	Pitt	79	33	31	64	24
77-78	Pitt	79	40	25	65	50
78-79	Atl	75	28	39	67	30
79-80	Atl	80	24	19	43	12
80-81	Wash	80	22	36	58	67
81-82	Wash	10	1	2	3	4
Totals		998	391	383	774	419
Playoff Totals		35	11	9	20	14

PRONOVOST, Rene Marcel *6-0 190 D*
B. Lac la Tortue, Que., June 15, 1930

Season	Team	GP	G	A	Pts.	PIM
50-51	Det	37	1	6	7	20
51-52	Det	69	7	11	18	50
52-53	Det	68	8	19	27	72
53-54	Det	57	6	12	18	50
54-55	Det	70	9	25	34	90
55-56	Det	68	4	13	17	46
56-57	Det	70	7	9	16	38
57-58	Det	62	2	18	20	52
58-59	Det	69	11	21	32	44
59-60	Det	69	7	17	24	38
60-61	Det	70	6	11	17	44
61-62	Det	70	4	14	18	30
62-63	Det	69	4	9	13	48
63-64	Det	67	3	17	20	20
64-65	Det	68	1	15	16	45
65-66	Tor	54	2	8	10	34
66-67	Tor	58	2	12	14	28
67-68	Tor	70	3	17	20	48
68-69	Tor	34	1	2	3	20
69-70	Tor	7	0	1	1	4
Totals		1206	88	257	345	821
Playoff Totals		134	8	23	31	104

PROPP, Brian Philip *5-10 195 LW*
B. Lanigan, Sask., Feb. 15, 1959

Season	Team	GP	G	A	Pts.	PIM
79-80	Phil	80	34	41	75	54
80-81	Phil	79	26	40	66	110
81-82	Phil	80	44	47	91	117
82-83	Phil	80	40	42	82	72
83-84	Phil	79	39	53	92	37
84-85	Phil	76	43	53	96	43
85-86	Phil	72	40	57	97	47
86-87	Phil	53	31	36	67	45
87-88	Phil	74	27	49	76	76
88-89	Phil	77	32	46	78	37
89-90	Phil-Bos	54	16	24	40	41
90-91	Minn	79	26	47	73	58
91-92	Minn	51	12	23	35	49
Totals		934	410	558	968	786
Playoff Tot.		160	64	84	148	151

PROVOST, Joseph Antoine (Claude)
5-9,
175 RW
B. Montreal, Que., Sept. 17, 1933

Season	Team	GP	G	A	Pts.	PIM
55-56	Mont	60	13	16	29	30
56-57	Mont	67	16	14	30	24
57-58	Mont	70	19	32	51	71
58-59	Mont	69	16	22	38	37
59-60	Mont	70	17	29	46	42
60-61	Mont	49	11	4	15	32
61 62	Mont	70	33	29	62	22
62-63	Mont	67	20	30	50	26
63-64	Mont	68	15	17	32	37

PROVOST, Joseph Antoine (Claude)
(Continued)

Season	Team	GP	G	A	Pts.	PIM
64-65	Mont	70	27	37	64	28
65 66	Mont	70	19	36	55	38
66-67	Mont	64	11	13	24	16
67-68	Mont	73	14	30	44	26
68-69	Mont	73	13	15	28	18
69-70	Mont	65	10	11	21	22
Totals		1005	254	335	589	469
Playoff Totals		126	25	38	63	86

PRYOR, Chris *5-11 210 D*
B. St. Paul, Minn., Jan. 23, 1961

Season	Team	GP	G	A	Pts.	PIM
84-85	Minn	4	0	0	0	16
85-86	Minn	7	0	1	1	0
86-87	Minn	50	1	3	4	49
87-88	Minn-NYI	4	0	0	0	8
88-89	NYI	7	0	0	0	25
89-90	NYI	10	0	0	0	24
Totals		82	1	4	5	122

PRYSTAI, Metro *5-9 170 C*
B. Yorkton, Sask., Nov. 7, 1927

Season	Team	GP	G	A	Pts.	PIM
47-48	Chi	54	7	11	18	25
48-49	Chi	59	12	7	19	19
49-50	Chi	65	29	22	51	31
50-51	Det	62	20	17	37	27
51-52	Det	69	21	22	43	16
52-53	Det	70	16	34	50	12
53-54	Det	70	12	15	27	26
54-55	Det-Chi	69	13	16	29	37
55-56	Chi-Det	71	13	19	32	18
56-57	Det	70	7	15	22	16
57-58	Det	15	1	1	2	4
Totals		674	151	179	330	231
Playoff Totals		43	12	14	26	8

PUDAS, Albert *LW*

Season	Team	GP	G	A	Pts.	PIM
26-27	Tor	3	0	0	0	0

PULFORD, Robert Jesse *5-11 188 LW*
B. Newton Robinson, Ont., Mar. 31, 1936

Season	Team	GP	G	A	Pts.	PIM
56-57	Tor	65	11	11	22	32
57-58	Tor	70	14	17	31	48
58-59	Tor	70	23	14	37	53
59-60	Tor	70	24	28	52	81
60-61	Tor	40	11	18	29	41
61-62	Tor	70	18	21	39	98
62-63	Tor	70	19	25	44	49
63-64	Tor	70	18	30	48	73
64-65	Tor	65	19	20	39	46
65-66	Tor	70	28	28	56	51
66-67	Tor	67	17	28	45	28
67-68	Tor	74	20	30	50	40
68-69	Tor	72	11	23	34	20
69-70	Tor	74	18	19	37	31
70-71	LA	59	17	26	43	53
71-72	LA	73	13	24	37	48
Totals		1079	281	362	643	792
Playoff Totals		89	25	26	51	126

PULKKINEN, David Joel John *6-0 175 D*
B. Kapuskasing, Ont., May 18, 1949

Season	Team	GP	G	A	Pts.	PIM
72-73	NYI	2	0	0	0	0

PURPUR, Clifford (Fido) *F*
B. Grand Forks, N.D., Sept. 26, 1916

Season	Team	GP	G	A	Pts.	PIM
34-35	StL E	25	2	1	3	8
41-42	Chi	8	0	0	0	0
42-43	Chi	50	13	16	29	14
43-44	Chi	40	9	10	19	13
44-45	Chi	21	2	7	9	11
Totals		144	26	34	60	46
Playoff Totals		16	1	2	3	4

PURVES, John *6-1 201 RW*
B. Toronto, Ont., Feb. 12, 1968

Season	Team	GP	G	A	Pts.	PIM
90-91	Wash	7	1	0	1	0

PUSIE, Jean Baptiste *6-0 205 D*
B. Montreal, Que., Oct. 15, 1910

Season	Team	GP	G	A	Pts.	PIM
30-31	Mont	6	0	0	0	0
31-32	Mont	1	0	0	0	0
33-34	NYR	19	0	2	2	17
34-35	Bos	4	1	0	1	0
35-36	Mont	31	0	2	2	11
Totals		61	1	4	5	28
Playoff Totals		7	0	0	0	0

PYATT, Frederick (Nelson) *6-0 175 C*
B. Port Arthur, Ont., Sept. 9, 1953

Season	Team	GP	G	A	Pts.	PIM
73-74	Det	5	0	0	0	0
74-75	Det-Wash	25	6	4	10	21
75-76	Wash	77	26	23	49	14
76-77	Col	77	23	22	45	20
77-78	Col	71	9	12	21	8

PYATT, Frederick (Nelson) *(Continued)*

Season	Team	GP	G	A	Pts.	PIM
78-79	Col	28	2	2	4	2
79-80	Col	13	5	0	5	2
Totals		296	71	63	134	67

QUACKENBUSH, Hubert George (Bill) *5-11 180 D*
B. Toronto, Ont., Mar. 2, 1922

Season	Team	GP	G	A	Pts.	PIM
42-43	Det	10	1	1	2	4
43-44	Det	43	4	14	18	6
44-45	Det	50	7	14	21	10
45-46	Det	48	11	10	21	6
46-47	Det	44	5	17	22	6
47-58	Det	58	6	16	22	17
48-49	Det	60	6	17	23	0
49-50	Bos	70	8	17	25	4
50-51	Bos	70	5	24	29	12
51-52	Bos	69	2	17	19	6
52-53	Bos	69	2	16	18	6
53-54	Bos	45	0	17	17	6
54-55	Bos	68	2	20	22	8
55-56	Bos	70	3	22	25	4
Totals		774	62	222	284	95
Playoff Totals		79	2	19	21	8

QUACKENBUSH, Maxwell Joseph *6-2 180 D*
B. Toronto, Ont., Aug. 29, 1928

Season	Team	GP	G	A	Pts.	PIM
50-51	Bos	47	4	6	10	26
51-52	Chi	14	0	1	1	4
Totals		61	4	7	11	30
Playoff Totals		6	0	0	0	4

QUENNEVILLE, Joel Norman *6-1 200 D*
B. Windsor, Ont., Sept. 15, 1958

Season	Team	GP	G	A	Pts.	PIM
78-79	Tor	61	2	9	11	60
79-80	Tor-Col	67	6	11	17	50
80-81	Col	71	10	24	34	86
81-82	Col	64	5	10	15	55
82-83	NJ	74	5	12	17	46
83-84	Hart	80	5	8	13	95
84-85	Hart	79	6	16	22	96
85-86	Hart	71	5	20	25	83
86-87	Hart	37	3	7	10	24
87-88	Hart	77	1	8	9	44
88-89	Hart	69	4	7	11	32
89-90	Hart	44	1	4	5	34
90-91	Wash	9	1	0	1	0
Totals		803	54	136	190	705
Playoff Totals		26	0	8	8	22

QUENNEVILLE, Leonard (Leo) *5-10 170 F*
B. St. Anicet, Que., June 15, 1900

Season	Team	GP	G	A	Pts.	PIM
29-30	NYR	25	0	3	3	10
Playoff Totals		3	0	0	0	0

QUILTY, John Francis *5-10 175 C*
B. Ottawa, Ont., Jan. 21, 1921

Season	Team	GP	G	A	Pts.	PIM
40-41	Mont	48	18	16	34	31
41-42	Mont	48	12	12	24	44
46-47	Mont	3	1	1	2	0
47-48	Mont-Bos	26	5	5	10	6
Totals		125	36	34	70	81
Playoff Totals		13	3	5	8	9

QUINN, Dan *5-10 175 C*
B. Ottawa, Ont., June 1, 1965

Season	Team	GP	G	A	Pts.	PIM
83-84	Calg	54	19	33	52	20
84-85	Calg	74	20	38	58	22
85-86	Calg	78	30	42	72	44
86-87	Calg-Pitt	80	31	49	80	54
87-88	Pitt	70	40	39	79	50
88-89	Pitt	79	34	60	94	102
89-90	Pitt-Van	78	25	38	63	49
90-91	Van-StL	78	22	38	60	66
91-92	Phil	67	11	26	37	26
Totals		658	232	363	595	433
Playoff Totals		53	21	22	43	56

QUINN, John Brian Patrick (Pat) *6-3 215 D*
B. Hamilton, Ont., Jan. 19, 1943

Season	Team	GP	G	A	Pts.	PIM
68-69	Tor	40	2	7	9	95
69-70	Tor	59	0	5	5	88
70-71	Van	76	2	11	13	149
71-72	Van	57	2	3	5	63
72-73	Atl	78	2	18	20	113
73-74	Atl	77	5	27	32	94
74-75	Atl	80	2	19	21	156
75-76	Atl	80	2	11	13	134
76-77	Atl	59	1	12	13	58
Totals		606	18	113	131	950
Playoff Totals		11	0	1	1	21

QUINNEY, Ken *5-10 186 RW*
B. New Westminster, B.C., May 23, 1965

Season	Team	GP	G	A	Pts.	PIM
86-87	Que	25	2	7	9	16
87-88	Que	15	2	2	4	5
90-91	Que	19	3	4	7	2
Totals		59	7	13	20	23

QUINTAL, Stephane *6-3 215 D*
B. Bouchervillle, Que., Oct. 22, 1968

Season	Team	GP	G	A	Pts.	PIM
88-89	Bos	26	0	1	1	29
89-90	Bos	38	2	2	4	22
90-91	Bos	45	2	6	8	89
91-92	Bos-StL	75	4	16	20	109
Totals		184	8	25	33	249
Playoff Totals		7	1	3	4	13

QUINTIN, Jean-Francois *6-1 180 C*
B. St. Jean, Que., May 28, 1969

Season	Team	GP	G	A	Pts.	PIM
91-92	SJ	8	3	0	3	0

RACINE, Yves *6-0 185 D*
B. Matane, Que., Feb. 7, 1969

Season	Team	GP	G	A	Pts.	PIM
89-90	Det	28	4	9	13	23
90-91	Det	62	7	40	47	33
91-92	Det	61	2	22	24	94
Totals		151	13	71	84	150
Playoff Totals		18	4	1	5	10

RADLEY, Harry John (Yip) *5-11 198 D*
B. Ottawa, Ont., June 27, 1910

Season	Team	GP	G	A	Pts.	PIM
30-31	NYA	1	0	0	0	0
36-37	Mont M	17	0	1	1	13
Totals		18	0	1	1	13

RAGLAN, Clarence Eldon (Rags) *6-1 177 D*
B. Pembroke, Ont., Sept. 4, 1927

Season	Team	GP	G	A	Pts.	PIM
50-51	Det	33	3	1	4	14
51-52	Chi	35	0	5	5	28
52-53	Chi	32	1	3	4	10
Totals		100	4	9	13	52
Playoff Totals		3	0	0	0	0

RAGLAN, Herb *6-0 205 RW*
B. Peterborough, Ont., Aug. 5, 1967

Season	Team	GP	G	A	Pts.	PIM
85-86	StL	7	0	0	0	5
86-87	StL	62	6	10	16	159
87-88	StL	73	10	15	25	190
88-89	StL	50	7	10	17	144
89-90	StL	11	0	1	1	21
90-91	StL-Que	47	4	6	10	82
91-92	Que	62	6	14	20	120
Totals		312	33	56	89	721
Playoff Totals		32	3	6	9	50

RALEIGH, James Donald (Don, Bones) *5-11 150 C*
B. Kenora, Ont., June 27, 1926

Season	Team	GP	G	A	Pts.	PIM
43-44	NYR	15	2	2	4	2
47-48	NYR	52	15	18	33	2
48-49	NYR	41	10	16	26	8
49-50	NYR	70	12	25	37	11
50-51	NYR	64	15	24	39	18
51-52	NYR	70	19	42	61	14
52-53	NYR	55	4	18	22	2
53-54	NYR	70	15	30	45	16
54-55	NYR	69	8	32	40	19
55-56	NYR	29	1	12	13	4
Totals		535	101	219	320	96
Playoff Totals		18	6	5	11	6

RAMAGE, George (Rob) *6-2 200 D*
B. Byron, Ont., Jan. 11, 1959

Season	Team	GP	G	A	Pts.	PIM
78-79	Birm (WHA)	80	12	36	48	165
79-80	Col	75	8	20	28	135
80-81	Col	79	20	42	62	193
81-82	Col	80	13	29	42	201
82-83	StL	78	16	35	51	193
83-84	StL	80	15	45	60	121
84-85	StL	80	7	31	38	178
85-86	StL	77	10	56	66	171
86-87	StL	59	11	28	39	108
87-88	StL-Calg	79	9	40	49	164
88-89	Calg	68	3	13	16	156
89-90	Tor	80	8	41	49	202
90-91	Tor	80	10	25	35	173
91-92	Minn	34	4	5	9	69
Totals		949	134	410	545	2061
Playoff Totals		77	8	42	50	214

RAMSAY, Beattie *D*

Season	Team	GP	G	A	Pts.	PIM
27-28	Tor	43	0	2	2	10

RAMSAY, Craig Edward *5-10 175 LW*
B. Weston, Ont., Mar. 17, 1951

Season	Team	GP	G	A	Pts.	PIM
71-72	Buf	57	6	10	16	0
72-73	Buf	76	11	17	28	15
73-74	Buf	78	20	26	46	0
74-75	Buf	80	26	38	64	26
75-76	Buf	80	22	49	71	34
76-77	Buf	80	20	41	61	20
77-78	Buf	80	28	43	71	18
78-79	Buf	80	26	31	57	10
79-80	Buf	80	21	39	60	18
80-81	Buf	80	24	35	59	12
81-82	Buf	80	16	35	51	8
82-83	Buf	64	11	18	29	7
83-84	Buf	76	9	17	26	17
84-85	Buf	79	12	21	33	16
Totals		1070	252	420	672	201
Playoff Totals		89	17	31	48	27

RAMSEY, Les *LW*
B. Montreal, Que., July 1, 1920

Season	Team	GP	G	A	Pts.	PIM
44-45	Chi	11	2	2	4	2

RAMSEY, Michael Allen *6-3 195 D*
B. Minneapolis, Minn., Dec. 3, 1960

Season	Team	GP	G	A	Pts.	PIM
79-80	Buf	13	1	6	7	6
80-81	Buf	72	3	14	17	56
81-82	Buf	80	7	23	30	56
82-83	Buf	77	8	30	38	55
83-84	Buf	72	9	22	31	82
84-85	Buf	79	8	22	30	102
85-86	Buf	76	7	21	28	117
86-87	Buf	80	8	31	39	109
87-88	Buf	63	5	16	21	77
88-89	Buf	56	2	14	16	84
89-90	Buf	73	4	21	25	47
90-91	Buf	71	6	14	20	46
91-92	Buf	66	3	14	17	67
Totals		878	71	248	319	904
Playoff Totals		72	8	18	26	158

RAMSEY, Wayne *6-0 185 D*
B. Hamiota, Man., Jan. 31, 1957

Season	Team	GP	G	A	Pts.	PIM
77-78	Buf	2	0	0	0	0

RANDALL, Kenneth *RW*

Season	Team	GP	G	A	Pts.	PIM
17-18	Tor	20	12	0	12	55
18-19	Tor	14	7	6	13	27
19-20	Tor	21	10	7	17	43
20-21	Tor	21	6	1	7	58
21-22	Tor	24	10	6	16	20
22-23	Tor	24	3	5	8	51
23-24	Ham	24	7	1	8	18
24-25	Ham	30	8	0	8	49
25-26	NYA	34	4	2	6	94
26-27	NYA	5	0	0	0	0
Totals		217	67	28	95	415
Playoff Totals		13	3	1	4	49

RANHEIM, Paul *6-0 195 LW*
B. St. Louis, Mo., Jan. 25, 1966

Season	Team	GP	G	A	Pts.	PIM
88-89	Calg	5	0	0	0	0
89-90	Calg	80	26	28	54	23
90-91	Calg	39	14	16	30	4
91-92	Calg	80	23	20	43	32
Totals		204	63	64	127	59
Playoff Totals		13	3	5	8	2

RANIERI, George Dominic *5-8 190 LW*
B. Toronto, Ont., Jan. 14, 1936

Season	Team	GP	G	A	Pts.	PIM
56-57	Bos	2	0	0	0	0

RATELLE, Joseph Gilbert Yvon (Jean) *6-1 180 C*
B. Lac St. Jean, Que., Oct. 3, 1940

Season	Team	GP	G	A	Pts.	PIM
60-61	NYR	3	2	1	3	0
61-62	NYR	31	4	8	12	4
62-63	NYR	48	11	9	20	8
63-64	NYR	15	0	7	7	6
64-65	NYR	54	14	21	35	14
65-66	NYR	67	21	30	51	10
66-67	NYR	41	6	5	11	4
67-68	NYR	74	32	46	78	18
68-69	NYR	75	32	46	78	26
69-70	NYR	75	32	42	74	28
70-71	NYR	78	26	46	72	14
71-72	NYR	63	46	63	109	4
72-73	NYR	78	41	53	94	12
73-74	NYR	68	28	39	67	16
74-75	NYR	79	36	55	91	26
75-76	NYR-Bos	80	36	69	105	18
76-77	Bos	78	33	61	94	22
77-78	Bos	80	25	59	84	10
78-79	Bos	80	27	45	72	12
79-80	Bos	67	28	45	73	8
80-81	Bos	47	11	26	37	16
Totals		1281	491	776	1267	276

RATELLE, Joseph Gilbert Yvon (Jean)
(Continued)

Season Team	GP	G	A	Pts.	PIM
Playoff Totals	123	32	66	98	24

RATHWELL, John Donald *6-0 190 RW*
B. Temiscaming, Que., Aug. 12, 1947

74-75 Bos	1	0	0	0	0

RAUSSE, Errol A. *5-10 181 LW*
B. Quesnel, B.C., May 18, 1959

79-80 Wash	24	6	2	8	0
80-81 Wash	5	1	1	2	0
81-82 Wash	2	0	0	0	0
Totals	31	7	3	10	0

RAUTAKALLIO, Pekka *5-11 185 D*
B. Pori, Finland, July 25, 1953

75-76 Phoe (WHA)	73	11	39	50	8
76-77 Phoe (WHA)	78	4	31	35	8
79-80 Atl	79	5	25	30	18
80-81 Calg	76	11	45	56	64
81-82 Calg	80	17	51	68	40
NHL Totals	235	33	121	154	122
WHA Totals	151	15	70	85	16
NHL Playoff Totals	23	2	5	7	8
WHA Playoff Totals	5	0	2	2	0

RAVLICH, Matthew Joseph *5-10 185 D*
B. Sault Ste. Marie, Ont., July 12, 1938

62-63 Bos	2	1	0	1	0
64-65 Chi	61	3	16	19	80
65-66 Chi	62	0	16	16	78
66-67 Chi	62	0	3	3	39
68-69 Chi	60	2	12	14	57
69-70 Det-LA	67	3	13	16	67
70-71 LA	66	3	16	19	41
71-72 Bos	25	0	1	1	2
72-73 Bos	5	0	1	1	0
Totals	410	12	78	90	364
Playoff Totals	24	1	5	6	16

RAY, Robert *6-0 210 LW*
B. Stirling, Ont., June 8, 1968

89-90 Buf	27	2	1	3	99
90-91 Buf	66	8	8	16	350
91-92 Buf	63	5	3	8	354
Totals	156	15	12	27	803
Playoff Totals	13	1	1	2	58

RAYMOND, Armand *D*
B. Mechanicsville, N.Y., Jan. 12, 1913

37-38 Mont	11	0	1	1	10
39-40 Mont	11	0	1	1	0
Totals	22	0	2	2	10

RAYMOND, Paul Marcel *5-7 138 RW*
B. Montreal, Que., Feb. 27, 1913

32-33 Mont	16	0	0	0	0
33-34 Mont	29	1	0	1	2
34-35 Mont	20	1	1	2	0
37-38 Mont	11	0	2	2	4
Totals	76	2	3	5	6
Playoff Totals	5	0	0	0	2

READ, Melvin Dean (Pee Wee)
5-6 165 C
B. Montreal, Que., Apr. 10, 1922

46-47 NYR	1	0	0	0	0

REARDON, Kenneth Joseph *5-10 180 D*
B. Winnipeg, Man., Apr. 1, 1921

40-41 Mont	34	2	8	10	41
41-42 Mont	41	3	12	15	93
45-46 Mont	43	5	4	9	45
46-47 Mont	52	5	17	22	84
47-48 Mont	58	7	15	22	129
48-49 Mont	46	3	13	16	103
49-50 Mont	67	1	27	28	109
Totals	341	26	96	122	604
Playoff Totals	31	2	5	7	62

REARDON, Terrance George *5-10 170 D*
B. Winnipeg, Man., Apr. 6, 1919

38-39 Bos	4	0	0	0	0
40-41 Bos	34	6	5	11	19
41-42 Mont	33	17	17	34	14
42-43 Mont	13	6	6	12	2
45-46 Bos	49	12	11	23	21
46-47 Bos	60	6	14	20	17
Totals	193	47	53	100	73
Playoff Totals	30	8	10	18	14

REAUME, Marc Avellin *6-1 185 D*
B. Lasalle, Que., Feb. 7, 1934

54-55 Tor	1	0	0	0	4
55-56 Tor	48	0	12	12	50
56-57 Tor	63	6	14	20	81
57-58 Tor	68	1	7	8	49
58-59 Tor	51	1	5	6	57
59-60 Tor-Det	45	0	2	2	8
60-61 Det	38	0	1	1	8
63-64 Mont	3	0	0	0	2
70-71 Van	27	0	2	2	4
Totals	344	8	43	51	263
Playoff Totals	21	0	2	2	8

REAY, William Tulip *5-7 155 C*
B. Winnipeg, Man., Aug. 21, 1918

43-44 Det	2	2	0	2	2
44-45 Det	2	0	0	0	0
45-46 Mont	44	17	12	29	10
46-47 Mont	59	22	20	42	17
47-48 Mont	60	6	14	20	24
48-49 Mont	60	22	23	45	33
49-50 Mont	68	19	26	45	48
50-51 Mont	60	6	18	24	24
51-52 Mont	68	7	34	41	20
52-53 Mont	56	4	15	19	26
Totals	479	105	162	267	204
Playoff Totals	63	13	16	29	43

RECCHI, Mark *5-10 185 RW*
B. Kamloops, B.C., Feb. 1, 1968

88-89 Pitt	15	1	1	2	0
89-90 Pitt	74	30	37	67	44
90-91 Pitt	78	40	73	113	48
91-92 Pitt-Phil	80	43	54	97	96
Totals	257	114	165	279	188
Playoff Totals	24	10	24	34	33

REDAHL, Gordon *5-11 170 RW*
B. Kinistino, Sask., Aug. 28, 1935

58-59 Bos	18	0	1	1	2

REDDING, George *D*

24-25 Bos	27	3	2	5	10
25-26 Bos	8	0	0	0	0
Totals	35	3	2	5	10

REDMOND, Craig *5-11 190 D*
B. Dawson Creek, B.C., Sept. 22, 1965

84-85 LA	79	6	33	39	57
85-86 LA	73	6	18	24	57
86-87 LA	16	1	7	8	8
87-88 LA	2	0	0	0	0
88-89 Edm	21	3	10	13	12
Totals	191	16	68	84	134
Playoff Totals	3	1	0	1	2

REDMOND, Michael Edward (Mickey)
5-11 185 RW
B. Kirkland Lake, Ont., Dec. 27, 1947

67-68 Mont	41	6	5	11	4
68-69 Mont	65	9	15	24	12
69-70 Mont	75	27	27	54	61
70-71 Mont-Det	61	20	24	44	42
71-72 Det	78	42	28	70	34
72-73 Det	76	52	41	93	24
73-74 Det	76	51	26	77	14
74-75 Det	29	15	12	27	18
75-76 Det	37	11	17	28	10
Totals	538	233	195	428	219
Playoff Totals	16	2	3	5	2

REDMOND, Richard John (Dick)
5-11 178 D
B. Kirkland Lake, Ont., Aug. 14, 1949

69-70 Minn	7	0	1	1	4
70-71 Minn-Cal	20	2	6	8	28
71-72 Cal	74	10	35	45	76
72-73 Cal-Chi	76	12	32	44	26
73-74 Chi	76	17	42	59	69
74-75 Chi	80	14	43	57	90
75-76 Chi	53	9	27	36	25
76-77 Chi	80	22	25	47	30
77-78 StL-Atl	70	11	22	33	32
78-79 Bos	64	7	26	33	21
79-80 Bos	76	14	33	47	39
80-81 Bos	78	15	20	35	60
81-82 Bos	17	0	0	0	4
Totals	771	133	312	445	504
Playoff Totals	66	9	22	31	27

REEDS, Mark *5-10 190 RW*
B. Burlington, Ont., Jan. 24, 1960

81-82 StL	9	1	3	4	0
82-83 StL	20	5	14	19	6
83-84 StL	65	11	14	25	23
84-85 StL	80	9	30	39	25

REEDS, Mark *(Continued)*

85-86 StL	78	10	28	38	28
86-87 StL	68	9	16	25	16
87-88 Hart	38	0	7	7	31
88-89 Hart	7	0	2	2	6
Totals	365	45	114	159	135
Playoff Totals	53	8	9	17	23

REEKIE, Joe *6-3 215 D*
B. Victoria, B.C., Feb. 22, 1965

85-86 Buf	3	0	0	0	14
86-87 Buf	56	1	8	9	82
87-88 Buf	30	1	4	5	68
88-89 Buf	15	1	3	4	26
89-90 NYI	31	1	8	9	43
90-91 NYI	66	3	16	19	96
91-92 NYI	54	4	12	16	85
Totals	255	11	51	62	414
Playoff Totals	2	0	0	0	4

REGAN, Lawrence Emmett *5-9 178 RW*
B. North Bay, Ont., Aug. 9, 1930

56-57 Bos	69	14	19	33	29
57-58 Bos	59	11	28	39	22
58-59 Bos-Tor	68	9	27	36	12
59-60 Tor	47	4	16	20	6
60-61 Tor	37	3	5	8	2
Totals	280	41	95	136	71
Playoff Totals	47	7	14	21	18

REGAN, William Donald *D*
B. Creighton Mines, Ont., Dec. 11, 1908

29-30 NYR	10	0	0	0	4
30-31 NYR	42	2	1	3	49
32-33 NYA	15	1	1	2	14
Totals	67	3	2	5	67
Playoff Totals	8	0	0	0	2

REGIER, Darcy John *5-11 190 D*
B. Swift Current, Sask., Nov. 27, 1956

77-78 Clev	15	0	1	1	28
82-83 NYI	6	0	0	0	7
83-84 NYI	5	0	1	1	0
Totals	26	0	2	2	35

REIBEL, Earl (Dutch) *5-8 160 C*
B. Kitchener, Ont., July 21, 1930

53-54 Det	69	15	33	48	18
54-55 Det	70	25	41	66	15
55-56 Det	68	17	39	56	10
56-57 Det	70	13	23	36	6
57-58 Det-Chi	69	8	17	25	10
58-59 Bos	63	6	8	14	16
Totals	409	84	161	245	75
Playoff Totals	39	6	14	20	4

REICHEL, Robert *5-11 180 C*
B. Litinov, Czechoslovakia, June 25, 1971

90-91 Calg	66	19	22	41	22
91-92 Calg	77	20	34	54	34
Totals	143	39	56	95	56
Playoff Totals	6	1	1	2	0

REID, Allan Thomas *6-1 200 D*
B. Fort Erie, Ont., June 24, 1946

67-68 Chi	56	0	4	4	25
68-69 Chi-Minn	48	0	7	7	50
69-70 Minn	66	1	7	8	51
70-71 Minn	73	3	14	17	62
71-72 Minn	78	6	15	21	107
72-73 Minn	60	1	13	14	50
73-74 Minn	76	4	19	23	81
74-75 Minn	74	1	5	6	103
75-76 Minn	69	0	15	15	52
76-77 Minn	65	0	8	8	52
77-78 Minn	36	1	6	7	21
Totals	701	17	113	130	654
Playoff Totals	42	1	13	14	49

REID, David *F*
B. Toronto, Ont., Jan. 11, 1934

52-53 Tor	2	0	0	0	0
54-55 Tor	1	0	0	0	0
55-56 Tor	4	0	0	0	0
Totals	7	0	0	0	0

REID, David *6-1 205 LW*
B. Toronto, Ont., May 15, 1964

83-84 Bos	8	1	0	1	2
84-85 Bos	35	14	13	27	27
85-86 Bos	37	10	10	20	10
86-87 Bos	12	3	3	6	0
87-88 Bos	3	0	0	0	0
88-89 Tor	77	9	21	30	22
89-90 Tor	70	9	19	28	9

REID, David *(Continued)*

Season	Team	GP	G	A	Pts.	PIM
90-91	Tor	69	15	13	28	18
91-92	Bos	43	7	7	14	27
Totals		354	68	86	154	115
Playoff Totals		25	3	5	8	4

REID, Gerald Roland *6-0 160 C*

B. Owen Sound, Ont., Oct. 13, 1928

Season	Team	GP	G	A	Pts.	PIM
48-49	Det	0	0	0	0	0
Playoff Totals		2	0	0	0	0

REID, Gordon J. *D*

B. Mt. Albert, Ont., Feb. 19, 1912

Season	Team	GP	G	A	Pts.	PIM
36-37	NYA	1	0	0	0	2

REID, Reginald S. *F*

Season	Team	GP	G	A	Pts.	PIM
24-25	Tor	28	2	0	2	2
25-26	Tor	12	0	0	0	2
Totals		40	2	0	2	4
Playoff Totals		2	0	0	0	0

REIERSON, David *6-0 185 D*

B. Bashaw, Alta., Aug. 30, 1964

Season	Team	GP	G	A	Pts.	PIM
88-89	Calg	2	0	0	0	2

REIGLE, Edmond (Rags) *5-8 180 D*

B. Winnipeg, Man., June 19, 1924

Season	Team	GP	G	A	Pts.	PIM
50-51	Bos	17	0	2	2	25

REINHART, Paul *5-11 200 D*

B. Kitchener, Ont., Jan. 6, 1960

Season	Team	GP	G	A	Pts.	PIM
79-80	Atl	79	9	38	47	31
80-81	Calg	74	18	49	67	52
81-82	Calg	62	13	48	61	17
82-83	Calg	78	17	58	75	28
83-84	Calg	27	6	15	21	10
84-85	Calg	75	23	46	69	18
85-86	Calg	32	8	25	33	15
86-87	Calg	76	15	53	68	22
87-88	Calg	14	0	4	4	10
88-89	Van	64	7	50	57	44
89-90	Van	67	17	40	57	30
Totals		648	133	426	559	277
Playoff Totals		83	23	54	77	42

REINIKKA, Oliver Mathias (Rocco) *F*

B. Shuswap, B.C., Aug. 2, 1901

Season	Team	GP	G	A	Pts.	PIM
26-27	NYR	16	0	0	0	0

REISE, Leo Charles, Jr. *D*

B. Stoney Creek, Ont., June 7, 1922

Season	Team	GP	G	A	Pts.	PIM
45-46	Chi	6	0	0	0	6
46-47	Chi-Det	48	4	6	10	32
47-48	Det	58	5	4	9	30
48-49	Det	59	3	7	10	60
49-50	Det	70	4	17	21	46
50-51	Det	68	5	16	21	46
51-52	Det	54	0	11	11	34
52-53	NYR	61	4	15	19	53
53-54	NYR	70	3	5	8	71
Totals		494	28	81	109	399
Playoff Totals		52	8	5	13	68

REISE, Leo Charles, Sr. *5-11 175 D*

B. Pembroke, Ont., June 1, 1892

Season	Team	GP	G	A	Pts.	PIM
20-21	Ham	6	2	0	2	8
21-22	Ham	24	9	14	23	8
22-23	Ham	24	6	6	12	35
23-24	Ham	4	0	0	0	0
26-27	NYA	40	7	6	13	24
27-28	NYA	43	8	1	9	62
28-29	NYA	44	4	1	5	32
29-30	NYR	14	0	1	1	8
Totals		199	36	29	65	177
Playoff Totals		6	0	0	0	16

RENAUD, Mark Joseph *6-0 185 D*

B. Windsor, Ont., Feb. 21, 1959

Season	Team	GP	G	A	Pts.	PIM
79-80	Hart	13	0	2	2	4
80-81	Hart	4	1	0	1	0
81-82	Hart	48	1	17	18	39
82-83	Hart	77	3	28	31	37
83-84	Buf	10	1	3	4	6
Totals		152	6	50	56	86

REYNOLDS, Bobby *5-11 175 LW*

B. Flint, Mich., July 14, 1967

Season	Team	GP	G	A	Pts.	PIM
89-90	Tor	7	1	1	2	0

RIBBLE, Patrick Wayne *6-4 210 D*

B. Leamington, Ont., Apr. 26, 1954

Season	Team	GP	G	A	Pts.	PIM
75-76	Atl	3	0	0	0	0
76-77	Atl	23	2	2	4	31
77-78	Atl	80	5	12	17	68
78-79	Atl-Chi	78	6	19	25	77
79-80	Chi-Tor-Wash	55	2	9	11	52

RIBBLE, Patrick Wayne *(Continued)*

Season	Team	GP	G	A	Pts.	PIM
80-81	Wash	67	3	15	18	103
81-82	Wash-Calg	15	1	2	3	16
82-83	Calg	28	0	1	1	18
Totals		349	19	60	79	365
Playoff Totals		8	0	1	1	12

RICCI, Mike *6-0 190 C*

B. Scarborough, Ont., Oct. 27, 1971

Season	Team	GP	G	A	Pts.	PIM
90-91	Phil	68	21	20	41	64
91-92	Phil	78	20	36	56	93
Totals		146	41	56	97	157

RICE, Steven *6-0 215 RW*

B. Kitchener, Ont., May 26, 1971

Season	Team	GP	G	A	Pts.	PIM
90-91	NYR	11	1	1	2	4
91-92	Edm	3	0	0	0	2
Totals		14	1	1	2	6
Playoff Totals		2	2	1	3	6

RICHARD, Jacques *5-11 180 LW*

B. Quebec City, Que., Oct. 7, 1952

Season	Team	GP	G	A	Pts.	PIM
72-73	Atl	74	13	18	31	32
73-74	Atl	78	27	16	43	45
74-75	Atl	63	17	12	29	31
75-76	Buf	73	12	23	35	31
76-77	Buf	21	2	0	2	16
78-79	Buf	61	10	15	25	26
79-80	Que	14	3	12	15	4
80-81	Que	78	52	51	103	39
81-82	Que	59	15	26	41	77
82-83	Que	35	9	14	23	6
Totals		556	160	187	347	307
Playoff Totals		35	5	5	10	34

RICHARD, Jean-Marc *5-11 178 D*

B. St.-Raymond, Que., Oct. 8, 1966

Season	Team	GP	G	A	Pts.	PIM
87-88	Que	4	2	1	3	2
88-89	Que	1	0	0	0	0
Totals		5	2	1	3	2

RICHARD, Joseph Henri (Pocket Rocket)
5-7 160 C

B. Montreal, Que., Feb. 29, 1936

Season	Team	GP	G	A	Pts.	PIM
55-56	Mont	64	19	21	40	46
56-57	Mont	63	18	36	54	71
57-58	Mont	67	28	52	80	56
58-59	Mont	63	21	30	51	33
59-60	Mont	70	30	43	73	66
60-61	Mont	70	24	44	68	91
61-62	Mont	54	21	29	50	48
62-63	Mont	67	23	50	73	57
63-64	Mont	66	14	39	53	73
64-65	Mont	53	23	29	52	43
65-66	Mont	62	22	39	61	47
66-67	Mont	65	21	34	55	28
67-68	Mont	54	9	19	28	16
68-69	Mont	64	15	37	52	45
69-70	Mont	62	16	36	52	61
70-71	Mont	75	12	37	49	46
71-72	Mont	75	12	32	44	48
72-73	Mont	71	8	35	43	21
73-74	Mont	75	19	36	55	28
74-75	Mont	16	3	10	13	4
Totals		1256	358	688	1046	928
Playoff Totals		180	49	80	129	181

RICHARD, Joseph Henri Maurice (Rocket)
5-10 195 RW

B. Montreal, Que., Aug. 4, 1921

Season	Team	GP	G	A	Pts.	PIM
42-43	Mont	16	5	6	11	4
43-44	Mont	46	32	22	54	45
44-45	Mont	50	50	23	73	46
45-46	Mont	50	27	21	48	50
46-47	Mont	60	45	26	71	69
47-48	Mont	53	28	25	53	89
48-49	Mont	59	20	18	38	110
49-50	Mont	70	43	22	65	114
50-51	Mont	65	42	24	66	97
51-52	Mont	48	27	17	44	44
52-53	Mont	70	28	33	61	112
53-54	Mont	70	37	30	67	112
54-55	Mont	67	38	36	74	125
55-56	Mont	70	38	33	71	89
56-57	Mont	63	33	29	62	74
57-58	Mont	28	15	19	34	28
58-59	Mont	42	17	21	38	27
59-60	Mont	51	19	16	35	50
Totals		978	544	421	965	1285
Playoff Totals		133	82	44	126	188

RICHARD, Michael *5-10 190 C*

B. Scarborough, Ont., July 9, 1966

Season	Team	GP	G	A	Pts.	PIM
87-88	Wash	4	0	0	0	0
89-90	Wash	3	0	2	2	0
Totals		7	0	2	2	0

RICHARDS, Todd *6-0 194 D*

B. Robindale, Minn., Oct. 20, 1966

Season	Team	GP	G	A	Pts.	PIM
90-91	Hart	2	0	4	4	2
91-92	Hart	6	0	0	0	2
Totals		8	0	4	4	4
Playoff Totals		11	0	3	3	6

RICHARDSON, David George *5-8 175 LW*

B. Boniface, Man., Dec. 11, 1940

Season	Team	GP	G	A	Pts.	PIM
63-64	NYR	34	3	1	4	21
64-65	NYR	7	0	1	1	4
65-66	Chi	3	0	0	0	2
67-68	Det	1	0	0	0	0
Totals		45	3	2	5	27

RICHARDSON, Glen Gordon *6-2 200 LW*

B. Barrie, Ont., Sept. 20, 1955

Season	Team	GP	G	A	Pts.	PIM
75-76	Van	24	3	6	9	19

RICHARDSON, Kenneth William
6-0 190 C

B. North Bay, Ont., Apr. 12, 1951

Season	Team	GP	G	A	Pts.	PIM
74-75	StL	21	5	7	12	12
77-78	StL	12	2	5	7	2
78-79	StL	16	1	1	2	2
Totals		49	8	13	21	16

RICHARDSON, Luke *6-3 215 D*

Season	Team	GP	G	A	Pts.	PIM
87-88	Tor	78	4	6	10	80
88-89	Tor	55	2	7	9	106
89-90	Tor	67	4	14	18	122
90-91	Tor	78	1	9	10	238
91-92	Edm	75	2	19	21	118
Totals		353	13	55	68	674
Playoff Totals		23	0	5	5	67

RICHER, Robert Roger *5-10 175 C*

B. Cowansville, Que., Mar. 5, 1951

Season	Team	GP	G	A	Pts.	PIM
72-73	Buf	3	0	0	0	0

RICHER, Stephane J.J. *6-2 200 RW*

B. Ripon, Que., June 7, 1966

Season	Team	GP	G	A	Pts.	PIM
84-85	Mont	1	0	0	0	0
85-86	Mont	65	21	16	37	50
86-87	Mont	57	20	19	39	80
87-88	Mont	72	50	28	78	72
88-89	Mont	68	25	35	60	61
89-90	Mont	75	51	40	91	46
90-91	Mont	75	31	30	61	53
91-92	NJ	74	29	35	64	25
Totals		487	227	203	430	387
Playoff Totals		79	37	23	60	51

RICHMOND, Steve *6-1 205 D*

B. Chicago, Ill., Dec. 11, 1959

Season	Team	GP	G	A	Pts.	PIM
83-84	NYR	26	2	5	7	110
84-85	NYR	34	0	5	5	90
85-86	NYR-Det	46	1	4	5	145
86-87	NJ	44	1	7	8	143
88-89	LA	9	0	2	2	26
Totals		159	4	23	27	514
Playoff Totals		4	0	0	0	12

RICHTER, David *6-5 225 D*

B. St. Boniface, Man., Apr. 8, 1960

Season	Team	GP	G	A	Pts.	PIM
81-82	Minn	3	0	0	0	11
82-83	Minn	6	0	0	0	4
83-84	Minn	42	2	3	5	132
84-85	Minn	55	2	8	10	221
85-86	Minn-Phil	64	0	5	5	167
86-87	Van	78	2	15	17	172
87-88	Van	49	2	4	6	224
88-89	StL	66	1	5	6	99
89-90	StL	2	0	0	0	0
Totals		365	9	40	49	1030
Playoff Totals		22	1	0	1	80

RIDLEY, Mike *6-1 200 C*

B. Winnipeg, Man., July 8, 1963

Season	Team	GP	G	A	Pts.	PIM
85-86	NYR	80	22	43	65	69
86-87	NYR-Wash	78	31	39	70	40
87-88	Wash	70	28	31	59	22
88-89	Wash	80	41	48	89	49
89-90	Wash	74	30	43	73	27
90-91	Wash	79	23	48	71	26
91-92	Wash	80	29	40	69	38
Totals		541	204	292	496	271
Playoff Totals		75	20	38	58	60

RILEY, Jack *5-10 160 C*

B. Berckenia, Ireland, Dec. 29, 1910

Season	Team	GP	G	A	Pts.	PIM
32-33	Det	1	0	0	0	0
33-34	Mont	48	6	11	17	4
34-35	Mont	47	4	11	15	4
35-36	Mont	8	0	0	0	0
Totals		104	10	22	32	8

Season	Team	GP	G	A	Pts.	PIM
RILEY, Jack *(Continued)*						
Playoff Totals		4	0	3	3	0
RILEY, James Norman *LW*						
B. Bayfield, N.B., May 25, 1897						
26-27	Det	17	0	2	2	14
RILEY, James William (Bill) *5-11 195 RW*						
B. Amherst, N.S., Sept. 20, 1950						
74-75	Wash	1	0	0	0	0
76-77	Wash	43	13	14	27	124
77-78	Wash	57	13	12	25	125
78-79	Wash	24	2	2	4	64
79-80	Winn	14	3	2	5	7
Totals		139	31	30	61	320
RIOPELLE, Howard Joseph (Rip)						
5-11 165 LW						
B. Ottawa, Ont., Jan. 30, 1922						
47-48	Mont	55	5	2	7	12
48-49	Mont	48	10	6	16	34
49-50	Mont	66	12	8	20	27
Totals		169	27	16	43	73
Playoff Totals		8	1	1	2	2
RIOUX, Gerard (Gerry) *5-11 195 RW*						
B. Iroquois Falls, Ont., Feb. 17, 1959						
79-80	Winn	8	0	0	0	6
RIOUX, Pierre *5-9 165 RW*						
B. Quebec City, Que., Feb. 1, 1962						
82-82	Calg	14	1	2	3	4
RIPLEY, Victor Merrick *5-7 170 LW*						
B. Elgin, Ont., May 30, 1906						
28-29	Chi	34	11	2	13	31
29-30	Chi	40	8	8	16	33
30-31	Chi	37	8	4	12	9
31-32	Chi	46	12	6	18	47
32-33	Chi-Bos	38	4	9	13	27
33-34	Bos-NYR	48	7	13	20	16
34-45	NYR-StL E	35	1	7	8	10
Totals		278	51	49	100	173
Playoff Totals		20	4	1	5	10
RISEBROUGH, Douglas *5-11 180 C*						
B. Guelph, Ont., Jan. 29, 1954						
74-75	Mont	64	15	32	47	198
75-76	Mont	80	16	28	44	180
76-77	Mont	78	22	38	60	132
77-78	Mont	72	18	23	41	97
78-79	Mont	48	10	15	25	62
79-80	Mont	44	8	10	18	81
80-81	Mont	48	13	21	34	93
81-82	Mont	59	15	18	33	116
82-83	Calg	71	21	37	58	138
83-84	Calg	77	23	28	51	161
84-85	Calg	15	7	5	12	49
85-86	Calg	62	15	28	43	169
86-87	Calg	22	2	3	5	66
Totals		740	185	286	471	1542
Playoff Totals		124	21	37	58	238
RISSLING, Gary Daniel *5-9 175 LW*						
B. Saskatoon, Sask., Aug. 8, 1956						
78-79	Wash	26	3	3	6	127
79-80	Wash	11	0	1	1	49
80-81	Pitt	25	1	0	1	143
81-82	Pitt	16	0	0	0	55
82-83	Pitt	40	5	4	9	128
83-84	Pitt	47	4	13	17	297
84-85	Pitt	56	10	9	19	209
Totals		221	23	30	53	1008
Playoff Totals		5	0	1	1	4
RITCHIE, David *F*						
17-18	Mont W-Ott	17	9	0	9	12
18-19	Tor	4	0	0	0	9
19-20	Que	21	6	3	9	18
20-21	Mont	5	0	0	0	0
24-25	Mont	5	0	0	0	0
25-26	Mont	2	0	0	0	0
Totals		54	15	3	18	39
Playoff Totals		1	0	0	0	0
RITCHIE, Robert *5-10 170 LW*						
B. Laverlochere, Que., Feb. 20, 1955						
76-77	Phil-Det	18	6	2	8	10
77-78	Det	11	2	2	4	0
Totals		29	8	4	12	10
RITSON, Alexander Clive *5-11 172 C*						
B. Peace River, Alta., Mar. 7, 1922						
44-45	NYR	1	0	0	0	0

Season	Team	GP	G	A	Pts.	PIM
RITTINGER, Alan Wilbur *5-9 155 LW*						
B. Regina, Sask., Jan. 28, 1925						
43-44	Bos	19	3	7	10	0
RIVARD, Joseph Robert (Bob)						
5-8 155 LW						
B. Sherbrooke, Que., Aug. 1, 1939						
67-68	Pitt	27	5	12	17	4
RIVERS, George (Gus) *F*						
B. Winnipeg, Man., Nov. 19, 1909						
29-30	Mont	19	1	0	1	2
30-31	Mont	44	2	5	7	6
31-32	Mont	25	1	0	1	4
Totals		88	4	5	9	12
Playoff Totals		16	2	0	2	2
RIVERS, John Wayne *5-10 180 RW*						
B. Hamilton, Ont., Feb. 1, 1942						
61-62	Det	2	0	0	0	0
63-64	Bos	12	2	7	9	6
64-65	Bos	58	6	17	23	72
65-66	Bos	2	1	1	2	2
66-67	Bos	8	2	1	3	6
67-68	StL	22	4	4	8	8
68-69	NYR	4	0	0	0	0
72-73	NY (WHA)	75	37	40	77	47
73-74	NY-NJ (WHA)	73	30	27	57	20
74-75	SD (WHA)	78	54	53	107	52
75-76	SD (WHA)	71	19	25	44	24
76-77	SD (WHA)	60	18	31	49	40
NHL Totals		108	15	30	45	94
WHA Totals		357	158	176	334	183
WHA Playoff Totals	23	8	6	14	14
RIZZUTO, Garth Alexander *5-11 180 C*						
B. Trail, B.C., Sept. 11, 1947						
70-71	Van	37	3	4	7	16
72-73	Winn (WHA)	61	10	10	20	32
73-74	Winn (WHA)	41	3	4	7	8
NHL Totals		37	3	4	7	16
WHA Totals		102	13	14	27	40
WHA Playoff Totals	14	0	1	1	14
ROACH, Mickey *C*						
B. Boston, Mass., 1895						
19-20	Tor	20	10	2	12	4
20-21	Tor-Ham	22	9	7	16	2
21-22	Ham	24	14	3	17	7
22-23	Ham	23	17	8	25	8
23-24	Ham	21	5	3	8	0
24-25	Ham	30	6	4	10	4
25-26	NYA	25	3	0	3	4
26-27	NYA	44	11	0	11	14
Totals		209	75	27	102	43
ROBERGE, Mario *5-11 185 LW*						
B. Quebec City, Que., Jan. 23, 1964						
90-91	Mont	5	0	0	0	21
91-92	Mont	20	2	1	3	62
Totals		25	2	1	3	83
Playoff Totals		12	0	0	0	24
ROBERGE, Serge *6-1 195 RW*						
B. Quebec City, Que., Mar. 31, 1965						
90-91	Que	9	0	0	0	24
ROBERT, Claude *5-11 175 LW*						
B. Montreal, Que., Aug. 10, 1928						
50-51	Mont	23	1	0	1	9
ROBERT, Rene Paul *5-10 184 RW*						
B. Trois-Rivieres, Que., Dec. 31, 1948						
70-71	Tor	5	0	0	0	0
71-72	Pitt-Buf	61	13	14	27	44
72-73	Buf	75	40	43	83	83
73-74	Buf	76	21	44	65	71
74-75	Buf	74	40	60	100	75
75-76	Buf	72	35	52	87	53
76-77	Buf	80	33	40	73	46
77-78	Buf	67	25	48	73	25
78-79	Buf	68	22	40	62	46
79-80	Col	69	28	35	63	79
80-81	Col-Tor	42	14	18	32	38
81-82	Tor	55	13	24	37	37
Totals		744	284	418	702	597
Playoff Totals		50	22	19	41	73
ROBERT, Samuel *F*						
17-18	Ott	1	0	0	0	0
ROBERTO, Phillip Joseph *6-1 190 RW*						
B. Niagara Falls, Ont., Jan. 1, 1949						
69-70	Mont	8	0	1	1	8

Season	Team	GP	G	A	Pts.	PIM
ROBERTO, Phillip Joseph *(Continued)*						
70-71	Mont	39	14	7	21	76
71-72	Mont-StL	76	15	15	30	98
72-73	StL	77	20	22	42	99
73-74	StL	15	1	1	2	10
74-75	StL-Det	53	13	29	42	32
75-76	Det-KC	74	8	22	30	110
76-77	Col-Clev	43	4	9	13	31
77-78	Birm (WHA)	53	8	20	28	91
NHL Totals		385	75	106	181	464
WHA Totals		53	8	20	28	91
NHL Playoff Totals	31	9	8	17	69
WHA Playoff Totals	4	1	0	1	20
ROBERTS, Douglas William *6-2 190 D*						
B. Detroit, Mich., Oct. 28, 1942						
65-66	Det	1	0	0	0	0
66-67	Det	13	3	1	4	25
67-68	Det	37	8	9	17	12
68-69	Oak	76	1	19	20	79
69-70	Oak	76	6	25	31	107
70-71	Cal	78	4	13	17	94
71-72	Bos	3	1	0	1	0
72-73	Bos	45	4	7	11	7
73-74	Bos-Det	64	12	26	38	35
74-75	Det	26	4	4	8	8
75-76	NE (WHA)	76	4	13	17	51
76-77	NE (WHA)	64	3	18	21	33
NHL Totals		419	43	104	147	367
WHA Totals		140	7	31	38	84
NHL Playoff Totals	16	2	3	5	46
WHA Playoff Tot.	19	1	1	2	8
ROBERTS, Gary *6-1 190 LW*						
B. North York, Ont., May 23, 1966						
86-87	Calg	32	5	10	15	85
87-88	Calg	74	13	15	28	282
88-89	Calg	71	22	16	38	250
89-90	Calg	78	39	33	72	222
90-91	Calg	80	22	31	53	252
91-92	Calg	76	53	37	90	219
Totals		411	154	142	296	1310
Playoff Totals		46	10	18	28	149
ROBERTS, Gordon (Gordie) *6-0 190 D*						
B. Detroit, Mich., Oct. 2, 1957						
75-76	NE (WHA)	77	3	19	22	102
76-77	NE (WHA)	77	13	33	46	169
77-78	NE (WHA)	78	15	46	61	118
78-79	NE (WHA)	79	11	46	57	113
79-80	Hart	80	8	28	36	89
80-81	Hart-Minn	77	8	42	50	175
81-82	Minn	79	4	30	34	119
82-83	Minn	80	3	41	44	103
83-84	Minn	77	8	45	53	132
84-85	Minn	78	6	36	42	112
85-86	Minn	76	2	21	23	101
86-87	Minn	67	3	10	13	68
87-88	Minn-Phil-StL	70	3	15	18	143
88-89	StL	77	2	24	26	90
89-90	StL	75	3	14	17	140
90-91	StL-Pitt	64	3	13	16	78
91-92	Pitt	73	2	22	24	87
NHL Totals		973	55	341	396	1437
WHA Totals		311	42	144	186	502
NHL Playoff Totals	137	10	46	56	259
WHA Playoff Totals	46	4	20	24	81
ROBERTS, James Drew *6-1 198 LW*						
B. Toronto, Ont., June 8, 1956						
76-77	Minn	53	11	8	19	14
77-78	Minn	42	4	14	18	19
78-79	Minn	11	2	1	3	0
Totals		106	17	23	40	33
Playoff Totals		2	0	0	0	0
ROBERTS, James Wilfred *5-10 185 RW*						
B. Toronto, Ont., Apr. 9, 1940						
63-64	Mont	15	0	1	1	2
64-65	Mont	70	0	13	13	40
65-66	Mont	70	5	5	10	20
66-67	Mont	63	3	0	3	16
67-68	StL	74	14	23	37	66
68-69	StL	72	14	19	33	81
69-70	StL	76	13	17	30	51
70-71	StL	72	13	18	31	77
71-72	StL-Mont	77	12	22	34	57
72-73	Mont	77	14	18	32	28
73-74	Mont	67	8	16	24	39
74-75	Mont	79	5	13	18	52
75-76	Mont	74	13	8	21	35
76-77	Mont	45	5	14	19	18
77-78	StL	75	4	10	14	39
Totals		1006	126	194	320	621
Playoff Totals		153	20	16	36	160

Season	Team	GP	G	A	Pts.	PIM
ROBERTSON, Fred	5-10 198 D					
B. Carlisle, England, Oct. 22, 1911						
31-32	Tor	8	0	0	0	23
33-34	Tor-Det	26	1	0	1	12
Totals		34	1	0	1	35
Playoff Totals		7	0	0	0	0
ROBERTSON, Geordie	6-0 165 RW					
B. Victoria, B.C., Aug. 1, 1959						
82-83	Buf	5	1	2	3	7
ROBERTSON, George Thomas (Robbie)	C					
B. Winnipeg, Man., May 11, 1928						
47-48	Mont	1	0	0	0	0
48-49	Mont	30	2	5	7	6
Totals		31	2	5	7	6
ROBERTSON, Torrie Andrew						
5-11 200 LW						
B. Victoria, B.C., Aug. 2, 1961						
80-81	Wash	3	0	0	0	0
81-82	Wash	54	8	13	21	204
82-83	Wash	5	0	2	2	4
83-84	Hart	66	7	13	20	198
84-85	Hart	74	11	30	41	337
85-86	Hart	76	13	24	37	358
86-87	Hart	20	1	0	1	98
87-88	Hart	63	2	8	10	293
88-89	Hart-Det	39	4	6	10	147
89-90	Det	42	1	5	6	112
Totals		442	49	99	148	1751
Playoff Totals		22	2	1	3	90
ROBIDOUX, Florent	6-2 190 LW					
B. Treheme, Man., May 5, 1960						
80-81	Chi	39	6	2	8	75
81-82	Chi	4	1	2	3	0
83-84	Chi	9	0	0	0	0
Totals		52	7	4	11	75
ROBINSON, Douglas Garnet	6-2 197 LW					
B. Catharines, Ont., Aug. 27, 1940						
64-65	Chi-NYR	61	10	23	33	10
65-66	NYR	51	8	12	20	8
66-67	NYR	1	0	0	0	0
67-68	LA	34	9	9	18	6
68-69	LA	31	2	10	12	2
70-71	LA	61	15	13	28	8
Totals		239	44	67	111	34
Playoff Totals		11	4	3	7	0
ROBINSON, Douglas Scott	6-2 180 RW					
B. 100 Mile House, B.C., Mar. 29, 1964						
89-90	Minn	1	0	0	0	2
ROBINSON, Earl Henry	5-10 160 RW					
B. Montreal, Que., Mar. 11, 1907						
28-29	Mont M	33	2	1	3	2
29-30	Mont M	35	1	2	3	10
31-32	Mont M	28	0	3	3	2
32-33	Mont M	43	15	9	24	6
33-34	Mont M	47	12	16	28	14
34-35	Mont M	47	17	18	35	23
35-36	Mont M	40	6	14	20	27
36-37	Mont M	48	16	18	34	19
37-38	Mont M	38	4	7	11	13
38-39	Chi	48	9	6	15	13
39-40	Mont	11	1	4	5	4
Totals		418	83	98	181	133
Playoff Totals		25	5	4	9	0
ROBINSON, Larry Clark	6-4 225 D					
D. Winchester, Ont., June 2, 1951						
72-73	Mont	36	2	4	6	20
73-74	Mont	78	6	20	26	66
74-75	Mont	80	14	47	61	76
75-76	Mont	80	10	30	40	59
76-77	Mont	77	19	66	85	45
77-78	Mont	80	13	52	65	39
78-79	Mont	67	16	45	61	33
79-80	Mont	72	14	61	75	39
80-81	Mont	65	12	38	50	37
81-82	Mont	71	12	47	59	41
82-83	Mont	71	14	49	63	33
83-84	Mont	74	9	34	43	39
84-85	Mont	76	14	33	47	44
85-86	Mont	78	19	63	82	39
86-87	Mont	70	13	37	50	44
87-88	Mont	53	6	34	40	30
88-89	Mont	74	4	26	30	22
89-90	LA	64	7	32	39	34
90-91	LA	62	1	22	23	16
91-92	LA	56	3	10	13	37
Totals		1384	208	750	958	793
Playoff Totals		227	28	116	144	211
ROBINSON, Morris (Moe)	6-4 175 D					
B. Winchester, Ont., May 29, 1957						
79-89	Mont	1	0	0	0	0
ROBINSON, Robert	6-1 214 D					
B. St. Catharines, Ont., Apr. 19, 1967						
91-92	StL	22	0	1	1	8
ROBITAILLE, Luc	6-1 190 LW					
B. Montreal, Que., Feb. 17, 1966						
86-87	LA	79	45	39	84	28
87-88	LA	80	53	58	111	82
88-89	LA	78	46	52	98	65
89-90	LA	80	52	49	101	38
90-91	LA	76	45	46	91	68
91-92	LA	80	44	63	107	95
Totals		473	285	307	592	376
Playoff Totals		49	25	28	53	66
ROBITAILLE, Michael James David						
5-11 195 D						
B. Midland, Ont., Feb. 12, 1948						
69-70	NYR	4	0	0	0	8
70-71	NYR-Det	34	5	9	14	29
71-72	Buf	31	2	10	12	22
72-73	Buf	65	4	17	21	40
73-74	Buf	71	2	18	20	60
74-75	Buf-Van	66	2	23	25	31
75-76	Van	71	8	19	27	69
76-77	Van	40	0	9	9	21
Totals		382	23	105	128	280
Playoff Totals		13	0	1	1	4
ROCHE, Earl	5-11 175 LW					
B. Prescott, Ont., Feb. 22, 1910						
30-31	Mont M	42	2	0	2	18
32-33	Mont M-Bos-Ott	28	4	5	9	6
33-34	Ott	44	13	16	29	22
34-35	StL E-Det	32	6	6	12	2
Totals		146	25	27	52	48
Playoff Totals		2	0	0	0	0
ROCHE, Ernest Charles	6-1 170 D					
B. Montreal, Que., Feb. 4, 1930						
50-51	Mont	4	0	0	0	2
ROCHE, Michael Patrick Desmond (Desse)						
5-6 188 RW						
B. Kemptville, Ont., Feb. 1, 1909						
30-31	Mont M	20	1	1	1	6
32-33	Mont M-Ott	21	3	6	9	6
33-34	Ott	44	14	10	24	22
34-35	StL E-Mont-Det	27	3	1	4	10
Totals		112	20	18	38	44
ROCHEFORT, David Joseph	6-0 180 C					
B. Red Deer, Alta., July 22, 1946						
66-67	Det	1	0	0	0	0
ROCHEFORT, Leon Joseph Fernand						
6-0 185 RW						
B. Cap-de-la-Madeleine, Que., May 4, 1939						
60-61	NYR	1	0	0	0	0
62-63	NYR	23	5	4	9	6
63-64	Mont	3	0	0	0	0
64-65	Mont	9	2	0	2	0
65-66	Mont	1	0	1	1	0
66-67	Mont	27	9	7	16	6
67-68	Phil	74	21	21	42	16
68-69	Phil	65	14	21	35	10
69-70	LA	76	9	23	32	14
70-71	Mont	57	5	10	15	4
71-72	Det	64	17	12	29	10
72-73	Det-Atl	74	11	22	33	12
73-74	Atl	56	10	12	22	13
74-75	Van	76	18	11	29	2
75-76	Van	11	0	3	3	0
Totals		617	121	147	268	93
Playoff Totals		39	4	4	8	16
ROCHEFORT, Normand	6-1 214 D					
B. Trois Rivieres, Que., Jan. 28, 1961						
80-81	Que	56	3	7	10	51
81-82	Que	72	4	14	18	115
82-83	Que	62	6	17	23	40
83-84	Que	75	2	22	24	47
84-85	Que	73	3	21	24	74
85-86	Que	26	5	4	9	30
86-87	Que	70	6	9	15	45
87-88	Que	46	3	10	13	49
88-89	NYR	11	1	5	6	18
89-90	NYR	31	3	1	4	24
ROCHEFORT, Normand	(Continued)					
90-91	NYR	44	3	7	10	35
91-92	NYR	26	0	2	2	31
Totals		592	39	119	158	560
Playoff Totals		69	7	5	12	82
ROCKBURN, Harvey	D					
29-30	Det	36	4	0	4	97
30-31	Det	42	0	1	1	118
32-33	Ott	16	0	1	1	39
Totals		94	4	2	6	254
RODDEN, Edmund Anthony (Eddie)	F					
B. Toronto, Ont., Mar. 22, 1901						
26-27	Chi	20	3	3	6	92
27-28	Chi-Tor	34	3	8	11	42
28-29	Bos	20	0	0	0	10
30-31	NYR	24	0	3	3	8
Totals		98	6	14	20	152
Playoff Totals		2	0	1	1	0
ROENICK, Jeremy	6-0 170 C					
B. Boston, Mass., Jan. 17, 1970						
88-89	Chi	20	9	9	18	4
89-90	Chi	78	26	40	66	54
90-91	Chi	79	41	53	94	80
91-92	Chi	80	53	50	103	98
Totals		257	129	152	281	236
Playoff Totals		54	27	25	52	31
ROGERS, Alfred John	5-11 175 RW					
B. Paradise Hill, Alta., Apr. 10, 1953						
73-74	Minn	10	2	4	6	0
74-75	Minn	4	0	0	0	0
75-76	Edm (WHA)	44	9	8	17	34
NHL Totals		14	2	4	6	0
WHA Totals		44	9	8	17	34
ROGERS, Michael	6-9 170 C					
B. Calgary, Alta., Oct. 24, 1954						
74-75	Edm (WHA)	78	35	48	83	2
75-76	EDM-NE (WHA)	80	30	29	59	20
76-77	NE (WHA)	78	25	57	82	10
77-78	NE (WHA)	80	28	43	71	46
78-79	NE (WHA)	80	27	45	72	31
79-80	Hart	80	44	61	105	10
80-81	Hart	80	40	65	105	32
81-82	NYR	80	38	65	103	43
82-83	NYR	71	29	47	76	28
83-84	NYR	78	23	38	61	45
84-85	NYR	78	26	38	64	24
85-86	NYR-Edm	17	2	3	5	2
NHL Totals		484	202	317	519	184
WHA Totals		396	145	222	367	109
NHL Playoff Totals		17	1	13	14	6
WHA Playoff Totals		46	13	21	34	14
ROHLICEK, Jeff	6-0 180 C					
B. Park Ridge, Ill., Jan. 27, 1966						
87-88	Van	7	0	0	0	4
88-89	Van	2	0	0	0	4
Totals		9	0	0	0	8
ROLFE, Dale Roland Carl	6-4 210 D					
B. Timmins, Ont., Apr. 30, 1940						
59-60	Bos	3	0	0	0	0
67-68	LA	68	3	13	16	84
68-69	LA	75	3	19	22	85
69-70	LA-Det	75	3	18	21	89
70-71	Det-NYR	58	3	16	19	71
71-72	NYR	68	2	14	16	67
72-73	NYR	72	7	25	32	74
73-74	NYR	48	3	12	15	56
74-75	NYR	42	1	8	9	30
Totals		509	25	125	150	556
Playoff Totals		71	5	24	29	89
ROMANCHYCH, Larry Brian	6-1 180 RW					
B. Vancouver, B.C., Sept. 7, 1949						
70-71	Chi	10	0	2	2	2
72-73	Atl	70	18	30	48	39
73-74	Atl	73	22	29	51	33
74-75	Atl	53	8	12	20	16
75-76	Atl	67	16	19	35	8
76-77	Atl	25	4	5	9	4
Totals		298	68	97	165	102
Playoff Totals		7	2	2	4	4
ROMANIUK, Russell	6-0 185 LW					
B. Winnipeg, Man., June 9, 1970						
91-92	Winn	27	3	5	8	18

Season	Team	GP	G	A	Pts.	PIM
ROMBOUGH, Douglas George *6-3 215 C*						
B. Fergus, Ont., July 8, 1950						
72-73	Buf	5	2	0	2	0
73-74	Buf-NYI	58	9	10	19	35
74-75	NYI-Minn	68	11	15	26	39
75-76	Minn	19	2	2	4	6
Totals		150	24	27	51	80
ROMNES, Elwin Nelson (Doc) *5-11 156 F*						
B. White Bear, Minn., Jan. 1, 1909						
30-31	Chi	30	5	7	12	8
31-32	Chi	18	0	1	1	6
32-33	Chi	47	10	12	22	2
33-34	Chi	47	8	21	29	6
34-35	Chi	35	10	14	24	8
35-36	Chi	48	13	25	38	6
36-37	Chi	28	4	14	18	2
37-38	Chi	44	10	22	32	4
38-39	Chi-Tor	48	7	20	27	0
39-40	NYA	14	0	1	1	0
Totals		359	67	137	204	42
Playoff Totals		43	7	18	25	4
RONAN, Edward *5-11 170 RW*						
B. Quincy, Mass., Mar. 21, 1968						
91-92	Mont	3	0	0	0	0
RONAN, Erskine (Skene) *D*						
18-19	Ott	11	0	0	0	0
RONNING, Cliff *5-8 175 C*						
B. Vancouver, B.C., Oct. 1, 1965						
86-87	StL	42	11	14	25	6
87-88	StL	26	5	8	13	12
88-89	StL	64	24	31	55	18
90-91	StL-Van	59	20	24	44	10
91-92	Van	80	24	47	71	42
Totals		271	84	124	208	88
Playoff Totals		35	16	13	29	20
RONSON, Leonard Keith (Len) *5-9 175 LW*						
B. Brantford, Ont., July 8, 1936						
60-61	NYR	13	2	1	3	10
68-69	Oak	5	0	0	0	0
Totals		18	2	1	3	10
RONTY, Paul *6-0 160 C*						
B. Toronto, Ont., June 12, 1928						
47-48	Bos	24	3	11	14	0
48-49	Bos	60	20	29	49	11
49-50	Bos	70	23	36	59	8
50-51	Bos	70	10	22	32	20
51-52	NYR	65	12	31	43	16
52-53	NYR	70	16	38	54	20
53-54	NYR	70	13	33	46	18
54-55	NYR-Mont	59	4	11	15	10
Totals		488	101	211	312	103
Playoff Totals		21	1	7	8	6
ROONEY, Steve *6-2 195 LW*						
B. Canton, Mass., June 28, 1962						
84-85	Mont	3	1	0	1	7
85-86	Mont	38	2	3	5	114
86-87	Mont-Winn	32	2	3	5	79
87-88	Winn	56	7	6	13	217
88-89	NJ	25	3	1	4	79
Totals		154	15	13	28	496
Playoff Totals		25	3	2	5	86
ROOT, William John *6-2 210 D*						
B. Toronto, Ont., Sept. 6, 1959						
82-83	Mont	46	2	3	5	24
83-84	Mont	72	4	13	17	45
84-85	Tor	35	1	1	2	23
85-86	Tor	27	0	1	1	29
86-87	Tor	34	3	3	6	37
87-88	StL-Phil	33	1	2	3	22
Totals		247	11	23	34	180
Playoff Totals		22	1	2	3	25
ROSS, Arthur Howey *D*						
B. Naughton, Ont., Jan.13, 1886						
17-18	Mont W	3	1	0	1	0
ROSS, James *6-3 190 D*						
B. Edinburgh, Scotland, May 20, 1926						
51-52	NYR	51	2	9	11	25
52-53	NYR	11	0	2	2	4
Totals		62	2	11	13	29
ROSSIGNOL, Roland *168 RW*						
B. Edmundston, N.B., Oct. 18, 1921						
43-44	Det	1	0	1	1	0

Season	Team	GP	G	A	Pts.	PIM
ROSSIGNOL, Roland *(Continued)*						
44-45	Mont	5	2	2	4	2
45-46	Det	8	1	2	3	4
Totals		14	3	5	8	6
Playoff Totals		1	0	0	0	2
ROTA, Darcy Irwin *5-11 180 LW*						
B. Vancouver, B.C., Feb. 16, 1953						
73-74	Chi	74	21	12	33	58
74-75	Chi	78	22	22	44	93
75-76	Chi	79	20	17	37	73
76-77	Chi	76	24	22	46	82
77-78	Chi	78	17	20	37	67
78-79	Chi-Atl	76	22	22	44	98
79-80	Atl-Van	70	15	14	29	78
80-81	Van	80	25	31	56	124
81-82	Van	51	20	20	40	139
82-83	Van	73	42	39	81	88
83-84	Van	59	28	20	48	73
Totals		794	256	239	495	973
Playoff Totals		60	14	7	21	147
ROTA, Randolph Frank (Randy) *5-8 170 LW*						
B. Creston, B.C., Aug. 16, 1950						
72-73	Mont	2	1	1	2	0
73-74	LA	58	10	6	16	16
74-75	KC	80	15	18	33	30
75-76	KC	71	12	14	26	14
76-77	Col	1	0	0	0	0
76-77	Edm (WHA)	40	9	6	15	8
77-78	Edm (WHA)	53	8	22	30	12
NHL Totals		212	38	39	77	60
WHA Totals		93	17	28	45	20
NHL Playoff Totals		5	0	1	1	0
WHA Playoff Totals		10	4	3	7	4
ROTHSCHILD, Samuel *F*						
B. Sudbury, Ont., Oct. 16, 1899						
24-25	Mont M	27	5	4	9	4
25-26	Mont M	33	2	1	3	8
26-27	Mont M	22	1	1	2	8
27-28	NYA	17	0	0	0	4
Totals		99	8	6	14	24
Playoff Totals		10	0	0	0	0
ROULSTON, Thomas *6-1 185 C/RW*						
B. Winnipeg, Man., Nov. 20, 1957						
80-81	Edm	11	1	1	2	2
81-82	Edm	35	11	3	14	22
82-83	Edm	67	19	21	40	24
83-84	Edm-Pitt	77	16	24	40	24
85-86	Pitt	5	0	0	0	2
Totals		195	47	49	96	74
Playoff Totals		21	2	2	4	2
ROULSTON, William Orville (Rolly) *6-0 180 D*						
B. Toronto, Ont., Apr. 12, 1911						
35-36	Det	1	0	0	0	0
36-37	Det	21	0	5	5	10
37-38	Det	2	0	1	1	0
Totals		24	0	6	6	10
ROUPE, Magnus *6-0 189 LW*						
B. Gislaved, Sweden, Mar. 23, 1963						
87-88	Phil	33	2	4	6	32
87-88	Phil	7	1	1	2	10
Totals		40	3	5	8	42
ROUSE, Robert *6-1 210 D*						
B. Surrey, B.C., June 18, 1964						
83-84	Minn	1	0	0	0	0
84-85	Minn	63	2	9	11	113
85-86	Minn	75	1	14	15	151
86-87	Minn	72	2	10	12	179
87-88	Minn	74	0	12	12	168
88-89	Minn-Wash	79	4	15	19	160
89-90	Wash	70	4	16	20	123
90-91	Wash-Tor	60	7	19	26	75
91-92	Tor	79	3	19	22	97
Totals		573	23	114	137	1066
Playoff Totals		24	4	3	7	53
ROUSSEAU, Guy *5-5 140 LW*						
B. Montreal, Que., Dec. 21, 1934						
54-55	Mont	2	0	1	1	0
56-57	Mont	2	0	0	0	2
Totals		4	0	1	1	2
ROUSSEAU, Bobby *5-10 178 RW*						
B. Montreal, Que., July 26, 1940						
60-61	Mont	15	1	2	3	4
61-62	Mont	70	21	24	45	26

Season	Team	GP	G	A	Pts.	PIM
ROUSSEAU, Bobby *(Continued)*						
62-63	Mont	62	19	18	37	15
63-64	Mont	70	25	31	56	32
64-65	Mont	66	12	35	47	26
65-66	Mont	70	30	48	78	20
66-67	Mont	68	19	44	63	58
67-68	Mont	74	19	46	65	47
68-69	Mont	76	30	40	70	59
69-70	Mont	72	24	34	58	30
70-71	Minn	63	4	20	24	12
71-72	NYR	78	21	36	57	12
72-73	NYR	78	8	37	45	14
73-74	NYR	72	10	41	51	4
74-75	NYR	8	2	2	4	0
Totals		942	245	458	703	359
Playoff Totals		128	27	57	84	69
ROUSSEAU, Roland (Roly) *5-8 160 D*						
B. Montreal, Que., Dec. 1, 1929						
52-53	Mont	2	0	0	0	0
ROUTHIER, Jean-Marc *6-2 190 RW*						
B. Quebec City, Que., Feb. 2, 1968						
89-90	Que	8	0	0	0	9
ROWE, Mike *6-1 210 D*						
B. Kingston, Ont., Mar. 8, 1965						
84-85	Pitt	6	0	0	0	7
85-86	Pitt	3	0	0	0	4
86-87	Pitt	2	0	0	0	0
Totals		11	0	0	0	11
ROWE, Robert *D*						
24-25	Bos	4	1	0	1	0
ROWE, Ronald Nickolas *5-8 170 LW*						
B. Toronto, Ont., Nov. 30, 1924						
47-48	NYR	5	1	0	1	0
ROWE, Thomas John *6-0 190 RW*						
B. Lynn, Mass., May 23, 1956						
76-77	Wash	12	1	2	3	2
77-78	Wash	63	13	8	21	82
78-79	Wash	69	31	30	61	137
79-80	Wash-Hart	61	16	21	37	106
80-81	Hart	74	13	28	41	190
81-82	Hart-Wash	27	5	1	6	54
82-83	Det	51	6	10	16	44
Totals		357	85	100	185	615
Playoff Totals		3	2	0	2	0
ROY, Stephane *6-0 190 C*						
B. Ste. Foy, Que., June 29, 1967						
87-88	Minn	12	1	0	1	0
ROZZINI, Gino *5-8 150 C*						
B. Shawinigan Falls, Que., Oct. 24, 1918						
44-45	Bos	31	5	10	15	20
Playoff Totals		6	1	2	3	6
RUCINSKI, Mike *5-11 190 C*						
B. Wheeling, Ill., Dec. 12, 1963						
88-89	Chi	1	0	0	0	0
Playoff Totals		2	0	0	0	0
RUCINSKY, Martin *5-11 178 LW*						
B. Most, Czechoslovakia, Mar. 11, 1971						
91-92	Edm-Que	6	1	1	2	2
RUELLE, Bernard Edward *5-9 165 LW*						
B. Houghton, Mich., Nov. 23, 1920						
43-44	Det	2	1	0	1	0
RUFF, Lindy Cameron *6-2 201 D/LW*						
B. Warburg, Alta., Feb. 17, 1960						
79-80	Buf	63	5	14	19	38
80-81	Buf	65	8	18	26	121
81-82	Buf	79	16	32	48	194
82-83	Buf	60	12	17	29	130
83-84	Buf	58	14	31	45	101
84-85	Buf	39	13	11	24	45
85-86	Buf	54	20	12	32	158
86-87	Buf	50	6	14	20	74
87-88	Buf	77	2	23	25	179
88-89	Buf-NYR	76	6	16	22	117
89-90	NYR	56	3	6	9	80
90-91	NYR	14	0	1	1	27
Totals		691	105	195	300	1264
Playoff Totals		52	11	13	24	193
RUHNKE, Kent *6-1 180 RW*						
B. Toronto, Ont., Sept. 18, 1952						
75-76	Bos	2	0	1	1	0
76-77	Winn (WHA)	51	11	11	22	2

Season	Team	GP	G	A	Pts.	PIM

RUHNKE, Kent (Continued)

Season	Team	GP	G	A	Pts.	PIM
77-78	Winn (WHA)	21	8	9	17	2
NHL Totals		2	0	1	1	0
WHA Totals		72	19	20	39	4
WHA Playoff Totals		5	2	0	2	0

RUMBLE, Darren 6-1 200 D
B. Barrie, Ont., Jan. 23, 1969

90-91	Phil	3	1	0	1	0

RUNDQVIST, Thomas 6-3 195 C
B. Vimmerby, Sweden, May 4, 1960

84-85	Mont	2	0	1	1	0

RUNGE, Paul 5-11 167 LW
B. Edmonton, Alta., Sept. 10, 1908

30-31	Bos	2	0	0	0	0
31-32	Bos	14	0	1	1	8
33-34	Mont M	4	0	0	0	0
34-35	Mont	3	0	0	0	2
35-36	Mont-Bos	45	8	4	12	18
36-37	Mont-Mont M	34	5	10	15	8
37-38	Mont M	41	5	7	12	21
Totals		143	18	22	40	57
Playoff Totals		7	0	0	0	6

RUOTSALAINEN, Reijo 5-8 170 D
B. Oulu, Finland, Apr. 1, 1960

81-82	NYR	78	18	38	56	27
82-83	NYR	77	16	53	69	22
83-84	NYR	74	20	39	59	26
84-85	NYR	80	28	45	73	32
85-86	NYR	80	17	42	59	47
86-87	Edm	16	5	8	13	6
89-90	NJ-Edm	41	3	12	15	20
Totals		446	107	237	344	180
Playoff Totals		86	15	32	47	44

RUPP, Duane Edward Franklin 6-1 185 D
B. Macnutt, Sask., Mar. 29, 1938

62-63	NYR	2	0	0	0	0
64-65	Tor	2	0	0	0	0
65-66	Tor	2	0	1	1	0
66-67	Tor	3	0	0	0	0
67-68	Tor	71	1	8	9	42
68-69	Minn-Pitt	59	5	11	16	32
69-70	Pitt	64	2	14	16	18
70-71	Pitt	59	5	28	33	34
71-72	Pitt	34	4	18	22	32
72-73	Pitt	78	7	13	20	68
74-75	Van (WHA)	72	3	26	29	45
75-76	Calg (WHA)	42	0	16	16	33
NHL Totals		374	24	93	117	226
WHA Totals		114	3	42	45	78
NHL Playoff Totals		10	2	2	4	8
WHA Playoff Totals		7	0	2	2	0

RUSKOWSKI, Terry Wallace 5-9 190 C
B. Prince Albert, Sask., Dec. 31, 1954

74-75	Hou (WHA)	71	10	36	46	134
75-76	Hou (WHA)	65	14	35	49	100
76-77	Hou (WHA)	80	24	60	84	146
77-78	Hou (WHA)	78	15	57	72	170
78-79	Winn (WHA)	75	20	66	86	211
79-80	Chi	74	15	55	70	252
80-81	Chi	72	8	51	59	225
81-82	Chi	60	7	30	37	120
82-83	Chi-LA	76	14	32	46	139
83-84	LA	77	7	25	32	89
84-85	LA	78	16	33	49	144
85-86	Pitt	73	26	37	63	162
86-87	Pitt	70	14	37	51	145
87-88	Minn	47	5	12	17	76
88-89	Minn	11	1	2	2	2
NHL Totals		630	113	313	426	1354
WHA Totals		369	83	254	337	761
NHL Playoff Totals		21	1	6	7	86
WHA Playoff Totals		52	18	36	54	174

RUSSELL, Cam 6-4 174 D
B. Halifax, N.S., Jan. 12, 1969

89-90	Chi	19	0	1	1	27
90-91	Chi	3	0	0	0	5
91-92	Chi	19	0	0	0	34
Totals		41	0	1	1	66
Playoff Totals		12	0	2	2	2

RUSSELL, Churchill Davidson (Church) 5-11 175 LW
B. Winnipeg, Man., Mar. 16, 1923

45-46	NYR	17	0	5	5	2

RUSSELL, Churchill Davidson (Church) (Continued)

46-47	NYR	54	20	8	28	8
47-48	NYR	19	0	3	3	2
Totals		90	20	16	36	12

RUSSELL, Phillip Douglas 6-2 205 D
B. Edmonton, Alta., July 21, 1952

72-73	Chi	76	6	19	25	156
73-74	Chi	75	10	25	35	184
74-75	Chi	80	5	24	29	260
75-76	Chi	74	9	29	38	194
76-77	Chi	76	9	36	45	233
77-78	Chi	57	6	20	26	139
78-79	Chi-Atl	79	9	29	38	150
79-80	Atl	80	5	31	36	115
80-81	Calg	80	6	23	29	104
81-82	Calg	71	4	25	29	110
82-83	Calg	78	13	18	31	112
83-84	NJ	76	9	22	31	96
84-85	NJ	66	4	16	20	110
85-86	NJ-Buf	42	4	6	10	63
86-87	Buf	6	0	2	2	12
Totals		1016	99	325	424	2038
Playoff Totals		73	4	22	26	202

RUUTTU, Christian 5-11 194 C
B. Lappeenranta, Finland, Feb. 20, 1964

86-87	Buf	76	22	43	65	62
87-88	Buf	73	26	45	71	85
88-89	Buf	67	14	46	60	98
89-90	Buf	75	19	41	60	66
90-91	Buf	77	16	34	50	96
91-92	Buf	70	4	21	25	76
Totals		438	101	230	331	483
Playoff Totals		23	3	8	11	45

RUZICKA, Vladimir 6-3 212 C
B. Most, Czechoslovakia, June 6, 1963

89-90	Edm	25	11	6	17	10
90-91	Bos	29	8	8	16	19
91-92	Bos	77	39	36	75	48
Totals		131	58	50	108	77
Playoff Totals		30	4	14	18	2

RYCHEL, Warren 6-0 190 LW
B. Tecumseh, Ont., May 12, 1967

88-89	Chi	2	0	0	0	17
Playoff Totals		3	1	3	4	2

RYMSHA, Andrew 6-3 210 D
B. St. Catharines, Ont., Dec. 10, 1968

91-92	Que	6	0	0	0	23

SAARINEN, Simo 5-8 185 D
B. Helsinki, Finland, Feb. 14, 1963

84-85	NYR	8	0	0	0	0

SABOL, Shaun 6-3 230 D
B. Minneapolis, Minn., July 13, 1966

89-90	Phil	2	0	0	0	0

SABOURIN, Gary Bruce 5-11 180 RW
B. Parry Sound, Ont., Dec. 4, 1943

67-68	StL	50	13	10	23	50
68-69	StL	75	25	23	48	58
69-70	StL	72	28	14	42	61
70-71	StL	59	14	17	31	56
71-72	StL	77	28	17	45	52
72-73	StL	76	21	27	48	30
73-74	StL	54	7	23	30	27
74-75	Tor	55	5	18	23	26
75-76	Cal	76	21	28	49	33
76-77	Clev	33	7	11	18	4
Totals		627	169	188	357	397
Playoff Totals		62	19	11	30	58

SABOURIN, Ken 6-3 205 D
B. Scarborough, Ont., Apr. 28, 1966

88-89	Calg	6	0	1	1	26
89-90	Calg	5	0	0	0	10
90-91	Calg-Wash	44	2	7	9	117
91-92	Wash	19	0	0	0	48
Totals		74	2	8	10	201
Playoff Totals		12	0	0	0	34

SABOURIN, Robert 5-9 205 RW
B. Sudbury, Ont., Mar. 17, 1933

51-52	Tor	1	0	0	0	2

SACCO, Joseph 6-1 180 LW
B. Medford, Mass., Feb. 4, 1969

90-91	Tor	20	0	5	5	2
91-92	Tor	17	7	4	11	6
Totals		37	7	9	16	8

SACHARUK, Lawrence William (Satch) 6-0 200 D
B. Saskatoon, Sask., Oct. 16, 1952

72-73	NYR	8	1	0	1	0
73-74	NYR	23	2	4	6	4
74-75	StL	76	20	22	42	24
75-76	NYR	42	6	7	13	14
76-77	NYR	2	0	0	0	0
78-79	Ind (WHA)	15	2	9	11	25
NHL Totals		151	29	33	62	42
WHA Totals		15	2	9	11	25
NHL Playoff Totals		2	1	1	2	0

SAGANIUK, Rocky 5-8 185 RW/C
B. Myrnam, Alta., Oct. 15, 1957

78-79	Tor	16	3	5	8	9
79-80	Tor	75	24	23	47	52
80-81	Tor	71	12	18	30	52
81-82	Tor	65	17	16	33	49
82-83	Tor	3	0	0	0	2
83-84	Pitt	29	1	3	4	37
Totals		259	57	65	122	201
Playoff Totals		6	1	0	1	15

ST. LAURENT, Andre 5-10 180 C
B. Rouyn-Noranda, Que., Feb. 16, 1953

73-74	NYI	42	5	9	14	18
74-75	NYI	78	14	27	41	60
75-76	NYI	67	9	17	26	56
76-77	NYI	72	10	13	23	55
77-78	NYI-Det	79	31	39	70	110
78-79	Det	76	18	31	49	124
79-80	LA	77	6	24	30	88
80-81	LA	22	10	6	16	63
81-82	LA-Pitt	34	10	9	19	32
82-83	Pitt	70	13	9	22	105
83-84	Pitt-Det	27	3	3	6	38
Totals		644	129	187	316	749
Playoff Totals		59	8	12	20	48

ST. LAURENT, Dollard Herve 5-11 180 D
B. Verdun, Que., May 12, 1929

50-51	Mont	3	0	0	0	0
51-52	Mont	40	3	10	13	30
52-53	Mont	54	2	6	8	34
53-54	Mont	53	3	12	15	43
54-55	Mont	58	3	14	17	24
55-56	Mont	46	4	9	13	58
56-57	Mont	64	1	11	12	49
57-58	Mont	65	3	20	23	68
58-59	Chi	70	4	8	12	28
59-60	Chi	68	4	13	17	60
60-61	Chi	67	2	17	19	58
61-62	Chi	64	0	13	13	44
Totals		652	29	133	162	496
Playoff Totals		92	2	22	24	87

ST. MARSEILLE, Francis Leo (Frank) 5-11 180 RW
B. Levack, Ont., Dec. 14, 1939

67-68	StL	57	16	16	32	12
68-69	StL	72	12	26	38	22
69-70	StL	74	16	43	59	18
70-71	StL	77	19	32	51	26
71-72	StL	78	16	36	52	32
72-73	StL-LA	74	14	22	36	10
73-74	LA	78	14	36	50	40
74-75	LA	80	17	36	53	46
75-76	LA	68	10	16	26	20
76-77	LA	49	6	22	28	16
Totals		707	140	285	425	242
Playoff Totals		88	20	25	45	18

ST. SAUVEUR, Claude 6-0 170 LW
B. Sherbrooke, Que., Jan. 2, 1952

72-73	Phil (WHA)	2	1	0	1	0
73-74	Van (WHA)	70	38	30	68	55
74-75	Van (WHA)	76	24	23	47	32
75-76	Atl	79	24	24	48	23
76-77	Calg-Edm (WHA)	32	5	10	15	4
77-78	Ind (WHA)	72	36	42	78	24
78-79	Ind-Cin (WHA)	33	8	7	15	16
NHL Totals		79	24	24	48	23
WHA Totals		285	112	112	224	131
NHL Playoff Totals		2	0	0	0	0
WHA Playoff Totals		5	1	0	1	0

SAKIC, Joe 5-11 185 C
B. Burnaby, B.C., July 7, 1969

88-89	Que	70	23	39	62	24
89-90	Que	80	39	63	102	27
90-91	Que	80	48	61	109	24
91-92	Que	69	29	65	94	20
Totals		299	139	228	367	95

SALESKI, Donald Patrick (Big Bird) *6-3 205 RW*

B. Moose Jaw, Sask., Oct. 10, 1949

Season	Team	GP	G	A	Pts.	PIM
71-72	Phil	1	0	0	0	0
72-73	Phil	78	12	9	21	205
73-74	Phil	77	15	25	40	131
74-75	Phil	63	10	18	28	107
75-76	Phil	78	21	26	47	68
76-77	Phil	74	22	16	38	33
77-78	Phil	70	27	18	45	44
78-79	Phil-Col	51	13	5	18	18
79-80	Col	51	8	8	16	23
Totals		543	128	125	253	629
Playoff Totals		82	13	17	30	131

SALMING, Anders Borje *6-1 193 D*

B. Kiruna, Sweden, Apr. 17, 1951

Season	Team	GP	G	A	Pts.	PIM
73-74	Tor	76	5	34	39	48
74-75	Tor	60	12	25	37	34
75-76	Tor	78	16	41	57	70
76-77	Tor	76	12	66	78	46
77-78	Tor	80	16	60	76	70
78-79	Tor	78	17	56	73	76
79-80	Tor	74	19	52	71	94
80-81	Tor	72	5	61	66	154
81-81	Tor	69	12	44	56	170
82-83	Tor	69	7	38	45	104
83-84	Tor	68	5	38	43	92
84-85	Tor	73	6	33	39	76
85-86	Tor	41	7	15	22	48
86-87	Tor	56	4	16	20	42
87-88	Tor	66	2	24	26	82
88-89	Tor	63	3	17	20	86
89-90	Det	49	2	17	19	52
Totals		1148	150	637	787	1344
Playoff Totals		81	12	37	49	91

SALOVAARA, John Barry *5-8 175 D*

B. Cookesville, Ont., Jan. 7, 1948

Season	Team	GP	G	A	Pts.	PIM
74-75	Det	27	0	2	2	18
75-76	Det	63	2	11	13	52
Totals		90	2	13	15	70

SALVIAN, David Clifford *5-10 170 RW*

B. Toronto, Ont., Sept. 9, 1955

Season	Team	GP	G	A	Pts.	PIM
76-77	NYI	0	0	0	0	0
Playoff Totals		1	0	1	1	2

SAMIS, Philip Lawrence *5-10 180 D*

B. Edmonton, Alta., Dec. 28, 1927

Season	Team	GP	G	A	Pts.	PIM
49-50	Tor	2	0	0	0	0
Playoff Totals		5	0	1	1	2

SAMPSON, Gary Edward *6-0 190 LW*

B. Atikokan, Ont., Aug. 24, 1959

Season	Team	GP	G	A	Pts.	PIM
83-84	Wash	15	1	1	2	6
84-85	Wash	46	10	15	25	13
85-86	Wash	19	1	4	5	2
86-87	Wash	25	1	2	3	4
Totals		105	13	22	35	25
Playoff Totals		12	1	0	1	0

SAMUELSSON, Kjell *6-6 235 D*

B. Tyngsryd, Sweden, Oct. 18, 1958

Season	Team	GP	G	A	Pts.	PIM
85-86	NYR	9	0	0	0	10
86-87	NYR-Phil	76	3	12	15	136
87-88	Phil	74	6	24	30	184
88-89	Phil	69	3	14	17	140
89-90	Phil	66	5	17	22	91
90-91	Phil	78	9	19	28	82
91-92	Phil-Pitt	74	5	11	16	110
Totals		446	31	97	128	753
Playoff Totals		76	3	16	19	92

SAMUELSSON, Ulf *6-1 195 D*

B. Fagersta, Sweden, Mar. 26, 1964

Season	Team	GP	G	A	Pts.	PIM
84-85	Hart	41	2	6	8	83
85-86	Hart	80	5	19	24	174
86-87	Hart	78	2	31	33	162
87-88	Hart	76	.8	33	41	159
88-89	Hart	71	9	26	35	181
89-90	Hart	55	2	11	13	177
90-91	Hart-Pitt	76	4	22	26	211
91-92	Pitt	62	1	14	15	208
Totals		539	33	162	195	1353
Playoff Totals		72	5	9	14	166

SANDELIN, Scott *6-0 200 D*

B. Hibbing, Minn., Aug. 8, 1964

Season	Team	GP	G	A	Pts.	PIM
86-87	Mont	1	0	0	0	0
87-88	Mont	8	0	1	1	2
90-91	Phil	15	0	3	3	0
91-92	Minn	1	0	0	0	0
Totals		25	0	4	4	2

SANDERSON, Derek Michael (Turk) *6-0 185 C*

B. Niagara Falls, Ont., June 16, 1946

Season	Team	GP	G	A	Pts.	PIM
65-66	Bos	2	0	0	0	0
66-67	Bos	2	0	0	0	0
67-68	Bos	71	24	25	49	98
68-69	Bos	61	26	22	48	146
69-70	Bos	50	18	23	41	118
70-71	Bos	71	29	34	63	130
71-72	Bos	78	25	33	58	108
72-73	Phil (WHA)	8	3	3	6	69
72-73	Bos	25	5	10	15	38
73-74	Bos	29	8	12	20	48
74-75	NYR	75	25	25	50	106
75-76	NYR-StL	73	24	43	67	63
76-77	StL-Van	48	15	22	37	56
77-78	Pitt	13	3	1	4	0
NHL Totals		598	202	250	452	911
WHA Totals		8	3	3	6	69
NHL Playoff Totals		56	18	12	30	187

SANDERSON, Geoff *6-0 185 C*

B. Hay River, Northwest Territory, Feb. 1, 1972

Season	Team	GP	G	A	Pts.	PIM
90-91	Hart	2	1	0	1	0
91-92	Hart	64	13	18	31	18
Totals		66	14	18	32	18
Playoff Totals		10	1	0	1	2

SANDFORD, Edward Michael (Sandy) *6-1 190 LW*

B. New Toronto, Ont., Aug. 20, 1928

Season	Team	GP	G	A	Pts.	PIM
47-48	Bos	59	10	15	25	25
48-49	Bos	56	16	20	36	57
49-50	Bos	17	1	4	5	6
50-51	Bos	51	10	13	23	33
51-52	Bos	65	13	12	25	54
52-53	Bos	61	14	21	35	44
53-54	Bos	70	16	31	47	42
54-55	Bos	60	14	20	34	38
55-56	Det-Chi	61	12	9	21	56
Totals		500	106	145	251	355
Playoff Totals		42	13	11	24	27

SANDLAK, Jim *6-4 219 RW*

B. Kitchener, Ont., Dec. 12, 1966

Season	Team	GP	G	A	Pts.	PIM
85-86	Van	23	1	3	4	10
86-87	Van	78	15	21	36	66
87-88	Van	49	16	15	31	81
88-89	Van	72	20	20	40	99
89-90	Van	70	15	8	23	104
90-91	Van	59	7	6	13	125
91-92	Van	66	16	24	40	176
Totals		417	90	97	187	661
Playoff Totals		22	5	8	13	24

SANDS, Charles Henry *5-9 160 C*

B. Fort William, Ont., Mar. 23, 1910

Season	Team	GP	G	A	Pts.	PIM
32-33	Tor	3	0	3	3	0
33-34	Tor	45	8	8	16	2
34-35	Bos	43	15	12	27	0
35-36	Bos	41	6	4	10	8
36-37	Bos	46	18	5	23	6
37-38	Bos	46	17	12	29	12
38-39	Bos	39	7	5	12	10
39-40	Mont	47	9	20	29	10
40-41	Mont	43	5	13	18	4
41-42	Mont	39	11	16	27	6
42-43	Mont	31	3	9	12	0
43-44	NYR	9	0	2	2	0
Totals		432	99	109	208	58
Playoff Totals		44	6	6	12	4

SANDSTROM, Tomas *6-2 200 RW*

B. Jakobstad, Finland, Sept. 4, 1964

Season	Team	GP	G	A	Pts.	PIM
84-85	NYR	74	29	29	58	51
85-86	NYR	73	25	29	54	109
86-87	NYR	64	40	34	74	60
87-88	NYR	69	28	40	68	95
88-89	NYR	79	32	56	88	148
89-90	NYR-LA	76	32	39	71	128
90-91	LA	68	45	44	89	106
91-92	LA	49	17	22	39	70
Totals		552	248	293	541	767
Playoff Totals		55	17	23	40	93

SANIPASS, Everett *6-2 204 LW*

B. Big Cove, N.B., Feb. 13, 1968

Season	Team	GP	G	A	Pts.	PIM
86-87	Chi	7	1	3	4	2
87-88	Chi	57	8	12	20	126
88-89	Chi	50	6	9	15	164
89-90	Chi-Que	21	5	5	10	25
90-91	Que	29	5	5	10	41
Totals		164	25	34	59	358
Playoff Totals		5	2	0	2	4

SARGENT, Gary Alan *5-10 210 D*

B. Red Lake, Minn,. Feb. 8, 1954

Season	Team	GP	G	A	Pts.	PIM
75-76	LA	63	8	16	24	36
76-77	LA	80	14	40	54	65
77-78	LA	72	7	34	41	52
78-79	Minn	79	12	32	44	39
79-80	Minn	52	13	21	34	22
80-81	Minn	23	4	7	11	36
81-82	Minn	15	0	5	5	18
82-83	Minn	18	3	6	9	5
Totals		402	61	161	222	273
Playoff Totals		20	5	7	12	8

SARNER, Craig Brian *5-11 185 RW*

B. St. Paul, Minn., June 20, 1949

Season	Team	GP	G	A	Pts.	PIM
74-75	Bos	7	0	0	0	0
75-75	Minn (WHA)	1	0	0	0	0

SARRAZIN, Richard (Dick) *6-0 185 RW*

B. St. Gabriel de Brandon, Que., Jan. 22, 1946

Season	Team	GP	G	A	Pts.	PIM
68-69	Phil	54	16	30	46	14
69-70	Phil	18	1	1	2	4
71-72	Phil	28	3	4	7	4
72-73	NE-Chi (WHA)	68	7	15	22	2
NHL Totals		100	20	35	55	22
WHA Totals		68	7	15	22	2
NHL Playoff Totals		4	0	0	0	0

SASKAMOOSE, Fred *5-9 165 C*

B. Sandy Lake Reserve, Sask., Dec. 24, 1934

Season	Team	GP	G	A	Pts.	PIM
53-54	Chi	11	0	0	0	6

SASSER, Grant *5-10 175 C*

B. Portland, Ore., Feb. 13, 1964

Season	Team	GP	G	A	Pts.	PIM
83-84	Pitt	3	0	0	0	0

SATHER, Glen Cameron (Slats) *5-11 180 LW*

B. High River, Alta., Sept. 2, 1943

Season	Team	GP	G	A	Pts.	PIM
66-67	Bos	5	0	0	0	0
67-68	Bos	65	8	12	20	34
68-69	Bos	76	4	11	15	67
69-70	Pitt	76	12	14	26	114
70-71	Pitt-NYR	77	10	3	13	148
71-72	NYR	76	5	9	14	77
72-73	NYR	77	11	15	26	64
73-74	NYR-StL	71	15	29	44	82
74-75	Mont	63	6	10	16	44
75-76	Minn	72	9	10	19	94
76-77	Edm(WHA)	81	19	34	53	77
NHL Totals		658	80	113	193	724
WHA Totals		81	19	34	53	77
NHL Playoff Totals		72	1	5	6	86
WHA Playoff Totals		5	1	1	2	2

SAUNDERS, Bernard *6-0 190 LW*

B. Montreal, Que., June 21, 1956

Season	Team	GP	G	A	Pts.	PIM
79-80	Que	4	0	0	0	0
80-81	Que	6	0	1	1	8
Totals		10	0	1	1	8

SAUNDERS, David *6-1 195 LW*

B. Ottawa, Ont., May 20, 1966

Season	Team	GP	G	A	Pts.	PIM
87-88	Van	56	7	13	20	10

SAUNDERS, Edward (Bud) *5-10 168 RW*

B. Ottawa, Ont., Aug. 29, 1912

Season	Team	GP	G	A	Pts.	PIM
33-34	Ott	19	1	3	4	4

SAUVE, Jean-Francois *5-6 175 C*

B. Ste-Genevieve, Que., Jan. 23, 1960

Season	Team	GP	G	A	Pts.	PIM
80-81	Buf	20	5	9	14	12
81-82	Buf	69	19	36	55	49
82-83	Buf	9	0	4	4	9
83-84	Que	39	10	17	27	2
84-85	Que	64	13	29	42	21
85-86	Que	75	16	40	56	20
86-87	Que	14	2	3	5	4
Totals		290	65	138	203	117
Playoff Totals		36	9	12	21	10

SAVAGE, Gordon (Tony) *5-11 170 D*

B. Calgary, Alta., July 18, 1906

Season	Team	GP	G	A	Pts.	PIM
34-35	Bos-Mont	49	1	5	6	6
Playoff Totals		2	0	0	0	0

SAVAGE, Joel *5-11 205 RW*

B. Surrey, B.C., Dec. 25, 1969

Season	Team	GP	G	A	Pts.	PIM
90-91	Buf	3	0	1	1	0

SAVAGE, Reginald *5-10 187 C*
B. Montreal, Que., May 1, 1970

Season	Team	GP	G	A	Pts.	PIM
90-91	Wash	1	0	0	0	0

SAVARD, Andre *6-1 185 C*
B. Temiscamingue, Que., Feb. 9, 1953

Season	Team	GP	G	A	Pts.	PIM
73-74	Bos	72	16	14	30	39
74-75	Bos	77	19	25	44	45
75-76	Bos	79	17	23	40	60
76-77	Buf	80	25	35	60	30
77-78	Buf	80	19	20	39	40
78-79	Buf	65	18	22	40	20
79-80	Buf	33	3	10	13	16
80-81	Buf	79	31	43	74	63
81-82	Buf	62	18	20	38	24
82-83	Buf	68	16	25	41	28
83-84	Que	60	20	24	44	38
84-85	Que	35	9	10	19	8
Totals		790	211	271	482	411
Playoff Totals		85	13	18	31	77

SAVARD, Denis Joseph *5-10 175 C*
B. Pointe Gatineau, Que., Feb. 4, 1961

Season	Team	GP	G	A	Pts.	PIM
80-81	Chi	76	28	47	75	47
81-82	Chi	80	32	87	119	82
82-83	Chi	78	35	86	121	99
83-84	Chi	75	37	57	94	71
84-85	Chi	79	38	67	105	56
85-86	Chi	80	47	69	116	111
86-87	Chi	70	40	50	90	108
87-88	Chi	80	44	87	131	95
88-89	Chi	58	23	59	82	110
89-90	Chi	60	27	53	80	56
90-91	Mont	70	28	31	59	52
91-92	Mont	77	28	42	70	73
Totals		883	407	735	1142	960
Playoff Totals		123	58	89	147	232

SAVARD, Jean *5-11 172 C*
B. Verdun, Que., Apr. 26, 1957

Season	Team	GP	G	A	Pts.	PIM
77-78	Chi	31	7	11	18	2
78-79	Chi	11	0	1	1	9
79-80	Hart	1	0	0	0	2
Totals		43	7	12	19	13

SAVARD, Serge *6-2 210 D*
B. Montreal, Que., Jan. 22, 1946

Season	Team	GP	G	A	Pts.	PIM
66-67	Mont	2	0	0	0	0
67-68	Mont	67	2	13	15	34
68-69	Mont	74	8	23	31	73
69-70	Mont	64	12	19	31	38
70-71	Mont	37	5	10	15	30
71-72	Mont	23	1	8	9	16
72-73	Mont	74	7	32	39	58
73-74	Mont	67	4	14	18	49
74-75	Mont	80	20	40	60	64
75-76	Mont	71	8	39	47	38
76-77	Mont	78	9	33	42	35
77-78	Mont	77	8	34	42	24
78-79	Mont	80	7	26	33	30
79-80	Mont	46	5	8	13	18
80-81	Mont	77	4	13	17	30
81-82	Winn	47	2	5	7	26
82-83	Winn	76	4	16	20	29
Totals		1040	106	333	439	592
Playoff Totals		130	19	49	68	88

SCAMURRA, Peter Vincent *6-3 185 D*
B. Buffalo, N.Y., Feb. 23, 1955

Season	Team	GP	G	A	Pts.	PIM
75-76	Wash	58	2	13	15	33
76-77	Wash	21	0	2	2	8
78-79	Wash	30	3	5	8	12
79-80	Wash	23	3	5	8	6
Totals		132	8	25	33	59

SCEVIOUR, Darin *5-10 185 RW*
B. Lacombe, Alta., Nov. 30, 1965

Season	Team	GP	G	A	Pts.	PIM
86-87	Chi	1	0	0	0	0

SCHAEFFER, Paul (Butch) *D*

Season	Team	GP	G	A	Pts.	PIM
36-37	Chi	5	0	0	0	6

SCHAMEHORN, Kevin Dean *5-9 185 RW*
B. Calgary, Alta., July 28, 1956

Season	Team	GP	G	A	Pts.	PIM
76-77	Det	3	0	0	0	9
79-80	Det	2	0	0	0	4
80-81	LA	5	0	0	0	4
Totals		10	0	0	0	17

SCHELLA, John Edward *6-0 180 D*
B. Port Arthur, Ont., May 9, 1947

Season	Team	GP	G	A	Pts.	PIM
70-71	Van	38	0	5	5	58
71-72	Van	77	2	13	15	166
72-73	Hou(WHA)	77	2	24	26	239
73-74	Hou (WHA)	73	12	19	31	170
74-75	Hou (WHA)	78	10	42	52	176
75-76	Hou (WHA)	74	6	32	38	106

SCHELLA, John Edward *(Continued)*

Season	Team	GP	G	A	Pts.	PIM
76-77	Hou (WHA)	20	0	6	6	28
77-78	Hou(WHA)	63	9	20	29	125
NHL Totals		115	2	18	20	224
WHA Totals		385	39	143	182	844
WHA Playoff Totals		66	4	25	29	143

SCHERZA, Charles (Chuck) *5-10 190 C*
B. Brandon, Man., Feb. 15, 1923

Season	Team	GP	G	A	Pts.	PIM
43-44	Bos-NYR	34	4	3	7	17
44-45	NYR	22	2	3	5	18
Totals		56	6	6	12	35

SCHINKEL, Kenneth Calvin *5-10 172 RW*
B. Jansen, Sask., Nov. 27, 1932

Season	Team	GP	G	A	Pts.	PIM
59-60	NYR	69	13	16	29	27
60-61	NYR	38	2	6	8	18
61-62	NYR	65	7	21	28	17
62-63	NYR	69	6	9	15	15
63-64	NYR	4	0	0	0	0
66-67	NYR	20	6	3	9	0
67-68	Pitt	57	14	25	39	19
68-69	Pitt	76	18	34	52	18
69-70	Pitt	72	20	25	45	19
70-71	Pitt	50	15	19	34	6
71-72	Pitt	74	15	30	45	10
72-73	Pitt	42	11	10	21	16
Totals		636	127	198	325	165
Playoff Totals		19	7	2	9	4

SCHLEGEL, Brad *5-10 181 D*
B. Kitchener, Ont., July 22, 1968

Season	Team	GP	G	A	Pts.	PIM
91-92	Wash	15	0	1	1	0
Playoff Totals		7	0	1	1	2

SCHLIEBENER, Andreas (Andy)
6-0 200 D
B. Ottawa, Ont., Aug. 16, 1962

Season	Team	GP	G	A	Pts.	PIM
81-82	Van	22	0	1	1	10
83-84	Van	51	2	10	12	48
84-85	Van	11	0	0	0	16
Totals		84	2	11	13	74
Playoff Totals		6	0	0	0	0

SCHMAUTZ, Clifford Harvey *5-7 161 RW*
B. Saskatoon, Sask., Mar. 17, 1939

Season	Team	GP	G	A	Pts.	PIM
70-71	Buf-Phil	56	13	19	32	33

SCHMAUTZ, Robert James *5-9 172 RW*
B. Saskatoon, Sask., Mar. 28, 1945

Season	Team	GP	G	A	Pts.	PIM
67-68	Chi	13	3	2	5	6
68-69	Chi	63	9	7	16	37
70-71	Van	26	5	5	10	14
71-72	Van	60	12	13	25	82
72-73	Van	77	38	33	71	137
73-74	Van-Bos	76	33	32	65	89
74-75	Bos	56	21	30	51	63
75-76	Bos	75	28	34	62	116
76-77	Bos	57	23	29	52	62
77-78	Bos	54	27	27	54	87
78-79	Bos	65	20	22	42	77
79-80	Bos-Edm-Col	69	25	18	43	81
80-81	Van	73	27	34	61	137
Totals		764	271	286	557	988
Playoff Totals		73	28	33	61	92

SCHMIDT, Clarence *5-11 165 RW*
B. Williams, Minn., 1923

Season	Team	GP	G	A	Pts.	PIM
43-44	Bos	7	1	0	1	2

SCHMIDT, John R. (Jackie) *5-10 155 LW*
B. Odessa, Sask., Nov. 11, 1924

Season	Team	GP	G	A	Pts.	PIM
42-43	Bos	45	6	7	13	6
Playoff Totals		5	0	0	0	0

SCHMIDT, Joseph *5-9 157 LW*
B. Odessa, Sask., Nov. 5, 1926

Season	Team	GP	G	A	Pts.	PIM
43-44	Bos	2	0	0	0	0

SCHMIDT, Milton Conrad *5-11 180 C*
B. Kitchener, Ont., Mar. 5, 1918

Season	Team	GP	G	A	Pts.	PIM
36-37	Bos	26	2	8	10	15
37-38	Bos	44	13	14	27	15
38-39	Bos	41	15	17	32	13
39-40	Bos	48	22	30	52	37
40-41	Bos	45	13	25	38	23
41-42	Bos	36	14	21	35	34
45-46	Bos	48	13	18	31	21
46-47	Bos	59	27	35	62	40
47-48	Bos	33	9	17	26	28
48-49	Bos	44	10	22	32	25
49-50	Bos	68	19	22	41	41
50-51	Bos	62	22	39	61	33
51-52	Bos	69	21	29	50	57
52-53	Bos	68	11	23	34	30

SCHMIDT, Milton Conrad *(Continued)*

Season	Team	GP	G	A	Pts.	PIM
53-54	Bos	64	14	18	32	28
54-55	Bos	23	4	8	12	26
Totals		778	229	346	575	466
Playoff Totals		86	24	25	49	60

SCHMIDT, Norm *5-11 190 D*
B. Sault Ste. Marie, Ont., Jan. 24, 1963

Season	Team	GP	G	A	Pts.	PIM
83-84	Pitt	34	6	12	18	12
85-86	Pitt	66	15	14	29	57
86-87	Pitt	20	1	5	6	4
87-88	Pitt	5	1	2	3	0
Totals		125	23	33	56	73

SCHNARR, Werner *F*

Season	Team	GP	G	A	Pts.	PIM
24-25	Bos	24	0	0	0	0
25-26	Bos	1	0	0	0	0
Totals		25	0	0	0	0

SCHNEIDER, Mathieu *5-11 189 D*
B. New York, N.Y., June 12, 1969

Season	Team	GP	G	A	Pts.	PIM
87-88	Mont	4	0	0	0	2
89-90	Mont	44	7	14	21	25
90-91	Mont	69	10	20	30	63
91-92	Mont	78	8	24	32	72
Totals		195	25	58	83	162
Playoff Totals		32	4	14	18	55

SCHOCK, Daniel Patrick *5-11 180 LW*
B. Terrace Bay, Ont., Dec. 30, 1948

Season	Team	GP	G	A	Pts.	PIM
70-71	Bos-Phil	20	1	2	3	0
Playoff Totals		1	0	0	0	0

SCHOCK, Ronald Lawrence *5-11 180 C*
B. Chapleau, Ont., Dec. 19, 1943

Season	Team	GP	G	A	Pts.	PIM
63-64	Bos	5	1	2	3	0
64-65	Bos	33	4	7	11	14
65-66	Bos	24	2	2	4	6
66-67	Bos	66	10	20	30	8
67-68	StL	55	9	9	18	17
68-69	StL	67	12	27	39	14
69-70	Pitt	76	8	21	29	40
70-71	Pitt	71	14	26	40	20
71-72	Pitt	77	17	29	46	22
72-73	Pitt	78	13	36	49	23
73-74	Pitt	77	14	29	43	22
74-75	Pitt	80	23	63	86	36
75-76	Pitt	80	18	44	62	28
76-77	Pitt	80	17	32	49	10
77-78	Buf	40	4	4	8	0
Totals		909	166	351	517	260
Playoff Totals		55	4	16	20	29

SCHOENFELD, James Grant *6-2 210 D*
B. Galt, Ont., Sept. 4, 1952

Season	Team	GP	G	A	Pts.	PIM
72-73	Buf	66	4	15	19	178
73-74	Buf	28	1	8	9	56
74-75	Buf	68	1	19	20	184
75-76	Buf	56	2	22	24	114
76-77	Buf	65	7	25	32	97
77-78	Buf	60	2	20	22	89
78-79	Buf	46	8	17	25	67
79-80	Buf	77	9	27	36	72
80-81	Buf	71	8	25	33	110
81-82	Buf-Det	52	8	11	19	99
82-83	Det	57	1	10	11	18
83-84	Bos	39	0	2	2	20
84-85	Buf	34	0	3	3	28
Totals		719	51	204	255	1132
Playoff Totals		75	3	13	16	151

SCHOFIELD, Dwight Hamilton *6-3 195 D*
B. Waltham, Mass., Mar. 25, 1956

Season	Team	GP	G	A	Pts.	PIM
76-77	Det	3	1	0	1	2
82-83	Mont	2	0	0	0	7
83-84	StL	70	4	10	14	219
84-85	StL	43	1	4	5	184
85-86	Wash	50	1	2	3	127
86-87	Pitt	25	1	6	7	59
87-88	Winn	18	0	0	0	33
Totals		211	8	22	30	631
Playoff Totals		9	0	0	0	55

SCHREIBER, Wally *5-11 180 RW*
B. Edmonton, Alta., Apr. 15, 1962

Season	Team	GP	G	A	Pts.	PIM
87-88	Minn	16	6	5	11	2
88-89	Minn	25	2	5	7	10
Totals		41	8	10	18	12

SCHRINER, David (Sweeney) *LW*
B. Calgary, Alta., Nov. 30, 1911

Season	Team	GP	G	A	Pts.	PIM
34-35	NYA	48	18	22	40	6
35-36	NYA	48	19	26	45	8
36-37	NYA	48	21	25	46	17
37-38	NYA	48	21	17	38	22
38-39	NYA	48	13	31	44	20

SCHRINER, David (Sweeney) *(Continued)*

Season	Team	GP	G	A	Pts.	PIM
39-40	Tor	39	11	15	26	10
40-41	Tor	48	24	14	38	6
41-42	Tor	47	20	16	36	21
42-43	Tor	37	19	17	36	13
44-45	Tor	26	27	15	42	10
45-46	Tor	47	13	6	19	15
Totals		484	206	204	410	148
Playoff Totals		60	18	11	29	54

SCHULTZ, David William (Hammer)
6-1 190 LW
B. Waldheim, Sask., Oct. 14, 1949

Season	Team	GP	G	A	Pts.	PIM
71-72	Phil	1	0	0	0	0
72-73	Phil	76	9	12	21	259
73-74	Phil	73	20	16	36	348
74-75	Phil	76	9	17	26	472
75-76	Phil	71	13	19	32	307
76-77	LA	76	10	20	30	232
77-78	LA-Pitt	74	11	25	36	405
78-79	Pitt-Buf	75	6	12	18	243
79-80	Buf	13	1	0	1	28
Totals		535	79	121	200	2294
Playoff Totals		73	8	12	20	412

SCHURMAN, Maynard F. *6-3 205 LW*
B. Summerdale, P.E.I., July 16, 1957

Season	Team	GP	G	A	Pts.	PIM
79-80	Hart	7	0	0	0	0

SCHUTT, Rodney *5-10 185 LW*
B. Bancroft, Ont., Oct. 13, 1956

Season	Team	GP	G	A	Pts.	PIM
77-78	Mont	2	0	0	0	0
78-79	Pitt	74	24	21	45	33
79-80	Pitt	73	18	21	39	43
80-81	Pitt	80	25	35	60	55
81-82	Pitt	35	9	12	21	42
82-83	Pitt	5	0	0	0	0
83-84	Pitt	11	1	3	4	4
85-86	Tor	6	0	0	0	0
Totals		286	77	92	169	177
Playoff Totals		22	8	6	14	26

SCISSONS, Scott *6-1 201 C*
B. Saskatoon, Sask., Oct. 29, 1971

Season	Team	GP	G	A	Pts.	PIM
90-91	NYI	1	0	0	0	0

SCLISIZZI, Enio James *5-10 168 LW*
B. Milton, Ont., Aug. 1, 1925

Season	Team	GP	G	A	Pts.	PIM
47-48	Det	4	1	0	1	0
48-49	Det	50	9	8	17	24
49-50	Det	4	0	0	0	2
51-52	Det	9	2	1	3	0
52-53	Chi	14	0	2	2	0
Totals		81	12	11	23	26
Playoff Totals		13	0	0	0	6

SCOTT, Ganton *RW*

Season	Team	GP	G	A	Pts.	PIM
22-23	Tor	17	0	0	0	0
23-24	Tor-Ham	8	0	0	0	0
24-25	Mont M	28	1	1	2	0
26-27	Tor	1	0	0	0	0
Totals		54	1	1	2	0

SCOTT, Lawrence (Laurie) *5-6 155 F*
B. South River, Ont., June 19, 1900

Season	Team	GP	G	A	Pts.	PIM
26-27	NYA	39	6	2	8	22
27-28	NYR	23	0	1	1	6
Totals		62	6	3	9	28

SCREMIN, Claudio *6-2 205 D*
B. Burnaby, B.C., May 28, 1968

Season	Team	GP	G	A	Pts.	PIM
91-92	SJ	13	0	0	0	25

SCRUTON, Howard *6-3 190 D*
B. Toronto, Ont., Oct. 6, 1962

Season	Team	GP	G	A	Pts.	PIM
82-83	LA	4	0	4	4	9

SEABROOKE, Glen *6-0 190 C*
B. Peterborough, Ont., Sept. 11, 1967

Season	Team	GP	G	A	Pts.	PIM
86-87	Phil	10	1	4	5	2
87-88	Phil	6	0	1	1	2
88-89	Phil	3	0	1	1	0
Totals		19	1	6	7	4

SECORD, Alan William *6-1 205 LW*
B. Sudbury, Ont., Mar. 3, 1958

Season	Team	GP	G	A	Pts.	PIM
78-79	Bos	71	16	7	23	125
79-80	Bos	77	23	16	39	170
80-81	Bos-Chi	59	13	12	25	187
81-82	Chi	80	44	31	75	303
82-83	Chi	80	54	32	86	180
83-84	Chi	14	4	4	8	77
84-85	Chi	51	15	11	26	193
85-86	Chi	80	40	36	76	201
86-87	Chi	77	29	29	58	196
87-88	Tor	74	15	27	42	221

SECORD, Alan William *(Continued)*

Season	Team	GP	G	A	Pts.	PIM
88-89	Tor-Phil	60	6	10	16	109
89-90	Chi	43	14	7	21	131
Totals		766	273	222	495	2093
Playoff Totals		102	21	34	55	382

SEDLBAUER, Ronald Andrew
6-3 200 LW
B. Burlington, Ont., Oct. 22, 1954

Season	Team	GP	G	A	Pts.	PIM
74-75	Van	26	3	4	7	17
75-76	Van	56	19	13	32	66
76-77	Van	70	18	20	38	29
77-78	Van	62	18	12	30	25
78-79	Van	79	40	16	56	26
79-80	Van-Chi	77	23	14	37	21
80-81	Chi-Tor	60	22	7	29	26
Totals		430	143	86	229	210
Playoff Totals		19	1	3	4	27

SEGUIN, Daniel G. *5-8 165 LW*
B. Sudbury, Ont., June 7, 1948

Season	Team	GP	G	A	Pts.	PIM
70-71	Minn-Van	36	1	6	7	50
73-74	Van	1	1	0	1	0
Totals		37	2	6	8	50

SEGUIN, Steve *6-2 200 RW*
B. Cornwall, Ont., Apr. 10, 1964

Season	Team	GP	G	A	Pts.	PIM
84-85	LA	5	0	0	0	9

SEIBERT, Earl Walter *6-2 198 D*
B. Kitchener, Ont., Dec. 7, 1911

Season	Team	GP	G	A	Pts.	PIM
31-32	NYR	44	4	6	10	88
32-33	NYR	45	2	3	5	92
33-34	NYR	48	13	10	23	66
34-35	NYR	48	6	19	25	86
35-36	NYR-Chi	44	5	9	14	27
36-37	Chi	43	9	6	15	46
37-38	Chi	48	8	13	21	38
38-39	Chi	48	4	11	15	57
39-40	Chi	36	3	7	10	35
40-41	Chi	46	3	17	20	52
41-42	Chi	46	7	14	21	52
42-43	Chi	44	5	27	32	48
43-44	Chi	50	8	25	33	40
44-45	Chi-Det	47	12	17	29	23
45-46	Det	18	0	3	3	18
Totals		655	89	187	276	768
Playoff Totals		66	11	8	19	66

SEILING, Richard James (Ric)
6-1 180 RW/C
B. Elmira, Ont., Dec. 15, 1957

Season	Team	GP	G	A	Pts.	PIM
77-78	Buf	80	19	19	38	33
78-79	Buf	78	20	22	42	56
79-80	Buf	80	25	35	60	54
80-81	Buf	74	30	27	57	80
81-82	Buf	57	22	25	47	58
82-83	Buf	75	19	22	41	41
83-84	Buf	78	13	22	35	42
84-85	Buf	73	16	15	31	86
85-86	Buf	69	12	13	25	74
86-87	Det	74	3	8	11	49
Totals		738	179	208	387	573
Playoff Totals		62	14	14	28	36

SEILING, Rodney Albert (Rod) *6-0 195 D*
B. Elmira, Ont., Nov. 14, 1944

Season	Team	GP	G	A	Pts.	PIM
62-63	Tor	1	0	1	1	0
63-64	NYR	2	0	1	1	0
64-65	NYR	68	4	22	26	44
65-66	NYR	52	5	10	15	24
66-67	NYR	12	1	1	2	6
67-68	NYR	71	5	11	16	44
68-69	NYR	73	4	17	21	75
69-70	NYR	76	5	21	26	68
70-71	NYR	68	5	22	27	34
71-72	NYR	78	5	36	41	62
72-73	NYR	72	9	33	42	36
73-74	NYR	68	7	23	30	32
74-75	NYR-Wash-Tor	65	5	13	18	40
75-76	Tor	77	3	16	19	46
76-77	StL	79	3	26	29	36
77-78	StL	78	1	11	12	40
78-79	StL-Atl	39	0	5	5	16
Totals		979	62	269	331	603
Playoff Totals		77	4	8	12	55

SEJBA, Jiri *5-10 185 LW*
B. Pardubice, Czechoslovakia, July 22, 1962

Season	Team	GP	G	A	Pts.	PIM
90-91	Buf	11	0	2	2	8

SELBY, Robert Briton (Brit) *5-10 175 LW*
B. Kingston, Ont., Mar. 27, 1945

Season	Team	GP	G	A	Pts.	PIM
64-65	Tor	3	2	0	2	2
65-66	Tor	61	14	13	27	26

SELBY, Robert Briton (Brit) *(Continued)*

Season	Team	GP	G	A	Pts.	PIM
66-67	Tor	6	1	1	2	0
67-68	Phil	56	15	15	30	24
68-69	Phil-Tor	77	12	15	27	42
69-70	Tor	74	10	13	23	40
70-71	Tor-StL	67	1	5	6	29
71-72	StL	6	0	0	0	8
72-73	Que-NE (WHA)	72	13	30	43	52
73-74	Tor (WHA)	64	9	17	26	21
74-75	Tor (WHA)	17	1	4	5	0
NHL Totals		350	55	62	117	171
WHA Totals		153	23	51	74	73
NHL Playoff Totals		16	1	1	2	8
WHA Playoff Totals		23	4	7	11	15

SELF, Steven *5-9 170 C*
B. Peterborough, Ont., May 9, 1950

Season	Team	GP	G	A	Pts.	PIM
76-77	Wash	3	0	0	0	0

SELWOOD, Bradley Wayne *6-1 200 D*
B. Leamington, Ont., Mar. 18, 1948

Season	Team	GP	G	A	Pts.	PIM
70-71	Tor	28	2	10	12	13
71-72	Tor	72	4	17	21	58
72-73	NE (WHA)	75	13	21	34	114
73-74	NE (WHA)	76	9	28	37	91
74-75	NE (WHA)	77	4	35	39	117
75-76	NE (WHA)	40	2	10	12	28
76-77	NE (WHA)	41	4	12	16	71
77-78	NE (WHA)	80	6	25	31	88
78-79	NE (WHA)	42	4	12	16	47
79-80	LA	63	1	13	14	82
NHL Totals		163	7	40	47	153
WHA Totals		431	42	143	185	556
NHL Playoff Totals		6	0	0	0	4
WHA Playoff Totals		63	6	12	18	81

SEMAK, Alexander *5-10 185 C*
B. Ufa, Soviet Union, Feb. 11, 1966

Season	Team	GP	G	A	Pts.	PIM
91-92	NJ	25	5	6	11	0
Playoff Totals		1	0	0	0	0

SEMENKO, David *6-3 200 LW*
B. Winnipeg, Man., July 12, 1957

Season	Team	GP	G	A	Pts.	PIM
77-78	Edm (WHA)	65	6	6	12	140
78-79	Edm (WHA)	77	10	14	24	158
79-80	Edm	67	6	7	13	135
80-81	Edm	58	11	8	19	80
81-82	Edm	59	12	12	24	194
82-83	Edm	75	12	15	27	141
83-84	Edm	52	6	11	17	118
84-85	Edm	69	6	12	18	172
885-86	Edm	69	6	12	18	141
86-87	Edm-Hart	56	4	8	12	87
87-88	Tor	70	2	3	5	107
NHL Totals		575	65	88	153	1175
WHA Totals		142	16	20	36	298
NHL Playoff Totals		73	6	6	12	208
WHA Playoff Totals		16	4	2	6	37

SEMENOV, Anatoli *6-2 190 C/LW*
B. Moscow, Soviet Union, Mar. 5, 1962

Season	Team	GP	G	A	Pts.	PIM
90-91	Edm	57	15	16	31	26
91-92	Edm	59	20	22	42	16
Totals		116	35	38	73	42
Playoff Totals		22	6	6	12	12

SENICK, George *5-10 175 LW*
B. Saskatoon, Sask., Sept. 16, 1929

Season	Team	GP	G	A	Pts.	PIM
52-53	NYR	13	2	3	5	8

SEPPA, Jyrki *6-1 190 D*
B. Tampere, Finland, Nov. 14, 1961

Season	Team	GP	G	A	Pts.	PIM
83-84	Winn	13	0	2	2	6

SERAFINI, Ronald William *5-11 185 D*
B. Detroit, Mich., Oct. 31, 1953

Season	Team	GP	G	A	Pts.	PIM
73-74	Cal	2	0	0	0	2
75-76	Cin (WHA)	16	0	2	2	15

SEROWIK, Jeff *6-0 190 D*
B. Manchester, N.H., Oct. 1, 1967

Season	Team	GP	G	A	Pts.	PIM
90-91	Tor	1	0	0	0	0

SERVINIS, George *5-11 180 LW*
B. Toronto, Ont., Apr. 29, 1962

Season	Team	GP	G	A	Pts.	PIM
87-88	Minn	5	0	0	0	0

SEVCIK, Jaroslav *5-9 170 LW*
B. Brno, Czechoslovakia, May 15, 1965

Season	Team	GP	G	A	Pts.	PIM
89-90	Que	13	0	2	2	2

SEVERYN, Brent *6-2 210 LW*
B. Vegreville, Alta., Feb. 22, 1966

Season	Team	GP	G	A	Pts.	PIM
89-90	Que	35	0	2	2	42

SHACK, Edward Steven Phillip *6-1 200 RW*
B. Sudbury, Ont., Feb. 11, 1937

Season	Team	GP	G	A	Pts.	PIM
58-59	NYR	67	7	14	21	109
59-60	NYR	62	8	10	18	110
60-61	NYR-Tor	67	15	16	31	107
61-62	Tor	44	7	14	21	62
62-63	Tor	63	16	9	25	97
63-64	Tor	64	11	10	21	128
64-65	Tor	67	5	9	14	68
65-66	Tor	63	26	17	43	88
66-67	Tor	63	11	14	25	58
67-68	Bos	70	23	19	42	107
68-69	Bos	50	11	11	22	74
69-70	LA	73	22	12	34	113
70-71	LA-Buf	67	27	19	46	101
71-72	Buf-Pitt	68	16	23	39	46
72-73	Pitt	74	25	20	45	84
73-74	Tor	59	7	8	15	74
74-75	Tor	26	2	1	3	11
Totals		1047	239	226	465	1437
Playoff Totals		74	6	7	13	151

SHACK, Joseph *5-10 170 LW*
B. Winnipeg, Man., Dec. 3, 1915

Season	Team	GP	G	A	Pts.	PIM
42-43	NYR	20	5	9	14	6
44-45	NYR	50	18	4	22	14
Totals		70	23	13	36	20

SHAKES, Paul Steven *5-10 172 D*
B. Collingwood, Ont., Sept. 4, 1952

Season	Team	GP	G	A	Pts.	PIM
73-74	Cal	21	0	4	4	12

SHANAHAN, Brendan *6-3 210 RW*
B. Mimico, Ont., Jan. 23, 1969

Season	Team	GP	G	A	Pts.	PIM
87-88	NJ	65	7	19	26	131
88-89	NJ	68	22	28	50	115
89-90	NJ	73	30	42	72	137
90-91	NJ	75	29	37	66	141
91-92	StL	80	33	36	69	171
Totals		361	121	162	283	695
Playoff Totals		31	10	12	22	90

SHANAHAN, Sean Bryan *6-3 210 LW*
B. Toronto, Ont., Feb. 8, 1951

Season	Team	GP	G	A	Pts.	PIM
75-76	Mont	4	0	0	0	0
76-77	Col	30	1	3	4	40
77-78	Bos	6	0	0	0	7
78-79	Cin (WHA)	4	0	0	0	7
NHL Totals		40	1	3	4	47
WHA Totals		4	0	0	0	7

SHAND, David Alistair *6-2 200 D*
B. Cold Lake, Alta., Aug. 11, 1956

Season	Team	GP	G	A	Pts.	PIM
76-77	Atl	55	5	11	16	62
77-78	Atl	80	2	23	25	94
78-79	Atl	79	4	22	26	64
79-80	Atl	74	3	7	10	104
80-81	Tor	47	0	4	4	60
82-83	Tor	1	0	1	1	2
83-84	Wash	72	4	15	19	124
84-85	Wash	13	1	1	2	34
Totals		421	19	84	103	544
Playoff Totals		26	1	2	3	83

SHANK, Daniel *5-10 190 RW*
B. Montreal, Que., May 12, 1967

Season	Team	GP	G	A	Pts.	PIM
89-90	Det	57	11	13	24	143
90-91	Det	7	0	1	1	14
91-92	Hart	13	2	0	2	18
Totals		77	13	14	27	175
Playoff Totals		5	0	0	0	22

SHANNON, Charles Kitchener *5-10 192 D*
B. Campbellford, Ont., Mar. 22, 1916

Season	Team	GP	G	A	Pts.	PIM
39-40	NYA	4	0	0	0	2

SHANNON, Darrin *6-2 200 LW*
B. Barrie, Ont., Dec. 8, 1969

Season	Team	GP	G	A	Pts.	PIM
88-89	Buf	3	0	0	0	0
89-90	Buf	17	2	7	9	4
90-91	Buf	34	8	6	14	12
91-92	Buf-Winn	69	13	27	40	41
Totals		123	23	40	63	57
Playoff Totals		21	1	4	5	18

SHANNON, Darryl *6-2 195 D*
B. Barrie, Ont., June 21, 1968

Season	Team	GP	G	A	Pts.	PIM
88-89	Tor	14	1	3	4	6
89-90	Tor	10	0	1	1	12
90-91	Tor	10	0	1	1	0
91-92	Tor	48	2	8	10	23
Totals		82	3	13	16	41

SHANNON, Gerald Edmund (Gerry) *5-11 170 F*
B. Campbellford, Ont., Oct. 25, 1910

Season	Team	GP	G	A	Pts.	PIM
33-34	Ott	48	11	15	26	0
34-35	StL-Bos	42	3	3	6	15
35-36	Bos	25	0	1	1	6
36-37	Mont M	32	9	7	16	20
37-38	Mont M	36	0	3	3	80
Totals		183	23	29	52	121
Playoff Totals		9	0	1	1	2

SHARPLES, Jeff *6-1 195 D*
B. Terrace, B.C., July 28, 1967

Season	Team	GP	G	A	Pts.	PIM
86-87	Det	3	0	1	1	2
87-88	Det	56	10	25	35	42
88-89	Det	46	4	9	13	26
Totals		105	14	35	49	70
Playoff Totals		7	0	3	3	6

SHARPLEY, Glen Stuart *6-0 187 C*
B. Yotk, Ont., Sept. 6, 1956

Season	Team	GP	G	A	Pts.	PIM
76-77	Minn	80	25	32	57	48
77-78	Minn	79	22	33	55	42
78-79	Minn	80	19	34	53	30
79-80	Minn	51	20	27	47	38
80-81	Minn-Chi	63	22	28	50	30
81-82	Chi	36	9	7	16	11
Totals		389	117	161	278	199
Playoff Totals		27	7	11	18	24

SHAUNESSY, Scott *6-4 220 D/LW*
B. Newport, R.I., Jan. 22, 1964

Season	Team	GP	G	A	Pts.	PIM
86-87	Que	3	0	0	0	7
88-89	Que	4	0	0	0	16
Totals		7	0	0	0	23

SHAW, Brad *6-0 190 D*
B. Cambridge, Ont., Apr. 28, 1964

Season	Team	GP	G	A	Pts.	PIM
85-86	Hart	8	0	2	2	4
86-87	Hart	2	0	0	0	0
87-88	Hart	1	0	0	0	0
88-89	Hart	3	1	0	1	0
89-90	Hart	64	3	32	35	30
90-91	Hart	72	4	28	32	29
91-92	Hart	62	3	22	25	44
Totals		212	11	84	95	107
Playoff Totals		19	4	8	12	6

SHAW, David *6-2 204 D*
B. St. Thomas, Ont., May 25, 1964

Season	Team	GP	G	A	Pts.	PIM
82-83	Que	2	0	0	0	0
83-84	Que	3	0	0	0	0
84-85	Que	14	0	0	0	11
85-86	Que	73	7	19	26	78
86-87	Que	75	0	19	19	69
87-88	NYR	68	7	25	32	100
88-89	NYR	63	6	11	17	88
89-90	NYR	22	2	10	12	22
90-91	NYR	77	2	10	12	89
91-92	NYR-Edm-Minn	59	1	9	10	72
Totals		456	25	103	128	529
Playoff Totals		17	2	4	6	51

SHAY, Norman *F*

Season	Team	GP	G	A	Pts.	PIM
24-25	Bos	18	1	1	2	14
25-26	Bos-Tor	35	4	1	5	20
Totals		53	5	2	7	34

SHEA, Francis (Pat) *D*
B. Potlatch, Idaho, Oct. 29, 1912

Season	Team	GP	G	A	Pts.	PIM
31-32	Chi	14	0	1	1	0

SHEDDEN, Douglas Arthur *6-0 185 C*
B. Wallaceburg, Ont., Apr. 29, 1961

Season	Team	GP	G	A	Pts.	PIM
81-82	Pitt	38	10	15	25	12
82-83	Pitt	80	24	43	67	54
83-84	Pitt	67	22	35	57	20
84-85	Pitt	80	35	32	67	30
85-86	Pitt-Det	78	34	37	71	34
86-87	Det-Que	49	6	14	20	14
88-89	Tor	1	0	0	0	2
90-91	Tor	23	8	10	18	10
Totals		416	139	186	325	176

SHEEHAN, Robert Richard *5-7 155 C*
B. Weymouth, Mass., Jan. 11, 1949

Season	Team	GP	G	A	Pts.	PIM
69-70	Mont	16	2	1	3	2
70-71	Mont	29	6	5	11	2
71-72	Cal	78	20	26	46	12
72-73	NY (WHA)	75	35	53	88	17
73-74	NY-NJ-Edm (WHA)	60	13	11	24	14
74-75	Edm (WHA)	77	19	39	58	8
75-76	Chi	78	11	20	31	18

SHEEHAN, Robert Richard *(Continued)*

Season	Team	GP	G	A	Pts.	PIM
76-77	Det	34	5	4	9	2
77-78	Ind (WHA)	29	8	7	15	6
79-80	Col	30	3	4	7	2
80-81	Col	41	1	3	4	10
81-82	LA	4	0	0	0	2
NHL Totals		310	48	63	111	50
WHA Totals		241	75	110	185	45
NHL Playoff Totals		25	4	3	7	8
WHA Playoff Totals		5	1	3	4	0

SHEEHY, Neil *6-2 214 D*
B. International Falls, Minn., Feb. 9, 1960

Season	Team	GP	G	A	Pts.	PIM
83-84	Calg	1	1	0	1	2
84-85	Calg	31	3	4	7	109
85-86	Calg	65	2	16	18	271
86-87	Calg	54	4	6	10	151
87-88	Calg-Hart	62	3	10	13	189
88-89	Wash	72	3	4	7	179
89-90	Wash	59	1	5	6	291
91-92	Calg	35	1	2	3	119
Totals		379	18	47	65	1311
Playoff Totals		54	0	3	3	241

SHEEHY, Timothy Kane *6-1 185 RW*
B. Fort Francis, Ont., Sept. 3, 1948

Season	Team	GP	G	A	Pts.	PIM
72-73	NE (WHA)	78	33	38	71	30
73-74	NE (WHA)	77	29	29	58	22
74-75	NE-Edm (WHA)	81	28	33	61	22
75-76	Edm (WHA)	81	34	31	65	17
76-77	Edm-Birm (WHA)	78	41	29	70	48
77-78	Birm-NE (WHA)	38	12	13	25	17
77-78	Det	15	0	0	0	0
79-80	Hart	12	2	1	3	0
NHL Totals		27	2	1	3	0
WHA Totals		433	177	173	350	156
WHA Playoff Totals		39	16	21	37	26

SHELTON, Wayne Douglas (Doug) *5-9 175 RW*
B. Woodstock, Ont., June 27, 1945

Season	Team	GP	G	A	Pts.	PIM
67-68	Chi	5	0	1	1	0

SHEPPARD, Joseph Francis Xavier (Frank) *5-6 157 C*
B. Montreal, Que., Oct. 19, 1907

Season	Team	GP	G	A	Pts.	PIM
27-28	Det	8	1	1	2	0

SHEPPARD, Gregory Wayne *5-8 170 C*
B. North Battleford, Sask., Apr. 23, 1949

Season	Team	GP	G	A	Pts.	PIM
72-73	Bos	64	24	26	50	18
73-74	Bos	75	16	31	47	21
74-75	Bos	76	30	48	78	19
75-76	Bos	70	31	43	74	28
76-77	Bos	77	31	36	67	20
77-78	Bos	54	23	36	59	24
78-79	Pitt	60	15	22	37	9
79-80	Pitt	76	13	24	37	20
80-81	Pitt	47	11	17	28	49
81-82	Pitt	58	11	10	21	35
Totals		657	205	293	498	243
Playoff Totals		92	32	40	72	31

SHEPPARD, Jake O. (Johnny) *5-7 165 LW*
B. Montreal, Que., Oct. 19, 1907

Season	Team	GP	G	A	Pts.	PIM
26-27	Det	43	13	8	21	60
27-28	Det	44	10	10	20	40
28-29	NYA	43	5	4	9	38
29-30	NYA	43	14	15	29	32
30-31	NYA	42	5	8	13	16
31-32	NYA	8	1	0	1	2
32-33	NYA	46	17	9	26	32
33-34	Bos-Chi	42	3	4	7	4
Totals		311	68	58	126	224
Playoff Totals		10	0	0	0	0

SHEPPARD, Ray *6-1 182 RW*
B. Pembroke, Ont., May 27, 1966

Season	Team	GP	G	A	Pts.	PIM
87-88	Buf	74	38	27	65	14
88-89	Buf	67	22	21	43	15
89-90	Buf	18	4	2	6	0
90-91	NYR	59	24	23	47	21
91-92	Det	74	36	26	62	27
Totals		292	124	99	223	77
Playoff Totals		18	7	4	11	6

SHERF, John Harold *5-11 178 LW*
B. Calumet, Mich., Apr. 8, 1914

Season	Team	GP	G	A	Pts.	PIM
35-36	Det	1	0	0	0	0
36-37	Det	1	0	0	0	0
37-38	Det	6	0	0	0	2

SHERF, John Harold *(Continued)*

Season	Team	GP	G	A	Pts.	PIM
38-39	Det	3	0	0	0	0
43-44	Det	8	0	0	0	6
Totals		19	0	0	0	8
Playoff Totals		8	0	1	1	2

SHERO, Frederick Alexander (Fog)
5-10 185 D
B. Winnipeg, Man., Oct. 23, 1925

Season	Team	GP	G	A	Pts.	PIM
47-48	NYR	19	1	0	1	2
48-49	NYR	59	3	6	9	64
49-50	NYR	67	2	8	10	71
Totals		145	6	14	20	137
Playoff Totals		13	0	2	2	8

SHERRITT, Gordon Ephraim (Moose)
6-1 195 D
B. Oakville, Man., Apr. 8, 1922

Season	Team	GP	G	A	Pts.	PIM
43-44	Det	8	0	0	0	12

SHERVEN, Gord *6-0 185 C*
B. Gravelbourg, Sask., Aug. 21, 1963

Season	Team	GP	G	A	Pts.	PIM
83-84	Edm	2	1	0	1	0
84-85	Edm-Minn	69	11	19	30	18
85-86	Minn-Edm	18	1	3	4	15
86-87	Hart	7	0	0	0	0
87-88	Hart	1	0	0	0	0
Totals		97	13	22	35	33
Playoff Totals		3	0	0	0	0

SHEWCHUK, John Michael (Jack)
6-1 190 D
B. Brantford, Ont., June 19, 1917

Season	Team	GP	G	A	Pts.	PIM
38-39	Bos	3	0	0	0	2
39-40	Bos	47	2	4	6	55
40-41	Bos	20	2	2	4	8
41-42	Bos	22	2	0	2	14
42-43	Bos	48	2	6	8	50
44-45	Bos	47	1	7	8	31
Totals		187	9	19	28	160
Playoff Totals		20	0	1	1	19

SHIBICKY, Alexi (Alex) *6-0 180 RW*
B. Winnipeg, Man., May 19, 1914

Season	Team	GP	G	A	Pts.	PIM
35-36	NYR	18	4	2	6	6
36-37	NYR	47	14	8	22	30
37-38	NYR	43	17	18	35	26
38-39	NYR	48	24	9	33	24
39-40	NYR	43	11	21	32	33
40-41	NYR	40	10	14	24	14
41-42	NYR	45	20	14	34	16
45-46	NYR	33	10	5	15	12
Totals		317	110	91	201	161
Playoff Totals		40	12	12	24	12

SHIELDS, Allen *6-0 188 D*
B. Ottawa, Ont., May 10, 1907

Season	Team	GP	G	A	Pts.	PIM
27-28	Ott	6	0	1	1	2
28-29	Ott	42	0	1	1	10
29-30	Ott	44	6	3	9	32
30-31	Phil Q	43	7	3	10	98
31-32	NYA	48	4	1	5	45
32-33	Ott	48	4	7	11	119
33-34	Ott	48	4	7	11	44
34-35	Mont M	43	4	8	12	45
35-36	Mont M	45	2	7	9	81
36-37	NYA-Bos	45	3	4	7	94
37-38	Mont M	48	5	7	12	67
Totals		460	39	49	88	637
Playoff Totals		17	0	1	1	14

SHILL, John Walker (Jack) *5-8 175 D*
B. Toronto, Ont., Jan. 12, 1913

Season	Team	GP	G	A	Pts.	PIM
33-34	Tor	7	0	1	1	0
34-35	Bos	45	4	4	8	22
35-36	Tor	3	0	1	1	0
36-37	Tor	32	4	4	8	26
37-38	NYA-Chi	48	5	6	11	18
38-39	Chi	28	2	4	6	4
Totals		163	15	20	35	70
Playoff Totals		27	1	6	7	13

SHILL, William Roy *6-1 175 RW*
B. Toronto, Ont., Mar. 6, 1923

Season	Team	GP	G	A	Pts.	PIM
42-43	Bos	7	4	1	5	4
45-46	Bos	45	15	12	27	12
46-47	Bos	27	2	0	2	2
Totals		79	21	13	34	18
Playoff Totals		7	1	2	3	2

SHINSKE, Richard Charles (Rick)
5-11 165 C
B. Weyburn, Sask., May 31, 1955

Season	Team	GP	G	A	Pts.	PIM
76-77	Clev	5	0	0	0	2

SHINSKE, Richard Charles (Rick)
(Continued)

Season	Team	GP	G	A	Pts.	PIM
77-78	Clev	47	5	12	17	6
78-79	StL	11	0	4	4	2
Totals		63	5	16	21	10

SHIRES, James Arthur *6-0 180 LW*
B. Edmonton, Alta., Nov. 15, 1945

Season	Team	GP	G	A	Pts.	PIM
70-71	Det	20	2	1	3	22
71-72	StL	18	0	3	3	8
72-73	Pitt	18	1	2	3	2
Totals		56	3	6	9	32

SHMYR, Paul *5-11 170 D*
B. Cudworth, Sask., Jan. 28, 1946

Season	Team	GP	G	A	Pts.	PIM
68-69	Chi	3	1	0	1	8
69-70	Chi	24	0	4	4	26
70-71	Chi	57	1	12	13	41
71-72	Cal	69	6	21	27	156
72-73	Clev (WHA)	73	5	43	48	169
73-74	Clev (WHA)	78	13	31	44	165
74-75	Clev (WHA)	49	7	14	21	103
75-76	Clev (WHA)	70	6	44	50	101
76-77	SD (WHA)	81	13	37	50	103
77-78	Edm (WHA)	80	9	40	49	100
78-79	Edm (WHA)	80	8	39	47	119
79-80	Minn	63	3	15	18	84
80-81	Minn	61	1	9	10	79
81-82	Hart	66	1	11	12	134
NHL Totals		343	13	72	85	528
WHA Totals		511	61	248	309	860
NHL Playoff Totals		34	3	3	6	44
WHA Playoff Totals		43	5	18	23	107

SHOEBOTTOM, Bruce *6-2 200 D*
B. Windsor, Ont., Aug. 20, 1965

Season	Team	GP	G	A	Pts.	PIM
87-88	Bos	3	0	1	1	0
88-89	Bos	29	1	3	4	44
89-90	Bos	2	0	0	0	4
90-91	Bos	1	0	0	0	5
Totals		35	1	4	5	53
Playoff Totals		14	1	2	3	77

SHORE, Edward William *5-11 190 D*
B. Ft. Qu'Appelle, Sask., Nov. 25, 1902

Season	Team	GP	G	A	Pts.	PIM
26-27	Bos	41	12	6	18	130
27-28	Bos	44	11	6	17	165
28-29	Bos	39	12	7	19	96
29-30	Bos	43	12	19	31	105
30-31	Bos	44	15	16	31	105
31-32	Bos	44	9	13	22	80
32-33	Bos	48	8	27	35	102
33-34	Bos	30	2	10	12	57
34-35	Bos	48	7	26	33	32
35-36	Bos	46	3	16	19	61
36-37	Bos	19	3	1	4	12
37-38	Bos	47	3	14	17	42
39-39	Bos	46	4	14	18	47
39-40	Bos-NYA	14	4	4	8	13
Totals		553	105	179	284	1047
Playoff Totals		55	6	13	19	187

SHORE, Sam Hamilton (Hamby) *LW*
B. Ottawa, Ont., 1886

Season	Team	GP	G	A	Pts.	PIM
17-18	Ott	18	3	0	3	0

SHORES, Aubrey *F*

Season	Team	GP	G	A	Pts.	PIM
30-31	Phil Q	1	0	0	0	0

SHORT, Steven *6-2 210 LW*
B. Roseville, Minn., Apr. 6, 1954

Season	Team	GP	G	A	Pts.	PIM
77-78	LA	5	0	0	0	2
78-79	Det	1	0	0	0	0
Totals		6	0	0	0	2

SHUCHUK, Gary *5-10 185 RW*
B. Edmonton, Alta., Feb. 17, 1967

Season	Team	GP	G	A	Pts.	PIM
90-91	Det	6	1	2	3	6
Playoff Totals		3	0	0	0	0

SHUDRA, Ron *6-2 192 D*
B. Winnipeg, Man., Nov. 28, 1967

Season	Team	GP	G	A	Pts.	PIM
87-88	Edm	10	0	5	5	6

SHUTT, Stephen John *5-11 185 LW*
B. Toronto, Ont., July 1, 1952

Season	Team	GP	G	A	Pts.	PIM
72-73	Mont	50	8	8	16	24
73-74	Mont	70	15	20	35	17
74-75	Mont	77	30	35	65	40
75-76	Mont	80	45	34	79	47
76-77	Mont	80	60	45	105	28
77-78	Mont	80	49	37	86	24
78-79	Mont	72	37	40	87	31
79-80	Mont	77	47	42	89	34
80-81	Mont	77	35	38	73	51

SHUTT, Stephen John *(Continued)*

Season	Team	GP	G	A	Pts.	PIM
81-82	Mont	57	31	24	55	40
82-83	Mont	78	35	22	57	26
83-84	Mont	63	14	23	37	29
84-85	Mont-LA	69	18	25	43	19
Totals		930	424	393	817	410
Playoff Totals		99	50	48	98	65

SIEBERT, Albert Charles (Babe)
5-10 182 LW
B. Plattsville, Que., Jan. 14, 1904

Season	Team	GP	G	A	Pts.	PIM
25-26	Mont M	35	16	8	24	108
26-27	Mont M	42	5	3	8	116
27-28	Mont M	40	8	9	17	109
28-29	Mont M	39	3	5	8	82
29-30	Mont M	41	14	19	33	94
30-31	Mont M	42	16	12	28	76
31-32	Mont M	48	21	18	39	64
32-33	NYR	42	9	10	19	38
33-34	NYR-Bos	45	5	7	12	49
34-35	Bos	48	6	18	24	80
35-36	Bos	46	12	9	21	66
36-37	Mont	44	8	20	28	38
37-38	Mont	37	8	11	19	56
38-39	Mont	44	9	7	16	26
Totals		593	140	156	296	1002
Playoff Totals		54	8	7	15	62

SILK, David *5-11 190 RW*
B. Scituate, Mass., Jan. 1, 1958

Season	Team	GP	G	A	Pts.	PIM
79-80	NYR	2	0	0	0	0
80-81	NYR	59	14	12	26	58
81-82	NYR	64	15	20	35	39
82-83	NYR	16	1	1	2	15
83-84	Bos	35	13	17	30	64
84-85	Bos-Det	41	9	5	14	32
85-86	Winn	32	2	4	6	63
Totals		249	54	59	113	271
Playoff Totals		13	2	4	6	13

SILLINGER, Mike *5-10 191 C*
B. Regina, Sask., June 29, 1971

Season	Team	GP	G	A	Pts.	PIM
90-91	Det	3	0	1	1	0
91-92	Det	0	0	0	0	0
Totals		3	0	1	1	0
Playoff Totals		11	2	3	5	2

SILTALA, Michael *5-9 170 RW*
B. Toronto, Ont., Aug. 5, 1963

Season	Team	GP	G	A	Pts.	PIM
81-82	Wash	3	1	0	1	2
86-87	NYR	1	0	0	0	0
87-88	NYR	3	0	0	0	0
Totals		7	1	0	1	2

SILTANEN, Risto *5-9 180 D*
B. Tampere, Finland, Oct. 31, 1958

Season	Team	GP	G	A	Pts.	PIM
78-79	Edm (WHA)	20	3	4	7	4
79-80	Edm	64	6	29	35	26
80-81	Edm	79	17	36	53	54
81-82	Edm	63	15	48	63	26
82-83	Hart	74	5	25	30	28
83-84	Hart	75	15	38	53	34
84-85	Hart	76	12	33	45	30
85-86	Hart-Que	65	10	27	37	36
86-87	Que	66	10	29	39	32
NHL Totals		562	90	265	355	266
WHA Totals		20	3	4	7	4
NHL Playoff Tot.		32	6	12	18	30
WHA Playoff Tot.		11	0	9	9	4

SIM, Trevor *6-2 192 RW*
B. Calgary, Alta., June 9, 1970

Season	Team	GP	G	A	Pts.	PIM
89-90	Edm	3	0	1	1	2

SIMARD, Martin *6-3 215 RW*
B. Montreal, Que., June 25, 1966

Season	Team	GP	G	A	Pts.	PIM
90-91	Calg	16	0	2	2	53
91-92	Calg	21	1	3	4	119
Totals		37	1	5	6	172

SIMMER, Charles Robert *6-3 210 LW*
B. Terrace Bay, Ont., Mar. 20, 1954

Season	Team	GP	G	A	Pts.	PIM
74-75	Cal	35	8	13	21	26
75-76	Cal	21	1	1	2	22
76-77	Clev	24	2	0	2	16
77-78	LA	3	0	0	0	2
78-79	LA	38	21	27	48	16
79-80	LA	64	56	45	101	65
80-81	LA	65	56	49	105	62
81-82	LA	50	15	24	39	42
82-83	LA	80	29	51	80	51
83-84	LA	79	44	48	92	78
84-85	LA-Bos	68	34	30	64	39
85-86	Bos	55	36	24	60	42

SIMMER, Charles Robert *(Continued)*

Season	Team	GP	G	A	Pts.	PIM
86-87	Bos	80	29	40	69	59
87-88	Pitt	50	11	17	28	24
Totals		712	342	369	711	544
Playoff Totals		24	9	9	18	32

SIMMONS, Allan Kenneth *6-0 170 D*
B. Winnipeg, Man., Sept. 25, 1951

Season	Team	GP	G	A	Pts.	PIM
71-72	Cal	1	0	0	0	0
73-74	Bos	3	0	0	0	0
75-76	Bos	7	0	1	1	21
Totals		11	0	1	1	21
Playoff Totals		1	0	0	0	0

SIMON, John Cullen (Cully) *5-10 190 D*
B. Brockville, Ont., May 8, 1918

Season	Team	GP	G	A	Pts.	PIM
42-43	Det	34	1	1	2	34
43-44	Det	46	3	7	10	52
44-45	Det-Chi	50	0	3	3	35
Totals		130	4	11	15	21
Playoff Totals		14	0	1	1	6

SIMON, Thain Andrew *6-0 200 D*
B. Brockville, Ont., Apr. 24, 1922

Season	Team	GP	G	A	Pts.	PIM
46-47	Det	3	0	0	0	0

SIMONETTI, Frank *6-1 190 D*
B. Melrose, Mass., Sept. 11, 1962

Season	Team	GP	G	A	Pts.	PIM
84-85	Bos	43	1	5	6	26
85-86	Bos	17	1	0	1	14
86-87	Bos	25	1	0	1	17
87-88	Bos	30	2	3	5	19
Totals		115	5	8	13	76
Playoff Totals		12	0	1	1	8

SIMPSON, Clifford Vernon *5-11 175 C*
B. Toronto, Ont., Apr. 4, 1923

Season	Team	GP	G	A	Pts.	PIM
46-47	Det	6	0	1	1	0
Playoff Totals		2	0	0	0	2

SIMPSON, Craig *6-2 195 LW*
B. London, Ont., Feb. 15, 1967

Season	Team	GP	G	A	Pts.	PIM
85-86	Pitt	76	11	17	28	49
86-87	Pitt	72	26	25	51	57
87-88	Pitt-Edm	80	56	34	90	77
88-89	Edm	66	35	41	76	80
89-90	Edm	80	29	32	61	180
90-91	Edm	75	30	27	57	66
91-92	Edm	79	24	37	61	80
Totals		528	211	213	424	589
Playoff Totals		67	36	32	68	56

SIMPSON, Harold Joseph (Bullet Joe) *D*
B. Selkirk, Man., Aug. 13, 1893

Season	Team	GP	G	A	Pts.	PIM
25-26	NYA	32	2	2	4	2
26-27	NYA	43	4	2	6	39
27-28	NYA	24	2	0	2	32
28-29	NYA	43	3	2	5	29
29-30	NYA	44	8	13	21	41
30-31	NYA	42	2	0	2	13
Totals		228	21	19	40	156
Playoff Totals		2	0	0	0	0

SIMPSON, Reid *6-1 211 LW*
B. Flin Flon, Man., May 21, 1969

Season	Team	GP	G	A	Pts.	PIM
91-92	Phil	1	0	0	0	0

SIMPSON, Robert (Bobby) *6-0 190 LW*
B. Caughnawa, Que., Nov. 17, 1956

Season	Team	GP	G	A	Pts.	PIM
76-77	Atl	72	13	10	23	45
77-78	Atl	55	10	8	18	49
79-80	StL	18	2	2	4	0
81-82	Pitt	26	9	9	18	4
82-83	Pitt	4	1	0	1	0
Totals		175	35	29	64	98
Playoff Totals		6	0	1	1	2

SIMMS, Allan Eugene *6-0 180 D*
B. Toronto, Ont., Apr. 18, 1953

Season	Team	GP	G	A	Pts.	PIM
73-74	Bos	77	3	9	12	22
74-75	Bos	75	4	8	12	73
75-76	Bos	48	4	3	7	43
76-77	Bos	1	0	0	0	0
77-78	Bos	43	2	8	10	6
78-79	Bos	67	9	20	29	28
79-80	Hart	76	10	31	41	30
80-81	Hart	80	16	36	52	68
81-82	LA	8	1	1	2	16
82-83	LA	1	0	0	0	0
Totals		476	49	116	165	384
Playoff Totals		41	0	2	2	14

SINCLAIR, Reginald Alexander (Reg)
6-0 165 RW
B. Lachine, Que., Mar. 6, 1925

Season	Team	GP	G	A	Pts.	PIM
50-51	NYR	70	18	21	39	70

SINCLAIR, Reginald Alexander (Reg)
(Continued)

Season	Team	GP	G	A	Pts.	PIM
51-52	NYR	69	20	10	30	33
52-53	Det	69	11	12	23	36
Totals		208	49	43	92	139
Playoff Totals		3	1	0	1	0

SINGBUSH, E. Alexander (Alex) *D*
B. Winnipeg, Man., 1915

Season	Team	GP	G	A	Pts.	PIM
40-41	Mont	32	0	5	5	15
Playoff Totals		3	0	0	0	4

SINISALO, Ilkka *6-0 200 RW*
B. Valeakoski, Finland, July 10, 1958

Season	Team	GP	G	A	Pts.	PIM
81-82	Phil	66	15	22	37	22
82-83	Phil	61	21	29	50	16
83-84	Phil	73	29	17	46	29
84-85	Phil	70	36	37	73	16
85-86	Phil	74	39	37	76	31
86-87	Phil	42	10	21	31	8
87-88	Phil	68	25	17	42	30
88-89	Phil	13	1	6	7	2
89-90	Phil	59	23	23	46	26
90-91	Minn-LA	53	5	12	17	26
91-92	LA	3	0	1	1	2
Totals		582	204	222	426	208
Playoff Totals		68	21	11	32	6

SIREN, Ville *6-2 191 D*
B. Tampere, Finland, Feb. 11, 1964

Season	Team	GP	G	A	Pts.	PIM
85-86	Pitt	60	4	8	12	32
86-87	Pitt	69	5	17	22	50
87-88	Pitt	58	1	20	21	62
88-89	Pitt-Minn	50	3	10	13	72
89-90	Minn	53	1	13	14	60
Totals		290	14	68	82	276
Playoff Totals		15	1	1	2	43

SIROIS, Robert *6-0 178 RW*
B. Montreal, Que., Feb. 6, 1954

Season	Team	GP	G	A	Pts.	PIM
74-75	Phil	3	1	0	1	4
75-76	Phil-Wash	44	10	19	29	6
76-77	Wash	45	13	22	35	2
77-78	Wash	72	24	37	61	6
78-79	Wash	73	29	25	54	6
79-80	Wash	49	15	17	32	18
Totals		286	92	120	212	42

SITTLER, Darryl Glen *6-0 190 C*
B. Kitchener, Ont., Sept. 18, 1950

Season	Team	GP	G	A	Pts.	PIM
70-71	Tor	49	10	8	18	37
71-72	Tor	74	15	17	32	44
72-73	Tor	78	29	48	77	69
73-74	Tor	78	38	46	84	55
74-75	Tor	72	36	44	80	47
75-76	Tor	79	41	59	100	90
76-77	Tor	73	38	52	90	89
77-78	Tor	80	45	72	117	100
78-79	Tor	70	36	51	87	69
79-80	Tor	73	40	57	97	62
80-81	Tor	80	43	53	96	77
81-82	Tor-Phil	73	32	38	70	74
82-83	Phil	80	43	40	83	60
83-84	Phil	76	27	36	63	38
84-85	Det	61	11	16	27	37
Totals		1096	484	637	1121	948
Playoff Totals		76	29	45	74	137

SJOBERG, Lars-Erik *5-8 179 D*
B. Falun, Sweden, Apr. 5, 1944

Season	Team	GP	G	A	Pts.	PIM
74-75	Winn (WHA)	75	7	53	60	30
75-76	Winn (WHA)	81	5	36	41	12
76-77	Winn (WHA)	52	2	38	40	31
77-78	Winn (WHA)	78	11	39	50	72
78-79	Winn (WHA)	9	0	3	3	2
79-80	Winn	79	7	27	34	48
NHL Totals		79	7	27	34	48
WHA Totals		295	25	169	194	147
WHA Playoff Totals		52	1	22	23	42

SKAARE, Bjorne *6-0 180 C*
B. Oslo, Norway, Oct. 29, 1948

Season	Team	GP	G	A	Pts.	PIM
78-79	Det	1	0	0	0	0

SKALDE, Jarrod *6-0 170 C*
B. Niagara Falls, Ont., Feb. 26, 1971

Season	Team	GP	G	A	Pts.	PIM
90-91	NJ	1	0	1	1	0
91-92	NJ	15	2	4	6	4
Totals		16	2	5	7	4

SKARDA, Randy *6-1 205 D*
B. St. Paul, Minn., May 5, 1968

Season	Team	GP	G	A	Pts.	PIM
89-90	StL	25	0	5	5	11
91-92	StL	1	0	0	0	0
Totals		26	0	5	5	11

SKILTON, Raymond (Raymie) *D*

Season	Team	GP	G	A	Pts.	PIM
17-18	Mont W	1	1	0	1	0

SKINNER, Alfred (Alf) *RW*

Season	Team	GP	G	A	Pts.	PIM
17-18	Tor	19	13	0	13	20
18-19	Tor	17	12	3	15	26
24-25	Bos-Mont M	27	1	1	2	28
25-26	Pitt Pi	7	0	0	0	2
Totals		70	26	4	30	76
Playoff Totals		7	8	1	9	0

SKINNER, Laurence Foster (Larry)
5-11 180 C
B. Vancouver, B.C., Apr. 21, 1956

Season	Team	GP	G	A	Pts.	PIM
76-77	Col	19	4	5	9	6
77-78	Col	14	3	5	8	0
78-79	Col	12	3	2	5	2
79-80	Col	2	0	0	0	0
Totals		47	10	12	22	8
Playoff Totals		2	0	0	0	0

SKOV, Glen Frederick *6-1 185 C*
B. Wheatley, Ont., Jan. 26, 1931

Season	Team	GP	G	A	Pts.	PIM
49-50	Det	2	0	0	0	0
50-51	Det	19	7	6	13	13
51-52	Det	70	12	14	26	48
52-53	Det	70	12	15	27	54
53-54	Det	70	17	10	27	95
54-55	Det	70	14	16	30	53
55-56	Chi	70	7	20	27	26
56-57	Chi	67	14	28	42	69
57-58	Chi	70	17	18	35	35
58-59	Chi	70	3	5	8	4
59-60	Chi	69	3	4	7	16
60-61	Mont	3	0	0	0	0
Totals		650	106	136	242	413
Playoff Totals		53	7	7	14	48

SKRIKO, Petri *5-10 175 LW*
B. Lappeenranta, Finland, Mar. 12, 1962

Season	Team	GP	G	A	Pts.	PIM
84-85	Van	72	21	14	35	10
85-86	Van	80	38	40	78	34
86-87	Van	76	33	41	74	44
87-88	Van	73	30	34	64	32
88-89	Van	74	30	36	66	57
89-90	Van	77	15	33	48	36
90-91	Van-Bos	48	9	18	27	17
91-92	Bos-Winn	24	3	3	6	10
Totals		524	179	219	398	240
Playoff Totals		28	5	9	14	4

SKRUDLAND, Brian *6-0 196 C*
B. Peace River, Alta., July 31, 1963

Season	Team	GP	G	A	Pts.	PIM
85-86	Mont	65	9	13	22	57
86-87	Mont	79	11	17	128	107
87-88	Mont	79	12	24	36	112
88-89	Mont	71	12	29	41	84
89-90	Mont	59	11	31	42	56
90-91	Mont	57	15	19	34	85
91-92	Mont	42	3	3	6	36
Totals		452	73	136	209	537
Playoff Totals		101	14	37	51	261

SLEAVER, John *6-1 180 C*
B. Copper Cliff, Ont., Aug. 18, 1934

Season	Team	GP	G	A	Pts.	PIM
53-54	Chi	12	1	0	1	2
56-57	Chi	12	1	0	1	4
Totals		24	2	0	2	6

SLEIGHER, Louis *5-11 200 RW*
B. Nouvelle, Que., Oct. 23, 1958

Season	Team	GP	G	A	Pts.	PIM
78-79	Birm (WHA)	62	26	12	38	46
79-80	Que	2	0	1	1	0
81-82	Que	8	0	0	0	0
82-83	Que	51	14	10	24	49
83-84	Que	44	15	19	34	32
84-85	Que-Bos	76	13	21	34	45
85-86	Bos	13	4	2	6	20
NHL Totals		194	46	53	99	146
WHA Totals		62	26	12	38	46
NHL Playoff Totals		17	1	1	2	64

SLOAN, Aloysius Martin (Tod)
5-10 175 C
B. Vinton, Que., Nov. 30, 1927

Season	Team	GP	G	A	Pts.	PIM
47-48	Tor	1	0	0	0	0
48-49	Tor	29	3	4	7	0
50-51	Tor	70	31	25	56	105

SLOAN, Aloysius Martin (Tod)
(Continued)

Season	Team	GP	G	A	Pts.	PIM
51-52	Tor	68	25	23	48	89
52-53	Tor	70	15	10	25	76
53-54	Tor	67	11	32	43	100
54-55	Tor	63	13	15	28	89
55-56	Tor	70	37	29	66	100
56-57	Tor	52	14	21	35	33
57-58	Tor	59	13	25	38	58
58-59	Chi	59	27	35	62	79
59-60	Chi	70	20	20	40	54
60-61	Chi	67	11	23	34	48
Totals		745	220	262	482	831
Playoff Totals		47	9	12	21	47

SLOBODZIAN, Peter Paul *6-1 185 D*
B. Dauphin, Man., Apr. 24, 1918

Season	Team	GP	G	A	Pts.	PIM
40-41	NYA	41	3	2	5	54

SLOWINSKI, Edward Stanley *6-0 200 RW*
B. Winnipeg, Man., Nov. 18, 1922

Season	Team	GP	G	A	Pts.	PIM
47-48	NYR	38	6	5	11	2
48-49	NYR	20	1	1	2	2
49-50	NYR	63	14	23	37	12
50-51	NYR	69	14	18	32	15
51-51	NYR	64	21	22	43	18
52-53	NYR	37	2	5	7	14
Totals		291	58	74	132	63
Playoff Totals		16	2	6	8	6

SLY, Darryl Hayward *5-10 185 D*
B. Collingwood, Ont., Apr. 3, 1939

Season	Team	GP	G	A	Pts.	PIM
65-66	Tor	2	0	0	0	0
67-68	Tor	17	0	0	0	4
69-70	Minn	29	1	0	1	6
70-71	Van	31	0	2	2	10
Totals		79	1	2	3	20

SMAIL, Douglas *5-9 175 LW*
B. Moose Jaw, Sask., Sept. 2, 1957

Season	Team	GP	G	A	Pts.	PIM
80-81	Winn	30	10	8	18	45
81-82	Winn	72	17	18	35	55
82-83	Winn	80	15	29	44	32
83-84	Winn	66	20	17	37	62
84-85	Winn	80	31	35	66	45
85-86	Winn	73	16	26	42	32
86-87	Winn	78	25	18	43	36
87-88	Winn	71	15	16	31	34
88-89	Winn	47	14	15	29	52
89-90	Winn	79	25	24	49	63
90-91	Winn-Minn	72	8	15	23	48
91-92	Que	46	10	18	28	47
Totals		794	206	239	445	551
Playoff Totals		42	9	2	11	49

SMART, Alexander (Alec) *F*
B. Brandon, Man., May 29, 1918

Season	Team	GP	G	A	Pts.	PIM
42-43	Mont	8	2	5	7	0

SMEDSMO, Dale Darwin *6-1 195 LW*
B. Roseau, Minn., Apr. 23, 1951

Season	Team	GP	G	A	Pts.	PIM
72-73	Tor	4	0	0	0	0
75-76	Cin (WHA)	66	8	14	22	187
76-77	NE-Cin (WHA)	38	2	5	7	197
77-78	Ind (WHA)	6	0	3	3	7
NHL Totals		4	0	0	0	0
WHA Totals		110	10	22	32	291
WHA Playoff Totals		2	0	1	1	0

SMILLIE, Donald *F*

Season	Team	GP	G	A	Pts.	PIM
33-34	Bos	12	2	2	4	4

SMITH, Alexander (Alex) *5-11 176 D*
B. Liverpool, England, Apr. 2, 1902

Season	Team	GP	G	A	Pts.	PIM
24-25	Ott	7	0	0	0	2
25-26	Ott	36	0	0	0	36
26-27	Ott	42	4	1	5	58
27-28	Ott	44	9	4	13	90
28-29	Ott	44	1	7	8	36
29-30	Ott	43	2	6	8	91
30-31	Ott	37	5	6	11	73
31-32	Det	48	6	8	14	47
32-33	Ott-Bos	49	7	4	11	72
33-34	Bos	45	4	6	10	32
34-35	NYA	48	3	8	11	46
Totals		443	41	50	91	583
Playoff Totals		19	0	2	2	40

SMITH, Arthur *F*
B. 1907

Season	Team	GP	G	A	Pts.	PIM
27-28	Tor	15	5	3	8	22
28-29	Tor	43	5	0	5	91
29-30	Tor	43	3	3	6	75
30-31	Ott	36	2	4	6	61
Totals		137	15	10	25	249
Playoff Totals		4	1	1	2	8

SMITH, Barry Edward *5-11 178 C*
B. Surrey, B.C., Apr. 25, 1955

Season	Team	GP	G	A	Pts.	PIM
75-76	Bos	19	1	0	1	2
79-80	Col	33	2	3	5	4
80-81	Col	62	4	4	8	4
Totals		114	7	7	14	10

SMITH, Brad Allan *6-1 195 RW*
B. Windsor, Ont., Apr. 13, 1958

Season	Team	GP	G	A	Pts.	PIM
78-79	Van	2	0	0	0	2
79-80	Van-Atl	23	1	3	4	54
80-81	Calg-Det	65	12	6	18	158
81-82	Det	33	2	0	2	80
82-83	Det	1	0	0	0	0
83-84	Det	8	2	1	3	36
84-85	Det	1	1	0	1	5
85-86	Tor	42	5	17	22	84
86-87	Tor	47	5	7	12	172
Totals		222	28	34	62	591
Playoff Totals		20	3	3	6	49

SMITH, Brian Desmond *6-0 180 LW*
B. Ottawa, Ont., Sept. 6, 1940

Season	Team	GP	G	A	Pts.	PIM
67-68	LA	58	10	9	19	33
68-69	Minn	9	0	1	1	0
Totals		67	10	10	20	33
Playoff Totals		7	0	0	0	0

SMITH, Brian Stuart *6-0 180 LW*
B. Creighton Mine, Ont., Dec. 6, 1937

Season	Team	GP	G	A	Pts.	PIM
57-58	Det	4	0	1	1	0
59-60	Det	31	2	5	7	2
60-61	Det	26	0	2	2	10
Totals		61	2	8	10	12
Playoff Totals		5	0	0	0	0

SMITH, Carl David *F*
B. Cache Bay, Ont., Sept. 18, 1917

Season	Team	GP	G	A	Pts.	PIM
43-44	Det	7	1	1	2	2

SMITH, Clinton James (Snuffy)
5-8 165 C
B. Assiniboia, Sask., Dec. 12, 1913

Season	Team	GP	G	A	Pts.	PIM
36-37	NYR	2	1	0	1	0
37-38	NYR	48	14	23	37	0
38-39	NYR	48	21	20	41	2
39-40	NYR	41	8	16	24	2
40-41	NYR	48	14	11	25	0
41-42	NYR	47	10	24	34	4
42-43	NYR	47	12	21	33	4
43-44	Chi	50	23	49	72	4
44-45	Chi	50	23	31	54	0
45-46	Chi	50	26	24	50	2
46-47	Chi	52	9	17	26	6
Totals		483	161	236	397	24
Playoff Totals		44	10	14	24	2

SMITH, Dallas Earl *5-11 180 D*
B. Hamiota, Man., Oct. 10, 1941

Season	Team	GP	G	A	Pts.	PIM
59-60	Bos	5	1	1	2	0
60-61	Bos	70	1	9	10	79
61-62	Bos	7	0	0	0	10
65-66	Bos	2	0	0	0	0
66-67	Bos	33	0	1	1	24
67-68	Bos	74	4	23	27	65
68-69	Bos	75	4	24	28	74
69-70	Bos	75	7	17	24	119
70-71	Bos	73	7	38	45	68
71-72	Bos	78	8	22	30	132
72-73	Bos	78	4	27	31	72
73-74	Bos	77	6	21	27	64
74-75	Bos	79	3	20	23	84
75-76	Bos	77	7	25	32	103
76-77	Bos	58	2	20	22	40
77-78	NYR	29	1	4	5	23
Totals		890	55	252	307	957
Playoff Totals		86	3	29	32	128

SMITH, Dalton J. (Nakina) *5-10 150 C*
B. Cache Bay, Ont., June 26, 1915

Season	Team	GP	G	A	Pts.	PIM
36-37	NYA	1	0	0	0	0
43-44	Det	10	1	2	3	0
Totals		11	1	2	3	0

SMITH, Dennis *5-11 190 D*
B. Detroit, Mich., July 27, 1964

Season	Team	GP	G	A	Pts.	PIM
89-90	Wash	4	0	0	0	0
90-91	LA	4	0	0	0	4
Totals		8	0	0	0	4

SMITH, Derek Robert *5-11 180 C/LW*
B. Quebec City, Que., July 31, 1954

Season	Team	GP	G	A	Pts.	PIM
76-77	Buf	5	0	0	0	0
77-78	Buf	36	3	3	6	0
78-79	Buf	43	14	12	26	8
79-80	Buf	79	24	39	63	16

SMITH, Derek Robert *(Continued)*

Season	Team	GP	G	A	Pts.	PIM
80-81	Buf	69	21	43	64	12
81-82	Buf-Det	61	9	15	24	12
82-83	Det	42	7	4	11	12
Totals		335	78	116	194	60
Playoff Totals		30	9	14	23	13

SMITH, Derrick *6-2 215 LW*
B. Scarborough, Ont., Jan. 22, 1965

Season	Team	GP	G	A	Pts.	PIM
84-85	Phil	77	17	22	39	31
85-86	Phil	69	6	6	12	57
86-87	Phil	71	11	21	32	34
87-88	Phil	76	16	8	24	104
88-89	Phil	74	16	14	30	43
89-90	Phil	55	3	6	9	32
90-91	Phil	72	11	20	21	37
91-92	Minn	33	2	4	6	33
Totals		527	82	91	173	371
Playoff Totals		82	14	11	25	79

SMITH, Desmond Patrick (Des)
6-0 185 D
B. Ottawa, Ont., Feb. 22, 1914

Season	Team	GP	G	A	Pts.	PIM
37-38	Mont M	41	3	1	4	47
38-39	Mont	16	3	3	6	8
39-40	Chi-Bos	42	3	6	9	50
40-41	Bos	48	6	8	14	61
41-42	Bos	48	7	7	14	70
Totals		195	22	25	47	236
Playoff Totals		25	1	4	5	18

SMITH, Donald *C*
B. 1889

Season	Team	GP	G	A	Pts.	PIM
19-20	Mont	10	1	0	1	4

SMITH, Donald Arthur *5-10 165 C*
B. Regina, Sask., May 4, 1929

Season	Team	GP	G	A	Pts.	PIM
49-50	NYR	11	1	1	2	0
Playoff Totals		1	0	0	0	0

SMITH, Douglas Eric *5-11 186 C*
B. Ottawa, Ont., May 17, 1963

Season	Team	GP	G	A	Pts.	PIM
81-82	LA	80	16	14	30	64
82-83	LA	42	11	11	22	12
83-84	LA	72	16	20	36	28
84-85	LA	62	21	20	41	58
85-86	LA-Buf	78	18	20	38	129
86-87	Buf	62	16	24	40	106
87-88	Buf	70	9	19	28	117
88-89	Edm-Van	29	4	5	9	13
89-90	Van-Pitt	40	4	5	9	97
Totals		535	115	138	253	624
Playoff Totals		18	4	2	6	21

SMITH, Floyd Robert Donald
5-10 180 RW
B. Perth, Ont., May 16, 1935

Season	Team	GP	G	A	Pts.	PIM
54-55	Bos	3	0	1	1	0
56-57	Bos	23	0	0	0	6
60-61	NYR	29	5	9	14	0
62-63	Det	51	9	17	26	10
63-64	Det	52	18	13	31	22
64-65	Det	67	16	29	45	44
65-66	Det	66	21	28	49	20
66-67	Det	54	11	14	25	8
67-68	Det-Tor	63	24	22	46	14
68-69	Tor	64	15	19	34	22
69-70	Tor	61	4	14	18	13
70-71	Buf	77	6	11	17	46
71-72	Buf	6	0	1	1	2
Totals		616	129	178	307	207
Playoff Totals		48	12	11	23	16

SMITH, Geoff *6-3 200 D*
B. Edmonton, Alta., Mar. 7, 1969

Season	Team	GP	G	A	Pts.	PIM
89-90	Edm	74	4	11	15	52
90-91	Edm	59	1	12	13	55
91-92	Edm	74	2	16	18	43
Totals		207	7	39	46	150
Playoff Totals		12	0	1	1	6

SMITH, George *F*

Season	Team	GP	G	A	Pts.	PIM
21-22	Tor	9	0	0	0	0

SMITH, Glen *F*

Season	Team	GP	G	A	Pts.	PIM
50-51	Chi	2	0	0	0	0

SMITH, Glenn *D*

Season	Team	GP	G	A	Pts.	PIM
22-23	Tor	9	0	0	0	0

SMITH, Gordon Joseph *5-10 175 D*
B. Perth, Ont., Nov. 17, 1949

Season	Team	GP	G	A	Pts.	PIM
74-75	Wash	63	3	8	11	56
75-76	Wash	25	1	2	3	28
76-77	Wash	79	1	12	13	92
77-78	Wash	80	4	7	11	78

Season	Team	GP	G	A	Pts.	PIM
SMITH, Gordon Joseph *(Continued)*						
78-79	Wash	39	0	1	1	22
79-80	Winn	13	0	0	0	8
Totals		299	9	30	39	284
SMITH, Gregory James 6-0 195 D						
B. Ponoka, Alta., July 8, 1955						
75-76	Cal	1	0	1	1	2
76-77	Clev	74	9	17	26	65
77-78	Clev	80	7	30	37	92
78-79	Minn	80	5	27	32	147
79-80	Minn	55	5	13	18	103
80-81	Minn	74	5	21	26	126
81-82	Det	69	10	22	32	79
82-83	Det	73	4	26	30	79
83-84	Det	75	3	20	23	108
84-85	Det	73	2	18	20	117
85-86	Det-Wash	76	5	22	27	94
86-87	Wash	45	0	9	9	31
87-88	Wash	54	1	6	7	67
Totals		829	56	232	288	1110
Playoff Totals		63	4	7	11	106
SMITH, James Stephen (Steve) 6-4 215 D						
B. Glasgow, Scotland, Apr. 30, 1963						
84-85	Edm	2	0	0	0	2
85-86	Edm	55	4	20	24	166
86-87	Edm	62	7	15	22	165
87-88	Edm	79	12	43	55	286
88-89	Edm	35	3	19	22	97
89-90	Edm	75	7	34	41	171
90-91	Edm	77	13	41	54	193
91-92	Chi	76	9	21	30	304
Totals		461	55	193	248	1384
Playoff Totals		105	11	40	51	232
SMITH, Kenneth Alvin 5-7 150 LW						
B. Moose Jaw, Sask., May 8, 1924						
44-45	Bos	49	20	14	34	2
45-46	Bos	23	2	6	8	0
46-47	Bos	60	14	7	21	4
47-48	Bos	60	11	12	23	14
48-49	Bos	59	20	20	40	6
49-50	Bos	66	10	31	41	12
50-51	Bos	14	1	3	4	11
Totals		331	78	93	171	49
Playoff Totals		30	8	13	21	6
SMITH, Randy 6-4 200 C						
B. Saskatoon, Sask., July 7, 1965						
85-86	Minn	1	0	0	0	0
86-87	Minn	2	0	0	0	0
Totals		3	0	0	0	0
SMITH, Reginald Joseph (Hooley) D						
B. Toronto, Ont., Jan. 7, 1905						
24-25	Ott	30	10	3	13	81
25-26	Ott	28	16	9	25	53
26-27	Ott	43	9	6	15	125
27-28	Mont M	34	14	5	19	72
28-29	Mont M	41	10	9	19	120
29-30	Mont M	42	21	9	30	83
30-31	Mont M	39	12	14	26	48
31-32	Mont M	43	11	33	44	49
32-33	Mont M	48	20	21	41	66
33-34	Mont M	47	18	19	37	58
34-35	Mont M	46	5	22	27	41
35-36	Mont M	47	19	19	38	75
36-37	Bos	44	8	10	18	36
37-38	NYA	47	10	10	20	23
38-39	NYA	48	8	11	19	18
39-40	NYA	47	7	8	15	41
40-41	NYA	41	2	7	9	4
Totals		715	200	215	415	993
Playoff Totals		54	11	8	19	109
SMITH, Richard Allan (Rick) 5-11 200 D						
B. Kingston, Ont., June 29, 1948						
68-69	Bos	48	0	5	5	29
69-70	Bos	69	2	8	10	65
70-71	Bos	67	4	19	23	44
71-72	Bos-Cal	78	3	16	19	72
72-73	Cal	64	9	24	33	77
73-74	Minn (WHA)	71	10	28	38	98
74-75	Minn (WHA)	78	9	29	38	112
75-76	Minn (WHA)	51	1	32	33	50
75-76	StL	24	1	7	8	18
76-77	StL-Bos	64	6	17	23	36
77-78	Bos	79	7	29	36	69
78-79	Bos	65	7	18	25	46
79-80	Bos	78	8	18	26	62
80-81	Det-Wash	51	5	6	11	42
NHL Totals		687	52	167	219	560

Season	Team	GP	G	A	Pts.	PIM
SMITH, Richard Allan (Rick) *(Continued)*						
WHA Totals		200	20	89	109	260
NHL Playoff Totals		78	3	23	26	73
WHA Playoff Totals		23	2	8	10	28
SMITH, Robert David (Bobby) 6-4 210 C						
B. North Sydney, N.S., Feb. 12, 1958						
78-79	Minn	80	30	44	74	39
79-80	Minn	61	27	56	83	24
80-81	Minn	78	29	64	93	73
81-82	Minn	80	43	71	114	82
82-83	Minn	77	24	53	77	81
83-84	Minn-Mont	80	29	43	72	71
84-85	Mont	65	16	40	56	59
85-86	Mont	79	31	55	86	55
86-87	Mont	80	28	47	75	72
87-88	Mont	78	27	66	93	78
88-89	Mont	80	32	51	83	69
89-90	Mont	53	12	14	26	35
90-91	Mont	73	15	31	46	60
91-92	Minn	68	9	37	46	111
Totals		1032	352	672	1024	909
Playoff Totals		184	64	96	160	245
SMITH, Roger 6-0 175 D						
B. 1898						
25-26	Pitt Pi	36	9	1	10	22
26-27	Pitt Pi	36	4	0	4	16
27-28	Pitt Pi	43	1	0	1	30
28-29	Pitt Pi	44	4	2	6	49
29-30	Pitt Pi	42	2	1	3	55
30-31	Phil Q	9	0	0	0	0
Totals		210	20	4	24	172
Playoff Totals		4	3	0	3	0
SMITH, Ronald Robert 6-0 185 D						
B. Port Hope, Ont., Nov. 19, 1952						
72-73	NYI	11	1	1	2	14
SMITH, Sidney James 5-10 177 LW						
B. Toronto, Ont., July 11, 1925						
46-47	Tor	14	2	1	3	0
47-48	Tor	31	7	10	17	10
48-49	Tor	1	0	0	0	0
49-50	Tor	68	22	23	45	6
50-51	Tor	70	30	21	51	10
51-52	Tor	70	27	30	57	6
52-53	Tor	70	20	19	39	6
53-54	Tor	70	22	16	38	28
54-55	Tor	70	33	21	54	14
55-56	Tor	55	4	17	21	8
56-57	Tor	70	17	24	41	4
57-58	Tor	12	2	1	3	2
Totals		601	186	183	369	94
Playoff Totals		44	17	10	27	2
SMITH, Stanford George (Stan) 5-10 165 C						
B. Coal Creek, B.C., Aug. 13, 1917						
39-40	NYR	1	0	0	0	0
40-41	NYR	8	2	1	3	0
Totals		9	2	1	3	0
SMITH, Steve 5-9 215 D						
B. Trenton, Ont., Apr. 4, 1963						
81-82	Phil	8	0	1	1	0
84-85	Phil	2	0	0	0	7
85-86	Phil	2	0	0	0	0
86-87	Phil	2	0	0	0	6
87-88	Phil	1	0	0	0	0
88-89	Buf	3	0	0	0	2
Totals		18	0	1	1	15
SMITH, Stuart Ernest (Stu) RW						
40-41	Mont	16	2	3	5	2
41-42	Mont	1	0	1	1	0
Totals		17	2	4	6	2
SMITH, Stuart Gordon 6-1 205 D						
B. Toronto, Ont., Mar. 17, 1960						
79-80	Hart	4	0	0	0	0
80-81	Hart	38	1	7	8	55
81-82	Hart	17	0	3	3	15
82-83	Hart	18	1	0	1	25
Totals		77	2	10	12	95
SMITH, Thomas J. LW						
B. Ottawa, Ont., Sept. 27, 1885						
19-20	Que	10	0	0	0	9
SMITH, Vern 6-1 190 D						
B. Winnipeg, Man., May 30, 1964						
84-85	NYI	1	0	0	0	0

Season	Team	GP	G	A	Pts.	PIM
SMITH, Wayne Clifford 6-0 195 D						
B. Kamsack, Sask., Feb. 12, 1943						
66-67	Chi	2	1	1	2	2
Playoff Totals		1	0	0	0	0
SMRKE, John 5-11 205 LW						
B. Chicoutimi, Que., Feb. 25, 1956						
77-78	StL	18	2	4	6	11
78-79	StL	55	6	8	14	20
79-80	Que	30	3	5	8	2
Totals		103	11	17	28	33
SMRKE, Stanley 5-11 180 LW						
B. Belgrade, Yugoslavia, Sept. 2, 1928						
56-57	Mont	4	0	0	0	0
57-58	Mont	5	0	3	3	0
Totals		9	0	3	3	0
SMYL, Stanley Phillip 5-8 185 RW						
B. Glendon, Alta., Jan. 28, 1958						
78-79	Van	62	14	24	38	89
79-80	Van	77	31	47	78	204
80-81	Van	80	25	38	63	171
81-82	Van	80	34	44	78	144
82-83	Van	74	38	50	88	114
83-84	Van	80	24	43	67	136
84-85	Van	80	27	37	64	100
85-86	Van	73	27	35	62	144
86-87	Van	66	20	23	43	84
87-88	Van	57	12	25	37	110
88-89	Van	75	7	18	25	102
89-90	Van	47	1	15	16	71
90-91	Van	45	2	12	14	87
Totals		896	262	411	673	1556
Playoff Totals		41	16	17	33	64
SMYLIE, Roderick (Rod) LW						
20-21	Tor	23	2	0	2	2
21-22	Tor	21	0	0	0	2
22-23	Tor	2	0	0	0	0
23-24	Ott	14	1	1	2	6
24-25	Tor	11	0	0	0	0
25-26	Tor	5	0	0	0	0
Totals		76	3	1	4	10
Playoff Totals		9	1	2	3	2
SMYTH, Greg 6-3 212 D						
B. Oakville, Ont., Apr. 23, 1966						
86-87	Phil	1	0	0	0	0
87-88	Phil	48	1	6	7	192
88-89	Que	10	0	1	1	70
89-90	Que	13	0	0	0	57
90-91	Que	1	0	0	0	0
91-92	Que-Calg	36	1	3	4	143
Totals		109	2	10	12	462
SNELL, Harold Edward (Ted) 5-9 190 RW						
B. Ottawa, Ont., May 28, 1946						
73-74	Pitt	55	4	12	16	8
74-75	KC-Det	49	3	6	9	14
Totals		104	7	18	25	22
SNELL, Ronald Wayne 5-10 158 RW						
B. Regina, Sask., Aug. 11, 1948						
68-69	Pitt	4	3	1	4	6
69-70	Pitt	3	0	1	1	0
73-74	Winn(WHA)	70	24	25	49	32
74-75	Winn(WHA)	20	0	0	0	8
NHL Totals		7	3	2	5	6
WHA Totals		90	24	25	49	40
WHA Playoff Totals		4	0	0	0	0
SNEPSTS, Harold John 6-3 210 D						
B. Demonton, Alta., Oct. 24, 1954						
74-75	Van	27	1	2	3	30
75-76	Van	78	3	15	18	125
76-77	Van	79	4	18	22	149
77-78	Van	75	4	16	20	118
78-79	Van	76	7	24	31	130
79-80	Van	79	3	20	23	202
80-81	Van	76	3	16	19	212
81-82	Van	68	3	14	17	153
82-83	Van	46	2	8	10	80
83-84	Van	79	4	16	20	152
84-85	Minn	71	0	7	7	232
85-86	Det	35	0	6	6	75
86-87	Det	54	1	13	14	129
87-88	Det	31	1	4	5	67
88-89	Van	59	0	8	8	69
89-90	Van-StL	46	1	4	5	36
90-91	StL	54	1	4	5	50
Totals		1033	38	195	233	2009
Playoff Totals		93	1	14	15	231

Season	Team	GP	G	A	Pts.	PIM
SNOW, William Alexander (Sandy)						
5-11 175 RW						
B. Glace Bay, N.S., Nov. 11, 1946						
68-69	Det	3	0	0	0	2
SNUGGERUD, Dave	*6-0 190 RW*					
B. Minnetonka, Minn., June 20, 1966						
89-90	Buf	80	14	16	30	41
90-91	Buf	80	9	15	24	32
91-92	Buf-SJ	66	3	16	19	45
Totals		226	26	47	73	118
Playoff Totals		12	1	3	4	6
SOBCHUK, Dennis James	*6-2 180 C*					
B. Lang, Sask., Jan. 12, 1954						
74-75	Phoe (WHA)	38	32	45	77	36
75-76	Cin (WHA)	79	32	40	72	74
76-77	Cin (WHA)	81	44	52	96	38
77-78	Cin-Edm (WHA)	36	11	12	23	26
78-79	Edm (WHA)	74	26	37	63	31
79-80	Det	33	4	6	10	0
82-83	Que	2	1	0	1	2
NHL Totals		35	5	6	11	2
WHA Totals		308	145	186	331	205
WHA Playoff Totals		25	11	8	19	12
SOBCHUK, Eugene	*5-9 160 LW*					
B. Lang, Sask., Jan. 2, 1951						
73-74	Van	1	0	0	0	0
74-75	Phoe (WHA)	3	1	0	1	0
75-76	Cin (WHA)	78	24	19	43	37
NHL Totals		1	0	0	0	0
WHA Totals		81	25	19	44	37
SOLHEIM, Kenneth Lawrence						
6-3 210 LW						
B. Hythe, Alta., Mar. 27, 1961						
80-81	Chi-Minn	10	4	1	5	0
81-82	Minn	29	4	5	9	4
82-83	Minn-Det	35	2	4	6	6
84-85	Minn	55	8	10	18	19
85-86	Edm	6	1	0	1	5
Totals		135	19	20	39	34
Playoff Totals		3	1	1	2	2
SOLINGER, Robert Edward	*5-10 190 LW*					
B. Star City, Sask., Dec. 23, 1925						
51-52	Tor	24	5	3	8	4
52-53	Tor	19	1	1	2	2
53-54	Tor	39	3	2	5	2
54-55	Tor	17	1	5	6	11
59-60	Det	1	0	0	0	0
Totals		100	10	11	21	19
SOMERS, Arthur E.	*5-5 167 F*					
B. Winnipeg, Man., Jan. 17, 1904						
29-30	Chi	44	11	13	24	74
30-31	Chi	33	3	6	9	33
31-32	NYR	48	11	15	26	45
32-33	NYR	48	7	15	22	28
33-34	NYR	8	1	2	3	5
34-35	NYR	41	0	5	5	4
Totals		222	33	56	89	189
Playoff Totals		30	1	5	6	20
SOMMER, Roy	*6-0 180 C*					
B. Oakland, Calif., Apr. 5, 1957						
80-81	Edm	3	1	0	1	7
SONGIN, Thomas David	*6-3 195 RW*					
B. Norwood, Mass., Dec. 20, 1953						
78-79	Bos	17	3	1	4	0
79-80	Bos	17	1	3	4	16
80-81	Bos	9	1	1	2	6
Totals		43	5	5	10	22
SONMOR, Glen Robert	*5-11 165 LW*					
B. Moose Jaw, Sask., Apr. 22, 1929						
53-54	NYR	15	2	0	2	17
54-55	NYR	13	0	0	0	4
Totals		28	2	0	2	21
SORRELL, John Arthur	*6-0 152 LW*					
B. Chesterville, Ont., Jan. 16, 1906						
30-31	Det	39	9	7	16	10
31-32	Det	48	8	5	13	22
32-33	Det	47	14	10	24	11
33-34	Det	47	21	10	31	8
34-35	Det	47	20	16	36	12
35-36	Det	48	13	15	28	8
36-37	Det	48	8	16	24	4
37-38	Det-NYA	40	11	9	20	9

Season	Team	GP	G	A	Pts.	PIM
SORRELL, John Arthur *(Continued)*						
38-39	NYA	48	13	9	22	10
39-40	NYA	48	8	16	24	4
40-41	NYA	30	2	6	8	2
Totals		490	127	119	246	100
Playoff Totals		42	12	15	27	10
SPARROW, Emory (Spunk)	*F*					
24-25	Bos	6	0	0	0	4
SPECK, Frederick Edmondstone						
5-9 160 C						
B. Thorold, Ont., July 22, 1947						
68-69	Det	5	0	0	0	2
69-70	Det	5	0	0	0	0
71-72	Van	18	1	2	3	0
72-73	Minn-LA (WHA)	75	16	29	45	74
73-74	LA (WHA)	18	2	5	7	4
74-75	Balt (WHA)	30	4	8	12	18
NHL Totals		28	1	2	3	2
WHA Totals		123	22	42	64	96
WHA Playoff Totals		6	3	2	5	2
SPEER, Francis William (Bill)	*5-11 200 D*					
B. Lindsay, Ont., Mar. 20, 1942						
67-68	Pitt	68	3	13	16	44
68-69	Pitt	34	1	4	5	27
69-70	Bos	27	1	3	4	4
70-71	Bos	1	0	0	0	4
72-73	NY (WHA)	69	3	23	26	40
73-74	NY-NJ (WHA)	66	1	3	4	30
NHL Totals		130	5	20	25	79
WHA Totals		135	4	26	30	70
NHL Playoff Totals		8	1	0	1	4
SPEERS, Ted	*5-11 200 RW*					
B. Ann Arbor, Mich., Jan. 28, 1961						
85-86	Det	4	1	1	2	0
SPENCER, Brian Roy	*5-11 185 LW*					
B. Fort St. James, B.C., Sept. 3, 1949						
69-70	Tor	9	0	0	0	12
70-71	Tor	50	9	15	24	115
71-72	Tor	36	1	5	6	65
72-73	NYI	78	14	24	38	90
73-74	NYI-Buf	67	8	18	26	69
74-75	Buf	73	12	29	41	77
75-76	Buf	77	13	26	39	70
76-77	Buf	77	14	15	29	55
77-78	Pitt	79	9	11	20	81
78-79	Pitt	7	0	0	0	0
Totals		553	80	143	223	634
Playoff Totals		37	1	5	6	29
SPENCER, Irvin James	*5-10 180 D*					
B. Sudbury, Ont., Dec. 4, 1937						
59-60	NYR	32	1	2	3	20
60-61	NYR	56	1	8	9	30
61-62	NYR	43	2	10	12	31
62-63	Bos	69	5	17	22	34
63-64	Det	25	3	0	3	8
67-68	Det	5	0	1	1	4
72-73	Phil (WHA)	54	2	27	29	43
73-74	Van (WHA)	19	0	1	1	6
NHL Totals		230	12	38	50	127
WHA Totals		73	2	28	30	49
NHL Playoff Totals		16	0	0	0	8
SPEYER, Christopher	*D*					
B. Toronto, Ont., June 1906						
23-24	Tor	3	0	0	0	0
24-25	Tor	2	0	0	0	0
33-34	NYA	9	0	0	0	0
Totals		14	0	0	0	0
SPRING, Donald Neil	*5-11 195 D*					
B. Maracaibo, Venezuela, June 15, 1959						
80-81	Winn	80	1	18	19	18
82-83	Winn	78	0	16	16	21
82-83	Winn	80	0	16	16	37
83-84	Winn	21	0	4	4	4
Totals		259	1	54	55	80
Playoff Totals		6	0	0	0	10
SPRING, Franklin Patrick	*6-3 216 RW*					
B. Cranbrook, B.C., Oct. 19, 1949						
69-70	Bos	1	0	0	0	0
73-74	StL	2	0	0	0	0
74-75	StL-Cal	31	3	8	11	6
75-67	Cal	1	0	2	2	0
76-77	Clev	26	11	10	21	6
77-78	Ind (WHA)	13	2	4	6	2
NHL Totals		61	14	20	34	12
WHA Totals		13	2	4	6	2

Season	Team	GP	G	A	Pts.	PIM
SPRING, Jesse	*D*					
B. Toronto, Ont.						
23-24	Ham	20	3	2	5	8
24-25	Ham	29	2	0	2	11
25-26	Pitt Pi	32	5	0	5	23
26-27	Tor	2	0	0	0	0
28-29	NYA-Pitt Pi	32	0	0	0	2
29-30	Pitt Pi	22	1	0	1	18
Totals		137	11	2	13	62
Playoff Totals		2	0	2	2	2
SPRUCE, Andrew William	*5-11 177 LW*					
B. London, Ont., Apr. 17, 1954						
76-77	Van	51	9	6	15	37
77-78	Col	74	19	21	40	43
78-79	Col	47	3	15	18	31
Totals		172	31	42	73	111
Playoff Totals		2	0	2	2	2
SRSEN, Tomas	*5-11 180 LW*					
B. Olomouc, Czechoslovakia, Aug. 25, 1966						
90-91	Edm	2	0	0	0	0
STACKHOUSE, Ronald Lorne	*6-3 210 D*					
B. Haliburton, Ont., Aug. 26, 1949						
70-71	Cal	78	8	24	32	73
71-72	Cal-Det	79	6	28	34	89
72-73	Det	78	5	29	34	82
73-74	Det-Pitt	69	6	29	35	66
74-75	Pitt	72	15	45	60	52
75-76	Pitt	80	11	60	71	76
76-77	Pitt	80	7	34	41	72
77-78	Pitt	50	5	15	20	36
78-79	Pitt	75	10	33	43	54
79-80	Pitt	78	6	27	33	36
80-81	Pitt	74	6	29	35	86
81-82	Pitt	76	2	19	21	102
Totals		889	87	372	459	824
Playoff Totals		32	5	8	13	38
STACKHOUSE, Theodore (Ted)	*D*					
21-22	Tor	12	0	0	0	2
Playoff Totals		5	0	0	0	0
STAHAN, Frank Ralph (Butch)	*D*					
B. Minnedosa, Man., Oct. 29, 1915						
44-45	Mont	0	0	0	0	0
Playoff Totals		3	0	1	1	2
STALEY, Allan R. (Red)	*6-0 160 C*					
B. Regina, Sask., Sept. 21. 1928						
48-49	NYR	1	0	1	1	0
STAMLER, Lorne Alexander	*6-0 190 LW*					
B. Winnipeg, Man., Aug. 9, 1951						
76-77	LA	7	2	1	3	2
77-78	LA	2	0	0	0	0
78-79	Tor	45	4	3	7	2
79-80	Winn	62	8	7	15	12
Totals		116	14	11	25	16
STANDING, George Michael						
5-10 175 RW						
B. Toronto, Ont., Aug. 3, 1941						
67-68	Minn	2	0	0	0	0
STANFIELD, Frederic William	*5-10 185 C*					
B. Toronto, Ont., May 4, 1944						
64-65	Chi	58	7	10	17	14
65-66	Chi	39	2	2	4	2
66-67	Chi	10	1	0	1	0
67-68	Bos	73	20	44	64	10
68-69	Bos	71	25	29	54	22
69-70	Bos	73	23	35	58	14
70-71	Bos	75	24	52	76	12
71-72	Bos	78	23	56	79	12
72-73	Bos	78	20	58	78	10
73-74	Minn	71	16	28	44	10
74-75	Minn-Buf	72	20	39	59	16
75-76	Buf	80	18	30	48	4
76-77	Buf	79	9	14	23	6
77-78	Buf	57	3	8	11	2
Totals		914	211	405	616	134
Playoff Totals		106	21	35	56	10
STANFIELD, James Boviard	*5-10 165 C*					
B. Toronto, Ont., Jan. 1, 1947						
69-70	LA	1	0	0	0	0
70-71	LA	2	0	0	0	0
71-72	LA	4	0	1	1	0
Totals		7	0	1	1	0

STANFIELD, John Gordon (Jack)
5-11 176 LW
B. Toronto, Ont., May 30, 1942

Season	Team	GP	G	A	Pts.	PIM
72-73	Hou (WHA)	71	8	12	20	8
73-74	Hou (WHA)	41	1	3	4	2
WHA Totals		112	9	15	24	10
NHL Playoff Totals		1	0	0	0	0
WHA Playoff Totals		16	1	0	1	2

STANKIEWICZ, Edward 5-9 175 RW
B. Kitchener, Ont., Dec. 1, 1929

Season	Team	GP	G	A	Pts.	PIM
53-54	Det	1	0	0	0	2
55-56	Det	5	0	0	0	0
Totals		6	0	0	0	2

STANKIEWICZ, Myron (Mike)
5-11 185 LW

Season	Team	GP	G	A	Pts.	PIM
68-69	StL-Phil	35	0	7	7	36
Playoff Totals		1	0	0	0	0

STANLEY, Allan Herbert 6-2 191 D
B. Timmins, Ont., Mar. 1, 1926

Season	Team	GP	G	A	Pts.	PIM
48-49	NYR	40	2	8	10	22
49-50	NYR	55	4	4	8	58
50-51	NYR	70	7	14	21	75
51-52	NYR	50	5	14	19	52
52-53	NYR	70	5	12	17	52
53-54	NYR	10	0	2	2	11
54-55	NYR-Chi	64	10	16	26	24
55-56	Chi	59	4	14	18	70
56-57	Bos	60	6	25	31	45
57-58	Bos	69	6	25	31	37
58-59	Tor	70	1	22	23	47
59-60	Tor	64	10	23	33	22
60-61	Tor	68	9	25	34	42
61-62	Tor	60	9	26	35	24
62-63	Tor	61	4	15	19	22
63-64	Tor	70	6	21	27	60
64-65	Tor	64	2	15	17	30
65-66	Tor	59	4	14	18	35
66-67	Tor	53	1	12	13	20
67-68	Tor	64	1	13	14	16
68-69	Phil	64	4	13	17	28
Totals		1244	100	333	433	792
Playoff Totals		109	7	36	43	80

STANLEY, Daryl 6-2 200 D/LW
B. Winnipeg, Man., Dec. 2, 1962

Season	Team	GP	G	A	Pts.	PIM
83-84	Phil	23	1	4	5	71
85-86	Phil	33	0	2	2	69
86-87	Phil	33	1	2	3	76
87-88	Van	57	2	7	9	151
88-89	Van	20	3	1	4	14
89-90	Van	23	1	1	2	27
Totals		189	8	17	25	408
Playoff Totals		17	0	0	0	30

STANLEY, Russell (Barney) F
B. Paisley, Ont., June 1, 1893

Season	Team	GP	G	A	Pts.	PIM
27-28	Chi	1	0	0	0	0

STANOWSKI, Walter Peter (Wally)
5-11 180 D
B. Winnipeg, Man., Apr. 28, 1919

Season	Team	GP	G	A	Pts.	PIM
39-40	Tor	27	2	7	9	11
40-41	Tor	47	7	14	21	35
41-42	Tor	24	1	7	8	10
44-45	Tor	34	2	9	11	16
45-46	Tor	45	3	10	13	10
46-47	Tor	51	3	16	19	12
47-48	Tor	54	2	11	13	12
48-49	NYR	60	1	8	9	16
49-50	NYR	37	1	1	2	10
50-51	NYR	49	1	5	6	28
Totals		428	23	88	111	160
Playoff Totals		60	3	14	17	13

STANTON, Paul 6-0 193 D
B. Boston, Mass., June 22, 1967

Season	Team	GP	G	A	Pts.	PIM
90-91	Pitt	75	5	18	23	40
91-92	Pitt	54	2	8	10	62
Totals		129	7	26	33	102
Playoff Totals		43	2	9	11	66

STAPLETON, Brian 6-2 190 D
B. Fort Erie, Ont., Dec. 25, 1951

Season	Team	GP	G	A	Pts.	PIM
75-76	Wash	1	0	0	0	0

STAPLETON, Mike 5-10 183 C
B. Sarnia, Ont., May 5, 1966

Season	Team	GP	G	A	Pts.	PIM
86-87	Chi	39	3	6	9	6
87-88	Chi	53	2	9	11	59
88-89	Chi	7	0	1	1	7

STAPLETON, Mike (Continued)

Season	Team	GP	G	A	Pts.	PIM
90-91	Chi	7	0	1	1	2
91-92	Chi	19	4	4	8	8
Totals		125	9	21	30	82
Playoff Totals		4	0	0	0	2

STAPLETON, Patrick James (Pat)
5-8 185 D
B. Sarnia, Ont., July 4, 1940

Season	Team	GP	G	A	Pts.	PIM
61-62	Bos	69	2	5	7	42
62-63	Bos	21	0	3	3	8
65-66	Chi	55	4	30	34	52
66-67	Chi	70	3	31	34	54
67-68	Chi	67	4	34	38	34
68-69	Chi	75	6	50	56	44
69-70	Chi	49	4	38	42	28
70-71	Chi	76	7	44	51	30
71-72	Chi	78	3	38	41	47
72-73	Chi	75	10	21	31	14
73-74	Chi (WHA)	78	6	52	58	44
74-75	Chi (WHA)	68	4	30	34	38
75-76	Ind (WHA)	80	4	40	44	48
76-77	Ind (WHA)	81	8	45	53	29
77-78	Cin (WHA)	65	4	45	49	28
NHL Totals		635	43	294	337	353
WHA Totals		372	26	212	238	187
NHL Playoff Totals		65	10	39	49	38
WHA Playoff Totals		34	2	21	23	38

STARIKOV, Sergei 5-10 225 D
B. Chelyabinsk, Soviet Union, Dec. 4, 1958

Season	Team	GP	G	A	Pts.	PIM
89-90	NJ	16	0	1	1	8

STARR, Harold 5-11 176 D
B. Ottawa, Ont., July 6, 1906

Season	Team	GP	G	A	Pts.	PIM
29-30	Ott	27	2	1	3	12
30-31	Ott	36	2	1	3	48
31-32	Mont M	46	1	2	3	47
32-33	Ott-Mont	46	0	0	0	36
33-34	Mont M	1	0	0	0	0
34-35	NYR	32	1	1	2	31
35-36	NYR	15	0	0	0	12
Totals		203	6	5	11	186
Playoff Totals		17	1	0	1	2

STARR, Wilfred Peter (Wilf) 5-11 190 F
B. St. Boniface, Man., July 22, 1909

Season	Team	GP	G	A	Pts.	PIM
32-33	NYA	27	4	3	7	8
33-34	Det	28	2	2	4	17
34-35	Det	29	1	1	2	0
35-36	Det	5	1	0	1	0
Totals		89	8	6	14	25
Playoff Totals		7	0	2	2	2

STASIUK, Victor John 6-1 185 LW
B. Lethbridge, Alta., May 23, 1929

Season	Team	GP	G	A	Pts.	PIM
49-50	Chi	17	1	1	2	2
50-51	Chi-Det	70	8	13	21	18
51-52	Det	58	5	9	14	19
52-53	Det	3	0	0	0	0
53-54	Det	42	5	2	7	4
54-55	Det	59	8	11	19	67
55-56	Bos	59	19	18	37	118
56-57	Bos	64	24	16	40	50
57-58	Bos	70	21	35	56	55
58-59	Bos	70	27	33	60	63
59-60	Bos	69	29	39	68	121
60-61	Bos-Det	69	15	38	53	51
61-62	Det	59	15	28	43	45
62-63	Det	36	6	11	17	37
Totals		745	183	254	437	650
Playoff Totals		69	16	18	34	40

STASTNY, Anton 6-0 188 LW
B. Bratislava, Czechoslovakia, Aug. 5, 1959

Season	Team	GP	G	A	Pts.	PIM
80-81	Que	80	39	46	85	12
81-82	Que	68	26	46	72	16
82-83	Que	79	32	60	92	25
83-84	Que	69	25	37	62	14
84-85	Que	79	38	42	80	30
85-86	Que	74	31	43	74	19
86-87	Que	77	27	35	62	8
87-88	Que	69	27	45	72	14
88-89	Que	55	7	30	37	12
Totals		650	252	384	636	150
Playoff Totals		66	20	32	52	31

STASTNY, Marian 5-10 195 RW
B. Bratislava, Czechoslovakia, Jan. 8, 1953

Season	Team	GP	G	A	Pts.	PIM
81-82	Que	74	35	54	89	27
82-83	Que	60	36	43	79	32
83-84	Que	68	20	32	52	26

STASTNY, Marian (Continued)

Season	Team	GP	G	A	Pts.	PIM
84-85	Que	50	7	14	21	4
85-86	Tor	70	23	30	53	21
Totals		322	121	173	294	110
Playoff Totals		32	5	17	22	7

STASTNY, Peter 6-1 200 C
B. Bratislava, Czechoslovakia, Sept. 18, 1956

Season	Team	GP	G	A	Pts.	PIM
80-81	Que	77	39	70	109	37
81-82	Que	80	46	93	139	91
82-83	Que	75	47	77	124	78
83-84	Que	80	46	73	119	73
84-85	Que	75	32	68	100	95
85-86	Que	76	41	81	122	60
86-87	Que	64	24	53	77	43
87-88	Que	76	46	65	111	69
88-89	Que	72	35	50	85	117
89-90	Que-NJ	74	29	44	73	40
90-91	NJ	77	18	42	60	53
91-92	NJ	66	24	38	62	42
Totals		892	427	754	1181	798
Playoff Totals		84	33	70	103	119

STASZAK, Ray 6-0 200 RW
B. Philadelphia, Pa., Dec. 1, 1962

Season	Team	GP	G	A	Pts.	PIM
85-86	Det	4	0	1	1	7

STEELE, Frank D

Season	Team	GP	G	A	Pts.	PIM
30-31		1	0	0	0	0

STEEN, Anders F
B. Nykoping, Sweden, Apr. 28, 1955

Season	Team	GP	G	A	Pts.	PIM
80-81	Winn	42	5	11	16	22

STEEN, Thomas 5-10 195 C
B. Grums, Sweden, June 8, 1960

Season	Team	GP	G	A	Pts.	PIM
81-82	Winn	73	15	29	44	42
82-83	Winn	75	26	33	59	60
83-84	Winn	78	20	45	65	69
84-85	Winn	79	30	54	84	80
85-86	Winn	78	17	47	64	76
86-87	Winn	75	17	33	50	59
87-88	Winn	76	16	38	54	53
88-89	Winn	80	27	61	88	80
89-90	Winn	53	18	48	66	35
90-91	Winn	58	19	48	67	49
91-92	Winn	38	13	25	38	29
Totals		763	218	461	679	632
Playoff Totals		50	11	29	40	50

STEFANIW, Morris Alexander 5-11 170 C
B. North Battleford, Sask., Jan. 10, 1948

Season	Team	GP	G	A	Pts.	PIM
72-73	Atl	13	1	1	2	2

STEFANSKI, Edward Stanley Michael (Bud)
5-10 170 C
B. South Porcupine, Ont., Apr. 28, 1955

Season	Team	GP	G	A	Pts.	PIM
77-78	NYR	1	0	0	0	0

STEMKOWSKI, Peter David (Stemmer)
6-1 210 C
B. Winnipeg, Man., Aug. 25, 1943

Season	Team	GP	G	A	Pts.	PIM
63-64	Tor	1	0	0	0	2
64-65	Tor	36	5	15	20	33
65-66	Tor	56	4	12	16	55
66-67	Tor	68	13	22	35	75
67-68	Tor-Det	73	10	21	31	86
68-69	Det	71	21	31	52	81
69-70	Det	76	25	24	49	114
70-71	Det-NYR	78	18	31	49	69
71-72	NYR	59	11	17	28	53
72-73	NYR	78	22	37	59	71
73-74	NYR	78	25	45	70	74
74-75	NYR	77	24	35	59	63
75-76	NYR	75	13	28	41	49
76-77	NYR	61	2	13	15	8
77-78	LA	80	13	18	31	33
Totals		967	206	349	555	866
Playoff Totals		83	25	29	54	136

STENLUND, Kenneth Vern (Vern) 6-1 178 C
B. Thunder Bay, Ont., Nov. 4, 1956

Season	Team	GP	G	A	Pts.	PIM
76-77	Clev	4	0	0	0	0

STEPHENS, Philip D
B. 1895

Season	Team	GP	G	A	Pts.	PIM
17-18	Mont W	4	1	0	1	0
21-22	Mont	4	0	0	0	0
Totals		8	1	0	1	0

STEPHENSON, Robert 6-1 187 D
B. Saskatoon, Sask., Feb. 1, 1954

Season	Team	GP	G	A	Pts.	PIM
77-78	Birm (WHA)	39	7	6	13	33

STEPHENSON, Robert *(Continued)*

Season	Team	GP	G	A	Pts.	PIM
78-79	Birm (WHA)	78	23	24	47	72
79-80	Hart-Tor	18	2	3	5	4
NHL Totals		18	2	3	5	4
WHA Totals		117	30	30	60	105

STERN, Ronald *6-0 195 RW*
B. Ste. Agathe, Que., Jan. 11, 1967

Season	Team	GP	G	A	Pts.	PIM
87-88	Van	15	0	0	0	52
88-89	Van	17	1	0	1	49
89-90	Van	34	2	3	5	208
90-91	Van-Calg	44	3	6	9	240
91-92	Calg	72	13	9	22	338
Totals		182	19	18	37	887
Playoff Totals		10	1	4	5	31

STERNER, Ulf *6-2 187 LW*
B. Deje, Sweden, Feb. 11, 1941

Season	Team	GP	G	A	Pts.	PIM
64-65	NYR	4	0	0	0	0

STEVENS, John *6-1 195 D*
B. Campbeltoh, N.B., May 4, 1966

Season	Team	GP	G	A	Pts.	PIM
86-87	Phil	6	0	2	2	14
87-88	Phil	3	0	0	0	0
90-91	Hart	14	0	1	1	11
91-92	Hart	21	0	4	4	19
Totals		44	0	7	7	44

STEVENS, Kevin *6-3 217 LW*
B. Brockton, Mass., Apr. 15, 1965

Season	Team	GP	G	A	Pts.	PIM
87-88	Pitt	16	5	2	7	8
88-89	Pitt	24	12	3	15	19
89-90	Pitt	76	29	41	70	171
90-91	Pitt	80	40	46	86	133
91-92	Pitt	80	54	69	123	252
Totals		276	140	161	301	583
Playoff Totals		56	33	38	71	97

STEVENS, Mike *5-11 195 LW*
B. Kitchener, Ont., Dec. 30, 1965

Season	Team	GP	G	A	Pts.	PIM
84-85	Van	6	0	3	3	6
87-88	Bos	7	0	1	1	9
88-89	NYI	9	1	0	1	14
89-90	Tor	1	0	0	0	0
Totals		23	1	4	5	29

STEVENS, Paul *D*

Season	Team	GP	G	A	Pts.	PIM
25-26	Bos	17	0	0	0	0

STEVENS, Scott *6-2 215 D*
B. Kitchener, Ont., Apr. 1, 1964

Season	Team	GP	G	A	Pts.	PIM
82-83	Wash	77	9	16	25	195
83-84	Wash	78	13	32	45	201
84-85	Wash	80	21	44	65	221
85-86	Wash	73	15	38	53	165
86-87	Wash	77	10	51	61	283
87-88	Wash	80	12	60	72	184
88-89	Wash	80	7	61	68	225
89-90	Wash	56	11	29	40	154
90-91	StL	78	5	44	49	150
91-92	NJ	68	17	42	59	124
Totals		747	120	417	537	1902
Playoff Totals		87	11	48	59	245

STEVENSON, Shayne *6-1 190 RW*
B. Newmarket, Ont., Oct. 28, 1970

Season	Team	GP	G	A	Pts.	PIM
90-91	Bos	14	0	0	0	26
91-92	Bos	5	0	1	1	2
Totals		19	0	1	1	28

STEWART, Allan *6-0 195 LW*
B. Fort St. John, B.C., Jan. 31, 1964

Season	Team	GP	G	A	Pts.	PIM
85-86	NJ	4	0	0	0	21
86-87	NJ	7	1	0	1	26
87-88	NJ	1	0	0	0	0
88-89	NJ	6	0	2	2	15
90-91	NJ	41	5	2	7	159
91-92	NJ-Bos	5	0	0	0	22
Totals		64	6	4	10	243

STEWART, Blair James *5-11 185 LW*
B. Winnipeg, Man., Mar. 15, 1953

Season	Team	GP	G	A	Pts.	PIM
73-74	Det	17	0	4	4	16
74-75	Det-Wash	21	1	5	6	40
75-76	Wash	74	13	14	27	113
76-77	Wash	34	5	2	7	85
77-78	Wash	8	0	1	1	9
78-79	Wash	45	7	12	19	48
79-80	Que	30	8	6	14	15
Totals		229	34	44	78	326

STEWART, James (Gaye) *5-11 175 LW*
B. Fort William, Ont., June 28, 1923

Season	Team	GP	G	A	Pts.	PIM
42-43	Tor	48	24	23	47	20
45-46	Tor	50	37	15	52	8

STEWART, James (Gaye) *(Continued)*

Season	Team	GP	G	A	Pts.	PIM
46-47	Tor	60	19	14	33	15
47-48	Tor-Chi	61	27	29	56	83
48-49	Chi	54	20	18	38	57
49-50	Chi	70	24	19	43	43
50-51	Det	67	18	13	31	18
51-52	NYR	69	15	25	40	22
52-53	NYR-Mont	23	1	3	4	8
Totals		502	185	159	344	274
Playoff Totals		25	2	9	11	16

STEWART, John Alexander *6-0 180 LW*
B. Eriksdale, Man., May 16, 1950

Season	Team	GP	G	A	Pts.	PIM
70-71	Pitt	15	2	1	3	9
71-72	Pitt	25	2	8	10	23
72-73	Atl	68	17	17	34	30
73-74	Atl	74	18	15	33	41
74-75	Cal	76	19	19	38	55
75-76	Clev (WHA)	79	12	21	33	43
76-77	Minn-Birm (WHA)	16	3	3	6	2
77-78	Birm (WHA)	48	13	26	39	52
78-79	Birm (WHA)	70	24	26	50	108
79-80	Que	2	0	0	0	0
NHL Totals		260	58	60	118	158
WHA Totals		213	52	76	128	205
NHL Playoff Totals		4	0	0	0	10
WHA Playoff Totals		3	0	0	0	0

STEWART, John Sherratt (Black Jack) *5-11 185 D*
B. Pilot Mound, Man., May 6, 1917

Season	Team	GP	G	A	Pts.	PIM
38-39	Det	32	0	1	1	18
39-40	Det	48	1	0	1	40
40-41	Det	47	2	6	8	56
41-42	Det	44	4	7	11	93
42-43	Det	44	2	9	11	68
45-46	Det	47	4	11	15	73
46-47	Det	55	5	9	14	83
47-48	Det	60	5	14	19	83
48-49	Det	60	4	11	15	96
49-50	Det	65	3	11	14	86
50-51	Chi	26	0	2	2	49
51-52	Chi	37	1	3	4	12
Totals		565	31	84	115	757
Playoff Totals		80	5	14	19	143

STEWART, Kenneth *D*
B. Port Arthur, Ont., 1915

Season	Team	GP	G	A	Pts.	PIM
41 42	Chi	6	1	1	2	2

STEWART, Nelson Robert (Nels, Old Poison) *6-1 195 C*
B. Montreal, Que., Dec. 29, 1902

Season	Team	GP	G	A	Pts.	PIM
25-26	Mont M	36	34	8	42	119
26-27	Mont M	43	17	4	21	133
27-28	Mont M	41	27	7	34	104
28-29	Mont M	44	21	8	29	74
29-30	Mont M	44	39	16	55	81
30-31	Mont M	43	25	14	39	75
31-32	Mont M	38	22	11	33	61
32-33	Bos	47	18	18	36	62
33-34	Bos	48	21	17	38	68
34-35	Bos	47	21	18	39	45
35-36	NYA	48	14	15	29	16
36-37	Bos-NYA	43	23	12	35	37
37-38	NYA	48	19	17	36	29
38-39	NYA	46	16	19	35	43
39-40	NYA	35	7	7	14	6
Totals		651	324	191	515	953
Playoff Totals		54	15	13	28	61

STEWART, Paul G. *6-1 205 LW*
B. Boston, Mass., Mar. 21, 1954

Season	Team	GP	G	A	Pts.	PIM
76-77	Edm (WHA)	2	0	0	0	2
77-78	Cin (WHA)	40	1	5	6	241
78-79	Cin (WHA)	23	2	1	3	45
79-80	Que	21	2	0	2	74
NHL Totals		21	2	0	2	74
WHA Totals		65	3	6	9	288
WHA Playoff Totals		3	0	0	0	0

STEWART, Ralph Donald *6-2 190 C*
B. Fort William, Ont., Dec. 2, 1948

Season	Team	GP	G	A	Pts.	PIM
70-71	Van	3	0	1	1	0
72-73	NYI	31	4	10	14	4
73-74	NYI	67	23	20	43	6
74-75	NYI	70	16	24	40	12
75-76	NYI	31	6	7	13	2
76-77	Van	34	6	8	14	4
77-78	Van	16	2	3	5	0
Totals		252	57	73	130	28
Playoff Totals		19	4	4	8	2

STEWART, Robert Harold *6-1 205 D*
B. Charlottetown, P.E.I., Nov. 10, 1950

Season	Team	GP	G	A	Pts.	PIM
71-72	Bos-Cal	24	1	2	3	59
72-73	Cal	63	4	17	21	181
73-74	Cal	47	2	5	7	69
74-75	Cal	67	5	12	17	93
75-76	Cal	76	4	17	21	112
76-77	Clev	73	1	12	13	108
77-78	Clev	72	2	15	17	84
78-79	StL	78	5	13	18	47
79-80	StL-Pitt	75	3	8	11	56
Totals		575	27	101	128	809
Playoff Totals		5	1	1	2	2

STEWART, Ronald George *6-1 197 RW*
B. Calgary, Alta., July 11, 1932

Season	Team	GP	G	A	Pts.	PIM
52-53	Tor	70	13	22	35	29
53-54	Tor	70	14	11	25	72
54-55	Tor	53	14	5	19	20
55-56	Tor	69	13	14	27	35
56-57	Tor	65	15	20	35	28
57-58	Tor	70	15	24	39	51
58-59	Tor	70	21	13	34	23
59-60	Tor	67	14	20	34	28
60-61	Tor	51	13	12	25	8
61-62	Tor	60	8	9	17	14
62-63	Tor	63	16	16	32	26
63-64	Tor	65	14	5	19	46
64-65	Tor	65	16	11	27	33
65-66	Bos	70	20	16	36	17
66-67	Bos	56	14	10	24	31
67-68	StL-NYR	74	14	12	26	30
68-69	NYR	75	18	11	29	20
69-70	NYR	76	14	10	24	14
70-71	NYR	76	5	6	11	19
71-72	Van-NYR	55	3	3	6	12
72-73	NYR-NYI	33	2	3	5	4
Totals		1353	276	253	529	560
Playoff Totals		119	14	21	35	60

STEWART, Ryan *6-1 175 C*
B. Houston, B.C., June 1, 1967

Season	Team	GP	G	A	Pts.	PIM
85-86	Winn	3	1	0	1	0

STEWART, William Donald (Bill) *6-2 180 D*
B. Toronto, Ont., Oct. 6, 1957

Season	Team	GP	G	A	Pts.	PIM
77-78	Buf	13	2	0	2	15
78-79	Buf	68	1	17	18	101
80-81	StL	60	2	21	23	114
81-82	StL	22	0	5	5	25
82-83	StL	7	0	0	0	8
83-84	Tor	56	2	17	19	116
84-85	Tor	27	0	2	2	32
85-86	Minn	8	0	2	2	13
Totals		261	7	64	71	424
Playoff Totals		13	1	3	4	11

STIENBURG, Trevor *6-1 200 RW*
B. Kingston, Ont., May 13, 1966

Season	Team	GP	G	A	Pts.	PIM
85-86	Que	2	1	0	1	0
86-87	Que	6	1	0	1	12
87-88	Que	8	0	1	1	24
88-89	Que	55	6	3	9	125
Totals		71	8	4	12	161
Playoff Totals		1	0	0	0	0

STILES, Tony *5-11 200 D*
B. Carstairs, Alta., Aug. 12, 1959

Season	Team	GP	G	A	Pts.	PIM
83-84	Calg	30	2	7	9	20

STODDARD, John Edward (Jack) *6-3 180 RW*
B. Stoney Creek, Ont., Sept. 26, 1926

Season	Team	GP	G	A	Pts.	PIM
51-52	NYR	20	4	2	6	2
52-53	NYR	60	12	13	25	29
Totals		80	16	15	31	31

STOLTZ, Roland *6-1 191 RW*
B. Oeverkalix, Sweden, Aug. 15, 1954

Season	Team	GP	G	A	Pts.	PIM
81-82	Wash	14	2	2	4	14

STONE, Stephen George *5-8 170 RW*
B. Toronto, Ont., Sept. 26, 1952

Season	Team	GP	G	A	Pts.	PIM
73-74	Van	2	0	0	0	0

STOTHERS, Michael Patrick *6-4 212 D*
B. Toronto, Ont., Feb. 22, 1962

Season	Team	GP	G	A	Pts.	PIM
84-85	Phil	1	0	0	0	0
85-86	Phil	6	0	1	1	6
86-87	Phil	2	0	0	0	4
87-88	Phil-Tor	21	0	1	1	55
Totals		30	0	2	2	65
Playoff Totals		5	0	0	0	11

Season	Team	GP	G	A	Pts.	PIM
STOUGHTON, Blaine	5-11 185 RW					
B. Gilbert Plains, Man., Mar. 13, 1953						
73-74	Pitt	34	5	6	11	8
74-75	Tor	78	23	14	37	24
75-76	Tor	43	6	11	17	8
76-77	Cin (WHA)	81	52	52	104	39
77-78	Cin-Ind (WHA)	77	19	26	45	64
78-79	Ind-NE (WHA)	61	18	12	30	18
79-80	Hart	80	56	44	100	16
80-81	Hart	71	43	30	73	56
81-82	Hart	80	52	39	91	57
82-83	Hart	72	45	31	76	27
83-84	Hart-NYR	68	28	16	44	8
NHL Totals		526	258	191	449	204
WHA Totals		219	89	90	179	121
NHL Playoff Totals		8	4	2	6	2
WHA Playoff Totals		11	4	6	10	3
STOYANOVICH, Steve	6-2 205 C					
B. London, Ont., May 2, 1957						
83-84	Hart	23	3	5	8	11
STRAIN, Neil Gilbert	5-9 165 LW					
B. Kenora, Ont., Feb. 24, 1926						
52-53	NYR	52	11	13	24	12
STRATE, Gordon Lynn	6-1 190 D					
B. Edmonton, Alta., May 28, 1935						
56-57	Det	5	0	0	0	4
57-58	Det	45	0	0	0	24
58-59	Det	11	0	0	0	6
Totals		61	0	0	0	34
STRATTON, Arthur	6-1 175 C					
B. Winnipeg, Man., Oct. 8, 1935						
59-60	NYR	18	2	5	7	2
63-64	Det	5	0	3	3	2
65-66	Chi	2	0	0	0	0
67-68	Pitt-Phil	70	16	25	41	20
Totals		95	18	33	51	24
Playoff Totals		5	0	0	0	0
STROBEL, Arthur George	5-6 160 LW					
B. Regina, Sask., Nov. 28, 1922						
43-44	NYR	7	0	0	0	0
STRONG, Ken	5-11 185 LW					
B. Toronto, Ont., May 9, 1963						
82-83	Tor	2	0	0	0	0
83-84	Tor	2	0	2	2	2
84-85	Tor	11	2	0	2	4
Totals		15	2	2	4	6
STRUEBY, Todd Kenneth	6-1 185 LW					
B. Lannigan, Sask., June 15, 1963						
81-82	Edm	3	0	0	0	0
82-83	Edm	1	0	0	0	0
83-84	Edm	1	0	1	1	2
Totals		5	0	1	1	2
STUART, William (Red)	D					
B. Amherst, N.S., 1899						
20-21	Tor	18	2	1	3	4
21-22	Tor	24	3	6	9	16
22-23	Tor	23	7	3	10	16
23-24	Tor	24	4	3	7	16
24-25	Tor-Bos	29	5	2	7	32
25-26	Bos	33	6	1	7	41
26-27	Bos	42	3	1	4	20
Totals		193	30	17	47	145
Playoff Totals		17	1	0	1	12
STUMPEL, Jozef	6-1 187 RW					
B. Nitra, Czechoslovakia, June 20, 1972						
91-92	Bos	4	1	0	1	0
STUMPF, Robert	6-1 195 RW					
B. Milo, Alta., Apr. 25, 1953						
74-75	StL-Pitt	10	1	1	2	20
STURGEON, Peter Alexander	6-2 205 LW					
B. Whitehorse, Yukon, Feb. 12, 1954						
79-80	Col	2	0	0	0	0
80-81	Col	4	0	1	1	2
Totals		6	0	1	1	2
SUIKKANEN, Kai	6-2 205 D					
B. Opiskelija, Finland, Sept. 29, 1960						
81-82	Buf	1	0	0	0	0
82-83	Buf	1	0	0	0	0
Totals		2	0	0	0	0

Season	Team	GP	G	A	Pts.	PIM
SULLIMAN, Simon Douglas (Doug)	5-9 195 RW					
B. Glace Bay, N.S., Aug. 29, 1959						
79-80	NYR	31	4	7	11	2
80-81	NYR	32	4	1	5	32
81-82	Hart	77	29	40	69	39
82-83	Hart	77	22	19	41	14
83-84	Hart	67	6	13	19	20
84-85	NJ	57	22	16	38	4
85-86	NJ	73	21	22	43	20
86-87	NJ	78	27	26	53	14
87-88	NJ	59	16	14	30	22
88-89	Phil	52	6	6	12	8
89-90	Phil	28	3	4	7	0
Totals		631	160	168	328	175
Playoff Totals		16	1	3	4	2
SULLIVAN, Barry Carter	6-0 205 RW					
B. Preston, Ont., Sept. 21, 1926						
47-48	Det	1	0	0	0	0
SULLIVAN, Frank Taylor (Sully)	5-11 178 D					
B. Toronto, Ont., June 16, 1929						
49-50	Tor	1	0	0	0	0
52-53	Tor	5	0	0	0	2
54-55	Chi	1	0	0	0	0
55-56	Chi	1	0	0	0	0
Totals		8	0	0	0	2
SULLIVAN, George James (Red)	5-11 160 C					
B. Peterborough, Ont., Dec. 24, 1929						
49-50	Bos	3	0	1	1	0
51-52	Bos	67	12	12	24	24
52-53	Bos	32	3	8	11	8
54-55	Chi	70	19	42	61	51
55-56	Chi	63	14	26	40	58
56-57	NYR	42	6	17	23	36
57-58	NYR	70	11	35	46	61
58-59	NYR	70	21	42	63	56
59-60	NYR	70	12	25	37	81
60-61	NYR	70	9	31	40	66
Totals		557	107	239	346	441
Playoff Totals		18	1	2	3	7
SULLIVAN, Michael	6-2 185 C					
B. Marshfield, Mass., Feb. 27, 1968						
91-92	SJ	64	8	11	19	15
SULLIVAN, Peter Gerald (Silky)	5-9 170 C					
B. Toronto, Ont., July 25, 1951						
75-76	Winn (WHA)	78	32	39	71	22
76-77	Winn (WHA)	78	31	52	83	18
77-78	Winn (WHA)	77	16	39	55	43
78-79	Winn (WHA)	80	46	40	86	24
79-80	Winn	79	24	35	59	20
80-81	Winn	47	4	19	23	20
NHL Totals		126	28	54	82	40
WHA Totals		313	125	170	295	107
WHA Playoff Totals		52	21	32	53	8
SULLIVAN, Robert James	6-0 210 LW					
B. Noranda, Que., Nov. 29, 1957						
82-83	Hart	62	18	19	37	18
SUMMANEN, Raimo	5-11 191 LW					
B. Jyvaskyla, Finland, Mar. 2, 1962						
83-84	Edm	2	1	4	5	2
84-85	Edm	9	0	4	4	0
85-86	Edm	73	19	18	37	16
86-87	Edm-Van	58	14	11	25	15
87-88	Van	9	2	3	5	2
Totals		151	36	40	76	35
Playoff Totals		10	2	5	7	0
SUMMERHILL, William Arthur (Pee Wee)	5-9 170 RW					
B. Toronto, Ont., July 9, 1915						
38-39	Mont	43	6	10	16	28
39-40	Mont	13	3	2	5	24
41-42	Brk	16	5	5	10	18
Totals		72	14	17	31	70
Playoff Totals		3	0	0	0	2
SUNDIN, Mats	6-2 189 C/RW					
B. Sollentuna, Sweden, Feb. 13, 1971						
90-91	Que	80	23	36	59	58
91-92	Que	80	33	43	76	105
Totals		160	56	79	135	163

Season	Team	GP	G	A	Pts.	PIM
SUNDSTROM, Patrik	6-1 200 C					
B. Skelleftea, Sweden, Dec. 14, 1961						
82-83	Van	74	23	23	46	30
83-84	Van	78	38	53	91	37
84-85	Van	71	25	43	68	46
85-86	Van	79	18	48	66	28
86-87	Van	72	29	42	71	40
87-88	NJ	78	15	36	51	42
88-89	NJ	65	28	41	69	36
89-90	NJ	74	27	49	76	34
90-91	NJ	71	15	31	46	48
91-92	NJ	17	1	3	4	8
Totals		679	219	369	588	349
Playoff Totals		37	9	17	26	25
SUNDSTROM, Peter	6-0 180 LW					
B. Skelleftea, Sweden, Dec. 14, 1961						
83-84	NYR	77	22	22	44	24
84-85	NYR	76	18	25	43	34
85-86	NYR	53	8	15	23	12
87-88	Wash	76	8	17	25	34
88-89	Wash	35	4	2	6	12
89-90	NJ	21	1	2	3	4
Totals		338	61	83	144	120
Playoff Totals		23	3	3	6	8
SUOMI, Alfred	F					
36-37	Chi	5	0	0	0	0
SUTER, Gary	6-0 190 D					
B. Madison, Wisc., June 24, 1964						
85-86	Calg	80	18	50	68	141
86-87	Calg	68	9	40	49	70
87-88	Calg	75	21	70	91	124
88-89	Calg	63	13	49	62	78
89-90	Calg	76	16	60	76	97
90-91	Calg	79	12	58	70	102
91-92	Calg	70	12	43	55	126
Totals		511	101	370	471	738
Playoff Totals		43	4	30	34	54
SUTHERLAND, Ronald	5-8 180 D					
B. Eston, Sask., Feb. 8, 1913						
31-32	Bos	2	0	0	0	0
SUTHERLAND, William Fraser	5-10 176 C					
B. Regina, Sask., Nov. 10, 1934						
67-68	Phil	60	20	9	29	6
68-69	Tor-Phil	56	14	8	22	18
69-70	Phil	51	15	17	32	30
70-71	Phil-StL	69	19	20	39	41
71-72	StL-Det	14	2	4	6	4
72-73	Winn (WHA)	48	6	16	22	34
73-74	Winn (WHA)	12	4	5	9	6
NHL Totals		250	70	58	128	99
WHA Totals		60	10	21	31	40
NHL Playoff Totals		14	2	4	6	0
WHA Playoff Totals		18	5	9	14	13
SUTTER, Brent Colin	5-11 180 C					
B. Viking, Alta., June 10, 1962						
80-81	NYI	3	2	2	4	0
81-82	NYI	43	21	22	43	114
82-83	NYI	80	21	19	40	128
83-84	NYI	69	34	15	49	69
84-85	NYI	72	42	60	102	51
85-86	NYI	61	24	31	55	74
86-87	NYI	69	27	36	63	73
87-88	NYI	70	29	31	60	55
88-89	NYI	77	29	34	63	77
89-90	NYI	67	33	35	68	65
90-91	NYI	75	21	32	53	49
91-92	NYI-Chi	69	22	38	60	36
Totals		755	305	355	660	791
Playoff Totals		106	27	40	67	142
SUTTER, Brian Louis Allen	5-11 175 LW					
B. Viking, Alta., Oct. 7, 1956						
76-77	StL	35	4	10	14	82
77-78	StL	78	9	13	22	123
78-79	StL	77	41	39	80	165
79-80	StL	71	23	35	58	156
80-81	StL	78	35	34	69	232
81-82	StL	74	39	36	75	239
82-83	StL	79	46	30	76	254
83-84	StL	76	32	51	83	162
84-85	StL	77	37	37	74	121
85-86	StL	44	19	23	42	87
86-87	StL	14	3	3	6	18
87-88	StL	76	15	22	37	147
Totals		779	303	333	636	1786
Playoff Totals		65	21	21	42	249

SUTTER, Darryl John *5-11 180 LW*
B. Viking, Alta., Aug. 19, 1958

Season	Team	GP	G	A	Pts.	PIM
79-80	Chi	8	2	0	2	2
80-81	Chi	76	40	22	62	86
81-82	Chi	40	23	12	35	31
82-83	Chi	80	31	30	61	53
83-84	Chi	59	20	20	40	44
84-85	Chi	49	20	18	38	12
85-86	Chi	50	17	10	27	44
86-87	Chi	44	8	6	14	16
Totals		406	161	118	279	288
Playoff Totals		51	24	19	43	26

SUTTER, Duane Calvin *6-1 185 RW*
B. Viking, Alta., Mar. 16, 1960

Season	Team	GP	G	A	Pts.	PIM
79-80	NYI	56	15	9	24	55
80-81	NYI	23	7	11	18	26
81-82	NYI	77	18	35	53	100
82-83	NYI	75	13	19	32	118
83-84	NYI	78	17	23	40	94
84-85	NYI	78	17	24	41	174
85-86	NYI	80	20	33	53	157
86-87	NYI	80	14	17	31	169
87-88	Chi	37	7	9	16	70
88-89	Chi	75	7	9	16	214
89-90	Chi	72	4	14	18	156
Totals		731	139	203	342	1333
Playoff Totals		161	26	32	58	405

SUTTER, Richard *5-11 188 RW*
B. Viking, Alta., Dec. 2, 1963

Season	Team	GP	G	A	Pts.	PIM
82-83	Pitt	4	0	0	0	0
83-84	Pitt-Phil	75	16	12	28	93
84-85	Phil	56	6	10	16	89
85-86	Phil	78	14	25	39	199
86-87	Van	74	20	22	42	113
87-88	Van	80	15	15	30	165
88-89	Van	75	17	15	32	122
89-90	Van-StL	74	11	9	20	155
90-91	StL	77	16	11	27	122
91-92	StL	77	9	16	25	107
Totals		670	124	135	259	1165
Playoff Totals		57	13	4	17	119

SUTTER, Ronald *6-0 180 C*
B. Viking Alta., Dec. 2, 1963

Season	Team	GP	G	A	Pts.	PIM
82-83	Phil	10	1	1	2	9
83-84	Phil	79	19	32	51	101
84-85	Phil	73	16	29	45	94
85-86	Phil	75	18	42	60	159
86-87	Phil	39	10	17	27	69
87-88	Phil	69	8	25	33	146
88-89	Phil	55	26	22	48	80
88-90	Phil	75	22	26	48	104
90-91	Phil	80	17	28	45	92
91-92	StL	68	19	27	46	91
Totals		623	156	249	405	945
Playoff Totals		75	7	30	37	157

SUTTON, Kenneth *6-0 195 D*
B. Edmonton, Alta., May 11, 1969

Season	Team	GP	G	A	Pts.	PIM
90-91	Buf	15	3	6	9	13
91-92	Buf	64	2	18	20	71
Totals		79	5	24	29	84
Playoff Totals		13	0	3	3	6

SUZOR, Mark Joseph *6-1 212 D*
B. Windsor, Ont., Nov. 5, 1956

Season	Team	GP	G	A	Pts.	PIM
76-77	Phil	4	0	1	1	4
77-78	Col	60	4	15	19	56
Totals		64	4	16	20	60

SVENSSON, Leif *6-3 190 D*
B. Harnosand, Sweden, July 8, 1951

Season	Team	GP	G	A	Pts.	PIM
78-79	Wash	74	2	29	31	28
79-80	Wash	47	4	11	15	21
Totals		121	6	40	46	49

SVOBODA, Petr *6-1 174 D*
B. Most, Czechoslovakia, Feb. 14, 1966

Season	Team	GP	G	A	Pts.	PIM
84-85	Mont	73	4	27	31	65
85-86	Mont	73	1	18	19	33
86-87	Mont	70	5	17	22	63
87-88	Mont	69	7	22	29	149
88-89	Mont	71	8	37	45	147
89-90	Mont	60	5	31	36	98
90-91	Mont	60	4	22	26	52
91-92	Mont-Buf	71	6	22	28	146
Totals		537	40	196	236	813
Playoff Totals		79	3	32	35	86

SWAIN, Garth Frederick Arthur (Garry) *5-9 164 C*
B. Welland, Ont., Sept. 11, 1947

Season	Team	GP	G	A	Pts.	PIM
68-69	Pitt	9	1	1	2	0
74-75	NE (WHA)	66	7	15	22	18

SWAIN, Garth Frederick Arthur (Garry) *(Continued)*

Season	Team	GP	G	A	Pts.	PIM
75-76	NE (WHA)	79	10	16	26	46
76-77	NE (WHA)	26	5	2	7	6
NHL Totals		9	1	1	2	0
WHA Totals		171	22	33	55	70
WHA Playoff Totals		25	3	5	8	56

SWARBRICK, George Raymond *5-10 180 RW*
B. Moose Jaw, Sask., Feb. 16, 1942

Season	Team	GP	G	A	Pts.	PIM
67-68	Oak	49	13	5	18	62
68-69	Oak-Pitt	69	4	19	23	101
69-70	Pitt	12	0	1	1	8
70-71	Phil	2	0	0	0	0
Totals		132	17	25	42	171

SWEENEY, Don *5-11 170 D*
B. St. Stephen, N.B., Aug. 17, 1966

Season	Team	GP	G	A	Pts.	PIM
88-89	Bos	36	3	5	8	20
89-90	Bos	58	3	5	8	58
90-91	Bos	77	8	13	21	67
91-92	Bos	75	3	11	14	74
Totals		246	17	34	51	219
Playoff Totals		55	4	5	9	53

SWEENEY, Robert *6-3 200 C/RW*
B. Concord, Mass., Jan. 25, 1964

Season	Team	GP	G	A	Pts.	PIM
86-87	Bos	14	2	4	6	21
87-88	Bos	80	22	23	45	73
88-89	Bos	75	14	14	28	99
89-90	Bos	70	22	24	46	93
90-91	Bos	80	15	33	48	115
91-92	Bos	63	6	14	20	103
Totals		382	81	112	193	504
Playoff Totals		87	13	16	29	185

SWEENEY, Tim *5-11 180 LW*
B. Boston, Mass., Apr. 12, 1967

Season	Team	GP	G	A	Pts.	PIM
90-91	Calg	42	7	9	16	8
91-92	Calg	11	1	2	3	4
Totals		53	8	11	19	12

SWEENEY, William *5-10 165 C*
B. Guelph, Ont., Jan. 30, 1937

Season	Team	GP	G	A	Pts.	PIM
59-60	NYR	4	1	0	1	0

SYDOR, Darryl *6-0 200 D*
B. Edmonton, Alta., May 13, 1972

Season	Team	GP	G	A	Pts.	PIM
91-92	LA	18	1	5	6	22

SYKES, Phil *6-0 175 LW*
B. Dawson Creek, B.C., Mar. 18, 1959

Season	Team	GP	G	A	Pts.	PIM
82-83	LA	7	2	0	2	2
83-84	LA	3	0	0	0	2
84-85	LA	79	17	15	32	38
85-86	LA	76	20	24	44	97
86-87	LA	58	6	15	21	133
87-88	LA	40	9	12	21	82
88-89	LA	23	0	1	1	8
89-90	Winn	48	9	6	15	26
90-91	Winn	70	12	10	22	59
91-92	Winn	52	4	2	6	72
Totals		456	79	85	164	519
Playoff Totals		26	0	3	3	29

SYKES, Robert John William *6-0 200 LW*
B. Sudbury, Ont., Sept. 26, 1951

Season	Team	GP	G	A	Pts.	PIM
74-75	Tor	2	0	0	0	0

SZURA, Joseph Boleslaw *6-2 198 C*
B. Fort William, Ont., Dec. 18, 1938

Season	Team	GP	G	A	Pts.	PIM
67-68	Oak	20	1	3	4	10
68-69	Oak	70	9	12	21	20
72-73	LA (WHA)	72	13	32	45	25
73-74	Hou (WHA)	42	8	7	15	4
NHL Totals		90	10	15	25	30
WHA Totals		114	21	39	60	29
NHL Playoff Totals		7	2	3	5	2
WHA Playoff Totals		10	0	0	0	0

TAFT, John Philip *6-2 185 D*
B. Minneapolis, Minn., Mar. 8, 1954

Season	Team	GP	G	A	Pts.	PIM
78-79	Det	15	0	2	2	4

TAGLIANETTI, Peter *6-2 200 D*
B. Framingham, Mass., Aug. 15, 1963

Season	Team	GP	G	A	Pts.	PIM
84-85	Winn	1	0	0	0	0
85-86	Winn	18	0	0	0	48
86-87	Winn	3	0	0	0	12
87-88	Winn	70	6	17	23	182
88-89	Winn	66	1	14	15	226
89-90	Winn	49	3	6	9	136
90-91	Minn-Pitt	55	3	9	12	107
91-92	Pitt	44	1	3	4	57
Totals		306	14	49	63	768

TAGLIANETTI, Peter *(Continued)*

Season	Team	GP	G	A	Pts.	PIM
Playoff Totals		33	1	4	5	69

TALAFOUS, Dean Charles *6-4 190 RW*
B. Duluth, Minn., Aug. 25, 1953

Season	Team	GP	G	A	Pts.	PIM
74-75	Atl-Minn	61	9	21	30	19
75-76	Minn	79	18	30	48	18
76-77	Minn	80	22	27	49	10
77-78	Minn	75	13	16	29	25
78-79	NYR	68	13	16	29	29
79-80	NYR	55	10	20	30	26
80-81	NYR	50	13	17	30	28
81-82	NYR	29	6	7	13	8
Totals		497	104	154	258	163
Playoff Totals		21	4	7	11	11

TALAKOSKI, Ron *6-3 220 RW*
B. Thunder Bay, Ont., June 1, 1962

Season	Team	GP	G	A	Pts.	PIM
86-87	NYR	3	0	0	0	21
87-88	NYR	6	0	1	1	12
Totals		9	0	1	1	33

TALBOT, Jean-Guy *5-11 170 D*
B. Cap-de-la-Madeleine, Que., July 11, 1932

Season	Team	GP	G	A	Pts.	PIM
54-55	Mont	3	0	1	1	0
55-56	Mont	66	1	13	14	80
56-57	Mont	59	0	13	13	70
57-58	Mont	55	4	15	19	65
58-59	Mont	69	4	17	21	77
59-60	Mont	69	1	14	15	60
60-61	Mont	70	5	26	31	143
61-62	Mont	70	5	42	47	90
62-63	Mont	70	3	22	25	51
63-64	Mont	66	1	13	14	83
64-65	Mont	67	8	14	22	64
65-66	Mont	59	1	14	15	50
66-67	Mont	68	3	5	8	51
67-68	Minn-Det-StL	59	0	7	7	16
68-69	StL	69	5	4	9	24
69-70	StL	75	2	15	17	40
70-71	StL-Buf	62	0	7	7	42
Totals		1056	43	242	285	1006
Playoff Totals		150	4	26	30	142

TALLON, Michael Dale Lee (Dale) *6-1 205 D*
B. Noranda, Que., Oct. 19, 1950

Season	Team	GP	G	A	Pts.	PIM
70-71	Van	78	14	42	56	58
71-72	Van	69	17	27	44	78
72-73	Van	75	13	24	37	83
73-74	Chi	65	15	19	34	36
74-75	Chi	35	5	10	15	28
75-76	Chi	80	15	47	62	101
76-77	Chi	70	5	16	21	65
77-78	Chi	75	4	20	24	66
78-79	Pitt	63	5	24	29	35
79-80	Pitt	32	5	9	14	18
Totals		642	98	238	336	568
Playoff Totals		33	2	10	12	45

TAMBELLINI, Steven Anthony *6-0 184 C*
B. Trail, B.C. May 14, 1958

Season	Team	GP	G	A	Pts.	PIM
78-79	NYI	1	0	0	0	0
79-80	NYI	45	5	8	13	4
80-81	NYI-Col	74	25	29	54	19
81-82	Col	79	29	30	59	14
82-83	NJ	73	25	18	43	14
83-84	Calg	73	15	10	25	16
84-85	Calg	47	19	10	29	4
85-86	Van	48	15	15	30	12
86-87	Van	72	16	20	36	14
87-88	Van	41	11	10	21	8
Totals		553	160	150	310	105
Playoff Totals		2	0	1	1	0

TANCILL, Chris *5-10 185 C*
B. Livonia, Mich., Feb. 7, 1968

Season	Team	GP	G	A	Pts.	PIM
90-91	Hart	9	1	1	2	4
91-92	Hart-Det	11	0	0	0	2
Totals		20	1	1	2	6

TANGUAY, Christian (Chris) *5-10 190 RW*
B. Beauport, Que., Aug. 4, 1962

Season	Team	GP	G	A	Pts.	PIM
81-82	Que	2	0	0	0	0

TANNAHILL, Donald Andrew *5-11 175 LW*
B. Penetang, Ont., Feb. 21, 1949

Season	Team	GP	G	A	Pts.	PIM
72-73	Van	78	22	21	43	21
73-74	Van	33	8	12	20	4
74-75	Minn (WHA)	72	23	30	53	20
75-76	Calg (WHA)	78	25	24	49	10

TANNAHILL, Donald Andrew
(Continued)

Season Team	GP	G	A	Pts.	PIM
76-77 Calg (WHA)	72	10	22	32	4
NHL Totals	111	30	33	63	25
WHA Totals	222	58	76	134	34
WHA Playoff Totals	20	4	9	13	8

TANTI, Tony 5-9 184 RW
B. Toronto, Ont., Sept. 7, 1963

Season Team	GP	G	A	Pts.	PIM
81-82 Chi	2	0	0	0	0
82-83 Chi-Van	40	9	8	17	16
83-84 Van	79	45	41	86	50
84-85 Van	68	39	20	59	45
85-86 Van	77	39	33	72	85
86-87 Van	77	41	38	79	84
87-88 Van	73	40	37	77	90
88-89 Van-Pitt	77	24	25	49	69
89-90 Pitt-Buf	78	28	36	64	72
90-91 Pitt-Buf	56	7	19	26	50
91-92 Buf	70	15	16	31	100
Totals	697	287	273	560	661
Playoff Totals	30	3	12	15	27

TARDIF, Marc 6-0 195 LW
B. Granby, Que., June 12, 1949

Season Team	GP	G	A	Pts.	PIM
69-70 Mont	18	3	2	5	27
70-71 Mont	76	19	30	49	133
71-72 Mont	75	31	22	53	81
72-73 Mont	76	25	25	50	48
73-74 LA (WHA)	75	40	30	70	47
74-75 Mich-Que (WHA)	76	50	39	89	79
75-76 Que (WHA)	81	71	77	148	79
76-77 Que (WHA)	62	49	60	109	65
77-78 Que (WHA)	78	65	89	154	50
78-79 Que (WHA)	74	41	55	96	98
79-80 Que	58	33	35	68	30
80-81 Que	63	23	31	54	35
81-82 Que	75	39	31	70	55
82-83 Que	76	21	31	52	34
NHL Totals	517	194	207	401	443
WHA Totals	446	316	350	666	418
NHL Playoff Totals	62	13	15	28	75
WHA Playoff Totals	44	27	32	59	35

TATARINOV, Mikhail 5-10 195 D
B. Angarsk, Soviet Union, July 16, 1966

Season Team	GP	G	A	Pts.	PIM
90-91 Wash	65	8	15	23	82
91-92 Que	66	11	27	38	72
Totals	131	19	42	61	154

TAYLOR, David Andrew 6-0 190 RW
B. Levack, Ont., Dec. 4, 1955

Season Team	GP	G	A	Pts.	PIM
77-78 LA	64	22	21	43	47
78-79 LA	78	43	48	91	124
79-80 LA	61	37	53	90	72
80-81 LA	72	47	65	112	130
81-82 LA	78	39	67	106	130
82-83 LA	46	21	37	58	76
83-84 LA	63	20	49	69	91
84-85 LA	79	41	51	92	132
85-86 LA	76	33	38	71	110
86-87 LA	67	18	44	62	84
87-88 LA	68	26	41	67	129
88-89 LA	70	26	37	63	80
89-90 LA	58	15	26	41	96
90-91 LA	73	23	30	53	148
91-92 LA	77	10	19	29	63
Totals	1030	421	626	1047	1512
Playoff Totals	70	23	28	51	114

TAYLOR, Edward Wray (Ted) 6-0 175 LW
B. Brandon, Man., Feb. 25, 1942

Season Team	GP	G	A	Pts.	PIM
64-65 NYR	4	0	0	0	4
65-66 NYR	4	0	1	1	2
66-67 Det	2	0	0	0	0
67-68 Minn	31	3	5	8	34
70-71 Van	56	11	16	27	53
71-72 Van	69	9	13	22	88
72-73 Hou (WHA)	72	34	42	76	103
73-74 Hou (WHA)	75	21	23	44	143
74-75 Hou (WHA)	73	26	27	53	130
75-76 Hou (WHA)	68	15	26	41	80
76-77 Hou (WHA)	78	16	35	51	90
77-78 Hou (WHA)	54	11	11	22	46
NHL Totals	166	23	35	58	181
WHA Totals	420	123	164	287	592
WHA Playoff Totals	63	18	21	39	147

TAYLOR, Harry 5-8 165 C
B. St. James, Man., Mar. 28, 1926

Season Team	GP	G	A	Pts.	PIM
46-47 Tor	9	0	2	2	0
48-49 Tor	42	4	7	11	30
51-52 Chi	15	1	1	2	0
Totals	66	5	10	15	30

TAYLOR, Harry (Continued)

Season Team	GP	G	A	Pts.	PIM
Playoff Totals	1	0	0	0	0

TAYLOR, Mark 5-11 185 C
B. Vancouver, B.C., Jan. 26, 1958

Season Team	GP	G	A	Pts.	PIM
81-82 Phil	2	0	0	0	0
82-83 Phil	61	8	25	33	24
83-84 Phil-Pitt	60	24	31	55	24
84-85 Pitt-Wash	56	8	11	19	21
85-86 Wash	30	2	1	3	4
Totals	209	42	68	110	73
Playoff Totals	6	0	0	0	0

TAYLOR, Ralph F. (Bouncer) 5-9 180 D
B. Toronto, Ont., Oct. 2, 1905

Season Team	GP	G	A	Pts.	PIM
27-28 Chi	22	1	1	2	39
28-29 Chi	38	0	0	0	56
29-30 Chi-NYR	39	3	0	3	74
Totals	99	4	1	5	169
Playoff Totals	4	0	0	0	10

TAYLOR, Robert F
B. Newton, Mass., Aug. 12, 1904

Season Team	GP	G	A	Pts.	PIM
29-30 Bos	8	0	0	0	6

TAYLOR, William Gordon 6-1 184 C
B. Winnipeg, Man., Oct. 14, 1942

Season Team	GP	G	A	Pts.	PIM
64-65 NYR	2	0	0	0	0

TAYLOR, William James 5-9 150 C
B. Winnipeg, Man., May 3, 1919

Season Team	GP	G	A	Pts.	PIM
39-40 Tor	29	4	6	10	9
40-41 Tor	47	9	26	35	15
41-42 Tor	48	12	26	38	20
42-43 Tor	50	18	42	60	2
45-46 Tor	48	23	18	41	14
46-47 Det	60	17	46	63	35
47-48 Bos-NYR	41	4	16	20	25
Totals	323	87	180	267	120
Playoff Totals	33	6	18	24	13

TEAL, Allen Leslie (Skip) C
B. Ridgeway, Ont., July 17, 1933

Season Team	GP	G	A	Pts.	PIM
54-55 Bos	1	0	0	0	0

TEAL, Jeffrey Brad 6-3 205 RW
B. Edina, Minn., May 30, 1960

Season Team	GP	G	A	Pts.	PIM
84-85 Mont	6	0	1	1	0

TEAL, Victor (Skeeter) 6-1 160 RW
B. St. Catharines, Ont., Aug. 10, 1949

Season Team	GP	G	A	Pts.	PIM
73-74 NYI	1	0	0	0	0

TEBBUTT, Gregory 6-2 215 D
B. North Vancouver, B.C., May 11, 1957

Season Team	GP	G	A	Pts.	PIM
78-79 Birm (WHA)	38	2	5	7	83
79-80 Que (WHA)	2	0	1	1	4
83-84 Pitt	24	0	2	2	31
NHL Totals	26	0	3	3	35
WHA Totals	38	2	5	7	83

TERBENCHE, Paul Frederick 5-10 190 D
B. Cobourg, Ont., Sept. 16, 1945

Season Team	GP	G	A	Pts.	PIM
67-68 Chi	68	3	7	10	8
70-71 Buf	3	0	0	0	2
71-72 Buf	9	0	0	0	2
72-73 Buf	42	0	7	7	8
73-74 Buf	67	2	12	14	8
74-75 Van (WHA)	60	3	14	17	10
75-76 Calg (WHA)	58	2	4	6	22
76-77 Calg (WHA)	80	9	24	33	30
77-78 Birm (WHA)	11	1	0	1	0
78-79 Winn (WHA)	68	3	22	25	12
NHL Totals	189	5	26	31	28
WHA Totals	277	18	64	82	74
NHL Playoff Totals	12	0	0	0	0
WHA Playoff Totals	26	2	8	10	10

TERRION, Greg Patrick 5-11 190 LW
B. Marmora, Ont., May 2, 1960

Season Team	GP	G	A	Pts.	PIM
80-81 LA	73	12	25	37	99
81-82 LA	61	15	22	37	23
82-83 Tor	74	16	16	32	59
83-84 Tor	79	15	24	39	36
84-85 Tor	72	14	17	31	20
85-86 Tor	76	10	22	32	31
86-87 Tor	67	7	8	15	6
87-88 Tor	59	4	16	20	65
Totals	561	93	150	243	339
Playoff Totals	35	2	9	11	41

TERRY, Bill 5-8 170 C
B. Toronto, Ont., July 13, 1961

Season Team	GP	G	A	Pts.	PIM
87-88 Minn	5	0	0	0	0

TESSIER, Orval Roy 5-8 160 C
B. Cornwall, Ont., June 30, 1933

Season Team	GP	G	A	Pts.	PIM
54-55 Mont	4	0	0	0	0
55-56 Bos	23	2	3	5	6
60-61 Bos	32	3	4	7	0
Totals	59	5	7	12	6

THATCHELL, Spencer Harold (Spence) D
B. Lloydminster, Sask., July 16, 1924

Season Team	GP	G	A	Pts.	PIM
42-43 NYR	1	0	0	0	0

THEBERGE, Greg Ray 5-10 185 D
B. Peterborough, Ont., Sept. 3, 1959

Season Team	GP	G	A	Pts.	PIM
79-80 Wash	12	0	1	1	0
80-81 Wash	1	1	0	1	0
81-82 Wash	57	5	32	37	49
82-83 Wash	70	8	28	36	20
83-84 Wash	13	1	2	3	4
Totals	153	15	63	78	73
Playoff Totals	4	0	1	1	0

THELIN, Mats 5-10 185 D
B. Stockholm, Sweden, Mar. 30, 1961

Season Team	GP	G	A	Pts.	PIM
84-85 Bos	73	5	13	18	9
85-86 Bos	31	2	3	5	29
86-87 Bos	59	1	3	4	69
Totals	163	8	19	27	107
Playoff Totals	5	0	0	0	6

THELVEN, Michael 5-11 185 D
B. Stockholm, Sweden, Jan. 7, 1961

Season Team	GP	G	A	Pts.	PIM
85-86 Bos	60	6	20	26	48
86-87 Bos	34	5	15	20	18
87-88 Bos	67	6	25	31	57
88-89 Bos	40	3	18	21	71
89-90 Bos	6	0	2	2	23
Totals	207	20	80	100	217
Playoff Totals	34	4	10	14	34

THERRIEN, Gaston 5-10 185 D
B. Montreal, Que., May 27, 1960

Season Team	GP	G	A	Pts.	PIM
80-81 Que	3	0	1	1	2
81-82 Que	14	0	7	7	6
82-83 Que	5	0	0	0	4
Totals	22	0	8	8	12
Playoff Totals	9	0	1	1	4

THIBAUDEAU, Gilles 5-10 165 C
B. Montreal, Que., Mar. 4, 1963

Season Team	GP	G	A	Pts.	PIM
86-87 Mont	9	1	3	4	0
87-88 Mont	17	5	6	11	0
88-89 Mont	32	6	6	12	6
89-90 NYI-Tor	41	11	15	26	30
90-91 Tor	20	2	7	9	4
Totals	119	25	37	62	40
Playoff Totals	8	3	3	6	2

THIBEAULT, Laurence Lorrain 5-7 180 LW
B. Charleton, Ont., Oct. 2, 1918

Season Team	GP	G	A	Pts.	PIM
44-45 Det	4	0	2	2	0
45-46 Mont	1	0	0	0	0
Totals	5	0	2	2	0

THIFFAULT, Leo Edmond 5-10 175 LW
B. Drummondville, Que., Dec. 16, 1944

Season Team	GP	G	A	Pts.	PIM
67-68 Minn	0	0	0	0	0
Playoff Totals	5	0	0	0	0

THOMAS, Cyril James (Cy) 5-10 185 F
B. Dowlais, Wales, Aug. 5, 1926

Season Team	GP	G	A	Pts.	PIM
47-48 Chi-Tor	14	2	2	4	12

THOMAS, Reginald Kenneth 5-10 185 LW
B. Lambeth, Ont., Apr. 21, 1953

Season Team	GP	G	A	Pts.	PIM
73-74 LA (WHA)	77	14	21	35	22
74-75 Balt (WHA)	50	8	13	21	42
75-76 Ind (WHA)	80	23	17	40	23
76-77 Ind (WHA)	79	25	30	55	34
77-78 Ind-Cin (WHA)	67	19	18	37	56
78-79 Cin (WHA)	80	32	39	71	22
79-80 Que	39	9	7	16	6
NHL Totals	39	9	7	16	6
WHA Totals	433	121	138	259	199
WHA Playoff Totals	19	9	10	19	8

THOMAS, Steve 5-11 185 LW
B. Stockport, England, July 15, 1963

Season Team	GP	G	A	Pts.	PIM
84-85 Tor	18	1	1	2	2
85-86 Tor	65	20	37	57	36

THOMAS, Steve *(Continued)*

Season	Team	GP	G	A	Pts.	PIM
86-87	Tor	78	35	27	62	114
87-88	Chi	30	13	13	26	40
88-89	Chi	45	21	19	40	69
89-90	Chi	76	40	30	70	91
90-91	Chi	69	19	35	54	129
91-92	Chi-NYI	82	30	48	78	97
Totals		463	179	210	389	578
Playoff Totals		64	20	26	46	86

THOMLINSON, Dave *6-1 196 LW*
B. Edmonton, Alta., Oct. 22, 1966

Season	Team	GP	G	A	Pts.	PIM
89-90	StL	19	1	2	3	12
90-91	StL	3	0	0	0	0
91-92	Bos	12	0	1	1	17
Totals		34	1	3	4	29
Playoff Totals		9	3	1	4	4

THOMPSON, Brent *6-2 175 D*
B. Calgary, Alta., Jan. 9, 1971

Season	Team	GP	G	A	Pts.	PIM
91-92	LA	27	0	5	5	89
Playoff Totals		4	0	0	0	4

THOMPSON, Clifford B. *5-11 185 D*
B. Winchester, Mass., Dec. 9, 1918

Season	Team	GP	G	A	Pts.	PIM
41-42	Bos	3	0	0	0	2
48-49	Bos	10	0	1	1	0
Totals		13	0	1	1	2

THOMPSON, Kenneth *F*

Season	Team	GP	G	A	Pts.	PIM
17-18	Mont W	1	0	0	0	0

THOMPSON, Loran Errol (Errol) *5-8 180 LW*
B. Summerside, P.E.I., May 28, 1950

Season	Team	GP	G	A	Pts.	PIM
70-71	Tor	1	0	0	0	0
72-73	Tor	68	13	19	32	8
73-74	Tor	56	7	8	15	6
74-75	Tor	65	25	17	42	12
75-76	Tor	75	43	37	80	26
76-77	Tor	41	21	16	37	8
77-78	Tor-Det	73	22	23	45	12
78-79	Det	70	23	31	54	26
79-80	Det	77	34	14	48	22
80-81	Det-Pitt	73	20	20	40	64
Totals		599	208	185	393	184
Playoff Totals		34	7	5	12	11

THOMPSON, Paul Ivan *5-10 180 LW*
B. Calgary, Alta., Nov. 2, 1906

Season	Team	GP	G	A	Pts.	PIM
26-27	NYR	43	7	3	10	12
27-28	NYR	41	4	4	8	22
28-29	NYR	44	10	7	17	38
29-30	NYR	44	7	12	19	36
30-31	NYR	44	7	7	14	36
31-32	Chi	48	8	14	22	34
32-33	Chi	48	13	20	33	27
33-34	Chi	48	20	16	36	17
34-35	Chi	48	16	23	39	20
35-36	Chi	46	17	23	40	19
36-37	Chi	47	17	18	35	28
37-38	Chi	48	22	22	44	14
38-39	Chi	37	5	10	15	33
Totals		586	153	179	332	336
Playoff Totals		48	11	11	22	54

THOMS, William D. *5-9 170 C*
B. Newmarket, Ont., Mar. 5, 1910

Season	Team	GP	G	A	Pts.	PIM
32-33	Tor	29	3	9	12	15
33-34	Tor	47	8	18	26	24
34-35	Tor	47	9	13	22	19
35-36	Tor	48	23	15	38	29
36-37	Tor	48	10	9	19	14
37-38	Tor	48	14	24	38	14
38-39	Tor-Chi	48	7	15	22	20
39-40	Chi	46	9	13	22	4
40-41	Chi	48	13	19	32	8
41-42	Chi	48	15	30	45	8
42-43	Chi	47	15	28	43	11
43-44	Chi	7	3	5	8	2
44-45	Chi-Bos	38	6	8	14	8
Totals		549	135	206	341	176
Playoff Totals		44	6	10	16	6

THOMSON, Floyd Harvey *6-0 190 LW*
B. Sudbury, Ont., June 14, 1949

Season	Team	GP	G	A	Pts.	PIM
71-72	StL	49	4	6	10	48
72-73	StL	75	14	20	34	71
73-74	StL	77	11	22	33	58
74-75	StL	77	9	27	36	106
75-76	StL	58	8	10	18	25
76-77	StL	58	7	8	15	11
77-78	StL	6	1	1	2	4
79-80	StL	11	2	3	5	18
Totals		411	56	97	153	341
Playoff Totals		10	0	2	2	6

THOMSON, James Richard *6-0 190 D*
B. Winnipeg, Man., Feb. 23, 1927

Season	Team	GP	G	A	Pts.	PIM
45-46	Tor	5	0	1	1	4
46-47	Tor	60	2	14	16	97
47-48	Tor	59	0	29	29	82
48-49	Tor	60	4	16	20	56
49-50	Tor	70	0	13	13	56
50-51	Tor	69	3	33	36	76
51-52	Tor	70	0	25	25	86
52-53	Tor	69	0	22	22	73
53-54	Tor	61	2	24	26	86
54-55	Tor	70	4	12	16	68
55-56	Tor	62	0	7	7	96
56-57	Tor	62	0	12	12	50
57-58	Chi	70	4	7	11	75
Totals		787	19	215	234	905
Playoff Totals		63	2	13	15	135

THOMSON, Jim *6-1 205 RW*
B. Edmonton, Alta., Dec. 30, 1965

Season	Team	GP	G	A	Pts.	PIM
86-87	Wash	10	0	0	0	35
88-89	Wash-Hart	19	2	0	2	67
89-90	NJ	3	0	0	0	31
90-91	LA	8	1	0	1	19
91-92	LA	45	1	2	3	162
Totals		85	4	2	6	314

THOMSON, John F. *D*
B. Bixbridge, England, Jan. 31, 1918

Season	Team	GP	G	A	Pts.	PIM
39-40	NYA	12	1	1	2	0
40-41	NYA	3	0	0	0	0
Totals		15	1	1	2	0
Playoff Totals		2	0	0	0	0

THOMSON, Rhys G. *D*
B. Toronto, Ont., Aug. 9, 1918

Season	Team	GP	G	A	Pts.	PIM
39-40	Mont	7	0	0	0	16
42-43	Tor	18	0	2	2	22
Totals		25	0	2	2	38

THOMSON, William Ferguson *5-9 162 C*
B. Ayshire, Scotland, Mar. 23, 1914

Season	Team	GP	G	A	Pts.	PIM
38-39	Det	4	0	0	0	0
43-44	Chi-Det	6	2	2	4	0
Totals		10	2	2	4	0
Playoff Totals		2	0	0	0	0

THORNBURY, Tom *5-11 175 D*
B. Lindsay, Ont., Mar. 17, 1963

Season	Team	GP	G	A	Pts.	PIM
83-84	Pitt	14	1	8	9	16

THORNTON, Scott *6-2 200 C*
B. London, Ont., Jan. 9, 1971

Season	Team	GP	G	A	Pts.	PIM
90-91	Tor	33	1	3	4	30
91-92	Edm	15	0	1	1	43
Totals		48	1	4	5	73
Playoff Totals		1	0	0	0	0

THORSTEINSON, Joseph *F*
B. Winnipeg, Man.

Season	Team	GP	G	A	Pts.	PIM
32-33	NYA	4	0	0	0	0

THURIER, Alfred Michael (Fred) *5-10 160 C*
B. Granby, Que., Jan. 11, 1918

Season	Team	GP	G	A	Pts.	PIM
40-41	NYA	3	2	1	3	0
41-42	Brk	27	7	7	14	4
44-45	NYR	50	16	19	35	14
Totals		80	25	27	52	18

THURLBY, Thomas Newman *5-10 180 D*
B. Kingston, Ont., Nov. 9, 1938

Season	Team	GP	G	A	Pts.	PIM
67-68	Oak	20	1	2	3	4

THYER, Mario *5-11 170 C*
B. Montreal, Que., Sept. 29, 1966

Season	Team	GP	G	A	Pts.	PIM
89-90	Minn	5	0	0	0	0
Playoff Totals		1	0	0	0	2

TIDEY, Alexander *6-0 188 RW*
B. Vancouver, B.C., Jan. 5, 1955

Season	Team	GP	G	A	Pts.	PIM
75-76	SD (WHA)	74	16	11	27	46
76-77	Buf	3	0	0	0	0
77-78	Buf	1	0	0	0	0
79-80	Edm	5	0	0	0	8
NHL Totals		9	0	0	0	8
WHA Totals		74	16	11	27	46
NHL Playoff Totals		2	0	0	0	0
WHA Playoff Totals		11	3	6	9	10

TIKKANEN, Esa *6-1 200 LW*
B. Helsinki, Finland, Jan. 25, 1965

Season	Team	GP	G	A	Pts.	PIM
85-86	Edm	35	7	6	13	28
86-87	Edm	76	34	44	78	120
87-88	Edm	80	23	51	74	153
88-89	Edm	67	31	47	78	92

TIKKANEN, Esa *(Continued)*

Season	Team	GP	G	A	Pts.	PIM
89-90	Edm	79	30	33	63	161
90-91	Edm	79	27	42	69	85
91-92	Edm	40	12	16	28	44
Totals		456	164	239	403	683
Playoff Totals		114	51	46	97	173

TILLEY, Tom *6-0 189 D*
B. Trenton, Ont., Mar. 28, 1965

Season	Team	GP	G	A	Pts.	PIM
88-89	StL	70	1	22	23	47
89-90	StL	34	0	5	5	6
90-91	StL	22	2	4	6	4
Totals		126	3	31	34	57
Playoff Totals		10	1	2	3	17

TIMGREN, Raymond Charles *5-9 161 LW*
B. Windsor, Ont., Sept. 29, 1928

Season	Team	GP	G	A	Pts.	PIM
48-49	Tor	36	3	12	15	9
49-50	Tor	68	7	18	25	9
50-51	Tor	70	1	9	10	20
51-52	Tor	50	2	4	6	11
52-53	Tor	12	0	0	0	4
54-55	Chi-Tor	15	1	1	2	4
Totals		251	14	44	58	57
Playoff Totals		30	3	9	12	6

TINORDI, Mark *6-4 205 D*
B. Red Deer, Alta., May 9, 1966

Season	Team	GP	G	A	Pts.	PIM
87-88	NYR	24	1	2	3	50
88-89	Minn	47	2	3	5	107
89-90	Minn	66	3	7	10	240
90-91	Minn	69	5	27	32	189
91-92	Minn	63	4	24	28	177
Totals		269	15	63	78	763
Playoff Totals		46	6	9	15	105

TIPPETT, Dave *5-10 180 LW*
B. Moosomin, Sask., Aug. 25, 1961

Season	Team	GP	G	A	Pts.	PIM
83-84	Hart	17	4	2	6	2
84-85	Hart	80	7	12	19	12
85-86	Hart	80	14	20	34	18
86-87	Hart	80	9	22	31	42
87-88	Hart	80	16	21	37	32
88-89	Hart	80	17	24	41	45
89-90	Hart	66	8	19	27	32
90-91	Wash	61	6	9	15	24
91-92	Wash	30	2	10	12	16
Totals		574	83	139	222	223
Playoff Totals		50	5	12	17	20

TITANIC, Morris S. *6-1 180 LW*
B. Toronto, Ont., Jan. 7, 1953

Season	Team	GP	G	A	Pts.	PIM
74-75	Buf	17	0	0	0	0
75-76	Buf	2	0	0	0	0
Totals		19	0	0	0	0

TKACHUK, Keith *6-2 200 LW*
B. Melrose, Mass., Mar. 28, 1972

Season	Team	GP	G	A	Pts.	PIM
91-92	Winn	17	3	5	8	28
Playoff Totals		7	3	0	3	30

TKACZUK, Walter Robert *6-0 190 C*
B. Emstedetten, West Germany, Sept. 29, 1947

Season	Team	GP	G	A	Pts.	PIM
67-68	NYR	2	0	0	0	0
68-69	NYR	71	12	24	36	28
69-70	NYR	76	27	50	77	38
70-71	NYR	77	26	49	75	48
71-72	NYR	76	24	42	66	65
72-73	NYR	76	27	39	66	59
73-74	NYR	71	21	42	63	58
74-75	NYR	62	11	25	36	34
75-76	NYR	78	8	28	36	56
76-77	NYR	80	12	38	50	38
77-78	NYR	80	26	40	66	30
78-79	NYR	77	15	27	42	38
79-80	NYR	76	12	25	37	36
80-81	NYR	43	6	22	28	28
Totals		945	227	451	678	556
Playoff Totals		93	19	32	51	119

TOAL, Michael James (Toaler) *6-0 175 C*
B. Red Deer, Alta., Mar. 23, 1959

Season	Team	GP	G	A	Pts.	PIM
79-80	Edm	3	0	0	0	0

TOCCHET, Rick *6-0 205 RW*
B. Scarborough, Ont., Apr. 9, 1964

Season	Team	GP	G	A	Pts.	PIM
84-85	Phil	75	14	25	39	181
85-86	Phil	69	14	21	35	284
86-87	Phil	69	21	26	47	288
87-88	Phil	65	31	33	64	301
88-89	Phil	66	45	36	81	183
89-90	Phil	75	37	59	96	196

Season Team	GP	G	A	Pts.	PIM
TOCCHET, Rick *(Continued)*					
90-91 Phil	70	40	31	71	150
91-92 Phil-Pitt	61	27	32	59	151
Totals	550	229	263	492	1734
Playoff Totals	85	28	39	67	318
TODD, Kevin *5-10 175 C*					
B. Winnipeg, Man., May 4, 1968					
88-89 NJ	1	0	0	0	0
90-91 NJ	1	0	0	0	0
91-92 NJ	80	21	42	63	69
Totals	82	21	42	63	69
Playoff Totals	8	3	2	5	14
TOMALTY, Glenn *D*					
79-80 Winn	1	0	0	0	0
TOMLAK, Mike *6-3 205 C/LW*					
B. Thunder Bay, Ont., Oct. 17, 1964					
89-90 Hart	70	7	14	21	48
90-91 Hart	64	8	8	16	55
91-92 Hart	6	0	0	0	0
Totals	140	15	22	37	103
Playoff Totals	10	0	1	1	4
TOMLINSON, Dave *5-11 177 C*					
B. North Vancouver, B.C., May 8, 1969					
91-92 Tor	3	0	0	0	2
TOMLINSON, Kirk *5-10 175 C*					
B. Toronto, Ont., May 2, 1968					
87-88 Minn	1	0	0	0	0
TONELLI, John *6-1 200 LW*					
B. Milton, Ont., Mar. 23, 1957					
75-76 Hou (WHA)	79	17	14	31	66
76-77 Hou (WHA)	80	24	31	55	109
77-78 Hou (WHA)	65	23	41	64	103
78-79 NYI	73	17	39	56	44
79-80 NYI	77	14	30	44	49
80-81 NYI	70	20	32	52	57
81-82 NYI	80	35	58	93	57
82-83 NYI	76	31	40	71	55
83-84 NYI	73	27	40	67	66
84-85 NYI	80	42	58	100	95
85-86 NYI-Colg	74	23	45	68	60
86-87 Colg	78	20	31	51	72
87-88 Colg	74	17	41	58	84
88-89 LA	77	31	33	64	110
89-90 LA	73	31	37	68	62
90-91 LA	71	14	16	30	49
91-92 Chi-Que	52	3	11	14	51
NHL Totals	1028	325	511	836	911
WHA Totals	224	64	86	150	278
NHL Playoff Totals	172	40	75	115	200
WHA Playoff Totals	34	11	14	25	38
TOOKEY, Timothy Raymond *5-11 185 C*					
B. Edmonton, Alta., Aug. 29, 1960					
80-81 Wash	29	10	13	23	18
81-82 Wash	28	8	8	16	35
82-83 Que	12	1	6	7	4
83-84 Pitt	8	0	2	2	2
86-87 Phil	2	0	0	0	0
87-88 LA	20	1	6	7	8
88-89 LA	7	2	1	3	4
Totals	106	22	36	58	71
Playoff Totals	10	1	3	4	2
TOOMEY, Sean *6-1 200 LW*					
B. St. Paul, Minn., June 27, 1965					
86-87 Minn	1	0	0	0	0
TOPPAZZINI, Gerald (Jerry, Topper)					
5-11 180 RW					
B. Copper Cliff, Ont., July 29, 1931					
52-53 Bos	69	10	13	23	36
53-54 Bos-Chi	51	5	8	13	42
54-55 Chi	70	9	18	27	20
55-56 Det-Bos	68	8	14	22	53
56-57 Bos	55	15	23	38	26
57-58 Bos	64	25	24	49	51
58-59 Bos	70	21	23	44	61
59-60 Bos	69	12	33	45	26
60-61 Bos	67	15	35	50	35
61-62 Bos	70	19	31	50	26
62-63 Bos	65	17	18	35	6
63-64 Bos	65	7	4	11	15
Totals	783	163	244	407	397
Playoff Totals	40	13	9	22	13
TOPPAZZINI, Zellio Louis Peter (Topper)					
5-11 180 RW					
B. Copper Cliff, Ont., Jan. 5, 1930					
48-49 Bos	5	1	1	2	0
49-50 Bos	36	5	5	10	18
50-51 Bos-NYR	59	14	14	28	27

Season Team	GP	G	A	Pts.	PIM
TOPPAZZINI, Zellio Louis Peter (Topper)					
(Continued)					
51-52 NYR	16	1	1	2	4
56-57 Chi	7	0	0	0	0
Totals	123	21	21	42	49
Playoff Totals	2	0	0	0	0
TORKKI, Jari *5-11 185 LW*					
B. Rauma, Finland, Aug. 11, 1965					
88-89 Chi	4	1	0	1	0
TOUHEY, William J. *5-9 155 LW*					
B. Ottawa, Ont., Mar. 23, 1906					
27-28 Mont M	29	2	0	2	2
28-29 Ott	44	9	3	12	28
29-30 Ott	44	10	3	13	24
30-31 Ott	44	15	15	30	8
31-32 Bos	26	5	4	9	12
32-33 Ott	47	12	7	19	12
33-34 Ott	46	12	8	20	21
Totals	280	65	40	105	107
Playoff Totals	2	1	0	1	0
TOUPIN, J. Jacques *F*					
B. Trois Rivieres, Que.					
43-44 Chi	8	1	2	3	0
Playoff Totals	4	0	0	0	0
TOWNSEND, Arthur Gordon *F*					
26-27 Chi	5	0	0	0	0
TOWNSHEND, Graeme *6-2 225 RW*					
B. Kingston, Jamaica, Oct. 2, 1965					
89-90 Bos	4	0	0	0	7
90-91 Bos	18	2	5	7	12
91-92 NYI	7	1	2	3	0
Totals	29	3	7	10	19
TRADER, Larry *6-1 180 D*					
B. Barry's Bay, Ont., July 7, 1963					
82-83 Det	15	0	2	2	6
84-85 Det	40	3	7	10	39
86-87 StL	5	0	0	0	8
87-88 StL-Mont	31	2	4	6	21
Totals	91	5	13	18	74
Playoff Totals	3	0	0	0	0
TRAINOR, Thomas Weston (Wes)					
5-8 180 LW					
B. Charlottetown, P.E.I., Sept. 11, 1922					
48-49 NYR	17	1	2	3	6
TRAPP, Albert Robert (Bobby) *D*					
B. 1898					
26-27 Chi	44	4	2	6	92
27-28 Chi	38	0	2	2	37
Totals	82	4	4	8	129
Playoff Totals	2	0	0	0	4
TRAPP, Doug *6-0 180 LW*					
B. Balcarres, Sask., Nov. 28, 1965					
86-87 Buf	2	0	0	0	0
TRAUB, Percy (Puss) *D*					
26-27 Chi	42	0	2	2	93
27-28 Det	44	3	1	4	75
28-29 Det	44	0	0	0	46
Totals	130	3	3	6	214
Playoff Totals	4	0	0	0	6
TREDWAY, Brock *6-0 180 RW*					
B. Highland Creek, Ont., June 23, 1959					
81-82 LA	0	0	0	0	0
Playoff Totals	5	0	0	0	0
TREMBLAY, Brent Francis *6-2 192 D*					
B. North Bay, Ont., Nov. 1, 1957					
78-79 Wash	1	0	0	0	0
79-80 Wash	9	1	0	1	6
Totals	10	1	0	1	6
TREMBLAY, Jean Claude (J.C.)					
5-11 190 D					
B. Bagotville, Que., Jan. 22, 1939					
59-60 Mont	11	0	1	1	0
60-61 Mont	29	1	3	4	18
61-62 Mont	70	3	17	20	18
62-63 Mont	69	1	17	18	10
63-64 Mont	70	5	16	21	24
64-65 Mont	68	3	17	20	22
65-66 Mont	59	6	29	35	8
66-67 Mont	60	8	26	34	14
67-68 Mont	73	4	26	30	18
68-69 Mont	75	7	32	39	18
69-70 Mont	58	2	19	21	7
70-71 Mont	76	11	52	63	23

Season Team	GP	G	A	Pts.	PIM
TREMBLAY, Jean Claude (J.C.)					
(Continued)					
71-72 Mont	76	6	51	57	24
72-73 Que (WHA)	76	14	75	89	32
73-74 Que (WHA)	68	9	44	53	10
74-75 Que (WHA)	68	16	56	72	18
75-76 Que (WHA)	80	12	77	89	16
76-77 Que (WHA)	53	4	31	35	16
77-78 Que (WHA)	54	5	37	42	26
78-79 Que (WHA)	56	6	38	44	8
NHL Totals	794	57	306	363	204
WHA Totals	455	66	358	424	126
NHL Playoff Totals	108	14	51	65	58
WHA Playoff Totals	34	2	23	25	4
TREMBLAY, Joseph Jean-Gilles (Gilles)					
5-10 175 LW					
B. Montmorency, Que., Dec. 17, 1938					
60-61 Mont	45	7	11	18	4
61-62 Mont	70	32	22	54	28
62-63 Mont	60	25	24	49	42
63-64 Mont	61	22	15	37	21
64-65 Mont	26	9	7	16	16
65-66 Mont	70	27	21	48	24
66-67 Mont	62	13	19	32	16
67-68 Mont	71	23	28	51	8
68-69 Mont	44	10	15	25	2
Totals	509	168	162	330	161
Playoff Totals	48	9	14	23	4
TREMBLAY, Marcel *F*					
B. Winnipeg, Man., July 4, 1915					
38-39 Mont	10	0	2	2	0
TREMBLAY, Mario *6-0 190 RW*					
B. Alma, Que., Sept. 2, 1956					
74-75 Mont	63	21	18	39	108
75-76 Mont	71	11	16	27	88
76-77 Mont	74	18	28	46	61
77-78 Mont	56	10	14	24	44
78-79 Mont	76	30	29	59	74
79-80 Mont	77	16	26	42	105
80-81 Mont	77	25	38	63	123
81-82 Mont	80	33	40	73	66
82-83 Mont	80	30	37	67	87
83-84 Mont	67	14	25	39	112
84-85 Mont	75	31	35	66	120
85-86 Mont	56	19	20	39	55
Totals	852	258	326	584	1043
Playoff Totals	100	20	29	49	187
TREMBLAY, Nelson (Nels) *5-9 170 C*					
B. Quebec City, Que., July 26, 1923					
44-45 Mont	1	0	1	1	0
45-46 Mont	2	0	0	0	0
Totals	3	0	1	1	0
Playoff Totals	2	0	0	0	0
TRIMPER, Timothy Edward *5-9 185 LW*					
B. Windsor, Ont., Sept. 28, 1959					
79-80 Chi	30	6	10	16	10
80-81 Winn	56	15	14	29	28
81-82 Winn	74	8	8	16	100
82-83 Winn	5	0	0	0	0
83-84 Winn	5	0	0	0	0
84-85 Minn	20	1	4	5	15
Totals	190	30	36	66	153
Playoff Totals	2	0	0	0	2
TROTTIER, Bryan John *5-11 195 C*					
B. Val Marie, Sask., July 17, 1956					
75-76 NYI	80	32	63	95	21
76-77 NYI	76	30	42	72	34
77-78 NYI	77	46	77	123	46
78-79 NYI	76	47	87	134	50
79-80 NYI	78	42	62	104	68
80-81 NYI	73	31	72	103	74
81-82 NYI	80	50	79	129	88
82-83 NYI	80	34	55	89	68
83-84 NYI	68	40	71	111	59
84-85 NYI	68	28	31	59	47
85-86 NYI	78	37	59	96	72
86-87 NYI	80	23	64	87	50
87-88 NYI	77	30	52	82	48
88-89 NYI	73	17	28	45	44
89-90 NYI	59	13	11	24	29
90-91 Pitt	52	9	19	28	24
91-92 Pitt	63	11	18	29	54
Totals	1238	520	890	1410	876
Playoff Totals	209	66	113	184	277
TROTTIER, David T. *5-10 170 LW*					
B. Pembroke, Ont., June 25, 1906					
28-29 Mont M	37	2	4	6	60
29-30 Mont M	41	17	10	27	73
30-31 Mont M	43	9	8	17	58
31-32 Mont M	48	26	18	44	94

Season	Team	GP	G	A	Pts.	PIM
TROTTIER, David T. *(Continued)*						
32-33	Mont M	48	16	15	31	38
33-34	Mont M	48	9	17	26	47
34-35	·Mont M	34	10	9	19	22
35-36	Mont M	46	10	10	20	25
36-37	Mont M	43	12	11	23	33
37-38	Mont M	47	9	10	19	42
38-39	Det	11	1	1	2	16
Totals		446	121	113	234	508
Playoff Totals		31	4	3	7	41
TROTTIER, Guy 5-8 165 RW						
B. Hull, Que., Apr. 1, 1941						
68-69	NYR	2	0	0	0	0
70-71	Tor	61	19	5	24	21
71-72	Tor	52	9	12	21	16
72-73	Ott (WHA)	72	26	32	58	25
73-74	Tor (WHA)	71	27	35	62	58
74-75	Tor-Mich (WHA)	23	7	6	13	4
NHL Totals		115	28	17	45	37
WHA Totals		166	60	73	133	87
NHL Playoff Totals		9	1	0	1	16
WHA Playoff Totals		17	6	7	13	4
TROTTIER, Rocky 5-11 185 RW						
B. Climax, Sask., Apr. 11, 1964						
83-84	NJ	5	1	1	2	0
84-85	NJ	33	5	3	8	2
Totals		38	6	4	10	2
TRUDEL, Louis Napoleon 5-11 167 LW						
B. Salem, Mass., July 21, 1913						
33-34	Chi	31	1	3	4	13
34-35	Chi	47	11	11	22	28
35-36	Chi	47	3	4	7	27
36-37	Chi	45	6	12	18	11
37-38	Chi	42	6	16	22	15
38-39	Mont	31	8	13	21	2
39-40	Mont	47	12	7	19	24
40-41	Mont	16	2	3	5	2
Totals		306	49	69	118	122
Playoff Totals		24	1	3	4	6
TRUDELL, Rene Joseph 5-9 165 RW						
B. Mariapolis, Man., Jan. 31, 1919						
45-46	NYR	16	3	5	8	4
46-47	NYR	59	8	16	24	38
47-48	NYR	54	13	7	20	30
Totals		129	24	28	52	72
Playoff Totals		5	0	0	0	2
TUCKER, John 6-0 200 C						
B. Windsor, Ont., Sept. 29, 1964						
83-84	Buf	21	12	4	16	4
84-85	Buf	64	22	27	49	21
85-86	Buf	75	31	34	65	39
86-87	Buf	54	17	34	51	21
87-88	Buf	45	19	19	38	20
88-89	Buf	60	13	31	44	31
89-90	Buf-Wash	46	10	21	31	12
90-91	Buf-NYI	38	4	7	11	8
Totals		403	128	177	305	156
Playoff Totals		29	10	18	28	22
TUDIN, Cornell (Connie) D						
41-42	Mont	4	0	1	1	4
TUDOR, Robert Alan 5-11 190 RW/C						
B. Cupar, Sask., June 30, 1956						
78-79	Van	24	4	4	8	19
79-80	Van	2	0	0	0	0
82-83	StL	2	0	0	0	0
Totals		28	4	4	8	19
Playoff Totals		3	0	0	0	0
TUER, Allan 6-0 190 D						
B. North Battleford, Sask., July 19, 1963						
85-86	LA	45	0	1	1	150
87-88	Minn	6	1	0	1	29
88-89	Hart	4	0	0	0	23
89-90	Hart	2	0	0	0	6
Totals		57	1	1	2	208
TURCOTTE, Alfie 5-11 185 C						
B. Gary, Ind., June 5, 1965						
83-84	Mont	30	7	7	14	10
84-85	Mont	53	8	16	24	35
85-86	Mont	2	0	0	0	0
87-88	Winn	3	0	0	0	0
88-89	Winn	14	1	3	4	2
89-90	Wash	4	0	2	2	0
90-91	Wash	6	1	1	2	0
Totals		112	17	29	46	49
Playoff Totals		5	0	0	0	0

Season	Team	GP	G	A	Pts.	PIM
TURCOTTE, Darren 6-0 185 C						
B. Boston, Mass., Mar. 2, 1968						
88-89	NYR	20	7	3	10	4
89-90	NYR	76	32	34	66	32
90-91	NYR	74	26	41	67	37
91-92	NYR	71	30	23	53	57
Totals		241	95	101	196	130
Playoff Totals		25	6	8	14	10
TURGEON, Pierre 6-1 203 C						
B. Rouyn, Que., Aug. 29, 1969						
87-88	Buf	76	14	28	42	34
88-89	Buf	80	34	54	88	26
89-90	Buf	80	40	66	106	29
90-91	Buf	78	32	47	79	26
91-92	Buf-NYI	77	40	55	95	20
Totals		391	160	250	410	135
Playoff Totals		23	12	13	25	14
TURGEON, Sylvain 6-0 200 LW						
B. Noranda, Que., Jan. 17, 1965						
83-84	Hart	76	40	32	72	55
84-85	Hart	64	31	31	62	67
85-86	Hart	76	45	34	79	88
86-87	Hart	41	23	13	36	45
87-88	Hart	71	23	26	49	71
88-89	Hart	42	16	14	30	40
89-90	NJ	72	30	17	47	81
90-91	Mont	19	5	7	12	20
91-92	Mont	56	9	11	20	39
Totals		417	222	185	407	506
Playoff Totals		36	4	7	11	22
TURLICK, Gordon F						
B. Mickel, B.C., Sept. 17, 1939						
59-60	Bos	2	0	0	0	2
TURNBULL, Ian Wayne 6-0 200 D						
B. Montreal, Que., Dec. 22, 1953						
73-74	Tor	78	8	27	35	74
74-75	Tor	22	6	7	13	44
75-76	Tor	76	20	36	56	90
76-77	Tor	80	22	57	79	84
77-78	Tor	77	14	47	61	77
78-79	Tor	80	12	51	63	80
79-80	Tor	75	11	28	39	90
80-81	Tor	80	19	47	66	104
81-82	Tor-LA	54	11	17	28	89
82-83	Pitt	6	0	0	0	4
Totals		628	123	317	440	753
Playoff Totals		55	13	32	45	94
TURNBULL, Perry John 6-2 200 C						
B. Rimbey, Alta., Mar. 9, 1959						
79-80	StL	80	16	19	35	124
80-81	StL	75	34	22	56	209
81-82	StL	79	33	26	59	161
82-83	StL	79	32	15	47	172
83-84	StL-Mont	72	20	15	35	140
84-85	Winn	66	22	21	43	130
85-86	Winn	80	20	31	51	183
86-87	Winn	26	1	5	6	44
87-88	StL	51	10	9	19	82
Totals		608	188	163	351	1245
Playoff Totals		34	6	7	13	86
TURNBULL, Randy Layne 5-11 185 D						
B. Bentley, Alta., Feb. 7, 1962						
81-82	Calg	1	0	0	0	2
TURNER, Brad 6-2 205 D						
B. Winnipeg, Man., May 25, 1968						
91-92	NYI	3	0	0	0	0
TURNER, Dean Cameron 6-2 215 D						
B. Dearborn, Mich., June 22, 1958						
78-79	NYR	1	0	0	0	0
79-80	Col	27	1	0	1	51
80-81	Col	4	0	0	0	4
82-83	LA	3	0	0	0	4
Totals		35	1	0	1	59
TURNER, Robert George 6-0 178 D						
B. Regina, Sask., Jan. 31, 1934						
55-56	Mont	33	1	4	5	35
56-57	Mont	58	1	4	5	48
57-58	Mont	66	0	3	3	30
58-59	Mont	68	4	24	28	66
59-60	Mont	54	0	9	9	40
60-61	Mont	60	2	2	4	16
61-62	Chi	69	8	2	10	52
62-63	Chi	70	3	3	6	20
Totals		478	19	51	70	307
Playoff Totals		68	1	4	5	44

Season	Team	GP	G	A	Pts.	PIM
TUSTIN, Norman Robert 5-11 175 LW						
B. Regina, Sask., Jan. 3, 1919						
41-42	NYR	18	2	4	6	0
TUTEN, Audley K. 5-10 180 D						
B. Enterprise, Alta., Jan. 14, 1915						
41-42	Chi	5	1	1	2	10
42-43	Chi	34	3	7	10	38
Totals		39	4	8	12	48
TUTT, Brian 6-1 195 D						
B. Small Well, Alta., June 9, 1962						
89-90	Wash	7	1	0	1	2
TUTTLE, Steve 6-1 197 RW						
B. Vancouver, B.C., Jan. 5, 1966						
88-89	StL	53	13	12	25	6
89-90	StL	71	12	10	22	4
90-91	StL	20	3	6	9	2
Totals		144	28	28	56	12
Playoff Totals		17	1	6	7	2
TWIST, Anthony (Tony) 6-0 212 D						
B. Sherwood Park, Alta., May 9, 1968						
89-90	StL	28	0	0	0	124
90-91	Que	24	0	0	0	104
91-92	Que	46	0	1	1	164
Totals		98	0	1	1	392
UBRIACO, Eugene Stephen 5-8 157 LW						
B. Sault Ste. Marie, Ont., Dec. 26, 1937						
67-68	Pitt	65	18	15	33	16
68-69	Pitt-Oak	75	19	18	37	28
69-70	Oak-Chi	37	2	2	4	6
Totals		177	39	35	74	50
Playoff Totals		11	2	0	2	4
ULANOV, Igor 6-1 205 D						
B. Perm, Soviet Union, Oct. 1, 1969						
91-92	Winn	27	2	9	11	67
Playoff Totals		7	0	0	0	39
ULLMAN, Norman Victor Alexander 5-10 185 C						
B. Provost, Alta., Dec. 26, 1935						
55-56	Det	66	9	9	18	26
56-57	Det	64	16	36	52	47
57-58	Det	69	23	28	51	38
58-59	Det	69	22	36	58	42
59-60	Det	70	24	34	58	46
60-61	Det	70	28	42	70	34
61-62	Det	70	26	38	64	54
62-63	Det	70	26	30	56	53
63-64	Det	61	21	30	51	55
64-65	Det	70	42	41	83	70
65-66	Det	70	31	41	72	35
66-67	Det	68	26	44	70	26
67-68	Det-Tor	71	35	37	72	28
68-69	Tor	75	35	42	77	41
69-70	Tor	74	18	42	60	37
70-71	Tor	73	34	51	85	24
71-72	Tor	77	23	50	73	26
72-73	Tor	65	20	35	55	10
73-74	Tor	78	22	47	69	12
74-75	Tor	80	9	26	35	8
75-76	Edm (WHA)	77	31	56	87	12
76-77	Edm (WHA)	67	16	27	43	28
NHL Totals		1410	490	739	1229	712
WHA Totals		144	47	83	130	40
NHL Playoff Totals		106	30	53	83	67
WHA Playoff Totals		9	1	6	7	2
UNGER, Garry Douglas 6-0 185 C						
B. Edmonton, Alta., Dec. 7, 1947						
67-68	Tor-Det	28	6	11	17	6
68-69	Det	76	24	20	44	33
69-70	Det	76	42	24	66	67
70-71	Det-StL	79	29	28	56	104
71-72	StL	78	36	34	70	104
72-73	StL	78	41	39	80	119
73-74	StL	78	33	35	68	96
74-75	StL	80	36	44	80	123
75-76	StL	80	39	44	83	95
76-77	StL	80	30	27	57	56
77-78	StL	80	32	20	52	66
78-79	StL	80	30	26	56	44
79-80	StL	79	17	16	33	39
80-81	LA-Edm	71	10	10	20	46
81-82	Edm	46	7	13	20	69
82-83	Edm	16	2	0	2	8
Totals		1105	413	391	804	1075
Playoff Totals		52	12	18	30	105

VADNAIS, Carol Marcel 6-1 210 D
B. Montreal, Que., Sept. 25, 1945

Season	Team	GP	G	A	Pts.	PIM
66-67	Mont	11	0	3	3	35
67-68	Mont	31	1	1	2	31
68-69	Oak	76	15	27	42	151
69-70	Oak	76	24	20	44	212
70-71	Cal	42	10	16	26	91
71-72	Cal-Bos	68	18	26	44	143
72-73	Bos	78	7	24	31	127
73-74	Bos	78	16	43	59	123
74-75	Bos	79	18	56	74	129
75-76	Bos-NYR	76	22	35	57	121
76-77	NYR	74	11	37	48	131
77-78	NYR	80	6	40	46	115
78-79	NYR	77	8	37	45	86
79-80	NYR	66	3	20	23	118
80-81	NYR	74	3	20	23	91
81-82	NYR	50	5	6	11	45
82-83	NJ	51	2	7	9	64
Totals		1087	169	418	587	1813
Playoff Totals		106	10	40	50	185

VAIL, Eric Douglas (Big Train) 6-2 210 LW
B. Timmins, Ont., Sept. 16, 1953

Season	Team	GP	G	A	Pts.	PIM
73-74	Atl	23	2	9	11	30
74-75	Atl	72	39	21	60	46
75-76	Atl	60	16	31	47	34
76-77	Atl	78	32	39	71	22
77-78	Atl	79	22	36	58	16
78-79	Atl	80	35	48	83	53
79-80	Atl	77	28	25	53	22
80-81	Calg	64	28	36	64	23
81-82	Calg-Det	58	14	15	29	35
Totals		591	216	260	476	281
Playoff Totals		20	5	6	11	6

VAIL, Melville (Sparky) 6-0 185 D
B. Meaford, Ont., July 5, 1906

Season	Team	GP	G	A	Pts.	PIM
28-29	NYR	18	3	0	3	16
29-30	NYR	32	1	1	2	2
Totals		50	4	1	5	18
Playoff Totals		10	0	0	0	2

VAIVE, Richard Claude 6-0 200 RW
B. Ottawa, Ont., May 14, 1959

Season	Team	GP	G	A	Pts.	PIM
78-79	Birm (WHA)	75	26	33	59	248
79-80	Van-Tor	69	22	15	37	188
80-81	Tor	75	33	29	62	229
81-82	Tor	77	54	35	89	157
82-83	Tor	78	51	28	79	105
83-84	Tor	76	52	41	93	114
84-85	Tor	72	35	33	68	112
85-86	Tor	61	33	31	64	85
86-87	Tor	73	32	34	66	61
87-88	Chi	76	43	26	69	108
88-89	Chi-Buf	58	31	26	57	124
89-90	Buf	70	29	19	48	74
90-91	Buf	71	25	27	52	74
91-92	Buf	21	1	3	4	14
NHL Totals		877	441	347	788	1445
WHA Totals		75	26	33	59	248
NHL Playoff Totals		54	27	16	43	111

VALENTINE, Christopher William 6-0 190 C
B. Belleville, Ont., Dec. 6, 1961

Season	Team	GP	G	A	Pts.	PIM
81-82	Wash	60	30	37	67	92
82-83	Wash	23	7	10	17	14
83-84	Wash	22	6	5	11	21
Totals		105	43	52	95	127
Playoff Totals		2	0	0	0	4

VALIQUETTE, John Joseph (Jack) 6-2 195 C
B. St. Thomas, Ont., Mar. 18, 1956

Season	Team	GP	G	A	Pts.	PIM
74-75	Tor	1	0	0	0	0
75-76	Tor	45	10	23	33	30
76-77	Tor	66	15	30	45	7
77-78	Tor	60	8	13	21	15
78-79	Col	76	23	34	57	12
79-80	Col	77	25	25	50	8
80-81	Col	25	3	9	12	7
Totals		350	84	134	218	79
Playoff Totals		23	3	6	9	4

VALK, Garry 6-1 190 LW
B. Edmonton, Alta., Nov. 27, 1967

Season	Team	GP	G	A	Pts.	PIM
90-91	Van	59	10	11	21	67
91-92	Van	65	8	17	25	56
Totals		124	18	28	46	123
Playoff Totals		9	0	0	0	25

VAN ALLEN, Shaun 6-1 200 C
B. Shaunavon, Sask., Aug. 29, 1967

Season	Team	GP	G	A	Pts.	PIM
90-91	Edm	2	0	0	0	0

VAN BOXMEER, John Martin 6-0 190 D
B. Petrolia, Ont., Nov. 20, 1952

Season	Team	GP	G	A	Pts.	PIM
73-74	Mont	20	1	4	5	18
74-75	Mont	9	0	2	2	0
75-76	Mont	46	6	11	17	31
76-77	Mont-Col	45	2	12	14	32
77-78	Col	80	12	42	54	87
78-79	Col	76	9	34	43	46
79-80	Buf	80	11	40	51	55
80-81	Buf	80	18	51	69	69
81-82	Buf	69	14	54	68	62
82-83	Buf	65	6	21	27	53
83-84	Que	18	5	3	8	12
Totals		588	84	274	358	465
Playoff Totals		38	5	15	20	37

VAN DORP, Wayne 6-4 225 LW
B. Vancouver, B.C., May 19, 1961

Season	Team	GP	G	A	Pts.	PIM
86-87	Edm	3	0	0	0	25
87-88	Pitt	25	1	3	4	75
88-89	Chi	8	0	0	0	23
89-90	Chi	61	7	4	11	303
90-91	Que	4	1	0	1	30
91-92	Que	24	3	5	8	109
Totals		125	12	12	24	565
Playoff Totals		27	0	1	1	42

VAN IMPE, Edward Charles 5-10 205 D
B. Saskatoon, Sask., May 27, 1940

Season	Team	GP	G	A	Pts.	PIM
66-67	Chi	61	8	11	19	111
67-68	Phil	67	4	13	17	141
68-69	Phil	68	7	12	19	112
69-70	Phil	65	0	10	10	117
70-71	Phil	77	0	11	11	80
71-72	Phil	73	4	9	13	78
72-73	Phil	72	1	11	12	76
73-74	Phil	77	2	16	18	119
74-75	Phil	78	1	17	18	109
75-76	Phil-Pitt	52	0	13	13	76
76-77	Pitt	10	0	3	3	6
Totals		700	27	126	153	1025
Playoff Totals		66	1	12	13	131

VASKE, Dennis 6-2 210 D
B. Rockford, Ill., Oct. 11, 1967

Season	Team	GP	G	A	Pts.	PIM
90-91	NYI	5	0	0	0	2
91-92	NYI	39	0	1	1	39
Totals		44	0	1	1	41

VASKO, Elmer (Moose) 6-3 220 D
B. Duparquet, Que., Dec. 11, 1935

Season	Team	GP	G	A	Pts.	PIM
56-57	Chi	64	3	12	15	31
57-58	Chi	59	6	20	26	51
58-59	Chi	63	6	10	16	52
59-60	Chi	69	3	27	30	110
60-61	Chi	63	4	18	22	40
61-62	Chi	64	2	22	24	87
62-63	Chi	64	4	9	13	70
63-64	Chi	70	2	18	20	65
64-65	Chi	69	1	10	11	56
65-66	Chi	56	1	7	8	44
67-68	Minn	70	1	6	7	45
68-69	Minn	72	1	7	8	68
69-70	Minn	3	0	0	0	0
Totals		786	34	166	200	719
Playoff Totals		78	2	7	9	73

VASKO, Richard John (Rick) 6-0 185 D
B. St. Catharines, Ont., Jan. 12, 1957

Season	Team	GP	G	A	Pts.	PIM
77-78	Det	3	0	0	0	7
79-80	Det	8	0	0	0	2
80-81	Det	20	3	7	10	20
Totals		31	3	7	10	29

VAUTOUR, Yvon 6-0 200 RW
B. St. John, N.B., Sept. 10, 1956

Season	Team	GP	G	A	Pts.	PIM
79-80	NYI	17	3	1	4	24
80-81	Col	74	15	19	34	143
81-82	Col	14	1	2	3	18
82-83	NJ	52	4	7	11	136
83-84	NJ	42	3	4	7	78
84-85	Que	5	0	0	0	2
Totals		204	26	33	59	401

VAYDIK, Gregory 6-0 185 C
B. Yellowknife, N.W.T., Oct. 9, 1955

Season	Team	GP	G	A	Pts.	PIM
76-77	Chi	5	0	0	0	0

VEITCH, Darren William 5-11 195 D
B. Saskatoon, Sask., Apr. 24, 1960

Season	Team	GP	G	A	Pts.	PIM
80-81	Wash	59	4	21	25	46
81-82	Wash	67	9	44	53	54
82-83	Wash	10	0	8	8	0

VEITCH, Darren William (Continued)

Season	Team	GP	G	A	Pts.	PIM
83-84	Wash	46	6	18	24	17
84-85	Wash	75	3	18	21	37
85-86	Wash-Det	75	3	14	17	29
86-87	Det	77	13	45	58	52
87-88	Det	63	7	33	40	45
88-89	Tor	37	3	7	10	16
90-91	Tor	2	0	1	1	0
Totals		511	48	209	257	296
Playoff Totals		33	4	11	15	33

VELISCHEK, Randy 6-0 200 D
B. Montreal, Que., Feb. 10, 1962

Season	Team	GP	G	A	Pts.	PIM
82-83	Minn	3	0	0	0	2
83-84	Minn	33	2	2	4	10
84-85	Minn	52	4	9	13	26
85-86	NJ	47	2	7	9	39
86-87	NJ	64	2	16	18	52
87-88	NJ	51	3	9	12	66
88-89	NJ	80	4	14	18	70
89-90	NJ	62	0	6	6	72
90-91	Que	79	2	10	12	42
91-92	Que	38	2	3	5	22
Totals		509	21	76	97	401
Playoff Totals		44	2	5	7	32

VENASKY, Victor William 5-11 177 C
B. Thunder Bay, Ont., June 3, 1951

Season	Team	GP	G	A	Pts.	PIM
72-73	LA	77	15	19	34	10
73-74	LA	32	6	5	11	12
74-75	LA	17	1	2	3	0
75-76	LA	80	18	26	44	12
76-77	LA	80	14	26	40	18
77-78	LA	71	3	10	13	6
78-79	LA	73	4	13	17	8
Totals		430	61	101	162	66
Playoff Totals		21	1	5	6	12

VENERUZZO, Gary Raymond 5-9 165 LW
B. Fort William, Ont., June 28, 1943

Season	Team	GP	G	A	Pts.	PIM
67-68	StL	5	1	1	2	0
71-72	StL	2	0	0	0	0
72-73	LA (WHA)	78	43	30	73	34
73-74	LA (WHA)	78	39	29	68	68
74-75	Balt (WHA)	77	33	27	60	57
75-76	Cin-Phoe (WHA)	75	22	26	48	35
76-77	SD (WHA)	40	14	11	25	18
NHL Totals		7	1	1	2	0
WHA Totals		348	151	123	274	212
NHL Playoff Totals		9	0	2	2	2
WHA Playoff Totals		18	5	0	5	11

VERBEEK, Patrick 5-9 190 LW/RW
B. Sarnia, Ont., May 24, 1964

Season	Team	GP	G	A	Pts.	PIM
82-83	NJ	6	3	2	5	8
83-84	NJ	79	20	27	47	158
84-85	NJ	78	15	18	33	162
85-86	NJ	76	25	28	53	79
86-87	NJ	74	35	24	59	120
87-88	NJ	73	46	31	77	227
88-89	NJ	77	26	21	47	189
89-90	Hart	80	44	45	89	228
90-91	Hart	80	43	39	82	246
91-92	Hart	76	22	35	57	243
Totals		699	279	270	549	1660
Playoff Totals		40	9	14	23	129

VERMETTE, Mark 6-1 203 RW
B. Cochenour, Ont., Oct. 3, 1967

Season	Team	GP	G	A	Pts.	PIM
88-89	Que	12	0	4	4	7
89-90	Que	11	1	5	6	8
90-91	Que	34	3	4	7	10
91-92	Que	10	1	0	1	8
Totals		67	5	13	18	33

VERRET, Claude 5-9 165 C
B. Lachine, Que., Apr. 20, 1963

Season	Team	GP	G	A	Pts.	PIM
83-84	Buf	11	2	5	7	2
84-85	Buf	3	0	0	0	0
Totals		14	2	5	7	2

VERSTRAETE, Leigh 5-11 185 RW
B. Pincher Creek, Alta., Jan. 6, 1962

Season	Team	GP	G	A	Pts.	PIM
82-83	Tor	3	0	0	0	5
84-85	Tor	2	0	0	0	0
87-88	Tor	3	0	1	1	0
Totals		8	0	1	1	14

VERVERGAERT, Dennis Andrew 6-0 195 RW
B. Hamilton, Ont., Mar. 30, 1953

Season	Team	GP	G	A	Pts.	PIM
73-74	Van	78	26	31	57	25
74-75	Van	57	19	32	51	25
75-76	Van	80	37	34	71	53
76-77	Van	79	27	18	45	38

VERVERGAERT, Dennis Andrew *(Continued)*

Season	Team	GP	G	A	Pts.	PIM
77-78	Van	80	21	33	54	23
78-79	Van-Phil	72	18	24	42	19
79-80	Phil	58	14	17	31	24
80-81	Wash	79	14	27	41	40
Totals		583	176	216	392	247
Playoff Totals		8	1	2	3	6

VESEY, Jim *6-1 202 C/RW*
B. Columbus, Mass., Oct. 29, 1965

Season	Team	GP	G	A	Pts.	PIM
88-89	StL	5	1	1	2	7
89-90	StL	6	0	1	1	0
91-92	Bos	4	0	0	0	0
Totals		15	1	2	3	7

VEYSEY, Sidney *5-11 175 C*
B. Sherbrooke, Que., July 3, 1955

Season	Team	GP	G	A	Pts.	PIM
77-78	Van	1	0	0	0	0

VIAL, Dennis *6-1 215 D*
B. Sault Ste. Marie, Ont., Apr. 10, 1969

Season	Team	GP	G	A	Pts.	PIM
90-91	NYR-Det	30	0	0	0	77
91-92	Det	27	1	0	1	72
Totals		57	1	0	1	149

VICKERS, Stephen James *6-0 185 LW*
B. Toronto, Ont., Apr. 21, 1951

Season	Team	GP	G	A	Pts.	PIM
72-73	NYR	61	30	23	53	37
73-74	NYR	75	34	24	58	18
74-75	NYR	80	41	48	89	64
75-76	NYR	80	30	53	83	40
76-77	NYR	75	22	31	53	26
77-78	NYR	79	19	44	63	30
78-79	NYR	66	13	34	47	24
79-80	NYR	75	29	33	62	38
80-81	NYR	73	19	39	58	40
81-82	NYR	34	9	11	20	13
Totals		698	246	340	586	330
Playoff Totals		68	24	25	49	58

VIGNEAULT, Alain *5-11 195 D*
B. Quebec City, Que., May 14, 1961

Season	Team	GP	G	A	Pts.	PIM
81-82	StL	14	1	2	3	43
82-83	StL	28	1	3	4	39
Totals		42	2	5	7	82
Playoff Totals		4	0	1	1	26

VILGRAIN, Claude *6-1 205 RW*
B. Port-au-Prince, Haiti, Mar. 1, 1963

Season	Team	GP	G	A	Pts.	PIM
87-88	Van	6	1	1	2	0
89-90	NJ	6	1	2	3	4
91-92	NJ	71	19	27	46	74
Totals		83	21	30	51	78
Playoff Totals		11	1	1	2	17

VINCELETTE, Daniel *6-2 202 LW*
B. Verdun, Que., Aug. 1, 1967

Season	Team	GP	G	A	Pts.	PIM
87-88	Chi	69	6	11	17	109
88-89	Chi	66	11	4	15	119
89-90	Chi-Que	13	0	1	1	29
91-92	Chi	29	3	5	8	56
Totals		177	20	21	41	313
Playoff Totals		12	0	0	0	4

VIPOND, Peter John *5-10 175 LW*
B. Oshawa, Ont., Dec. 8, 1949

Season	Team	GP	G	A	Pts.	PIM
72-73	Cal	3	0	0	0	0

VIRTA, Hannu *5-11 180 D*
B. Turku, Finland, Mar. 22, 1963

Season	Team	GP	G	A	Pts.	PIM
81-82	Buf	3	0	1	1	4
82-83	Buf	74	13	24	37	18
83-84	Buf	70	6	30	36	12
84-85	Buf	51	1	23	24	16
85-86	Buf	47	5	23	28	16
Totals		245	25	101	126	66
Playoff Totals		26	5	5	10	10

VIVEIROS, Emanuel *6-0 175 D*
B. St. Albert, Alta., Jan. 8, 1966

Season	Team	GP	G	A	Pts.	PIM
85-86	Minn	4	0	1	1	0
86-87	Minn	1	0	1	1	0
87-88	Minn	24	1	9	10	6
Totals		29	1	11	12	6

VOKES, Ed *F*

Season	Team	GP	G	A	Pts.	PIM
30-31	Chi	5	0	0	0	0

VOLCAN, Michael Stephen (Mickey) *6-0 190 D*
B. Edmonton, Alta., Mar. 3, 1962

Season	Team	GP	G	A	Pts.	PIM
80-81	Hart	49	2	11	13	26
81-82	Hart	26	1	5	6	29

VOLCAN, Michael Stephen (Mickey) *(Continued)*

Season	Team	GP	G	A	Pts.	PIM
82-83	Hart	68	4	13	17	73
83-84	Calg	19	1	4	5	18
Totals		162	8	33	41	146

VOLEK, David *6-0 185 LW/RW*
B. Prague, Czechoslovakia, June 18, 1966

Season	Team	GP	G	A	Pts.	PIM
88-89	NYI	77	25	34	59	24
89-90	NYI	80	17	22	39	41
90-91	NYI	77	22	34	56	57
91-92	NYI	74	18	42	60	35
Totals		308	82	132	214	157
Playoff Totals		5	1	4	5	0

VOLMAR, Douglas Steven *6-1 215 RW*
B. Cleveland Heights, Ohio, Jan. 9, 1945

Season	Team	GP	G	A	Pts.	PIM
70-71	Det	2	0	1	1	2
71-72	Det	39	9	5	14	8
72-73	LA	21	4	2	6	16
74-75	SD (WHA)	10	0	1	1	4
NHL Totals		62	13	8	21	26
WHA Totals		10	0	1	1	4
NHL Playoff Totals		2	1	0	1	0

VOSS, Carl Potter *5-8 168 C*
B. Chelsea, Mass., Jan. 6, 1907

Season	Team	GP	G	A	Pts.	PIM
26-27	Tor	12	0	0	0	0
28-29	Tor	2	0	0	0	0
32-33	NYR-Det	48	8	15	23	10
33-34	Det-Ott	48	7	18	25	12
34-35	StL E	48	13	18	31	14
35-36	NYA	46	3	9	12	10
36-37	Mont M	20	0	2	2	4
37-38	Mont M-Chi	37	3	8	11	0
Totals		261	34	70	104	50
Playoff Totals		24	5	3	8	0

VUJTEK, Vladimir *6-0 190 LW*
B. Ostrava Czechoslovakia, Feb. 17, 1972

Season	Team	GP	G	A	Pts.	PIM
91-92	Mont	2	0	0	0	0

VUKOTA, Mick *6-2 195 RW*
B. Saskatoon, Sask., Sept. 14, 1966

Season	Team	GP	G	A	Pts.	PIM
87-88	NYI	17	1	0	1	82
88-89	NYI	48	2	2	4	237
89-90	NYI	76	4	8	12	290
90-91	NYI	60	2	4	6	238
91-92	NYI	74	0	6	6	293
Totals		275	9	20	29	1140
Playoff Totals		3	0	0	0	40

VYAZMIKIN, Igor *6-1 194 RW/LW*
B. Moscow, Soviet Union, Jan. 8, 1966

Season	Team	GP	G	A	Pts.	PIM
90-91	Edm	4	1	0	1	0

WADDELL, Donald *5-10 178 D*
B. Detroit, Mich., Aug. 19, 1958

Season	Team	GP	G	A	Pts.	PIM
80-81	LA	1	0	0	0	0

WAITE, Frank E. (Deacon) *5-11 150 F*
B. Qu'Appelle, Sask., Apr. 9, 1906

Season	Team	GP	G	A	Pts.	PIM
30-31	NYR	17	1	3	4	4

WALKER, Gord *6-0 175 RW*
B. Castiegar, B.C., Aug. 12, 1965

Season	Team	GP	G	A	Pts.	PIM
86-87	NYR	1	1	0	1	4
87-88	NYR	18	1	4	5	17
88-89	LA	11	1	0	1	2
89-90	LA	1	0	0	0	0
Totals		31	3	4	7	23

WALKER, Howard *6-0 205 D*
B. Grande Prairie, Alta., Aug. 5, 1958

Season	Team	GP	G	A	Pts.	PIM
80-81	Wash	64	2	11	13	100
81-82	Wash	16	0	2	2	26
82-83	Calg	3	0	0	0	7
Totals		83	2	13	15	133

WALKER, John Phillip (Jack) *LW*
B. Silver Mountain, Ont., Nov. 28, 1888

Season	Team	GP	G	A	Pts.	PIM
26-27	Det	37	3	4	7	6
27-28	Det	43	2	4	6	12
Totals		80	5	8	13	18

WALKER, Kurt Adrian *6-3 200 D*
B. Weymouth, Mass., June 10, 1954

Season	Team	GP	G	A	Pts.	PIM
75-76	Tor	5	0	0	0	49
76-77	Tor	26	2	3	5	34
77-78	Tor	40	2	2	4	69
Totals		71	4	5	9	152
Playoff Totals		16	0	0	0	34

WALKER, Russell *6-2 185 RW*
B. Red Deer, Alta., May 24, 1953

Season	Team	GP	G	A	Pts.	PIM
73-74	Clev (WHA)	76	15	14	29	117
74-75	Clev (WHA)	66	14	11	25	80
75-76	Clev (WHA)	72	23	15	38	122
76-77	LA	16	1	0	1	35
77-78	LA	1	0	0	0	6
NHL Totals		17	1	0	1	41
WHA Totals		214	52	40	92	319
WHA Playoff Totals		13	2	0	2	46

WALL, Robert James Albert *5-10 202 D*
B. Richmond Hill, Ont., Dec. 1, 1942

Season	Team	GP	G	A	Pts.	PIM
64-65	Det	1	0	0	0	0
65-66	Det	8	1	1	2	8
66-67	Det	31	2	2	4	26
67-68	LA	71	5	18	23	66
68-69	LA	71	13	13	26	16
69-70	LA	70	5	13	18	26
70-71	StL	25	2	4	6	4
71-72	Det	45	2	4	6	9
72-73	Alb (WHA)	78	16	29	45	20
73-74	Edm (WHA)	74	6	31	37	46
74-75	SD (WHA)	33	0	9	9	15
75-76	SD (WHA)	68	1	20	21	32
NHL Totals		322	30	55	85	155
WHA Totals		253	23	89	112	113
NHL Playoff Totals		22	0	3	3	2
WHA Playoff Totals		26	1	8	9	8

WALLIN, Peter *5-9 170 RW*
B. Stockholm, Sweden, Apr. 30, 1957

Season	Team	GP	G	A	Pts.	PIM
80-81	NYR	12	1	5	6	2
81-82	NYR	40	2	9	11	12
Totals		52	3	14	17	14
Playoff Totals		14	2	6	8	6

WALSH, James *6-1 185 D*
B. Norfolk, Va., Oct. 26, 1956

Season	Team	GP	G	A	Pts.	PIM
81-82	Buf	4	0	1	1	4

WALSH, Mike *6-2 195 LW*
B. New York, N.Y., Apr. 3, 1962

Season	Team	GP	G	A	Pts.	PIM
87-88	NYI	1	0	0	0	0
88-89	NYI	13	2	0	2	4
Totals		14	2	0	2	4

WALTER, Ryan William *6-0 200 C/LW*
B. New Westminster, B.C., Apr. 23, 1958

Season	Team	GP	G	A	Pts.	PIM
78-79	Wash	69	28	28	56	70
79-80	Wash	80	24	42	66	106
80-81	Wash	80	24	44	68	150
81-82	Wash	78	38	49	87	142
82-83	Mont	80	29	46	75	40
83-84	Mont	73	20	29	49	83
84-85	Mont	72	19	19	38	59
85-86	Mont	69	15	34	49	45
86-87	Mont	76	23	23	46	34
87-88	Mont	61	13	23	36	39
88-89	Mont	78	14	17	31	48
89-90	Mont	70	8	16	24	59
90-91	Mont	25	0	1	1	12
91-92	Van	67	6	11	17	49
Totals		978	261	382	643	936
Playoff Totals		113	16	35	51	62

WALTON, Michael Robert (Shakey) *5-10 175 C*
B. Kirkland Lake, Ont., Jan. 3, 1945

Season	Team	GP	G	A	Pts.	PIM
65-66	Tor	6	1	3	4	0
66-67	Tor	31	7	10	17	13
67-68	Tor	73	30	29	59	48
68-69	Tor	66	22	21	43	34
69-70	Tor	58	21	34	55	68
70-71	Tor-Bos	45	6	15	21	31
71-72	Bos	76	28	28	56	45
72-73	Bos	56	25	22	47	37
73-74	Minn (WHA)	78	57	60	117	88
74-75	Minn (WHA)	75	48	45	93	33
75-76	Minn (WHA)	58	31	40	71	27
75-76	Van	10	8	8	16	9
76-77	Van	40	7	24	31	32
77-78	Van	65	29	37	66	30
78-79	StL-Bos-Chi	62	17	16	33	10
NHL Totals		588	201	247	448	357
WHA Totals		211	136	145	281	148
NHL Playoff Totals		47	14	10	24	45
WHA Playoff Totals		23	20	15	35	26

WALTON, Robert Charles *5-9 165 C*
B. Ottawa, Ont., Aug. 5, 1917

Season	Team	GP	G	A	Pts.	PIM
43-44	Mont	4	0	0	0	0

WALZ, Wes *5-10 180 C*
B. Calgary, Alta., May 15, 1970

Season	Team	GP	G	A	Pts.	PIM
89-90	Bos	2	1	1	2	0
90-91	Bos	56	8	8	16	32
91-92	Bos-Phil	17	1	3	4	12
Totals		75	10	12	22	44
Playoff Totals		2	0	0	0	0

WAPPEL, Gordon Alexander *6-2 203 D*
B. Regina, Sask., July 26, 1958

Season	Team	GP	G	A	Pts.	PIM
79-80	Atl	2	0	0	0	0
80-81	Calg	7	0	1	1	4
81-82	Calg	11	1	0	1	6
Totals		20	1	1	2	10
Playoff Totals		2	0	0	0	4

WARD, Donald Joseph *6-2 210 D*
B. Sarnia, Ont., Oct. 19, 1935

Season	Team	GP	G	A	Pts.	PIM
57-58	Chi	3	0	0	0	0
59-60	Bos	31	0	1	1	160
Totals		34	0	1	1	160

WARD, James William *5-11 167 RW*
B. Fort William, Ont., Sept. 1, 1906

Season	Team	GP	G	A	Pts.	PIM
27-28	Mont M	44	10	2	12	44
28-29	Mont M	44	14	8	22	46
29-30	Mont M	43	10	7	17	54
30-31	Mont M	42	14	8	22	52
31-32	Mont M	48	19	19	38	39
32-33	Mont M	48	16	17	33	52
33-34	Mont M	48	14	9	23	46
34-35	Mont M	42	9	6	15	24
35-36	Mont M	48	12	19	31	30
36-37	Mont M	41	14	14	28	34
37-38	Mont M	48	11	15	26	34
38-39	Mont	36	4	3	7	0
Totals		532	147	127	274	455
Playoff Totals		31	4	4	8	18

WARD, Joseph Michael *6-0 178 C*
B. Sarnia, Ont., Feb. 11, 1961

Season	Team	GP	G	A	Pts.	PIM
80-81	Col	4	0	0	0	2

WARD, Ronald Leon *5-10 180 C*
B. Cornwall, Ont., Sept. 12, 1944

Season	Team	GP	G	A	Pts.	PIM
69-70	Tor	18	0	1	1	2
71-72	Van	71	2	4	6	4
72-73	NY (WHA)	77	51	67	118	28
73-74	Van-LA-Clev (WHA)	70	33	28	61	25
74-75	Clev (WHA)	73	30	32	62	18
75-76	Clev (WHA)	75	32	50	82	24
76-77	Minn-Winn-Calg (WHA)	64	24	33	57	8
NHL Totals		89	2	5	7	6
WHA Totals		359	170	210	380	103
WHA Playoff Totals		13	3	4	7	4

WARE, Michael *6-5 216 RW*
B. York, Ont., Mar. 22, 1967

Season	Team	GP	G	A	Pts.	PIM
88-89	Edm	2	0	1	1	11
89-90	Edm	3	0	0	0	4
Totals		5	0	1	1	15

WARES, Edward George *5-10 182 D*
B. Calgary, Alta., Mar. 19, 1915

Season	Team	GP	G	A	Pts.	PIM
36-37	NYR	2	2	0	2	0
37-38	Det	21	9	7	16	2
38-39	Det	28	8	8	16	10
39-40	Det	33	2	6	8	19
40-41	Det	42	10	16	26	34
41-42	Det	43	9	29	38	31
42-43	Det	47	12	18	30	10
45-46	Chi	45	4	11	15	34
46-47	Chi	60	4	7	11	21
Totals		321	60	102	162	161
Playoff Totals		45	5	7	12	34

WARNER, James Francis *5-11 180 RW*
B. Minneapolis, Minn., Mar. 26, 1954

Season	Team	GP	G	A	Pts.	PIM
78-79	NE (WHA)	41	6	9	15	20
79-80	Hart	32	0	3	3	10
NHL Totals		32	0	3	3	10
WHA Totals		41	6	9	15	20
WHA Playoff Totals		1	0	0	0	0

WARNER, Robert Norman *5-11 180 D*
B. Grimsby, Ont., Dec. 13, 1950

Season	Team	GP	G	A	Pts.	PIM
76-77	Tor	10	1	1	2	4
Playoff Totals		4	0	0	0	0

WARWICK, Grant David (Knobby) *5-6 165 RW*
B. Regina, Sask., Oct. 11, 1921

Season	Team	GP	G	A	Pts.	PIM
41-42	NYR	44	16	17	33	36

WARWICK, Grant David (Knobby)
(Continued)

Season	Team	GP	G	A	Pts.	PIM
42-43	NYR	50	17	18	35	31
43-44	NYR	18	8	9	17	14
44-45	NYR	42	20	22	42	25
45-46	NYR	45	19	18	37	19
46-47	NYR	54	20	20	40	24
47-48	NYR-Bos	58	23	17	40	38
48-49	Bos	58	22	15	37	14
49-50	Mont	30	2	6	8	19
Totals		399	147	142	289	220
Playoff Totals		16	2	4	6	6

WARWICK, William Harvey *5-6 165 LW*
B. Regina, Sask., Nov. 17, 1924

Season	Team	GP	G	A	Pts.	PIM
42-43	NYR	1	0	1	1	4
43-44	NYR	13	3	2	5	12
Totals		14	3	3	6	16

WASNIE, Nicholas *5-10 174 RW*
B. Winnipeg, Man., Jan. 1, 1904

Season	Team	GP	G	A	Pts.	PIM
27-28	Chi	14	1	0	1	22
29-30	Mont	44	12	11	23	64
30-31	Mont	44	9	2	11	26
31-32	Mont	48	10	2	12	16
32-33	NYA	48	11	12	23	36
33-34	Ott	37	11	6	17	10
34-35	StL E	13	3	1	4	2
Totals		248	57	34	91	176
Playoff Totals		14	6	3	9	20

WATSON, Bryan Joseph (Bugsy)
5-10 175 D
B. Bancroft, Ont., Nov. 14, 1942

Season	Team	GP	G	A	Pts.	PIM
63-64	Mont	39	0	2	2	18
64-65	Mont	5	0	1	1	7
65-66	Det	70	2	7	9	133
66-67	Det	48	0	1	1	66
67-68	Mont	12	0	1	1	9
68-69	Oak-Pitt	68	2	7	9	132
69-70	Pitt	61	1	9	10	189
70-71	Pitt	43	2	6	8	119
71-72	Pitt	75	3	17	20	212
72-73	Pitt	69	1	17	18	179
73-74	Pitt-StL-Det	70	1	9	10	255
74-75	Det	70	1	13	14	238
75-76	Det	79	0	18	18	322
76-77	Det-Wash	70	1	15	16	130
77-78	Wash	79	3	11	14	167
78-79	Wash	20	0	1	1	36
78-79	Cin (WHA)	21	0	2	2	56
NHL Totals		878	17	135	152	2212
WHA Totals		21	0	2	2	56
NHL Playoff Totals		32	2	0	2	70
WHA Playoff Totals		3	0	1	1	2

WATSON, David *6-2 190 LW*
B. Kirkland Lake, Ont., May 19, 1958

Season	Team	GP	G	A	Pts.	PIM
79-80	Col	5	0	0	0	2
80-81	Col	13	0	1	1	8
Totals		18	0	1	1	10

WATSON, Harry Percival (Whipper)
6-1 203 LW
B. Saskatoon, Sask., May 6, 1923

Season	Team	GP	G	A	Pts.	PIM
41-42	Brk	47	10	8	18	6
42-43	Det	50	13	18	31	10
45-46	Det	44	14	10	24	4
46-47	Tor	44	19	15	34	10
47-48	Tor	57	21	20	41	16
48-49	Tor	60	26	19	45	0
49-50	Tor	60	19	16	35	11
50-51	Tor	68	18	19	37	18
51-52	Tor	70	22	17	39	18
52-53	Tor	63	16	8	24	8
53-54	Tor	70	21	7	28	30
54-55	Tor-Chi	51	15	17	32	4
55-56	Chi	55	11	14	25	6
56-57	Chi	70	11	19	30	9
Totals		809	236	207	443	150
Playoff Totals		62	16	9	25	27

WATSON, James Arthur (Watty)
6-2 195 D
B. Malartic, Que., June 28, 1943

Season	Team	GP	G	A	Pts.	PIM
63-64	Det	1	0	0	0	0
64-65	Det	1	0	0	0	2
65-66	Det	2	0	0	0	4
67-68	Det	61	0	3	3	87
68-69	Det	8	0	1	1	4
69-70	Det	4	0	0	0	0
70-71	Buf	78	2	9	11	147
71-72	Buf	66	2	6	8	101
72-73	LA (WHA)	75	5	15	20	123
73-74	LA-Chi (WHA)	71	0	11	11	50

WATSON, James Arthur (Watty)
(Continued)

Season	Team	GP	G	A	Pts.	PIM
74-75	Chi (WHA)	57	3	6	9	31
75-76	Que (WHA)	28	0	1	1	24
NHL Totals		221	4	19	23	345
WHA Totals		231	8	33	41	228
WHA Playoff Totals		22	2	4	6	20

WATSON, James Charles *6-0 195 D*
B. Smithers, B.C., Aug. 19, 1952

Season	Team	GP	G	A	Pts.	PIM
72-73	Phil	4	0	1	1	5
73-74	Phil	78	2	18	20	44
74-75	Phil	68	7	18	25	72
75-76	Phil	79	2	34	36	66
76-77	Phil	71	3	23	26	35
77-78	Phil	71	5	12	17	62
78-79	Phil	77	9	13	22	52
79-80	Phil	71	5	18	23	51
80-81	Phil	18	2	2	4	6
81-82	Phil	76	3	9	12	99
Totals		613	38	148	186	492
Playoff Totals		101	5	34	39	89

WATSON, Joseph John *5-10 185 D*
B. Smithers, B.C., July 6, 1943

Season	Team	GP	G	A	Pts.	PIM
64-65	Bos	4	0	1	1	0
66-67	Bos	69	2	13	15	38
67-68	Phil	73	5	14	19	56
68-69	Phil	60	2	8	10	14
69-70	Phil	54	3	11	14	28
70-71	Phil	57	3	7	10	50
71-72	Phil	65	3	7	10	38
72-73	Phil	63	2	24	26	46
73-74	Phil	74	1	17	18	34
74-75	Phil	80	6	17	23	42
75-76	Phil	78	2	22	24	28
76-77	Phil	77	4	26	30	39
77-78	Phil	65	5	9	14	22
78-79	Col	16	0	2	2	12
Totals		835	38	178	216	447
Playoff Totals		84	3	12	15	82

WATSON, Phillipe Henri (Phil)
5-11 165 RW
B. Montreal, Que., Apr. 24, 1914

Season	Team	GP	G	A	Pts.	PIM
35-36	NYR	24	0	2	2	24
36-37	NYR	48	11	17	28	22
37-38	NYR	48	7	25	32	52
38-39	NYR	48	15	22	37	42
39-40	NYR	48	7	28	35	42
40-41	NYR	40	11	25	36	49
41-42	NYR	48	15	37	52	58
42-43	NYR	46	14	28	42	44
43-44	Mont	44	17	32	49	61
44-45	NYR	45	11	8	19	24
45-46	NYR	49	12	14	26	43
46-47	NYR	48	6	12	18	17
47-48	NYR	54	18	15	33	54
Totals		590	144	265	409	532
Playoff Totals		45	10	25	35	67

WATSON, William (Bill) *6-0 185 RW*
B. Pine Falls, Man., Mar. 30, 1964

Season	Team	GP	G	A	Pts.	PIM
85-86	Chi	52	8	16	24	2
86-87	Chi	51	13	19	32	6
87-88	Chi	9	2	0	2	0
88-89	Chi	3	0	1	1	4
Totals		115	23	36	59	12
Playoff Totals		6	0	2	2	0

WATTERS, Timothy J. *5-11 185 D*
B. Kamloops, B.C., July 25, 1959

Season	Team	GP	G	A	Pts.	PIM
81-82	Winn	69	2	22	24	97
82-83	Winn	77	5	18	23	98
83-84	Winn	74	3	20	23	169
84-85	Winn	63	2	20	22	74
85-86	Winn	56	6	8	14	97
86-87	Winn	63	3	13	16	119
87-88	Winn	36	0	0	0	106
88-89	LA	76	3	18	21	168
89-90	LA	62	1	10	11	92
90-91	LA	45	0	4	4	92
91-92	LA	37	0	7	7	92
Totals		658	25	140	165	1204
Playoff Totals		60	1	3	4	85

WATTS, Brian Alan *6-0 180 LW*
B. Hagersville, Ont., Sept. 10, 1947

Season	Team	GP	G	A	Pts.	PIM
75-76	Det	4	0	0	0	0

WEBSTER, Aubrey *5-9 168 F*
B. Fort William, Ont., Sept. 25, 1910

Season	Team	GP	G	A	Pts.	PIM
30-31	Phil Q	1	0	0	0	0
34-35	Mont M	4	0	0	0	0
Totals		5	0	0	0	0

Season	Team	GP	G	A	Pts.	PIM
WEBSTER, Donald	*5-7 180 LW*					
B. Toronto, Ont., July 3, 1924						
43-44	Tor	27	7	6	13	28
Playoff Totals		5	0	0	0	12
WEBSTER, John Robert (Chick)						
5-10 160 C						
B. Toronto, Ont., Nov. 3, 1921						
49-50	NYR	14	0	0	0	4
WEBSTER, Thomas Ronald	*5-10 170 RW*					
B. Kirkland Lake, Ont., Oct. 4, 1948						
68-69	Bos	9	0	2	2	9
69-70	Bos	2	0	1	1	2
70-71	Det	78	30	37	67	40
71-72	Det-Cal	12	3	2	5	10
72-73	NE (WHA)	77	53	50	103	89
73-74	NE (WHA)	64	43	27	70	28
74-75	NE (WHA)	66	40	24	64	52
75-76	NE (WHA)	55	33	50	83	24
76-77	NE (WHA)	70	36	49	85	43
77-78	NE (WHA)	20	15	5	20	5
79-80	Det	1	0	0	0	0
NHL Totals		102	33	42	75	61
WHA Totals		352	220	205	425	241
NHL Playoff Totals		1	0	0	0	0
WHA Playoff Totals		43	28	26	54	19
WEIGHT, Doug	*5-11 185 C*					
B. Warren, Mich., Jan. 21, 1971						
90-91	NYR	0	0	0	0	0
91-92	NYR	53	8	22	30	23
Totals		53	8	22	30	23
Playoff Totals		8	2	2	4	0
WEILAND, Ralph C. (Cooney)	*5-7 150 C*					
B. Seaforth, Ont., Nov. 5, 1904						
28-29	Bos	40	11	7	18	16
29-30	Bos	44	43	30	73	27
30-31	Bos	44	25	13	38	14
31-32	Bos	47	14	12	26	20
32-33	Ott	48	16	11	27	4
33-34	Ott-Det	46	13	19	32	10
34-35	Det	48	13	25	38	10
35-36	Bos	48	14	13	27	15
36-37	Bos	48	6	9	15	6
37-38	Bos	48	11	12	23	16
38-39	Bos	47	7	9	16	9
Totals		508	173	160	333	147
Playoff Totals		45	12	10	22	12
WEINRICH, Eric	*6-1 210 D*					
B. Roanoke, Virg., Dec. 19, 1966						
88-89	NJ	2	0	0	0	0
89-90	NJ	19	2	7	9	11
90-91	NJ	76	4	34	38	48
91-92	NJ	76	7	25	32	55
Totals		173	13	66	79	114
Playoff Totals		20	2	7	9	27
WEIR, Stanley Brian	*6-1 180 C*					
B. Ponoka, Alta., Mar. 17, 1952						
72-73	Cal	78	15	24	39	16
73-74	Cal	58	9	7	16	10
74-75	Cal	80	18	27	45	12
75-76	Tor	64	19	32	51	22
76-77	Tor	65	11	19	30	14
77-78	Tor	30	12	5	17	4
78-79	Edm (WHA)	68	31	30	61	20
79-80	Edm	79	33	33	66	40
80-81	Edm	70	12	20	32	40
81-82	Edm-Col	61	5	16	21	23
82-83	Det	57	5	24	29	2
NHL Totals		642	139	207	346	183
WHA Totals		68	31	30	61	20
NHL Playoff Totals		37	6	5	11	4
WHA Playoff Totals		13	2	5	7	2
WEIR, Wally	*6-2 205 D*					
B. Verdun, Que., June 3, 1954						
76-77	Que (WHA)	69	3	17	20	197
77-78	Que (WHA)	13	0	0	0	47
78-79	Que (WHA)	68	2	7	9	166
79-80	Que	73	3	12	15	133
80-81	Que	54	6	8	14	77
81-82	Que	62	3	5	8	173
82-83	Que	58	5	11	16	135
83-84	Que	25	2	3	5	17
84-85	Hart-Pitt	48	2	6	8	90
NHL Totals		320	21	45	66	625
WHA Totals		150	5	24	29	410
NHL Playoff Totals		23	0	1	1	96
WHA Playoff Totals		32	2	8	10	67
WELLINGTON, Duke	*D*					
19-20	Que	1	0	0	0	0

Season	Team	GP	G	A	Pts.	PIM
WELLS, Gordon (Jay)	*6-1 210 D*					
B. Paris, Ont., May 18, 1959						
79-80	LA	43	0	0	0	113
80-81	LA	72	5	13	18	155
81-82	LA	60	1	8	9	145
82-83	LA	69	3	12	15	167
83-84	LA	69	3	18	21	141
84-85	LA	77	2	9	11	185
85-86	LA	79	11	31	42	226
86-87	LA	77	7	29	36	155
87-88	LA	58	2	23	25	159
88-89	Phil	67	2	19	21	184
89-90	Phil-Buf	60	3	17	20	129
90-91	Buf	43	1	2	3	86
91-92	Buf-NYR	52	2	9	11	181
Totals		826	42	190	232	2026
Playoff Totals		69	3	13	16	183
WENSINK, John	*6-0 200 LW*					
B. Cornwall, Ont., Apr. 1, 1953						
73-74	StL	3	0	0	0	0
76-77	Bos	23	4	6	10	32
77-78	Bos	80	16	20	36	181
78-79	Bos	76	28	18	46	106
79-80	Bos	69	9	11	20	110
80-81	Que	53	6	3	9	124
81-82	Col	57	5	3	8	152
82-83	NJ	42	2	7	9	135
Totals		403	70	68	138	840
Playoff Totals		43	2	6	8	86
WENTWORTH, Marvin (Cy)	*5-9 170 D*					
B. Grimsby, Ont., Jan. 24, 1905						
27-28	Chi	44	5	5	10	31
28-29	Chi	44	2	1	3	44
29-30	Chi	39	3	4	7	28
30-31	Chi	43	4	4	8	12
31-32	Chi	48	3	10	13	30
32-33	Mont M	47	4	10	14	48
33-34	Mont M	48	2	5	7	31
34-35	Mont M	48	4	9	13	28
35-36	Mont M	48	4	5	9	24
36-37	Mont M	44	3	4	7	29
37-38	Mont M	48	4	5	9	32
38-39	Mont	45	0	3	3	12
39-40	Mont	32	1	3	4	6
Totals		578	39	68	107	355
Playoff Totals		35	5	6	11	22
WESLEY, Glen	*6-1 195 D*					
B. Red Deer, ALta., Oct. 2, 1968						
87-88	Bos	79	7	30	37	69
88-89	Bos	77	19	35	54	61
89-90	Bos	78	9	27	36	48
90-91	Bos	80	11	32	43	78
91-92	Bos	78	9	37	46	54
Totals		392	55	161	216	310
Playoff Totals		88	12	29	41	97
WESLEY, Trevor (Blake)	*6-1 200 D*					
B. Red Deer, Alta., July 10, 1959						
79-80	Phil	2	0	1	1	2
80-81	Phil	50	3	7	10	107
81-82	Hart	78	9	18	27	123
82-83	Hart-Que	74	4	9	13	130
83-84	Que	46	2	8	10	75
84-85	Que	21	0	2	2	28
85-86	Tor	27	0	1	1	21
Totals		298	18	46	64	486
Playoff Totals		19	2	2	4	30
WESTFALL, Vernon Edwin (Ed)						
6-1 197 RW						
B. Belleville, Ont., Sept. 19, 1940						
61-62	Bos	63	2	9	11	53
62-63	Bos	48	1	11	12	34
63-64	Bos	55	1	5	6	35
64-65	Bos	68	12	15	27	65
65-66	Bos	59	9	21	30	42
66-67	Bos	70	12	24	36	26
67-68	Bos	73	14	22	36	38
68-69	Bos	70	18	24	42	22
69-70	Bos	72	14	22	36	28
70-71	Bos	78	25	34	59	48
71-72	Bos	78	18	26	44	19
72-73	NYI	67	15	31	46	25
73-74	NYI	68	19	23	42	28
74-75	NYI	73	22	33	55	28
75-76	NYI	80	25	31	56	27
76-77	NYI	79	14	33	47	8
77-78	NYI	71	5	19	24	14
78-79	NYI	55	5	11	16	4
Totals		1227	231	394	625	544
Playoff Totals		95	22	37	59	41

Season	Team	GP	G	A	Pts.	PIM
WHARRAM, Kenneth Malcolm						
5-9 165 RW						
B. Ferris, Ont., July 2, 1933						
51-52	Chi	1	0	0	0	0
53-54	Chi	29	1	7	8	8
55-56	Chi	3	0	0	0	0
58-59	Chi	66	10	9	19	14
59-60	Chi	59	14	11	25	16
60-61	Chi	64	16	29	45	12
61-62	Chi	62	14	23	37	29
62-63	Chi	55	20	18	38	17
63-64	Chi	70	39	32	71	18
64-65	Chi	68	24	20	44	27
65-66	Chi	69	26	17	43	28
66-67	Chi	70	31	34	65	21
67-68	Chi	74	27	42	69	18
68-69	Chi	76	30	39	69	19
Totals		766	252	281	533	227
Playoff Totals		80	16	27	43	38
WHARTON, Leonard (Len)	*F*					
B. Winnipeg, Man., Dec. 13, 1927						
44-45	NYR	1	0	0	0	0
WHEELDON, Simon	*5-11 170 C*					
B. Vancouver, B.C., Aug. 30, 1966						
87-88	NYR	5	0	1	1	4
88-89	NYR	6	0	1	1	2
90-91	Winn	4	0	0	0	4
Totals		15	0	2	2	10
WHELDON, Donald	*6-2 185 D*					
B. Falmouth, Mass., Dec. 28, 1954						
74-75	StL	2	0	0	0	0
WHELTON, William	*6-1 180 D*					
B. Everett, Mass., Aug. 28, 1959						
80-81	Winn	2	0	0	0	0
WHISTLE, Rob	*6-2 195 D*					
B. Thunder Bay, Ont., Apr. 4, 1961						
85-86	NYR	32	4	2	6	10
87-88	StL	19	3	3	6	6
Totals		51	7	5	12	16
Playoff Totals		4	0	0	0	2
WHITE, Anthony Raymond	*5-10 175 LW*					
B. Grand Falls, Nfld., June 16, 1954						
74-75	Wash	5	0	2	2	0
75-76	Wash	80	25	17	42	56
76-77	Wash	72	12	9	21	44
77-78	Wash	1	0	0	0	0
79-80	Minn	6	0	0	0	4
NHL Totals		164	37	28	65	104
WHA Playoff Totals		6	1	0	1	0
WHITE, Leonard Arthur (Moe)						
5-11 178 LW						
B. Verdun, Que., July 28, 1919						
45-46	Mont	4	0	1	1	2
WHITE, Sherman Beverly	*5-10 165 C*					
B. Amherst, N.S., May 12, 1923						
46-47	NYR	1	0	0	0	0
49-50	NYR	3	0	2	2	0
Totals		4	0	2	2	0
WHITE, Wilfred Belmont (Tex)						
5-11 155 F						
B. 1901						
25-26	Pitt Pi	35	7	1	8	22
26-27	Pitt Pi	43	5	4	9	21
27-28	Pitt Pi	44	5	1	6	54
28-29	Pitt Pi-NYA	43	5	5	10	26
29-30	Pitt Pi	29	8	1	9	16
30-31	Phil Q	9	3	0	3	2
Totals		203	33	12	45	141
Playoff Totals		4	0	0	0	2
WHITE, William Earl	*6-1 195 D*					
B. Toronto, Ont., Aug. 26, 1939						
67-68	LA	74	11	27	38	100
68-69	LA	75	5	28	33	38
69-70	LA-Chi	61	4	16	20	39
70-71	Chi	67	4	21	25	64
71-72	Chi	76	7	22	29	58
72-73	Chi	72	9	38	47	80
73-74	Chi	69	5	31	36	52
74-75	Chi	51	4	23	27	20
75-76	Chi	59	1	9	10	44
Totals		604	50	215	265	495
Playoff Totals		91	7	32	39	76

WHITELAW, Robert 5-11 185 D
B. Motherwell, Scotland, Oct. 5, 1916

Season Team	GP	G	A	Pts.	PIM
40-41 Det	23	0	2	2	2
41-42 Det	9	0	0	0	0
Totals	32	0	2	2	2
Playoff Totals	8	0	0	0	0

WHITLOCK, Robert Angus 5-10 175 C
B. Charlottetown, P.E.I., July 16, 1949

69-70 Minn	1	0	0	0	0
72-73 Chi (WHA)	75	23	28	51	53
73-74 Chi-LA (WHA)	66	20	29	49	48
74-75 Ind (WHA)	73	31	26	57	56
75-76 Ind (WHA)	30	7	15	22	16
NHL Totals	1	0	0	0	0
WHA Totals	244	81	98	179	173

WHITNEY, Ray 5-9 160 C
B. Edmonton, Alta., May 8, 1972

91-92 SJ	2	0	3	3	0

WHYTE, Sean 6-0 198 RW
B. Sudbury, Ont., May 4, 1970

91-92 LA	3	0	0	0	0

WICKENHEISER, Douglas Peter 6-1 200 C
B. Regina, SAsk., Mar. 30, 1961

80-81 Mont	41	7	8	15	20
81-82 Mont	56	12	23	35	43
82-83 Mont	78	25	30	55	49
83-84 Mont-StL	73	12	26	38	25
84-85 StL	68	23	20	43	36
85-86 StL	36	8	11	19	16
86-87 Stl	80	13	15	28	37
87-88 Van	80	7	19	26	36
88-89 NYR-Wash	17	3	5	8	4
89-90 Wash	27	1	8	9	20
Totals	556	111	165	276	286
Playoff Totals	41	4	7	11	18

WIDING, Juha Markku (Whitey) 6-1 190 C
B. Uleaborg, Finland, July 4, 1947

69-70 NYR-LA	48	7	9	16	12
70-71 LA	78	25	40	65	24
71-72 LA	78	27	28	55	26
72-73 LA	77	16	54	70	30
73-74 LA	71	27	30	57	26
74-75 LA	80	26	34	60	46
75-76 LA	67	7	15	22	26
76-77 LA-Clev	76	9	16	25	18
77-78 Edm (WHA)	71	18	24	42	8
NHL Totals	575	144	226	370	208
WHA Totals	71	18	24	42	8
NHL Playoff Totals	8	1	2	3	2
WHA Playoff Totals	5	0	1	1	0

WIEBE, Arthur Walter Ronald 5-10 180 D
B. Rosthern, Sask., Sept. 28, 1913

32-33 Chi	3	0	0	0	0
34-35 Chi	42	2	1	3	27
35-36 Chi	46	1	0	1	25
36-37 Chi	45	0	2	2	6
37-38 Chi	44	0	3	3	24
38-39 Chi	47	1	2	3	24
39-40 Chi	40	3	2	5	28
40-41 Chi	46	2	2	4	28
41-42 Chi	44	2	4	6	20
42-43 Chi	33	1	7	8	25
43-44 Chi	21	2	4	6	2
Totals	411	14	27	41	209
Playoff Totals	31	1	3	4	8

WIEMER, James Duncan 6-4 210 D
B. Sudbury, Ont., Jan. 9, 1961

83-84 Buf	64	5	15	20	48
84-85 Buf-NYR	32	7	5	12	34
85-86 NYR	7	3	0	3	2
87-88 Edm	12	1	2	3	15
88-89 LA	9	2	3	5	20
89-90 Bos	61	5	14	19	63
90-91 Bos	61	4	19	23	62
91-92 Bos	47	1	8	9	84
Totals	293	28	66	94	328
Playoff Totals	61	5	8	13	59

WILCOX, Archibald 187 D
B. Montreal, Que., May 9, 1903

29-30 Mont M	40	3	5	8	38
30-31 Mont M	40	2	2	4	42
31-32 Mont M	48	3	3	6	37
32-33 Mont M	47	0	3	3	37

WILCOX, Archibald (Continued)

33-34 Mont M-Bos	26	0	1	1	4
34-35 StL E	11	0	0	0	0
Totals	212	8	14	22	158
Playoff Totals	12	1	0	1	10

WILCOX, Barry Frederick 6-1 190 RW
B. New Westminster, B.C., Apr. 23, 1948

72-73 Van	31	3	2	5	15
74-75 Van	2	0	0	0	0
Totals	33	3	2	5	15

WILDER, Archibald 5-9 155 LW
B. Melville, Sask., Apr. 30, 1917

40-41 Det	18	0	2	2	2

WILEY, James Thomas 6-2 195 C
B. Sault Ste. Marie, Ont., Apr. 28, 1950

72-73 Pitt	4	0	1	1	0
73-74 Pitt	22	0	3	3	2
74-75 Van	1	0	0	0	0
75-76 Van	2	0	0	0	2
76-77 Van	34	4	6	10	4
Totals	63	4	10	14	8

WILKIE, Bob 6-2 200 D
B. Calgary, Alta., Feb. 11, 1969

90-91 Det	8	1	2	3	2

WILKINS, Barry James 5-11 190 D
B. Toronto, Ont., Feb. 28, 1947

66-67 Bos	1	0	0	0	0
68-69 Bos	1	0	1	1	0
69-70 Bos	6	0	0	0	2
70-71 Van	70	5	18	23	131
71-72 Van	45	2	5	7	65
72-73 Van	76	11	17	28	133
73-74 Van	78	3	28	31	123
74-75 Van-Pitt	66	5	30	35	103
75-76 Pitt	75	0	27	27	106
76-77 Edm(WHA)	51	4	24	28	75
77-78 Ind (WHA)	79	2	21	23	79
NHL Totals	418	27	125	152	663
WHA Totals	130	6	45	51	154
NHL Playoff Totals	6	0	1	1	4
WHA Playoff Totals	4	0	1	1	2

WILKINSON, John H. D

43-44 Bos	9	0	0	0	3

WILKINSON, Neil 6-3 190 D
B. Selkirk, Man., Oct. 16, 1967

89-90 Minn	36	0	5	5	100
90-91 Minn	50	2	9	11	117
91-92 SJ	60	4	15	19	97
Totals	146	6	29	35	314
Playoff Totals	29	3	5	8	23

WILKS, Brian 5-11 175 C
B. North York, Ont., Feb. 27, 1966

84-85 LA	2	0	0	0	0
85-86 LA	43	4	8	12	25
86-87 LA	1	0	0	0	0
88-89 LA	2	0	0	0	2
Totals	48	4	8	12	27

WILLARD, Rod Stephen 6-0 190 LW
B. New Liskeard, Ont., May 1, 1960

82-83 Tor	1	0	0	0	0

WILLIAMS, Burr 5-10 183 D
B. Okemah, Okla., Aug. 30, 1909

33-34 Det	1	0	1	1	12
34-35 StL E-Bos	16	0	0	0	12
36-37 Det	2	0	0	0	4
Totals	19	0	1	1	28
Playoff Totals	2	0	0	0	8

WILLIAMS, David 6-2 195 D
B. Plainfield, N.J., Aug. 25, 1967

91-92 SJ	56	3	25	28	40

WILLIAMS, David James (Tiger) 5-11 190 LW
B. Weyburn, Sask., Feb. 3, 1954

74-75 Tor	42	10	19	29	187
75-76 Tor	78	21	19	40	299
76-77 Tor	77	18	25	43	338
77-78 Tor	78	19	31	50	351
78-79 Tor	77	19	20	39	298
79-80 Tor-Van	78	30	23	53	278
80-81 Van	77	35	27	62	343
81-82 Van	77	17	21	38	341
82-83 Van	68	8	13	21	265
83-84 Van	67	15	16	31	294
84-85 Det-LA	67	7	11	18	201

WILLIAMS, David James (Tiger) (Continued)

85-86 LA	72	20	29	49	320
86-87 LA	76	16	18	34	358
87-88 LA-Hart	28	6	0	6	93
Totals	962	241	272	513	3966
Playoff Totals	83	12	23	35	455

WILLIAMS, Frederick Richard 5-11 178 C
B. Saskatoon, Sask., July 1, 1956

76-77 Det	44	2	5	7	10

WILLIAMS, Gordon James 5-11 190 RW
B. Saskatoon, Sask., Apr. 10, 1960

81-82 Phil	1	0	0	0	2
82-83 Phil	1	0	0	0	0
Totals	2	0	0	0	2

WILLIAMS, Sean 6-1 182 C
B. Oshawa, Ont., Jan. 28, 1968

91-92 Chi	2	0	0	0	4

WILLIAMS, Thomas Charles 6-0 187 LW
B. Windsor, Ont., Feb. 7, 1951

71-72 NYR	3	0	0	0	2
72-73 NYR	8	0	1	1	0
73-74 NYR-LA	60	12	19	31	10
74-75 LA	74	24	22	46	16
75-76 LA	70	19	20	39	14
76-77 LA	80	35	39	74	14
77-78 LA	58	15	22	37	9
78-79 LA	44	10	15	25	8
Totals	397	115	138	253	73
Playoff Totals	29	8	7	15	4

WILLIAMS, Thomas Mark 5-11 185 C
B. Duluth, Minn., Apr. 17, 1940

61-62 Bos	26	6	6	12	2
62-63 Bos	69	23	20	43	11
63-64 Bos	37	8	15	23	8
64-65 Bos	65	13	21	34	28
65-66 Bos	70	16	22	38	31
66-67 Bos	29	8	13	21	2
67-68 Bos	68	18	32	50	14
68-69 Bos	26	4	7	11	19
69-70 Minn	75	15	52	67	18
70-71 Minn-Cal	59	17	23	40	24
71-72 Cal	32	3	9	12	2
72-73 NE (WHA)	69	10	21	31	14
73-74 NE (WHA)	70	21	37	58	6
74-75 Wash	73	22	36	58	12
75-76 Wash	34	8	13	21	6
NHL Totals	663	161	269	430	177
WHA Totals	139	31	58	89	20
NHL Playoff Totals	10	2	5	7	2
WHA Playoff Totals	19	6	14	20	12

WILLIAMS, Warren Milton (Butch) 5-11 195 RW
B. Duluth, Minn., Sept. 11, 1952

73-74 StL	31	3	10	13	6
74-75 Cal	63	11	21	32	118
75-76 Cal	14	0	4	4	7
76-77 Edm (WHA)	29	3	10	13	16
NHL Totals	108	14	35	49	131
WHA Totals	29	3	10	13	16

WILLSON, Donald Arthur F
B. Chatham, Ont., Jan. 1, 1914

37-38 Mont	18	2	7	9	0
38-39 Mont	4	0	0	0	0
Totals	22	2	7	9	0
Playoff Totals	3	0	0	0	0

WILSON, Behn Bevan 6-3 210 D
B. Toronto, Ont., Dec. 19, 1958

78-79 Phil	80	13	36	49	197
79-80 Phil	61	9	25	34	212
80-81 Phil	77	16	47	63	237
81-82 Phil	59	13	23	36	135
82-83 Phil	62	8	24	32	92
83-84 Chi	59	10	22	32	143
84-85 Chi	76	10	23	33	185
85-86 Chi	69	13	37	50	113
87-88 Chi	58	6	23	29	166
Totals	601	98	260	358	1480
Playoff Totals	67	12	29	41	190

WILSON, Bertwin Hilliard (Bert) 6-0 190 LW
B. Orangeville, Ont., Oct. 17, 1949

73-74 NYR	5	1	1	2	2
74-75 NYR	61	5	1	6	66
75-76 StL-LA	58	2	3	5	64
76-77 LA	77	4	3	7	64

WILSON, Bertwin Hilliard (Bert) *(Continued)*

Season	Team	GP	G	A	Pts.	PIM
77-78	LA	79	7	16	23	127
78-79	LA	73	9	10	19	138
79-80	LA	75	4	3	7	91
80-81	Calg	50	5	7	12	94
Totals		478	37	44	81	646
Playoff Totals		22	0	2	2	42

WILSON, Carey *6-2 195 C*
B. Winnipeg, Man., May 19, 1962

Season	Team	GP	G	A	Pts.	PIM
83-84	Calg	15	2	5	7	2
84-85	Calg	74	24	48	72	27
85-86	Calg	76	29	29	58	24
86-87	Calg	80	20	36	56	42
87-88	Calg-Hart	70	27	41	68	40
88-89	Hart-NYR	75	32	45	77	59
89-90	NYR	41	9	17	26	57
90-91	Hart-Calg	57	11	18	29	18
91-92	Calg	42	11	12	23	37
Totals		530	165	251	416	306
Playoff Totals		52	11	13	24	14

WILSON, Carol (Cully) *RW*
B. 1893

Season	Team	GP	G	A	Pts.	PIM
19-20	Tor	23	21	5	26	79
20-21	Tor-Mont	17	8	2	10	16
21-22	Ham	23	7	9	16	21
22-23	Ham	23	16	3	19	46
26-27	Chi	39	8	4	12	40
Totals		125	60	23	83	202
Playoff Totals		2	1	0	1	6

WILSON, Douglas Jr. *6-1 187 D*
B. Ottawa, Ont., July 5, 1957

Season	Team	GP	G	A	Pts.	PIM
77-78	Chi	77	14	20	34	72
78-79	Chi	56	5	21	26	37
79-80	Chi	73	12	49	61	70
80-81	Chi	76	12	39	51	80
81-82	Chi	76	39	46	85	54
82-83	Chi	74	18	51	69	58
83-84	Chi	66	13	45	58	64
84-85	Chi	78	22	54	76	44
85-86	Chi	79	17	47	64	80
86-87	Chi	69	16	32	48	36
87-88	Chi	27	8	24	32	28
88-89	Chi	66	15	47	62	69
89-90	Chi	70	23	50	73	40
90-91	Chi	51	11	29	40	32
91-92	SJ	44	9	19	28	26
Totals		982	234	573	807	790
Playoff Totals		95	19	61	80	88

WILSON, Gordon Allan *6-1 185 LW*
B. Port Arthur, Ont., Aug. 13, 1932

Season	Team	GP	G	A	Pts.	PIM
54-55	Bos	0	0	0	0	0
Playoff Totals		2	0	0	0	0

WILSON, James (Hub) *5-10 180 LW*
B. Ottawa, Ont., May 13, 1909

Season	Team	GP	G	A	Pts.	PIM
31-32	NYA	2	0	0	0	0

WILSON, Jerold (Jerry) *6-2 200 F*
B. Edmonton, Alta., Apr. 10, 1937

Season	Team	GP	G	A	Pts.	PIM
56-57	Mont	3	0	0	0	2

WILSON, John Edward (Iron Man) *5-10 175 LW*
B. Kincardine, Ont., June 14, 1929

Season	Team	GP	G	A	Pts.	PIM
49-50	Det	1	0	0	0	0
51-52	Det	28	4	5	9	18
52-53	Det	70	23	19	42	22
53-54	Det	70	17	17	34	22
54-55	Det	70	12	15	27	14
55-56	Chi	70	24	9	33	12
56-57	Chi	70	18	30	48	24
57-58	Det	70	12	27	39	14
58-59	Det	70	11	17	28	18
59-60	Tor	70	15	16	31	8
60-61	Tor-NYR	59	14	13	27	24
61-62	NYR	40	11	3	14	14
Totals		688	161	171	332	190
Playoff Totals		66	14	13	27	11

WILSON, Lawrence *5-11 170 C*
B. Kincardine, Ont., Oct. 23, 1930

Season	Team	GP	G	A	Pts.	PIM
49-50	Det	1	0	0	0	2
51-52	Det	5	0	0	0	4
52-53	Det	15	0	4	4	6
53-54	Chi	66	9	33	42	22
54-55	Chi	63	12	11	23	39
55-56	Chi	2	0	0	0	2
Totals		152	21	48	69	75
Playoff Totals		4	0	0	0	0

WILSON, Mitch *5-8 199 RW*
B. Kelowna, B.C., Feb. 15, 1962

Season	Team	GP	G	A	Pts.	PIM
84-85	NJ	9	0	2	2	21
86-87	Pitt	17	2	1	3	83
Totals		26	2	3	5	104

WILSON, Murray Charles *6-1 185 LW*
B. Ottawa, Ont., Aug. 3, 1951

Season	Team	GP	G	A	Pts.	PIM
72-73	Mont	52	18	9	27	16
73-74	Mont	72	17	14	31	26
74-75	Mont	73	24	18	42	44
75-76	Mont	59	11	24	35	36
76-77	Mont	60	13	14	27	26
77-78	Mont	12	0	1	1	0
78-79	LA	58	11	15	26	14
Totals		386	94	95	189	162
Playoff Totals		53	5	14	19	32

WILSON, Richard Gordon (Rick) *6-1 195 D*
B. Prince Albert, Sask., Aug. 10, 1950

Season	Team	GP	G	A	Pts.	PIM
73-74	Mont	21	0	2	2	6
74-75	StL	76	2	5	7	83
75-76	StL	65	1	6	7	20
76-77	Det	77	3	13	16	56
Totals		239	6	26	32	165
Playoff Totals		3	0	0	0	0

WILSON, Richard William (Rik) *6-0 185 D*
B. Long Beach, Cal., June 17, 1962

Season	Team	GP	G	A	Pts.	PIM
81-82	StL	48	3	18	21	24
82-83	StL	56	3	11	14	50
83-84	StL	48	7	11	18	53
84-85	StL	51	8	16	24	39
85-86	StL-Calg	34	0	4	4	48
87-88	Chi	14	4	5	9	6
Totals		251	25	65	90	220
Playoff Totals		22	0	4	4	23

WILSON, Robert Wayne *5-9 178 D*
B. Sudbury, Ont., Feb. 18, 1934

Season	Team	GP	G	A	Pts.	PIM
53-54	Chi	1	0	0	0	0

WILSON, Roger Sidney *6-2 210 D*
B. Sudbury, Ont., Sept. 18, 1946

Season	Team	GP	G	A	Pts.	PIM
74-75	Chi	7	0	2	2	6

WILSON, Ronald Lawrence *5-10 170 D*
B. Windsor, Ont., May 28, 1955

Season	Team	GP	G	A	Pts.	PIM
77-78	Tor	13	2	1	3	0
78-79	Tor	46	5	12	17	4
79-80	Tor	5	0	2	2	2
84-85	Minn	13	4	8	12	2
85-86	Minn	11	1	3	4	8
86-87	Minn	65	12	29	41	36
87-88	Minn	24	2	12	14	16
Totals		177	26	67	93	68
Playoff Totals		20	4	13	17	8

WILSON, Ronald Lee *5-9 180 C*
B. Toronto, Ont., May 13, 1956

Season	Team	GP	G	A	Pts.	PIM
79-80	Winn	79	21	36	57	28
80-81	Winn	77	18	33	51	55
81-82	Winn	39	3	13	16	49
82-83	Winn	12	6	3	9	4
83-84	Winn	51	3	12	15	12
84-85	Winn	75	10	9	19	31
85-86	Winn	54	6	7	13	16
86-87	Winn	80	3	13	16	13
87-88	Winn	69	5	8	13	28
89-90	StL	33	3	17	20	23
90-91	StL	73	10	27	37	54
91-92	StL	64	12	17	29	46
Totals		708	100	195	295	359
Playoff Totals		48	10	12	22	52

WILSON, Wallace Lloyd *5-11 165 C*
B. Berwick, N.S., May 25, 1921

Season	Team	GP	G	A	Pts.	PIM
47-48	Bos	53	11	8	19	18
Playoff Totals		1	0	0	0	0

WING, Murray Allan *5-11 180 D*
B. Thunder Bay, Ont., Oct. 14, 1950

Season	Team	GP	G	A	Pts.	PIM
73-74	Det	1	0	1	1	0

WINNES, Christopher *6-0 170 RW*
B. Ridgefield, Conn., Feb. 12, 1968

Season	Team	GP	G	A	Pts.	PIM
90-91	Bos	0	0	0	0	0
91-92	Bos	24	1	3	4	6
Totals		24	1	3	4	6
Playoff Totals		1	0	0	0	0

WISEMAN, Edward Randall *5-7 160 RW*
B. Newcastle, N.B., Dec. 28, 1912

Season	Team	GP	G	A	Pts.	PIM
32-33	Det	47	8	8	16	16

WISEMAN, Edward Randall *(Continued)*

Season	Team	GP	G	A	Pts.	PIM
33-34	Det	47	5	9	14	13
34-35	Det	40	11	13	24	14
35-36	Det-NYA	43	12	15	27	16
36-37	NYA	43	14	19	33	12
37-38	NYA	48	18	14	32	32
38-39	NYA	45	12	21	33	8
39-40	NYA-Bos	49	7	19	26	8
40-41	Bos	47	16	24	40	10
41-42	Bos	45	12	22	34	8
Totals		454	115	164	279	137
Playoff Totals		45	10	10	20	16

WISTE, James Andrew *5-10 185 C*
B. Moose Jaw, Sask., Feb. 18, 1946

Season	Team	GP	G	A	Pts.	PIM
68-69	Chi	3	0	0	0	0
69-70	Chi	26	0	8	8	8
70-71	Van	23	1	2	3	0
72-73	Clev (WHA)	70	28	43	71	24
73-74	Clev (WHA)	76	23	35	58	26
74-75	Ind (WHA)	75	13	28	41	30
75-76	Ind (WHA)	7	0	2	2	0
NHL Totals		52	1	10	11	8
WHA Totals		228	64	108	172	80
WHA Playoff Totals		14	3	9	12	13

WITHERSPOON, James Douglas *6-3 205 D*
B. Toronto, Ont., Oct. 3, 1951

Season	Team	GP	G	A	Pts.	PIM
75-76	LA	2	0	0	0	2

WITIUK, Stephen *5-7 165 RW*
B. Winnipeg, Man., Jan. 8, 1929

Season	Team	GP	G	A	Pts.	PIM
51-52	Chi	33	3	8	11	14

WOIT, Benedict Francis (Benny) *5-11 190 D*
B. Fort William, Ont., Jan. 7, 1928

Season	Team	GP	G	A	Pts.	PIM
50-51	Det	2	0	0	0	0
51-52	Det	58	3	8	11	20
52-53	Det	70	1	5	6	40
53-54	Det	70	0	2	2	38
54-55	Det	62	2	3	5	22
55-56	Chi	63	1	8	9	46
56-57	Chi	9	0	0	0	2
Totals		334	7	26	33	168
Playoff Totals		41	2	6	8	18

WOJCIECHOWSKI, Stephen (Wochy) *5-8 160 RW*
B. Fort William, Ont., Dec. 25, 1922

Season	Team	GP	G	A	Pts.	PIM
44-45	Det	49	19	20	39	17
46-47	Det	5	0	0	0	0
Totals		54	19	20	39	17
Playoff Totals		6	0	1	1	0

WOLANIN, Craig *6-3 205 D*
B. Grosse Pointe, Mich., July 27, 1967

Season	Team	GP	G	A	Pts.	PIM
85-86	NJ	44	2	16	18	74
86-87	NJ	68	4	6	10	109
87-88	NJ	78	6	25	31	170
88-89	NJ	56	3	8	11	69
89-90	NJ-Que	50	1	10	11	57
90-91	Que	80	5	13	18	89
91-92	Que	69	2	11	13	80
Totals		445	23	89	112	648
Playoff Totals		18	2	5	7	51

WOLF, Bennett Martin *6-3 205 D*
B. Kitchener, Ont., Oct. 23, 1959

Season	Team	GP	G	A	Pts.	PIM
80-81	Pitt	24	0	1	1	94
81-82	Pitt	1	0	0	0	2
82-83	Pitt	5	0	0	0	37
Totals		30	0	1	1	133

WONG, Michael Anthony *6-3 205 C*
B. Minneapolis, Minn., Jan. 14, 1955

Season	Team	GP	G	A	Pts.	PIM
75-76	Det	22	1	1	2	12

WOOD, Randy *6-0 195 LW/C*
B. Princeton, N.J., Oct. 12, 1963

Season	Team	GP	G	A	Pts.	PIM
86-87	NYI	6	1	0	1	4
87-88	NYI	75	22	16	38	80
88-89	NYI	77	15	13	28	44
89-90	NYI	74	24	24	48	39
90-91	NYI	76	24	18	42	45
91-92	NYI-Buf	78	22	18	40	86
Totals		386	108	89	197	298
Playoff Totals		30	5	5	10	30

WOOD, Robert Owen *6-1 185 D*
B. Lethbridge, Alta., July 9, 1930

Season	Team	GP	G	A	Pts.	PIM
50-51	NYR	1	0	0	0	0

Season	Team	GP	G	A	Pts.	PIM
WOODLEY, Dan	*5-11 185 RW*					
B. Oklahoma City, Okla., Dec. 29, 1967						
87-88	Van	5	2	0	2	17
WOODS, Paul William	*5-10 170 LW*					
B. Hespeler, Ont., Apr. 12, 1955						
77-78	Det	80	19	23	42	52
78-79	Det	80	14	23	37	59
79-80	Det	79	6	20	26	24
80-81	Det	67	8	16	24	45
81-82	Det	75	10	17	27	48
82-83	Det	63	13	20	33	30
83-84	Det	57	2	5	7	18
Totals		501	72	124	196	276
Playoff Totals		7	0	5	5	4
WOOLLEY, Jason	*6-0 186 D*					
B. Toronto, Ont., July 27, 1969						
91-92	Wash	1	0	0	0	0
WOYTOWICH, Robert Ivan	*5-11 195 D*					
B. Winnipeg, Man., Aug. 18, 1941						
64-65	Bos	21	2	10	12	16
65-66	Bos	68	2	17	19	75
66-67	Bos	64	2	7	9	43
67-68	Minn	66	4	17	21	63
68-69	Pitt	71	9	20	29	62
69-70	Pitt	68	8	25	33	49
70-71	Pitt	78	4	22	26	30
71-72	Pitt-LA	67	1	8	9	14
72-73	Winn (WHA)	62	2	4	6	47
73-74	Winn (WHA)	72	6	28	34	43
74-75	Winn-Ind (WHA)	66	0	12	12	36
75-76	Ind (WHA)	42	1	7	8	14
NHL Totals		503	32	126	158	352
WHA Totals		242	9	51	60	140
NHL Playoff Totals		24	1	3	4	20
WHA Playoff Totals		18	1	1	2	4
WRIGHT, John Gilbert Brereton	*5-11 175 C*					
B. Toronto, Ont., Nov. 9, 1948						
72-73	Van	71	10	27	37	32
73-74	Van-StL	52	6	9	15	33
74-75	KC	4	0	0	0	2
Totals		127	16	36	52	67
WRIGHT, Keith Edward	*6-0 180 LW*					
B. Newmarket, Ont., Apr. 13, 1944						
67-68	Phil	1	0	0	0	0
WRIGHT, Larry Dale	*6-1 180 C*					
B. Regina, Sask., Oct. 8, 1951						
71-72	Phil	27	0	1	1	2
72-73	Phil	9	0	1	1	4
74-75	Cal	2	0	0	0	0
75-76	Phil	2	1	0	1	0
77-78	Det	66	3	6	9	13
Totals		106	4	8	12	19
WYCHERLEY, Ralph H. (Bus)	*6-0 185 LW*					
B. Saskatoon, Sask., Feb. 26, 1920						
40-41	NYA	26	4	5	9	4
41-42	Brk	2	0	2	2	2
Totals		28	4	7	11	6
WYLIE, Duane Steven	*5-8 170 C*					
B. Spokane, Wash., Nov. 10, 1950						
74-75	Chi	6	1	3	4	2
76-77	Chi	8	2	0	2	0
Totals		14	3	3	6	2
WYLIE, William Vance (Wiggie)	*5-8 145 C*					
B. Galt, Ont., July 15, 1928						
50-51	NYR	1	0	0	0	0
WYROZUB, William Randall (Randy)	*5-11 170 C*					
B. Lacombe, Alta., Apr. 8, 1950						
70-71	Buf	16	2	2	4	6
71-72	Buf	34	3	4	7	0
72-73	Buf	45	3	3	6	4
73-74	Buf	5	0	1	1	0
75-76	Ind (WHA)	55	11	14	25	8
NHL Totals		100	8	10	18	10
WHA Totals		55	11	14	25	8
YACKEL, Kenneth James	*F*					
B. St. Paul, Minn., Mar. 5, 1932						
58-59	Bos	6	0	0	0	2
Playoff Totals		2	0	0	0	0

Season	Team	GP	G	A	Pts.	PIM
YAKE, Terry	*5-11 185 C*					
B. New Westminster, B.C., Oct. 22, 1968						
88-89	Hart	2	0	0	0	0
89-90	Hart	2	0	1	1	0
90-91	Hart	19	1	4	5	10
91-92	Hart	15	1	1	2	4
Totals		38	2	6	8	14
Playoff Totals		6	1	1	2	16
YAREMCHUK, Gary	*6-0 185 C*					
B. Edmonton, Alta., Aug. 15, 1961						
81-82	Tor	18	0	3	3	10
82-83	Tor	3	0	0	0	2
83-84	Tor	1	0	0	0	0
84-85	Tor	12	1	1	2	16
Totals		34	1	4	5	28
YAREMCHUK, Ken	*5-11 185 C*					
B. Edmonton, Alta., Jan. 1, 1964						
83-84	Chi	47	6	7	13	19
84-85	Chi	63	10	16	26	16
85-86	Chi	78	14	20	34	43
86-87	Tor	20	3	8	11	16
87-88	Tor	16	2	5	7	10
88-89	Tor	11	1	0	1	2
Totals		235	36	56	92	106
Playoff Totals		31	6	8	14	49
YATES, Richard (Ross)	*6-0 180 C*					
B. Montreal, Que., June 18, 1959						
83-84	Hart	7	1	1	2	4
YAWNEY, Trent	*6-3 192 D*					
B. Hudson Bay, Sask., Sept. 29, 1965						
87-88	Chi	15	2	8	10	15
88-89	Chi	69	5	19	24	116
89-90	Chi	70	5	15	20	82
90-91	Chi	61	3	13	16	77
91-92	Calg	47	4	9	13	45
Totals		262	19	64	83	335
Playoff Totals		41	6	15	21	55
YOUNG, Brian Donald	*6-1 183 D*					
B. Jasper, Alta., Oct. 2, 1958						
80-81	Chi	8	0	2	2	6
YOUNG, Douglas G.	*5-9 190 D*					
B. Medicine Hat, Alta., Oct. 1, 1908						
31-32	Det	47	10	2	12	45
32-33	Det	48	5	6	11	59
33-34	Det	48	4	0	4	36
34-35	Det	48	4	6	10	37
35-36	Det	48	5	12	17	54
36-37	Det	10	0	0	0	6
37-38	Det	48	3	5	8	24
38-39	Det	44	1	5	6	16
39-40	Mont	47	3	9	12	22
40-41	Mont	3	0	0	0	4
Totals		391	35	45	80	303
Playoff Totals		28	1	5	6	16
YOUNG, Howard John Edward	*6-0 190 D*					
B. Toronto, Ont., Aug. 2, 1937						
60-61	Det	29	0	8	8	108
61-62	Det	30	2	2	2	67
62-63	Det	64	4	5	9	273
63-64	Chi	39	0	7	7	99
66-67	Det	44	3	14	17	100
67-68	Det	62	2	17	19	112
68-69	Chi	57	3	7	10	67
70-71	Van	11	0	2	2	25
74-75	Phoe-Winn (WHA)	72	16	22	38	86
76-77	Phoe (WHA)	26	1	3	4	23
NHL Totals		336	12	62	74	851
WHA Totals		98	17	25	42	109
NHL Playoff Totals		19	2	4	6	46
YOUNG, Scott	*6-0 190 RW*					
B. Clinton, Mass., Oct. 1, 1967						
87-88	Hart	7	0	0	0	2
88-89	Hart	76	19	40	59	27
89-90	Hart	80	24	40	64	47
90-91	Hart-Pitt	77	17	25	42	41
Totals		240	60	105	165	117
Playoff Totals		32	6	6	12	8
YOUNG, Timothy Michael	*6-1 190 C*					
B. Scarborough, Ont., Feb. 22, 1955						
75-76	Minn	63	18	33	51	71
76-77	Minn	80	29	66	95	58
77-78	Minn	78	23	35	58	64
78-79	Minn	73	24	32	56	46
79-80	Minn	77	31	43	74	24
80-81	Minn	74	25	41	66	40
81-82	Minn	49	10	31	41	67

Season	Team	GP	G	A	Pts.	PIM
YOUNG, Timothy Michael	*(Continued)*					
82-83	Minn	70	18	35	53	31
83-84	Winn	44	15	19	34	25
84-85	Phil	20	2	6	8	12
Totals		628	195	341	536	438
Playoff Totals		36	7	24	31	27
YOUNG, Warren Howard	*6-3 195 C*					
B. Toronto, Ont., Jan. 11, 1956						
81-82	Minn	1	0	0	0	0
82-83	Minn	4	1	1	2	0
83-84	Pitt	15	1	7	8	19
84-85	Pitt	80	40	32	72	174
85-86	Det	79	22	24	46	161
86-87	Pitt	50	8	13	21	103
87-88	Pitt	7	0	0	0	15
Totals		236	72	77	149	472
YOUNGHANS, Thomas	*5-11 RW*					
B. St. Paul, Minn., Jan. 22, 1953						
76-77	Minn	78	8	6	14	35
77-78	Minn	72	10	8	18	100
78-79	Minn	76	8	10	18	50
79-80	Minn	79	10	6	16	92
80-81	Minn	74	4	6	10	79
81-82	Minn-NYR	50	4	5	9	17
Totals		429	44	41	85	373
Playoff Totals		24	2	1	3	21
YSEBAERT, Paul	*6-1 190 C*					
B. Sarnia, Ont., May 15, 1966						
88-89	NJ	5	0	4	4	0
89-90	NJ	5	1	2	3	0
90-91	NJ-Det	62	19	21	40	22
91-92	Det	79	35	40	75	55
Totals		151	55	67	122	77
Playoff Totals		12	1	2	3	10
YZERMAN, Steve	*5-11 183 C*					
B. Cranbrook, B.C., May 9, 1965						
83-84	Det	80	39	48	87	33
84-85	Det	80	30	59	89	58
85-86	Det	51	14	28	42	16
86-87	Det	80	31	59	90	43
87-88	Det	64	50	52	102	44
88-89	Det	80	65	90	155	61
89-90	Det	79	62	65	127	79
90-91	Det	80	51	57	108	34
91-92	Det	79	45	58	103	64
Totals		673	387	516	903	432
Playoff Totals		50	22	33	55	34
ZABROSKI, Martin	*D*					
44-45	Chi	1	0	0	0	0
ZAHARKO, Miles	*6-0 197 D*					
B. Mannville, Alta., Apr. 30, 1957						
77-78	Atl	71	1	19	20	26
78-79	Chi	1	0	0	0	0
80-81	Chi	42	3	11	14	40
81-82	Chi	15	1	2	3	18
Totals		129	5	32	37	84
Playoff Totals		3	0	0	0	0
ZAINE, Rodney Carl (Zainer)	*5-10 180 C*					
B. Ottawa, Ont., May 18, 1946						
70-71	Pitt	37	8	5	13	21
71-72	Buf	24	2	1	3	4
72-73	Chi (WHA)	74	3	14	17	25
73-74	Chi (WHA)	78	5	13	18	17
74-75	Chi (WHA)	68	3	6	9	16
NHL Totals		61	10	6	16	25
WHA Totals		220	11	33	44	58
WHA Playoff Totals		18	2	1	3	2
ZALAPSKI, Zarley	*6-1 211 D*					
B. Edmonton, Alta., Apr. 22, 1968						
87-88	Pitt	15	3	8	11	7
88-89	Pitt	58	12	33	45	57
89-90	Pitt	51	6	25	31	37
90-91	Pitt-Hart	77	15	39	54	65
91-92	Hart	79	20	37	57	116
Totals		280	56	142	198	282
Playoff Totals		24	4	14	18	27
ZAMUNER, Rob	*6-2 202 C*					
B. Oakville, Ont., Sept. 17, 1969						
91-92	NYR	9	1	2	3	2
ZANUSSI, Joseph Lawrence	*5-10 180 D*					
B. Rossland, B.C., Sept. 25, 1947						
72-73	Winn (WHA)	73	4	21	25	53
73-74	Winn (WHA)	76	3	22	25	53
74-75	NYR	8	0	2	2	4

ZANUSSI, Joseph Lawrence *(Continued)*

Season	Team	GP	G	A	Pts.	PIM
75-76	Bos	60	1	7	8	30
76-77	Bos-StL	19	0	4	4	12
NHL Totals		87	1	13	14	46
WHA Totals		149	7	43	50	106
NHL Playoff Totals		4	0	1	1	2
WHA Playoff Totals		18	2	5	7	6

ZANUSSI, Ronald Kenneth *5-11 180 RW*
B. Toronto, Ont., Aug. 31, 1956

Season	Team	GP	G	A	Pts.	PIM
77-78	Minn	68	15	17	32	89
78-79	Minn	63	14	16	30	82
79-80	Minn	72	14	31	45	93
80-81	Minn-Tor	53	9	11	20	95
81-82	Tor	43	0	8	8	14
Totals		299	52	83	135	373
Playoff Totals		17	0	4	4	17

ZEIDEL, Lazarus (Larry) *5-11 185 D*
B. Montreal, Que., June 1, 1928

Season	Team	GP	G	A	Pts.	PIM
51-52	Det	19	1	0	1	14
52-53	Det	9	0	0	0	8
53-54	Chi	64	1	6	7	102
67-68	Phil	57	1	10	11	68
68-69	Phil	9	0	0	0	6
Totals		158	3	16	19	198
Playoff Totals		12	0	1	1	12

ZELEPUKIN, Valeri *5-11 180 RW*
B. Voskresensk, Soviet Union, Sept. 17, 1968

Season	Team	GP	G	A	Pts.	PIM
91-92	NJ	44	13	18	31	28
Playoff Totals		4	1	1	2	2

ZEMLAK, Richard Andrew *6-2 190 RW*
B. Wynard, Sask., Mar. 3, 1963

Season	Team	GP	G	A	Pts.	PIM
86-87	Que	20	0	2	2	47
87-88	Minn	54	1	4	5	307
88-89	Minn-Pitt	34	0	0	0	148
89-90	Pitt	19	1	5	6	43
91-92	Calg	5	0	1	1	42
Totals		132	2	12	14	587
Playoff Totals		1	0	0	0	10

ZENIUK, Edward William *5-11 180 D*
B. Landis, Sask., Mar. 8, 1933

Season	Team	GP	G	A	Pts.	PIM
54-55	Det	2	0	0	0	0

ZETTERSTROM, Lars *6-1 198 D*
B. Stockholm, Sweden, Nov. 6, 1953

Season	Team	GP	G	A	Pts.	PIM
78-79	Van	14	0	1	1	2

ZETTLER, Rob *6-3 190 D*
B. Sept Iles, Que., Mar. 8, 1968

Season	Team	GP	G	A	Pts.	PIM
88-89	Minn	2	0	0	0	0
89-90	Minn	31	0	8	8	45
90-91	Minn	47	1	4	5	119
91-92	SJ	74	1	8	9	103
Totals		154	2	20	22	267

ZEZEL, Peter *5-11 200 C*
B. Toronto, Ont., Apr. 22, 1965

Season	Team	GP	G	A	Pts.	PIM
84-85	Phil	65	15	46	61	26
85-86	Phil	79	17	37	54	76
86-87	Phil	71	33	39	72	71
87-88	Phil	69	22	35	57	42
88-89	Phil-StL	78	21	49	70	42
89-90	StL	73	25	47	72	30
90-91	Wash-Tor	52	21	19	40	14
91-92	Tor	64	16	33	49	26
Totals		551	170	305	475	327

ZEZEL, Peter *(Continued)*

Season	Team	GP	G	A	Pts.	PIM
Playoff Totals		78	17	34	51	57

ZOMBO, Richard *6-1 195 D*
B. Des Plaines, Ill., May 8, 1963

Season	Team	GP	G	A	Pts.	PIM
84-85	Det	1	0	0	0	0
85-86	Det	14	0	1	1	16
86-87	Det	44	1	4	5	59
87-88	Det	62	3	14	17	96
88-89	Det	75	1	20	21	106
89-90	Det	77	5	20	25	95
90-91	Det	77	4	19	23	55
91-92	Det-StL	67	3	15	18	61
Totals		417	17	93	110	488
Playoff Totals		48	1	10	11	102

ZUKE, Michael *6-0 180 C*
B. Sault Ste. Marie, Ont., Apr. 16, 1954

Season	Team	GP	G	A	Pts.	PIM
76-77	Ind (WHA)	15	3	4	7	2
77-78	Edm (WHA)	71	23	34	57	47
78-79	StL	34	9	17	26	18
79-80	StL	69	22	42	64	30
80-81	StL	74	24	44	68	57
81-82	StL	76	13	40	53	41
82-83	StL	43	8	16	24	14
83-84	Hart	75	6	23	29	36
84-85	Hart	67	4	12	16	12
85-86	Hart	17	0	2	2	12
NHL Totals		455	86	196	282	220
WHA Totals		86	26	38	64	49
NHL Playoff Totals		26	6	6	12	12
WHA Playoff Totals		5	2	3	5	0

ZUNICH, Ralph (Ruby) *D*
B. Calumet, Mich., Nov. 24, 1910

Season	Team	GP	G	A	Pts.	PIM
43-44	Det	2	0	0	0	2

GOALIES

Season	Team	GP	Min.	GA	SO.	Avg.
ABBOTT, George						
43-44	Bos	1	60	7	0	7.00
ADAMS, John Matthew		*6-0 200*				
B. Port Arthur, Ont., July 27, 1946						
72-73	Bos	14	780	39	1	3.00
74-75	Wash	8	400	46	0	6.90
Totals		22	1180	85	1	4.32
AIKEN, Donald						
B. Arlington, Mass., Jan. 1, 1932						
57-58	Mont	1	34	6	0	10.59
AITKENHEAD, Andrew						
B. Glasgow, Scotland, Mar. 6, 1904						
32-33	NYR	48	2970	107	3	2.23
33-34	NYR	48	2990	113	7	2.35
34-35	NYR	10	610	37	1	3.70
Totals		106	6570	257	11	2.35
Playoff Totals		10	608	15	3	1.48
ALMAS, Ralph Clayton (Red)		*5-9 160*				
B. Saskatoon, Sask., Apr. 26, 1924						
46-47	Det	1	60	5	0	5.00
50-51	Chi	1	60	5	0	5.00
52-53	Det	1	60	3	0	3.00
Totals		3	180	13	0	4.33
Playoff Totals		5	263	13	0	2.97
ANDERSON, Lawrence Lorne		*5-11 166*				
B. Renfrew, Ont., July 26, 1931						
51-52	NYR	3	180	18	0	6.00
ASTROM, Hardy		*6-0 170*				
B. Skelleftea, Sweden, Mar. 29, 1951						
77-78	NYR	4	240	14	0	3.50
79-80	Col	49	2574	161	0	3.75
80-81	Col	30	1642	103	0	3.76
Totals		83	4456	278	0	3.74
BAKER, Steven		*6-3 200*				
B. Boston, Mass., May 6, 1957						
79-80	NYR	27	1391	79	1	3.41
80-81	NYR	21	1260	73	2	3.48
81-82	NYR	6	328	33	0	6.04
82-83	NYR	3	102	5	0	2.94
Totals		57	3081	190	3	3.70
BANNERMAN, Murray		*5-11 184*				
B. Fort Francis, Ont., Apr. 27, 1957						
77-78	Van	1	20	0	0	0.00
80-81	Chi	15	865	62	0	4.30
81-82	Chi	29	1671	116	1	4.17
82-83	Chi	41	2460	127	4	3.10
83-84	Chi	56	3335	188	2	3.38
84-85	Chi	60	3371	215	0	3.83
85-86	Chi	48	2689	201	1	4.48
86-87	Chi	39	2059	142	0	4.14
Totals		289	16470	1051	8	3.83
Playoff Totals		40	2322	165	0	4.26
BARON, Marco Joseph		*5-11 179*				
B. Montreal, Que., Apr. 8, 1959						
79-80	Bos	1	40	2	0	3.00
80-81	Bos	10	507	24	0	2.84
81-82	Bos	44	2515	144	1	3.44
82-83	Bos	9	516	33	0	3.84
83-84	LA	21	1211	87	0	4.31
84-85	Edm	1	33	2	0	3.64
Totals		86	4822	292	1	3.63
Playoff Totals		1	20	3	0	9.00
BARRASSO, Thomas		*6-3 207*				
B. Boston, Mass., Mar. 31, 1965						
83-84	Buf	42	2475	117	2	2.84
84-85	Buf	54	3248	144	5	2.66
85-86	Buf	60	3561	214	2	3.61
86-87	Buf	46	2501	152	2	3.65

Season	Team	GP	Min.	GA	SO.	Avg.
BARRASSO, Thomas	*(Continued)*					
87-88	Buf	54	3133	173	2	3.31
88-89	Buf-Pitt	54	2951	207	0	4.21
89-90	Pitt	24	1294	101	0	4.68
90-91	Pitt	48	2754	165	1	3.59
91-92	Pitt	57	3329	196	1	3.53
Totals		439	25246	1469	15	3.49
Playoff Totals		64	3702	192	2	3.12
BASSEN, Henry (Hank)		*5-10 170*				
B. Calgary, Alta., Dec. 6, 1932						
54-55	Chi	21	1260	63	0	3.00
55-56	Chi	12	720	42	1	3.50
60-61	Det	35	2120	102	0	2.89
61-62	Det	27	1620	76	3	2.81
62-63	Det	17	980	53	0	3.24
63-64	Det	1	60	4	0	4.00
65-66	Det	11	406	17	0	2.51
66-67	Det	8	384	22	1	3.44
67-68	Pitt	25	1299	62	1	2.86
Totals		157	8849	441	6	2.99
Playoff Totals		5	274	11	0	2.41
BASTIEN, Aldege (Baz)		*5-7 160*				
B. Timmins, Ont., Aug. 29, 1920						
45-46	Tor	5	300	20	0	4.00
BAUMAN, Gary Glenwood		*5-11 175*				
B. Innisfail, Alta., July 21, 1940						
66-67	Mont	2	120	5	0	2.50
67-68	Minn	26	1294	75	0	3.48
68-69	Minn	7	304	22	0	4.34
Totals		35	1718	102	0	3.56
BEAUPRE, Donald William		*5-8 150*				
B. Waterloo, Ont., Sept. 19, 1961						
80-81	Minn	44	2585	138	0	3.20
81-82	Minn	29	1634	101	0	3.71
82-83	Minn	36	2011	120	0	3.58
83-84	Minn	33	1791	123	0	4.12
84-85	Minn	31	1770	109	1	3.69
85-86	Minn	52	3073	182	1	3.55
86-87	Minn	47	2622	174	1	3.98
87-88	Minn	43	2288	161	0	4.22
88-89	Minn-	12	637	31	1	2.92
	Wash					
89-90	Wash	48	2793	150	2	3.22
90-91	Wash	45	2572	113	5	2.64
91-92	Wash	54	3108	166	1	3.20
Totals		474	26884	1568	12	3.50
Playoff Totals		60	3375	188	2	3.34
BEAUREGARD, Stephane		*5-11 185*				
B. Cowansville, Que., Jan. 10, 1968						
89-90	Winn	19	1079	59	0	3.28
90-91	Winn	16	836	55	0	3.95
91-92	Winn	26	1267	61	2	2.89
Totals		61	3182	175	2	3.30
Playoff Totals		4	238	12	0	3.03
BEDARD, James Arthur		*5-10 181*				
B. Niagara Falls, Ont., Nov. 14, 1956						
77-78	Wash	43	2492	152	1	3.66
78-79	Wash	30	1740	126	0	4.34
Totals		73	4232	278	1	3.94
BEHREND, Marc		*6-1 180*				
B. Madison, Wisc., Jan 11, 1961						
83-84	Winn	6	351	32	0	5.47
84-85	Winn	23	1173	87	1	4.45
85-86	Winn	9	422	41	0	5.83
Totals		38	1946	160	1	4.93
Playoff Totals		7	312	19	0	3.65
BELANGER, Yves		*5-11 170*				
B. Baie Comeau, Que., Sept. 30, 1952						
74-75	StL	11	640	29	1	2.72
75-76	StL	31	1763	113	0	3.85
76-77	StL	3	140	7	0	3.00

Season	Team	GP	Min.	GA	SO.	Avg.
BELANGER, Yves	*(Continued)*					
77-78	StL-Atl	20	1081	70	1	3.89
78-79	Atl	5	182	21	0	6.92
79-80	Bos	8	328	19	0	3.48
Totals		78	4134	259	2	3.76
BELFOUR, Ed		*6-0 175*				
B. Carmen, Man., Apr. 21, 1965						
88-89	Chi	23	1148	74	0	3.87
89-90	Chi	0	0	0	0	0.00
90-91	Chi	74	4127	170	4	2.47
91-92	Chi	52	2928	132	5	2.70
Totals		149	8203	376	9	2.75
Playoff Totals		33	1722	79	1	2.75
BELHUMEUR, Michel		*5-10 160*				
B. Sorel, Que., Sept. 2, 1949						
72-73	Phil	23	1117	60	0	3.22
74-75	Wash	35	1812	162	0	5.36
75-76	Wash	7	377	32	0	5.09
Totals		65	3306	254	0	4.61
BELL, Gordon		*5-10 164*				
B. Portage La Prairie, Man., Mar. 13, 1925						
45-46	Tor	8	480	31	0	3.88
Playoff Totals		1	10	1	0	6.00
BENEDICT, Clinton Stephen (Benny)						
B. Ottawa, Ont., 1891						
17-18	Ott	22	1337	114	1	5.18
18-19	Ott	18	1113	53	2	2.94
19-20	Ott	24	1443	64	5	2.67
20-21	Ott	24	1457	75	2	3.13
21-22	Ott	24	1508	84	2	3.50
22-23	Ott	24	1486	54	4	2.25
23-24	Ott	22	1356	45	3	2.05
24-25	Mont M	30	1843	65	2	2.17
25-26	Mont M	36	2288	73	6	2.03
26-27	Mont M	43	2748	65	13	1.51
27-28	Mont M	44	2690	76	6	1.73
28-29	Mont M	37	2300	57	11	1.54
29-30	Mont M	14	752	38	0	2.71
Totals		362	22321	863	57	2.32
Playoff Totals		48	2907	87	15	1.80
BENNETT, Harvey A.		*6-0 175*				
B. Edington, Sask., July 23, 1925						
44-45	Bos	24	1470	106	0	4.33
BERGERON, Jean-Claude		*6-2 192*				
B. Hauterive, Que., Oct. 14, 1968						
90-91	Mont	18	941	59	0	3.76
BERNHARDT, Timothy John		*5-9 160*				
B. Sarnia, Ont., Jan. 17, 1958						
82-83	Calg	6	280	21	0	4.50
84-85	Tor	37	2182	136	0	3.74
85-86	Tor	23	1266	107	0	5.07
86-87	Tor	1	20	3	0	9.00
Totals		67	3748	267	0	4.27
BERTHIAUME, Daniel		*5-9 150*				
B. Longueuil, Que., Jan. 26, 1966						
86-87	Winn	31	1758	93	1	3.17
87-88	Winn	56	3010	176	2	3.51
88-89	Winn	9	443	44	0	5.96
89-90	Winn-	29	1627	100	1	3.69
	Minn					
90-91	LA	37	2119	117	1	3.31
91-92	LA-Bos	27	1378	87	0	3.79
Totals		189	10335	617	5	3.58
Playoff Totals		14	807	50	0	3.72
BESTER, Allan J.		*5-7 150*				
B. Hamilton, Ont., Mar. 26, 1964						
83-84	Tor	32	1848	134	0	4.35
84-85	Tor	15	767	54	1	4.22
85-86	Tor	1	20	2	0	6.00

BESTER, Allan J. *(Continued)*

Season	Team	GP	Min.	GA	So.	Avg.
86-87	Tor	36	1808	110	2	3.65
87-88	Tor	30	1607	102	2	3.81
88-89	Tor	43	2460	156	2	3.80
89-90	Tor	42	2506	165	0	4.49
90-91	Tor-Det	9	425	31	0	4.38
91-92	Det	1	31	2	0	3.87
Totals		209	11472	756	7	3.95
Playoff Totals		11	508	37	0	4.37

BEVERIDGE, William S. *5-8 170*
B. Ottawa, Ont., July 1, 1909

Season	Team	GP	Min.	GA	So.	Avg.
29-30	Det	39	2410	109	2	2.79
30-31	Ott	9	520	32	0	3.56
32-33	Ott	35	2195	95	5	2.71
33-34	Ott	48	3000	143	3	2.98
34-35	St L E	48	2990	144	3	3.00
35-36	Mont M	32	1970	71	1	2.22
36-37	Mont M	21	1290	47	1	2.24
37-38	Mont M	48	2980	149	2	3.10
42-43	NYR	17	1020	89	1	5.24
Totals		297	18375	879	18	2.87
Playoff Totals		5	300	11	0	2.20

BIBEAULT, Paul *5-9 160*
B. Montreal, Que., Apr. 13, 1919

Season	Team	GP	Min.	GA	So.	Avg.
40-41	Mont	4	210	15	0	4.29
41-42	Mont	38	2380	131	1	3.45
42-43	Mont	50	3010	191	1	3.81
43-44	Tor	29	1740	87	5	3.00
44-45	Bos	26	1530	113	0	4.43
45-46	Bos-Mont	26	1560	75	2	2.88
46-47	Chi	41	2460	170	1	4.15
Totals		214	12890	782	10	3.64
Playoff Totals		20	1237	71	2	3.44

BILLINGTON, Craig *5-10 170*
B. London, Ont., Sept. 11, 1966

Season	Team	GP	Min.	GA	So.	Avg.
85-86	NJ	18	901	77	0	5.13
86-87	NJ	22	1114	89	0	4.79
88-89	NJ	3	140	11	0	4.71
91-92	NJ	26	1363	69	2	3.04
Totals		69	3518	246	2	4.20

BINETTE, Andre *5-7 165*
B. Montreal, Que., Dec. 2, 1933

Season	Team	GP	Min.	GA	So.	Avg.
54-55	Mont	1	60	4	0	4.00

BINKLEY, Leslie John (Les) *6-0 175*
B. Owen Sound, Ont., June 6, 1936

Season	Team	GP	Min.	GA	So.	Avg.
67-68	Pitt	54	3141	151	6	2.88
68-69	Pitt	50	2885	158	0	3.29
69-70	Pitt	27	1477	79	3	3.21
70-71	Pitt	34	1870	89	2	2.86
71-72	Pitt	31	1673	98	0	3.51
72-73	Ott (WHA)	30	1709	106	0	3.72
73-74	Tor (WHA)	27	1412	77	1	3.27
74-75	Tor (WHA)	17	772	46	0	3.58
75-76	Tor (WHA)	7	335	32	0	5.73
NHL Totals		196	11046	575	11	3.12
WHA Totals		81	4228	261	1	3.70
NHL Playoff Totals		7	428	15	0	2.10
WHA Playoff Tot.		10	464	40	0	5.17

BITTNER, Richard J. *6-0 170*
B. New Haven, Conn., Jan. 12, 1922

Season	Team	GP	Min.	GA	So.	Avg.
49-50	Bos	1	60	3	0	3.00

BLAKE, Michael W. *6-0 185*
B. Kitchener, Ont., Apr. 6, 1956

Season	Team	GP	Min.	GA	So.	Avg.
81-82	LA	2	51	2	0	2.35
82-83	LA	9	432	30	0	4.17
83-84	LA	29	1634	118	0	4.33
Totals		40	2117	150	0	4.25

BOISVERT, Gilles *5-8 152*
B. Trois-Rivieres, Que., Feb. 15, 1933

Season	Team	GP	Min.	GA	So.	Avg.
59-60	Det	3	180	9	0	3.00

BOUCHARD, Daniel Hector *6-0 175*
B. Val d'Or, Que., Dec. 12, 1950

Season	Team	GP	Min.	GA	So.	Avg.
72-73	Atl	34	1944	100	2	3.09
73-74	Atl	46	2660	123	5	2.77
74-75	Atl	40	2400	111	3	2.78
75-76	Atl	47	2671	113	2	2.54
76-77	Atl	42	2378	139	1	3.51
77-78	Atl	58	3340	153	2	2.75
78-79	Atl	64	3624	201	3	3.33
79-80	Atl	53	3076	163	2	3.18
80-81	Calg-Que	43	2500	143	2	3.43
81-82	Que	60	3572	230	1	3.86
82-83	Que	50	2947	197	1	4.01
83-84	Que	57	3373	180	1	3.20

BOUCHARD, Daniel Hector *(Continued)*

Season	Team	GP	Min.	GA	So.	Avg.
84-85	Que	29	1738	101	0	3.49
85-86	Winn	32	1696	107	2	3.79
Totals		655	37919	2061	27	3.26
Playoff Totals		43	2549	147	1	3.46

BOURQUE, Claude Hennessey *5-6 140*
B. Oxford, N.S., Mar. 31, 1915

Season	Team	GP	Min.	GA	So.	Avg.
38-39	Mont	25	1560	69	2	2.76
39-40	Mont-Det	37	2270	123	3	3.25
Totals		62	3830	192	5	3.01
Playoff Totals		3	188	8	1	2.55

BOUTIN, Roland (Rollie) *5-9 179*
B. Westlock, Atla., Nov. 6, 1957

Season	Team	GP	Min.	GA	So.	Avg.
78-79	Wash	2	90	10	0	6.67
79-80	Wash	18	927	54	0	3.50
80-81	Wash	2	120	11	0	5.50
Totals		22	1137	75	0	3.96

BOUVRETTE, Lionel *5-9 165*
B. Hawsbury, Ont., June 10, 1914

Season	Team	GP	Min.	GA	So.	Avg.
42-43	NYR	1	60	6	0	6.00

BOWER, John William (China Wall)
5-11 189
B. Prince Albert, Sask., Nov. 8, 1924

Season	Team	GP	Min.	GA	So.	Avg.
53-54	NYR	70	4200	182	5	2.60
54-55	NYR	5	300	13	0	2.60
56-57	NYR	2	120	7	0	3.50
58-59	Tor	39	2340	107	3	2.74
59-60	Tor	66	3960	180	5	2.73
60-61	Tor	58	3480	145	2	2.50
61-62	Tor	59	3540	152	2	2.58
62-63	Tor	42	2520	110	1	2.62
63-64	Tor	51	3009	106	5	2.11
64-65	Tor	34	2040	81	3	2.38
65-66	Tor	35	1998	75	3	2.25
66-67	Tor	24	1431	63	2	2.64
67-68	Tor	43	2239	84	4	2.25
68-69	Tor	20	779	37	2	2.85
69-70	Tor	1	60	5	0	5.00
Totals		549	32016	1347	37	2.52
Playoff Totals		74	4350	184	5	2.54

BRANNIGAN, Andrew John *5-11 190*
B. Winnipeg, Man., Apr. 11, 1922

Season	Team	GP	Min.	GA	So.	Avg.
40-41	NYA	1	7	0	0	0.00

BRIMSEK, Francis Charles (Mr. Zero)
5-9 170
B. Eveleth, Minn., Sept. 26, 1915

Season	Team	GP	Min.	GA	So.	Avg.
38-39	Bos	43	2610	68	10	1.58
39-40	Bos	48	2950	98	6	2.04
40-41	Bos	48	3040	102	6	2.13
41-42	Bos	47	2930	115	3	2.45
42-43	Bos	50	3000	176	1	3.52
45-46	Bos	34	2040	111	2	3.26
46-47	Bos	60	3600	175	3	2.92
47-48	Bos	60	3600	168	3	2.80
48-49	Bos	54	3240	147	1	2.72
49-50	Chi	70	4200	244	5	3.49
Totals		514	31210	1404	40	2.70
Playoff Totals		68	4365	186	2	2.56

BRODA, Walter (Turk) *5-9 180*
B. Brandon, Man., May 15, 1914

Season	Team	GP	Min.	GA	So.	Avg.
36-37	Tor	45	2770	106	3	2.36
37-38	Tor	48	2980	127	6	2.65
38-39	Tor	48	2990	107	8	2.23
39-40	Tor	47	2900	108	4	2.30
40-41	Tor	48	2970	99	5	2.06
41-42	Tor	48	2960	136	6	2.83
42-43	Tor	50	300	159	1	3.18
45-46	Tor	15	900	53	0	3.53
46-47	Tor	60	3600	172	4	2.87
47-48	Tor	60	3600	143	5	2.38
48-49	Tor	60	3600	161	5	2.68
49-50	Tor	68	4040	167	9	2.48
50-51	Tor	31	1827	68	6	2.23
51-52	Tor	1	30	3	0	6.00
Totals		629	38167	1609	62	2.53
Playoff Totals		102	6406	211	13	1.98

BRODERICK, Kenneth Lorne *5-10 178*
B. Toronto, Ont., Feb. 16, 1942

Season	Team	GP	Min.	GA	So.	Avg.
69-70	Minn	7	360	26	0	4.33
73-74	Bos	5	300	16	0	3.20
74-75	Bos	15	804	32	1	2.39
76-77	Edm (WHA)	40	2301	134	4	3.49
77-78	Edm-Que (WHA)	33	1637	125	0	4.58
NHL Totals		27	1464	74	1	3.03
WHA Totals		73	3938	259	4	3.95
WHA Playoff Totals		5	227	12	0	3.17

BRODERICK, Len
B. Toronto, Ont., Oct. 11, 1930

Season	Team	GP	Min.	GA	So.	Avg.
57-58	Mont	1	60	2	0	2.00

BRODEUR, Martin *6-0 190*
B. Montreal, Que., May 6, 1972

Season	Team	GP	Min.	GA	So.	Avg.
91-92	NJ	4	179	10	0	3.35
Playoff Totals		1	32	3	0	5.63

BRODEUR, Richard *5-7 160*
B. Longeuil, Que., Sept. 15, 1952

Season	Team	GP	Min.	GA	So.	Avg.
72-73	Que (WHA)	24	1288	102	0	4.75
73-74	Que (WHA)	30	1607	89	1	3.32
74-75	Que (WHA)	51	2938	191	2	3.90
75-76	Que (WHA)	69	3967	244	2	3.69
76-77	Que (WHA)	53	2906	167	2	3.45
77-78	Que (WHA)	36	1962	121	0	3.70
78-79	Que (WHA)	42	2433	126	3	3.11
79-80	NYI	2	80	6	0	4.50
80-81	Van	52	3024	177	0	3.51
81-82	Van	52	3010	168	2	3.35
82-83	Van	58	3291	208	0	3.79
83-84	Van	36	2110	141	1	4.01
84-85	Van	51	2930	228	0	4.67
85-86	Van	64	3541	240	2	4.07
86-87	Van	53	2972	178	1	3.59
87-88	Van-Hart	17	1010	64	0	3.80
NHL Totals		385	21968	1410	6	3.85
WHA Totals		305	17101	1040	10	3.65
NHL Playoff Tot.		33	2009	111	1	3.32
WHA Playoff Tot.		51	2948	177	3	3.60

BROMLEY, Gart Bert *5-10 160*
B. Edmonton, Alta., Jan. 19, 1950

Season	Team	GP	Min.	GA	So.	Avg.
73-74	Buf	12	598	33	0	3.31
74-75	Buf	50	2787	144	4	3.10
75-76	Buf	1	60	7	0	7.00
76-77	Calg (WHA)	28	1237	79	0	3.83
77-78	Winn (WHA)	39	2252	124	1	3.30
78-79	Van	38	2144	136	2	3.81
79-80	Van	15	860	43	1	3.00
80-81	Van	20	978	62	0	3.80
NHL Totals		136	7427	425	7	3.43
WHA Totals		67	3489	203	1	3.49
NHL Playoff Totals		7	360	25	0	4.17
WHA Playoff Totals		5	268	7	0	1.57

BROOKS, Arthur

Season	Team	GP	Min.	GA	So.	Avg.
17-18	Tor	4	220	23	0	5.75

BROOKS, Donald Ross *5-8 173*
B. Toronto, Ont., Oct. 17, 1937

Season	Team	GP	Min.	GA	So.	Avg.
72-73	Bos	16	910	40	1	2.64
73-74	Bos	21	1170	46	3	2.36
74-75	Bos	17	967	48	0	2.98
Totals		54	3047	134	4	2.64

BROPHY, Frank

Season	Team	GP	Min.	GA	So.	Avg.
19-20	Que	21	1247	148	0	7.05

BROWN, Andrew Conrad (Andy) *6-0 185*
B. Hamilton, Ont., Feb. 15, 1944

Season	Team	GP	Min.	GA	So.	Avg.
71-72	Det	10	560	37	0	3.96
72-73	Det-Pitt	16	857	61	0	4.27
73-74	Pitt	36	1956	115	1	3.53
74-75	Ind (WHA)	52	2979	206	2	4.15
75-76	Ind (WHA)	24	1368	82	1	3.60
76-77	Ind (WHA)	10	430	26	0	3.63
NHL Totals		62	3373	213	1	3.79
WHA Totals		86	4777	314	3	3.94

BROWN, Kenneth Murray (Ken) *5-11 175*
B. Port Arthur, Ont., Feb. 15, 1944

Season	Team	GP	Min.	GA	So.	Avg.
70-71	Chi	1	18	1	0	3.33
72-73	Alb (WHA)	20	1034	63	1	3.66
74-75	Edm (WHA)	32	1466	85	2	3.48
NHL Totals		1	18	1	0	3.33
WHA Totals		52	2500	148	3	3.55

BRUNETTA, Mario *6-3 180*
B. Quebec City, Que., Jan. 25, 1967

Season	Team	GP	Min.	GA	So.	Avg.
87-88	Que	29	1550	96	0	3.72

BRUNETTA, Mario *(Continued)*

Season	Team	GP	Min.	GA	So.	Avg.
88-89	Que	5	226	19	0	5.04
89-90	Que	6	191	13	0	4.08
Totals		40	1967	128	0	3.90

BULLOCK, Bruce John *5-7 160*
B. Toronto, Ont., May 9, 1949

Season	Team	GP	Min.	GA	So.	Avg.
72-73	Van	14	840	67	0	4.79
74-75	Van	1	60	4	0	4.00
76-77	Van	1	27	3	0	6.67
Totals		16	927	74	0	4.79

BURKE, Sean *6-4 210*
B. Windsor, Ont., Jan. 29, 1967

Season	Team	GP	Min.	GA	So.	Avg.
87-88	NJ	13	689	35	1	3.05
88-89	NJ	62	3590	230	3	3.84
89-90	NJ	52	2914	175	0	3.60
90-91	NJ	35	1870	112	0	3.59
Totals		162	9063	552	4	3.65
Playoff Totals		19	1126	65	0	3.46

BUZINSKI, Stephen
B. Dunblane, Sask., Oct. 15, 1917

Season	Team	GP	Min.	GA	So.	Avg.
42-43	NYR	9	560	55	0	5.89

CALEY, Donald Thomas *5-10 165*
B. Dauphin, Man., Oct. 9, 1945

Season	Team	GP	Min.	GA	So.	Avg.
67-68	St L	1	30	3	0	6.00

CAPRICE, Frank *5-9 160*
B. Hamilton, Ont., May 2, 1962

Season	Team	GP	Min.	GA	So.	Avg.
82-83	Van	1	20	3	0	9.00
83-84	Van	19	1098	62	1	3.39
84-85	Van	28	1523	122	0	4.81
85-86	Van	7	308	28	0	5.46
86-87	Van	25	1390	89	0	3.84
87-88	Van	22	1250	87	0	4.18
Totals		102	5589	391	1	4.20

CARON, Jacques Joseph *6-2 185*
B. Noranda, Que., Apr. 21, 1940

Season	Team	GP	Min.	GA	So.	Avg.
67-68	LA	1	60	4	0	4.00
68-69	LA	3	140	9	0	3.86
71-72	St L	28	1619	68	1	2.52
72-73	St L	30	1562	92	1	3.53
73-74	Van	10	465	38	0	4.90
75-76	Clev (WHA)	2	130	8	1	3.69
76-77	Cin (WHA)	24	1292	61	3	2.83
NHL Totals		72	3846	211	2	3.29
WHA Totals		26	1422	69	4	2.91
NHL Playoff Totals		12	639	34	0	3.19
WHA Playoff Totals		1	14	3	0	12.86

CARTER, Lyle Dwight *6-1 185*
B. Truro, N.S., Apr. 29, 1945

Season	Team	GP	Min.	GA	So.	Avg.
71-72	Cal	15	721	50	0	4.16

CASEY, Jon *5-9 155*
B. Grand Rapids, Minn., Aug. 29, 1962

Season	Team	GP	Min.	GA	So.	Avg.
83-84	Minn	2	84	6	0	4.29
85-86	Minn	26	1402	91	0	3.89
87-88	Minn	14	663	41	0	3.71
88-89	Minn	55	2961	151	1	3.06
89-90	Minn	61	3407	183	3	3.22
90-91	Minn	55	3185	158	3	2.98
91-92	Minn	52	2911	165	2	3.40
Totals		265	14613	795	9	3.26
Playoff Totals		41	2268	120	2	3.17

CHABOT, Frederic *5-11 175*
B. Hebertville, Que., Feb. 12, 1968

Season	Team	GP	Min.	GA	So.	Avg.
90-91	Mont	3	108	6	0	3.33

CHABOT, Lorne (Chabotsky) *6-1 185*
B. Montreal, Que., Oct. 5, 1900

Season	Team	GP	Min.	GA	So.	Avg.
26-27	NYR	36	2307	56	10	1.56
27-28	NYR	44	2730	79	11	1.80
28-29	Tor	43	2458	67	12	1.56
29-30	Tor	42	2620	113	6	2.69
30-31	Tor	37	2300	80	6	2.16
31-32	Tor	44	2698	106	4	2.41
32-33	Tor	48	2948	111	5	2.31
33-34	Mont	47	2928	101	8	2.15
34-35	Chi	48	2940	88	8	1.83
35-36	Mont M	16	1010	35	2	2.19
36-37	NYA	6	370	25	1	4.17
Totals		411	25309	861	73	2.04
Playoff Totals		37	2558	64	5	1.50

CHADWICK, Edwin Walter *5-11 184*
B. Fergus, Ont., May 8, 1933

Season	Team	GP	Min.	GA	So.	Avg.
55-56	Tor	5	300	3	2	0.60
56-57	Tor	70	4200	192	5	2.74
57-58	Tor	70	4200	226	4	3.23
58-59	Tor	31	1800	93	3	3.10

CHADWICK, Edwin Walter *(Continued)*

Season	Team	GP	Min.	GA	So.	Avg.
59-60	Tor	4	240	15	0	3.75
61-62	Bos	4	240	22	0	5.50
Totals		184	10980	551	14	3.01

CHAMPOUX, Robert Joseph *5-10 175*
B. St. Hilaire, Que., Dec. 2, 1942

Season	Team	GP	Min.	GA	So.	Avg.
63-64	Det	0	0	0	0	0
73-74	Cal	17	923	80	0	5.20
Playoff Totals		1	40	4	0	6.00

CHEEVERS, Gerald Michael (Cheesey) *5-11 175*
B. St. Catharines, Ont., Dec. 7, 1940

Season	Team	GP	Min.	GA	So.	Avg.
61-62	Tor	2	120	7	0	3.50
65-66	Bos	7	340	34	3	6.00
66-67	Bos	22	1298	72	1	3.33
67-68	Bos	47	2646	125	3	2.83
68-69	Bos	52	3112	145	3	2.80
69-70	Bos	41	2384	108	4	2.72
70-71	Bos	40	2400	109	3	2.73
71-72	Bos	41	2420	101	2	2.50
72-73	Clev (WHA)	52	3144	149	5	2.84
73-74	Clev (WHA)	59	3562	180	4	3.03
74-75	Clev (WHA)	52	3076	167	4	3.26
75-76	Clev (WHA)	28	1570	95	1	3.63
75-76	Bos	15	900	41	1	2.73
76-77	Bos	45	2700	137	3	3.04
77-78	Bos	21	1086	48	1	2.65
78-79	Bos	43	2509	132	1	3.16
79-80	Bos	42	2479	116	4	2.81
NHL Totals		418	24394	1175	26	2.89
WHA Totals		191	11352	591	14	3.12
NHL Playoff Tot.		88	5396	242	7	2.69
WHA Playoff Tot.		19	1151	63	0	3.28

CHEVELDAE, Timothy *5-11 175*
B. Melville, Sask., Feb. 15, 1968

Season	Team	GP	Min.	GA	So.	Avg.
88-89	Det	2	122	9	0	4.43
89-90	Det	28	1600	101	0	3.79
90-91	Det	65	3615	214	2	3.55
91-92	Det	72	4236	226	2	3.20
Totals		167	9573	550	4	3.45
Playoff Totals		18	1017	49	2	2.89

CHEVRIER, Alain *5-8 180*
B. Cornwall, Ont., Apr. 23, 1961

Season	Team	GP	Min.	GA	So.	Avg.
85-86	NJ	37	1862	143	0	4.61
86-87	NJ	58	3153	227	0	4.32
87-88	NJ	45	2354	148	1	3.77
88-89	Winn-Chi	49	2665	170	1	3.83
89-90	Chi-Pitt	42	2060	146	0	4.25
90-91	Det	3	108	11	0	6.11
Totals		234	12202	845	2	4.16
Playoff Totals		16	1013	44	0	2.61

CLANCY, Francis Michael (King) *5-9 184*
B. Ottawa, Ont., Feb. 25, 1903

Season	Team	GP	Min.	GA	So.	Avg.
32-33	Tor	1	1	0	0	0.00

CLEGHORN, Ogilvie (Odie)
B. Montreal, Que.

Season	Team	GP	Min.	GA	So.	Avg.
25-26	Pitt Pi	1	60	2	0	2.00

CLOUTIER, Jacques *5-7 167*
B. Noranda, Que., Jan. 3, 1960

Season	Team	GP	Min.	GA	So.	Avg.
81-82	Buf	7	311	13	0	2.51
82-83	Buf	25	1390	81	0	3.50
84-85	Buf	1	65	4	0	3.69
85-86	Buf	15	872	49	1	3.37
86-87	Buf	40	2167	137	0	3.79
87-88	Buf	20	851	67	0	4.72
88-89	Buf	36	1786	108	0	3.63
89-90	Chi	43	2178	112	2	3.09
90-91	Chi-Que	25	1232	85	0	4.14
91-92	Que	26	1345	88	0	3.93
Totals		238	12197	744	3	3.66
Playoff Totals		8	413	18	1	2.62

COLVIN, Les *5-6 150*
B. Oshawa, Ont., Feb. 8, 1921

Season	Team	GP	Min.	GA	So.	Avg.
48-49	Bos	1	60	4	0	4.00

CONACHER, Charles William (The Bomber) *6-1 195*
B. Toronto, Ont., Dec. 20, 1910

Season	Team	GP	Min.	GA	So.	Avg.
32-33	Tor	1	2	0	0	0.00
34-35	Tor	1	3	0	0	0.00
38-39	Det	1	4	0	0	0.00
Totals		3	9	0	0	0.00

CONNELL, Alex (The Ottawa Fireman) *5-9 150*
B. Ottawa, Ont., Feb. 8, 1902

Season	Team	GP	Min.	GA	So.	Avg.
24-25	Ott	30	1852	66	7	2.20
25-26	Ott	36	2231	42	15	1.17
26-27	Ott	44	2782	69	13	1.57
27-28	Ott	44	2760	57	15	1.30
28-29	Ott	44	2820	67	7	1.52
29-30	Ott	44	2780	118	3	2.68
30-31	Ott	36	2190	110	3	3.06
31-32	Det	48	3050	108	6	2.25
32-33	Ott	15	845	36	1	2.57
33-34	NYA	1	40	2	0	3.00
34-35	Mont M	48	2970	92	9	1.92
36-37	Mont M	27	1710	63	2	2.33
Totals		417	26030	830	81	1.91
Playoff Totals		21	1309	26	4	1.19

CORSI, James *5-10 180*
B. Montreal, Que., June 19, 1954

Season	Team	GP	Min.	GA	So.	Avg.
77-78	Que (WHA)	23	1089	82	0	4.52
78-79	Que (WHA)	40	2291	126	3	3.30
79-80	Edm	26	1366	83	0	3.65
NHL Totals		26	1366	83	0	3.65
WHA Totals		63	3380	208	3	3.69

COURTEAU, Maurice Laurent *5-8 162*
B. Quebec City, Que., Feb. 18, 1920

Season	Team	GP	Min.	GA	So.	Avg.
43-44	Bos	6	360	33	0	5.50

COX, Abbie

Season	Team	GP	Min.	GA	So.	Avg.
29-30	Mont M	1	60	2	0	2.00
33-34	Det-NYA	3	133	8	0	3.61
35-36	Mont	1	70	1	0	0.86
Totals		5	263	11	0	2.51

CRAIG, James *6-1 190*
B. North Easton, Me., May 31, 1957

Season	Team	GP	Min.	GA	So.	Avg.
79-80	Atl	4	206	13	0	3.79
80-81	Bos	23	1272	78	0	3.68
83-84	Minn	3	110	9	0	4.92
Totals		30	1588	100	0	3.78

CRHA, Jiri *5-11 170*
B. Pardubice, Czechoslovakia, Apr. 13, 1950

Season	Team	GP	Min.	GA	So.	Avg.
79-80	Tor	15	830	50	0	3.61
80-81	Tor	54	3112	211	0	4.07
Totals		69	3942	261	0	3.97
Playoff Totals		5	186	21	0	6.77

CROZIER, Roger Allan *5-8 140*
B. Bracebridge, Ont., Mar. 16, 1942

Season	Team	GP	Min.	GA	So.	Avg.
63-64	Det	15	900	51	2	3.40
64-65	Det	70	4167	168	6	2.42
65-66	Det	64	3734	173	7	2.78
66-67	Det	58	3256	182	4	3.35
67-68	Det	34	1729	95	1	3.30
68-69	Det	38	1820	101	0	3.33
69-70	Det	34	1877	83	0	2.65
70-71	Buf	44	2198	135	1	3.69
71-72	Buf	63	3654	214	2	3.51
72-73	Buf	49	2633	121	3	2.76
73-74	Buf	12	615	39	0	3.80
74-75	Buf	23	1260	55	3	2.62
75-76	Buf	11	620	27	1	2.61
76-77	Wash	3	103	2	0	1.17
Totals		518	28566	1446	30	3.04
Playoff Totals		31	1769	82	1	2.78

CUDE, Wilfred *5-9 146*
B. Barrie, England, July 4, 1910

Season	Team	GP	Min.	GA	So.	Avg.
30-31	Phil Q	29	1750	127	1	4.38
31-32	Bos-Chi	3	161	15	1	5.59
33-34	Det-Mont	30	1920	47	5	1.47
34-35	Mont	48	2960	145	1	3.02
35-36	Mont	47	2940	122	6	2.60
36-37	Mont	44	2730	99	5	2.25
37-38	Mont	47	2990	126	3	2.68
38-39	Mont	23	1440	77	2	3.35
39-40	Mont	7	415	24	0	3.43
40-41	Mont	3	180	13	0	4.33
Totals		281	17486	795	24	2.73
Playoff Totals		19	1317	51	1	2.32

CUTTS, Donald Edward *6-3 190*
B. Edmonton, Alta., Feb. 24, 1953

Season	Team	GP	Min.	GA	So.	Avg.
79-80	Edm	6	269	16	0	3.57

CYR, Claude
B. Montreal, Que., Mar. 27, 1939

Season	Team	GP	Min.	GA	So.	Avg.
58-59	Mont	1	20	1	0	3.00

Season	Team	GP	Min.	GA	So.	Avg.
DADSWELL, Doug	*5-10 180*					
B. Scarborough, Ont., Feb. 7, 1964						
86-87	Calg	2	125	10	0	4.80
87-88	Calg.	25	1221	89	0	4.37
Totals		27	1346	99	0	4.41
DALEY, Thomas Joseph (Joe)	*5-10 160*					
B. Winnipeg, Man., Feb. 20, 1943						
68-69	Pitt	29	1615	87	2	3.23
69-70	Pitt	9	528	26	0	2.95
70-71	Buf	38	2073	128	1	3.70
71-72	Det	29	1620	85	0	3.15
72-73	Winn (WHA)	29	1718	83	2	2.90
73-74	Winn (WHA)	41	2454	163	0	3.99
74-75	Winn (WHA)	51	2902	175	1	3.62
75-76	Winn (WHA)	62	3612	171	5	2.84
76-77	Winn (WHA)	65	3818	206	3	3.24
77-78	Winn (WHA)	37	2075	114	1	3.30
78-79	Winn (WHA)	23	1256	90	0	4.30
NHL Totals		105	5836	326	3	3.35
WHA Totals		308	17835	1002	12	3.37
WHA Playoff Tot.		49	2706	149	2	3.30
DAMORE, Nicholas	*5-6 160*					
B. Niagara Falls, Ont., July 10, 1916						
41-42	Bos	1	60	3	0	3.00
D'AMOUR, Marc	*5-9 185*					
B. Sudbury, Ont., Apr. 29, 1961						
85-86	Calg	15	560	32	0	3.43
DASKALAKIS, Cleon	*5-9 175*					
B. Boston, Mass., Sept. 29, 1962						
84-85	Bos	8	289	24	0	4.98
85-86	Bos	2	120	10	0	5.00
86-87	Bos	2	97	7	0	4.33
Totals		12	506	41	0	4.86
DAVIDSON, John Arthur	*6-3 205*					
B. Ottawa, Ont., Feb. 27, 1953						
73-74	St L	39	2300	118	0	3.08
74-75	St L	40	2360	144	0	3.66
75-76	NYR	56	3207	212	3	3.97
76-77	NYR	39	2116	125	1	3.54
77-78	NYR	34	1848	98	1	3.18
78-79	NYR	39	2232	131	0	3.52
79-80	NYR	41	2306	122	0	3.17
80-81	NYR	10	560	48	0	5.14
81-82	NYR	1	60	1	0	1.00
82-83	NYR	2	120	5	0	2.50
Totals		301	17109	1004	7	3.52
Playoff Totals		31	1862	77	1	2.48
DECOURCY, Robert Phillip	*5-11 160*					
B. Toronto, Ont., June 12, 1927						
47-48	NYR	1	29	6	0	12.41
DEFELICE, Norman	*5-10 150*					
B. Schumacher, Ont., Jan. 19, 1933						
56-57	Bos	10	600	30	0	3.00
DeJORDY, Denis Emile	*5-9 185*					
B. St. Hyacinthe, Que., Nov. 12, 1938						
62-63	Chi	5	290	12	0	2.48
63-64	Chi	6	360	19	0	3.17
64-65	Chi	30	1760	74	3	2.52
66-67	Chi	44	2536	104	4	2.46
67-68	Chi	50	2838	128	4	2.71
68-69	Chi	53	2981	156	2	3.14
69-70	Chi-LA	31	1704	87	0	3.06
70-71	LA	60	3375	214	1	3.80
71-72	LA-Mont	12	623	48	0	4.62
72-73	Det	24	1331	83	1	3.74
73-74	Det	1	20	4	0	12.00
Totals		316	17818	929	15	3.13
Playoff Totals		18	946	55	0	3.49
DELGUIDICE, Matthew	*5-9 170*					
B. West Haven, Conn., Mar. 5, 1967						
90-91	Bos	1	10	0	0	0.00
91-92	Bos	10	424	28	0	3.96
Totals		11	434	28	0	3.87
DESJARDINS, Gerard Ferdinand	*5-11 190*					
B. Sudbury, Ont., July 22, 1944						
68-69	LA	60	3499	190	4	3.26
69-70	LA-Chi	47	2693	167	3	3.72
70-71	Chi	22	1217	49	0	2.42
71-72	Chi	6	360	21	0	3.50
72-73	NYI	44	2498	195	0	4.68
DESJARDINS, Gerard Ferdinand *(Continued)*						
73-74	NYI	36	1945	101	0	3.12
74-75	Balt (WHA)	41	2282	162	0	4.26
74-75	Buf	9	540	25	0	2.78
75-76	Buf	55	3280	161	2	2.95
76-77	Buf	49	2871	126	3	2.63
77-78	Buf	3	111	7	0	3.78
NHL Totals		331	19014	1042	12	3.29
WHA Totals		41	2282	162	0	4.26
NHL Playoff Totals		35	1874	108	0	3.46
DICKIE, William						
41-42	Chi	1	60	3	0	3.00
DION, Conrad	*5-4 140*					
B. St. Remi de Tingwick, Que., Aug. 11, 1918						
43-44	Det	26	1560	80	1	3.08
44-45	Det	12	720	39	0	3.25
Totals		38	2280	119	1	3.13
Playoff Totals		5	300	17	0	3.40
DION, Michel	*5-10 184*					
B. Granby, Que., Feb. 11, 1954						
74-75	Ind (WHA)	1	60	4	0	4.00
75-76	Ind (WHA)	31	1860	85	0	2.74
76-77	Ind (WHA)	42	2286	128	1	3.36
77-78	Cin (WHA)	45	2356	140	4	3.57
78-79	Cin (WHA)	30	1681	93	0	3.32
79-80	Que	50	2773	171	2	3.70
80-81	Que-Winn	26	1445	122	0	5.07
81-82	Pitt	62	3580	226	0	3.79
82-83	Pitt	49	2791	198	0	4.26
83-84	Pitt	30	1553	138	0	5.33
84-85	Pitt	10	553	43	0	4.67
NHL Totals		227	12695	898	2	4.24
WHA Totals		149	8243	450	5	3.28
NHL Playoff Totals		5	304	22	0	4.34
WHA Playoff Totals		7	371	22	0	3.56
DOLSON, Clarence (Dolly)						
28-29	Det	44	2750	63	10	1.43
29-30	Det	5	320	24	0	4.80
30-31	Det	44	2750	105	6	2.39
Totals		93	5820	192	16	1.98
Playoff Totals		2	120	7	0	3.50
DOWIE, Bruce	*5-10 170*					
B. Oakville, Ont., Dec. 9, 1962						
83-84	Tor	2	72	4	0	3.33
DRAPER, Thomas	*5-11 180*					
B. Outremont, Que., Nov. 20, 1966						
88-89	Winn	2	120	12	0	6.00
89-90	Winn	6	359	26	0	4.35
91-92	Buf	26	1403	75	1	3.21
Totals		34	1882	113	1	3.60
Playoff Totals		7	433	19	1	2.63
DRYDEN, David Murray	*6-2 180*					
B. Hamilton, Ont., Sept. 5, 1941						
61-62	NYR	1	40	3	0	4.50
65-66	Chi	11	453	23	0	3.05
67-68	Chi	27	1268	69	1	3.26
68-69	Chi	30	1479	79	3	3.20
70-71	Buf	10	409	23	1	3.37
71-72	Buf	20	1026	68	0	3.98
72-73	Buf	37	2018	89	3	2.65
73-74	Buf	53	2987	148	1	2.97
74-75	Chi (WHA)	45	2728	176	1	3.87
75-76	Edm (WHA)	62	3567	235	1	3.95
76-77	Edm (WHA)	24	1416	77	1	3.26
77-78	Edm (WHA)	48	2578	150	2	3.49
78-79	Edm (WHA)	63	3531	170	3	2.89
79-80	Edm	14	744	53	0	4.27
NHL Totals		203	10424	555	9	3.19
WHA Totals		242	13820	808	8	3.51
NHL Playoff Tot.		3	133	9	0	4.06
WHA Playoff Tot.		18	958	63	0	3.95
DRYDEN, Kenneth Wayne	*6-4 210*					
B. Hamilton, Ont., Aug. 8, 1947						
70-71	Mont	6	327	9	0	1.65
71-72	Mont	64	3800	142	8	2.24
72-73	Mont	54	3165	119	6	2.26
74-75	Mont	56	3320	149	4	2.69
DRYDEN, Kenneth Wayne *(Continued)*						
75-76	Mont	62	3580	121	8	2.03
76-77	Mont	56	3275	117	10	2.14
77-78	Mont	52	3071	105	5	2.05
78-79	Mont	47	2814	108	5	2.30
Totals		397	23352	870	46	2.24
Playoff Totals		112	6846	274	10	2.40
DUMAS, Michel	*5-9 180*					
B. St. Antoine-de-Pontbriand, Que., July 8, 1949						
74-75	Chi	3	121	7	0	3.47
76-77	Chi	5	241	17	0	4.23
Totals		8	362	24	0	3.98
Playoff Totals		1	19	1	0	3.16
DUPUIS, Robert						
79-80	Edm	1	60	4	0	4.00
DURNAN, William	*6-0 190*					
B. Toronto, Que., Jan. 22, 1916						
43-44	Mont	50	3000	109	2	2.18
44-45	Mont	50	3000	121	1	2.42
45-46	Mont	40	2400	104	4	2.60
46-47	Mont	60	3600	138	4	2.30
47-48	Mont	59	3505	162	5	2.77
48-49	Mont	60	3600	126	10	2.10
49-50	Mont	64	3840	141	8	2.20
Totals		383	22945	901	34	2.36
Playoff Totals		45	2851	99	2	2.08
DYCK, Edwin Paul	*5-11 160*					
B. Warman, Sask., Oct. 29, 1950						
71-72	Van	12	573	35	0	3.66
72-73	Van	25	1297	98	1	4.53
73-74	Van	12	583	45	0	4.63
74-75	Ind (WHA)	32	1692	123	0	4.36
NHL Totals		49	2453	178	1	4.35
WHA Totals		32	1692	123	0	4.36
EDWARDS, Donald Laurie	*5-9 160*					
B. Hamilton, Ont., Sept. 28, 1955						
76-77	Buf	25	1480	62	2	2.51
77-78	Buf	72	4209	185	5	2.64
78-79	Buf	54	3160	159	2	3.02
79-80	Buf	49	2920	125	2	2.57
80-81	Buf	45	2700	133	3	2.96
81-82	Buf	62	3500	205	0	3.51
82-83	Calg	39	2209	148	1	4.02
83-84	Calg	41	2303	157	0	4.09
84-85	Calg	34	1691	115	1	4.08
85-86	Tor	38	2009	160	0	4.78
Totals		459	26181	1449	16	3.32
Playoff Totals		42	2302	132	1	3.44
EDWARDS, Gary William						
B. Toronto, Ont., Oct. 5, 1947						
68-69	St L	1	4	0	0	0.00
69-70	St L	1	60	4	0	4.00
71-72	LA	44	2503	150	2	3.60
72-73	LA	27	1560	94	1	3.62
73-74	LA	18	929	50	1	3.23
74-75	LA	27	1561	61	3	2.34
75-76	LA	29	1740	103	0	3.55
76-77	LA-Clev	27	1500	107	2	4.28
77-78	Clev	30	1700	128	0	4.52
78-79	Minn	25	1337	83	0	3.72
79-80	Minn	26	1539	82	0	3.20
80-81	Edm	15	729	44	0	3.62
81-82	St L-Pitt	16	840	67	1	4.79
Totals		286	16002	973	10	3.65
Playoff Totals		11	537	34	0	3.80
EDWARDS, Marvin Wayne	*5-8 155*					
B. St. Catharines, Ont., Aug. 15, 1935						
68-69	Pitt	1	60	3	0	3.00
69-70	Tor	25	1420	77	1	3.25
72-73	Cal	21	1207	87	1	4.32
73-74	Cal	14	780	51	0	3.92
Totals		61	3467	218	2	3.77
EDWARDS, Roy Allen	*5-8 165*					
B. Seneca Township, Ont., Mar. 12, 1937						
67-68	Det	41	2177	127	0	3.50
68-69	Det	40	2099	89	4	2.54
69-70	Det	47	2683	116	2	2.59
70-71	Det	38	2104	119	0	3.39
71-72	Pitt	15	847	36	0	2.55
72-73	Det	52	3012	132	6	2.63
73-74	Det	4	187	18	0	5.78
Totals		236	13109	637	12	2.92
Playoff Totals		4	206	11	0	3.20
ELIOT, Darren	*6-1 175*					
B. Hamilton, Ont., Nov. 26, 1961						
84-85	LA	33	1882	137	0	4.37

Season	Team	GP	Min.	GA	So.	Avg.

ELIOT, Darren *(Continued)*

Season	Team	GP	Min.	GA	So.	Avg.
85-86	LA	27	1481	121	0	4.90
86-87	LA	24	1404	103	1	4.40
87-88	Det	3	97	9	0	5.57
88-89	Buf	2	67	7	0	6.27
Totals		89	4931	377	1	4.59
Playoff Totals		1	40	7	0	10.50

ELLACOTT, Kenneth   *5-8 160*
B. Paris, Ont., Mar. 3, 1959

Season	Team	GP	Min.	GA	So.	Avg.
82-83	Van	12	555	41	0	4.43

ERICKSON, Chad   *5-9 175*
B. Minneapolis, Minn., Aug. 21, 1970

Season	Team	GP	Min.	GA	So.	Avg.
91-92	NJ	2	120	9	0	4.50

ESPOSITO, Anthony James (Tony O)
5-11 185
B. Sault Ste. Marie, Ont., Apr. 23, 1943

Season	Team	GP	Min.	GA	So.	Avg.
68-69	Mont	13	746	34	2	2.73
69-70	Chi	63	3763	136	15	2.17
70-71	Chi	57	3325	126	6	2.27
71-72	Chi	48	2780	82	9	1.76
72-73	Chi	56	3340	140	4	2.51
73-74	Chi	70	4143	141	10	2.04
74-75	Chi	71	4219	193	6	2.74
75-76	Chi	68	4003	198	4	2.97
76-77	Chi	69	4067	234	2	3.45
77-78	Chi	64	3840	168	5	2.63
78-79	Chi	63	3780	206	4	3.27
79-80	Chi	69	4140	205	6	2.97
80-81	Chi	66	3935	246	0	3.75
81-82	Chi	52	3069	231	1	4.52
82-83	Chi	39	2340	135	1	3.46
83-84	Chi	18	1095	88	1	4.82
Totals		886	52585	2563	76	2.92
Playoff Totals		99	6017	308	6	3.07

ESSENSA, Robert   *6-0 160*
B. Toronto, Ont., Jan. 14, 1965

Season	Team	GP	Min.	GA	So.	Avg.
88-89	Winn	20	1102	68	1	3.70
89-90	Winn	36	2035	107	1	3.15
90-91	Winn	55	2916	153	4	3.15
91-92	Winn	46	2627	126	5	2.88
Totals		157	8680	454	11	3.14
Playoff Totals		5	239	15	0	3.77

EVANS, Claude   *5-8 165*
B. Longueuil, Que., Apr. 28, 1933

Season	Team	GP	Min.	GA	So.	Avg.
54-55	Mont	4	220	12	0	3.27
57-58	Bos	1	60	4	0	4.00
Totals		5	280	16	0	3.43

EXELBY, Randy   *5-9 170*
B. Toronto, Ont., Aug. 13, 1965

Season	Team	GP	Min.	GA	So.	Avg.
88-89	Mont	1	3	0	0	0.00
89-90	Edm	1	60	5	0	5.00
Totals		2	63	5	0	4.76

FARR, Norman Richard (Rocky)   *5-11 180*
B. Toronto, Ont., Apr. 7, 1947

Season	Team	GP	Min.	GA	So.	Avg.
72-73	Buf	1	29	3	0	6.21
73-74	Buf	11	480	25	0	3.13
74-75	Buf	7	213	14	0	3.94
Totals		19	722	42	0	3.49

FAVELL, Douglas Robert   *5-10 172*
B. St. Catharines, Ont., Apr. 5, 1945

Season	Team	GP	Min.	GA	So.	Avg.
67-68	Phil	37	2192	83	4	2.27
68-69	Phil	21	1195	71	1	3.56
69-70	Phil	15	820	43	1	3.15
70-71	Phil	44	2434	108	2	2.66
71-72	Phil	54	2993	140	5	2.81
72-73	Phil	44	2419	114	3	2.83
73-74	Tor	32	1752	79	0	2.71
74-75	Tor	39	2149	145	1	4.05
75-76	Tor	3	160	15	0	5.63
76-77	Col	30	1614	105	0	3.90
77-78	Col	47	2663	159	1	3.58
78-79	Col	7	380	34	0	5.37
Totals		373	20771	1096	18	3.17
Playoff Totals		21	1270	66	1	3.12

FISET, Stephane   *6-0 175*
B. Montreal, Que., June 17, 1970

Season	Team	GP	Min.	GA	So.	Avg.
89-90	Que	6	342	34	0	5.96
90-91	Que	3	186	12	0	3.87
91-92	Que	23	1133	71	1	3.76
Totals		32	1661	117	1	4.23

FITZPATRICK, Mark   *6-2 190*
B. Toronto, Ont., Nov. 13, 1968

Season	Team	GP	Min.	GA	So.	Avg.
88-89	LA-NYI	28	1584	105	0	3.98
89-90	NYI	47	2653	150	3	3.39

FITZPATRICK, Mark   *(Continued)*

Season	Team	GP	Min.	GA	So.	Avg.
90-91	NYI	2	120	6	0	3.00
91-92	NYI	30	1743	93	0	3.20
Totals		107	6100	354	3	3.48
Playoff Totals		4	152	13	0	5.13

FLAHERTY, Wade   *6-0 170*
B. Terrace. B.C., Jan. 11, 1968

Season	Team	GP	Min.	GA	So.	Avg.
91-92	SJ	3	178	13	0	4.38

FORBES, Vernon (Jake)   *5-6 140*
B. Toronto, Ont.

Season	Team	GP	Min.	GA	So.	Avg.
19-20	Tor	5	300	21	0	4.20
20-21	Tor	20	1221	78	0	3.90
22-23	Ham	24	1469	110	0	4.58
23-24	Ham	24	1483	68	1	2.83
24-25	Ham	30	1833	60	6	2.00
25-26	NYA	36	2241	86	2	2.39
26-27	NYA	44	2715	91	8	2.07
27-28	NYA	16	980	51	2	3.19
28-29	NYA	1	60	3	0	3.00
29-30	NYA	1	70	1	0	1.00
30-31	Phil Q	2	120	7	0	3.50
31-32	NYA	6	360	16	0	2.67
32-33	NYA	2	70	2	0	2.00
Totals		210	12922	594	19	2.76
Playoff Totals		2	120	7	0	3.50

FORD, Brian   *5-10 170*
B. Edmonton, Alta., Sept. 22, 1961

Season	Team	GP	Min.	GA	So.	Avg.
83-84	Que	3	123	13	0	6.34
84-85	Pitt	8	457	48	0	6.30
Totals		11	580	61	0	6.31

FOSTER, Norm   *5-9 175*
B. Vancouver, B.C., Feb. 10, 1965

Season	Team	GP	Min.	GA	So.	Avg.
90-91	Bos	3	184	14	0	4.57
91-92	Edm	10	439	20	0	2.73
Totals		13	623	34	0	3.27

FOWLER, Norman (Hec)

Season	Team	GP	Min.	GA	So.	Avg.
24-25	Bos	7	420	43	0	6.14

FRANCIS, Emile Percy (The Cat)   *5-6 145*
B. North Battleford, Sask., Sept. 13, 1926

Season	Team	GP	Min.	GA	So.	Avg.
46-47	Chi	19	1140	104	0	5.47
47-48	Chi	54	3240	183	1	3.39
48-49	NYR	2	120	4	0	2.00
49-50	NYR	1	60	8	0	8.00
50-51	NYR	5	260	14	0	3.23
51-52	NYR	14	840	42	0	3.00
Totals		95	5660	355	1	3.76

FRANKS, James Reginald   *5-11 156*
B. Melville, Sask., Nov. 8, 1914

Season	Team	GP	Min.	GA	So.	Avg.
37-38	Det	1	60	3	0	3.00
42-43	NYR	23	1380	103	0	4.48
43-44	Det-Bos	19	1140	79	1	4.16
Totals		43	2580	185	1	4.30
Playoff Totals		1	30	2	0	2.00

FREDERICK, Raymond   *6-0 154*
B. Fort Francis, Ont., July 31, 1929

Season	Team	GP	Min.	GA	So.	Avg.
54-55	Chi	5	300	22	0	4.40

FRIESEN, Kari   *6-0 185*
B. Winnipeg, Man., June 30, 1958

Season	Team	GP	Min.	GA	So.	Avg.
86-87	NJ	4	130	16	0	7.38

FROESE, Robert Glenn   *5-11 180*
B. St. Catharines, Que., June 30, 1958

Season	Team	GP	Min.	GA	So.	Avg.
82-83	Phil	25	1407	59	4	2.52
83-84	Phil	48	2863	150	2	3.14
84-85	Phil	17	923	37	1	2.41
85-86	Phil	51	2728	116	5	2.55
86-87	Phil-NYR	31	1654	100	0	3.63
87-88	NYR	25	1443	85	0	3.53
88-89	NYR	30	1621	102	1	3.78
89-90	NYR	15	812	45	0	3.33
Totals		242	13451	694	13	3.10
Playoff Totals		18	830	55	0	3.98

FUHR, Grant   *5-10 186*
B. Spruce Grove, Alta., Sept. 28, 1962

Season	Team	GP	Min.	GA	So.	Avg.
81-82	Edm	48	2847	157	0	3.31
82-83	Edm	32	1803	129	0	4.29
83-84	Edm	45	2625	171	1	3.91
84-85	Edm	46	2559	165	1	3.87
85-86	Edm	40	2184	143	0	3.93
86-87	Edm	44	2388	137	0	3.44
87-88	Edm	75	4304	246	4	3.43
88-89	Edm	59	3341	213	1	3.83
89-90	Edm	21	1081	70	1	3.89

FUHR, Grant   *(Continued)*

Season	Team	GP	Min.	GA	So.	Avg.
90-91	Edm	13	778	39	1	3.01
91-92	Tor	65	3774	230	2	3.66
Totals		488	27684	1700	11	3.68
Playoff Totals		111	6528	330	2	3.03

GAGNON, David   *6-0 185*
B. Windsor, Ont., Oct. 31, 1967

Season	Team	GP	Min.	GA	So.	Avg.
90-91	Det	2	35	6	0	10.29

GAMBLE, Bruce George   *5-9 200*
B. Port Arthur, Ont., May 24, 1938

Season	Team	GP	Min.	GA	So.	Avg.
58-59	NYR	2	120	6	0	3.00
60-61	Bos	52	3120	195	0	3.75
61-62	Bos	28	1680	123	1	4.39
65-66	Tor	10	501	21	4	2.51
66-67	Tor	23	1185	67	0	3.39
67-68	Tor	41	2201	85	5	2.31
68-69	Tor	61	3446	161	3	2.80
69-70	Tor	52	3057	156	5	3.06
70-71	Tor-Phil	34	1946	120	2	3.78
71-72	Phil	24	1186	58	2	2.93
Totals		327	18442	992	22	3.23
Playoff Totals		4	206	25	0	7.28

GAMBLE, Troy   *5-11 190*
B. New Glasgow, N.S., Apr. 7, 1967

Season	Team	GP	Min.	GA	So.	Avg.
86-87	Van	1	60	4	0	4.00
88-89	Van	5	302	12	0	2.38
90-91	Van	47	2433	140	1	3.45
91-92	Van	19	1009	73	0	4.34
Totals		72	3804	229	1	3.61
Playoff Totals		4	249	16	0	3.86

GARDINER, Charles Robert (Chuck)
B. Edinburgh, Scotland, Dec. 31, 1904

Season	Team	GP	Min.	GA	So.	Avg.
27-28	Chi	40	2420	114	3	2.85
28-29	Chi	44	2758	85	5	1.93
29-30	Chi	44	2750	111	3	2.52
30-31	Chi	44	2710	78	12	1.77
31-32	Chi	48	2989	92	4	1.92
32-33	Chi	48	3010	101	5	2.10
33-34	Chi	48	3050	83	10	1.73
Totals		316	19687	664	42	2.02
Playoff Totals		21	1532	35	5	1.37

GARDINER, Wilbert (Bert)   *5-11 160*
B. Saskatoon, Sask., Mar. 25, 1913

Season	Team	GP	Min.	GA	So.	Avg.
35-36	NYR	1	60	1	0	1.00
40-41	Mont	42	2600	119	1	2.83
41-42	Mont	10	620	42	0	4.20
42-43	Chi	50	3020	180	1	3.58
43-44	Bos	41	2460	212	1	5.17
Totals		144	8760	554	3	3.79
Playoff Totals		9	647	20	0	1.85

GARDNER, George Edward (Bud)
5-10 160
B. Lachine, Que., Oct. 8, 1942

Season	Team	GP	Min.	GA	So.	Avg.
65-66	Det	1	60	1	0	1.00
66-67	Det	11	560	36	0	3.86
67-68	Det	12	534	32	0	3.60
70-71	Van	18	922	52	0	3.38
71-72	Van	24	1237	86	0	4.17
72-73	LA (WHA)	49	2713	149	1	3.30
73-74	LA-Van (WHA)	30	1710	138	0	4.84
NHL Totals		66	3313	207	0	3.75
WHA Totals		79	4423	287	1	3.89
WHA Playoff Totals		3	116	11	0	5.69

GARRETT, John Murdock   *5-8 175*
B. Trenton, Ont., June 17, 1951

Season	Team	GP	Min.	GA	So.	Avg.
73-74	Minn (WHA)	40	2290	137	1	3.59
74-75	Minn (WHA)	58	3294	180	2	3.28
75-76	Minn-Tor (WHA)	61	3730	210	3	3.38
76-77	Birm (WHA)	65	3803	224	4	3.53
77-78	Birm (WHA)	58	3306	210	4	3.81
78-79	NE (WHA)	41	2496	149	2	3.58
79-80	Hart	52	3046	202	0	3.98
80-81	Hart	54	3152	241	0	4.59
81-82	Hart-Que	28	1618	125	0	4.64
82-83	Que-Van	34	1887	112	1	3.56
83-84	Van	29	1653	113	0	4.10
84-85	Van	10	407	44	0	6.49
NHL Totals		207	11763	837	1	4.27
WHA Totals		323	18919	1110	14	3.52
NHL Playoff Tot.		9	461	33	0	4.30
WHA Playoff Tot.		32	1816	124	1	4.10

Season	Team	GP	Min.	GA	So.	Avg.

GATHERUM, David L. *5-8 170*
B. Fort William, Ont., Mar. 28, 1932

Season	Team	GP	Min.	GA	So.	Avg.
53-54	Det	3	180	3	1	1.00

GAUTHIER, Paul *5-5 125*
B. Winnipeg, Man., Mar. 6, 1915

37-38	Mont	1	70	2	0	1.71

GELINEAU, John Edward (Jack) *6-0 180*
B. Toronto, Ont., Nov. 11, 1924

48-49	Bos	4	240	12	0	3.00
49-50	Bos	67	4020	220	3	3.28
50-51	Bos	70	4200	197	4	2.81
53-54	Chi	2	120	18	0	9.00
Totals		143	8580	447	7	3.13
Playoff Totals		4	260	7	1	1.62

GIACOMIN, Edward (Fast Eddie) *5-11 180*
B. Sudbury, Ont., June 6, 1939

65-66	NYR	36	2096	128	0	3.66
66-67	NYR	68	3981	173	9	2.61
67-68	NYR	66	3940	160	8	2.44
68-69	NYR	70	4114	175	7	2.55
69-70	NYR	70	4148	163	6	2.36
70-71	NYR	45	2641	95	8	2.16
71-72	NYR	44	2551	115	1	2.70
72-73	NYR	43	2580	125	4	2.91
73-74	NYR	56	3286	168	5	3.07
74-75	NYR	37	2069	120	1	3.48
75-76	NYR-Det	33	1980	119	2	3.61
76-77	Det	33	1791	107	3	3.58
77-78	Det	9	516	27	0	3.14
Totals		610	35693	1675	54	2.82
Playoff Totals		65	3834	180	1	2.82

GILBERT, Gilles Joseph *6-1 175*
B. St. Esprit, Que., Mar. 31, 1949

69-70	Minn	1	60	6	0	6.00
70-71	Minn	17	931	59	0	3.80
71-72	Minn	4	218	11	0	3.03
72-73	Minn	22	1320	67	2	3.05
73-74	Bos	54	3210	158	6	2.95
74-75	Bos	53	3029	158	3	3.13
75-76	Bos	55	3123	151	3	2.90
76-77	Bos	34	2040	97	1	2.85
77-78	Bos	25	1326	56	2	2.53
78-79	Bos	23	1254	74	0	3.54
79-80	Bos	33	1933	88	1	2.73
80-81	Det	48	2618	175	0	4.01
81-82	Det	27	1478	105	0	4.26
82-83	Det	20	1137	85	0	4.49
Totals		416	23677	1290	18	3.27
Playoff Totals		22	1919	97	3	3.03

GILL, Andre *5-7 145*
B. Sorel, Que., Sept. 19, 1941

67-68	Bos	5	270	13	1	2.89
72-73	Chi (WHA)	33	1709	118	0	4.14
73-74	Chi (WHA)	13	803	46	0	3.44
NHL Totals		5	270	13	1	2.89
WHA Totals		46	2512	164	0	3.92
WHA Playoff Tot.		11	614	38	0	3.71

GOODMAN, Paul *5-9 165*
B. Selkirk, Man., Nov. 4, 1908

39-40	Chi	31	1920	62	4	1.94
40-41	Chi	21	1320	55	2	2.50
Totals		52	3240	117	6	2.17
Playoff Totals		3	187	10	0	3.21

GORDON, Scott *5-10 175*
B. Brockton, Mass., Feb. 6, 1963

89-90	Que	10	597	53	0	5.33
90-91	Que	13	485	48	0	5.94
Totals		23	1082	101	0	5.60

GOSSELIN, Mario *5-8 165*
B. Thetford Mines, Que., June 15, 1963

83-84	Que	3	148	3	1	1.21
84-85	Que	35	1960	109	1	3.34
85-86	Que	31	1726	111	2	3.86
86-87	Que	30	1625	86	0	3.18
87-88	Que	54	3002	189	2	3.78
88-89	Que	39	2064	146	0	4.24
89-90	LA	26	1226	79	0	3.87
Totals		218	11751	723	6	3.81
Playoff Totals		32	1815	99	0	3.27

GOVERDE, David *6-1 205*
B. Toronto, Ont., Apr. 9, 1970

91-92	LA	2	120	9	0	4.50

GRAHAME, Ronald Ian *5-11 175*
B. Victoria, B.C., June 7, 1950

73-74	Hou (WHA)	4	250	5	1	1.20
74-75	Hou (WHA)	43	2590	131	4	3.03
75-76	Hou (WHA)	57	3343	182	3	3.27
76-77	Hou (WHA)	39	2345	107	4	2.74
77-78	Bos	40	2328	107	3	2.76
78-79	LA	34	1940	136	0	4.21
79-80	LA	26	1405	98	2	4.19
80-81	LA-Que	14	799	68	0	5.11
NHL Totals		114	6472	409	5	3.79
WHA Totals		143	8528	425	12	2.99
NHL Playoff Tot.		4	202	7	0	2.08
WHA Playoff Tot.		36	2158	116	4	3.23

GRANT, Benjamin Cameron *5-11 160*
B. Owen Sound, Ont., July 14, 1908

28-29	Tor	3	110	4	0	1.33
29-30	Tor-NYA	9	550	36	0	3.93
30-31	Tor	7	430	19	2	2.71
31-32	Tor	5	320	18	1	3.60
33-34	NYA	5	320	18	1	3.60
43-44	Tor-Bos	21	1260	93	0	4.43
Totals		50	2990	188	4	3.77

GRANT, Doug Munro *6-1 200*
B. Corner Brook, Nfld., July 27, 1948

73-74	Det	37	2018	140	1	4.16
74-75	Det	7	380	34	0	5.37
75-76	Det	2	120	8	0	4.00
76-77	StL	17	960	50	1	3.13
77-78	StL	9	500	24	0	2.88
78-79	StL	4	190	23	0	7.26
79-80	StL	1	31	1	0	1.94
Totals		77	4199	280	2	4.00

GRATTON, Gilles *5-11 160*
B. La Salle, Que., July 28, 1952

72-73	Ott (WHA)	51	3021	187	0	3.71
73-74	Tor (WHA)	57	3200	188	2	3.53
74-75	Tor (WHA)	53	2881	185	2	3.85
75-76	StL	6	265	11	0	2.49
76-77	NYR	41	2034	143	0	4.22
NHL Totals		47	2299	154	0	4.02
WHA Totals		161	9102	560	4	3.69
WHA Playoff Tot.		13	662	37	0	3.35

GRAY, Gerald Robert (Gerry) *6-0 168*
B. Brantford, Ont., Jan. 28, 1948

70-71	Det	7	380	30	0	4.74
72-73	NYI	1	60	5	0	5.00
Totals		8	440	35	0	4.77

GRAY, Harrison Leroy *5-11 165*
B. Calgary, Alta., Sept. 5, 1941

63-64	Det	1	40	5	0	7.50

GREENLAY, Michael *6-3 200*
B. Vitoria, Brazil, Sept. 15, 1968

89-90	Edm	2	20	4	0	12.00

GUENETTE, Steve *5-10 175*
B. Gloucester, Ont., Nov. 13, 1965

86-87	Pitt	2	113	8	0	4.25
87-88	Pitt	19	1092	61	1	3.35
88-89	Pitt	11	574	41	0	4.29
89-90	Calg	2	119	8	0	4.03
90-91	Calg	1	60	4	0	4.00
Totals		35	1958	122	1	3.74

HACKETT, Jeff *6-1 175*
B. London, Ont., June 1, 1968

88-89	NYI	13	662	39	0	3.53
90-91	NYI	30	1508	91	0	3.62
91-92	SJ	42	2314	148	0	3.84
Totals		85	4484	278	0	3.72

HAINSWORTH, George *5-6 150*
B. Toronto, Ont., June 26, 1895

26-27	Mont	44	2732	67	14	1.52
27-28	Mont	44	2730	48	13	1.09
28-29	Mont	44	2800	43	22	0.98
29-30	Mont	42	3008	108	4	2.57
30-31	Mont	44	2740	89	8	2.02
31-32	Mont	48	2998	110	6	2.29
32-33	Mont	48	2980	115	8	2.40
33-34	Tor	48	3010	119	3	2.48
34-35	Tor	48	2957	111	8	2.31

HAINSWORTH, George *(Continued)*

35-36	Tor	48	3000	106	8	2.21
36-37	Tor-Mont	7	460	21	0	2.74
Totals		465	29415	937	94	1.91
Playoff Totals		52	3486	112	8	1.93

HALL, Glenn Henry (Mr. Goalie) *6-0 160*
B. Humboldt, Sask., Oct. 3, 1931

52-53	Det	6	360	10	1	1.67
54-55	Det	2	120	2	0	1.00
55-56	Det	70	4200	148	12	2.11
56-57	Det	70	4200	157	4	2.24
57-58	Chi	70	4200	202	7	2.89
58-59	Chi	70	4200	208	1	2.97
59-60	Chi	70	4200	180	6	2.57
60-61	Chi	70	4200	180	6	2.57
61-62	Chi	70	4200	186	9	2.66
62-63	Chi	66	3910	166	5	2.55
63-64	Chi	65	3840	148	7	2.31
64-65	Chi	41	2440	99	4	2.43
65-66	Chi	64	3747	164	4	2.63
66-67	Chi	32	1664	66	2	2.38
67-68	StL	49	2858	118	5	2.48
68-69	StL	41	2354	85	8	2.17
69-70	StL	18	1010	49	1	2.91
70-71	StL	32	1761	71	2	2.42
Totals		906	53464	2239	84	2.51
Playoff Totals		115	6899	321	6	2.79

HAMEL, Pierre *5-9 170*
B. Montreal, Que., Sept. 16, 1952

74-75	Tor	4	195	18	0	5.54
78-79	Tor	1	1	0	0	0.00
79-80	Winn	35	1947	130	0	4.01
80-81	Winn	29	1623	128	0	4.73
Totals		69	3766	276	0	4.40

HANLON, Glen *6-0 185*
B. Brandon, Man., Feb. 20, 1957

77-78	Van	4	200	9	0	2.70
78-79	Van	31	1821	94	3	3.10
79-80	Van	57	3341	193	0	3.47
80-81	Van	17	798	59	1	4.44
81-82	Van-StL	30	1686	114	1	4.06
82-83	StL-NYR	35	1844	117	0	3.81
83-84	NYR	50	2837	166	1	3.51
84-85	NYR	44	2510	175	0	4.18
85-86	NYR	23	1170	65	0	3.33
86-87	Det	36	1963	104	1	3.18
87-88	Det	47	2623	141	4	3.23
88-89	Det	39	2092	124	1	3.56
89-90	Det	45	2290	154	1	4.03
90-91	Det	19	862	46	0	3.20
Totals		477	26037	1561	13	3.60
Playoff Totals		35	1756	92	4	3.14

HARRISON, Paul Douglas *6-1 175*
B. Timmons, Ont., Feb. 11, 1955

75-76	Minn	6	307	28	0	5.47
76-77	Minn	2	120	11	0	5.50
77-78	Minn	27	1555	99	1	3.82
78-79	Tor	25	1403	82	1	3.51
79-80	Tor	30	1492	110	0	4.42
81-82	Pitt-Buf	19	929	78	0	5.04
Totals		109	5806	408	2	4.22
Playoff Totals		4	157	9	0	3.44

HASEK, Dominik *6-0 175*
B. Pardubice, Czechoslovakia, Jan. 29, 1965

90-91	Chi	5	195	8	0	2.46
91-92	Chi	20	1014	44	1	2.60
Totals		25	1209	52	1	2.58
Playoff Totals		6	227	11	0	2.91

HAYWARD, Brian *5-10 180*
B. Weston, Ont., June 25, 1960

82-83	Winn	24	1440	89	1	3.71
83-84	Winn	28	1530	124	0	4.86
84-85	Winn	61	3436	220	0	3.84
85-86	Winn	52	2721	217	0	4.79
86-87	Mont	37	2178	102	1	2.81
87-88	Mont	39	2247	107	2	2.86
88-89	Mont	36	2091	101	1	2.90
89-90	Mont	29	1647	94	1	3.37
90-91	Minn	26	1473	77	2	3.14
91-92	SJ	7	305	25	0	4.92
Totals		339	19068	1156	8	3.64
Playoff Totals		37	1803	104	0	3.46

HEAD, Donald Charles
B. Mount Dennis, Ont., June 30, 1933

61-62	Bos	38	2280	161	2	4.24

HEALY, Glenn *5-10 185*
B. Pickering, Ont., Aug. 23, 1962

85-86	LA	1	51	6	0	7.06

HEALY, Glenn *(Continued)*

Season	Team	GP	Min.	GA	So.	Avg.
87-88	LA	34	1869	135	1	4.33
88-89	LA	48	2699	192	0	4.27
89-90	NYI	39	2197	128	2	3.50
90-91	NYI	53	2999	166	0	3.32
91-92	NYI	37	1960	124	1	3.80
Totals		212	11775	751	4	3.83
Playoff Totals		11	503	35	0	4.17

HEBERT, Guy *5-11 180*

B. Troy, N.Y., Jan. 7, 1967

Season	Team	GP	Min.	GA	So.	Avg.
91-92	StL	13	738	36	0	2.93

HEBERT, Sammy

B. 1894

Season	Team	GP	Min.	GA	So.	Avg.
17-18	Tor-Ott	2	80	10	0	7.50
23-24	Ott	2	120	9	0	4.50
Totals		4	200	19	0	5.70

HEINZ, Richard *5-10 165*

B. Essex, Ont., May 30, 1955

Season	Team	GP	Min.	GA	So.	Avg.
80-81	StL	4	220	8	0	2.18
81-82	StL-Van	12	613	44	1	4.31
82-83	StL	9	335	24	1	4.30
83-84	StL	22	1118	80	0	4.29
84-85	StL	2	70	3	0	2.57
Totals		49	2356	159	2	4.05

HENDERSON, John Duncan (Long John) *6-1 174*

B. Toronto, Ont., Mar. 25, 1933

Season	Team	GP	Min.	GA	So.	Avg.
54-55	Bos	44	2628	109	5	2.49
55-56	Bos	1	60	4	0	4.00
Totals		45	2688	113	5	2.52
Playoff Totals		2	120	8	0	4.00

HENRY, Gordon David (Red) *6-0 185*

B. Owen Sound, Ont., Aug. 17, 1926

Season	Team	GP	Min.	GA	So.	Avg.
48-49	Bos	1	60	0	1	0.00
49-50	Bos	2	120	5	0	2.50
Totals		3	180	5	1	1.67
Playoff Totals		5	283	21	0	4.45

HENRY, Samuel James (Sugar Jim) *5-9 165*

B. Winnipeg, Man., Oct. 23, 1920

Season	Team	GP	Min.	GA	So.	Avg.
41-42	NYR	48	2960	143	1	2.98
45-46	NYR	11	623	41	1	3.95
46-47	NYR	2	120	9	0	4.50
47-48	NYR	48	2880	153	2	3.19
48-49	Chi	60	3600	211	0	3.52
51-52	Bos	70	4200	176	7	2.51
52-53	Bos	70	4200	172	7	2.46
53-54	Bos	70	4200	181	8	2.59
54-55	Bos	26	1532	79	1	3.09
Totals		405	24315	1165	27	2.87
Playoff Totals		29	1741	81	2	2.79

HERRON, Denis *5-11 165*

B. Chambly, Que., Juen 18, 1952

Season	Team	GP	Min.	GA	So.	Avg.
72-73	Pitt	18	967	55	2	3.41
73-74	Pitt	5	260	18	0	4.15
74-75	Pitt-KC	25	1388	91	0	3.93
75-76	KC	64	3620	243	0	4.03
76-77	Pitt	34	1920	94	1	2.94
77-78	Pitt	60	3534	210	0	3.57
78-79	Pitt	56	3208	180	0	3.37
79-80	Mont	34	1909	80	0	2.51
80-81	Mont	25	1147	67	1	3.50
81-82	Mont	27	1547	68	3	2.64
82-83	Pitt	31	1707	151	1	5.31
83-84	Pitt	38	2028	138	1	4.08
84-85	Pitt	42	2193	170	1	4.65
85-86	Pitt	3	180	14	0	4.67
Totals		462	25608	1579	10	3.70
Playoff Totals		15	901	50	0	3.33

HEXTALL, Ron *6-3 192*

B. Winnipeg, Man., May 3, 1964

Season	Team	GP	Min.	GA	So.	Avg.
86-87	Phil	66	3799	190	1	3.00
87-88	Phil	62	3561	208	0	3.50
88-89	Phil	64	3756	202	0	3.23
89-90	Phil	8	419	29	0	4.15
90-91	Phil	36	2035	106	0	3.13
91-92	Phil	45	2668	151	3	3.40
Totals		281	16238	886	4	3.27
Playoff Totals		48	2805	150	2	3.21

HIGHTON, Hector Salisbury *6-0 175*

B. Medicine Hat, Alta., Dec. 10, 1923

Season	Team	GP	Min.	GA	So.	Avg.
43-44	Chi	24	1440	108	0	4.50

HIMES, Norman *5-9 145*

B. Galt, Ont., Apr. 13, 1903

Season	Team	GP	Min.	GA	So.	Avg.
27-28	NYA	1	19	0	0	0.00
28-29	NYA	1	60	3	0	3.00
Totals		2	79	3	0	2.28

HODGE, Charles Edward *5-6 150*

B. Lachine, Que., July 28, 1933

Season	Team	GP	Min.	GA	So.	Avg.
54-55	Mont	14	800	31	1	2.33
57-58	Mont	12	720	31	1	2.58
58-59	Mont	2	120	6	0	3.00
59-60	Mont	1	60	3	0	3.00
60-61	Mont	30	1800	76	4	2.53
63-64	Mont	62	3720	140	8	2.26
64-65	Mont	53	3120	135	3	2.60
65-66	Mont	26	1301	56	1	2.58
66-67	Mont	37	2055	88	3	2.57
67-68	Oak	58	3311	158	3	2.86
68-69	Cal	14	781	48	0	3.69
69-70	Oak	14	738	43	0	3.50
70-71	Van	35	1967	112	0	3.42
Totals		358	20593	927	24	2.70
Playoff Totals		16	804	31	2	2.31

HOFFORT, Bruce *5-10 185*

B. North Battleford, Sask., July 30, 1966

Season	Team	GP	Min.	GA	So.	Avg.
89-90	Phil	7	329	20	0	3.65
90-91	Phil	2	39	3	0	4.62
Totals		9	368	23	0	3.75

HOGANSON, Paul Edward *5-11 175*

B. Toronto, Ont., Nov. 12, 1949

Season	Team	GP	Min.	GA	So.	Avg.
70-71	Pitt	2	57	7	0	7.37
73-74	LA (WHA)	27	1308	102	0	4.68
74-75	Balt (WHA)	32	1776	121	2	4.09
75-76	NE-Cin (WHA)	49	2616	161	2	3.69
76-77	Cin-Ind (WHA)	28	1218	88	1	4.33
77-78	Cin (WHA)	7	326	24	0	4.42
NHL Totals		2	57	7	0	7.37
WHA Totals		143	7244	496	5	4.11
WHA Playoff Totals		5	348	17	1	2.93

HOGOSTA, Goran *6-1 179*

B. Appelbo, Sweden, Apr. 15, 1954

Season	Team	GP	Min.	GA	So.	Avg.
77-78	NYI	1	9	0	0	0.00
79-80	Que	21	1199	83	1	4.15
Totals		22	1208	83	1	4.12

HOLDEN, Mark *5-10 165*

B. Weymouth, Mass., June 12, 1957

Season	Team	GP	Min.	GA	So.	Avg.
81-82	Mont	1	20	0	0	0.00
82-83	Mont	2	87	6	0	4.14
83-84	Mont	1	52	4	0	4.60
84-85	Winn	4	213	15	0	4.23
Totals		8	372	25	0	4.03

HOLLAND, Kenneth Mark *5-8 160*

B. Vernon, B.C., Nov. 10, 1955

Season	Team	GP	Min.	GA	So.	Avg.
80-81	Hart	1	60	7	0	7.00

HOLLAND, Robert (Robbie) *6-1 182*

B. Montreal, Que., Sept, 19, 1957

Season	Team	GP	Min.	GA	So.	Avg.
79-80	Pitt	34	1974	126	1	3.83
80-81	Pitt	10	539	45	0	5.01
Totals		44	2513	171	1	4.08

HOLMES, Harold (Hap)

B. Aurora, Ont., Apr. 15, 1889

Season	Team	GP	Min.	GA	So.	Avg.
17-18	Tor	16	965	76	0	4.75
18-19	Tor	2	120	9	0	4.50
26-27	Det	43	2685	100	6	2.33
27-28	Det	44	2740	79	11	1.80
Totals		105	6510	264	17	2.43
Playoff Totals		7	420	26	0	3.71

HORNER, Reginald (Red) *6-0 190*

B. Lynden, Ont., May 28, 1909

Season	Team	GP	Min.	GA	So.	Avg.
32-33	Tor	1	1	1	0	60.00

HRIVNAK, Jim *6-2 185*

B. Montreal, Que., May 28, 1968

Season	Team	GP	Min.	GA	So.	Avg.
89-90	Wash	11	609	36	0	3.55
90-91	Wash	9	432	26	0	3.61
91-92	Wash	12	605	35	0	3.47
Totals		32	1646	97	0	3.54

HRUDEY, Kelly Stephen *5-10 180*

B. Edmonton, Alta., Jan. 13, 1961

Season	Team	GP	Min.	GA	So.	Avg.
83-84	NYI	12	535	28	0	3.14
84-85	NYI	41	2335	141	2	3.62
85-86	NYI	45	2563	137	1	3.21
86-87	NYI	46	2634	145	0	3.30

HRUDEY, Kelly Stephen *(Continued)*

Season	Team	GP	Min.	GA	So.	Avg.
87-88	NYI	47	2751	153	3	3.34
88-89	NYI-LA	66	3774	230	1	3.66
89-90	LA	52	2860	194	2	4.07
90-91	LA	47	2730	132	3	2.90
91-92	LA	60	3509	197	1	3.39
Totals		416	23691	1357	13	3.44
Playoff Totals		64	3882	208	0	3.21

ING, Peter *6-2 165*

B. Toronto, Ont., Apr. 28, 1969

Season	Team	GP	Min.	GA	So.	Avg.
89-90	Tor	3	182	18	0	5.93
90-91	Tor	56	3162	200	1	3.84
91-92	Edm	12	463	33	0	4.28
Totals		71	3807	251	1	3.96

INNESS, Gary George *6-0 195*

B. Toronto, Ont., May 28, 1949

Season	Team	GP	Min.	GA	So.	Avg.
73-74	Pitt	20	1032	56	0	3.26
74-75	Pitt	57	3122	161	2	3.09
75-76	Pitt-Phil	25	1332	85	0	3.83
76-77	Phil	6	210	9	0	2.57
77-78	Ind (WHA)	52	2850	200	0	4.21
78-79	Ind (WHA)	9	609	51	0	5.02
78-79	Wash	37	2107	130	0	3.70
79-80	Wash	14	727	44	0	3.63
80-81	Wash	3	180	9	0	3.00
NHL Totals		162	8710	494	2	3.40
WHA Totals		61	3459	251	0	4.35
NHL Playoff Totals		9	540	24	0	2.67

IRBE, Arturs *5-8 172*

B. Riga, Soviet Union, Feb. 2, 1967

Season	Team	GP	Min.	GA	So.	Avg.
91-92	SJ	13	645	48	0	4.47

IRELAND, Randolph *6-0 165*

B. Rosetown, Sask., Apr. 5, 1957

Season	Team	GP	Min.	GA	So.	Avg.
78-79	Buf	2	30	3	0	6.00

IRONS, Robert Richard (Robbie) *5-8 150*

B. Toronto, Ont., Nov. 19, 1946

Season	Team	GP	Min.	GA	So.	Avg.
68-69	StL	1	3	0	0	0.00

IRONSTONE, Joseph

B. 1897

Season	Team	GP	Min.	GA	So.	Avg.
25-26	NYA	1	40	3	0	4.50
27-28	Tor	1	70	0	1	0.00
Totals		2	110	3	1	1.64

JABLONSKI, Pat *6-0 175*

B. Toledo, Ohio, June 20, 1967

Season	Team	GP	Min.	GA	So.	Avg.
89-90	StL	4	208	17	0	4.90
90-91	StL	8	492	25	0	3.05
91-92	StL	10	468	38	0	4.87
Totals		22	1168	80	0	4.11
Playoff Totals		3	90	5	0	3.33

JACKSON, Douglas *5-10 150*

B. Winnipeg, Man., Dec. 12, 1924

Season	Team	GP	Min.	GA	So.	Avg.
47-48	Chi	6	360	42	0	7.00

JACKSON, Percy *5-9 165*

B. Canmore, Alta., Sept. 21, 1908

Season	Team	GP	Min.	GA	So.	Avg.
31-32	Bos	4	232	8	0	2.07
33-34	NYA	1	60	9	0	9.00
34-35	NYR	1	60	8	0	8.00
35-36	Bos	1	40	1	0	1.50
Totals		7	392	26	0	3.98

JANASZAK, Steven *6-1 210*

B. St. Paul, Minn., Jan. 7, 1957

Season	Team	GP	Min.	GA	So.	Avg.
79-80	Minn	1	60	2	0	2.00
81-82	Col	2	100	13	0	7.80
Totals		3	160	15	0	5.63

JANECYK, Robert *6-1 180*

B. Chicago, Ill., May 18, 1957

Season	Team	GP	Min.	GA	So.	Avg.
83-84	Chi	8	412	28	0	4.08
84-85	LA	51	3002	183	2	3.66
85-86	LA	38	2083	162	0	4.67
86-87	LA	7	420	34	0	4.86
87-88	LA	5	303	23	0	4.55
88-89	LA	1	30	2	0	4.00
Totals		110	6250	432	2	4.15
Playoff Totals		3	184	10	0	3.26

JENKINS, Joseph Roger *5-11 173*

B. Appleton, Wis., Nov. 18, 1911

Season	Team	GP	Min.	GA	So.	Avg.
38-39	NYA	1	30	7	0	14.00

JENSEN, Allan Raymond *5-10 180*

B. Hamilton, Ont., Nov. 27, 1958

Season	Team	GP	Min.	GA	So.	Avg.
80-81	Det	1	60	7	0	7.00
81-82	Wash	26	1274	81	0	3.81

Season	Team	GP	Min.	GA	So.	Avg.

JENSEN, Allan Raymond *(Continued)*

Season	Team	GP	Min.	GA	So.	Avg.
82-83	Wash	40	2358	135	1	3.44
83-84	Wash	43	2414	117	4	2.91
84-85	Wash	14	803	34	1	2.54
85-86	Wash	44	2437	129	2	3.18
86-87	Wash-LA	11	628	54	0	5.16
Totals		179	9974	557	8	3.35
Playoff Totals		12	598	32	0	3.21

JENSEN, Darren Aksel *5-9 165*
B. Creston, B.C., May 27, 1960

84-85	Phil	1	60	7	0	7.00
85-86	Phil	29	1436	88	2	3.68
Totals		30	1496	95	2	3.81

JOHNSON, Robert Martin *6-1 185*
B. Farmington, Mich., Nov. 12, 1948

72-73	StL	12	583	26	0	2.68
74-75	Pitt	12	476	40	0	5.04
75-76	Ott-Clev	42	2377	144	1	3.63
	(WHA)					
NHL Totals		24	1059	66	0	3.74
WHA Totals		42	2377	144	1	3.63
WHA Playoff Totals		2	120	8	0	4.00

JOHNSTON, Edward Joseph *6-0 190*
B. Montreal, Que., Nov. 23, 1935

62-63	Bos	50	2880	196	1	4.05
63-64	Bos	70	4200	211	6	3.01
64-65	Bos	47	2820	163	3	3.47
65-66	Bos	33	1743	108	1	3.72
66-67	Bos	34	1880	116	0	3.70
67-68	Bos	28	1524	73	0	2.87
68-69	Bos	24	1440	74	2	3.08
69-70	Bos	37	2176	108	3	2.98
70-71	Bos	38	2280	96	4	2.53
71-72	Bos	38	2260	102	2	2.71
72-73	Bos	45	2510	137	5	3.27
73-74	Tor	26	1516	78	1	3.09
74-75	StL	30	1800	93	2	3.10
75-76	StL	38	2152	130	1	3.62
76-77	StL	38	2111	108	1	3.07
77-78	StL-Chi	16	890	62	0	4.18
Totals		591	34182	1854	32	3.25
Playoff Totals		18	1023	57	1	3.34

JOSEPH, Curtis *5-10 182*
B. Keswick, Ont., Apr. 29, 1967

89-90	StL	15	852	48	0	3.38
90-91	StL	30	1710	89	0	3.12
91-92	StL	60	3494	175	2	3.01
Totals		105	6056	312	2	3.09
Playoff Totals		12	706	41	0	3.48

JUNKIN, Joseph Brian *5-11 180*
B. Lindsay, Ont., Sept. 8, 1946

68-69	Bos	1	8	0	0	0.00
73-74	NY-NJ	53	3122	197	1	3.79
	(WHA)					
74-75	SD	16	839	46	1	3.29
	(WHA)					
NHL Totals		1	8	0	0	0.00
WHA Totals		69	3961	243	2	3.68

KAARELA, Jari Pekka *5-10 165*
B. Tampere, Finland, Aug. 8, 1958

| 80-81 | Col | 5 | 220 | 22 | 0 | 6.00 |

KAMPURRI, Hannu *6-0 175*
B. Helsinki, Finland, June 1, 1957

| 84-85 | NJ | 13 | 645 | 54 | 0 | 5.02 |

KARAKAS, Michael *5-11 147*
B. Aurora, Minn., Dec. 12, 1911

35-36	Chi	48	2990	92	9	1.92
36-37	Chi	48	2978	131	5	2.73
37-38	Chi	48	2980	139	1	2.90
38-39	Chi	48	2988	132	5	2.75
39-40	Chi-Mont	22	1360	76	0	3.45
43-44	Chi	26	1560	79	3	3.04
44-45	Chi	48	2880	187	4	3.90
45-46	Chi	48	2880	166	1	3.46
Totals		336	20616	1002	28	2.92
Playoff Totals		23	1434	72	3	3.01

KEANS, Douglas Frederick *5-7 175*
B. Pembroke, Ont., Jan. 7, 1958

79-80	LA	10	559	23	0	2.47
80-81	LA	9	454	37	0	4.89
81-82	LA	31	1436	103	0	4.30
82-83	LA	6	304	24	0	4.73
83-84	Bos	33	1779	92	2	3.10
84-85	Bos	25	1497	82	1	3.29
85-86	Bos	30	1757	107	0	3.65
86-87	Bos	36	1942	108	0	3.34
87-88	Bos	30	1660	90	1	3.25
Totals		210	11388	666	4	3.51

KEANS, Douglas Frederick *(Continued)*

| Playoff Totals | | 9 | 432 | 34 | 0 | 4.72 |

KEENAN, Donald

| 58-59 | Bos | 1 | 60 | 4 | 0 | 4.00 |

KERR, David Alexander *5-10 160*
B. Toronto, Ont., Jan. 11, 1910

30-31	Mont M	28	1649	76	1	2.71
31-32	NYA	1	60	6	0	6.00
32-33	Mont M	25	1520	58	4	2.32
33-34	Mont M	48	3060	122	6	2.54
34-35	NYR	37	2290	94	4	2.54
35-36	NYR	47	2980	95	8	2.02
36-37	NYR	48	3020	106	4	2.21
37-38	NYR	48	2960	96	8	2.00
38-39	NYR	48	2970	105	6	2.19
39-40	NYR	48	3000	77	8	1.60
40-41	NYR	48	3010	125	2	2.60
Totals		426	26519	960	51	2.17
Playoff Totals		40	2616	76	8	1.74

KIDD, Trevor *6-2 176*
B. Dugald, Man., Mar. 29, 1972

| 91-92 | Calg | 2 | 120 | 8 | 0 | 4.00 |

KING, Scott *6-1 170*
B. Thunder Bay, Ont., June 25, 1967

90-91	Det	1	45	2	0	2.67
91-92	Det	1	16	1	0	3.75
Totals		2	61	3	0	2.95

KLEISINGER, Terry *6-0 190*
B. Regina, Sask., Oct. 10, 1960

| 85-86 | NYR | 4 | 191 | 14 | 0 | 4.40 |

KLYMKIW, Julian *5-11 180*
B. Winnipeg, Man., July 16, 1933

| 58-59 | NYR | 1 | 19 | 2 | 0 | 6.32 |

KOLZIG, Olaf *6-3 204*
B. Johannesburg, South Africa, Apr. 6, 1970

| 89-90 | Wash | 2 | 120 | 12 | 0 | 6.00 |

KURT, Gary David *6-3 205*
B. Kitchener, Ont., Mar. 9, 1947

71-72	Cal	16	838	60	0	4.30
72-73	NY	36	1881	150	0	4.78
	(WHA)					
73-74	NY-NJ	20	1009	75	0	4.13
	(WHA)					
74-75	Phoe	47	2841	156	0	3.29
	(WHA)					
75-76	Phoe	40	2369	147	1	3.72
	(WHA)					
76-77	Phoe	33	1752	162	0	5.55
	(WHA)					
NHL Totals		16	838	60	0	4.30
WHA Totals		176	9932	690	3	4.17
WHA Playoff Totals		4	207	12	0	3.48

LACROIX, Alphonse

| 25-26 | Mont | 5 | 280 | 16 | 0 | 3.20 |

LaFERRIERE, Richard *5-9 170*
B. Hawksbury, Ont., Jan. 3, 1961

| 81-82 | Col | 1 | 20 | 1 | 0 | 3.00 |

LaFOREST, Mark Andrew *5-11 190*
B. Welland, Ont., July 10, 1962

85-86	Det	28	1383	114	1	4.95
86-87	Det	5	219	12	0	3.29
87-88	Phil	21	972	60	1	3.70
88-89	Phil	17	933	64	0	4.12
89-90	Tor	27	1343	87	0	3.89
Totals		98	4850	337	2	4.17
Playoff Totals		2	48	1	0	1.25

LAROCQUE, Michel Raymond (Bunny) *5-10 185*
B. Hull, Que., Apr. 16, 1952

73-74	Mont	27	1431	69	0	2.89
74-75	Mont	25	1480	74	3	3.00
75-76	Mont	22	1220	50	2	2.46
76-77	Mont	26	1525	53	0	2.09
77-78	Mont	30	1729	77	1	2.67
78-79	Mont	34	1986	94	3	2.84
79-80	Mont	29	2259	125	3	3.32
80-81	Mont-Tor	36	2083	122	1	3.51
81-82	Tor	50	2647	207	0	4.69
82-83	Tor-Phil	18	955	76	0	4.77
83-84	StL	5	300	31	0	6.20
Totals		312	17615	978	17	3.33
Playoff Totals		14	759	37	1	2.92

LASKOWSKI, Gary *6-1 175*
B. Ottawa, Ont., June 6, 1959

82-83	LA	46	2227	173	0	4.56
83-84	LA	13	665	55	0	4.96
Totals		59	2942	228	0	4.65

LAXTON, Gordon *5-10 195*
B. Montreal, Que., Mar. 16, 1955

75-76	Pitt	8	414	31	0	4.49
76-77	Pitt	6	253	26	0	6.17
77-78	Pitt	2	73	9	0	7.40
78-79	Pitt	1	60	8	0	8.00
Totals		17	800	74	0	5.55

LeBLANC, Raymond *5-10 170*
B. Fitchburg, Mass., Oct. 24, 1964

| 91-92 | Chi | 1 | 60 | 1 | 0 | 1.00 |

LeDUC, Albert (Battleship) *5-9 180*
B. Valleyfield, Que., Nov. 12, 1902

| 31-32 | Mont | 1 | 2 | 1 | 0 | 30.00 |

B. LEGRIS, Claude *5-9 160*
B. Verdun, Que., Nov. 6, 1956

80-81	Det	3	63	4	0	3.81
81-82	Det	1	28	0	0	0.00
Totals		4	91	4	0	2.64

LEHMAN, Hugh
B. Pembroke, Ont., Oct. 27, 1895

26-27	Chi	44	2797	116	5	2.64
27-28	Chi	4	250	20	1	5.00
Totals		48	3047	136	6	2.68
Playoff Totals		2	120	10	0	5.00

LEMELIN, Rejean *5-11 160*
B. Sherbrooke, Que. Nov. 19, 1954

78-79	Atl	18	994	55	0	3.32
79-80	Atl	3	150	15	0	6.00
80-81	Calg	29	1629	88	2	3.24
81-82	Calg	34	1866	135	0	4.34
82-83	Calg	39	2211	133	0	3.61
83-84	Calg	51	2568	150	0	3.50
84-85	Calg	56	3176	183	1	3.46
85-86	Calg	60	3369	229	1	4.08
86-87	Calg	34	1735	94	2	3.25
87-88	Bos	49	2828	138	3	2.93
88-89	Bos	40	2392	120	0	3.01
89-90	Bos	43	2310	108	2	2.81
90-91	Bos	33	1829	111	1	3.64
91-92	Bos	8	407	23	0	3.39
Totals		497	27364	1582	12	3.47
Playoff Totals		59	3119	186	2	3.58

LESSARD, Mario *5-9 177*
B. East Broughton, Que., June 25, 1954

78-79	LA	49	2860	148	4	3.10
79-80	LA	50	2836	185	0	3.91
80-81	LA	64	3746	203	2	3.25
81-82	LA	52	2933	213	2	4.36
82-83	LA	19	888	68	1	4.59
83-84	LA	6	266	26	0	5.87
Totals		240	13529	843	9	3.74
Playoff Totals		20	1136	83	0	4.38

LEVASSEUR, Jean-Louis *5-10 160*
B. Noranda, Que., June 16, 1949

75-76	Minn	4	193	10	0	3.11
	(WHA)					
76-77	Minn-Edm	51	2928	166	2	3.40
	(WHA)					
77-78	NE	27	1655	91	3	3.30
	(WHA)					
78-79	Que	3	140	14	0	6.00
	(WHA)					
79-80	Minn	1	60	7	0	7.00
NHL Totals		1	60	7	0	7.00
WHA Totals		85	4916	281	5	3.43
WHA Playoff Tot.		15	911	49	0	3.23

LEVINSKY, Alexander *5-10 184*
B. Syracuse, N.Y., Feb. 2, 1910

| 32-33 | Tor | 1 | 1 | 1 | 0 | 60.00 |

LINDBERGH, Per-Erik (Pelle) *5-9 160*
B. Stockholm, Sweden, May 24, 1959

81-82	Phil	8	480	35	0	4.38
82-83	Phil	40	2334	116	3	2.98
83-84	Phil	36	1999	135	1	4.05
84-85	Phil	65	3858	194	2	3.02
85-86	Phil	8	480	23	1	2.88
Totals		157	9151	503	7	3.30
Playoff Totals		23	1214	63	3	3.11

LINDSAY, Bert A.

Season	Team	GP	Min.	GA	So.	Avg.
17-18	Mont W	4	240	35	0	8.75
18-19	Tor	16	979	83	0	5.19
Totals		20	1219	118	0	5.81

LITTMAN, David 6-0 172
B. Cranston, R.I., June 13, 1967

Season	Team	GP	Min.	GA	So.	Avg.
90-91	Buf	1	36	3	0	5.00
91-92	Buf	1	60	4	0	4.00
Totals		2	96	7	0	4.38

LIUT, Michael 6-2 195
B. Weston, Ont., Jan. 7, 1956

Season	Team	GP	Min.	GA	So.	Avg.
77-78	Cin (WHA)	27	1215	86	0	4.25
78-79	Cin (WHA)	54	3181	184	3	3.47
79-80	StL	64	3661	194	2	3.18
80-81	StL	61	3570	199	1	3.34
81-82	StL	64	3691	250	2	4.06
82-83	StL	68	3794	235	1	3.72
83-84	StL	58	3425	197	3	3.45
84-85	StL-Hart	44	2600	155	2	3.58
85-86	Hart	57	3282	198	2	3.62
86-87	Hart	59	3476	187	4	3.23
87-88	Hart	60	3532	187	2	3.18
88-89	Hart	35	2006	142	1	4.25
89-90	Hart-Wash	37	2161	91	4	2.53
90-91	Wash	35	1834	114	0	3.73
91-92	Wash	21	1123	70	1	3.74
NHL Totals		663	38155	2219	25	3.49
WHA Totals		81	4396	270	3	3.69
NHL Playoff Totals		67	3814	215	2	3.38
WHA Playoff Totals		3	179	12	0	4.02

LOCKETT, Kenneth Richard 6-0 160
B. Toronto, Ont., Aug. 30, 1947

Season	Team	GP	Min.	GA	So.	Avg.
74-75	Van	25	912	48	2	3.16
75-76	Van	30	1436	83	0	3.47
76-77	SD (WHA)	45	1144	148	1	7.76
NHL Totals		55	2348	131	2	3.35
WHA Totals		45	1144	148	1	7.76
NHL Playoff Totals		1	60	6	0	6.00
WHA Playoff Totals		5	260	19	0	4.38

LOCKHART, Howard (Holes)

Season	Team	GP	Min.	GA	So.	Avg.
19-20	Tor-Que	6	328	31	0	5.67
20-21	Ham	24	1454	132	1	5.50
21-22	Ham	24	1409	103	0	4.29
23-24	Tor	1	60	5	0	5.00
24-25	Bos	2	120	11	0	5.50
Totals		57	3371	282	1	5.02

LoPRESTI, Peter Jon 6-1 195
B. Virginia, Minn., May 23, 1954

Season	Team	GP	Min.	GA	So.	Avg.
74-75	Minn	35	1964	137	1	4.19
75-76	Minn	34	1789	123	1	4.13
76-77	Minn	44	2590	156	1	3.61
77-78	Minn	53	3065	216	2	4.23
78-79	Minn	7	345	28	0	4.87
80-81	Edm	2	105	8	0	4.57
Totals		175	9858	668	5	4.07
Playoff Totals		2	77	6	0	4.68

LoPRESTI, Samuel 5-11 200
B. Eveleth, Minn., Jan. 30, 1917

Season	Team	GP	Min.	GA	So.	Avg.
40-41	Chi	27	1670	84	1	3.11
41-42	Chi	47	2860	152	3	3.23
Totals		74	4530	236	4	3.13
Playoff Totals		8	530	17	1	1.92

LORENZ, Danny 5-10 170
B. Murrayville, B.C., Dec. 12, 1969

Season	Team	GP	Min.	GA	So.	Avg.
90-91	NYI	2	80	5	0	3.75
91-92	NYI	2	120	10	0	5.00
Totals		4	200	15	0	4.50

LOUSTEL, Ron 5-11 185
B. Winnipeg, Man., Mar. 7, 1962

Season	Team	GP	Min.	GA	So.	Avg.
80-81	Winn	1	60	10	0	10.00

LOW, Ronald Albert 6-1 205
B. Birtle, Man., June 21, 1950

Season	Team	GP	Min.	GA	So.	Avg.
72-73	Tor	42	2343	152	1	3.89
74-75	Wash	48	2588	235	1	5.45
75-76	Wash	43	2289	208	0	5.45
76-77	Wash	54	2918	188	0	3.87
77-78	Det	32	1816	102	1	3.37
79-80	Que-Edm	26	1478	88	0	3.57
80-81	Edm	24	1260	93	0	4.43
81-82	Edm	29	1554	100	0	3.86
82-83	Edm-NJ	14	712	51	0	4.30

LOW, Ronald Albert *(Continued)*

Season	Team	GP	Min.	GA	So.	Avg.
83-84	NJ	44	2218	161	0	4.35
84-85	NJ	26	1326	85	1	3.85
Totals		382	20502	1463	4	4.28
Playoff Totals		7	452	29	0	3.85

LOZINSKI, Larry Peter 5-11 175
B. Hudson Bay, Sask., Mar. 11, 1958

Season	Team	GP	Min.	GA	So.	Avg.
80-81	Det	30	1459	105	0	4.32

LUMLEY, Harry (Apple Cheeks) 6-0 195
B. Owen Sound, Ont., Nov. 11, 1926

Season	Team	GP	Min.	GA	So.	Avg.
43-44	Det-NYR	3	140	13	0	5.57
44-45	Det	37	2220	119	1	3.22
45-46	Det	50	3000	159	2	3.18
46-47	Det	52	3120	159	3	3.06
47-48	Det	60	3592	147	7	2.46
48-49	Det	60	3600	145	6	2.42
49-50	Det	63	3780	148	7	2.35
50-51	Chi	64	3785	246	3	3.90
51-52	Chi	70	4180	241	2	3.46
52-53	Tor	70	4200	167	10	2.39
53-54	Tor	69	4140	128	13	1.86
54-55	Tor	69	4140	134	8	1.94
55-56	Tor	59	3520	159	3	2.71
57-58	Bos	25	1500	71	3	2.84
58-59	Bos	11	660	27	1	2.45
59-60	Bos	42	2520	147	2	3.50
Totals		804	48097	2210	71	2.76
Playoff Totals		76	4778	199	7	2.50

MacKENZIE, Shawn 5-10 175
B. Bedford, N.S., Aug. 22, 1962

Season	Team	GP	Min.	GA	So.	Avg.
82-83	NJ	4	130	15	0	6.92

MALARCHUK, Clint 6-0 187
B. Grand Prairie, Alta., May 1, 1961

Season	Team	GP	Min.	GA	So.	Avg.
81-82	Que	2	120	14	0	7.00
82-83	Que	15	900	71	0	4.73
83-84	Que	23	1215	80	0	3.95
85-86	Que	46	2657	142	4	3.21
86-87	Que	54	3092	175	1	3.40
87-88	Wash	54	2926	154	4	3.16
88-89	Wash-Buf	49	2754	154	2	3.36
89-90	Buf	29	1596	89	0	3.35
90-91	Buf	37	2131	119	1	3.35
91-92	Buf	29	1639	102	0	3.73
Totals		338	19030	1100	11	3.47
Playoff Totals		16	781	56	0	4.30

MANELUK, George 5-11 185
B. Winnipeg, Man., July 25, 1967

Season	Team	GP	Min.	GA	So.	Avg.
90-91	NYI	4	140	15	0	6.43

MANIAGO, Cesare 6-3 195
B. Trail, B.C., Jan. 13, 1939

Season	Team	GP	Min.	GA	So.	Avg.
60-61	Tor	7	420	18	0	2.57
62-63	Mont	14	820	42	0	3.07
65-66	NYR	28	1613	94	2	3.50
66-67	NYR	6	219	14	0	3.84
67-68	Minn	52	2877	133	6	2.77
68-69	Minn	64	3599	198	1	3.30
69-70	Minn	50	2887	163	2	3.39
70-71	Minn	40	2380	107	5	2.70
71-72	Minn	43	2539	112	3	2.65
72-73	Minn	47	2736	132	5	2.89
73-74	Minn	40	2378	138	1	3.48
74-75	Minn	37	2129	149	1	4.20
75-76	Minn	47	2704	151	2	3.35
76-77	Van	47	2699	151	1	3.36
77-78	Van	46	2570	172	1	4.02
Totals		568	32570	1774	30	3.27
Playoff Totals		36	2245	100	3	2.67

MAROIS, Jean

Season	Team	GP	Min.	GA	So.	Avg.
43-44	Tor	1	60	4	0	4.00
53-54	Chi	2	120	11	0	5.50
Totals		3	180	15	0	5.00

MARTIN, Seth 5-11 180
B. Rossland, B.C., May 4, 1933

Season	Team	GP	Min.	GA	So.	Avg.
67-68	StL	30	1552	67	1	2.59
Playoff Totals		2	73	5	0	4.11

MATTSSON, Rainer Markus 6-0 180
B. Suoneiemi, Finland, July 30, 1957

Season	Team	GP	Min.	GA	So.	Avg.
77-78	Que-Winn (WHA)	16	777	60	0	4.63
78-79	Winn (WHA)	52	2990	181	0	3.63
79-80	Winn	21	1200	65	2	3.25
80-81	Winn	31	1707	128	1	4.50
82-83	Minn-LA	21	999	71	2	4.26
83-84	LA	19	1101	79	1	4.31
NHL Totals		92	5007	343	6	4.11
WHA Totals		68	3767	241	0	3.84

MASON, Robert 6-1 180
B. International Falls, Minn., Apr. 22, 1961

Season	Team	GP	Min.	GA	So.	Avg.
83-84	Wash	2	120	3	0	1.50
84-85	Wash	12	661	31	1	2.81
85-86	Wash	1	16	0	0	0.00
86-87	Wash	45	2536	137	0	3.24
87-88	Chi	41	2312	160	0	4.15
88-89	Que	22	1168	92	0	4.73
89-90	Wash	16	822	48	0	3.50
90-91	Van	6	353	29	0	4.93
Totals		145	7988	500	1	3.76
Playoff Totals		5	369	12	1	1.95

MAY, Darrell Gerald 6-0 175
B. Edmonton, Alta., Mar. 6, 1962

Season	Team	GP	Min.	GA	So.	Avg.
85-86	StL	3	184	13	0	4.24
87-88	StL	3	180	18	0	6.00
Totals		6	364	31	0	5.11

MAYER, Gilles 5-6 135
B. Ottawa, Ont., Aug. 24, 1930

Season	Team	GP	Min.	GA	So.	Avg.
49-50	Tor	1	60	2	0	2.00
53-54	Tor	1	60	3	0	3.00
54-55	Tor	1	60	1	0	1.00
55-56	Tor	6	360	19	0	3.17
Totals		9	540	25	0	2.78

McAULEY, Kenneth Leslie (Tubby) 5-10 190
B. Edmonton, Alta., Jan. 9, 1921

Season	Team	GP	Min.	GA	So.	Avg.
43-44	NYR	50	2980	310	0	6.20
44-45	NYR	46	2760	227	1	4.93
Totals		96	5740	537	1	5.61

McCARTAN, John William (Jack) 6-1 195
B. St. Paul, Minn., Aug. 5, 1935

Season	Team	GP	Min.	GA	So.	Avg.
59-60	NYR	4	240	7	0	1.75
60-61	NYR	8	440	36	1	4.91
72-73	Minn (WHA)	38	2160	129	1	3.58
73-74	Minn (WHA)	2	42	5	0	7.14
74-75	Minn (WHA)	2	61	5	0	4.92
NHL Totals		12	680	43	1	3.79
WHA Totals		42	2263	139	1	3.69
WHA Playoff Tot.		4	213	14	0	3.94

McCOOL, Frank 6-0 170
B. Calgary, Alta., Oct. 27, 1918

Season	Team	GP	Min.	GA	So.	Avg.
44-45	Tor	50	3000	161	4	3.22
45-46	Tor	22	1320	81	0	3.68
Totals		72	4320	242	4	3.36
Playoff Totals		13	807	30	4	2.23

McDUFFE, Peter Arnold 5-9 180
B. Milton, Ont., Feb. 16, 1948

Season	Team	GP	Min.	GA	So.	Avg.
71-72	StL	10	467	29	0	3.73
72-73	NYR	1	60	1	0	1.00
73-74	NYR	6	340	18	0	3.18
74-75	KC	36	2100	148	0	4.23
75-76	Det	4	240	22	0	5.50
77-78	Ind (WHA)	12	539	39	0	4.34
NHL Totals		57	3207	218	0	4.08
WHA Totals		12	539	39	0	4.34
NHL Playoff Totals		1	60	7	0	7.00

McGRATTON, Thomas 6-2 170
B. Brantford, Ont., Oct. 19, 1927

Season	Team	GP	Min.	GA	So.	Avg.
47-48	Det	1	8	0	0	0.00

McKAY, Ross Lee 5-11 175
B. Edmonton, Alta., Mar. 3, 1964

Season	Team	GP	Min.	GA	So.	Avg.
90-91	Hart	1	35	3	0	5.14

McKENZIE, William Ian 5-11 180
B. St. Thomas, Ont., Mar. 12, 1949

Season	Team	GP	Min.	GA	So.	Avg.
73-74	Det	13	720	43	1	3.58
74-75	Det	13	740	58	0	4.70
75-76	KC	22	1120	97	0	5.20
76-77	Col	5	200	8	0	2.40
77-78	Col	12	654	42	0	3.85
79-80	Col	26	1342	78	1	3.49
Totals		91	4776	326	2	4.10

McKICHAN, Steve 5-11 180
B. Strathroy, Ont., May 29, 1967

Season	Team	GP	Min.	GA	So.	Avg.
90-91	Van	1	20	2	0	6.00

McLACHLAN, Murray 6-0 195
B. London, Ont., Oct. 20, 1948

Season	Team	GP	Min.	GA	So.	Avg.
70-71	Tor	2	25	4	0	9.60

McLEAN, Kirk *6-0 185*
B. Willowdale, Ont., June 26, 1966

Season	Team	GP	Min.	GA	So.	Avg.
85-86	NJ	2	111	11	0	5.95
86-87	NJ	4	160	10	0	3.75
87-88	Van	41	2380	147	1	3.71
88-89	Van	42	2477	127	4	3.08
89-90	Van	63	3739	216	0	3.47
90-91	Van	41	1969	131	0	3.99
91-92	Van	65	3852	176	5	2.74
Totals		258	14688	818	10	3.34
Playoff Totals		20	1210	58	2	2.88

McLELLAND, David *5-9 165*
B. Penticton, B.C., Nov. 20, 1952

Season	Team	GP	Min.	GA	So.	Avg.
72-73	Van	2	120	10	0	5.00

McLEOD, Donald Martin *6-0 190*
B. Trail, B.C., Aug. 24, 1946

Season	Team	GP	Min.	GA	So.	Avg.
70-71	Det	14	698	60	0	5.16
71-72	Phil	4	181	14	0	4.64
72-73	Hou (WHA)	41	2410	145	1	3.61
73-74	Hou (WHA)	49	2971	127	3	2.56
74-75	Van (WHA)	72	4184	233	1	3.34
75-76	Calg (WHA)	63	3534	206	1	3.50
76-77	Calg (WHA)	67	3701	210	3	3.40
77-78	Que-Edm (WHA)	40	2126	130	2	3.67
NHL Totals		18	879	74	0	5.05
WHA Totals		332	18926	1051	11	3.33
WHA Playoff Tot.		31	1786	96	0	3.23

McLEOD, James Bradley *5-8 170*
B. Port Arthur, Ont., Apr. 7, 1937

Season	Team	GP	Min.	GA	So.	Avg.
71-72	StL	16	880	44	0	3.00
72-73	Chi (WHA)	54	2996	166	1	3.32
73-74	NJ-LA (WHA)	27	1486	105	1	4.24
74-75	Balt (WHA)	16	694	53	0	4.58
NHL Totals		16	880	44	0	3.00
WHA Totals		97	5176	324	2	3.76

McNAMARA, Gerald *6-2 190*
B. Sturgeon Falls, Ont., Sept. 22, 1934

Season	Team	GP	Min.	GA	So.	Avg.
60-61	Tor	5	300	13	0	2.60
69-70	Tor	2	23	2	0	5.22
Totals		7	323	15	0	2.79

McNEIL, Gerard George *5-7 155*
B. Quebec City, Que., Apr. 17, 1926

Season	Team	GP	Min.	GA	So.	Avg.
47-48	Mont	2	95	7	0	4.42
49-50	Mont	6	360	9	1	1.50
50-51	Mont	70	4200	184	6	2.63
51-52	Mont	70	4200	164	5	2.34
52-53	Mont	66	3960	140	10	2.12
53-54	Mont	53	3180	114	6	2.15
56-57	Mont	9	540	32	0	3.56
Totals		276	16535	650	28	2.36
Playoff Totals		35	2284	72	5	1.89

McRAE, Gordon Alexander *6-0 180*
B. Sherbrooke, Que., Apr. 12, 1948

Season	Team	GP	Min.	GA	So.	Avg.
72-73	Tor	11	620	39	0	3.77
74-75	Tor	20	1063	57	0	3.22
75-76	Tor	20	956	59	0	3.70
76-77	Tor	2	120	9	0	4.50
77-78	Tor	18	1040	57	1	3.29
Totals		71	3799	221	1	3.49
Playoff Totals		8	454	22	0	2.91

MELANSON, Roland Joseph (Rollie) *5-10 180*
B. Moncton, N.B., June 28, 1960

Season	Team	GP	Min.	GA	So.	Avg.
80-81	NYI	11	620	32	0	3.10
81-82	NYI	36	2115	114	0	3.23
82-83	NYI	44	2460	109	1	2.66
83-84	NYI	37	2019	110	0	3.27
84-85	NYI-Minn	28	1567	113	0	4.33
85-86	Minn-LA	28	1571	111	0	4.24
86-87	LA	46	2734	168	1	3.69
87-88	LA	47	2676	195	2	4.37
88-89	LA	4	178	19	0	6.40
90-91	NJ	1	20	2	0	6.00
91-92	Mont	9	492	22	2	2.68
Totals		291	16452	995	6	3.63
Playoff Totals		23	801	59	0	4.42

MELOCHE, Gilles *5-10 170*
B. Montreal, Que., July 12, 1950

Season	Team	GP	Min.	GA	So.	Avg.
70-71	Chi	2	120	6	0	3.00
71-72	Cal	56	3121	173	4	3.33

MELOCHE, Gilles *(Continued)*

Season	Team	GP	Min.	GA	So.	Avg.
72-73	Cal	59	3473	235	1	4.06
73-74	Cal	47	2800	198	1	4.24
74-75	Cal	47	2771	186	1	4.03
75-76	Cal	41	2440	140	1	3.44
76-77	Clev	51	2961	171	2	3.47
77-78	Clev	54	3100	195	1	3.77
78-79	Minn	53	3118	173	2	3.33
79-80	Minn	54	3141	160	1	3.06
80-81	Minn	38	2215	120	2	3.25
81-82	Minn	51	3026	175	1	3.47
82-83	Minn	47	2689	160	1	3.57
83-84	Minn	52	2883	201	2	4.18
84-85	Minn	32	1817	115	0	3.80
85-86	Pitt	34	1989	119	0	3.59
86-87	Pitt	43	2343	134	0	3.43
87-88	Pitt	27	1394	95	0	4.09
Totals		788	45401	2756	20	3.64
Playoff Totals		45	2464	143	2	3.48

MICALEF, Corrado *5-8 172*
B. Montreal, Que., Apr. 20, 1961

Season	Team	GP	Min.	GA	So.	Avg.
81-82	Det	18	809	63	0	4.67
82-83	Det	34	1756	106	2	3.62
83-84	Det	14	808	52	0	3.86
84-85	Det	36	1856	136	0	4.40
85-86	Det	11	565	52	0	5.52
Totals		113	5794	409	2	4.24

MIDDLEBROOK, Lindsay *5-7 160*
B. Collingwood, Ont., Sept. 7, 1955

Season	Team	GP	Min.	GA	So.	Avg.
79-80	Winn	10	580	40	0	4.14
80-81	Winn	14	653	65	0	5.97
81-82	Minn	3	140	7	0	3.00
82-83	NJ-Edm	10	472	40	0	5.08
Totals		37	1845	152	0	4.94

MILLAR, Joseph *5-11 175*
B. Winnipeg, Man., Sept. 18, 1929

Season	Team	GP	Min.	GA	So.	Avg.
57-58	Bos	6	360	25	0	4.17

MILLEN, Greg H. *5-9 175*
B. Toronto, Ont., June 25, 1957

Season	Team	GP	Min.	GA	So.	Avg.
78-79	Pitt	28	1532	86	2	3.37
79-80	Pitt	44	2586	157	2	3.64
80-81	Pitt	63	3721	258	0	4.16
81-82	Hart	55	3201	229	0	4.29
82-83	Hart	60	3520	282	1	4.81
83-84	Hart	60	3583	221	2	3.70
84-85	Hart-StL	54	3266	222	1	4.08
85-86	StL	36	2168	129	1	3.57
86-87	StL	42	2482	146	0	3.53
87-88	StL	48	2854	167	1	3.51
88-89	StL	52	3019	170	6	3.38
89-90	StL-Que-Chi	49	2900	188	1	3.89
90-91	Chi	3	58	4	0	4.14
91-92	Det	10	487	22	0	2.71
Totals		604	35347	2281	17	3.87
Playoff Totals		59	3383	193	0	3.42

MILLER, Joseph *5-9 170*
B. Morrisburgh, Ont., Oct. 6, 1900

Season	Team	GP	Min.	GA	So.	Avg.
27-28	NYA	28	1721	77	5	2.75
28-29	Pitt Pi	44	2780	80	11	1.82
29-30	Pitt Pi	43	2630	179	0	4.16
30-31	Phil Q	15	850	50	0	3.33
Totals		130	7981	386	16	2.90
Playoff Totals		3	180	3	1	1.00

MIO, Edward *5-10 180*
B. Windsor, Ont., Jan. 31, 1954

Season	Team	GP	Min.	GA	So.	Avg.
77-78	Ind (WHA)	17	900	64	0	4.27
78-79	Ind-Edm (WHA)	27	1310	84	2	3.85
79-80	Edm	34	1711	120	1	4.21
80-81	Edm	43	2393	155	0	3.89
81-82	NYR	25	1500	89	0	3.56
82-83	NYR	41	2365	136	2	3.45
83-84	Det	24	1295	95	1	4.40
84-85	Det	7	376	27	0	4.31
85-86	Det	18	788	83	0	6.32
NHL Totals		192	12299	822	6	4.01
WHA Totals		44	2210	148	2	4.02
NHL Playoff Totals		17	986	63	0	3.83
WHA Playoff Totals		3	90	6	0	4.00

MITCHELL, Ivan

Season	Team	GP	Min.	GA	So.	Avg.
19-20	Tor	15	872	65	0	4.33
20-21	Tor	4	240	22	0	5.50
21-22	Tor	2	120	6	0	3.00
Totals		21	1232	93	0	4.53

MOFFAT, Michael *5-10 165*
B. Galt, Ont., Feb. 4, 1962

Season	Team	GP	Min.	GA	So.	Avg.
81-82	Bos	2	120	6	0	3.00

MOFFAT, Michael *(Continued)*

Season	Team	GP	Min.	GA	So.	Avg.
82-83	Bos	13	673	49	0	4.37
83-84	Bos	4	186	15	0	4.84
Totals		19	979	70	0	4.29
Playoff Totals		11	663	38	0	3.44

MOOG, Donald Andrew (Andy) *5-8 170*
B. Penticton, B.C., Feb. 18, 1960

Season	Team	GP	Min.	GA	So.	Avg.
80-81	Edm	7	313	20	0	3.83
81-82	Edm	8	399	32	0	4.81
82-83	Edm	50	2833	167	1	3.54
83-84	Edm	38	2212	139	1	3.77
84-85	Edm	39	2019	111	1	3.30
85-86	Edm	47	2664	164	1	3.69
86-87	Edm	46	2461	144	0	3.51
87-88	Bos	6	360	17	1	2.83
88-89	Bos	41	2482	133	1	3.22
89-90	Bos	46	2536	122	3	2.89
90-91	Bos	51	2844	136	4	2.87
91-92	Bos	62	3640	196	1	3.23
Totals		441	24763	1381	14	3.35
Playoff Tot.		104	5845	290	3	2.98

MOORE, Alfred Ernest (Alfie)
B. Toronto, Ont.

Season	Team	GP	Min.	GA	So.	Avg.
36-37	NYA	18	1110	64	1	3.56
38-39	NYA	2	120	14	0	7.00
39-40	Det	1	60	3	0	3.00
Totals		21	1290	81	1	3.77
Playoff Totals		3	180	7	0	2.33

MOORE, Robert David (Robbie) *5-5 155*
B. Sarnia, Ont., May 3, 1954

Season	Team	GP	Min.	GA	So.	Avg.
78-79	Phil	5	237	7	2	1.77
82-83	Wash	1	20	1	0	3.00
Totals		6	257	8	2	1.87
Playoff Totals		5	268	18	0	4.03

MORRISSETTE, Jean Guy *5-6 140*
B. Causapscal, Que., Dec. 19, 1937

Season	Team	GP	Min.	GA	So.	Avg.
63-64	Mont	1	36	4	0	6.67

MOWERS, John Thomas *5-11 185*
B. Niagara Falls, Ont., Oct. 29, 1916

Season	Team	GP	Min.	GA	So.	Avg.
40-41	Det	48	3040	102	4	2.13
41-42	Det	47	2880	144	5	3.06
42-43	Det	50	3010	124	6	2.47
46-47	Det	7	420	29	0	4.14
Totals		152	9350	399	15	2.56
Playoff Totals		32	2000	85	2	2.55

MRAZEK, Jerome John *5-9 160*
B. Prince Albert, Sask., Oct. 15, 1951

Season	Team	GP	Min.	GA	So.	Avg.
75-76	Phil	1	6	1	0	10.00

MUMMERY, Harry

Season	Team	GP	Min.	GA	So.	Avg.
19-20	Que	3	142	18	0	6.00
21-22	Ham	1	49	2	0	2.00
Totals		4	191	20	0	6.28

MURPHY, Harold (Hal)
B. Montreal, Que., July 6, 1927

Season	Team	GP	Min.	GA	So.	Avg.
52-53	Mont	1	60	4	0	4.00

MURRAY, Thomas Mickey

Season	Team	GP	Min.	GA	So.	Avg.
29-30	Mont	1	60	4	0	4.00

MYLLYS, Jarmo *5-8 150*
B. Sovanlinna, Finland, May 29, 1965

Season	Team	GP	Min.	GA	So.	Avg.
88-89	Minn	4	238	22	0	5.55
89-90	Minn	4	156	16	0	6.15
90-91	Minn	2	78	8	0	6.15
91-92	SJ	27	1374	115	0	5.02
Totals		39	1846	161	0	5.23

MYLNIKOV, Sergei *5-10 176*
B. Chelyabinski, Soviet Union, Oct. 6, 1958

Season	Team	GP	Min.	GA	So.	Avg.
89-90	Que	10	568	47	0	4.96

MYRE, Louis Philippe (Phil) *6-1 185*
B. Ste.-Anne-de-Bellevue, Que., Nov. 1, 1948

Season	Team	GP	Min.	GA	So.	Avg.
69-70	Mont	10	503	19	0	2.27
70-71	Mont	30	1677	87	1	3.11
71-72	Mont	9	528	32	0	3.64
72-73	Atl	46	2736	138	2	3.03
73-74	Atl	36	2020	112	0	3.33
74-75	Atl	40	2400	114	5	2.85
75-76	Atl	37	2129	123	1	3.47
76-77	Atl	43	2422	124	3	3.07
77-78	Atl-StL	53	3143	202	1	3.86
78-79	StL	39	2259	163	1	4.33
79-80	Phil	41	2367	141	0	3.57
80-81	Phil-Col	26	1480	94	0	3.81

MYRE, Louis Philippe (Phil) *(Continued)*

Season	Team	GP	Min.	GA	So.	Avg.
81-82	Col	24	1256	112	0	5.35
82-83	Buf	5	300	21	0	4.20
Totals		439	25220	1482	14	3.53
Playoff Totals		12	747	41	1	3.29

NEWTON, Cameron Charles (Cam) *5-11 170*

B. Peterborough, Ont., Feb. 25, 1950

Season	Team	GP	Min.	GA	So.	Avg.
70-71	Pitt	5	281	16	0	3.42
72-43	Pitt	11	533	35	0	3.94
73-74	Chi (WHA)	45	2732	143	1	3.14
74-75	Chi (WHA)	32	1905	126	0	3.97
75-76	Ott-Clev (WHA)	25	1469	83	1	3.39
NHL Totals		16	814	51	0	3.76
WHA Totals		102	6106	352	2	3.46
WHA Playoff Tot.		11	546	40	0	4.40

NORRIS, Jack Wayne *5-10 175*

B. Saskatoon, Sask., Aug. 5, 1942

Season	Team	GP	Min.	GA	So.	Avg.
64-65	Bos	23	1380	86	1	3.74
67-68	Chi	7	334	22	1	3.95
68-69	Chi	3	100	10	0	6.00
70-71	LA	25	1305	85	0	3.91
72-73	Alb (WHA)	64	3702	189	1	3.06
73-74	Edm (WHA)	53	2954	158	2	3.21
74-75	Phoe (WHA)	33	1962	107	1	3.27
75-76	Phoe (WHA)	41	2412	128	1	3.18
NHL Totals		58	3119	203	2	3.91
WHA Totals		191	11030	582	5	3.17
WHA Playoff Tot.		10	509	36	0	4.24

OLESCHUK, William Stephen *6-3 194*

B. Edmonton, Alta., July 20, 1955

Season	Team	GP	Min.	GA	So.	Avg.
75-76	KC	1	60	4	0	4.00
77-78	Col	2	100	9	0	5.40
78-79	Col	40	2118	136	1	3.85
79-80	Col	12	557	39	0	4.20
Totals		55	2835	188	1	3.98

OLESEVICH, Daniel

B. Port Colburne, Ont., Aug. 16, 1937

Season	Team	GP	Min.	GA	So.	Avg.
61-62	NYR	1	40	2	0	3.00

O'NEILL, Michael *5-7 155*

B. LaSalle, Que., Nov. 3, 1967

Season	Team	GP	Min.	GA	So.	Avg.
91-92	Winn	1	13	1	0	4.62

OUIMET, Edward John (Ted) *6-0 175*

B. Noranda, Que., July 6, 1947

Season	Team	GP	Min.	GA	So.	Avg.
68-69	StL	1	60	2	0	2.00
74-75	NE (WHA)	1	20	3	0	9.00

PAGEAU, Paul *5-9 160*

B. Montreal, Que., Oct. 1, 1959

Season	Team	GP	Min.	GA	So.	Avg.
80-81	LA	1	60	8	0	8.00

PAILLE, Marcel *5-8 185*

B. Shawinigan Falls, Que., Dec. 8, 1932

Season	Team	GP	Min.	GA	So.	Avg.
57-58	NYR	33	1980	102	1	3.09
58-59	NYR	1	60	4	0	4.00
59-60	NYR	17	1020	67	1	3.94
60-61	NYR	4	240	16	0	4.00
61-62	NYR	10	600	28	0	2.80
62-62	NYR	3	180	10	0	3.33
64-65	NYR	39	2262	135	0	3.58
72-73	Phil (WHA)	15	611	49	0	4.81
NHL Totals		107	6342	362	2	3.42
WHA Totals		15	611	49	0	4.81
WHA Playoff Totals		1	26	5	0	11.54

PALMATEER, Michael *5-9 170*

B. Toronto, Ont., Jan 13, 1954

Season	Team	GP	Min.	GA	So.	Avg.
76-77	Tor	50	2877	154	4	3.21
77-78	Tor	63	3760	172	5	2.74
78-79	Tor	58	3396	167	4	2.95
79-80	Tor	38	2039	125	2	3.68
80-81	Wash	49	2679	173	2	3.87
81-82	Wash	11	584	47	0	4.83
82-83	Tor	53	2965	197	0	3.99
83-84	Tor	34	1831	149	0	4.88
Totals		356	20131	1183	17	3.53
Playoff Totals		29	1765	89	2	3.03

PANG, Darren *5-5 155*

B. Meaford, Ont., Feb. 17, 1964

Season	Team	GP	Min.	GA	So.	Avg.
84-85	Chi	1	60	4	0	4.00

PANG, Darren *(Continued)*

Season	Team	GP	Min.	GA	So.	Avg.
87-88	Chi	45	2548	163	0	3.84
88-89	Chi	35	1644	120	0	4.38
Totals		81	4252	287	0	4.05
Playoff Totals		6	250	18	0	4.32

PARENT, Bernard Marcel (Bernie) *5-10 180*

B. Montreal, Que., Apr. 3, 1945

Season	Team	GP	Min.	GA	So.	Avg.
65-66	Bos	39	2083	128	1	3.69
66-67	Bos	18	1022	62	0	3.64
67-68	Phil	38	2248	93	4	2.48
68-69	Phil	58	3365	151	1	2.69
69-70	Phil	62	3680	171	3	2.79
70-71	Phil-Tor	48	2626	119	3	2.72
71-72	Tor	47	2715	116	3	2.56
72-73	Phil (WHA)	63	3653	220	2	3.61
73-74	Phil	73	4314	136	12	1.89
74-75	Phil	68	4041	137	12	2.03
75-76	Phil	11	615	24	0	2.34
76-77	Phil	61	3525	159	5	2.71
77-78	Phil	49	2923	108	7	2.22
78-79	Phil	36	1979	89	4	2.70
NHL Totals		608	35136	1493	55	2.55
WHA Totals		63	3653	220	2	3.61
NHL Playoff Totals		71	4302	174	6	2.43
WHA Playoff Totals		1	70	3	0	2.57

PARENT, Robert John *5-9 175*

B. Windsor, Ont., Feb. 19, 1958

Season	Team	GP	Min.	GA	So.	Avg.
81-82	Tor	2	120	13	0	6.50
82-83	Tor	1	40	2	0	3.00
Totals		3	160	15	0	5.63

PARRO, David *5-10 155*

B. Saskatoon, Sask., Apr. 30, 1957

Season	Team	GP	Min.	GA	So.	Avg.
80-81	Wash	18	811	49	1	3.63
81-82	Wash	52	2942	206	1	4.20
82-83	Wash	6	261	19	0	4.37
83-84	Wash	1	1	0	0	0.00
Totals		77	4015	274	2	4.09

PATRICK, Lester *6-1 180*

B. Drummondville, Que., Dec. 30, 1883

Season	Team	GP	Min.	GA	So.	Avg.
27-28	NYR	0	0	0	0	0.00
Playoff Totals		1	46	1	0	1.30

PEETERS, Peter *6-0 170*

B. Edmonton, Alta., Aug. 1, 1957

Season	Team	GP	Min.	GA	So.	Avg.
78-79	Phil	6	280	16	0	3.43
79-80	Phil	40	2373	108	1	2.73
80-81	Phil	40	2333	115	2	2.96
81-82	Phil	44	2591	160	0	3.71
82-83	Bos	62	3611	142	8	2.36
83-84	Bos	50	2868	151	0	3.16
84-85	Bos	51	2975	172	1	3.47
85-86	Bos-Wash	42	2506	144	1	3.45
86-87	Wash	37	2002	107	0	3.21
87-88	Wash	35	1896	88	2	2.78
88-89	Wash	33	1854	88	4	2.85
89-90	Phil	24	1140	72	1	3.79
90-91	Phil	26	1270	61	1	2.88
Totals		489	27699	1424	21	3.08
Playoff Totals		71	4200	232	2	3.31

PELLETIER, Marcel *5-11 180*

B. Drummondville, Que., Dec. 6, 1927

Season	Team	GP	Min.	GA	So.	Avg.
50-51	Chi	6	355	29	0	4.90
62-63	NYR	2	40	4	0	6.00
Totals		8	395	33	0	5.01

PENNEY, Steven *6-1 190*

B. Ste-Foy, Que., Feb. 2, 1961

Season	Team	GP	Min.	GA	So.	Avg.
83-84	Mont	4	240	19	0	4.75
84-85	Mont	54	3252	167	1	3.08
85-86	Mont	18	990	72	0	4.36
86-87	Winn	7	327	25	0	4.59
87-88	Winn	8	385	30	0	4.68
Totals		91	5194	313	1	3.62
Playoff Totals		27	1604	72	4	2.69

PERREAULT, Robert (Miche) *5-8 170*

B. Trois-Rivieres, Que., Jan. 28, 1931

Season	Team	GP	Min.	GA	So.	Avg.
55-56	Mont	6	360	12	1	2.00
58-59	Det	3	180	9	0	3.00
62-63	Bos	22	1320	85	1	3.86
72-73	LA (WHA)	1	60	2	0	2.00
NHL Totals		31	1860	106	2	3.42
WHA Totals		1	60	2	0	2.00

PETTIE, James *6-0 195*

B. Toronto, Ont., Oct. 24, 1953

Season	Team	GP	Min.	GA	So.	Avg.
76-77	Bos	1	60	3	0	3.00

PETTIE, James *(Continued)*

Season	Team	GP	Min.	GA	So.	Avg.
77-78	Bos	1	60	6	0	6.00
78-79	Bos	19	1037	62	1	3.59
Totals		21	1157	71	1	3.68

PIETRANGELO, Frank *5-10 182*

B. Niagara Falls, Ont., Dec. 17, 1964

Season	Team	GP	Min.	GA	So.	Avg.
87-88	Pitt	21	1207	80	1	3.98
88-89	Pitt	15	669	45	0	4.04
89-90	Pitt	21	1066	77	0	4.33
90-91	Pitt	25	1311	86	0	3.94
91-92	Pitt-Hart	10	531	32	0	3.62
Totals		92	4784	320	1	4.01
Playoff Totals		12	713	34	1	2.86

PLANTE, Joseph Jacques (Jake the Snake) *6-0 175*

B. Mont Carmel, Que., Jan. 17, 1929

Season	Team	GP	Min.	GA	So.	Avg.
52-53	Mont	3	180	4	0	1.33
53-54	Mont	17	1020	27	5	1.59
54-55	Mont	52	3080	110	5	2.14
55-56	Mont	64	3840	119	7	1.86
56-57	Mont	61	3660	123	9	2.02
57-58	Mont	57	3386	119	9	2.11
58-59	Mont	67	4000	144	9	2.16
59-60	Mont	69	4140	175	3	2.54
60-61	Mont	40	2400	112	2	2.80
61-62	Mont	70	4200	166	4	2.37
62-63	Mont	56	3320	138	5	2.49
63-64	NYR	65	3900	220	3	3.38
64-65	NYR	33	1938	109	2	3.37
68-69	StL	37	2139	70	5	1.96
69-70	StL	32	1839	67	5	2.19
70-71	Tor	40	2329	73	4	1.88
71-72	Tor	34	1965	86	2	2.63
72-73	Tor-Bos	40	2197	103	4	2.81
74-75	Edm (WHA)	31	1592	88	1	3.32
NHL Totals		837	49533	1965	82	2.38
WHA Totals		31	1592	88	1	3.32
NHL Playoff Totals		112	6651	241	15	2.17

PLASSE, Michel Pierre *5-11 172*

B. Montreal, Que., June 1, 1948

Season	Team	GP	Min.	GA	So.	Avg.
70-71	StL	1	60	3	0	3.00
72-73	Mont	17	932	40	0	2.58
73-74	Mont	15	839	57	0	4.08
74-75	KC-Pitt	44	2514	169	0	4.03
75-76	Pitt	55	3096	178	2	3.45
76-77	Col	54	2986	190	0	3.82
77-78	Col	25	1383	90	0	3.90
78-79	Col	41	2302	152	0	3.96
79-80	Col	6	327	26	0	4.77
80-81	Que	33	1933	118	0	3.66
81-82	Que	8	388	35	0	5.41
Totals		299	16760	1058	2	3.79
Playoff Totals		4	195	9	1	2.77

PLAXTON, Hugh John

B. Barrie, Ont., May 16, 1904

Season	Team	GP	Min.	GA	So.	Avg.
32-33	Mont M	1	59	5	0	5.08

POTVIN, Felix *6-1 183*

B. Anjou, Que., June 23, 1971

Season	Team	GP	Min.	GA	So.	Avg.
91-92	Tor	4	210	8	0	2.29

PRONOVOST, Claude

B. Shawinigan Falls, Que., July 22, 1935

Season	Team	GP	Min.	GA	So.	Avg.
55-56	Bos	1	60	0	1	0.00
58-59	Mont	2	60	7	0	7.00
Totals		3	120	7	1	3.50

PUPPA, Daren *6-3 205*

B. Kirkland Lake, Ont., Mar. 23, 1963

Season	Team	GP	Min.	GA	So.	Avg.
85-86	Buf	7	401	21	1	3.14
86-87	Buf	3	185	13	0	4.22
87-88	Buf	17	874	61	0	4.19
88-89	Buf	37	1908	107	1	3.36
89-90	Buf	56	3241	156	1	2.89
90-91	Buf	38	2092	118	2	3.38
91-92	Buf	33	1757	114	0	3.89
Totals		191	10458	590	5	3.38
Playoff Totals		11	593	36	0	3.64

PUSEY, Chris *6-0 180*

B. Brantford, Ont., June 30, 1965

Season	Team	GP	Min.	GA	So.	Avg.
85-86	Det	1	40	3	0	4.50

RACICOT, Andre *5-11 165*

B. Rouyn, Que., June 9, 1969

Season	Team	GP	Min.	GA	So.	Avg.
89-90	Mont	1	13	3	0	13.85
90-91	Mont	21	975	52	1	3.20
91-92	Mont	9	436	23	0	3.17
Totals		31	1424	78	1	3.29
Playoff Totals		3	13	2	0	9.23

RANFORD, Bill *5-10 170*
B. Brandon, Man., Dec. 14, 1966

Season	Team	GP	Min.	GA	So.	Avg.
85-86	Bos	4	240	10	0	2.50
86-87	Bos	41	2234	124	3	3.33
87-88	Bos	6	325	16	0	2.95
88-89	Edm	29	1509	88	1	3.50
89-90	Edm	56	3107	165	1	3.19
90-91	Edm	60	3415	182	0	3.20
91-92	Edm	67	3822	228	1	3.58
Totals		263	14652	813	6	3.33
Playoff Totals		45	2688	133	2	2.97

RAYMOND, Alain *5-10 177*
B. Rimouski, Que., June 24, 1965

Season	Team	GP	Min.	GA	So.	Avg.
87-88	Wash	1	40	2	0	3.00

RAYNER, Claude Earl (Chuck) *5-11 190*
B. Sutherland, Sask., Aug. 11, 1920

Season	Team	GP	Min.	GA	So.	Avg.
40-41	NYA	12	773	44	0	3.67
41-42	NYA	36	2230	129	1	3.58
45-46	NYR	41	2377	150	5	3.79
46-47	NYR	58	3480	177	5	3.05
47-48	NYR	12	691	42	0	3.65
48-49	NYR	58	3480	168	7	2.90
49-50	NYR	69	4140	181	6	2.62
50-51	NYR	66	3940	187	6	2.85
51-52	NYR	53	3180	159	2	3.00
52-53	NYR	20	1200	58	1	2.90
Totals		425	25491	1295	33	3.05
Playoff Totals		18	1135	46	1	2.43

REAUGH, Daryl *6-4 200*
B. Prince George, B.C., Feb. 13, 1965

Season	Team	GP	Min.	GA	So.	Avg.
84-85	Edm	1	60	5	0	5.00
87-88	Edm	6	176	14	0	4.77
90-91	Hart	20	1010	53	1	3.15
Totals		27	1246	72	1	3.47

REDDICK, Eldon (Pokey) *5-8 170*
B. Halifax, N.S., Oct. 6, 1964

Season	Team	GP	Min.	GA	So.	Avg.
86-87	Winn	48	2762	149	0	3.24
87-88	Winn	28	1487	102	0	4.12
88-89	Winn	41	2109	144	0	4.10
89-90	Edm	11	604	31	0	3.08
90-91	Edm	2	120	9	0	4.50
Totals		130	7082	435	0	3.69
Playoff Totals		4	168	10	0	3.57

REDQUEST, Greg *5-10 190*
B. Toronto, Ont., July 30, 1956

Season	Team	GP	Min.	GA	So.	Avg.
77-78	Pitt	1	13	3	3	13.85

REECE, David Barrett *6-1 190*
B. Troy, N.Y., Sept. 13, 1948

Season	Team	GP	Min.	GA	So.	Avg.
75-76	Bos	14	777	43	2	3.32

REESE, Jeff *5-9 170*
B. Brantford, Ont., Mar. 24, 1966

Season	Team	GP	Min.	GA	So.	Avg.
87-88	Tor	5	249	17	0	4.10
88-89	Tor	10	486	40	0	4.94
89-90	Tor	21	1101	81	0	4.41
90-91	Tor	30	1430	92	1	3.86
91-92	Tor-Calg	20	1000	57	1	3.42
Totals		86	4266	287	2	4.04
Playoff Totals		2	108	6	0	3.33

RESCH, Glenn Allan (Chico) *5-9 165*
B. Moose Jaw, Sask., July 10, 1948

Season	Team	GP	Min.	GA	So.	Avg.
73-74	NYI	2	120	6	0	3.00
74-75	NYI	25	1432	59	3	2.47
75-76	NYI	44	2546	88	7	2.07
76-77	NYI	46	2711	103	4	2.28
77-78	NYI	45	2637	112	3	2.55
78-79	NYI	43	2539	106	2	2.50
79-80	NYI	45	2606	132	3	3.04
80-81	NYI-Col	40	2266	121	3	3.20
81-82	Col	61	3424	230	0	4.03
82-83	NJ	65	3650	242	0	3.98
83-84	NJ	51	2641	184	1	4.18
84-85	NJ	51	2884	200	0	4.16
85-86	NJ-Phil	36	1956	136	0	4.17
86-87	Phil	17	867	42	0	2.91
Totals		571	32279	1761	26	3.27
Playoff Totals		41	2044	85	2	2.50

RHEAUME, Herbert

Season	Team	GP	Min.	GA	So.	Avg.
25-26	Mont	31	1889	92	0	2.92

RHODES, Damian *6-0 165*
B. St. Paul, Minn., May 28, 1969

Season	Team	GP	Min.	GA	So.	Avg.
90-91	Tor	1	60	1	0	1.00

RICCI, Joseph Nick *5-10 160*
B. Niagara Falls, Ont., June 3, 1959

Season	Team	GP	Min.	GA	So.	Avg.
79-80	Pitt	4	240	14	0	3.50
80-81	Pitt	9	540	35	0	3.88

RICCI, Joseph Nick *(Continued)*

Season	Team	GP	Min.	GA	So.	Avg.
81-82	Pitt	3	160	14	0	5.25
82-83	Pitt	3	147	16	0	6.53
Totals		19	1087	79	0	4.36

RICHARDSON, Terrance Paul *6-1 190*
B. Powell River, B.C., May 7, 1953

Season	Team	GP	Min.	GA	So.	Avg.
73-74	Det	9	315	28	0	5.33
74-75	Det	4	202	23	0	6.83
75-76	Det	1	60	7	0	7.00
76-77	Det	5	269	18	0	4.01
78-79	Det	1	60	9	0	9.00
Totals		20	906	85	0	5.63

RICHTER, Mike *5-11 185*
B. Philadelphia, Pa., Sept. 22, 1966

Season	Team	GP	Min.	GA	So.	Avg.
89-90	NYR	23	1320	66	0	3.00
90-91	NYR	45	2596	135	0	3.12
91-92	NYR	41	2298	119	3	3.11
Totals		109	6214	320	3	3.09
Playoff Totals		20	1113	61	2	3.29

RIDLEY, Charles Curtis (Curt) *6-0 190*
B. Minnedosa, Man., Oct. 24, 1951

Season	Team	GP	Min.	GA	So.	Avg.
74-75	NYR	2	81	7	0	5.19
75-76	Van	9	500	19	1	2.28
76-77	Van	37	2074	134	0	3.88
77-78	Van	40	2010	136	0	4.06
79-80	Van-Tor	13	709	47	0	3.98
80-81	Tor	3	124	12	0	5.81
Totals		104	5498	355	1	3.87
Playoff Totals		2	120	8	0	4.00

RIENDEAU, Vincent *5-10 185*
B. St. Hyacinthe, Que., Apr. 20, 1966

Season	Team	GP	Min.	GA	So.	Avg.
87-88	Mont	1	36	5	0	8.33
88-89	StL	32	1842	108	0	3.52
89-90	StL	43	2551	149	1	3.50
90-91	StL	44	2671	134	3	3.01
91-92	StL-Det	5	244	13	0	3.20
Totals		125	7344	409	4	3.34
Playoff Totals		23	1157	63	1	3.27

RIGGIN, Denis Melville *5-11 156*
B. Kincardine, Ont., Apr. 11, 1936

Season	Team	GP	Min.	GA	So.	Avg.
59-60	Det	9	540	32	1	3.56
62-63	Det	9	445	22	0	2.97
Totals		18	985	54	1	3.29

RIGGIN, Patrick Michael *5-9 163*
B. Kincardine, Ont., May 26, 1959

Season	Team	GP	Min.	GA	So.	Avg.
78-79	Birm (WHA)	46	2511	158	1	3.78
79-80	Atl	25	1368	73	2	3.20
80-81	Calg	42	2411	154	0	3.83
81-82	Calg	52	2934	207	2	4.23
82-83	Wash	38	2161	121	0	3.36
83-84	Wash	41	2299	102	4	2.66
84-85	Wash	57	3388	168	2	2.98
85-86	Wash-Bos	46	2641	150	1	3.41
86-87	Bos-Pitt	27	1501	84	0	3.36
87-88	Pitt	22	1169	76	0	3.90
Totals		350	19872	1135	11	3.43
Playoff Totals		25	1336	72	0	3.23

RING, Robert

Season	Team	GP	Min.	GA	So.	Avg.
65-66	Bos	1	34	4	0	7.06

RIVARD, Fernand Joseph *5-9 160*
B. Grand Mere, Que., Jan. 18, 1946

Season	Team	GP	Min.	GA	So.	Avg.
68-69	Minn	13	657	48	0	4.38
69-70	Minn	14	800	42	1	3.15
73-74	Minn	13	701	50	1	4.28
74-75	Minn	15	707	50	0	4.24
Totals		55	2865	190	2	3.98

ROACH, John Ross *5-5 130*
B. Fort Perry, Ont., June 23, 1900

Season	Team	GP	Min.	GA	So.	Avg.
21-22	Tor	22	1340	91	0	4.14
22-23	Tor	24	1469	88	1	3.67
23-24	Tor	23	1380	80	1	3.48
24-25	Tor	30	1800	84	1	2.80
25-26	Tor	36	2210	114	2	3.17
26-27	Tor	44	2764	94	4	2.14
27-28	Tor	43	2690	88	4	2.05
28-29	NYR	44	2760	65	13	1.48
29-30	NYR	44	2770	143	1	3.25
30-31	NYR	44	2760	87	7	1.98
31-32	NYR	48	3020	112	9	2.33
32-33	Det	48	2970	93	10	1.94
33-34	Det	18	1030	45	1	2.50
34-35	Det	23	1460	62	4	2.70
Totals		491	30423	1246	58	2.46
Playoff Totals		34	2206	69	8	1.88

ROBERTS, Maurice (Moe) *5-9 165*
B. Waterbury, Conn., Dec. 13, 1907

Season	Team	GP	Min.	GA	So.	Avg.
25-26	Bos	2	90	5	0	2.50
31-32	NYA	1	60	1	0	1.00
33-34	NYA	6	336	25	0	4.17
51-52	Chi	1	20	0	0	0.00
Totals		10	506	31	0	3.68

ROBERTSON, Earl Cooper *5-10 165*
B. Bingorgh, Sask., Nov. 24, 1910

Season	Team	GP	Min.	GA	So.	Avg.
37-38	NYA	48	3000	111	6	2.31
38-39	NYA	46	2850	136	3	2.96
39-40	NYA	48	2960	140	6	2.92
40-41	NYA	36	2260	142	1	3.94
41-42	NYA	12	750	46	0	3.83
Totals		190	11820	575	16	2.92
Playoff Totals		15	995	29	2	1.75

ROLLINS, Elwin Ira (Al) *6-2 175*
B. Vanguard, Sask., Oct. 9, 1926

Season	Team	GP	Min.	GA	So.	Avg.
49-50	Tor	2	120	4	1	2.00
50-51	Tor	40	2373	70	5	1.77
51-52	Tor	70	4170	154	5	2.22
52-53	Chi	70	4200	175	6	2.50
53-54	Chi	66	3960	213	5	3.23
54-55	Chi	44	2640	150	0	3.41
55-56	Chi	58	3480	174	3	3.00
56-57	Chi	70	4200	225	3	3.21
59-60	NYR	8	480	31	0	3.88
Totals		428	25623	1196	28	2.80
Playoff Totals		13	798	30	0	2.26

ROMANO, Roberto *5-6 170*
B. Montreal, Que., Oct. 10, 1962

Season	Team	GP	Min.	GA	So.	Avg.
82-83	Pitt	3	155	18	0	6.97
83-84	Pitt	18	1020	78	1	4.59
84-85	Pitt	31	1629	120	1	4.42
85-86	Pitt	46	2684	159	2	3.55
86-87	Pitt-Bos	26	1498	93	0	3.72
Totals		125	7046	474	4	4.04

ROUSSEL, Dominic *6-1 185*
B. Hull, Que., Feb. 22, 1970

Season	Team	GP	Min.	GA	So.	Avg.
91-92	Phil	17	992	40	1	2.60

ROY, Patrick *6-0 182*
B. Quebec City, Que., Oct. 5, 1965

Season	Team	GP	Min.	GA	So.	Avg.
84-45	Mont	1	20	0	0	0.00
85-86	Mont	47	2651	148	1	3.35
86-87	Mont	46	2686	131	1	2.93
87-88	Mont	45	2586	125	3	2.90
88-89	Mont	48	2744	113	4	2.47
89-90	Mont	54	3173	134	3	2.53
90-91	Mont	48	2835	128	1	2.71
91-92	Mont	67	3935	155	6	2.36
Totals		356	20630	934	18	2.72
Playoff Totals		88	5296	223	5	2.53

RUPP, Patrick Lloyd
B. Detroit, Mich., Aug. 12, 1942

Season	Team	GP	Min.	GA	So.	Avg.
63-64	Det	1	60	4	0	4.00

RUTHERFORD, James Earl (Jim) *5-8 168*
B. Beeton, Ont., Feb. 17, 1949

Season	Team	GP	Min.	GA	So.	Avg.
70-71	Det	29	1498	94	1	3.77
71-72	Pitt	40	2160	116	1	3.22
72-73	Pitt	49	2660	129	3	2.91
73-74	Pitt-Det	51	2852	168	0	3.53
74-75	Det	59	3478	217	2	3.74
75-76	Det	44	2640	158	4	3.59
76-77	Det	48	2740	180	0	3.94
77-78	Det	43	2468	134	1	3.26
78-79	Det	32	1892	103	1	3.27
79-80	Det	23	1326	92	1	4.16
80-81	Det-Tor-LA	31	1741	135	0	4.65
81-82	LA	7	380	43	0	6.79
82-83	Det	1	60	7	0	7.00
Totals		457	25895	1576	14	3.65
Playoff Totals		8	440	28	0	3.82

RUTLEDGE, Wayne Alvin *6-2 200*
B. Barrie, Ont., Jan. 5, 1942

Season	Team	GP	Min.	GA	So.	Avg.
67-68	LA	45	2444	117	2	2.87
68-69	LA	17	921	56	0	3.65
69-70	LA	20	960	68	0	4.25
72-73	Hou (WHA)	36	2163	108	0	3.00
73-74	Hou (WHA)	25	1509	84	0	3.34
74-75	Hou (WHA)	35	2098	113	2	3.23
75-76	Hou (WHA)	25	1456	77	1	3.17
76-77	Hou (WHA)	42	2512	132	3	3.15

RUTLEDGE, Wayne Alvin *(Continued)*

Season	Team	GP	Min.	GA	So.	Avg.
77-78	Hou (WHA)	12	634	47	0	4.45
NHL Totals		82	4325	241	2	3.34
WHA Totals		175	10372	561	6	3.25
NHL Playoff Tot.		8	378	20	0	3.17
WHA Playoff Tot.		16	874	42	0	2.88

St. CROIX, Richard *5-10 160*

B. Kenora, Ont., Jan. 3, 1955

Season	Team	GP	Min.	GA	So.	Avg.
77-78	Phil	7	395	20	0	3.04
78-79	Phil	2	117	6	0	3.08
79-80	Phil	1	60	2	0	2.00
80-81	Phil	27	1567	65	2	2.49
81-82	Phil	29	1729	112	0	3.89
82-83	Phil-Tor	33	1860	112	0	3.61
Totals		99	5728	317	2	3.32
Playoff Totals		11	562	29	1	3.10

ST. LAURENT, Sam *5-10 190*

B. Arvida, Que., Feb. 16, 1959

Season	Team	GP	Min.	GA	So.	Avg.
85-86	NJ	4	188	13	1	4.15
86-87	Det	6	342	16	0	2.81
87-88	Det	6	294	16	0	3.27
88-89	Det	4	141	9	0	3.83
89-90	Det	14	607	38	0	3.76
Totals		34	1572	92	1	3.51
Playoff Totals		1	10	1	0	6.00

SANDS, Charlie *5-9 160*

B. Fort William, Ont., Mar. 23, 1911

Season	Team	GP	Min.	GA	So.	Avg.
39-40	Mont	1	25	5	0	12.00

SANDS, Michael *5-9 155*

B. Mississauga, Ont., April 6, 1963

Season	Team	GP	Min.	GA	So.	Avg.
84-85	Minn	3	139	14	0	6.04
86-87	Minn	3	163	12	0	4.42
Totals		6	302	26	0	5.17

SAUVE, Robert *5-8 165*

B. Ste. Genevieve, Que., June 17, 1955

Season	Team	GP	Min.	GA	So.	Avg.
76-77	Buf	4	184	11	0	3.59
77-78	Buf	11	480	20	2	2.50
78-79	Buf	29	1610	100	0	3.73
79-80	Buf	32	1880	74	4	2.36
80-81	Buf	35	2100	111	2	3.17
81-82	Buf-Det	55	3125	200	0	3.84
82-83	Buf	54	3110	179	1	3.45
83-84	Buf	40	2375	138	0	3.49
84-85	Buf	27	1564	84	0	3.22
85-86	Chi	38	2099	138	0	3.95
86-87	Chi	46	2660	159	1	3.59
87-88	NJ	34	1804	107	0	3.56
Totals		405	22991	1321	8	3.45
Playoff Totals		34	1850	95	4	3.08

SAWCHUK, Terrance Gordon (Terry) *6-0 195*

B. Winnipeg, Man., Dec. 28, 1929

Season	Team	GP	Min.	GA	So.	Avg.
49-50	Det	7	420	16	1	2.29
50-51	Det	70	4200	139	11	1.99
51-52	Det	70	4200	133	12	1.90
52-53	Det	63	3780	120	9	1.90
53-54	Det	67	4000	129	12	1.94
54-55	Det	68	4040	132	12	1.96
55-56	Bos	68	4080	181	9	2.66
56-57	Bos	34	2040	81	2	2.38
57-58	Det	70	4200	207	3	2.96
58-59	Det	67	4020	209	5	3.12
59-60	Det	58	3480	156	5	2.69
60-61	Det	37	2080	113	2	3.05
61-62	Det	43	2580	143	5	3.33
62-63	Det	48	2775	119	3	2.48
63-64	Det	53	3140	138	5	2.60
64-65	Tor	36	2160	92	1	2.56
65-66	Tor	27	1521	80	1	2.96
66-67	Tor	28	1409	66	2	2.81
67-68	LA	36	1936	99	2	3.07
68-69	Det	13	641	28	0	2.62
69-70	NYR	8	412	20	1	2.91
Totals		971	57114	2401	103	2.52
Playoff Totals		106	6311	267	12	2.54

SCHAEFER, Joseph

B. Long Island City, N.Y., Dec. 21, 1924

Season	Team	GP	Min.	GA	So.	Avg.
59-60	NYR	1	39	5	0	7.69
60-61	NYR	1	47	3	0	3.83
Totals		2	86	8	0	5.58

SCOTT, Ron *5-8 155*

B. Guelph, Ont., July 21, 1960

Season	Team	GP	Min.	GA	So.	Avg.
83-84	NYR	9	485	29	0	3.59
85-86	NYR	4	156	11	0	4.23
86-87	NYR	1	65	5	0	4.62

SCOTT, Ron *(Continued)*

Season	Team	GP	Min.	GA	So.	Avg.
87-88	NYR	2	90	6	0	4.00
89-90	LA	12	654	40	0	3.67
Totals		28	1450	91	0	3.77
Playoff Totals		1	32	4	0	7.50

SEVIGNY, Richard *5-8 172*

B. Montreal, Que., Apr. 11, 1957

Season	Team	GP	Min.	GA	So.	Avg.
79-80	Mont	11	632	31	0	2.94
80-81	Mont	33	1777	71	2	2.40
81-82	Mont	19	1027	53	0	3.10
82-83	Mont	38	2130	122	1	3.44
83-84	Mont	40	2203	124	1	3.38
84-85	Que	20	1104	62	1	3.37
85-86	Que	11	468	33	0	4.23
86-87	Que	4	144	11	0	4.58
Totals		176	9485	507	5	3.21
Playoff Totals		6	208	13	0	3.75

SHARPLES, Warren *6-0 180*

B. Calgary, Alta., Mar. 1, 1965

Season	Team	GP	Min.	GA	So.	Avg.
91-92	Calg	1	65	4	0	3.69

SHIELDS, Allen *6-0 188*

B. Ottawa, Ont., May 10, 1907

Season	Team	GP	Min.	GA	So.	Avg.
31-32	NYA	2	41	9	0	13.17

SIDORKIEWICZ, Peter *5-9 180*

B. Dabrown Bialostocka, Poland, June 29, 1963

Season	Team	GP	Min.	GA	So.	Avg.
87-88	Hart	1	60	6	0	6.00
88-89	Hart	44	2635	133	4	3.03
89-90	Hart	46	2703	161	1	3.57
90-91	Hart	52	2953	164	1	3.33
91-92	Hart	35	1995	111	2	3.34
Totals		178	10346	575	8	3.33
Playoff Totals		15	912	55	0	3.62

SIMMONS, Donald *5-10 150*

B. Port Colborne, Ont., Sept. 13, 1931

Season	Team	GP	Min.	GA	So.	Avg.
56-57	Bos	26	1560	63	4	2.42
57-58	Bos	38	2228	93	5	2.50
58-59	Bos	58	3480	184	3	3.17
59-60	Bos	28	1680	94	2	3.36
60-61	Bos	18	1080	59	1	3.28
61-62	Tor	9	540	21	1	2.33
62-63	Tor	28	1680	70	1	2.50
63-64	Tor	21	1191	63	3	3.17
65-66	NYR	11	491	37	0	4.52
67-68	NYR	5	300	13	0	2.60
68-69	NYR	5	206	8	0	2.33
Totals		247	14436	705	20	2.93
Playoff Totals		24	1436	64	3	2.67

SIMMONS, Gary Byrne *6-2 200*

B. Charlottetown, P.E.I., July 19, 1944

Season	Team	GP	Min.	GA	So.	Avg.
74-75	Cal	34	2029	124	2	3.67
75-76	Cal	40	2360	131	2	3.33
76-77	Clev-LA	19	1080	67	1	3.72
77-78	LA	14	693	44	0	3.81
Totals		107	6162	366	5	3.56
Playoff Totals		1	20	1	0	3.00

SKIDMORE, Paul *6-0 185*

B. Smithtown, N.Y., July 22, 1956

Season	Team	GP	Min.	GA	So.	Avg.
81-82	StL	2	120	6	0	3.00

SKORODENSKI, Warren *6-1 180*

B. Winnipeg, Man., Mar. 22, 1960

Season	Team	GP	Min.	GA	So.	Avg.
81-82	Chi	1	60	5	0	5.00
84-85	Chi	27	1396	75	2	3.22
85-86	Chi	1	60	6	0	6.00
86-87	Chi	3	155	7	0	2.71
87-88	Edm	3	61	7	0	6.89
Totals		35	1732	100	2	3.46
Playoff Totals		2	33	6	0	10.91

SMITH, Allan Robert (Al) *6-1 200*

B. Toronto, Ont., Nov. 10, 1945

Season	Team	GP	Min.	GA	So.	Avg.
65-66	Tor	2	62	2	0	1.94
66-67	Tor	1	60	5	0	5.00
68-69	Tor	7	335	16	0	2.87
69-70	Pitt	46	2555	129	2	3.03
70-71	Pitt	46	2472	128	2	3.11
71-72	Det	43	2500	135	4	3.24
72-73	NE (WHA)	51	3059	162	3	3.18
73-74	NE (WHA)	55	3194	164	2	3.08
74-75	NE (WHA)	59	3494	202	2	3.47
75-76	Buf	14	840	43	0	3.07
76-77	Buf	7	265	19	0	4.30
77-78	NE (WHA)	55	3246	174	2	3.22
78-79	NE (WHA)	40	2396	132	1	3.31

SMITH, Allan Robert (Al) *(Continued)*

Season	Team	GP	Min.	GA	So.	Avg.
79-80	Hart	30	1754	107	2	3.66
80-81	Col	37	1909	151	0	4.75
NHL Totals		233	12752	735	10	3.46
WHA Totals		260	15389	834	10	3.25
NHL Playoff Tot.		6	317	21	0	3.97
WHA Playoff Tot.		35	1947	124	1	3.82

SMITH, Gary Edward (Suitcase) *6-4 215*

B. Ottawa, Ont., Feb. 4, 1944

Season	Team	GP	Min.	GA	So.	Avg.
65-66	Tor	3	118	7	0	3.56
66-67	Tor	2	115	7	0	3.65
67-68	Oak	21	1129	60	1	3.19
68-69	Oak	54	2993	148	4	2.97
69-70	Oak	65	3762	195	2	3.11
70-71	Cal	71	3975	256	2	3.86
71-72	Chi	28	1540	62	5	2.42
72-73	Chi	23	1340	79	0	3.54
73-74	Van	66	3632	208	3	3.44
74-75	Van	72	3823	197	6	3.09
75-76	Van	51	2864	167	2	3.50
76-77	Minn	36	2090	139	1	3.99
77-78	Wash-Minn	20	1160	77	0	3.98
78-79	Ind-Winn (WHA)	22	1290	92	0	4.28
79-80	Winn	20	1073	73	0	4.08
NHL Totals		532	29614	1675	26	3.39
WHA Totals		22	1290	92	0	4.28
NHL Playoff Tot.		20	1153	62	1	3.23
WHA Playoff Tot.		10	563	35	0	3.73

SMITH, Norman *5-7 165*

Toronto, Ont., Mar. 18, 1908

Season	Team	GP	Min.	GA	So.	Avg.
31-32	Mont M	21	1267	62	0	2.95
34-35	Det	25	1550	52	2	2.08
35-36	Det	48	3030	103	6	2.15
36-37	Det	48	2980	102	6	2.13
37-38	Det	47	2930	130	3	2.77
38-39	Det	4	240	12	0	3.00
43-44	Det	5	240	11	0	2.75
44-45	Det	1	60	3	0	3.00
Totals		199	12297	475	17	2.32
Playoff Totals		12	880	18	3	1.23

SMITH, William John (Billy) *5-10 185*

B. Perth, Ont., Dec. 12, 1950

Season	Team	GP	Min.	GA	So.	Avg.
71-72	LA	5	300	23	0	4.60
72-73	NYI	37	2122	147	0	4.16
73-74	NYI	46	2615	134	0	3.07
74-75	NYI	58	3368	156	3	2.78
75-76	NYI	39	2254	98	3	2.61
76-77	NYI	36	2089	87	2	2.50
77-78	NYI	38	2154	95	2	2.65
78-79	NYI	40	2261	108	1	2.87
79-80	NYI	38	2114	104	2	2.95
80-81	NYI	41	2363	129	2	3.28
81-82	NYI	46	2685	133	0	2.97
82-83	NYI	41	2340	112	1	2.87
83-84	NYI	42	2279	130	2	3.42
84-85	NYI	37	2090	133	0	3.82
85-86	NYI	41	2308	143	1	3.72
86-87	NYI	40	2252	132	1	3.52
87-88	NYI	38	2107	113	2	3.22
88-89	NYI	17	730	54	0	4.44
Totals		680	38426	2031	22	3.17
Playoff Totals		132	7645	348	5	2.73

SNEDDON, Robert Allan *6-2 190*

B. Montreal, Que., May 31, 1944

Season	Team	GP	Min.	GA	So.	Avg.
70-71	Cal	5	225	21	0	5.60

SOETAERT, Douglas Henry *6-0 185*

B. Edmonton, Alta., Apr. 21, 1955

Season	Team	GP	Min.	GA	So.	Avg.
75-76	NYR	8	273	24	0	5.27
76-77	NYR	12	570	28	1	2.95
77-78	NYR	6	360	20	0	3.33
78-79	NYR	17	900	57	0	3.80
79-80	NYR	8	435	33	0	4.55
80-81	NYR	39	2320	152	0	3.93
81-82	Winn	39	2157	155	2	4.31
82-83	Winn	44	2533	174	0	4.12
83-84	Winn	47	2530	182	0	4.30
84-85	Mont	28	1606	91	0	3.40
85-86	Mont	23	1215	56	3	2.77
86-87	NYR	13	675	58	0	5.16
Totals		284	15583	1030	6	3.97
Playoff Totals		5	180	14	0	4.67

SPOONER, Andy (Red)

Season	Team	GP	Min.	GA	So.	Avg.
29-30	Pitt Pi	1	60	6	0	6.00

STANIOWSKI, Edward *5-9 170*

B. Moose Jaw, Sask., July 7, 1955

Season	Team	GP	Min.	GA	So.	Avg.
75-76	StL	11	620	33	0	3.19
76-77	StL	29	1589	108	0	4.08
77-78	StL	17	886	57	0	3.86
78-79	StL	39	2291	146	0	3.82

Season	Team	GP	Min.	GA	So.	Avg.
STANIOWSKI, Edward *(Continued)*						
79-80	StL	22	1108	80	0	4.33
80-81	StL	19	1010	72	0	4.28
81-82	Winn	45	2643	174	1	3.95
82-83	Winn	17	827	65	1	4.72
83-84	Winn-Hart	19	1081	82	0	4.55
84-85	Hart	1	20	1	0	3.00
Totals		219	12075	818	2	4.06
Playoff Totals		8	428	28	0	3.92
STARR, Harold *5-11 176*						
B. Ottawa, Ont., July 6, 1906						
31-32	Mont M	1	3	0	0	0.00
STAUBER, Robb *5-10 165*						
B. Duluth, Minn., Nov. 25, 1967						
89-90	LA	2	83	11	0	7.95
STEFAN, Gregory Steven *5-11 180*						
B. Brantford, Ont., Feb. 11, 1961						
81-82	Det	2	120	10	2	5.00
82-83	Det	35	1847	139	0	4.52
83-84	Det	50	2600	152	2	3.51
84-85	Det	46	2635	190	0	4.33
85-86	Det	37	2068	155	1	4.50
86-87	Det	43	2351	135	1	3.45
87-88	Det	33	1854	96	1	3.11
88-89	Det	46	2499	167	0	4.01
89-90	Det	7	359	24	0	4.01
Totals		299	16333	1068	5	3.92
Playoff Totals		30	1681	99	1	3.53
STEIN, Phillip J.						
B. Toronto, Ont., Sept. 13, 1913						
39-40	Tor	1	70	2	0	1.71
STEPHENSON, Frederick Wayne *5-9 175*						
B. Fort William, Ont., Jan. 29, 1945						
71-72	StL	2	100	9	0	5.40
72-73	StL	45	2535	128	1	3.03
73-74	StL	40	2360	123	2	3.13
74-75	Phil	12	639	29	1	2.72
75-76	Phil	66	3819	164	1	2.58
76-77	Phil	21	1065	41	3	2.31
77-78	Phil	26	1482	68	3	2.75
78-79	Phil	40	2187	122	2	3.35
79-80	Wash	56	3146	187	0	3.57
80-81	Wash	20	1010	66	1	3.92
Totals		328	18343	937	14	3.06
Playoff Totals		26	1522	79	2	3.11
STEVENSON, Douglas *5-8 170*						
B. Regina, Sask., Apr. 6, 1924						
44-45	NYR-Chi	6	360	27	0	4.50
45-46	Chi	2	120	12	0	6.00
Totals		8	480	39	0	4.88
STEWART, Charles (Doc)						
24-25	Bos	21	1266	65	2	3.10
25-26	Bos	35	2168	80	6	2.29
26-27	Bos	21	1303	49	2	2.33
Totals		77	4737	194	10	2.46
STEWART, Jim						
79-80	Bos	1	20	5	0	15.00
STUART, Herbert						
26-27	Det	3	180	5	0	1.67
SYLVESTRI, Don *6-0 180*						
B. Sudbury, Ont., June 2, 1961						
84-85	Bos	3	102	6	0	3.53
TABARACCI, Richard *5-10 185*						
B. Toronto, Ont., Jan. 2, 1969						
88-89	Pitt	1	33	4	0	7.27
90-91	Winn	24	1093	71	1	3.90
91-92	Winn	18	966	52	0	3.23
Totals		43	2092	127	1	3.64
Playoff Totals		7	387	26	0	4.03
TAKKO, Kari *6-2 185*						
B. Uusikaupunki, Finland, June 23, 1963						
85-86	Minn	1	60	3	0	3.00
86-87	Minn	38	2075	119	0	3.44
87-88	Minn	37	1919	143	1	4.47
88-89	Minn	32	1603	93	0	3.48
89-90	Minn	21	1012	68	0	4.03
90-91	Minn	2	119	12	0	6.05
Totals		131	6788	438	1	3.87
Playoff Totals		4	109	7	0	3.85
TANNER, John *6-3 182*						
B. Cambridge, Ont., Mar. 17, 1971						
89-90	Que	1	60	3	0	3.00

Season	Team	GP	Min.	GA	So.	Avg.
TANNER, John *(Continued)*						
90-91	Que	6	228	16	0	4.21
91-92	Que	14	796	46	1	3.47
Totals		21	1084	65	1	3.60
TATARYN, David Nathan *5-9 160*						
B. Sudbury, Ont., July 17, 1950						
75-76	Tor	23	1261	100	0	4.76
	(WHA)					
76-77	NYR	2	80	10	0	7.50
TAYLOR, Robert Ian *6-1 180*						
B. Calgary, Alta., Jan. 24, 1945						
71-72	Phil	6	320	16	0	3.00
72-73	Phil	23	1144	78	0	4.09
73-74	Phil	8	366	26	0	4.26
74-75	Phil	3	120	13	0	6.50
75-76	Phil-Pitt	6	318	22	0	4.15
Totals		46	2268	155	0	4.10
TENO, Harvey						
B. Windsor, Ont.						
38-39	Det	5	300	15	0	3.00
TERRERI, Chris *5-9 160*						
B. Providence, R.I., Nov. 15, 1964						
86-87	NJ	7	286	21	0	4.41
88-89	NJ	8	402	18	0	2.69
89-90	NJ	35	1931	110	0	3.42
90-91	NJ	53	2970	144	1	2.91
91-92	NJ	54	3169	169	1	3.20
Totals		157	8758	462	2	3.17
Playoff Totals		18	1052	57	0	3.25
THOMAS, Robert Wayne *6-2 195*						
B. Ottawa, Ont., Oct. 9, 1947						
72-73	Mont	10	583	23	1	2.37
73-74	Mont	42	2410	111	1	2.76
75-76	Tor	64	3684	196	2	3.19
76-77	Tor	33	1803	116	1	3.86
77-78	NYR	41	2352	141	4	3.60
78-79	NYR	31	1668	101	1	3.63
79-80	NYR	12	668	44	0	3.95
80-81	NYR	10	600	34	0	3.40
Totals		243	13768	766	10	3.34
Playoff Totals		15	849	50	1	3.53
THOMPSON, Cecil R. (Tiny) *5-10 160*						
B. Sandon, B.C., May 31, 1905						
28-29	Bos	44	2710	52	12	1.18
29-30	Bos	44	2680	98	3	2.23
30-31	Bos	44	2730	90	3	2.05
31-32	Bos	43	2698	103	9	2.40
32-33	Bos	48	3000	88	11	1.83
33-34	Bos	48	2980	130	5	2.71
34-35	Bos	48	2970	112	8	2.33
35-36	Bos	48	2930	82	10	1.71
36-37	Bos	48	2970	110	6	2.29
37-38	Bos	48	2970	89	7	1.85
38-39	Bos-Det	44	2706	109	4	2.42
39-40	Det	46	2830	120	3	2.61
Totals		553	34174	1183	81	2.08
Playoff Totals		44	2970	93	7	1.88
THOMPSON, Vincent *5-11 185*						
B. Quebec City, Que., Oct. 21, 1959						
79-80	Tor	10	329	28	0	5.11
80-81	Tor	3	143	16	0	6.71
81-82	Tor	40	2033	153	1	4.52
82-83	Tor	1	40	2	0	3.00
83-84	Pitt	4	240	24	0	6.00
Totals		58	2785	223	1	4.80
TUCKER, Ted *5-11 165*						
B. Fort William, Ont., May 7, 1949						
73-74	Cal	5	177	10	0	3.39
TUGNUTT, Ron *5-11 155*						
B. Scarborough, Ont., Oct. 22, 1967						
87-88	Que	6	284	16	0	3.38
88-89	Que	26	1367	82	0	3.60
89-90	Que	35	1978	152	0	4.61
90-91	Que	56	3144	212	0	4.05
91-92	Que-Edm	33	1707	116	1	4.08
Totals		156	8480	578	1	4.09
Playoff Totals		2	60	3	0	3.00
TURNER, Joseph						
41-42	Det	1	60	3	0	3.00
VACHON, Rogatien (Rogie) *5-7 165*						
B. Palmarolle, Que., Sept. 8, 1945						
66-67	Mont	19	1137	47	1	2.48
67-68	Mont	39	2227	92	4	2.48
68-69	Mont	36	2051	98	2	2.87
69-70	Mont	64	3697	162	4	2.63
70-71	Mont	47	2676	118	2	2.65

Season	Team	GP	Min.	GA	So.	Avg.
VACHON, Rogatien (Rogie) *(Continued)*						
71-72	Mont-LA	29	1606	111	0	4.15
72-73	LA	53	3120	148	4	2.85
73-74	LA	65	3751	175	5	2.80
74-75	LA	54	3239	121	6	2.24
75-76	LA	51	3060	160	5	3.14
76-77	LA	68	4059	184	8	2.72
77-78	LA	70	4107	196	4	2.86
78-79	Det	50	2908	189	0	3.90
79-80	Det	59	3474	209	4	3.61
80-81	Bos	53	3021	168	1	3.34
81-82	Bos	38	2165	132	1	3.66
Totals		795	46298	2310	51	2.99
Playoff Totals		48	2876	133	2	2.77
VANBIESBROUCK, John *5-7 175*						
B. Detroit, Mich., Sept. 4, 1963						
81-82	NYR	1	60	1	0	1.00
83-84	NYR	3	180	10	0	3.33
84-85	NYR	42	2358	166	1	4.22
85-86	NYR	61	3326	184	3	3.32
86-87	NYR	50	2656	161	0	3.64
87-88	NYR	56	3319	187	2	3.38
88-89	NYR	56	3207	197	0	3.69
89-90	NYR	47	2734	154	1	3.38
90-91	NYR	40	2257	126	3	3.35
91-92	NYR	45	2526	120	2	2.85
Totals		401	22623	1306	12	3.46
Playoff Totals		38	1940	105	2	3.25
VEISOR, Michael David *5-9 158*						
B. Toronto, Ont., Aug. 25, 1952						
73-74	Chi	10	537	20	1	2.23
74-75	Chi	9	460	36	0	4.70
76-77	Chi	3	180	13	0	4.33
77-78	Chi	12	720	31	2	2.58
78-79	Chi	17	1020	60	0	3.53
79-80	Chi	11	660	37	0	3.36
80-81	Hart	29	1588	118	1	4.46
81-82	Hart	13	701	53	0	4.54
82-83	Hart	23	1280	118	1	5.53
83-84	Hart-Winn	12	660	46	0	4.18
Totals		139	7806	532	5	4.09
Playoff Totals		4	180	15	0	5.00
VERNON, Michael *5-9 170*						
B. Calgary, Alta., Feb. 24, 1963						
82-83	Calg	2	100	11	0	6.60
83-84	Calg	1	11	4	0	22.22
85-86	Calg	18	921	52	1	3.39
86-87	Calg	54	2957	178	1	3.61
87-88	Calg	64	3565	210	1	3.53
88-89	Calg	52	2938	130	0	2.65
89-90	Calg	47	2795	146	0	3.13
90-91	Calg	54	3121	172	1	3.31
91-92	Calg	63	3640	217	0	3.58
Totals		355	20048	1120	4	3.35
Playoff Totals		70	4157	202	0	2.92
VEZINA, Georges						
B. Chicoutimi, Que., Jan., 1887						
17-18	Mont	22	1282	84	1	3.82
18-19	Mont	18	1097	78	1	4.33
19-20	Mont	24	1454	113	0	4.71
20-21	Mont	24	1436	99	1	4.13
21-22	Mont	24	1468	94	0	3.92
22-23	Mont	24	1488	61	2	2.54
23-24	Mont	24	1459	48	3	2.00
24-25	Mont	30	1860	56	5	1.87
25-26	Mont	1	20	0	0	0.00
Totals		191	11564	633	13	3.28
Playoff Totals		26	1596	74	4	2.78
VILLEMURE, Gilles *5-8 185*						
B. Trois-Rivieres, Que., May 30, 1940						
63-64	NYR	5	300	18	0	3.60
67-68	NYR	4	200	8	1	2.40
68-69	NYR	4	240	9	0	2.25
70-71	NYR	34	2039	78	4	2.30
71-72	NYR	37	2129	74	3	2.09
72-73	NYR	34	2040	78	3	2.29
73-74	NYR	21	1054	62	0	3.53
74-75	NYR	45	2470	130	2	3.16
75-76	Chi	15	797	57	0	4.29
76-77	Chi	6	312	28	0	5.38
Totals		205	11581	542	13	2.81
Playoff Totals		14	656	32	0	2.93
WAITE, Jimmy *6-0 165*						
B. Sherbrooke, Que., Apr. 15, 1969						
88-89	Chi	11	494	43	0	5.22
89-90	Chi	4	183	14	0	4.59
90-91	Chi	1	60	2	0	2.00
91-92	Chi	17	877	54	0	3.69
Totals		33	1614	113	0	4.20

WAKALUK, Darcy *5-11 180*
B. Pincher Creek, Alta., Mar. 14, 1966

Season	Team	GP	Min.	GA	So.	Avg.
88-89	Buf	6	214	15	0	4.21
90-91	Buf	16	630	35	0	3.33
91-92	Minn	36	1905	104	1	3.28
Totals		58	2749	154	1	3.36
Playoff Totals		2	37	2	0	3.24

WAKELY, Ernest Alfred (Ernie) *5-11 160*
B. Flin Flon, Man., Nov. 27, 1940

Season	Team	GP	Min.	GA	So.	Avg.
62-63	Mont	1	60	3	0	3.00
68-69	Mont	1	60	4	0	4.00
69-70	StL	30	1651	58	4	2.11
70-71	StL	51	2859	133	3	2.79
71-72	StL	30	1614	92	1	3.42
72-73	Winn (WHA)	49	2889	152	2	3.16
73-74	Winn (WHA)	37	2254	123	3	3.27
74-75	Winn-SD (WHA)	41	2417	131	3	3.25
75-76	SD (WHA)	67	3824	208	3	3.26
76-77	SD (WHA)	46	2506	129	2	3.09
77-78	Cin-Hou (WHA)	57	3381	192	2	3.41
78-79	Birm (WHA)	37	2060	129	0	3.76
NHL Totals		113	6244	290	8	2.79
WHA Totals		334	19331	1064	15	3.30
NHL Playoff Tot.		10	509	37	1	4.36
WHA Playoff Tot.		31	1740	109	0	3.76

WALSH, James Patrick (Flat) *5-11 175*
B. Kinston, Ont., Mar. 23, 1897

Season	Team	GP	Min.	GA	So.	Avg.
26-27	Mont M	1	60	3	0	3.00
27-28	Mont M	1	40	1	0	1.00
28-29	NYA-Mont M	11	710	9	4	0.76
29-30	Mont M	30	1897	74	2	2.47
30-31	Mont M	16	781	30	2	1.88
31-32	Mont M	27	1670	77	2	2.85
32-33	Mont M	22	1303	56	2	2.55
Totals		108	6461	250	12	2.32
Playoff Totals		8	570	16	2	1.68

WAMSLEY, Richard *5-11 185*
B. Simcoe, Ont., May 25, 1959

Season	Team	GP	Min.	GA	So.	Avg.
80-81	Mont	5	253	8	1	1.90
81-82	Mont	38	2206	101	2	2.75
82-83	Mont	46	2583	151	0	3.51
83-84	Mont	42	2333	144	2	3.70
84-85	StL	40	2319	126	0	3.26
85-86	StL	42	2517	144	1	3.43
86-87	StL	41	2410	142	0	3.54
87-88	StL-Calg	33	1891	108	2	3.43
88-89	Calg	35	1927	95	2	2.96
89-90	Calg	36	1969	107	2	3.26
90-91	Calg	29	1670	85	0	3.05
91-92	Calg-Tor	17	885	61	0	4.14
Totals		404	22963	1272	12	3.32
Playoff Totals		27	1397	73	0	3.14

WATT, James Magnus *5-11 180*
B. Duluth, Minn., May 11, 1950

Season	Team	GP	Min.	GA	So.	Avg.
73-74	StL	1	20	2	0	6.00

WEEKS, Stephen *5-11 165*
B. Scarborough, Ont., June 30, 1958

Season	Team	GP	Min.	GA	So.	Avg.
80-81	NYR	1	60	2	0	2.00
81-82	NYR	49	2852	179	1	3.77
82-83	NYR	18	1040	68	0	3.92
83-84	NYR	26	1361	90	0	3.97
84-85	Hart	24	1457	93	2	3.82
85-86	Hart	27	1544	99	1	3.85
86-87	Hart	25	1367	78	1	3.42
87-88	Hart-Van	27	1468	86	0	3.51
88-89	Van	35	2056	102	0	2.98
89-90	Van	21	1142	79	0	4.15

WEEKS, Stephen *(Continued)*

Season	Team	GP	Min.	GA	So.	Avg.
90-91	Van	1	59	6	0	6.10
91-92	NYI-LA	30	1284	79	0	3.69
Totals		284	15690	961	5	3.67
Playoff Totals		12	486	27	0	3.33

WETNEL, Carl David *6-1 170*
B. Detroit, Mich., Dec. 12, 1938

Season	Team	GP	Min.	GA	So.	Avg.
64-65	Det	2	33	4	0	7.27
67-68	Minn	5	269	18	0	4.01
72-73	Minn (WHA)	1	60	3	0	3.00
NHL Totals		7	302	22	0	4.37
WHA Totals		1	60	3	0	3.00

WHITMORE, Kay *5-11 175*
B. Sudbury, Ont., Apr. 10, 1967

Season	Team	GP	Min.	GA	So.	Avg.
88-89	Hart	3	180	10	0	3.33
89-90	Hart	9	442	26	0	3.53
90-91	Hart	18	850	52	0	3.67
91-92	Hart	45	2567	155	3	3.62
Totals		75	4039	243	3	3.61
Playoff Totals		3	154	11	0	4.29

WILSON, Duncan Shepherd (Dunc) *5-11 175*
B. Toronto, Ont., Mar. 22, 1948

Season	Team	GP	Min.	GA	So.	Avg.
69-70	Phil	1	60	3	0	3.00
70-71	Van	35	1791	128	0	4.29
71-72	Van	53	2870	173	1	3.62
72-73	Van	43	2423	159	1	3.94
73-74	Tor	24	1412	68	1	2.89
74-75	Tor-NYR	28	1573	99	0	3.78
75-76	NYR	20	1080	76	0	4.22
76-77	Pitt	45	2627	129	5	2.95
77-78	Pitt	21	1180	95	0	4.83
78-79	Van	17	835	58	0	4.17
Totals		287	15851	988	8	3.74

WILSON, Ross Ingram (Lefty) *5-11 178*
B. Toronto, Ont., Oct. 15, 1919

Season	Team	GP	Min.	GA	So.	Avg.
53-54	Det	1	20	0	0	0.00
55-56	Tor	1	13	0	0	0.00
57-58	Bos	1	52	1	0	1.15
Totals		3	85	1	0	0.71

WINKLER, Harold Lang (Hal) *5-8 150*
B. Gretna, Man., Mar. 20, 1892

Season	Team	GP	Min.	GA	So.	Avg.
26-27	NYR-Bos	31	1959	56	6	1.72
27-28	Bos	44	2780	70	15	1.59
Totals		75	4739	126	21	1.60
Playoff Totals		10	640	18	2	1.69

WOLFE, Bernard Ronald *5-9 165*
B. Montreal, Que., Dec. 18, 1951

Season	Team	GP	Min.	GA	So.	Avg.
75-76	Wash	40	2134	148	0	4.16
76-77	Wash	37	1779	114	1	3.84
77-78	Wash	25	1328	94	0	4.25
78-79	Wash	18	863	68	0	4.73
Totals		120	6104	424	1	4.17

WOODS, Alec
B. Falkirk, Sask.

Season	Team	GP	Min.	GA	So.	Avg.
36-37	NYA	1	70	3	0	2.57

WORSLEY, Lorne John (Gump) *5-7 180*
B. Montreal, Que., May 14, 1929

Season	Team	GP	Min.	GA	So.	Avg.
52-53	NYR	50	3000	153	2	3.06
54-55	NYR	65	3900	197	4	3.03
55-56	NYR	70	4200	203	4	2.90
56-57	NYR	68	4080	220	3	3.24
57-58	NYR	37	2220	86	4	2.32
58-59	NYR	67	4001	205	2	3.07
59-60	NYR	41	2301	137	0	3.57
60-61	NYR	58	3473	193	1	3.33
61-62	NYR	60	3520	174	2	2.97
62-63	NYR	67	3980	219	2	3.30
63-64	Mont	8	444	22	1	2.97
64-65	Mont	19	1080	50	1	2.78

WORSLEY, Lorne John (Gump) *(Continued)*

Season	Team	GP	Min.	GA	So.	Avg.
65-66	Mont	51	2899	114	2	2.36
66-67	Mont	18	888	47	1	3.18
67-68	Mont	40	2213	73	6	1.98
68-69	Mont	30	1703	64	5	2.55
69-70	Mont-Minn	14	813	34	1	2.51
70-71	Minn	24	1369	57	0	2.50
71-72	Minn	34	1923	68	2	2.12
72-73	Minn	12	624	30	0	2.88
73-74	Minn	29	1601	86	0	3.22
Totals		862	50232	2432	43	2.90
Playoff Totals		70	4079	192	5	2.82

WORTERS, Roy (Shrimp) *5-3 135*
B. Toronto, Ont., Oct. 19, 1900

Season	Team	GP	Min.	GA	So.	Avg.
25-26	PittPi	35	2145	68	7	1.94
26-27	PittPi	44	2711	108	4	2.45
27-28	PittPi	44	2740	76	10	1.73
28-29	NYA	38	2390	46	13	1.21
29-30	NYA-Mont	37	2330	137	2	3.53
30-31	NYA	44	2760	74	8	1.68
31-32	NYA	40	2459	110	5	2.75
32-33	NYA	47	2970	116	5	2.47
33-34	NYA	36	2240	75	4	2.08
34-35	NYA	48	3000	142	3	2.96
35-36	NYA	48	3000	122	3	2.54
36-37	NYA	23	1430	69	2	3.00
Totals		484	30175	1143	66	2.27
Playoff Totals		11	690	24	3	2.09

WORTHY, Christopher John *6-0 180*
B. Bristol, England, Oct. 23, 1947

Season	Team	GP	Min.	GA	So.	Avg.
68-69	Oak	14	786	54	0	4.12
69-70	Oak	1	60	5	0	5.00
70-71	Cal	11	480	39	0	4.88
73-74	Edm (WHA)	29	1452	92	0	3.80
74-75	Edm (WHA)	29	1660	99	1	3.58
75-76	Edm (WHA)	24	1256	98	1	4.68
NHL Totals		26	1326	98	0	4.43
WHA Totals		82	4368	289	2	3.97
WHA Playoff Totals		4	206	15	0	4.37

WREGGET, Kenneth *6-1 195*
B. Brandon, Man., Mar. 25, 1964

Season	Team	GP	Min.	GA	So.	Avg.
83-84	Tor	3	165	14	0	5.09
84-85	Tor	23	1278	103	0	4.84
85-86	Tor	30	1566	113	0	4.33
86-87	Tor	56	3026	200	0	3.97
87-88	Tor	56	3000	222	2	4.44
88-89	Tor-Phil	35	2018	152	0	4.52
89-90	Phil	51	2961	169	0	3.42
90-91	Phil	30	1484	88	0	3.56
91-92	Phil-Pitt	32	1707	106	0	3.73
Totals		316	17205	1167	2	4.07
Playoff Totals		31	1784	86	3	2.89

YOUNG, Douglas G. *5-9 190*
B. Medicine Hat, Alta., Oct. 1, 1908

Season	Team	GP	Min.	GA	So.	Avg.
33-34	Det	1	21	1	0	2.86

YOUNG, Wendell *5-9 185*
B. Halifax, N.S., Aug. 1, 1963

Season	Team	GP	Min.	GA	So.	Avg.
85-86	Van	22	1023	61	0	3.58
86-87	Van	8	420	35	0	5.00
87-88	Phil	6	320	20	0	3.75
88-89	Pitt	22	1150	92	0	4.80
89-90	Pitt	43	2318	161	1	4.17
90-91	Pitt	18	773	52	0	4.04
91-92	Pitt	18	838	53	0	3.79
Totals		137	6842	474	1	4.16
Playoff Totals		2	99	6	0	3.64

ZANIER, Michael *5-11 183*
B. Trail, B.C., Aug. 22, 1962

Season	Team	GP	Min.	GA	So.	Avg.
84-85	Edm	3	185	12	0	3.89

NHL COACH DIRECTORY

On your feet all game, pacing back and forth in cramped quarters. Coast-to-coast road trips. Countless bus rides and practices. And little, if any, job security. That's the lot of the coach in the National Hockey League.

Still, some have thrived on it. Dick Irvin, for example. A member of the Hockey Hall of Fame, he coached for 26 years in the NHL, which added up to a record total of 1,437 regular-season games until the New York Islanders' Al Arbour broke it by one in the season's finale in 1991–92. Irvin's 690 wins are second to Scotty Bowman, who has 778 victories (1,355 games) through 1991–92.

Billy Reay, known for the hat he wore behind the bench, coached for 16 years (1,102 games) with the Chicago Blackhawks and Toronto Maple Leafs and held on to his job despite the fact that he never guided a Stanley Cup winner.

Other coaches have not been so fortunate. As the saying goes, "Coaches are hired to be fired," and it's as true in hockey as it is in other major sports.

In exceptional cases—as it was with baseball's legendary Billy Martin and the Yan-

《 *The New York Islanders' Al Arbour had reason to cheer in 1983: Four straight Stanley Cups.*

kees—hockey coaches sometimes resurface with their old teams. Art Ross coached the Boston Bruins four separate times between 1924 and 1945, and Emile Francis took over the coaching reins of the New York Rangers three times in the 1960s and '70s.

Roger Neilson holds the league's "suitcase award," having served as coach in five different cities—Toronto, Buffalo, Vancouver, Los Angeles and New York. Bowman has been head coach in four cities, as was Sid Abel.

The following is a list of the coaches who have served in the history of the current NHL franchises:

NHL COACHES

Boston—Art Ross, 1924–25 to 1927–28; Cy Denneny, 1928–29; Art Ross, 1929–30 to 1933–34; Frank Patrick, 1934–35 to 1935–36; Art Ross, 1936–37 to 1938–39; Ralph (Cooney) Weiland, 1939–40 to 1940–41; Art Ross, 1941–42 to 1944–45; Dit Clapper, 1945–46 to 1948–49; George (Buck) Boucher, 1949–50; Lynn Patrick, 1950–51 to 1953–54; Lynn Patrick and Milt Schmidt, 1954–55; Milt Schmidt, 1955–56 to 1960–61; Phil Watson, 1961–62; Phil Watson

and Milt Schmidt, 1962–63; Milt Schmidt, 1963–64 to 1965–66; Harry Sinden, 1966–67 to 1969–70; Tom Johnson, 1970–71 to 1971–72; Tom Johnson and Bep Guidolin, 1972–73; Bep Guidolin, 1973–74; Don Cherry, 1974–75 to 1978–79; Fred Creighton and Harry Sinden, 1979–80; Gerry Cheevers, 1980–81 to 1983–84; Gerry Cheevers and Harry Sinden, 1984–85; Butch Goring, 1985–86; Butch Goring and Terry O'Reilly, 1986–87; Terry O'Reilly, 1987–88 to 1988–89; Mike Milbury, 1989–90 to 1990–91; Rick Bowness, 1991–92.

Buffalo—Punch Imlach, 1970–71; Punch Imlach, Floyd Smith and Joe Crozier, 1971–72; Joe Crozier, 1972–73 to 1973–74; Floyd Smith, 1974–75 to 1976–77; Marcel Pronovost, 1977–78; Marcel Pronovost and Bill Inglis, 1978–79; Scotty Bowman, 1979–80; Roger Neilson, 1980–81; Jim Roberts and Scotty Bowman, 1981–82; Scotty Bowman, 1982–83 to 1984–85; Jim Schoenfeld and Scotty Bowman, 1985–86; Scotty Bowman, Craig Ramsay and Ted Sator, 1986–87; Ted Sator, 1987–88 to 1988–89; Rick Dudley, 1989–90 to 1990–91; Rick Dudley and John Muckler, 1991–92.

Calgary (Atlanta 1972–73 to 1979–80)—Bernie Geoffrion, 1972–73 to 1973–74; Bernie Geoffrion and Fred Creighton, 1974–75; Fred Creighton, 1975–76 to 1978–79; Al MacNeil, 1979–80; 1980–81 to 1981–82; Bob Johnson, 1982–83 to 1986–87; Terry Crisp, 1987–88 to 1989–90; Doug Risebrough, 1990–91 to 1991–92.

Chicago—Pete Muldoon, 1926–27; Barney Stanley and Hugh Lehman, 1927–28; Herb Gardiner, 1928–29; Tom Shaughnessy and Bill Tobin, 1929–30; Dick Irvin, 1930–31; Dick Irvin and Bill Tobin, 1931–32; Godfrey Matheson, Emil Iverson and Tommy Gorman, 1932–33; Tommy Gorman, 1933–34; Clem Loughlin, 1934–35 to 1936–37; Bill Stewart, 1937–38; Bill Stewart and Paul Thompson, 1938–39; Paul Thompson, 1939–40 to 1943–44; Paul Thompson and Johnny Gottselig, 1944-45; Johnny Gottselig, 1945–46 to 1946–47; Johnny Gottselig and Charlie Conacher, 1947–48; Charlie Co-

nacher, 1948–49 to 1949–50; Ebbie Goodfellow, 1950–51 to 1951–52; Sid Abel, 1952–53 to 1953–54; Frank Eddolls, 1954–55; Dick Irvin, 1955–56; Tommy Ivan, 1956–57; Tommy Ivan and Rudy Pilous, 1957–58; Rudy Pilous, 1958–59 to 1962–63; Billy Reay, 1963–64 to 1975–76; Billy Reay and Bill White, 1976–77; Bob Pulford, 1977–78 to 1978–79; Eddie Johnston, 1979–80; Keith Magnuson, 1980–81; Keith Magnuson and Bob Pulford, 1981–82; Orval Tessier, 1982–83 to 1983–84; Orval Tessier and Bob Pulford, 1984–85; Bob Pulford, 1985–86 to 1986–87; Bob Murdoch, 1987–88; Mike Keenan, 1988–89 to 1991–92.

Detroit—Art Duncan, 1926–27; Jack Adams, 1927–28 to 1946–47; Tommy Ivan, 1947–48 to 1953–54; Jimmy Skinner, 1954–55 to 1956–57; Jimmy Skinner and Sid Abel, 1957–58; Sid Abel, 1958–59 to 1967–68; Bill Gadsby, 1968–69; Bill Gadsby and Sid Abel, 1969–70; Ned Harkness and Doug Barkley, 1970–71; Doug Barkley and John Wilson, 1971–72; John Wilson, 1972–73; Ted Garvin and Alex Delvecchio, 1973–74; Alex Delvecchio, 1974–75; Doug Barkley and Alex Delvecchio, 1975–76; Alex Delvecchio and Larry Wilson, 1976–77; Bobby Kromm, 1977–78 to 1978–79; Bobby Kromm and Ted Lindsay, 1979–80; Ted Lindsay and Wayne Maxner, 1980–81; Wayne Maxner and Billy Dea, 1981–82; Nick Polano 1982–83 to 1984–85; Harry Neale and Brad Park, 1985–86; Jacques Demers, 1986–87 to 1989–90; Bryan Murray 1990–91 to 1991–92.

Edmonton—Glen Sather, 1979–80; Bryan Watson and Glen Sather, 1980–81; Glen Sather, 1981–82 to 1988–89; John Muckler, 1989–90 and 1990–91; Ted Green, 1991–92.

Hartford—Don Blackburn, 1979–80; Don Blackburn and Larry Pleau, 1980–81; Larry Pleau, 1981–82; Larry Kish and Larry Pleau, 1982–83; Tex Evans, 1983–84 to 1986–87; Tex Evans and Larry Pleau, 1987–88; Larry Pleau, 1988–89; Rick Ley, 1989–90 to 1990–91; Jim Roberts, 1991–92.

Scotty Bowman can look back on an illustrious coaching and general-manager career that has taken him from St. Louis to Montreal to Buffalo to Pittsburgh, where his team added a Stanley Cup in 1991-1992.

Los Angeles—Leonard (Red) Kelly, 1967–68 to 1968–69; Hal Laycoe and John Wilson, 1969–70; Larry Regan, 1970–71; Larry Regan and Fred Glover, 1971–72; Bob Pulford, 1972–73 to 1976–77; Ron Stewart, 1977–78; Bob Berry, 1978–79 to 1980–81; Parker MacDonald and Don Perry, 1981–82; Don Perry, 1982–83; Don Perry, Rogatien Vachon and Roger Neilson, 1983–84; Pat Quinn, 1984–85 to 1985–86; Pat Quinn and Mike Murphy, 1986–87; Mike Murphy and Robbie Ftorek, 1987–88; Robbie Ftorek, 1988–89; Tom Webster, 1989–90 to 1991–92.

Minnesota—Wren Blair, 1967–68; John Muckler and Wren Blair, 1968–69; Wren Blair and Charlie Burns, 1969–70; Jackie Gordon, 1970–71 to 1972–73; Jackie Gordon and Parker MacDonald, 1973–74; Jackie Gordon and Charlie Burns, 1974–75; Ted Harris, 1975–76 to 1976–77; Ted Harris, Andre Beaulieu and Lou Nanne, 1977–78; Harry Howell and Glen Sonmor, 1978–79; Glen Sonmor, 1979–80 to 1981–82; Glen Sonmor and Murray Oliver, 1982–83; Bill Mahoney, 1983–84 to 1984–85; Lorne Henning, 1985–86; Lorne Henning and Glen Sonmor, 1986–87; Herb Brooks, 1987–88; Pierre Page, 1988–89 to 1989–90; Bob Gainey, 1990–91 to 1991–92.

Montreal—George Kennedy, 1917–18 to 1919–20; Leo Dandurand, 1920–21 to 1924–25; Cecil Hart, 1925–26 to 1931–31; Newsy Lalonde, 1932–33 to 1933–34; Newsy Lalonde and Leo Dandurand, 1934–35; Sylvio Mantha, 1935–36; Cecil Hart, 1936–37 to 1937–38; Cecil Hart and Jules Dugal, 1938–39; Pit Lepine, 1939–40; Dick Irvin,

1940–41 to 1954–55; Toe Blake, 1955–56 to 1967–68; Claude Ruel, 1968–69 to 1969–70; Claude Ruel and Al MacNeil, 1970–71; Scotty Bowman, 1971–72 to 1978–79; Bernie Geoffrion and Claude Ruel, 1979–80; Claude Ruel, 1980–81; Bob Berry, 1981–82 to 1982–83; Bob Berry and Jacques Lemaire, 1983–84; Jacques Lemaire, 1984–85; Jean Perron, 1985–86 to 1987–88; Pat Burns, 1988–89 to 1991–92.

New Jersey (Kansas City 1974–75 to 1975–76; Colorado 1976–77 to 1982–82)—Bep Guidolin, 1974–75; Bep Guidolin, Sid Abel and Eddie Bush, 1975–76; John Wilson, 1976–77; Pat Kelly, 1977–78; Pat Kelly and Bep Guidolin, 1978–79; Don Cherry, 1979–80; Bill MacMillan, 1980–81; Bert Marshall and Marshall Johnston, 1981–82; Bill MacMillan, 1982–83; Bill MacMillan and Tom McVie, 1983–84; Doug Carpenter, 1984–85 to 1986–87; Doug Carpenter and Jim Schoenfeld, 1987–88; Jim Schoenfeld, 1988–89; Jim Schoenfeld and John Cunniff, 1989–90; John Cunniff and Tom McVie, 1990–91; Tom McVie, 1991–92.

New York Islanders—Phil Goyette and Earl Ingerfield, 1972–73; Al Arbour, 1973–74 to 1985–86; Terry Simpson, 1986–87 to 1987–88; Terry Simpson and Al Arbour, 1988–89; Al Arbour, 1989–90 to 1991–92.

New York Rangers—Lester Patrick, 1926–27 to 1938–39; Frank Boucher, 1939–40 to 1947–48; Frank Boucher and Lynn Patrick, 1948–49; Lynn Patrick, 1949–50; Neil Colville, 1950–51; Neil Colville and Bill Cook, 1951–52; Bill Cook, 1952–53; Frank Boucher and Murray Patrick, 1953–54; Murray Patrick, 1954–55; Phil Watson, 1955–56 to 1958–59; Phil Watson and Alf Pike, 1959–60; Alf Pike, 1960–61; Doug Harvey, 1961–62; Murray Patrick and George Sullivan, 1962–63; George Sullivan, 1963–64 to 1964–65; George Sullivan and Emile Francis, 1965–66; Emile Francis, 1966–67 to 1967–68; Bernie Geoffrion and Emile Francis, 1968–69; Emile Francis, 1969–70 to 1972–73; Larry Popein and Emile Francis, 1973–74; Emile Francis, 1974–75; Ron Stew-

art and John Ferguson, 1975–76; John Ferguson, 1976–77; Jean-Guy Talbot, 1977–78; Fred Shero, 1978–79 to 1979–80; Fred Shero and Craig Patrick, 1980–81; Herb Brooks, 1981–82 to 1983–84; Herb Brooks and Craig Patrick, 1984–85; Ted Sator, 1985–86; Ted Sator, Tom Webster and Phil Esposito, 1986–87; Michel Bergeron, 1987–88; Michel Bergeron and Phil Esposito, 1988–89; Roger Neilson, 1989–90 to 1991–92.

Philadelphia—Keith Allen, 1967–68 to 1968–69; Vic Stasiuk, 1969–70 to 1970–71; Fred Shero, 1971–72 to 1977–78; Bob McCammon and Pat Quinn, 1978–79; Pat Quinn, 1979–80 to 1980–81; Pat Quinn and Bob McCammon, 1981–82; Bob McCammon, 1982–83 to 1983–84; Mike Keenan, 1984–85 to 1987–88; Paul Holmgren, 1988–89 to 1990–91; Paul Holmgren and Bill Dineen, 1991–92.

Pittsburgh—George Sullivan, 1967–68 to 1968–69; Red Kelly, 1969–70 to 1971–72; Red Kelly and Ken Schinkel, 1972–73; Ken Schinkel and Marc Boileau, 1973–74; Marc Boileau, 1974–75; Marc Boileau and Ken Schinkel, 1975–76; Ken Schinkel, 1976–77; John Wilson, 1977–78 to 1979–80; Eddie Johnston, 1980–81 to 1982–83; Lou Angotti, 1983–84; Bob Berry, 1984–85 to 1986–87; Pierre Creamer, 1987–88; Gene Ubriaco, 1988–89; Gene Ubriaco and Craig Patrick, 1989–90; Bob Johnson, 1990–91; Scotty Bowman, 1991–92.

Quebec—Jacques Demers, 1979–80; Maurice Filion and Michel Bergeron, 1980–81; Michel Bergeron, 1981–82 to 1986–87; Andre Savard and Ron Lapointe, 1987–88; Ron Lapointe and Jean Perron, 1988–89; Michel Bergeron, 1989–90; Dave Chambers, 1990–91; Dave Chambers and Pierre Page, 1991–92.

St. Louis—Lynn Patrick and Scotty Bowman, 1967–68; Scotty Bowman, 1968–69 to 1969–70; Al Arbour and Scotty Bowman, 1970–71; Sid Abel, Bill McCreary and Al Arbour, 1971–72; Al Arbour and Jean-Guy Talbot, 1972–73; Jena-Guy Talbot and Lou Angotti, 1973–74; Lou Angotti, Lynn Patrick and Garry Young, 1974–75; Garry Young,

Lynn Patrick and Leo Boivin, 1975–76; Emile Francis, 1976–77; Leo Boivin and Barclay Plager, 1977–78; Barclay Plager, 1978–79; Barclay Plager and Red Berenson, 1979–80; Red Berenson, 1980–81; Red Berenson and Emile Francis, 1981–82; Barclay Plager and Emile Francis, 1982–83; Jacques Demers, 1983–84 to 1985–86; Jacques Martin, 1986–87 to 1987–88; Brian Sutter, 1988–89 to 1991–92.

San Jose—George Kingston, 1991–92.

Toronto—Conn Smythe, 1927–28 to 1929–30; Conn Smythe and Art Duncan, 1930–31; Art Duncan and Bill Irvin, 1931–32; Dick Irvin, 1932–33 to 1939–40; Hap Day, 1940–41 to 1949–50; Joe Primeau, 1950–51 to 1952–53; King Clancy, 1953–54 to 1955–56; Howie Meeker, 1956–57; Billy Reay, 1957–58; Billy Reay and Punch Imlach, 1958–59; Punch Imlach, 1959–60 to 1968–69; John McLellan, 1969–70 to 1970–71; John McLellan and King Clancy, 1971–72; John McLellan, 1972–73; Red Kelly, 1973–74 to 1976–77; Roger Neilson, 1977–78 to 1978–79; Floyd Smith, Dick Duff and Punch Imlach, 1979–80; Punch Imlach, Joe Crozier and Mike Nykoluk, 1980–81; Mike Nykoluk, 1981–82 to 1983–84; Dan Maloney, 1984–85 to 1985–86; John Brophy, 1986–87 to 1987–88; John Brophy and George Armstrong, 1988–89; Doug Carpenter, 1989–90; Doug Carpenter and Tom Watt, 1990–91; Tom Watt, 1991–92.

Vancouver—Hal Laycoe, 1970–71 to 1971–72; Vic Stasiuk, 1972–73; Bill McCreary and Phil Maloney, 1973–74; Phil Maloney, 1974–75 to 1975–76; Phil Maloney and Orland Kurtenbach, 1976–77; Orland Kurtenbach, 1977–78; Harry Neale, 1978–79 to 1980–81; Harry Neale and Roger Neilson, 1981–82; Roger Neilson, 1982–83; Roger Neilson and Harry Neale, 1983–84; Bill Laforge, 1984–85; Tom Watt, 1985–86 to 1986–87; Bob McCammon, 1987–88 to 1989–90; Bob McCammon and Pat Quinn, 1990–91; Pat Quinn, 1991–92.

Washington—Jim Anderson, George Sullivan and Milt Schmidt, 1974–75; Milt Schmidt and Tom McVie, 1975–76; Tom McVie, 1976–77 to 1977–78; Danny Belisle, 1978–79; Danny Belisle and Gary Green, 1979–80; Gary Green, 1980–81; Gary Green and Bryan Murray, 1981–82; Bryan Murray, 1982–83 to 1988–89; Bryan Murray and Terry Murray, 1989–90; Terry Murray, 1990–91 to 1991–92.

Winnipeg—Tom McVie, 1979–80; Tom McVie and Bill Sutherland, 1980–81; Tom Watt, 1981–82 to 1982–83; Tom Watt, John Ferguson and Barry Long, 1983-84; Barry Long, 1984–85; Barry Long and John Ferguson, 1985–86; Dan Maloney, 1986–87 to 1987–88; Dan Maloney and Rick Bowness, 1988–89; Bob Murdoch, 1989–90 to 1990–91; John Paddock, 1991–92.

GLOSSARY

Attacking Zone—Area from an opponent's blue line to goal line.

Back-Checking—A forward coming back into his defensive zone to check an opponent off the puck.

Backhander—Any shot or pass made with the stick turned around.

Blue Lines—Two lines, one at each end of the rink, that are 60 feet from the goal line and define the attacking zone. They are also used to determine offsides. No attacking player may precede the puck over the defending team's blue line.

Boarding—To ride or drive an opponent into the dasher boards. Can result in a minor or major penalty.

Bodycheck—To use one's body to block an opponent. Legal only when the man hit has the puck or was the last player to have touched it.

Charging—Skating three strides or more and crashing into an opponent. Illegal and calls for a penalty.

Checking—Defending against or guarding an opponent. On a line, a right wing checks the other team's left wing and a left wing checks the opposing right wing. Centers check each other. Checking requires harassing an opposing skater with the aim of making him surrender the puck.

Crease—The rectangular area marked off in front of each net. Only a goalie is permitted in the crease and no player may score from there unless he is being pinned in by a defending player.

Cross-Checking—To hit an opponent with both hands on the stick and no part of the stick on the ice. Illegal and calls for a penalty.

Curved Stick—A stick with a concave rather than flat blade.

Defending Zone—The area from a team's goal line to its blue line.

Deke—To feint or shift an opponent out of position.

Delay of Game—An intentional stoppage in play (i.e., shooting the puck into the stands, pinning a puck against the boards when unchecked, etc.). Illegal and calls for a minor penalty.

Elbowing—Hitting an opponent with the elbow. Illegal and calls for a minor penalty.

Empty-Netter—A goal scored after the opposition has pulled its goalie for an extra skater.

Faceoff—The dropping of the puck between two opposing players to start play. Faceoffs follow goals or other stoppages in action and are to hockey what the jump ball is to basketball.

Forechecking—Checking an opponent in his own zone.

Freezing the Puck—Pinning the puck against the boards with a skate or stick in order to force a stoppage in play. Can result in delay of game penalty if no opposing player is on the puck.

Goal Judge—Game official who sits in booth directly behind net and signals when a goal has been scored by turning on a red light.

Hat Trick—Three (or more) goals by a single player in a game.

Head-Manning—Always advancing the puck to a teammate up ice. Never retreating.

High-Sticking—The carrying of the stick above shoulder level. Always illegal and calls for a penalty if one player hits another in this way or a faceoff if no other infraction occurs.

Holding—To use your hands on an opponent or his equipment. Illegal and calls for a minor penalty.

Hooking—To impede an opponent with the blade of your stick. Illegal and calls for a minor penalty.

Icing the Puck—Shooting the puck from behind the center red line across an opponent's goal line. Usually done to break up an attack and ease pressure. The puck is brought back and a faceoff takes place in the defensive zone of the team that iced the puck. No icing is called against a team that is shorthanded because of a penalty.

Interference—Body contact with a man not in possession of the puck or who was not the last man to touch the puck. Also called for knocking an opponent's fallen stick out of his reach. Illegal and calls for a minor penalty.

Kneeing—Using the knee to check an opponent. Illegal and calls for a minor penalty.

Linesman—Secondary official who makes determinations on icing and offsides calls and is empowered to call a minor penalty if a team has too many men on the ice.

Major Penalty—A five-minute penalty. (For example, for fighting or spearing.)

Match Penalty—Suspension for the balance of the game.

Minor Penalty—A two-minute penalty. Most penalties are minors.

Misconduct Penalty—A 10-minute penalty against an individual, not a team. A substitute is permitted. Called for various forms of unacceptable behavior or when a player incurs a second major penalty in a game.

Neutral Zone—That area between blue lines. The center ice area.

Offsides—Called when an attacking player precedes the puck across the opponent's blue line. Illegal and calls for a faceoff.

Offsides Pass—Called when the puck is passed to a teammate across two or more lines. Illegal and calls for a faceoff from point where the pass originated.

Penalty-Killer—A player whose job it is to use up time while a teammate is serving a penalty. The best penalty-killers are fast skaters who can break up a power play. Once in possession of the puck, the penalty-killer tries to hold onto it and seldom tries to attack. He is content to waste time until his team is at full strength again.

Playmaker—Usually a center whose skating and puck-carrying ability enable him to set up or make a play that can lead to a goal.

Pokecheck—The quick thrust of the stick to take a puck away from an opposing player. Usually done best by defensemen rather than forwards. Legal.

Power Play—A manpower advantage resulting from a penalty to the opposing team.

Puck—The vulcanized rubber disc used in hockey.

Red Line—The line that divides the ice in half.

Referee—Head official in the game who has general supervision of play.

Roughing—Minor fisticuffs or shoving. Illegal and calls for a minor penalty.

Shorthanded—What a team is when it is trying to kill a penalty.

Slapshot—When a player winds and slaps his stick at the puck. Usually a hard but erratic shot.

Slashing—To swing stick at an opponent. Illegal and calls for a minor penalty.

Slot—The area extending from in front of the net out about 30 feet. Many goals are scored from this area.

Spearing—To use the stick as one would a spear. Illegal and calls for a major penalty.

Stickhandling—The art of carrying the puck with the stick.

Sudden-Death Goal—Any goal scored in overtime of a game. Overtime is only played if a game is tied after three periods.

Sweep Check—To swing the stick along the ice to intercept the puck or hamper an opponent. It is legal.

Tip-In—A goal scored from just outside the goalie's crease.

Wash-Out—Disallowing of a goal by a referee, or disallowing of icing or offsides by a linesman.

OFFICIAL NHL RULES

(Courtesy of the National Hockey League)

SECTION ONE—THE RINK

Rule 1. Rink

The game of "Ice Hockey" shall be played on an ice surface known as the "RINK."

(NOTE) *There shall be no markings on the ice except as provided under these rules without the express written permission of the League.*

Rule 2. Dimensions of Rink

(a) The official size of the rink shall be two hundred feet (200') long and eighty-five feet (85') wide. The corners shall be rounded in the arc of a circle with a radius of twenty-eight feet (28').

The rink shall be surrounded by a wooden or fibreglass wall or fence known as the "boards" which shall extend not less than forty inches (40") and not more than forty-eight inches (48") above the level of the ice surface. The ideal height of the boards above the ice surface shall be forty-two inches (42"). Except for the official markings provided for in these rules, the entire playing surface and the boards shall be white in color except the kick plate at the bottom of the board which shall be light blue or light yellow in colour.

Any variations from any of the foregoing dimensions shall require official authorization by the League.

(b) The boards shall be constructed in such manner that the surface facing the ice shall be smooth and free of any obstruction or any object that could cause injury to players.

All doors giving access to the playing surface must swing away from the ice surface.

All glass or other types of protective screens and gear used to hold them in position shall be mounted on the boards on the side away from the playing surface.

Rule 3. Goal Posts and Nets

(a) Eleven feet (11') from each end of the rink and in the center of a red line two inches (2") wide drawn completely across the width of the ice and continued vertically up the side of the boards, regulation goal posts and nets shall be set in such manner as to remain stationary during the progress of a game. The goal posts shall be kept in position by means of flexible pegs affixed in the ice or floor.

Where the length of the playing surface exceeds two hundred feet (200'), the goal line and goal posts may be placed not more than fifteen feet (15') from the end of the rink.

(b) The goal posts shall be of approved design and material, extending vertically four feet (4') above the surface of the ice and set six feet (6') apart measured from the inside of the posts. A cross bar of the same material as the goal posts shall extend from the top of one post to the top of the other.

(c) There shall be attached to each goal frame a net of approved design made of white nylon cord which shall be draped in such manner as to prevent the puck coming to rest on the outside of it.

A skirt of heavy white nylon fabric or heavy-weight white canvas shall be laced around the base plate of the goal frame in such a way as to protect the net from being cut or broken. This skirt shall not project more than one inch (1") above the base plate.

(NOTE) *The frame of the goal shall be draped with a nylon mesh net so as to completely enclose the back of the frame. The net shall be made of three-ply twisted twine (0.130 inch diameter) or equivalent braided twine of multifilament white nylon with an*

appropriate tensile strength of 700 pounds. The size of the mesh shall be two and one-half inches (2½")(inside measurement) from each knot to each diagonal knot when fully stretched. Knotting shall be made as to ensure no sliding of the twine. The net shall be laced to the frame with medium white nylon cord no smaller in size than No. 21.

(d) The goal posts and cross bar shall be painted in red and all other exterior surfaces shall be painted in white.

(e) The red line, two inches (2") wide, between the goal posts on the ice and extended completely across the rink, shall be known as the "GOAL LINE."

Rule 4. Goal Crease

(a) In front of each goal, a "GOAL CREASE" area shall be marked by a red line two inches (2") in width.

(b) The goal crease shall be laid out as follows: A semicircle six feet (6') in radius and two inches (2") in width shall be drawn using the center of the goal line as the center point. In addition, an 'L'-shaped marking of five inches (5") in length (both lines) at each front corner will be painted on the ice.
   The location of the 'L'-shaped marking is measured by drawing an imaginary four foot (4') line from the goal line to the edge of the semi-circle. At that point, the 'L' may be drawn.

(c) The goal crease area shall include all the space outlined by the crease lines and extending vertically four feet (4') to the level of the top of the goal frame.

(d) The goal area, enclosed by the goal line and the base of the goal, as well as the goal crease area shall be painted in a different colour than the remainder of the ice surface, i.e., a more prominent white color or a light blue color.

Rule 5. Division of Ice Surface

(a) The ice area between the two goals shall be divided into three parts by lines, twelve inches (12") in width, and blue in color, drawn sixty feet (60') out from the goal lines, and extended completely across the rink, parallel with the goal lines, and continued vertically up the side of the boards.

(b) That portion of the ice surface in which the goal is situated shall be called the "DEFENDING ZONE" of the team defending that goal; the central portion shall be known as the "NEUTRAL ZONE", and the portion farthest from the defended goal as the "ATTACKING ZONE."

(c) There shall also be a line, twelve inches (12") in width and red in color, drawn completely across the rink in center ice, parallel with the goal lines and continued vertically up the side of the boards, known as the "CENTER LINE". This line shall contain at regular interval markings of a uniform

distinctive design which will easily distinguish it from the two blue lines . . . the outer edges of which must be continuous.

Rule 6. Center Ice Spot and Circle

A circular blue spot, twelve inches (12") in diameter, shall be marked exactly in the center of the rink; and with this spot as a center, a circle of fifteen feet (15') radius shall be marked with a blue line two inches (2") in width.

Rule 7. Faceoff Spots in Neutral Zone

Two red spots two feet (2') in diameter shall be marked on the ice in the neutral zone five feet (5') from each blue line. The spots shall be forty-four feet (44') apart and each shall be a uniform distance from the adjacent boards.

Rule 8. End Zone Faceoff Spots and Circles

(a) In both end zones and on both sides of each goal, red face-off spots and circles shall be marked on the ice. The face-off spots shall be two feet (2') in diameter. Within the faceoff spot, draw two parallel lines three inches (3") from the top and bottom of the spot. The area within the two lines shall be painted red, the remainder shall be painted white.
   The circles shall be two inches (2") wide with a radius of fifteen feet (15') from the center of the face-off spots. At the outer edge of both sides of each face-off circle and parallel to the goal line shall be marked two red lines, two inches (2") wide and two feet (2') in length and three feet (3') apart.

(b) The location of the faceoff spots shall be fixed in the following manner:
   Along a line twenty feet (20') from each goal line and parallel to it, mark two points twenty-two feet (22') on both sides of the straight line joining the center of the two goals. Each such point shall be the center of a faceoff spot and circle.

Rule 9. Players' Benches

(a) Each rink shall be provided with seats or benches for the use of players of both teams and the accommodations provided including benches and doors shall be uniform for both teams. Such seats or benches shall have accommodation for at least fourteen persons of each team, and shall be placed immediately alongside the ice, in the neutral zone, as near to the center of the rink as possible with doors opening in the neutral zone and convenient to the dressing rooms.
   Each players' bench should be twenty-four feet (24') in length and when situated in the spectator area, they shall be separated from the spectators by a protective glass of sufficient height so as to afford the necessary protection for the players. The players' benches shall be on the same side of the playing surface opposite the penalty bench and should be separated by a substantial distance.
   (NOTE) *Where physically possible, each players' bench shall have two doors opening in the neutral*

zone and all doors opening to the playing surface shall be constructed so that they swing inward.

(b) No one but players in uniform, the Manager, Coach and Trainer shall be permitted to occupy the benches so provided.

Rule 10.　　　Penalty Bench

(a) Each rink must be provided with benches or seats to be known as the "PENALTY BENCH." These benches or seats must be capable of accommodating a total of ten persons including the Penalty Timekeepers. Separate penalty benches shall be provided for each team and they shall be situated on opposite sides of the Timekeeper's area, directly across the ice from the players' benches. The penalty bench(es) must be situated in the neutral zone.

(b) On the ice immediately in front of the Penalty Timekeeper's seat there shall be marked in red on the ice a semi-circle of ten feet (10') radius and two inches (2") in width which shall be known as the "REFEREE'S CREASE."

(c) Each Penalty Bench shall be protected from the spectator area by means of a glass partition which shall not be less than five feet (5') above the height of the boards.

Rule 11.　　　Signal and Timing Devices

(a) Each rink must be provided with a siren, or other suitable sound device, for the use of Timekeepers.

(b) Each rink shall be provided with some form of electrical clock for the purpose of keeping the spectators, players and game officials accurately informed as to all time elements at all stages of the game including the time remaining to be played in any period and the time remaining to be served by at least five penalized players on each team.

Time recording for both game time and penalty time shall show time remaining to be played or served.

The game time clock shall measure the time remaining in tenths of a second during the last minutes of each period.

(c) Behind each goal, electrical lights shall be set up for the use of the Goal Judges. A red light will signify the scoring of a goal and a green light will signify the end of a period or a game.

(NOTE) *A goal cannot be scored when a green light is showing.*

Rule 12.　　　Police Protection

All clubs shall provide adequate police or other protection for all players and officials at all times.

The Referee shall report to the President any failure of this protection observed by him or reported to him with particulars of such failure.

SECTION TWO—TEAMS

Rule 13.　　　Composition of Team

(a) A team shall be composed of six players who shall be under contract to the club they represent.

(b) Each player and each goalkeeper listed in the line-up of each team shall wear an individual identifying number at least ten inches (10") high on the back of his sweater and, in addition, each player and goalkeeper shall wear his surname in full, in block letters three inches (3") high, across the back of his sweater at shoulder height.

All players of each team shall be dressed uniformly in conformity with approved design and colour of their helmets, sweaters, short pants, stockings and boots. Any player or goalkeeper not complying with this provision shall not be permitted to participate in the game.

Each Member Club shall design and wear distinctive and contrasting uniforms for their home and road games, no parts of which shall be interchangeable except the pants.

Rule 14.　　　Captain of Team

(a) One Captain shall be appointed by each team, and he alone shall have the privilege of discussing with the Referee any questions relating to interpretation of rules which may arise during the progress of a game. He shall wear the letter "C", approximately three inches (3") in height and in contrasting colour, in a conspicuous position on the front of his sweater.

In addition, if the permanent Captain is not on the ice, Alternate Captains (not more than two) shall be accorded the privileges of the Captain. Alternate Captains shall wear the letter "A" approximately three inches (3") in height and in contrasting colour, in a conspicuous position on the front of their sweaters.

(b) The Referee and Official Scorer shall be advised prior to the start of each game, of the name of the Captain of the team and the Alternate Captains.

(c) Only the Captain, when invited to do so by the Referee, shall have the privilege of discussing any point relating to the interpretation of rules. Any Captain or player who comes off the bench and makes any protest or intervention with the officials for any purpose must be assessed a misconduct penalty in addition to a minor penalty under Rule 42(b)–Abuse of Officials.

A complaint about a penalty is NOT a matter "relating to the interpretation of the rules" and a minor penalty shall be imposed against any Captain or other player making such a complaint.

(d) No playing Coach or playing Manager or goalkeeper shall be permitted to act as Captain or Alternate Captain.

Rule 15.　　　Players in Uniform

(a) At the beginning of each game, the Manager or Coach of each team shall list the players and

goalkeepers who shall be eligible to play in the game. Not more than eighteen players, exclusive of goalkeepers, shall be permitted.

(b) A list of names and numbers of all eligible players and goalkeepers must be handed to the Referee or Official Scorer before the game, and no change shall be permitted in the list or addition thereto shall be permitted after the commencement of the game.

    i) If a goal is scored when an ineligible player is on the ice, the goal will be disallowed.

    ii) The ineligible player will be removed from the game and the club shall not be able to substitute another player on its roster.

(c) Each team shall be allowed one goalkeeper on the ice at one time. The goalkeeper may be removed and another player substituted. Such substitute shall not be permitted the privileges of the goalkeeper.

(d) Each team shall have on its bench, or on a chair immediately beside the bench, a substitute goalkeeper who shall, at all times, be fully dressed and equipped ready to play.

The substitute goalkeeper may enter the game at any time following a stoppage of play, but no warm-up shall be permitted.

(e) Except when both goalkeepers are incapacitated, no player in the playing roster in that game shall be permitted to wear the equipment of the goalkeeper.

(f) In regular League and playoff games, if both listed goalkeepers are incapacitated, that team shall be entitled to dress and play any available goalkeeper who is eligible. No delay shall be permitted in taking his position in the goal, and he shall be permitted a two-minute warm-up. However, the warm-up is not permitted in the event a goalkeeper is substituted for a penalty shot.

(g) The Referee shall report to the President for disciplinary action any delay in making a substitution of goalkeepers.

Rule 16.   Starting Line-Up

(a) Prior to the start of the game, at the request of the Referee, the Manager or Coach of the visiting team is required to name the starting line-up to the Referee or Official Scorer. At any time in the game, at the request of the Referee made to the Captain, the visiting team must place a playing line-up on the ice and promptly commence play.

(b) Prior to the start of the game, the Manager or Coach of the home team, having been advised by the Official Scorer or the Referee the names of the starting line-up of the visiting team, shall name the starting line-up of the home team which information shall be conveyed by the Official Scorer or the Referee to the Coach of the visiting team.

(c) No change in the starting line-up of either team as given to the Referee or Official Scorer, or in the playing line-up on the ice, shall be made until the game is actually in progress. For an infraction of this rule, a bench minor penalty shall be imposed upon the offending team, provided such infraction is called to the attention of the Referee before the second face-off in the first period takes place.

Rule 17.   Equalizing of Teams

DELETED

Rule 18.   Change of Players

(a) Players may be changed at any time from the players' bench provided that the player or players leaving the ice shall be within five feet (5') of his players' bench and out of the play before the change is made.

A goalkeeper may be changed for another player at any time under the conditions set out in this section.

(NOTE 1) *When a goalkeeper leaves his goal area and proceeds to his players' bench for the purpose of substituting another player, the rear Linesman shall be responsible to see that the substitution made is not illegal by reason of the premature departure of the substitute from the bench (before the goalkeeper is within five feet (5') of the bench). If the substitution is made prematurely, the Linesman shall stop the play immediately by blowing his whistle unless the nonoffending team has possession of the puck in which event the stoppage will be delayed until the puck changes hands. There shall be no time penalty to the team making the premature substitution but the resulting face-off will take place on the center "face-off spot".*

(NOTE 2) *The Referee shall request that the public address announcer make the following announcement: "Play has been stopped due to premature entry of a player from the players' bench." If in the course of making a substitution, the player entering the game plays the puck with his stick, skates or hands or who checks or makes any physical contact with an opposing player while the retiring player is actually on the ice, then the infraction of "too many men on the ice" will be called.*

If in the course of a substitution either the player entering the play or the player retiring is struck by the puck accidentally, the play will not be stopped and no penalty will be called.

(b) If by reason of insufficient playing time remaining, or by reason of penalties already imposed, a bench minor penalty is imposed for deliberate illegal substitution (too many men on the ice) which cannot be served in its entirety within the legal playing time, a penalty shot shall be awarded against the offending team.

(c) A player serving a penalty on the penalty bench, who is to be changed after the penalty has been served, must proceed at once by way of the ice and be at his own players' bench before any change can be made.

For any violation of this rule, a bench minor penalty shall be imposed.

(d) Following the stoppage of play, the visiting team shall promptly place a line-up on the ice ready for play and no substitution shall be made from that time until play has been resumed. The home team

may then make any desired substitution which does not result in the delay of the game.

If there is any undue delay by either team in changing lines, the Referee shall order the offending team or teams to take their positions immediately and not permit a line change.

(NOTE) *When a substitution has been made under the above rule, no additional substitution may be made until play commences.*

(e) The Referee shall give the visiting team a reasonable amount of time to make their change after which he shall put up his hand to indicate that no further change shall be made by the visiting club. At this point, the home team may change immediately. Any attempt by the visiting team to make a change after the Referee's signal shall result in the assessment of a bench minor penalty for delay of game.

Rule 19.   Injured Players

(a) When a player other than a goalkeeper is injured or compelled to leave the ice during a game, he may retire from the game and be replaced by a substitute, but play must continue without the teams leaving the ice.

(b) If a goalkeeper sustains an injury or becomes ill, he must be ready to resume play immediately or be replaced by a substitute goalkeeper and NO additional time shall be allowed by the Referee for the purpose of enabling the injured or ill goalkeeper to resume his position. The substitute goalkeeper shall be allowed a two-minute warm-up during all pre-season games. No warm-up shall be permitted for a substitute goalkeeper in all regular season or playoff games. (See also Section (d).)

(c) The Referee shall report to the President for disciplinary action any delay in making a goalkeeper substitution.

The substitute goalkeeper shall be subject to the regular rules governing goalkeepers and shall be entitled to the same privileges.

(d) When a substitution for the regular goalkeeper has been made, such regular goalkeeper shall not resume his position until the first stoppage of play thereafter.

(e) If a penalized player has been injured, he may proceed to the dressing room without the necessity of taking a seat on the penalty bench. If the injured player receives a minor penalty, the penalized team shall immediately put a substitute player on the penalty bench, who shall serve the penalty without change. If the injured player receives a major penalty, the penalized team shall place a substitute player on the penalty bench before the penalty expires and no other replacement for the penalized player shall be permitted to enter the game except from the penalty bench. For violation of this rule, a bench minor penalty shall be imposed.

The penalized player who has been injured and been replaced on the penalty bench shall not be eligible to play until his penalty has expired.

(f) When a player is injured so that he cannot continue play or go to his bench, the play shall not be stopped until the injured player's team has secured possession of the puck; if the player's team is in possession of the puck at the time of injury, play shall be stopped immediately unless his team is in a scoring position.

(NOTE) *In the case where it is obvious that a player has sustained a serious injury, the Referee and/or Linesman may stop the play immediately.*

(g) When play has been stopped by the Referee or Linesman due to an injured player, such player must be substituted for immediately (except goalkeeper).

If when the attacking team has control of the puck in its attacking zone, play is stopped by reason of any injury to a player of the defending team, the faceoff shall take place in the defending team's end zone faceoff spot.

SECTION THREE—EQUIPMENT

Rule 20.   Sticks

(a) The sticks shall be made of wood, or other material approved by the Rules Committee, and must not have any projections. Adhesive tape of any colour may be wrapped around the stick at any place for the purpose of reinforcement or to improve control of the puck. In the case of a goalkeeper's stick, there shall be a knob of white tape or some other protective material approved by the League not less than one-half inch ($\frac{1}{2}$") thick at the top of the shaft.

(b) No stick shall exceed sixty inches (60") in length from the heel to the end of the shaft nor more than twelve and one-half inches (12$\frac{1}{2}$") from the heel to the end of the blade.

The blade of the stick shall not be more than three inches (3") in width at any point nor less than two inches (2"). All edges of the blade shall be bevelled. The curvature of the blade of the stick shall be restricted in such a way that the distance of a perpendicular line measured from a straight line drawn from any point at the heel to the end of the blade to the point of maximum curvature shall not exceed one-half inch ($\frac{1}{2}$").

(c) The blade of the goalkeeper's stick shall not exceed three and one-half inches (3$\frac{1}{2}$") in width at any point except at the heel where it must not exceed four and one-half inches (4$\frac{1}{2}$") in width; nor shall the goalkeeper's stick exceed fifteen and one-half inches (15$\frac{1}{2}$") in length from the heel to the end of the blade.

The widened portion of the goalkeeper's stick extending up the shaft from the blade shall not extend more than twenty-six inches (26") from the heel and shall not exceed three and one-half inches (3$\frac{1}{2}$") in width.

(d) A minor penalty plus a fine of two hundred dollars ($200) shall be imposed on any player or goalkeeper who uses a stick not conforming to the provisions of this rule.

(NOTE 1) *When a formal complaint is made by the Captain, or Alternate Captain of a team, against the dimensions of any stick, the Referee shall take the stick to the Timekeeper's bench where the necessary measurement shall be made immediately. The result shall be reported to the Penalty Timekeeper who shall record it on the back of the penalty record.*

If the complaint is not sustained, a bench minor penalty shall be imposed against the complaining club in addition to a fine of one hundred dollars ($100).

(NOTE 2) *A player who participates in the play while taking a replacement stick to his goalkeeper shall incur a minor penalty under this rule but the automatic fine of two hundred dollars ($200) shall not be imposed. If his participation causes a foul resulting in a penalty, the Referee shall report the incident to the President for disciplinary action.*

(e) In the event that a player scores on a penalty shot while using an illegal stick, the goal shall be disallowed and no further penalty imposed. However, if no goal is scored, the player taking the penalty shot shall receive a minor penalty.

(f) A minor penalty plus a ten-minute misconduct penalty shall be imposed on any player who refuses to surrender his stick for measurement when requested to do so by the Referee. In addition, this player shall be subject to a two hundred dollar ($200) fine.

Rule 21.   Skates

(a) All hockey skates shall be of a design approved by the Rules Committee. All skates worn by players (but not goalkeepers) and by the Referee and Linesmen shall be equipped with an approved safety heel.

When the Referee becomes aware that any person is wearing a skate that does not have the approved safety heel, he shall direct its replacement at the next intermission. If such replacement is not carried out, the Referee shall report the incident to the President for disciplinary action.

(b) The use of speed skates or fancy skates or any skate so designed that it may cause injury is prohibited.

Rule 22.   Goalkeeper's Equipment

(a) With the exception of skates and stick, all the equipment worn by the goalkeeper must be constructed solely for the purpose of protecting the head or body, and he must not wear any garment or use any contrivance which would give him undue assistance in keeping goal.

(NOTE) *Cages on gloves and abdominal aprons extending down the front of the thighs on the outside of the pants are prohibited. "Cage" shall mean any lacing or webbing or other material in the goalkeeper's glove joining the thumb and index finger which is in excess of the minimum necessary to fill the gap when the goalkeeper's thumb and forefinger in the glove are fully extended and spread and includes any pocket or pouch effect produced by excess lacing or webbing or other material between*

the thumb and forefinger when fully extended or spread.

Protective padding attached to the back or forming part of goalkeeper's gloves shall not exceed eight inches (8") in width nor more than sixteen inches (16") in length at any point.

(b) The leg guards worn by goalkeepers shall not exceed twelve inches (12") in extreme width when on the leg of the player.

(NOTE) *At the commencement of each season or at random during the season and prior to playoffs, goalkeepers' leg guards and gloves shall be checked by League staff and any violation of this rule shall be reported to the club involved and to the President of the League.*

(c) Protective masks of a design approved by the Rules Committee may be worn by goalkeepers.

Rule 23.   Protective Equipment

(a) All protective equipment, except gloves, headgear and goalkeepers' leg guards must be worn under the uniform. For violation of this rule, after warning by the Referee, a minor penalty shall be imposed.

(NOTE) *Players including the goalkeeper violating this rule shall not be permitted to participate in game until such equipment has been corrected or removed.*

(b) All players of both teams shall wear a helmet of design, material and construction approved by the Rules Committee at all time while participating in a game, either on the playing surface or the players' or the penalty benches.

Players who have been under Standard Player's Contract to a Member Club of the League at any time prior to June 1, 1979, may elect for exemption from the operation of this sub-section (b) by execution of an approved Request and Release form and filing it with the League office.

(c) A glove from which all or part of the palm has been removed or cut to permit the use of the bare hand shall be considered illegal equipment and if any player wears such a glove in play, a minor penalty shall be imposed on him.

When a complaint is made under this rule, and such complaint is not sustained, a bench minor penalty shall be imposed against the complaining club.

Rule 24.   Dangerous Equipment

(a) The use of pads or protectors made of metal, or of any other material likely to cause injury to a player, is prohibited.

(NOTE) *All elbow pads which do not have a soft protective outer covering of sponge rubber or similar material at least one-half inch (½") thick shall be considered dangerous equipment.*

(b) A mask or protector of a design approved by the Rules Committee may be worn by a player who has sustained a facial injury.

In the first instance, the injured player shall be entitled to wear any protective device prescribed by the club doctor. If any opposing club objects to

the device, it may record its objection with the President.

(NOTE) *The Officiating Department is specifically authorized to make a check of each team's equipment to ensure the compliance with this rule. It shall report its findings to the President for his disciplinary action.*

Rule 25. Puck

(a) The puck shall be made of vulcanized rubber, or other approved material, one inch (1") thick and three inches (3") in diameter and shall weigh between five and one-half ounces (5½ oz.) and six ounces (6 oz.). All pucks used in competition must be approved by the Rules Committee.

(b) The home team shall be responsible for providing an adequate supply of official pucks which shall be kept in a frozen condition. This supply of pucks shall be kept at the penalty bench under the control of one of the regular Off-ice Officials or a special attendant.

(NOTE TO SECTION THREE) *A request for measurement of any equipment covered by this section shall be limited to one request by each club during the course of any stoppage of play.*

SECTION FOUR—PENALTIES

Rule 26. Penalties

Penalties shall be actual playing time and shall be divided in the following classes:
  (1) Minor penalties
  (2) Bench minor penalties
  (3) Major penalties
  (4) Misconduct penalties
  (5) Match penalties and
  (6) Penalty shot
When coincident penalties are imposed on players of both teams, the penalized players of the visiting team shall take their positions on the penalty bench first in the place designated for visiting players.

(NOTE) *When play is not actually in progress and an offense is committed by any player, the same penalty shall apply as though play was actually in progress.*

Rule 27. Minor Penalties

(a) For a "MINOR PENALTY" any player, other than a goalkeeper, shall be ruled off the ice for two minutes during which time no substitute shall be permitted.

(b) A "BENCH MINOR" penalty involves the removal from the ice of one player of the team against which the penalty is assessed for a period of two minutes. Any player except a goalkeeper of the team may be designated to serve the penalty by the Manager or Coach through the playing Captain and such player shall take his place on the penalty bench promptly and serve the penalty as if it was a minor penalty imposed upon him.

(c) If while a team is "short-handed" by one or more minor or bench minor penalties, the opposing team scores a goal, the first of such penalties shall automatically terminate.

(NOTE) *"Short-handed" means that the team must be below the numerical strength of its opponents on the ice at the time the goal is scored. The minor or bench minor penalty which terminates automatically is the one which causes the team scored against to be "short-handed". Thus coincident minor penalties to both teams do NOT cause either side to be "short-handed".*

This rule shall also apply when a goal is scored on a penalty shot, or when an awarded goal is given.

When the minor penalties of two players of the same team terminate at the same time, the Captain of that team shall designate to the Referee which of such players will return to the ice first and the Referee will instruct the Penalty Timekeeper accordingly.

When a player receives a major penalty and a minor penalty at the same time, the major penalty shall be served first by the penalized player, except under Rule 28(c) in which case the minor penalty will be recorded and served first.

(NOTE) *This applies to the case where BOTH penalties are imposed on the SAME player. See also Note to Rule 33.*

(d) When coincident major penalties or coincident minor penalties of equal duration are imposed against players of both teams, the penalized players shall all take their places on the penalty benches and such penalized players shall not leave the penalty bench until the first stoppage of play following the expiry of their respective penalties. Immediate substitution shall be made for an equal number of minor penalties OR coincident minor penalties of equal duration to each team so penalized and the penalties of the players for which substitutions have been made shall not be taken into account for the purposes of the Delayed Penalty Rule (Rule 33).

Rule 28. Major Penalties

(a) For the first "MAJOR PENALTY" in any one game, the offender, except the goalkeeper, shall be ruled off the ice for five minutes during which time no substitute shall be permitted.

An automatic fine of fifty dollars ($50) shall also be added when a major penalty is imposed for any foul causing injury to the face or head of an opponent by means of a stick.

(b) For the third major penalty in the same game to the same player, or for a major for butt-ending, cross-checking, high-sticking, slashing or spearing, he shall be ruled off the ice for the balance of the playing time, but a substitute shall be permitted to replace the player so suspended after five minutes shall have elapsed. (Major penalty plus game misconduct penalty with automatic fine of one hundred dollars ($100).)

(NOTE) *In accordance with Rule 58(c) a goalkeeper shall not be assessed a game misconduct penalty when he is being assessed a major penalty for highsticking.*

(c) When coincident major penalties or coincident penalties of equal duration, including a major penalty, are imposed against players of both teams, the penalized players shall all take their places on the penalty benches and such penalized players shall not leave the penalty benches until the first stoppage of play following the expiry of their respective penalties. Immediate substitutions shall be made for an equal number of major penalties, or coincident penalties of equal duration including a major penalty to each team so penalized, and the penalties of the players for which substitutions have been made shall not be taken into account for the purposes of the delayed penalty rule, (Rule 33).

Where it is required to determine which of the penalized players shall be designated to serve the delayed penalty under Rule 33, the penalized team shall have the right to make such designation not in conflict with Rule 27.

Rule 29.   Misconduct Penalties

(a) "MISCONDUCT" penalties to all players except the goalkeeper involve removal from the game for a period of ten minutes each. A substitute player is permitted to immediately replace a player serving a misconduct penalty. A player whose misconduct penalty has expired shall remain in the penalty box until the next stoppage of play.

When a player receives a minor penalty and a misconduct penalty at the same time, the penalized team shall immediately put a substitute player on the penalty bench and he shall serve the minor penalty without change.

When a player receives a major penalty and a misconduct penalty at the same time, the penalized team shall place a substitute player on the penalty bench before the major penalty expires and no replacement for the penalized player shall be permitted to enter the game except from the penalty bench. Any violation of this provision shall be treated as an illegal substitution under Rule 18 calling for a bench minor penalty.

(b) A misconduct penalty imposed on any player at any time shall be accompanied with an automatic fine of fifty dollars ($50).

(c) A "GAME MISCONDUCT" penalty involves the suspension of a player for the balance of the game but a substitute is permitted to replace immediately the player so removed. A player incurring a game misconduct penalty shall incur an automatic fine of one hundred dollars ($100) and the case shall be reported to the President who shall have full power to impose such further penalties by way of suspension or fine on the penalized player or any other player involved in the altercation.

(d) The Referee may impose a "GROSS MISCONDUCT" penalty on any player, Manager, Coach or Trainer who is guilty of gross misconduct of any kind. Any person incurring a "gross misconduct" penalty shall be suspended for the balance of the game and shall incur an automatic fine of one hundred dollars ($100) and the case shall be referred to the President of the League for further disciplinary action.

(NOTE) *For all game misconduct and gross misconduct penalties regardless of when imposed, a total of ten minutes shall be charged in the records against the offending player.*

(e) In regular League games, any player who incurs a total of three game misconduct penalties shall be suspended automatically for the next League game of his team. For each subsequent game misconduct penalty, the automatic suspension shall be increased by one game. For each suspension of a player, his club shall be fined one thousand dollars ($1,000).

In playoff games, any player who incurs a total of two game misconduct penalties shall be suspended automatically for the next playoff game of his team. For each subsequent game misconduct penalty during the playoffs, the automatic suspension shall be increased by one game. For each suspension of a player during playoffs, his club shall be fined one thousand dollars ($1,000).

(f) In regular League games, any player who incurs a total of two game misconduct penalties for stick related infractions penalized under Rule 28(b) shall be suspended automatically for the next League game of his team. For each subsequent game misconduct penalty, the automatic suspension shall be increased by one game.

In playoff games any player who incurs a total of two game misconduct penalties for stick related infractions penalized under Rule 28(b) shall be suspended automatically for the next playoff game of his team. For each subsequent game misconduct penalty during the playoffs the automatic suspension shall be increased by one game.

(NOTE) *Any game misconduct penalty for which a player has been assessed an automatic suspension or supplementary discipline in the form of game suspension(s) by the President shall NOT be taken into account when calculating the total number of offenses under this subsection.*

The automatic suspensions incurred under this subsection in respect to League games shall have no effect with respect to violations during playoff games.

Rule 30.   Match Penalties

A "MATCH" penalty involves the suspension of a player for the balance of the game and the offender shall be ordered to the dressing room immediately. A substitute player is permitted to replace the penalized played after ten minutes playing time has elapsed when the penalty is imposed under Rule 49, and after five minutes actual playing time has elapsed when the penalty is imposed under Rule 44.

(NOTE 1) *Regulations regarding additional penalties and substitutes are specifically covered in individual Rules 44, 49 and 64. Any additional penalty shall be served by a player to be designated by the Manager or Coach of the offending team through the playing Captain, such player to take his place in the penalty box immediately.*

For all match penalties, regardless of when imposed, or prescribed additional penalties, a total of ten minutes shall be charged in the records against the offending player.

(NOTE 2) *When coincident match penalties have been imposed under Rule 44, Rule 49 or Rule 64 to a*

player on both teams, Rule 28(c) covering coincident major penalties will be applicable with respect to player substitution.

(NOTE 3) *The Referee is required to report all match penalties and the surrounding circumstances to the President of the League immediately following the game in which they occur.*

Rule 31. Penalty Shot

(a) Any infraction of the rules which calls for a "PENALTY SHOT" shall be taken as follows:

The Referee shall ask to announce over the public address system the name of the player designated by him or selected by the team entitled to take the shot (as appropriate) and shall then place the puck on the center faceoff spot and the player taking the shot will, on the instruction of the Referee, play the puck from there and shall attempt to score on the goalkeeper. The player taking the shot may carry the puck in any part of the neutral zone or his own defending zone but once the puck has crossed the attacking blue line, it must be kept in motion towards the opponent's goal line and once it is shot, the play shall be considered complete. No goal can be scored on a rebound of any kind and any time the puck crosses the goal line, the shot shall be considered complete.

Only a player designated as a goalkeeper or alternate goalkeeper may defend against the penalty shot.

(b) The goalkeeper must remain in his crease until the player taking the penalty shot has touched the puck and in the event of violation of this rule or any foul committed by a goalkeeper, the Referee shall allow the shot to be taken and if the shot fails, he shall permit the penalty shot to be taken over again.

The goalkeeper may attempt to stop the shot in any manner except by throwing his stick or any object, in which case a goal shall be awarded.

(NOTE) *See Rule 81.*

(c) In cases where a penalty shot has been awarded under Rule 50(c), deliberately displacing goal post during course of a breakaway; under Rule 62(g), interference; under Rule 66(k), illegal entry into the game; under Rule 81(a) for throwing a stick; and under Rule 84(b), fouling from behind, the Referee shall designate the player who has been fouled as the player who shall take the penalty shot.

In cases where a penalty shot has been awarded under Rule 18(b), deliberate illegal substitution with insufficient playing time remaining; under Rule 50(d), deliberately displacing goal post; under Rule 53(c), falling on the puck in the crease; under Rule 57(d), picking up the puck from the crease area, the penalty shot shall be taken by a player selected by the Captain of the non-offending team from the players on the ice at the time when the foul was committed. Such selection shall be reported to the Referee and cannot be changed.

If by reason of injury, the player designated by the Referee to take the penalty shot is unable to do so within a reasonable time, the shot may be taken by a player selected by the Captain of the non-offending team from the players on the ice when the foul was committed. Such selection shall be reported to the Referee and cannot be changed.

(d) Should the player in respect to whom a penalty shot has been awarded himself commit a foul in connection with the same play or circumstances, either before or after the penalty shot has been awarded, be designated to take the shot, he shall first be permitted to do so before being sent to the penalty bench to serve the penalty except when such penalty is for a game misconduct, gross misconduct or match penalty in which case the penalty shot shall be taken by a player selected by the Captain of the non-offending team from the players on the ice at the time when the foul was committed.

If at the time a penalty shot is awarded, the goalkeeper of the penalized team has been removed from the ice to substitute another player, the goalkeeper shall be permitted to return to the ice before the penalty shot is taken.

(e) While the penalty shot is being taken, players of both sides shall withdraw to the sides of the rink and beyond the center red line.

(f) If, while the penalty shot is being taken, any player of the opposing team shall have by some action interfered with or distracted the player taking the shot and, because of such action, the shot should have failed, a second attempt shall be permitted and the Referee shall impose a misconduct penalty on the player so interfering or distracting.

(g) If a goal is scored from a penalty shot, the puck shall be faced-off at center ice in the usual way. If a goal is not scored, the puck shall be faced-off at either of the end faceoff spots in the zone in which the penalty shot was tried.

(h) Should a goal be scored from a penalty shot, a further penalty to the offending player shall not be applied unless the offense for which the penalty shot was awarded was such as to incur a major or match penalty or misconduct penalty, in which case the penalty prescribed for the particular offense shall be imposed.

If the offense for which the penalty shot was awarded was such as would normally incur a minor penalty, then regardless of whether the penalty shot results in a goal or not, no further minor penalty shall be served.

(i) If the foul upon which the penalty shot is based occurs during actual playing time, the penalty shot shall be awarded and taken immediately in the usual manner notwithstanding any delay occasioned by a slow whistle by the Referee to permit the play to be completed, which delay results in the expiry of the regular playing time in any period.

The time required for the taking of a penalty shot shall not be included in the regular playing time or overtime.

Rule 32. Goalkeeper's Penalties

(a) A goalkeeper shall not be sent to the penalty bench for an offense which incurs a minor

penalty, but instead, the minor penalty shall be served by another member of his team who was on the ice when the offense was committed, said player to be designated by the Manager or Coach of the offending team through the Playing Captain and such substitute shall not be changed.

(b) A goalkeeper shall not be sent to the penalty bench for an offense which incurs a major penalty, but instead, the major penalty shall be served by another member of his team who was on the ice when the offense was committed, said player to be designated by the Manager or Coach of the offending team through the playing Captain and such substitute shall not be changed.

(c) Should a goalkeeper incur three major penalties in one game penalized under Rule 28(b), he shall be ruled off the ice for the balance of the playing time and his place will be taken by a member of his own club, or by a regular substitute goalkeeper who is available. (Major penalty plus game misconduct penalty and automatic fine of one hundred dollars ($100).)

(d) Should a goalkeeper on the ice incur a misconduct penalty, this penalty shall be served by another member of his team who was on the ice when the offense was committed, said player to be designated by the Manager or Coach of the offending team through the Captain and, in addition, the goalkeeper shall be fined fifty dollars ($50).

(e) Should a goalkeeper incur a game misconduct penalty, his place will then be taken by a member of his own club, or by a regular substitute goalkeeper who is available, and such player will be allowed the goalkeeper's full equipment. In addition, the goalkeeper shall be fined one hundred dollars ($100).

(f) Should a goalkeeper incur a match penalty, his place will then be taken by a member of his own club, or by a substitute goalkeeper who is available, and such player will be allowed the goalkeeper's full equipment. However, any additional penalties as specifically called for by the individual rules covering match penalties will apply, and the offending team shall be penalized accordingly, such additional penalties to be served by other members of the team on the ice when the offenses were committed, said players to be designated by the Manager or Coach of the offending team through the Captain. (See Rules 44, 49 and 64.)

(g) Should a goalkeeper incur a match penalty, the case shall be investigated promptly by the President who shall have full power to fine or suspend the penalized goalkeeper or any other players in the altercation.

(h) A minor penalty shall be imposed on a goalkeeper who leaves the immediate vicinity of his crease during an altercation. In addition, he shall be subject to a fine of one hundred dollars ($100) and this incident shall be reported to the President for such further disciplinary action as may be required.

(NOTE) *All penalties imposed on a goalkeeper, regardless of who serves the penalty or any substitution, shall be charged in the records against the goalkeeper.*

(i) If a goalkeeper participates in the play in any manner when he is beyond the center red line, a minor penalty shall be imposed upon him.

Rule 33.   Delayed Penalties

(a) If a third player of any team shall be penalized while two players of the same team are serving penalties, the penalty time of the third player shall not commence until the penalty time of one of the two players already penalized has elapsed. Nevertheless, the third player penalized must at once proceed to the penalty bench but may be replaced by a substitute until such time as the penalty time of the penalized player shall commence.

(b) When any team shall have three players serving penalties at the same time and because of the delayed penalty rule, a substitute for the third offender is on the ice, none of the three penalized players on the penalty bench may return to the ice until play has stopped. When play has been stopped, the player whose full penalty has expired may return to the play.

Provided however that the Penalty Timekeeper shall permit the return to the ice in the order of expiry of their penalties, of a player or players when, by reason of the expiration of their penalties, the penalized team is entitled to have more than four players on the ice.

(c) In the case of delayed penalties, the Referee shall instruct the Penalty Timekeeper that penalized players whose penalties have expired shall only be allowed to return to the ice when there is a stoppage of play.

When the penalties of two players of the same team will expire at the same time, the Captain of that team will designate to the Referee which of such players will return to the ice first and the Referee will instruct the Penalty Timekeeper accordingly.

When a major and a minor penalty are imposed at the same time on players of the same team, the Penalty Timekeeper shall record the minor as being the first of such penalties.

(NOTE) *This applies to the case where the two penalties are imposed on DIFFERENT players of the same team. See also Note to Rule 27.*

Rule 34.   Calling of Penalties

(a) Should an infraction of the rules which would call for a minor, major, misconduct, game misconduct or match penalty be committed by a player of the side in possession of the puck, the Referee shall immediately blow his whistle and penalize the deserving players.

The resulting faceoff shall be made at the place where the play was stopped unless the stoppage occurs in the attacking zone of the player penalized in which case the faceoff shall be made at the nearest faceoff spot in the neutral zone.

(b) Should an infraction of the rules which would call for a minor, major, misconduct, game misconduct or match penalty be committed by a player of the team not in possession of the puck, the Referee will blow his whistle and impose the penalty on the offending player upon completion of the play by the team in possession of the puck.

(NOTE) *There shall be no signal given by the Referee for a misconduct or game misconduct penalty under this section.*

The resulting faceoff shall be made at the place where the play was stopped, unless during the period of a delayed whistle due to a foul by a player of the side NOT in possession, the side in possession ices the puck, shoots the puck so that it goes out of bounds or is unplayable, then the faceoff following the stoppage shall take place in the neutral zone near the defending blue line of the team shooting the puck.

If the penalty or penalties to be imposed are minor penalties and a goal is scored on the play by the non-offending side, the minor penalty or penalties shall not be imposed but major and match penalties shall be imposed in the normal manner regardless of whether or not a goal is scored.

(NOTE 1) *"Completion of the play by the team in possession" in this rule means that the puck must have come into the possession and control of an opposing player or has been "frozen". This does not mean a rebound off the goalkeeper, the goal or the boards, or any accidental contact with the body or equipment of an opposing player.*

(NOTE 2) *If after the Referee has signalled a penalty but before the whistle has been blown, the puck shall enter the goal of the non-offending team as the direct result of a player of that team, the goal shall be allowed and the penalty signalled shall be imposed in the normal manner.*

If when a team is "short-handed" by reason of one or more minor or bench minor penalties, the Referee signals a further minor penalty or penalties against the "short-handed" team and a goal is scored by the non-offending side before the whistle is blown, then the goal shall be allowed, the penalty or penalties signalled shall be washed out and the first of the minor penalties already being served shall automatically terminate under Rule 27(c).

(c) Should the same offending player commit other fouls on the same play, either before or after the Referee has blown his whistle, the offending player shall serve such penalties consecutively.

Rule 34A. Supplementary Discipline

In addition to the automatic fines and suspensions imposed under these rules, the President may, at his discretion, investigate any incident that occurs in connection with any exhibition, league or playoff game and may assess additional fines and/or suspensions for any offence committed during the course of a game or any aftermath thereof by a player, Trainer, Manager, Coach or club executive, whether or not such offence has been penalized by the Referee.

(NOTE) *If an investigation is requested by a club or by the league on its own initiative, it must be initiated within seventy-two (72) hours following the* completion of the game in which the incident occurred.

Rule 34B. Suspensions Arising from Exhibition Games

Whenever suspensions are imposed as a result of infractions occurring during exhibition games, the President shall exercise his discretion in scheduling the suspensions to ensure that no team shall be short more players in any regular league game than it would have been had the infractions occurred in regular league games.

SECTION FIVE—OFFICIALS

Rule 35. Appointment of Officials

(a) The President shall appoint a Referee, two Linesmen, Game Timekeeper, Penalty Time-keeper, Official Scorer and two Goal Judges for each game.

(b) The President shall forward to all clubs a list of Referees, Linesmen, and Off-ice Officials, all of whom must be treated with proper respect at all times during the season by all players and officials of clubs.

Rule 36. Referee

(a) The REFEREE shall have general supervision of the game and shall have full control of all game officials and players during the game, including stoppages; and in case of any dispute, his decision shall be final. The Referee shall remain on the ice at the conclusion of each period until all players have proceeded to their dressing rooms.

(b) All Referees and Linesmen shall be garbed in black trousers and official sweaters.

They shall be equipped with approved whistles and metal tape measures with minimum length of six feet.

(c) The Referee shall order the teams on the ice at the appointed time for the beginning of a game and at the commencement of each period. If for any reason, there is more than fifteen minutes' delay in the commencement of the game or any undue delay in resuming play after the fifteen-minute intervals between periods, the Referee shall state in his report to the President the cause of the delay and the club or clubs which were at fault.

(d) It shall be his duty to see to it that all players are properly dressed, and that the approved regulation equipment is in use at all times during the game.

(e) The Referee shall, before starting the game, see that the appointed Game Timekeeper, Penalty Timekeeper, Official Scorer and Goal Judges are in their respective places and satisfy himself that the timing and signalling equipment are in order.

(f) It shall be his duty to impose such penalties as are prescribed by the rules for infractions thereof and he shall give the final decision in matters of disputed goals. The Referee may consult with the Linesmen or Goal Judge before making his decision.

(g) The Referee shall announce to the Official Scorer or Penalty Timekeeper all goals legally scored as well as penalties and for what infractions such penalties are imposed.

The Referee shall cause to be announced over the public address system the reason for not allowing a goal every time the goal signal light is turned on in the course of play. This shall be done at the first stoppage of play regardless of any standard signal given by the Referee when the goal signal light was put on in error.

The Referee shall report to the Official Scorer the name or number of the goal scorer but he shall not give any information or advice with respect to assist.

(NOTE) *The name of the scorer and any player entitled to an assist will be announced on the public address system. In the event that the Referee disallows a goal for any violation of the rules, he shall report the reason for disallowance to the Official Scorer who shall announce the Referee's decision correctly over the public address system.*

The infraction of the rules for which each penalty has been imposed will be announced correctly, as reported by the Referee, over the public address system. Where players of both teams are penalized on the same play, the penalty to the visiting player will be announced first.

Where a penalty is imposed by the Referee which calls for a mandatory or automatic fine, only the time portion of the penalty will be reported by the Referee to the Official Scorer and announced on the public address system, and the fine will be collected through the League office.

(h) The Referee shall see to it that players of opposing teams are separated on the penalty bench to prevent feuding.

(i) He shall not halt the game for any infractions of the rules concerning off-side play at the blue line or center line, or any violation of Rule 61, icing the puck. Determining infractions of these rules is the duty of the Linesmen unless, by virtue of some accident, the Linesman is prevented from doing so in which case the duties of the Linesman shall be assumed by the Referee until play is stopped.

(j) Should a Referee accidentally leave the ice or receive an injury which incapacitates him from discharging his duties while play is in progress, the game shall be automatically stopped.

(k) If, through misadventure or sickness, the Referee and Linesmen appointed are prevented from appearing, the Managers or Coaches of the two clubs shall agree on a Referee and Linesman. If they are unable to agree, they shall appoint a player from each side who shall act as Referee and Linesman; the player of the home club acting as Referee and the player of the visiting club as Linesman.

(l) If the regularly appointed officials appear during the progress of the game, they shall at once replace the temporary officials.

(m) Should a Linesman appointed be unable to act at the last minute or through sickness or accident be unable to finish the game, the Referee shall have the power to appoint another in his stead, if he deems it necessary, or if required to do so by the Manager or Coach of either of the competing teams.

(n) If, owing to illness or accident, the Referee is unable to continue to officiate, one of the Linesmen shall perform the duties of the Referee during the balance of the game, the Linesman to be selected by the Referee. In the event that an NHL Supervisor is in attendance at a game where a spare official is present, he shall have the authority to substitute the injured Referee with the spare official.

(o) The Referee shall check club rosters and all players in uniform before signing reports of the game.

(p) The Referee shall report to President promptly and in detail the circumstances of any of the following incidents:

(1) When a stick or part thereof is thrown outside the playing area—Rule 81(c);

(2) Every obscene gesture made by any person involved in the playing or conduct of the game whether as a participant or as an official of either team or of the League, which gesture he has personally observed or which has been brought to his attention by any game official—Rule 68(a);

(3) When any player, Trainer, Coach or club executive becomes involved in an altercation with a spectator—Rule 63(b);

(4) Every infraction under Rule 28(b) major and game misconducts.

(q) In the event of failure by a club to comply with a provision of the League constitution, by-laws, resolutions, rules or regulations affecting the playing of a game, the Referee shall, if so directed by the President or his designee, refuse to permit the game to proceed until the offending club comes into compliance with such provision.

Should the offending club persist in its refusal to come into compliance, the Referee shall, with the prior approval of the President or his designee, declare the game forfeited and the non-offending club the winner. Should the Referee declare the game forfeited because both clubs have refused to comply with such a provision, the visiting club shall be declared the winner.

If the game is declared forfeited prior to its having commenced, the score shall be recorded as 1-0 and no player shall be credited with any personal statistics.

If the game was in progress at the time it is declared forfeited, the score shall be recorded as zero for the loser and 1, or such greater number of goals that had been scored by it, for the winner;

however, the players on both clubs shall be credited with all personal statistics earned up to the time the forfeit was declared.

Rule 37. Linesman

(a) The duty of the LINESMAN is to determine any infractions of the rules concerning off-side play at the blue line or center line, or any violation of Rule 61, icing the puck.

He shall stop the play when the puck goes outside the playing area, when it is interfered with by any ineligible person, when it is struck above the height of the shoulder and when the goal post has been displaced from its normal position. He shall stop the play for off-sides occurring on faceoffs and for premature entry into faceoff circles. He shall stop the play when he has observed that a goal has been scored which has not been observed by the Referee. He shall stop the play when there has been a premature substitution for a goalkeeper under Rule 18(a), for injured players under Rule 19(f), for a player batting the puck forward to a teammate under Rule 57(e), the calling of a double-minor penalty for accidental high sticks, under Rule 58(c), interference by spectators under Rule 63(a), the calling of a double-minor penalty to a player who attempts to poke, jab or spear an opponent, under Rule 79(c), and the calling of a penalty under Rule 81(a) for deliberately throwing a stick in the defensive zone.

(b) He shall faceoff the puck at all times, except at the start of the game, at the beginning of each period and after a goal has been scored.

The Referee may call upon a Linesman to conduct a faceoff at any time.

(c) He shall, when requested to do so by the Referee, give his version of any incident that may have taken place during the playing of the game.

(d) He shall not stop the play to impose any penalty except when a major penalty is warranted to a player on the ice when a serious incident has been observed by him but not by the Referee and/or when he observes any violation of Rules 18(a) and (c), change of players (too many men on the ice); Rule 42(k), articles thrown on the ice from vicinity of players' or penalty bench; Rule 42(l), interference with game officials by player, Coach, Trainer or club executive; and Rule 46(c), stick thrown on ice from players' bench. He shall report such violation to the Referee who shall impose a bench minor penalty against the offending team.

In addition, when assessing a major penalty to a player, he may, at his discretion, assess a minor penalty to a player of the opposing team that he deems instigated the incident for which the major penalty was assessed.

He shall report immediately to the Referee his version of the circumstances with respect to Rule 50(c)—Delaying the game by deliberately displacing post from its normal position. He shall report immediately to the Referee his version of the circumstances with regard to interference on a goaltender when a goal is scored.

He shall report immediately to the Referee his version of any infraction of the rules constituting a major or match foul or game misconduct or any conduct calling for a bench minor penalty or misconduct penalty under these rules.

Rule 38. Goal Judge

(a) There shall be one GOAL JUDGE at each goal. They shall not be members of either club engaged in a game, nor shall they be replaced during its progress, unless after the commencement of the game it becomes apparent that either Goal Judge, on account of partisanship or any other cause, is guilty of giving unjust decision, when the Referee may appoint another Goal Judge to act in his stead.

(b) Goal Judges shall be stationed behind the goals during the progress of play, in properly protected areas, so that there can be no interference with their activities; and they shall not change goals during the game.

(c) In the event of a goal being claimed, the Goal Judge of that goal shall decide whether or not the puck has passed between the goal posts and entirely over the goal line.

Rule 39. Penalty Timekeeper

(a) The PENALTY TIMEKEEPER shall keep, on the official forms provided, a correct record of all penalties imposed by the officials including the names of the players penalized, the infractions penalized, the duration of each penalty and the time at which each penalty was imposed. He shall report in the Penalty Record each penalty shot awarded, the name of the player taking the shot and the result of the shot.

(b) The Penalty Timekeeper shall check and ensure that the time served by all penalized players is correct. He shall be responsible for the correct posting of penalties on the scoreboard at all times and shall promptly call to the attention of the Referee any discrepancy between the time recorded on the clock and the official correct time and he shall be responsible for making any adjustments ordered by the Referee.

He shall upon request, give a penalized player correct information as to the unexpired time of his penalty.

(NOTE 1) *The infraction of the rules for which each penalty has been imposed will be announced twice over the public address system as reported by the Referee. Where players of both teams are penalized on the same play, the penalty to the visiting player will be announced first.*

(NOTE 2) *Misconduct penalties and coincident major penalties should not be recorded on the timing device but such penalized players should be alerted and released at the first stoppage of play following the expiration of their penalties.*

(c) Upon the completion of each game, the Penalty Timekeeper shall complete and sign four copies of the Penalty Record to be distributed as quickly as possible to the following persons:

(1) One copy to the Official Scorer for transmission to the League President;

(2)   One copy to the visiting Coach or Manager;

(3)   One copy to the home Coach or Manager;

(4)   One copy to the home team Public Relations Department.

(d)   The Officiating Department shall be entitled to inspect, collect and forward to League headquarters the actual work sheets used by the Penalty Timekeeper in any game.

Rule 40.   Official Scorer

(a)   Before the start of the game, the Official Scorer shall obtain from the Manager or Coach of both teams a list of all eligible players and the starting line-up of each team which information shall be made known to the opposing Manager or Coach before the start of play, either personally or through the Referee.

The Official Scorer shall secure the names of the Captain and Alternate Captains from the Manager or Coach at the time the line-ups are collected and will indicate those nominated by placing the letter "C" or "A" opposite their names on the Referee's Report of Match. All this information shall be presented to the Referee for his signature at the completion of the game.

(b)   The Official Scorer shall keep a record of the goals scored, the scorers, the players to whom assists have been credited and shall indicate those players on the lists who have actually taken part in the game. He shall also record the time of entry into the game of any substitute goalkeeper. He shall record on the Official Score Sheet a notation where a goal is scored when the goalkeeper has been removed from the ice.

(c)   The Official Scorer shall award the points for goals and assists and his decision shall be final. The awards of points for goals and assists shall be announced twice over the public address system and all changes in such awards shall also be announced in the same manner.

No requests for changes in any award of points shall be considered unless they are made at or before the conclusion of actual play in the game by the team Captain.

(d)   At the conclusion of the game, the Official Scorer shall complete and sign four copies of the Official Score Sheet for distribution as quickly as possible to the following persons:

(1)   One copy to the Official Scorer to be transmitted to the League President;

(2)   One copy to the visiting Coach or Manager;

(3)   One copy to the home Coach or Manager;

(4)   One copy to the home team Public Relations Department.

(e)   The Official Scorer shall also prepare the Official Report of Match for signature by the Referee and forward it to the League President together with the Official Score Sheet and the Penalty Record.

(f)   The Official Scorer should be in an elevated position, well away from the players' benches, with house telephone communication to the public address announcer.

Rule 41.   Game Timekeeper

(a)   The Game Timekeeper shall record the time of starting and finishing of each period in the game. During the game the game timekeeper will start the clock with the drop of the puck and stop the clock upon hearing the Official's whistle or the scoring of a goal.

(b)   The Game Timekeeper shall signal the Referee and the competing teams for the start of the game and each succeeding period and the Referee shall start the play promptly in accordance with Rule 82.

To assist in assuring the prompt return to the ice of the teams and the officials, the Game Timekeeper shall give preliminary warnings five and two minutes prior to the resumption of play in each period.

(c)   If the rink is not equipped with an automatic signalling device or, if such device fails to function, the Game Timekeeper shall signal the end of each period by blowing a whistle.

(d)   He shall cause to be announced on the public address system at the nineteenth minute in each period that there is one minute remaining to be played in the period.

(e)   In the event of any dispute regarding time, the matter shall be referred to the Referee for adjustment and his decision shall be final.

Rule 41A.   Statistician

(a)   There shall be appointed for duty at every game played in the League a Statistician and such assistants or alternates as may be deemed necessary.

(b)   The duty of the Statistician(s) is to correctly record on the official League forms supplied all the data therein provided for concerning the performances of individual players and the participating teams.

(c)   These records shall be compiled and recorded in strict conformity with the instructions printed on the forms supplied and shall be completed as to totals where required and with such accuracy as to ensure that the data supplied is "in balance".

(d)   At the conclusion of each game, the Statistician shall sign and distribute four copies of the final and correct Statistician's Report to each of the following persons:

(1)   One copy to the Official Scorer for transmission to the League President;

(2)   One copy to the visiting Coach or Manager;

(3) One copy to the home Coach or Manager;

(4) One copy to the home team Public Relations Department.

SECTION SIX—PLAYING RULES

Rule 42. Abuse of Officials and other Misconduct

(NOTE) *In the enforcement of this rule, the Referee has, in many instances, the option of imposing a misconduct penalty or a bench minor penalty. In principle, the Referee is directed to impose a bench minor penalty in respect to the violations which occur on or in the immediate vicinity of the players' bench but off the playing surface and in all cases affecting non-playing personnel or players. A misconduct penalty should be imposed for violations which occur on the playing surface or in the penalty bench area and where the penalized player is readily identifiable.*

(a) A misconduct penalty shall be imposed on any player who uses obscene, profane or abusive language to any person or who intentionally knocks or shoots the puck out of the reach of an official who is retrieving it or who deliberately throws any equipment out of the playing area.

(b) A minor penalty shall be assessed to any player who challenges or disputes the rulings of any official during a game. If the player persists in such challenge or dispute, he shall be assessed a misconduct penalty and any further dispute will result in a game misconduct penalty being assessed to the offending player.

In the event that a teammate of a penalized player challenges or disputes the ruling of the official in assessing the penalty, a misconduct penalty shall be imposed.

(c) A misconduct penalty shall be imposed on any player or players who bang the boards with their sticks or other instruments at any time.

In the event that the Coach, Trainer, Manager or club executive commits an infraction under this rule, a bench minor penalty shall be imposed.

(d) A bench minor penalty shall be imposed on the team of any penalized player who does not proceed directly and immediately to the penalty box and take his place on the penalty bench or to the dressing room when so ordered by the Referee.

Where coincident penalties are imposed on players of both teams, the penalized players of the visiting team shall take their positions on the penalty bench first in the place designated for visiting players.

(e) Any player who, following a fight or other altercation in which he has been involved is broken up and for which he is penalized, fails to proceed directly and immediately to the penalty bench, or who causes any delay by retrieving his equipment (gloves, sticks, etc. shall be delivered to him at the penalty bench by teammates), shall incur an automatic fine of one hundred dollars ($100) in addition to all other penalties or fines incurred.

(f) Any player who persists in continuing or attempting to continue the fight or altercation after he has been ordered by the Referee to stop, or who resists a Linesman in the discharge of his duties shall, at the discretion of the Referee, incur a misconduct or game misconduct penalty in addition to any penalties imposed.

(g) A misconduct penalty shall be imposed on any player who, after warning by the Referee, persists in any course of conduct (including threatening or abusive language or gestures or similar actions) designed to incite an opponent into incurring a penalty.

If, after the assessment of a misconduct penalty, a player persists in any course of conduct for which he was previously assessed a misconduct penalty, he shall be assessed a game misconduct penalty.

(h) A bench minor penalty shall be imposed against the offending team if any player, club executive, Manager, Coach or Trainer uses obscene, profane or abusive language or gesture to any person or uses the name of any official coupled with any vociferous remarks.

(i) In the case of any club executive, Manager, Coach or Trainer being guilty of such misconduct, he is to be removed from the bench by order of the Referee and his case reported to the President for further action.

(j) If any club executive, Manager, Coach or Trainer is removed from the bench by order of the Referee, he must not sit near the bench of his club nor in any way direct or attempt to direct the play of his club.

(k) A bench minor penalty shall be imposed against the offending team if any player, Trainer, Coach, Manager or club executive in the vicinity of the players' bench or penalty bench throws anything on the ice during the progress of the game or during stoppage of play.

(NOTE) *The penalty provided under this rule is in addition to any penalty imposed under Rule 46(c)— "Broken Stick."*

(l) A bench minor penalty shall be imposed against the offending team if any player, Trainer, Coach, Manager or club executive interferes in any manner with any game official including Referee, Linesmen, Timekeepers or Goal Judges in the performance of their duties.

The Referee may assess further penalties under Rule 67 (Abuse of Officials) if he deems them to be warranted.

(m) A misconduct penalty shall be imposed on any player or players who, except for the purpose of taking their positions on the penalty bench, enter or remain in the Referee's crease while he is reporting to or consulting with any game official including Linesmen, Timekeeper, Penalty Timekeeper, Official Scorer or Announcer.

(n) A minor penalty shall be imposed on any player who is guilty of unsportsmanlike conduct

including, but not limited to hair-pulling, biting, grabbing hold of face mask, etc.

(NOTE) *If warranted the Referee may apply Rule 29(d)—gross misconduct.*

Rule 43. Adjustment to Clothing or Equipment

(a) Play shall not be stopped nor the game delayed by reasons of adjustments to clothing, equipment, skates or sticks.

For an infringement of this rule, a minor penalty shall be given.

(b) The onus of maintaining clothing and equipment in proper condition shall be upon the player. If adjustments are required, the player shall retire from the ice and play shall continue with a substitute.

(c) No delay shall be permitted for the repair or adjustment of goalkeeper's equipment. If adjustments are required, the goalkeeper will retire from the ice and his place will be taken by the substitute goalkeeper immediately.

(d) For an infraction of this rule by a goalkeeper, a minor penalty shall be imposed.

Rule 44. Attempt to Injure

(a) A match penalty shall be imposed on any player who deliberately attempts to injure an opponent and the circumstances shall be reported to the President for further action. A substitute for the penalized player shall be permitted at the end of the fifth minute.

(b) A game misconduct penalty shall be imposed on any player who deliberately attempts to injure an Official, Manager, Coach or Trainer in any manner and the circumstances shall be reported to the President for further action.

(NOTE) *The President, upon preliminary investigation indicating the probable imposition of supplementary disciplinary action, may order the immediate suspension of a player who has incurred a match penalty under this rule, pending the final determination of such supplementary disciplinary action.*

Rule 45. Board Checking
and Checking from Behind

(a) A minor or major penalty, at the discretion of the Referee based upon the degree of violence of the impact with the boards, shall be imposed on any player who bodychecks, cross-checks, elbows, charges or trips an opponent in such a manner that causes the opponent to be thrown violently into the boards.

(NOTE) *Any unnecessary contact with a player playing the puck on an obvious "icing" or "off-side" play which results in that player being knocked into the boards is "boarding" and must be penalized as such. In other instances where there is no contact with the boards, it should be treated as "charging".*

"Rolling" an opponent (if he is the puck carrier) along the boards where he is endeavouring to go through too small an opening is not boarding.

However, if the opponent is not the puck carrier, then such action should be penalized as boarding, charging, interference or, if the arms or stick are employed, it should be called holding or hooking.

(b) When a major penalty is imposed under this rule, an automatic fine of fifty dollars ($50) shall be imposed.

(c) When a major penalty is imposed under this rule for a foul resulting in an injury to the face or head of an opponent, an automatic game misconduct shall be imposed.

(d) Any player who cross-checks or pushes a player from behind into the boards when the player is unable to defend himself, shall be assessed a major and a game misconduct penalty.

(e) In regular season games any player who incurs a total of two game misconduct penalties for board-checking under Rule 45(c) and (d) shall be suspended automatically for the next League game of his team. For each subsequent game misconduct penalty the automatic suspension shall be increased by one game.

In playoff games, any player who incurs a total of two game misconduct penalties for board-checking under Rule 45(c) and (d) shall be suspended automatically for the next playoff game of his team. For each subsequent game misconduct penalty during the playoffs the automatic suspension shall be increased by one game.

Rule 46. Broken Stick

(a) A player without a stick may participate in the game. A player whose stick is broken may participate in the game provided he drops the broken portion. A minor penalty shall be imposed for an infraction of this rule.

(NOTE) *A broken stick is one which, in the opinion of the Referee, is unfit for normal play.*

(b) A goalkeeper may continue to play with a broken stick until stoppage of play or until he has been legally provided with a stick.

(c) A player whose stick is broken may not receive a stick thrown on the ice from any part of the rink but must obtain same at his players' bench. A goalkeeper whose stick is broken may not receive a stick thrown on the ice from any part of the rink but may receive a stick from a teammate without proceeding to his players' bench. A minor penalty shall be imposed on the player or goalkeeper receiving a stick illegally under this rule.

(d) A goalkeeper whose stick is broken or illegal may not go to the players' bench for a replacement but must receive his stick from a teammate.

For an infraction of this rule, a minor penalty shall be imposed on the goalkeeper.

Rule 47. Charging

(a) A minor or major penalty shall be imposed on a player who runs or jumps into or charges an opponent.

(b) When a major penalty is imposed under this rule for a foul resulting in injury to the face or head of an opponent, an automatic fine of fifty dollars ($50) shall be imposed.

(c) A minor or major penalty shall be imposed on a player who charges a goalkeeper while the goalkeeper is within his goal crease.

(NOTE) *If more than two steps or strides are taken, it shall be considered a charge.*

A goalkeeper is NOT "fair game" just because he is outside the goal crease area. A penalty for interference or charging (minor or major) should be called in every case where an opposing player makes unnecessary contact with a goalkeeper.

Likewise, Referees should be alert to penalize goalkeepers for tripping, slashing or spearing in the vicinity of the goal.

Rule 48.   Cross-Checking and Butt-Ending

(a) A minor or major penalty, at the discretion of the Referee, shall be imposed on a player who "cross-checks" an opponent.

(NOTE 1) *Cross-check shall mean a check delivered with both hands on the stick and no part of the stick on the ice.*

(NOTE 2) *When a major penalty is assessed for cross-checking, an automatic game misconduct penalty shall be imposed on the offending player.*

(b) A major penalty and a game misconduct penalty shall be imposed on any player who "butt-ends" or attempts to "butt-end" an opponent.

(NOTE) *Attempt to "butt-end" shall include all cases where a "butt-end" gesture is made regardless whether body contact is made or not.*

(c) When a major penalty is imposed under this rule, an automatic fine of fifty dollars ($50) shall also be imposed.

Rule 49.   Deliberate Injury of Opponents

(a) A match penalty shall be imposed on a player who deliberately injures an opponent in any manner.

(NOTE) *Any player wearing tape or any other material on his hands who cuts or injures an opponent during an altercation shall receive a match penalty under this rule.*

(b) In addition to the match penalty, the player shall be automatically suspended from further competition until the President has ruled on the issue.

(c) No substitute shall be permitted to take the place of the penalized player until ten minutes actual playing time have elapsed from the time the penalty was imposed.

(d) A game misconduct penalty shall be imposed on any player who deliberately injures an official, Manager, Coach or Trainer in any manner and the circumstances shall be reported to the President for further action.

Rule 50.   Delaying the Game

(a) A minor penalty shall be imposed on any player or goalkeeper who delays the game by deliberately shooting or batting the puck with his stick outside the playing area.

(NOTE) *This penalty shall also apply when a player or goalkeeper deliberately bats or shoots the puck with his stick outside the playing area after a stoppage of play.*

(b) A minor penalty shall be imposed on any player or goalkeeper who throws or deliberately bats the puck with his hand or stick outside the playing area.

(c) A minor penalty shall be imposed on any player (including goalkeeper) who delays the game by deliberately displacing a goal post from its normal position. The Referee or Linesmen shall stop play immediately when a goal post has been displaced.

If the goal post is deliberately displaced by a goalkeeper or player during the course of a "breakaway", a penalty shot will be awarded to the nonoffending team, which shot shall be taken by the player last in possession of the puck.

(NOTE) *A player with a "breakaway" is defined as a player in control of the puck with no opposition between him and the opposing goal and with a reasonable scoring opportunity.*

In the event that a goalpost is deliberately displaced by a defending player or goalkeeper, prior to the puck crossing the goal line between the normal position of the goalposts, the Referee, at his discretion, may assess a minor penalty under Rule 50(c) (paragraph 1), a penalty shot under Rule 50(d), or award a goal.

(d) If by reason of insufficient time in the regular playing time or by reason of penalties already imposed, the minor penalty assessed to a player for deliberately displacing his own goal post cannot be served in its entirety within the regular playing time of the game or at any time in overtime, a penalty shot shall be awarded against the offending team.

(e) A bench minor penalty shall be imposed upon any team which, after warning by the Referee to its Captain or Alternate Captain to place the correct number of players on the ice and commence play, fails to comply with the Referee's direction and thereby causes any delay by making additional substitutions, by persisting in having its players off-side, or in any other manner.

Rule 51. Elbowing, Kneeing and Head-Butting

(a) A minor or major penalty, at the discretion of the Referee, shall be imposed on any player who uses his elbow or knee in such a way as to in any way foul an opponent.

(b) When a major penalty is imposed under this rule for a foul resulting in an injury to an opponent, an automatic fine of fifty dollars ($50) shall also be imposed.

(c) A match penalty shall be imposed on any player who deliberately "head-butts" or attempts to "head-butt" or knees an opponent during an altercation and the circumstances shall be reported to the President for further action. A substitute shall be permitted at the end of the fifth minute. In the event there is an injury to an opponent resulting from the foul, no substitute shall be permitted to take the place of the penalized player until ten minutes actual time has elapsed.

Rule 52.   Faceoffs

(a) The puck shall be "faced-off" by the Referee or the Linesman dropping the puck on the ice between the sticks of the players "facing-off". Players facing-off will stand squarely facing their opponent's end of the rink approximately one stick length apart with the blade of their sticks on the ice.

When the faceoff takes place in any of the end faceoff circles, the players taking part shall take their position so that they will stand squarely facing their opponent's end of the rink. The sticks of both players facing-off shall have the blade on the ice within the designated white area. The visiting player shall place his stick within the designated white area first.

No other player shall be allowed to enter the faceoff circle or come within fifteen feet of the players facing-off the puck and must stand on side on all faceoffs.

If a violation of this sub-section of this rule occurs, the Referee or Linesman shall re-face the puck.

(b) If after warning by the Referee or Linesman, either of the players fails to take his proper position for the faceoff promptly, the official shall be entitled to faceoff the puck notwithstanding such default.

(c) In the conduct of any faceoff anywhere on the playing surface, no player facing-off shall make any physical contact with his opponent's body by means of his own body or by his stick except in the course of playing the puck after the faceoff has been completed.

For violation of this rule, the Referee shall impose a minor penalty or penalties on the player(s) whose action(s) caused the physical contact.

(NOTE) *"Conduct of any faceoff" commences when the Referee designates the place of the faceoff and he (or the Linesman) takes up his position to drop the puck.*

(d) If a player facing-off fails to take his proper position immediately when directed by the official, the official may order him replaced for that faceoff by any teammate then on the ice.

No substitution of players shall be permitted until the faceoff has been completed and play has resumed except when a penalty is imposed which affects the on-ice strength of either team.

(e) A second violation of any of the provisions of subsection (a) hereof by the same team during the same faceoff shall be penalized with a minor penalty to the player who commits the second violation of the rule.

(f) When an infringement of a rule has been committed or a stoppage of play has been caused by any player of the attacking side in the attacking zone, the ensuing faceoff shall be made in the neutral zone on the nearest faceoff spot.

(NOTE) *This includes stoppage of play caused by a player of the attacking side shooting the puck on the back of the defending team's net without any intervening action by the defending team.*

(g) When an infringement of a rule has been committed by players of both sides in the play resulting in the stoppage, the ensuing faceoff will be made at the place of such infringement or at the place where play is stopped.

(h) When stoppage occurs between the end faceoff spots and near end of the rink, the puck shall be faced-off at the end faceoff spot on the side where the stoppage occurs unless otherwise expressly provided by these rules.

(i) No faceoff shall be made within fifteen feet of the goal or sideboards.

(j) When a goal is illegally scored as a result of a puck being deflected directly from an official anywhere in the defending zone, the resulting faceoff shall be made at the end faceoff spot in the defending zone.

(k) When the game is stopped for any reason not specifically covered in the official rules, the puck must be faced-off where it was last played.

(l) The whistle will not be blown by the official to start play. Playing time will commence from the instant the puck is faced-off and will stop when the whistle is blown.

(m) Following a stoppage of play, should one or both defensemen who are the point players or any player coming from the bench of the attacking team, enter into the attacking zone beyond the outer edge of the corner faceoff circle, the ensuing faceoff shall take place in the neutral zone near the blue line of the defending team.

Rule 53.   Falling on Puck

(a) A minor penalty shall be imposed on a player other than the goalkeeper who deliberately falls on or gathers the puck into his body.

(NOTE) *Any player who drops to his knees to block a shot should not be penalized if the puck is shot under him or becomes lodged in his clothing or equipment but any use of the hands to make the puck unplayable should be penalized promptly.*

(b) A minor penalty shall be imposed on a goalkeeper who, when he is in his own goal crease, deliberately falls on or gathers the puck into his body or who holds or places the puck against any part of the goal in such a manner as to cause a stoppage of play unless he is actually being checked by an opponent.

(NOTE) *Refer to Rule 74(c) for rule governing freezing of the puck by a goalkeeper outside of his crease area.*

(c) No defending player, except the goalkeeper, will be permitted to fall on the puck, hold the puck or gather the puck into the body or hands when the puck is within the goal crease.

For infringement of this rule, play shall immediately be stopped and a penalty shot shall be ordered against the offending team, but no other penalty shall be given.

(NOTE) *The rule shall be interpreted so that a penalty shot will be awarded only when the puck is in the crease at the instant the offense occurs. However, in cases where the puck is outside the crease. Rule 53(a) may still apply and a minor penalty may be imposed, even though no penalty shot is awarded.*

(a) A major penalty shall be imposed on any player who engages in fisticuffs.

In addition, a minor or a major and/or a game misconduct penalty, at the discretion of the Referee, shall be imposed on any player who starts fisticuffs and, if such player is wearing a face shield, he shall be assessed an additional minor penalty. These penalties are in addition to any other penalty incurred in the same incident.

Also, any player assessed a minor and a major penalty under this rule on two occasions in a game shall receive automatically a misconduct penalty. A player assessed an additional major penalty under this rule on one occasion in a game shall receive automatically a misconduct penalty.

(b) A minor penalty shall be imposed on a player who, having been struck, shall retaliate with a blow or attempted blow. However, at the discretion of the Referee, a major or a double-minor penalty or a game misconduct penalty may be imposed if such player continues the altercation.

(NOTE 1) *It is the intent and purpose of this rule that the Referee shall impose the "major and game misconduct" penalty in all cases where the instigator or retaliator of the fight is the aggressor and is plainly doing so for the purpose of intimidation or punishment.*

(NOTE 2) *The Referee is provided very wide latitude in the penalties which he may impose under this rule. This is done intentionally to enable him to differentiate between the obvious degrees of responsibility of the participants either for starting the fighting or persisting in continuing the fighting. The discretion provided should be exercised realistically.*

(NOTE 3) *Referees are directed to employ every means provided by these rules to stop "brawling" and should use this rule and Rules 42(e) and (f) for this purpose.*

(NOTE 4) *Any player wearing tape or any other material on his hands who cuts or injures an opponent during an altercation will receive a match penalty under Rule 49(a).*

(c) A misconduct or game misconduct penalty shall be imposed on any player involved in fisticuffs off the playing surface or with another player who is off the playing surface.

(d) A game misconduct penalty, at the discretion of the Referee, shall be imposed on any player or goalkeeper who is the first to intervene in an altercation then in progress except when a match penalty is being imposed in the original altercation. This penalty is in addition to any other penalty incurred in the same incident.

(e) When a fight occurs, all players not engaged shall go immediately to the area of their players' bench and in the event the altercation takes place at a players' bench, the players on the ice from that team shall go to their defensive zone.

Failure to comply with the Rule shall, in addition to the other penalties that may be assessed, result in a fine to the team of $1,000 and the Coach of said team in the amount of $1,000.

(f) A game misconduct penalty shall be imposed on any player who is assessed a major penalty for fighting after the original altercation.

Notwithstanding this rule, at the discretion of the Referee, the automatic game misconduct penalty may be waived for a player in the altercation if the opposing player was clearly the instigator of the altercation.

(g) Any teams whose players become involved in an altercation, other than during the periods of the game, shall be fined automatically twenty-five thousand dollars ($25,000) in addition to any other appropriate penalties that may be imposed upon the participating players by supplementary discipline or otherwise.

Any player who would be deemed to be an instigator pursuant to Rule 54(a) at a time other than during the periods of the game shall be suspended automatically for ten (10) games. Such determination may be made by the Referee at the time of the incident or subsequently by the President or his designee based upon such reports and other information as he deems sufficient, including but not limited to television tapes.

(NOTE) *In the case of altercations taking place after the period or game the fine under this rule shall be assessed only in the event that an altercation is commenced after the period or game has terminated.*

(h) Any player who incurs two fighting majors in the same game, the second of which includes an instigator penalty, shall receive an automatic game misconduct penalty.

Rule 55.   Goals and Assists

(NOTE) *It is the responsibility of the Official Scorer to award goals and assists, and his decision in this respect is final notwithstanding the report of the Referee or any other game official. Such awards shall be made or withheld strictly in accordance with the provisions of this rule. Therefore, it is essential that the Official Scorer be thoroughly familiar with every aspect of this rule, be alert to observe all actions which could affect the making of an award and, above all, the awards must be made or withheld with absolute impartiality.*

In case of an obvious error in awarding a goal or an assist which has been announced, it should be corrected promptly but changes should not be made in the official scoring summary after the Referee has signed the Game Report.

(a) A goal shall be scored when the puck shall have been put between the goal posts by the stick of a player of the attacking side, from in front and

below the cross bar, and entirely across a red line the width of the diameter of the goal posts drawn on the ice from one goal post to the other.

(b) A goal shall be scored if the puck is put into the goal in any way by a player of the defending side. The player of the attacking side who last played the puck shall be credited with the goal but no assist shall be awarded.

(c) If an attacking player kicks the puck and it is deflected into the net by any player of the defending side except the goalkeeper, the goal shall be allowed. The player who kicked the puck shall be credited with the goal but no assist shall be awarded.

(d) If the puck shall have been deflected into the goal from the shot of an attacking player by striking any part of the person of a player of the same side, a goal shall be allowed. The player who deflected the puck shall be credited with the goal. The goal shall not be allowed if it has been kicked, thrown or otherwise deliberately directed into the goal by any means other than a stick.

(e) If a goal is scored as a result of being deflected directly into the net from an official, the goal shall not be allowed.

(f) Should a player legally propel a puck into the goal crease of the opponent club and the puck should become loose and available to another player of the attacking side, a goal scored on the play shall be legal.

(g) Any goal scored, other than as covered by the official rules, shall not be allowed.

(h) A "goal" shall be credited in the scoring records to a player who shall have propelled the puck into the opponent's goal. Each "goal" shall count one point in the player's record.

(i) When a player scores a goal, an "assist" shall be credited to the player or players taking part in the play immediately preceding the goal, but no more than two assists can be given on any goal. Each "assist" shall count one point in the player's record.

(j) Only one point can be credited to any one player on a goal.

Rule 56. Gross Misconduct

Refer to Rule 29—Misconduct Penalty

Rule 57. Handling Puck with Hands

(a) If a player, except a goalkeeper, closes his hand on the puck, the play shall be stopped and a minor penalty shall be imposed on him. A goalkeeper who holds the puck with his hands for longer than three seconds shall be given a minor penalty unless he is actually being checked by an opponent.

(b) A goalkeeper must not deliberately hold the puck in any manner which, in the opinion of the Referee, causes a stoppage of play, nor throw the puck forward towards the opponent's net, nor deliberately drop the puck into his pads or onto the goal net, nor deliberately pile up snow or obstacles at or near his net, that in the opinion of the Referee, would tend to prevent the scoring of a goal.

(NOTE) *The object of this entire rule is to keep the puck in play continuously and any action taken by the goalkeeper which causes an unnecessary stoppage must be penalized without warning.*

(c) The penalty for infringement of this rule by the goalkeeper shall be a minor penalty.

(NOTE) *In the case of the puck thrown forward by the goalkeeper being taken by an opponent, the Referee shall allow the resulting play to be completed, and if goal is scored by the non-offending team, it shall be allowed and no penalty given; but if a goal is not scored, play shall be stopped and a minor penalty shall be imposed against the goalkeeper.*

(d) A minor penalty shall be imposed on a player, except the goalkeeper, who, while play is in progress, picks up the puck off the ice with his hand.

If a player, except a goalkeeper, while play is in progress, picks up the puck with his hand from the ice in the goal crease area, the play shall be stopped immediately and a penalty shot shall be awarded to the non-offending team.

(e) A player shall be permitted to stop or "bat" a puck in the air with his open hand, or push it along the ice with his hand, and the play shall not be stopped unless, in the opinion of the Referee, he has deliberately directed the puck to a teammate in any zone other than the defensive zone, in which case the play shall be stopped and the puck faced-off at the spot where the offense occurred. Play will not be stopped for any hand pass by players in their own defensive zone.

(NOTE) *The object of this rule is to ensure continuous action and the Referee should NOT stop play unless he is satisfied that the directing of the puck to a teammate was, in fact, DELIBERATE.*

The puck may not be "batted" with the hand directly into the net at any time, but a goal shall be allowed when the puck has been legally "batted" or is deflected into the goal by a defending player except the goalkeeper.

Rule 58. High Sticks

(a) The carrying of sticks above the normal height of the shoulders is prohibited and a minor, double-minor or major penalty may be imposed on a player violating this rule, at the discretion of the Referee.

(b) A goal scored from a stick so carried shall not be allowed, except by a player of the defending team.

(c) When a player carries or holds any part of his stick above the height of his shoulders so that injury to the face or head of an opposing player results, the Referee shall:

(1) assess a double-minor penalty when it is deemed to be accidental in nature by the officials;

(2) assess a major and game-misconduct when the high stick is deemed to be careless by the officials. Refer to Rule 29(f) and 28(b).

When a major penalty is imposed under this rule for a foul resulting in injury to the face or head of an opponent, an automatic fine of fifty dollars ($50) shall also be imposed. Also when a major penalty is imposed under this rule, the player, excluding goalkeepers, shall receive automatically a game misconduct penalty.

(d) Batting the puck above the normal height of the shoulders with the stick is prohibited and when it occurs, there shall be a whistle and ensuing faceoff at the spot where the offense occurred or at the spot where the puck is touched when a territorial advantage has been gained by the offending team, unless:

(1) the puck has been batted to an opponent in which case the play shall continue;

(2) a player of the defending side shall bat the puck into his own goal in which case the goal shall be allowed.

(NOTE) *When a player bats the puck to an opponent under sub-section 1, the Referee shall give the "washout" signal immediately. Otherwise, he will stop the play.*

(e) When either team is below the numerical strength of its opponent and a player of the team of greater numerical strength causes a stoppage of play by striking the puck with his stick above the height of his shoulder, the resulting faceoff shall be made at one of the end faceoff spots adjacent to the goal of the team causing the stoppage.

Rule 59.　　　　Holding an Opponent

A minor penalty shall be imposed on a player who holds an opponent with hands or stick or in any other way.

Rule 60.　　　　Hooking

(a) A minor penalty shall be imposed on a player who impedes or seeks to impede the progress of an opponent by "hooking" with his stick.

(b) A major penalty shall be imposed on any player who injures an opponent by "hooking".

When a major penalty is imposed under this rule for a foul resulting in injury to the face or head of an opponent, an automatic fine of fifty dollars ($50) shall also be imposed.

(NOTE) *When a player is checking another in such a way that there is only stick-to-stick contract, such action is neither hooking or holding.*

Rule 61.　　　　Icing the Puck

(a) For the purpose of this rule, the center red line will divide the ice into halves. Should any player of a team equal or superior in numerical strength to the opposing team shoot, bat or deflect the puck from his own half of the ice beyond the goal line of the opposing team, play shall be stopped and the puck faced-off at the end faceoff spot of the offending team, unless on the play, the puck shall have entered the net of the opposing team, in which case the goal shall be allowed.

For the purpose of this rule, the point of last contact with the puck by the team in possession shall be used to determine whether icing has occurred or not.

(NOTE 1) *If during the period of a delayed whistle due to a foul by a player of the side NOT in possession, the side in possession "ices" the puck, then the faceoff following the stoppage of play shall take place in the neutral zone near the defending blue line of the team icing the puck.*

(NOTE 2) *When a team is "short-handed" as the result of a penalty and the penalty is about to expire, the decision as to whether there has been an "icing" shall be determined at the instant the penalty expires. The action of the penalized player remaining in the penalty box will not alter the ruling.*

(NOTE 3) *For the purpose of interpretation of the rule, "icing the puck" is completed the instant the puck is touched first by a defending player (other than the goalkeeper) after it has crossed the goal line and if in the action of so touching the puck, it is knocked or deflected into the net, it is NO goal.*

(b) A minor penalty shall be imposed on any player on the players' bench or on the penalty bench who, by means of his stick or his body, interferes with the movements of the puck or of any opponent on the ice during the progress of the play.

(c) If when the goalkeeper has been removed from the ice, any member of his team (including the goalkeeper) not legally on the ice, including the Manager, Coach or Trainer, interferes by means of his body, stick or any other object with the movements of the puck or an opposing player, the Referee shall immediately award a goal to the non-offending team.

(d) When a player in control of the puck on his opponent's side of the center red line and having no other opponent to pass than the goalkeeper is interfered with by a stick or any part thereof or any other object thrown or shot by any member of the defending team including the Manager, Coach or Trainer, a penalty shot shall be awarded to the non-offending team.

(NOTE) *The attention of Referees is directed particularly to three types of offensive interference which should be penalized:*

(1) When the defending team secures possession of the puck in its own end and the other players of that team run interference for the puck carrier by forming a protective screen against forecheckers;

(2) When a player facing-off obstructs his opposing number after the faceoff when the opponent is not in possession of the puck;

(3) When the puck carrier makes a drop pass and follows through so as to make bodily contact with an opposing player.

Defensive interference consists of bodily contact with an opposing player who is not in possession of the puck.

Rule 63. Interference by/with Spectators

(a) In the event of a player being held or interfered with by a spectator, the Referee or Linesman shall blow the whistle and play shall be stopped unless the team of the player interfered with is in possession of the puck at this time when the play shall be allowed to be completed before blowing the whistle and the puck shall be faced-off at the spot where last played at time of stoppage.

(b) Any player who physically interferes with the spectators shall automatically incur a gross misconduct penalty and the Referee shall report all such infractions to the President who shall have full power to impose such further penalty as he shall deem appropriate.

(c) In the event that objects are thrown on the ice which interfere with the progress of the game, the Referee shall blow the whistle and stop the play and the puck shall be faced-off at the spot play is stopped.
(NOTE) *The Referee shall report to the President for disciplinary action all cases in which a player becomes involved in an altercation with a spectator.*

Rule 64. Kicking a Player

A match penalty shall be imposed on any player who kicks or attempts to kick another player.
(NOTE) *Whether or not an injury occurs, the Referee may, at his own discretion, impose a ten-minute time penalty under this rule.*

Rule 65. Kicking the Puck

Kicking the puck shall be permitted in all zones, but a goal may not be scored by the kick of an attacking player except if an attacking player kicks the puck and it is deflected into the net by any players of the defending side except the goalkeeper.

Rule 66. Leaving Players' or Penalty Bench

(a) No player may leave the players' or penalty bench at any time during an altercation or for the purpose of starting an altercation. Substitutions made prior to the altercation shall be permitted provided the players so substituting do not enter the altercation.

(b) For the violation of this rule, a game misconduct penalty shall be imposed on the player who was the first or second player to leave the players' bench or penalty bench from either or both teams.

(c) The first player to leave the players' or penalty bench from either or both teams shall be suspended automatically without pay for the next ten (10) regular League and/or playoff games of his team.

(d) The second player to leave the bench from either or both teams shall be suspended automatically without pay for the next five (5) regular league and/or playoff games.

(NOTE) *The determination as to the players penalized under (c) and (d) of this rule shall be made by the Referee in consultation with the Linesmen and off-ice officials. In the event that he is unable to identify the offending players, the matter will be referred to the President or his designee and such determinations may be made subsequently based or reports and other information including but not limited to television tapes.*

(e) Any team that has a player penalized under (a) shall be fined ten thousand dollars ($10,000) for the first instance. This fine shall be increased by five thousand dollars ($5,000) for each subsequent occurrence over the next following three-year period.

(f) All players including the first and second players who leave the bench during an altercation shall be subject to an automatic fine in the amount equal to the maximum permitted under the collective bargaining agreement.

(g) Any player who leaves the penalty bench during an altercation and is not the first player, shall be suspended automatically without pay for the next five (5) regular League and/or playoff games.

(h) Except at the end of each period or on expiration of his penalty, no player may, at any time, leave the penalty bench.

(i) A penalized player who leaves the penalty bench before his penalty has expired, whether play is in progress or not, shall incur an additional minor penalty, after serving his unexpired penalty.

(j) Any penalized player leaving the penalty bench during stoppage of play and during an altercation shall incur a minor penalty plus a game misconduct penalty after serving his unexpired time.

(k) If a player leaves the penalty bench before his penalty is fully served, the Penalty Timekeeper shall note the time and signal the Referee who will immediately stop play.

(l) In the case of a player returning to the ice before his time has expired through an error of the Penalty Timekeeper, he is not to serve an additional penalty, but must serve his unexpired time.

(m) If a player of the attacking side in possession of the puck shall be in such a position as to have no opposition between him and the opposing goalkeeper, and while in such position he shall be interfered with by a player of the opposing side who shall have illegally entered the game, the Referee shall impose a penalty shot against the side to which the offending player belongs.

(n) If the opposing goalkeeper has been removed and an attacking player in possession of the puck shall have no player of the defending team to pass and a stick or a part thereof or any other object is thrown or shot by an opposing player, or the player is fouled from behind thereby being prevented from having a clear shot on an open

goal, a goal shall be awarded against the offending team.

If when the opposing goalkeeper has been removed from the ice, a player of the side attacking the unattended goal is interfered with by a player who shall have entered the game illegally, the Referee shall immediately award a goal to the non-offending team.

(o) If a Coach or Manager gets on the ice after the start of a period and before that period is ended, the Referee shall impose a bench minor penalty against the team and report the incident to the President for disciplinary action.

(p) Any club executive or Manager committing the same offense will be automatically fined two hundred dollars ($200).

(q) If a penalized player returns to the ice from the penalty bench before his penalty has expired by his own error or the error of the Penalty Timekeeper, any goal scored by his own team while he is illegally on the ice shall be disallowed but all penalties imposed on either team shall be served as regular penalties.

(r) If a player shall illegally enter the game from his own players' bench or from the penalty bench, any goal scored by his own team while he is illegally on the ice shall be disallowed but all penalties imposed on either team shall be served as regular penalties.

(s) A bench minor penalty shall be imposed on a team whose player(s) leave the players' bench for any purpose other than a change of players and when no altercation is in progress.

(t) Any player who has been ordered to the dressing room by the Referee and returns to his bench or to the ice for any reason before the appropriate time shall be assessed a game misconduct penalty and shall be suspended automatically without pay for the next ten (10) regular League and/or playoff games.

(u) The Coach of the team whose player was the first to leave the players' or penalty bench during an altercation shall be suspended automatically for the next five (5) regular League and/or playoff games of his club and shall be fined one thousand dollars ($1,000). The Coach of the team whose players came off the bench subsequently shall be suspended automatically for the next three (3) regular League and/or playoff games of his club and shall be fined one thousand dollars ($1,000). For each subsequent offense of this rule by either or both Coaches over a three-year period, the fines and suspensions shall be doubled.

(v) For all suspensions imposed on players under this rule, the club of the player shall pay to the League a sum equal to the pro-rata of that player's salary covered by the suspension. For purposes of computing amounts due for a player's suspension, the player's fixed salary shall be divided by the number of days in the regular season and then, said result shall be multiplied by the number of games suspended.

In addition, any club that is deemed by the President to pay or reimburse to the player the amount of the fine or loss of salary assessed under this rule shall be fined automatically one hundred thousand dollars ($100,000).

(NOTE) *In the event that suspensions imposed under this rule cannot be completed in regular League and/or playoff games in any one season, the remainder of the suspension shall be served the following season.*

Rule 67. Physical Abuse of Officials

(a) Any player who deliberately applies physical force in any manner against an official, in any manner attempts to injure an official, deliberately makes contact with an official, physically demeans an official or deliberately applies physical force to an official solely for the purpose of getting free of such an official during or immediately following an altercation shall receive a game misconduct penalty.

In addition, the following disciplinary penalties shall apply:
CATEGORY I
Any player who deliberately strikes an official and causes injury or who deliberately applies physical force in any manner against an official with intent to injure, or who in any manner attempts to injure an official shall be automatically suspended for not less than 20 games. (For the purpose of the rule, "intent to injure" shall mean any physical force which a player knew or should have known could reasonably be expected to cause injury.)
CATEGORY II
Any player who deliberately applies physical force to an official in any manner (excluding actions as set out in Category One), which physical force is applied without intent to injure shall be automatically suspended for not less than 10 games.
CATEGORY III
Any player who, by his actions physically demeans an official or who deliberately applies physical force to an official solely for the purpose of getting free of such an official during or immediately following an altercation shall be suspended for not less than 3 games.

Immediately after the game in which such game misconduct penalty is imposed, the Referee shall, in consultation with the Linesmen, decide the category of the offense. He shall make an oral report to the President and advise of the category and of the offense. In addition, he shall file a written report to the President in which he may request a review as to the adequacy of the suspension. The player and club involved shall be notified of the decision of the Referee on the morning following the game and the player may request the President to review, subject to the provisions of this rule, the penalty imposed by the Referee. Such request must be filed with the President by TWX not later than 72 hours following notification of the penalty. No appeal to the Board of Governors pursuant to By-Law 17 shall be available to the player unless a review has been conducted as provided herein.

If a review of the incident is requested by either the player or by the official, a hearing will be conducted by the President as soon as practical prior to the fourth game of any suspension. The

player's suspension shall continue pending the outcome of the hearing by the President.

After any review as called for hereby, the President shall issue an order either:

(1) sustaining the minimum suspension

or

(2) increasing the number of games within the category

or

(3) changing to a lower category

or

(4) changing to a lower category and increasing the number of games within the category.

A player shall have the right of appeal from any such order pursuant to By-Law 17.11. Upon such appeal, the Board of Governors' determination shall be one of the four alternatives listed above.

The penalties imposed under this rule shall not be deemed to limit the right of the President with respect to any action that he might otherwise take under By-Law 17.

In the event that the player has committed more than one offense under this rule, in addition to the penalties imposed under this offense, his case shall be referred to the President of the League for consideration of supplementary disciplinary action.

(In all instances where the President is referred to in this rule, it shall mean the President or his designee.)

(b) Any club executive, Manager, Coach or Trainer who holds or strikes an official shall be automatically suspended from the game, ordered to the dressing room and a substantial fine shall be imposed by the President.

Rule 68. Obscene or Profane Language or Gestures

(a) Players shall not use obscene gestures on the ice or anywhere in the rink before, during or after the game. For a violation of the rule, a game misconduct penalty shall be imposed and the Referee shall report the circumstances to the President of the League for further disciplinary action.

(b) Players shall not use profane language on the ice or anywhere in the rink before, during or after a game. For violation of this rule, a misconduct penalty shall be imposed except when the violation occurs in the vicinity of the players' bench in which case a bench minor penalty shall be imposed.

(NOTE) *It is the responsibility of all game officials and all club officials to send a confidential report to the President setting out the full details concerning the use of obscene gestures or language by any player, Coach or other official. The President shall take such further disciplinary action as he shall deem appropriate.*

(c) Club executives, Managers, Coaches and Trainers shall not use obscene or profane language or gestures anywhere in the rink. For violation of this rule, a bench minor penalty shall be imposed.

Rule 69. Off-Sides

(a) The position of the player's skates and not that of his stick shall be the determining factor in all instances in deciding an "off-side". A player is off-side when both skates are completely over the outer edge of the determining center line or blue line involved in the play.

(NOTE 1) *A player is "on-side" when either of his skates are in contact with or on his own side of the line at the instant the puck completely crosses the outer edge of that line regardless of the position of his stick. However, if while an off-side call is delayed, players of the offending team clear the zone, the Linesman shall drop his arm and the play is no longer off-side.*

(NOTE 2) *It should be noted that while the position of the player's skates is what determines whether a player is "off-side", nevertheless, the question of an "off-side" never arises until the puck has completely crossed the outer edge of the line at which time the decision is to be made.*

(b) If in the opinion of the Linesman, an intentional off-side play has been made, the puck shall be faced-off at the end faceoff spot in the defending zone of the offending team.

(NOTE 1) *An intentional off-side is one which is made for the purpose of securing a stoppage of play regardless of the reason.*

(NOTE 2) *If, while an off-side call is delayed, a player of the offending team deliberately touches the puck to create a stoppage of play, the Linesman will signal an intentional off-side.*

(c) If a Linesman errs in calling an off-side pass infraction (regardless of whether either team is short-handed), the puck shall be faced-off on the center ice faceoff spot.

Rule 70. Passes

(a) The puck may be passed by any player to a player of the same side within any one of the three zones into which the ice is divided, but it may not be passed forward from a player in one zone to a player of the same side in another zone, except by players of the defending team who may make and take forward passes from their own defending zone to the center line without incurring an off-side penalty. This forward pass from the defending zone must be completed by the pass receiver who is preceded by the puck across the center line, otherwise the play shall be stopped and the faceoff shall be at the point from which the pass was made.

(NOTE 1) *The position of the puck and not that of the player's skates shall be the determining factor in deciding from which zone the pass was made.*

(NOTE 2) *Passes may be completed legally at the center red line in exactly the same manner as passes at the attacking blue line.*

(NOTE 3) *In the event the player has preceded the puck at the center line he may become eligible to play the puck if he makes skate contact with the line prior to playing the puck.*

(b) Should the puck having been passed contact any part of the body, stick or skates of a player of the same side who is legally on-side, the pass shall be considered to have been completed.

(c) The player last touched by the puck shall be deemed to be in possession.

Rebounds off goalkeepers' pads or other equipment shall not be considered as a change of possession or completion of the play by the team when applying Rule 34(b).

(d) If a player in the neutral zone is preceded in the attacking zone by the puck passed from the neutral zone, he shall be eligible to take possession of the puck anywhere in the attacking zone except when the "Icing the Puck" rule applies.

(e) If a player in the same zone from which a pass is made is preceded by the puck into succeeding zones, he shall be eligible to take possession of the puck in that zone except where the "Icing the Puck" rule applies.

(f) If an attacking player passes the puck backward toward his own goal from the attacking zone, an opponent may play the puck anywhere regardless of whether the opponent was in the same zone at the time the puck was passed. (No "slow whistle".)

Rule 71. Preceding Puck into Attacking Zone

(a) Players of the attacking team must not precede the puck into the attacking zone.

(b) For violation of this rule, the play is stopped and the puck shall be faced-off in the neutral zone at the faceoff spot nearest the attacking zone of the offending team.
    (NOTE) *A player actually controlling the puck who shall cross the line ahead of the puck shall not be considered "off-side".*

(c) If however, notwithstanding the fact that a member of the attacking team shall have preceded the puck into the attacking zone, the puck be cleanly intercepted by a member of the defending team at or near the blue line and be carried out or passed by them into the neutral zone, the "off-side" shall be ignored and play permitted to continue.
    (Officials will carry out this rule by means of the "slow whistle".)

(d) If a player legally carries or passes the puck back into his own defending zone while a player of the opposing team is in such defending zone, the "off-side" shall be ignored and play permitted to continue. (No "slow whistle".)

Rule 72.   Protection of Goalkeeper

(a) A minor penalty for interference shall be imposed on a player who, by means of his stick or his body, interferes with or impedes the movements of the goalkeeper by actual physical contact.
    (NOTE) *A goalkeeper is not "fair game" just because he is outside the goal crease area. A penalty for interference or charging (minor or major) should be called in every case where an opposing player makes unnecessary contact with the goalkeeper.*
    Likewise, referees should be alert to penalize goalkeepers for tripping, slashing, or spearing in the vicinity of the goal.

(b) Unless the puck is in the goal crease area, a player of the attacking side may not stand on the goal crease line or in the goal crease nor hold his stick in the goal crease area and, if the puck should enter the net while such conditions prevail, the goal shall not be allowed and the offending player will be assessed a minor penalty for interference. The ensuing faceoff shall be taken in the neutral zone at the faceoff spot nearest the attacking zone of the offending team.

(c) If a player of the attacking side has been physically interfered with by the action of any defending player so as to cause him to be in the goal crease and the puck should enter the net while the player so interfered with is still in the goal crease, the goal shall be allowed.

(d) A minor penalty shall be assessed to a player of the attacking side who having been interfered with fails to avoid making contact with the goalkeeper. In addition, if a goal is scored it shall be disallowed.

(e) A minor penalty for interference shall be imposed on any attacking player, who makes deliberate contact with a goalkeeper whether in or out of the crease. At the discretion of the Referee a major penalty may be imposed under Rule 47(c).

(f) A minor and misconduct penalty shall be imposed on an attacking player, not in possession of the puck, who is tripped or caused to fall and fails to attempt to avoid contact with the goalkeeper whether he is in or out of his crease.

(g) In the event that a goalkeeper has been pushed into the net together with the puck after making the stop, the goal will be disallowed. If applicable, the appropriate penalties will be assessed.

Rule 73.   Puck Out of Bounds or Unplayable

(a) When the puck goes outside the playing area at either end or either side of the rink, or strikes any obstacles above the playing surface other than the boards, glass or wire, it shall be faced-off from where it was shot or deflected unless otherwise expressly provided in these rules.

(b) When the puck becomes lodged in the netting on the outside of either goal so as to make it unplayable, or if it is frozen between opposing players intentionally or otherwise, the Referee shall stop the play and face-off the puck at either of the adjacent faceoff spots unless in the opinion of the Referee, the stoppage was caused by a player of the attacking team, in which case the resulting faceoff shall be conducted in the neutral zone.
    (NOTE) *This includes a stoppage of play caused by a player of the attacking side shooting the puck onto the back of the defending team's net without any intervening action by the defending team.*
    The defending team and/or the attacking team may play the puck off the net at any time. However, should the puck remain on the net for more than three seconds, play shall be stopped and the faceoff shall take place in the end faceoff zone except when the stoppage is caused by the attacking team, then the

faceoff shall take place on a faceoff spot in the neutral zone.

(c) A minor penalty shall be imposed on a goalkeeper who deliberately drops the puck on the goal netting to cause a stoppage of play.

(d) If the puck comes to rest on top of the boards surrounding the playing area, it shall be considered to be in play and may be played legally by hand or stick.

Rule 74.   Puck Must be Kept in Motion

(a) The puck must at all times be kept in motion.

(b) Except to carry the puck behind its goal once, a side in possession of the puck in its own defense area shall always advance the puck towards the opposing goal except if it shall be prevented from doing so by players of the opposing side.
    For the first infraction of this rule, play shall be stopped and a faceoff shall be made at either end faceoff spot adjacent to the goal of the team causing the stoppage and the Referee shall warn the Captain or designated substitute of the offending team of the reason for the faceoff. For a second violation by any player of the same team in the same period, a minor penalty shall be imposed on the player violating the rule.

(c) A minor penalty shall be imposed on any player including the goalkeeper who holds, freezes or plays the puck with his stick, skates or body in such a manner as to deliberately cause a stoppage of play.
    (NOTE) *With regard to a goalkeeper, this rule applies outside of his goal crease area.*

Rule 75.   Puck Out of Sight and Illegal Puck

(a) Should a scramble take place or a player accidentally fall on the puck and the puck be out of sight of the Referee, he shall immediately blow his whistle and stop the play. The puck shall then be faced-off at the point where the play was stopped unless otherwise provided for in the rules.

(b) If at any time while play is in progress, a puck other than the one legally in play shall appear on the playing surface, the play shall not be stopped but shall continue with the legal puck until the play then in progress is completed by change of possession.

Rule 76.   Puck Striking Official

Play shall not be stopped if a puck touches the official anywhere on the rink, regardless of whether a team is shorthanded or not.

Rule 77.   Refusing to Start Play

(a) If when both teams are on the ice, one team for any reason shall refuse to play when ordered to do so by the Referee, he shall warn the Captain and allow the team so refusing fifteen seconds within which to begin the play or resume play. If at the end of that time, the team shall still refuse to play,

the Referee shall impose a two-minute penalty on a player of the offending team to be designated by the Manager or Coach of that team through the playing Captain. Should there be a repetition of the same incident, the Referee shall notify the Manager or Coach that he has been fined the sum of two hundred dollars ($200). Should the offending team still refuse to play, the Referee shall have no alternative but to declare that the game be forfeited to the non-offending club and the case shall be reported to the President for further action.

(b) If a team, when ordered to do so by the Referee through its club executive, Manager or Coach, fails to go on the ice and start play within five minutes, the club executive, Manager or Coach shall be fined five hundred dollars ($500), the game shall be forfeited and the case shall be reported to the President for further action.
    (NOTE) *The President of the League shall issue instructions pertaining to records, etc., of a forfeited game.*

Rule 78.   Slashing

(a) A minor or major penalty, at the discretion of the Referee, shall be imposed on any player who impedes or seeks to impede the progress of an opponent by "slashing" with his stick.

(b) A major and a game misconduct penalty shall be imposed on any player who injures an opponent by slashing. In addition, a fine of fifty dollars ($50) shall be imposed for each major penalty assessed under this rule.
    (NOTE) *Referees should penalize as "slashing" any player who swings his stick at any opposing player (whether in or out of range) without actually striking him or where a player, on the pretext of playing the puck, makes a wild swing at the puck with the object of intimidating an opponent.*

(c) Any player who swings his stick at another player in the course of an altercation shall be subject to a fine of not less than two hundred dollars ($200), with or without suspension, to be imposed by the President.
    (NOTE) *The Referee shall impose the normal appropriate penalty provided in the other sections of this rule and shall, in addition, report promptly to the President all infractions under this section.*

Rule 79.   Spearing

(a) A major penalty and a game misconduct penalty shall be imposed on a player who spears an opponent.

(b) In addition to the major penalty imposed under this rule, an automatic fine of fifty dollars ($50) will also be imposed.
    (NOTE 1) *"Spearing" shall mean stabbing an opponent with the point of the stick blade while the stick is being carried with one hand or both hands.*
    (NOTE 2) *Spearing may also be treated as a "deliberate attempt to injure" under Rule 44.*

(c) A double-minor penalty will be imposed by the officials on a player who attempts to spear, poke, or jab an opponent.

(NOTE) *Attempts to spear will include all cases where a spearing gesture is made without contact.*

Rule 80. Start of Game and Periods

(a) The game shall be commenced at the time scheduled by a "faceoff" in the center of the rink and shall renewed promptly at the conclusion of each intermission in the same manner.

No delay shall be permitted by reason of any ceremony, exhibition, demonstration or presentation unless consented to reasonably in advance by the visiting team.

(b) Home clubs shall have the choice of goals to defend at the start of the game except where both players' benches are on the same side of the rink, in which case the home club shall start the game defending the goal nearest to its own bench. The teams shall change ends for each succeeding regular or overtime period.

(c) During the pre-game warm-up (which shall not exceed twenty minutes in duration) and before the commencement of play in any period, each team shall confine its activity to its own end of the rink so as to leave clear an area thirty feet wide across the center of the neutral zone.

(NOTE 1) *The Game Timekeeper shall be responsible for signalling the commencement and termination of the pre-game warm-up and any violation of this rule by the players shall be reported to the President by the supervisor when in attendance at the game.*

(NOTE 2) *Players shall not be permitted to come on the ice during a stoppage of play or at the end of the first and second periods for the purpose of warming-up. The Referee will report any violation of this rule to the President for disciplinary action.*

(d) Twenty minutes before the time scheduled for the start of the game, both teams shall vacate the ice and proceed to their dressing rooms while the ice is being flooded. Both teams shall be signalled by the Game Timekeeper to return to the ice together in time for the scheduled start of the game.

(e) At the beginning of the game, if a team fails to appear on the ice promptly without proper justification, a fine shall be assessed against the offending team, the amount of the fine to be decided by the President.

At the beginning of the second and third periods, and overtime periods in playoffs (0:00 on the clock), clubs must be on the ice or be observed to be proceeding to the ice. For failure to comply, a bench minor penalty for delay of game shall be imposed.

(f) At the end of each period, the home team players must proceed directly to their dressing room while the visiting team players must wait for a signal from the Referee to proceed only if they have to go on the ice to reach their dressing room. Failure to comply with this regulation will result in a two-minute bench minor for delay of game.

Rule 81. Throwing Stick

(a) When any player of the defending side or Manager, Coach or Trainer, deliberately throws or shoots a stick or any part thereof or any other object at the puck in his defending zone, the Referee shall allow the play to be completed and if a goal is not scored, a penalty shot shall be awarded to the non-offending side, which shot shall be taken by the player designated by the Referee as the player fouled.

If however, the goal being unattended and the attacking player having no defending player to pass and having a chance to score on an "open net", a stick or any part thereof or any other object be thrown or shot by a member of the defending team, including the Manager, Coach or Trainer, thereby preventing a shot on the "open net", a goal shall be awarded to the attacking side.

(NOTE 1) *If the officials are unable to determine the person against whom the offense was made, the offended team, through the Captain, shall designate a player on the ice at the time the offense was committed to take the shot.*

(NOTE 2) *For the purpose of this rule, an open net is defined as one from which a goalkeeper has been removed for an additional attacking player.*

(b) A major penalty shall be imposed on any player on the ice who throws his stick or any part thereof or any other object in the direction of the puck in any zone, except when such act has been penalized by the assessment of a penalty shot or the award of a goal.

(NOTE) *When the player discards the broken portion of a stick by tossing it to the side of the ice (and not over the boards) in such a way as will not interfere with play or opposing player, no penalty will be imposed for so doing.*

(c) A misconduct or game misconduct penalty, at the discretion of the Referee, shall be imposed on a player who throws his stick or any part thereof outside the playing area. If the offense is committed in protest of an official's decision, a minor penalty for unsportsmanlike conduct plus a game misconduct penalty shall be assessed to the offending player.

Rule 82. Time of Match

(a) The time allowed for a game shall be three twenty-minute periods of actual play with a rest intermission between periods.

Play shall be resumed promptly following each intermission upon the expiry of fifteen minutes from the completion of play in the preceding period. A preliminary warning shall be given by the Game Timekeeper to the officials and to both teams five minutes prior to the resumption of play in each period and the final warning shall be given two minutes prior to resumption of play to enable the teams to start play promptly.

(NOTE) *For the purpose of keeping the spectators informed as to the time remaining during intermissions, the Game Timekeeper will use the electric clock to record length of intermissions.*

(b) The team scoring the greatest number of goals during the three twenty-minute periods shall be

the winner and shall be credited with two points in the League standing.

(c) In the interval between periods, the ice surface shall be flooded unless mutually agreed to the contrary.

(d) If any unusual delay occurs within five minutes of the end of the first or second periods, the Referee may order the next regular intermission to be taken immediately and the balance of the period will be completed on the resumption of play with the teams defending the same goals after which, the teams will change ends and resume play of the ensuing period without delay.

(NOTE) *If a delay takes place with more than five minutes remaining in the first or second period, the Referee will order the next regular intermission to be taken immediately only when requested to do so by the home club.*

Rule 83.   Tied Games

(a) If at the end of the three regular twenty-minute periods the score shall be tied, the teams will play an additional period of not more than five (5) minutes with the team scoring first being declared the winner. If at the end of the overtime period, the score remains tied, each team shall be credited with one point in the League standing.

(NOTE) *The overtime period will be commenced immediately following a two-minute rest period during which the players will remain on the ice. The teams will not change ends for the overtime period.*

(b) Special conditions for the duration and number of periods of Playoff games shall be arranged by the Board of Governors.

Rule 84.   Tripping

(a) A minor penalty shall be imposed on any player who shall place his stick, knee, foot, arm, hand or elbow in such a manner that it shall cause his opponent to trip or fall.

(NOTE 1) *If in the opinion of the Referee, a player is unquestionably hook-checking the puck and obtains possession of it thereby tripping the puck carrier, no penalty shall be imposed.*

(NOTE 2) *Accidental trips occurring simultaneously with or after a stoppage of play will not be penalized.*

(b) When a player, in control of the puck on the opponent's side of the center red line and having no other opponent to pass than the goalkeeper, is tripped or otherwise fouled from behind thus preventing a reasonable scoring opportunity, a penalty shot shall be awarded to the non-offending side. Nevertheless, the Referee shall not stop play until the attacking side has lost possession of the puck to the defending side.

(NOTE) *The intention of this rule is to restore a reasonable scoring opportunity which has been lost by reason of a foul from behind when the foul is committed on the opponent's side of the center red line.*

"Control of the puck" means the act of propelling the puck with the stick. If while it is being propelled, the puck is touched by another player or his equipment, hits the goal or goes free, the player shall no longer be considered to be "in control of the puck".

(c) If when the opposing goalkeeper has been removed from the ice, a player in control of the puck is tripped or otherwise fouled with no opposition between him and the opposing goal thus preventing a reasonable scoring opportunity, the Referee shall immediately stop the play and award a goal to the attacking team.

Rule 85.   Unnecessary Roughness

At the discretion of the Referee, a minor penalty or a double-minor penalty may be imposed on any player deemed guilty of unnecessary roughness.

Rule 86.   Time-Outs

Each team shall be permitted to take one thirty second time-out during the course of regular time or overtime in the case of a playoff game. This time-out must be taken during a normal stoppage of play. Any player designated by the Coach will indicate to the Referee that his team is exercising its option and the Referee will report the time-out to the Game Timekeeper who shall be responsible for signalling the termination of the time-out.

(NOTE) *All players including goalkeepers on the ice at the time of the time-out will be allowed to go to their respective benches. Only one team is allowed a time-out per stoppage and no time-out will be allowed after a reasonable amount of time has elapsed during a normal stoppage of play.*

OFFICIAL SIGNALS

BOARDING

Pounding the closed fist of one hand into the open palm of the other hand.

CHARGING

Rotating clenched fists around one another in front of chest.

CROSS-CHECKING

A forward and backward motion with both fists clenched extending from the chest.

DELAYED CALLING OF PENALTY

Referee extends arm and points to penalized player.

ELBOWING

Tapping the elbow of the "whistle hand" with the opposite hand.

HIGH-STICKING

Holding both fists, clenched, one above the other at the side of the head.

HOLDING

Clasping the wrist of the "whistle hand" well in front of the chest.

HOOKING

A tugging motion with both arms, as if pulling something toward the stomach.

ICING

Linesman's arms folded across the upper chest.

INTERFERENCE

Crossed arms stationary in front of chest with fists closed.

KNEEING

Slapping the knee with palm of hand while keeping both skates on the ice.

MISCONDUCT

Place both hands on hips.

ROUGHING

A thrusting motion with the arm extending from the side.

SLASHING

A chopping motion with the edge of one hand across the opposite forearm.

SLOW WHISTLE

Arm in which whistle is not held extended above head. If play returns to neutral zone without stoppage of play, arm is drawn down the instant the puck crosses the line.

SPEARING

A jabbing motion with both hands thrust out in front of the body.

TRIPPING

Strike the right leg with the right hand below the knee, keeping both skates on the ice.

UNSPORTSMANLIKE CONDUCT

Use both hands to form a "T" in front of the chest.

WASH-OUT

Both arms swung laterally across the body with palms down. When used by the Referee it means goal disallowed.

WASH-OUT

Both arms swung laterally at shoulder level with palms down. When used by the Linesman, it means no icing or no off-side.

INDEX

This index includes all persons, associations, leagues and teams appearing in the encyclopedia with the exception of those whose names appear only in the NHL All-Time Player Register and the NHL Coach Directory (Chapter 18); and in any other tabular material. **Boldface numerals** denote references to photos.

Dorey, Jim, 379
Douglas, Kent, 99, 110
Drillon, Gordon (Gordie), 45, **45,** 50, 55, 322
Drinkwater, Charles Graham, 322
Drury, Herb, **33**
Dryden, Ken, 109, **115,** 135, **225,** 322
  on All-Star team, 120, 129, 132, 134
  awards, 116, 117, 128, 128, 132
  career of, 224-26
  in Stanley Cup playoffs, 116
Duchesne, Steve, 273
Dudley, George, 338
Duff, Dick, 284, 285
Duggan, Thomas J., 17
Dumart, Woody, 45, **50,** 52, 55, **66,** 202, 208, 322
  in All-Star game, 278
Duncan, Art, 34
Dunderdale, Thomas, 322
Dunn, Jimmie, 338
Dunn, Richie, 267
Dupont, Andre, 120
Dupont, Arthur, 24
Durnan, Ronald (Bill), 63, **74,** 93, **227,** 323
  on All-Star team, 62, 64, 67, 69, 73, 75
  awards, 62, 64, 67, 69, 73, 75
  career of, 226-29
  in Stanley Cup playoffs, 70, 75, 76, 82
Dutton, Mervyn (Red), 12, 55, 59, 60, 68, 310, 323
Dwyer, Bill, 43
Dye, Cecil (Babe), 9, 12, **13,** 13, 18, 323

E
Eagleson, Robert Alan, 338-39
Eastern Canadian Amateur Hockey Association, 241
Edmonton Oilers, 137, 138, 149, 169, 267-68, 269, 271-73
  Avco Cup playoffs, 387
  greatest players with, 188-89, 197-98, 232
  Stanley Cup playoffs, 139, 143, 147, 149, 150, 153-54,
    156, 159, 162, 167, 170, 172, 173-74, 180, 248,
    248-49
Edmonton (Pacific Coast Hockey Association team), 14
Edmonton (Western Canada Hockey League team), 12
Edwards, Don, **142,** 267, 268, 295
Elliott, Chaucer, 337
Emms, Hap, 36
Errey, Bob, 274
Eruzione, Mike, 395
Esposito, Patsy, 267
Esposito, Phil, 109, 113, **114,** 117, 125, 127, 139, 141,
  151, 161, **187,** 188, 212, 214, 224, 226, 229, **244,**
  265, 265-66, 267, **276,** 323
  in All-Star game, 293
  on All-Star team, 113, 114, 116, 117
  awards, 112, 122
  career of, 186-88
  as leading scorer, 111-12, 115, 117, 118, 121
  in Stanley Cup playoffs, 112
Esposito, Tony, 113, **114,** 186, 187, **228,** 323, 391
  in All-Star game, 290
  on All-Star team, 114, 117
  awards, 113, 114, 117, 122
  career of, 229-30
Ezinicki, Bill, 78, 185

F
Farrell, Arthur, 323
Faulkner, Alex, 263

Faulkner, Steve, 227
Favell, Doug, 110
Federov, Sergei, 180
Ferguson, Elmer, 24
Ferguson, John, 287
Fitzpatrick, Mark, 180
Flaman, Ferdinand Charles (Fernie), 323
Fletcher, Cliff, 271
Fontinato, Louie, 87, **88,** 97, 99, 191
Forbes, Dave, 125
Fowler, Norm, 12, 18
Foyston, Frank, 7, **8,** 11-12, 21, 323
Francis, Emile (The Cat), 79, 102-03, **105,** 106, 259, 339,
  555
Francis, Ron, 274
Fredrickson, Frank, 13, 18, 21, 323
Ftorek, Robbie, 385
Fuhr, Grant, 150, **161,** 161, 167, 170, 172
  in All-Star game, 298
  on All-Star team, 163
  in Stanley Cup playoffs, 156

G
Gadsby, Bill, 87, 100, **101,** 263, 323-24
  on All-Star team, 87, 91, 92
  in Stanley Cup playoffs, 106
Gagnon, Johnny, 43
Gainey, Bob, 134, 173, 324
Gainor, Dutch, 207
Gallinger, Don, 72
Gallivan, Dan, 315
Gardiner, Charles (Chuck), 34, 35, 38, 39, 324
Gardiner, Herbert Martin (Herb), 21, 323
Gardner, James Henry (Jimmy), 324
Gee, George, 79, 260
Gelinas, Martin, 165
Gelineau, Jack, 75
Geoffrion, Bernie (Boom Boom), 85, 89, 91, 95, 96, 104,
  105, 106, 231, 263, 264, **323,** 324
  in All-Star game, 283
  on All-Star team, 95
  awards, 79-80, 95
  as leading scorer, 85, 95
  in Stanley Cup playoffs, 89
Gerard, Eddie, 10, 23, 245, 255, 324
German Olympic team (1932), **393**
Giacomin, Ed, 106, 116, 265, 324
Gibson, J. L. (Jack), 339
Gilbert, Rod, 103, 106, 110-11, 117, **324,** 325
Gillies, Clark, 132, 134, 203
Gilmour, Doug, 161, 167, 179, 271
Gilmour, Hamilton Livingstone (Billy), 325
Goalies' masks, 31, 93-94, 262, **316**
Gobuty, Michael, 387
Goheen, Frank (Moose), 325
Goldham, Bob, 71, 77, 279
Goodenow, Bob, 179
Goodfellow, Ebenezer R. (Ebbie), **33,** 34, 44, 52, 221, 325
Goodman, Paul, 47
Goring, Butch, 132, 138, **140,** 140, 247
Gorman, Thomas Patrick (Tommy), 68, 200, 339
Gosselin, Mario, 273
Gottselig, Johnny, **31**
Goulet, Michel, 149, 150, 157, **159,** 160
Goyette, Phil, 106, **110,** 114
Graham, Dirk, 176
Grahame, Ron, 381

Hynes, Gordon Ross, **397**

I
Iafrate, Al, 391
Imlach, George (Punch), 91, 99, 102, 103, 212, 339
Indianapolis Racers, 189, 381, 383, 387
 greatest players with, 189, 197
Ingarfield, Earl, 203
Ion, Fred J. (Mickey), 2, **306,** 306, 307, 309, 337
Irvin, James Dickenson (Dick), 12, 19, 21, 34-35, 38, 39, 52-53, 62, 68, 76, 82, 84, 87, 147, 153, 179, 282, 326, **326,** 555
Ivan, Tommy, 96, 339

J
Jackson, Don, 156
Jackson, Harvey (Busher), 35, 38, 39, 43, 55, 162, 321, 326, 331
 on All-Star team, 35, 40, 44
 as leading scorer, 35
Jagr, Jaromir, **179,** 180, 249, 274
Janney, Craig, 391
Jarvis, Doug, 150, 158
Jenkins, Roger, 38
Jennings (William M.) Award, 354-55, **355**
Jennings, William M. (Bill), 339
Jensen, David A., 396
Jersey Knights, 381
Johnson, Bob, 177, **274,** 274, 339
Johnson, Ernie (Moose), **9,** 10, 326
Johnson, Ivan (Ching), **210,** 220, 326
 on All-Star team, 35, 36
 career of, 209-10
Johnson, Jim, 274
Johnson, Mark, 297
Johnson, Paul, **394**
Johnson, Terry, 156
Johnson, Thomas Christian (Tom), 92, 99, 327
Joliat, Aurel, **12,** 13, 17, 35, 36, 43, 327
 on All-Star team, 34
 awards, 38
Juckes, Gordon, 339
Juneau, Joe, 396

K
Kansas City Scouts, 125, 127, 129
Karakas, Mike, 42, 47
Keats, Gordon (Duke), 327
Kehoe, Rick, 140
Kelley, Jack, 379
Kelly, Leonard Patrick (Red), 106, 110, **211,** 221, **243,** 267, 327
 in All-Star game, 281, 283
 on All-Star team, 77, 79, 82, 83, 85, 89
 awards, 77, 82, 83, 95
 career of, 210-12
 in Stanley Cup playoffs, 98
Kennedy, George, 10
Kennedy, Theodore (Ted), 76, 85, 191, 258, 280, 327
Kenora Thistles, 243
Keon, David Michael (Dave), **94,** 95, 98, 107, 327, 377
Kerr, Davey, 47, **51,** 52, 156
Kerr, Tim, 153, **156**
Kilcoursie, Lord, 239
Kilpatrick, Gen. John Reed, 339
Kilrea, Hec, 31, 256
Kitchener Rangers, 219

Klima, Petr, 172, 173-74
Koharski, Don, 162
Kroc, Ray, 386-87
Krushelnyski, Mike, 165
Kurry, Jari, 149, 151, 153, 158, 170, 269
 on All-Star team, 154, 160
 awards, 154
 in Stanley Cup playoffs, 154
Kurtenbach, Orland, **108**

L
Labine, Leo, 80
Lach, Elmer James, 62-63, **71,** 82, 257, 318, 327
 on All-Star team, 64, 73, 79
 awards, 64, 69
 as leading scorer, 64, 71
 Stanley Cup playoffs, 67
Lacroix, Andre, 379, 381, **382**
Lady Byng Trophy, 18, 356-57, **356**
Lafleur, Guy, 109, 126, **126,** 129, 146, 151, 165, **327,** 327
 on All-Star team, 125, 128, 129, 132, 134, 139
 awards, 130, 132
 as leading scorer, 126, 130
 in Stanley Cup playoffs, 126, 130, 132
LaFontaine, Pat, 158, 248, 391, 396
Laidlaw, Tom, 273
Lalonde, Edouard (Newsy), 1, 4, 5, 7, 9, 10, 12-13, 17, **36,** 36, 271, 327-28
Langway, Rod, 147, 150 **150,** 197
Laperriere, Jacques, 101-02, 103, 105, **244,** 289, 328
Lapointe, Guy, 120, 129
Laprade, Edgar, 67, 75, 221
Larmer, Steve, 147
Larocque, Michel, 132
Larose, Claude, 195-96, 288
Laviolette, Jean Baptiste (Jack), 328
Laycoe, Hal, 85
Leach, Reggie, 128, 160, 257, 271, 294
Leader, G. A. (Al), 339
LeBel, Robert, 339
LeBlanc, Ray, 396
Leduc, Albert (Battleship), **19**
Leetch, Brian, 167, **168,** 179, 180, 391
Lehman, Hughie, 12, 15, 23, 328
Lemaire, Jacques (Gerard), 130, 328, **328**
Lemieux, Claude, 159, 271
Lemieux, Mario, 150, 151-52, **153,** 156, **160,** 165, 167, 169, 172, 174, **175,** 177, **178, 179,** 189, **194,** 269-71, 274, 275
 in All-Star game, 298, 299, 300, 301
 on All-Star team, 163, 169
 awards, 153, 160, 176, 180
 career of, 193-95
 as leading scorer, 160, 179
 in Stanley Cup playoffs, 156, 180, 249
LeSueur, Percy, 328
Leswick, Tony, 84
Lewis, Bryan, 305-06, **312**
Lewis, Herbert (Herbie), 256, 317, 328
Ley, Rick, 379
Lichtenhein, Sam, 3
Lindbergh, Pelle, 153, **154,** 154, 156
Lindros, Eric, 177-78, **180,** 180, 396, **397**
Lindsay, Theodore (Ted), **64,** 71-72, 73, 74-75, 78, 82, 90, **102,** 196, 231, 328
 in All-Star game, 278, 279, 280, 282
 on All-Star team, 72, 75, 77, 79, 82, 83, 87, 89

Montreal Nationals, 1
Montreal Royals, 231
Montreal Shamrocks, 1, **240**
Montreal Victorias, 239
Montreal Wanderers, 1, 2-3, 5, 8-9, 10
Moog, Andy, 170, 172, 269, 298, 301
Moore, Alfie, 47
Moore, Hammy, 220
Moore, Richard (Dickie), 89, 91, 92, 231, 264, 284, 329-30
Moran, Patrick Joseph (Paddy), **242**, 330
Morenz, Howie, 15, 17, 21, 31, 35, 39, 42, 43, 128, 193, **199**, 327, 330
   on All-Star team, 34, 35
   awards, 23, 24, 34, 35
   career of, 198-99
   death of, 43, 199
   as leading scorer, 23, 34
Morris, Bernie, 5, 18
Morrison, Don, 77
Morrison, Doug, 241
Morrison, Ian P. (Scotty), **310,** 313, 315
Morrison, Jim, 91
Morrow, Ken, 269, 391
Morrow, Steve, 149
Mortson, Gus, 75, 78, 280, 281
Mosdell, Ken, 83, 84, 280
Mosienko, William (Bill), 71, 79, 259-60, **260,** 318, 330
   awards, 64
   in All-Star game, 278, 280
Mowers, Johnny, 53, 60
Muldoon, Pete, 22-23, 101, 241
Mullen, Joey, 156, 169, 180, 274
Mullenix, Ivan, 383
Mummery, Harry, 10
Munro, Scotty, 379
Murdoch, Bob, **123**
Murphy, Dennis, 377
Murphy, Joe, 170
Murphy, Larry, 274
Murphy, Ron, 87, 265
Murray, Troy, 157

N
Naslund, Mats, 162, 248, **248,** 299
Nassau Veterans Memorial Coliseum, 117
National Collegiate Athletic Association, 391
National Hockey Association, 1, 2, 4, 241
National Hockey League, 1, 241
   all-time player register, 401-553
   beginnings of radio broadcasts, 13, 24
   entry draft, 365-75
   expansion, 16, 20-21, 103-04; 109-10, 117, 125
   final standings: 1917-18, 4; 1918-19, 7; 1919-20, 8; 1920-21, 10; 1921-22, 12; 1922-23, 14; 1923-24, 15; 1924-25, 18; 1925-26, 20; 1926-27, 22; 1927-28, 24; 1928-29, 27; 1929-30, 32; 1930-31, 34; 1931-34, 35; 1932-33, 37; 1933-34, 38; 1934-35, 40; 1935-36, 42; 1936-37, 44; 1937-38, 47; 1938-39, 50; 1939-40, 52; 1940-41, 55; 1941-42, 56; 1942-43, 60; 1943-44, 63; 1944-45, 66; 1945-46, 67; 1946-47, 70; 1947-48, 73; 1948-49, 74; 1949-50, 76; 1950-51, 79; 1951-52, 81; 1952-53, 82; 1953-54, 84; 1954-55, 87; 1955-56, 89; 1956-57, 90; 1957-58, 91; 1958-59, 93; 1959-60, 95; 1960-61, 96; 1961-62, 98; 1962-63, 99; 1963-64, 102; 1964-65, 103; 1965-66, 106; 1966-67, 107; 1967-68, 111; 1968-69, 113; 1969-70, 114; 1970-71, 117;

1971-72, 118; 1972-73, 120; 1973-74, 122, 125; 1974-75, 126; 1975-76, 129; 1976-77, 130; 1977-78, 132; 1978-79, 134; 1979-80, 139; 1980-81, 140; 1981-82, 145; 1982-83, 147, 149; 1983-84, 150; 1984-85, 154; 1985-86, 157; 1986-87, 160; 1987-88, 163; 1988-1989, 169; 1989-90, 172; 1990-91, 176-77; 1991-92, 181
   against foreign teams, 399
   founding of, 2
   leading scorers: 1917-18, 5; 1918-19, 7; 1919-20, 8; 1920-21, 10; 1921-22, 12; 1922-23, 14; 1923-24, 15; 1924-25, 18; 1925-26, 20; 1926-27, 22; 1927-28, 24; 1928-29, 27; 1929-30, 32; 1930-31, 34; 1931-34, 36; 1932-33, 37; 1933-34, 39; 1934-35, 40; 1935-36, 42; 1936-37, 44; 1937-38, 47; 1938-39, 52; 1939-40, 52; 1940-41, 55; 1941-42, 56; 1942-43, 61; 1943-44, 63; 1944-45, 66; 1945-46, 67; 1946-47, 70; 1947-48, 73; 1948-49, 74; 1949-50, 76; 1950-51, 79; 1951-52, 81; 1952-53, 82; 1953-54, 84; 1954-55, 87; 1955-56, 89; 1956-57, 90; 1957-58, 91; 1958-59, 93; 1959-60, 95; 1960-61, 96; 1961-62, 99; 1962-63, 99; 1963-64, 102; 1964-65, 103; 1965-66, 106; 1966-67, 107; 1967-68, 111; 1968-69, 113; 1969-70, 114; 1970-71, 117; 1971-72, 118; 1972-73, 120; 1973-74, 125; 1974-75, 126; 1975-76, 129; 1976-77, 130; 1977-78, 132; 1978-79, 135; 1979-80, 139; 1980-81, 141; 1981-82, 145; 1982-83, 149; 1983-84, 151; 1984-85, 155; 1985-86, 157; 1986-87, 160; 1987-88, 163; 1988-1989, 169; 1989-90, 172; 1990-91, 177; 1991-92, 181
   merger with World Hockey Association, 137-38, 387
   pension plan, 71
   players' strike, 179
   rules, 4, 5, 24, 29, 59-60, 62, 67, 89, 563-90
   television contract, 106
   use of video replay, 180
National Hockey League Players' Association, 90, 179
Neilson, Roger, 169, 555
Nelson, Francis, 340
Nesterenko, Eric, 264, 285
New England Whalers, 379, 381
New Jersey Devils, 161-62, 174
New Jersey Knights, 381
New Westminster (Pacific Coast Hockey Association team), 1
New York Americans, 18, 20, 43
   greatest players with, 210, 220
   Stanley Cup playoffs, 24, 42, 46, 50, 52
New York Golden Blades, 381
New York Islanders, 117, 118, 130, 137, 138, 139, 269
   greatest players with, 185-86, 203-04, 215-17
   Stanley Cup playoffs, 125, 130, 131, 133, 139, 140, 145-46, 146-47, 149, 150, 153, 156, 158, 162, 247-48, 248
New York Raiders, 381
New York Rangers, 20, **53,** 102, **105,** 106, 133, 153, 158, 255-56, 259-60, 260-62, 263-64, 386
   greatest players with, 186-88, 197, 199, 209, 210, 214-15, 232, 233, 234-35
   Stanley Cup playoffs, 23-24, 24, 31, 34, 35, 37, 38, 40, 44, 46, 50, 52, 53, 56, 75-76, 89, 91, 98, 106, 111, 112, 113, 116, 121, 125, 133-34, 140, 146, 150, 153, 156, 169-70, 180, 245
New York Rovers, 235, 259
Nicholls, Bernie, 167, 169, 178, 197, 273
Nieuwendyk, Joe, 161, **162,** 167

Prystai, Metro, 77
Pulford, Bob, 98, 107, 283, 284, 285, 331
Pulford, Harvey, 331

Q

Quackenbush, Bill, 72, 73, 77, 80, 221, 331
Quebec Aces, 183
Quebec Bulldogs, 2, 5, 7, 8
Quebec (Canadian Hockey Association team), 1
Quebec (National Hockey Association team), 2
Quebec Nordiques, 137, 177, 180, 379, 385
  Avco Cup playoffs, 381, 385
  Stanley Cup playoffs, 153, 156
Quebec Senior League, 183
Quilty, Johnny, 53
Quinn, Pat, 180

R

Raleigh, Don, **74, 84**
Ramage, Rob, 157, 161
Ramsey, Craig, 154
Ramsey, Mike, 391
Ranford, Bill, 169, 170, 172, 248-49, **249,** 273
Ranheim, Paul, 167
Rankin, Frank, 331
Ratelle, Jean, 103, 110-11, 214, 331, 333, **332**
  in All-Star game, 290
  awards, 117, 128
Raymond, Donat, 17, 340
Rayner, Claude Earl (Chuck), 55, 75, 79, 279, 333
Reardon, Kenneth (Ken), 55, **69** , 69, 75, 333
Reardon, Terry, 55
Reaume, Marc, 91
Reay, Billy, 91, 555
Recchi, Mark, 174, 179, 274
Redmond, Mickey, 120
Reece, Dave, 267
Regan, Larry, 89, 106
Regina (Western Canada Hockey League team), 12
Reibel, Earl (Dutch), 87, 282
Renfrew (National Hockey Association team), 1
Resch, Chico, 293
Rice, Steven, 197
Richard, Henri, 87, **88,** 231, 262-63, **333,** 333
  in All-Star game, 287
  on All-Star team, 91
Richard, Maurice (Rocket), 53, 59, 60, 63, 64, 67, 77, 78-
  79, **80,** 82, 85, 89, 90-91, **93,** 95, 96, 99, 101, 104,
  139, 141, 188, 191, 193, **201,** 227, 230, **245,** 257,
  258, 262, 263, 267, 271, 284, 285, 287, 318, 327,
  333, 385
  in All-Star game, 278, 280, 281, 282, 283, 284
  on All-Star team, 64, 67, 69, 73, 75, 85, 87
  awards, 69
  career of, 200
  in Stanley Cup playoffs, 63, 67, 70, 79, 80-81, 89, 91,
    92, 247
Richardson, George, 333
Ridley, Mike, 158
Riley, Jack, 106
Riley, Jim, 11-12
Risebrough, Doug, **248**
Rivers, Wayne, 381
Roach, John Ross, 36
Roach, Mickey, 9
Roberts, Gordon, 333
Robertson, Earl, 44, 223

Robertson, John Ross, 340
Robinson, Claude C., 340-41
Robinson, Larry, **128, 218**
  in All-Star game, 301-02
  on All-Star team, 129, 134, 139
  awards, 130, 132, 139
  career of, 217-19
Robinson, Major Frank, 2
Robitaille, Luc, **159,** 273
  in All-Star game, 300
  on All-Star team, 163, 169, 172, 176
  awards, 160
  in Stanley Cup playoffs, 173
Rodden, Michael J. (Mike), 306, **308,** 337
Rollins, Al, 78, 82-83, 281
Romnes, Doc, 41, 47
Ronty, Paul, 279
Ross (Art) Trophy, 350-51, **350**
Ross, Arthur Howey (Art), 17, 48, 62, 202, 334, 350, 555
Ross, Philip D., 239, 341
Rousseau, Bobby, 98, 287
Roy, Patrick, **155,** 179
  on All-Star team, 169, 172, 180
  awards, 157, 167, 172, 180
  in Stanley Cup playoffs, 248
Ruel, Claude, 112, 229
Ruskowski, Terry, 387
Russell, Blair, 334
Russell, Ernie, 334
Russia-Team Canada series, 118
Ruttan, J. D. (Jack), 334

S

St. Louis Blues, 106, 110, 157
  greatest players with, 209, 230-31, 232
  Stanley Cup playoffs, 111, 112, 113, 149, 156, 170, 173,
    180
St. Louis Eagles, 39, 41
Salming, Borje, 129
Samuelsson, Kjell, 179
Samuelsson, Ulf, 274
San Diego Mariners, 381, 387
San Jose Sharks, 178
Sanderson, Derek, 111, **378,** 379
Sandford, Ed, 82
Saskatoon (Western Canada Hockey League team), 12
Sather, Glen, 197
Sator, Ted, 153, 269
Savard, Serge Aubrey, 334, **335**
Sawchuk, Terry, 77, 78, **81,** 87, 89, 90, 93, **101,** 103, **108,**
  110, **233,** 334
  in All-Star game, 279, 280, 281, 282
  on All-Star team, 77, 79, 82, 89
  awards, 77, 79, 82, 85, 103
  career of, 232-35
  in Stanley Cup playoffs, 81, 106
Scanlan, Fred, 334
Schaefer, Joe, 262
Schmautz, Bobby, 205, 290
Schmidt, Milton Conrad (Milt), 45, 52, 55, **66, 81, 202,** 208,
  322, 334
  on All-Star team, 52, 69, 77
  awards, 77
  career of, 200, 202-03
  as leading scorer, 52
  in Stanley Cup playoffs, 55
Schoenfeld, Jim, 162

79, 83, 87, 89, 92, 95, 96, 98, 99, 102, 103, 105, 106-07, 112, 121, 131, 159, 245, 247
Toronto (National Hockey Association team), 2
Toronto St. Patrick's, 7, 12, 21
Toronto Toros, 380, 385
Torrey, Bill, 131, 186, 203, 269
Tremblay, Gilles, 100, 263
Tremblay, J. C., 116, 377
Tretiak, Vladislav, 336
Trihey, Harry, 336
Trottier, Bryan, 131, 137, 176, **204,** 269
  in All-Star game, 298
  on All-Star team, 132, 134
  awards, 128, 134, 139
  career of, 203-04
  as leading scorer, 133
  in Stanley Cup playoffs, 158
Turner, Lloyd, 341
Tutt, W. Thayer, 341

U

Udvari, Frank, **304,** 309, 311, 337
Ullman, Norm, 103, 285, 287, 336
Unger, Garry, 158, 290
United States Amateur League, 19
United States Olympic teams, **390,** 394-96

V

Vachon, Rogatien (Rogie), 111, 228
Vadnais, Carol, 214
Vail, Eric, **123,** 125
Vaive, Rick, 297
Valtonen, Jorma, **395**
Van Impe, Ed, 120
Vanbiesbrouck, John, 157
Vancouver Blazers, 381, 383
Vancouver Canucks, 116, 143, 156, 167, 173, 179, 247
Vancouver Millionaires, 1, 4, 10, 12, 14, 15, 245
VanHellemond, Andy, 306, 309, 310, 312
Vasko, Elmer (Moose), **93**
Verdun Black Hawks, 205
Vernon, Mike, 156, 167, 248
Vezina, Georges, 4, 15, 18, 19, 21, 24, **234,** 336, 351
  career of, 235
  death of, 19
Vezina Trophy, 21, 351-52, **351**
Vickers, Jack, 129
Vickers, Steve, 120
Victoria (Pacific Coast Hockey Association team), 1, 5, 18
Victoria (Western Hockey League team), 19-20
Villemure, Gilles, 116
Voss, Carl V., 41, 341

W

Waghorne, Fred, 341
Walker, John Phillip (Jack), 18, 336
Walsh, Martin (Marty), 336
Walters, Ryan, 167, 271
Walton, Mike (Shakey), 381, **384**

Ward, Jimmy, 256
Warwick, Grant, 56
Washington Capitals, 125
  Stanley Cup playoffs, 146, 150, 153, 156, 158, 162, 167, 170, 174, 179, 248
Watson, Harry, 258, 336
Watson, Jim, 120
Watson, Joe, 120
Watson, Phil, 87, 236
Webster, Tom, 169
Weiland, Ralph (Cooney), 31, **31,** 207, 336-37
Wensink, John, **133**
Western Canada Hockey League, 12
Western Hockey League, 19, 20
Westfall, Ed, **104**
Westwick, Harry, 337
Wharram, Ken, 101, 106, 288
Whitcroft, Fred, 337
Williams, Tiger, 185, 186
Williams, Tommy, 391
Wilson, Cully, 5, 7, 10
Wilson, Doug, 143
Wilson, Gordon Allan (Phat), 337
Wilson, Rik, 156
Winnipeg Jets, 118, 137, 140, 377, 383, 386, 387
  Avco Cup playoffs, 379, 383, 385, 387
  greatest players with, 192-93
  Stanley Cup playoffs, 159, 170, 180
Wirtz, Arthur M., 341
Wirtz, William, 341
Wiseman, Eddie, 55
World championships, 397-99
World Hockey Association, 109, 117, 133, 189, 192, 197, 377-89
  final standings of: 1972-73, 379; 1973-74, 381; 1974-75, 381; 1975-76, 383; 1976-77, 385; 1977-78, 387; 1978-79, 389
  founding of, 118
  leading scorers: 1972-73, 380; 1973-74, 381; 1974-75, 383; 1975-76, 383; 1976-77, 386; 1977-78, 387; 1978-79, 389
  merger with National Hockey League, 137-38, 387
World War I, 5, 7
World War II, 52, 55, 61, 66
Worsley, Lorne (Gump), 229, **236, 244,** 263, 337
  in All-Star game, 290
  on All-Star team, 111
  awards, 82, 105, 111
  career of, 235-37
  in Stanley Cup playoffs, 98, 103
Worters, Roy, 24, **32,** 34, 337

Y

Young, Howie, 99, 103
Yukon Klondikes, 239-40
Yzerman, Steve, 167, 169

Z

Ziegler, John A., Jr., 109, **132,** 132, 179, 180, 273, 341